ISBN 978-0-260-06729-6
PIBN 11022610

FB &c Ltd, Dalton House, 60 Windsor Avenue, London, SW19 2RR.
Company number 08720141. Registered in England and Wales.

For support please visit www.forgottenbooks.com

THE INTERNATIONAL

naturalists universal

SCIENTIST'S DIRECTORY.

CONTAINING

THE NAMES, ADDRESSES, SPECIAL DEPARTMENTS OF STUDY, ETC., OF AMATEUR AND PROFESSIONAL NATURALISTS, CHEMISTS, PHYSICISTS, ASTRONOMERS, ETC., ETC.,

IN AMERICA, EUROPE, ASIA, AFRICA AND OCEANICA.

COMPILED BY
SAMUEL E. CASSINO.

BOSTON:
S. E. CASSINO,
1888

NOTICE.

In this edition of the Directory, all names which have been heard from since the last edition are followed by an (*). In the American portion of the Directory, names which are followed by an (?) have not replied to the blanks sent them for at least two years, and all such will be dropped from the next edition of the work, unless heard from in the meantime. Names which are not followed by an (*) or an (?) are, without doubt, correct, but have failed to reply to the last blanks sent to their address.

For convenience, an index has been placed in the front of the book, and the list of abbreviations will be found immediately following the index. The editor is indebted to many persons for assistance in the compiling of the work, especially to the following, who have taken much trouble and pains to forward corrections, changes of address and lists of new names: Frazer S. Crawford, Adelaide, So. Australia; G. J. Symons, London, England; J. Palisa, Vienna, Austro-Hungary; J. E. Gore, Beltra, Ireland; G. J. Cassimati, Athens, Greece; N. C. Kindberg, Linköping, Sweden; J. Hopkinson, St. Albans, England.

Another edition of the Directory will be made in about two years, and the editor will be very glad to receive from any one interested, notices of errors, as well as new names.

INDEX.

PART I.

INDEX.

PART II.

ABBREVIATIONS.

Acad., Academy.
Agric., Agriculture.
Ala., Alabama.
Am., American.
Anat., Anatomy.
Analyt., Analytical.
Anth., Anthropology.
Antiq , Antiquities.
Arach., Arachnida.
Arch., Archæology.
Ariz., Arizona.
Ark., Arkansas.
Ast., Astronomy.
Asst., Assistant.
Biol., Biology.
Bot., Botany.
Bryol., Bryology.
C., Collection.
Cal., California.
Carab., Carabidæ.
Carb., Carboniferous.
Ceramb., Cerambycidæ.
Chem., Chemistry.
Cicind., Cicindelidæ.
Cin., Cincinnati.
Colo., Colorado.
Coleopt., Coleoptera.
Coll., College.
Comp , Comparative.
Con., Conchology.
Conn., Connecticut.
Crypt., Cryptogamic.
Crystal., Crystallography.
Cur., Curator.
Cus., Custodian.
Dak., Dakota.
D. C., District of Columbia.
Del., Delaware.
Dept., Department.
Devon., Devonian.
Dipt., Diptera.
Dir., Director.
Dist., Distribution.
Econ., Economic.
Elect., Electricity.
Emb., Embryology.
Ent., Entomology.
Esp., Especially.
Eth., Ethnology.
Ethnog., Ethnography.
Ex., Exchange.
Fla., Florida.
Ga., Georgia.
Gen., General.
Geog., Geographical.
Geol., Geology.
Held., Helderberg.
Hemipt., Hemiptera.
Herpetol., Herpetology.
Histol., Histology.
Hort., Horticulture.
Hymenop., Hymenoptera.
Ia., Iowa.
Ichth., Ichthyology.
Ill , Illinois.
Ind., Indiana.
Invert., Invertebrates.
Inorg., Inorganic.
Inst., Institute.
Kan., Kansas.
Ky., Kentucky.
L., Lower
La., Louisiana.
L. & F. W., Land and Fresh Water.
Lepid., Lepidoptera.
Lithol., Lithology.
M., Marine.
Mam., Mammalogy.
Mass., Massachusetts.
Math., Mathematics.
Md., Maryland.
Me., Maine.
Med., Medical.
Meteo., Meteorology.
Met., Metallurgy.
Mic., Microscopy.
Mich., Michigan.
Min., Mineralogy.
Minn., Minnesota.
Miss., Mississippi.
Mo., Missouri.
Moll., Molluscs.
Mont., Montana.
Mus., Museum.
Nat. Hist., Natural History.
N. C., North Carolina.

Neb., Nebraska.
Neuropt., Neuroptera.
Nev., Nevada.
N. H., New Hampshire.
Niag., Niagara.
N. J., New Jersey.
N. M., New Mexico.
N. Y., New York.
O., Ohio.
Obs., Observatory.
Ool., Oology.
Ophthal. Ophthalmology.
Ore., Oregon.
Org., Organic.
Orn., Ornithology.
Orthopt., Orthoptera.
Osteol., Osteology.
Palæo., Palæontology.
Pathol., Pathological.
Penn., Pennsylvania.
Phæn., Phænogamic.
Philol., Philology.
Phil., Philosophy.
Photog., Photography.
Phys., Physics.
Piscol., Piscology.
Pres., President.
Prof., Professor.
R. I., Rhode Island.
S. C., South Carolina.
Sec., Secretary.
Sci., Science.
Sil., Silurian.
So., Southern.
Soc., Society.
Sp., Species.
Spec., Specimens or Specialty.
Strat., Stratigraphical.
Surv., Survey.
Syst., Systematic.
Tax., Taxidermy.
Tech., Technical, Technology.
Tenn., Tennessee.
Tex., Texas.
U., Upper.
Univ., University.
Va., Virginia.
Vasc., Vascular.
Veg., Vegetable.
Vert., Vertebrates.
Vt., Vermont.
Wis., Wisconsin.
Wash. Ter., Washington Territory.
W. T., Wyoming Territory.
W. Va., West Virginia.
Zool., Zoology.

THE

NATURALISTS' DIRECTORY.

UNITED STATES AND CANADA.

An asterisk (*) indicates that parties have been heard from since issue of last Directory. Names followed by a question mark (?) have not been heard from for three years and will be dropped from the next edition.

1 Aaron, Chas. E., A.M., 4118 Ogden St., W. Philadelphia, Pa. *Phæn. Bot., Ferns, Diurnal Lepid.**

2 Aaron, Eugene M., P. O. Box 916, Philadelphia, Pa. *Diurnal Lepid. Highest cash for Hesperidæ.* C. Ex.*

3 Abbe, Cleveland, Prof. and Assistant, Army Signal Office, Washington, D. C. *Meteorology; Terrestrial Physics; Astronomy; Atmospheric Electricity; Standard Time; Aeronautics; Solar Physics; Sky colors; Mathematical Physics; Bibliography of Meteorology.**

4 Abbe, Frank B., San Juan, San Benito Co., Calif. *Min., Lepid., Coleopt., Geol., Con.* C. Ex.*

5 Abbott, C. C., M.D., Trenton, N. J., or Peabody Mus., Cambridge, Mass. *N. A. Arch., Comp. Psychology, Local Zool.**

6 Abbott, Charles S., Antrim, N. H. C. Ex.?

7 Abbott, E. K., M.D., Salinas, Monterey Co., Calif. *Bot., Met.* C.*

8 Abbott, Helen C. De S., 1509 Locust St., Philadelphia, Pa. *Plant Chem.* C. Ex.*

9 Abbott, J. T., D.D.S., Manchester, Iowa. *Palæo.* C.*

10 Abbott, Wm. H., Waukegan, Ill. *Bot., Arch.*

11 Achert, E. E., Denver, Col. *Min.**

12 Acheson, Geo., M.A., M.B.P.S.O., cor. McCaul and College Sts., Toronto, Canada. *Chem., Gen. Biol., Pathology.**

13 Achilles, F. W., M.D., Evansville, Ind. *Chem.*?

14 Ackerill, Daniel, Belleville, Ont., Canada. *Mic.*

15 Ackerman, W. A., Marengo, Iowa. *Min., Zool., Arch., Orn., Ool., Ichth., Tax., Ent.* C. Ex.*

16 Acklin, Graff M., Toledo, Lucas Co., Ohio. *Geol., Min., Arch., Crustacea, Moll., Sponges.* C. Ex.*

17 Adams, Chas. F., A.M., A.B., Asst. Chem. Lab., Univ. of Mich., Ann Arbor, Mich.?

18 Adams, E. F., Middletown, N. Y. *Min., Arch., Ool., Ent., Moll.* C.*

19 Adams, Miss E. Isidore, Park St., Roxbury, Mass. *Bot.**

20 Adams, Edw. P., C.E., Box 444, Medford, Mass. *Geol.*, *Bot.*, especially in relation to landscape and sanitary engineering.*
21 Adams, Frank Dawson, Geol. Survey, Ottawa, Can. *Lith.*, *Inorg. Chem.* C.*
22 Adams, Fred., B.S., Elmore, Ill. *Arch.*, *Geol.* C. Ex. Indian relics, Mound Builders' relics and coal measure fossils for rare U. S. coins or fractional currency.*
23 Adams, J. M., Watertown, N. Y. *Mic*, *Fungi*, *Algæ*, *Desmids*, *Diatoms*, *Geol.*, *Min.*, *Chem.*, *Histol.*, *Path.*, *Urinalysis*, *Ent.*, *Worms*, *Infusoria*, *Bacteria*. C. Ex.*
24 Adams, Rev. Myron, 9 Washington St., Rochester, N. Y. *Mic.*, *Ent.*, *Photog.* ?
25 Adams, Capt. Robert C., Box 6, Montreal, P. Q. Phosphate and Mica Mines. *Geol.*, *Min.* C. Ex.*
26 Adams, W. H., Elmore, Peoria Co., Ill. *Arch.*, *Palæo.* Offers fossil fruits and other fossils of the Coal Measures, in ex. for Arch. Spec. Send for check list.*
27 Adel, E. E., Groveport, Franklin Co., Ohio. *Mic.*, *Photog.*, *Zool.* C. Ex.?
28 Adkins, Chapman, Wayne C. H., W. Va. *Med. and Gen. Sci.**
29 Agard, A. H., M.D., 1259 Alice St., Oakland, Cal. *Bot.*, *Palæo.*, *Geol.*, *Min.*, *Mic.*, *Ent.* C.*
30 Agassiz, Alexander, Museum of Comparative Zoology at Harvard College, Cambridge, Mass. *Zoology.**
31 Aiken, Charles E., Colorado Springs, Colo. *Orn.*, *Ool.*, *Mam.*, *Min.* C. Nat. Hist. Store.*
32 Aiken, W. E. A., M.D., LL.D., Emer. Prof. Chem., Univ. of Md., 110 East Baltimore St., Baltimore, Md. *Phæn. Bot.*, *Ferns*, *Chem.* C.*
33 Ainslie, Charles N., A.M., Rochester, Minn. *Mic.*, *Ent.*, *Arachnida.* C. Ex.*
34 Akhurst, John, 32 Nassau St., Brooklyn, N. Y. *Ent: Lepid.*, *Coleopt.*, *Tax.* C. Ex. and Dealer.*
35 Albrecht, Dr. Jos., 219 Elysianfield St., New Orleans, La. *Bot.: Ferns*, *Hort.*, *Geol.*, *Min.*, *Chem.*, *Metal.*, *Phys.*, *Elect.*, *Photog.*, *Anat.*, *Ent.**
36 Albrook, Rev. J. B., A.M., Ph.D., Waverly, Iowa. *Invert. Palæo.*, *Geol.*, *Min.* C. Ex. fossils of Maquoketa and Rockford Shales.*
37 Alden, John, Lawrence, Mass. *Chem.**
38 Alden, Levi, Madison, Wis. *Ast.**
39 Aldrich, Chas. W., Webster City, Hamilton Co., Iowa Interested in Bibliography, Autographs, MSS. C. Ex.*
40 Aldrich, John D., 41 College Ave., Indianapolis, Ind. *Con.*, *Lepid.* C. Ex. Desires correspondents in So. States and Foreign Countries.*
41 Aldrich, T. H., M.E., Southern Ave., Cincinnati, Ohio. *Moll.* Specialty, Tertiary fossils of N. A. Exchanges desired.*
42 Allan, Alex., Box 369, Pawtucket, R. I. *Chem.*, *Mic.*, *Ent.* C.*
43 Allard, Memminger, M.D., Prof. Chem. and Hygiene in State Medical Coll. of S. C., Address, 34 Broad St., Charleston, S. C. *Org. Chem.**

44 Allbee, Burton H., Perkinsville, Windsor Co., Vt. *Bot.*, *Gen. Geol.*, *Min.*, *Crystall.*, *Lithol.*, *Metall.*, *Elec.*, *Meteo.*, *Bibliog.*, *Tax*, *Ent.* C. Ex.*

45 Allbright, Leo H., Hutchinson, Kansas. *Palæo.*, *Min.*, *Vert.*, *Emb.*, *Arch.* C. Ex.*

46 Allen, Dr. Amos, Grafton, Rensselaer Co., N. Y. *Phæn. Bot. Ferns a specialty.**

47 Allen, A. T., 415 16th St., Denver, Colo. *Gen. Zool.*, *Coll. and Tax.**

48 Allen, C. A., Nicasio, Marin Co., Calif. *Orn.*, *Ool.*, *Tax.* C.*

49 Allen, Dr. Charles Slover, 21 East 28th St., N. Y. City. *Orn.*, *Ool.*, *Mic.*, *Photog.*, *Tax.* C. Ex.*

50 Allen, Chas. C., Orlando, Fla. C. Ex. Desires to collect for others in different branches of Nat. Hist.*

51 Allen, Prof. C. H., State Normal School, San José, Calif.

52 Allen, Frank H., Norwich, Conn. *Photo.*, *Mollusks*, *Radiates*, *Sponges.* C. Ex.*

53 Allen, Fred P., 30 Park Ave., Rochester, N. Y. *Mic.*

54 Allen, Prof. H. C., M.D., Ann Arbor, Mich. *Bot.*, *Experimental Drug Provings.* C. Ex.*

55 Allen, Harrison, M.D., 117 South 20th St., Philadelphia, Pa. *Mam.*, *Morph.*, *Anat.*, *Osteol.*, *Myol.**

56 Allen, J. A., Cur. Depts. Mam. and Orn., Am. Mus. of Nat. Hist., 77th St., and 8th Ave., New York, N. Y. *Mam.*, *Orn.**

57 Allen, James E., Omer, Arenac Co., Mich. *Ent.* C.*

58 Allen, Mrs. Juliette B., Camden, N. J. *Bot.*, *Min.**

59 Allen, Jno. K., Assoc. Ed. *The Sanitary News*, 217-225 Dearborn St., Chicago, Ill.*

60 Allen, J. M., President Hartford Steam Boiler Inspection and Insurance Co., Hartford, Ct. *Mic.*, *Mech. Engineering.**

61 Allen, Mary E., M.D. (late Prof. Physiol. and Hygiene, Vassar Coll., Poughkeepsie, N. Y.), 346 S. 16th St., Phila., Pa.

62 Allen, Prof. O. D., Yale University, New Haven, Ct. *Chem.*, *Phæn. Bot.*, *Musci.* C. Ex.

63 Allen, R. L., Providence, R. I. *Ast.* Manufacturer Ast. Telescopes.*

64 Allen, Richard, 62 No. Third St., Troy, N. Y. *Micros.?*

65 Allen, Richard H., P. O. Box 43, Chatham, N. J. *Orn.* C.*

66 Allen, Timothy F., M.D., 10 E. 36th St., New York, N. Y. *Bot.*, *Characeæ.**

67 Alling, Charles E., 45 Tremont St., Rochester, N. Y. *Mic.* C. Ex.*

68 Alling, Jas. Carey, Hasbrouck Inst., Jersey City, N. J.?

69 Allis, E. W., Adrian, Lenawee Co., Mich. *Ool.*, *Arch.*, *Econ. Ent.*, *Parasitism.**

70 Allis, James W., Rochester, N. Y. *Ent: Lepid.*, *Coleopt.* C.*

71 Allis, Solon M., C.E. *Geol.* C. Ex. Box 964, Malden, Mass.*

72 Allison, Chas. R., Ph.D. (Berlin), Oswego, N. Y. *Diatoms*, *Mic.*, *Arch.*, *Articulates.?*

73 Allison, J. F., Mount Carroll, Carroll Co., Ill. *Geol.*, *Prehistoric relics.* C.*

74 Allison, W. E., Oriskany, Oneida Co., N. Y. *Orn.**
75 Allmendinger, Miss E. C., Ann Arbor, Mich. *Bot.* C. Ex.*
76 Alvord, Major Henry E., Prof. Agric., Mass. Agric. Coll., Amherst, Mass. *Agric.**
77 Ames, Mary E. P., Auburn, Calif. *Bot.* C. Ex.*
78 Ami, Henry M., M.A., F.G.S., Asst. Paleont., Geol. Surv. of Can., Ottawa, Ont., Canada. *Palæo., Geol., Bot.* C.*
79 Ammon, W. Harring von, 523 Clay St., Bosqui Print. Co., San Francisco, Calif. *Ent.* C. Ex.*
80 Anderson, C. L., M.D., Santa Cruz, Calif. *Bot: Algæ.* C.*
81 Anderson, D. G., Keokuk, Ia. *Geol., Palæo.* C.*
82 Anderson, Edgar S., Richmond, Ind. *Photog.* C. Ex.?
83 Anderson, Mrs. E. J., Trenton, N. J. *Gen. Nat. Hist.* C. Ex.*
84 Anderson, Fred. W., Great Falls, Choteau Co., Montana. *Bot., Ichth., Arach., Lower Invert.**
85 Anderson, Rev. Joseph, D.D., Waterbury, Ct. *Am. Eth., Arch., Philology.* C. Ex. Desires Aboriginal Stone Implements, Pottery, etc.*
86 Anderson, Mrs. Louisa P., M.S., Prof. Bot. and Zool., Whitman College, Walla Walla, Wash. Ter. *Bot., Zool., Moll.* C. Ex.?
87 Anderson, Newton M., Prin. Cleveland Manual Training School, Cleveland, O. *Phys., Elect., Photog., Meteorol.**
88 Anderson, William P., Engineer of Marine Dept., Ottawa, Ont., Canada. *Geol.**
89 Anderzen, James A., P. O. Box 93, College Springs, Page Co. Iowa. *Ool.* Would like to exchange eggs and coins with collectors. C. Ex.*
90 Andras, J. C., Manchester, Scott Co., Ill. *Bot.* C. Ex. native plants of this locality.*
91 Andrews, D. M., Farina, Ill. *Palæo., Arch., Min.* C. Ex.*
92 Andrews, E., LL.D., M.D., Prof. Surg., Chic. Med. Coll., 6 Sixteenth St., Chicago, Ill. *Geol., Anth.**
93 Andrews, Ellen D., Southington, Ct. *Bot.* C. Ex.*
94 Andrews, Frank D., Vineland, N. J. *Geol., Min., Palæo., Arch.* C.*
95 Andrews, Mrs. Geo., Knoxville, Tenn. *L. and F. W. Shells.**
96 Andrews, Horace, jr., City Engineer and Surveyor, Albany, N. Y.*
97 Andrews, L., Southington, Hartford Co., Ct. *Geol., Min., Met., Palæo., Arch.* C. Ex. Spec. *Fucoid* upon the Triassic Sandstone.*
98 Andrews, Q. E., M.D., Moorhead, Minn. *Min., Cryst., Geol.* C. Ex.*
99 Andrews, Dr. R. R. 432 Harvard St., Cambridge, Mass. *Mic., Dental Histol.**
100 Andrews, T. L., M.D., Wichita, Sedgwick Co., Kansas. *Bot.* C. Ex.*
101 Andrews, T. P., Farina, Fayette Co., Ill. *Bot., Geol., Min., Mic.* C. Ex.*

102 Andriessen, Hugo, Beaver, Beaver Co., Pa. *Min., Chem., Pharm., Bot.* C. Ex. birds, plants, minerals, shells, rare drugs, etc. Desires herbarium and mineralogical spec. in ex.
103 Andros, F. W., 35 Cedar St., Taunton, Mass., Civil Engineer and Surveyor. *Orn., Ool.**
104 Andros, Chas. H., Box 54, Taunton, Mass. *Orn., Ool.* C. Ex.*
105 Andrus, D. A. K., 107 N. Church St., Rockford, Ill. *Arch., Min.* C. Ex. Correspondence solicited.*
106 Angell, George W. J., 44 Hudson St., New York City. *Coleopt. espec. Buprestidæ.* Will purchase desirable Coleopt. from U. S. and Canada. C. Ex. A fine collection of South American Coleoptera to exchange for Buprestidæ or native Coleoptera.*
107 Angus, J., West Farms, New York City, N. Y. *Indian relics, Lepid: Catocala and Sphingidæ* a specialty. C. Ex.*
108 Ansley, Clark F., Swedona, Mercer Co., Ill. *Palæo., Geol., Min., Arch.* C. Ex.*
109 Anthony, Arthur C., 285 Marlboro St., Boston, Mass. *Ent: Coleopt.**
110 Anthony, Mrs. Emilia C., Gouverneur, St. Lawrence Co., N. Y. *Bot.**
111 Anthony, William A., Prof. of Physics, Cornell Univ., Ithaca N. Y. *Elect.**
112 Apgar, Austin C., State Normal Sch., Trenton, N. J. *Zool.* C.*
113 Apgar, Ellis A., Trenton, N. J. *Bot., Orn., Mic.* C.
114 Appleton, Francis H., A.M., Peabody, Mass. *Agric.*
115 Appleton, John Howard, Prof. Chem., Brown Univ., Providence, R. I.*
116 Appleton, John S., West Newbury, Mass. *Ool.* C. Ex.*
117 Archbold, George, Ph.D., M.D., F.C.S., Chem. Laboratory, Phœnix, Oswego Co., N. Y. *Org. Chem., Phys., Elect., Mic.* C. Germ Theory of disease a specialty. Correspondence solicited.*
118 Arms, J. M., East Cambridge, Mass. *Geol., Zool.**
119 Armstrong, J. E., Englewood, Ill. *Gen. Biol., Tax., Osteol., Chem.**
120 Armstrong, Dr. J. T., Beatrice, Neb. *Crypt. Bot., Mic., Gen. Biol., Anat., Protozoa, Infusoria.**
121 Arnold, Benj. W., jr., 11 Tenbrœck St., Albany, N. Y. *Orn., Min., Lepid., Ool.**
122 Arnold, Craig R., Sharon Hill, Pa. *Orn., Ool., Tax., Elect.* C. Ex.*
123 Arnold, Delos, Pasadena, Cal. *Min., Fossils, Palæo., Geol., Ferns, Lithol., Arch., Ethnol.* C. Ex.*
124 Arnold, James E., Elmira, N. Y. *Tax., Orn., Ool., Bot.* C. Ex. botany, skins and eggs.*
125 Arnold, J. M., 376 Washington St., Boston, Mass. *Math.**
126 Arthur, J. C., N. Y. Agric. Expr. Station, Geneva, N. Y. *Bot.* C.*

127 Aschman, T., Ph. B., Analyt. Chem., Sharon, Mercer Co., Pa. *Chem., Phœn. Bot., Mic., Tax.* C. Ex. Correspondence in English, French and German. South American, Asiatic, and herbarium specimens particularly desired.*

128 Ash, Thos. S., 2052 Rush St., Phila., Pa. *Min., Crystall., Inorg. Chem.* Correspondence solicited. C. Ex.*

129 Ashburner, Charles A., C. E., M. S., Geologist in charge Geol. Survey of Pa., and Ass't in charge coal statistics, U. S. Geol. Survey, Pittsburgh, Pa. *Mining, Geol., Min., Phys.**

130 Ashburner, William, 1014 Pine St., San Francisco, Calif. *Mic., Mining Eng.**

131 Ashby, Geo. E., 108 Maiden Lane, New York City. *Mic. objects.**

132 Ashe, W. A., F.R.A.S., R.N., Dir. Quebec Observ., Quebec, Can. *Meteo., Ast.*

133 Ashman, Geo., 11 E. Liberty St., Cincinnati, Ohio. *Palæo., Lamellibranchiata, Brachiopods.* C. Ex.?

134 Ashmead, William H., Jacksonville, Fla. *Hemiptera and Hymenopt.* C.*

135 Ashton, Miss Margaret, Tonganoxie, Leavenworth Co., Kan. *Lepid: Butterflies and Sphingidæ.* C. Ex.

136 Ashton, T. B., Tonganoxie, Leavenworth Co., Kan. *Ent: Coleopt.* C.*

137 Asire, Merwin E., Marquette, Mich. *Orn., Ent: Coleopt., Lepid.* C.*

138 Asquith, A. W., 77 Lexington Ave., Brooklyn, N. Y. *Coleopt.**

139 Atkins, Charles G., Bucksport, Me. *Hort., Ichth.**

140 Atkins, Dr. H. A., Locke, Ingham Co., Mich. *Orn.* C. ?

141 Atkinson. Archer, M.D., 311 N. Charles St., Baltimore, Md. *Chem., Mic., Zool., Anat.* C. Ex.*

142 Atkinson, Geo. F., Prof. Ent. and Gen. Zool., Univ. of N. C., Chapel Hill, N. C. *Fungi, Econ. and Biol. Ent., Orn.*, C. Ex. for Carolina Butterflies and Birds.*

143 Attwater, Henry P., Chatham, Ontario, Canada. *Arch., Mam., Orn., Ool., Herpetol., Ichth., Tax., Indian relics and Curiosities.* C. Ex.*

144 Atwater, Richard M., A. M., Millville, Cumberland Co., N. J. *Inorg. Chem., Glass, Mic.*

145 Atwater, W. O., Prof. Chem., Wesleyan Univ., Middletown, Ct. *Chem.**

146 Atwell, Charles B., Ph.M., Evanston, Ill. *Bot., Phys.**

147 Atwood, Carl C., Albion, Dane Co., Wis. *Orn., Ool.* C. Ex. ?

148 Atwood, Charles, M.D., Moravia, Cayuga Co., N. Y. *Phœn. Bot., Ferns, Mosses.* C. Ex.

149 Atwood, E. S., East Orange, Essex Co., N. J. *Mic.* ?

150 Atwood, H. F., F.R.M.S., Rochester, N. Y. *Mic., Infusoria, Parasites.**

151 Atwood, W. P., S.B., 81 Appleton St., Lowell, Mass. *Bot., Chem.* C.*

152 Austen, Peter Townsend, Ph.D., F.C.S., Prof. Gen. and Applied Chem., Rutgers Coll. (the N. J. State Scientific School), New Brunswick, N. J. *Chem.**

153 **Austin, A. C., 818 Jefferson St., Kansas City, Mo.** *Geol., Min., Crystall.* C. Ex.*
154 **Austin, E. P., Assayer, 70 Vine St., Salt Lake City, Utah.** *Ent: Coleoptera.* C.*
155 **Austin, Laura A., Salina, Salina Co., Kan.** *Palæo., Min., Crystall.* C. Ex.
156 **Auxer, Samuel, 150 S. Prince St., Lancaster, Pa.** *Ent: Lepid., Coleopt.* C. Ex. only in Coleopt.*
157 **Averell, Wm. D., Chestnut Hill, Philadelphia, Pa.** *Mic., Moll., spec. Cypræidæ, Unionidæ and Helicidæ.* Desires foreign correspondents. Will buy named collections of shells and conchological works. Editor and Publisher of "Conchologists' Exchange."*
158 **Averill, Charles K., jr., Bridgeport, Ct.** *Orn., Ool., Bot.* C.*
159 **Avery, Chas., Ridgeway, Welland Co., Ont., Canada.** *Ent: Lepid., Coleopt.* C. Ex.
160 **Avery, George R., Locke, Mich.** *Bot.* C. Ex.*
161 **Avery, Gerritt S., 11 Nonotuck St., Holyoke, Mass.** *Ent., Fungi, Min., Mic., Geol., Chem., Elect.* C. Ex.*
162 **Avery, W. Cushman, M.D., Greensboro', Hale Co., Alabama.** *Phæn. Bot., Orn., Ool., Tax.* C. Ex.*
163 **Ayres, Brown, Prof. Phys., Tulane Univ., New Orleans, La.** *Phys., Elect., Photog., Ast.**
164 **Ayres, S. G., Moriah, N. Y.** *Geol., Min.* C. Ex.
165 **Ayres, Rev. William W., Wickford, R. I.** *Bot.* C. Ex.?
166 **Babbitt, Frane E., Box 75, Little Falls, Morrison Co., Minn.** *Bibliog., Anth., Arch., Ethnol., Ethnog., Philol.* C. Ex.?
167 **Babcock, A. L. Sherborn, Mass.** *Orn., Ent.* C. Ex.*
168 **Babcock, H. P., General Bird Store, 23 7th St., New Bedford, Mass.** *Orn., Mam., Gen. Zool., Tax.* C. Ex.*
169 **Babcock, James F., State Assayer for Mass., 1151 Washington St., Boston, Mass.** *Chem., Mic., Photog., Bibliog.**
170 **Babcock, S. E., M.D., Chester, S. C.** Collects relics of Catawba Indians.
171 **Babcock, S. Moulton, Chem., N. Y. Agr'l Exp. Station, Geneva, N. Y.***
172 **Bacon, Chas. A., Dir. Smith Observatory, Beloit, Wis.** *Meteo., Ast.*
173 **Baetz, Wm., 96 Fulton St., Room 11 New York, N. Y.** *Chem., Phys. and Elect. Glass apparatus* *
174 **Bagg, Egbert, jr., 187 Genesee St., Utica N.Y.** *Orn., Ool.* C. Ex.
175 **Bagg, Mrs. Helen M., Locust Grove, Lewis Co., N. Y.** *Bot: Phæn. and Crypt., Plants, Ferns, Hort.* C.*
176 **Bagley, John A., C.E., 45 East 28th St., New York, N. Y.** *Mic., Diatoms.**
177 **Bailey, Albert, Chepatchet, Herkimer Co., N. Y.** *Con.* C. Ex. Offers L. and F. W. shells of N. Y. Desires L., F. W. and Marine shells of other localities. List of duplicates sent on application.*
178 **Bailey, E. H. S., Prof. State Univ., Lawrence, Kan.** *Chem., Min.* Ex.*

179 Bailey, George Irving, 95 Eagle St., Albany, N. Y. *Lepid.**
180 Bailey, L. H., jr., Agric. College, Mich. *Bot.* C. Exchanges and notes on Carex esp. desired, also botanical and live specimens of native fruits.
181 Bailey, L. W., Prof. Chem. and Nat. Hist., Univ. of New Brunswick, Fredericton, N. B., Canada. *Geol.* C. Ex.*
182 Bailey, Dr. Theodore P., 95 Eagle St., Albany, New York. *Ent: Lepid.* C. Ex.*
183 Bailey, Wm. Whitman, Prof. Botany, Brown Univ., Providence, R. I. *Gen. Bot.**
184 Bailly, J. F. D., 348 Alexander St., Rochester, N. Y. *Nat. Hist.* Preparator of Osteol *Geol., Osteol., Con., Bot.* C.?
185 Baily, Alfred W., M.D., Box 712, Atlantic City, N. J. *Min., Arch., Pathological Microscopy, Bot., Morbid Anat., Osteol., Con.* C. Ex. in Con. for Con., Min., Osteol.*
186 Baily, Wm. L., S.B., 1624 Arch St., Philadelphia, Pa. *Orn., Ool.* C. Ex.*
187 Bair, Robert C., York Furnace, York Co., Pa. *Min., Arch., Histol.* C.*
188 Baird, Prof. John F., A.M., Hanover, Jeff. Co., Ind. *Phæn. Bot., Ferns.* C. Ex.?
189 Baird, J. W., M.A., Ph.C., Prof. Anal. Chem., Mass. Coll. Pharmacy, Boston, Mass.*
190 Baird, William R., M.E., Memb. Soc. Min. de France, 243 Broadway, New York, N. Y. *Min.* C. Ex. Offers American minerals, especially N. J. zinc ores and minerals. Desires only good specimens, foreign preferred. No fossils wanted.*
191 Baker, A. B., Banner, Trego Co., Kan. *Vert. Palæo., Mam.* Cretaceous reptiles, fishes, skins, skeletons and skulls of prairie mammals for ex.*
192 Baker, A. L., Scranton, Pa. *Mic., Nat. Hist.* C.*
193 Baker, B. N., Baltimore, Md. *Min., Chem.* C. Ex.
194 Baker, Frank, M.D., Prof. Anat., Univ. of Georgetown, 1315 Corcoran St., N. W., Washington, D. C. *Gen. Biol., Morph., Emb., Anat. and Histol. of Vert.**
195 Baker, Henry B., M.D., Lansing, Mich. *Gen. Biol., Micros., Meteo., Sanitary Sci.**
196 Baker, Ira O., Prof. C. E., Ills. Univ., Champaign, Ill. *Phys., Ast.?*
197 Baker, L. H., Bridgeport, Ct. *Phæn. Bot.**
198 Baker, Marcus, M.A., Geographer, U. S. Geol. Survey, Washington, D. C.
199 Baker, P.S., A.M., M.D., Greencastle, Ind. *Min., Lithol., Chem.*
200 Baker, Thos. R., Ph.D., Orlando, Fla. *Min., Chem., Phys.**
201 Baker, W. Fred., Savannah, Ga. *Orn., Ool.* C. Ex.*
202 Baker, W. H., M.D. 1610 Summer St., Philadelphia, Pa. *Mic., Histol.* C. Ex.*
203 Balch, Wm E., Lunenburg, Essex Co., Vt. *Mam., Orn., Ool., Tax.* C. Ex. Sample orders in tax. solicited.*
204 Baldwin, Evelyn B., Oswego, Kansas. *Geol., Min., Arch., Eth.* C. Ex.*

205 Baldwin, David, Midland Park, Bergen Co., N. J.
206 Baldwin, von Herff, Ph.D., Chemist in Agric. Expr. Station. Raleigh, N. C. *Geol.*, *Min.*, *Chem.**
207 Baldwin, H. B., Analytical and Consulting Chemist, 215 Market St., Newark, N. J. *Chem.*, *Mic.*, *Biol.*, *Photog.* C. Ex.*
208 Baldwin, H. L., C.E., 1280 Logan St., Denver, Colo. *Elect.*, *Ast.*, *Geol.* Topographer on Geol. Survey, Washington, D. C.*
209 Baldy, Stephen, So. Bethlehem, Northampton Co., Pa. *Ent: Lepid.* C. Ex.*
210 Ball, Rev. E. H., Tangier, N. S, Can. *Phæn. Bot.*, *Ferns of N. S.* C.*
211 Ball, Joseph P., 4533 Frankford Ave., Frankford, Phila., Pa. *Gen. Nat. Science.* C. Ex. in Geol., Invertebrate Zool.*
212 Ballard, H. H., A.M., Pres. of Agassiz Assoc., Pittsfield, Mass.*
213 Ballard, Mrs. Julia P., Easton, Pa. *Ent: Lepid.* C. Ex.*
214 Ballard, W. A., Richburg, N. Y. Histological slides exchanged for mounting materials or *vice versa.*
215 Balliet, L. D., M.D., Du Bois, Clearfield Co., Pa. *Prac. Tax.**
216 Ballou, Willard E., 13 Merrick St., Worcester, Mass. *Orn.*, *Mam.*, *Tax.* C. Ex.*
217 Bangs, C. B. Fisk, North Lansing, Mich. *Hort.*, *Hymenoptera.**
218 Bannister, H. M., M.D., Kankakee, Ill. *Palæo.*, *Geol.*, *Gen. Biol.*
219 Bannister, Marshal J., Willimansett, Mass. *Ent.*, *Tax.* Ex.*
220 Barbeck, Wm., San Antonio, Texas. *Crypt. Bot.*, *Mic.**
221 Barber, Edwin A., A.M., 522 Walnut St., Philadelphia, Pa. *Arch.*, *Eth.**
222 Barber, S. W., 404 Market St., St. Louis, Mo.*
223 Barbour, Fred F., 14 Cottage St., Cambridgeport, Mass. *Elect.*, *Coleopt.* C. Ex.*
224 Barbour, Prof. O. F., Rockford, Ill. *Geol.**
225 Barclay, Alex., St. Paul, Minn. *Mic.*, *Diatoms.* C. Ex.*
226 Barclay, Robert, A.M., M.D., 12 W. 35th St., New York City. *Chem.*, *Biol.*, *Emb.*, *Anat.*, *Anth.*, *Histol.*
227 Barlow, Joseph C., Cadet, Washington Co., Mo. *Bot.*, *Hort.*, *Geol.*, *Elect.*, *Mic.*, *Meteo.*, *Ast.*, *Ent: Coleopt.*, *Gen. Zool.* C.?
228 Barnard, Arthur F., Student, P. O. Box 152, Oberlin, Ohio. *Desmids*, *Diatoms*, *Lithol.*, *Mic.*, *Histol.*, *Zool.* (Minute forms of animal life). C. Ex.*
229 Barnard, Edw. E., Vanderbilt University Observ., Nashville, Tenn. *Ast.*, *Phys.*, *Photog.**
230 Barnard, F. A. P., D.D., LL.D., D.C.L., Pres. Columbia Coll., New York, N. Y. *Math.*, *Phys.*, *Mic.*, *Micro.*, *Biol.**
231 Barnard, M. P., Kennett Square, Pa. *Orn.*, *Ool.*, *Tax.* C.*
232 Barnard, Prof. W. S., B.S., Ph.D., Canton, Ill., and University Place, Des Moines, Iowa. *Fungi*, *Org. Chem.*, *Mic.*, *Zool.*, *Vert. and Invert. Emb.*, *Anat.*, *Morph.*, *Ent.* C. Ex.*
233 Barnes, A. E., Topeka, Kan. *Geol.*, *Min.*, *Crystall.*, *Chem.*, *Met.* C. Ex.?
234 Barnes, Chas. E., Battle Creek, Mich. *Arch.*, *Geol.*, *Mound Builders.* C. Ex.*

235 Barnes, Chas. J., 263 Wabash Ave., Chicago, Ill. *Bibliog.*, *Early Am. Hist.*, *early printing, rare books et al, Gen. Biol.*, *Arch.* C.*
236 Barnes, C. R., Prof. Bot., Univ. of Wisconsin, Editor Botanical Gazette, Madison, Wis. *Bot.*, *Mosses.* C.*
237 Barnes, Ella L., 1961 Madison Ave., New York, N. Y. *Phæn. Bot.*, *Invert. Palæo.* C. Ex.*
238 Barnes, George William, M.D., San Diego, Calif. *Geol.*, *Meteo.**
239 Barnes, J. W., Plattsmouth, Cass Co , Neb. *Geol.*, *Min.*, *Crystall.*, *Meteo.* C. Ex.?
240 Barnes, R. M., Attorney-at-law Lacon, Ills. *Orn.*, *Ool.* C. Ex.*
241 Barnes, Wm., S.B., Decatur, Ill. *Emb.*, *Lepid.* C.
242 Barnett, J. Davis, Port Hope, Ont., Canada. *Inorg. Chem.*, *Metal.*, *Phys.*, *Elect.*, *Bibliog.**
243 Barns, Dr. John, Milford, Mass. *Mic.*
244 Barnum, Eugene E., A.M., M.D., Waterport, Orleans Co., N. Y. *Bot.*, *Min.*, *Mic.*, *Histol.* C.?
245 Barnum, Morgan K., 94 E. Jefferson St., Syracuse, N. Y. *Orn.*, *Ool.*, *Tax.* C. Ex.?
246 Barnwell, James G., A.M., Librarian, Ridgway Branch, Phila. Library, Broad and Christian Sts., Phila., Pa. *Bibliog.**
247 Baron, Oscar F., C.E , Alameda, Alameda Co., Calif. *Orn.* (*Trochilidæ*), *Lepid.*, *Coleopt.* C.*
248 Barrell, H. F., New Providence, N. J. *Min.*, *Photog.*, *Orn.*, *Ool.*, *Ent.* C. Ex.*
249 Barrett, Jno. B., jr., Henderson, Ky. *Woods, Mins. and Eggs* to ex. for eggs.*
250 Barrett, S. T., Port Jervis, N. Y. *Geol.*, *Palæo.*
251 Barrett, Wm. C., M.D., 208 Franklin St., Buffalo, N. Y. *Mic.*, *Histol.*, *Experimental Physiol.**
252 Barris, Rev. W. H., Prof. Griswold Coll., Davenport, Ia. *Geol.*, *Palæo.*
253 Barrow, James M., Columbus, Miss. *Bot.*, *Mic.**
254 Barrows, Walter B., S.B., U. S. Dept. Agric., Washington, D. C. *Zool.*, *Bot.* C.*
255 Barry, W. C., Nurseryman, Rochester, N. Y. *Bot.**
256 Bartholomew, Rev. E. F., A.M., Pres. and Prof. Mental and Moral Sci., Carthage Coll., Carthage, Ill.*
257 Bartholomew, Robert, 1521 Poplar St., Philadelphia, Pa. *Lepid.* C. ?
258 Bartlett, Rev. E. N., 221 North Webber St., Colorado Springs, Colo. *Min.*, *Fossils.* Coll. for sale. Correspondence desired. Ex.
259 Bartlett, Edward P., La Moille, Bureau Co., Ill. *Min.*, *Lepid.*, *Coleopt*, *Woods.* C. Ex.*
260 Bartlett, Edwin J., M.D., Prof. of Chem., Dartmouth College, Hanover, N. H.*
261 Bartlett, Frank L., Portland, Me. *Stratigraphical and Physical Geol.*, *Min.*, *Crystall.*, *Lithol.*, *Org. and Inorg. Chem.*, *Met.*, *Phys.*, *Elect.*, *Mic.*, *Photog.**

262 Bartley, Elias Hudson, B.S., M.D., Prof. of Chem. and Toxicology, L. I. College Hospital, Chief Chemist to Health Dept., City of Brooklyn, N. Y. Chem. N. Y. State Dairy Comm., and Pres. Am. Soc. Pub. Analysts. *Medicine. Chem. Elect., Mic., Sanitary Science.**

263 Bartol, William C., A.M., Prof. Math. and Ast., Bucknell Univ., Lewisburg, Pa.*

264 Barton, Bolling W., M.D., 2008 Maryland Ave., Baltimore, Md. *Bot.* C. Ex.*

265 Barton, George H., Mass. Inst. Technol., Boston, Mass. *Geol., Min.* C. Ex.*

266 Barus, Carl, Ph.D., Physicist, U. S. Geol. Survey, Washington, D. C. *Physical and Inorg. Chem., Met., Phys., Elect.**

267 Bass, W. L., Randolph, Fremont Co., Iowa. *Arch.* C. Ex. ?

268 Bassett, Frank L., Little Silver, N. J. *Bot. esp. of N. J. plants.* C.*

269 Bassett, Homer F., Waterbury, Ct. *Ent: Hymenop., Gall insects and their parasites.* C. Ex.*

270 Bassett, Norman C., B. Sc., Prof. Mech. Engin. Iowa Coll. of Agric. and Mechanic Arts, Ames, Iowa. *Mechan. Engineering.**

271 Bassett, Wm. F., Hammonton, N. J. *Bot.* C.*

272 Bassett, Wilson T., M.D., Cooperstown, N. Y. *Chem., Elect., Mic., Anat.* ?

273 Bassler, Thomas, Geuda Springs, Kan. *Bot., Coleopt.* C. Ex.*

274 Bastin, E. S., Prof. Bot., Chicago College of Pharmacy, Chicago, Ill. *Crypt. Bot., Veg. Phys.**

275 Batchelder, C. F., Cambridge, Mass. *Orn.* C. Ex.*

276 Bates, Frank A., with F. B. Webster, Naturalists' Supply Dépot, 409 Washington St., Boston, Mass., So. Braintree, Mass. *Gen. Nat. Hist., Pictography, Ool., Ent., Arch.* C. Curiosities. Wishes Sphingidæ of the world.*

277 Bates, George A., Salem, Mass. *Marine Invertebrates; Hydroid medusæ.* Desires spec. of Hydroids from all parts of the world, for which will ex. mic. preparations.

278 Bates, J. Elwyn, Hawkinsville, Orange Co., Fla. *Lepid.* C.?

279 Bates, H. Wm., M.D., F.R.M.S., 175 Remsen St., Brooklyn, N. Y. *Gen. Biol., Histol. of Vert., Infusoria.* C. Ex.*

280 Battershall, Fletcher W., Cornell Univ., Ithaca, N. Y. *Bot., Elect.* C.

281 Battey, T. J., Friends School, Providence, R. I. *Bot., Min.* C. Ex.*

282 Battle, H. B., Ph.D., Chemist, Agric. Exper. Station, Raleigh, N. C. *Chem., Min., Met.**

283 Batty, Joseph H., Parkville, Kings Co., N. Y. *Tax., Orn., Ool., Zool.* C. Ex. ?

284 Baur, Dr. G., Yale College, Asst. in Osteol. Museum, New Haven, Ct. *Morphology and Morphogeny of vertebrates (skeletons).* C.*

285 Bausch, Edw., Bausch and Lomb Opt. Co., Rochester, N. Y. *Mic.**

286 Bausch, J. J., B. and Lomb Opt. Co., Rochester, N. Y. *Mic.**
287 Baxter, Edward K., M.D., Sharon, Windsor Co., Vt. *Bot., Min., Mic., Orn., Diatoms.* C.*
288 Baxter, Florus R., care of Vacuum Oil Co., Rochester, N. Y. *Ent.* C.*
289 Baxter, R. T., Glens Falls, Warren Co., N. Y. *Min., Crystall.* C. Ex.*
290 Baylor, W. L., M.D., Petersburg, Va. *Bot., Chem., Phys.?*
291 Beach, Horace, Prairie du Chien, Wis. *General. Nat. Hist.* C. Ex.
292 Beach, William H., Madison, Wis. *Palæo., Mic., Geol.* C.*
293 Beachel, L. A., Antiquarian, Box 338, Kenosha, Wis. *Min.* C. Ex.*
294 Beadle, D. W., St. Catharine's, Ont., Can. *Ent.**
295 Beadle, Rev. H. H., Bridgeton, N. J. *Min., Con., Arch.* C. Ex.*
296 Beal, William J., M.S., Ph.D., Prof. of Bot. and Forestry. Post Office, Agric. Coll., Mich. *Phæn. Bot., Mic., Grasses.**
297 Bean, Tarleton H., M.D., M.S., Curator, Dept. of Fishes, U. S. Nat. Mus., Asst. U. S. Fish Comm., Smithsonian Inst., Washington, D. C. *Ichth; Alaskan, Arctic and deep sea fishes.**
298 Bean, Thomas E., Galena, Ill. *Lepid.**
299 Bean, Wm. H., Lebanon, Warren Co., Ohio. *Hort., Invert., Min., Arch., Moll.* C. Have L. S. fossils and local L. and F. W. shells for ex.
300 Bearce, Gideon, West Minot, Me. *Min.* C. Ex.*
301 Beard, John, Attica, Ohio. *Gen. Nat. Sci.* C. in *Geol., Palæo., Recent and Fossil Ent., Algæ, Con., Min.*, etc., etc. Ex.*
302 Beard, Richard O., M.D., 1221 Nicollet Ave., Minneapolis, Minn. *Palæo., Elect., Mic., Zool., Gen. Biol., Emb. Anat., Anth., Vert., Mammals, Osteol., Histol.**
303 Beardsley, Prof. Arthur, C.E., Swarthmore College, Del. Co., Pa. *Civil and Mechanical Eng.**
304 Beath, James W., Lapidist, 111 So. 10th St., Philadelphia, Pa. *Min.?*
305 Beatty, Chas., N. W. T. Co.'s office, Sarnia, Ontario, Canada. *Orn., Ool., Tax.* C. Ex.*
306 Beatty, Prof. James, Haverford College, Montgomery Co., Pa. *Strat. Geol., Min., Inorg. Chem., Metall.*
307 Beauchamp, Miss Virginia, Baldwinsville, N. Y. *Ferns, Algæ,* C. Ex.
308 Beauchamp, Rev. W. M., S.T.D., Baldwinsville, N. Y. *Arch., Con., Bot.* C. Ex. in Con.*
309 Beaudry, J. A. M., Civil Eng., 112 St. Frs. Xavier St., Montreal, Can. *Geol., Min., Org. Chem., Ent.* C. Ex.*
310 Beaver, Daniel, B.D., M.D., 150 North 6th St., Reading, Pa. *Phæn. Bot., Ferns.* C. Ex.*
311 Bebb, M. S., 926 Grant Ave., Rockford, Ill. *Bot: Salices.* C.*
312 Bechdolt, Adolf F., Supt. City Schools, Mankato, Minn. *Phæn. Bot., Palæo., Geol., Phys., Philol.**
313 Beckett, W. W., San Luis Obispo, Calif. *Palæo., Min.* C. Ex.

314 **Beckham, Charles Wickliffe, Bardstown, Nelson Co., Ky.** *Orn.* C. Ex.*

315 **Beckwith, Edwin F., M.D., Muir, Ionia Co., Mich.** *Mic., Histol.* C.*

316 **Beckwith, H. C., P.A., Eng'r U. S. Navy, Chesterfield, New London Co., Ct.** *Geol.* C.?

317 **Beckwith, Will, Danville, Vermilion Co., Ill.** *Arch.* C. Ex.*

318 **Beckford, P. W., Ed. Pharmaceutical Record, 5 Beekman St., P. O. Box 1807, Prof. Pharmacy, New York, N. Y.** *Mic., Inorg. Chem.*

319 **Beebe, William, Tutor, Yale College, 83 Wall St., New Haven, Ct.** *Math., Ast.?*

320 **Beebe, William S., Maj. U. S. Army, Thompson, Ct.** *Anth., Arch.**

321 **Beecher, Charles E., in charge dept. of** *Invert. Palæo.* **Yale College Museum, New Haven, Ct** *

322 **Beekman, W. S., Ph.C., Box 108, West Medford, Mass.** *Min.* Will exchange fine crystallized minerals and cut gems, such as moonstones, India; opals, Mexico; ruby spinels, Ceylon; and others; for fine minerals. Send for lists.*

323 **Beeman, Dr. T. W., Perth, Ont., Can.** *Arch., Orn., Tax., Ent.* C Ex.*

324 **Behr, Hermann H., M.D., Prof. California Acad. of Sci., San Francisco, Calif.** *Ent., Bot.**

325 **Behrens, James, 1812 Stockton St., San Francisco, Calif.** *Coleopt., Lepid., Gen. Ent.**

326 **Bel, Alphonse, Prof. Middletown, Ct.** *Algæ, Biol., Coleopt., Lepid.* Native and foreign coll. Ex. buys and sells.*

327 **Bel, Mrs. Alphonse, Middletown, Ct.** *Lepid.* C. Ex.*

328 **Bell, Alex. Graham, Scott Circle, Washington, D. C.***

329 **Bell, Clara, Chicopee, Mass.** *Bot., Ferns.* C. Ex.?

330 **Bell, Rev. Geo., B.A., LL.D., Queen's College, Kingston, Ont., Can.** *Arch., Anth., Psychol., Geol.**

331 **Bell, James T., Sc.D., Prof. Mining and Agric., Albert Univ., Box 104, Belleville, Ont., Can.** *Geol., Zool., Palæo.**

332 **Bell, Prof. Robert, B.A., Sc., LL.D., M.D., Senior Asst. Director Geol. Surv. of Can., Ottawa, Can.** *Geol., Zool., Am. Arch.**

333 **Bell, Sam'l N., Manchester, N. H.** *Bot., Geol., Meteor.**

334 **Bell, W. T. R., jr., Kings Mountain, Cleveland Co., N. C.** *Geol., Min., Crystall., Chem.* Will ex. crystals of tin. C.?

335 **Bellamy, Wm., Mt. Bowdoin, Dorchester, Mass.** *Ast.*

336 **Bement, Clarence S., 1804 Spring Garden St., Philadelphia, Pa.** *Min.* C.*

337 **Bendire, Charles E., Capt. U. S. A., Fort Custer, Montana, or care Nat. Museum, Washington, D. C.** *Mam., Fossils, Fishes, Reptiles, Orn., Ool.*

338 **Benedict, A. L., 35 Rowley St., Rochester, N. Y.** *Strat. Geol., Arch., Osteol.* C. Ex.?

339 **Benedict, N. W., D.D., 47 So. Clinton St., Rochester, N. Y.** *Mic.**

340 Benjamin, Edm. B., Fellow Geog. Soc.; 6 Barclay St., New York City. *Chem.*, *Phys.*, *Elect.**
341 Benjamin, Marcus, Ph.B., F.C.S., 48 E. 67th Street, New York, N. Y. *Chem.*, *Min.* C.*
342 Benner, Franklin, Minneapolis, Minn. *Orn.*, *Ool.* C.*
343 Benners, Geo. B., 2048 Arch St., Philadelphia, Pa. *Orn.*, *Ool.* C. Ex. rare Texan eggs for those of other localities.
344 Bennet, Frank A., Morrisville, N. Y. *Gen. Nat. Hist.* C.*
345 Bennett, A. A., Prof. Chem., Ames Coll., Ames, Iowa.*
346 Bennett, Arthur F., Keene, N. H. *Mosses*, *Orn.* C. Ex.*
347 Bennett, J. B., Salinas, Monterey Co., Calif. *Min.*, *Crust.*, *Moll.*, *Radiates.* C. Ex.*
348 Bennett, Mrs. J. B., Salinas, Monterey Co., Calif. *Bot.*, *Chem.*, *Lepid.* C. Ex.*
349 Bennett, James L., Providence, R. I. *Bot: Filices.* Ex.?
350 Bennett, Wm. Z., Ph.D., Prof. Univ., Wooster, Wayne Co., O. *Phys.*, *Chem.* C.*
351 Benson, R. F., M.D., 108 Second St., Troy, N. Y.*
352 Bent, Arthur C., Taunton, Mass. *Orn.*, *Ool.*, *Tax.* C. Ex. *
353 Bereman, T. A., Mount Pleasant, Henry Co., Iowa. *Geol.*, *Meteor.*, *Arch.* C. Ex.?
354 Berendsohn, Theo., 86 Fulton St., New York, N. Y. Dealer in Books on Nat. Hist.*
355 Bergen, Mrs. Fanny, Peabody, Mass. *Bot.*, *Mic.* C. Ex.*
356 Bergen, J. Y., jr., Peabody, Mass. *Chem.*, *Min.*, *Geol.*, C. Ex.*
357 Berger, Martin Luther, D D., Prof. of Nat. and Mental Sci., Straight Univ., New Orleans, La. 1380 Euclid Ave., Cleveland, Ohio. *Min.*, *Meteo.*, *Ast.*, *Ent.*, *Moll.* C. Ex.*
358 Berlug, J. Edw., C.E., Decatur, Ill. *Min.*, *Mic.* C.*
359 Beringer, Geo. M., 932 So. 3rd St., Camden, N. J. *Bot.*, *Chem.* C. Ex.*
360 Berlin, A. F., Allentown, Pa. *Arch.* C. Ex.*
361 Berliner, E., Columbia Road, betw. 14th and 15th Sts., Washington, D. C. *Phys.**
362 Bernays, Augustus C., A.M., M.D., M.R.C.S., Eng., F.R.M.S., Lond., Prof. Anat., College of Phys. and Surg., 903 Olive St., St. Louis, Mo. *Mic.*, *Zool*, *Morph.*, *Emb.*, *Vert. Anat.*, *Herpet.*, *Ichth.*, *Osteol.*, *Histol.* C. Ex.*
363 Berry, Henry N., Surveyor, Box 649, Iowa City, Johnson Co., Iowa. *Bot.*, *Min.*, *Orn.*, *Ool.*, *Tax.* C.*
364 Bessels, Dr. Emil, Smithsonian Institution, Washington, D. C. *Gen. Biol.*, *Anth.*, *Geography.*?
365 Bessey, Charles E., Ph.D., Prof. Bot., University of Nebraska. Lincoln, Neb. Botanical Editor *Am. Naturalist*, *Bot.* C. Ex. Desires parasitic fungi.*
366 Best, Wm. F., 74 Germain St., St. John, N. B., Can. *Chem.*, *Metal.**
367 Bethune, Rev. Chas. J. S., Trinity Coll. School, Port Hope, Ont., Can. Editor of "The Canadian Entomologist." C. *Ent.*, *especially in its practical relation to Agric.**

368 Beuttenmüller, Wm., jr., 182 E. 76th St., New York City. *Lepid., Coleopt., Orthopt.* Desires Acrididæ and Micro-Lepidoptera of N. Am. 3000 Coleopt. from Florida for sale, also Hymenoptera, Dipt., Neuropt., Hemipt. C. Ex.*

369 Beveridge, David. 145 Griswold St., Detroit, Mich. *Bibliog., Philol.* C. Ex.*

370 Beyer, Henry Gustav., M.D., Ph.D., M.R.C.S., Bureau Med. and Surgery, Navy Dept., Washington, D. C. *Chem., Mic., Emb., Morph., Histol., Gen. Biol.**

371 Bickmore, Prof. Albert S., Sec'y of Amer. Mus. of Nat. Hist., 8th Ave. and 77th St., Central Park, New York, N. Y. Cur. Ethnol. and Prof. in charge of Dept. Public Instruction.*

372 Bicknell, Eugene P., Riverdale on-Hudson, New York, N. Y. *Orn., Bot.* C.*

373 Biddlecome, Miss H. J., 28 Keifer Avenue, Columbus, Ohio. *Crypt. Bot.* C.*

374 Bidwell, Nathan D., St. Johnsville, Montgomery Co, N. Y. *Bot., Zool.* ?

375 Biedenmeister, Frank A., Indianapolis, Ind. *Ent: Lepid.* C. Ex.

376 Bierwirth, L. C., M. E., Dover, N. J. *Min.* C. Ex.*

377 Bigelow, Horatio R., M.D., Washington, D. C. *Elect., Mic., Bibliog., Emb., Eth., Philol.* ?

378 Bigelow, Otis, Avenel, Montgomery Co., Maryland. *Gen. Biol., Anth., Arch.* C.*

379 Bigelow, Robert Payne, 605 7th St., Washington, D. C. *Zoology.**

380 Bigler, E. A., Auburn, Sangamon Co., Ill. *Bot., Ent: Lepid.* C.*

381 Bilgram, Hugo, 440 N. 12th St., Phila., Pa. *Mic., Fungi.* C. Ex.*

382 Billin, C. E., C.E., 115 Dearborn St., Chicago, Ill. *Geol., Engineering.**

383 Billings, Hosmer H., Elmira, N. Y. *Ent., Orn.**

384 Billings, John S., Surg. General's Office, U. S. Army, Washington, D. C. *Mic., Fungi, Bibliog., Gen. Biol., Anat., Pathol., Basteriology, Anth., Eth.**

385 Billings, Walter R., Ottawa, Can. *Invert. Palæo.**

386 Binley, A. J., 319 Clinton Ave., Albany, N. Y. *Lepid.* C. Ex. ?

387 Binney, W. G., Burlington, N. J. *Am. Land Shells.* C.*

388 Birdsall, E. T., 107 East 70th St., New York, N. Y. *Mic., Ent: Coleopt., Elect., Photography.* C. Ex. insects and mic.

389 Birdseye, R. Pomeroy, 67 Lansing St., Utica, N. Y. *Nat. Hist.* C.*

390 Birge, Charles P., Keokuk, Ia. *Geol.* C.*

391 Birge, Edward A., Prof. Zool., Univ. Wis., Madison, Wis. *Zool., Histol.**

392 Birkman, Rev. Gotthilf, Giddings, Lee Co., Texas. *Bot., Min., Lithol., Ent., Hymen. a specialty, Coleopt., Mollusks.* Coll. of Insects and Shells. Ex.*

393 Birney, Herman H., Johns Hopkins Univ., Baltimore, Md. *Orn., Ool., Tax., Lepid., Coleopt.* C. Ex.?

394 Biscoe, T. D., Prof. Nat. Sci., Marietta, Ohio. *Bot.* C.?
395 Bishop, Chas. L., Antiquarian, 304 East 3d St., Jamestown, N. Y. *Fungi, Vert., Palæo., Geol., Reptiles, Lepid., Radiates, Numismatics.* C. Ex.*
396 Bishop, James N., Plainville, Ct. *Bot., Mic.* C. Ex.*
397 Bitner, Henry F., A.M., Prof. Chem. and Physics, State Normal School, Millersville, Lancaster Co., Pa. *Bot: Phæn. and Cryptog. Plants, Ferns, Chem.* C. Ex.*
398 Bixby, William E., Haverhill, Mass. *Lepid., Coleopt.* C. Ex.*
399 Blachly, Chas. P., Manhattan, Kan. *Orn., Tax.* C. Foreign ex. desired.*
400 Blackford, Eugene G., 80 Fulton Market, New York, N. Y. *Ichth.* C.*
401 Blackham, Geo. E., M.D., F.R.M.S., etc., Dunkirk, N. Y. *Mic.**
402 Blackwell, Mrs. A. B., A.M., Elizabeth, N. J. *Chem., Phys., Gen. Biol.* C.*
403 Blair, Jas. R., Warren, Mass. Collector of botanical specimens of all kinds. C. Ex.*
404 Blaisdell, Frank E., Poway, San Diego Co., Calif. *Orn., Tax., Ool., Ent: Coleopt., Biol.* C.*
405 Blake, Chas. A., 2346 Catherine St., Phila., Pa. *Ent: Lepid.* C.*
406 Blake, Clarence J., M.D., 226 Marlborough St., Boston, Mass. Assoc. Editor Annales des Maladies de l'Oreille, etc. *Acoustics, Otology.* Would like to receive Otological papers for review.*
407 Blake, Eli W., Prof. Physics, Brown Univ., Providence, R. I. *
408 Blake, F. C., Pennsylvania Lead Co., Mansfield Valley, Allegheny Co., Pa. *Chem., Metal.* C. Ex.*
409 Blake, J. Henry, Zoological artist, Cambridge, Mass. *Con.* C. Ex.*
410 Blake, Prof. J. R., Greenwood, S. C. *Phys., Ast.**
411 Blake, John M., Photographer on wood, New Haven, Ct. *Chem., Optics, Scientific application of Photog.**
412 Blake, Rev. Joseph, Andover, Mass. *Bot.* C. Ex. for Southern, Western or foreign.*
413 Blake, Joseph A., New Haven, Ct. *Biol., Orn., Ool.**
414 Blake, Wm. P., Mill Rock, New Haven, Ct. *Geol., Min., Mining.* C.*
415 Blanchard, Ferdinand, M.D., Peacham, Vt. *Gen. Bot.* C. Ex. in Phænogams, Ferns, Musci and Hepaticæ.
416 Blanchard, Frederick, Lowell, Mass. *Coleopt.* C. Ex.*
417 Blanchard, Herbert W., Millville, N. J. *Min., Photog., Arch., Ool., Tax.* C. Ex.*
418 Blankinship, Joseph W., North Springfield, Greene Co., Mo. *Bot.* C. Ex.*
419 Blatchford, E. W., 375 La Salle Ave., Chicago, Ill.*
420 Bliss, H. D., M.D., 57 Madison St., Brooklyn, N. Y. *Microscopic Pathol.**
421 Bliss, Richard, Newport, R. I. *Geog., Cartog., Bibliog.**

422 Blitz, Adolph, M.D., 418 Second Ave. So., Minneapolis, Minn. *Vert. Palæo.. Min., Phys., Elect., Gen. Biol., Anat., Anth.* C Ex. ?

423 Blochman, Lucien A., San Diego, Calif. *Min.* C. Ex. Offers specimens found at San Diego or northern part of Lower California.*

424 Block, P.D., A.M., St. Vincent's Coll., Beatty, Pa. *Bot., Ent.* C.*

425 Blodgett, Hiram A., Middleburgh, Schoharie Co., N. Y. *Bot., Phæn. and Crypt. Plants, Ferns, Mosses, Fungi, Lichens, Algæ, Horticulture, Geol., Min., Phys., Elect., Mic., Photog., Meteo., Ast., Zool., Eth., Ethnog., Orn., Ool., Tax., Ent., Hymen., Lepid., Dipt., Coleopt., Hemipt., Orthopt., Neuropt., Arach., Myriop.* C. Ex.*

426 Blodgett, J. H., Rockford, Ill. *Geol.* C. Ex. ?

427 Blood, Chas. L., Taunton, Mass. *Tax., Orn.* Gen. collector for ex.*

428 Bluthner, S., Lockford, San Joaquin Co., Calif. *Coleopt.* C.

429 Boardman, Mrs. Alice L., 38 Kenilworth St., Roxbury, Mass. *Invert. Palæo., Geol., Arch., Eth.* C.*

430 Boardman, E. O., M.D., Osceola, Stark Co., Ill. *Bot., Orn., Ool.* C. Ex.*

431 Boardman, E. R., M.D., Elmira, Ill. *Bot., Ent.* C. Ex. Am. plants and coleoptera for European.*

432 Boardman-Pulsifer, Mrs. C., M.D., 1837 Kennett Pl., St. Louis, Mo. *Med., Biol.**

433 Bock, H. P., London, Ontario, Can. *Ent.* C.*

434 Bodley, A. R., M.D., Ottawa, Can. *Geol., Min., Palæo., Arch., Ent.* C. Ex. fossils for Indian relics.

435 Boerner, Chas. G., Vevay, Switzerland Co., Ind. *Ast., Met., Mic., Geol., Bot.**

436 Bohl, Otto, Kansas City, Mo. *Orn., Ool., Tax.* C. Ex. ?

437 Boies, Capt. Albert H., Hudson, Lenawee Co., Mich. *Elect., Meteo., Orn., Ool., Tax., Ent.* C. Ex.*

438 Boker, Mollie, A.B., Winnebago Agency, Dakota Co., Neb. *Phæn. Bot., Geol., Min., Ent.* C. Ex.

439 Bolles, Rev. E. C., The Washington, 29 Washington Sq., New York, N. Y. *Crypt. Bot., Mic.* C.

440 Bollman, Chas. H., Indiana Univ., Bloomington, Ind. *Ent., (Myriapoda, Arachnida), Ichth.**

441 Bolter, A., 172–4 Van Buren St., Chicago, Ill. *Ent.* C. Ex.*

442 Bolton, David A., A.M., Prof. Math. and Sec. of Grant Memorial Univ., Athens, Tenn.*

443 Bolton, H. Carrington, Ph.D., Prof. Chem., Trinity College, Hartford, Ct *Chem. and Bibliog. of Sci.**

444 Bolton, W. P., Liberty Sq., Pa. *Bot., Min., Geol., Orn.* C.*

445 Boltwood, H. L , Evanston, Ill. *Bot.* C.*

446 Bolze, Prof. Gustave, New Haven, Ct. *Orn.* C. Ex.

447 Bonbright, Lt. Col. Stephe S., Prof. Bonbright's Museum, and Cur. Drake Univ., Des Moines, Ia. *Orn., Ool., Strat. Geol., Crystall., Palæo., L. and F. W. Shells, War, Historical and Mound Builders' relics, Numismatics, Philatry.**

448 Booth, Clarence F., Chemist, residence 370 Herkimer St., Brooklyn, N. Y. *Bot., Diatoms, Hort., Chem., Mic.* C. Ex.*
449 Booth, J. C., Melter and Refiner, U. S. Mint, Philadelphia, Pa. *Chem.**
450 Booth, M. A., Longmeadow, Mass. *Marine Algæ, Diatoms, Gen. Mic.* C. Ex. Want diatomaceous and other material (prepared preferred) from all parts of the world.*
451 Booth, S. C., Longmeadow, Mass. *Nat. Hist., Min., Indian Implements.* C. Ex.*.
452 Borgstrom, E. W., 706 W. 4th St., Des Moines, Ia. *Bot., Nat. Hist., Floriculture.*
453 Boring, C. O., Market and Monroe Sts., Chicago, Ill. *Fungi.**
454 Borst, Prof. Chas. A. R., A.M., Astronomer, Clinton, Oneida Co., N. Y. *Geol., Phys., Ast.**
455 Boshart, C. F., Lowville, N. Y. *Orn., Oöl., Ent., Bot.* C. Ex.*
456 Boss, Lewis, Asst. Dir. Dudley Obs., Albany, N. Y. *Ast.**
457 Boutwell, R. L., Theresa, Jefferson Co., N. Y. *Palæo., Geol., Min.* C. Ex.*
458 Boutwell, W. L., B.S., Leverett, Mass. *Bot: Ferns.* C.*
459 Bouvé, T. T., 18 Post Office Sq., Boston, Mass. *Min., Bot.* C.*
460 Bowden, Charles, 612 N. 2nd St., Camden, N. J. *Mic., Ast.* C.*
461 Bowditch, Fred. C., Tappan St., Brookline, Mass. *Coleopt.* C.*
462 Bowditch, H. P., Prof. Physiol., Harvard Med. Sch., Boston, Mass. *Physiol.**
463 Bowen, Edward S., Pawtucket, R. I. *Min., Ent.* C.*
464 Bowen, Henry C., Columbia Coll., New York City. *Chem.**
465 Bowers, Mrs. Maggie, San Buenaventura, Calif. *Bot.* C.
466 Bowers, Rev. Stephen, Ph.D., Editor of Daily Free Press, San Buenaventura, Calif. *Geol., Min., Arch., Palæo., Marine and Terr. Moll.* C. Ex. for good specimens.*
467 Bowler, E. S., 124 Main St., Bangor, Me., Nat. Hist. Store. *Tax., Orn., Ool.* C. Ex. Coast birds in flesh to sell or ex. during winter.*
468 Bowles, G. J., 1466 Catherine St., Montreal, Can. *Ent: Lepid., Neuroptera.* C.
469 Bowles, George, 259 E. Ohio St., Chicago, Ill. *Gen. Zool., Geol., Ent.* C.*
470 Bowles, Margaretta, The Institute, Columbia, Tenn. *Palæo., Gen. Biol., Anat., Eth., Philol.* C. Ex.?
471 Bowman, Edw. S., Rock Island, Ill. *Gen. Zool., Geol., Palæo., Orn., Ool.* Ex.*
472 Bowman, Geo. A., Vienna, Fairfax Co., Va. *Met., Min.* C.?
473 Bowron, William M., South Pittsburgh, Marion Co., Tenn. *Invert. Palæo., Strat. Geol., Inorg. Chem., Met.**
474 Boyce, Thos. E., Middlebury, Vt. *Mic., Bot.* C. Ex. Good specimens desired.*
475 Boyd, C. R., Geologist, Wytheville, Va., author of Geological essays and maps of southwest Virginia.*

476 Boyden, Arthur C., A.M., Prof. Nat. Sci., State Normal School, Bridgewater, Mass. *Zool.*, *Ent.*, *Crust.* C. Ex.

477 Boyer, C. S., A.M., Elm, Camden Co., N. J. *Phæn. Bot.*, *Diatoms*, *Mic.* C. Ex.*

478 Brackett, A. S., 2729 Jackson St., San Francisco, Calif. *Mic.*, *Anth.* C.*

479 Brackett, Prof. C. F., Princeton, N. J.*

480 Brackett, S. H., A.M., Prof. Nat. Sci., Academy, St. Johnsbury, Vt. *Phys.*, *Tax.* C.*

481 Bradbury, Henry K., Santa Barbara, Calif. *Palæo.*, *Geol.*, *Ast.*, *Gen. Biol.*, *Philol.**

482 Braddock, W. James, 1117 North 10th St., Springfield, Ill. *Orn.*, *Tax.*, *Gen. Ent.* C. Ex.*

483 Brady, John, Aledo, Mercer Co., Ill. *Moll.*, *Arch.* Miss. river shells in ex. for Helix.*

484 Bragg, Everett B., Agawam, Mass. *Chem.*, *Nat. Hist.* C.*

485 Bragg, Luther C., Taxidermist, San Diego, Calif. *Geol.*, *Min.*, *Crystall.*, *Lithol.*, *Zool.*, *Gen. Biol.*, *Anat.*, *Vert.*, *Orn.*, *Tax.* C. Ex.*

486 Brainerd, Ezra, Prof. Middlebury Coll., Middlebury, Vt. *Bot.* C. Ex. for good specimens only.*

487 Braman, Benj., 44 E. 30th St., New York City. *Mic.*, *Bot.*, *Ent.**

488 Braman, Chas. B., Brockport, Monroe Co., N. Y. *Orn.*, *Tax.*, *Ent: Lepid.* C. Ex. especially in bird skins fit for mounting.

489 Brandegee, T. S., Canyon City, Colo. *Bot.* C. ?

490 Branner, John C., Ph.D., Prof. of Geol., State Geologist of Arkansas, Little Rock, Ark. *Geol.* C. Ex.*

491 Branson, Joseph, 176 Ashmead St., Germantown, Pa. *Min.* C. Ex.*

492 Brashear, J. A., Allegheny, Pa. Telescopes, spectroscopes, plane and concave diffraction gratings, and instruments of precision for astronomical and physical research.*

493 Brastow, S. D., care Wells, Fargo & Co., San Francisco, Calif. *Paleo.*, *Min.* C. Ex.*

494 Braun, Prof. Carl, 77½ State St., Bangor, Me. *Ent: Hymen.*, *Lepid.*, *Dipt.*, *Coleopt.* C. Ex. *N. A. Lepid. for European and exotic. N. A. species always fresh and in large quantities on hand.* Live cocoons of diurnal and nocturnal Lepid. Buys and sells Papilionidæ, *Sphingidæ*, and *Catocala* of the World, Microscope, and Lectures on the Insect World, illustrated by the Stereopticon.*

495 Braverman, Max., Visalia, Calif. *Min.*, *Crystall.*, *Fossils*, *Medals.* C. Ex.*

496 Bray, Frank E., 45 Fort Ave., Boston Highlands, Mass. *Orn.*, *Ool.*, *Tax.* C. ?

497 Bray, Mrs. Maria H., West Gloucester, Mass. *Marine Algæ*, *Ferns.* C. Ex.

498 Braymer, F. H., M.D., West Pawlet, Vt. *Palæo.*, *Geol.*, *Min.*, *Orn.*, *Crystall.*, *Con.* C. Ex.*

499 Brayton, A. W., M.D., M.S., Prof. Chem. and Toxicol., Med. Coll. of Ind., 19 W. Ohio St., Indianapolis, Ind.

500 Brayton, Mrs. Jessie M., 4 Ruckle St., Indianapolis, Ind. *Orn.*, *Tax.* C. Ex.
501 Breckenfeld, A. H., 1701 Buchanan St., San Francisco, Calif. *Mic.*, *F. W. Algæ.* C. Ex.*
502 Breedon, Jacob, Adrian, Mich. *Ast.*, *Meteo.**
503 Breese, Arthur B., M.D., 52 Gifford St., Syracuse, N. Y. *Diatomaceæ*, *Histol.* C. Ex.*
504 Breidenbaugh, Edward S., A.M., Sc.D., Prof. Chem. and Min., Penn. Coll., Gettysburg, Pa. Ex. in Min. and Lithol.*
505 Bremer, Ludwig, 2023 Park Ave., St. Louis, Mo. *Mic.*, *Gen. Biol.*, *Emb.*, *Histol.**
506 Brendel, Emil, M.D., Cedar Rapids, Ia. *Coleopt.*, C.*
507 Brendel, F., M.D., Peoria, Ill. *Bot.*, *Meteo.*, *Osteol.*, *Geog. Dist.* C.*
508 Breneman, A. A., Analyt. Chem., 97 Water St., New York City. *Indus. and Sanitary Chem.**
509 Brentano, Clemens, M.D., Easton, Northampton Co., Pa. *Bot: Phæn. and Crypt. Plants*, *Ferns*, *Mic.* C. Ex.*
510 Bretherton, S. E., Leadville, Colo. *Chem.*, *Metal.**
511 Brett, Frank W., Principal of Academy, Hanover, Mass. *Bot: Ferns and Mosses*, *Geol.*, *Min.*, *Crystall.*, *Chem.*, *Phys.*, *Mic.**
512 Brewer, Wm. H., Prof. Agric., Sheffield Scientific School, Yale Univ., New Haven, Ct. *Bot.*, *Mic.*, *Phys.*, *Geog.*, *Heredity.**
513 Brewster, J. R., Windsor, Vt. *Min.*, *Orn.*, *Ool.*, *Tax.* C. Ex. L. and F. W. Shells for Min. or Eggs.*
514 Brewster, Wm., 61 Sparks St., Cambridge, Mass. *Orn.*, *Ool.* C. Ex. for first-class specimens only.*
515 Brice, Albert G., 122 Gravier St., New Orleans, La.*
516 Bridge, H. A., Columbus, Ohio *Ool.*, *Con.* C. Ex.*
517 Bridgham, Mrs. S. W., 24 Waverly Place, New York, N. Y. *Lepid.**
518 Briggs, Chas. E, Norwich, New London Co., Ct. *Invert.*, *Min.*, *Moll.* C. Ex.*
519 Briggs, Mrs. S., 48 Cedar Ave., Cleveland, Ohio. *Ent.: Lepid.* C.*
520 Briggs, S. A., 21 Cortlandt St., New York, N. Y. *Diatoms*, *Desmids.* C. Ex.*
521 Brigham, Alma S., Jamaica Plain, Mass. *Bot.*, *Zool.**
522 Brigham, George L., Bolton, Mass. *Ool.*, *Min.* C. Ex. Desires correspondents from all localities.*
523 Brigham, Wm. T., Boston, Mass. *Anth.* C.*
524 Brimley, Clement S, Raleigh, N. C. *Mammals*, *Orn.*, *Ool.*, *Tax.**
525 Brimley, Herbert H., Raleigh, N. C. *Mammals*, *Orn.*, *Ool.*, *Tax.**
526 Brinckley, W. J., jr., A.B., Prof. Nat. Sci., Hayward Collegiate Inst., Fairfield, Ill. *Min.*, *Geol.*, *Palæo.*, *Con.* C. Ex.*
527 Brinton, C. H., Thornbury, Chester Co., Pa. *Orn.*, *Ool.* C. Ex.
528 Brinton, D. G., M.D., 115 So. 7th St., Philadelphia, Pa. *Arch.*, *Eth.*, *Philol.*

529 Brinton, Dr. J. Bernard, 755 Corinthian Ave., Philadelphia, Pa. *Phæn. and Cryptogamic* (*Myxomycetes*) *Bot.*, *Mic.* Ex. N. J. pine barren plants for southern.*
530 Bristow, Arthur, Dept., of the Interior, Ottawa, Canada, C. E. and D. L. Surveyor. *Anthropology*, *Arch.*, *Phys. Geol.* C.*
531 Brittain, John, Petitcodiac, New Brunswick, Can. *Botany*, *Ornithology*, *Mineralogy*.*
532 Britton, Elizabeth G., Editor of the Bulletin of the Torrey Botanical Club, Columbia Coll., New York City. *Ferns*, *Mosses*. C. Ex.*
533 Britton, J. Blodget, 339 Walnut St., Philadelphia, Pa. *Chem.*?
534 Britton, N. L., E.M., Ph.D., Instructor in Botany, Columbia Coll., New York, N. Y.; Asst. Geologist and Botanist, Geol. Surv. of New Jersey. *Bot.*, *Geol.* C. Ex.*
535 Broad, Wallace, A.B., St. Stephen, N. B., Min. and Geol. Surveyor, late of the Geol. Surv. of Canada. *Geol.*, *Lithol.*, *Mic.*
536 Broadhead, Garland C., Prof. Geol. Mo. Univ., Columbia, Mo. *Geol.*, *Bot.*, *Arch.* Coll. in Palæo., Bot., Min., Con.*
537 Brock, R. A., Cor. Sec. Southern Historical Society, Cor. Sec. and Lib. Va. Historical Soc., Richmond, Va.*
538 Brockenbrough, J. C., 203 W. Franklin St., Richmond, Va. *Diatoms*, *Mic.* C. Ex.*
539 Brocklesby, John, LL.D., Prof. Emeritus, Nat. Philos. and Ast., Trinity Coll., Hartford, Ct.*
540 Broadbent, F. V., Dept. of Agric., Washington, D. C. *Chem.*
541 Brodhead, L. W., Delaware Water Gap, Pa. *Indian Relics*, *Fossils*.*
542 Brodie, Wm., L.D.S., 425 Parliament St., Toronto, Canada. *Gen. Biol.*, *Ent: Hymen.*, *Dipt.*, *Coleopt.*, *Hemipt.*, *Orthop.* C. Ex.*
543 Bromfield, E. T., Glenbrook, Ct., and 658 Broadway, N. Y. City. *Bot.*
544 Brooks, Charles Wolcott, Union Club, San Francisco, Calif. *Eth.*
545 Brooks, E., 1725 Sutter St., San Francisco, Calif. *Ferns*. C.*
546 Brooks, Major Thomas B., Newburgh, N. Y. *Geol.*
547 Brooks, W. K., Associate in Biology; and Director Marine Laboratory of Johns Hopkins Univ., Baltimore, Md. *Zool.*
548 Brooks, W. R., D.D., Madison Univ., Hamilton, N. Y. *Geol.*, *Zool.* (*Invert.*).
549 Brooks, Wm. R., Red House Observ., Phelps, N. Y. *Ast.*, *Mic.*
550 Broomall, John M., Media, Del. Co., Pa.; Pres. Del. Co. Inst. of Sci.*
551 Brosius, Lewis W., Cochranville, Chester Co., Pa. *Phæn. Bot.*, *Ferns*, *Mic.* C. Ex.
552 Bross, Mason, 550 Dearborn Ave., Chicago, Ill. *Phæn. Bot.*, *Ferns*, *Mic.*
553 Brous, H. A., M.D., 507 Pine St,, Phila., Pa. *Coleopt.* C.*
554 Brower, George G., Lee Centre, N. Y. *Bot.* C. Ex., especially Vascular Cryptogams.*
555 Brown, Addison, Judge, 238 East 48th St., New York City, *Bot.* C.*

556 Brown, Albert P., Ph.D., 501 Federal St., Camden, N. J. *Chem.*, *Ent.*, *Mic.* C. Ex.*
557 Brown, Arthur Erwin, Supt. Zool. Garden, Philadelphia, Pa.*
558 Brown, Chas. S., B.Ph., Ludden, Dickey Co., Dakota Terr. *Mic.*, *Bot.*, *Lepid.* C. Ex.*
559 Brown, Daniel S., 1801 Lami St., St. Louis, Mo. *Bot: Ferns, Mosses*, *Hort.* C. Ex.*
560 Brown, E. L., Durand, Pepin Co., Wis. *Geol.*, *Min.*, *Arch.*, *Orn.*, *Ool.*, *Tax.** C. Ex.*
561 Brown, Ewing, M.D., Prof. Anat., Omaha Med. Coll., Creighton Block, corner 15th and Douglas Sts., Omaha, Neb. *Mic.*, *Anat.*, *Osteol.*, *Myol. and Histol. of Vert.*, *Protozoa.**
562 Brown, F. W., Glen Rock, Pa. *Min.*, *Fossils*, *Coins*, *Mound Builders' Relics.* C. Ex.*
563 Brown, Geo. C., D.D.S., Elizabeth, N. J. *Orn.*, *Ool.*, *Ent.* C.*
564 Brown, G. P., Ed. *The Sanitary News*, 217-225 Dearborn St., Chicago, Ill. *Sanitary Science.**
565 Brown, Harry A., Salmon Falls, Stafford Co., N. H. *Min.*, *Ool.* C. Ex.*
566 Brown, John J., M.D., Sheboygan, Wis. *Con.*, *Bot.* C. Ex.*
567 Brown, Jos. Stanford, care Sawyer Manuf. Electric Co., New York, N. Y. *Marine Algæ.* C. Ex.*
568 Brown, L. E., M.S., Cur. Coll. Mus., Hillsdale, Mich. *Palæo.* Ex.*
569 Brown, Merton W., Cedarville, Herkimer Co., N. Y. *Orn.*, *Ool.*, *Con.*, *Min.* C. Ex.*
570 Brown, Nathan Clifford, 85 Vaughan St., Portland, Me. *Orn.* C.*
571 Brown, R. J., Pres. Nat. Hist. Soc., Leavenworth, Kan.*
572 Brown, R. T., M.D., Indianapolis, Ind. *Geol.**
573 Brown, Robert, A.M., Sec. Yale College Obs., New Haven, Ct. *Diatoms*, *Hort.*, *Mic.*, *Ent.*
574 Brown, Prof. Stimson J., U. S. Naval Observ., Washington, D.C.*
575 Brooks, Henry, 97 Beacon St., Boston, Mass. *Palæo.*, *Invert.*, *Mic.*, *Photog.**
576 Brown, Wesley E., M.D., Gilbertville, Mass. *Diatoms*, *Min.*, *Mic.*, *Photog.*, *Anat.*, *Hist.* C. Ex.*
577 Brown, W. O., M.D., Barton, Vt. *Bot.*, *Geol.*, *Min.**
578 Brown, Wm. G., B.S., Washington and Lee Univ., Lexington, Va. *Chem.*, *Min.**
579 Brown, Wm. H., M.D., Cedarville, Herkimer Co., N. Y. *Con.*, *Min.* C. Ex. 500 dup. species of L., F. W. and Marine Shells for ex. Will name N. A. Land and F. W. shells.*
580 Browne, Frank C., Framingham, Mass. *N. A. Orn.* C. Con., Ex., *Numis.**
581 Brownell, Rev. J. T., A.M., Mansfield, Pa. *Mic.*, *Bot.*, *Philol.*?
582 Brownell, W. A., A.M., Ph.D., High School, Syracuse, N. Y. *Geol.*, *Min.* C. A large and extensive list of fossils and minerals from America and Europe for ex. Also transparencies of fossils for magic lanterns, and a private geol. and mineralogical collection for sale in whole or in part.*

583 Bruce, David, Rockport, Monroe Co., N. Y. *Orn., Ent., Bot.* Spec. Flora and Fauna of Rocky Mts. C. In Colorado from May 1 to Sept. 1.*
584 Brugler, Albert, Franklin Furnace, New Jersey. *Min., Crystall.* Large collection of Franklin Minerals. Ex.*
585 Brumell, H. P., Geol. and Nat. Hist. Surv., Ottawa, Canada. *Min.* C. Ex.*
586 Bruner, Lawrence, West Point, Neb. *Ent., specialty Orthop.* C. Ex. Specimens of Orthoptera wanted from all countries.*
587 Bruner, Thos. K., Salisbury, Rowan Co., N. C. *Geol., Min.* C.*
588 Brunn, A. E., South Woodstock, Ct. *Economic Entomology,* C. Ex.*
589 Brush, George J., Prof. Min., Yale College, New Haven, Ct. *Min.* C.
590 Bryant, D. S., Healdsburg, Sonoma Co., Calif. *Orn.* C.*
591 Bryant, F. W., Teacher, 25th Ward, Cincinnati, O. *Geol., Min., Con.* C. Ex.
592 Bryant, Walter E., Calif. Acad Sci., San Francisco, Calif. *Mam., Orn., Ool., Tax.* C.*
593 Bryant, Wm. S., 61 Beacon St., Boston, Mass. *Orn.* C. Ex.*
594 Buchanan, Andrew H., Lebanon, Wilson Co., Tenn. Prof. Math., Cumberland Univ., Tenn. *Physics, Math., Geodesy, Meteo., Ast.**
595 Buchanan, J. R., M.D., 6 James St., Boston, Mass. *Anth., Psychometry.**
596 Buckham, Jas. N., Ph.C., M.D., Flint, Mich. *Bot., Orn., Ool.,* C.*
597 Buckhout, Wm. A., Prof. Bot. and Hort., State College, Centre Co., Pa. *Bot., Ent.* C.*
598 Budd, Harry S., Electrician, Lock Box 227, El Paso, Texas. *Elect., Bibliog. of Phil. Lit., Geog. Dist., Coleopt., Philol. of N. A. Indians, Coleopt. Mex. and Rocky Mts.* C. Ex.*
599 Budd, Henry I., Mount Holly, N. J. *Geol., Min., Elect.**
600 Buffum, Fannie A., Linden, Mass. *Geol., Chem.*
601 Bull, James H., Lt. U. S. Navy, Naval Acad., Annapolis, Md. ?
602 Bull, Wm. T., M.D., Columbia Coll., New York, N. Y. *Anat.?*
603 Bulloch, W. H., F.R.M.S., Manufacturer of Microscopes, 99-101 W. Munroe St., Chicago, Ill. *Optics, Lithol.* C.*
604 Bullock, C., 528 Arch St., Philadelphia, Pa. *Chem.**
605 Bumpus, H. C., Olivet College, Olivet, Mich. *Zool.* Ex.*
606 Bumpus, L. Insley, Auburn, Androscoggin Co., Maine. *Geol., Min., Lithol., Meteo.* C. Ex. Crystallized specimens preferred.*
607 Bundy, John, Cheshire, Ont. Co., N. Y. *Orn., Bot., Tax.* C. Ex.
608 Bundy, W. F., M.D., Prof. Nat. Sci. and Drawing, State Normal School, Whitewater, Wis. *Bot: Higher Fungi, Zool., F. W. Crustacea.* C. Ex.?
609 Bunker, R., 26 Jay St., Rochester, N. Y. *Ent: Lepid., Diptera.* Ex.*
610 Bunn, G. B., 1320 Savery St., Philadelphia, Pa. *Ent: Coleopt., Tax.* C. Ex.

611 Bunn, Jacob G., 1320 Savery St., Philadelphia, Pa. *Coleopt.* C. Ex.*
612 Bunn, W. C., 1320 Savery St., Phila., Pa. *Ent.*, *Min.* C.
613 Burbridge, J. R., Crawfordsville, Ind. *Min.*, *Ool.* C. Ex.*
614 Burchard, Wm. M., M.D., Uncasville, Ct. *Phys.*, *Elect.*, *Mic.*?
615 Burchfield, S. E., M.D., Latrobe, Pa. *Bot.*, *Geol.* C.
616 Burdick, A. Hall, Prin. Union School, St. Johnsville, Montgomery Co., N. Y. *Phæn Bot.*, *Ferns.* C. Ex.
617 Burdick, E. A., Pension Office, Washington, D. C. *Mic.* C. Ex.?
618 Burdick, Justin H., M.D., Utica, Dane Co., Wis. *Bot.* C.*
619 Burdick, Wm. L., A.M., Ph.D., Prin. Natchaug School, Willimantic, Ct. *Bot.*, *Geol.*, *Inorg. Chem.*, *Ast.* C. Ex.*
620 Burgess, Edward Sandford, A.M., Washington High School, Washington, D. C. *Bot.*, *Algæ.* C.*
621 Burgess, Robert, Ames, Story Co., Ia. *Bot.* C.?
622 Burgess, Thomas J. W., M.D., F.R.S.C., Asst. Supt. Asylum for Insane, London, Ont., Can. *Bot: Can. Phænogams and N. A. Crypt.* C. Ex.*
623 Burke, Jas. H., Ukiah, Mendocino Co., Calif. *Diatoms*, *Mic.*, *Ent.*, *Agric.*, *Phyclopoda.**
624 Burland, Jeffrey H., B.A. Sc., F.C.S., Secretary British Am. Bank Note Co., Montreal, Quebec, Can. *Min.*, *Pract. Chem.*, *Invert.* C. Ex.*
625 Burnett, H. S., Kendall, Orleans Co., N. Y. *Phæn. Bot.*, *Ferns*, *Lepid.* C.*
626 Burney, Prof. Wm. B., Ph.D., Univ. of S. C., Columbia, S. C. *Chem.**
627 Burnham, J. P., 456 W. 15th St., Chicago, Ill., Prof. of *Mechanical refrigeration*, *Mic.*, *Bacteria.*
628 Burnham, S. W., 3573 Vincennes Ave., Chicago, Ill. *Ast.**
629 Burnham, Miss Sarah M., East Cambridge, Mass. *Geol.*, *Min.* C.*
630 Burns, James A., A.M., Ph.D., Prof. Chem., So. Med. Coll., Box 456, Atlanta, Ga. *Geol*, *Min.*, *Chem.*, *Metal.* C. Ex.*
631 Burrill, T. J., Prof. Bot., Univ. of Ill., Champaign, Ill. *Gen. Bot.*, *Fungi*, *Mic.* C. Ex.*
632 Burr, Catherine S., Cazenovia, Madison Co., N. Y. *Ent: Lepid.* C. Ex.*
633 Burrington, Albert H., Windsor, Vt. *Bot.*, *Ool.* C. Ex.*
634 Burroughs, Dr. J. B., Shortsville, Ont. Co., N. Y. *Mic.**
635 Burrowes, J. C., 523 E. King St., Lancaster, Pa. *Bot.*, *Orn.* C. Ex.?
636 Burt, Prof. E. A., State Normal School, Albany, N. Y. *Phæn. Bot.*, *Lichens.* C. Ex.*
637 Burtch, Verdi, Branchport, Yates Co., N. Y. *Orn.*, *Ool.* C. Ex.*
638 Busey, Prof. Samuel C., M.D., 1545 I St., N. W., Washington, D. C. *Medicine.**
639 Bush, Mrs. A. E., Curator State Normal School Museum, San José, Calif. *Con.*, *Marine Algæ*, *Palæo.*, *Ent.*, *Moll.* C. Ex.*

640 Bush, Benjamin E., C.E., Grand Blanc, Mich. *Min.*, *Arch.* C. Ex.*

641 Bush, C. G., Claremont, N. H. *Microscopy.**

642 Bush, Frank, Independence, Mo. *Phæn. Bot.*, *Con.* C. Ex.?

643 Bush, Miss Jennie R., San José, Calif. *Ent.* C. Ex.*

644 Bush, Walter D., Wilmington, Del. *Orn.*, *Ent.* C. Ex.*

645 Busteed, John B., 103 Bellingham St., Chelsea, Mass. *Bot.*, *Min.*, *Zool.* C. Ex.*

646 Butler, Amos W., Sec. Soc. Nat. Hist., Brookville, Ind. *Orn.*, *Con.*, *Herpetology.* C. Exchange for spec. and publications relating to specialties.*

647 Butler, Cyrus W., Point Pinellas, Fla. *Gen. Zool.*, *Tax.*, *Osteol.**

648 Butler, E. H., Rushville, Rush Co., Ind. *Palæo.*, *Geol.*, *Chem.*, *Mic.*, *Arch.*, *Eth.*, *Ent.* C. Ex.*

649 Butler, Wm. D., Principal of the Blow School, 6706 Virginia Ave., St. Louis, Mo. *Hort.*, *Geol.*, *Mic.*, *Meteo.*, *Forestry.**

650 Butterfield, Ralph, A.M., M.D., Kansas City, Mo. *Geol.*, *Palæo.*, *Min* C.*

651 Butterfield, W. Webster, M.Sc., M.D., Prof. of Human and Comparative Histology and Microscopical Technology in Central Coll. of Physicians and Surgeons, Indianapolis, Ind. *Phænerogamic Histology.**

652 Butterfield, Mrs. Zula N., B.Sc., Indianapolis, Ind. *Zygosporeæ.**

653 Buttles, Prof. Edwin K., Hobart College, Geneva, N. Y. *Chem.*, *Mic.**

654 Button, Fred. L., 969 Broadway, Oakland, Calif. *Con.*, *Moll.* C. Ex.*

655 Button, Henry M., Norwich, N. Y. *Ent.*, *Geol.**

656 Buxton, Wm. W., Milo Centre, Yates Co., N. Y. *Palæo.*, *Geol.* C. Ex. L. and F. W. and Marine Shells, Crystals and Fossils. Wishes Indian Relics.*

657 Buzby, F. T., South Bend, Ind. *Orn.* C.?

658 Byerly, Wm. E., Prof. Math., Harvard College, Cambridge, Mass.

659 Byington, E. L., A.M., Supt. City Schools, 321 N. Weber St., Colorado Springs, Colorado. *Bot.*, *Ferns*, *Phys.*, *Mic.* C. Ex.*

660 Byrkit, J. W., Indianapolis, Ind. *Tax.*, *Moll.* C.*

661 Cabeen, T. B., Keithsburg, Mercer Co., Ill. *Arch.*, *Palæo.* C. Ex.*

662 Cabell, James Alston, C.E., M.E., B.S., Richmond, Va. *Diatoms*, *Geol.*, *Min.*, *Chem.*, *spec. fossils, ores, minerals of Va. and W. Va.* C.*

663 Caffrey, G. W., Bethlehem, Pa. *Ent.*, *Con.* C. Ex.

664 Cahoon, John C., 2 Morton St., Taunton, Mass. *Zool.*, *Vert.*, *Mammals*, *Orn.*, *Ool.*, *Tax.* C. Ex.*

665 Calder, Edwin E., Analyt. and Consult. Chemist, Prof. Chem., Boston Univ., School of Med., Board of Trade, Providence, R. I. *Chem.*, *Ent: Coleopt.* C. Ex.

666 Caldwell, G. C., Ithaca, N. Y. *Chem.**
667 Caldwell, J. E., B.Ph., M.D., Emerson, Ia. *Bot.* C.
668 Caldwell, Rev. Lisle B., M.D., Ph.D., D.D., Prof. Physics, E. Tenn. Wesleyan Univ., Athens, Tenn. *Min.*, *Geol.*, *Chem.* C. Ex.*
669 Calef, Horace W., 327 Produce Exchange, New York, N. Y. *Mic.* C. Ex.*
670 Callahan, Thos. F., C.E., 532 Tracy Ave., Kansas City, Mo. *Photog.*, *Geol.*, *Ent.* C. Ex.*
671 Callender, John H., M.D., Prof. Physiol., Vanderbilt Univ., Nashville, Tenn.?
672 Calvert, B. T., Cornersville, Ind. *Con.*, *Rep* C. Ex. Lower and F. W. and Marine shells; also snakes of Indiana and Ohio.*
673 Calvin, Samuel, Prof. Geol. and Zool., State Univ. of Iowa. Iowa City, Ia. *Geol.*, *Zool.* C. Ex. for invertebrate fossils.*
674 Cameron, Rev. James G., Syracuse, N. Y. *Bot.?*
675 Camp, David N., New Britain, Ct. *Geol.*, *Org. Chem.* C.*
676 Campbell, Andrew B., Kendall Creek, Pa. *Min.*, *Chem.*, *Elect.* C. Ex.*
677 Campbell, A. M., Perth, Ont., Canada. *Geol.*, *Min.*, *Metall.*, *Zool.*, *Orn*, *Ool.* C. Ex.?
678 Campbell, Arthur W., West Walnut Lane, Germantown, Phila., Pa. *Photog.**
679 Campbell, Rev. E. V., St. Cloud, Stearns Co., Minn. *Gen. Bot: Ferns.* C. Ex.*
680 Campbell, Harry D., A.M., Ph.D., Prof. Geol. and Biol., Wash. and Lee Univ., Lexington, Va. *Palæo.*, *Geol.*, *Min.*, *Lithol.*, *Chem*, *Zool.* C. Ex.*
681 Campbell, J. Addison, Pulaski and Logan Sts., Germantown, Phila., Pa. *Mic.*, *Ast.*, *Gen. Sci.* C.*
682 Campbell, Rev. John, M.A., Presbyterian Coll., Montreal, Canada. *Anth.*, *Philol.?*
683 Campbell, Capt. John T., Rockville, Ind. Civil and Topographical Engineer. Field Student of Topographical Geol.*
684 Canby, William M., 1101 Delaware Ave., Wilmington, Del. *Bot.* Ex.*
685 Canfield, Frederick A., A.M., E.M., Dover, N. J. *Min.* C.*
686 Canoll, Rev. Henry, LL.D., D.Æ., Dean of Coll. of Arch., and Æsthetics, 120 East 105th St., New York City. *Photog.*, *Eth.*, *Mnemonics applied to scientific data*, *Scientific and art analogies.* C. Ex.*
687 Capen, E. A., Canton, Mass. *Orn.*, *Ool.* C.*
688 Cardeza, John T. M., A.M., M.D., Claymont, New Castle Co., Del. *Min.* C. Ex.*
689 Cardwell, John C., 17 Lawton St., Brooklyn, N. Y. *Gen. Biol.*, *Physiol.*, *Histol.**
690 Carhart, H. S., Prof. Phys., Ann Arbor, Mich. *Phys.*, *Elect.**
691 Carleton, Mark A., B.Sc., Scottsville, Mitchell Co., Kansas. *Bot: Phæn. & Crypt. Plants*, *Fungi*, *Algæ*, *Hort.*, *Mic. Emb. Crustacea*, *Mollusks.* C. Ex.*

692 Carll, J. F., Ass't Geol. Survey, Pleasantville, Pa. *Geol.**
693 Carman, Henry D., "Canadian" Office, Samia, Ontario, Can. *Orn.*, *Ool.*, *Tax.* C. A few choice local specimens for ex.*
694 Carman, Lewis, Bangall, Dutchess Co., N. Y. *Geol.*, *Min.*, *Chem.* C. Ex.*
695 Carmichael, Prof., Bowdoin Coll., Brunswick, Me. *Chem.*, *Phys.?*
696 Carney, John P. R., 314 West St., Camden, N. J. *Gen. Nat. Hist*, *Lepid.* C. Ex.*
697 Carpenter, F.H., 409 Washington St., Boston, Mass. *Photog.*, *Orn.*, *Ool.*, *Tax.* C.*
698 Carpenter, H, F., Gold and Silver Refiner, Chemist, 29 Page St., Providence, R. I. *Min.*, *Con.* C. Ex.*
699 Carpenter, Louis G., Ass't Prof. Math., Agric. Coll., Lansing, Mich. *Phys.*, *Meteo.*, *Ast.**
700 Carpenter, R. C., Prof. Math. and Eng., Agric. Coll., Lansing, Mich. *Geol.*, *Phys.*, *Elect.*, *Ast.**
701 Carr, Charles F., 531 State St., Madison, Wis. *Min.*, *Zool.*, *Gen. Biol.*, *Vert.*, *Mam.*, *Orn.*, *Ool.*, *Tax.*, *Osteol.*, *Mollusks*, *Radiates*, *Sponges.* C. Ex.*
702 Carr, Hattie, Morris, Ill. *Geol.*, *Con.*, *Fossil ferns from Mazon Creek to ex. for Marine Shells.* C. Ex*.
703 Carr, J. C., Morris, Ill. *Geol.*, *Con.* Fossil ferns from Mazon Creek a specialty. Ex.*
704 Carr, Lucien, Ass't Cur. Peabody Mus. Am. Arch. and Eth., Cambridge, Mass. *Anth.**
705 Carruth, Prof. J. H., State Botanist, Lawrence, Kan. *Bot.**
706 Carson, C. J. R., Curator High School Collection, New Bedford, Mass. *Con.*, *fossil and recent*, *Min.*, *Geol.*, *Arch.*, *Lithol.*, *Radiates.* C. Ex. Would like horns of all kinds of animals in exchange for shells *
707 Carter, Chas. W., Aledo, Mercer Co., Ill. *Mam.*, *Orn.*, *Ool.*, *Tax.* C. Ex.*
708 Carter, Rev. F. B., Montclair, New Jersey. *Mic.*, *Algæ.* Ex.*
709 Carter, John E., Knox and Coulter Sts., Germantown, Phila., Pa. *Inorg. Chem.*, *Mic.**
710 Carter, Mrs. M. C., Hesper, Winneshelk Co., Ia. *Phæn. Bot.*, *Ferns.**
711 Carter, Rev. N. F., Queechee, Vt. *Bot.**
712 Carter, Warren, 1225 Market St., Philadelphia, Pa. *Orn.*, *Ool.**
713 Carry, D. S., B.S., Weston, Mo. *Geol.*, *Phys.* C. Ex.*
714 Case, Geo. R., 188 Sigourney St., Hartford, Ct. *Phæn. Bot.*, *Lichens*, *Diatoms*, *Mic.*, *Orn.**
715 Case, H. B., Londonville, Ashland Co., Ohio. *Arch.*, *Geol.*, *Paleo.*, *Min.* Desires fossils of all ages in ex. for Arch. spec.*
716 Case, Theodore S., Kansas City, Mo. *Gen. Sci.**
717 Casey, Thos. L., U. S. Army, Newport, R. I. *Coleopt.* C.*
718 Casseber, Henry A., 292 Sixth Ave., New York, N. Y. C. Ex.*
719 Cassino, Samuel Edson, Peabody, Mass. *Bibliog.*, *Hemiptera.* C.*

720 Castle, D. M., M.D., 2007 Arch St., Philadelphia, Pa. *Coleopt.* C. Ex.*

721 Castle, F. A., M.D., 55 East 52nd St., New York, N. Y. *Med. Bot.*, *Photog*, *Bibliog.* C.

722 Castle, Wm. P., Inst. of Technology, Boston, Mass. *Orn.*, *Ool.*, *Tax.* C. Ex.*

723 Castle, Wm. W., Wellesley Hills, Mass. *Zool.*, *Mam.*, *Orn.*, *Ool.*, *Tax.* C. Ex.*

724 Cate, Will. A., B.S., Prof. of Science and the Art of Teaching, Maryville Coll., Maryville, Tenn. *Geol.*, *Ent.*, *Moll.*, *Min.*, *Palæo.* C.*

725 Caswell, John H., 11 W. 48th St., New York, N. Y. *Min.*, *Crystall.*, *Microscopical Petrography.* C. Ex.*

726 Catlin, Chas. A., Ph.B., 133 Hope St., Providence, R. I. *Min.*, *Chem.*, *Met.*, *Mic.* C. Ex.*

727 Catlin, J. C., Ravenna, Ohio. *Mic.*, *Orn.*, *Gen. Collector.* Desires skins of the *Tetraonidæ* of the world, purchase or ex. C. Ex.*

728 Caton, John Dean, 1900 Calumet Ave., Chicago, Ill. *Mam.*, *Cervidæ of America.**

729 Cauch, Robert, M.D., Carpenteria, Santa Barbara Co., Calif. *Algæ*, *Diatoms*, *Mic.*, *Histol. of Vert.*, *Infusoria.* C. Ex. marine algæ of Pacific coast for mins., marine algæ from any part of the world or for mic. material.*

730 Cawein, John D., 1828 West Market St., Louisville, Ky. *Min.*, *Crystall.*, *Metal.* C. Ex.*

731 Carr, Frank A., Editor the Western Naturalist, Pres. Madison Nat. Hist. Soc., Madison, Wis. *Zool.*, *Gen. Biol.*, *Emb.*, *Anat.*, *Vert.*, *Mammals*, *Orn.*, *Ool.*, *Tax.*, *Gen. Ent: Arachnida*, *Myriapoda*, *Crustacea.* C. Ex.*

732 Chadbourne, Arthur P., Cambridge, Mass. *Orn.* C. Ex. for first-class North Am. specimens only.*

733 Chalmers, Robert, Geol. Survey, Ottawa, Canada. *Bot.*, *Geol.**

734 Chamberlain, Arthur, 284 Pavonia Ave., Jersey City, N. J. Dealer in *Min.* Editor of "The Exchangers' Monthly." C. Ex.*

735 Chamberlain, Chauncy W., 51 Lincoln St., Boston, Mass. *Orn.*, *Ool.*, *Lepid.*, *Coleopt.* C. Ex.*

736 Chamberlain, Montague, St. John, N. B., Can. *Orn.* C.*

737 Chamberlain, Thos., jr., Publisher of "The Exchangers' Monthly," 284 Pavonia Ave., Jersey City, N. J. *Min.* C.*

738 Chamberlin, B. B., 247 W. 125th St, New York, N. Y. *Min.*, *Algæ.**

739 Chamberlin, H. B., 1664 Lawrence St., Denver, Colo. *Mic.* C. Ex.*

740 Chamberlin, J. K. P., Pomfret, Vt. *Hort.*, *Min.*, *Crystall.* *Mic.* C. Ex.?

741 Chamberlin, Lewis C., Portland, Ind. *Phæn.Bot.*, *Min.*, *Palæo.* *Geol.*, *Ool.* C. Ex.?*

742 Chamberlin, Samuel M., Wells River, Orange Co., Vt. *Orn* Ex. skins.?

743 Chamberlin, T. C., Univ. of Wis., Madison, Wis. *Glacial Geol.**
744 Chambers, Robert W., 126 Fort Green Place, Brooklyn, N. Y. *Lepid., Coleopt.* C. Ex.?
745 Chance, Dr. H. M., Hokendauqua, Pa. *Geol., Mining.**
746 Chandler, C. F., Prof. of Chem., Columbia Coll; Coll. of Physicians and Surgeons; N. Y. Coll. Pharm., N. Y. City.
747 Chandler, Charles H, Prof. Phys. and Math., Ripon Coll., Ripon, Wis.*
748 Chandler, Eli H., White Oaks, Lincoln Co., New Mex. *Min.* C.
749 Chandler, Seth C., jr., Cambridge, Mass. *Ast* *
750 Chandler, W. H., Ph D., South Bethlehem, Pa. Prof. of Chem. in Lehigh Univ.*
751 Chaney, L. W., jr., M.Sc., Prof. Biol. and Geol., Carleton College, Northfield, Minn. *Biol., Geol., specialty Gen. Biol.* C.*
752 Chapin, J. H., Prof. Geol., St. Lawrence Univ., N. Y., Meriden, Ct. *Palæo., Geol., Min., Crystall.. Lithol.* C. Ex.*
753 Chapman, A. W., Apalachicola, Fla. *Bot.?*
754 Chapman, Chas. H., 160 Hicks St., Brooklyn, N. Y. *Geol., Min., Palæo., Arch.* C. Ex.?
755 Chapman, E. C., 1107 Bedford Ave., Brooklyn, N. Y. *Specialties in Chem. Apparatus, Mic.**
756 Chapman, Frank M., Englewood, N. J. *Orn.* C.*
757 Chapman, Geo. W., M.D., Cawker City, Kansas. *Geol., Min., Anat., Osteol.* C. Ex.*
758 Chapman, H. C., M.D., Prof. Insts. of Med. and Med. Jurisprudence in Jeff. Med. Coll.
759 Chapman, John H., Box 728, Newburgh, N. Y. *Orn., Ool.* C. Ex.*
760 Chapman, Warren H., M.D., Peoria, Ill. *Geol., Palæo.**
761 Chapman, W. Albert (Assayer), Okolona, Clarke Co., Ark. *Geol., Min., Arch.* C. Ex. Works on Geol., Min., Chem. and Assaying, desired in exchange for specimens or cash. Arkansites a specialty; fine samples for sale or exchange.*
762 Chase, F. A., Prof. Phys. Sci., Fisk Univ., Nashville, Tenn.*
763 Chase, F. D., Box 724, Altoona, Pa. *Geol., Chem., Met.**
764 Chase, H. H., M.D., Lock Box 73, Geneva, N. Y. *Mic. esp. Diatoms.* C. Ex.?
765 Chase, Henry S., M.D., St. Louis, Mo. *Microscopy.**
766 Chase, Joseph E., Lakeville, Orange Co., Fla. *Lepid., Coleopt., Ool.* Collection to sell, or will exchange for rare cancelled postage stamps.*
767 Chase, Mrs. Mariné J., 1662 Locust St., Philadelphia, Pa. *Mic., Min., Con.* C.*
768 Chase, Robert H., A.M., M.D., State Hosp. for Insane, Norristown, Pa. *Mic., Histol., Pathol.**
769 Chase, Theodore R., 31 Edmund Place, Detroit, Mich. *Geol., Min., Eth.* C.*
770 Chase, R. Stuart, Haverhill, Mass. *Mic.**
771 Chase, Wm. Earl, Franklin, Essex Co., N. J. *Mic., Nat. Sci.* C. Ex.?

772 Chatfield, A. F., Albany, N. Y. *Ent: Lepid.* C. Ex.
773 Chatfield, D. S., 73 Gifford St., Syracuse, N. Y. *Min., Geol., Palæo.* C. Exchange for fossils, minerals, or for Geol. and Palæo. reports of other States or will sell entire collection which will now cover a space of four hundred square feet, closely packed.*
774 Chatterton, F. W., New Haven, Ct. *Bot.* (*Phæn. & Crypt.*) *Mic., Photog., Ent.* C. Ex. Desires Mosses, Lichens and Algæ.*
775 Chauvenet, W. M., St. Louis, Mo. *Chem., Geol.?*
776 Cheeseman, E. L., Knowlesville, Orleans Co., N. Y. *Micro. Fungi, W. Algæ.* C. Ex.*
777 Cheney, Amos P., Natick, Mass. *Ent.* C. Ex.*
778 Cheney, Chas. A., 21 N. Butler St., Madison, Wis. *Palæo., Strat. Geol., Min., Crystall., Arch.* C. Ex.*
779 Cheney, Eston S., Huron, Beadle Co., Dakota. *Min., Photog., Arch., Orn., Ool., Tax.* C. Ex.*
780 Chesebro, Denison S., Box 327, Syracuse, N. Y. *Crustacea, Moll.* Desires to buy fine marine shells. C.*
781 Chester, Albert H., E.M., Ph.D., Prof. Chem. and Min., Hamilton Coll., Clinton, Oneida Co., N. Y. *Chem., Min., Mic.* C. Ex.*
782 Cheyney, J. S., 649 N. 44th St., Philadelphia, Pa. *Mic., Gen. Histol., Bot.**
783 Chickering, J. J., Deaf Mute Coll., Washington, D. C.*
784 Chickering, Prof. J. W., Deaf Mute Coll., Washington, D. C. *Bot.* C. Ex.*
785 Child, Arthur A., Needham, Mass. *Orn., Ool.* C. Ex.
786 Child, Harry P., Kansas City, Mo. *Palæo., Herpetol., Numismatics.* C.
787 Childs, Mrs. Mollie, Santa Barbara, Calif. *Ferns, Min., Crystall.* C. Ex.*
788 Chittenden, F. H., Ithaca, N. Y. *Ent: specialty, Biol. of Coleopt.* C. Ex.
789 Chittenden, Geo. H., Dorchester, Mass. *Elect., Photog., Zool., Orn., Ool.* C. Ex.*
790 Chittenden, Prof. R. H., Ph.D., Yale University, New Haven, Ct. *Physiological Chem., Toxicology.**
791 Chope, Ed. B., 1013 Cherry St., Milwaukee, Wis. *Coleopt.* C. Ex.*
792 Choquette, Rev. C. P., M.A., College St. Hyacinthe, Can. *Geol., Chem., Physics.* C. Ex.*
793 Christian, Thomas, 1418 Main St., Richmond, Va. *Diatoms, Mic.* C. Ex. Postage stamps of Confederate States for ex. for other stamps. Also Indian arrowpoints and spears.*
794 Christie, James, Pencoyd, Pa. Mechanical Engineer. *Metall., Phys.**
795 Christie, Wm. M., Mumford, Monroe Co., N. Y. *Geol., Min., Arch.* C. Ex.*
796 Christy, S. B., Prof. Mining and Met., Univ. of Calif., Berkeley, Calif. *Mining, Met., Geol., Mic., Lithol.* C.*

797 Chubb, H. E., 235 Viaduct, Cleveland, Ohio. *Orn.*, *Tax.* C. Ex.*
798 Church, Royal T., Turin, Lewis Co., N. Y. *Chem.*, *Metall.*, *Ent.* C. Ex.*
799 Churchill, Mrs. F. C., Lebanon, N. H. *Min.*, *Fossils*, *Con.* C. N. E. and Bermuda specimens in ex.*
800 Churchill, Jos. R., 82 Devonshire St., Boston, Mass. *Bot.* C.*
801 Chute, H. N., Prof. of Physics and Chem., Ann Arbor, Mich.*
802 Cisco, J. G., Jackson, Tenn. *Am. Arch.*, *Anth.*, *Lepid.* C. Ex.*
803 Clapp, Miss Cornelia M., Mt. Holyoke Seminary, South Hadley, Mass. *Zool.*
804 Clapp, E F., M.D., Prof. Anat., Iowa City, Ia. *Anat.* C*.
805 Clapp, Geo. H., 98 Fourth Ave., Pittsburg, Pa. *Inorg. Chem.*, *Metal.*, *Anth.*, *Arch.* C.*
806 Clapp, Henry L., Prin. Geo. Putnam's School, 70 West Cottage St., Roxbury, Mass. *Bot.*, *Min.* C. Ex.*
807 Clark, A. C., Wausau, Marathon Co., Wis. *Geol.*, *Crystall.*, *Lithol.*, *Coleopt.*
808 Clark, A. Howard, Smithsonian Institution, Washington, D. C. *Eth.*, *Ethnog.*, *Fisheries.**
809 Clark, Benjamin Preston, care of B. C. Clark & Co., 55 Kilby St., Boston, Mass. *Phæn. Bot.*, *Ferns.* C.*
810 Clark, Daniel, Tyringham, Berkshire Co., Mass. *Geol.*, *Min.*, *Lithol.*, *Arch.*, *Eth.*, *Ethnog.* C. Ex.*
811 Clark, Daniel B., Webster, Wayne Co., Ind. *Orn.*, *Ool.*, *Tax.* C. Ex.*
812 Clark, Edw. E. M.D., Acad. of Sci., San Francisco, Cal. *Palæo.*, *Invert.*, *Mic.*, *Photog.* C. Ex.*
813 Clark, Fred C., Earlville, Ill. *Geol.*, *Min.*, *Arch.*, *Tax.*, *Palæo.*, *Orn.*, *Ool.* C. Ex.*
814 Clark, H. L., P. O. Box 317, Providence, R. I. *Lepid.* C. Ex.*
815 Clark, J. N., Saybrook, Ct. *Orn.*, *Ool.* C.*
816 Clark, John E., Prof. Math., Yale Coll., 30 Trumbull St., New Haven, Ct. *Math.**
817 Clark, Nathan Mendall, 103 Genesee St., Lockport, N. Y. *Ent.*
818 Clark, Oscar A., C.E., Gov't Insp. in charge construction of levee at Jeffersonville, Ind. *Geol.*
819 Clark, Patrick, C. E., Rahway, N. J. *Geol.*, *Lithol.*, *Chem.*, *Metall.*, *Phys.*, *Elect.*, *Gen. Biol.*, *Ent.* C.?
820 Clark, S. M., Vineland, N. J. *Ferns*, *Mosses*, *Algæ*, *Min.* C. Ex.?
821 Clark, Simeon Tucker, A.M., M.D., 103 Genesee St., Lockport, N. Y. *Con.* C. Ex. Wishes mitres and volutes for Gulf species.*
822 Clark, Thomas H., Asst. in Chem., Wesleyan Univ., Middletown, Ct. *Chem.**
823 Clark, U. S., Rawlinsville, Lancaster Co., Pa. *Phæn. Bot.*, *Geol.*, *Min.*, *Chem.*, *Ast.*, *Zool.*, *Anat.*, *Philol.*, *Histol.*, *Invert.* C. Ex.*

824 Clarke, Miss Cora H., Jamaica Plain, Mass. *Bot: Cryptogamia, Ent: Larval cases of Trichoptera, Insect Galls.**
825 Clarke, Frank W., Chief Chemist U. S. Geol. Survey, Curator of Min., Nat. Mus., Washington, D. C. C. Ex.*
826 Clarke, F. W., Chief Chemist, U. S. Geol. Survey, Washington, D. C. *Min., Chem.**
827 Clarke, James Freeman, Jamaica Plain, Boston, Mass. *Anat.**
828 Clarke, John M., N. Y. State Museum of Natural History, Albany, N. Y. *Palæo.**
829 Clarke, Robert, Cincinnati, Ohio. *Bibliog., Arch., Ethnol. Ethnog., Ichth.**
830 Clarke, Samuel F., Prof. Nat. Hist., Williams College, Williamstown, Mass. *Gen. Biol.**
831 Clarke, W. P., Milton, Rock Co., Wis. *Arch.* Ex.*
832 Clarkson, A., Potsdam, N. Y. *Ent: specialty Lepid.* C. Ex.*
833 Clarkson, Edw H., 30 Boardman St., Newburyport, Mass. *Min., Orn., Ool.* C. Ex.*
834 Clarkson, Frederick, 30 Pine St., New York City.*
835 Claussen, F. F., S.B., U. S. Mint, New Orleans, La. *Chem., Metal., Mic., Photog.**
836 Clay, Miss Jennie E., Cobden, Ill. *Ent: Lepid.*?
837 Claypole, Edw. W., B.A., B.Sc. (Lond.), F.G.S., Buchtel College, Akron, Ohio. *Bot., Palæo., Geol., Meteo., Zool., Anat., Ent.* C. Ex.*
838 Clayton, J. R., D.D.S., Prof. Histol. and Dental Pathol., Indiana Dental College, Indianapolis; P. O. address Shelbyville, Ind. *Mic. of dental tissues.* C.?
839 Claywall, Robert, Morgantown, N. C. *Min., Crystall., Tax.* C. Ex.*
480 Cleaveland, J. R., E. Lebanon, Grafton Co., N. H. *Fossils, Min.**
841 Clemons, Oscar E., McGregor, Clayton Co., Ia. *Geol., Min., Con., Mollusks.* C. Ex.*
842 Clement, Asa, Pawtucketville, Lowell, Mass. *Hort., Orn., Ent., Agric.*
843 Clement, Jabish H., 121 Capp St., San Francisco, Calif. *Ool.* C. Ex.*
844 Clementi, Rev. Vincent, B.A., Peterboro, Ontario, Canada.
845 Cleveland, Daniel, San Diego, Calif. *Bot: Ferns, Marine Algæ.* C. Ex.*
846 Clevenger, S. V., M.D., 95 Fifth Ave., Chicagó, Ill. *Gen. Biol., Morph., Histol.**
847 Clifford, F. S., 23 School St., Boston, Mass. *Sponges, Corals, Shells, Marine Curiosities.**
848 Close, J. A., M B., L.R.C.P.E., L.R.C.S.E., F R.M S. Lond., F.O.S. Lond., Summerfield, St. Clair Co., Ill. *Elect., Mic.,* Ex. Pathol., Helminth.*
849 Clough, J. P., Junction, Lemhi Co.. Idaho. Ex.?
850 Coale, H. K., 3564 Vernon Ave., Chicago, Ill. *Orn.* C. Ex. Land birds' skins for small birds in flesh; will identify land birds gratis (sender paying postage).*

851 Coale, R. Dorsey, Ph.D., Prof. of Chem. and Toxicol., Univ. of Md., 918 Madison Ave., Baltimore, Md. *Analyt. Chem.**
852 Coates, W. B., Lenover, Chester Co., Pa. *Orn., Ool., Tax.* C.*
853 Coburn, H. P., Box 919, Michigan City, Laporte Co., Ind. *Orn.**
854 Cobb, Charles Newell, 108 Wall St., Auburn, N. Y. *Bot., Geol., Min., Chem., Phys., Gen. Biol.* C.*
855 Cochrane, J. D., A.M., M.D., East Corinth, Me. *Bot., Min.* C. Ex.*
856 Cockey, Charles H., M.D., 210 N. Gilmor St., Prof. Mic., Balt. Univ. School of Medicine, Baltimore, Md. *Histol.* Ex. in other branches of microscopy.*
857 Coe, Emily M., Prin. Am. Kindergarten Normal School, Room 72, Bible House, New York, N. Y. *Zool.* C. Ex.*
858 Coe, Hon. Henry W., M.D., Mandan, Dakota. *Mic., Anth., Arch., Eth.* C. Ex.*
859 Coe, W. W., Portland, Ct. *Mam., Orn., Ool., Ichth.* C. Ex.
860 Coffin, Selden J., Ph.D., Prof Math. and Ast., Lafayette College, Easton, Pa. *Ast., Met.**
861 Coffman, Joseph H., Augusta, Ill. *Min., Geol.* C. Ex.*
862 Cogswell, Chas. P., jr., Norwich, Ct. *Coleopt., Lepid., Gen. Curiosities.* C.
863 Cogswell, Wm. B., Syracuse, N. Y. *Mechanical Engineering.**
864 Cohen, S. Solis, M.D., 219 So. 17th St., Phila., Pa. *Elect., Anth.**
865 Coit, Rev. C. P., 165 Hudson St., Rochester, N. Y. *Mic.* ?
866 Coit, Jos. M., M.A., Ph.D., St Paul's School, Concord, N. H. *Org. and Inorg. Chem., Phys., Elect.**
867 Coit, Judson B., Ph.D., Newton Centre, Mass. *Ast.**
868 Cole, Norman, Glen Falls, Warren Co., N. Y. *Geol., Min., Crystall., Arch.* C. Ex.*
869 Colburn, Edwin M., M.D., Ionia, Ill. *Anth.?*
870 Cole, Otto B., 57 Chester Park, Boston, Mass. *Meteo., Elect.**
871 Cole, Palmer C., M.D., 254 W. 42nd St., New York, N. Y. *Diatoms, Mic., Histol.* C. Ex.*
872 Coleman, Prof. A. P., Ph.D., Victoria Univ., Cobourg, Ont., Can. *Geol., Zool., Bot.**
873 Coleman, Thos. D., A.B., 563 Greene St., Augusta, Ga. *Mic., Emb., Vert., Histol.**
874 Collett, John, A.M , Ph.D., late State Geol. of Ind., Indianapolis, Ind. *Stratigraphic Geol., Am. Arch.* C.*
875 Collier, Peter, Dept. of Agric., Washington, D. C. *Min.*
876 Collier, Mrs. S. A., Eugene City, Ore. *Bot.* C.
877 Colling, Thomas R., Utica, N. Y. *Bot: Mycology.* C. Ex.*
878 Collin, Alonzo, Prof. Chem. and Phys., Cornell Coll., Mt. Vernon, Iowa. *Chem., Phys., Elect., Mic., Zool.**
879 Collins, George K., 14 Bastable Block, Syracuse, N. Y. *Bot., Mic., Photog., Orn.**
880 Collins, Frank S., 25 Dexter St., Malden, Mass. *Bot: Algæ, Ferns, Characeæ.* C. Ex.*
881 Collins, J. Franklin, 10 Carroll St., Providence, R. I. *Bot., Phæn. Plants, Ferns, Mosses.* C. Ex.*

882 Collins, W. H., 56 Cadillac Sq., Detroit, Mich. *Orn.*, *Mam.* C.*
883 Collins, W. P., F.R.M.S., 157 Gt. Portland St., London, W., England. *Mic. and Mic. Literature, Diatoms, Desmids, etc.**
884 Collis, R. O., Loveland, Ohio. *Arch.* C.
885 Colman, Henry, M.D., 34 Nahant St., Lynn, Mass. *Anat.*, *Histol.**
886 Colton, Prof. Charles A., E.M., Dir. Newark Technical School, 21 West Park St., Newark, N. J. *Min.*, *Technical Chem.**
887 Colton, George H., M.S., Prof. Nat. Sci., Hiram Coll., Hiram, Portage Co., Ohio.*
888 Colvin, Verplanck, Supt. N. Y. State Land Surv., Adirondack Region, Albany, N. Y. *Astron.*, *Geodesy*, *Geol.*, *Chem.*, *Phys.**
889 Colwell, Walter E., St. Louis, Mo. *Chem.* ?
890 Colyer, Walter, Albion, Edwards Co., Ill. *Palæo.*, *Ast.*, *Gen. Biol.*, *Arch.*, *Eth.* C. Ex. ?
891 Comer, Harris, 624 Locust St., Phila., Pa. *Invert. Palæo.*, *Min.*, *Chem.*, *Arch.* C.*
892 Commons, Albert, Faulkland, New Castle Co., Del. *Phæn. Bot.*, *Ferns*, *Mosses*, *Hepaticæ*, *Lichens*, *Fungi.* C.*
893 Comstock, Frank M. A.M., C.E., LeRoy, Genesee Co., N. Y. *Lithol.*, *Vert.*, *Orn.*, *Arch.* C. Ex.*
894 Comstock, J. Henry, Prof. of Ent. and Gen. Invert. Zool., Cornell University, Ithaca, N. Y. *Economic Ent.**
895 Comstock, Theo. B., Prof. of Mining Engineering, Univ. of Ill., Champaign, Ill. Desires ex. *Min.*, *Lithol.*, *Palæo; also esp. metallic ores, coals and economic mins.*
896 Comstock, T. Griswold, A.M., M.D., Ph.D., 507 N. 14th St., St. Louis, Mo. *Elect.*, *Anat.**
897 Conant, Woodbury P., Wenham, Mass. *Bot: Cyperaceæ.* C.
898 Cone, James B. 640 Farmington Ave., Hartford, Ct. *Min.* C. Ex.*
899 Congdon, Ernest A., 111 Broadway, New York, N. Y. *Chem.*, *Zool.*, *Mic.*, *Diatoms.**
900 Conklin, Wm. A., Ph.D., Director Central Park Menagerie, New York, N. Y. *Vert.* Ex. Annual Reports of Menagerie for those of other societies.*
901 Conklin, W. J., M.D., Dayton, Ohio. *Lepid.* C.*
902 Conn, H. W., Ph.D., Prof. Biol., Wesleyan University, Middletown, Ct. *Zool.*, *Bot*, *Mic.* Ex.*
903 Conrad, A. H, Prof. Nat. Sci., Western Normal Coll., Shenandoah, Iowa *Palæo.*, *Geol.* C. Desirable fossils of Hamilton and Coal-measure Groups for ex. Correspondence solicited.*
904 Conradi, Adolph, Box 4, Bethlehem, Pa. *Native and foreign Lepid.* C. Ex. and for sale.*
905 Converse, J. H., M.D., M.D.S., Danville, Ill. *Orn.*, *Gen. Mic.*
906 Conyngton, Hugh R., S. W. cor. 22nd and P. O. Sts., Galveston, Texas. *Min.*, *Crystall.*, *Lithol.*, *Chem.*, *Met.* C. Ex.
907 Cook, Albert J., Prof. Zool. and Ent., Agricultural College, Mich. *Ent.**
908 Cook, Chas., Odin, Ill. *Zool.*, *Orn.*, *Ool.*, *Tax.* C. Ex.*

909 Cook, Geo. H., Rutgers Coll., New Brunswick, N. J. State Geologist. *Geol.*, *Agric.**
910 Cook, Marcus, Brockport, Monroe Co., N. Y. *Min.*, *Tax.* C. Will exchange birds for birds of other localities, or minerals.*
911 Cook, O. F., jr., Clyde, N. Y. *Cryptogamic Botany.* C. Ex. especially Musci and Hepaticæ.
912 Cooke, Mrs. Belle W., Salem, Ore. *Ferns.* C. Ex.*
913 Cooke, Clinton T., Salem, Ore. *Orn.*, *Ool*, *Tax.* C.*
914 Cooke, Josiah P., Prof. Chem. and Min., Harvard Coll., Cambridge, Mass.*
915 Cooke, V. A., Boulder Valley, Jefferson Co., Montana. *Min.* C. Ex.*
916 Cooke, Wm. T., Providence, R. I. *Min.* C. Ex.?
917 Cooley, Geo. W., C.E., 42 S. 3d St., Minneapolis, Minn. *Geol.*, *Min.* C. Ex.*
918 Cooley, Grace E., Wellesley College, Wellesley, Mass. *Phæn. Histology*, *Bot.* C. Will exchange Phæn. Plants.*
919 Cooley, Prof. LeRoy C., Ph.D., Vassar Coll., Poughkeepsie N. Y. *Chem.*, *Phys.**
920 Coomes, Martin F., M.D., Prof. Physiol., etc., Ky. School of Med., 423 W. Chestnut St., Louisville, Ky. *Hort.*, *Agric.*, *Palæo.*, *Geol.*, *Phys.*, *Elect.*, *Mic.*, *Gen. Biol.*, *Anat.*, *Arch.*, *Eth.* C.*
921 Coon, H. C., A.M., M.D., Alfred Univ., Alfred Centre, Allegany Co., N. Y. *Physics*, *Chem.* C. Ex.*
922 Coon, J. S., 604 Main St., Cambridgeport, Mass. *Bot.*, *Phys.*, *Elect.*, *Ast.*, *Orn.*?
923 Cooper, Ed. M., 164 Walnut St., Cincinnati, Ohio. *Palæo.*, *Con.*, *Recent Marine Zool.* C. Ex.?
924 Cooper, Ellwood, Santa Barbara, Calif. *Hort.*, *Diseases peculiar and destructive to semi-tropical fruits.*
925 Cooper, Ellwood Mrs., Santa Barbara, Calif. *Bot.* C.
926 Cooper, J. C., Topeka, Kan. *Min.* C. Ex.*
927 Cooper, J. G., Hayward, Alameda Co., Calif. *Bot.*, *Zool.*, *Geol.*, *Palæo.*, *Anth.*, *Arch.*, *Mam.*, *Orn.*, *Herpetol.*, *Moll.* Ex. for books only.*
928 Cooper, W. H., 560 Grand St., Brooklyn, N. Y. *Chem.*
929 Cooper, W. T., Exr. and Man. of estate of Henry Whitall, 307 Race St., Philadelphia, Pa., or P. O. Box 141, Woodbury, N. J. *Movable Planispheres*, *Heliotelles.* C. Ex.*
930 Cope, Prof. Edw. D., 2102 Pine St., Philadelphia, Pa. *Vert. Palæo.*, *Vert. Zool.*, *Geol.* C. Ex.*
931 Copeland, Prof. M. S., Siloam Springs, Arkansas.
932 Coquillett, D. W., Los Angeles, Calif. *Econ. and Biol. Ent: Dipt.* Wishes to ex. Diptera. C.*
933 Corbusier, Wm. H., M.D., Asst. Surg. U. S. A., care of Surg. Gen. U. S. A., Washington, D. C. *Eth.* C.*
934 Corey, Thos. W., Fredonia, Kans. *Phæn. Bot*, *Ferns.* C. Ex.
935 Corning, Erastus, sr., Albany, N. Y. *Bot.*, *Ent.* C.*
936 Corning, Erastus, jr., Albany, N. Y. *Ent.*, *Ool.* C.*
937 Corser, D. B., 38 Rumford St., Concord, N. H. *Min.* C.*

938 Corson, E. H., East Rochester, N. H. *Hort.*, *Geol.*, *Chem.*, *Elect.*, *Ast.*, *Anat.*, *Eth.*, *Ethnog.?*
939 Corson, Ellwood M., M.D., Morristown, Pa. *Phæn. Bot.*, *Mic.**
940 Corthell, W. G., Tremont Temple, Boston, Mass. *Mic.* C.*
941 Cory, Chas. B., 8 Arlington St., Boston, Mass. *Orn.*, *Zool.* C. Ex.*
942 Cottlow, B. A., Shelbyville, Shelby Co., Ills. *Palæo.*, *Min.*, *Chem.*, *Arch.*, *Ool.* *
943 Cottmann, John M., 722 No. Madison St., Rome, N. Y. *Min.*, C. Ex.*
944 Cottrell, E. W., 18 Willcut Ave., Cleveland, Ohio. *Tax.* C. Ex.*
945 Couch, Edw. J., Ridgefield, Ct. *Orn.*, *Ent.* C. Ex.*
946 Coues, Elliott, Washington, D. C. *Bibliog. of Sci.*, *Gen. Biol.*, *Geog. Dist.*, *Vert. Emb.*, *Vertebrates*, *Protozoa*, *etc.* C.*
947 Coulter, J. M., Prof. Botany, Ed. *Bot. Gazette*, Wabash Coll., Crawfordsville, Ind.*
948 Coulter, Stanley, Terre Haute, Ind. *Bot.*, *Mic.**
949 Coulter, S. E. M., A.B., Terre Haute, Ind. *Bot.* C. Ex.*
950 Couper, William, 518 Whipple Ave., Lansingburgh, N. Y. *Tax.*, *Ent: Hymen.*, *Solitary Wasps.* C.
951 Courtis, William M., 449 4th Ave., Detroit, Mich. *Bot.*, *Mic.*, *Min.*, *Geol*, *Met.* C.*
952 Cousins, Marshall, Eau Claire, Wis. *Orn.*, *Ool.* C. Ex.*
953 Coville, A. L., Oxford, N. Y. *Bot.*, *Geol.* C. Ex.*
954 Coville, Fred. V., Oxford, Chenango Co., N. Y. *Bot.*, *Hepaticæ*, *Apidæ.* C. Ex.*
955 Cowan, Frank, M.D., Attorney at Law, Greensburg, Pa. *Palæo.*, *Zool.*, *Arch.*, *Philol.*, *Ent.*, *Moll.* C.*
956 Cowdry, N. H., Macleod, Alberta, Can.*
957 Cowing, Philo, Omaha, Neb. *Geol.*, *Min.*, *Chem.*, *Phys.*, *Elect.*, C. Ex.
958 Cowles, Dr. Burt, 4 Harrison St., Syracuse, N. Y. *Ool.*
959 Cowles, Calvin J., Wilkesborough, N. C. Corres. solicited.*
960 Cowles, Samuel N., Otisco, Onondaga Co., N. Y. *Bot.*, *Ent.*, *Mic.* C.*
961 Cox, C. F., 55 Broadway, New York, N. Y. *Mic.*, *Veg. Anat.**
962 Cox, Daniel G., 217 Ontario St, Toronto, Can. *Orn.*, *Ent.**
963 Cox, George H., 2 Central Sq., Cambridgeport, Mass. *Min.*, *Crystall.*, *Lake Superior Specimens.* C. Ex.*
964 Cox, Joseph, Judge Circuit Court, Cincinnati, Ohio. *Arch.*, *Nat. Hist.* C. Ex.
965 Cox, Lisbon A., Keokuk, Ia. *Palæo: Crinoids.* C. Ex. Would like to ex. for good crinoids, especially European.*
966 Cox, William J., Supt. Public Schools, Hancock, Mich. *Min.*, *Geol.* C.*
967 Coxe, Eckley B., Drifton, Luzerne Co., Pa. *Mining Engineer.**
968 Cozzens, Fred. T., Leominster, Mass. *Geol.*, *Min.* C. Ex. Foreign and Western correspondence desired. Ex. Mins. for Mins., perfect fossils and Indian relics. Send lists.*

969 Crafts, Samuel D., 17 Exchange Place, Boston, Mass. *Orn.*
970 Cragin, F. W., Sc.B., Prof. Nat. Hist., Washburn Coll., Topeka, Kan. Editor Bull. Washb. Lab. Nat. Hist. *Biol.*, *Herpetol.*, *Carcinology*, *Crypt. Bot.* C. Ex. Desires N. A. Lacertilia and F. W. Crust. Will be glad to receive notes, short articles, and descriptions of new species relating to Nat. Hist. of territory west of the Miss. river, for publication in the *Bulletin of the Washburn Laboratory of Nat. Hist.*; also specimens and notes from Kansas in aid of the Washburn Biological Survey of Kansas.*
971 Craig, J. W., M.D., Mansfield, Richland Co., Ohio. *Geol.*, *Arch.* C.*
972 Cramer, A. W. P., 808 Macon St., Brooklyn, N. Y. *Lepid.* C. Ex.*
973 Cramer, N. L., Oneida, N. Y. *Bot.*, *Geol.*, *Mic.*, *Elect.*, *Ent.**
974 Crampton, Chas. A., M.D., Dept. of Agric., Wash., D.C. *Chem.**
975 Cranch, Edward, M.D., Box 111, Erie, Pa. *Mic.* C. Ex.*
976 Crandall, A. R., Prof. Ag. and Mech. Coll. of Ky., Lexington, Ky. *Geol.*, *Palæo.*, *Bot.*, *Mic.*, *Photo-micrography.*
977 Crandall, Chauncey W., Woodside, Queen's Co., N. Y. *Orn.*, *Ool.*, *Tax.* C. Ex.*
978 Crandall, O. A., Sedalia, Pettis Co., Mo. *Min.*, *L. and F. W. Shells.* C. Ex.*
979 Crane, Alfred J., Montclair, Essex Co., N. J. *Phæn. Bot.*, *Ferns.* C. Ex.?
980 Crane, Will. E., C.E., A.M., Civil Eng., C. M. and St. P. Ry., Milwaukee, Wis. *Palæo.*, *Invert.*, *Min.* C. Will buy, sell or exchange.*
981 Crannell, Charles E., Pittston, Pa. *Orn.*, *Min.*, *Herpetol.*, *Ichth.*, *Worms*, *Numismatics.* C.*
982 Crans, James T., New Britton, Hamilton Co., Ind. *L. and F. W. Shells of N. A.* C. Ex.
983 Cratty, R. I., Armstrong, Emmet Co., Iowa. *Phæn. Bot.*, *Ferns*, *Mosses.**
984 Crawford, H. D., 127 Lincoln Ave., Ottumwa, Ia. *Palæo.*, *Geol.*, *Mic.*, *Gen. Biol.* Offers desirable ex. in Invert. Palæo.?
985 Crawford, J. C., A.M., Green Bay, Wisconsin. *Mic.*, *Diatoms*, *Desmids*, *Ent.*, *Bacteria*, *Crypt. Bot.* C.*
986 Crawford, Marion, Wayland, Clark Co., Mo. *Geol.*, *Min.*, *Photog.*, *Arch.*, *Orn.*, *Ool.*, *Tax.*, *Ent.* C. Ex. Collects in all branches, esp. Ool.
987 Crawford, M. B , A.M., Middletown, Ct. *Phys.**
988 Cregoe, Jas. Plomer, 26 Rutledge Ave., Charleston, S. C. *Lepid.* C. Ex.*
989 Cressman, N. F., Chestnut Hill, Philadelphia, Pa. *Bot.**
990 Cressman, Philip, A.M., 1623 Poplar St., Philadelphia, Pa. *Bot.* C.*
991 Cresson, Ezra T., Box 1577, Phila., Pa. *Ent: Hymenop.**
992 Cresson, George B., Custodian of the Am. Ent. Soc., Acad. of Nat. Sciences, Phila., Pa. *Hymenoptera of the world; Aculeata especially.* C. Ex.*

993 Crim, A. B., Middleville, Herkimer Co , N. Y. *Min.*, *Crystall.* Have for sale fine doubly terminated quartz crystals found only at this locality. Price list sent on application.*
994 Crittenden, A. R., Middletown, Ct. *Geol.*, *Con.**
995 Croissant, Rev. J. D., Washington, D. C. *Geol.* C. Ex. foreign for home specimens.*
996 Crooks, Will. A., Gilman, Ill. *Min.*, *Photog.*, *Zool.*, *Orn.*, *Ool.*, *Tax.* C. Ex.*
997 Crosby, Eugene C., 909 Campbell St., Kansas City, Mo. *Chem.*, *Phys.* C.?
998 Crosby, W. O., Boston Soc. Nat. Hist., Boston, Mass. *Geol.*, *Min.* C. Ex. Desires crystalline rocks.*
999 Crosier, Dr. E. S., New Albany, Ind. *Bot.*, *Zool.*, *Mic.*, *Anth.**
1000 Cross, Charles R., Thayer Prof. Physics, Mass. Inst. Tech., Boston, Mass.*
1001 Cross, C. Whitman, Ph.D., U. S. Geol. Survey, Denver, Colo. *Geol.*, *Min.*, *Petrography.**
1002 Cross, John E., Chana, Ill. *Phænogamous Plants*, *Zool.* C. Ex. Will exchange local plants for Leguminosæ.*
1003 Cross, Rev. R. T., Denver, Colo. *Min.* C. Small cabinets furnished at low prices.*
1004 Cross, Wm., 183 Queen St., west, Toronto, Can. *Orn.*, *Ool.*, *Tax.* C. Ex. Birds of India, Africa and Australia wanted in exchange for birds or mammals of N. A.*
1005 Cross, Whitman, Ph.D., U. S. Geol. Survey, Denver, Colo. *Geol.*, *Min.*, *Lithol.**
1006 Crotsenberg, C. N., Clinton, Rock Co., Wis. *Phys.*, *Elect.*, *Orn.*, *Ool.*, *Tax.* C. Ex.*
1007 Crowner, Walter E., Watsonville, Santa Cruz Co., Calif. *Mosses*, *Min.*, *Crystall.*, *Vertebrates*, *Orn.*, *Articulates*, *Worms*, *Moll.*, *Radiates.* C. Ex. Stuffed Birds, Postage Stamps, Coins, etc.
1008 Crowther, John, Journalist, 320 Pleasant St., Fall River, Mass. *Palæo.*, *Strat. Geol.*, *Min.*, *Physics*, *Mic.*, *Gen. Biol.*, *Philol.* Ex.*
1009 Crozier, A. A., M.Sc., Asst. Botanist, Dept. Agric., Washington, D. C. *Agricultural Botany.**
1010 Crump, M. H., Bowling Green, Ky. *Geol.*, *Palæo.*, *Min.* C. Ex.
1011 Cullmann, John G., Cullmann, Cullmann Co., Alabama. *Phæn. Bot.*, *Hort.*, *Geol.*, *Min.*, *Forestry.**
1012 Culver, Howard, 217 Fifth Ave., Eau Claire, Wis. *Orn.*, *Ool.* C. Ex.*
1013 Culver, W. W., West Lĕbanon, N. H. *Geol.*, *Min.* C. Ex. Alpine plants of the White Mts. to ex. for Mins.*
1014 Cummins, Adley H., A.M., Prof. Calif. Acad. of Sci., San Francisco, Calif. *Comp. Philology.**
1015 Cummings, Clara E., Associate Prof. of Bot., Wellesley Coll., Wellesley, Mass. *Bot.* C. Ex. for mosses and lichens.*
1016 Cummings, Geo. J., Howard Univ., Washington, D. C. *Min.*, *Gen. Nat. Hist.*, *Orn.* C. Ex.*

1017 Cunningham, J. C., Terre Haute, Ind.
1018 Cunningham, Mrs. K M., Blairsville, Indiana Co., Pa. *Bot.* C.*
1019 Cunningham, Seymour, Civil Engineer, 1723 K St., N. W., Washington, D. C. *Ool.* C. Ex.*
1020 Cunningham, T. L., Oak Hill, Volusia Co., Fla. *L., F. W. and Marine Shells of Fla.* C. Ex.
1021 Cunningham, W. M., Newark, Licking Co., Ohio. *Arch., Geol., Palæo.* C.*
1022 Curran, Mary K., Curator Botany, Calif. Acad. of Sciences, San Francisco, Calif.*
1023 Currie, Rev. Hector, B.A., Thedford P. O., Ont., Can. *Geol., Palæo.* C. Ex.*
1024 Currier, Edw. H., M.D., 782 Elm St., Manchester, N. H. *Gen. Nat. Hist.**
1025 Currier, John M., M.D., Newport, Orleans Co., Vt., Sec. Rut. Co. Hist. Soc. *Arch., Min., Eth., Palæo., Anth.**
1026 Curtis, F. S., B.S., Moravia, Cayuga Co., N. Y. *Phæn. Bot., Ent: Coleopt.* C. Ex.
1027 Curtis, Geo. Edw., Prof. Math., Washburn Coll., Topeka, Kan. *Meteo., Ast.**
1028 Curtis, John Green, M.D., Prof. of Physiol. in the College of Physicians and Surgeons, N. Y. City, 127 E. 35th St., New York, N. Y. *Gen. Biol., Anat., Phys., Vertebrates.**
1029 Curtis, Wm. H., Box 66, Haverhill, Mass. *Mic., Diatoms.* C. Ex.*
1030 Curtiss, A. H., Jacksonville, Fla. *Bot., Spec. southern trees.* C.*
1031 Curtiss, Mrs. F. A., Jacksonville, Fla. *Bot., Marine Algæ,* Spec. Florida.*
1032 Curtiss, Geo. F., Lynn, Mass. *Elect., Coleopt., Lepid.* C. Ex.*
1033 Curtiss, L. R., Mendota, Ill. *Phys. Sci.**
1034 Curtman, Chas. O., 3718 North 9th St., St. Louis, Mo. *Min., Crystall., Chem., Mic.* C. Ex.*
1035 Cushing, Frank H., Smithsonian Institution, Washington, D. C. *Arch., Eth.* C.
1036 Cusick, Wm. C., Crowell, Ore. *Bot.* C.?
1037 Cuthbert, Alfred, Beaufort, S. C. *Bot., Orn.* C. Ex.*
1038 Cutler, Andrew S., D.D.S., Kankakee, Ill. *Bot., Orn.**
1039 Cutler, E. A., 192 N. Pearl St., Albany, N. Y. *Ent.* C. Ex.*
1040 Cutter, Geo. R., M.D., 52 Bedford Ave., Brooklyn, N. Y. *Histol., Pathology, Mic.* C.*
1041 Cutting, Hiram A., A.M., M.D., Ph D., Geologist Curator Natural History; Vermont Committee of U. S. Forestry Congress; Prof. of Natural Science, Norwich University, Northfield; Lecturer on Science in Vermont Conference Seminary and Female College, Montpelier, and at the Seminary, Newbury, Vt.; Lunenburgh, Essex Co., Vt. *Geol., Meteo., Agric., Fungi.* Collection 25,000 specimens. Will exchange Vermont specimens for others.*

1042 Dabney, Charles Wm., jr., Ph.D. State Chem, and Director N. C. Agric. Experiment Station, Raleigh, N. C. *Organic Agric.*, *Chem.*, *Min.*, *Met.**
1043 Daggett, Frank S., Duluth, Minn. *Ent: Lepid.*, *Coleopt.* C. C. Ex.*
1044 D'Ailly, Richard, Malvern, Ark. *Bot.*, *Forestry*, *Hort.*, *Orn.*?
1045 Daily, M. A., Fargo, Dakota. *Ent.*, *Herpetol.* C. Ex.*
1046 Dale, T. Nelson, U. S. Geog. Surv., Newport, R. I. *Stratigraghical Geol.*, *Palæo.**
1047 Dall, Mrs. Caroline H., fellow of Am. Assoc. for Adv. of Sci. Depts. Arch. and Eth., 1603 O St., N. W., Washington, D. C.*
1048 Dall, Wm. H., Hon. Curator U. S. Nat. Mus., Palæontologist, U. S. Geol. Surv., care Smithsonian Institution, Washington, D. C. *Malacol.*, *Anth.*, *Arctic Geog.*
1049 Dame, L. L., Medford, Mass. *Bot.*, *Trees and Shrubs.* C.*
1050 Dammer, Henry G., 1726 Preston Place, St. Louis, Mo. *Ent: Lepid.* C. Ex.?
1051 Damon, Wm. E., Ph.D., M.D., Univ. of Mich., Ann Arbor, Mich. *Bot.*, *Geol.*, *Inorg. Chem.*, *Mic.*, *Emb.*, *Anat. of Vert.*, *Ool.*, *Histol.* C. Ex.
1052 Dana, Edw. S., Ph.D., New Haven, Ct. *Min.*, *Crystall.**
1053 Dana, J. D., Prof. Min. and Geol., Yale Coll, New Haven, Ct. *Min.*, *Geol.*, *Crustacea*, *Corals.**
1054 Danby, W. H., 144 Kosciosco St., Brooklyn, N. Y. *Lepid.*, C. Ex.*
1055 Dancy, Frank B., A.B., Chemist Agr. Expr. Station, Raleigh, N. C.*
1056 Daniel, F. W., St. John, N. B., Can., care Daniel & Boyd. *Orn.**
1057 Daniel, John, Tuscaloosa, Ala. *Geol.*, *Min*, *Phys.*, *Elect.*, *Mic.*, *Ast.*
1058 Darrow, Charles E., M.D., 74 East Ave., Rochester, N. Y. *Mic.*?
1059 Darton, Nelson H., U. S. Geol. Survey, Washington, D. C. *Geol.**
1060 Darwin, Charles C., U. S. Geol. Survey, Washington, D. C. *Geol.*, *Bibliog.*, *Eth.*
1061 Davenport, Dr. Bennett F., State Analyst, 161 Tremont St., Boston, Mass. *Med.*, *Chem.*, *Tax.*, *Adult.* C. Member of the Am. Chem. Soc., also, of London, Paris and Berlin; of the British Soc. of Public Analysts; also of German Soc. of Analytical Chemists.*
1062 Davenport, George E., Medford, Mass. *Vascular Crypt.**
1063 Davenport, W. H., D.D.S., Lee, Berkshire Co., Mass. *Geol.*, *Min.* Cabinet exchange. Desires fine specimens only. Correspondence solicited.*
1064 Davidson, Prof. George, A.M., Ph.D., U. S. Coast and Geodetic Survey; Member Nat. Acad. Sci.; Calif. Acad. Sci. Pres. Geog. Soc. Pac., Davidson Observatory, San Francisco, Calif. *Phys.**

1065 Davidson, H. M., Box 415, Ogdensburg, N. Y. *Chem.*, *Min.*, *Orn.*, *Tax.* C. F. W. Shells from St. Lawrence in ex. for small sea shells.*

1066 Davidson, Mrs. Jas., Monticello, Jones Co., Iowa. *Palæo.*, *Geol.*, *Arch.* C. Ex.*

1067 Davidson, Miss Mary, care J. D. Davidson, Lexington, Rockbridge Co., Va. *Numismatics*, *Bot.*, *Ferns*, *Bibliog.* C. Ex.*

1068 Davie, Oliver, 170 No. High St., Columbus, O. *Tax.*, *Orn.*, *Ool.* C. Ex.*

1069 Davis, A. J., M.D., West 11th St., New York City. *Psychol.*

1070 Davis, C. H. S., M.D., Meriden, Ct. *Palæo.*, *Anth.*, *Arch.*, *Eth.* C.*

1071 Davis, Chas. T., 330 Wood St., Reading, Pa. *Min.*, *Arch.* C. Ex.*

1072 Davis, E. G., Curator Pub. Mus., Leominster, Mass. *Min.*, *Photog.*, *Tax.* C. Ex.*

1073 Davis, Frank M., 404 N. Carroll St., Madison, Dane Co., Wis. *Bot.*, *Palæo.*, *Geol.*, *Min.*, *Chem.*, *Phys.*, *Mic.*, *Photog.*, *Meteor.*, *Ast.*, *Gen. Zool.*, *Geographical Distribution*, *Arch.*, *Philol.*, *Orn.*, *Ool.*, *Tax.*, *Ent.*, *Crust.* C. Ex.*

1074 Davis, G. Pierrepont, M.D., Hartford, Ct. *Phæn. Bot.* C.*

1075 Davis, G. A., Mexico, N. Y. *Orn.*, *Tax.*, *Mam.*, *Ool.* C. Ex.*

1076 Davis, Graham, Pres. A. A. 153, 3000 Groveland Ave., Chicago, Ill. *Palæo.*, *Min.*, *Orn.*, *Tax.* C. Ex.*

1077 Davis, Henry, McGregor, Ia. *Ferns*, *Mosses*, *Fungi*, *Geol.*, *Min.*, *Arch.*, *Myriopoda*, *Worms.*

1078 Davis, Howard B., 330 Wood St., Reading, Pa. *Min.*, *Anth.*, *Arch.* C. Ex. Desires shells from all parts of the U. S.*

1079 Davis, H. W., Box 34, North Granville, Ky. *Orn.*, *Ool.* C. Ex.*

1080 Davis, Rev. J. C., Athens, Ga. *Lepid.*, *Dipt.* C. Ex.?

1081 Davis, J. J., Racine, Wis. *Bot.* C.*

1082 Davis, Lorenzo M., Ph.C., Analytical Chemist, Cleveland, Ohio. *Strat. Geol.*, *Min.*, *Org. and Inorg. Chem.*, *Mic.*, *Ichth.* C. Ex.*

1083 Davis, Lyndall L., D.D.S., Lecturer, Hist. and Mic., Chicago Coll. of Dental Surgery, Chicago, Ill. *Mic.*, *Gen. Biol.*, *Emb.*, *Hist.* C. Ex. Address, 524 W. Van Buren St.*

1084 Davis, N. S., jr., A M., M.D., Member of Chicago Acad. of Sciences, 65 Randolph St., Chicago, Ill. *Herpetol.**

1085 Davis, R. S., M.D., LaCentre, Clark Co., Wash. Ter. *Orn.* C. Ex.*

1086 Davis, Wm. M., 2 Bond St., Cambridge, Mass. Ass't Prof. in Harvard Coll. *Geol.*, *Phys. Geog.*, *Meteorol.**

1087 Davis, W. T., Tompkinsville, Staten Island, N. Y. *Ent.* C. Will ex. Orthopt. from Staten Island.*

1088 Davis, William J., Centre and Walnut Sts., Louisville, Ky. *Palæo.*, *Corals (Polypi) of Silurian and Devonian periods.* C. ' Ex.

1089 Davison, A. H., Rock Rapids, Lyon Co., Iowa. *Geol.*, *Ethnol.**

1090 Davison, Henry H., 20 Sumner St., Pawtucket, R. I. *Mic.* C. Ex.*
1091 Davison, John L., Lockport, Niagara Co., N. Y. *Orn.*, *Ool.* C. Ex. of bird's eggs.*
1092 Davy, Robert Ballard, M.D., San Diego, California. *Gen. Biol.*, *Emb.*, *Anth.**
1093 Dawson, George M., D.S., F.G.S., Assoc. Royal School of Mines, Asst. Director Geol. Survey of Canada, Ottawa, Can. *Geol.*, *esp. Western Geol.*, *Eth.**
1094 Dawson, Sir J. William, C.M.G., LL.D., F.R.S., Prin. McGill Coll., Montreal, Can. *Geology*, *Palæontology.**
1095 Dawson, William, Spiceland, Henry Co., Ind. *Ast.*, *Meteo.**
1096 Day, David F., 69 Cottage St., Buffalo, N. Y. *Bot.* C. Ex.*
1097 Day, David S., U. S. Geol. Survey, Washington, D. C. *Org. and Inorg. Chem.* C. of minerals. Ex *
1098 Day, Edward G., Riverside Station, Fairfield Co., Ct. *Mic.*, *Gen. Biol.*, *Spec. Prep of Mic. slides.* C.?
1099 Day, L. T., M.D., Westport, Ct. *Vert. Palæo.*, *Diptera of N. A.* C.*
1100 Day, Mary C., San Luis Obispo, Calif. *Ferns*, *Con.*, *Min.*, *Crystall.* C. Ex.*
1101 Day, Robert S., 50 Union St., New Orleans, La. Ex. *Ichth. spec. for Geol.?*
1102 Day, Wm. C., Ph.D., Prof. Chem. Swarthmore Coll., Swarthmore, Pa.*
1103 Dayan, C. F., Lowville, Lewis Co., N. Y. *Ool.*, *Orn.*, *Tax.* C.?
1104 Dean, Rev. Artemas, Muncy, Lycoming Co., Pa. *Min.*, *Arch.*, *Palæo.*, *Zool.* C. Ex.*
1105 Dean, D. V., M.D., Grand Ave., and Olive Sts., St. Louis, Mo. *Bot.*, *Palæo.*, *Mic.*, *Emb.*, *Anth.*, *Ent.*, *Chem.**
1106 Dean, Edwin A., Scytheville, Merrimac Co., N. H. *Geol.*, *Min.* C. Ex.*
1107 Dean, Geo. W., Box 92, Fall River, Mass. *Elect.*, *Ast.**
1108 Dean, Geo. W., Kent, Portage Co., Ohio. *Hort.*, *Palæo.*, *Min.*, *Arch.*, *Moll.* C. Ex.*
1109 Dean, John, Entomologist; Chem. and Micros. Analyzer of Silk Fabrics, Silk Culturist, 216 Court St., Brooklyn, N. Y. *Mic.*, *Silk Culture.**
1110 Dean, W. Smith, Cortland, N. Y. *Geol.* C.
1111 Deane, Ruthven, 2 Wabash Ave., Chicago, Ill. *Orn.**
1112 Deane, Walter, Brewster Place, Cambridge, Mass. *Phæn. Bot.*, *Vascular Cryptogams.* C. Ex.*
1113 Dearing, Wm. S., Pedagogue, Valley Center, San Diego Co., Calif. *Bot.*, *Phæn. Plants*, *Org. Chem.*, *Physics*, *Mic.**
1114 Dearsall, Rich. F., 16 & 18 Broad St., New York City. *Zool.*, *Orn.*, *Ool.*, *Ent: Lepid.*, *Coleopt.* C. Ex. in Ent.*
1115 Deatrick, Rev. W. W., A.M., Prin. Clarion Coll. Inst., Rimersburg, Clarion Co., Pa *Bot.*, *Min.* C. Ex.*
1116 DeBeck, D., M.D., Med. Coll of O., Cincinnati, Ohio. *Histol. and Comp. Anat. of the Eye.* C.*

1117 DeCamp, Wm. H., M.D., Grand Rapids, Mich. *Am. Con., Min.* C. Ex. for land and fresh water shells of Am.
1118 DeCew, Edmund, P.L.S., DeCewville, Ont., Can. *Geol., Palæo.* A few sets of Devonian fossils for sale. C.*
1119 Decker, Miss Edith, Marysville, Union Co., O. *Sericulture.**
1120 DeForest, Eugene, Waterville, Me. *Ent: Diptera.**
1121 DeGarmo, James M., Ph D., Prin. DeGarmo Inst., Rhinebeck, N. Y. *Macro-Lepid., Orn.* C.?
1122 Degge, Prof. A. R., Petersburg, Ill. *Arch., Geol., Min., Anat.* C. Ex.?
1123 Degni, Rev. J. M., Prof. Phys., Woodstock Coll., Howard Co., Md.*
1124 DeKalb, Courtenay, Syracuse, N. Y. *Physical Geology, Min., Assaying.* C. Ex.*
1125 De La Cour, J. L., Camden, N. J. *Mic., Chem., Gen. Ent.**
1126 Delafontaine, Prof. M., Ph.D., 64 Park Ave., Chicago, Ill. *Chem., Geol., Min.* C.
1127 Delamater, N. D., A.M., M.D., Prof. mental and nervous diseases, 125 State St., Chicago, Ill. *Elect., Gen. Biol., Morphol.**
1128 DeLand, Levi J., Fairport, N. Y. *Mic., Soda.**
1129 DeLisle, A. A., Grand Rapids, Mich. *Ent: Lepid., Coleopt.* C Ex. Foreign and native.*
1130 DeMar, J. A., Brighton District, Boston, Mass. *Phæn. Bot., Hort., Org. Chem.* C. Ex.*
1131 Demarest, P. E., Dover, Morris Co., N. J. *Phæn. Bot., Ferns, Bot., Mic.* C. Ex.*
1132 Demerest, John M., Newton, N. J. *Orn., Tax.* C. Ex.*
1133 Deming, Dr. Lucius P., Syracuse, N. Y. *Mic.* C.*
1134 DeMotte, John B., Prof. of Phys., DePauw Univ., Greencastle, Ind. *Phys.**
1135 Denham, Chas. S., East Pepperell, Middlesex Co., Mass. *Bot., Orn., Ool., Tax.* C. Ex.*
1136 Denison, Charles, A.M., M.D., Denver, Colo. *Climatology.**
1137 Dennis, David W., Prof. Geol. in Earlham College, Richmond, Ind. *Palæo., Invert., Geol., Min.* C. Ex.*
1138 Denslow, Rev. H. M., Seneca Falls, N. Y. *Bot: N. A. Orchids.* C. Ex.*
1139 Denton, Wm. D., Wellesley, Mass. *Orn., Ent.* C. Ex.*
1140 Denton, S. W., Wellesley, Mass. *Orn., Tax., Ool., Ent., Con., Crypt. Bot., Photog.* Large collections of bird skins, eggs, shells, fossils and insects from New Zealand, Tasmania, Australia, New Guinea and America, for sale or to exchange for specimens desired. Send for catalogues of the above. Correspondence solicited. C. Ex.*
1141 Derby, Eugene C., New London, Merrimac Co., N. H. *Geol., Min.* C. Ex.
1142 Derousse, Louis T., Camden, N. J. *Agric., Mic., Ent.**
1143 Detmers, Prof. H. J., Champaign, Ill. *Pathol., Biol., Mic.* C.?
1144 Detwiller, J. W., M.D., 122 S. Main St., Bethlehem, Pa. *Min., Orn., Ool.* C. Ex.*

1145 De Veny, Miss Mary M., B.S., 790 Case Ave., Cleveland, Ohio. *Chem.*, *Phys.**

1146 Devereaux, W. L, Clyde, Wayne Co., N. Y. *Ent: Coleopt.*, *Lepid.*, *especially Rhyncophora and Noctuidæ.* C. Ex. limited *

1147 Dewey, A. H., 42 Monroe Ave., Rochester, N. Y. *Min.*, *Geol.*, *Arch.* C. Ex.*

1148 Dewey, Frederic P., Cur. Met., Nat. Mus., Smithsonian Inst., Washington, D. C. *Geol.* (*economic*), *Min.*, *Inorg. Chem.*, *Met.**

1149 Dexter, Ransom, A.M., M.D., LL.D., formerly Prof. Zool., Comp. and Human Anat. and Physiol., Univ. of Chicago, 76 East Madison St., Chicago, Ill. C.*

1150 Dexter, S. Frank, Pawtucket, R. I. *Orn.* C.*

1151 Dickel, George, Louisville, Ky. *Lepid.* C.

1152 Dickerson, W., 118 E. 7th St., Chattanooga, Tenn. *Min.* C Ex.*

1153 Dickinson, E., 73 Spring St., Springfield, Mass. *Orn.*, *Ool.* C.*

1154 Dickinson, Dr. E. E. Fairport, Monroe Co., N. Y. *Bot.*, *Min.*, *Elect.*, *Anat.*, *Osteol.* C. Ex.*

1155 Dickinson, Prof. John, University P. O., Los Angeles, Calif. *Min.*, *Phys.*, *Gen. Biol.* C. Ex.*

1156 Dickinson, J. E., 1108 Winnebago St., Rockford, Ill. *Orn.*, *Ool.*, *Tax.**

1157 Dickinson, Mrs. W. P., 893 Main St., Dubuque, Iowa. *Bot.*, *Palæo.* C.*

1158 Dickinson, Wm., A.M., M.D., 1322 Olive St., St. Louis, Mo. *Bibliog.*, *Ethnol.*, *Philol.*, *Numismatics.**

1159 Dietz, Ottomar J. L., 431 East 80th St., New York, N. Y. *Coleopt.* C. Ex.*

1160 Dietz, William G., M.D., Hazleton, Luzerne Co., Pa. *Coleopt. of U. S.* C. Ex. Desires to exchange N. A. Coleopt. for Rhynchophora (Curculionidæ) from all parts of the world. Correspondents (in English, German or French), from home and abroad desired.*

1161 Diller, Joseph S., S.B., U. S. Geol. Survey, Washington, D. C. *Geol.*, *Lithol.**

1162 Dillingham, Edwin, Moscow, Lamoille Co., Vt. *Bot.*, *Geol.*, *Min.* C. Ex.*

1163 Dimmock, George, Ph.D., Cambridge, Mass. *Ent.*, *Zool.* C.*

1164 Dinwiddie, H. H., Prof. Chem., College Station, Brazos Co., Tex. *Chem.*, *Min.*, *Agric.*, *Geol*, *Lithol.**

1165 Dinsmore, Thos. H., jr., Prof. Phys. and Chem., State Normal School, Emporia, Kans. *Chem.*, *Phys*, *Elect.**

1166 Dionne, C. E., Cur. du Mus. Zool. de l'Univ. Laval, Quebec Ca. *Zool.* C. Ex.*

1167 Dixwell, John, A.B., M.D. (Harv.) Mass. Med. Soc., etc. 52 W. Cedar St., Boston, Mass. *Osteology*, *Zoology.* C. Ex.*

1168 Doan, Abel, Westfield, Hamilton Co., Ind. *Forest Bot.*, *Geol.* C.*

1169 Doan, Wm. D., Box 206, Coatesville, Chester Co., Pa. *Zool.*, *Orn.*, *Ool.*, *Tax.*, *Ent.* C. Ex.*
1170 Dobbin, Geo. W.. St. Denis, Md. *Gen. Mic.**
1171 Dodd, Frank G., Nutley, Essex Co., N. J. *Bot.*, *Min.*, *Inorg. Chem.* C. Ex.*
1172 Dodds, Prof. Geo., Panquitots, Garfield Co., Utah. *Ent.*, *Geol.*, *Phys.*, *Philol.*, *Bot.*
1173 Dodge, Chas., B.Sc., 81 Pine St., Detroit, Mich. *Bot.*, *Zool.*, *Gen. Biol.**
1174 Dodge, Chas. Richards, Box 1362, Boston, Mass. *Econ. Ent.*, *Vegetable Fibres.* C.*
1175 Dodge, E. A , Glencoe, Dodge Co., Neb. *Lepid.* for sale.*
1176 Dodge, James A., Prof. Chem. Univ. of Minn., Minneapolis, Minn. *Min.*, *Chem.*, *Metall.*, *Crystall.**
1177 Dodge, S. C., Chattanooga, Tenn. *Chem.*, *Elect.*, *Eng.*, *Bot.* C.*
1178 Dolbear, Prof. A. E., College Hill, Mass. *Physics.*
1179 Dolley, C. S., M.D., Biological Dep't, University of Pa. *Gen. Biol.*, *Bacteriology.**
1180 Dolley, S. R. A., M.D., 52 East Ave., Rochester, N. Y. *Mic.*, *Biol.*
1181 Donaldson, Henry M., Fellow Johns Hopkins Univ., 123 W. Madison St., Baltimore, Md. *Mic.*, *Bot.*, *Ent.* C. Ex.?
1182 Doney, Chas. P., Cambridge City, Ind. *Palæo.?*
1183 Donnelly, Hon. Ignatius, Hastings, Minn. *Palæo.*, *Geol.*, *Meteo.*, *Ast.*, *Anth.*, *Arch.*, *Eth.**
1184 Doolittle, Chas. L., Prof. Math. and Ast., Lehigh Univ., So. Bethlehem, Pa.*
1185 Doremus, C. A , M.D., Ph.D., Adj. Prof. Chem. & Toxicology, Bellevue Hosp., Med. College, N. Y., Prof. Chem., Am. Veterinary College, N. Y., 92 Lexington Ave., New York, N. Y. *Chem.**
1186 Doremus, Robert Ogden, M.D., LL.D., Prof. Chem. and Phys.; "Coll. of the City of New York," N. Y., and Prof. Chem. Toxicol. and Medical Jurisprudence in "Bellevue Hosp. Medical College," N. Y.*
1187 Dorsch, E., M.D., Monroe, Mich. *Eth.*, *Palæo.*, *Bot.*, *Coleopt.*, *Con.* C.?
1188 Dorsett, A. D., Rushville, Schuyler Co., Ill. *Min.*, *Arch.* C. Geodes in ex. for other specimens. C. Ex.
1189 Dorsey, Rev. James Owen, Box 591, Washington, D. C. *Anth.*, *Eth.*, *Ethnog. and Philol. of N. A. Indians.**
1190 Douglas, H. F., Fenton, Genesee Co., Mich. *Diatoms*, *Mic.*, *Ast.*, *Infusoria.**
1191 Douglas, I., M.D., D.D.S., Romeo, Mich. *Bot.*, *Geol.*, *Min. Met.*, *Mic.*, *Histol.* Geol. C.*
1192 Dow, John M., F.Z.S., 69 Seventh Ave., New York City N. Y.*
1193 Downs, H. M., 7 Grove St., Rutland, Vt. *Min.*, *Radiates*, *Tax.* C. Ex.*
1194 Dowse, W. B., 11 Central St., Boston, Mass. *Orn.*, *Ool.* C.*

1195 Drake, F. S., B.S., Galesburg, Ill. *Geol.*, *Palæo.* C. Ex.*
1196 Draper, Daniel, Ph.D., Dir. N. Y. Met. Observ., New York City, N. Y. *Meteo* *
1197 Draper, Herbert E., Norwich, Conn. *Ent.* C. Ex.*
1198 Drew, Frank M., Bunker Hill, Ill. *Orn.*, *Ool.*
1199 Drown, Edw. D., Fern Hill, Weldon, Pa. *Ool.*, *Bot.*, *Palæo.*, *Geol.*, *Min.* Buys and sells good Mins. C. Ex.*
1200 Drown, Thomas M., Prof. Analyt. Chem , Mass. Inst. Technology, Boston, Mass.*
1201 Drumheller, Rev. C. K , Tamaqua, Pa. *Geol.*, *Min.*, *Ast.* All kinds of fossils. C. Ex.
1202 Dryer, C. R., M.D., Prof. Chem. and Toxicol., Fort Wayne, Ind. *Chem.*, *Geol.**
1203 Drysdale, Wm., 232 St. James St., Montreal, Can. *Mic.**
1204 DuBois, Patterson, Asst. Editor of "The Sunday School Times," Philadelphia, Pa. *Chem.*, *Met.*, *Arch.*, *Phil.**
1205 Dudleston, J. J., Frankfort, Herkimer Co., N. Y. *Geol.*, *Min.*?
1206 Dudley, Chas. B., Altoona, Blair Co., Pa. *Bot.*, *Chem.*, *Technology*, *Met.**
1207 Dudley, P. H., 66½ Pine St., New York City. *Engineering*, *Structure of Wood*, *Fungi*, *Metall.*, *Mic.**
1208 Dudley, Wm. L., Prof. Chem., Vanderbilt Univ., Nashville, *Chem.*, *Metall.**
1209 Dudley, Wm. R., Asst. Prof. Crypt. Bot., Cornell Univ., Ithaca, N. Y. C. Ex.*
1210 Duenkel, Wm., Seattle, W. T. *Coleoptera of Northern Calif.* Ex.?
1211 Duffield, George, M.D., 480 Woodward Ave., Detroit, Mich. *Mic.*, *Diatoms*, *Emb.*, *Anat.*, *Tax.*, *Pathol.*, *Histol.* C. Ex.*
1212 Dufresne, D.O.R., Chicoutimi, Quebec, Can. *Bot.*, *Ent.* C.*
1213 Duggan, J. R., Prof. of Chem., Wake Forest Coll., Wake Forest, N. C. *Chem.**
1214 Dumm, James F., Fleetwood, Berks Co., Pa. *Geol.*, *Min.*, *Crystall.* *Fine iridescent limonite equal if not superior to the foreign crystallizations of calcite and iron pyrites, zeolites, globular pyrites, a variety of zinc, copper, lead and iron ores, fœtid baryta, doubly terminated quartz crystals, etc. Will exfor good spec. only.*?
1215 Dumond, A. M., 70 Mt. Hope Ave., Rochester, N. Y. *Mic.**
1216 Dunham, Carroll, M.D., Irvington-on-Hudson, N. Y. *Path.*, *Public Health.**
1217 Dunham, Edw. K., Irvington-on-Hudson, N. Y. *Org. Chem.*, *Mic.*, *Gen. Biol.*?
1218 Dunlop, W. W., Box 1145, Montreal, Can. *Orn.*, *Ool.* C. Ex.?
1219 Dunn, E. C., M.D., Rockford, Ill. *Coins.* C.*
1220 Dunn, G. W., 629 Washington St., San Francisco, Calif. *Ferns*, *Con.*, *Coleopt.* Ex. in Con. and Coleopt.*
1221 Dunnington, F. P., B.Sc., Prof. Analyt. Chem., Univ. of Virginia, Va. *Min.*, *Inorg. Chem.*, *Met.* C. Ex.*

1222 DuPont, Francis G., Wilmington, Del. *Elect.*, *Ast.**

1223 DuPre, Col. L. J , 207 4½ St., Washington, D. C. *Am. Arch.?*

1224 Durbin, Thos., Weedsport, Cayuga Co., N. Y. *Orn.*, *Ool.* C. Ex.?

1225 Durfee, C. A., Springfield, Mass. *Geol.*, *Min.*, *Arch.* C. Ex.?

1226 Durfee, Matthew C., Bedford, Ohio. *Geol.*, *Zool.*, *Ool.*, *Tax.*, *Ent.* C.*

1227 Durfee, T. C., 44 Sabin St., Providence, R. I. *Geol.*, *Min.* C. Ex.*

1228 Durfee, W. F., C. & M.E., Birdsboro, Pa. *Min.*, *Chem.*, *Metall.*, *Phys.*, *Elect.*, *Photog.*, *Engineering* *

1229 During, Prof. Chas. A. A., 123 W. 41st St , New York City. *Ent: Lepid.* C.*

1230 Dury, Henry M., 707 Woodland St., Nashville, Tenn. *Metall.*, *Phys.*, *Elect.*, *Ent.* C. Ex.*

1231 Dustin, M. H., South Monmouth, Me. *Geol.*, *Min.*, *Crystall.*, *Arch.*, *Ool.* C. Ex.*

1232 Dutton, Capt. C. E., U.S.A., Ordnance Corps, U. S. Geol. Survey, Washington, D. C. *Geol.*, *Lithol.**

1233 Dwight, Thomas, M.D., Parkman Prof. of Anat., Harvard Med. School, Boston, Mass.*

1234 Dwight, William B., Prof. Nat. Hist., Vassar Coll., Poughkeepsie, N Y. *Geol.*, *Invert. Palæo.*, *Zool.* C.*

1235 Dwinelle, Charles H., Ph.B., Lecturer on Prac. Agric., Univ. of Cal., Berkeley, Alameda Co., Calif. *Ent.*, *Bot.?*

1236 Dyar, Harrison G., Rhinebeck, Dutchess Co., N. Y. *Lepid.*, C. Ex.*

1237 Dyche, D. T. D., Lebanon, O. *Palæo.*, *Geol.*, *Arch.* C. Ex?

1238 Eakin, Chas. H., 237 West Wayne St., Ft. Wayne, Ind. *Palæo.*, *Geol.*, *Min.* C. Ex.

1239 Earl, Thomas M., 401 East Naghten St., Columbus, Ohio. *Arch.*, *Tax.*, *Ool.*, *Orn.* C. Ex.*

1240 Earll, R. Edward, Smithsonian Inst., Washington, D. C. *Phæn. Bot.*, *Orn.*, *Ichth.* C.*

1241 Easby, Francis H., Media, Pa. *Min.**

1242 Eastman, Fred, Box 20, Salina, Kansas. *Geol.*, *Min.*, *Archæology.* C. Ex.*

1243 Eastman, Prof. J. R , Naval Obs., Washington, D. C. *Ast.**

1244 Eastman, Lewis M., A.M., M.D., 349 Lexington St., Baltimore, Md., *Mic.* Well mounted histological and pathological slides in exchange for other *first-class* slides, in any department of microscopy.*

1245 Easton, D. M., East Weymouth, Mass. *Geol.* C. Ex.

1246 Eastwick, Chas. H., 4053 Sansome St., Philadelphia, Pa. *Orn.*, *Ool.*

1247 Eastwood, Miss Alice, High School, Denver, Colo. *Bot.* C.*

1248 Eaton, Daniel C., Prof. Botany, Yale Coll , New Haven, Ct. *Bot.* C.*

1249 Eaton, D. G., Ph.D., late Prof. Phys. Sci., Packer Inst., 55 Pineapple St., Brooklyn, N. Y.*

1250 Eaton, D. H., Box 1235, Woburn, Mass. *Orn.*, *Ool.*, *Tax.*, *Geol.*, *Min.*, *Con.*, *L. and F. W. Shells desired.* Wishes foreign correspondence.*

1251 Eaton, Louis H., 147½ Union St., New Bedford, Mass. *Algæ*, *Desmids.* C. Ex.?

1252 Eberhart, Noble M., Box 1, Chicago Lawn, Ill. *Phæn. Bot.*, *Geol.*, *Min.*, *Zool.*, *Arch.*, *Orn.* , *Tax.*, *Ent.* C. Ex.

1253 Eckfeldt, Jacob B., Assayer, U. S. Mint, Philadelphia, Pa. *Min.*, *Inorg. Chem.*, *Metall.*, *Photog.* C.*

1254 Eckfeldt, John W., M.D., 6320 Vine St., West Philadelphia, Pa. *Lichens.* C. Ex.*

1255 Eddy, N. A., 509 N. Grand St., Bay City, Mich. *Orn.*, *Ool.* C. Ex.*

1256 Eddy, Wm. B., Granville, Licking Co., O. *Tax.* C. Ex.?

1257 Edison, Thomas Alva, Electrician, 40 and 42 Wall St., New York City, N. Y. *Org. and Inorg. Chem.*, *Metall.*, *Elect.* *

1258 Edmunds, J. Rayner, Harv. Coll. Obs., Cambridge, Mass. *Ast.*, *Geodesy*, *Phys.*, *Math.**

1259 Edmiston, Joseph L., Box 143, Riverside, San Bernardino Co., Calif. *Min.*, *Orn.*, *Ool.* C.*

1260 Edmond, E., Leger, West Redding, Fairfield Co., Ct. *Ent.* C. Ex.*

1261 Edwards, Carrie S. H , Argusville, Cass Co., Dakota. *Bot.*, *Orn.*, *Min.*, *Ferns*, *Mosses*, *Lichens*, *Zool.*, *Lepid.**

1262 Edwards, Charles L., 500 8th St., So. Minneapolis, Minn. *Zool.* C.*

1263 Edwards, E. Junius, 512 S. 7th St., Minneapolis, Minn. *Ent.* C.*

1264 Edwards, Miss Hattie E., Mendota, Ill. *Bot.* C. Ex.?

1265 Edwards, Henry, Wallack's Theatre, New York, N. Y. *Ent.*, *chiefly Lepid.*, *Ægeriadæ*, *Cossidæ*, *Hepialidæ and Plusias of the world.* Will purchase examples of these groups. C. Ex.*

1266 Edwards, James T., Pres. Chamberlain Inst., Randolph, N. Y. *Chem.* C. Ex.*

1267 Edwards, John M., Marlborough, Mass. *Mic.*, *Photo-Mic.**

1268 Edwards, Mrs. Mary J., 512 S. 7th St., Minneapolis, Minn. *Bot: Algæ.**

1269 Edwards, S. M., Argusville, Cass Co., Dak. *Hort.*, *Min.*, *Orn.* *Zool.**

1270 Edwards, Prof. Wm., Teacher of Tax. and Cur. Museum, Wellesley Coll., Wellesley, Mass.

1271 Edwards, Wm. H., Coalburgh, W. Va. *Diurnal Lepid. of N. A.* C.*

1272 Egan, W. C., 620 Dearborn Ave., Chicago, Ill. *Palæo.* C.*

1273 Egbert, H. V., A.M., Ass't Ast., Dudley Obs., Albany, N. Y. *Ast.**

1274 Egeling, Gustavus, Ph.D., Ph.G., Member Deutsche bot. Ges., Berlin, Bot. Verein. Landshut, Ver. f. Naturkunde Cassel, Larned, Kansas. *Bot: Phæn. and Crypt. Plants*, *Lichens*, *Org. and Inorg. Chem.*, *Mic.* C. Ex.*

1275 Eggert, H., 918 Wash St., St. Louis, Mo. *Phæn. Bot.*, *Ferns.* C.*

1276 Egleston, T., Engineer of Mines, Prof. of Mineralogy and Metallurgy, School of Mines, Columbia Coll., New York, N. Y. *Min.* C. Ex.*

1277 Ehinger, Geo. E., M.D., Keokuk, Ia. *Bot.* C. Ex.*

1278 Ehrman, Artis H., 1325 No. Cary St., Baltimore, Md. *Mic.*, *Elect.*, *Min.* C. Ex.*

1279 Ehrman, Geo. Alex., 2002 So. Josephine St., Pittsburg, Pa. Desires Macrolepidoptera of the World. Papilionidæ especially wanted.*

1280 Eisen, Gustav, Calif. Acad. of Sci., San Francisco, Calif. *Annelida*, *Oligochæta*, *Hort.*, *Central Am. Arch. and Hieroglyphics.* C.*

1281 Elder, Ella C., Florence, Mass. *Min.* C.

1282 Eldredge, Frank B., Attleboro, Mass. *Ool.* C. Ex.*

1283 Ellinwood, C. M., Prof. Natural Science, Indianola, Ia. C. Ex.*

1284 Elliot, S. Lowell, 466 Eighth St., near 8th Ave., Brooklyn, N. Y. *Ent.* C. Eggs, Larvæ, Pupæ, and Cocoons. American scientific books and pamphlets; Early Travel and Exploration; Government reports; Agriculture; Entomological publications of the world. Library. Exchange. Publications of Agricultural, Scientific and Historical Societies and Institutions. Town, County and General History of N. A. Periodicals.*

1285 Elliott, George W., 39 Rowley St., Rochester, N. Y. *Mic.*, *Meteo.*, *Ast.*?

1286 Elliott, Robert, Hannibal, Mo. *Mic.*, *Ast.**

1287 Ellis, A. L., Pawtucket, R. I. *Orn.*, *Ool.*, *Zool.* C.?

1288 Ellis, J. B., Newfield, N. J. *Fungi.* C. Ex.*

1289 Ellis, Prof. S. A., A.M., Ph.D., 13 Clifton St., Rochester, N. Y. *Mic.*, *Ent.**

1290 Ells, N. W., M.A., LL.D., Geol. Surv., Ottawa, Can. *Geol.*, *Lithol.**

1291 Ellsworth, Addison, New Berlin, N. Y. *Lepid.* C. Ex.*

1292 Ellsworth, E. W., East Windsor Hill, Ct. *Ool.*, *Arch.**

1293 Ellsworth, Wm., H., 450 Case St, Milwaukee, Wis. *Palæo.*, *Invert.*, *Arch.* Will ex. fossils and minerals for Indian relics and Trilobites. C. Ex.*

1294 Elmore, Norman, Breeder of English Beagle Hounds, Granb y Hartford Co., Ct. *Tax.* C. Ex.*

1295 Elmore, Samuel E., Hartford, Ct. *Orn.*, *Bot.**

1296 Elsner, John, A.B., M.D., Box 2282, Denver, Colo. *Chem. especially Min.* C. Ex. Only characteristic crystallized specimens wanted.*

1297 Ely, Charles A., Perrineville, Monmouth Co., N. J. *Fungi*, *Orn.*, *Ool.* C. Ex.*

1298 Emerson, Benj. K., Ph.D., Prof. Geol. and Min., Amherst Coll., Amherst, Mass.

1299 Emerson, Charles F., Appleton Prof. Nat. Phil., Dartmouth Coll., Hanover, N. H. *Phys.**

4

1300 Emerson, W. Otto, Hayward, Alameda Co., Calif. *Ool.*, *Orn.*, *Gen. Nat. Hist.*, *Numis.* C. Exchange only for perfect sets of Ool., and first-class skins with data and names, in all cases. Correspondence desired throughout the U. S., regarding the distribution of Birds.*

1301 Emmons, S. F., U. S. Geol. Survey, Washington, D. C. *Geol.*, *Mining Engineering.*

1302 Emswiler, George P., Richmond, Ind. *Palæo.* C.*

1303 Endemann, Herman, Ph.D., 33 Nassau St., New York, N. Y. *Chem.**

1304 Engelhardt, Francis E., Ph.D., Chem. for state salines, Syracuse, N. Y. *Chem.**

1305 Engelmann, George J., M.D., 3003 Locust St., St. Louis, Mo. *Arch.*, *Mic.**

1306 Engle, Robert H., Electrician and Metallurgist, Moorestown, Burlington Co., N. J., P. O. Box 862, Philadelphia, Pa. *Chem.*, *Min.*, *Arch.*, *Electric Lighting and application* *

1307 Engstrom, Aug., M.D., McPherson, Kans. *Elect.*, *Met.*, *Emb.*, *Osteol.**

1308 Enos, C. O., Connersville, Fayette Co., Ind. *Con.* C. Ex.

1309 Enos, Edw. A., Connersville, Fayette Co., Ind *Con.* C. Ex.*

1310 Ensign, William O., M.D., Rutland, La Salle Co., Ill. *Osteol.*, *Mic.*, *Gen. Biol.**

1311 Ernst, Chas. H., Box 345, Kenosha, Wis. *Min.* C. Ex.*

1312 Ernst, C. W., M.A., 298 Commonwealth Ave., Boston, Mass. *Anth.*, *Eth.*, *Ethnog.*, *Philol.**

1313 Estabrook, S. Adelle, Worcester, Mass. *Bot: Ferns.* C.*

1314 Evans, Edwin, M.D., Streator, La Salle Co., Ill. *Geol.*, *Palæo.* C. Ex.

1315 Evans, Geo. Wm., Instructor in Math., Eng. High Sch., Boston, Mass. *Phys.*, *Elect.*, *Math* *

1316 Evans, John D., P. L.S., Trenton, Ont., Can. *Ent: Coleopt.*, *Mic.* C. Ex. in Coleopt. desired. Foreign Corres. solicited.*

1317 Evans, S. G., 712 Walnut St., Evansville, Ind. *Lepid.* for sale or ex.*

1318 Everett, M. H., M.D., Troy Grove, Ill. *Arch.*, *Geol.* C. ?

1319 Everhart, Benj. M., West Chester, Pa. *Bot.**

1320 Evermann, Barton W., Prof. Nat. Sci., Ind. State Normal School, Terre Haute, Indiana. *Orn.*, *Ool.* C. Ex.*

1321 Evermann, Mrs. Meadie, Terre Haute, Ind. *Orn.*, *Bot.* C. Ex.*

1322 Evers, Edw., M.D., Lect. on Histol., St. Louis Medical Coll., 1861 North Market St., St. Louis, Mo. *Mic.*, *Zool.*, *Arch.*, *Histol.**

1323 Ewart, J. G., Yarker P. O., Addington Co., Ont., Can. *Mam.*, *Orn.* C. Ex.*

1324 Ewing, A. L., Teacher of Science, Working Man's School, 39 W. 65th St., New York City.*

1325 Eyerman, John, Easton, Pa. *Geol.*, *Min.*, *Crystall.*, *Petrog.*, *Anal. Chem.* C. Ex.*

1326 Eyster, Geo. S., A. M., Ph.D., Gettysburg, Pa. *Ferns, Mosses, Metall., Chem.*

1327 Faber, Chas. L., 397 Race St., Cincinnati, Ohio. *Palæo.* Ex. *Crinoidea, Cystoidea, Spongida; also Geol. Surveys* for Ex. Lists sent upon application.*

1328 Fahlberg, Constantin, Ph.D., Gray's Ferry Chemical Works, Philadelphia, Pa. *Chem.* C. Ex.?

1329 Fahs, Rev. R. Z., Olney, Richland Co., Ill. *Geol., Palæo.* C. Ex.*

1330 Failyer, G. A., Prof. of Chem., State Agric. Coll., Manhattan, Kan. *Chem., Min.* C. Ex.*

1331 Fairbanks, Arthur, St. Johnsbury, Vt. *Phæn. Bot., Ferns.* C. Ex.

1332 Fairbanks, F., St. Johnsbury, Vt. *Orn., Ool., Ent., Min., Curiosities.* C.*

1333 Fairbanks, Rev. Henry, Ph.D., St. Johnsbury, Vt. *Orn., Ool.**

1334 Fairchild, A. K., Whippany, N. J. *Min., Orn., Ool., Con.* C. Ex.*

1335 Fairchild, Davis S., M.D., Prof. Iowa Agric. Coll., Ames, Ia. *Histol., Phys., Mic., Gen. Biol.**

1336 Fairchild, Prof. Herman L., Secretary of N. Y. Acad. of Sciences, New York, N. Y. *Palæo., Geol., Zool.* C. Ex.*

1337 Fairman, Charles, LL.D., Upper Alton, Ill. *Chem., Geol.* C.*

1338 Falconer, William, Glen Cove, L. I., N. Y. *Hort.* C.*

1339 Fales, J. C., Prof. Nat. Sci., Centre Coll., Danville, Ky. *Geol., Palæo., Zool.* C. Ex.*

1340 Fall, Delos, M.S., Prof. Chem. and Biol., Albion Coll., Albion, Mich. A fine collection of minerals, 300 specimens, for sale or exchange for books.*

1341 Fall, H. C., Farmington, N. H. *Ent: Lepid., Coleopt.* C. Ex.*

1342 Fanning, J. T., Manchester, N. H. *Min., Phys., Meteo.?*

1343 Farlow, W. G., Prof. Crypt. Bot., Cambridge, Mass.*

1344 Farnam, Chas. H., Asst. in Arch., Yale Coll., Hillhouse Ave., New Haven, Ct.*

1345 Farnsworth, P. J., M.D., Clinton, Ia., Prof. Materia Medica, State University. *Geol.* C. Drugs, Niagara fossils.*

1346 Farquhar, Edward, Patent Office Library, Washington, D. C. *Anth., Philol.**

1347 Farr, Henry L., 14 Chestnut Ave., Rutland, Vt. *Geol., Min.* C.*

1348 Farwell, Oliver A., Phenix, Keweenaw Co., Mich. *Bot: Ferns.* C. and ex. in Phæn. and Crypt. Bot.*

1349 Faucher, G. L., West Winsted, Ct. *Palæo., Anth., Arch., Eth.* C. Ex.*

1350 Faught, V. R., Hamilton, Ill. *Geol., Orn., Ent.* C. Ex.*

1351 Faxon, Charles E., Boston, Mass. *Bot.?*

1352 Faxon, Walter, Assistant in Mus. Comp. Zool., Cambridge, Mass. *Gen. Zool., Crustacea.**

1353 Fearing, Clarence W., Mass. Inst. Tech., Boston, Mass. *Bot., Min.* C. Ex.*

1354 Fearn, R. Lee, Summit, N. J. *Photog.* C. Ex.
1355 Featherstone, J. E., Elk River, Sherburne Co., Minn. *Min.*?
1356 Febiger, Christian, Wilmington, Del. *Diatoms.*
1357 Feely, Laura C., Patchen, Santa Clara Co., Calif. *Con.* C. Ex.?
1358 Fell, Geo. E., M.D., F.R.M.S., 72 Niagara St., Buffalo, N. Y. *Mic.* C.*
1359 Fellows, Charles S., 38 Throop St., Chicago, Ill. *Gen. Nat. Hist., Crustacea.* C.*
1360 Fellows, Dana W., M.D., 23 Free St., Portland, Me. *Min., Odontology, Histol.* C.*
1361 Ferguson, D. W., 138 Wilson St., Brooklyn, E. D., N. Y. *Con., Radiates.* C. Ex.*
1362 Ferguson, Miss E. D., Stamford, Ct. *Ferns.* C.*
1363 Ferguson, Maj. T. B., Washington, D. C. *Ass't Comm. of Fish and Fisheries.*
1364 Fernald, C. H., Prof. of Zoology, State Coll., Amherst, Mass. *Nat. Hist.* C. Will purchase or ex. for Tortricidæ of all parts of the world. Correspondence with collectors of Tortricidæ desired. Wishes N. A. *Pyralidæ, Tineina* and *Pterophoridæ.**
1365 Fernald, Henry T., Amherst, Mass. *Hemiptera.* C. Ex. Desires American Hemiptera.*
1366 Fernald, M. C., Pres. Me. State Coll., Orono, Me. *Physics, Ast.**
1367 Ferrel, William, Prof., Ph.D., 1641 Broadway, Kansas City, Mo.*
1368 Ferrer, Henry, M.D., Calif. Acad. of Sci., San Francisco, Calif. *Comp. Ophthalmology and Mic.**
1369 Ferrier, Walter F., B.A.Sc., 144 Metcalfe St., Montreal, Canada. *Palæo., Min.* C. Ex. Will exchange for the rarer lead minerals.*
1370 Fewkes, A. A., Newton Highlands, Mass. *Bot., Hymenop.* C.*
1371 Fewkes, J. Walter, In charge Newport Marine Laboratory, Ass't Mus. Comp. Zool., Cambridge, Mass. *Marine Zool., Cœlenterates, Echinoderms, Worms, Molluscs.*
1372 Ficklin, Joseph, LL.D., Prof. Math. and Ast., State Univ., Columbia, Mo.*
1373 Fillion, Prof. F., 1005 Halsey St., Brooklyn, N. Y. *Coleopt.* C. Ex.*
1374 Finkelnburg, William A., Winona, Winona Co., Minn. *Arch., Geol., Palæo.* Will exchange Potsdam fossils for those from other groups. C. Ex.*
1375 Fischer, Moritz, Frankfort, Franklin Co., Ky. *Palæo., Arch.* C. Ex.*
1376 Fischer, Philip, 514 Dodge St., Buffalo, N. Y. *Ent: Am. and exotic Lepid., local Coleopt.* C. Ex. for perfect spec. in Lepidoptera. Bombycidæ and Catocalæ of U. S. desired.*
1377 Fish, Azel H., 26 Nevada Block, San Francisco, Calif. *Molluscs.* C. Ex.

1378 Fish, George T., 174 Meigs St., Rochester, N. Y. *Bot.* C.*
1379 Fish, M. W., M.D., San Francisco, Calif.
1380 Fisher, A. K., M.D., Sing Sing, N. Y. *Orn.*, *Vertebrates.* C.
1381 Fisher, C. H., M.D., Providence, R. I. *Crypt. Bot.*, *Mic.*, *Gen. Biol.*, *Protozoa*, *Infusoria.**
1382 Fisher, Davenport. Wauwatosa, Wis. *Chem.**
1383 Fisher, Ellen F., Lake Erie Seminary, Painesville, Ohio. *Phys.*, *Elect.*, *Ast.*
1384 Fisher, Frank G., Mount Repose, Ohio. *Orn.*, *Min.*, *Palæo.*, *Ent.* C. Ex.*
1385 Fisher, Dr. Herschel, Des Moines, Iowa. *Arch.* C.*
1386 Fisher, Orville, Civil and Sanitary Engineer, P. O. Box 644, Providence, R. I. *Org. Chem.*, *Phys.*, *Elect.*, *Meteo.*, *Emb.**
1387 Fisher, William Hubbell, Rooms 12 and 18 Wiggin's Block, Cincinnati, Ohio. *Orn.*, *Anat. of birds.* C. Ex. Birds of prey, of especial interest.*
1388 Fisk, Lyman B., Charlestown, Mass. *Bot.*, *Geol.*, *Min.**
1389 Fiske, Edw. H., Naturalist, Santa Cruz, Calif. *Ast.*, *Orn.*, *Ool.* C. Ex.*
1390 Fitch, E. Henry. Ed. Journal of Science and Art, Cleveland, Ohio. *Orn.*, *Ool.* Ex.*
1391 Fitch, Mrs. H. M., Sheridan, Madison Co., Montana. *Geol.*, *Min.* C. Ex.*
1392 Fitch, J. H., Lexington, Mass. *Min.*, *Zool.*, *Orn.*, *Ool.*, *Ichth.*, *Tax.* C. Ex.*
1393 Fitz, Geo. Wells, Normal Park, Cook Co., Ill. (Permanent address Peconic, Suff. Co., N. Y.) *Phys.*, *Mic.*, *Photog.*, *Meteo.* Ex.*
1394 Fitzgibbon, Thos., Sparksville, Jackson Co., Indiana. *Zool.*, *Ool.* C. Ex.*
1395 Fleming, John, Readington, Hunterdon Co., N. J.*
1396 Fletcher, Frank F., L.B. 83, St. Johnsbury, Vt. *Arch.*, *Numismatics.* *Geol.*, *Bot.*
1397 Fletcher, Hugh, B. A., Geolog. Surv., Ottawa, Can. *Geol.**
1398 Fletcher, James, Library of Parliament, Ottawa, Can. *Bot.*, *Con.*, *Spec. Econ. Ent: Lepid.*, *Aquatic plants*, *Ent.* Ex.*
1399 Fletcher, M. H., M.D., D.D.S., Cincinnati, Ohio.*
1400 Fletcher, Robert, M.D., Surgeon General's Office, U.S.A., Washington, D. C. *Bibliog.*, *Gen. Biol.*, *Anth.**
1401 Fletcher, S. L., Charlestown, N. H. *Geol.*, *Min.* C. Ex.*
1402 Fletcher, S., M.D., Pepperell, Mass. *Mic.*, *Bot.*, *Hist.* C. Ex.*
1403 Flett, John B., Groton, N. Y. *Geol.**
1404 Flint, Albert S., U. S. Naval Obs., Washington, D. C. *Ast.**
1405 Flint, James M., Surg. U. S. Navy, Smithsonian Inst., Washington, D. C. *Mic.* C.*
1406 Flint, Martha B., A.M., Amenia, N. Y. *Phæn. Bot.* C. Ex.*
1407 Flint, Weston, A.M., LL.M., Ph.D., Librarian, Sci. Lib. U. S. Patent Office, chairman Board of Examiners, U. S. Civil Service Commission, residence 1101 K. St., N. W., Washington, D. C. *Anth.*, *Arch.*, *Bibliography.**

1408 Flint, William C., 216 Sansome St., San Francisco, Calif. *Orn.*, *Ool.* C. Ex.*

1409 Flint, William F., B.S., Winchester, N. H., Comm. of Forestry for N. H. *Bot.* C.*

1410 Flood Bros., Oologists, Clinton, Mass. Ex. Eggs in sets, with data with any native or foreign collectors. Correspondence solicited.*

1411 Flood, Milton J., Naturalist and Taxidermist, Clinton, Mass. *Min.*, *Ent.*, *Ool.*, *Geol. and Gen. Zool.* Will exchange Fossils from the Phosphate beds of S. C. with other collectors. C. Ex.*

1412 Foerste, Aug. Fred., A.B., 348 Richard St., Dayton, Ohio. *Phæn. and Crypt. Bot.*, *Hepatica*, *Dalmontology*, *Invert.*, *Geol.*, *Arch.*, *Herpetol*, *Stratigraphical Palæo.*, *Clinton group and the lower part of the Upper Silurian Strata generally.* C. Ex.*

1413 Folsom, David, Chicopee, Mass. *Mic: esp. insect preparations.* C.*

1414 Folsom, John G., Winchendon, Mass. *Geol.*, *Min.*, *Arch.* C. Ex.*

1415 Fonta, Jules, Horticulturist, New Orleans, La. *Bot: Ferns*, *Ent.* C.

1416 Fontaine, William M., Prof. Geol. and Nat. Hist., Univ. of Va., Va. *Fossil Bot* *

1417 Foote, Albert E., M.D., Prof. Chem. and Min., 1223 Belmont Ave., Philadelphia, Pa. *Scientific Bibliog.*, *Min.*, *Gen. Nat. Hist.* See Advertisement. C. Ex.*

1418 Foote, Edward B., sr., M.D., 120 Lexington Ave., New York, N. Y. *Physics*, *Elect.*, *Anth.**

1419 Foote, E. B., jr., M.D., 120 Lexington Ave., New York, N. Y. *Mic.**

1420 Foote, Dr. Herbert C., F.C.S., Prof. Chem., Central High Sch., and Homœopathic Hosp. Coll., 87 Arlington Court, Cleveland, O. *Chem.*, *Photog.* C. Ex.*

1421 Foote, Lewis, Civil Engineer, Worthington, Nobles Co., Minn. *Bot.* C.*

1422 Forbes, S. A., State Entomologist and Prof. Zool. and Ent., Univ. of Ill., Champaign, Ill. *Zool.*, *Ent.**

1423 Forbush, Edw. H., Nat. Exchange, 424 Main St., Worcester, Mass. *Taxidermy*, *Orn.*, *Gen. Zool.* Ex.*

1424 Ford, Frank, Wichita, Kansas. Fine collection of Fresh Water Mollusca.*

1425 Ford, Henry C., Pres. Santa Barbara Soc. of Nat. Hist., Santa Barbara, Calif. *Bot.*, *Hort.*, *Meteo.*, *Arch.* C.*

1426 Ford, John, Vice Dir. Con. Section, Acad. Nat. Sci., Philadelphia, Pa. *Con.**

1427 Ford, J. H., Ravenna, Ohio. *Arch.*, *Bot.*, *Con.*, *Ent.*, *Geol.* C. Ex. eggs for shells, Indian relics or insects.*

1428 Ford, R. W., Bristol, Ct. *Orn.*, *Ool.* C. Ex. Desires foreign and Am. correspondence.*

1429 Fore, C. P., Wayland, Clark Co., Mo. *Geol.*, *Min.*, *Crystall.*, *Arch.* C. Ex.*

1430 Forehand, F., Box 349, Worcester, Mass. *Orn.*, *Ool.*, *Tax.* C. Ex.

1431 Forrer, A., Santa Cruz, Calif. Collector of specimens of Nat. Hist. of West Coast of N. A. *Zool.*, *Coll. of West Coast bought and sold.* Correspondence solicited. C. Ex.*

1432 Forrest, Will. H., Logansport, Ind. *Marine Bot.* Ex. Coll. Mosses and Ferns.*

1433 Forster, Edward J., M.D., 22 Monument Square, Charlestown District, Boston, Mass. *Fungi* (*North American Agarics and Boleti only*). Interested in North American Agaricini and Boleti and desirous of literature relating thereto.*

1434 Fortimer, Harry S., Camden, N. J. *Mic.*, *Chem.*, *Crystals.**

1435 Fosgate, Blanchard, M.D., Auburn, N. Y. *Eth. in Social Institutions.**

1436 Foster, Frank H., P. O. Box 557, Keene, N. H. *Ent: Lepid.*, *Coleopt.* C. Ex.*

1437 Foster, Granville F., Prin. Cal. Normal and Sci. School, Vacaville, Solano Co., Calif. *Anat*, *Physiol.*, *Meteo.* ?

1438 Foster, J. Herbert, 187 Crown St., Meriden, Ct. *General collection esp. Min.* C. Ex. Offers local spec. of barytes.*

1439 Foster, L. S., 35 Pine St., New York, N. Y. *Orn.**

1440 Foster, Richard, Howard Univ., Washington, D. C. *Bot.*, *Geol.*, *Zool.**

1441 Foulke, Sara G., 1827 Pine St., Philadelphia, Pa. *Mic.*, *Protozoa.*

1442 Foulkes, Albert E., Keokuk, Ia. *Crinoids.* C.*

1443 Fowler, Augustus, Danvers, Mass. *Ool.**

1444 Fowler, Rev. James, M.A., Lecturer on Nat. Sci., Queens Coll., Kingston, Can. *Geol.*, *Zool.*, *Bot.* C. Ex. plants only.*

1445 Fowler, John W., M.D., Dubuque, Iowa. *Orn.*, *Ool.* C. Ex.*

1446 Fowler, Samuel P., Danvers, Mass. *Orn.**

1447 Fox, Samuel L., 924 Chestnut St., Phila., Pa. *Ophthalmology.*

1448 Foye, James C., A.M., Ph.D., Prof. Chem. and Physics in Lawrence Univ., Appleton, Wis.*

1449 Fradenburgh, Rev. J. N., Ph.D., D.D., Oil City, Pa. *Anth.*, *Bot.*, *Geol.* C.*

1450 Fraine, Thomas W., 16 Joslyn Park, Rochester, N. Y. *Zool.*, *Orn. and Gen. Tax.* C. Ex.*

1451 Francis, George E., M.D., 79 Elm St., Worcester, Mass. *Elect.*, *Hort.*, *Photog.**

1452 Frank, Geo., 293 Ewen St., Brooklyn, E. D., N. Y. *Lepid.**

1453 Frankenburg, Prof. Otto, M.D., 248 E. Rich St., Columbus, Ohio. Prof. of Anat. Starling Medical College.*

1454 Franklin, G. S., A.M., M.D., Chillicothe, O. *Ent.*, *Arch.* C.?

1455 Frawley, J. A., Stromsberg, Neb. *Herpetol.*, *Geol.*, *Arch.**

1456 Frazer, John, 80 Burnet Ave., Cincinnati, Ohio. *Geol.*, *Hort.*, *Pomology.* C. Ex.?

1457 Frazer, Persifor, A.M., Dr. ès. Sci. Nat. (Univ. de France), Prof. Chem., Franklin Inst., 201 S. 5th St., Philadelphia, Pa. *Geol.*, *Lithol*, *Mic.*, *Chem.**

1458 Frazier, B. W., Prof. of Mineralogy and Metallurgy, Bethlehem, Pa. *Min.*, *Metall.* C. Ex.?
1459 Frazier, J. V., M.D., Viola, Mercer Co., Ill. *Palæo.*, *Geol.**
1460 Frear, Wm., Ph.D., Prof. of Agric. Chem., Pa. State College, Centre Co., Pa. *Chem.*, *Bibliog.* C.*
1461 Free, Rev. Alfred, Toms River, N. J. *Min*, *Geol.*, *Bot.* C.*
1462 Freed, A., Lancaster, Fairfield Co., Ohio. *Zool.*, *Min.*, *Geol.*, *Con.* C.*
1463 Freeman, H. C., Civil and Mining Engineer, Alto Pass, Union Co., Ill. *Geol.*, *Metall.*, *Mining.* C. Examines and reports on mining property. Long and extensive experience.*
1464 French, Alfred J., Lawrence, Mass.*
1465 French, Prof. G. H., Mus. of South Ill. Normal Univ., Carbondale, Ill. *Bot.*, *Ent: Lepid.* C. Ex. Have few sets of Colo. plants to ex. for insects.*
1466 French, Thomas, jr., A.M., Ph.D., Prof. of Physics, Univ. of Cincinnati, Ohio.*
1467 Freshwater, John, Loudonville, Ashland Co., Ohio. *Arch.*, *Geol.* C. Ex.?
1468 Fretz, C. D., M.D., Sellersville, Bucks Co., Pa. *Bot.* C. 1200 Eastern Pa., and N. J. Pine Barren plants for ex.*
1469 Frick, Jno. H., A.M., Prof. Nat. Sci., Central Wesleyan Coll., Warrenton, Mo. *Geol.*, *Bot.* C. Ex.*
1470 Frick, Moses L., San Diego, Calif. *Con.* C. Ex.?
1471 Fries, George W., B.P., Friendship, N. Y. *Mic.* C. Ex.*
1472 Frisbie, Dr. J. F., Newton, Mass. *Geol.*, *Arch.**
1473 Frisby, Prof Edgar, U. S. Naval Observ., Washington, D. C.*
1474 Fristoe, Edward T., A.M., LL.D., Prof. Chemistry in the Collegiate and Medical Depts., and Prof. Chemistry and Dean of the Faculty in the Corcoran School of Science and Arts, of the Columbian University, 1484 N. St., N. W. Washington, D. C. *Agric.*, *Geol.*, *Min.*, *Chem.*, *Phys.*, *Elect.*, *Meteo.*, *Ast.*, *Zool.*, *Gen. Biol.* ?
1475 Fritts, Chas. E., Electrician, 42 Nassau St., New York City. *Elect.*, *Phys.*, *Chem.*, *Photog.*, *Metall.**
1476 Froehling, Dr. Henry, Analyt. Chem., 17 S. 12th St., Richmond, Va. *Mic.*, *Chem.*, *Min.* C.*
1477 Frohock, Roscoe, Malden, Mass. *Crypt. Bot.* C. Ex.*
1478 Frossard, Edw., Prof., 787 and 789 Broadway, New York, N. Y. *Numismatics*, *Arch.* Collection of Coins. Ex.*
1479 Fry, T. M., 216 East Genesee St., Syracuse, N. Y. *Palæo.*, *Min.*, *Moll.* L. and F. W. Shells desired from all parts of the world. C. Ex.*
1480 Fuchs, Chas., 23 Post St., San Francisco, Calif. *Coleopt: Scarabidæ of the world.* C. Ex.?
1481 Fuchs, Charles, 6 Great Jones St., New York, N. Y. *Coleopt.*
1482 Fuller, A. S., Ridgewood, N. J. *Phæn. Bot.*, *Coleopt.* C. Ex.*
1483 Fuller, C. B., Portland, Me. *Zool.**
1484 Fuller, Mrs. C. E., Needham, Mass. *Bot.*, *Ent.*, *Orn.**
1485 Fuller, Chas. G., M.D., F.R.M.S., 38 Central Music Hall, Chicago, Ill. *Hist.*, *Mic.* C. Ex.*

1486 **Fuller, Chas. H.**, Turners, Orange Co., N. Y. *Bot.* C. Ex.*
1487 **Fuller, Frank H.**, Fruitland, Putnam Co., Fla. *Coleopt.*, *Lepid.* C.
1488 **Fuller, H. W.**, care Fuller & Fuller, Chicago, Ill. *Mic.*, *Chem.*, *Ast.* ?
1489 **Fuller, L. A.**, Supt. Pacific Ex. Co., 1829 Rutger St., St. Louis, Mo. *Palæo.* C.*
1490 **Fuller, Mrs. R. E.**, M.D., Macon, Ga. *Bot: Ferns.* C. Ex.*
1491 **Fuller, T. O.**, Needham, Norfolk Co., Mass. *Gen. Bot.*, *Orn.*, *Ool.**
1492 **Furness, H. B.**, 567 McMillen St., Walnut Hills, Cincinnati, Ohio. *Chem.*, *Min.*, *Metall.*, *Phys.**
1493 **Fyles, Rev. Thos. W.**, South Quebec, Canada. *Bot.*, *Mic.*, *Gen. Biol.*, *Ent.* C.?
1494 **Gabriel, R.**, Milford Centre, Ohio. *Lens and Speculæ grinding.**
1495 **Gade, George**, Fordham Station, New York, N. Y. *Nocturnal Lepid.*, *Mic.* C. Ex.?
1496 **Gaffield, Thomas**, 54 Allen St., Boston, Mass. *Chem.*, *Phys.*, *Glass making.**
1497 **Gage, Simon H.**, B.S., Ass't Prof. Phys. and Lect. on Mic. Tech., Cornell Univ., Ithaca, N. Y. *Morphology and Physiology of Vert.**
1498 **Gaillard, Edw.**, 11th and Montgomery Ave., Philadelphia, Pa. *Mic.*, *Chem.* C.*
1499 **Gaines, J. T.**, Broadway near Shelley, Louisville, Ky. *Palæo.* C. Ex.*
1500 **Gaines**, Richard H., Norfolk, Va. *Analyt. Chem.**
1501 **Galen, James**, Rawlinsville, Lancaster Co., Pa. *Bot.*, *Geol.*, *Min.*, *Orn.*, *Ool.*, *Emb.*, *Arch.*, *Con.*, *Philately*, *Numismatics*, *Chem.* Polished wood specimens a specialty. C. Ex.
1502 **Gallagher**, William C., Ross, Lake Co., Ind. *Ent.* C.*
1503 **Galloway**, B. T., Columbia, Mo. *Fungi.**
1504 **Gannett**, Henry, S.B., A. Met. B., U. S. Geol. Survey, Washington, D. C. *Geography.**
1505 **Ganong, Wm. F.**, A.M., St. Stephen, New Brunswick, Can. *Phæn. Plants*, *Zool.*, *Gen. Biol.*, *Geog. Dist.*, *Morph.*, *Vert.*, *Invert.*, *Moll.*, *Radiates.* C. Ex.*
1506 **Gardiner, Edw. G.**, Mass. Inst. Technology, 289 Marlboro St., Boston, Mass. *Emb.*, *Anat of Vert.**
1507 **Gardiner, F.**, jr., A.B., Sioux Falls, Dakota. *Ent.*, *Ichth.*, *Emb.* C. Dakota Coleopt. and Lepid. in ex. for Orn. specimens.*
1508 **Gardiner, Rev. F.**, D.D., Middletown, Ct.*
1509 **Gardiner, Hermon C.**, M.D., 111 Fourth St., Troy, N. Y. *Phæn. Bot.* Ex.*
1510 **Gardiner, James T.**, 21 Elk St., Albany, N. Y.*
1511 **Gardner, Rev. Corliss B.**, 8 New York St., Rochester, N. Y. *Phys.*, *Elect.*, *Mic.*, *Ast.*, *Anth.**
1512 **Gardner, J.**, M.D., 115 Mulberry St., Toledo, Ohio. *Phys.*, *Mic.*, *Histol.* C. Ex.

1513 Gardner, Leonard, South Weymouth, Mass. *Math.*, *Ast.*
1514 Gardner, W. Samuel, West Burlington, N. Y. *Tax.* C. Ex.
1515 Garlock, F. R., M.D., Racine, Wis. *Mic.*, *Anat.* C.*
1516 Garman, H., Champaign, Ill. *Biol.*, *Ent.*, *Emb.**
1517 Garman, Samuel, care Mus. Comp. Zool., Cambridge, Mass. *Herpetol.*, *Ichth.**
1518 Garnett, Algernon S., M.D., A.M., Hot Springs, Ark. *Gen. Biol.*, *Emb.*, *Anat.**
1519 Garrett, C. H., 102 West Main St., Kalamazoo, Mich. *Min.* C. Ex. Postage Stamp Collector.*
1520 Garrett, Philip C., Logan P. O., Philá., Pa. *Phys.*, *Geol.*, *Orn.* C. Ex. in Orn.*
1521 Garrett, Thomas H., 919 Chant St., Philadelphia, Pa. *Chem.* ?
1522 Garrison, H. D., 76 31st St., Prof. Chem., Chicago, Ill. *Chem.*, *Toxicol.*, *Photog.*, *Biol.* C.*
1523 Garver, M. M., Supt. U. S. Electric Lighting Co. of Pa., Chester and Maple Sts., Phila., Pa. *Elect.*, *Magnetism.*
1524 Gascoyne, Dr. Wm. J., Chemist, Va. Dept. Agric., Richmond, Va. *Geol.*, *Min.*, *Chem.*, *Metall.*, *Mic.*, *Photog.* C. Ex.*
1525 Gaskin, Helena C., Normal Coll., 69th St. and 4th Ave., New York City. *Bot*
1526 Gastman, E. A., Supt. City Schools, Decatur, Ill. *Ent.*, *Orn.* C. Ex. Can furnish live crayfish.*
1527 Gatschet, Albert S., Bureau of Eth., Washington, D. C. *Anth.*, *Indian Linguist*, *Philol.*, *Arch.*, *Eth.* Requests publications for review.*
1528 Gattinger, A., M.D., Nashville, Tenn. *Bot.* C.*
1529 Gaul, Charles F., 124 Lee Ave., Brooklyn, E. D., N. Y. *Gen. Biol.*, *Vert. Anat.*, *Geol.* C.*
1530 Gault, B. T., 878 Washington Boulevard, Chicago, Ill. *Orn.*, *Ool.*, *Tax.* C.*
1531 Gaumer, Geo. F., Lawrence, Kan. *Diptera*, *Birds.* C. Will exchange or purchase named Diptera of the world. Will sell objects of Natural History from Yucatan. ?
1532 Gavit, W. E., Box 3006, New York, N. Y. *Elect.*, *Mic.*, *Ent.*, *Fish Culture.* C.*
1533 Gay, Dr. Fred. A., 173 Westminster St., Providence, R. I. *Min.* C.*
1534 Geddes, Capt. Gamble, 3 Leader Lane, Toronto, Can. *General Ent.* Species from Ont. and Quebec in ex. for those of other N. A. localities. Diurnals from the Rocky Mts. a specialty.*
1535 Gee, Frank W., New Orleans, La. *Mic.* C. Ex.
1536 Gehring, J. G., M.D., 16 Church St., Cleveland, Ohio. *Ent: Coleopt.**
1537 Geisler, Joseph Frank, Ph C., F.C.S., Mercantile Exchange Building cor. Hudson and Harrison Sts., New York, N. Y. *Phæn. Bot.*, *Lithol.*, *Chem.**
1538 Genth, Prof. Fred. A., Ph.C., West Philadelphia, Pa. *Min.*, *Chem.* C. Ex.*
1539 Genth, Fred., jr., Prof. Univ. Pa., Philadelphia, Pa. *Chem.**

1540 Gentry, A. F., Acad. Nat. Sci., Philadelphia, Pa. *Ool., Herpetol., Osteol.* C. Ex.*
1541 Gentry, Thomas G., U. S. Grant Boys' Grammar School, N. E. corner of 17th and Pine Sts., Phila., Pa. *Orn., Ool., Mosses, Fungi.* C. Ex.*
1542 George, F. W., Williamstown, Iowa. *Inorg. Chem., Zool., Orn.**
1543 George, James N., 37 Pearl St., Boston, Mass. *Elect.**
1544 George, Wm. R., Keene, N. H. *Min.* C. Ex.*
1545 Gerard, Chas. B., Anderson, Ind. *Arch.**
1546 Gerard, W. R., 61 Clinton Place, New York, N. Y. *Bot.**
1547 Gerber, John M., Columbia, Lancaster Co., Pa. *Min., Elect., Meteorol., Ast.*
1548 Gerend, John, Sheboygan, Wis. *Orn., Ool., Lepid., Herpetol.* C.*
1549 Germer, Dr. E. W., Erie, Pa. *Mic.?*
1550 Gernerd, J. M. M., Muncy, Lycoming Co., Pa. *Arch., Min., Con., Palæo.* C.*
1551 Gerrish, Wm. L., 675 Congress St., Portland, Me. *Min., Zool., Vert., Anat., Orn., Ool.?*
1552 Gerry, A. M., Taxidermist, 2 Odd Fellows' Block, So. Paris, Me. *Orn., Ool., Ichth., Tax., Mammals.* C. Ex.*
1553 Gesner, William. M.D., Birmingham, Ala. *Min.* C.*
1554 Getchell, Ellen P., Newburyport, Mass. *Palæo., Min., Arch., Eth.* C. Ex.*
1555 Getman, M. J., Gloversville, Fulton Co., N. Y. *Min., Phæn. Bot.* C.
1556 Giauque, Florien, Attorney, 4th and Walnut Sts., Cincinnati, O. *Am. Arch.**
1557 Gibbes, Prof. L. R., 28 Coming St., Charleston, S. C. *Bot., Con.* C. Ex.
1558 Gibbs, Edwin A., M.D., Pension Office, Washington, D. C. *Mic.* C. Ex.*
1559 Gibbs, J. Stanley, M.D., Health Retreat, St. Helena, Calif. *Geol., Orn., Ool., Tax.* C.*
1560 Gibbs, J. Willard, Ph.D., Prof. Mathematical Phys., Yale Coll., 121 High St., New Haven, Ct.*
1561 Gibbs, Morris, M.D., Kalamazoo, Mich. *Orn., Ool., Herpetol.**
1562 Gibbs, P. H., Oshawa, Ont., Can. *Mam., Orn., Min., Geol.?*
1563 Gibbs, William, Helena, Montana. *Orn., Ool.* C. Ex.*
1564 Gibbs, Wolcott, Rumford Prof., Cambridge. Mass. *Chem.**
1565 Gibson, Chas. B., M.D., Prof. Inorg. Chem., Coll. of Physicians and Surgeons, Room 15, 81 Clarke St., Chicago, Ill., Analyt. Consulting Chemist, Collector of Minerals. *Crystall., Lithol., Physics.* C. Ex.*
1566 Gibson, Charles D., Dover, Kent Co., Del. *Orn., Ool., Tax.**
1567 Gifford, William E., 54 Pine St., New York, N. Y. *Analyt. Chem.**
1568 Gilbert, Chas. H., Ph.D., Prof. of Biol., Univ. of Cincinnati, Ohio. *Ichth.**

1569 Gilbert, D. W., Keene, N. H. *Con., Min.* C. Ex.*
1570 Gilbert, E C., Woodland, Yolo Co., Calif. *Natural history specimens in general.* C. Ex.*
1571 Gilbert, Eliza J. C., Keene, N. H. *Bot.* C. Ex.*
1572 Gilbert, Frank H., Woodland, Yolo Co., Calif. *Orn., Ool., Stamps.* C. Ex.*
1573 Gilbert, Geo. H., 237 Main St., Charlestown, Mass. *Min., Spec. Marbles and Serpentines.* C. Ex.*
1574 Gilbert, G. K., U. S. Geologist, Box 591, Washington, D. C. *Geol., Barometric Hypsometry.**
1575 Gilbert, Harold, St. John, N. B., Can. *Orn.**
1576 Gilbert, Warner W., 11 Jay St., Rochester, N. Y. *Ent.?*
1577 Gilchrist, Maude, Instructor in Botany, Wellesley College, Wellesley, Mass.*
1578 Gilham, Frank M., 422 Eighth St., Oakland, Calif. I have the finest collection of Indian goods to be had. Prices given on application.*
1579 Gill, John Kaye, 254 Alder St., Portland, Oregon. *Eth., Palæo., Philol: Aboriginal Am. dialects, Geol.**
1580 Gill, Theo. N., M.D., Ph.D., Smithsonian Inst., Washington, D. C. *Gen. Zool., Mam., Ichth., Con.* C.*
1581 Gill, William L., 20 So. Prince St., Lancaster, Pa. *Palæo., Geol., Ast.**
1582 Gillett, Edw., Southwick, Mass. *Cultivation of wild flowers.* Collector of and dealer in N. A. wild flowers. Catalogues sent. Foreign correspondence solicited. C.*
1583 Gillett, W. W., Buncomb, Fayette Co., Wis. *Geol., Min.* C.?
1584 Gillhan, Robert, Kansas City, Mo. *Engineering and Geology.**
1585 Gillin, Thos. S., C.E., Ambler, Montgomery Co., Pa. *Orn., Ool., Tax.* C. Ex.*
1586 Gilman, Daniel C., Pres. Johns Hopkins Univ., Baltimore, Md.*
1587 Gilman, Henry A., M.D., Supt. Iowa Hospital for Insane, Mt. Pleasant, Iowa. *Bot., Geol., Chem., Physics, Anat.**
1588 Gilpin, Edwin, A.M., F.G.S., Government Inspector of Mines, Halifax, N. S., Can. *Mining Engineer, Local Geol.?*
1589 Gilson, F. H., 159 High St., Boston, Mass. *Bot.* C.*
1590 Gilson, J. C., Supt. of Schools, 1964 San Pablo Avenue, Oakland, Alameda Co., Calif. *Min.* C.
1591 Girling, Robt. N., Chemist, Cor. St. Charles and Washington Ave., New Orleans, La. *Bot., Hort., Agric., Org. and Inorg. Chem., Mic.* C. Ex.*
1592 Gisborne, Frederic N., F.R.S.C., M.S.C.C.E., M.I.T.E. and E., General Supt. Govt. Telh. and Signal Service, Canada, C. E. and Electrician, Ottawa, Can.*
1593 Gissler, Carl F., Ph.D., 15 Adams St., Brooklyn, E. D., N. Y., *Zool., Crustacea.**
1594 Glasgow, Frank A., A M., M.D., Lecturer on Gynæcology, St. Louis Med. College, 3016 Glasgow Place, St. Louis, Mo. *Org. and Inorg. Chem., Elect., Mic., Emb., Vert., Eth., Ethnog., Histol.**

1595 Gleason, E. B., Elmira, N. Y. *Nat. Hist.*
1596 Gleason, Herbert, 51 Commercial St., Boston, Mass. *Geol.**
1597 Gleason, Rev. H. W., Minneapolis, Minn. *Bot.*, *Min.*
1598 Gleason, S. O., M.D., Elmira, N. Y. *Mic.*, *Desmids*, *Gen. Biol.*, *Histol.*
1599 Gleason, Thos. W., Volta Laboratory, Washington, D. C. *Chem.*, *Phys.*, *Elect.*
1600 Glover, T. W., Hanson, Mass. *Orn.*, *Ool.*, *Tax.* C. Ex.*
1601 Gochenour, Wm., Oregon, Ogle Co., Ills. *Phæn. Bot.* C. Ex.*
1602 Godbey, Prof. S. M., Prof. Nat. Science, Pacific Methodist College, Santa Rosa, Calif. *Geol.*, *Min.*, *Con.* C. Ex.*
1603 Goddard, Anson M., Augusta, Me. *Orn.* C. Ex.
1604 Goddard, Chas., M.D, Harvard, Ill. *Photo-Micrography.**
1605 Godfrey, Chas. C., M.D., 254 State St., Bridgeport, Fairfield Co., Ct.*
1606 Goehring, G. H. M., Phar. G., Wittenburg, Mo. *Bot.*, *Mic.* C. Ex.*
1607 Goessmann, C. A., Ph.D., Dir. Mass. Agric. Expr. Station, and Prof. Chem., Mass. Agric. Coll., Amherst, Mass.*
1608 Goff, Emmett S, N. Y. Agric. Experiment Station, Geneva, N. Y. *Hort.*, *Experimental Agric.**
1609 Gold, T. S., Sec. Conn. Board of Agric., West Cornwall, Ct. *Bot.*, *Hort.*, *Min.* C.*
1610 Goldschmidt, S. A., E.M., Ph.D., 55 Broadway, New York, N. Y. *Chem.**
1611 Goldthorp, George J., Mineral Point, Wis. *Palæo.*, *Min.* C. Ex. Photog. work, lantern slides, etc., for fossils, mounted diatoms, etc.
1612 Gooch, F. A., Ph.D., Prof. Yale Univ., New Haven, Ct. *Chem.**
1613 Goodale, Mrs. Annie M., 1114 N. 3d St., St Joseph, Missouri. *Coleoptera* C. Ex.*
1614 Goodale, Prof. George L., Cambridge, Mass. *Bot.**
1615 Goode, G. Brown, Ass't Sec. Smithsonian Institution; in charge U. S. National Museum, Washington, D. C. *Geog. Dist.*, *Ichth.*, *Nat. Hist. of Bermudas.* History and Bibliography of American Science. Museum Administration. C. Ex.*
1616 Goodell, J. H., M.D., Marseilles, La Salle Co., Ill. *Osteol.* C.?
1617 Goodell, L. W., Amherst, Mass. *Bot.*, *Hort.*, *Floriculture*, *Ent: Lepid.*, *Photog.* C.*
1618 Goodenough, H. B., Bristol, Ct. *Min.* C. Ex.*
1619 Goodfellow, Edward, Assistant U. S. Coast and Geodetic Survey, Washington, D. C.*
1620 Goodfellow, G. E., M.D., Tombstone, Ariz. *Bot.*, *Emb.**
1621 Goodhue, Charles F., Webster, N. H. *Orn.*, *Lepid.*, *Sphingidæ Catocalæ.* C. Ex.*
1622 Goodrich, Joseph K., Smithsonian Inst., Washington, D. C. *Geog.*, *Ethnol.*, *Sinology.*
1623 Goodrich, L. L., Mrs., Pres. Bot. Club, 99 Willow St., Syracuse, N. Y. *Flora of Onondaga Co.**

1624 Goodrich, Wilbur F., C.E., Leominster, Mass. *Con.*, *Min.*, *Fossils.* C. Ex.* Desires Helices, F. W. shells, crystals and fossils.*
1625 Goodwillie, D. H., M.D., 160 W. 34th St., New York City.*
1626 Goodwillie, J. M., M.A., Georgetown, Ont., Can. *Arch.*, *Geol.*, *Palæo.* C. Ex.*
1627 Goodwin, A. C., Superintendent City Schools, Owensboro', Ky. *Geol.*, *Palæo.*, *Bot.* C. Lower Sil. and upper Helderberg fossils for ex. Wants only perfect fossils.*
1628 Goodwin, E. J., M.D., Solitude, Ind. *Phys.**
1629 Goodwin, E. M., Hartland, Vt. *Min.*, *L. and F. W. Shells*, *Indian relics, curiosities, etc.* C. Ex.*
1630 Goodwin, F. M., Hartland, Vt. *Orn.*, *Ool.* C. Ex.*
1631 Goodyear, W. H., New Haven, Ct. *Min.* C. Ex.
1632 Goold, C. H., Morris, Ill. *Palæo: Fossil flora of Mazon Creek, Grundy Co.* C. Ex.*
1633 Gorden, Wm. J., 53 Water St., Cleveland, Ohio.*
1634 Gordon, J. C., Prof. Nat. Coll. for the Deaf, Kendall Green, Washington, D. C. *Chem.**
1635 Gordon, T. Winslow, M. D., Georgetown, Brown Co., Ohio. *Mic.*, *Meteo.*, *Gen. Biol.* ?
1636 Gordon, W. E., Patchogue, Suffolk Co., N. Y. *Algæ*, *Local Arch.*, *Con.* C.*
1637 Gordon, Mrs. W. L., Chelmsford, Mass. *Geol.*, *Min.* C. Ex.*
1638 Gore, J. Howard, Prof. Math., Columbian Univ., Washington, D. C. *Ceremonial Government and Geodesy.**
1639 Gorton, L. G., Detroit, Mich. *Geol.*, *Mic.*, *Phys.*, *Physiol.* C. Ex. mic. slides.*
1640 Goss, B. F., Pewaukee, Waukesha Co., Wis. *Ool.* C. Ex. in sets.*
1641 Goss, Col. N. S., Topeka, Shawnee Co., Kan. *Orn.* C.*
1642 Gottschalk, Chas. F. A., 193 N. Salina St., Syracuse, N. Y. *Mic.*, *Bot.* C. Ex.*
1643 Gould, Dr. B. A., 29 Kirkland St., Cambridge, Mass. *Ast.**
1644 Gould, S. Clark, Manchester, N. H. *Gen. Sci.* Ex.*
1645 Grady, John H., Natick, Mass. *Orn.*, *Ool.*, *Min.*, *Coins*, *Curiosities, etc.* C. Ex. Will buy eggs and coins. Correspondents desired in all countries.*
1646 Graef, Edw. L., 40 Court St., Brooklyn, N. Y. *Lepid.* C. Liberal returns in exchange or cash for new N. A. species. Ex.*
1647 Graf, L., Van Buren, Ark. *Geol.*, *Invert. Palæo.* C. Ex.*
1648 Graham, C. W., Museum of Tax and Curios., St. Johnsbury, Vt. *Tax.*, *Orn.*, *Zool.*, *Curiosities and war relics wanted.* C.*
1649 Grannis, Hial S., Plantsville, Ct. *Lepid.*, *Coleopt.* C. Ex. N. A. Coleopt.*
1650 Grant, G. B., Box 580, Leominster, Mass. *Orn.*, *Ool.* C. ?
1651 Grant, H. L., Prof. of Chem., Dakota School of Mines, Rapid City, Dakota.*
1652 Grant, J. M., Pt. Angeles, Washing Terr. *Bot.*, *Hort.*, *Min.*, *Lith.*, *Zool.*, *Eth.*, *Orn.*, *Ent.*, *Molluscs.* C. Ex.*

1653 Gratacap, L. P., Ph.B., M.A., Am. Mus. Nat. Hist., New York, N. Y. *Chem.*, *Min.**
1654 Graves, G. H., Kankakee, Ill. *Indian relics.**
1655 Gray, Arthur F., C.E., Lawrence, Mass. *Mollusca.* C. Desires exotic Land and F. W. Shells, esp. those of West Indies, Mexico, Central and So. Am.; also Pupadæ and Unionidæ from all sources. Ex. offered in Am. L. and F. W. shells. Correspondents desired.*
1656 Gray, Prof. Asa, M.D., Bot. Gardens, Cambridge, Mass. *Bot.**
1657 Gray, Edward, M.D., A.B., Hoopa Valley, Humboldt Co., Calif. *Mic.*, *Bot.*, *Histol.* C. Ex.?
1658 Gray, Elisha, Highland Park, Ill. *Electrician.**
1659 Gray, John R., North East, Erie Co., Pa. *Geol.*, *Bot.* C. "Cone in Cone" to ex.
1660 Gray, Louis F., Boston Public Library, Boston, Mass. *Min.*
1661 Gray, Mrs. Mary T., 339 Washington Ave., Wyandotte, Kan. *Con.*, *Geol.* C. Ex.*
1662 Gray, Wm. M., M.D., Army Med. Mus., Washington, D. C. *Emb.*, *Mycology*, *Pathol.*, *Photog.*, *Histol.* C. Ex.*
1663 Graybill, J. K., M.D., Lebanon, O. *Diatoms*, *Palæo.*, *Min.*, *Chem.*, *Mic.*, *Histol.* C. Ex.?
1664 Greany, Wm. F., 827 Brannan St., San Francisco, Calif. *Orn.*, *Ool.*, *Tax.* C. Ex.*
1665 Greegor, Isaiah, 61 Laura St., Jacksonville, Fla. *Con.**
1666 Green, Caleb, A.M., M.D., Homer, Cortland Co., N. Y. *Bot.*, *Mic.*, *Gen. Biol.* C.*
1667 Green, Edgar M., A.M., M.D., 222 Spring Garden St., Easton, Pa. *Bot.*, *Mic.*, *Gen. Biol.**
1668 Green, Fred. C., Milwaukee, Wis. *Orn.*?
1669 Green, H. A., Prof. Nat. Sci., Brainerd Inst., Chester, S. C. *Min.*, *Chem.*, *Bot.* Spec. *Ferns*, *Lichens*, *Mosses and Algæ.* Ex. botanical specimens, particularly lichens, mosses and algæ, Am. and foreign.*
1670 Green, J. B., Box 549, Des Moines, Ia. *Orn.*, *Ool.* C. Ex.*
1671 Green, Dr. Jesse C., West Chester, Pa. *Met.*, *Mic.* C. Ex.*
1672 Green, Milbrey, M.D., 1 Columbus Sq., Boston, Mass. *Phys.*, *Mic.*, *Meteo.*, *Gen. Biol.*, *Anth.**
1673 Green, N. Y., Battle Creek, Mich. *Orn.*, *Tax.* C. Ex.*
1674 Green, Samuel A., M.D., Boston, Mass. *Arch.* C.*
1675 Greene, Caleb, A.M., M.D., Homer, Cortland Co., N. Y. *Gen. Nat. Hist.*, *Mic.* C.*
1676 Greene, Charles Augustus, M.D., 22 N. 2d St., Harrisburg, Pa. General C. Ex.*
1677 Greene, Prof. Edw. L., Berkeley, Calif. *Bot.* C.*
1678 Greene, Geo. K., New Albany, Floyd Co., Ind. *Palæo.* C.*
1679 Greene, Thomas A., Milwaukee, Wis. *Min.*, *Fossils from Niagara and Hamilton groups.**
1680 Greenleaf, Orlando C., Belleville, Ont., Can. *Machinist*, *Amateur Elect.*?
1681 Greenleaf, R. C., 33 Summer St., Boston, Mass. *Diatoms*, *Mic.* C.*

1682 Greenleaf, R. P., M.D., 803 Market St., Wilmington, Del. *Hort., Agric., Chem.**

1683 Greenleaf, R. W., A.M., M.D., 341 Boylston St., Boston, Mass. *Bot.**

1684 Greenwood, E. C., Ipswich, Mass. *Orn., Tax., Osteol.* C. Ex.

1685 Gregg, Wm. H., M.D., 43 Cambridge Place, Brooklyn, N. Y. *Orn., Ichth.* C.*

1686 Gregory, James C., Nyack-on-Hudson, N. Y. *Bot., Palæo., Geol., Min., Mic., Ent.* C. Ex.*

1687 Gregory, J. J. H., Marblehead, Mass. *Min., Con., Indian Antiquities.* C.*

1688 Gregory, W. D., Susquehanna, Pa. *Chem., Phys., Elect.*

1689 Grey, William, Kenwood, Albany Co., N. Y. *Bot., Ent.**

1690 Grice, J. T., Waterburgh, Tompkins Co., N. Y. *Mic.* C.*

1691 Gridlay, Rev. A. L., Benzonia, Mich. *Cosmogony.**

1692 Griffin, Rev. L. J., Albion, Calhoun Co., Mich. *Tax.* C. Ex.*

1693 Griffin, W. W., 32 Johnson St., Lynn, Mass. *Mic., Gen. Biol., Histol.**

1694 Griffing, Moses B., Shelter Island, N. Y. *Orn., Ool., Tax., Indian relics.* C. Ex.?

1695 Griffith, Mrs. B. M., Springfield. *Crypt. Bot: Ferns, Geol., Mic.?*

1696 Griffith, E. H., A. M, F.R.M.S., Fairport, Monroe Co., N. Y. *Mic.**

1697 Griffith, Dr. J. P. Crozer, Ass't Demonstrator of Histol., Univ. of Pa., 1420 Chestnut St., Philadelphia, Pa.?

1698 Griffith, Richard, Box 521, Kenosha, Wis. *Min.* C. Ex.*

1699 Griffith, S. H., Passed Ass't Surg. U.S.N., Navy Dept., Washington, D. C. *Mic.?*

1700 Grim, W. H., Hamburgh, Pa. *Min., Ool., Orn., Indian relics.* C. Ex.?

1701 Grinnell, George Bird, Ph.D., Station M, New York, N. Y. *Osteol., Vert., Palæo., Orn.**

1702 Groesel, Charles E., Akron, Summit Co., Ohio. *Ent., Geol.* C. Ex.*

1703 Groff, Prof. George G., M.D., Lewisburg, Pa. *Nat. Hist.* C.*

1704 Gross, C. A., Landisville, Atlantic Co., N. J. *Bot.* C. Ex. Coll. of pine barren plants for herb.*

1705 Gross, L. N., Deadwood, D. T. *Strat. Geol., Min., Chem., Metall.*

1706 Gross, Oran R, M.D., Truro, Mass. *Phæn. Bot., Crypt. Bot., Moll., Ichth., Orn.* C.?

1707 Grossman, Prof. John H., Shannon, Carroll Co., Ill. *Bot., Phys., Geol.* C. Ex.*

1708 Gruber, F., Naturalist, Inventor of Zoögraphicon, 407 Dolores St., San Francisco, Calif. *Zool., Orn., Ool.* Museum of Nat. Hist. for sale containing 15,000 specimens of Zool.; all specimens, lifelike mounted and in best condition. Price, $10,000.

1709 **Gruhlke**, A. C., Waterloo, DeKalb Co., Ind. *Arch.*, *Palæo.*, *Min.*, *Numismatics*. C. Ex.*
1710 **Grumbling**, Christian M., A.M., Prof. Nat. Sci., Iowa Wesleyan University, Mt. Pleasant, Ia. *Chem.*, *Phys.*, *Geol.*, *Zool.*, *Bot.**
1711 **Grundell**, Julius G., 2012 Folsom St., San Francisco, Calif. *Lepid.* ?
1712 **Grunow**, J., Microscopes, Microscope Objectives, and other Optical Instruments, 621 6th Ave., New York, N. Y. *Optics in general.**
1713 **Guelf**, Charles P., Lock Box 6, Brockport, N. Y. *Geol.*, *Min.*, *Zool.*, *Arch.*, *Orn.*, *Ool.*, *Tax.*, *Ent.*, *Lepid.**
1714 **Guignard**, J. A., B.A., 36 Daly St., Ottawa, Can. *Bot.*, *Hymenoptera.**
1715 **Guild**, A. S., Lowell, Mass. *Bot.* C. Ex.?
1716 **Guldenschuh**, Isaac P., Rochester, N. Y. *Elect.*, *Meteo.*, *Ast.**
1717 **Gulley**, Prof. F. A., M.S., Agricultural College P. O., Miss. *Agric.**
1718 **Gunckel**, L. W., 121 W. 2nd St., Dayton, Ohio. *Palæo.*, *Geol.*, *Anth.*, *Arch.*, *Ethnol.* C. Ex. rare fossils, mins., etc., for rare Arch. spec. of all kinds. Correspondence solicited.*
1719 **Gundlach**, Ernst, care Gundlach Optical Co., Rochester, N. Y. *Elect.*, *Mic.*, *Ast.**
1720 **Gunn**, Robert A., M.D., 45 E. 22 St., New York City. *Anat.**
1721 **Gurley**, Mrs. Anna S., Danville, Ill. *Con.*, *Crust.*, *Invert. Zool.* C. Ex. fossils for above.*
1722 **Gurley**, William F. E., Danville, Ill. *Invert. Palæo.* C. Fossils to ex.*
1723 **Guthrie**, Ezra L., Adams, Decatur Co., Ind. *Arch.*, *Orn.*, *Tax.* C. Desires to exchange good skins of this locality for the same of other localities.*
1724 **Guttenberg**, Gustavus, Erie, Pa. *Bot.*, *Min.*, *Geol.* C. Ex.*
1725 **Haanel**, Prof. E., Ph.D., F.R.S.C., Victoria Univ., Cobourg, Ont., Can. *Phys.*, *Min.**
1726 **Haberer**, Joseph V., M.D., 66 Miller St , Utica, N. Y. *Bot.: Cyperaceæ* (*spec. carex*), *Comp. Anat.*, *Osteol.* C. Rare plants for ex. Solicits correspondence. Desires Caricæ from all parts of the world.*
1727 **Habirshaw**, Fred., F.R.M.S., 113 Maiden Lane, New York, N. Y. *Diatomaceæ.* C. Ex.
1728 **Habirshaw**, John, M.D., F.R.M.S., 260 W. 57th St., New York, N. Y. *Mic.*, *Vert.* C.*
1729 **Hack**, Arthur H., 30 Harrison St., Taunton, Mass. *Orn.*, *Ool.*, *Tax.* C. Ex ?
1730 **Hacker**, Wm., 233 So. 4th St., Philadelphia, Pa. *Orn.*, *Bot.* C. Ex.*
1731 **Hackman**, H. S., Peru, La Salle Co., Ill. *Algæ*, *Fungi*, *Mosses*, *Hort.*, *Palæo.*, *Geol.*, *Min.*, *Arch.*, *Ent.*, *Moll.* C. Ex.*
1732 **Hadaway**, W. S., Jr., Plymouth, Mass. *Org. Chem.*, *Physics*, *Elect.*, *Mic.* C. Ex.*
1733 **Hafstein**, L. M., Belvidere, N. J. *Min.*, *Tax.* ?

1734 Hagemann, John, 106 Bank St., Cincinnati, O. *Min.*, *Chem. Metall.*, *Phys.* C.*
1735 Hagen, H. A., M.D., Ph.D., Prof. Harvard Univ., Ass't, Mus. Comp. Zool., 7 Putnam Ave., Cambridge, Mass. *Ent.* Ex *Biological specimens. Neuroptera, Pseudo-neuroptera.**
1736 Hager, Albert D., 463 S. Leavitt St., Sec. and Librarian of the Chicago Historical Soc., Chicago, Ill. *Geol.* C.*
1737 Hague, Arnold, U. S. Geol. Surv., Washington, D. C. *Geol.*, *Lithol.**
1738 Hague, James D., Mining Engineer, 18 Wall St., New York, N. Y. *Geol.*, *Mining Engineering.**
1739 Hahn, H. C., Ph.D., Lansing, Mich. *Crystall.*, *Chem.*, *Gen. Biol.*, *Vert. Emb.*, *Hist.*, *Philol.* C. Ex.*
1740 Haight, E. M., Riverside, Calif. Dealer in *Gen. Nat. Hist. spec.*, *Coins*, *Stamps*, *Relics*, *and Curiosities.* C. Ex.*
1741 Hailes, Wm., M.D., 197 Hamilton St., Albany, N. Y. *Embryology*, *Normal and Pathological Histol.* C. Ex.?
1742 Haines, Benjamin, Elizabeth, N. J. *Min.*, *Arch.* C. Ex.
1743 Haines, H. Cope, Haines St., Germantown, Pa. *Bot.*?
1744 Haines, H. F., 1259 Waverly Place, Elizabeth, N. J. *Ool.* C. Ex.?
1745 Haines, Reuben, 123 W. Chelten Ave., Germantown, and 738 Sansom St., Philadelphia, Pa. *Analyt. Chem.*
1746 Haines, Wm. J., A.B., Cheltenham, Montgomery Co., Pa. *Elect.*, *Orn.*, *Ool.* C. Ex.*
1747 Hake, E. G., M.D., New Cumberland, Cumberland Co., Pa. *Bot.* (*Crypt.*), *Zool.*, *Geol.*, *Mic.*, *Photog.**
1748 Halberstadt, A. G., 270 Seventh St., New York, N. Y. *Am. and Foreign Stamps.**
1749 Halberstadt, Baird, Penn. Geol. Survey, Pottsville, Pa. *Geol.*, *Ethnog.*, *Neuropt.* C. Ex.?
1750 Halbrook, F. M., Box 107, El Paso, Texas. *Min.*, *Metall.*, *Photog.* C. Ex.
1751 Hale, Dr. Edwin M., Emeritus Prof. Materia Med. and Therap., Chicago Hom. Med. Coll., 65 22nd St., Chicago, Ill. *Med. Bot.*, *Materia Medica.*
1752 Hale, Horatio, Clinton, Ont., Can. *Anth.*, *Arch.*, *Eth.*, *Ethnog.*, *Philol.**
1753 Hale, John P., M.D., Charlton, Kanawha Co., W. Va. *Ethnog.*, *Ethnol.*, *Arch.*
1754 Hale, William H., Ph.D., 50 Clinton Ave., Albany, N. Y. *Gen. Biol.*, *Anth.*, *Comp. Philol.**
1755 Hall, A., Naturalist and Taxidermist, East Rockport, Ohio.*
1756 Hall, Alex. P., M.D., Mobile, Ala. *Microscope in Medicine.**
1757 Hall, Asa F., Hudson, Mass. *Min.*, *Geol.* C Ex.*
1758 Hall, Prof. Asaph, U. S. Naval Observ., Washington, D. C.*
1759 Hall, Rev. C. H., D.C., 157 Montague St., Brooklyn, N. Y. *Bot.* Ex.*
1760 Hall, C. W., Prof. Univ. Minn., 803 Univ. Ave., S. Minneapolis, Minn. *Geol.*, *Min.*, *Lithol.* C. Ex.*
1761 Hall, D. K., Rutland, Vt. *Geol.*, *Min.* C. Ex.*

1762 Hall, Edwin B., Wellsville, Alleghany Co., N. Y. *Ferns.*
1763 Hall, Edwin H., 5 Avon St., Cambridge, Mass. *Phys.**
1764 Hall, Henry G., Savoy, Champaign Co., Ill. *Arch.*, *Orn.*, *Min.*, *Bot.*, *Ool.*, *Tax.*, *Ent.*, *Fossils.* C. Ex. or sell birds, reptiles and mammals, mounted or skins; eggs; imitations and casts of fruit, arrow and spear heads; foreign and U. S. stamps, old type; casts and stubbed specimens made to order. Correspondence desired.*
1765 Hall, Isaac H., Metropolitan Museum of Art, New York, N. Y. *Bot: Ferns*, *Orchids.**
1766 Hall, James, State Geologist and Director of State Mus. Nat. Hist., Albany, N. Y. *Geol.*, *Palæo.* C. Ex.*
1767 Hall, John W., jr., Covington, Ky. *Palæo.*, *Min.* C. Ex.?
1768 Hall, Lyman B., Ph.D., Haverford Coll., Montgomery Co., Pa. *Chem.*, *Phys.**
1769 Hall, Dr. L. Brewer, 17 So. 16th St., Philadelphia, Pa. *Crypt. Bot.*, *Mic.**
1770 Hall, Newton, 2nd, A.B., L. Box 8, Syracuse, N. Y. *Diatoms*, *Phys.*, *Ferns*, *Geol.*, *Mic.* C. Ex.?
1771 Hall, Orvis W., M.D., Atlanta, Idaho. *Phæn. Bot.*, *Ferns*, *Mosses*, *Chem.*, *Elect.*, *Osteol.*, *Myol.*, *Histol.**
1772 Hall, T. P., B.A., F.C.S., Prof. Nat. Sci., Woodstock Coll., Woodstock, Ont., Canada.*
1773 Hall, Wm. C. J., Jamestown, Chautauqua Co., N. Y. Director of Chaut. Univ. *Mic.* C. Ex.?
1774 Hall, Capt. W. P., Acad. Nat. Sciences, Davenport, Ia. *Arch.*?
1775 Hallock, A. P., Ph.D., Consolidated Gas Co., 21st St. and Ave. A, New York, N. Y.*
1776 Hallock, Chas., 1827 I St. N. W., Washington, D. C. *Physical*, *Gen. Biol.*, *Geog. Dist.*, *Ichth.**
1777 Hallock, Prof. E. J., Ph.D., Peekskill, N. Y. *Chem.**
1778 Hallock, Wm., A.B., Ph.D., U. S. Geol. Survey, Washington, D. C. *Phys.*, *Elect.**
1779 Hallowell, Susan M., Prof. Bot., Wellesley Coll., Wellesley, Mass.*
1780 Halsted, Byron D., office of "American Agriculturist," 751 Broadway, New York, N. Y. *Crypt. Bot.*?
1781 Halsted, Geo. B., Prof. Math., Univ. of Tex., 2004 Matilde St., Austin, Tex. *Crystall.*, *Phys.*, *Ast.**
1782 Ham, G. E., 7 Silver St., Worcester, Mass. *Coleopt.*
1783 Hambach, G., M.D., 1319 Lami St., St. Louis, Mo. *Palæo.*, *Bot.* C. Ex. fossils and minerals.*
1784 Hamblin, F., 33 South St., Utica, N.Y. *Min*, *Geol.*, *Arch.* C.*
1785 Hamel, Thomas E., M.A., F.R.S.C., Prof. Faculty of Arts, Laval Univ., Quebec, Can. *Nat. Phil.**
1786 Hamill, Alex., M.D., Baldwinsville, N. Y. *Arch.* C. Ex.*
1787 Hamilton, C. W., Brimfield, Ill. *Orn.*, *Geol.*, *Ferns*, *Palæo.*, *Min.*, *Herpetol.*, *Moll.* C. Ex.*
1788 Hamilton, Edwin H., Petersburg, Ill. *Ool.*, *Arch.*, *Nat. Hist.*
1789 Hamilton, Hugh, M.Sc., M.D., 212 So. 2d St., Harrisburgh, Pa. *Chem.*, *Geol.* C.*

1790 Hamilton, John, M.D., 18 Ohio St., Allegheny, Pa. *Coleopt.* C. Ex.*

1791 Hamilton, Leonidas Le Cenci, 6 James St., Franklin Sq., Boston. *Bot.: Fungi., Algæ, Diatoms, Palæo., Geol., Min., Crystall., Org. and Inorg. Chem., Phys., Elect., Meteo., Ast., Zool., Gen. Biol., Emb., Anth., Arch., Phil.**

1792 Hamilton, W. N., Greencastle, Ind. *Math.?*

1793 Hamlin, Augustus C., M.D., Bangor, Me. *Palæo., Geol., Min., Crystall., Chem., Metall., Arch., Eth.* C.*

1794 Hamlin, D. A., Training School, Boston, Mass. *Bot., Mic.**

1795 Hamlin, F. M., M.D., 9 William St., Auburn, N. Y. *Mic., Con.* C. Ex. Bermuda and W. I. sea-shells in ex. for L. and F. W. and other marine shells. Also mic. objects generally.*

1796 Hamlin, Thomas, Exeter, Ont., Canada. C. Ex.*

1797 Hammond, H. A., jr., Nicollett, Wis. *Orn.?*

1798 Hampton, C. J., Junius, Seneca Co., N. Y. *Orn., Min., Moll.* C.*

1799 Hanaman, C. E., F.R.M.S., 108 First St., Troy, N. Y. *Biol., Histol.* C.*

1800 Hancock, E. M., Waukon, Ia. *Orn.**

1801 Hancock, Joseph L., 3120 Vernon Ave., Chicago, Ill. *Orn., Zool., Biol., Medicine.**

1802 Hanke, Henry C., Minneapolis, Minn. *Orn., Ool.* C. Ex.*

1803 Hankenson, E. L., Newark, Wayne Co., N. Y. *Bot: Salices, Carices.* C. Ex. local for other plants.*

1804 Hanks, Henry G., F.G.S., 1124 Greenwich St., San Francisco, Calif. Ex.*

1805 Hanna, George B., Ass't Assayer U. S. Assay Office, Charlotte, N. C. *Min. Engineering, Met and Min., Chem.* C.*

1806 Hanna, H. W., Warsaw, Ind. *Palæo., Geol., Min., Con., Arch.* C. Ex.

1807 Hannum, Frank A., Easthampton, Mass. *Orn., Ool., Bot.* C.*

1808 Hansom, James F., Fremont, Neb. *Bot., Geol.**

1809 Harbison, W. F., Spencerville, Allen Co., Ohio. *Arch., Geol., Moll., Palæo.* C. Ex.*

1810 Harbron, George, P. O. Box 1381, Hamilton, Ohio. *Orn., Tax.* Ex.*

1811 Hard, M. E., M.A., Supt. Pub. Instruction, Gallipolis, O. *Geol., Min., Crystall., Lithol.* C. Ex.*

1812 Hardaway, R. A., Prof. of Civil Engineering, University of Alabama, Ala *Engineering.**

1813 Harden, Edw. B., M.E., Ass't Geol. Surv. Pa., 907 Walnut St., Phila., Pa. *Struct. Geol., Geol. models, Inorg. Chem., Photog.**

1814 Harden, John H., M.E., Phœnixville, Pa. *Expert in Min. Eng.* C. Ex.*

1815 Harden, Oliver B., Asst. State Survey, 907 Walnut St., Philadelphia, Pa. *Top Eng. and Stenographer.**

1816 Hardin, Robert A., M.D., Cor. 5th Ave. and Russell St., Nashville, Tenn. *Mic., Zool., Gen. Biol.* C. Ex.*

1817 Hardy, Arthur S., Ph.D., Dartmouth Coll., Hanover, N. H. *Math.**

1818 Hardy, E. R., 420 Congress St., Portland, Me. *Mam.*, *Orn.*, *Reptiles.* C.

1819 Hardy, Manly, Brewer, Me. *Orn.* C. Ex.*

1820 Hare, Sidney J., C.E., 1634 Wyandotte St., Kansas City, Mo. *Palæo.*, *Ent.*, *Min.*, *Geol.*, *Arch.* Collector and exchanger for Washington Park Museum, Kansas City, Mo.*

1821 Haren, Wm. A., 1400 Hickory St., St. Louis, Mo. *Mic.*, *Ast.*, *Diatoms*, *Phys.*, *Ent.* C. Ex.*

1822 Harger, Oscar, 14 University Place, New Haven, Ct. *Isopod Crustacea*, *Palæo.**

1823 Hargrave, C., Sec. of the Central Normal Coll., Danville, Ind. *Land and Fresh Water shells. Those from White River a specialty.* C. Ex.*

1824 Hargreaves, H. B., Box 19, Garnerville, Rockland Co., N. Y. *Mic: Sections of wood.* C. Ex.

1825 Harkness, Chas. W., Elmwood, Peoria Co., Ill. *Geol.*, *Lithol.*, *Chem.* C. Ex.

1826 Harkness, H. W., M.D., Pres. Calif. Academy of Science, San Francisco, Calif. *Micros.*, *Fungi.* C.*

1827 Harper, Esmondé, 2035 Wallace St., Philadelphia, Pa. *Orn.*, *Ool.* C. Ex.*

1828 Harper, George W., Principal Woodward High School, Cincinnati, Ohio. *Geol.*, *Con*, *Palæo.* C. L. Sil. fossils and F. W. and L. Shells of Ohio, Ky. and Tenn. for ex.*

1829 Harr, W. H., Att'y at Law, Hamilton, Butler Co., O. *Arch.*, *Geol.*, *Palæo.* C. Ex.*

1830 Harriman, M. C., Elizabeth, N. J. *Min.*, *Orn.*, *Ent.*, *Photography.* C. Ex.*

1831 Harring, Wm., 523 Clay St., San Francisco, Calif. *Lepid.* C. Ex. and purchase.

1832 Harrington, B. J., B.A., Ph.D., Prof. Chem. and Min., McGill College, Montreal, Can. *Min.* C. Ex.*

1833 Harrington, Chas., M.D., Instructor in Hygiene and Ass't Chem., Harvard Med. Coll., Boston, Mass. *Med. Chem.*, *Tox. and Hygiene.**

1834 Harrington, M., York Centre, Iowa Co., Ia. *Ool.* C. Ex.*

1835 Harrington, Prof. Mark W., Dir. of Obs., Ann Arbor, Mich. *Ast.*, *Meteo.**

1836 Harrington, W. Hague, P. O. Dept., Ottawa, Can. *Ent: Coleoptera*, *Hymenoptera.* C.

1837 Harris, DeWitt S., Cuba, Fulton Co., Ill. *Mic.*, *Arch.*, *Ent.* C. Ex.*

1838 Harris, Elijah P., Ph.D., Prof. Chem., Amherst Coll., Amherst, Mass.*

1839 Harris, Gilbert D., Ph.B., Ithaca, N. Y. *Invert.*, *Lithol.*, *Molluscs*, *Geol.*, *Palæo.* C.*

1840 Harris, I. H., Waynesville, Ohio. *Geol.*, *Palæo.*, *Arch.* C. Ex.*

1841 Harris, Sarah C., M.D., Galena, Ill. *Bot.*, *Min.*, *Palæo.* C.

1842 Harris, Thaddeus W., Asst. in Geol., Harvard College, Divinity Hall, 40, Cambridge, Mass. *Strat. and Physical Geol.**
1843 Harris, Thos. C., Cur. N. C. Geol. Museum, Dept. Agric., Raleigh, N. C. *Min., Phys., Elect., Photog.**
1844 Harrison, Edwin, B.S., St. Louis, Mo. *Geol.**
1845 Harrison, Frank S., Princeton, Ill. *Bot., Geol., Arch.* C.*
1846 Harrison, George B., 520 East Mulberry St., Bloomington, Ill. *Geol.* C. Ex.*
1847 Harrison, G. E., M.D , Ottawa, Ohio. *Elect., Mic.* C. Ex.?
1848 Harrison, J. B., Franklin Falls, N. H. *Bot., Geol.* C. Ex.*
1849 Harrison, Wm. G., M.D., 26 Mt. Vernon Place, Baltimore, Md. *Mic., Biol.**
1850 Harrod, P., M.D., Avon, Fulton Co., Ill. *Ool.* C. Ex.*
1851 Hart, Chas. A., 550 E. University Ave., Champaign. Ill. *Ent., Bot., Con.* C.*
1852 Hart, C. P., Wyoming, Ohio. *Biol., Alienist and Neurologist.**
1853 Hart, Edward, Ph.D., Prof. Chem., Easton, Pa. *Chem.**
1854 Hartman, John H., Lebanon, Warren Co., Ohio. *L. and F. W. Shells, Cin. Fossils*, for ex. in *Palæo., Ferns, Min.* C.?
1855 Hartman, Walter, Belleville, Ont., Can. *Orn., Tax.* C. Ex.*
1856 Hartman, W. D., M.D., Westchester, Pa. *Con.* C.*
1857 Hartmann, Leopold, Hockley, Harris Co., Texas. *Ent.**
1858 Hartshorne, Dr. Henry, A.M., M.D., LL.D., Germantown, Phila., Pa. *Gen. Biol.**
1859 Hartwell, Edw. M., Ph.D., M.D., Associate in Phys. Training and Dir. Gymnasium, Johns Hopkins Univ., Baltimore, Md. *Biol.*?
1860 Hartwell, Samuel, Lincoln, Mass. *Hort.**
1861 Hartzell, L. B., Harper, Harper Co., Kan. *Orn., Ool.* C. Ex.
1862 Hartzler, Prof. J. C., Newark, O. *Arch., Geol., Palæo.*
1863 Harvey, F. L., B.S., Prof. Biology and Geology, Ark. Indust. Univ., Fayetteville, Ark. *Bot., Zool., Geol., Min.* C. Ex.?
1864 Harvey, Leon F., M.D., Buffalo, N. Y. *Lepid.* C.*
1865 Harvey, William, Bradford, Stark Co., Ill. *Bot.* C.*
1866 Haskell, Charles H., Holland Patent, Oneida Co., N. Y. *Palæo., Min.* C. Ex. fossils from Utica slate for fossils or fine minerals.
1867 Haskins, J. P., Proprietor Saratoga Co. Mus. of Nat. Hist., Seltzer Building, Saratoga Springs, N. Y. *Geol., Min., Arch., Palæo.* C. Ex.?
1868 Haslam, Rev. Geo. E., M.A., Trinity College, Toronto, Can. *Bot., Geol., Zool.* C. Ex.
1869 Hasse, H. E., M.D., Los Angeles, Calif. *Bot.* C. Ex.*
1870 Hassler, Ferdinand A., M.D., Ph.D., Santa Ana, Los Angeles Co., Calif. *Phæn. Bot., Geog. Dist., Mollusca.* C.*
1871 Hastings, Wm. N., Rochester, Strafford Co., N. H. *Desmids, Diatoms, Mic., Protozoa, Infusoria.* C.*
1872 Hatch, C C., Community, N. Y. *Orn.* C. Ex.*
1873 Hatch, Delos, Oak Centre, Wis. *Orn.* C. Ex. birds' eggs and skins for same, and mins., shells, etc.*

1874 Hatch, James H., D.D.S., 28 Geary St., San Francisco, Calif. *Diatoms, Mic., Hist.**

1875 Hatch, P. L., M.D., Minneapolis, Minn. *Microscopist.**

1876 Hatch, S. R., Milford, Mass. *Diatoms, Min., Mic., Photog., Infusoria, Electricity.* C. Ex.

1877 Hatch, W. H., Rock Island, Ill. *Phæn. Bot.* C. Ex.*

1878 Hathaway, H. S., 118 Elmwood Ave., Providence, R. I. *Min., Orn., Ool., Tax., Ent.* C. Ex.*

1879 Hathaway, T. F., So. Parish, Oxford Co., Me. *Bot: Woods a specialty.* C. Ex.

1880 Haupt, H., jr., M.D., Ph.D., Patent Att'y, St. Paul, Minn. *Geol., Bot.* C.*

1881 Hawkes, Wm. H., B.A., M.D., 1330 N. Y. Ave., Washington, D. C. *Philology, Arch., Anthropology.**

1882 Hawkins, Hiram B., Box 190, Oneonta, Otsego Co., N. Y. *Min., Ent: Lepid., Coleopt.* C. Ex.*

1883 Hawkins, James, 212 So. Leavitt St., Chicago, Ill.

1884 Hawkins. Thomas H., M.D., Denver, Colo. *Physiol.*

1885 Hawley, Geo. D., Augusta, Hancock Co., Ill. *Palæo., Geol., Min., Ent.* C. Ex.*

1886 Hawley, Geo. P., Round Grove, Whiteside Co., Ill. *Ent.* C.?

1887 Hawley, Mrs. Helen D., Round Grove, Whiteside Co., Ill. *Bot: Ferns, Mosses, Geol., Min., spec. Arch.* C. Ex.?

1888 Hawley, Rev. R. E., M.A., Washington, Ind. *Indian Relics, Cin. and Carb. Fossils and Goniatites.* C.*

1889 Hawley, R. V., 117 Jefferson St., Cleveland, Ohio. *Ent.?*

1890 Haworth, Alphonso, Mayport, Fla. *Marine Shells.* C. Ex.?

1891 Haworth, Erasmus, Prof. Physical Sciences, Oskaloosa, Iowa.?

1892 Hay, George U., St. John, N. B., Can. *Bot: Ferns, Fungi, Algæ.*

1893 Hay, J. Marley, F.S.A. Scot., 912 Sixth Ave., New York, N. Y. *Arch.*

1894 Hay, O. P., Prof. Nat. Hist., Butler Univ., Indianapolis, Ind. *Comp. Anat., Fishes, Crustacea.* C. Ex.

1895 Hay, Robert, Geologist, Junction City, Kansas. *Geol., Lith.* C. Would like to sell.*

1896 Hayden, Everett, Hydrographic Office, Navy Dept., Washington, D. C. *Physical Geol., Meteo.**

1897 Hayden, Rev. Horace Edwin, Wilkes-Barré, Pa. *Bibliog., Arch., Numismatics.* C. Ex.*

1898 Hayden, N. W., Windsor, Hartford Co., Ct. *Bot.* C.*

1899 Hayes, Charles E., cor. Main and Dyre Sts., Frankford, Philadelphia, Pa. *Orn., Ool.* C. Ex.

1900 Hayes, Prof. E. A., Randolph, N. Y. *Geol., Min., Phys., Ast.* C. Ex.

1901 Haynes, Ernest E., Oberlin, O. *Orn., Ool.* C. Ex.?

1902 Haynes, Prof. Henry W., 239 Beacon St., Boston, Mass. *Arch.**

1903 Haynes, Hiram, Taxidermist, 4 Caulkins Ct., Water St., Lawrence, Mass. *Orn., Herpetol., Tax., Ent.* C.*

1904 Hayt, H. W., Med. Electrician, Lowville, N. Y. *Mam., Orn.* C. Ex.*

1905 Hayward, Roland, 346 Marlboro St., Boston, Mass. *Ent: Coleopt.* C. Ex.*
1906 Hazard, Fred'k R., Syracuse, N. Y. *Min.*, *Inorg. Chem.* C. Ex.*
1907 Hazard, John N., Peace Dale, R. I. *Analyt. Chem.**
1908 Hazard, R. G., 2d, Peace Dale, R. I. *Ool.* C.*
1909 Hazard, Willis P., West Chester, Chester Co., Pa. *Agric.*, *Mic.*, *Bibliog.*, *Zool.*, *Gen. Biol.*, *Mammals*, *Orn.**
1910 Hazen, Miss Frances M., Mt. Holyoke Female Seminary, South Hadley, Mass.?
1911 Hazen, Henry Allen, A.M., Washington, D. C. *Meteorol.*, *Elect.*, *Ast.**
1912 Hazen, Levi, West Hartford, Vt. *Min.* C.*
1913 Head, W. R., Chicago, Ill. *Spongiadæ.* Examples for determination and classification, promptly returned free of expense.*
1914 Heading, Alice L., Peoria, Ill. *Bot.* C. Ex.*
1915 Hecox, Laura J. F., Santa Cruz, Calif. *Con.* C. Calif. shells in ex. for L. and F. W. shells and fossils.*
1916 Hedden, R. T., 33 Battles Ave., Columbus, Ohio. *Orn.*, *Ool.*,* *Arch.* C. Ex.?
1917 Hedge, Fred'k H., jr., Public Library, Lawrence, Mass. *Bot.**
1918 Hedges, Sidney M., 178 Devonshire St., Boston, Mass.*
1919 Hedley, Carl W., Medina, N. Y. *Ool.*, *Postage Stamps.* C. Ex.*
1920 Hedley, Chas. H., Medina, N. Y. *Orn.*, *Ool.*, *Ast.*, *Photog.*, *Tax.*, *Bot.* C. Pitcher plants and sundew for ex. Foreign correspondence solicited. Local mammals in ex. for bird skins.*
1921 Hedley, W. Edgar, Medina, N. Y. *Orn.*, *Ool.* Buy, sell or ex., also postage stamps for ex.*
1922 Heighway, A. E., M.D., 88 W. 7th St., Cincinnati, Ohio. *Chem*, *Geol.**
1923 Heighway, A. E., jr., M.D., 88 W. 7th St., Cincinnati, Ohio. *Geol.*, *Mic.*, *Photog.*, *Anat.* C.?
1924 Heighway, S. C., 88 W. 7th St., Cincinnati, Ohio. *Relics.* C. Ex.*
1925 Heiligbrodt, L., Bastrop, Texas. *Lepid.*, *Hymenop.*, *Coleopt.*, *Reptiles.* C.?
1926 Heilprin, Angelo, Prof. Invert. Palæo. and Curator-in-charge, Acad. Nat. Sci., Philadelphia, Pa. Prof. Geol., Wagner Free Inst. of Sci.*
1927 Heimstreet, Thomas B., M.D., 132 2d St., Troy, N. Y. *Orn.*, *Gen. Zool.* C. Ex.?
1928 Heistand, George W., Marysville, Union Co., Ohio. *Orn.*, *Ent.* C. Ex.?
1929 Heitzmann, Dr. Carl, 39 W. 45th St., New York City, N. Y. *Biol.*, *Mic.*, *Dermatol.**
1930 Heitzmann, Louis, M.D., 39 West 45th St., New York, N. Y. *Fungi*, *Mic.*, *Gen. Biol.*, *Morph.*, *Hist.**
1931 Helme, James W., jr., Adrian, Mich. *Orn.*, *Tax.* C.?

1932 Helmuth, Dr. Carl A., 218 Chicago Ave., Chicago, Ill. *Zool.*, *Bot.*, *Mic.**
1933 Hemiup, N. H., 604 S. E. Fifth St., Minneapolis, Minn. *Ast.*, *Gen. Zool.*, *Mam.*?
1934 Hemphill, Henry, San Diego, Calif.*
1935 Henderson, George A., Decatur, Ill. Manufacturer of Scientific instruments and novelties.*
1936 Henderson, J. L., M.D., Three Runs, Clearfield Co., Pa. *Mic.*, *Bibliog.*, *Orn.*, *Ent: esp. Lepid.* C. Ex.*
1937 Henderson, Dr. J. P., Newville, Richland Co., Ohio. *Arch.*, *Eth.* C.?
1938 Henderson, Louis F., 471 7th St., Portland, Ore. *Phæn. Bot.*, *Ferns, Mosses and Lichens.* C. Ex.*
1939 Hennig, Miss L. Ida, Principal Mount Gardner Sem., Gardner, Mass.?
1940 Henning, Carl Fritz, Boone, Boone Co., Iowa. *Orn.*, *Ool.*, *Tax.* C. Ex.*
1941 Henry, Joseph, P. O. Box 785, Salina, Kan. *Bot.*, *Hort.*, *Grasses of the World, Ferns and Mosses.* C. Ex.*
1942 Henry, W. A., Prof. Agric., and Director Expt. Station, Univ. Wisconsin, Madison, Wis.*
1943 Henshall, J. A., M.D., Cynthiana, Ky. *Ichth.**
1944 Henshall, Mrs. J. A., Cynthiana, Ky. *Palæo.*, *Con.*, *Ent.**
1945 Henshaw, H. W., Smithsonian Institution, Washington, D. C. *Orn.*, *Eth.* C. Ex.*
1946 Henshaw, Samuel, 77 Newbury St., Boston, Mass. *Ent: Myriopoda*, *Orthop.*, *Coleopt.**
1947 Hensoldt, H., Cedar, Fayette Co., Texas. Specialty, *Microscopic investigation of Rocks and Minerals.* *Gen. Mic.* C. Ex.*
1948 Herbert, W. S., Lynn, Mass. *Mic.*, *Ent: Coleopt.**
1949 Hermann, Henry W., M.D., 2330 Washington Ave., St. Louis, Mo. *Elect.*, *Mic.*, *Anat.*, *Histol.**
1950 Hermann, Richard, Dubuque, Ia. *Geol.*, *Palæo.*, *Min.*, *Arch.* C. Ex.*
1951 Herpers, Henry, 18 Crawford St., Newark, N. J. *Ent: Lepid.* C. Ex.*
1952 Herrick, C. L., M.S., Prof. Geol. and Nat. Hist. in Denison Univ., Granville, O. Desires literature of Rotifera and Paleontology of Sub-carboniferous.*
1953 Herrick, Francis H., Tilton, N. H. *Orn.*, *Bot.* C. Ex.
1954 Herrick, Harold, Lawrence, Queens Co., N. Y. *Orn.* C.*
1955 Herron, R. B., Colton, San Bernardino Co., Calif. *Mam.*, *Ool.*, *Orn.*, *Tax* C. Large collection of Calif. birds. Desires to ex. for game birds of N. A.*
1956 Herron, W. M., M.D., 165 Robinson St., Allegheny City, Pa. *Phys.*, *Mic.*, *Spectroscopy*, *Ast.**
1957 Hervey, Rev. A. B., Ph.D., Taunton, Mass. *Mic.*, *Crypt. Bot.*, *Marine Algæ in particular.* C. Ex.*
1958 Herzer, Rev. H., Berea, Ohio. *Mosses*, *Palæo.*, *Geol.* C. Ex.*
1959 Hess, Frank W., 3d Artillery, U. S. A., address Allegheny College, Meadville, Pa. *Orn.* C. Ex.

1960 Heuser, H. J., Chemist and Druggist, Wytheville, Wythe Co., Va. *Antiquities, Geol., Min.* C. Ex.*
1961 Heustis, Mrs. Caroline E., Parrsboro', Nova Scotia, Can. *Ent: Lepid.* C.?
1962 Hewston, George, Prof., A.M., M.D., 1132 Sutter St., San Francisco, Calif. *Zool., Orn., Ool., Radiates, Sponges, Protozoa.* C. Ex*
1963 Hexamer, C. John, B.S., C.E., 2313 Green St., Philadelphia, Pa. *Anth., Arch., Eth., Ethnog.* C. Ex.?
1964 Hexamer, F. M., M.D., New Rochelle, N. Y. *Bot.**
1965 Heyer, W. D., 1141 East Broad St., Elizabeth, N. J. *Phys., Ast.**
1966 Heys, Thomas, Toronto, Canada. *Bot., Min., Chem.?*
1967 Heyward, James S., A.M., Prof. Nat. Sci., State Agric. Coll., Orangeburg, S. C.*
1968 Hibbard, William N., Hyde Park, Ill. *Coleopt.* C.
1969 Hickman, John Bale, Watsonville, Santa Cruz Co., Calif. *Tax., Phæn. Bot., Ferns, Hort.* C. for sale.*
1970 Hicks, Gilbert H., Grayling, Michigan. *Bot., Gen. Biol.* C. Ex. Correspondence solicited on botanical subjects.*
1971 Hicks, John S., Roslyn, L. I., N. Y. *Hort., Photog., Meteo.**
1972 Hicks, Prof. L. E., Lincoln, Neb. *Strat. Geol., Palæo.* C. Ex.*
1973 Hicks, Milton A., Weathersfield, Windsor Co., Vt. *Bot., Geol., Min., Physics, Elect., Gen. Biol., Geog. Dist., Arch.* C. Ex. Desires fossils, minerals, Palæolithic and Neolithic relics.*
1974 Hidden, Wm. Earl, 25 Orleans St., Newark, N. J., and Stony Point, Alexander Co., N. C. *Min., Cryst., Gen. Sci., Gems.* C. Ex. Meteorites espec. desired.*
1975 Higgins, Sam'l, Susquehanna, Pa. *Metall., Elect., Phys., Geol.*
1976 Higginson, Charles M., care C. B. & Q. R. R., Chicago, Ill. *Min.* C. Ex.*
1977 Higley, W. Kerr, Ph.D., Prof. Bot., Northwestern Univ., Department of Pharmacy, 40 Dearborn St., Chicago, Ill. *Bot.* C.*
1978 Hildebrand, Charles, Yale Coll., 34 Chestnut St., New Haven, Ct. *Math.*
1979 Hilgard, Eug. W., Prof. of Agric. Chem., Univ. of Calif., Berkeley, Calif. *Agric. Chem., Geol.* Col. in Bot.*
1980 Hill, Alfred J., 406 Maria Ave., St. Paul, Minn. *Geog., Cartog., Anth.**
1981 Hill, Alonzo E., Norwich, Ct. *Orn., Tax., Ent.* Desires foreign skins for native. C. Ex.*
1982 Hill, Chas. S., Washington, D. C. *Political Economy, Geol., Min., Metall., Phys., Anth.* C. Ex.
1983 Hill, Rev. E. J., Normal Park, Cook Co., Ill. *Bot., Geol.* C.*
1984 Hill, Edwin A., New Haven, Ct. *Min., Mic.* C. Ex.
1985 Hill, F. A., Prin. English High School, Cambridge, Mass. *Am. Arch.**

1986 Hill, Frank A., Geologist in charge Anthracite District, Geol. Surv. of Pa., 907 Walnut St., Philadelphia, Pa.*

1987 Hill, Franklin C., Box 338, Princeton, N. J. *Geol.*, *Ent.**

1988 Hill, Frederick A., P. O. Box 155, Valley Falls, R. I. *Pharmacy*, *Chem.*, *Bot.*, *Mic.*, *Metall.*, *Phys.*, *Meteo.**

1989 Hill, G. W., Nautical Almanac Office, Navy Dept., Washington, D. C. *Bot.*, *Ast.*, *Math.**

1990 Hill, Henry B., Prof. Chem., Harvard Coll., Cambridge, Mass.

1991 Hill, Herbert M., A.M., 30 William St., Watertown, N. Y. *Chem.*, *Min.*, *Geol.*, *Mic.* C. Ex.*

1992 Hill, J. Stewart, M.D., 151 Lake St., Elmira, N. Y. *Orn.* C.*

1993 Hill, Homer D., Morris, Ill. *Palæo.*, *Geol.*, *Min.*, *Arch.* Dealer in fossils and min. Buys, sells and exchanges.*

1994 Hill, Louis C., Box 2598, Ann Arbor, Mich. *Tax.* C. Ex.

1995 Hill, Lucy A., Belmont, Mass. C.*

1996 Hill, Rev. Winfield E., East Liverpool, Ohio. *Bot: Phæn. and Crypt. Plants*, *Ferns*, *Mosses*, *Orn.*, *Ool.**

1997 Hill, Rev. W. K., A.M., Prof. Phys. and Nat. Sci., Carthage Coll., Carthage, Ill.*

1998 Hill, W. W., Albany, N. Y. *Lepid.* C. Ex. Only perfect examples desired, and the same given in return.*

1999 Hiller, Chas. A., A.M., Salina, Kan. *Elect.*, *Ast.*

2000 Hiller, P. C., Conestoga, Lancaster Co., Pa. *Arch.* C. Ex. 3d Annual Report, Bureau of Ethnology, and Geol. Reports, U. S. and Indian Relics for Indian Relics from other localities to ex. Correspondence solicited.*

2001 Hills, W. D., Odin, Marion Co., Ill. *Ool.*, *Hort.*, *Pomology.* C. Ex.*

2002 Himes, Charles F., Ph.D., Prof. Phys., Dickinson Coll., Carlisle, Pa. *Phys.*, *Chem.*, *Photog.**

2003 Himes, Isaac N., M.D., Prof. Med. Coll. of West. Reserve Univ., Cleveland, Ohio. *Pathol. and Morbid Anat.**

2004 Hinde, B. C., A.M., Prof. Phys. Sci., Howard Female Coll., Fayette, Mo. C.?

2005 Hindman, Wm., P. O. Box 366, La Salle, Ill. *Palæo.*, *Geol.*, *Min.*, *Anat.*, *Moll.*, *Radiates*, *Protozoa.* C. Ex.

2006 Hinds, J. I. D., A.M., C.E., Ph.D., Prof. Chem. and Biology, Cumberland Univ., Lebanon, Tenn. *Chem.*, *Geol.*, *Bot.**

2007 Hinds, Wm. A., Community, Madison Co., N. Y. *Bot.* C.*

2008 Hinkley, A. A., Dubois, Washington Co., Ill. *L. and F. W. Shells.* C. Ex.*

2009 Hinkley, Holmes, 14 Kirkland Place, Cambridge, Mass. *Ent: Lepid.* Ex.*

2010 Hinman, C. W., S.B., 32 Hawley St., Boston, Mass. *Chem.* Gas Inspector for Mass.*

2011 Hinman, Chas. D., Columbus Savings Bank Co., Box 600, Columbus, Ohio. *Anat.*, *Zool.*, *Orn.*, *Ool.* C. Ex.*

2012 Hinrichs, G., A.M., M.D., LL.D., Iowa City, Ia. *Meteo.*, *Director Ia. weather service.**

2013 Hirschfelder, Chas. A., U. S. Vice-Consul, Toronto, Can. *Min.*, *Anth.*, *Arch.*, *Eth.* C. Ex.?

2014 Hiscox, Gardner D., 435 Greene Ave., Brooklyn, N. Y. *C. and M. Eng.*, *Ast.*, *Geol.*, *Physical Sciences*, *Micro-Min.*, *Mic.* C. Ex.*

2015 Hitchcock, A. M., Williamstown, Mass. *Mam.*, *Vert.**

2016 Hitchcock, C. H., Prof. Geol., Dartmouth Coll., Hanover, N. H. *Geol.*, *Lithol.*, *Ichnol.* C. Ex.*

2017 Hitchcock, Chas. A., Northeast, Erie Co., Pa. *Geol.*, *Min.* C. Ex.*

2018 Hitchcock, Fanny R. M., 41 West 73d St., New York City. *Invert. Palæo.*, *Min.*, *Inorg. Chem.* C. Ex.*

2019 Hitchcock, Geo. E., Woodland, Yolo Co., Calif. *Ool.* C. Ex.*

2020 Hitchcock, Geo. N., San Diego, Calif. *Astronomy.*

2021 Hitchcock, H. S., Broad and Pine Sts., Philadelphia, Pa. *Mic.*, *Anat.*, *Phys.*

2022 Hitchcock, Prof. R., F.R.M.S., National Museum, Washington, D. C. *Mic.*, *F. W. Algæ.* C.*

2023 Hittell, Mrs. Theo. H., Calif. Acad. of Sci., San Francisco, Calif. *Sericulture.**

2024 Hoadley, A. E., M.D., Prof. Anat., Coll. Phys. and Surgeons of Chicago, 683 Washington Boulevard, Chicago, Ill. *Zool.*, *Vert. Anat.*, *Osteol.* Ex. in Osteol and Anat.*

2025 Hoadley, John C., 28 State St., Boston, Mass. Engineer and Expert in patent cases. *Geol*, *Phys.*, *Elect.* C.

2026 Hoaglind, Cornelius N., M.D., 410 Clinton Ave., Brooklyn, N. Y. *Mic.*, *Photog*, *Gen. Biol.*, *Histol.**

2027 Hobble, C. S., Hampton, Iowa.

2028 Hobbs, Orlando, Jeffersonville, Clarke Co., Ind. *Photography*, *Assay of Minerals and Ores*, *Geol.*, *Palæo.* C. Lower Silurian to the Hamilton of the Devon. to ex. for Carb. and overlying formations.*

2029 Hobby, C. M., M.D., Iowa City, Ia. *F. W. Algæ*, *Mic.* C. Ex.

2030 Hobson, Geo. W., 4555 Wakefield St., Germantown, Pa. *Min.* C. Ex.*

2031 Hochstein, A., Botanical Artist, 58 Seventh St., Hoboken, N. J. *Bot.?*

2032 Hodge, F., A.B., A.M., M.D., Hudson, Ohio. *Coleopt.* C. Ex.

2033 Hodges, Edw. F., Prof. Pathol., Med. Coll. of Ind., Indianapolis, Ind. *Mic.*, *Histol.* C. Ex.

2034 Hodges, N. D. C., 47 Lafayette Pl., New York, N. Y. *Phys.**

2035 Hodgin, J. N., 1020 Main St., Richmond, Wayne Co., Ind. *Geol.*, *Min.*, *Arch.* C. Ex.*

2036 Hoffman, Theo. C., Rockville, Ct. *Orn.*, *Ool.*, *Tax.* C. Ex.*

2037 Hoffman, D. A, M.D., Oskaloosa, Ia. *Geol.*, *Palæo.*, *Ool.*, *Ent.*, *Arch.* C.?

2038 Hoffman, Walter J., M.D., Bureau of Ethnology, Washington, D. C. *Anth.*, *Vert. Zool.*, *Min.**

2039 Hoffman, G. C., F. Inst. Chem., F.R.S.C., Chemist, Mineralogist and Ass't Dir. Geological and Natural History Surv. of Canada, Ottawa, Can.*

2040 Hogg, Alex., Supt. City Schools, Fort Worth, Tex.*

2041 Holbrook, Alfred, Pres. Nat. Normal Univ., Lebanon, Ohio. *Bot.*, *Palæo.*, *Geol.*, *Min.* C. Ex.?

2042 Holbrook, Francis N., C.E., care of Holbrook & Foucar, El Paso, Texas. *Mining and Met.**

2043 Holbrook, M. L., M.D., 13 Laight St., New York, N. Y., Editor Herald of Health, Prof. of Hygiene in New York Med. Coll., and Hospital for women, N. Y.*

2044 Holcomb, Benton, West Granby, Hartford Co., Ct. *Con.*, *Ool.*, *Min.* C. Ex.?

2045 Holden, Chas. N., 106 Warren Ave., Chicago, Ill. *Photog.*, *Arch.*, *Orn.*, *Ool.*, *Tax.*, *Osteol.* C. Ex.*

2046 Holden, E. G. D., Grand Rapids, Mich. *Arch.**

2047 Holden, E S., Pres. Univ. of Calif., and Dir. Lick Obs., Berkeley, Calif. *Ast.**

2048 Holden, Isaac, A.M., Bridgeport, Ct. *Pteridophyta*, *Musci*, *Algæ.* C. Ex.*

2049 Holder, J. B., M.D., Cur. Invert. Zool., Fishes and Reptiles, Am. Museum, Central Park, New York, N. Y.*

2050 Holder, Mary H., Berlin, Mass. *Bot.* C.

2051 Holland, Rev. F. R., Hope, Ind. *Bot.*, *Con.* C.*

2052 Holland, Frank, Manchester, N. H. *Mic.* C.*

2053 Holland, Rev. W. J., M.A., Ph.D., Member Ent. Soc. of France, London, etc., Pittsburg, Pa. *Bot.*, *Ent: Lepid.*, *Coleopt.* Large collection, including types of T. L. Mead and W. H. Edwards. Desires to ex. or buy insects from all parts of the world, esp. N. A. Also rare books on Lepid.*

2054 Hollick, Arthur, Ph.B., Box 105, New Brighton, Staten Island, N. Y. *Phæn. and Crypt. Bot.* C. Ex.*

2055 Holman, David S., Lock Box 519, 15 S. 7th St., Philadelphia, Pa. *Mic.*

2056 Holman, Silas W., S.B., Assoc. Prof. of Physics, Mass. Inst. Tech., Boston, Mass. *Phys.*, *Elect.*, *Thermometry.**

2057 Holmes, E. S., D.D.S., Grand Rapids, Mich. *Zool.**

2058 Holmes, J. C., 55 Moffat Block, Detroit, Mich. *Ent.* C.*

2059 Holmes, Prof. Joseph A., Chapel Hill, N. C. *Geol.*, *Bot.* C. Ex.*

2060 Holmes, Miss Mary E., 201 S. 1st St., Rockford, Winnebago Co., Ill. *Bot.*, *Orn.*, *Geol.*, *Mic.* C. Ex.*

2061 Holmes, W. H., U. S. Geol. Survey, Washington, D. C. *Geol.*, *Arch.*?

2062 Holstein, Geo. Wolf, Belvidere, N. J. *Invert. Palæo.*, *Bot.*, *Anth.*, *Arch.* C. Ex.*

2063 Holt, Alfred F., M.D., 5 Pleasant St., Cambridgeport, Mass. *Pathol.*, *and Histol.*, *Mic. slides of same in ex. for any Mic. objects.**

2064 Holt, James P., M.D., Claremont, N. H. *Mic.*, *Bot.*, *Fungi*, *Diatoms*, *Chem.*, *Anat.*, *Hist.* C. Ex.*

2065 Holterhoff, G., jr., San Diego, Calif. *Orn.*, *Ool.* C.*

2066 Holway, E. W. D., Decorah, Ia. *Fungi, Phæn. Bot., Mic.* C. fungi.*
2067 Holzinger, John M., Prof. Nat. Hist., State Normal School, Winona, Minn. *Phæn. Bot.* Desires to ex. corals, mins., plants, fossils and shells.*
2068 Homsher, Geo. W., M.D., Cur. Arch., Dublin Nat. Hist. Soc., Dublin, Wayne Co., Ind. *Arch.* C.?
2069 Honeyman, Rev. David, D.C.L., F.R.S.C., Provincial Geologist and Cur. Prov. Mus., Halifax, N. S., Can. *Geol.?*
2070 Hood, E. Lyman, Minneapolis, Minn. *Orn., Ool., Ent., Mic.* C. Ex. for European species.?
2071 Hood, Harvey P., Derry, Rockingham Co., N. H.?
2072 Hooper, Franklin W., Prof. Chem. and Geol., Adelphi Acad., 71 St. James Pl., Brooklyn, N. Y.*
2073 Hooper, John R., M.D., 1425 Linden Ave., Baltimore, Md. *Ast.* Collection of Telescopes.*
2074 Hooper, Josiah, West Chester, Pa. *Bot., Coniferæ.* C.?
2075 Hoopes, Wm. L., Ass't Prof. Phys., Tufts College, College Hill, Mass. *Phys., Elect.**
2076 Hope, Henry W., Paint P. O., Highland Co., Ohio. *Geol., Arch.* C. Ex.*
2077 Hopkins, Florence M., Care of University, Vincennes, Ind. *Ferns, Algæ, Paleo., Geol.* C. Ex.*
2078 Horn, George H., M.D., 874 North 4th St., Philadelphia, Pa. *Coleoptera of U. S.* C.*
2079 Horn, H. B., M.D., Atchison, Kan.*
2080 Hornaday, William T., Chief Taxidermist U. S. Nat. Mus., Pres. Soc. Am. Taxidermists, Washington, D. C. *Mam.* Coll. and Tax. in all branches.*
2081 Horne, A. R., D.D., Ed. "Nat. Educator," Allentown, Pa. *Bot., Geol., Min., Chem., Phys., Meteo.* C. Ex.*
2082 Horne, Edwin W., 12 E. Main St., Rochester, N. Y. *Mic., Photog.?*
2083 Horne, Henry E., McGregor, Ia. *Min.* C. Ex. Also offers curiosities from the Miss. River.
2084 Horr, Asa, M.D., Dubuque, Ia. *Bot.* C.*
2085 Horsford, F. H., Charlotte, Vt. *Bot.**
2086 Hoskins, William, La Grange, Cook Co., Ill. *Min., Analyt. Chem., Mic.* C. Ex.*
2087 Hotchkiss, Jed., Ed. of "The Virginias," the mining and industrial journal of Va. and W. Va.; Geologist and consulting Mining Engineer, 346 East Main St., Staunton, Augusta Co., Va. *Geol., Meteo., Physics, Arch., Bibliog., Eth., Ethnog.* C.*
2088 Hough, G. W., Dir. Dearborn Observatory, Evanston, Ill. *Physics, Elect., Meteorol., Ast.**
2089 Hough, Prof. Jacob Brenneman, M D., Waynesville, Warren Co., Ohio. *Bot of Aquatic plants, Chem., Phys., Mic.* Wants living water plants for Aquariculture and gratis distribution. Lists furnished. Ex.*
2090 Hough, Romeyn B., Lowville, N. Y. *Orn., Bot., Dendrol.* C.*

2091 Houghton, Chas. A , W. Medway, Mass. *Orn.*, *Tax.* C. Ex.*
2092 Houghton, John N., Grinnell, Iowa. *Orn.*, *Ool.* C. Ex.
2093 Houston, George M., Harrisonville, Mo. *Min.*, *Mic.* C. Ex.*
2094 Hovey, C. H., 69 Tremont St., Boston, Mass. *Floriculture, Pomology, Horticulture.* C. Ex.?
2095 Hovey, C. M., Boston, Mass. *Ferns, Mosses, Horticulture.*?
2096 Hovey, Edmund Otis, Yale Coll., New Haven, Ct. *Geol., Min.* C. Ex.*
2097 Hovey, Rev. Horace C., D.D., 14 Park St., Bridgeport, Ct. *Geol., Anth.* C. Ex. crinoids, corals and cave specimens.*
2098 Howard, Curtis C., M.Sc., Prof. Chem., Starling Med. Coll., Columbus, Ohio. *Chem., Phys., Mic.* C. Ex.*
2099 Howard, E. M., M.D., B.S., 401 Linden St., Camden, N. J. *Bot., Min., Mic., Myology of Vert.* C. Ex.?
2100 Howard, Harry T., 196 Felicity St., New Orleans, La. *Photog., Mic., Anth.* *
2101 Howard, L. A., Petersburg, Monroe Co., Mich. *Bot., Min., Zool., Geol., Orn., Ool.* Ex. in Ool. Eggs in sets only.*
2102 Howard, L. O., M.S., Ass't Entomologist, Dept. Agric., Washington, D. C. *Econ. Ent., esp. parasitic Hymenoptera.**
2103 Howard, Prof. Orson, A.M., Desert Univ., Salt Lake City, Utah. *Moll.* C. Ex.*
2104 Howard, Sophie E., M.D., Auburn, N. Y. *Gen. Biol., Mic.* Ex.*
2105 Howard, W. H., B.S., B.Ph., Prof. of Phys. Sci., Adrian Coll., Adrian, Mich. *Phys. Geol., Chem., Phys.**
2106 Howe, Albion S., Box 2160, U. S. Geol. Survey, San Francisco, Calif. *Chem., Met.**
2107 Howe, Allen B., Ph D., Yale Coll., 188 College St., New Haven, Ct. *Analyt. Chem.*?
2108 Howe, Elliot C., M.D., Yonkers, N. Y. *Bot: Cyperaceæ, Ferns, Ent., Biol.* C. Ex. in Bot.?
2109 Howe, Prof. H. A., Denver, Colo. *Math., Ast.**
2110 Howe, James Lewis, M.D., Ph.D., F.C.S., Scientist to the Polytechnic Soc., Prof. Med. Chem. and Tox., Hospital Coll. of Med., Louisville, Ky. *Chem.**
2111 Howe, Lucien, M.D., 64 W. Huron St., Buffalo, N. Y. *Mic., Anat.* C. Ex. desired in slides illustrating anatomy and pathology of the eye and ear.*
2112 Howe, Oliver H., Dedham, Mass. *Bot.*?
2113 Howell, Edwin E., A.M., Ward's Nat. Sci. Estab., 18 College Ave., Rochester, N. Y. *Geol., Min., Meteorites.**
2114 Howell, Geo. Rogers, M.A., N. Y. State Library, Albany, N. Y. *Arch, Eth., Philol.**
2115 Howell, Joseph, Arthur, Multnomah Co., Ore. *Bot.* C.*
2116 Howell, Robert, Nichols, Tioga Co., N. Y. *Geol., Palæo., Zool., Arch.* C. Ex.*
2117 Howell, Samuel B., M.D., 1513 Green St. Philadelphia, Pa. Prof. Min. and Geol., Univ. of Pa. *Palæo., Geol., Chem., Min., Lithol., Mic., Photog., Invert.* C. Ex Particularly desires to obtain Polyzoa, recent and fossil.
2118 Howell, Thomas, Arthur, Multnomah Co., Ore. *Bot.* Collects native seeds, bulbs, ferns, etc.*

2119 Howes, Geo. H., Box 187, Braintree, Mass. *Ent., Orn., Ool., Tax.* C. Ex.*
2120 Howes, R. A., Coll. of Phys. and Surgeons, 813 W. Harrison St., Chicago, Ill. *Osteol.* Skeletons for sale or exchange.*
2121 Howland, E. P., M.D., 211 4½ St., N. W., Washington, D. C. *Phys., Elect., Mic., Photog.**
2122 Hoxie, Walter, Frogmore, S. C. *Tax., Ool., Orn.* (*Crust., Moll., Batrachians and Snakes in spirit*). Coll. made to order.*
2123 Hoy, Philo R., M.D., Racine, Wis. *Ent., Herpetol. and Orn. of Wisconsin.* C.*
2124 Hoyt, D. B., Lynn, Mass. *Bot., Orn., Ool., Ent.**
2125 Hoyt, E. C., Seneca Falls, N. Y. *Diatoms, Min., Org. Chem., Metall., Mic.* C. Ex.*
2126 Huart, Rev. Victor A., A.M., Prof. Zool., Sem., Chicoutimi, P. Q., Can. *Ent., Gen. Nat. Hist.* C. Ex.*
2127 Hubbard, G. W., M.D., Prof. of Nat. Sci., Central Tenn Coll., Nashville, Tenn. *Bot., Geol., Min.* C. Tenn. plants for ex.*
2128 Hubbard, H. G., 114 Griswold St., Detroit, Mich. Winter address Crescent City, Fla. *Coleopt.* C. Ex.*
2129 Hubbard, Lucius, South Bend, Ind. *Ent., L. and F. W. Shells.* C. Ex.*
2130 Hubbard, Oliver Payson, M.D., LL.D., Emer. Prof. Chem. and Pharm., Dartmouth Coll., Hanover, N. H., 65 W. 19th St., New York City.*
2131 Hubbard, W. C., 27 West Ninth St., New York, N. Y. *Phys., Chem., Mic.*
2132 Huber, Rev. E., 1412 E. Fayette St., Baltimore, Md. *Mic.* Ex.*
2133 Hubregtse, Adrian, 37 Cypress St., Rochester, N. Y. *Bot.* C. Will buy or exchange, especially Ferns.*
2134 Huckel, Rev. William, 161 Maiden Lane, New York, N. Y. *Bot., Mic.**
2135 Huckins, D. T., M.D., Watertown, Mass. *Marine, L. and F. W. Moll.* C. Ex.*
2136 Hudson, B., Peterboro', Can. *Mam., Orn., Tax.**
2137 Hudson, Geo. H., Plattsburg, Clinton Co., N. Y. *Lepid., Coleopt., Con., L. and F. W. Shells.* C. Ex.*
2138 Huett, John W., Ottawa, La Salle Co., Ill. *Bot., Geol., Con., Ent.* C. Ex.*
2139 Hughes, W. H., 188 So. Union St., Grand Rapids, Mich. *Geol.* C.*
2140 Hulbert, E. M., New Britain, Ct. *Ent: Lepid., Coleopt.* C. Ex.*
2141 Huling, Ray Greene, A.M., New Bedford, Mass. *Anth., Arch., Eth., Philol., Ethnog.**
2142 Hull, Chas. G., Wallingford, Ct. *Geol., Min., Crystall., Photog.* C. Ex.*
2143 Hull, G. Fred., Wallingford, Ct. *Mic.*
2144 Hull H. V., M.D., P. O. Box 1199, Schenectady, N. Y. *Mic.**
2145 Hulst, Geo. D., 15 Himrod St., Brooklyn, E.D., N. Y. *North Am. Lepid., esp. Geometridæ, Pyralidæ and Tineidæ.* C. Ex.*
2146 Hume, John, Eglinton Place, Davenport, Ia. *Geol., Palæo., Arch., Eth.* C. Ex.*

2147 Humphrey, D., M.D., Lawrence, Mass. *Gen. Biol., Mic.**
2148 Humphrey, Fred., Colorado Springs, Col. *Orn., Arch.* C.*
2149 Humphrey, George W., Dedham, Mass. *Bot., Zool.* C.*
2150 Humphrey, James E., Harvard Univ., Cambridge, Mass. *Bot., esp. Algæ, Biology.* C. Ex.*
2151 Humphrey, Wm., Adrian, Mich. *Mic., Micro-Photog.* C. Ex.*
2152 Humphreys, A. W., 71 Columbia Heights, Brooklyn, N. Y. *Geol., Min., Bibliog.* C.*
2153 Hunt, David, A.M., M.D., 149 Boylston St., Boston, Mass. *Vert. Emb.**
2154 Hunt, Fred M., Swartzwood, Sussex Co., New Jersey. *Bot: Phæn. and Crypt. Plants, Ferns.* C. Ex.*
2155 Hunt, George M., C.E., No. Argyle, Washington Co., N. Y. *Geol., Min., Bot.* C.
2156 Hunt, Joseph H., M.D., 1065 Bedford Ave., Brooklyn, N. Y. *Palæo., Geol., Min., Lithol., Chem., Elect., Mic., Gen. Biol., Morphology, Emb., Anat., Anth., Arch., Eth., Histol.* C. Ex.*
2157 Hunt, T. Sterry, LL.D., F.R.S., Montreal, Can. *Geol., Min., Chem.**
2158 Hunter, D. E., A.M., Terrell, Kaufman Co., Tex. *Ast.*
2159 Hunter, John L., 35 Grover St., Auburn, N. Y. *Orn., Ool.* C. Ex.*
2160 Hunting, A. J., Natick, Mass. *Orn., Ool., Ent.* C. Ex.*
2161 Huntington, Alfred T., 166 Maverick St., Chelsea, Mass. *Bot., Geol., Marine Zool., Ent.* C. Botanical specimens for exchange.*
2162 Huntington, C. M., Utica, Oneida Co., N. Y. *Geol.**
2163 Huntington, George S., C.E., 245 Browne St., Cincinnati, O. *Native and foreign land shells. Coleopt.* C. Ex.*
2164 Huntington, Oliver W., 12 Ware St., Cambridge, Mass. *Min., Chem.* C. Ex.*
2165 Hurlburt, Edward, Utica, N. Y. *Geol., Palæo.* C. Ex.*
2166 Hurlburt, John E., A.M., M.D., 138 Park Ave., Chicago, Ill. *Mic.* C. Ex.*
2167 Hurter, J., 2346 So. 10th St., St. Louis, Mo. *Orn.* C. Herpetol. Ex.*
2168 Hurty, John, 104 N. Penn St., Indianapolis, Ind. *Chem.**
2169 Huston, Henry A., A.M., A.C., Purdue Univ., Lafayette, Ind. *Physics and Chemistry.**
2170 Huston, Sam., B.S., Steubenville, Ohio *Geol., Palæo.* Desires geological papers, books and reports, in. ex. for coal measure fossils from Linton, etc.*
2171 Hutcheson, David, Library of Congress, Washington, D. C. *Bibliog., Anth.**
2172 Hutcheson, James M., Young Hickory, Muskingum Co., O. *Bot., Agric., Mic.* C. Ex.*
2173 Hutchins, J. P., Santa Ana, Calif. *Orn., Tax.**
2174 Hutchinson, Chas. W., Utica, N. Y. *Arch., Eth.* C. Ex.*
2175 Hutchinson, Edw. S., C.E., M.E., Arkansas City, Kans. *Mic.**

2176 Huttinger, J. Wm., Beverly, Burlington Co., N. J. *Geol., Min., Lithol., Mic., Philol.* C. Ex.*

2177 Hyams, C. W., Statesville, N. C. *Min., Arch., Con., Ool.* C. Ex.?

2178 Hyams, F. D., Charlotte, N. C. *Ool., Con.* C. Ex.*

2179 Hyams, M. E., Charlotte, N. C. *Bot.* C. Ex. and for sale.*

2180 Hyatt, Alpheus, Prof. of Palæo. and Zool., Mass. Inst. of Technol., Curator Boston Soc. of Nat. Hist., Ass't Mus. Comp. Zool., Boston, Mass. *Zool., Palæo.**

2181 Hyatt, J. D., Station R., N. Y. City. *Bot., Mic.**

2182 Hyatt, James, Stanfordville, Dutchess Co., N. Y. *Chem., Bot., Min., Palæo.* C.*

2183 Hyde, Alton H., Berkeley, Alameda Co., Calif. *Orn., Ool.* C. Ex.*

2184 Hyde, G. A., Cleveland, Ohio.*

2185 Hyde, Henry C., 411½ California St., San Francisco, Calif. *Diatoms, Mic.* C.*

2186 Hynds, F. P., Ralston Station, Weakley Co., Tenn. *Bot.**

2187 Iddings, J. P., U. S. Geol. Surv., Washington, D. C. *Geol. Petrog.**

2188 Ingalls, Chas. E., East Templeton, Mass. *Orn., Mam., Tax.* C. Ex.*

2189 Ingalls, M. W., M.D., LaGrange, Lorain Co., Ohio. *Fungi, Gen. Biol., Histol. of Vert.?*

2190 Ingals, A. O., Murray, Shoshone Co., Idaho. *Bot., Chem.**

2191 Ingersoll, A. M., Santa Cruz, Calif. *Orn., Ool.* C. Ex. in Ool.

2192 Ingersoll, Ernest, 71 Mackay St., Montreal, Can.*

2193 Ingersoll, R. G., 1421 New York Ave., Washington, D. C. *Eth.?*

2194 Ingersoll, Seymour R., 792 Bolton Ave., Cleveland, Ohio. *Orn., Ool., Tax.**

2195 Ingersoll, T. Dwight, 702 State St., Erie, Pa. *Geol.* C. Ex.*

2196 Ingham, Chas. F., 2 Union St., Wilkes Barré, Pa. *Veg. Palæo., Geol., Min., Moll.**

2197 Ingraham, D. P., M.S., Elmira, N. Y. *Geol., Orn., Ool., Con., Gen. Collection in Nat Hist. in North and South American spec.* Ex.*

2198 Ingraham, Rollin H., Youngstown, Ohio. *Bot., Mic., Ast.* C. Ex.*

2199 Ingram, W. E., Box 155, Odin, Ill. *Ool.* C. Ex.?

2200 Irelan, Wm., jr., Chemist and State Mineralogist, San Francisco, Calif. *Phys. Geol., Crystall., Lithol., Chem., Metall.**

2201 Irish, Charles W., Iowa City, Ia. *Civil Engineer. Bot., Min.* C. Ex.

2202 Irving, Prof. Roland Duer, Geologist in charge Lake Superior Division U. S. Geol. Survey, also, Prof. Geol. and Min., Univ. of Wis., Madison, Wis. *Archæan Geol., Microscopic Lithol.**

2203 Isom, J. F., M.D., Cleveland, Ohio. *Ent: Lepid.* C. Ex.*

2204 Ives, W. W., Norwich, Ct. *Min.* C. Ex.*

2205 Jack, John G., Chateauguay Basin, P. Q., Can. *Ent.* C. Ex.*

2206 **Jackson, A. W.**, Prof. of Mineralogy, Petrography and Economic Geol., Univ. of Calif., Berkeley, Calif. *Min.*, *Mic.*, *Lithol.*, *Geol.* C. Ex.*

2207 **Jackson, Prof. C. L.**, Holworthy 11, Cambridge, Mass. *Chem.**

2208 **Jackson, E. E.**, Columbia, S. C. *Mic.**

2209 **Jackson, Halliday**, West Chester, Pa. *Bot.: Ferns, Algæ.* C. Ex.?

2210 **Jackson, J. A.**, Des Moines, Ia. *Ent.*, *Con.* C. Ex.*

2211 **Jackson, Joseph**, Worcester, Mass. *Bot.*, *Mic.* C. Ex.*

2212 **Jackson, Lawson**, So. Hadley Falls, Mass. *Geol.*, *Chem.*, *Phys.*, *Histol.* C. Ex.*

2213 **Jackson, Robert Tracy**, 89 Charles St., Boston, Mass. *Hort.*, *Palæo.*, *Invert.* C. (Hort.). Ex.*

2214 **Jacobs, Chas. P.**, A.M., Indianapolis, Ind. *Ast.*, *Bibliog.**

2215 **Jacobs, F. O.**, D.D.S., Newark, Licking Co., Ohio. *Phæn. Bot.*, *Mic.* C. of Native Seeds, Sections of teeth mounted for mic. Ex.*

2216 **Jacques, William W.**, Ph.D., 95 Milk St., Boston, Mass. *Phys.**

2217 **Jæger, H. F.**, Riverside, Cook Co., Ill. *Bot.*

2218 **James, Bushrod W.**, A.M., M.D., 18th and Green Sts., Philadelphia, Pa. *Anat.*, *Mam.**

2219 **James, Davis L.**, 177 Race St., Cincinnati, O. *Bot.**

2220 **James, Frank L.**, Ph.D., M.D., 615 Locust St., or Box 568, St. Louis, Mo. *Mic.*, *Animal Histol.* C. Ex.*

2221 **James, I. E.** (C. & M.E.), Tombstone, Ariz. *Min.*, *Geol.*, *Mic.* C. Ex.?

2222 **James, Joseph F.**, Oxford, Butler Co., O. Prof. of Bot. and Geol. in Miami Univ. Ex. for Univ. in Bot., Palæo. and Min. *Bot.* C.*

2223 **James, U. P.**, 177 Race St., Cincinnati, Ohio. *Palæo.*, *Local Con.* C.*

2224 **Janney, Reynold**, A.M., Prof. Math., Ast. and Geol., Wilmington Coll., Wilmington, O. *Phys.*, *Elect.* C.*

2225 **Jasper, Theo.**, A.M., M.D., Columbus, Ohio. *Zool.*, *Orn.* C.?

2226 **Jay, J. W.**, M.D., D.D.S., Richmond, Ind. *Palæo.*, *Arch.* C. Ex. L. Silurian fossils for those of other periods.*

2227 **Jayne, Horace**, M.D., Prof. Vert. Morph., Univ. of Pa., 1826 Chestnut St., Philadelphia, Pa. *Comp. Anat.*, *Zool.*?

2228 **Jefferis, W. W.**, 1836 Green St., Philadelphia, Pa. *Bot.*, *Min.* C. Ex.*

2229 **Jeffries, J. Amory**, M.D., 91 Newbury St., Boston, Mass. *Morph.*, *Orn.* C.*

2230 **Jencks, F. T.**, Drownville, R. I. *Orn.*, *Ool.*, *Tax.* C. Ex.*

2231 **Jenkins, Benj.**, St. Paul, Ind. *Geol.* C. Niagara fossils from the famous Waldron Beds, and Mound Builders' Relics for ex.*

2232 **Jenkins, Oliver P.**, A.M., Prof. Biol., De Pauw Univ., Greencastle, Ind. *Zool.*, *Physiol.*, *Histol.* C. Ex.*

2233 **Jenkins, Wm.**, Mendota, La Salle Co., Ill. *Palæo.*, *Geol.*, *Phys.*, *Eth.*, *Phil.*, *Orn.*, *Tax.* C. Ex.*

2234 Jenks, Charles W., Boston, Suffolk Co., Mass. *Bot.**
2235 Jenks, John W. P., Prof. and Cur. Mus., Brown Univ., Providence, R. I. or Middleboro', Mass.*
2236 Jenney, Herbert, N. W. cor. 5th and Walnut Sts., Cincinnati, Ohio. *Bot.**
2237 Jennings, C. G., M.D., Prof. Chem. Detroit Coll. of Med., 544 Jefferson Ave., Detroit, Mich. *Chem.*, *Mic.**
2238 Jennings, T. Buttolph, Signal Service, Lebo, Kansas. *Mic.*, *Dipt.*, *Protozoa.* C. Ex.*
2239 Jeremiah, William H., Silver Springs Park, Marion Co., Fla. *Orn.*, *Tax.* C. Ex.
2240 Jesup, Rev. H. G., Prof. Nat. Hist., Hanover, N. H. *Bot.**
2241 Jesup, Morris K., Pres. Am. Mus. Nat. Hist., 197 Madison Ave., New York City. *Geol.*, *Min.*, *Zool.*, *Orn.**
2242 Jewell, Commander Theo. F., Commanding U. S. S., "Essex" Asiatic Squadron, care of Navy Dept., Washington, D. C. *Physics.**
2243 Jewett, Charles, M.D., 307 Gates Ave., Brooklyn, N. Y. *Mic.*, *Micro-Photography.* C.*
2244 Jewett, F. R., Woodstock, Vt. *Ent.* C. ?
2245 Jewett, Fred A., M.D., 334 Madison St., Brooklyn, N. Y. *Bot.*, *Mic.* C.*
2246 Jewett, Prof. F. F., A.M., Oberlin Coll., Oberlin, O. *Chem.*, *Min.**
2247 Jewett, H. S., M.A., M.D., 21 So. Ludlow St., Dayton, Ohio. *Chem.*, *Lepid.*, *Bot.*, *Geol.* C.*
2248 Job, H. K., 1631 Tremont St., Boston, Mass. *Orn.*, *Ool.* C. ?
2249 Johnson, Albert I., Hydeville, Rutland Co., Vt. *Tax.*, *Orn.*, *Ool.* C. Ex.*
2250 Johnson, Dr. Anna H., Hampton Institute, Hampton, Va. *Bot.*, *Phys.**
2251 Johnson, A. S., Topeka, Kan. *Min.* C.
2252 Johnson, C. A., 174 Lagrave St., Grand Rapids, Mich. *Geol.*, *Arch.*, *Min.*, *Palæo.* C. Ex. Gypsum polished or natural for other spec. Fractional, colonial, continental and confederate currency to ex.*
2253 Johnson, C. B., 186 No. Maine St., Providence, R. I. *Mic.* C. Ex.*
2254 Johnson, C. E., Salt Lake City, Utah. *Bot.*, *Chem.*, *Physics*, *Elect.*, *Mic.*, *Photog.*, *Meteo.*, *Mic.*, *Ast.* C. Ex.*
2255 Johnson, E. G., Bantam, Cleremont Co., Ohio. *Palæo.* Cin. fossils, L. and F. W. shells for ex.?
2256 Johnson, F. S., A. M., M.D., Prof. Gen. Path. and Pathological Anat., Chicago Med. College, 4 16th St., Chicago, Ill. *Mic.* *Gen. Biol.*, *Emb.*, *Histol.**
2257 Johnson, George A., Taxidermist, Marshall, Mich. *Nat. Hist.**
2258 Johnson, Geo. H., C.E., S.D., Engineer's Office B. & M. R. R., Lincoln, Neb. *Metallurgy*, *Meteo.*, *Ast.**
2259 Johnson, Prof. H. A., M.D., LL.D., Chicago Medical Coll., 4 16th St., Chicago, Ill. *Biol.**

2260 **Johnson, James J.**, Johnsonville, Wayne Co., Ill. *Bot.*, *Fungi*, *Hort.*, *Zool.*, *Orn.* C. Ex.*

2261 **Johnson, James S.**, 4900 Frankford Ave., Frankford, Philadelphia, Pa. *Lepid.*, *specialty Catocalæ and Sphingidæ.* C. Ex.*

2262 **Johnson, Jos. T.**, A.M., M.D., 926 17th St., Washington, D.C. Prof. Obstet. and Gynecol., to several Hospitals and Dispensaries.*

2263 **Johnson, Lawrence C.**, Holly Springs, Miss. *Geol.*, *Palæo.*, *Zool.*, *Orn.*, *Ent.*?

2264 **Johnson, O. B.**, Prof. Nat. Hist., Univ., Seattle, W. T. *Orn.*, *Ool.*, *Con.*, *Ent.*, *Zool.* C. Ex.*

2265 **Johnson, Samuel W.**, Prof. Chem., Yale Coll., 54 Trumbull St., New Haven, Ct.*

2266 **Johnson, Sarah E.**, Community, Madison Co., N. Y. *Bot.*, *Orn.*

2267 **Johnston, Prof. Christopher**, M.D., 201 W. Franklin St., Baltimore, Md. *Mic.**

2268 **Jones, A. W.**, L. B. 499, Salina, Kan. *Geol.*, *Arch.*, *Ent.*, *esp. Coleopt.* C.*

2269 **Jones, Rev. C. M.**, Eastford, Ct. *Orn.*, *Ool.* C. Ex.

2270 **Jones, George C.**, Brookfield Centre, Fairfield Co., Ct. *Gen. Nat. Hist.*, *Orn.*, *Arch.* C. Ex. Ancient and modern Indian articles and implements of savage tribes especially desired. Western and Southern correspondence solicited.*

2271 **Jones, George Wheeler**, M.D., Danville, Vermilion Co., Ill. *Phys.*, *Psych.**

2272 **Jones, Henry L.**, Wellsville, N. Y. *Geol.* C. Ex.*

2273 **Jones, Howard**, A.M., M.D., Circleville, Ohio. *Orn.*, *Ool.*, *Gen. Nat. Hist.**

2274 **Jones, Jesse**, Martin's Ferry, Belmont Co., Ohio. *Orn.*, *Ool.* C. Ex.?

2275 **Jones, J. E.**, 28 Cliff St., St. Johnsbury, Vt. *Bot.*, *Palæo.*, *Geol.*, *Min.*, *Mic.*, *Orn.*, *Ool.*, *Tax.*, *Invert.*

2276 **Jones, J. Matthew**, Halifax, N. S., Can. *Gen. Zool. and Nat. Hist. of the Bermudas.**

2277 **Jones, Joseph**, M.D., 156 Washington St., New Orleans, La. *Palæo.*, *Geol.*, *Min.*, *Chem.*, *Metall.*, *Mic.*, *Meteo.*, *Bibliog.*, *Zool.*, *Gen. Biol.*, *Vert. Anat.*, *Anth.*, *Arch.*, *Eth.*, *Herpet.* C. Ex.?

2278 **Jones, L.**, Box 523, Grinnell, Ia. *Orn.*, *Ool.*, *Tax.* C. Ex. in Ool. only.*

2279 **Jones, Marcus E.**, A.M., 125 W. Third South, Salt Lake City, Utah. *Bot: Ferns*, *Fungi*, *Diatoms*, *Orn.*, *Ool.*, *Ent.* C. Ex.*

2280 **Jones, Mrs. N. E.**, Author of "Illustrations of the Nests and Eggs of Birds of Ohio," Circleville, Ohio. *Emb.*, *Orn.*, *Ool.* C. Ex.*

2281 **Jones, Richard W.**, M.A., LL.D., Pres. Miss. Ind. Inst. and College, Columbus, Miss. *Chem.*, *Min.**

2282 **Jones, W. Martin**, Rochester, N. Y.*

2283 **Jones, Woodruff**, Germantown, Phila., Pa. *Chem.**

2284 Joor, J. F., M.D., 92 Prairie St., Houston, Texas. *Phæn. Bot.*, *Ferns*, *Mosses*. C.?
2285 Jordan, David S., Prof. Zool. and Pres. Indiana Univ., Ass't U. S. Fish Comm., Bloomington, Ind. *Fishes*, *Vertebrates generally*, *Bot.* C.*
2286 Joseph, Nathan, 641 Clay St., San Francisco, Calif. *Min.*, *Crystall.*, *Arch.* C. Ex.*
2287 Josselyn, Clara F., South Hanson, Mass. *Phæn. Bot.**
2288 Judd, James W., 528 Willoughby Ave., Brooklyn, N. Y. *Zool.*, *Orn.*, *Ool.*, *Ent.*, *Moll.* C. Ex.*
2289 Judge, J. F., Prof. Chem., Cinn. Coll. of Pharmacy, Cincinnati, O. *Con.* C. Ex.*
2290 Julich, Wilhelm, 450 Water St., New York, N. Y. *Ent: Coleopt.* C.*
2291 Julien, Alexis A., Ph.D., School of Mines, Columbia College, New York, N. Y. *Lithol.*, *Chem.*, *Biol.* C.*
2292 Jump, R. E., Oberlin, Ohio. *Zool.*, *Ool.*, *Orn.*, *Tax.**
2293 Justice, A. R., 321 N. 33d St., West Philadelphia, Pa. *Ool.* C.?
2294 Kain, Henry C., Camden, N. J. *Mic.*, *Diatoms.**
2295 Kaldenburg, Fred. Robert, Ivory Sculptor, 371 Broadway, New York, N. Y. *Arch.**
2296 Kaucher, Mrs. Samuel, Yankton, Dak. *Min.*, *Geol.*, *F. W. Shells*, *Indian Relics*. C. Ex.
2297 Kaufmann, Ferdinand, jr., 285 Lincoln Ave., Chicago, Ill. *Coleopt.*, *Orn.*, *Ool.* C. Ex.*
2298 Keen, Eugene L., 816 Charlotte St., Philadelphia, Pa. *Bot.*, *Orn.*, *Gen. Ent.* C. Correspondence solicited.*
2299 Keen, W. W., M.D., 1729 Chestnut St., Philadelphia, Pa. *Anat.*, *Mic.* C. Ex.*
2300 Keener, W. T., 96 Washington St., Chicago, Ill. *Books on Mic.*, *Chem. and Nat. Hist.*
2301 Keep, Prof. Josiah, Mill's College, Alameda Co., Calif. *Con.* Author of "West Coast Shells," describing Marine, L. and F. W. species, west of the Rocky Mts.*
2302 Keim, Edw. T., Dubuque, Ia. *Geol.*, *Orn.* C. Ex. Have full line of minerals and fossils of Galena limestone.*
2303 Keller, Alex., Auburn, Placer Co., Calif. Practical Mineralogist and Min. claim agent. *Palæo.*, *Geol.*, *Min.*, *Elect.*, *Mining*, *Mic.*, *Arch.*
2304 Keller, Prof. Edward, Humboldt School, 26th Ward, Pittsburg, Pa. *Bot.*, *Lepid.* C. Ex.
2305 Keller, Harry F., 257 N. 6th St., Philadelphia, Pa. *Inorg. and Analyt. Chem.*, *Min.*, *Metall.* C. Ex.*
2306 Kellerman, Mrs. W. A., Manhattan, Kan. *Bot.* C. Ex.*
2307 Kellerman, Prof. William A., Ph.D., Agr. College, Manhattan, Kan. *Fungi.* C. Ex.*
2308 Kelley, W. L., Harwichport, Cape Cod, Mass. *Palæo.*, *Con.*, C.*
2309 Kellicott, D. S., Sec. Am. Soc. of Microscopists, 119 Fourteenth St., Buffalo, N. Y. *Ent.* C.*

2310 Kellogg, D. S., A.M., M.D., Plattsburgh, Clinton Co., N. Y. *Anth., Arch., Eth.* C. Ex.*
2311 Kellogg, J. H., M.D., Battle Creek, Mich. *Biol., Histol.**
2312 Kellogg, J. H., 1 Ida Terrace, Troy, N. Y. *Mic.**
2313 Kellogg, Justin, 62 Second St., Troy, N. Y. *Min., Emb.* C.*
2314 Kellogg, Mrs. Olive A., Community, Madison Co., N. Y. *Bot., Orn.**
2315 Kellogg, Theo. S., De Pere, Brown Co., Wis. *Bot: Phænogamous Plants, Cryptogamous Plants, Ferns, Mosses, Lichens, Fungi, Algæ.* C. Ex.*
2316 Kellogg, V. L., Lawrence, Kan. *Bot., Micro-Photography, Orn., Tax. (skins).* C. Ex.*
2317 Kelly, Dorman S., Department of Nat. Hist., State Normal School, Emporia, Kans. *Bot., Zool., Geol.* C. Ex.*
2318 Kelly, Henry A., Custodian Nat. Hist. Soc., Worcester, Mass. *Coleopt.* C. Ex. Florida Coleoptera for ex.*
2319 Kelsey, C. A., Theresa, Jefferson Co., N. Y. *Palæo., Geol., Min.* C. Ex.*
2320 Kemp, J. F., Cornell Univ., Geol. Lab., Ithaca, N. Y. *Phys., Geol., Min., Lithol.* C. Ex.*
2321 Kendall, T. A., Reading, Pa. *Min., Arch.* C. Ex. Have fine local spec. to ex. for western, southern and foreign spec. Fine spec. of Vanadainite and Descloizite for ex. Correspondence solicited with advanced collectors.*
2322 Kendig, Rev. A. B., D.D., 11' Hanson Place, Brooklyn, N. Y. *Moll.* C. Ex. Correspondence solicited.*
2323 Kneer, F. G., M.D., 85 Charles St., New York, N. Y. *Chem., Phys., Elect., Mic., Photog., Anat. and Histol. of Vert.**
2324 Keeney, Miss M. J., LeRoy, N. Y. *Bot.**
2325 Kelsey, Rev. Francis D., Helena, Montana. *Bot: Phæn., and Crypt. Plants, Ferns, Mosses, Fungi, Lichens, Algæ, Palæo., Geol., Min., Mic., Philol.* C.*
2326 Kennan, George, 1318 Mass. Ave., Washington, D. C. *Anth., Arch., Eth., Ethnog.**
2327 Kennedy, George T., A.M., B.A.Sc., F.G.S., Prof. Chem., Geol. and Min., Kings College, Windsor, N. S., Can. *Geol., Min., Palæo., Zool.* Ex.*
2328 Kennicut, Dr. L. P., Worcester, Mass. *Chem.* ?
2329 Kent, Perley E., Poway, San Diego Co., Calif. *Orn., Ool.* C. Ex.*
2330 Kenyon, C. A., 63 Linden St., Rochester, N. Y. *Mic.**
2331 Kepler, William, Ph.D., Baldwin Univ., Berea, Ohio.?
2332 Kerr, James, Prof. Surgery and Dean of Faculty, Manitoba Med. Coll., Winnipeg, Manitoba Co., Canada. *Eth.* ?
2333 Kerr, Prof. J. H., Acting Pres. of Colo. College, Colorado Springs, Colo. *Chem., Geol.**
2334 Kershner, Jefferson E., Prof. of Math. and Ast., Franklin and Marshall Coll., Lancaster, Pa. *Ast.**
2335 Kersting, Rud., Palatka, Fla. *Bot., Ent: Coleopt., Lepid., Dipt., N. A. Reptiles.* C.*

2336 Kervey, H. R., Box 1982, West Chester, Pa. *Arch.*, *Eth.* C. Ex.*
2337 Ketchum, Henry, Hartland, Vt.
2338 Keutgen, Charles, Stapleton, N. Y. *Met.**
2339 Keyes, Charles R., 926 Ninth St., Des Moines, Iowa. *Palæo.*, *Mic.*, *Moll.* C. Ex.*
2340 Keyes, W. H., East Saugus, Mass. *Min.*, *Geol.*, *Orn.*, *Ool.*, *Tax.*, *Ent.* C. Would like to ex. in Ent., Tax. and Min. for the same, or Books, Pamphlets and Sci. Pub.*
2341 Keyes, W. S., Mining Engineer and Metallurgist, Trustee Calif. State Mining Bureau, P. O. Box 1716, San Francisco, Calif. *Geol.*, *Min.*, *Crystall.*, *Lithol.*, *Inorg. Chem.*, *Metall.*, *Photog.* C. Ex.*
2342 Kidder, Dr. J. H., Smithsonian Institution, Washington, D. C. *Chem.*, *Biol.*, *Mic.**
2343 Kiechler, Geo., 495 Walnut St., Cincinnati, Ohio. *Palæo.*, *L. and F. W. Shells*, *Arch.* C. Ex.
2344 Kief, E. G., Inst. in Tax., Fla. Univ., Tallahassee, Fla. *Tax.*, *Gen. Collection.* C. Ex.?
2345 Kiehel, C. D., Rochester, N. Y. *Mic.*, *Anat.*, *Vert.*, *Histol. of Vert.**
2346 Kilborne, Fred. L., B.Agr., B.U.S., Director U. S. Vet. Exp. Station, Dept. of Agric., Washington, D. C. *Veterinary.**
2347 Kilman, Alva H., Ridgeway, Welland Co., Ont., Can. *Ent: Coleopt.*, *Lepid.* Canadian species in exchange for southern and exotic. Correspondence solicited.*
2348 Kilpatrick, Joshua W., Prof. Central Coll., Fayette, Mo. *Nat. Hist.*, *Min.**
2349 Kimball, Arthur L., Johns Hopkins Univ., Baltimore, Md. Associate in Physics. *Elect.*, *Phys.**
2350 Kimball, James P., Director of the Mint, Washington, D. C. *Geol.*, *Met.**
2351 Kimball, John Cone, Revere House, Boston, Mass. *Arch.**
2352 Kimball, Walter H., 230 Broadway, Providence, R. I. *Palæo.*, *Geol.*, *Min.*, *Crystall.*, *Chem.*, *Metall.*, *Physics*, *Elect.*, *Mic.*, *Photog.*, *Meteo.*, *Ast.*, *Zool.*, *Emb.*, *Anat.*, *Arch.*, *Vert.*, *Mammals*, *Orn.*, *Ool.*, *Ichth.*, *Tax.*, *Ent: Hymen.*, *Lepid.*, *Dipt.*, *Coleopt.*, *Hemipt.*, *Orthopt.*, *Neuropt.*, *Arach.*, *Myriop.*, *Crustacea*, *Worms*, *Molluscs*, *Radiates*, *Sponges*, *Protozoa.* C.*
2353 King, Chas. F., Chem. of Pa. Steel Co., Steelton, Pa. *Analyt. Chem.*
2354 King, Clarence, U. S. Geologist, 18 Wall St., Room 45, New York, N. Y. *Geol.*
2355 King, Edw. W., M.D., Ukiah, Mendocino Co., Calif. *Gen. Biol.**
2356 King, F. H., Dept. Nat. Sci., Normal School, River Falls, Wis. *Orn.*, *Geol.*, *Phys. Geog.**
2357 King, G. B., Entomologist, Lawrence, Mass. *Palæo.*, *Geol.*, *Min.*, *Zool.*, *Ent: Hymenop.*, *Lepid.*, *Dipt.*, *Coleopt.*, *Hemipt.*, *Orthopt.*, *Neuropt.*, *Arach.* C. Ex.*

2358 King, J. D., Cottage City (Dept. of Mic., Martha's Vineyard Summer Institute, Cottage City), Mass. *Moll.*, *Algæ*, *Mic.* C.

2359 King, John, M.D., North Bend, Hamilton, Co., Ohio. *Mosses*, *Fungi*, *Algæ*, *Desmids*, *Diatoms*, *Invert. Palæo.*, *Elect.*, *Mic.*, *Meteor.*, *Ast.*, *Zool.*, *Crust.*, *Protozoa*, *Infusoria*. C.*

2360 King, L. M., Santa Rosa, Calif. *Algæ*, *Desmids*, *Diatoms*.*

2361 King, Mrs. Mary B. A., Rochester, N. Y. *Con.?*

2362 King, Robert, M.D., Prof. of Nat. Sci., College of Emporia, Emporia, Kansas. *Mic.*, *Spec. Fungi and Histol.**

2363 King, Thos. W., Ass't Chem. to Pa. S. Co., Steelton, Pa. *Chem.?*

2364 King, W. H. H., M.D., Jacksonville, Ill. *Orn.*, *Ool.*, *Indian Relics*. C. Desires to purchase collections of either.*

2365 King, W. P., Lancaster, Pa. *Bot.* Ex.?

2366 Kingsbury, C. Irwin, Lansing, Oswego Co., N. Y. *Ent.* C. Ex.*

2367 Kingsbury, Howard, Ph.G., Terre Haute, Ind. *Ent.*, *Min.* C. Ex.*

2368 Kingsbury, Joseph T., Univ. of Deseret, Salt Lake City, Utah, *Phys.*, *Chem.**

2369 Kingsley, J. S., Bloomington, Ind. Editor of "American Naturalist." *Morphology*.*

2370 Kinnaman, A. J., Ass't Teacher of Mathematics C. N. C., Danville, Hendricks Co., Ind. *Coleopt.* C. Ex.*

2371 Kinne, C. Mason, 422 California St., San Francisco, Calif. *Mic.* C.*

2372 Kinne, F. W., 243 Fourth Ave. S., Minneapolis, Minn. *Arch.*, *Ool.* C. Ex.*

2373 Kinne, Frank M., Knoxville, Marion Co., Iowa. *Min.*, *Ool.*, C. Ex. Coins to exchange for eggs in sets.*

2374 Kinner, Hugo, M.D., 1101 Autumn St., St. Louis, Mo. *Eth.*, *Arch.*, *Zool.* C.*

2375 Kinnicutt, Prof. Leonard P., 5 Chestnut St., Worcester, Mass. *Chem.**

2376 Kirk, Mrs. Carrie A., Richland, Union Co., Dak. *Geol.*, *Min.*, *Con.*, *Modern Indian Relics*. C. Ex.*

2377 Kirk, Hyland C., Phelps, Ontario Co., N. Y. *Gen. Biol.**

2378 Kirk, Isaac S., Fremont, Chester Co., Pa. *Min.*, *Arch.* C. Ex.*

2379 Kirk, Lauretta A., Wakefield, Pa. *Min.*, *Bot.* C.*

2380 Kirkwood, Daniel, Bloomington, Ind.*

2381 Kistler, Rev. Amos H., Channahon, Will Co., Ill. C. Ex.*

2382 Kitchel, H. S., South Bethlehem, Pa. *Crypt. Bot.*, *Ferns*, *Mosses*, *Algæ*, *Diatoms*, *Desmids*.*

2383 Kizer, Frank, Teacher Nat. Sci., Downs, Osborne Co., Kansas. *Bot.*, *Geol.*, *Chem.*, *Zool.*, *Emb.*, *Tax.*, *Ent.* C.*

2384 Klages, H. G., 130 S. 11th St., Pittsburgh, Pa. *Coleopt.* C. Ex. Desires Carabidæ and Cerambycidæ of the world.*

2385 Kleeberger, Prof. George R., State Normal School, San Jose, Calif. C.*

2386 Kleine, Charles B., 274 Eighth Ave., New York, N. Y. *Mic.**
2387 Klock, Edgar J., East Schuyler, Herkimer Co., N. J. *Palæo., Geol., Min., Lithol.* C. Ex.*
2388 Knab, Ferdinand, Box 249, Chicopee, Mass. *Ent: Lepid.* C. Ex.*
2389 Knapp, Ezra B., Skaneateles, Onondaga Co., N. Y. *Geol., Palæo.* C. Ex.*
2390 Knapp, Geo. S., 189 John St., Bridgeport, Ct. *Min., Chem., Mic., Bibliog., Zool.**
2391 Knauss, Warren, M.Sc., McPherson, Kan. *Economic Ent: spec. Coleopt.* C. Ex.*
2392 Knight, Charles M., A.M., Prof. Chem. and Phys., Buchtel Coll., Akron, O.*
2393 Knight, Wilbur C., B.Sc., 307 West 16th St., Cheyenne, Wyo. *Invert. Palæo., Strat. Geol., Min., Inorg. Chem., Met., Elect.* C. Ex.*
2394 Knipe, Rev. S. W., Oceanic, Monmouth Co., N. J. *Bot., Min.* Ex.*
2395 Knorr, Aug. E., Dept. of Agric., Washington, D. D. *Chem.*
2396 Knott, W. T., Lebanon, Ky. *Geol., L. and F. W. Shells, Palæo., Min.* C. Ex. fossils of Devon., Sub. Carb. and L Sil.?
2397 Knowlton, E. J. M., Big Lake, Sherburne Co., Minn. *Numismatics.**
2398 Knowlton, Prof. F. H., M.S., U. S. Nat. Museum, Washington, D. C. *General Botany: Fossil Wood.* C. Ex.*
2399 Knowlton, W. J., S.B., 168 Tremont St., Boston, Mass., Dealer in Minerals, Gems, and Precious Stones. *Geol., Chem., Min.* C. Ex.*
2400 Kny, Richard, 135 Clermont Ave, Brooklyn, N. Y. *Min., Chem.* C. Ex.*
2401 Koch, August, Williamsport, Pa. *Orn., Tax.* C. Ex.*
2402 Kocher, J. F., M.D., Guths Station, Lehigh Co., Pa. *Orn., Ool., Tax.* C. Ex.*
2403 Koebele, Albert, Ass't Ent., Dept. Agric., Washington, D. C. *N. A. Noctuidæ.* Will purchase or ex. inflated larvæ of such. C. Ex.*
2404 Koehler, Fred., Litchfield, Ct. *Tax., Orn.* C.*
2405 Kost, Prof. J., M.D., LL.D., Chancellor of the Univ. of Fla., Tallahassee, Fla., and State Geologist. *Nat. Hist., Geol.* Ex. Min., Fossil Shells, Bird and other skins. Fish and reptiles dessicated and in skins. Small alligator skins by mail in ex. Also med. books in ex. for others. A large lot of sharks' teeth, of many species, in stock.*
2406 Krause, Joseph, Lebanon, Pa. *Min., Crystall., Lithol.* C. Ex.*
2407 Krebs, T. L., Anniston, Ala. *Ent: Lepid., Coleopt.* C. Ex. Desires correspondents in all parts of the world.*
2408 Kress, Oscar De, Evansville, Vanderburgh Co., Ind. *Mic. Histol., Ent., Fungi.*?
2409 Kruttschnitt, J., Box 144, New Orleans, La. *Veg. Phys. and Histol., Mic.**

2410 Knechler, 26 E. Liberty St., Cincinnati, Ohio. *Brachiopoda.* C. Ex.?

2411 Kuetzing, P., 1027 Third St. N., Minneapolis, Minn. *Orn., Ent.* Tropical bird-skins or remnants of skins wanted for plumes. Good Canadian skins in ex.

2412 Kuhn, Maria L., Box 213, Peoria, Ill. *Phæn. Bot.* C.*

2413 Kuithan, E. F., Burlington, Ia. *Orn., Ool.* C.*

2414 Kuithan, Dr. F., Burlington, Ia. *Orn., Mam.**

2415 Kunze, Richard E., M.D., Pharm. D., 606 Third Ave., New York, N. Y. *Med. Bot., Arch.* Cacti of the genera *Phyllocactus and Cereus. Ent., Psychology and Pharmacy.**

2416 Kunz, George F., Gemmist, Tiffany & Co., N. Y., 402 Garden St., Hoboken, N. J. *Min.* C. Ex. Desires information or new or interesting gems especially from Am. localities. Will buy or ex. for Meteorites, finely crystallized or rare minerals, Jade and Jadeite objects, only aboriginal, especially from Mexico, New Zealand, Alaska, etc. Buys everything ever published on gems, in all languages. Early manuscripts especially desired.*

2417 Kyle, Geo. G., M.D., Granville, Licking Co., O. *Orn., Ool.* C. Ex.

2418 La Bar, Gilbert, Delaran, Wisconsin. *Min., Orn.* C.*

2419 Lacoe, R. D., Pittston, Luzerne Co., Pa. *Palæo., Min.* C. Fossils of all kinds wanted by purchase or in exchange for minerals or other fossils. Correspondence solicited with parties having well-selected collections for sale, or good specimens of Palæozoic Plants, Annelids, Crustaceans, Arachnids, Myriopods, Insects, Fish and Batrachians, singly or in numbers. Both American and European wanted.*

2420 *Lacy, William H., Ripon, Wis. *Bot.: Ferns, Fungi.* C. Ex.?

2421 Ladd, Samuel B., West Chester, Pa. *Ool.* C. Ex.*

2422 Ladd, W. H., Prin. Chauncey Hall School, 259 Boylston St., Boston, Mass. *Phys. Geog.**

2423 Laflamme, S., Cl.K., D.D., Prof. Univ. Laval, Quebec, Can. *Min., Geol.**

2424 Lakes, Prof. Arthur, State School of Mines, Golden, Colo. *Geol.* C. Ex. Geological and Mineralogical spec.*

2425 Lamb, Mrs. Martha J., 743 Broadway, New York City, N. Y. Ed. Mag. of Am. Hist. *Bot., Mosses, Geol., Min., Chem., Elect., Photog., Ast., Gen. Biol., Anth., Arch.**

2426 Lamb, Thomas F., 56 Spruce St., Portland, Me. *Geol., Min.* C. Ex. Tourmalines and accompanying minerals from Mt. Apatite, Auburn, Me., for sale.*

2427 Lamb, W. F., 93 Front St., Holyoke, Mass. *Tax., Orn., Ool., Arch.* C. Ex. for eggs of extreme northern species.*

2428 Lambert, Thomas, Lonsdale, R. I. *Orn., Ool., Mam., Tax.* Coll. of 1000 spec. Ex. or sell.*

2429 Lamoreux, Chas. G., Center Hill, Fla. *Geol., Min.* C.*

2430 Lanborn, George S., Liberty Square, Lancaster Co., Pa. *Min., Geol., Palæo., Con., Arch.,* *Philatelist.* C. Ex.*

2431 Lanborn, Robert H , Ph.D., 32 Nassau St., New York City, N. Y. *Metall.*, *Anth.* C.*
2432 Landis, Dr. Henry G., 105 S. 6th St., Columbus, Ohio. *Diurnal Lepid.* C.
2433 Landis, H. K., Landis Valley, Lancaster Co., Pa. *Min.*, *Geol.* C. Ex.*
2434 Landreth, Olin H., A.M., C.E., Vanderbilt Univ., Nashville, Tenn. *Engineering*, *Geodesy.**
2435 Landry, S. F., M.D., Logansport, Cass Co., Ind. *Pollenography and Phæn. Bot.*, *Palæo.*, *Phys.* Specimens of foreign and Native medicinal plants desired. Exchanges effected, when possible, for plants and fossils. *Discoverer of the laws of Pollen-strumenality; Evolution of New Orders and Species of Plants; and of a new and effective germicide, etc.**
2436 Lane, A. Church, 623 Tremont St., Boston, Mass. *Invert.*, *Geol.*, *Min.*, *Crystall.*, *Lithol.*, *Mic.* C. Ex.*
2437 Lane, Alvin V., C.E., Ph.D., Univ. of Texas, Austin, Texas. *Engineering*, *Math.**
2438 Langdon, Daniel W., jr., B.A., Assistant Chemist and Geologist, Ala. Geol. Survey, University, Tuscaloosa Co., Ala.*
2439 Langdon, F. W., M.D., 65 W. 7th St., Cincinnati, Ohio. *Orn.*, *Anth.*, *Human and Comp. Anat.**
2440 Langguth, J. G., 1830 Fred'k St., Lake View, Ill. *Mic.* C.*
2441 Langille, J. H., Box 63, Smithsonian Institution, Washington, D. C. *Orn.* C.*
2442 Langley, Jno. W., Prof. Gen. Chem., Ann Arbor, Mich. *Inorg. Chem.*, *Metall.*, *Elect.**
2443 Langley, Samuel P., Astronomer, Observatory, Allegheny City, Pa. *Ast.*
2444 Langlois, Rev. A. B., St. Martinsville P. O., La. *Bot: Ferns, Mosses, Lichens, Fungi.* C. Ex.*
2445 Langshaw, John P., Lawrence, Mass. *Palæo.*, *Geol.*, *Min.*, *Arch.*, *Ent.* C. Ex.*
2446 Langstroth, J. A., 532 Calif. St., San Francisco, Calif. *Mic.**
2447 Lanphere, Alvin T., Coldwater, Mich. *Geol.*, *Arch.* C.*
2448 Lanza, Gætano, Prof. of Theoretical and Applied Mechanics, in charge Dept. of Mechanical Engineering, Mass. Inst. Technology, Boston, Mass.*
2449 Larison, Cornelius W., M.D., Prof. Zool., Univ. Lewisburg, Pa., Prin. Acad. Sci. and Arts, Ringoes, N. J. *Zool.*, *Biol.* C. Ex. Fishes.*
2450 Latchford, Francis R., B.A., Ottawa, Ont., Can. *Moll.* C. Ex. Desires Limnæidæ of Northwestern and Pacific States and Territories.?
2451 Latham, Woodville, W. Va. Univ., Morgantown, W. Va. *Min.*, *Chem.* C. Ex.?
2452 Lathrop, James C., Bridgeport, Ct. *Palæo.*, *Geol.*, *Min.*, *Crystall.*, *Mic.*, *Infusoria.* C. Ex.?
2453 Latimer, A. W., Lumpkin, Stewart Co., Ga. *Mic.*, *Lepid.*, *Ool.*, *Bot.* C. Ex *
2454 Latimer, Charles, Civil Eng., Cleveland, Ohio.*

2455 Latour-Huguet, Maj. L.A., M.A., N.P., 36 McGill College Ave., Montreal, Canada. *Hort.*, *Meteo.*, *Arch.*, *Histol.*

2456 Lattimore, S. A., Ph.D., LL.D., Prof. Chem., Univ. of Rochester, Rochester, N. Y. *Chem.*, *Mic.**

2457 Lattin, Frank H., Albion (formerly of Gaines), Orleans Co., N. Y. Publisher "Oologist." Thousands of duplicates for sale or ex. *Ool.* C. Ex.*

2458 Laubach, Chas., Practical Geologist, Riegelsville, Bucks Co., Pa. *Gen. Geol.*, *Min.*, *Crystall.*, *Lithol.*, *Elect.*, *Mic.*, *Meteo.*, *Anth.*, *Arch.*, *Eth*, *Ethnog.* C.*

2459 Laubach, S. H., Surveyor and Civil Eng., Riegelsville, Bucks Co., Pa. *Bot.*, *Geol.*, *Min.*, *Arch.* C. Ex.*

2460 Laudy, DeLucien Charles, Am. Mus. Nat. Hist., 77th St. and 8th Ave., Central Park, New York, N. Y. *Technical Photog.**

2461 Laudy, Louis H., Ph.D., Asst in Gen. Chem., Asst. Instruct. in App. Chem., School of Mines, New York, N. Y.*

2462 Lauerhering, Rudolph, Phar. G., M.D., Mayville, Dodge Co., Wis. *Crypt. Bot.*, *Chem.*, *Elect.*, *Mic.* C.

2463 Laurent, Emil, 621 Marshall St., Philadelphia, Pa. *Elect.**

2464 Laurent, Philip, 621 Marshall St., Philadelphia, Pa. *Orn.*, *Coleopt.*, *Lepid.* C. Ex.*

2465 Lautenbach, Rob't, Ph.D.,M.D., Pharmacist, 69 N. Eutaw, cor. Saratoga St., Baltimore, Md. *Bot.*, *Chem.*, *Elect.*, *Mic.* Ex.*

2466 Lawrence, Frank W., Saratoga Springs, N. Y. *Orn.*, *Ool.*, *Chem.* C.*

2467 Lawrence, G. N., 45 E. 21st St., New York, N. Y. *Orn.**

2468 Lawrence, Harry H., Saratoga Springs, N. Y. *Orn.*, *Ool.*, *Min.* C. Ex.*

2469 Lawrence, N. T., 45 E. 29th St., New York, N. Y. *Orn.* C. Ex.?

2470 Lawrence, Robert B., 35 Wall St., New York, N. Y. *Orn.*, *Ool.*, *Bot.* C. Ex.*

2471 Lawton, Joseph G., De Pere, Browne Co., Wis. *Palæo.*, *Geol.*, *Min.*, *Crystall.*, *Lithol.*, *Meteo.*, *Anth.*, *Eth.* C. Ex.*

2472 Lazenby, William R., Prof. Bot. and Hort., Ohio State Univ., Columbus, Ohio, and Dir. of the Ohio Experiment Station. *Bot.*, *Hort.*, *Agric.* C. Ex.*

2473 Lazier, W. D., 25 E. Main St., Xenia, Ohio. *Arch.*, *Geol.* C. Ex.*

2474 Leach, M. L., M.D., Traverse City, Mich. *Palæo.*, *Geol.*, *Moll.* Collector of Mich. L. and F. W. shells. C.*

2475 Leal, Malcolm, M.D., "The Albany" 52d St. and Broadway, New York, N. Y. *Chem.*, *Gen. Biol.**

2476 Leavenworth, F. P., Cincinnati Observatory, Mt. Lookout, Hamilton Co., Ohio. *Ast.*?

2477 Lebold, Jno. F., Attica, Seneca Co., Ohio. *Bot.*, *Palæo.*, *Geol.*, *Min.*, *Chem.*, *Ent.*, *Zool.*, *Arch.* C. Ex.*

2478 Leckenby, A. B., A.M., P. O. Brighton, N. Y. *Bot: Ferns*, *Mosses*, *Algæ*, *Desmids*, *Diatoms*, *Hort.*, *Mic.*, *Ent.**

2479 LeConte, Prof. John, M.D., LL.D., Univ. of California, Berkeley, Calif. *Phys.*, *Elect.*, *Meteo.**

2480 LeConte, Joseph, M.D., LL.D., Univ. of Calif., Berkeley, Calif. *Geol.*, *Biol.**
2481 Ledoux, A. R., 10 Cedar St., New York, N. Y. *Agric. Chem.**
2482 Lee, F. S., Ph.D., Bryn Mawr College, Bryn Mawr, Pa. *Animal Physiology.**
2483 Lee, John W., 118 Pearl St., Baltimore, Md. *Min.*, *Lithol.*, *Mic.* C. Ex.*
2484 Lee, Leslie A., Ph.D., Prof. Geol. and Biol., Bowdoin Coll., Brunswick, Me. *Gen. Zool.*, *Crust.*, *Foraminifera* C. Ex.*
2485 Lee, Thomas G., M.D., Lecturer on Histology, Yale Univ., New Haven, Ct. *Mic.*, *Hist.* C Ex.*
2486 Lee, William, M.D., Prof. of Physiology, Med. Dept., Columbian Univ., Washington, D. C. (2111 Penn. Ave.). *Elect.*, *Mic.*, *Photog.*, *Bibliog.*, *Biol.*, *Anth.*, *Arch.*, *Eth.*, *Ethnog.**
2487 Lee, Will. S., Trenton, N. J. *Bot., and all branches of plant structure.* C. Ex. all plants on Eastern coast for ferns and orchids. Correspondence in French and German. ?
2488 Leeds, B. Frank, Santa Clara, Santa Clara Co., Calif. *Bot.: Phæn. Plants.* C. Ex.*
2489 Leffman, Henry, M.D., Box 791, Phila., Pa. *Chem.*, *Mic.**
2490 Legro, John I., New Britain, Ct. *Min.* C. Ex.*
2491 Leiberg, John B., Rathdrum, Kootenai Co., Idaho. *Bot., Fungi peculiar and destructive to the wheat plants and grain. Mic. Min. of the western slope of the Bitteroot Mts.* C. Ex.*
2492 Leibig, J. E., Cornwall, Pa. *Min.*, *Lepid.*, *Coleopt.* C. Ex. ?
2493 Leidy, Joseph, M.D., Prof. Anat., Univ. Pa., 1302 Filbert St., Phila., Pa. *Zool.*, *Comp. Anat.**
2494 Leland, George H., Civil Engineer, 74 Westminster St., Providence, R. I. *Bot.* C. Ex. Desires Ferns.*
2495 Lemmon, Prof. J. G., Snell Seminary, Oakland, Calif. *Bot.*, *Ent.*, *Mic.* C. Plants for sale in sets or per desiderata.*
2496 Lemmon, Mrs. J. G., Snell Seminary, Oakland, Calif. *Bot., and flower painting.**
2497 Leng, Chas. W., B.S., Box 3565, New York, N. Y. *Coleopt.* Wants Cerambycidæ of the world by exchange or purchase. Corresponds in French, German and Spanish. C. Ex.*
2498 Lennon, W. H., State Normal School, Brockport, N. Y. *Ferns*, *Mosses.* C. Ex. N. A. ferns for foreign.*
2499 Leonard, Arthur G., Oberlin, O. *Invert. Palæo.*, *Geol.*, *Min.* C. Ex.*
2500 Leonard, F. E., Oberlin, O. *Phæn. Bot.*, *Ferns.* C. Ex.*
2501 Leonard, M. H., Pittsford, Hillsdale Co., Mich. *Min.*, *Palæo.*, *Numismatics.* C.*
2502 Leonard, R., M.D., Mauch Chunk, Carbon Co., Pa. *Bot.*, *Gen. Biol.* C.*
2503 Leonard, Wm. E., Minneapolis, Minn. *Bot.*, *Mic.**
2504 Leonard, William H., Minneapolis, Minn. *Ferns.*
2505 Leonhard, Cæsar, Carlstadt, Bergen Co., N. J. *Lepid.* C. Ex.*
2506 Lesley, J. P., State Geologist, 1008 Clinton St., Philadelphia, Pa. *Geol.**

2507 Lesquereux, Leo, Columbus, Ohio. *Palæo-botany, Bot., Bryology.**

2508 Letterman, George W., Allentown, Mo. *Phæn. Bot., Ferns, Anth., Arch., Ent.* C. Ex. for herb spec. in general.*

2509 LeVean, Axel Magnus, Assaria, Kan. *Chem., Phys., Elect., Mic., Meteo., Ast., Anat.*

2510 Levette, G. M., M.D., Indianapolis, Ind. *N. A. Con., Coleopt.* C. Ex.*

2511 Levison, Wallace Goold, Pres. Brooklyn Acad. of Photography, Lib. Am. Ast. Soc., Fellow N. Y. Acad. of Sci., Res. 314 Livingston St., Brooklyn, N. Y. *Inorg. Chem., Metall., Phys., Elect., Photog., Ast., Celestial Chem.**

2512 Lewis, Arthur P., Kerr City, Marion Co., Fla. *Photog., Chem., Ent: Lepid., Coleopt.* C. Ex.*

2513 Lewis, E. G., Wilmington, N. C. *Zool., Tax., Orn., Ool.* C. Ex.?

2514 Lewis, Frank, Downs, Kan. *Tax.*

2515 Lewis, Miss Grace Anna, Acad. Nat. Sciences, Phila., Pa. *Gen. Nat. Hist.**

2516 Lewis, H. Carvill, Prof. Min., Acad. Nat. Sci., Philadelphia, Pa. Prof. Geol., Haverford Coll., Germantown, Pa. *Min., Geol., Chem.* C.*

2517 Lewis, Rev. H. J. S., Grafton, Rensselaer Co., N. Y. *Bot., Ast., Geol.?*

2518 Lewis, L. L., P. O. Box 174, Copenhagen, N. Y. Collect, sell and ex. Nat. Hist. Spec., Price Lists desired.*

2519 Lewis, Miss M. V., High St., Germantown, Pa. *Bot: Ferns.* C. Ex.*

2520 Lewis, T. H., 406 Maria Ave., St. Paul, Minn. *Arch. and Archæological Surveys.* C. Ex.*

2521 Lewis, Thos. J., 710 No. 22d St., Philadelphia, Pa. *Min., Inorg. Chem.* C. Ex.

2522 Lewis, W. H., Katonah, West Chester Co., N. Y. *Arch.* C.

2523 Lewis, Wm. H., 61 Old Boston Road, Pawtucket, R. I. *Orn., Ool., Tax.* C. Ex. of skins and eggs.*

2524 Lewis, Wm. J., A.M., M.D., 30 Gillett St., Hartford, Ct. *Mic., Gen. Biol.* C.*

2525 Liautard, A. F., M.D., 141 West 54th St., New York, N. Y. *Mic.**

2526 Libbey, Wm., jr., A.M., Sc.D., F.G.S., F.R.G.S., etc., Prof. Princeton Coll., N. J. Director of the E. M. Museum of Geology and Archæology. *Phys. Geog., Normal Histol., Palæo., Mic., Photog., Meteor., Geog. Dist.* C. Ex.*

2527 Lichtenthaler, G. W., Bloomington, Ill. *General Con., Algæ.* Marine Algæ and shells from Cal., Oregon, and B. C., Alaska and Sandwich Islands. C. Ex.*

2528 Liefeld, E. Theophilus, 36 Orchard St., New Haven, Ct. *Geol., Min., Philology.* C.*

2529 Lientz, Montgomery P., Fayette, Howard Co., Mo. *Geol., Orn.**

2530 Lightfoot, J. C., jr., 307 Walnut St., Philadelphia, Pa. *Min.* C. Ex.*

2531 Lilliendahl, A. W., Mining Eng., Guanajuato, Mex. *Min.* C. Ex.
2532 Lilliendahl, Henry T., 82 Danforth Ave., Jersey City, N. J. *Ool.* C. Ex.*
2533 Lilliendahl, William, 82 Danforth Ave., Jersey City, N. J. *Ent.* C. Ex.*
2534 Lincoln, Chas. E., Gildersleeve, Ct. *Orn., Ool.* C. Ex.*
2535 Lind, G. Dallas, Danville, Ind. *Nat. Hist., F. W. and L. Shells.* C. Ex. Ind spec. for others.?
2536 Lindahl, Josua, P.D., Prof. Nat. Hist., Augustana Coll., Rock Island, Ill. *Gen. Zool., Palæo.* C. Ex.*
2537 Lindsley, J. Berrien, M.D., Nashville, Tenn. *Con. of Tenn.**
2538 Line, J. Edw., D.D.S., F.R.M.S., 50 Rowley St., Rochester, N. Y. *Dental Histol.**
2539 Linell, Martin L., 271 Bergen St., Brooklyn, N. Y. *Ent: Coleopt.* C. Ex.*
2540 Ling, Chas. J., 12 Fort St., Auburn, N. Y. *Phys. Geol., Min.* C. Ex*
2541 Lingle, David J., B.S., Univ. of Chicago, Chicago, Ill. *Mic., Gen. Biol.*
2542 Lintner, J. A., Ph.D., N. Y. State Entomologist, Room 27, Capitol, Albany, N. Y. *Gen. and Econ. Ent.* C.*
2543 Linton, Edwin, Prof. Geol. and Biol., Washington and Jefferson Coll., Washington, Pa. *Geol., Zool., Entozoa.* C.*
2544 Linton, Robert, Rich Valley, Dakota Co., Minn. *Ool.* C. Ex.*
2545 Lippincott, Geo. A., Huntsville, Ala. *Ent: Lepid., Geol.* C.*
2546 Litton, A., Prof. Chem., 2220 Eugenia St., St. Louis, Mo. *Min., Palæo.* C. Ex.*
2547 Livermore, Mrs. M. A. C., 24 North Ave., Cambridge, Mass. *Bot., Ent.**
2548 Livezey, Jos. B., Clarksboro', N. J. *Geol.* C. Ex.?
2549 Livingston, Luther S., 310 Sheldon St., Grand Rapids, Mich. *Lepid.* C. Ex.*
2550 Lloyd, C. G., 345 Race St., Cincinnati, O. *Bot.* C. Ex.*
2551 Lloyd, J. U., Court and Plum Sts., Cincinnati, O. *Chem.**
2552 Lloyd, Mrs. Rachel, Ph.D., Assoc. Prof. Chem., Univ. of Neb., Lincoln, Neb. *Min.* C.*
2553 Lochman, Charles L., Bethlehem, Pa. *Med., Bot., Materia Medica; Specialty, photographs of medicinal plants from life.* Will send list if desired.*
2554 Locke, J. H., North Charlestown, Sullivan Co., N. H. *Ferns, Mosses, Geol., Min., Hist.* C. Ex.*
2555 Lockhart, B., Lake George, Warren Co., N. Y. *Ool., Orn.* C. Ex.*
2556 Lockington, Wm. Neale, Philadelphia, Pa. *Marine Zoology of the Pacific coast.*?
2557 Lockwood, Prof. Samuel, Ph.D., Freehold, N. J. *Phæn. Bot., Arch., Geol., Zool., Mic.* C.*
2558 Loeber, John, 119 Nassau St., New York, N. Y. *Bot., Chem., Photog.**
2559 Loeffler, Jacob, 45 Bedford St., Newark, N. J. *Coleopt.*

2560 Loer, Z. T., Lebanon, Ohio. *Palæo.*, *Min.*, *Ent.* C. Ex.
2561 Loftus, John P., Dorchester District, Boston, Mass. *Bot.** Lower Silurian fossils to exchange for good minerals.*
2562 Logan, James H., Penn Building, Pittsburg, Pa. *Desmids*, *Diatoms*, *Mic.*, *Histol.*, *Protozoa.**
2563 Loitloff, H., Greenville, Hudson Co., N. J. *Lepid.* C. Ex.?
2564 Lomb, C. F. (Bausch and L. Opt. Co.), Rochester, N. Y. *Mic.**
2565 Lomb, H. (Bausch and L. Opt. Co.), Rochester, N. Y. *Mic.**
2566 Long, Horace B., West Upton, Mass. *Mam.*, *Orn.*, *Tax.* C. Ex.*
2567 Long, John H., Prof. Chem., Chicago Med. Coll. and Illinois Coll. of Pharmacy (Med. and Pharm. Dept., N. W. Univ.), Chicago, Ill.*
2568 Long, Judge Thos. B., 320½ Ohio St., Terre Haute, Ind. *Arch.*, *Min.*, *Palæo.* C.*
2569 Longenecker, C. B., 289 Washington St., Newark, N. J. *Mic.*, *Photog.**
2570 Longfellow, Richard K., 37 South St., Portland, Me. *Orn.*, *Ool.* C.?
2571 Longley, Fred E., Scytheville, Merrimac Co., N. H. *Geol.*, *esp. Ool.*, *Tax.*, *Ent: Min.* (*a specialty*). C. Ex.*
2572 Look, Miss Fanny H., Florence, Hampshire Co., Mass. *Bot.*, *Min.* C.
2573 Loomis, Elias, New Haven, Ct. *Meteorology.**
2574 Loomis, J. C., Pharmacist, Jeffersonville, Ind. *Mic.*, *Meteorology.**
2575 Loomis, Leverett M., Chester, S. C. *Bibliog. of Mam. and Orn.*, *Mam.*, *Orn.*, *Ool. of S. C.* C. Desires publications.*
2576 Loop, D. D., M.D., Northeast, Erie Co., Pa. C. Ex.
2577 Lopp, Wm. T., Valley City, Harrison Co., Ind. *Phæn. and Crypt. Bot.*, *Palæo.*, *Arch.*, *Ichth.*, *Lepid.* C. Ex.
2578 Lorber, Anton S., Alameda, Alameda Co., Calif. *Orn.*, *Ool.*, *Moll.* C. Ex.
2579 Lord, Maud M., 75 Lamberton St., New Haven, Ct. *Min.* C. Ex.*
2580 Lord, Nat. W., E.M., Prof. Mining and Met., Ohio State Univ., Columbus, Ohio.
2581 Loucks, Casper, York, Pa. Collection of U. S. and Foreign Coins, Min. and Indian Relics. *Sea Shells*, *Ool.* Ex. or buy.*
2582 Loud, Prof. F. H., Colorado Springs, Colo. *Meteo.*, *Ast.**
2583 Loudon, James, Prof. Math. and Phys., University Coll., Toronto, Can. *Phys.**
2584 Loughridge, R. H., Ph.D., Prof. Min. and Agric., South Carolina Coll., Columbus, S. C. *Geol.*, *Min.*, *Chem.**
2585 Love, Rev. Archibald L., Putnam, Ct. *Lichens*, *Ent.*, *Lepid.*, (*native and foreign*). C. Ex.*
2586 Love, Edw. G., Ph.D., School of Mines, Columbia College, 49th St., near 4th Ave., New York, N. Y. *Chem.*, *Min.**
2587 Love, James, Burlington, Ia. *Crinoidæ.* C. Ex.*

2588 Love, Samuel G., A.M., Jamestown, N. Y. *Orn.*, *Min.*, *Articulates.* C.

2589 Lovering, Joseph, Prof. Nat. Phil., Dir. of Jefferson Physical Laboratory, Harvard Univ., Cambridge, Mass.*

2590 Lovett, J. W., Brandon, Rutland Co., Vt. *Min.*, *Zool.*, *Orn.* C. Ex.*

2591 Lovewell, Charles H., M.D., Englewood, Cook Co., Ill. *Gen. Biol.*, *Diatoms*, *Mic.* C. Ex.*

2592 Lovewell, Prof. Joseph T., Ph.D., Prof. Chem. and Phys. Wash. Coll., Topeka, Kan. *Chem.*, *Metall.*, *Phys.*, *Meteo.*, *Elect.* C. Ex. for Coll. Mus.*

2593 Lowder, Fred. W., Sioux City, Iowa. *Geol.*, *Mic.* C. Ex.*

2594 Lowe, Chas. B. E., Augusta, Ga. *Analyt. Chem.*, *Elect.*, *Mic.*, *Bibliog.* Ex.*

2595 Lown, Clarence, Poughkeepsie, N. Y. *Ferns*, *Mic.*, *Thin Rock Sections.* C. Ex. Would like European Ferns in ex. for American.*

2596 Lucas, Fred'k A., U. S. Nat. Mus., Washington, D. C. *Osteol.*

2597 Lucy, Thomas F., M.D., 215 Mt. Zoar St., Elmira, N. Y. *Mic.* (pollen), *Gen. Nat. Hist.*, *Phæn. Bot.*, *Photog.* C. Bot. especies for sale, or ex. for N. and S. Amer. desiderata. Special, N. Y. State Flora.*

2598 Lüders, H. F , Sauk City, Sauk Co., Wis. *Phæn. and Crypt. Bot.*, *Ferns*, *Palæo.*, *Coleopt.* C. Ex.*

2599 Ludwick, H. E., Connersville, Ind. *Ool.*, *Moll.* C. Ex. Western and Southern specimens desired in exchange.*

2600 Luetgens, Augustus (Box 328) 207 E. 15th St., New York City. *Ent: Am. and European Coleopt.* C. Ex.*

2601 Lufkin, Albert, Civil Engineer, Newton, Jasper Co., Iowa. *Geol.*, *Min.*, *Chem.*, *Metall.* C. Ex.*

2602 Lufkin, Frank, Pigeon Cove, Rockport, Mass.*

2603 Lugger, Otto, N. W. Cor. of Lorman and Gilmor Sts., Baltimore, Md. Ass't Ent., Dept. Agric., Washington, D. C. *Coleopt. of the world.* C.*

2604 Lummis, Henry, Lawrence Univ., Appleton, Wis. *Phæn. and Crypt. Bot.*, *Geol.*, *Min.*, *Zool.*, *Moll.*

2605 Lumsden, George R., 54 Second St., Norwich, Ct. *Bot.*, *Ent.*, *Mic.*, *Moll.* C. Ex.*

2606 Lupton, N. T., M.D., LL.D., Prof. Chem. and State Chemist, Agricultural Coll., Auburn, Ala. *Chem.*, *Met.* C. Ex.*

2607 Lusignan, Alphonse, Advocate, Mem. Royal Soc. of Canada, Officer of Academy France, Ottawa, Can. Collection of Canadian books. *Bibliography*, *Arch.*, *Philol.*

2608 Luthe, F. Henry, McGregor, Ia. *Minerals*, *Fossils.* C. Ex.*

2609 Luther, S. M., Garretsville, Ohio. *Arch.*, *Moll.* C. Ex. in L. and F. W. Shells.*

2610 Luthy, Otto, 2336 Fairmount Ave., Philadelphia, Pa. *Chem.*

2611 Lyford, Chas. C., M.D., Pres. N. W. Veterinary Coll., 309 Second Ave., S. Minneapolis, Minn. *Mic.*, *Anat.* C. Ex.?

2612 Lyford, Edwin F., Springfield, Mass. *Min.*, *Chem.*, *Elect.*, *Ast.*, *Anth.* C. Ex.*

2613 Lykins, Wm. H. R., Kansas City, Mo. *Geol.*, *Palæo.*, *Mic.* C.*
2614 Lyle, David A., Capt. of Ordnance, U. S. A., Box 2253, Boston, Mass. *Orn.*, *Eth.*, *Ast.*, *Phys.*, *Metall. and Mining.* ?
2615 Lyman, A. C., M.A., 84 Victoria St., Montreal, Can. *Phys.*, *Elect.*, *Ast.*
2616 Lyman, Benj. Smith, Northampton, Mass. *Geol.**
2617 Lyman, Prof. Chester S., M.A., Yale Coll., New Haven, Ct. *Ast.*, *Physics.**
2618 Lyman, H. H., M.A., 74 McTavish St., Montreal, Can. *Lepid.*, *Geol.*, *Bot.* C.*
2619 Lyman, Theodore, Brookline, Mass. *Radiata*, *Pisciculture.**
2620 Lynch, Wm. H., Author of "Sci. Dairy Practice," Danville, P. Q., Can. *Agric.*, *Economic Sci. and Statistics*, *Hygiene and Sanitation.**
2621 Lyon, Victor W., C.E. and Geologist, Jeffersonville, Clark Co., Ind. *Invert. Palæo.* C. Ex. Crinoids for Crinoids only.*
2622 Lyons, A. B., M.D., F.C.S., Ed. "Pharmaceutical Era," 428 Second St., Detroit, Mich. *Min.*, *Bot.*, *Con.* C. Ex. ferns.*
2623 Mabery, C. F., S.D., Prof. Chem., Case School of Applied Science, Cleveland, Ohio.*
2624 Machesney, Chas. P., 65 Broadway, New York, N. Y., care of Am. Ex. Co. *Gen. Ent.*, *especially Lepid.* C. Ex.*
2625 Mason, Mrs. Adella, Oregon, Ogle Co., Ills. *Bot.*, *Algæ.* Desires Ranunculaceæ. C. Ex.*
2626 Mann, Thos. S., Ambler, Montgomery Co., Pa. *Orn.*, *Ool.* C. Ex.*
2627 Manton, W. P., M.D., F.R.M.S., Managing Editor of "The Microscope," 83 Lafayette Ave., Detroit, Mich. *Mic.*, *Zool.*, *Emb.*, *Tax.*, *Histol.**
2628 Martin, Edward, Kenosha, Wis.
2629 Marlatt, C. L., Manhattan, Kansas. *Hymen.*, *Economic Ent.**
2630 McAdam, Howard H., Oak Bay, Charlotte Co., N. B., Canada. *Orn.*, *Ool.*, *Tax.* C.*
2631 McAdams, Hon. Wm., jr., Alton, Madison Co., Ill. *Arch.*, *Geol.*, *Palæo.* Desires to ex. mollusca.
2632 McAllister, Frank W., 3 N. Charles St., Baltimore, Md. *Mic.*, *Photog.*, *Optics.* C.*
2633 McAllister, T. H., 49 Nassau St., New York, N. Y. *Mic.**
2634 McAlvin, J. H., C.E., Cur. Min and Geol spec., Land Dept., U. P. Ry., Omaha, Nebraska. C. Ex.*
2635 McAndrew, W. A., 5101 Lake Ave., Chicago, Ill. *Chem. and Mental Sci.**
2636 McBride, F. E., Mansfield, Ohio. *Min.* C. Ex.?
2637 McBride, R. Wes, Waterloo, DeKalb Co., Ind. *Arch.*, *Ent.*, *Orn.*, *Ool.*, *Min.* C. Ex.*
2638 McBride, Prof. T. H., Iowa City, Ia. *Bot.*, *Zool.* Ex. ferns and mosses.*
2639 McBryde, John M., Ph.D., Pres. South Carolina College, and Prof. Bot., Columbia, S. C.*

2640 McCalla, Albert, Ph.D., Prof. Math. and Ast., Lake Forest Univ., Lake Forest, Ill. *Ast.*, *Mic.* C. Ex.*
2641 McCallum, G. A., M.D., Dunnville, Ont., Canada. *Orn.*, *Ool.* C. Ex.*
2642 McCallum, Wm. G., Dunnville, Ont., Canada. *Herpet.*, *Ent: Lepid.*, *Coleopt.* C. Ex.*
2643 McCarthy, T. J., N. W. cor. 6th and Olive Sts., Los Angeles, Calif. *Geol.*, *Min.*, *Chem.* C.*
2644 McCaskey, G. W., A.M., M.D., 24 W. Berry St., Fort Wayne, Ind. *Mic.*, *Gen. Biol.*, *Emb.*, *Histol.**
2645 McCleery, Jennie A., Douglass, Fayette Co., Iowa. *Geol.*, *Min.*, *Zool.*, *Orn.* C. Ex.*
2646 McClintock, Andrew H., Wilkes-Barré, Pa. *Arch.* Ex. for Wyoming Hist. and Geological Soc.*
2647 McClintock, Chas. T., Prof. Biol., Chautauqua Coll. of Liberal Arts, Millersburg, Bourbon Co., Ky.*
2648 McClintock, Emory, Actuary, Milwaukee, Wis. *Math.**
2649 McClintock, F., West Union, Fayette Co., Ia. *Ast.*, *Physics*, *Elect.*, *Meteorol.*
2650 McClung, C. M., Knoxville, Knox Co., Tenn. *Min.*, *Orthop.* C. Ex.*
2651 McConnell, J. B., M.D., 141 Bleury St., Montreal, Can. *Bacteriology*, *Mic.*, *Histol.* C.*
2652 McConnell, R. G., B.A., Geol. Surv., Ottawa, Can. *Western Geol.**
2653 McCook, Henry C., Acad. Nat. Sci., Philadelphia, Pa. *Hymenoptera.**
2654 McCord, D. A., Oxford, Butler Co., Ohio. *Palæo.*, *Min.*, *Fossils of the Hudson River group for Fossils, Shells and Mins.* C. Ex.*
2655 McCowen, Jennie, A.M., M.D., Sec. Davenport Acad. Nat. Sci., Davenport, Ia. *Gen. Biol.*, *Anth.**
2656 McCourt, Peter J., M.D., 233 W. 23d St., New York, N. Y. *Histol. and Pathological Anatomy.**
2657 McCown, F. O., Oregon City, Ore. *Arch.*, *Geol.* C.*
2658 McCoy, Solon, Red Bluff, Calif. *Geol.*, *Min.*, *Arch.**
2659 McCracken, S. B., Delphi, Ind. *Phæn. Bot.* C. Ex.
2660 McCreath, Andrew S., Analyt. Chemist, 2d Geol. Surv. of Pa., Harrisburg, Pa. *Inorg. Chem.*, *Iron and Steel.?*
2661 McCutchen, Aug. R., Geologist for Dept. of Agric., Atlanta, Ga. *Geol.* C. Ex.*
2662 McDaniel, Rev. Benjamin F., San Diego, Calif. *Min.* C. Fossils and minerals in ex. for minerals.*
2663 McDonald, J. L., V.D.M., Ottawa, Ohio. *Bibliog.?*
2664 McDonald, Marshall, Ass't in Ch. Fish Culture, U. S. F. C., 1515 R St., Washington, D. C. Desires correspondence in relation to the Nat. Hist., distribution and migration of fishes.*
2665 McDowell, Chas., 150 West 11th St., New York, N. Y. *Histol.* C.*
2666 McFadden, Prof. L. H., Otterbein University, Westerville, O. *Chem.*, *Phys.*, *Gen. Biol.**

2667 McGee, Emma R., Farley, Iowa. *Bot.?*
2668 McGee, W. J., U. S. Geol. Surv., Washington, D. C. *Geol.**
2669 McGill, John T., Ph.D., Vanderbilt Univ., Nashville, Tenn. *Chem.**
2670 MacGregor, James Gordon, M.A., D.Sc., F.R.S.S.E. and C., Prof. of Physics, Dalhousie College, Halifax, Nova Scotia, Canada. *Physics, Electricity.**
2671 McIlwraith, K. C., Hamilton, Can. *Orn.* C. Ex.*
2672 McIlwraith, Thomas, Hamilton, C. W., Can. *Orn.* C. Ex.*
2673 McInnis, Louis L., Prof. Math., A. and M., Coll. of Tex., College Station, Tex. *Ast., Anth., Arch., Eth., Ethnog.**
2674 Mackay, A. H., B.A., B.Sc., F.S.Sc., Prin. Pictou Acad., Pictou, N. S., Can. *Gen. Biol*, *Local Diatomaceæ and Fresh-Water Sponges.* C. Ex.*
2675 McKay, Joseph, 245 Eighth St., Troy, N. Y. *Mic., Invertebrates.* C. Ex.*
2676 Mackay, Wm., Thorndale, Ont., Canada. *Tax.* C. Ex.
2677 McKeown, S. W., Youngstown, Ohio. *Min., Crystall., Chem., Elect., Mic.**
2678 McKim, Rev. Haslett, New Haven, Ct. *Bot.**
2679 Mackintosh, James B., E.M., C.E., Lehigh Univ., South Bethlehem, Pa. *Min., Chem.* C.*
2680 McKnight, Dr. Chas. S., Saranac Lake, N. Y. *Ent: Lepid.* C. Ex.
2681 McLane, Miss Kittie, 418 12th St., Oakland, Calif. *Mosses, Ferns, Lichens, Algæ.* C. Ex.*
2682 McLaughlin, Rev. Daniel D. Tompkins, Litchfield, Ct. *Geol., Min.* C.*
2683 McLaughlin, Prof. Wm. M., Spencer, Mass. *Min., Geol., Arch., Bot.* C.*
2684 McLean, J. B., Simsbury, Hartford Co., Ct. *Geol., Bot., Ent., Min.* C.*
2685 MacLean, J. P., Hamilton, Butler Co., Ohio. *Arch., Geol., Palæo.* C. Ex.*
2686 McLennan, L. P., Pictou, N. S., Canada. *Ent.* C. Ex.*
2687 MacLean, Frank P., M.D., Chemist and Examiner, U. S. Patent Office, Washington, D. C. *Bot., Inorg. Chem., Met., Electro-Met., Mic.**
2688 Macloskie, George, D.Sc., LL.D., Prof. Princeton Coll., Princeton, N. J. *Biol.* C.*
2689 McLouth, Lewis, A.M., Ph.D., Pres. and Prof. Chem., Dakota Agric Coll., Brookings, Dak. *Chem., Physics.*
2690 McMurrich, J. Playfair, M.A., Ph.D., Prof. of Biol., Haverford College, Pa. *Gen. Biol., Morph., Emb., Actinozoa.**
2691 McMurtrie, Wm., E.M., Ph.D., Prof. Chem., Univ. of Ills., Champaign, Ill. *Chem.**
2692 McNair, A. R., Lieut. Commander U. S. N., 588 North Broadway, Saratoga Springs, N. Y. *Geol., Deep sea-soundings.**
2693 McNeal, Albert T., Bolivar, Tenn.?
2694 McNeill, Jerome, Indiana University, Bloomington, Ind. *Ent: Hymen., Orthopt., Lepid., Coleopt., Myriapods.* C. Ex.

2695 McNeill, M., Ass't Prof., Princeton, N. J.*
2696 McNeill, Wm. S., Mobile, Ala. *Mic., Diatoms, especially cleaning and mounting marine soundings.* C. Ex.?
2697 MacNider, V. St. Clair, M.D., Jackson, Northampton Co., N. C. *Bot., Mic., Zool., Gen. Biol.**
2698 Macomber, Isaac B., Portsmouth, R. I. *Hort., Agric., Chem., Geol.**
2699 Macoun, Prof. J., A.M., F.L.S., F.R.S.C., Geol. and Nat. Hist. Survey, Ottawa, Ont., Can. *Bot., Orn.* C. Ex.*
2700 Macoun, J. M., Geol. Museum, Ottawa, Ont., Can. *Bot: Ferns, Mosses, Fungi, Algæ, Lichens, Mam., Orn.* C. Ex.*
2701 McQuesten, C. B., M.D., Dobbs Ferry, N. Y. *Nat. Hist., Eth.**
2702 McShane, J. T., M.D., Carmel, Hamilton Co., Ind. *Arch.* C. Ex. or buy.*
2703 MacSwain, L. S., Pres. So. Ga. Coll., Thomasville, Thomas Co., Ga. *Diatoms, Mic.*
2704 McWhorter, Tyler, Aledo, Ill. *Geol., Palæo., Vegetable Phys.* C.*
2705 Maddox, Chas. K., Atlanta, Ga. *Bot., Min., Phys., Philol.* C. Ex.*
2706 Madtes, Henry, Chester, Pa. *Bot., Min.* Ex.?
2707 Maeser, Karl G., Principal Brigham Young Acad., Provo City, Utah Co., Utah. *Theory of Teaching, Ast.?*
2708 Mailloux, C. Odillon, Electrical Engineer, 120 Broadway, New York City. *Phys., Elect.**
2709 Main, J. T., M.D., Pres. Mic. Soc., Jackson, Mich. *Mic.* C. Ex. animal tissue.*
2710 Maisch, J. M., Prof. of Materia Medica and Botany, Philadelphia College of Pharm., 143 No. 10th St., Philadelphia, Pa. *Phæn. Bot., Ferns.* C.*
2711 Maitre, R., Seedsman and Florist, Grower of Southern Fruit, Shade and Ornamental Plants, etc., New Orleans, La. *Agric.?*
2712 Malleis, W. B., Cedar Mill, Portland, Oregon. *Orn.* Ex. or sell.*
2713 Mallery, Garrick, Bvt. Lt. Col. U. S. A., 1323 N. St., N. W., Washington, D. C. *Anth.**
2714 Mallet, J. W., Prof. Chem., Univ. of Virginia, Albemarle Co., Va. *Chem., Phys., Min.* C. Ex.*
2715 Mallinckrodt, Edw., St. Louis, Mo. *Chem.* C.*
2716 Maloney, James A., Box 491, Washington, D. C. *Elect., Acoustics, Chem.**
2717 Mancheé, Sidney H., 146 Adelaide St. W., Toronto, Canada. *General Ent.* C. Ex.?
2718 Mandeville, Wm. R., M.D., Ph.D., 142 Canal St., New Orleans, La. *Diatoms, Mic., Photog., Gen. Biol., Histol.* C. Ex.*
2719 Manigault, G. E., M.D., Cur. Mus., Charleston, S. C. C. Ex.*
2720 Mann, B: Pickman, of Cambridge, Mass., Managing and Bibliographical Ed. *Psyche;* 1918 Sunderland Place, Washington, D. C. Autobiographies, lists of writings of Entomologists and contributions to the Bibliographical Record of *Psyche* desired. References, transcripts and translations upon all subjects furnished. *Ent., Bibliog.**

2721 Mann, Charles L., 124 Farwell Ave., Milwaukee, Wis. *Orn.*, *Arch.* (Copper Age). C. Exotic orchids wanted. Will give bird and mammal skins, living native plants, or copper and iron ores in ex.*

2722 Manning, George F., Coshocton, Ohio. *Gen. Collector, Dealer and Exchanger of Curiosities.* C. Ex. Wanted: Old arms and Indian relics in exchange for other specimens.*

2723 Manning, J. W., jr., Reading, Mass. *Ent.*, *Bot.* C. Ex. Coniferous specimens and rare deciduous trees and plants.*

2724 Manning, Rufus P., Youngstown, Ohio. *Agric.*, *Palæo.*, *Geol.*, *Lithol.*, *Min.*, *Arch.*, *Con.* C. Ex. selenite crystals, fossil fruits of L. Coal Meas. Iron ores and Lithological spec. for ex. Has a very large collection of correctly identified fossils, in which many geol. periods are represented, for sale at very reasonable prices; also another large collection of ores, minerals and metals.*

2725 Manning, Warren H., Reading, Mass. *Bot.* C. of N. A. plants for herbarium, specialty, introduced plants and orchids, and also live plants. Exchanges wanted.*

2726 Mansfield, F. A., Camden, Knox Co., Me. *Gen. Nat. Hist.* C.?

2727 Mansfield, Hon. Ira F., Cannelton, Beaver Co., Pa. *Bot: Ferns*, *Hort.*, *Palæo.* C.

2728 Mansfield, J, M., Ph.D., Mt. Pleasant, Iowa. *Chem.*, *Mic.*, *Gen. Biol.* C.?

2729 Marble, Sarah, Woonsocket, R. I. *Min.*, *Chem.* C.*

2730 Marburg, C. L., Baltimore, Md. *Zool.**

2731 Marcou, John Belknap, Ass't U. S. Geol. Surv., Smithsonian Inst., Washington, D. C. (and 42 Garden St., Cambridge, Mass.).*

2732 Marcou, Jules, 42 Garden St., Cambridge, Mass. (and at Salins, Jura, France).*

2733 Marcy, Henry O., M.D., 116 Boylston St., Boston, Mass. *Emb. of Vert.*, *Osteol.*, *Gen. Biol.*, *Bacteriology.**

2734 Marcy, Oliver, Prof. Nat. Hist., Northwestern Univ., Evanston, Cook Co., Ill. *Zool.*, *Geol.*, *Bot.* C.*

2735 Marden, Geo. H., 7 Parker St., Charlestown, Mass. *Geol.* C.*

2736 Mariner, Prof. Geo. A., M.D., 81 S. Clark St., Chicago, Ill. *Analyt. and Consulting Chem.* C. of Mins.*

2737 Mark, Edw. L., Ph.D., Hersey Prof. of Anat., Harvard Univ., Ass't Mus. Comp. Zool., Cambridge, Mass. *Zool.*, *Emb.*, *Worms.**

2738 Mark, Edw. S., M.D., Calif. Acad. of Sci., San Francisco, Calif. *Palæo.*, *Mic.**

2739 Markoe, Francis H., M.D., Columbia Coll., New York, N. Y. *Anat.**

2740 Markoe, George F. H., Ph.G., Prof. Chem., Mass. Coll. Pharmacy, 61 Warren St., Boston, Mass. *Pharm.*

2741 Marks, R., Dodgeville, Iowa Co., Wis. *Geol.*, *Min.* C. Ex.*

2742 Marlatt, C. L., Manhattan, Riley Co., Kansas. *Bot.*, *Hort.*, *Ent.: Hymen.*, *Econ. Ent.* C. Ex.*

2743 Marrett, W. H., Brunswick, Me. *Min.*, *Palæo.* C. Good specimens for ex.*
2744 Marsden, Samuel, 907 Clay Ave., St. Louis, Mo. *Ast.?*
2745 Marsh, C. Dwight, Prof. Chem. and Biol., Ripon, Wis. *Ent.*, *Geol.* C. Desires coleoptera and fossils.*
2746 Marsh, Charles H., Dulzura, San Diego, Calif. *Ool.*, *Orn.* C. New Mexico and Southern Cal. skins and eggs for sale. Do not ex. Price-list sent on application.*
2747 Marsh, Rev. Dwight Whitney, D.D., Amherst, Mass. *Orn.**
2748 Marsh, O. C., Prof. Yale Coll., New Haven, Ct. *Palæo.*, *Comp. Anat.**
2749 Marsh, Philip, Aledo, Ill. *Con.*, *Orn.*, *Ool.*, *Palæo.* C. Ex. L. and F. W. shells; Unionidæ and Helicidæ esp. desired.*
2750 Marsh, Wm. A., Box 31, Aledo, Mercer Co., Ill. *Bot.*, *Palæo.*, *Min.*, *Geog. Dist.*, *Arch.*, *Moll.*, *Coins*, *Woods.* Ex.*
2751 Marsh, Wm. D., Box 274, Amherst, Mass. *Min.*, *Orn.*, *Ool.* C. Ex.*
2752 Marshall, Dyer M., Fruit Valley, Oswego Co., N. Y. *Orn.*, *Ool.*, *Tax.* C.
2753 Marshall, John P., Prof. Min. and Geol., Tufts Coll., College Hill, Mass., Dir. of Barnum Museum. Ex.*
2754 Marston, Ira D., Cambridge, Ill. *Geol.?*
2755 Marten, John, Albion, Edwards Co., Ill. *Dipt.* Ex.
2756 Martens, Jas. Wm., jr., Mohegan, Westchester Co., N. Y. *Bot: Phæn. Plants*, *Crypt. Plants*, *Ferns*, *Mosses.* C. Ex.*
2757 Martin, Prof. Daniel S., 236 W. 4th St., New York, N. Y. *Geol.*, *Min.*, *Con.* C. Ex.*
2758 Martin, Henry Newell, M.A., D.Sc., M.D., F.R.S., Prof. Johns Hopkins Univ., Baltimore, Md. *Gen. Biol.*, *Physiology.**
2759 Martin, John A., Wallingford, Ct. *Orn.*, *Ool.* C. Ex.
2760 Martin, Lillie J., Teacher of Sci., High School, Indianapolis, Ind. *Plant Chemistry.**
2761 Martin, William J., Prof. Davidson Coll., Mecklenberg Co., N. C. *Chem.*, *Geol.* C. Min. and Lower Sil. fossils to ex. for other minerals or fossils.*
2762 Martindale, Isaac C., Camden, N. J. *Bot.* C.*
2763 Marvin, D. S., Watertown, N. Y. *Min.*, *Fossils.* C. Ex.*
2764 Marvin, J. B., M.D., 903 4th Ave., Louisville, Ky. *Chem.*, *Mic.**
2765 Maryatt, D. P., jr., Weiser, Idaho. *Civil Eng.**
2766 Mason, Henry H., Farmington, Ct. *Lepid.* C.*
2767 Mason, Norman N., Box 949, Providence, R. I. *Algæ*, *Desmids*, *Diatoms*, *Mic.*, *Histol.* C. Ex.*
2768 Mason, Otis Tufton, Curator of Dept. of Ethnology, National Museum, Washington, D. C. *Anth.**
2769 Mason, Stephen G., Oregon, Ogle Co., Ill. *Phænogamous Plants.* C. Ex. Will ex. local plants for Compositæ.*
2770 Mason, O. G., Sec. Am. Mic. Soc., Sec. Photo. Sect., Am. Inst., N. Y. City, Official Photog. to Dept. Public Charities and Correction, Photographic Department Bellevue Hospital, New York, N. Y. *App. of Photog. to the illust. of science.* C. Ex.*

2771 Mather, Fred., Ass't U. S. Fish. Comm., Fishery editor "Forest and Stream," New York, Supt. N. Y. Fish Commission, Cold Spring Harbor, Suffolk Co., N. Y.*

2772 Mathews, Frank, A.M., Denver, Colo. *Geol., Min., Lithol.*

2773 Matlack, J. Hoopes, West Chester, Pa. *Ool.* C.*

2774 Matthew, Geo. F., Chief Clerk of Customs, St. John, N. B. *Bot: Phæn. Plants, Invert. Palæo., Strat. Geol., Min., Geog. Distribution, Emb., Arch., Crustacea, Moll.* C. Ex.*

2775 Matthews, Washington, Capt. and Ass't Surgeon U. S. Army, Army Medical Museum, Washington, D. C. *Bot., Anth., Arch., Eth., Ethnog., Philol. of American Aborigines.* C.*

2776 Mattison, I. W., Oberlin, Ohio. *Chem., Phys., Mic., Elect.*?

2777 Matz, F. P., A.M., Sc.M., Ph.D., formerly of the Johns Hopkins Univ., Prof. of Higher Math. and Chem. in Bell's Military Univ. School, King's Mountains, N. C. *Math., Chem., Mathematical Ast.**

2778 Maxson, Edwin R., A.M., M.D., LL.D., 208 Madison St., Syracuse, N. Y. *Bot., Diatoms, Elect., Mic., Ast., Anat., Philol.**

2779 Maxwell, A. W., 127 Euclid Ave., Cleveland, O. *Ent.* C. Ex.*

2780 Maxwell, Geo. M., Bond Hill, Ohio. *Palæo., Geol., Min., Anth.* C. Ex.?

2781 Maxwell, Mary K., North Market St., Meadville, Pa. *Ent.* C. Ex.*

2782 Maxwell, Prof. S. A., Rock Falls, Ill. *Meteorol., Min., Bot.* C. Ex.*

2783 May, A. M., Waukon, Ia. *Geol., Arch.* C. Ex.*

2784 Mayall, Rev. J. M., Ohio, Bureau Co., Ill. *Geol., Zool.* C. Ex.*

2785 Maycock, Prof. M. M., Buffalo, N. Y. *Gen. Nat. Hist.**

2786 Mayer, Prof. Alfred M., Stevens Inst. Tech., Hoboken, N. J. *Experimental Physiology.*

2787 Maynard, C. J., 339 Washington St., Boston, Mass. *Zool., Mammals, Orn., Ool., Tax.* C. Ex.*

2788 Maynard, S. T., Prof. Mass. Agric. Coll., Amherst, Mass. *Bot.* Hampshire Co. plants and dups. for ex.*

2789 Mayo, E. R., 35 Upton St., Boston, Mass. *Molluscs.* C. Ex.*

2790 Mazyck, W. G., 56 Montague St., Charleston, S. C. *Con.* C. Ex.*

2791 McAdam, D. J., Prof. Applied Math. and Astronomy, Washington and Jefferson College, Washington, Pa.*

2792 McGregor, Richard, 2841 Champa St., Denver, Col. *Orn., Ool.* C. Ex.*

2793 McIntire, Dr. H. E., Middletown, Middlesex Co., Ct. *Bot., Org. and Inorg. Chem., Phys., Elect., Photog., Emb., Anat., Vert., Invert., Orn., Ool., Tax.* C. Ex.*

2794 McKee, John F., Att'y-at-Law, Brookville, Franklin Co. Indiana. *Palæo. (Vert. and Invert.), Geol., Min., Crystall. Lithol., Ast., Hymen., Lepid., Dipt., Coleopt., Hemipt. Orthopt., Neuropt., Myriop.**

2795 McLain, Byron W., A.M., Ph.D., Prof. Nat. Sci. and Dean of Applied Sci. and Industrial Art, Grant Memorial Univ., Athens, Tenn.*

2796 McRae, Austin L., U. S. Signal Service, Terre Haute, Ind. *Phys.*, *Elect.*, *Meteo.**
2797 Mead, George G., Ferris, Carbon Co., Wyoming Terr. Dealer in Rocky Mt. curiosities. *Min.*, *Mic.*, *Zool.*, *Orn.*, *Ool.*, *Tax.* C. Ex.*
2798 Mead, J. R., Wichita, Kansas. *Anth.*, *Arch.*, *Fresh Water Molluscs.* C. Ex.*
2799 Mead, T. L., Lake Charm, Fla. *Bot.*, *specialty*, *Palms*, *also introduction of new plants.**
2800 Mead, Walter H., 65 Wall St., New York, N. Y. *Mic.**
2801 Mearns, Edgar A., M.D., Ass't Surg. U. S. Army, Fort Verde, Arizona. *Vertebrates*, *Zool.* C. Ex.*
2802 Mears, Ellis, Accomac Co., Va. *Phæn. Bot.**
2803 Meddock, Dora, 66 Virginia Ave., Indianapolis, Ind. *Palæo.*, *Geol.*, *Min.*, *Arch.*, *Orn.*, *Ool.*, *Tax.*, *Ent.*, *Moll.* C. Ex.
2804 Meech, Rev. Wm. W., A.M., Vineland, N. J. *Hort.*, *Min.*, *Ent.* C.*
2805 Meehan, Thomas, State Botanist, Germantown, Pa. *Phæn. Bot.*, *Ferns*, *Horticulture.* C.*
2806 Meeker, John Willard, M.D., Nyack-on-Hudson, N. Y. *Mic.*, *Emb.*, *Histol.* C. Ex.*
2807 Meisky, John C., Washington Borough, Lancaster Co., Pa. *Mam.*, *Orn.* C. Desires to ex. with all parts of the world.*
2808 Meissner, Carl A., Ph.B., Brier Hill, Mahoning Co., Ohio. *Inorg Chem.*, *Min.*, *Crypt. Bot: esp. Lichens.* C. Ex.?
2809 Mell, P. H., jr., M.E., Ph.D., Prof. Nat. Hist. and Geol., State Polytechnic Inst. and Dir. of Ala. Weather Service, Auburn, Ala. *Palæo.*, *Geol.*, *Min.*, *Zool.* Large supply of fossils from the Claiborne group, Tertiary formation, Alabama. C. Minerals for exchange. Desires all kinds of scientific spec. to rebuild a museum recently burned.*
2810 Mellor, C. C., Pittsburgh, Pa. *Bot.*, *Mic.*, *Photog.* C.*
2811 Melville, Wm. Harlow, Ph.D., U. S. Geol. Survey, San Francisco, Calif. *Min.*, *Crystall.*, *Chem.**
2812 Melville, Wm. P., 14 Cottingham St., Toronto, Can. *Mammals*, *Orn.*, *Ool.*, *Tax.* C. Ex.*
2813 Melzer, James P., Milford, N. H. *Orn.*, *Ool.*, *Tax.*, *Ent.* C. Ex. lepidoptera.*
2814 Mendenhall, Prof. Thomas C., Ph.D., Prof. Phys., Ohio State Univ., and Dir. State Weather Service, Columbus, Ohio. *Phys.?*
2815 Menefee, C. A., San José, Santa Clara Co., Calif. *Bot.*, *Orn.*, *Ent.* C. Ex.*
2816 Menefee, E. L., San José, Santa Clara Co., Calif. *Ool.* C. Ex.*
2817 Menges, Franklin, B.S., Ass't in Chem., Pa. College, Gettysburg, Pa. *Inorg. Chem.*, *Met.* C.*
2818 Menough, Wm. C., 2232 Sharswood St., Philadelphia, Pa. *Orn.*, *Mam.*, *Herpet.* C. Buys or ex.*
2819 Mepham, George S., 1823 Mississippi Ave., St. Louis, Mo. *Arch.*, *Min.* C. Ex.*

2820 Mercer, A. Clifford, M.D., F.R.M.S., Prof. of Pathol., College of Med., Syracuse Univ., N. Y., Health Officer. *Pathol., Histol., Mic., Photo-Microg., Hygiene, Photography.**

2821 Mercer, Frederick Wentworth, M.D., F.R.M.S., 2600 Calumet Ave., Chicago, Ill. *Micro-Histol. and Pathol., Photo-micrography.* Ex.*

2822 Mercer, R. W., 147 Central Ave., Cincinnati, Ohio. Dealer in *Mound Pipes and Pottery, Stone and Flint Indian Relics, Old Arms, Old Coins, Confederate money, Autographs, State and U. S. Surveys, Minerals, Fossils, etc.* Send stamps for price-lists and prices paid for rare coins, etc.*

2823 Merck, Fred'k, Box 63, Attleboro' Falls, Mass. *Orn., Ool., Tax., Ent., Coleopt., Hemipt.* C. Ex.*

2824 Mergler, Marie J., M.D., Women's Med. College, Chicago, Ill. *Mic.**

2825 Merkel, Aug., P. O. Box 1429, 13 Broadway, New York City, N. Y. *Coleoptera of N. A.* C.*

2826 Merkel, G. H., M.D., 86 Boylston St., Boston, Mass. *Anth., Histol.* Ex.

2827 Merriam, Bessie G., 68 Dayle Ave., Providence, R. I. *Bot: Ferns.* C. Ex.*

2828 Merriam, C. Hart, M.D., Washington, D. C. *Mam., Orn.* C. Ex. for bats, mammals, skins and skeletons.*

2829 Merriam, Florence A., Locust Grove, Lewis Co., New York. *Orn.**

2830 Merrick, Edwin T., LL.D., Ex. Chief Justice of La., Fellow New Orleans Acad. Sci., 29 Carondelet St., New Orleans, La. *Palæo., Geol., Ast.**

2831 Merrill, F. J. H., Columbia College, New York City. *Bot., Palæo., Geol., Min., Lithol.* C. Ex.*

2832 Merrill, George P., Cur. Dept. Lithol. and Phys. Geol., U. S. National Museum, Washington, D. C. *Min., Crystall., Petrography, Lithol., Mic.**

2833 Merrill, Harry, Bangor, Me. *Orn., Ool.* C. Ex.*

2834 Merriman, C. C., Rochester, N. Y. *Mic., Algæ.* ?

2835 Merriman, Geo. B., Rutgers Coll., New Brunswick, N. J. *Ast.**

2836 Merriman, Mansfield, Prof. Civil Eng., Lehigh Univ., Bethlehem, Pa. *Math., Goedesy, Bibliog.* ?

2837 Mertz, Henry N., Supt. Pub. Schools, Steubenville, O. *Bot: Ferns, Geol., Chem.* C. Ex.*

2838 Merwin, Orange, 244 Kossuth St., Bridgeport, Ct. *Palæo., Geol., Min.* C.*

2839 Mesick, John C., M.D., Niverville, N. Y. *Anat., Orn., Ool., Tax* C. Ex.?

2840 Messenger, F. Lawrence, Melrose Highlands, Mass. *Geol., Min.* C. Ex.*

2841 Metcalf, F. H., 75 Appleton St., Holyoke, Mass. *Orn., Ool., Palæo.* C.*

2842 Metcalfe, H., Capt. of Ordnance, West Point, N. Y.*

2843 Meusebach, J. O., Loyal Valley, Texas. *Bot., Hort., Invert. Palæo. (Cretaceous and Silurian).* C.*

2844 Meyer, Jacob, 393 Race St., Cincinnati, Ohio. Cin. Group fossils to ex. for others.?

2845 Meyer, Otto, P.D., Geol., Mus. Yale Coll., New Haven, Ct. *Lithol.*, *Vert. and Invert. Palæo.* C.?

2846 Meyncke, O. M., Brookville, Ind. *Bot.* C. Ex.

2847 Michael, Arthur, College Hill, Mass. *Organic Chem.**

2848 Michael, George W., jr., Morro, San Luis Obispo Co., Calif. *Geol.*, *Palæo.*, *Min.*, *Moll.*, *Bot.* C. Ex. in Mollusca for same, minerals, fossils or prehistoric remains. Corres. desired.*

2849 Michel, Chas. E., Prof. Oph., Mo. Med. Coll., St. Louis Post Graduate School of Med., 2925 Washington Ave., St. Louis, Mo. *Mic.*, *Photog.* C. Ex.*

2850 Michels, John, Box 3413, New York, N. Y. *Mic.**

2851 Michelson, Albert A., Ph.D., Prof. Phys., Case School of Applied Sciences, Cleveland, Ohio. *Phys.**

2852 Mickleborough, John, Brooklyn, N. Y. *Palæo.*, *Geol.*, *Zool.* Will exchange fine lots of Low. Sil. fossils for zool. specimens or minerals.*

2853 Middagh, Wm., Rollag, Clay Co., Minn. *Arch.*, *Phys.*, *Bot.* Wishes to ex. seeds and plants of vegetables and flowers. Will. ex. papers and books, magazines, etc.*

2854 Middleton, Robert M., jr., F.L.S., F.Z.S., So. Pittsburg, Tennessee. *Bot.*, *Zool.*, *Arch.* C.*

2855 Midlam, L. W., Marquette, Mich. *Ent.**

2856 Miellez, A., Horticulturist, Springfield, Mass. *Bot: Ferns*, *Orchids*, *Roses*, *Exotics.* C. Ex.

2857 Mignault, Dr. Louis D., Prof. Anat., Victoria Univ., 155 Bleury St., Montreal, Can. *Phæn. Bot.*, *Ferns.* C.

2858 Miles, Miss Mabel M., San Luis Obispo, Calif. *Ferns*, *Shells*, *Lepid.* C. Ex.

2859 Miles, Manly, M.D., D.V.S., Prof. Agric., Mass. Agric. Coll., Amherst, Mass. *Experimental Agric.*, *Biol.* C.

2860 Milgate, W. H., Biddeford Pool, Me. *Sea Birds.*?

2861 Millard, L. S., Gatesville, Coryell Co., Tex. *Geol.*, *Bot.*, *General.* C. Ex. Indian relics and Bot. spec. of Austin Co. to ex. for books.

2862 Milier, A. W., M.D., N. W. cor. 3d and Callowhill Sts., Philadelphia, Pa. *Bot.**

2863 Miller, Benjamin, Georgetown Station, D. C. *Phæn. Bot.*, *Gen. Biol.**

2864 Miller, Chas. R., 932 Avery St., Reading, Pa. *Geol.*, *Min.* C. Ex.

2865 Miller, E. S., Wading River, L. I., N. Y. *Bot.*, *Hort.*, *Min.*, *Palæo.*, *Con.*, *Arch.* C.*

2866 Miller, George, 117 So. Queen St., York, York Co., Pa. *Orn.*, *Ool.*, *Tax.*, *Ent.* C. Ex.*

2867 Miller, H. D., Plainville, Ct. *Min.* C. Ex. for good crystallized specimens only. Fine Nova Scotia and other minerals in ex. for equivalents. Minerals from England and Scotland particularly desired. Correspondence solicited Cash paid for fine spec.*

2868 Miller, Jacob, Princeton, Ill. *Geol.* C.*
2869 Miller, J. H., Lowville, N. Y. *Orn.*, *Tax.* C. Ex.*
2870 Miller, John, jr., 122 W. 21st St., Erie, Pa. *Bot.* C. Ex.*
2871 Miller, Maurice Norton, M.D., Instructor in Histol. in Univ. Med. Coll., 410 E. 26th St., New York, N. Y. *Min.*, *Crystall.*, *Mic.*, *Photog.*, *Gen. Biol.*, *Photo-Micrography.* Will ex. slides in histol. and pathol. for quartz, tourmaline, etc., crystals for lapidary work. C.
2872 Miller, Morris B., Media, Del. Co., Pa. *Palæo.*, *Min.*, *Mic.*, *Bot.*, *Orn.* C. Ex. for good specimens of above. Correspondence desired.*
2873 Miller, Ryell T., D.D.S , South Bend, Ind. *Geol.*, *Min.*, *Arch.* C. Ex. rare fossils, casts, photos., minerals, etc., for good minerals, fossils, Indian relics, or books. Casts of rare archæological spec. and images esp. desired.*
2874 Miller, S. A., 8 W. 3d St., Cincinnati, Ohio. *Palæo.*, *Geol.* C. Ex.*
2875 Miller, W. M., State Univ., Reno, Nevada. *Min.**
2876 Miller, Dr. W. S., 3 Castle St., Worcester, Mass. *Mic.*, *Hist.*, *Pathology.**
2877 Milligan, Mrs. J. M., Jacksonville, Morgan Co., Ill. *Bot.*, *Palæo.* C. Ex.*
2878 Millman, Thomas, M.D., M.R.C.S., etc., Asylum for Insane, Kingston, Ont., Can. *Bot.* C. Ex.*
2879 Mills, Henry, 162 Fargo Ave., Buffalo, N. Y. *Mic.*, *Fresh Water Sponges.**
2880 Mills, Henry, Natick, Mass. *Orn.*, *Ool.*, *Min.*, *Bot.* C. Ex. eggs.
2881 Mills, James C. C., M.A., Prof. of Chem., Ont. Agric. Coll., Guelph, Ont., Can.*
2882 Mills, Jas., M.A., Pres. Ont. Agric. College, Guelph, Ont., Can.
2883 Millspaugh, C. F., M.D., Waverly, N. Y. *Gen. and Medical Bot.*, *esp. Euphorbiaceæ.* C. Ex. Correspondence desired on N. A. (including Mexican) species of the genus Euphorbia.
2884 Miner, Randolph H., Ensign U. S. Navy, Mem. Biol. Soc. of Washington, U. S. S. Iroquois, San Francisco, Calif. *Ichth.*, *Tax.**
2885 Miner, W. W., M.D., Ware, Mass. *Hist.* C. Ex.*
2886 Minns, Miss S., 14 Louisburg Sq., Boston, Mass. *Bot.*, *Gramineæ*, *Umbelliferæ.**
2887 Minot, Charles Sedgwick, Harvard Med. School, Boston, Mass. *Biology.*
2888 Mitchell, George O., Raleigh, N. C. *Mic.*, *Gen. Biol.*, *Histol. of Vert.* C. Ex.?
2889 Mitchell, Mrs. Isa M., Rose Hill, Johnson Co., Mo. *Moll.* C. Ex.
2890 Mitchell, Louis J., M.D., 45 Macalester Place, Chicago, Ill. *Physical Geog. in its Biol. and Eth. aspects. Spec. Northern America and Asia.* C.*

2891 Mitchell, Melville A., Jasper, Mo. Shells of Fla. and Mo. to Ex. Desires other shells of Fla. and Mo. and fine cabinet spec. from all parts of the world.*

2892 Mixter, Wm. G., Prof. Chem., Yale University, 144 Edwards St., New Haven, Ct. *Chem.**

2893 Miyabe, Kingo, Sapporo Agric. College, Sapporo, Japan. Temporary address 7 Story St., Cambridge, Mass. *Bot: Phæn. Plants, Fungi, Algæ.**

2894 Moffat, J. Alston, Hamilton, Ont., Can. *Coleopt., Lepid.* C.*

2895 Moffat, J. L., M.D., O. et A. Chir., 17 Schermerhorn St., Brooklyn, N. Y. *Oculist.**

2896 Moffatt, Ansil, Indianapolis, Ind. *Bot., Chem.**

2897 Moffatt, Will S., M.D., 94 La Salle St., Chicago, Ill. *Cactaceæ of U. S. and Mex. and Phæn. Plants of N. Ill.* C. Ex.*

2898 Moffitt, Jacob W., Chillicothe, Ill. *Palæo.* C.*

2899 Mohns, Julius, 715 165th St., New York City. *Lepid.* C.*

2900 Mohr, Chas., Mobile, Ala. *Bot: Forestry.**

2901 Mohr, Charles A., Prof. Chem., Med. Coll. of Ala., Mobile, Ala. *Chem.**

2902 Mohr, Emily, Cullman, Cullman Co., Ala. *Bot.**

2903 Mohr, Marie, Cullman, Cullman Co., Ala. *Bot.**

2904 Mohr, Paul, Cullman, Cullman Co., Ala. *Geol., Palæo., Min.**

2905 Moler, Wm. G., B.S., Greenfield, Ohio. *Math., Ast.* C. Ex.*

2906 Molera, E. J., Civil and Electrical Engineer, P. O. Box No. 107, Branch A, San Francisco, Calif. *Physics, Elect., Mic., Photog., Meteo., Ast., Bibliog., Arch., Eth., Philol.* C.*

2907 Monks, Sarah P., A.M., Cold Spring, Putnam Co., N. Y. *Herpet., Comp. Osteol., spec. Batrachia.* C. Ex.?

2908 Monroe, Frederic S., 200 Kempton St., New Bedford, Mass. *Phæn. Bot., Ferns.* C. Ex.*

2909 Montgomery, Prof. Henry, M.A., B.Sc., Ph.B., University of North Dakota, Grand Forks, Dakota. *Spec. Subjects:—Zool., Comp. Anat., Physiol., Bot., Palæo., Geol.* C.*

2910 Montgomery, James H., Prof. Physics and Chem., Allegheny Coll., Meadville, Pa. *Min., Mic., Phys., Zool.* C. Ex.*

2911 Montgomery, S., A.M., Prof. Chem. and Physiology, Olivet Coll., Olivet, Eaton Co., Mich. *Chem., Phys.**

2912 Moody, Prof. Edw. F., C.E., Ph.D., Camden, N. J. *Chem.**

2913 Moody, J. D., Mendota, Ill. *Am. Antiquities.* C.*

2914 Moody, Mary Blair, M.D., Fair Haven Heights, New Haven, Ct.*

2915 Moore, Addie, 620 North 5th St., Terre Haute, Ind. *Geol., Zool., Molluscs.**

2916 Moore, Alex., 3 School St., Boston, Mass. *General.**

2917 Moore, Dr. Chas. D., Rooms 1, 2, 3, & 4 Parry Block, N. W. cor. 7th & Walnut Sts., Des Moines, Iowa. *Mic., Anat.* C.*

2918 Moore, E. C., care Tiffany & Co., Union Sq., New York City. *Antique, Greek or Roman Glass, Mex. Antiquities, Curios, Gold or Silver Work.* C. Purchase.*

2919 Moore, George, Antiquarian, Cambridge, Turnas Co., Nebraska. *Min., Arch., Ent.* C. Ex.*

2920 Moore, George, Muscatine, Ia. *Con.* C. Ex.*
2921 Moore, James W., A.M., M.D., Lafayette College, Easton, Pa. *Phys.**
2922 Moore, Rich. M., M.D., 74 South Fitzhugh St., Rochester, N. Y. *Coleopt., Chiefly the Chrysomelidæ.* C. Ex.*
2923 Moores, Henry, 109 W. Rich St., Columbus, Ohio. *Palæo., Moll.* C. Ex.*
2924 Morcom, G. Frean, 870 North Park Ave., Chicago, Ill. *Orn., Ool.* Desires only rare N. A. and Humming birds.*
2925 Morden, John A., Hyde Park, Ont., Can. *Orn., Ool., Arch., Geol., Mam.* C. Ex.
2926 Moreau, Timothy, Box 488, Chicopee, Mass. *Coleopt.* C. Ex.*
2927 Morehead, Mrs. H. B., 1042 Gilbert Ave., Cincinnati, Ohio. *Land, Fresh-water and Marine Molluscs.* C. Ex.*
2928 Morehouse, G. R., A.M., M.D., 227 So. 9th St., Philadelphia, Pa. *Biol.**
2929 Moreland, Sidney T., Prof. W. and L. Univ., Lexington, Va. *Phys.**
2930 Morgan, A. P., Preston, Hamilton Co., Ohio. *Bot.* C. Ex.*
2931 Morgan, Henry, 45 Bradford St., Springfield, Mass. *Orn.**
2932 Morgan, Thomas, Conchologist, Somerville, Somerset Co., N. J. *Molluscs.* C. Ex. in shells.*
2933 Morgan, W., A.M., Ass't Ast., Observ., Haverford Coll., Pa.?
2934 Morison Harrison G. O., Minneapolis, Minn. *Geol., Chem., Ast.**
2935 Morley, Edw. W., M.D., Ph.D., Prof. Chem., Adelbert College, Prof. Chem., Cleveland Med. Coll., Cleveland, Ohio. *Chem., especially Gas Analysis.**
2936 Morong, Rev. Thomas, Ashland, Mass. *Phæn. Bot., Vascular Cryptogams, Specialty of Naiadaceæ and Aquatics generally.* C. Ex.*
2937 Morrell, H. K., Gardiner, Me. *Min., Con., Bot.* C.*
2938 Morrell, Jas. J., Nyack-on-Hudson, N. Y. *Min., Mic.* C. Ex.*
2939 Morrill, Albro D., Prof Chem. and Biology, Belmont College, College Hill, Hamilton Co., Ohio. *Biol.* C. Ex.*
2940 Morris, Miss Cornelia F., 123 So. Salina St., Syracuse, N. Y. *Geol., Lithol., Min., Invert. Palæo., Arch., Con.* C. Ex.*
2941 Morris, Galloway, C. E., Tulpohocken St., Germantown, Philadelphia, Pa. *Mic., Diatoms, Desmids, Algæ.* Ex.*
2942 Morris, Rev. Geo. K., Vineland, N. J. *Biol. of Ants.**
2943 Morris, Gouveneur, M.E., Ardsley, N. Y. *Hort., Geol., Min., Metall.**
2944 Morris, J. Cheston, M.D., 1514 Spruce St., Philadelphia, Pa. *Biol. and Hygiene.* C.*
2945 Morris, Rev. John G., D.D., LL.D., 406 N. Green St., Baltimore, Md. *Ent., Mic.* C.*
2946 Morris, Robert T., M.D., New Haven, Ct. *Vertebrates of N. A.* Ex. *Entozoa.*

2947 Morris, Wm., 36 Twelfth St., Norwich, Ct. *Bot., Geol., Physical Min., Molluscs, Radiates.* C. Ex.*
2948 Morrisey, Alfred, St. John, N. B., Can. *Orn.**
2949 Morrison, Chas. F., Pres. Col. State Orn. Ass'n, Vice Pres. Bristol Orn. Club of Mass., Fort Lewis, La Plata Co., Colorado. *Orn., Ool., Mammals, Tax., Osteol.* C.*
2950 Morrison, Leo, S.M., Marshall, Calhoun Co., Ala. *Gen. Nat. Hist.* C. Ex.
2951 Morse, Edw. S., Director Peabody Acad. Sci., Salem, Mass. *Zool., Ethnol.**
2952 Morse, Harmon N., Johns Hopkins Univ., Baltimore, Md. Associate Prof. of Chem.*
2953 Morse, Hobart A., Morristown, St. Lawrence Co., N. Y. *Orn., Ool., Tax.* C. Ex.*
2954 Morse, S. R., County Supt. of Public Instruction, Atlantic City, N. J. *Bot: Marine Algæ, Geol., Min., Ool.* C. Ex.*
2955 Morse, Mrs. Walter, Eaton, Madison Co., N. Y. *Palæo., Geol., Zool., Crust., Molluscs.* C. Ex.*
2956 Morse, Wm. L., Syracuse, N. Y. *Geol., Min., Crystall., Lithol., Orn., Ool.* C. Ex.
2957 Morton, Miss Emily L., P. O. Box 228, Newburgh, N. Y. *Ent: Lepid., Coleopt.* C. Ex.*
2958 Morton, Henry, Ph.D., Pres. Stevens Inst. of Tech., Hoboken, N. J. *Physics, Chem.**
2959 Moser, J. F., Coast Survey Office, Washington, D. C. *Geol., Min.* C. Ex.*
2960 Moses, Alfred J., Instructor in Min., School of Mines, Columbia College, New York, N. Y. *Min.* C. Ex.*
2961 Moses, T. F., A.M., Prof. Nat. Sci., Univ., Urbana, O. *Geol., Gen. Biol., Arch.* C.*
2962 Mosey, E. Richard, 47 Gloucester St., Toronto, Can. *Ent., Ool., Herpetol.* C. Ex.*
2963 Mosgrove, Dr. S. M., 18 Miami St., Urbana, Ohio. *Mic., Histol., and Pathol.?*
2964 Moss, J. Clark, P. C., Mid Lothian P. O., Harper Co., Kans. *Geol., Orn., Ool.* C.
2965 Mote, E. J., Richmond, Ind. *Meteo., Photog., Palæo., Anth., Geol.* C. Ex. L. Sil. fossils for those of other periods.
2966 Moyer, I. S., M.D., Richland Centre, Bucks Co., Pa. *Bot.* C. Will purchase plants from Alaska and Mex. border.*
2967 Mueller, Otto E., Shelby and Madison Sts., Louisville, Ky. *Bot.* C. Ex.*
2968 Mundorff, Edgar A., M.D., 2312 Carson St., Pittsburgh, Pa. *Histol. and Pathology.**
2969 Mundy, Rev. Ezekiel W., Syracuse, N. Y.*
2970 Munroe, Charles E., Prof. Chem. to Torpedo Corps, U. S. A., Torpedo Station, Newport, R. I. *Chem.* Specialty, the Chem. of explosives.*
2971 Munroe, H. S., E.M., Ph.D., Prof. School of Mines, Columbia Coll., 49th St., and 4th Ave., New York, N. Y. *Econ., Geol.**

2972 Munroe, Henry F., 821 West Jackson St., Chicago, Ill. *Bot.* C. Ex.*

2973 Munroe, William C., M.D., Douglass, Butler Co., Kan. *Dermatology, Mic., Diatoms, Infusoria, Bot., Ast., Orn.* C. Ex.

2974 Munson, W. W., M.D., Otisco, Onondaga Co., N. Y. *Gen. Nat. Hist., Mic.**

2975 Murdoch, John, Smithsonian Inst., Washington, D. C. *Zool., Ethnog. (Eskimo), Orn., Arctic Crust.**

2976 Murdock, D. H., Capt. U. S. Army, Fort Douglass, Utah. *Lepid., Coleopt.* C. Ex.?

2977 Murdock, J. B., Lieut. U. S. Navy, Care Navy Dept., Washington, D. C. *Min., Elect.**

2978 Murphy, Edw., 836 Dorchester St., Montreal, Canada. *Mic.* C.*

2979 Murphy, M., Provincial Government Engineer of N. S., Halifax, N. S, Can. *Geol.**

2980 Murphy, P. J., A.M., M.D., Columbia Hospital, Washington, D. C.*

2981 Murray, David J., 1533 Summit St., Kansas City, Mo. *Ool., Geol.* C. Ex.?

2982 Murray, J. Clark, LL D., F.R.S.C., Montreal, Can. *Anth.**

2983 Murray, Seward H., L. B. 3, Sewickey, Pa. *Mic., Protozoa.* C. Ex.

2984 Murray, T. R., 2 Akron Place, Roxbury, Mass. *Mic., Ent., Bot.* C.*

2985 Murtfeldt, Mary E., Kirkwood, Mo. *Ent: Micro-Lepid., Phæn. Bot.**

2986 Musso, George W., jr., Waltham, Mass. *Min.* C. Ex. for good characteristic spec., cabinet size. Correspondence solicited.*

2987 Myers, John A., State Chemist, Prof. Chem., Agricultural College, Oktibbeha Co., Miss. *Min., Chem., Metall.**

2988 Myers, Justus M. T., Fort Madison, Ia. *Gen. Nat. Hist., Coleopt., Lepid., Geol.* C. Ex.*

2989 Myrick, L., Northborough, Mass. *Hort., Agric., Agric. Chem., Spec., Chem. of mineral phosphates and fertilizers.**

2990 Nachtrieb, Henry F., Prof. of Animal Biol., Univ. of Minn., Minneapolis, Minn.*

2991 Naffziger, Wm., Dakota City, Nebraska. *Geol., Min., Inorg. Chem., Zool., Anat.* C. Ex.

2992 Nash, George V., Clifton, N. Y. *Min.* C. Ex.*

2993 Nash, H. W., Pueblo, Colo. *Orn., Tax., Lepid., Photog.* C.*

2994 Nason, Rev. Elias, North Billerica, Mass. *Bot., Met., Acoustics.**

2995 Nason, H. B., Prof. Chem. and Min., R. P. Inst., Troy, N. Y., Dir. of Technical Museum, Pratt Institute, Brooklyn, N. Y. C.*

2996 Nason, William A., A.M., M.D., Algonquin, Ill. *Ent: Coleopt., Invert. Palæo., Moll.* C. Ex. Offers his extensive collections of shells and insects for sale. Desires western and southern plants in ex.*

2997 Naylor, Joseph, Prof. Physics, State Univ., Bloomington, Ind. *Physics* *

2998 Naysmith, Geo., Natchez St., 32nd Ward, Pittsburg, Pa. *Ent.* Desires Macro-lepidoptera of the world, Sphingidæ and Bombycidæ especially.*

2999 Nealis, T. J., 719 Olive St., St. Louis, Mo. *Hort.*, *Min.*, *Elect.* C. Ex.*

3000 Neff, Charles H., Portland, Ct. *Arch.*, *Orn.*, *Ool.* C. Ex.*

3001 Nell, Philip, 437 N. 7th St., Phila., Pa. *Ent: Arach.* C. Ex.*

3002 Nelson, E. T., Ph.D., Prof. Nat. Hist. and Cur. in charge of Univ. Mus., Ohio Wesleyan Univ., Delaware, Ohio. *Geol.*, *Zool.* C. Desires ex. for Museum from all parts of the world. Offers Unionidæ, Strepomatidæ and other F. W. Shells, Helices, Cincinnati Fossils, etc.*

3003 Nelson, E. W., Springersville, Arizona. *Orn.*, *Eth.*?

3004 Nelson, Julius, Baltimore, Md. *Zool.*, *Protozoa and Sponges Sex heredity*, *Fish Embryol.**

3005 Nesbit, Thomas M., Box 316, Lewisburg, Pa. *Anth.*, *Arch.*, *Ent.* C. Ex.*

3006 Nettleton, Chas., 115 Broadway, New York, N. Y. *Palæo.*, *Agric.*, *Geol.*, *Anth.*, *Arch.**

3007 Neüington, Harry M., Washington Univ., St. Louis, Mo. *Geol.*, *Min.*, *Phys.*, *Anat.**

3008 Neumogen, B., Box 2581, New York, N. Y. Purchase and exchange of Lepidoptera of the world. Collectors wanted in all parts of the world. Liberal payments.*

3009 Nevin, Rev. J. C., Los Angeles, Calif. *Bot.* C. Ex. only for Pacific Coast, Arizona and New Mexico at present.*

3010 Newberry, J. S., M.D., LL.D., Prof. Geol. and Palæo., Columbia Coll., New York, N. Y. *Geol.*, *Palæo.*, *Bot.* C.*

3011 Newbury, Prof. Spencer B., Cornell Univ., Ithaca, N. Y. *Chem.*, *Photog.* C. Ex.*

3012 Newby, Dr. J. B., 2640 Washington Ave., St. Louis, Mo. *Ool.*, *Arch.* C. Ex.*

3013 Newcomb, Arthur, Waterbury Centre, Vt. *Bot: Ferns*, *Mosses*, *Fungi*, *Geol*, *Min.*, *Ast.* C. Ex.*

3014 Newcomb, Simon, Nautical Almanac Office, Washington, D. C. *Mathematical Ast.**

3015 Newcomb, W., M.D., Cur. Cornell Univ., Ithaca, N. Y. *Con.**

3016 Newcomb, Wilmon W., 1085 Woodward Ave., Detroit, Mich. *Lepid.* C. Ex. Cocoons, chrysalides and images for ex. First-class specimens only.*

3017 Newcomer, Frisby S., M.D., 82 W. North St., Indianapolis, Ind. *Algæ*, *arranged Diatoms*, *Mic.*, *Infusoria.* C. Ex.*

3018 Newcomer, J. W., M.D., Petersburg, Ill. *Bot.*, *Ent.*, *Mic.* *Orn.*, *Geol. of Coal Measures.**

3019 Newcommer, George, Franklin Groves, Lee Co., Ill. *Arch.* C. Ex.*

3020 Newlin, Prof. Chas. E., Frankport, Clinton Co., Ind. *Bot.*, *Crystall.*, *Metall.*, *Elect.*, *Ast.*, *Orn.*, *Ool.*, *Tax.*, *Coleopt.*, *Orthopt.*, *Crustacea*, *Sponges.* C. Ex.*

3021 Newlon, W. S., M.D., Oswego, Kan. *Med. Bot., Chem., Geol., Min., Palæo., Ent., Arch., Vert.**

3022 Newton, Prof. H. A., Yale Coll., New Haven, Ct. *Ast.**

3023 Nichols, Austin P., S.B., Editor Popular Science News and Boston Journal of Chemistry, 19 Pearl St., Boston, Mass. *Chem., Physics, Min.**

3024 Nichols, D. A. A., Ed. "Journal," Dunkirk, N. Y. *Bot.*

3025 Nichols, Edw. L., Ph.D., University of Kansas, Lawrence, Kan. *Phys, Elect., Ast.**

3026 Nichols, J. H., Easton, Pa. *Ast., Geog., Meteo.**

3027 Nichols, Jason E., Lansing, Mich. *Orn., Ool.* C. Ex.*

3028 Nichols, Wm. Ripley, Mass. Inst. of Tech., Boston, Mass. *Inorg. Chem., Water Supply.?*

3029 Nicholson, H. H., M.A., Prof. Chem., Nebraska State Univ., Lincoln, Neb. *Min.* C. Ex.*

3030 Nickerson, George Y., 28 Pleasant St., New Bedford, Mass. *Con.**

3031 Nickles, J. M., Sparta, Randolph Co., Ill. *Bot., Zool., Palæo., Specialty, fossil Bryozoa.* C. Ex.*

3032 Niedham, Wladimir F. de, Ph.D., M.D., Omaha and Winnebago Indian Agency, Nebraska. *Bot., Hort., Min., Chem., Phys., Elect., Mic., Anat., Histol. Specialty Gramineæ.* C. Ex.

3033 Niles, Wm. H. (Prof. Mass. Inst. Tech.), Boston, Mass. *Geol., Phys. Geog.**

3034 Nipher, Francis E., Prof. Phys., Washington Univ., Pres. St. Louis Acad. Sci., Dir Mo. Weather Service, St. Louis, Mo. *Meteorol., Phys.**

3035 Nissley, J. R., Collector during the winter, Ada, Hardin Co., Ohio. *Geol., Min., Arch.* Coll. of 5000 Spec. Ex.*

3036 Nix, Robert, New Ulm, Minn. *Min., Crystall., Lithol., Phys.* C. Ex.*

3037 Nixon, Chas. F., Pharmacist, Pres. Leominster Botanical Soc., Leominster, Mass. *Min., Bot.* C. Ex.*

3038 Noble, Geo., Savannah, Ga. *Tax., Ool., Orn.* C. Ex.*

3039 Noe, Fletcher M., 130 East New York St., Indianapolis, Ind. Prac. Tax. and dealer in bird skins, lepid., Indian relics, etc. Desires to ex. with foreign correspondents.*

3040 Nolan, Edw. J., M.D., Acad. Nat. Sci., Philadelphia, Pa. *Biol., Bibliog. of Nat. Sci.**

3041 Nolen, Wm. W., Harvard College, Cambridge, Mass. *Bot., Phænogamous Plants, Cryptogamous Plants, Ferns, Lichens, Algæ, Zool., Osteol., Radiates.* C. Ex.*

3042 Nordino, J. N., Broad and N. J. Sts., Mobile, Ala. *Palæo., Bibliog., Anth., Arch., Philol.**

3043 Norris, Basil, M.D., Surgeon U. S. A., 1733 G St., Washington, D. C. *Bot: Hort., Agric., Plants, Elect., Gen. Biol., Anth.?*

3044 Norris, J. W., M.D., Oregon City, Ore. *Arch.**

3045 Norris, William, 516 California St., San Francisco, Calif. *Mic.* C.?

3046 Norton, Alice J., Bristol, Ct. *Bot: Ferns, Orchids.**
3047 Norton, Edw., Farmington, Ct. *Ent: Hymenoptera.**
3048 Norton, Edw. E., 419 Washington St., Boston, Mass. *Gen. Nat. Hist.*
3049 Norton, J. H., Plainville, Onondaga Co., N. Y. *Eth., Arch.* Ex. Prehistoric relics of Iroquois or Six Nations wanted.*
3050 Norton, Mary E. B., San Jose, Calif. *Bot.* C.*
3051 Norton, Oliver D., M.D., 286 W. 4th St., Cincinnati, O. *Bot.?*
3052 Norton, Samuel, 67 Carver St., Boston, Mass.
3053 Norton, Sidney A., Ph.D., LL.D., Prof. Chem., Ohio State Univ., 299 E. Town St., Columbus, Ohio. *Chem.**
3054 Norton, William H., Prof. Cornell Coll., Mt Vernon, Ia., Cur. Museum. *Invert. Palæo., Geol., Min.* Sil. and Devon. fossils of Iowa to ex. List of duplicates for exchange sent on application. C. Ex.*
3055 Nowle, C. Robbins, Chestnut Hill, Phila., Pa. *Min., Arch.* C. Ex.*
3056 Noyes, Wm. A., Ph.D., Prof. of Chem., Rose Polytechnic Institute, Terre Haute, Ind. *Chem., Min.**
3057 Noyes, W. H., D.M.D., Newburyport, Mass. *Mic., Aquaria.* C.*
3058 Numsen, W. H., 18 Light St., Baltimore, Md. *Ast.**
3059 Nunn, R. J., M.D., 119 York St., Savannah, Ga. *Mic., Anth.**
3060 Nutter, Frank H., C.E., Room 14, Johnston Block, Minneapolis, Minn. *Min., Ool., Con.* C. Ex. shells or any desired spec. of this vicinity for birds' eggs.*
3061 Nye, H. B., 101 St. Clair St., Cleveland, Ohio. *Analyt. Chem.**
3062 Oakes, Walter, cor. 9th and Penn Sts., Kansas City, Mo. *Con., Ool.* C.?
3063 Ober, Frederick A., Beverly, Mass. *Orn.**
3064 Oberholtzer, Mrs. S. L., Norristown, Pa. *Ferns, Algæ, Orn., Ool.* C. Ex.*
3065 O'Brien, William D. A., 178 W. North St., Springfield, Ohio. *Marine Objects.* C.*
3066 Obst, C. L., Pittsfield, Pike Co., Ill. *Arch., Prehistoric remains, Min.* C. Ex. Hoeflichst erbitte einen vertausch aller Vorgeschichtlichen Geraetschaften von Stein, Hörn, Kupfer, Thon, Knochen, und Mineralien von den U. S. Europa, und aller Länder. Would sell my entire (fine and rare) collections. Würsche meine grosse und ueberauss feine colection Americanisch vorgeschichtlicher Waffen und Geraetschaften zu verkaufen.*
3067 Odendall, Godfrey, jr., Ph.D., P.O.Box 520, Stapleton, Richmond Co., N. Y. *Bot., Min., Gen. Chem., Physics, Mic., Ast., Zool., Hist., Mathematics, Latin, Greek.**
3068 Odlum, Edw., M.A., B.Sc., Prin. High School, Pembroke, Ont., Canada. *Phæn. Bot., Palæo., Geol., Min., Chem., Elect.* C. Ex.

3069 Ohlendorf, Dr. W. C., Ph.G., 645 Blue Island Ave., Chicago, Ill. *Phæn. and Crypt. Bot: Ferns, Mosses.* C. Ex.*
3070 Ohman-Dumesnil, H. H., A.M., M.D., Editor St. Louis Medical and Surgical Journal, 903 Olive St., St. Louis, Mo. *Mic., Specialty, Human Skin, normal and pathological; general histology.* C. Ex.*
3071 Oliver, Chas. A., M.D., 1507 Locust St., Philadelphia, Pa. *Special Sense Morphology.**
3072 Oliver, J. C., 828 Hope St., Los Angeles, Calif. *Phæn. Bot., Mic., Ool.* C. Ex.
3073 Olmsted, Will. H., Syracuse, N. Y. *Mic.* C. Ex.*
3074 Onderdonk, Cornelius, Rugby, Tenn. *Bot., Diatoms, Hort., Mic., Infusoria.**
3075 Ong, P. L., Hennepin, Ill. *Orn.*
3076 O'Niel, J. D., West Elizabeth, Pa. *Bot., Min., Orn., Ool., Ichth.* C. Ex.?
3077 Orcutt, Charles R., San Diego, Calif. *Ed. "West Am. Scientist" and "The Young Men's Journal," Gen. Sci., Bot., Moll.* Plants, Seeds, Shells, etc., from So. and L. Calif., furnished or collected to order. C. Ex. for books, etc. Young men wanted to assist in scientific work. Correspondence solicited.*
3078 Orcutt, John H., San Diego, Calif. *Con., Ool.* C.*
3079 Ordway, Mrs. E. W., S.B., Newcomb College, Tulane University, New Orleans, La. *Chem.**
3080 Ordway, John M., Tulane Univ., New Orleans, La. *Chem., Biol.**
3081 Orne, John, jr., Cambridge, Mass. *Ast., Phys., Bot., Ent.* C.*
3082 Orton, Prof. Edward, Columbus, Ohio. *Strat. Geol.* C.*
3083 Osband, L. A., A.M., Prof. Biol. and Geol., State Normal School, Ypsilanti, Mich. *Bot., Geol., Zool.**
3084 Osborn, Mrs. Ada M., Waterville, Oneida Co., N. Y. *Palæo., Con.* C.*
3085 Osborn, A. O., Waterville, Oneida Co., N. Y. *Geol., Devonian and Lower Helderberg.**
3086 Osborn, B. F., A.M., Rippey, Greene Co., Ia. *Palæo., Geol., Herpetol.* C. Ex.
3087 Osborn, Chas. E., 1421 Fairmont Ave., Philadelphia, Pa. *Con., Min.* C. Ex. Dealer.*
3088 Osborn, Francis A., 43 Milk St., Boston, Mass. *Bot., Mic.**
3089 Osborn, Prof. Henry Fairfield, Princeton, N. J. *Comp. Anat., Palæo., Emb., Vertebrates.**
3090 Osborn, Henry Leslie, Ph.D. (Johns Hopkins Univ.), Purdue Univ., Lafayette, Ind. Editor American Monthly Microscopical Journal. *Animal Morphology.* C. Ex.*
3091 Osborn, Prof. H. S., LL.D., Oxford, Ohio. *Min., Chem.**
3092 Osborn, Herbert, M.Sc., Prof. Ent. and Zool., Ag. Coll., Ames, Ia. *Ent.* C. Ex. Desires Hemiptera and espec. Mallophaga.*
3093 Osborn, J. A., 141 Austin St., Cambridgeport, Mass. *Min., Emb., Gen. Nat. Hist.* C. Ex.?
3094 Osborn, Lucian M., LL.D., Prof. Phys. Sci., Madison Univ., Hamilton, N. Y.*

3095 Osborne, James H., M.D., Southington, Hartford Co., Ct. *Elect.*, *Mic.*, *Bibliog.*, *Herpetol.*
3096 Osborne, John W., 212 Delaware Ave., N. E., Washington, D. C. *Chem.*, *Photog.*, *Meteo.**
3097 Osgood, F. Story, Box 517, Newburyport, Mass. *Min.*, *Arch.* C.*
3098 Osgood, John W., Cincinnatus, Cortland Co., N. Y. *Mic.*, *Ast.*
3099 Osler, William, M.D., F.R.C.P. Lond., Prof. Clin. Medicine, Univ. of Penn., Philadelphia, Pa. *Gen. Biol.*, *Entozoa*, *Protozoa.*?
3100 Osmond, I. Thornton, A.M., Prof. Physics, State College, Centre Co., Pa *Physics.**
3101 Osmun, Gilbert R., Detroit, Mich. *Astronomy.**
3102 Owen, David A., Prof. Biol., Franklin, Ind. *Bot.*, *Geol.* C.*
3103 Owen, Prof. E. T., Madison, Dane Co., Wis. *Native and Exotic Lepid.* C. Ex. Desires price-lists of Lepid. Will send list of nearly one thousand duplicates on application. Many species from Mexico, Japan, etc.*
3104 Owen, Prof. Richard, M.D., LL.D., New Harmony, Ind. *Phys.*, *Dynam.*, *Geol.*, *Physiography*, *Seismology.**
3105 Owen, S. J., North Turner Bridge, Me. *Min.*, *Ool.* C. Ex.?
3106 Owens, Chas. S., 94 Steuben St., Utica, N. Y. *Eth.*, *Am. Arch.* C.
3107 Owens, Mary E., 270 W. 7th St., Cincinnati, Ohio. *Chem.*, *Phys.*?
3108 Owens, Wm. G., A.M., Prof. Chem. and Phys., Bucknell Univ., Lewisburgh, Pa. *Chem.*, *Phys.*, *Elect.**
3109 Oyster, Dr. J. H., Paola, Kan. *Med. Bot.* Ex. for Herbarium specimens from all parts of the world. Wish to accumulate a complete and general botanical library.*
3110 Packard, A. S., Prof. Zool. and Geol., Brown Univ., Providence, R. I. *Gen. Zool.* Desires Thysanura and Bombycidæ.*
3111 Page, Prof. John R., M.D., Univ. of Virginia, Va. *Zool.*, *Agric.*, *Bot.* C. Ex.
3112 Page, John W., Metamora, Woodford Co., Ill. *Geol.* C.*
3113 Paine, Rev. Prof. J. A., Ph.D., Tarrytown, N. Y. *Phæn. Bot.*, *Ferns.* C. Ex.*
3114 Palmer, Asher, Kennett Square, Chester Co., Pa. *Ool.*, *Tax.* C.*
3115 Palmer, Chase, Ph.D., Chemist, Tufts College, College Hill, Mass.
3116 Palmer, F. S., Naturalist, Berkeley, Alameda Co., Calif. *Orn.*, *Ool.*, *Stamps.* C. Ex.*
3117 Palmer, F. W., Theol. Sem., Auburn, N. Y. *Bot.* C.*
3118 Palmer, T. C., jr., 22 N. Front St., Philadelphia, Pa. *Bot.* C. *Analyt. Chem.*, *Chemistry of veg. coloring matters and dyers' chemicals.**
3119 Palmer, Wm., Modeler and Taxidermist, Nat. Museum, Washington, D. C. *Orn.*, *Ferns*, *Tax.* C. Ex.*

3120 Pammel, Louis H., La Crosse, Wis. *Phæn. Bot., Fungi.* C. Ex.

3121 Panton, J. H., M.A., F.G.S., Prof. Geol. and Nat. Hist., Agric. Coll., Guelph, Ontario, Canada. *Bot., Palæo., Geol., Ent.* C.*

3122 Panton, M. H., Oak Hill, Clay Co., Kan. *Phæn. Bot.**

3123 Pardee, Walter S., 1029 Emerson Ave., North Minneapolis, Minn. *Min., Inorg. Chem., Elect., Photog., Philol.* C. Ex.*

3124 Parish, Jennie L., M.D., Salem, Oregon. *Anat., Invert. and Vert.* ?

3125 Parish, Samuel B., San Bernardino, Calif. *Bot.* C. Ex.*

3126 Parish, Wm. H., M.D., 1435 Spruce St., Philadelphia, Pa. *Emb., Anat., Osteol.**

3127 Park, Austin F., 31 Boardman Building, Troy, N. Y. *Orn.* C. Ex.*

3128 Park, Frank E., 922 Broadway, So. Boston, Mass. *Ent.* C. Ex.*

3129 Park, John R., M.D., Pres. Univ. of Deseret, Salt Lake City, Utah. *Crypt. and Phæn. Bot., Zool.* C. Ex.*

3130 Park, Roswell, M.D., Prof. Surgery, Univ. of Buffalo, 510 Delaware Ave., Buffalo, N. Y. *Bacteriology.**

3131 Parke, Davis & Co., Herbarium, Detroit, Mich. *Bot.* C. Ex.*

3132 Parker, A. J., M.D., Acad. Nat. Sci., N. 9th St., Philadelphia, Pa. *Vert. Anat.**

3133 Parker, A. T., Lexington, Ky. *Mic., Histol., Photog.* C. Ex.?

3134 Parker, Chas. B., M.D., M.R.C.S. Eng., 352 Erie St., Cleveland, Ohio. *Crypt. Plants, Histol.* C. Ex.*

3135 Parker, Edw. Melville, M.A., St. Paul's School, Concord, N. H. *Phæn. Bot.* C.*

3136 Parker, Frederick A., 1258 Iowa St., Dubuque, Iowa. *Bot: Crypt. Plants, Palæo., Invert., Mic., Min.* C. Ex.*

3137 Parker, Geo. Howard, Academy of Natural Sciences, Phila., Pa. *Bot., Zool., Gen. Biol., Ent.*

3138 Parker, Harry G., The Roach Ship Works, Chester, Pa. *Orn., Ool.* C. Ex.*

3139 Parker, Prof. H. W., Iowa Coll., Grinnell, Iowa. *Mic., Geol., Gen. Zool.* C.*

3140 Parker, Harvey D., Greeley, Weld Co., Colo. *Min.* C.*

3141 Parker, Dr. J. C., State Fish Commissioner, Grand Rapids, Mich. *Ichth.* C. Ex.*

3142 Parker, John D., Ph.D., B.D., Fort Riley, Kansas. *Arch., Meteorol.**

3143 Parker, P. H., Washington, Tazewell Co., Ill. *Min., Palæo., Con., Coins.* C. Ex.*

3144 Parker, Thomas J., Supt. Kalbfleisch Chem. Works, Bergen Point, N. J. *Chem.* ?

3145 Parkes, Wm. J., 1 D'Arcy St., Toronto, Canada. C. Ex. *Ent: Hymenop., Lepid., Dipt., Coleopt., Hemipt., Orthopt., Neuropt.**

3146 Parkhurst, Alfred L., San Luis Obispo, Calif. *Orn.*, *Ool.*, *Tax.* C. Ex.*
3147 Parkhurst, Henry M., 173 Gates Ave., Brooklyn, N. Y. *Ast.**
3148 Parkhurst, V. P., East Templeton, Mass. *Gen. Nat. Hist.*, *Spec. Tropical Bot.*, Ed. Coll. for Schools and Colleges. Photographer and Publisher of "Picturesque Jamaica," selections of Tropical Scenery. Present address, 18 Church St., Kingston, Jamaica, W. I.*
3149 Parkinson, Daniel B., Carbondale, Ill. *Geol.*, *Phys.*, *Chem.*, *Min.*, *Tax.* C.*
3150 Parks, John K., 29 Mechanic St., Portland, Me. *Mic.*, *Botany.* C. Ex.*
3151 Parmele, George L., M.D., D.M.D., 17 Haynes St., Hartford, Ct. *Oral Sci.*, *Ent.*, *Gen. Biol.**
3152 Parmele, Mrs. G. L., 17 Haynes St., Hartford, Ct. *Ferns*, *Ent.*, *Con.**
3153 Parr, Thomas W., Barron, Wis. *Chem.*, *Phæn. Bot.* C. Ex.*
3154 Parry, Dr. C. C., Davenport, Ia. *Bot.**
3155 Parshall, S. E., Shortsville, Ont. Co., N. Y. *Tax.* C. of birds' eggs. Ex.*
3156 Parsons, Newell A., Enfield St., Thompsonville, Hartford Co., Ct. *Arch.*, *Ool.*, *Moll.* C.*
3157 Parvin, Prof. T. S., Iowa City, Ia. *Bot.*, *Geol.*, *Min.?*
3158 Patch, Edgar L., Ph.G., Prof. Theory and Practice of Pharm., Mass. Coll., 109 Green St., Boston, Mass. *Pharm.*, *Chem.**
3159 Paterson, Edw. M., M.D., Cor. Broadway and 12th St., Oakland, Calif. *Geol.*, *Chem.*, *Phys.*, *Gen. Biol.*, *Emb.*, *Anat.*, *Anth.* C. Ex.
3160 Patrick, G. E , 27 Kilby St., Boston, Mass. *Chem.*, *Min.**
3161 Patrick, J. J. R., D.D.S., Belleville, St. Clair Co., Ill. *Anth.*, *Arch.*, *Eth.* C. Ex.*
3162 Pattee, Asa F., M.D., 94 West Springfield St., Boston, Mass. Prof. Coll. of Physicians and Surgeons. *Bot.* C. Ex.*
3163 Patterson, H. N., Oquawka, Ill. *Bot.* C. Ex.*
3164 Patterson, John P., A.M., Supt. of Schools, Pensacola, Escambia Co., Florida. Gulf Shells. C. Ex.*
3165 Paton, Edw. A., M.D., 1228 Second Ave. South, Minneapolis, Minn. *Ool.*, *Lepid.* C. Ex
3166 Patten, Horace B., Mineralogist, Washington, D. C. Ass't in Min. at Heidelberg.*
3167 Patton, Robert M., 312 N. 33d St., Philadelphia, Pa. *Min.*, *Ent* , *Gen. Nat. Hist.* C.*
3168 Patton, W. H., Waterbury, Ct. *Bot.*, *Ent: Hymenop.* C.?
3169 Paul, Henry M., Ass't Astronomer at Naval Observ., Washington, D. C. *Ast.*, *Phys.*, *Meteo.**
3170 Paul, Willard A., M.D., Rock Island, Ill. *Geol.*, *Min.*, *Chem.*, *Vert. Anat.*, *Arch.*, *Orn.* C. Ex.*
3171 Payne, William B., Ph.D., Prof. Physical Sciences, Tabor College, Tabor, Fremont Co., Ia. *Min.*, *Chem.*, *Physics*, *Meteo.**

3172 Payne, William M., Teacher Chem. and Phys., West Division High School, Chicago, Ill. *Bot., Zool., Chem., Phys.**

3173 Payne, William W., Prof. Math. and Ast., and Director of Carleton Coll. Obs., Northfield, Rice Co., Minn. *Ast.**

3174 Peabody, Selim H., Ph.D., LL.D., Pres. University of Illinois, Champaign, Ill. *Phys., Ent.* C.*

3175 Peacock, William F., Marysville, Yuba Co., Calif. *Orn.* C. Ex.*

3176 Peale, A. C., M.D., U. S. Geol. Survey, Washington, D. C. *Geol.**

3177 Pearce, James H., 28 Front St. West, Toronto, Can. *Algæ, Desmids, Diatoms, Sponges, Protozoa, Infusoria.* C.*

3178 Pearce, Otis E., Ithaca, N. Y. *Bot., Mic., Orthopt.* C. Ex.

3179 Pearce, Robert E., North Hannibal, Oswego Co., N. Y. *Mammals, Orn., Ool., Tax.* C. Ex.*

3180 Pearshall, Richard F., 44 Monroe Place, Brooklyn, N. Y. *Coleopt., Lepid.* C. Ex.*

3181 Pearson, Fred. S., College Hill, Mass. *Chem., Met.?*

3182 Pearson, Gustavus C., Danville, Vermillion Co., Ills. *Min., Orn., Zool.* C.*

3183 Pease, Arthur D., A.M., Wilson, Niagara Co., N. Y. *Bot.* C. Desires to ex. Many duplicates. Carices and Filices especially desired.*

3184 Pease, Frederic N., Box 630, Altoona, Pa. *Bot., Chem., Mosses.* C. Ex.*

3185 Pease, James L , L. Box 164, Chicopee, Mass. Manufacturer of specialties for the Microscope. C.

3186 Peaslee, F. J., Colby Academy, New London, N. H. *Have fine Beryl, Tourmaline and Staurolite and many varieties of Quartz to ex. for Fossil Corals, etc.**

3187 Peck, Charles H., State Botanist, Albany, N. Y. *Bot: Fungi.* C.*

3188 Peck, Emmeline W., East Orange, New Jersey. *Bot., Min.* C. Ex.*

3189 Peck, Geo. D., La Porte City, Iowa. *Orn., Ool., Tax.**

3190 Peck, Harold S., 472 Broadway, Albany, N. Y. *Min.* C. Ex.*

3191 Peck, James I., Biol. Lab., Williamstown, Mass. *Org. Chem., Emb., Vert. Anat., Anth., Histol.**

3192 Peckham, B. J., Box 396, Westerly, R. I. *Ool., Gen. Nat. Hist.* C. Ex.*

3193 Peckham, Geo. W., Teacher Biol., High School, Milwaukee, Wis. *Comp. Anat., Arachnida.* C.*

3194 Peckham, Stephen Farnum, Chemist, 159 Olney St., Providence, R. I. *Bot., Min., Chem.* C. Ex.*

3195 Peckham, W. C., Adelphi Academy, Brooklyn, N. Y. *Bot., Phys., Elect., Ast.* C. Ex.*

3196 Pedrick, William R., Lawrence, Mass. *Geol., Min., Arch.**

3197 Peet, Stephen D., Editor American Antiquarian, Clinton, Wis. *Arch., Eth.*

3198 Peffer, Geo. P., Pewaukee, Waukesha Co., Wis. *Hort.**

3199 Peirce, Chas. S , 209 E. 15th St., New York, N. Y. Ass't U. S. Coast Surv. *Geodesy, Meteorology, Gravitation, Ast., Optics, Math., Logic, Bibliog.*

3200 Peirce, James Mills, Prof Math., Harvard University, Cambridge, Mass.*

3201 Peirce, Warren, Garrettsville, Ohio. *Con., Geol., Min., Ent.* C. Ex. L. and F. W. Shells and Ent. of Ohio, for Marine and other Shells.*

3202 Peirson, Miss Katherine, Zoological artist, 13 Barton Square, Salem, Mass. *Drawings made in ink or pencil for stone engraving or photo-lithography.**

3203 Pember, F. T., Granville, Washington Co., N. Y. *Ool.* C. Ex. A large quantity of duplicates in sets for exchange or for sale.*

3204 Pemberton, Henry, 1947 Locust St., Philadelphia, Pa. *Chem., Geol., Min., Crystall., Arch.**

3205 Pemberton, Henry, jr., 1947 Locust St., Philadelphia, Pa. *Chem.**

3206 Penfield, Saml. L., Sheffield Scientific School, New Haven, Ct. *Min., Chem.**

3207 Pengra, C., M.D., Ph.C., Prof. Mat. Med. and Bot., Mass. College of Pharmacy, and Prof. Hist., Boston Dent. Coll., Boston, Mass. *Mat. Med., Bot., Mic.**

3208 Penhallow, Prof. D. P., McGill Univ., Montreal, Can. *Bot., Veg. Physiol., and Diseases of Plants, Mic.* Dir. Montreal Bot. Gar.*

3209 Pennock, C. J., Kennett Square, Chester Co., Pa. *Orn., Ool.,* C. Ex.*

3210 Pennock, Edw., 805 Franklin St., Philadelphia, Pa. *Mic., Bot.**

3211 Pennock, T., M.D., Media, Pa. *Orn., Ool.**

3212 Pennypacker, Charles H., Memb. Acad. Nat. Sci., West Chester, Pa. *Min., Con, Arch., Mic., Bot.* Importer and Dealer in Fine Cabinet Minerals and rare Land and Marine Shells. Examples sent upon approval.*

3213 Pennypacker, Henry, 138 Mt. Auburn St., Cambridge, Mass. *Min.*

3214 Pennypacker, J. T., L. B. 13, Philadelphia, Pa. *Bot., Ent.*?

3215 Pepoon, Dr. H. S., B.S., Lewistown, Fulton Co., Ill. *Bot., Min., Phæn. and Crypt. Plants, Ferns, Orn., Tax., Ent., Lepid., Coleopt.* C. Ex.*

3216 Percy, Henry C., Norfolk, Va. *Hort., Photog* C.*

3217 Pergande, Theo., Ass't Ent., Dept. Agric., Washington, D. C. *Hymenop., Coleopt. Thripidæ a specialty.* C.

3218 Perkins, George H., Prof. Nat. Hist., Univ. of Vt., Burlington, Vt. *Bot., Palæo., Arch., Zool.* C. Ex.

3219 Perkins, Herbert B., S.B., Prof. Math. and Ast., Lawrence Univ., Appleton, Wis.

3220 Perkins, L. T., M.D., Salem, Mass. *Microscopy.*

3221 Perkins, Maurice, M.D., Union Coll. and Albany Med. Coll., Schenectady, N. Y. *Chem.**

3222 Perley, Dr. T. F., 116 Danforth St., Portland, Me. *Ent.*, *Bot.* C. ?
3223 Perot, Chas. P., 252 No. Broad St., Phila., Pa. *Gen. Sci.**
3224 Perot, Elliston J., 5103 Main St., Germantown, Phila., Pa. *Ent: Neuropt.*, *Lepid.*, *esp. Hemipt.**
3225 Perry, Mrs. E. R., South Paris, Oxford Co., Me. *Min.* C. Ex.*
3226 Perry, Rev. Edw. A., Fort Plain, N. Y. *Min.*, *Mic.* C. Ex.*
3227 Perry, Edw. F., P. O. Box 5, Putnam, Ct. *Ent: Lepid.* C. Ex.*
3228 Perry, Troup D., Savannah, Ga. *Ool.* C. Ex.*
3229 Perry, N. H., South Paris, Oxford Co., Me. *Min.* C. Collector and dealer in minerals, geological specimens and gems. List sent on application.*
3230 Perry, S. G., D.D.S., 46 W. 37th St., New York, N. Y. *Mic.**
3231 Peter, Alfred M., Lexington, Ky. *Analyt. Chem.*, *Phæn. Bot.**
3232 Peter, R., M.D., Chemist to Ky. Geol. Surv., and Prof. Chem. and Phys., Lexington, Ky. *Chem.**
3233 Peters, C. H. F., Clinton, N. Y. *Ast.**
3234 Peters, Rev. J. E., Mayo Landing, Atlantic Co., N. J. *Mic.*, *Bot.*, *Zool.*, *Geol.*, *Min.* C.*
3235 Peters, Thomas M., A.M., Ex-Judge, Moulton, Ala. *Bot.?*
3236 Peterson, J. P., Prof. in the Danish Theological Coll. of Am., Luck, Polk Co., Wis. *Bot.*, *Zool.*, *Geol.*, *Orn.* C. Ex.*
3237 Peticolas, C. L., 635 8th St., Richmond, Va. *Mic: Diatomaceæ.* C. Ex.*
3238 Pettee, Edw. F., C.E., LL.B., Room 10, 257 Washington St., Boston, Mass. *Elect.*, *Sponges.**
3239 Pettee, Wm. H., Prof. Min., Econ. Geol. and Mining Engineering, Univ. Mich., Ann Arbor, Mich. *Mining and Geol.**
3240 Pettet, J., A.M., M.D., Pettet Animal Vaccine Farm, Mayfield St., Cleveland, Ohio, also, National Union Vaccine Farm, Englewood, Ill.
3241 Pettingell, Alfred, Hudson, Summit Co., Ohio. *Molluscs*, *Coleopt.* C. Ex.
3242 Phares, David L., A.M., M.D., Agricultural College, Oktibbeha Co., Miss. *Gen. Bot.*, *Geol.*, *Mic.* C. Ex. in Botany.*
3243 Phelps, Albert H., M.D., Abilene, Dixon Co., Kans. Fine collection of coal from 25 mines in Kansas, Neb., Colo., Ind. Terr., Texas, Mo., Ill., Wyoming Terr. and Calif. to exchange for marine and land shells (attractive spec. only) perfect fossils, minerals or prehistoric relics.*
3244 Philips, G. M., A.M., Ph.D., State Normal Sch., West Chester, Chester Co., Pa. *Math.*, *Ast.*, *Min.* C. Ex.*
3245 Phillips, Andrew W., Ph.D., Ass't Prof. Math., Yale Coll., 184 York St., New Haven, Ct.*
3246 Phillips, Chas. D., Rome, Oneida Co., N. Y. *Palæo.*, *Arch.* C. Ex.
3247 Phillips, Henry, jr., A.M., Ph.D., Sec. Am. Philos. Soc., 320 S. 11th St., Philadelphia, Pa. *Bibliog.*, *Anth.*, *Arch.*, *Eth.* *Ethnog.*, *Philol.*, *Numis.**

3248 Phillips, T. S., German Inst. Building, Buffalo, N. Y. *Preparations of tooth Sections for Mic.* C. Ex.?
3249 Phillips, Victor E., M.S., Ph.B., Olney, Richland Co., Ill. *Palæo., Invert., Geol., Min., Crystall., Analyt. and Inorg. Chem., Mic., Molluscs, Radiates.* C. Ex.*
3250 Phin, John, 294 Broadway, New York, N. Y. *Mic.**
3251 Phinney, Arthur J., M.D., Asst. Ind. Geol. Survey, Muncie, Delaware Co., Ind. *Bot., Geol., Min., Palæo.* C.*
3252 Phippen, Geo. D., Treasurer of the Essex Institute, Salem, Mass. *Bot.**
3253 Pickering, E. C., Dir. Havard Coll. Obs., Cambridge, Mass. *Ast.**
3254 Pickering, Wm. H., Harvard Observatory, Cambridge, Mass. *Ast., Photog.**
3255 Pierce, A. J., Civil Eng., Aberdeen, Brown Co., Dakota. *Curios in general, Fonetic Alfabets a specialty.**
3256 Pierce, David F., South Britain, New Haven Co., Ct. *Geol., Min.* C. Ex.*
3257 Pierce, Edwin H., 16 Seminary St., Auburn, Cayuga Co., N. Y. *Ent: Lepid.* C. Ex.*
3258 Pierce, Ella V., Box 66, West Brookfield, Worcester Co., Mass. *Zool., Orn., Tax.* C. Ex.*
3259 Pierce, Granville T., A.M., 37 Austin St., Somerville, Mass. *Min., Arch.* C. Ex.*
3260 Pierce, James O., Minneapolis, Minn. *Min., Geog.**
3261 Pierce, John, Box 1063, Providence, R. I. *Mic.* C. Ex.?
3262 Pierce, Newton B., Ludington, Mason Co., Mich. *Ent., especially Neuroptera.* Desires to obtain species of the genus Myrmeleon by ex. or otherwise. C.*
3263 Piersol, G. A., 1110 Spring Garden St., Phila., Pa. *Histol., Photog.* C. Ex.
3264 Pierson, Allen, M.D., Spencer, Ind. *Mic., Vert. Anat., Histol.* C.*
3265 Pike, J. W., Vineland, N. J. *Geol.* C. Lectures on Geol., Min., Palæo.
3266 Pike, Nicolas, 575 Carlton Ave., Brooklyn, N. Y. *Algæ, Mic., Photog., Arachnol., Herpetol.* C. Ex.*
3267 Pilate, G. R., Palmer St., Dayton, Ohio. *Ent: Lepid.**
3268 Pilling, James C., Box 591, Washington, D. C. *Eth., Geol., Bibliog.**
3269 Pillsbury, F. I., Dubuque, Ia. *Bot.* C. Ex.
3270 Pillsbury, J. H., Prof. Biol., Smith Coll., Northampton, Mass. *Bot., Zool., Mic.**
3271 Pillsbury, Martha H., New London, N. H. *Min.* C. Ex.*
3272 Pilsbry, H. A., Acad. of Nat. Sci., Phila., Pa. *L. and F. W. Moll.* Alcoholic specimens of fresh water Molluscs especially desired. Offers shells of N. Miss. Valley and Texas, also mounted odontophores.*
3273 Pinckney, Eugene, Dixon, Lee Co., Ill. *Crypt. Bot., Mic., Emb., Histol.* C. Ex.*
3274 Pine, Geo., Trenton, N. J. *Gen.* C. Ex.*

3275 Pineo, A. J., A.B., Kentville, N. S., Can. Editor Canadian Science Monthly. *Geol.*, *Min.*, *Con.* C. Wishes Mins., M. L. and F. W. Shells and fossils from all parts of Am. in exchange for fine Zeolites, etc.

3276 Pindar, L. O., Hickman, Fulton Co., Ky. *Arch.*, *Mammals*, *Orn.*, *Ool.*, *Herpetol.**

3277 Pinkerton, T. H., M.D., Oakland, Calif.*

3278 Pirz, Anthony, Long Island City, N. Y. *Chem.*, *Geol.**

3279 Pitman, John, Capt. U. S. Ordnance, Fort A. Lincoln Ordnance Depot, D. T. *Analyt. Chem.**

3280 Pitman, Prof. Stephen M., A.M.B., 134 Mathewson St., Providence, R. I.*

3281 Pitt, Wm. H., M.D., 2 Arlington Pl., Buffalo, N. Y. *Chem.*, *Phys.*, *Geol.*, *Palæo.**

3282 Plank, E. N., Wyandotte, Kan. *Bot: Flora of Kan.* C.*

3283 Plank, Wm. H., Wyandotte, Kansas. *Bot.*, *Min.* Correspondence. Ex.*

3284 Plapp, F. W., A.B., 1331 Jackson St., Dubuque, Iowa. *Palæo.*, *Geol.*, *Min.*, *Physics.* C. Ex.*

3285 Platt, Franklin, 615 Walnut St., Philadelphia, Pa. *Geol.**

3286 Platt, Theron E., Redding Ridge, Fairfield Co., Ct. *Bot.*, *esp. Forestry and Woods*, *Min.*, *Indian Implements*, *Experimental Agriculture.* C. Ex. in specialties. Desires Central and South Am. wood specimens in ex. for those of U. S.*

3287 Playter, John B., Bristow, Butler Co., Iowa. *Crypt. Bot.*, *Min.*, *Mic.*, *Ent.* C. Ex.*

3288 Pleas, C. E., Spiceland, Indiana. *Tax.*, *Orn.*, *Ool.* C. Ex.*

3289 Pleas, Elwood, Dunreith, Henry Co., Ind. *Palæo.*, *Geol.*, *Min.*, *Arch.*, *Ent.*, *Con.* C. Ex.*

3290 Plimpton, Fannie O., Litchfield, Maine. *Bot.*, *Ferns*, *Mosses*, *Fungi*, *Min.* (*specialty Sodalite*, *Elæolite*). Sealed correspondence only. C. Ex.*

3291 Plimpton, F. S., San Diego, San Diego Co., Calif. *Filices*, *Orn.**

3292 Plummer, Gordon, 244 Purchase St., Boston, Mass. *Orn.* C.*

3293 Poggenburg, Justus F., 447 E. 57th St., New York City. *Bot.* C.*

3294 Pohlman, Dr. Julius, Dir. Mus. of Soc. Nat. Sci., Prof. Physiology, Univ. of Buffalo, Buffalo, N. Y. *Invert. Palæo.*, *Geol.* C.*

3295 Pond, Edwin J., Drawer 19, Austin, Texas. *Mosses*, *Invert.*, *Cretaceous and Stratigraphical Geol.*, *Sponges.* C. Ex.*

3296 Pond, Fred E. (Will Wildwood), 39 Park Row, New York City. *Bibliog.*, *Zool.*, *Mam.*, *Orn.*, *Ool.* C. Ex.*

3297 Pond, G. Gilbert, Instructor in Chem., Amherst College, Amherst, Mass. *Gen. Chem.**

3298 Pool, Isaac A., Escanaba, Delta Co., Mich. *Ent.*, *Min.*, *Con.* C. Ex.*

3299 Pope, T. E., Ames, Ia. *Chem.?*
3300 Popenoe, Edwin A., A.M., Prof. Hort. and Ent., State Agric. Coll., Manhattan, Kans. *Geog. Dist., Ent: Coleopt., Hemiptera.**
3301 Porter, Prof. Albert B., Richmond High School, Richmond, Ind. *Physics, Chem.*
3302 Porter, C. H., A.M., M.D., 55 Eagle St., Albany, N. Y. *Chem., Phys.**
3303 Porter, C. J. A., A.M., Oakland, Calif. *Geol., Nat. Hist.* C. Ex.*
3304 Porter, James A., B.A , M.D., Kemptville, Ont., Canada. *Phæn. Bot., Ferns, Orn., Ool., Ent: Lepid.* C. Ex.*
3305 Porter, Thos. C., Prof. of Bot. and Zool., Lafayette College, Easton, Pa. *N. Am. Bot.* C. Ex. Introduced plants desired.*
3306 Poteat, W. L., A.B., Prof. Nat. Hist., Wake Forest Coll., Wake Co., N. C.*
3307 Potter, B. S., Prof. Illinois Wesleyan Univ., Bloomington, Ill. *Bot., Mic.**
3308 Potter, Frederick G., 47 W. 83d St., between 8th and 9th Aves., New York, N. Y. *Geol., Ent.* C. Ex.*
3309 Potter, W. B., A.M., E.M., Prof. Mining and Met., Washington Univ., St. Louis, Mo. *Geol., Met.* C. Ex. minerals, ores and fossils.*
3310 Potter, Wm. P., 60 Prospect St., Norwich, Ct. *Physical Geol., Min., Lithol , Molluscs, Radiates.* C. Ex.*
3311 Potts, Edward, 228 S. 3d St., Philadelphia, Pa. *Mic., Invert. Zool.* Desires spec. of Am. and foreign F. W. sponges. C.*
3312 Powell, Jehu Z., Ph.D., M.D., 220 6th St., Logansport, Ind. *Bot., Chem., Mic., Anat.* C. Ex.*
3313 Powell, J. W., Ph.D., LL.D., 910 M St., N. W., Box 591, Washington, D. C. *Anth., Geol.**
3314 Power, Frederick B., Ph.D., Prof. Pharm. and Mat. Med., Univ. of Wis., Madison, Wis. *Phæn. Bot., Chem., Mic.**
3315 Powers, C. H., Manual Training School, 12th St. and Michigan Ave., Chicago, Ill. *Palæo., Philol.* C. Fine palæontological cabinet of 800 species, all mounted and named, for sale. Many new and undescribed Trenton species; also library on subjects for sale with cabinet.*
3316 Powers, Miss Hattie E., Litchfield, Kennebec Co., Me. *Min.* C. Ex.
3317 Powers, Jennie, P. O. Box 890, Brattleboro, Vt. *Min., Tax., Ent.* C.*
3318 Praeger, Wm. E., Keokuk, Iowa. *Orn., Ool.* C. Ex.*
3319 Pratt, Rev. Geo. B., Oak Park, Ill. *Orn.**
3320 Pratt, Stillman B., Marlboro, Mass. *Anth.**
3321 Pratt, W. H., Davenport, Ia. *Arch., Physics, Con.**
3322 Pratt, Wm. H., 49 Clifford St., Taunton, Mass. *Mic., Diatoms.* C. Ex.*
3323 Pray, Fannie Motley, care B. S. Pray & Co., 80 State St., Boston, Mass. *Ferns.* C. Ex.*

3324 Pride, Sub-Curator, Toronto Univ., Toronto, Can. *Zool.*
3325 Prentiss, Albert N., Prof. Bot., Hort., and Abor., Cornell Univ., Ithaca, N. Y. *Bot.**
3326 Prentiss, D. W., M.D., 1101 14th St., N. W., Washington, D. C. *Orn.*, *Nat. Hist.*, *Medicine.* C.*
3327 Prescott, A. B., Director Chem. Lab., Univ. of Mich., Ann Arbor, Mich. *Analyt. and Org. Chem.**
3328 Prescott, Cyrus D., Rome, N. Y. *Min.* C. Desires to sell collection.*
3329 Preston, Chas. H., S.B., 161 Tremont St., Boston, Mass. *Bot.*, *Min.*, *Chem.*, *Mic.* Bot. Coll.*
3330 Preston, C. S., South Hadley, Mass. *Tax.*, *Orn.* C.?
3331 Preston, H. L., Ward's Nat. Sci. Estab., Rochester, N. Y. *Min.**
3332 Preston, H. W., 63 Parade St., Providence, R. I. *Phæn. Bot.* C.
3333 Price, Cyrus A., A.M., M.D., 126 State St., Chicago, Ill. *Bot.*, *Mic.*, *Biol.*, *Anth.*, *Arch.*, *Photog.*, *esp. Ophthalmology and Otology.* C. Ex.
3334 Price, Justin L., Manston, Juneau Co., Wis. *Bot.*, *Hort.*, *Geol.*, *Arch.*, *Tax.**
3335 Price, Wm. W., Riverside, San Bernardino Co., Calif. *Orn.* C. Ex.*
3336 Pride, H. A., Holland Patent, N. Y. *Palæo.*, *Min.*, *Moll.*, *Corals*, *Arch.* C. Ex. fossils from Utica slate for other spec. Will buy.*
3337 Prime, Frederick, 222 S. 3d St., Philadelphia, Pa. *Geol.**
3338 Prime, Henry, Riverdale Station, New York, N. Y. *Geog. Dist.*, *Land Moll.* C. Ex.*
3339 Prime, Temple, 26 Broad St., New York, N. Y. *Con.**
3340 Prindle, M. S., Tucson, Ariz. *Fossil flora of Grundy Co.*, *Mazon Creek*), *Coal Measures.* C. Ex.?
3341 Pringle, C. G., A.M., East Charlotte, Vt. *Bot.* C. Ex. Offers for sale or exchange Plants of North Mexico.*
3342 Pringle, H. N., Thetford, Vt. *Ool.*, *Min.* C. Ex.*
3343 Pritchett, C. W., Dir. Morrison Observatory, Glasgow, Mo.*
3344 Pritchett, H. S., Dir. Obs. and Prof. Ast., Washington Univ., St. Louis, Mo. *Math.*, *Ast.**
3345 Prochazka, G. A., Ph.D., 219 E. 62nd St., New York, N. Y. *Chem.*?
3346 Proctor, Frank, Franklin Falls, N. H. *Min.*, *Indian Relics.* C. Ex.*
3347 Proctor, John R., State Geologist, Frankfort, Ky. *Geol.* Ex.*
3348 Proctor, Thomas, 31 Nassau St., New York City, N. Y. *Orn.**
3349 Prosser, Chas. S., M.S., Cornell Univ., Ithaca, N. Y. *Invert. Palæo.*, *Con.* C. Ex.*
3350 Proudfit, S. V., Interior Dept., Washington, D. C. *Arch.**
3351 Proudfoot, Alex, M.D., 2 Phillips Place, Montreal, Can. *Anat.*, *Anth.*, *Eth.*, *Osteol.**
3352 Prouty, Ira J., M.D., Keene, N. H. *Orn.*, *Min.* C. Ex.*
3353 Prouty, John Jay, Baldwinsville, Onondaga Co., N. Y. *Min.* C. Ex.*

3354 Provancher, L'Abbé, Caprouge, Can. *Gen. Nat. Hist.*, *Ent.*, *Con.*, *Bot.* C. Ex.*
3355 Provence, David M., Ridgeway, Fairfield Co., S. C. *Orn.**
3356 Puffer, Mrs. E. L. S., 3 Liberty St., Providence, R. I. *Palæo.*, *Geol.*, *Min.*, *Arch.* C. Ex.*
3357 Puissant, P. A., Prof. St. Joseph's Prov. Sem., Troy, N. Y. *Phæn. Bot.* C.*
3358 Pulsifer, C. L., M.D., 1837 Kennett Place, St. Louis, Mo. *Med.*, *Biol.**
3359 Pulsifer, W. H., 1837 Kennett Place, St. Louis, Mo. *Ast.*, *Arch.**
3360 Pumpelly, Raphael, U. S. Geological Survey, Newport, R. I. *Geol.* C.*
3361 Purdie, H. A., State House, Boston, Mass. *Orn.*, *Ool.* C. Ex.*
3362 Purdy, Carl, Ukiah, Calif. *Phæn. Bot.*, *Ferns*, *Orn.*, *Ool.* Pacific coast plants, bulbs and ferns. C.?
3363 Purdy, Mark S., B.S., M.D., 25 Washington Ave., Detroit, Mich. *Bot.*, *Mic.*, *Gen. Biol.* C.*
3364 Purdy, M. S., B.S., M.D., Corning, N. Y. *Bot.*, *Mic.* C.*
3365 Purinton, Geo. D., A.M., Prof. Chem., Min. and Biol., Arkansas Indust. Univ., Fayetteville, Ark. *Bot.*, *Min.*, *Chem.*, *Orn.*, *Tax.* C. Ex.*
3366 Purrington, Charles, Pequabuck, Litchfield Co., Ct. *Chem.*, *Min.* C. Ex. Will pay cash for fine minerals not already in cabinet. None but fine crystallized specimens desired.*
3367 Purviance, Amos T., Hennepin, Putnam Co., Ill. *Trees*, *Shrubs, etc.* C. Ex.*
3368 Puterbaugh, Geo. W., Greenfield, Hancock Co., Ind *Geol.*, *Moll.* C. Ex. fossils, shells. European corres. solicited.*
3369 Putnam, Mrs. Dora L., Waukesha, Waukesha Co., Wis. *Bot.*, *Geol.*, *Ent.* C. Ex.*
3370 Putnam, F. W., Peabody Prof. of Am. Arch. and Eth., Harvard Univ., and Curator Peabody Mus. Am. Arch. and Eth., Cambridge, Mass. Permanent Secretary American Association Advancement of Science. (Office, Salem, Mass.) Residence, Cambridge, Mass. *Anth.**
3371 Putnam, J. R., Portland Block, Chicago, Ill. *Min.* C. Ex.*
3372 Pycott, J. W., 33 Concord Sq. *Ast.*
3373 Pynchon, T. R., D.D., LL.D., Prof. Trinity Coll., Hartford, Ct. *Zool.**
3374 Queen, James W. & Co., 924 Chestnut St., Philadelphia, Pa. Makers of Microscopical and other scientific apparatus, etc.*
3375 Quick, Edgar R., Brookville, Ind. *Mam.*, *Orn.*, *Eth.* C.*
3376 Quimby, E. T., Prof Math., Hanover, N. H. Engaged in U. S. Coast and Geodetic Survey.*
3377 Quinn, Rev. J. C., M.A., Ph.B., Emerson, Man. *Bot.*, *Hort.*, *Physical Geol.*, *Min.*, *Phys.*, *Mic.*, *Bibliography*, *Philology*, *Orn.* C.*
3378 Quintard, C. A., Norwalk, Ct. *Min.*, *Crystall.*, *Met.*, *Arch.* C. Ex.*

3379 Rachford, Robert E. & Son, Collecting Naturalists, Beaumont, Jefferson Co., Texas. *Orn.*, *Ool.* C. Ex.*

3380 Rafter, George W., C.E., Rochester, N. Y. *Phys.**

3381 Ragsdale, G. H., Gainesville, Texas. *Orn.*, *Ool.* C. Ex. Collects Mammals, L. and F. W. Shells and Cretaceous Fossil Shells on orders. Orders taken for Taxidermic work.*

3382 Raine, Walter, Walton St., Toronto, Can., Oologist. British C. Can offer in exchange Birds' Eggs from Iceland, Europe, Asia Minor and Canada; makes a specialty of Eggs or Birds of Prey.*

3383 Rainey, William T., 1477 Euclid Ave., Cleveland, Ohio. *Min.*, *Orn.*, *Ool.*, *Tax.* C. Ex. eggs, bird-skins, and mounted birds for the same.?

3384 Rakestraw, G. G., 63d Hamilton St., Philadelphia, Pa. *Min.* *Mic.* C. Ex.*

3385 Rakestraw, H. H., Lock Box 410, Middletown, Dauphin Co., Pa. *Analyt. Chem.*, *Min.*, *Geol.* C. Ex.*

3386 Ralph, W. L., M.D., 26 Court St., Utica, N. Y. *Orn.*, *Ool.* *Bot.* C. Ex. in Ool. sets only.*

3387 Ralphy, Alfred J., M.D., Nashville, Brown Co., Ind. *Ent.*, C. Ex.*

3388 Ranch, John H., Sec. State Board of Health, Springfield, Ill.*

3389 Rand, A. J., Holyoke, Mass. *Zool.* C. Ex.*

3390 Rand, Herbert L., Worcester, Mass. *Orn.*, *Ent.*, *Tax.**

3391 Rand, Theo. D., 17 So. 3d St., Phila., Pa. *Min.* C. Ex.*

3392 Randall, O. E., W. Chesterfield, N. H. *Osteol.*, *Biol.*, *Zool.*, *Bot.**

3393 Randall, S. F., 120 Broadway, New York City. *Diatoms*, *Mic.*, *Photog.*, *Infusoria.* C. Ex.*

3394 Randolph, L. S., Susquehanna, Pa. *Org. Chem.*, *Mechanics.*?

3395 Randolph, N. A., M.D., Prof. Hygiene, Univ. of Pa., Philadelphia, Pa *Physiol. and Hygiene.**

3396 Rankin, Walter M., Princeton, N. J. *Gen. Biol.*

3397 Rappleye, W. G., Oswego, N. Y. *Phæn. Bot.*, *Ferns*, *Phys.* C. Ex.*

3398 Rasin, R. W. L, 35 Chamber of Commerce, Baltimore, Md. *Chem.*, *Hort.*, *Agric.**

3399 Rathbun, Frank R., Auburn, Cayuga Co., N. Y. *Orn.*, *Ent.*, *Gen. Nat. Hist.*, *Bibliog.* Will ex. publications.*

3400 Rathbun, Richard, Cur. U. S. Nat. Mus., Ass't U. S. Fish Comm., Smithsonian Inst., Washington, D. C. *Marine Invertebrates*, *Brazilian Palæo.**

3401 Rathbun, Samuel F., 9 Court St., Auburn, N. Y. *Orn.*, *Ool.*, *Tax.* C. Desires ex. Correspondence invited.*

3402 Rathvon, S. S., 506 N. Queen St., Lancaster, Pa. *Gen. Nat. Hist.*, *especially Ent.**

3403 Rattan, Volney, Girls' High School, San Francisco, Calif. *Phæn. Bot.* C.*

3404 Rattle, W. J., 101 St. Clair St., Cleveland, Ohio. *Mic.*, *Analyt. Chem.**

3405 Rattray, Rev. B. Franklin, Stillwater, Minn. *Mosses, Geol., Min., Crystall., Met., Arch.* C. Ex.

3406 Rau, Eugene A., Bethlehem, Pa. *Phæn. Bot., Musci, Fungi.* C.*

3407 Rauterberg, F., 1015 Cherry St., Milwaukee, Wis. *Coleopt.* Ex. only in U. S. Coleoptera.*

3408 Raymond, Chas. F., 739 Republic St., Cleveland, Ohio. *Ool.* C. Ex.*

3409 Raymond, Rossiter W., Ph.D., 123 Henry St., Brooklyn, N. Y. *Geol., Crystall., Lith., Min., Met., Elect.**

3410 Raymond, Wm. J., 26 13th St., Oakland, Alameda Co., Calif. *Moll.* C. Ex.*

3411 Read, Matthew C., A.M., Hudson, Ohio. *Geol., Zool., Arch.* C. Special attention given to examinations of mineral lands.*

3412 Reade, Frank M., Druggist, Boonville, Oneida Co., N. Y. *Geol., Min., Ent.**

3413 Reade, John, F.R.S. Can., 157 Laval Ave., Montreal, Can. *Anth., Eth., Philol.**

3414 Readio, William, Garnerville, Rockland Co., N. Y. *Nat. Hist., Mic.* C. Ex.*

3415 Ready, George H., Santa Cruz, Calif. *Orn., Ool., Tax.* C. Ex.

3416 Ream, Henry, Peru, La Salle Co., Ill. *Palæo., Orn., Ool., Tax., Ent.* C. Ex.*

3417 Reamer, William D., Greensburg, Westmoreland Co., Pa. *Min., Arch.* C. Ex.*

3418 Reasoner, P. W., Manatee, Manatee Co., Fla. *Phæn. Bot., Hort.* C. Ex.*

3419 Redding, T. B., A.M., Ph.D., F.R.M.S., Newcastle, Ind. *Mic., Biol.* C. Ex.*

3420 Redfield, John H., 216 W. Logan Square, Philadelphia, Pa. *Bot., Ferns.* C.*

3421 Redway, Jacques W., 17 So. 6th St., Philadelphia, Pa. *Phys. Geog., Geol., Mic.**

3422 Reed, Charles K., Worcester, Mass. *Orn., Tax.* C. Ex.*

3423 Reed, E. B., Ass't Editor Canadian Entomologist, London, Ont., Can. *Ent: Meteorology.*?

3424 Reed, J. Edward, Santa Clara, Oakland Co., Calif. *Assaying, Min., Filices.* C. Ex. local ferns and lichens for those of other localities.*

3425 Reed, R. C., A.M., M.D., Prof. Materia Med., etc., Cincinnati Coll. Med. and Surg., Stockton, Butler Co., Ohio. *Bot., Org. Chem.**

3426 Reed, W. H., Kansas City, Mo. *Upper local series.* C.*

3427 Rees, J. K., Prof. Geodesy and Pract. Ast., and Dir. of Observatory, Columbia College, New York, N. Y. *Ast., Geodesy.**

3428 Reese, Jacob, Pittsburgh, Pa. *Min., Chem., Metall., Phys., Elect.*?

3429 Reese, Lewis, Ast. and Telescope Maker, 300 S. Clark St., Chicago, Ill. *Ast.**

3430 Reeves, James A., Joplin, Mo. *Min.* Minerals of South West Missouri in ex. for good specimens of metallic minerals. C. Ex.*

3431 Refsnyder, E. A., Phœnixville, Pa. *Bot., Ferns, Geol., Min.* C. Ex.

3432 Regal, Edwin, Oberlin, Ohio. *Ent.* C. Ex.

3433 Reich, John C., Gundlach Opt. Co., Rochester, N. Y. *Mic.**

3434 Reiff, Isaac, 853 N. 13th St., Philadelphia, Pa. *Orn., Ool., Tax.* C. Ex. for eggs in sets only.*

3435 Reighard, Jacob, Ann Arbor, Mich., Ass't Prof. Zool. Univ. of Michigan.*

3436 Reinecke, Ottomar, 500 Main St., Buffalo, N. Y. *Coleopt.* C. Ex. in all orders of Coleopt., especially Cicindela and Cerambycidæ.*

3437 Reinhold, Eli S., Mahanoy City, Pa. *Min.* C. Fossils from Coal measures in ex. for minerals.*

3438 Reinhold, Wilhelm, M.D., 146 N. Clark St., Chicago, Ill. *Zool., Orn.* C.*

3439 Reisig, Augustus C., 389 Conti St., New Orleans, La. *Coleopt.* C. Ex. Only *Am. Cicindelidæ and Carabidæ* desired.*

3440 Remage, Geo. W., M.D., Jennings, Calcasieu Parish, La. *Invert. Palæo., Geol., Min., Radiates.* C. Ex.*

3441 Remington, Prof. J. P., Phila. Coll. of Pharmacy, 1233 Walnut St., Philadelphia, Pa. *Pharmacy, Chem.* C.?

3442 Remsen, Ira, Prof. Chem., Johns Hopkins Univ., Baltimore, Md. *Chem.**

3443 Renick, F. H., 44 Joy St., Detroit, Mich. *Orn., Ool., Birds' eggs and skins.* C. Ex.*

3444 Renninger, Miss Ida L., Findlay, Hancock Co., Ohio. *Ferns, Mosses, Lichens.* C. Ex.

3445 Renninger, John S., M.D., Marshall, Lyon Co., Minn. *Min., Arch., Eth., Geol.* C. Ex.*

3446 Renninger, Sam'l Findlay, Hancock Co., Ohio. *Meteo., Ast.* C.

3447 Renwick, Edward A., 57 Montauk Block, Chicago, Ill. *Phæn. Bot.**

3448 Reverchon, Julien, Dallas, Texas. *Bot.* C. Ex.*

3449 Rex, George A., M.D., 2023 Pine St., Philadelphia, Pa. *Mic., Fungi.* C Ex. Myxomycetes.*

3450 Reynolds, Arthur T., Canton, Oxford Co., Me. *Min., Geol.,* C. Ex. Mins., Geol., Garnet, Mica, etc.*

3451 Reynolds, Elmer R., M.D., Box 115, Smithsonian Inst., Washington, D. C. *Invert. Palæo., Bot., Bibliog., Arch., Eth.* C. Ex. Desires Botanical correspondents in Greece, Japan, Palestine, Persia, Portugal, Servia, Spain and Sweden.*

3452 Reynolds, Henry S., M.S., Willis, Montana. *Bot: Ferns, Mosses, Fungi, Lichens, Algæ, Ent.* C. Ex.*

3453 Reynolds, Miss Mary C., St. Augustine, Fla. Herbarium spec. Filices for sale. C.*

3454 Reynolds, R. N., Detroit, Mich. *Mic.* C. Ex.*

3455 Rhees, Wm. J., Chief Clerk, Smithsonian Inst., Washington, D. C. *Bibliog., Anth.**

3456 Rhoades, Mrs. M. A., Box 401, Clyde, Sandusky Co., Ohio. *Geol.* C. Ex. fossils, minerals, and F. W. shells for marine curiosities and F. W. Shells.*

3457 Rhoads, Joseph, jr., A.M., Principal of Central Academy, Spiceland, Ind.?

3458 Rhoads, Samuel N., Haddonfield, N. J. *Orn.*, *Ool.*, *Philol.* C. Ex.*

3459 Rice, Charles, Ph.D., Chemist, Dept. Char. Publ. and Corr., Bellevue Hosp , New York, N. Y. *Chem; Econ. and Med. Bot; History and Histol. of Drugs.**

3460 Rice, Frank L., Evanston, Cook Co , Ill. *Zool.*, *Vertebrates.**

3461 Rice, John Minot, Prof. Math., U. S. Naval Academy, Annapolis, Md. *Mathematics.**

3462 Rice, Wm., D.D., Springfield, Mass. *Bibliog.*, *Gen. Biol.* C. Ex.*

3463 Rice, William North, Prof. Geol., Wesleyan Univ., Middletown, Ct. *Geol.*, *Zool.* C. Ex.*

3464 Rich, Guy C., M.D., Box 372, Saratoga Springs, N. Y. *Orn.*, *Ool.*, *Tax.* C. Ex.

3465 Rich, Jacob M., E.M., C.E., 50 W. 38th St., New York City. *Min.*, *Geol.*, *Phys.*, *Photog.*, *Ast.* C. Ex.*

3466 Rich, W. E. C., 99 Moreland St., Roxbury, Mass. *Min.*, *Mic.* C. Ex.*

3467 Rich, William P., 3 N. Market St., Boston, Mass. *Bot.**

3468 Richards, Daniel, M.D., Marion, Wayne Co., N. Y. *Phæn. Bot.*, *Desmids*, *Mic.* C. Ex.*

3469 Richards, E. H., Woburn, Mass. *Microscopical materials and slides.* C. Ex.

3470 Richards, Eugene L., Ass't Prof. Math., Yale Coll., 315 York St., New Haven, Ct.*

3471 Richards, Herbert M., Sadsburyville, Chester Co., Pa. *Gen. Zool.*, *Mic.**

3472 Richards, J. B., Sec'y Y. O. A., Fall River, Mass. C. Ex.*

3473 Richards, Mrs. P. D., W. Medford, Mass. *Bot.*, *Ferns.* C. Ex.*

3474 Richards, Percival D., West Medford, Mass. *Elect.*, *Magnetism.**

3475 Richards, R. H., Prof. Mining and Metallurgy, Mass. Inst. Tech., Boston, Mass. *Min.* C.*

3476 Richards, Mrs. R. H., Inst. in Sanitary Chem., Mass. Inst. Tech., Boston, Mass. *Min.* C. Ex.

3477 Richards, Dr. T. Mason, Ebensburg, Cambria Co., Pa. *Ent: Macrolepidoptera.* C. Ex.*

3478 Richards, Theo. W., A.B., S.B., Chem. Lab., Harvard College, Cambridge, Mass. *Crystall.*, *Org. and Inorg. Chem.*, *Phys.*, *Ast.* C.*

3479 Richardson, Clifford, First Ass't Chem. to Dept. of Agric., Washington, D. C. *Agric. Chem.*, *Photo-Mic.**

3480 Richardson, C. A., Canandaigua, N. Y. *Bot.*, *Fungi.**

3481 Richardson, H. S., Concord, Mass. *Bot.*, *Con.* C.*

3482 Richardson, Jenness, in charge of the American Museum of Nat. Hist., Central Park, New York, N. Y. *Tax.* C. Ex.*

3483 **Richardson,** T. G., M.D., Univ. of La., New Orleans, La. *Amateur Florist, esp. Tropical Plants.**

3484 **Richmond,** A. G., Canajoharie, Montgomery Co., N. Y. *Arch.* C. Ex. Indian pottery, arrowheads, etc., for same from other localities. Desires correspondence. Ex. old coins and fractional currency for Indian relics.*

3485 **Richmond,** Charles W., 445 P St., N. W., Washington, D. C. *Orn., Ool., Tax.* C. Ex. Ornithological and Entomological Books and Pamphlets for Bird Skins.*

3486 **Richter,** Clemens Max, M.D., Late Staff Surgeon of German Army, 614 Geary St., San Francisco, Calif. *Meteo., Ethnog.**

3487 **Richter,** C. M., M.D., Calif. Acad. of Sci., San Francisco, Calif. *Climatology and Oceanography.**

3488 **Richter,** P. Geo., Prof. Phys., Beaumont Hosp., Med. Coll., 1432 So. Broadway, St. Louis, Mo. *Mic., Zool., Histol.* C. Ex.*

3489 **Ricker,** Everett W., 12 Harris Ave., Jamaica Plain, Mass. *Orn., Ool.* C. Ex.*

3490 **Ricketts,** P. de P., E. M., Ph.D., School of Mines, Columbia Coll., New York, N. Y. *Metall., Chem., Assaying.**

3491 **Ricksecker,** L. E., Sylvania, Occidental P. O., Sonoma Co., Calif. *Coleopt. and other insects of Western N. A. for sale.**

3492 **Rider,** Wheelock, B.Sc., M.D., 53 Fitzhugh St., Rochester, N. Y. *Bot.**

3493 **Ridgeway,** James A., Polo, Ogle Co., Ill. *Bot., Geol., Chem., Phys., Mic., Anat., Tax.* Desires Asclepidaceæ and Herbaceæ in ex.*

3494 **Ridgway,** Robert, Cur. Dept. Birds, U. S. Nat. Mus., Smithsonian Inst., Washington, D. C. *Orn.**

3495 **Ridings,** J. H., Rec. Sec., Am. Ent. Soc., 743 Holly St., Philadelphia, Pa. *Ent.**

3496 **Ridler,** C. E., A.M., Cor. Berkeley and Boylston Sts., Boston, Mass. *Bot., Min., Mic.* C.*

3497 **Riley,** C. V., M.A., Ph.D., U. S. Entomologist (Dept. of Agric.), Curator of Insects, U. S. National Museum. Residence 1700 18th St., N. W., Washington, D. C. *Articulates, General and Economic Ent., Bot.* Desires Diptera, Homoptera, Galls and Gall-insects of all orders, also larvæ of all orders: ex. for specimens in Meloidæ, Coccidæ, Psyllidæ, Tingidæ and Aleurodidæ.*

3498 **Rinedollar,** N., M.D., Mt. Carroll, Ill. *Geol., Min., Palæo.?*

3499 **Ringueberg,** E. N. S., M.D., Lockport, N. Y. *Palæo., spec. Niagara period and its foreign equivalent palæo., Arch., Histology of the eye.* C. Ex.*

3500 **Rippon,** Edrick, 60 Scollard St., Toronto, Ont., Can. *Orn., Ool., Herp.* C. Ex.*

3501 **Rising,** Willard B., Ph.D., M.E., Prof. Chem., and State Analyst, Univ. of Calif., Berkeley, Calif.*

3502 **Risley,** F. S., Rockledge, Brevard Co., Fla. *Tax.* Ex. Land and F. W. shells, also Marine and Indian relics for same, and books on Con., Orn. and Arch. C. Will collect in any dept. in ex. for books or papers on Architecture, Boat building, etc.

3503 Ritchie, John, jr., Box 2725, Boston, Mass. Cor. Sec. Boston Scientific Society; Editor Science Observer. *Min.*, *Con.*, *Ast.* C. Ex. Desires shells from all parts of the world. Helices a specialty.*

3504 Rivers, J. J., Curator of Organic Natural History, University of California, Berkeley, Alameda Co., Calif. *Ent.*, *West coast species of Reptilia, Coleopt and Lepid.**

3505 Rixford, Emmet, 1713 Pierce St., San Francisco, Calif. *Moll.* C. Ex.*

3506 Roach, Paul, M.D., Quaker St., Schenectady Co., N. Y. *Min.*, *Mic.* C. Ex. ?

3507 Robarts, John O. K., Phœnixville, Chester Co., Pa. *Min.* C. Ex.*

3508 Robb, Wm. L., Ph.D., Prof. Phys., Trinity Coll., Hartford, Ct.*

3509 Robbins, Wm. K., 290 McGregor St., Manchester, N. H. *Chem.*, *Elect.*, *Mic.**

3510 Roberts, Charlotte F., Wellesley College, Wellesley, Mass. *Min.*, *Lithol.*, *Chem.**

3511 Roberts, C. H., Rochester, Minn. *Bot.*, *Geol.*, *Chem.*?

3512 Roberts, Chris. H., 11 W. 123d St., New York, N. Y. *Ent: Coleopt.* C. Ex.*

3513 Roberts, Prof. G. S., E.M., C.E., Rockville Centre, Queens Co., L. I., N. Y. *Geol.*, *Min.**

3514 Roberts, Homer, Teacher, Lewistown, Ill. *Geol.*, *Arch.* C.*

3515 Roberts, Isaac P., Prof. Agric., Cornell Univ., Ithaca, N. Y. *Bot.*, *Hort.*, *Chem.*, *Ent.* C. Ex.*

3516 Roberts, Miss Mary E., Caledonia, Livingstone Co., N. Y. *Geol.*, *Min.*, *Ent.* C. Ex. fossils for Geol. or Min.*

3517 Roberts, Milton Josiah, M.D., 105 Madison Ave., New York, N. Y. *Anth.**

3518 Roberts, Otis S., Boswell, Benton Co., Ind. *Coleopt.* C. Ex.*

3519 Roberts, S. Raymond, Recorder Con. Section, Acad. Nat. Sci., 26 W. Johnson St., Germantown, Philadelphia, Pa. *Molluscs*, *Cypræidæ.* C.*

3520 Roberts, Thomas S., M.D., 27 N. 8th St., Minneapolis, Minn. *Orn.*, *Bot.**

3521 Roberts, Willis M., Duluth, Minn. *Phys.*, *Elect.*, *Min.* C. Ex.*

3522 Robertson, Chas., Carlinville, Ill. *Phæn. Bot.*, *Flower-loving Hymen.*, *Dipt.*, *Lepid.* Mutual relations of flowers and insects.*

3523 Robinson, Charles, Williamson, Wayne Co., N. Y. *Tax.*, *Ool.*

3524 Robinson, Rev. Edw. S., Enterprise, Clark Co., Miss. *Bot.*, *Geol.* C.?

3525 Robinson, Franklin C., Bowdoin Coll., Brunswick, Me., Prof. of *Chem.* and *Min.**

3526 Robinson, F. L., West Burlington, Otsego Co., N. Y. *Ool.* C. Ex.

3527 Robinson, Helen A., Huntsville, Schuyler Co., Ill. *Geol.*, *Min.* C. Ex.*

3528 Robinson, John, Treas. Peabody Academy of Science. In charge of Museum, East India Marine Hall, Salem, Mass. *Bot.**

3529 Robinson, L. M., E. Sumner, Me. *Org. and Inorg. Chem., Phys., Elect., Bibliog.**

3530 Robinson, Wm. F., Prin. 3d Ward Pub. Sch., Box 292, Bridgeton, N. J. *Lithol., Inorg. Chem., Ent., esp. Lepid., Coleopt.* C. Ex.?

3531 Robinson, Walter R., Huntsville, Schuyler Co., Ill. *Bot., Min., Geol., Mic.* C. Ex.*

3532 Rock, Miles, C.E., Jan. to June, Guatemala, Central America: June to Dec., 1430 Chapin St., N. W., Washington, D. C. Chief of the Boundary Comm. of Guatemala with Mex. *Ast., Geog., Anth.* C.*

3533 Rockey, A. E., M.D., Iowa City, Ia. *Histol. and Pathol.?*

3534 Rockwell, Charles H., Tarrytown, West Chester Co., N. Y. *Ast., Math.* (Double stars.)?

3535 Rockwell, George T., Box A, Kalamazoo, Mich. *Min., Arch., Palæo., Numis., Philately and Gen. curiosities, Autographs.* C. Ex. Desires Philatelic correspondents in foreign countries.

3536 Rockwood, Charles G., jr., Prof Math., Coll. of N. J., Princeton, N. J. *Meteo., Seismology.**

3537 Rockwood, Elbert W., Ithaca, N. Y. *Chem.**

3538 Roddy, H. Justin, M. E., Landisburg, Perry Co., Pa. *Bot: Ferns, Zool., Vert. Anat., Orn., Ool.* C. Ex.*

3539 Roe, John O., M.D., 28 N. Clinton St., Rochester, N. Y. *Laryngology.**

3540 Roesling, Fred., Cleveland, Ohio. *Palæo., Geol.* C. Ex.*

3541 Rogers, Abner, New Liberty, Ky. *Geol.* C. Ex.*

3542 Rogers, Henry Raymond, M.D., Dunkirk, N. Y.*

3543 Rogers, James E, Ph.D., Prof. Nat. Sci., French and German, member Soc. Bib. Archæology, London, Eng. Address, Maryville College, Maryville, Blount Co., Tenn. *Bot., Palæo., Geol., Min., Crystall., Lithol., Chem., Metall., Zool., Gen. Biol., Anat., Arch., Eth., Philol., Herpet.* C. Ex.*

3544 Rogers, Josephine E., 285 Bloomfield St., Hoboken, N. J. *Bot.* C. Ex.

3545 Rogers, MacLeod, Newburg, N. Y. *Ent: Coleopt., Lepid.* C.*

3546 Rogers, Prof. W. A., Cambridge, Mass. *Mic., Ast.*

3547 Rohmer, Dr. F. J. B., Spring Hill College, Mobile, Ala. *Phæn. and Crypt. Bot.?*

3548 Roland, Jacob D., Reading, Pa. *Min.* C. Ex.

3549 Rolfe, C. W., Prof. Geology and Physiology, Univ. of Ills., Urbana, Ill. *Geol., Gen. Biol.**

3550 Rolfe, George W., Geneva, Ill. *Chem., Elect., Min.**

3251 Rolfe, W. J., Assoc. Editor Popular Science News, 405 Broadway, Cambridgeport, Mass. *Chem., Phys. Sci.**

3552 Rominger, Charles, M.D., Ann Arbor, Mich. *Geol., Palæo.**

3553 Rommel, E., Lockport, N. Y. *Ent.* C. Ex.*

3554 Rood, Ogden N., A.M., Prof. Mech. and Phys., Columbia Coll., New York, N. Y.*
3555 Roosevelt, Clinton, 52 Exchange Place, New York, N. Y. *General Science, Eth.**
3556 Roosevelt, T., 422 Madison Ave., New York, N. Y. *Mam.* C. Ex.?
3557 Root, Mrs. E. H., M.D., Woman's Med. Coll., Chicago, Ill. *Gen. and Sanitary Science, Correspondence.**
3558 Roper, E. W., Revere, Mass. *North Am. L. and F. W. Shells.* C. Ex.*
3559 Rosamond, W. B., M.D., Milnersville, Guernsey Co., Ohio. *Geol., Min., Crystall., Palæo., Arch., Vert.* C. Ex.*
3560 Rose, D. L., Mankato, Minn. *Orn., Bot.* C.*
3561 Rose, John F., M.D., Oxford, Chester Co., Pa. *Geol., Min.* C. Ex. Pa. minerals.*
3562 Rosenthal, Jas., 628 Broadway, New York City.
3563 Ross, Dr. Alexander M., Toronto, Can. *Nat. Hist., especially Ornithology, Entomology and Ichthyology.**
3564 Ross, Frank W., M.D., 251 Baldwin St., Elmira, N. Y. *Geol., Nat. Hist. Pathol., and Histol.* C. Ex. Geol. spec. of Chemung Co.*
3565 Ross, Robert H., Atglen, Chester Co., Pa. *Mic., Elect., Arch.* C. Ex.*
3566 Rossiter, Luther N., Lake Forest, Lake Co., Ill. *Orn., Ool., Tax.* Collection of eggs. Ex.*
3567 Rotch, A. Lawrence, 3 Commonwealth Ave., Boston, Mass., Proprietor of Blue Hill Observ., Readville, Mass. *Met.**
3568 Rothrock, J. T., M.D., Prof. of Bot., Univ. of Pa., Phila., Pa. *Bot.**
3569 Rothwell, J. E., 100 Arch St., Boston, Mass. *Orn.* C. Ex.*
3570 Rothwell, Richard P., C.E., M.E., Editor of Engineering and Mining Journal, 27 Park Place, New York, N. Y. *Mining.**
3571 Rounds, Mrs. H. B., Box 876, Dover, N. H. *Geol., Min.*
3572 Rowell, Chas. E., M.D., Stamford, Ct. *Geol., Chem., Zool., Gen. Biol., Anat.* C.
3573 Rowland, Henry A., Prof. Physics, Johns Hopkins Univ., Baltimore, Md.*
3574 Rowley, Prof. Robert R., Curryville, Pike Co., Mo. *Invert., Palæo., Lepid., Coleopt.* C. Ex. Will give Burlington Crinoids and Kinderhook fossils in exchange for other Palæozoic remains. Desires Lepid. of the Gulf and Pacific States.*
3575 Rowley, Rev. C. H., F.R.M.S., Westford, Mass. *Mic., Sponges.* C. Ex.
3576 Royce, Chas. C., Columbus, Ohio. *Eth.**
3577 Rucker, P. H., Liter, Morgan Co., Ill. *Nat. Hist: Orn.* C. Ex. Ill. spec. for others.
3578 Rudd, Rev. Edw. H., M.A., Prof. of Sci., St. Mary's Sch., Knoxville, Ill. *Bot., Geol., Min., Chem., Phys., Elect., Photog., Ast., Zool., Philol.* C. Ex.*
3579 Rudkin, Wm. H., 74 William St., New York, N. Y. *Bot.* C.*

3580 Ruff, Lucius P., D.D.S., Jackson, Cape Girardeau Co., Mo. *Palæo., Geol., Min., Arch.**

3581 Rugg, Mrs. A. J., Leominster, Mass. *Geol., Min., Orn., Ool., Tax., Ent., Crust., Moll., Radiates.* C. Ex. Min.*

3582 Ruggles, Byron P., Hartland, Windsor Co., Vt. *Moll., Ent., Bot.* (*Cyperaceæ, Gramineæ and Filices.*) C. Ex. L. and F. W. shells.*

3583 Rumbold, Thos. F., M D., 2644 Washington Ave., St. Louis, Mo. *Mic., Anat., Vert., Histol.* C. Ex.*

3584 Rumney, Frank, No. Stoughton, Mass. *Nat. Hist., Orn.* Ex.?

3585 Rundstrom, John, M.D., Lindsborg, McPherson Co., Kan. *Bot.* C.*

3586 Runge, Carl, Corner of Goliad & Cherry Sts., San Antonio, Texas. *Botanist and Florist.* C. Ex. Cactaceæ, Yuccaceæ and Agave.*

3587 Rupp, Wm., F.C.S., 117 Pearl St., Hanover Sq., New York. N. Y. *Analyt. and Consulting Chem., Agric., Chem., Min.* C. Ex.*

3588 Rusby, Henry H., M.D., care Parke, Davis & Co., Detroit, Mich. *Bot., especially Medical.* Ex.*

3589 Rush, Wm. H., M.D., U. S. N., 1308 Green St., Philadelphia, Pa. *Moll.* C. Ex.*

3590 Rushby, George L., Franklin, Essex Co., N. J. *Orn., Ool.* C. Ex.

3591 Rushmore, Edward, M.D., Plainfield, N. J. *Desmids, Diatoms, Mic., Protozoa, Infusoria.**

3592 Russel, Hattie, Grassy Cove, Tenn. *Min., Bot.?*

3593 Russell, F. A., Bridgeport, Ct. *Mic., Ent.**

3594 Russell, I. C., U. S. Geol. Survey, Washington, D. C. *Geol.**

3595 Russell, L. E., M.D., Medico-legal expert, Springfield, Ohio. *Mic., Anth., Vert., Orn., Tax.* Ex. for rare spec.*

3596 Russell, L. W., Providence, R. I. *Forestry.**

3597 Rust, A. D., McGregor, Texas. *Cret and Carb. Fossils of Texas.* Correspondence solicited. C. Ex.*

3598 Rust, Horatio N., South Pasadena, Los Angeles Co., Calif. *Arch.* C.*

3599 Rust, Mary O., 112 E. Genesee St., Syracuse, N. Y. *Crypt. Bot.* C. Ex.?

3600 Ryan, John Henry, Sussex, King's Co., New Brunswick, Can. *Hort., Veg. Palæo., Chem., Elect., Mic., Anat.**

3601 Ryder, John A., Biological Dept., Univ. of Pa., Phila., Pa. *Embryology.**

3602 Sabin, A. H., Prof. Chem. and Physics, 579 Seigneurs St., Montreal, Canada. *Chem.**

3603 Sabine, Thomas T., M.D., Prof. Anat., Columbia Coll., New York, N. Y.*

3604 Sadtler, Saml. P., Prof. Gen. and Org. and Industrial Chem., Univ. of Pa., Philadelphia, Pa. *Org. and Industrial Chem.**

3605 Safford, James M., M.D., A.M., Ph.D., State Geologist, Prof. Vanderbilt Univ., Nashville, Tenn. *Nat. Hist., Geol., Chem.* C. Ex.*

3606 Safford, Mary J., M.D., Tarpon Springs. Fla. *Phæn. Bot., Ferns, Diurnal Lepid.**
3607 Safford, Truman H., Ph.D., Prof. Ast., Williams Coll., Williamstown, Mass.*
3608 Safford, Wm. E., Ensign U. S. Navy, care Navy Dept., Washington, D. C. *Phæn. Bot., Algæ, Geog. Dist.* C.
3609 Sage, Jno. H., Portland, Ct. C. Ex.*
3610 Saint-Cyr, Dominique, Napoléon Conservateur du Musée de l'Instruction Publique, Quebec, Can. *Bot: Phæn. and Crypt. Plants, Ferns, Mosses, Fungi, Lichens, Algæ, Min, Zool., Orn., Myol., Ent: Hymen., Lepid., Dipt., Coleopt., Hemipt., Orthopt., Neuropt., Crustacea, Molluscs, Radiates.* C.*
3611 Salisbury, Chas. M., 48 N. Main St., Providence, R. I. *Geol., Min., Con., Woods and Curiosities.* C. Ex.*
3612 Salisbury, James H., M.D., 9 West 29th St., New York City. *Bot., Palæo., Chem, Mic., Zool., Morphol., Emb., Anat., Histol., Arch., Geog. Dist.* C. Ex.*
3613 Salisbury, Rollin D., Ass't Geol., U. S. G. S., Quaternary Division, Prof. Geol., Beloit College, Beloit, Wis.*
3614 Salisbury, Stephen, Worcester, Mass. *Arch., Eth.* C.*
3615 Salmon, D. E., D.V.M., Dept. of Agric., Washington, D. C. *Fungi, Histol. of Vert., Pathol.**
3616 Sammis, Stephen D., 670 E. 142nd St., New York, N. Y. *Mic., Ent: Coleopt.* C. Ex.*
3617 Sampson, F. A., Sedalia, Mo. *Palæo., Con., Testudinata.* C. Cretaceous fossils of Texas, Turtles of Mo., and L. and F. W. shells for ex.*
3618 Sampson, Ira B., 157 Lancaster St., Albany, N. Y. *N. A. Sylva, Coll. of wood, bark, fruit, flowers and leaves.* Ex.*
3619 Sampson, Mrs. Mary C., 157 Lancaster St., Albany, N. Y. *Bot: Ferns, Mosses.* C. Ex.*
3620 Sampson, Wm. T., U.S.N., Supt. Naval Academy, Annapolis, Md. *Phys., Ast.**
3621 Samuels, Edw. A., 25 Congress St., Boston, Mass. *Orn., Ool.**
3622 Sanborn, J. W., Columbia, Mo.*
3623 Sandberg, John H., M.D., 501 Central Ave., E. Minneapolis, Minn. *Bot., Ool., Orn., Tax.* C. Ex.*
3624 Sander, Euno, 129 South Eleventh St., St. Louis, Mo. *Chem., Mineral Springs and Waters.**
3625 Sanford, James A., Stockton, Calif. *Bot.**
3626 Sanford, Leonard C., 216 Crown St., New Haven, Ct. *Orn., Ool.* C.*
3627 Sangster, J. H., A.M., M.D, Port Perry, Can. *Chem., Ent., Bot.**
3628 Sargent, Chas. S., Prof. Aboriculture, H. C., Director Arnold Arboretum, Brookline, Mass. *Bot.**
3629 Sargent, Erle H., Cornell Univ., Ithaca, N. Y. *Bot., Geol., Zool., Comp. Anat., Mic.* Correspondence desired upon Normal Pathological Histol. and Emb. C. Ex.*
3630 Sargent, F. L., care B. S. Bray, 80 State St., Boston, Mass. *Phæn. and Crypt. Bot., Lichens.* C. Ex.*

3631 **Sargent, Frank H.**, Claremont, N. H. *Geol.*, *Min.*, *Lithol.*, *Meteo.* C. Ex. local rocks and mins. for mins., fossils or rocks from other localities. Lists sent. Correspondence desired.*

3632 **Sargent, George H.**, Warner, N. H. *Geol.*, *Palæo.*, *Min.* Lists sent on application. C. Ex.*

3633 **Satterthwait, Thos. E.**, M.D., 17 E. 44th St., New York, N. Y. *Mic.*, *Hist.*, *Pathol.**

3634 **Saunders, R. T.**, 21 Orange St., Chelsea, Mass. *Ent.* C. Ex.*

3635 **Saunders, W. E.**, London, Ont. *Orn.*, *Ool.* C. Ex.*

3636 **Saunders, Wm.**, F.R.S.C., F.L.S., F.C.S., Director Canadian Experimental Farms, Ottawa, Can. *Agric.*, *Hort.*, *Ent.**

3637 **Saunders, Wm. H.**, A.M., M.D., Kenosha, Wis. *Chem.*, *Min.* C.*

3638 **Savage, Henry**, 431 Beacon St., Boston, Mass. *Ent: Coleopt.* C.?

3639 **Savage, Joseph**, Geologist, Lawrence, Kansas. *Hort.*, *Strat. Geol.*, *Min.* Large Coll. Ex.*

3640 **Saville, James H.**, 342 D St., N. W., Washington, D. C. *Forestry.*?

3641 **Sawyer, Edwin F.**, 58 Norfolk St., Cambridgeport, Mass. *Ast.**

3642 **Sawyer, F. C.**, Beauclerc, Fla. *Geol.*, *Min.*, *Con.* C. General Ex. Fla. curiosities of all kinds for ex. Wants all kinds of specimens.*

3643 **Sawyer, Geo. F.**, A.B., Carthage, N. Y. *Invert. Palæo.*, *Min.* C. Ex.*

3644 **Sawyer, Prof. Henry E.**, State Normal School, New Britain, Ct. *Bot.*, *Geol.*, *Chem.*, *Physics.*?

3645 **Sawyer, Louis J.**, East Templeton, Mass. *Bot.*, *Spec. Ferns.* C. Ex.

3646 **Sawyer, Mary**, Boxford, Mass. *Min.* C. Ex.*

3647 **Sayles, Ira**, A.M., Ph D., Dept. Interior, Geological Bureau, Washington, D. C. *Stratigraphy.**

3648 **Schäffer, Chas.**, M.D., 1309 Arch St., Philadelphia, Pa. *Phæn. Bot.**

3649 **Schaeffer, Edw. M.**, M.D., 323 Lexington St., Baltimore, Md. *Chem.*, *Mic.*, *Photog.* C. Ex.?

3650 **Schaffranck, A.**, Ph.D., Botanist, Palatka, Fla. Author of "Floral Almanac," "Florida Fruits," etc., etc. *Bot.*, *Ent.* C. Preparing an illustrated Flora of the United States and Canada. A limited number of good correspondents in the Dept. of Botany in English, German or French only desired.*

3651 **Schanck, Prof. J. S.**, M.D., LL.D., Princeton, N. J. *Chem.**

3652 **Scharar, C. H.**, C. & M.E., 2073 North Main Ave., Scranton, Pa. *Palæo.*, *Geol.*, *Anth.**

3653 **Schaufelberger, Fred'k J.**, M.D., Hastings, Adams Co., Nebraska. *Mic.*, *Min.*, *Hist. of Vert.*, *Bot.**

3654 **Scheller, Louis**, Green Bay, Wis. *Orn.*, *Tax.* C. Ex.*

3655 **Schenk, L. C.**, 300 Central Ave., Jersey City Heights, N. J. *Lepid.* C. Ex.?

3656 Schenk, W., 27 Bond St., New York City. *Lepid.* C. Ex.?
3657 Schick, W. H., M.D., 2933 Wentworth Ave., Chicago, Ill. *Orn.*, *Tax.* C.*
3658 Schimmel, J. O., Coopersburg, Pa. *Bot.*, *Mic.* C.*
3659 Schindler, O., Taxidermist, Galveston, Texas. C. Ex. shells and corals from Gulf Coast and Cab. spec. of mins. only.
3660 Schiener, John A., Minneapolis, Minn. *Orn.*, *Ool.*, *Nat. Hist.*, *Min.* C.*
3661 Schmidt, Erich F., 88 Travis St., Houston, Tex. *Geol.*, *Min.*, *Inorg. Chem.*, *Metall.* C. Ex.?
3662 Schmidt, H. D., M.D., 263½ Canal St., New Orleans, La. *Normal and Pathological Histology*, *Physiol.*, *Special branch: Nervous system.?*
3663 Schneck, J., M.D., Mt. Carmel, Ill. *Local Nat. Hist.* C. Ex. plants and shells.*
3664 Schneider, Julius, Anaheim, Los Angeles Co., Calif. *Orn.*, *Ool.*, *Tax.* C. Ex.*
3665 Schnupp, Henry C., 1821 Harcums Ave., Pittsburg, Pa. *Geol.*, *Min.*, *Lithol.* C. Ex.*
3666 Schock, Oliver D., Hamburg, Berks Co., Pa. *Coins and Indian relics.**
3667 Schoenborn, Henry F., 213 7th St., N. W., Washington, D. C. *Lepid.*, *Ool.* C. Ex.
3668 Schoney, L., M.D., 324 East 72nd St., New York, N. Y. *Biology*, *Mic.*, *Bot.* Ex. pathological and botanical specimens.*
3669 Schooley, W. D., Richmond, Ind. *Bot: Ferns*, *Mosses*, *Fungi*, *Algæ*, *Geol.*, *Min.*, *Arch.*, *Tax.* C. Ex. Will sell cabinet.*
3670 Schram, Nicholas H., Newburgh, Orange Co., N. Y. *Min.* C.
3671 Schrauer, L., 212 E. 34th St., New York, N. Y. *Mic.*, *Physical Apparatus.**
3672 Schrenk, Joseph, Hoboken, N. J. *Bot.*, *Pharmacognosy*, *Mic.* Ex.*
3673 Schuchert, C., Newport, Ky. Desires Brachiopoda from all parts of the world in exchange for Cincinnati group Fossils. C.*
3674 Schultze, C. E. L., 991 Sixth Ave., New York, N. Y. *Ent.*, *Bot.*
3675 Schultze, Edwin A., F.R.M.S. (Diatomist), P. O. Box 56, New York, N. Y. *Diatoms*, *Mic.* C.*
3676 Schuster, Moritz, 1808 Hickory St., St. Louis, Mo. *N. Am. Coleopt.* C. Ex.*
3677 Schuyler, Wm., St. Louis, Mo. *Phys.?*
3678 Schwarz, E. A., U. S. Dept. Agric., Washington, D. C. *Economic Ent: Coleopt.*, *Psyllidæ.* C. Ex.?
3679 Schweitzer, Paul, Ph.D., Prof. Chem., Mo. State Univ., Columbia, Boone Co., Mo. *Chem.**
3680 Schwensen, F. M., 977 Sixth Ave., New York, N. Y. *Coleopt.* C. Ex.*
3681 Schwimmer, A., 241 Hopkins St., Brooklyn, E.D., N. Y. *Elect.*

3682 Scofield, W. H., Cannon River Falls, Minn. *Palæo., Geol., Min., Crystall., Lithol., Chem., Metall.* C. Ex.*
3683 Scott, A. E., Lexington, Mass. *Bot.**
3684 Scott, Charles B., A.M., High School, St. Paul, Minn. *Bot: Crypt. Plants, Invert. and Veg. Palæo., Min., Zool., Gen. Biol.* C. Ex.*
3685 Scott, Chas. B., M. A., Univ. of Mich., Ann Arbor, Mich. *Geol., Min., Veg. and Invert. Palæo.* C. Ex.*
3686 Scott, J. T., Crawfish Springs, Walker Co., Ga. *Arch., Nat. Hist., Tax.?*
3687 Scott, N. S., 537 Prospect St., Cleveland, Ohio. *Ool.* C. Ex.*
3688 Scott, Rev. S. Henderson, White Plains, N. Y. *Min., Lithol., Orn., Ool.* C. Ex.
3689 Scott, Prof. William B., Princeton, N. J. *Palæo., Emb., Anat.**
3690 Scott, William Louis, 86 Spark St., Ottawa, Can. *Orn., Ool.**
3691 Scovell, J. T., Terre Haute, Ind. *Con.* C. Ex.*
3692 Scribner, F. Lamson, Agric. Dept., Washington, D. C. *Gramineæ, Economic Mycology and Vegetable Pathol.**
3693 Scribner, G. Hilton, Yonkers-on-Hudson, N. Y. *Ast., Zool., Gen. Biol., Anth., Eth.*
3694 Scribner, Rev. H. F. J., Strafford, Orange Co., Vt. *Meteor.**
3695 Scriven, Mrs. Abaline, Grafton, Rensselaer Co., N. Y. *Phæn. Bot., Ferns.**
3696 Scudder, John M., M.D., Dean of the Eclectic Medical Inst., 228 Court St., Cincinnati, Ohio.*
3697 Scudder, Newton P., Smithsonian Inst., Washington, D. C. *Comp. Anat., Vert.*
3698 Scudder, Samuel H., Cambridge, Mass. *Gen. Zool., Fossil, Insects, Orthoptera, Butterflies.**
3699 Seaman, Louis L., M.D., LL.B., 18 West 31st St., New York, N. Y. *Mic., Tax.**
3700 Seaman, W. H., Prof. Chem., 1424 11th St., N. W., Washington, D. C. *Mic.**
3701 Seamon, William H., B.S.A., Instructor Chem. and Nat. Hist., Miller Manual Labor School, Crozet, Albemarle Co., Va. *Min., Chem., Forestry.* C. Ex.*
3702 Searing, Dr. Anna H., 52 East Ave., Rochester, N. Y. *Bot: Ferns, Mosses, Fungi.* C. Ex.*
3703 Sears, J. F., Niagara Falls, N. Y. *Mic., Optics.* C.*
3704 Sears, John H., Ass't Peabody Acad. of Science, Salem, Mass. *Bot.* C. Ex. and for Ranunculaceæ E. N. and N. A.*
3705 Sedgwick, Wm. T., Ph.D., Mass. Inst. Tech., Boston, Mass. *Gen. Biol., Animal Physiol.**
3706 Seebach, B. G., Peru, La Salle Co., Ill. *Ferns, Mosses, Marine Animals, Geol., Elect., Zool., Arch., Tax., Moll., Sponges.* C. Ex. Have three large collections for public exhibition.*
3707 Seeber, Ernest, 939 So. 2d St., Philadelphia, Pa. *Coleopt. of the U. S. of A.* C. Ex.*
3708 Seely, Franklin A., Examiner U. S. Patent Office, Washington, D. C. *Anth., Spec., Eurematics (Philosophy of Invention).**

3709 Seely, Henry M., Prof. in Middlebury Coll., Middlebury, Vt. *Chem.*, *Bot.**

3710 Seelye, C. W., Rochester, N. Y. *Phæn. Bot.*, *Ferns*, *Horticulture.**

3711 Seever, Wm. J., 2856 N. Spring Ave., St. Louis, Mo. Collector of Archæology. Collection for sale. Can furnish collectors with fine spec. of Indian and Mound Implements of Stone, Copper and Pottery. Correspondence invited.*

3712 Seib, Simon, 20½ Holland St., Newark, N. J. *Lepid.* C. Ex.*

3713 Seidensticker, Frank J., Cambridge, Mass. *Diatoms*, *Mic.*, *Infusoria.* C.*

3714 Seiler, Carl, M.D., 1346 Spruce St., Phila., Pa. *Elect.*, *Mic.*, *Photog.* C.*

3715 Seiss, C. Few, 1338 Spring Garden St., Philadelphia, Pa. *Herpetology*, *Gen. Zool.* Reptiles and batrachians for ex.*

3716 Seiss, Ralph W., M.D.. 1338 Spring Garden St., Philadelphia, Pa. *Comp. Anat.*, *Vert. Zool.* C. Ex.*

3717 Seltzer, Jno. A., Lebanon, Pa. *Minerals.**

3718 Selwyn, Alfred R. C., LL.D., C.M.G , F.R.S., F.G.S., Can., Dir. Geol. and Nat. Hist. Surv. Can., Museum and Office, Sussex St., Ottawa, Can. *Geol.**

3719 Semans, William O , M.A., Prof. Chem. and Phys., Ohio Wesleyan Univ., Delaware, Ohio.*

3720 Sener, S. M., 124 N. Prince St., Lancaster, Pa. *Arch.**

3721 Senger, Robert, 5 Cedar St., New York City. *Chem.?*

3722 Sennett, George B., Am. Museum Nat. Hist., Central Park, New York City. *Orn.* C. Duplicates of Texas birds and eggs.*

3723 Sensenig, David M., Prof. State Normal School, West Chester, Pa. *Phæn. Bot.*, *Math.* C. Ex.*

3724 Setley, Cletus, 135 Second Ave., West Reading, Pa. *Geol.*, *Min.*, *Arch.*, *Photog.* C. Ex. A full line of Eastern and Southern Stereoscopic views for sale and ex.*

3725 Severance, Rev. M. L., Prin. of Burr and Burton Seminary, Manchester, Vt. *Geol.*, *Min.* C.*

3726 Sewall, Henry, Prof. of Physiol., Univ. of Mich., Ann Arbor, Mich.*

3727 Sewall, Joseph A., M.D., LL.D., Pres. and Prof. Chem. and Met., Univ. of Colo., Boulder, Colo.?

3728 Seymour, A. B., Bot. Garden, Cambridge, Mass. *Bot.*, *Fungi.* C. Ex.*

3729 Seymour, F. H., 163 Congress St., E. Detroit, Mich. *Numismatics.* C.*

3730 Seymour, George W., Taylor's Falls, Chisago Co., Minn. *Arch.*, *Coins.* C. Ex.*

3731 Seymour, John P., Ogdensburg, N. Y. *Min.* C.?

3732 Seymour, Wm. Pierce, M.D., 105 Third St., Troy, N. Y. *Obstetrics*, *Gynæcology.**

3733 Shafer, Harry C., Phœnixville, Chester Co., Pa. *Min.* C.*

3734 Shafer, J. A., Ph.G., Stoops, Pa. *Bot: Woods of N. A.*, *Veg. Palæo.*, *Min.* C. Ex.*

3735 Shaler, N. S., Prof. of Geology., Harvard Univ., Cambridge, Mass. *Geol., Palæo.**

3736 Shallcross, John, 4610 Frankford Ave., Philadelphia, Pa. *Ent., Min., Con., Mic.* C.*

3737 Shallenberger, Thomas M., Antiquarian, Bradshaw, Neb. *Arch., Min., Geol., Numis.* Will make collections in any department for ex. in above.*

3738 Shanks, Seth G., M.D., 547 Clinton Ave., Albany, N. Y. *Morph. Bot., Mic., Histol.* C. Ex.*

3739 Shannon, W. P., A.M., Greensburg, Decatur Co., Ind. *Invert. Palæo.* C. Cin. and Niag. fossils to ex. for those of other epochs.*

3740 Share, Wm. W., Ph.D., 336 Navy St., or P. O. Box 22, Brooklyn, N. Y., and Physical Dept., Columbia College, New York City. *Chem., Phys., Elect.**

3741 Sharp, A. P., Baltimore, Md. *Chem.**

3742 Sharp, Prof. Benj., M.D., Ph.D., Acad. Nat. Sci., 5th and Race Sts., Phila., Pa. *Emb. of Invert., Histol.**

3743 Sharp, S. Z., A.M., Mt. Morris, Ill. *Con., Geol.* C. Ex.*

3744 Sharples, S. P., S.B., Prof. Chem., Boston Dental Coll., 13 Broad St., Boston, Mass. *Geol., Lithol., Mic.**

3745 Sharpless, Alfred, West Chester, Pa. *Arch., Min.**

3746 Sharpless, Frederick F., West Charter, Pa. *Min., Chem.**

3747 Sharpless, Isaac, President, Haverford Coll., Pa. *Ast.**

3748 Shattuck, Miss Lydia W., Mt. Holyoke Seminary, South Hadley, Mass. *Phæn. Bot., Ferns, Mosses, Chem.**

3749 Shattuck, Samuel W., C.E., Urbana, Ill. *Math.**

3750 Shaw, Henry, Dir. Mo. Bot. Gardens, St. Louis, Mo. *Bot.**

3751 Shaw, James M., So. Waterford, Me. *Min.* C. Ex.*

3752 Sheafer, Arthur W., B. S., Mining Engineer and Geologist, Pottsville. Pa. *Geol., Mining.**

3753 Sheafer, P. W., Pottsville, Pa. *Iron, Coal, etc., Geol.* C.*

3754 Sheafer, Walter S., Pottsville, Pa. *Mining Engineer.**

3755 Sheaffer, Wm. E., 702 North 6th St., Reading, Pa. *Geol., Min., Arch.* C. Ex.

3756 Sheahan, J. P., A.M., M.D, Dennysville, Me. *Palæo., Lithol., Arch., Orn., Molluscs.* C. Ex.?

3757 Sheldon, Charles S., Normal School, Kirksville, Mo. *Bot., Con.* C. Eastern and Western plants for sale or ex.*

3758 Shepard, Edw., M., A.M., Prof. Biol. and Geol, Drury Coll,, Springfield, Mo. *Min., Bot: Vasc. Cryptogams.* C. Correspondence from Mo. botanists desired.*

3759 Shepard, Elmer E., Connersville, Ind. *Arch., Con., Anth., Crystall., Palæo.* Correspondence solicited from each of the States and Territories and Canada. C. Ex.*

3760 Shepard, Mrs. Harriet E., A.B., Springfield, Mo. *Phæn. Bot.* C.*

3761 Shepard, James, Box 1345, New Britain, Ct. *Min., Arch.* C. Ex.*

3762 Shepard, Rev. M. A., Lebanon, Ill. *Social Science, Fungi, Agric., Chem., Phys.* C. Ex.*

3763 Shepard, Miss Nettie, Box 1345, New Britain, Ct. *Min.*, *Molluscs*, *Bot.* C. Ex.*

3764 Sheperd, Mrs. Theodosia B., San Buenaventure, Calif. *Ferns*, *Cal. plants and curiosities.* Grower of plants, seeds and bulbs. Exchanges. Especially desires choice ferns and orchids and foreign seeds. C.*

3765 Sheppard, Edwin, Artist, 2036 Norris St., Philadelphia, Pa. *Vertebrates.* ?

3766 Sherman, B. F., M.D., Elizabeth St., Ogdensburg, N. Y. *Chem.*, *Mic.*, *Geol.**

3767 Sherman, Frank A., Prof. of Math., Chandler Scientific Department, Dartmouth College, Hanover, N. H *

3768 Sherman, John D., jr., Peekskill, N. Y. *Ent: especially Coleoptera.* C. Ex.*

3769 Sherman, Lewis, A.M., M.D., Milwaukee, Wis. *Bot.*, *Chem. Mic.**

3770 Sherman, O. T., Astronomer, Observatory, Yale Coll., 4 Library St., New Haven, Ct. *Astronomical Physics*, *Thermometry.**

3771 Sherwood, Andrew, Mansfield, Pa. *Geol.*, *Palæo.*, *Arch.*, *Hort.* C. Ex.*

3772 Sherwood, Ephraim, M.D., Dansville, Mich. *Chem.*, *Elect.*, *Mic.*, *Gen. Biol.*, *Emb.*, *Anat.*, *Histol. of Vert.*, *Protozoa*, *Infusoria.* C.*

3773 Sherwood, John N., 17 Holland St., Syracuse, N. Y. *Orn.*, *Ool.* C. Ex.*

3774 Sherwood, W. L., Box 55, Newark, N. J. Genealogy of Sherwood family. *Bibliography.* Would like to correspond and ex.*

3775 Shimek, B., C.E., Box 1692, Iowa City, Ia. *Phæn. Bot.*, *Ferns*, *Land, Fresh Water and Marine Shells.* C. U. S. Limnæidæ wanted in ex. for L. and F. W. Shells.*

3776 Shimer, Henry, A.M., M.D., Mt. Carroll, Ill. *Orn.*, *Ent.*, *Gen. Sci.* C. Ex. Has a good collection of birds, insects and plants.*

3777 Shimer, Porter W., M.E., College Hill, Easton, Pa. *Chem.*, *Metall.*, *Mic.**

3778 Shoemaker, Mary W., 45 Tulpehocken St., Germantown, Phila., Pa. *Bot.* C. Ex.*

3779 Shoop, Rev. Darius R., South Haven, Mich. *Bot.* ?

3780 Shores, E. I., M.D., Ass't Surg., Nat. Soldiers' Home, Hampton, Va. *Vert. Zool.*, *Anat.*, *Mic.*, *Photog.**

3781 Short, Sidney H., B.S., 71 North High St., Columbus, Ohio. Contractor for construction of Electric Railways. Inventor of Short's Overhead Series System Electric R. R.*

3782 Shorten, J. W., 191 W. 4th St., Cincinnati, Ohio. *Zool.*, *Tax.**

3783 Shriver, Howard, Wytheville, Va. *Phæn. Bot.*, *Ferns*, *Meteorol.**

3784 Shufeldt. Robert W., M.D., M.A.S.N., M.A.O.U., C.M.Q.S., Smithsonian Institution, Washington, D. C. *Gen. Biol.*, *Morph.*, *Anat. Vert.*, *Orn.*, *Osteol.*, *Vert.* C. Ex.*

3785 **Shulak, Rev. F. X.**, Prof. Min., Geol., and Nat. Hist., St. Ignatius Coll., 12th St., W. Chicago, Ill. *Min., Geol., Coleopt., Con.* C. Ex.?

3786 **Shultz, Charles S.**, Hoboken, N. J. *Mic., Gen. Biol., Infusoria.* C. Treasurer N. Y. Micros. Soc.*

3787 **Shultz, J. H.**, M.D., Box 332, Logansport, Ind. *Con., Geol.* C. Ex. Cal., also U. and L. Silurian fossils.*

3788 **Shumard, Sarah S.**, Richmond, Ind. *Lichens, Algæ, Palæo., Gen. Biol., Tax., Ent., Lower Invert.* C. Ex.*

3789 **Shurley, E. L.**, 25 Washington Ave., Detroit, Mich. *Mic.**

3790 **Shutt, Mrs. Ella V.**, Springfield, Sagamon Co., Ill. *Geol., Bot., Con.* C. Ex.*

3791 **Sias, Solomon**, A.M., M.D., Schoharie, N. Y. *Geol., Palæo., Met., Ast.* C.*

3792 **Siebel, J. E.**, Prof. Chem. and Tech., Zymotechnic Coll., Chicago, Ill. *Geol., Min., Chem., Phil.* C.?

3793 **Sigsbee, Charles D.**, Commander U. S. Navy, Navy Dept., Washington, D. C. *Practice and Economy of Deep-sea sounding, Dredging, etc.**

3794 **Siler, Andrew L.**, Ranch, Kane Co., Utah. *Bot: Bulbs, Cacti, L. and F. W. Shells, Arch., Anth.* Collects Indian relics of Cliff builders, and Pueblo Indians, coleoptera and insects generally.

3795 **Silliman, J. M.**, Prof. Mining Eng. and Graphics, Lafayette College, Easton, Pa. *Min., Mic.**

3796 **Silver, Wm. J.**, M.E., 149 W. North Temple St., Salt Lake City, Utah. *Metall., Phys., Elect.**

3797 **Silvester, Miss Martha**, Malden, Mass. *Bot.**

3798 **Simmons, D. Edgar, jr.**, Somerset, Bristol Co., Mass. *Chem., Pharmacology.**

3799 **Simmons, Geo. O.**, 352 Gates Ave., Brooklyn, N. Y. *Min., Lithol.* Proprietor of the "Diamond and Students' complete Mineral collections." Prepares collections for schools and private parties. Correspondence with view to exchanges solicited.*

3800 **Simmons, J. W.**, Dowagiac, Cass Co., Mich. *Phæn. Bot., Vertebrates, Invert., Physical and Stratigraphical Geol., Min., Lithol., Inorg. Chem., Phys., Elect., Mic., Meteo., Ast., Zool., Anat., Mam., Orn., Ool., Tax., Articulates, Ent: Hymenop., Lepid., Dipt., Coleopt., Hemipt., Orthopt., Neuropt.* C. Ex.*

3801 **Simmons, W. G.**, A.M., LL.D., Prof. of Physics and Applied Mathematics, Wake Forest Coll., Wake Co., N. C. C. Ex.*

3802 **Simon, H. L.**, Lancaster, Pa. *Min., Ool., Geol., Arch.* C. Ex.?

3803 **Simon, Wm.**, Ph.D., Prof. Chem., 1348 Block St., Baltimore, Md. *Chem., Min.* C.*

3804 **Simonds, O. C.**, Wright's Grove, Ill. *Phæn. Bot.**

3805 **Simonton, L.**, Lebanon, Warren Co., Ohio. *Palæo., Geol., Anth., Arch., Eth.* C. Ex. Ex. Lower Silurian fossils and arch. spec. for fossils and rare arch. spec. Correspondence solicited.*

3806 Simpson, Chas. T., Braidentown, Manatee Co., Fla. *Bot.*, *Con.* C. Ex. Fla. L., F. W. and M. shells for those of all parts of the world.
3807 Simpson, Joseph H., Manatee, Manatee Co., Fla. *Physics*, *Bot.* The Vitaceæ a specialty. C. Fla. Vitaceæ. Ex.*
3808 Singley, Mrs. Fannie L., Box 14, Giddings, Lee Co., Texas. *Orn.*, *Ool.*, *Con.*, *L. and F. W. Shells.* L. and F. W. Shells of Tex. in ex. for same.*
3809 Singley, J. A., Box 14, Giddings, Lee Co., Tex. *Orn.*, *Ool.*, *Tax.*, *Molluscs*, *L. and F. W. Shells.* C. Ex.*
3810 Sisson, Albert D., Westerly, R. I. *Ool.*, *Plants*, *Coins.* C. Ex.?
3811 Sizer, N. B., de S., B.Sc., M.D., 336 Greene Ave., Brooklyn, N. Y. *Hist.*, *Org. Chem.*, *Mic.*, *Ophthal.*, *Otology.**
3812 Skarstedt, Ernst, A.B., Mount Bell, Wash. Terr. *Phæn. Bot.*, *Zool.*, *Vert. Anat.*
3813 Skavlem, H. L., Janesville, Rock Co., Wisconsin. *Geol.*, *Gen. Biol.*, *Geog. Dist.*, *Orn.*, *Ichth.*, *Tax.* C. Ex.*
3814 Skelton, John L., 376 W. Monroe St., Chicago, Ill. *Orn.*, *Tax.*, *Ent.*, *Mic.* C. Ex.?
3815 Skidmore, Prof. S. T., Normal School, cor. 17th and Spring Garden Sts., Philadelphia, Pa. *Thermo and Electro Dynamics*, *Astron. and Chem.*, *Phys.**
3816 Skinner, Aaron N., Assistant Ast., U. S. N., Observatory, Washington, D. C. *Ast.*, *Mic.**
3817 Skinner, A. G., M.D., Youngstown, Niagara Co., N. Y. *Bot.**
3818 Skinner, Henry, M.D., 716 N. 20th St., Philadelphia, Pa. *Lepid.* C. Ex. Desires Am. moths.*
3819 Skirm, Joseph, Santa Cruz, Calif. *Orn.*, *Ool.* C. Ex.
3820 Slade, Daniel D., M.D., Ass't Mus. Comp. Zool., Cambridge, Mass. Lecturer on Comparative Osteology, Harvard Univ.*
3821 Slade, Elisha, Somerset, Mass. *Zool.*, *Nat. Hist. of the Farm*, *Meteo.*, *Heredity in Animals and Plants.**
3822 Slafter, Rev. Edmond F., 249 Berkeley St., Boston, Mass. *Bot.*, *Geol.*, *Bibliog.*, *Geog. Dist.*, *Anth.*, *Orn.**
3823 Sloan, John, M.D., New Albany, Ind. *Mic.*, *Gen. Pathol.*, *Diatoms of So. Ind.* C. Ex.*
3824 Sloan, Robert, Keosauqua, Van Buren Co., Iowa. *Geol.*, *Arch.* C. Ex.*
3825 Slocum, Chas. E., M.D., Ph.D., Defiance, Ohio. *Mic.*, *Biol.*, *Arch.**
3826 Slocum, Chas. E., jr., M.D., El Paso, Ill. *Mic.*, *Biol.*
3827 Small, H. Beaumont, M.D., Ottawa, Ont., Can. *Med.*, *Mic.*, *Bot.* C. Ex.*
3828 Small, L. Linn, Box 89, Auburn, Me. *Geol.*, *Min.*, *Crystall.* C. Ex.*
3829 Smiley, Chas. W., Editor of the publications of the U. S. Fish Commission, 1443 Mass. Ave., Washington, D. C. *Gen. Biol.*, *Bot.*, *Bibliog.*, *Anth.*, *Ichth.* C. Bot.*
3830 Smith, Arthur W., B.A., B.C.L., 2738 St. Catherine St., Montreal, Can. *Min.*, *Geol.*, *Palæo.**

3831 Smith, Benj. G., Cambridge, Mass. *Hort.*, *Orn.**
3832 Smith, Albert E., 251 Lewis Ave., Brooklyn, N. Y. *Ent.**
3833 Smith, Charles E., 215 So. 12th St., Philadelphia, Pa. *Bot.* C.*
3834 Smith, Prof. Emory C., Pres. So. Cal. Floral and Perfumery Co., Arcadia, Los Angeles Co., Cal. *Bot.*, *Crypt. Plants*, *Fungi*, *Hort.*, *Veg. Palæo.*, *Phys. Geol.*, *Elect.*, *Mic.* C. Ex.*
3835 Smith, E. C., Fort Wayne, Ind. *Orn.*, *Tax.* C. Ex.
3836 Smith, E. J., Natick, Mass. *Birds*, *Lepid.*, *Shells*, *Photography*. C. Desires Pacific Coast ex.*
3837 Smith, E. Kirby, Univ. of the South, Sewanee, Tenn. *Phæn. and Crypt. Bot.* Ex.*
3838 Smith, Edwin, Assistant Coast and Geodetic Survey, 2024 Hillyer Place, Washington, D. C. *Ast.**
3839 Smith, Miss Emma A., 185 Moss St., Peoria, Ill. (In Leipzig, Germany). *Econ. Ent: Hymenop.* Ex.
3840 Smith, Ellen E., Lake Erie Sem., Painsville, Ohio. *Phæn. Bot.*, *Ferns*, *Geol.*, *Min.* C. Ex.*
3841 Smith, Erwin F., Section of Vegetable Pathology, Dept. of Agric., Washington, D. C. Special Agt. in investigation of Peach " Yellows.*
3842 Smith, Eugene A., Ph.D., Prof. Chem and Geol., Univ. of Ala., State Geologist, P. O. Univ., Tuscaloosa Co., Ala. Ex.*
3843 Smith, F. C., Bridgeport, Ct. *Ent.*, *Mic.**
3844 Smith, Frank W., Mill St., Dorchester, Mass. *Organic Bot.**
3845 Smith, Frank, 25 S. Arlington St., Baltimore, Md. *Hort.**
3846 Smith, Fred. Sumner, M.D., West Hartford, Ct. *Orn.*, *Ool.*, *Herpetol.* C.*
3847 Smith, Geo. L., C.E., 1106 Madison Ave., Baltimore, Md. *Bot.*, *Phæn. Plants*, *Ferns*, *Mic.*, *Photog.**
3848 Smith, H. A., San Diego, Calif. *Geol*, *Min.*, *Zool.* C. Ex.*
3849 Smith, H. L., Prof. Nat. Phil. and Ast., Hobart College, Geneva, N. Y. *Ast.*, *Mic.*, *especially Diatoms.* C. Ex.*
3850 Smith, Herbert E., M.D., Med. Dept., Yale Univ., New Haven, Ct. *Chem.**
3851 Smith, Herbert H., 251 Lewis Ave., Brooklyn, N. Y. *Geog. Dist.*, *Ent.* C. Ex.*
3852 Smith, Herbert W., 222 E. 4th St., St. Paul, Minn. *Min.*, *Lithol.* C. Ex.*
3853 Smith, Hugh M., National Museum, Washington, D. C. *Bot.*, *Orn.*, *Ool.* C. Ex.*
3854 Smith, H. W., Truro, Colchester Co, N. S., Canada. *Phæn. Bot.*, *Hort.*, *Chem.*, *Zool.*, *Anat. of Vert.*, *Ent.**
3855 Smith, J. Alden, State Geologist, Denver, Colo. *Min.*, *Geol.* C. ?
3856 Smith, Prof. J. Edwards, M.D., 151 Windsor Ave, Cleveland, Ohio.*
3857 Smith, Jay L., 86 Beekman St., New York City, N. Y. *Mic.*, *Histol.*, *Pathol.*, *Embryol.* C. Ex.*
3858 Smith, John B., Ass't cur. of Ent., U. S. Nat. Mus., Washington, D. C., 290 3d Ave., Brooklyn, N. Y. *Coleopt.*, *Lepid.**

3859 Smith, John Donnell, 505 Park Ave., Baltimore, Md. *Bot.* C. Will purchase or exchange for desiderata.*
3860 Smith, Rev. Jos. L., Zanesville, O. *Palæo.*, *Geol.*, *Arch.* C.*
3861 Smith, Rev. J. Stewart, M.D., Elgin, Ill. *Histol.*, *Mic.*, *Chem.**
3862 Smith, Lee Herbert, M.D., 186 Allen St., Buffalo, N. Y. *Mic.*, *Anat.*, *Infusoria.* C. Ex.*
3863 Smith, Lewis L., Media, Pa. *Min.*, *Bot.* C.*
3864 Smith, M. Emory, A.M., Bennington, Switzerland Co., Ind. *Palæo.*, *Geol.* C. Ex.*
3865 Smith, Nettie, 265 West 11th St., Dubuque, Iowa. *Geol.*, *Min.*, *Lepid.*, *Coleopt.* Ex.*
3866 Smith, Norman A., M.D., C.M., Frelighsburg, Quebec, Can. *Gen. Nat. Hist.* C.*
3867 Smith, Oberlin, Bridgeton, N. J. *Phys.*, *Elect.**
3868 Smith, O. D., Ala. Agric. and Mech. Coll., Auburn, Ala. *Math. and Civil Engineering.**
3869 Smith, Q. C., M.D., 704 Congress Ave., Austin, Tex. *Bot.*, *Org. Chem.*, *Elect.*, *Mic.*, *Morph.*, *Emb.*, *Eth.*, *Herp.*, *Tax.**
3870 Smith, R. D., Pres. Columbia Athenæum, Columbia, Tenn. *Geol.* C. Ex.*
3871 Smith, Raymond W., Lebanon, Warren Co., Ohio. *Ast.*, *Orn.*, *Tax.* C. Ex.*
3872 Smith, Robert R., Berkeley, Alameda Co., Calif. *Ool.* C. Ex.*
3873 Smith, Miss Rosa, San Diego, Calif. *Algæ*, *Ferns*, *Fishes.* C.*
3874 Smith, Sidney I., Prof. Comp. Anat., Yale Coll., New Haven, Ct. *Gen. Biol.*, *Crustacea.*
3875 Smith, T. Berry, A.B., A.M., Prof. Chem. & Physics, Central College, Fayette, Howard Co., Mo.*
3876 Smith, Theobald, Ph.B., M.D., Dept. of Agric., Washington, D. C. *Hygiene*, *Bacteriology*, *Gen. Biol.**
3877 Smith, Uselma C., 1515 Green St., Philadelphia, Pa. *Algæ*, *Elect.*, *Mic.*, *Radiates.**
3878 Smith, Walter B., U. S. Geol. Survey, Denver, Colorado. C. Ex. *Min.*, *Crystall.*, *Lithol.**
3879 Smith, W. R., Belleville, Can. *Min.*, *Palæo.*, *Con.*
3881 Smith, Walter H., 31 Arcade St., Montreal, Canada, Pres. Astro-Meteor. Assoc., *Meteo.*, *Ast.*, *Diurnal Lepid.* C.*
3882 Smith, William A., M.A., M.D., Ph.D., Columbia, Tenn. *Nat. Hist.* C. Ex.*
3883 Smith, William R., Curator Botanic Gardens, Washington, D. C. *Bot.**
3884 Smock, John C., N. Y. State Museum, Albany, N. Y. *Geol.*, *Metal.*, *Meteo.**
3885 Smucker, Isaac, Newark, Ohio. *Arch.**
3886 Smyth, Chas. H., Clinton, Oneida Co., N. Y. *Inorg. Chem.*, *Mic.* C.*

3887 Smyth, Ellison A., jr., Charleston, So. Carolina. *Orn., Lepid., a specialty.* C. Ex.*

3888 Snell, Joseph A., Holyoke, Mass. *Ool., Tax.* C. Ex.*

3889 Snell, Merwin-Marie, U. S. Fish Commission, 732 Sixth St., N. W., Washington, D. C. *Asiatic Arch., Hierology, Ferns, Nat. Hist. of Palestine.**

3890 Snively, Z. T., Wayland, Clark Co., Mo. *Geol., Arch., Min., Crustacea, Zool., Palæo.* Specialty, crinoids and Indian Relics. C. Ex.*

3891 Snow, F. H., A.M., Ph.D., Prof. Nat. Hist., Univ. Kan., Lawrence, Kan. *Ent., Orn., Bot., Palæo., Min.* C. Kans. and N. Mex. coleopt., lepid., and plants for ex. Lists of duplicates sent free on application, also a fine series of western mins. and fossils for ex.*

3892 Snow, Norman G., La Salle, Ill. *Ast.**

3893 Snyder, Henry W., B.Sc., Prof. of Physics and Chemistry, Miami Univ., Oxford, Ohio. *Chem., Phys.**

3894 Snyder, John O., Waterloo, Ind. *Palæo., Orn., Ool.* C. Ex.*

3895 Snyder, M. B., Central High School, Philadelphia, Pa. *Ast.**

3896 Snyder, Z. X., Greensbury, Pa. *Min., Phys., Zool., Gen.Biol., Anat., Orn., Tax., Ent.* C. Ex.

3897 Somers, J., A.B., M.D., Halifax, N. S., Can. *Bot., Zool., Phys.**

3898 Sornberger, Samuel J., Ph.D., Cortland, N. Y. *Optics, Acoustics.**

3899 Soule, Wm., Ph.D., Mt. Union College, Mt. Union, Stark Co., Ohio. Prof. *Phys. and Chem.**

3900 Southwell, J. H., Rock Island, Ill. *Bot., Geol., Artesian Wells.* C. of fossils.*

3901 Southwick, Edmund B., Arsenal Building, 64th St. and 5th Ave., Central Park, New York, N. Y. Entomologist, Central Park, N. Y. and Curator of Ent., American Mus. of Nat. Hist., 77th St. and 8th Ave., New York, N. Y. *Forestry, Ent., Bot.* C. Ex.*

3902 Southwick, J. M., Naturalist, 258 Westminster St., Providence, R. I. *Mam., Orn., Ool., Con., Min.* Dealer.*

3903 Southworth, La Grande, Schuyler's Lake, Otsego Co., N. Y. *Bot., Orn., Ool., Ent.* C. Ex.

3904 Sowter, T. W. Edwin, Dept. of Interior, Ottawa, Canada. *Palæo., Stratigraphy.**

3905 Spalding, Volney M., Prof. Bot., Univ. Mich., Ann Arbor, Mich. *Bot.**

3906 Spang, Norman, Etna, Alleghany Co., Pa. *Min., Arch.* C.*

3907 Spangler, E. P., Clark City, Clark Co., Mo. *Geol., Palæo., Min., Crystall., Arch.*

3908 Sparks, Mrs. Mary Noble, Alton, Ill. *Tax., Snakes.* C.*

3909 Spaulding, Justin, Chicopee, Mass. *Mic.**

3910 Spayde, Wm. H., Steelton, Dauphin Co., Pa. *Min., Geol.* Wishes to exchange fine minerals for fossils, coral spec. and other minerals. Only fine spec. desired.*

3911 Speir, Francis, jr., So. Orange, N. J. *Vert. Palæo.**
3912 Spelman, Henry M., 62 Sparks St., Cambridge, Mass. *Orn.* C.*
3913 Spence, Mrs. E. Jane, Springfield, Ohio. *Bot: Ferns, Mosses.* C. Ex.*
3914 Spencer, A. H., E. Clarendon, Rutland Co., Vt. *Con., Min., Arch., Numis.* C. Ex.*
3915 Spencer, G. L., Ass't Chem., Department of Agriculture, Washington, D. C.
3916 Spencer, Herbert R. & Co., successors to Chas. A. Spencer & Sons, manufacturers of microscope objectives, Geneva, N.Y.*
3917 Spencer, John W., Paxton, Sullivan Co., Ind. *Bot., Geol., Palæo., Arch., Ent.* C. Ex.?
3918 Sperry, Joseph H., Clinton, Ct. *Phæn. and Crypt. Bot., Ferns.* C. Ex.*
3919 Sperry, Lyman B., M.A., M.D., Lecturer on Sanitary Science, Carleton Coll., Northfield, Minn.*
3920 Speyers, Clarence L., Mo. State University, Columbia, Mo. *Chem.**
3921 Spitzka, Edward C., M.D., 712 Lexington Ave., New York, N. Y. *Emb., Vertebrates, Anat. Vertebrates, Anth.**
3922 Sprague, F. H., Wollaston, Mass. *Ent.* C.*
3923 Sprague, Isaac, Wellesley Hills, Mass. *Botanical Artist.**
3924 Sprague, Isaac, jr., Wellesley Hills, Mass. *Lepid.* C. Ex.*
3925 Springhall, Joseph, M.D., Dexter, Me. *Min., Geol., Met., Fossils of Maine.**
3926 Springer, Alfred, A.M., Ph.D., Box 621, Cincinnati, Ohio. *Chem., Mic.* C.*
3927 Springer, Frank, Las Vegas, New Mexico. *Invert Palæontology.* C. Ex.*
3928 Springer, Phil. M., Springfield, Ill. *Ent., Con.* C.*
3929 Stacy, O. S., 794 Lafayette Ave., Brooklyn, N. Y. *Bot., Algæ, Hort., Geol., Min., Crystall., Lithol., Phys., Ichth., Lepid.* C. Ex *
3930 Stadmuller, L., Sheffield Scientific School, New Haven, Ct. *Min.* Sells, buys and exchanges.*
3931 Staebner, F. W., L.B. 322, State Normal School, Westfield, Mass. *Geol., Min., Gen. Biol.* C. Ex.*
3932 Stager, Walter, Sterling, Ill. *Geol.**
3933 Stahr, Prof. John S., Lancaster, Pa. *Phæn. Bot.* C. Ex.*
3934 Stakemiller, John A., Mt. Carroll, Carroll Co., Ill. *Geol., Min., Palæo.* C. Ex. fossils and corals and F. W. Shells from Mississippi River.*
3935 Stanley, Chas. H., Warner, N. H. *Phæn. and Crypt. Bot: Ferns.* C. Ex.*
3936 Stam, Colin F., Chestertown, Md. *Bot., Geol., Min., Chem.**
3937 Stanley, Prof. Richard C., Ph.D., Bates Coll., Lewiston, Me. *Geol.**
3938 Stanton, J. Y., Prof. Bates Coll., Lewiston, Me. *Orn.* C.*
3939 Stapleton, Rev. A., Seneca Falls, N. Y. *Geol.* C. Sil., Devon. and Carb. fossils for ex.?

3940 Starbird, N. W., jr., Danvers, Mass. *Min.*, *Lithol.*, *Photog.* C. Ex.*

3941 Starr, Mrs. Amory R., Marshall, Harrison Co., Texas. *Geol.* C. Ex.

3942 Starr, Prof. Frederick, M.S., Ph.D., 27 Seminary Ave., Auburn, N. Y., or Coe College, Cedar Rapids, Ia. *Geol.*, *Bot.*, *Anth.* C.*

3943 Starr, O. Stanley, 420 E. 118th St., New York, N. Y. *Coleopt.*, *Anat.*, *Mic.* C. Ex.

3944 Starrett, A. P., Warren, Me. *Ent: Coleopt.* C. Ex.?

3945 Startz, George, 277 Springfield Ave., Newark, N. J. *Lepid.*

3946 St. Cyr, D. N., Conservateur du Musie de l'Instruction Publique, Quebec, Can. *Bot.*, *Min.*, *Ent.*, *Con.**

3947 Steacy, W. H., Thonotosassa, Hillsboro' Co., Fla. *Orn.*, *Tax.**

3948 Stearns, Charles A., 33 Pearl St., Boston, Mass. *Min.*, *Con.**

3949 Stearns, Frederick, Detroit, Mich. *Pharmacy.* General collection; desires foreign correspondence and will purchase first-class specimens. *Arch.*, *Bot.*, *Eth.*, *Min.*, *Moll.* Bric à brac. Offers many ex. in same, lists furnished.*

3950 Stearns, Robert E. C., Ph.D., Ass't Curator Dept. Molluscs, U. S. Nat. Museum, Smithsonian Institution, Washington, D. C. Recent and Cenozoic Molluscs.*

3951 Stearns, Silas, Pensacola, Fla. *Ichth.* C.*

3952 Stearns, Winfrid A., Amherst, Mass. *Gen. Nat. Hist.*, *esp. Zool.*, *Specialty*, *Ornithology and Entomology.**

3953 Stebbins, Edward S., 507 Lumber Exchange, Minneapolis. Minn. *Arch.*, *Ool.* C. Ex. in sets with data.*

3954 Stebbins, E. J., Adrian, Mich. *Ent: Lepid.*, *Con.* C. Ex.*

3955 Stebbins, Fred. Briggs, Treasurer Adrian Sci. Soc., Adrian, Mich. *Arch.*, *Geol.*, *Philately*, *Gen. Sci.* C. I collect and ex. stamps, coins, seals, autographs, antiquities, etc. Many desirable spec. to ex. Correspondence on history of Stebbins, Briggs or Cossitt families desired.*

3956 Stebbins, W. D., 17 Maple St., Springfield, Mass. *Palæo.*, *Geol.*, *Min.*, *Zool.*, *Arch.*, *Con.* C. Ex.*

3957 Stebbins, James H., jr., Analyt. and Consulting Chemist, 117 Pearl St., New York, N. Y.*

3958 Stedman, John M., Cornell Univ., Ithaca, N. Y. *Biol.*, *Zool.*, *Emb.*, *Hist.*, *Mic.**

3959 Steele, Maria O., 138 Montague St., Brooklyn, N. Y. *Bot.*, *Ferns.* C. Ex.*

3960 Steele, Joseph, Scott's Bay, Nova Scotia. *Min.* C.

3961 Steere, J. B., Ph.D., Prof. Zool., Univ. Mich., Ann Arbor, Mich. *Syst. Zool.*, *Mich. Verts. and L. and F. W. Shells.* C. Ex.

3962 Stein, Fred., M.D., 25 W. McCarthy St., Indianapolis, Ind. *N. A. Coleopt.*, *Air-breathing Molluscs.**

3963 Steinbeck, Wm. P., Hollister, Calif. *Orn.*, *Ool.*, *Tax.**

3964 Steiner, L. H., M.D., Pratt Free Library, Baltimore, Md. *Chem.*, *Sanitary Sci.**

3965 Steinmeyer, F. A., M.D., Bonaparte, Van Buren Co., Iowa. *Geol.*, *Mic.*, *Arch.* C. Ex.*

3966 Stejneger, Leonhard, Smithsonian Institution, Washington, D. C. *Orn.**
3967 Stelle, Prof. J. P., Mobile, Ala. *Ent.*, *Bot.*, *Orn.*, *Geol.* C.*
3968 Stendicke, August, 60 Third Ave., New York, N. Y. *Optician.**
3969 Stephens, Frank, Ballena, San Diego Co., Calif. *Mam.*, *Orn.*, *Ool.* C. Ex.*
3970 Stephens, Hallie E., Cleves, Hamilton Co., Ohio. *Ferns*, *Mosses*, *Palæo.*, *Min.* C. Ex.*
3971 Stephenson, Wm., M.D., Ass't Surgeon U. S. Army, 119 State St., Portland, Me. *Ool.* C.*
3972 Steigerwalt, Chas., 130 E. King St., Lancaster, Pa. *Arch.*, *Numismatics.* Dealer.*
3973 Sterki, Victor, M.D., New Philadelphia, Tuscarawas Co., Ohio. *L. and F. W. Molluscs*, *Spec. Pupa*, *Vertigo*, *etc.* C. Ex.*
3974 Sterl, Alexander, M.D., 361 Blue Island Ave., Chicago, Ill. *Gen. Bot.* C. Ex.*
3975 Sternberg, Chas. N., 1038 Ky. St., Lawrence, Kansas. *Collection Dakota Group (Cretaceous) Plants for sale.**
3976 Sternberg, Geo. M., Maj. and Surgeon, U. S. A., care Surgeon Gen., U. S. A., Washington, D. C. *Fungi*, *Algæ*, *Mic.*, *Photog.*, *Gen. Biol.*, *Anth.*, *Arch.*, *Infusoria.**
3977 Stevens, George T., M.D., Ph.D., 33 W. 33d St., New York, N. Y. *Bot.* C. Ex.*
3978 Steward, J. F., 1135 Dunning St., Chicago, Ill. *Palæo. Arch.* C. Ex.*
3979 Stevens, H. C., Oregon City, Ore. *Arch.* C.*
3980 Stevens, W. LeConte, 170 Joralemon St., Brooklyn, N. Y. *Physical Geog.*, *Physiological optics*, *Physics.**
3981 Stevenson, Ernest, Walla Walla, Walla Walla Co., Washington Territory. *Bot.*, *Orn.*, *Tax.*, *Lepid.*, *Coleopt.* C. Ex.*
3982 Stevenson, James, Executive U. S. Geol. Surv., Washington, D. C. *Zool.*, *Anth.*, *Arch.*, *Eth.*, *Ethnog.*, *Philol.*
3983 Stevenson, James A., 160 Benjamin St., Akron, Ohio. *Con.* C. Ex.?
3984 Stevenson, John J., Prof. Univ. of City of New York, New York City, N. Y. *Geol.**
3985 Stevenson, W. G., M.D., 339 Mill St., Poughkeepsie, N. Y. *Biol.**
3986 Stevenson, William C., jr., 1525 Green St., Philadelphia, Pa. *Fungi.* C. Ex.*
3987 Stewart, Alex D., Wenonah, Gloucester Co., N. J. *Min.*, *Chem.* C. Ex.*
3988 Stewart, Bert, Decatur, Ill. *Eth.**
3989 Stewart, Prof. F. L., Murrysville, Westmoreland Co., Pa. *Saccharine Chem.*, *Geol.*, *Bot.*, *Orn.* C. Ex.
3990 Stewart, John, Department of the Interior, Ottawa, Ont., Can. *Geol.*, *Min.*, *Chem.*, *Metall.*, *Palæontology.** C. Ex.*
3991 Stewart, John H., Middletown, Middlesex Co., Ct. *Photog.*, *Orn.*, *Tax.* C. Ex.*
3992 Stewart, J. T., M.D., Peoria, Ill. *Bot.* C.*

3993 Stickney, Victor H., Tyson Furnace, Windsor Co., Vt. *Min.**

3994 Stidham, Rev. I. F., Ph.D., New Britain, Ct. *Palæo., Mic.**

3995 Stiles, E. P., 714 Congress Ave., Austin, Texas. *Ferns, Mic., Orn., Grasses.**

3996 Stiles, S. Edward, M.D., 51 Greene Ave., Brooklyn, N. Y. *Mic.* C. Ex. slides or good material.*

3997 Stillman, John M., Ph.D., Boston Sugar Refinery, Boston, Mass. *Chem.**

3998 Stillman, Thomas B., M.Sc., Ph.D., Prof. of Analytical Chem., Stevens Inst. of Tech., Hoboken, N. J. (Consulting Chemist, 40 Broadway, N. Y.). *Chem.**

3999 Stillman, Wm. O., A.M., M.D., 287 State St., Albany, N. Y. *Phys., Elect., Mic., Gen. Biol., Emb., Anth., Histol.**

4000 Stillson, Prof. Joseph O., A.M., M.D., Prof. Physiol. and Diseases of the Eye and Ear, Central Coll. of Phys. and Surgeons, 199 N. Delaware St., Indianapolis, Ind. *Mic., Physiol., Ophthal., Histol., Ent.* C. Ex.*

4001 Stillwell, Charles M., Box 1261 or 55 Fulton St., New York City, N. Y. *Inorg. Chem., Met.**

4002 Stilwel, Geo. E., 1811 Mercer St., Kansas City, Mo. *Tax., Orn., Ool.* Desires to buy or exchange Birds.*

4003 Stilwel, L. W., Deadwood, Dakota, wholesale and retail dealer in Minerals, Cretaceous and Tertiary Fossils and Sioux Indian Relics. Have 3,000 Oregon arrowheads. *Palæo., Vert., Invert., Min., Arch., Mammals, Molluscs.* C.*

4004 Stilwel, O. J., Alma, Mich. *Bot., Zool., Tax.* C. Ex.*

4005 Stimpson, Charles M., Peabody, Mass. *Bot.**

4006 Stinner, F. A., 3487 3rd Ave., New York City. *Ent: Lepid.* C. Ex.*

4007 Stejneger, Leonhard, Ass't Curator, Dep't of Birds, U. S. Nat. Mus., Washington, D. C.*

4008 St. John, E. P., Prattsburg, Steuben Co., N. Y. *Arch., Orn., Tax., Con.**

4009 St. John, Orestes, Topeka, Kansas. *Palæo., Strat. Geol.**

4010 St. John, Rob't P., Prattsburg, Steuben Co., N. Y. *Arch., Ool.* C. Ex.

4011 Stockbridge, Henry, jr., 12 N. Calhoun St., Baltimore, Md. *Mineral Microscopy.* C. Ex.

4012 Stockwell, John N., Ph.D., Cleveland, Ohio. *Ast., Lunar Theory in particular.**

4013 Stoddard, J. R., Newington Junction, Hartford Co., Ct. *Min.* C. Fine specimens for sale and exchange. Correspondence desired.*

4014 Stoddard, J. T., A.M., Ph.D. (Gott.), Prof. Chem. and Physics, Smith Coll., Northampton, Mass.*

4015 Stodder, James C., F.R.M.S., 5 W. Broadway, Bangor, Me. *Mic., Photog.**

4016 Stoker, Eug. E., Smithville, Lancaster Co., Pa. Collector of minerals, Indian relics, war relics, old arms, shells, polished wood specimens and curiosities. Ex.*

4017 Stoker, H. M., Florin, Lancaster Co. Pa. Collector of minerals, coins, stamps, Indian relics, books, old papers, shells, etc.*

4018 Stokes, A. C., M.D., 514 E. State St., Trenton, N. J. *Protozoa.**

4019 Stone, Charles E., P. O. Box 583, Spencer, Mass. *Min.* C. Ex.*

4020 Stone, Prof. Chas. S., Cooper Union, New York, N. Y. *Chem.*, *Min.* C.*

4021 Stone, Dwight D., cor. E. 10th and Oneida Sts., Oswego, N. Y. *Mam.*, *Orn.*, *Ool.*, *Tax.* C. Ex.*

4022 Stone, Frank M., 216 Sansome St., San Francisco, Calif. *Ool.* C. Ex.?

4023 Stone, George H., Prof. Geol., Colorado Coll., Colorado Springs, Colo. *Geol.*, *Min.* C.*

4024 Stone, Miss M. L., East Cambridge, Mass. *Geol.*, *Min.**

4025 Stone, Ormond, Dir. Leander McCormick Obs., University of Virginia. *Ast.**

4026 Stone, Winthrop E., Amherst, Mass. *Bot.*, *Hort.*, *Mic.*, *Gen. Biol.* C. Ex.

4027 Stone, Witmer, B.A., Fisher's Lane, Germantown, Pa. *Bot.*, *Orn.*, *Ent.* C.*

4028 Storer, Francis H., A.M., Prof. Agric. Chem., Bussey Inst., Jamaica Plain, Mass.*

4029 Storrs, C. H., Lebanon, N. H. *Orn.*, *Mam.*, *Tax.**

4030 Storrs, Henry E., Ph.D., Prof. Nat. Sci., Ill. Coll., Jacksonville, Ill. *Phys.*, *Chem.* C.*

4031 Stout, Arthur B., M.D., 729 Montgomery St., S. W. Corner Jackson St., San Francisco, Calif. *Anth.* C.*

4032 Stover, Albert, 40 State St., Boston, Mass. *Elect.*

4033 Stowell, C. H., M.D., F.R.M.S., Ann Arbor, Mich. *Mic.* C.*

4034 Stowell, Louisa R., M.S., F.R.M.S., Ann, Arbor, Mich. *Mic.*, *Bot.* C.*

4035 Stowell, T. B., A.M., Ph.D., State Normal School, Cortland, N. Y. *Comp. Anat.*, *Physiol.* C.*

4036 Straight, H. H., Normal School, Normal Park, Ill. *Anat. and Physiol. of Vert.*, *Gen. Biol.*, *Anth.* C. Ex.

4037 Stratton, F. A., Chattanooga, Tenn. *Min.*, *Arch.* C. Ex.?

4038 Stratton, Hattie R., Box 43, Grassy Cove, Cumberland Co., Tenn. *Gen. Nat. Hist.* C. Ex.?

4039 Streator, Clark, Garrettsville, Ohio. *Orn.*, *Tax.* C. Ex. of birds from all parts of the world.*

4040 Streator, Geo. J., Garrettsville, Portage Co., Ohio. *Bot.*, *L. and F. W. Shells.* C. Desires to exchange shells of Ohio for those of other states. Will correspond with persons in England and France in regard to exchange of L. and F. W. Shells.*

4041 Strecker, Herman, Box 111, Reading, Berks Co., Pa. *Ent.: Lepid.* C. Ex. Buys and sells Lepid. from all parts of the world.*

4042 Streeruwitz, W. H., Consulting Mining Engineer, Metallurgist and Assayer, Houston, Texas. C. Ex. Ores and rock specimens.*

4043 Streeter, Wm., 14 Scio St., Rochester, N. Y. *Mic.*, *Ast.**

4044 Streets, Thomas H., M.D., Surgeon, U. S. N., Navy Dept., Washington, D. C. *Amphidous Crustacea.**

4045 Streng, L. H., Grand Rapids, Mich. *Meteo.*, *Moll.* C. Ex. Desires anything in the line of Molluscs, espec. Hel., Bulimus, Helecina, Clausilia and F. W. shells, Ampullaria, Physa, Lymnæa, etc., from all parts of the world.*

4046 Stretch, R. H., P. O. Box 1905, San Francisco, Calif. *Zygænidæ*, *Bombycidæ of the world.*?

4047 Stringham, Irving, A.B. (Harv.), Ph.D. (Balt.), Prof. Math., Univ. Calif., Berkeley, Calif. *Math.**

4048 Strode, Wm. S., M.D., Bernadotte, Fulton Co., Illinois. *Arch.*, *Orn.*, *Ool.*, *Tax.* C. Ex.*

4049 Strong, Wm. C., A.M., Teacher Nat. Sci., Maine Wes. Sem. and F. C., Kent's Hill, Kennebec Co., Me. *Phys.*, *Meteorol.**

4050 Strumberg, C. W., Galesburg, Ill. *Coleopt. of N. A.* C. Ex. Wish to purchase or ex. rare Cincindelæ and Carabidæ. Correspondence solicited.*

4051 Stuart, Ernest B., Prof. Chem. Technology, Chicago College of Pharmacy, 465 & 467 State St. Chemist Phœnix Distillery Co., Chicago, Ill.*

4052 Stuart, Robert C., Tampa, Fla. *Orn.*, *Ool.*, *Tax.*, *Molluscs.**

4053 Stubbs, Chas. H., M.D., Wakefield, Pa. *Geol.*, *Min.*, *Arch.* C. Ex. minerals found in Hartford and Cecil counties, Md., and Lancaster and Chester counties, Pa. Would like to ex. minerals for stone relics.*

4054 Stubbs, Wm. C., Ph.D., State Chemist and Dir. State Experiment Station, Baton Rouge, La., and Dir. Sugar Experiment Station, Kenner, La.*

4055 Studer, Jacob Henry, Tribune Building, New York, N. Y. *Orn.* C.?

4056 Sturdy, Joseph, Niagara Falls, N. Y. *Phæn. Bot.*?

4057 Sturgis, Rev. Joseph R., Ashland, Va. *Crypt. Bot.*, *Mic.*, *Gen. Biol.*, *Emb.*, *Histol.*, *Lower Invert.* C. Ex.*

4058 Sturtevant, E. Lewis, South Framingham, Mass. *Agricultural Science.**

4059 Sudden, Mrs. Lorette C., Canton Point, Oxford Co., Me. *Bot.*, *Geol.*, *Min.*, *Ast.* C. Ex.*

4060 Sudworth, Geo. B., A.B., Dept. of Agric., Forestry Division, Washington, D. C. *Bot.*, *Phæn. and Crypt. Plants*, *Zool.*, *Orn.*, *Herpetol.* C. Ex.*

4061 Suksdof, W. N., Cambridge, Mass. *Bot.**

4062 Sulgrove, Leslie, Helena, Lewis and Clarke Cos., Mont. *Ent: Lepid.*, *Coleopt.* C. Ex. foreign and native.*

4063 Summers, Henry E., Cornell University, Ithaca, N. Y. *Mic.*, *Hemiptera-Heteroptera*, *Comparative Anatomy* C. Ex.*

4064 Summers, Rev. R. W., San Luis Obispo, Calif. *Geol.*, *Radiata*, *Moll.*, *Arch.* C. Ex.

4065 Summers, Mrs. R. W., San Luis Obispo, Calif. *Bot., Con., Ent., Radiates.* C. Will sell spec. or ex. for fossils, mins., mound builders' relics, etc.
4066 Summers, William H., 3450 Cottage Grove Ave., Chicago, Ill. *Mic., Diatoms, Ent.* C. Ex.*
4067 Sutton, William, 2514 Sacramento St., San Francisco, Calif. *Con.* Ex. Also desires correspondents in Southern States and foreign countries.
4068 Swain, Miss Emma, 1354 Eighth Ave., East Oakland, Calif. *Min., Moll.* C. Ex.*
4069 Swaine, Seorim, Rochester, N. H. *Desmids, Diatoms, Mic., Photog.* C. Ex.*
4070 Swallow, G. C., LL.D., Helena, Montana. *Geol., Zool., Bot.**
4071 Swan, Charles W., M.D., 32 Worcester St., Boston, Mass. *Bot.* C. Ex.*
4072 Swart, Walter G., 3 Fort St., Auburn, N. Y. *Palæo., Phys. Geol., Min.* C. Ex.*
4073 Sweeny, R. O., St. Paul, Minn. *Ichth.**
4074 Sweet, E. T., Silverton, Colo. *Min.* C.?
4075 Swezey, G. D., A.M., Prof. Doane Coll., Crete, Neb. *Ast., Nat. Hist., Geol.* C. Ex.*
4076 Swift, Edward, Taxidermist, 725 West 1st St., Elmira, N. Y. *Zool., Emb., Orn., Ool., Ichth., Tax., etc.* Correspondence with collectors of Birds solicited. C. Ex.*
4077 Swift, Lewis, F.R.A.S., Ph.D., Dir. Warner Obs., Rochester, N. Y. *Ast.**
4078 Swift, Robert, S.B., M.D., 23 Circuit St., Roxbury, Mass. *Geol., Comp. Anat.* C.*
4079 Sylvester, C. H., Boscobel, Grant Co., Wis. *Bot.**
4080 Taber, E. B., Journalist, "Times," New York, N. Y. *Lepid.?*
4081 Taggert, S. M., New Vienna, Clinton Co., Ohio. *Palæo., Geol., Moll.* C. Ex.
4082 Tainter, Sumner, 2020 F. St. N. W., Washington, D. C. *Phys., Elect., Ast.?*
4083 Talbot, D. H., Sioux City, Woodbury Co., Ia. *Nat. Hist. in Gen.* C. Cash paid for wild animals, birds, etc.; write particulars of what you wish to sell.*
4084 Talbott, Harry E., Mt. Auburn, Cincinnati, Ohio. *Orn., Ool., Palæo.* C.?
4085 Tallant, W.N., 73 Jefferson Ave., Columbus, O. *Lepid.* C. Ex.*
4086 Tallman, John L., Tecumseh, Mich. *Ool., Bot.* C.*
4087 Talmadge, Sam'l F., Berlin, Ct. *Photog., Arch., Ethnol., Ent.* C. Ex.*
4088 Talmadge, W. G., Plymouth, Ct. *Orn.**
4089 Talmage, James E., Provo City, Utah. *Min., Chem.?*
4090 Tammen, H. H., P. O. Box 1857, Denver, Colo. *Colorado Minerals and Indian relics.**
4091 Tandy, M., Dallas City, Hancock Co., Ill. *Tax.* C.*
4092 Tarbox, Miss Mary M., Bath, Me. *Bot.* C.*
4093 Tascott, Frank B., 19 So. Canal St., Chicago, Ill. *Ent., Min., Geol.* C. Ex.?

4094 Tatham, H. B., jr., 226–8 South 5th St., Philadelphia, Pa. Inventor and Patentee Automatic Electro-Hydraulic Heat Regulator and Appliances.*

4095 Tatnall, Edw., Wilmington, Del. *Bot.* C. Ex. Phænogams.*

4096 Taylor, A. O'D., Newport, R. I. [Honorary Curator of Newport Natural History Society.] *Orn., Con.**

4097 Taylor, Fred W., Lock Box 497, Washington, D. C. *Geol., Chem., Min., Met.**

4098 Taylor, Geo. C., Ex. 2nd V. Pres. Am. Soc. of Mic., 1882–3. Hon. Memb. Baltimore Mic. Soc., Thibodeaux, La Fourche Parish, La. *Mic.* in *Agric.* and sanitary matters. C. Ex.?

4099 Taylor, G. Morrison, Riverside, Burlington Co., N. J. *Min., Ent.* C. Ex.*

4100 Taylor, Prof. G. Washington, Cazenovia, N. Y. *Phæn. Bot., Ferns, Mosses, Fungi, Algæ, Geol., Palæo.* C.*

4101 Taylor, H. R., Alameda, Alameda Co., Calif. *Orn., Ool., Moll.* C.*

4102 Taylor, Julius S., M.D., Ph.D., Cur. and Dir. Mus. Nat. Hist., Blackburn Univ., Carlinville, Ill.*

4103 Taylor, Robert T., 4701 Leiper St., Frankford, Philadelphia, Pa. *Min., Lepid.* C. Ex.*

4104 Taylor, Thomas, M.D., Microscopist and plant pathologist, Dept. of Agriculture, Washington, D. C. *Mic., Fungi, Histol.* C. Ex.*

4105 Taylor, W. B., Mauch Chunk, Pa., Box 302. *Lepid.* C. Ex.*

4106 Taylor, Wm. B., Smithsonian Inst., Washington, D. C. *General Physics.**

4107 Teator, W. S., Upper Red Hook, Dutchess Co., N. Y. *Min., Geol., Indian Relics.* C. Ex. in minerals.*

4108 Teed, Ida, 235 Boyle Ave., Los Angeles, Calif. *Ferns, Molluscs.* C. Ex.*

4109 Teeter, C. W., Wyoming, Stark Co., Ill. *Pharm., Chem.**

4110 Tenney, Mrs. Ellen Le Gros, 484 Madison Ave., Albany, N. Y. *Bot: Ferns, Mosses and Fungi, Ent.* C. Ex.*

4111 Tenney, Jonathan, M.A., Ph.D., 484 Madison Ave., Albany, N. Y. *Hort., Geol., Min., Anat., Phys., Bibliog.* C. Will correspond.*

4112 Tepper, Fr., Box 3331, New York City. *Lepid.* C. Ex.?

4113 Terheun, Peter O., Hohokus, Bergen Co., N. J. *Min., Chem., Metall., Phys., Elect., Mic., Photog.* C. Ex.*

4114 Terry, N. M., Ph.D., U. S. Naval Academy, Annapolis, Md. *Phys.**

4115 Terry, Wm. A., Bristol, Hartford Co., Ct. *Algæ, Desmids, Diatoms, Mic., Photo.* C. Ex.*

4116 Teubner, Chas., Lexington, Lafayette Co., Mo. *Relics of the Mound Builders.* C. 6000 specimens. Duplicates for sale.*

4117 Thacher, James K., M.D., Prof. Physiol. and Clin.-Med., Yale College, 206 Crown St., New Haven, Ct. *Physiol.**

4118 Thacker, J. A., A.M., M.D., F.R.M.S., 121 W. 7th St., Cincinnati, Ohio. *Med. Mic.* Ed. Cin. Med. News.?

4119 Thatcher, A. R., Haydenville, Mass. *Min.* C.*
4120 Thatcher, Roscoe W., Chatham Centre, Medina Co., Ohio. *Embryology, Orn., Ool.* C. Ex.
4121 Thaxter, L. L., 13 Tremont St., Boston, Mass. *Molluscs.* C.*
4122 Thaxter, Roland, Kittery Point, Me. *Bot., Photog., Ent: Lepid.* C. Ex.
4123 Thayer, E. O., Atlanta, Ga.*
4124 Thayer, H. C., 813 Pearl St., Los Angeles, Calif. *Ferns, Min., Orn.* C. Ex.*
4125 Thayer, J. M., 1354 Euclid Ave., Cleveland, Ohio. *Orn., Ool., Tax., Min.* C. Ex.*
4126 Thayer, Samuel Proctor, No. Adams, Mass. *Bot.* C.*
4127 Thomas, Allen C., Haverford Coll., Pa. *History, Political Economy and Literature.**
4128 Thomas, Mrs. Annie N., 591 Bushwick Ave., Brooklyn, N. Y. *Bot.?*
4129 Thomas, Benj. F., A.M., Ph.D., Prof. Phys., Ohio State Univ., Dir. of Ohio Meteorological Bureau, Columbus, Ohio. *Elect., Light and Solar Physics.**
4130 Thomas, B. W., F.R.M.S., V. Pres. Chicago Acad. Sci., 1842 Indiana Ave., Chicago, Ill. *Mic., Diatoms, Boulder-clay Foraminifera, Crustaceans, F. W. Sponges.* C. Ex.*
4131 Thomas, Prof. Cyrus, 1246 11th St., N. W., Washington, D. C. *Am. Arch.?*
4132 Thomas, Dr. Flavel S., M.S., Hanson, Mass. *Zool., Orn., Ent., Comp. Anat., Comp. Pathol.**
4133 Thomas, Mrs. Flavel S., B.S., Hanson, Mass. *Bot., Zool., Ent.**
4134 Thomas, Fred. A., Mexico, N. Y. *Min., Arch.* C. Ex.*
4135 Thomas, Jos., M.D., Quakertown, Pa. *Bot., Orn., Ent., Hymen.* C. Ex.*
4136 Thomas, J. B., 2700 Wentworth Ave., Chicago, Ill. *Min., Geol.* C. Ex.*
4137 Thomas, W. H. B., Philadelphia, Pa. *Geol., Invert. Palæo., Anth., Am. Geog.**
4138 Thomas, Wm. Bailey, Athens, Ga. *Lepid., Dipt.* C. Ex.?
4139 Thomas, W. S., Little Rock, Ark. *Geol.**
4140 Thompson, Alton H., D.D.S., Topeka, Kan. *Anth.* C.*
4141 Thompson, Charles A., Quincy, Branch Co., Mich. *Geol., Arch.* C. Ex. Very fine gem arrowheads from Oregon. (Prehistoric).*
4142 Thompson, Everett A., A.M., North Woburn, Mass. *Min., Bot.* C. Ex.*
4143 Thompson, Gilbert, Geographer, U. S. Geol. Survey, Box 591, Washington, D. C. *Physical Geog.**
4144 Thompson, G. W., 712 President St., Brooklyn, N. Y. *Phæn. and Crypt. Bot., Chem.* C. Ex.*
4145 Thompson, Harry F., 17 Butler St., Indianapolis, Ind. *Palæo., Geol., Min., Arch.* C. Ex.
4146 Thompson, Harvey, A.M., Prof. Nat. Sci., Hastings, Nebraska. *Bot., Phæn. Plants, Geol., Zool.* C. Ex.*

4147 **Thompson, Richard J., M.D., 33 Rock St., Fall River, Mass.** *Phys. Geog., Min., Mic.* C.?

4148 **Thompson, Thos. H., L. Box 1082, Middletown, Ct.** *Orn., Ool.*

4149 **Thomson, John H., C.M.Z.S., Box 347, New Bedford, Mass.** *Con.* C. Ex. Wishes Foreign Helicidæ, for which American and Foreign L., F. W., and Marine species will be given in ex. South American species especially desired. Correspondence desired.*

4150 **Thomson, W. B., New Britain, Ct.** *Min.* C. Ex.*

4151 **Thornburg, Thos. E., Ashland, Ohio.** *Ent: Lepid.. Coleopt. of U. S.* Desires exchanges with all parts of the world. Correspondence solicited. List of duplicates on application.*

4152 **Thorburn, John, LL.D., Geol. Surv., Ottawa, Ont., Can.** *Arch., Philol.**

4153 **Thrasher, Allen B., M.A., M.D., 157 W. 9th St., Cincinnati, Ohio.** *Mic., Histol.* C. Ex.*

4154 **Thresher, Alfred A., Dayton, Ohio.** *Palæo., Geol., Min., Crystall., Photog., Arch.* C. Ex.*

4155 **Thum, H., Grand Rapids, Mich.** *Mic., Sanitarian Pharm., Chem.**

4156 **Thum, Mandeville, M.D., Louisville, Ky.** *Mic., Chem.**

4157 **Thurber, George, M.D., Passaic, N. J.** *Bot., especially Grasses.* C.*

4158 **Thurston, John H., Cambridge, Mass.** *Mic., Photog.* C. Ex.*

4159 **Thurston, R. C. Ballard, Ass't Ky. Geol. Survey, Louisville, Ky.** *Geol., Inorg. Chem., Metall.**

4160 **Thurston, Robert H., Director Sibley Coll., Cornell Univ., Ithaca, N. Y.** *Mechanical Engineering.**

4161 **Tibbals, Wm. H., A.M., Prof. Philos. and Sci., Park Co., Parkville, Platte Co., Mo.***

4162 **Tidswell, Thos. J., Independence, Jackson Co., Mo.** *Invert. Palæo., Ast., Arch.* C.*

4163 **Tiffany, Dr. Asa S., 901 W. 5th St., Davenport, Ia.** *Geol., Palæo., Eth.* C. Good fossils correctly named for ex.*

4164 **Tilden, John N., Peekskill, Westchester Co., N. Y.** *Min., Lithol.* C. Ex. Meteorites desired; ex. or purchase.*

4165 **Tilemann, J. N., Aurora, Kane Co., Ill.** *Chem.?*

4166 **Tillman, Samuel E., Prof. Chem., Min. and Geol., U. S. Military Acad., West Point, N. Y.** *Phys.**

4167 **Tillman, Walter, 426 So. 5th St., La Crosse, Wis.** *Min., Ool.* C. Ex.*

4168 **Tilton, John L., Nashua, N. H.** *Gen. Biol.**

4169 **Timmins, Geo., Syracuse, N. Y.** *Algæ, Desmids, Diatoms, Mic.* C. Ex.*

4170 **Tingley, Joseph, Ph.D., Prof. Nat. Sci., Pres. Marion Normal Coll., Marion, Ind.** *Phys.* C. Sub-carboniferous Nautilli, Orthocera, Fish teeth, etc. Fragments of meteorite of Dec. 26, 1876, very fine specimens.

4171 Todd, Aurelius, Oakland, Douglas Co., Ore. *Orn.*, *Ool.*, *Ent.*, *Mam.*, *Min.*, *Tax.* A good stock on hand for sale. Special rates to dealers. Will collect to order in other branches. Dealers' correspondence solicited.*

4172 Todd, David H., 1217 Cherry St., Kansas City, Mo. *Fossils.* C. Ex. Desires Fossils, Minerals and Sea Birds' eggs, Am. and foreign. Fossil Fish of the Green River Shale.*

4173 Todd, Prof. David P., Director Amherst College Observatory, Amherst, Mass., Nautical Almanac Office, Washington, D. C. *Ast.**

4174 Todd, J. E., Ass't Geologist, U. S. G. S., Prof. Nat Sci., Tabor Coll., Tabor, Ia. *Quarternary Geol.*, *Moll.*, *Forms of Flowers.**

4175 Tolman, Adams, Concord, Mass. *Coleopt.*, *Arch.* C.*

4176 Toner, J. M., M.D., Washington, D. C. *Anth.**

4177 Toker, William Wallace, Sag Harbor, N. Y. *Algæ*, *Eth.*, *Arch.* C.*

4178 Toppan, Geo. L , Rooms 306–307, 138 Jackson St., Chicago, Ill. *Orn.*, *Ool.* C. Ex.*

4179 Torrance, J. Frazer, 17 St. John St., Montreal, Canada. *Geol.*, *Min.*, *Crystall.*, *Lithol.*, *Chem.*, *Metall.*, *Sponges*, *Protozoa.**

4180 Torrey, Bradford, Melrose Highlands, Mass. *Bot.*, *Orn.**

4181 Townsend, A. C., Lincoln City, Colorado. *Min.* C. Large coll. of duplicates.*

4182 Townsend, Edw. W., Salmon Falls, N. H. *Min.* C. Ex.*

4183 Townsend, J., Durham, Ont., Canada. *Invert. Palæo.* C. Ex.

4184 Townshend, Louis J., Bloomsburg, Col. Co., Pa. *Geol.*, *Min.* C. Ex.*

4185 Townshend, N. S., State Univ., Columbus, Ohio. *Bot.*

4186 Tozer, Robert J., 263 Garden St., Cleveland, Ohio. *Orn.*, *Ool.*, *Tax.**

4187 Tracy, Mrs. Clarissa T., Ripon Coll., Ripon, Wis. *Bot.**

4188 Tracy, Cyrus M., Lynn, Mass. *Bot.*, *Min.* C.?

4189 Tracy, S. M , M.S., Prof. Bot., Mo. State Univ., Columbia, Mo. *Bot.* C Ex.*

4190 Traphagan, Frank W., Ph.D., F.C.C., Prof. Chem. and Assaying, College of Montana, Deer Lodge, Montana. *Min.*, *Chem.* C. Fossils of Silurian and Tertiary, in ex. for those of other groups or mins.*

4191 Treadwell, Geo. A., Phœnix, Ariz. *Diatoms*, *Chem.*, *Geol.*, *Min.*, *Met.*, *Mic.* C. Ex.?

4192 Treat, J. A., M.D., Stuart, Guthrie Co., Ia. *Chem.*, *Mic.*, *Photog.* C.*

4193 Treat, John Harvey, Lawrence, Mass. *Ent.*, *Neuroptera.* C.*

4194 Treat, Mrs. Mary, Vineland, N. J. *Bot.*, *Ent.*, *Mic.**

4195 Treat, Willard E., East Hartford, Ct. *Orn.*, *Ool.*, *Tax.* C. Ex.*

4196 Treherne, H. Sackville, C.E., Spokane Falls, Wash. Terr. *Coleopt.* Scientific drawings.*

4197 Trelease, Wm., Sc.D., Prof. Shaw School of Bot., St. Louis, Mo. *Mutual relations of Flowers and Insects, Parasitic fungi.* C. Ex. for material bearing on specialty.*
4198 Trembley, J. B., M.D., Oakland, Calif. *Bot., Meteorol.?*
4199 Tremper, R. H., M.D., Albion, Mich. *Geol., Arch.* C.*
4200 Trenholme, Chas. W., Mining Engineer, Osborne St., Montreal, Can. *Geol., Palæo., Min.?*
4201 Tribe, Paul, C.M., Oswego, N. Y. *Lepid., Coleopt.* C.*
4202 Trimble, Henry, 632 Marshall St., Prof. Analyt. Chem., Phila., Pa. *Analyt. and Tech. Chem.*
4203 Trimble, Wm., Concordville, Delaware Co., Pa. *Mic., Ferns. Phæn. Bot.* C. Ex *
4204 Tripp, Geo. W., Adrian, Mich. *Ool., Orn.* C. Ex.*
4205 Tripp, Henry O., 367 High St., Providence, R. I. *Min.* C.*
4206 Trippe, T. M., C.E., Howardsville, San Juan Co., Colo. *Orn., Mam.*
4207 Troop, James, Purdue Univ., La Fayette, Ind. *Phæn. Bot., Hort., Mic., Ent.* C. Ex. grasses.*
4208 Trombley, Jerome, Petersburg, Mich. *Bot., Orn., Ichth., Con.* C. Ex. Eggs, also L., F. W. and Marine Shells from all parts of the world. Desires books and publications for specimens.*
4209 Trotter, Dr. Spencer, Acad. Nat. Sci., 19th and Race Sts., Philadelphia, Pa. *Orn., Comp. Anat. of Vert.* C. Ex *
4210 Trouslot, B. B., Taxidermist, Publisher of Hoosier Naturalist, 39 Col. Ave., Valparaiso, Ind. *Orn., Ool., Coleopt.* C.*
4211 Troxler, C., sr., 363 E. Market St., Louisville, Ky. *Coleopt., Lepid.* C.*
4212 True, F. W., Cur. of Mammals, U. S. National Mus., Washington, D. C. *Zool., Morph., Anat. of Vert., Mammals, Tortoises.*
4213 Trumbull, Gurdon, 970 Asylum St., Hartford, Ct. *Orn.*
4214 Trumbull, J. Hammond, LL.D., Hartford, Ct. *Philol., Anth., Bibliog.*
4215 Tryon, A. Walter, M.D., 247 West 125th St., New York City, N. Y. *Con., Bot., Palæo.* C.*
4216 Tscharner, John B., Okawville, Washington Co., Ill. *Arch., Indian Relics.* C. Ex.*
4217 Tuck, Geo. H., Box 94, Chicopee, Hampden Co., Mass. *Orn., Tax., Ent: Coleopt., Lepid.* C.*
4218 Tucker, Gilbert M., Albany, N. Y. *Lexicog.*
4219 Tucker, Willis G., M.D., Ph.D., Prof. Inorg. and Analyt. Chem. and Med. Jurisprudence, Albany, Med. Coll., Prof. Chem., Albany Coll. of Pharmacy, Albany, N. Y. *Chem.*
4220 Tuckerman, Prof. L. B., Cleveland, Ohio. *Mic.*
4221 Tuckerman, Frederick, Amherst, Mass. *Histol. of Vert.*
4222 Tunison, Chas., 347 W. 92 St., New York, N. Y. *Coleopt.* C.
4223 Turner, Henry H., Gundlach Optical Co., Rochester, N. Y. *Ast., Mic.*
4224 Turner, Henry W., Ass't Geologist, U. S. Geol Surv., Office U. S. Geol Survey, San Francisco, Calif. *Gen. Geol.*

4225 Turnure, Milton, M.D., Tenafly, N. J. *Mic., Vert.* Ex.*
4226 Tustin, Prof. F. W., Ph.D., Univ., Lewisburgh, Pa.
4227 Tuttle, Albert H., Prof. Zool., State Univ., Columbus, Ohio. *Mic., Gen. Biol., Histol.**
4228 Tweedale, John B., M.D., St. Thomas, Ont., Can. *Palæo., Geol., Anth., Orn., Ent.* C. Ex.*
4229 Tweedy, Frank, C.E., Plainfield, N. J. *Phæn. Bot., Ferns.* C. Ex.*
4230 Tyler, Geo. F., Box 158, New Britain, Ct. *Mam., Orn., Tax.* C. Ex.
4231 Tyler, John M., Prof. Biol., Amherst Coll., Amherst, Mass. *Zool., Bot.* Ex. Con. and Marine Invert.*
4232 Tyrrell, J. B., B.A., F.G.S., Geol. Surv. of Can., Ottawa, Ont., Can. *Geol., Acaridæ, Arachnida.**
4233 Tyson, James, M.D., 4506 Spruce St., Philadelphia, Pa. *Pathol., Anat. and Histol.* C.*
4234 Tyson, Samuel, King of Prussia, Montgomery Co., Pa. *Min.* C.?
4235 Udden, J. A., Prof. Nat. Hist., Bethany College, Lindsborg, MacPherson Co., Kan. *Bot., Morph., Local Flora.* C. Ex.*
4236 Uhler, Philip R., Cor. Sec. Md. Acad. Sciences, 254 W. Hoffman St., Baltimore, Md. *Geol., Hemipt., Crayfish.* C. Ex.*
4237 Ulke, Henry, 411 15th St. N. W., Washington, D. C. *Coleopt. of temperate and Arctic Am.* C.*
4238 Ulrich, E. O., 280 Central Ave., Newport, Ky. *Invert. Palæo., especially Bryozoa.* C. Desires European and Am. fossil Bryozoa in ex. for Palæo. forms.*
4239 Ullrich, Lewis, Tiffin, Seneca Co., Ohio. *Lepid.* Raising pupa and collecting lepid., etc., for sale and ex. C. Ex.*
4240 Umholtz, F. H., Ph.D., North East, Erie Co., Pa. C. Ex.*
4241 Underhill, Wm. W., Poughkeepsie, N. Y. *Zool., Orn. Ool., Tax.* C. Ex.?
4242 Underwood, H. G., 66 Wisconsin St., Milwaukee, Wis. *Chemical and other Patents procured.**
4243 Underwood, Lucien M., Ph.D., Prof. Biol., Syracuse Univ., Syracuse, N. Y. *Bot., Ent* C. Ex. Hepaticæ and Myriapoda of N. A. desired particularly from south, southwest and Pacific coast.*
4244 Upham, Warren, Ass't on Geol. Surveys of N. H., Minn., and U. S., 21 Newbury St., Somerville, Mass. *Glacial and recent Geol.**
4245 Upson, J. B., Rockford, Ill. *L. and F. W. and Fla. Shells.* C. Ex.*
4246 Upton, Prof. Winslow, A.M., Brown University, Providence, R. I. *Ast., Meteo.**
4247 Upton, Will H., Ira, Vt. *Orn., Ool., Tax.* C. Ex *
4248 Vail, Albert W., Moores, Del. Co., Pa. *Fungi, Lichens, Mic.* C. Ex.*
4249 Valentine, Benj. B., Richmond, Va. *Anth., Arch.* C.*
4250 Valentine, Edw. P., Richmond, Va. *Geol., Min., Anth., Arch.* C.*

4251 Valentine, Ferdinand Charles, M.D., 215 West 48th St., New York, N. Y. *Meteo.*, *Ent.*, *Anat.*, *Anth.*, *Arch.*, *Eth.*, *Ethnog.*, *Philol.*, *Vert.* C. Ex.*
4252 Valentine, H. E., 70 Kilby St., Boston, Mass. *Ent.*, *Mic.**
4253 Valentine, Sterling G., B.S., M.A., Ph.D., Lebanon, Lebanon Co., Pa. *Bot.*, *Min.*, *Chem.*, *Met.**
4254 Valiant, W. S., Rome, N. Y. *Arch.*, *Min.*, *Geol.* Spec. fossils from Utica and Frankfort shales. C. Ex.*
4255 Van Aken, A. G., A.M., New Brunswick, N. J. *Orn.*, *Ool.**
4256 Van Alstyne, Clarence, Chatham Centre, Columbia Co., N. Y. *Orn.*, *Ool.*, *Tax.* C. Ex.?
4257 Van Brunt, Cornelius, 62 College Place, New York, N.Y. *Mic.**
4258 Van Cott, J. M., jr., M.D., 188 Henry St., or Long Island College Hospital, Brooklyn, N. Y. *Mic.*, *Photog.*, *Emb.*, *Histol.* C.*
4259 Van Cruyningham, D., Macedon, Wayne Co., N. Y. *Bot.*, *Mic.* C. Ex.?
4260 Van Den Bergh, F.P., B.S., M.D., City Chemist and Prof. of Chem., Univ. of Buffalo, Buffalo, N. Y. *Chem.**
4261 Van Denburg, M. W., A.M., M.D., Fort Edward, Wash. Co., N. Y. *Bot.*, *Orn.**
4262 Vanderpoole, Lew, Oyster Bay, L. I., N. Y. *Geol.*, *Min.*, *Meteo.*, *Ast.*, *Bibliog.*, *Geog. Dist.*, *Anth.*, *Arch.*, *Eth.*, *Ethnog.*, *Philol.*, *Orn.*, *Ool.*, *Tax.* C. Ex.*
4263 Van der Veer, A., M.D., Ph.D., Cor. State and Eagle Sts., Prof. Albany Med. Coll., Albany, N. Y. *Mic.*, *Pathol. and Surgery.* C.*
4264 Van der Weyde, P. H., M.D., 236 Duffield St., Brooklyn, N. Y. *Physics*, *Chem.*, *Elect.*, *Crystall.*, *Mic.*, *Photog.*, *Diatoms*, *Infusoria.* C.*
4265 Van Duzee, Edward P., Grosvenor Library, Buffalo, N. Y. *Bot.*, *Ent: Hemipt.* C. Ex. in Hemipt.*
4266 Van Duzee, M. C., Lancaster, Erie Co., N. Y. *Bot.*, *Orn.*, *Ent.* C.
4267 Van Dyck, Prof. F. C., Rutgers Coll., New Brunswick, N. J. *Mic.?*
4268 Van Eiff, Chas., jr., 160 Franklin St., Brooklyn, E.D., N. Y. *Micros. Zool. in Gen.* C. Ex.
4269 Van Hise, C. R., Prof. Metall., Univ. Wis., Madison, Wis. *Strat. Geol.*, *Petrog.*, *Metall.**
4270 Van Nuys, Thomas C., M.D., Prof. Chem., Ind. Univ., Indianapolis, Ind.?
4271 Van Rensselaer, H., 98 Columbia St., Albany, N. Y. *Arachnida.?*
4272 Vansant, Dr. John, Surgeon, United States Marine Hospital Service, St. Louis, Mo. *Chem.*, *Physics*, *Elect.*, *Mic.**
4273 Van Slyke, E., M.D., 320 So. Pearl St., Albany, N. Y. *Mic.* C.*
4274 Van Slyke, Lucius L., A.M., Ph.D., Government Chemist of the Hawaiian Islands and Prof. of Chemistry in Oahu College, Honolulu, H. I.*

4275 Van Vleck, Balfour H., Society Nat. Hist., Boston, Mass. *Comp. Anat.* C.*
4276 Van Vleck, John M., Prof. in Wesleyan Univ., Middletown, Ct. *Math.*, *Ast.**
4277 Vassey, George, A.M., M.D., Botanist, Dept. Agriculture, Washington, D. C. *Bot., especially Gramineæ.**
4278 Van Vleet, A. H., Peru, Nemaha Co., Nebraska. *Chem.**
4279 Van Winkle, A. S., Keota, Keokuk Co., Ia. *General and Historical Entomology, Bot., Invertebrate Palæontology. Geographical distribution of insects* a specialty; and desire both the living and fossil remains of insects from all known regions of the world with a view of completing my work upon this subject. Desires insects from all orders and correspondence with Entomologists throughout the entire world. Am a good entomological artist. C. Ex.*
4280 Van Yorx, Wilfred T., 428 Main St., Bridgeport, Ct. *Phæn. Bot., Geol.**
4281 Vaughan, Victor C., M.D., Ph.D., Lect. Med. Chem., Univ. Mich., Ann Arbor, Mich. *Phys., Chem.* C.?
4282 Vaupel, Ernst H., 183 Poplar St., Cincinnati, Ohio. *Palæo.* Corals and Bryozoa a specialty, including microscopic sections of same. Will sell or ex. for literature of Corals and Bryology. C.*
4283 Vaux, George, jr., 1715 Arch St., Philadelphia, Pa. *Min., Photog.* C.*
4284 Veeder, M. A., A.M., M.D., Lyons, Wayne Co., N. Y. *Histol.**
4285 Velie, J. W., M.D., Sec. and Cur. Chicago Acad. of Sci., Exposition Building, Michigan Ave., Chicago, Ill. *Arch., Orn., Con.* C.*
4286 Venable, F. P., Ph.D., Prof. Chem., Chapel Hill, N. C. *Chem.**
4287 Verbryck, Geo. G., M.D., Meshoppen, Wyoming Co., Pa.*
4288 Verrill, A. E., Prof. Zool., Yale Univ., New Haven, Ct. *Gen. Biol., Geol., Annelida, Moll., Radiates.**
4289 Vickery, Miss Helen P., Weymouth, Mass. *Mic.**
4290 Viele, G. E. L., Riverside Ave. and 88th St., New York, N. Y. *Bot., Horticulture, Min., Mic., Protozoa, Infusoria.* C. Ex.*
4291 Vining, Edward P., 175 Dearborn St, Chicago, Ill. *Anth., Eth., Philol.**
4292 Voelker, Charl A., Offices; 3419 Chestnut St., 618 Market St., Philadelphia, Pa. Residence, Sharon Hill, Del. Co., Pa. *Zool., Anat., Orn., Ool., Tax.**
4293 Vodges, A. W., 1st Lieut. 5th Art'y Fort Hamilton, N. Y. Harbor, N. Y. *Palæo.**
4294 Von Herff, Baldwin, Dept. of Agric., Raleigh, N. C. *Agric., Chem., Geol., Min., Phys., Elect., Photog.**
4295 Voorhees, Miss Belle, Daggett's Mills, Tioga Co., Pa. *Gen. Zool.* C. Ex.
4296 Voorhees, Charles H., M.D., New Brunswick, N. Y. *Nat. Hist., Palæo.**
4297 Vorce, C. M., 5 Rouse Block, Cleveland, Ohio. *Ent., Con., Moll., Mic., Photog.* C. Ex.*

4298 Votteler, William, 601 West Main St., Louisville, Ky. *Phæn. Bot.* C. Ex.*

4299 Vroom, James, St. Stephen, N. B., Canada. *Phæn. Bot.* C.*

4300 Wachsmuth, Chas., 111 Marietta St., Burlington, Ia. *Palæontology, Crinoids and Echinoderms generally.* C. Ex.*

4301 Wade, Jos. M., Boston, Mass. *Orn., Ool.**

4302 Wadsworth, Benjamin F., Oregon, Ill. *Mosses, Fungi, Zool.**

4303 Wadsworth, Dr. F. L., Prof. Physiol., 131 Dearborn Ave., Chicago, Ill. *Mic.* C.?

4304 Wadsworth, H. L., Ed. and Prop. "Mining and Scientific Review." *Geol., Min., Crystall., Lithol.**

4305 Wadsworth, M. E., Ph.D., Prof. Min. and Geol., Colby Univ., Waterville, Me. *Geol., Lithol., Min.* C.*

4306 Wadsworth, Samuel B., Oregon, Ogle Co., Ills. *Phæn. Bot., Ferns.* C. Ex.*

4307 Waid, J. T., M.D., Ridgway, Pa. *Diatoms, Mic., Gen. Biol., Anth., Histol.**

4308 Wait, Charles E., C.E., M.E., Dir. Mo. School of Mines and Met., Rolla, Mo. *Analyt. Chem., Met.**

4309 Wait, S. E., Traverse City, Mich. *Meteo.**

4310 Waite, M. B., Champaign, Ill. *Phæn. Bot., Ferns, Fungi.* C. Ex.*

4311 Wakefield, Julius Ross, Dedham, Mass. *Inorg. Chem., Ool., Orn.**

4312 Wakeman, Thaddeus B., 93 Nassau St., New York City. *Anth., Arch., Eth., Ethnog., Philol., Sociology.*

4313 Walbridge, O. D., Member Ottawa Acad. Sci., Marseilles, Ill. *Diatoms, Arch., Osteol.* Wishes to sell collection. Price-list on application.

4314 Walcott, Chas. D., Palæo. U. S. Geol. Surv., Hon. Cur. Palæo., U. S. National Museum, Washington, D. C. *Palæo., Geol.**

4315 Waldo, Prof. Clarence A., Rose Polytechnic Inst., Terre Haute, Ind. *Math.* C. Ex. crystallized minerals.*

4316 Waldo, Frank, Prof. Army Signal Office, Washington, D. C. *Ast., Meteorology.**

4317 Waldo, Gerald, Scotland, Ct. *Phæn. Bot., Ferns.* C.?

4318 Waldo, Leonard, Yale College Obs., New Haven, Ct. *Ast.?*

4319 Wale, George, Montclair, Essex Co., N. J. Photographic Instruments.*

4320 Wales, Rev. F. H., Tulare, Tulare Co., Calif. *Min.* C. Ex.*

4321 Walker, B. E., General Manager Canadian Bank of Commerce, Toronto, Ont., Can. *Palæo.* C.*

4322 Walker, Chas. W., 143 East Haverhill St., Lawrence, Mass. *Bot., Phæn. Plants, Hort., Arch., Eth., Lepid.**

4323 Walker, J. B., Pres. Am. Ind. Coll., 231 11th St., Louisville, Ky. *Geol.* C. Ex.?

4324 Walker, J. R., D.D S., Bay St. Louis, Miss. *Geol., Physiol.**

4325 Walker, Matthew, Barre, Mass. *Geol., Con., Min., Crystall., Lithol.* C. Ex.*

4326 Walker, Philip, Dep. of Agric., Washington, D. C. *Sericulturalist*, *Elect.*
4327 Walker, Richard W., C.E., Engineer Guatemala Boundary Survey with Mexico. Glen Moore, Chester Co., Pa. *Geol.*, *Min.* C.*
4328 Walker, W. C., Utica, N. Y. *Diatoms*, *Min.*, *Mic.**
4329 Walkley, Edwin N., Southington, Ct. *Lepid.*, *Coleopt.* C.*
4330 Walkley, Fannie S., Plantsville, Ct. *Lepid.*, *Coleopt.* C. Desires Lepid. not found in Ct.?
4331 Wall, John L., 338 Sixth Ave., New York, N. Y. *Bot.*, *Mic.**
4332 Wall, O M., M.D., Ph.G., 2113 South Second St., St. Louis, Mo. *Pharmacognosy.* C.*
4333 Wallace, Charles M., 1319 Cary St., Richmond, Va. *Arch.* Has explored the drift fields of Va. and will ex. their finds for equiv. Also has the largest collection of Va. finds in the U. S., which will be be exchanged for equivalents.*
4334 Wallace, Shippen, Analyt. and Consulting Chem., 113 Walnut St., Philadelphia, Pa. *Chem.**
4335 Wallace, Wm., Ansonia, Ct. *Metall.*, *Phys.*, *Elect.*, *Mic.**
4336 Waller, Elwyn, Ph.D., School of Mines, Columbia Coll., New York, N. Y. *Chem.*, *Filices.* C.?
4337 Walling, Henry F., Topographer, State Survey of Massachusetts, Cambridge, Mass. *Hypsometry*, *Struct. Geol.**
4338 Walmsley, William H., 1016 Chestnut St., Philadelphia, Pa. *Mic.*, *Photo-Micrography.**
4339 Walter, Bryant, 18 Moffat Block, Detroit, Mich. *Con.*, *L. and F. W. Shells only.* C. Ex.*
4340 Walter, M.D., Walters Park, Wernersville, Berks Co., Pa. *Hort.*, *Chem.*, *Gen. Biol.**
4341 Walton, John, Reynolds' Arcade, Rochester, N. Y. *Conchologist.**
4342 Walton, J. P., Box 1125, Muscatine, Ia. *Meteorol.*, *Ent.* C.*
4343 Walworth, A. W., Collamer, Ohio. *Min.*, *Orn.*, *Ool.*, *Tax.* C. Ex.*
4344 Walworth, Rev. Clarence A., Albany, N. Y. *N. A. Geol.*, *Arch.*?
4345 Ward, Mrs. Fannie B., Ravenna, Portage Co., Ohio. *Palæo.*, *Min.*, *Bibliog.*, *Arch.*, *Ethnol.* C. Ex.*
4346 Ward, Henry A., A.M., F.Z.S., F.G.S., Ward's Nat. Sci. Establishment, Rochester, N. Y. *Min.*, *Geol.*, *Zool.*, *Arch.* C.*
4347 Ward, Henry B., 53 Fourth St., Troy, N. Y. *Mic.*, *Zool.* C.*
4348 Ward, Henry L., 16 College Ave., Rochester, N. Y. *Zool.**
4349 Ward, James W., Sec. and Lib., Grosvenor Library, Buffalo, N. Y. *Mic.*, *Ast.*, *Bot.* C. Ex. dried plants for minerals, books, etc.*
4350 Ward, Lester F., A.M., U. S. National Mus., Washington, D. C. *Bot.*, *Veg. Palæo.*, *Gen. Biol.*, *Sociology.*?
4351 Ward, R. H., M.D., F.R.M.S., Prof. of Botany, Rensselaer Polytechnic Inst., 53 Fourth St., Troy, N.Y. *Mic.*, *Gen. Biol.* C.*

4352 Ward, Saml. B., M.D., Albany, N. Y. *Ast.*, *Vert. Anat.*, *Vert.**

4353 Ward, Rev. Wm. Hayes, D.D., "The Independent," New York, N. Y. *Bot.*, *Arch.*, *Philol.**

4354 Warder, Robert B., Purdue Univ., Lafayette, Ind. *Chemistry*, *Physics*, *esp. Dynamical Chem.* Correspondence invited upon the speed of Chem. action.*

4355 Waring, George E., jr., M. Inst., C.E., Newport, R. I. *Drainage Engineer.**

4356 Warne, H. A., Oneida, Madison Co., N. Y. *Bot.*, *Fungi*, *Algæ*, *Zool.*, *Mic.* C.*

4357 Warner, John DeWitt, 52 William St., New York City. *Anth.**

4358 Warner, W. R., Cleveland, O. *Ast.*, *Mic.**

4359 Warrell, M. J., South Bend, Ind. *Orn.*, *Tax.* C. Ex. in all branches. Wishes a White Whooping Crane and Ivory Billed Woodpecker.

4360 Warren, H. M., 3449 Walnut St., Philadelphia, Pa. *Orn.* C.*

4361 Warren, J. E., 74 West High St., Detroit, Mich. *Ent: Lepid.* C. Ex.*

4362 Warren, Jesse, 3449 Walnut St., Philadelphia, Pa. *Orn.*, *Ool.* C. Ex.?

4363 Warren, S. Edw., C.E., Nat. Hist. Soc., Newton, Mass. *Phæn. Bot.*, *Hort*, *Anth.**

4364 Warring, Chas. B., Ph.D., Poughkeepsie, N. Y. *Cosmology.**

4365 Washburn, F. L., Instructor in Zoology, Univ. of Mich., Ann Arbor, Mich.*

4366 Washburn, R.R., M.D., Waldron, Shelby Co., Ind. *Geol.* C. Niagara fossils for ex.*

4367 Watase, Sho., B.S., Johns Hopkins Univ., Baltimore, Md. (Address in Japan, Sapporo College, Japan). *Morphology*, *Embryology.**

4368 Waterhouse, A., M.D., Jamestown, N. Y. *Mic.*, *Bot.*, *Ent.* C.*

4369 Waterman, John R., Box 300, Woonsocket, R. I. *Min.*, *Geol.*, *Palæo.* C. Ex.?

4370 Waterman, S. C., 310 Madison Ave., Albany, N. Y. *Ent: Lepid.* C. Ex. Catocala desired.

4371 Waterman, Thomas, A.M., M.D., 172 Marlborough St., Boston, Mass. *Comp. Anat. and Phys.**

4372 Waterman, Wm. H., New Bedford, Mass. *Geol.*, *Min.* C. Ex. Specimens good size, massive or crystallized.*

4373 Waters, George Franklin, 8 Beacon St., Boston, Mass. *Crypt. Bot.*, *Ferns*, *Fungi*, *Hort.*, *Elect.*, *Mic.*, *Worms*, *Infusoria.**

4374 Waters, Wm., 103 Fulton St., New York City. *Lepid.* C.*

4375 Waters, Wm. E., Astronomer, 83 Highland Ave., Orange, N. J. *Ast.**

4376 Watson, B. A., A.M. M.D., 124 York St., Jersey City, N. J. *Bibliog.*, *Gen. Biol.* C. Ex.*

4377 Watson, Benjamin M., jr., A.B., Instructor in Horticulture, Bussey Inst. (Harvard Coll.), Jamaica Plain, Mass. *Bot.*, *Hort.*, *Agric.**

4378 Watson, George C., B. Agr., Clyde, Wayne Co., N. Y. *Phæn. Bot.*, *Ferns.* C. Ex.*

4379 Watson, John B., 164 Nassau St., New York, N. Y.*

4380 Watson, Louis, M.D., Ellis, Ellis Co., Kansas. *Bot.*, *Orn.*, *Ichth.**

4381 Watson, R. F., Grinnell, Iowa. *Ool.* C. Ex.

4382 Watson, Sereno, Curator Harvard Herbarium, Cambridge, Mass. *Bot.**

4383 Watt, David A. P., Montreal, Can. *Bot: Acrogens.* C. Desires West Coast species.*

4384 Watters, Henry, 188 Sparks St., Ottawa, Ont., Can. *Bot.*, *Min.* C.?

4385 Watters, Mrs. Mattie J., Sacramento, Calif. *Shells.* C. Ex.

4386 Wayne, Arthur T., 562 King St., Charleston, S. C. *Orn.*, *Ool.*, *Tax.* C. Ex.*

4387 Wayne, Prof. Edw. S., M.D., Cincinnati, Ohio. *Min.* C. Ex.?

4388 Wead, Charles K., 253 Main St., Hartford, Ct. *Physics.**

4389 Weaver, F. W., 434 Hart St., Brooklyn, N. Y. *Conchology*, *Entomology*, *Orn.*, *Zool.* C. Ex.*

4390 Webb, Prof. John Burkitt, C.E., Stevens Inst., Hoboken, N. J. *Mathematics*, *Physics* *

4391 Webber, F. W., M.D., Centre St., Newton, Mass. *Ool.* C. Ex.*

4392 Weber, H. K., Springfield, Ill.*

4393 Webster, C. E., M.D., 707 Opera House Block, Chicago, Ill. *Mic.*, *Ent.**

4394 Webster, F. M., Purdue Univ., Lafayette, Ind. *Economic Ent: Coleoptera of N. A.* C. Ex.*

4395 Webster, Frank B., Res. Hyde Park, Mass., Office 409 Washington St., Boston, Mass. *Orn.*, *Ool.*, *Mam.*, *Tax.* C.*

4396 Webster, Frederic S., Studio, 1345 Penn. Ave., Washington, D. C. *Mam.*, *Orn.*, *Tax. in every branch.* Models for drawing and study. Artistic decoration in Tax. a specialty. Wants fine skins of Grizzly and Black Bear, Tiger and of all kinds of fur-bearing animals. Choice specimens sold or purchased.*

4397 Webster, G. W., Botanist, Lake Helen, Volusia Co., Fla. *Bot.*, *Phæn. and Crypt. Plants*, *Ferns.**

4398 Webster, H. E., Prof. Nat. Hist., Rochester Univ., Rochester, N. Y.*

4399 Webster, Prof. N. B., Norfolk, Va. *Chem.*, *Phys.*, *Met.*, *Min.**

4400 Webster, Oscar B., Botanist and Conchologist, Lake Helen, Volusia Co., Fla. *Bot: Phæn. Plants*, *Crypt. Plants*, *Moll.* C. Ex.*

4401 Weed, Clarence M., M.Sc., Ent. Ass't Ill. State Lab. of Nat. Hist. and Ent., Champaign, Ill. *Braconidæ*, *Myriapoda*, *Phalangidæ.* Ex.*

4402 Weed, Walter H., E.M., Ass't Geol., U. S. Geol. Surv., Washington, D. C. *Geol.*, *Min.**

4403 Weeks, A. C, B.S., LL.B., 120 Broadway, New York City. *Ent: Lepid.*, *Hymen.*, *Coleopt.*, *Neuropt.*, *Hemipt.* C. Ex.*

4404 Weeks, Andrew G., jr., care Weeks & Potter, Boston, Mass. *Ent.: Diurnal Lepid.* C. Ex.*
4405 Wegener, Henry F., M.D., 1805 South 10th St., Denver, Colo. *Ent., Zool., Mic., Veg. Histol.* C. Ex.*
4406 Wehle, John, cor. Front and Mumford Sts., Rochester, N. Y. *Mic.* C. Ex.*
4407 Welman, Z. Lysander, Stoughton, Dane Co., Wis. *Geol., Min., Lithol., Arch., Orn., Ool.**
4408 Welsh, Thomas, Los Osos, S. L. O. Co., Cal. *Orn., Tax.* Coll. of Eggs and Shells. Ex.*
4409 Weller, Stuart, North Springfield, Mo. *Bot.* C. Ex.*
4410 Welles, Chas. S., Elwyn, Delaware Co., Pa. *Lepid.* C. Ex.*
4411 Welles, G. P., 117 So. Clark St., Chicago, Ill. *Coleopt.* C.
4412 Wellington, Charles, Ph.D., Assoc. Prof. Chem. Mass. Agr. Coll., Amherst, Mass. *Org. and Inorg. Chem.**
4413 Wells, Mrs. Charlotte Fowler, 775 Broadway, New York, N. Y. *Phrenology, Anth., Eth.* C. Ex.*
4414 Wells, Clarence, Topeka, Kan. *Min.* C. Ex.*
4415 Wells, E. H., A.M., M.D., Meshoppen, Wyoming Co., Pa.*
4416 Wells, Fred., Battle Creek, Mich. *Orn., Tax.* C.*
4417 Wells, Leonard H., Oskaloosa, Iowa. *Geol., Min., Ool., Moll.* C. Ex.?
4418 Wendall, O. C., Ass't Harvard Coll. Obs., Cambridge, Mass. *Ast.?*
4419 Wenzel, H. W., 808 McKean St., Philadelphia, Pa. *Ent: Coleopt. of U. S.* C. Ex.
4420 Wenzell, William T., Analytical Chemist, 532 Market St., San Francisco, Calif.*
4421 West, Frank E., Maywood, Ill. *Phæn. Bot., Ferns.*
4422 Westcott, O. S., Maywood, Ill. *Ent., Mic.* C. Ex.*
4423 Westermann, B. & Co., 838 Broadway, New York, N. Y. *Scientific Books.**
4424 Westervelt. Rev. W. D., Denver, Colo. *Min.* C. Ex.*
4425 Westgate, Wm. Walter, Curator, Texas Ass't State Geol. Washington St., opposite Glenwood, Houston, Harris Co., Texas. *Bot., Ferns, Geol., Vert., Invert., Orn., Ool., Herpetol., Ichth., Tax., Ent: Hymenop., Lepid., Dipt., Coleopt., Hemipt., Orthopt., Neuropt., Arach., Myriop., Crustacea, Worms, Moll., Radiates, Sponges, Protozoa.* C. Ex.*
4426 Weston, Edw., Chemist and Electrician, Newark, N. J. *Diatoms, Chem., Metall., Elect., Mic., Photog., Bibliog.* C. Ex.*
4427 Weston, Edw. B., A.M., M.D., Chicago, Ill. *Bot.* C.*
4428 Weston, Eugene, Canon City, Fremont Co., Colo. *Geol., Min.* C. Ex.*
4429 Westover, H. W., M.D., St. Joseph, Mo. *Mic., Diatoms, Hist.* C. Ex.*
4430 Wetherbee, I. J., D.D.S., Boston, Mass. *Mic.**
4431 Wetherby, Prof. A. G., Cincinnati, Ohio. *Geol., Ent., Con., Bot.* C. Duplicate fossils of Cin. group, L. and F. W. shells of Southern States; Desiderata, L. and F. W. Shells, Fossils, Orchids and Ferns. Has all the latest spec. N. A. Land Shells in duplicate.

4432 Wetherell, Frank E., Oskaloosa, Iowa. *Phæn. Bot., Min., Ool., Tax.* C. Ex.*
4433 Wettstein, Gustavus A., Mineral Store and Gem Workshop, Madison St. Bridge, Chicago, Ill. *Geol., Min., Chem., Elect.* C. Ex.*
4434 Wettstein, G. A., Negaunee, Marquette Co., Mich. *Min., Geol., Archæan rocks, Elect.* C. Ex. Large stock of L. Superior and other spec. cheap.
4435 Weyburn, L. A., Rockford, Ill. *Geol.* C. Ex.*
4436 Wharton, Joseph, Philadelphia, Pa. *Metallurgy.*?
4437 Wharton, Wm. R., Germantown, Philadelphia, Pa. *Nat. Hist., spec. Ool.* C.*
4438 Wheatland, Henry, M.D., Pres. Essex Inst., Salem, Mass. *Comp. Anat.**
4439 Wheeler, C. F., Hubbardston, Mich. *Bot. of Mich.* C. Ex.
4440 Wheeler, C. Gilbert, Prof. Chem., 81 Clark St., Chicago, Ill. *Chem., Min.* C. Ex. for rare minerals and chemicals.*
4441 Wheeler, Chas. P., Charlotte, N. C. *Geol., Min., Crystall., Chem.* C. Ex.?
4442 Wheeler, Erastus S., Berlin, Mass. *Phæn. Plants, Ferns, Orchids of N. E. Hort.* C. Ex. wild plants (living) of N. E.*
4443 Wheeler, Capt. George M., Corps of Engineers, U. S. Army, U. S. Geographical Survey, L. B. 93, Washington, D. C.?
4444 Wheeler, Herbert A., Wash. University, St. Louis, Mo. *Mining Eng., Min., Crystall., Lithol., Metall.* C. Ex.*
4445 Wheeler, John B., East Templeton, Mass. *Corals, Orn., Ool., Tax., Shells, Arch., Gen. Nat. Hist.* C. Ex. first-class spec. for Mound and Indian relics and works on Nat. Hist.*
4446 Wheeler, Mary H., Pittsfield, N. H. *Bot., Mic., Gen. Biol., Histol.**
4447 Wheeler, Orlando B., U. S. Ass't Eng., Office Mo. Riv. Comm. 1415 Washington Ave., St. Louis, Mo.*
4448 Wheeler, Stedman C., Waterbury Centre, Vt. *Min., Phys. Ast., Orn.* C. Ex.*
4449 Wheeler, S. J., 81 Clarke St., Chicago, Ill. *Min.*?
4450 Wheeler, Wm. M., Custodian Milwaukee Public Museum, Milwaukee, Wis. *Ent.**
4451 Wheelock, George A., Keene, N. H. *Crypt. Bot., Ent* *
4452 Whelpley, H. M., Ph.G., 510 Pine St., St. Louis, Mo. *Mic.* C. Ex.*
4453 Whipple, E., Reed's Ferry, N. H. *Zool.* C. Ex. mins., etc.
4454 Whipple, Jennie May, Box 1143, Norwich, Ct. *Orn., Ool.* C. Ex.*
4455 Whitcomb, Ansel H., Lawrence, Kan. *Geol., Con.* C.*
4456 White, Aug. J., 3842 Johnson Place, Chicago, Ill. *Orn., Ool.* C. Ex. local birds for others.*
4457 White, Miss Carrie D., W F.Seminary, Oxford, Ohio. *Bot.**
4458 White, Charles A., M.D., U. S. Geol. Surv., Cur. Palæo., U. S. Nat. Mus., Washington, D. C. *Geol., Palæo.**
4459 White, Chas. H., Surgeon U. S. Army, Navy Dept., Bureau Med. and Surg., Washington, D. C. *Chem., Mic.**

4460 White, Frances Emily, M.D., Prof. of Physiology in Woman's Med. Coll. of Pa., N. Coll. Ave. and 21st St., Philadelphia, Pa.*
4461 White, Geo. Rantoul, A.M., Wellesley Hills, Mass. *Chem.*, *General Biology.**
4462 White, Geo. R., P. O. Dept., Ottawa, Can. *Orn.* C. Ex.*
4463 White, I. C., Prof. Geol. and Nat. Hist., Univ. W. Va., Morgantown, W. Va., Ass't U. S. Geol. Survey. *Geol. and Fossil Bot.* C.*
4464 White, J. Fleming, S.B., Chemist, Buffalo Chem. Works, Buffalo, N. Y.*
4465 White, John D., Chicopee, Mass. *Mic.*, *Ent.* C. Ex.*
4466 White, LeRoy S., Waterbury, Ct. *Min.*, *Met.*, *Chem.*, *Phys.*, *Elect.*, *Mic.*, *Photog.*, *Meteo.**
4467 White, Moses C., M.D., Prof. Pathology, Med. Department of Yale Univ., New Haven, Ct.*
4468 White, Wm., Lieut. Col., Sec. to Post Office Dept., Ottawa, Ont., Can. *Bot.**
4469 White, W. S., F.R.M.S., 128 and 130 W. Main St., Kalamazoo, Mich. *Chem.*, *Mic.*, *Photog.* Manuf. Mic. Lantern slides. C. Ex.*
4470 Whiteaves, J. F., Palæontologist, Zoologist and Ass't Dir. Geol. Surv., Ottawa, Can. *Palæo.*, *Recent Marine Invert.**
4471 Whitehouse, Cope, 15 Fifth Ave., New York City. Spec. *The Oregraphy of the Libyan Desert and Mœris Basin.?*
4472 Whiteside, Albert, Allensboro, N. Y. *Bot.* C.*
4473 Whitesides, Jennie E., Harmonsburg, Pa. *Bot.* C. Ex.*
4474 Whitfield, Edw., Chemist, U. S. Geol. Survey, Washington, D. C. *Inorg. Chem.*, *Met.*, *Meteo.**
4475 Whitfield, Prof. R. P., Am. Mus. Nat. Hist., 77th St. and 8th Ave., New York, N. Y. *Geol.*, *Palæo.*, *Min.*, *Con.* C.*
4476 Whiting, Sarah F., Prof. Phys. and Ast., Wellesley Coll., Wellesley, Mass.*
4477 Whitley, Jas. D., M.D., Petersburg, Ill. *Zool.*, *Pathol.*, *Mic.**
4478 Whitman, C. O., M.A., Ph.D., Dir. of the Lake Laboratory, Milwaukee, Wis. *Emb.**
4479 Whitman, P. R., Box 1261, Ann Arbor, Mich. *Orn.*, *Ool.* C.?
4480 Whitney, Edw. L., Chatham Centre, Medina Co., Ohio. *Orn.*, *Ool.* C. Ex.*
4481 Whitney, James E., F.R.M.S., Rochester, N. Y. *Geol.*, *Hort.*, *Veg. Histol.*, *Ast.*, *Mic.* C. Ex. slides.*
4482 Whitney, Prof. J. D., Cambridge, Mass. *Geol.* C.
4483 Whitney, Solon F., Watertown, Mass. *Min.*, *Lepid.* C.*
4484 Whitney, Wm. F., M.D., Harvard Medical School, Boston, Mass. *Histol. of Vert.*, *Human Anat.* C.*
4485 Whiton, A. M., M.D., South Byron, Genesee Co., N. Y. *Elect.*, *Anat.*, *Hist.**
4486 Whittaker, D., M D., M.A., Tremont City, Clarke Co., Ohio. *Geol.*, *Chem.*, *Mic.**
4487 Whittelsey, Theodore, Williams Coll., Williamstown, Mass. *Ool.* C. Ex.*

4488 Whittlesey, Charles, M.E., 1305 Euclid Ave., Cleveland, Ohio. *Geol.*, *Lithol.*, *Meteo.*, *Arch.*, *Eth.*
4489 Whittemore, Chas. A., 53 Fourth St., Grand Rapids, Kent Co., Mich. *Min.**
4490 Whyte, R. B., 73 Rideau St., Ottawa, Can. *Bot.* C.*
4491 Wiard, Martin S., New Britain, Ct. *Mic.* C. A large variety of first-class slides to exchange for interesting and well-mounted objects in any department.*
4492 Wibbe, Rev. J. Herman, Ph.D., Schenectady, N. Y. *Bot.* C.*
4493 Wicksteed, Richard John, LL.D., B.A., B.C.L., House of Commons, Ottawa, Ont., Can. *Chem.*, *Physics*, *Elect.*, *Mic.*, *Photog.*, *Ast.*, *Zool.*, *Geog. Dist.*, *Anat. Vert.*, *Anth.*, *Eth.*, *Ethnog.*, *Philol.**
4494 Widmann, Otto, 3826 South Broadway, St. Louis, Mo. *Orn.**
4495 Weidensaul, H. A., 213 Wood St., Reading, Pa. *Min.*, *Anth.*, *Arch.* C. Ex.
4496 Wier, D. B., Lacon, Marshall Co., Ill. *Ent.*, *Zool.*, *Orn.*, *Hort.*, *Ichth.**
4497 Wight, Sidney B., Member Am. Inst. of Mining Engineers, Newberry, Mich. *Min.*, *Chem.*, *Metall.* C.*
4498 Wilber, G. M., 140 W. 20th St., New York, N. Y. *Bot.*, *Chem.* C. Ex.?
4499 Wilbour, Chas. Edwin, Summer, Little Compton, R. I. Spring and Fall, 164 Boulevard Haussman, Paris, France. Winter, Dehaberyeh Seven Hathors, Cairo, Egypt. *Arch.*, *Philol.* Wishes information of any unpublished Egyptian antiquities in private hands, esp. papyri and inscribed monuments *
4500 Wilber, F. A., M.S., Adjunct Prof. Analyt. Chem., Rutgers Coll., New Brunswick, N. J. *Analyt. Chem.**
4501 Wilcox, Mary A., Prof. Zool., Wellesley Coll., Wellesley, Mass. *Zool.*, *Morph.* C. Ex.*
4502 Wilcox, R. M., Gildersleeve, Middlesex Co., Ct. *Orn.*, *Ool.* C.*
4503 Wildberger, Maj. R. H., Clarksdale, Miss. *Agric. Bot.*, *Geol.**
4504 Wilder, Alex., M.D., F.A.S., 565 Orange St., Newark, N. J. *Bot.*, *Chem.*, *Bibliog.*, *Anth.*, *Eth.*, *Arch.*, *Philol.**
4505 Wilder, Burt G., M.D., Prof. Phys., Comp. Anat. and Zool., Curator of Vertebrate Museum, Cornell Univ., Ithaca, N. Y. *Comp. Anat. of Vertebrates.* C. Ex. *Branchiostoma*, or living or alcoholic *Necturus*, for brains and embryos of vertebrates, especially *Felidæ*.*
4506 Wiley, Chas. A., Care Detroit Safe Co., Detroit, Mich. *Ool.*, *esp. Lepid.* Live Cocoons of Cecropia, Polyphemus, Prometheus and other species of my locality for sale or exchange. C. Ex.*
4507 Wiley, H. W., Department of Agriculture, Bureau of Chem., Washington, D. C. *Agric.*, *Chem.**
4508 Wilkins, George, 898 Dorchester St., Montreal, Can., Prof. Med. Jurisprudence; Lecturer on Histol. and Demonstrator, Histol. Lab. McGill Univ. *Histol. and Gen. Mic.*, *Physiol.**

4509 **Wilkinson, E., jr., 78 W. Bloom St., Mansfield, Ohio.** *Botany, Ent.* **C. Ex.***
4510 **Willard, J. T., Chemist, Manhattan, Kansas.** *Min., Chem., Physics.**
4511 **Willcox, George W., 13 West 2nd St., Cincinnati, Ohio.** *Arch., Palæo., Min.* **C. Ex.***
4512 **Willet, Joseph E., Prof. Mercer Univ., Macon, Ga.** *Chem., Nat. Phil., Geol., Ent.* **C.***
4513 **Willetts, Joseph C., Skaneateles, Onondaga Co , N. Y.** *Ichth., Geol.* **C. Ex.***
4514 **Willey, Henry, New Bedford, Mass.** *Lichens.**
4515 **Williams, Rev. C. Foster, Ashwood, Maury Co., Tenn.** *Palæo., Arch.* **C. Ex.***
4516 **Williams, D. A., Newark, Ohio.** *Geol., Palæo., Min.* **C.?**
4517 **Williams, Edward H., jr., E.M., A.C., Prof. Mining and Geol., Lehigh Univ., South Bethlehem, Pa.***
4518 **Williams, F. H., M.D., L.B. 702, Bristol, Ct.** *Ent., Indian Relics, Stone Age implements and fossils.* **Ex. Desires correspondents in Europe or Asia, to exchange fine stone implements. French may be written.***
4519 **Williams, Geo. H., Ph.D., Assoc. Prof. in Min. and inorganic Geol., John Hopkins Univ., Baltimore, Md.** *Min., Crystall., Lithol.**
4520 **Williams, Dr. Harvey, East Saginaw, Mich.** *Diatoms, Chem., Elect., Mic., Anat., Histol.**
4521 **Williams, Henry S., Ph.D., Cornell Univ., Ithaca, N. Y.** *Geol., Palæo.**
4522 **Williams, H. U., Delaware Ave., Buffalo, N. Y.** *Palæo., Anth.* **C. Ex.***
4523 **Williams, James V. V., Chatham Centre, Columbia Co., N. Y.** *Mam., Orn., Ool., Tax.* **C. Ex.?**
4524 **Williams, John, Coralville, Johnson Co., Iowa.** *Zool., Orn., Ool.* **C. Ex.***
4525 **Williams, N. H., M.D., Jackson, Mich.** *Mic.**
4526 **Williams, Robert S., Great Falls, Mont.** *Orn., Bot.* **C.***
4527 **Williams, S. G., Ph.D., Prof. Cornell Univ., Ithaca, N. Y.** *Palæo , Geol.* **C. Ex.***
4528 **Williams, Violet S., Coralville, Johnson Co., Iowa.** *Bot., Zool., Orn., Tax* **C.***
4529 **Williams, Wm. J. B , Box 120, Holland Patent, Oneida Co., N. Y.** *Orn., Ool.* **C. Ex.***
4530 **Williamson, A. W., Prof. Math., Aug. Coll., Rock Island, Ill.** *Philol. of Dakota Languages.**
4531 **Willis, John L. M., M.D , Eliot, York Co., Me.** *Geol., Min., Crystall., Arch.* **C. Ex.***
4532 **Willis, Merritt, West Farms Station, New York, N. Y.** *Arch., Min.* **C. Ex.***
4533 **Willis, Oliver R., A.M., Ph.D., Prin. Alexander Inst., White Plains, N. Y.** *Bot., Geol., Phys., Chem.* **C. Ex.***
4534 **Willis, Snyder, Bloomsburg, Pa.** *Min., Ool.* **C. Ex.?**
4535 **Williston, S. W., Ph.D., M.D., Prof. Anat., Yale Univ., New Haven, Ct.** *Dipt., Vert. Anat.* **C.***

4536 Willmarth, Miss Harriet M., Hamilton, Burlington Co., N. J. *Bot.* C. Ex.?
4537 Wills, Wm. R., Lapidary and Mineralogist, 67 Adams St., Waltham, Mass.*
4538 Wilson, A. D., Topographical Engineer, Washington, D. C.?
4539 Wilson, A. H., M.D., Prof. Anat., M R.C.S. (Eng.), 504 East Broadway, South Boston, Mass. and 138 Boylston St., Boston, Mass. *Lithol.*, *Anat.* C. Ex.*
4540 Wilson, Chas. H., Rugby, Morgan Co., Tenn. *Geol.*, *Min.*, *Inorg. Chem.*, *Met.*, *Orn.*, *Lepid.*?
4541 Wilson, Chas. M., M.D., N. E., cor. 17th and Sansom Sts., Philadelphia, Pa. *Morph.*, *Emb.*, *Vert. Anat.*, *Anth.*, *Eth.*, *Osteol.*, *Histol.**
4542 Wilson, Edmund B., Prof. Bryn Mawr Coll., Bryn Mawr, Pa. *Gen. Biol.*, *Morph.*, *Emb.**
4543 Wilson, Harry, care of Marshall Field & Co., Wholesale, Chicago, Ill. *Ool.* C. Ex.*
4544 Wilson, H. G., Colton, Calif. *Mam.*, *Orn.*, *Ool.*, *Tax.* C. Ex.*
4545 Wilson, Dr. H. P. C., Baltimore, Md. *Mic.**
4546 Wilson, James, 924 Chestnut St., Philadelphia, Pa. *Elect.*?
4547 Wilson, James F., M.D., Plant City, Fla. *Geol.*, *Min.*, *Mic.*, *Meteo.*, *Tax.* C. Ex. Fla. curiosities.?
4548 Wilson, John, 707 Superior St., Toledo, Ohio. *Bot.*, *Ent.*, *Mic.**
4549 Wilson, John D., 285 Grape St., Syracuse, N. Y. *Palæo.*, *Geol.*, *Mic.* C. Ex.*
4550 Wilson, Prof. J. W. Syracuse, N. Y. *Geol.*, *Palæo.*?
4551 Wilson, Newman L., 237 Longwood Ave., Boston, Mass. *Bot.*, *Palæo.*, *Geol.*, *Min.*, *Crystall.*, *Arch.*, *Molluscs.* C. Ex.*
4552 Wilson, P. B, M.D., 304 Second St., Baltimore, Md. Prof. Chem. and Tox., Baltimore Univ. School of Medicine.*
4553 Wilson, Dr. Robt. T., 820 Park Ave., Baltimore, Md. *Mic.*, *Photog.*, *Arch.**
4554 Wilson, Dr. Thos. J., 87 Wall St., Auburn, N. Y. *Metall.*, *Zool.*, *Orn.*, *Ool.* C. Ex.?
4555 Wilson, Wm., M D., Anatomical and Pathological Phrenologist, 237 Longwood Ave., Boston, Mass. *Bot.*, *Chem.*, *Zool.*, *Anat.**
4556 Wilson, Wm. E., State Normal School, Providence, R. I. *Phæn. Bot.*, *Ferns*, *Algæ*, *Mic.*, *Zool.* C. Ex.*
4557 Wilson, Dr. W. P, Prof. of Physiological Botany, Dept. of Biology, Univ. of Penn., Phila., Pa. *Physiological Bot.**
4558 Wilson, W. W., 2120 Centre St., Little Rock, Ark. *Ool.* C. Ex.?
4559 Winchell, Alex., Prof. Geol. and Palæo., Univ. of Mich., Ann Arbor, Mich. *Geol.*, *Palæo.* C. Ex.*
4560 Winchell, Horace V., Minneapolis, Minn. *Geol.*, *Min.*, *Chem.*, *Ool.**
4561 Winchell, N. H., State Geologist, Prof. Minn. Univ., Minneapolis, Minn. *Geol.*, *Min.*, *Mic.*, *Lithol.**
4562 Windle, Miss S. C., Stamford, Ct. *Ferns.**

4563 Wing, A. R., Fort Edward, Washington Co., N. Y. *Bot.**
4564 Wing, H. H, Industrial Coll., Univ. of Neb., Lincoln, Neb. *Agric., Phæn. Bot., Hort.**
4565 Wingate, Harold, Box 1553, Philadelphia, Pa. *Fungi.* C. Myxomycetes for ex.*
4566 Winlock, Anna, Harvard College Observatory, Cambridge, Mass. *Ast.**
4567 Winlock, Wm. C., Ass't Astron., U. S. Naval Obs., Washington, D. C. *Ast.**
4568 Winslow, Arthur, Ass't Geologist in charge of Coal Field, Geol. Survey of Arkansas, Little Rock, Ark. *Geol., Metall.**
4569 Winslow, J. E., Virgil, N. Y. *Bot., Chem.* C. Ex.*
4570 Winslow, I. W., M.D., Waterloo, Ind. *Palæo., Min., Geol.* C. Ex.?
4571 Winters, E. C., Sterling, Whiteside Co., Ill. *Arch., Min., Geol.* C.?
4572 Wintringham, J. P., 36 Pine St., New York City. *Electric Battery.* Would like to meet other electricians.*
4573 Wise, Edwin A., Lake City, Wabasha Co., Minn. *Ool., Orn.* C. Ex.*
4574 Witherbee, Frank S., Port Henry, N. Y. *Lithol.* C. Ex.*
4575 Withers, W. A., A.M., Chemist, State Expr. Station, Raleigh, N. C. *Geol., Min., Chem.* C. Ex. N. C. mins. for those of other states.*
4576 Witmer, I. M., M.D., Conestoga, Lan. Co., Pa. *Indian relics, Fossils, Min., Bot.* C. Ex.*
4577 Witt, George M., Windsor, Windsor Co., Vt. *Orn., Ool.* C. in sets only. Ex.*
4578 Witter, F. M., Muscatine, Ia. *Con., Lepid.* C. Ex.*
4579 Wolcott, Robert H., 133 Clinton St, Grand Rapids, Mich. During college year, Oct. to June, Ann Arbor, Mich. *Gen. Zool, Lepid., Coleopt.* C. Ex.*
4580 Wolf, John, Canton, Ill. *Con., Bot.* C. Ex.*
4581 Wolford, William L, 59 Tenth St., So., Minneapolis, Minn. *Orn., Ool.* C. Ex.?
4582 Wolfe, Harry F., 922 S. Third St., Camden, N. J. *Bot., Ferns, Mic.* C. Ex*
4583 Wolfe, Walter M., Acad. of Sciences, San Francisco, Calif. *Bot.* C. Ex.?
4584 Woliston, R. T., M.E, Galena, Colo. *Metall., Chem.* C. Ex.?
4585 Wolle, Francis, Bethlehem, Pa. *Fresh Water Algæ.** C. Ex.*
4586 Wood, Charles H., Augusta, Ill. *Mineral Collection.**
4587 Wood, Chas. H., Winchester, Ind., Supt. City Schools. *Palæo., Geol., Min., Con., Bot., Herp., Ichth.* Correspondence on Phænogamous Botany solicited. C.*
4588 Wood, Edw. S., M.D., Prof. Chem., Harvard Med. School, Boston, Mass. *Med. Chem. and Toxicol.**
4589 Wood, Frank E., Hancock, Mich. *Crypt. Bot.* C. Ex. Phæn. and Crypt. plants of Lake Superior region for Crypt.?
4590 Wood, Joseph, Bar Harbor, Me. *Geol., Min., Fossils, Arch., Antiq., Eth.* C.*

4591 Wood, Mary E., Oskaloosa, Iowa. *Phæn. Bot.*, *Ferns*, *Geol.*, *Zool.*, *Gen. Biol.*, *Morph.*, *Emb.*, *Anat.* C. Ex.*
4592 Wood, Robert W., jr., Revere St., Jamaica Plain, Mass. *Geol.*, *Min.*, *Mic*, *Carboniferous ferns from Mazon and Lower Silurian crinoid heads, etc., in ex. for other fossils.* C. Ex.*
4593 Wood, Thos. F., M.D., Wilmington, N. C. *Bot.* C.*
4594 Wood, William S., Wilmington, Del. *Tax.*, *Orn.* C.?
4595 Woodbridge, S. H., Mass. Inst. Tech., Boston, Mass. *Physics*, *Heating and Ventilation of Buildings.**
4596 Woodbury, Milo, Attorney-at-Law, Court House, Madison, Wis. *Palæo.*, *Gen. Geol.*, *Min.*, *Crystall.*, *Lithol.*, *Arch.*, *Orn.*, *Herpetol.*, *Ent: Hymenop.*, *Dipt.*, *Coleopt.*, *Hemipt.*, *Orthopt.*, *Neuropt.*, *Arach.*, *Myriop.* C. Ex.*
4597 Woodend, D. C., 260 Park St, Denver, Colo. *Manufacturer of mineral curiosities and dealer in mins.* ?
4598 Woodman, Harvey T., 204 East 6th St., New York City. *Geol.*, *Zool.*, *Invert. Anat.*, *Ichth.*, *Moll.*, *Radiates*, *Sponges*, *Arch.*, *Min.* Will exchange fine corals, sea shells, starfish, sea urchins and other marine specimens for good perfect stone or copper implements.*
4599 Woodman, Henry S., P. O Box 87, Brooklyn, E D., N. Y. *Diatoms*, *Min.*, *Ent.* C. Ex.*
4600 Woods, Mrs. Deborah M., Leominster, Mass. *Geol.*, *Min.* C.?
4601 Woodward, A., Am. Museum of Nat Hist., 77th St. and 8th Ave., New York, N. Y. *Geol.*, *Mic.*, *Foraminifera.* C. Ex.*
4602 Woodward, A. J., M.D., Atlanta, Ga. *Herpetol.**
4603 Woodward, A. L., Utica, N. Y. *Veg. Histol.**
4604 Woodward, C. M., Hanover, N. H. *Bot.* ?
4605 Woodward, W. Elliot, 258 Dudley St., Roxbury, Mass. *Arch.*, *Mound builders' and Indian Antiquities*, *Coins*, *Prehistoric stone relics from Scandinavia, and medals*, *Bric-a-brac and rare books.* Always prepared to buy large or small collections for ready money. Holds auction sales in N. Y. and Boston monthly. Catalogues sent to collectors on application. C. Ex.*
4606 Woodworth, Charles, M.S., 610 Clark St., Champaign, Ill. *Ent.*, *Insect Histol.*, *Coleopt*, *Hemipt.* C. Ex.*
4607 Wooley, J. H., 865 West Monroe St., Chicago, Ill.*
4608 Woolman, Geo. S., 116 Fulton St., New York City. *Mic.* C.*
4609 Woolson, George C., Passaic, N. J. *Bot.*, *Hort.* Special Cultivation of native plants. C.*
4610 Woolverton, S., London, Ont., Can. *Gen. Collector of minerals, shells, coins, Indian relics, etc* *
4611 Wooster, L. C., Supt. City Schools, Eureka, Kan. *Geol.*, *Bot.* C.*
4612 Worcester, George W., Urbana, Champaign Co., Ohio. *Bot.*, *Spec. Fungi.* C.?
4613 Worden, T. D., Ph.B., M.D., Ph.M., Wilkesbarre, Pa. *Phys.*, *Min.* ?
4614 Worrall, Jno. Hunter, Ph.D., West Chester, Chester Co., Pa. *Physics*, *Meteo.*, *Ast.**

4615 Worthen, A. H., Geologist and Cur. State Museum of Nat. Hist., Springfield, Ill. C. Ex.*

4616 Worthen, Chas. K., Naturalist and Taxidermist, Warsaw, Ill. *Orn.*, *Tax.* C. Ex.*

4617 Worthen, Rev. Dr. H. W., Bradford, Vt. *Geol.*, *Min.*, *Lithol.*, *Molluscs.* C. Ex.*

4618 Worthington, Willis Woodford, Taxidermist and Collector, Shelter Island, Suffolk Co., N. Y. *Orn.*, *Ool.*, *Arch.*, *Min.*, *Tax.* Fine cabinet specimens collected to order. Correspondence solicited. C. Ex.*

4619 Wray, Chas. M., 228 East 19th St., New York City. *Zool.*, *Orn.*, *Ool.*, *Tax.* C. Ex.?

4620 Wright, Albert A., A.M., Ph.B., Prof. Geol. and Nat Hist., Oberlin Coll., Oberlin, Ohio. C.*

4621 Wright, Arthur W., Ph.D., Prof. Molecular Physics, Yale College, New Haven, Ct.*

4622 Wright, Berlin H., Lake Helen, Volusia Co., Fla. *Con.*, *Palæo.*, *Ast.* C. Unionidæ of Florida; new and rare forms for ex. in large quantities.*

4623 Wright, Chas. J., Peekskill Mil. Acad., Peekskill, N. Y. *Palæo.*, *Geol.*, *Min.*, *Crystall.*, *Lithol.*, *Mic.*, *Photog.*, *Ast.* C. Ex.?

4624 Wright, James C., Fredonia, Licking Co., Ohio. *Arch.*, *Palæo.*, *Min.*, *Con.*, *Old Coins, Medals and War Mottoes.* C. Ex.*

4625 Wright, Geo. M. (late Ass't Geologist, U. S. Geol. Surv.), Talmadge, Summit Co., Ohio. *Geol.*, *Lithol.*?

4626 Wright, Rev. G. Frederick, Oberlin, Ohio. *Glacialist.**

4627 Wright, Geo. M., Ass't Geol., U. S. Geol. Survey, Washington, D. C. *Geol.*, *Lithol.*?

4628 Wright, James A., 45 Waverly St., Brighton Dist., Boston, Mass. *Lepid.*, *Coleopt.*, *Gen. Nat. Hist.* C. Ex.*

4629 Wright, R. Ramsey, Prof. Biol., University of Toronto, Canada. *Anatomy of Vertebrates.**

4630 Wright, Samuel H., M.D., A.M., Ph.D., Penn Yan, Yates Co., N. Y. *Bot.*, *Con.*, *Mic.*, *Ast.* C. Specialty Carices and Unionidæ. Unios and Carex named gratis, and ex. in both wanted and Plants from Austria and U. S., for those of any other part of the world.*

4631 Wright, Walter E. C., A.M., Prof. Nat. Sci., Berea Coll., Berea, Ky.*

4632 Wright, W. G., B.S., San Bernardino, Calif. *Bot.*, *especially Palms, Cactuses and Seeds*, *Ent.*, *chiefly Lepid. and Coleopt.* C.*

4633 Wunderlich, Adolph, 35 Willcut St., Cleveland, Ohio. *Tax.*, *Elect.* C. Ex.*

4634 Wyman, Buyard, Perry, Lake Co., Ohio. *Hort.*, *Min.*, *Arch.*, *Orn.*, *Ool.* C. Ex.?

4635 Wyman, Vaughn, Perry, Lake Co., Ohio. *Ool.* C. Ex.*

4636 Wyman, Walter Channing, 158 Dearborn St., Chicago, Ill. *Arch.*, *Ethnol.* C. Ex.*

4637 Wyman, Wm. S., Prof. in Univ. of Ala., Tuscaloosa, Ala. *Am. Arch. and Eth.**
4638 Wynne, Samuel, Phœnixville, Chester Co., Pa. *Geol.*, *Min.*, *Indian relics.* C. Ex.*
4639 Yarrow, H. C., M.D., Cur. Dept. Reptiles, Nat. Mus., Smithsonian Inst., Army Med. Mus., Washington, D. C. *Eth.*, *Gen. Zool.*, *Herpetol.*, *Ichth.**
4640 Yates, Joseph, Mott Ave., near 138th St., New York City. *Geol.*, *Min.*, *Chem.*, *Physics*, *Elect.*, *Mic.*, *Meteo.*, *Ast.* C.*
4641 Yates, Dr. Lorenzo G., Santa Barbara, Calif., "Author of "All Known Ferns," etc." *Con.*, *Geol.*, *Min.* C. Ferns (living or dried) from foreign countries wanted by ex. or purchase. Send lists Tropical Plants.*
4642 Yeates, William S., Ass't Curator, Dept. of Minerals, U. S. Nat. Mus., Washington, D. C. *Min.*, *Crystall.*, *Inorg. Chem.**
4643 Yendall, Paul S., 419 Washington St., Boston, Mass. *Ast.**
4644 Yoakum, Prof. Franklin L., M.D., Sec. Acad. Sci., Texas, Palestine, Anderson Co., Tex. *Gen. Nat. Hist.* C. Ex. Texas invert., Gulf and F. W. shells for invert. fossils and recent shells, all named. Send for printed list.?
4645 Yocum, Wilbur F., Pres. Fort Wayne College, Ind. *Bot.*, *Mic.*, *Ent.**
4646 York, Wm. F., Nashua, N. H. *Geol.*, *Min.*, *Arch.* C. Ex.*
4647 Youmans, Miss Eliza, 2 East 15th St., New York, N. Y.?
4648 Youmans, William Jay, M.D., care Pop. Sci. Monthly, 1 Bond St., New York City. *Chem.*, *Physiol.**
4649 Young, Rev. Albert A., Boscobel, Wis. *Geol.*, *Mic.*, *Tax.* C. Ex.*
4650 Young, A. H., Hanover Coll., Hanover, Ind. *Bot.*, *Geol.* C. Ex.*
4651 Young, Dr. C. A., Coll. of N. J., Princeton, N. J. *Ast.**
4652 Young, E. Bentley, M.Sc., 104 Appleton St., Boston, Mass. *Bot.*, *Min.*, *Lithol.*, *Chem.*, *Phys.* C.*
4653 Young, H. A., Revere, Mass. *Bot: spec. Mosses.* C. Ex.*
4654 Young, Henry H., San Bernardino, Calif. *Bot: Phæn. and Crypt. Plants*, *Ferns*, *Tax.*, *Ent.*, *Hymen.*, *Lepid.*, *Coleopt.*, *Neuropt.* C. Ex.*
4655 Young, Rawlings, M.D., Corinth, Alcorn City, Miss. *Orn.*, *Ool.* C. Ex.*
4656 Young, Silas C., Edenville, N. Y. *Min.* C. Ex. Orange Co., N. Y., and Sussex Co., N. J., minerals for sale.*
4657 Youngs, Geo. R., C.E., Penn Yan, N. Y. *Bot.* C.*
4658 Zabriskie, Rev. J. L., Waverly Ave., Flatbush, L. I., N. Y. *Hymenoptera*, *Fungi*, *Mic.* *Preparations of Wood of N. A. for sale.* C. Ex.*
4659 Zahm, S. H., 443 W. Chestnut St., Lancaster, Pa. *Ool.*, *Arch.* C. Ex.*
4660 Zell, Mrs. Lydia D., Librarian Linnæan Society, Lancaster, Pa. *Phæn. and Crypt. Bot.**
4661 Zellweger, John, care Gundlach Optical Co., Rochester, N. Y. *Mic.**

4662 Zentmayer, Charles, 3021 Girard Ave., Philadelphia, Pa. *Mic.* ?

4663 Zentmayer, Joseph, 209 South 11th St., Philadelphia, Pa. *Manufacturer of Microscopes.**

4664 Zesch, Frank, 201 So. 11th St., Buffalo, N. Y. *Coleopt.* C. Ex. ?

4665 Zetlitz, Arne, Collector of Birds and Mammals for Museums, Dealers, Minneota, Lyon Co., Minn. *Zool.*, *Mammals*, *Orn.*, *Tax.*, *Ent.* C. Ex.*

4666 Zimmerman, Rev. Jeremiah, A.M., Syracuse, N. Y. *Mic.*, *Bibliog.*, *Arch.**

4667 Zimmerman, Wm., 164 Dearborn St., Chicago, Ill. *Phys.*, *Elect.*, *Gen. Biol.**

SCIENTIFIC SOCIETIES OF THE UNITED STATES AND CANADA.

American Association for the Advancement of Science. Organized, 1840; incorporated, Mar. 19, 1874. F. W. Putnam, Salem, Mass., Perm. Sec.*

American Institute of Mining Engineers. J. C. Bayles, New York City, Pres.; Rossiter W. Raymond, 13 Burling Slip, New York City, Sec.

American Postal Microscopical Club. Founded, 1875. Rev. Samuel Lockwood, Freehold, N. J., Pres.; Rev. A. B. Hervey, Taunton, Mass., Sec.*

American Society of Microscopists. Hamilton L. Smith, Geneva, N. Y., Pres.; D. S. Kellicott, Buffalo, N. Y., Sec.

National Academy of Sciences, Washington, D. C. Prof. O. C. Marsh, Pres.; Simeon Newcomb, Vice Pres.; Prof. Asaph Hall, Naval Observatory, Washington, D. C., Home Sec.; Wolcott Gibbs, Cambridge, Mass., Foreign Sec.*

Society of American Taxidermists (National). W. T. Hornaday, Pres.; F. A. Lucas, Sec., Office of the Executive Comm., U. S. National Museum, Washington, D. C.

CALIFORNIA.

California Academy of Sciences, San Francisco. H. W. Harkness, M.D., Pres.; Henry Ferrer, M.D., Cor. Sec. Publishes "Proceedings," "Memoirs" and "Bulletins." Has Collection, Museum and Library.*

California State Geological Society, San Francisco. Incorporated, Dec. 30, 1876. Henry G. Hanks, Pres.; S. Heydenfeldt, jr., Sec. Annual Meeting, first Monday in December.*

Geographical Society of the Pacific, San Francisco. ?

San Diego Society of Nat. Hist. Organized Nov. 2, 1874. Geo. W. Barnes, M.D., Pres.; Miss Rosa Smith, Cor. Sec. Library and Collection.*

San Diego Lyceum of Natural Sciences. Organized, June, 1873. Robert J. Gregg, M.D., Pres.; George N. Hitchcock, Cor. Sec. ?

San Francisco Microscopical Society, Rooms 120 Sutter St., Address Box 2244. E. J. Wickson, Pres.; Dr. C. P. Bates, Cor. Sec. Cabinet and Library.*

Santa Barbara Society of Natural History. Organized, Nov. 25, 1876. H. C. Ford, Pres.; Mrs. R. F. Bingham, Cor. Sec. Museum and Library.*

CANADA.

Canadian Institute, Toronto. Alan Macdougall, C.E., F.R.S.E., M.Inst.C.E., Sec. Library and Publishes Proceedings.*

Entomological Society, London, Ontario. William Saunders, Pres.; E. Baynes Reed, Sec. and Treas.

Hamilton Association, Hamilton, Ontario. Established 1857. Literary and Scientific. Museum. Library. Publishes Transactions. Exchange. John McDonald, M.D., Pres.; Geo. Dickinson, Cor. Sec.

Kentville Naturalists' Club, Kentville, N. S., Can. Col. L. DeV. Chipman, Pres.; A. J. Pineo, A.B., Sec. Forty-five Members. Library, Museum, Monthly Meetings and Summer Excursions.*

Murchison Scientific Society, Belleville, Ont. Organized, 1873. Thos. Wills, Pres.; W. R. Smith, Cor. Sec. Annual Meeting, second Monday in September.

Natural History Society, Montreal. Dr. Dawson, Pres.; Dr. Edwards, Sec. Collection. Publishes the "Canadian Naturalist and Geologist."

Natural History Society of Toronto, Canada. W. Brodie, Pres.; W. E. Middleton. Rec. Sec.; S. Hollingworth, Cor. Sec. Collections. Library.

Nova Scotia Institute of Natural Science, Halifax. Prof. J. Somers, M.D., F.R.M.S., Pres; Prof. D. Honeyman, D.C.L., F.R.S. Can., Sec.*

Ottawa Field Naturalists' Club, Ottawa, Canada. Organized, March, 1879. H. Beaumont Small, M.D., Pres.; W. H. Harrington, Sec. Publishes Transactions.

Ottawa Literary and Scientific Society, Ottawa. Organized, 1869. J. R Armstrong, Pres.; F. K. Bennetts, Sec.*

Colorado Scientific Society, Denver, Col. Organized, Dec. 8, 1882; incorporated, Jan., 1885. P. H. Van Dierst, Pres.; Whitman Cross, Sec. Museum. Ex. of Minerals especially desired. Publishes "Proceedings."*

CONNECTICUT.

Bridgeport Scientific Society. Isaac Holden, Pres.; C. H. Russell, Cor. Sec. Library.*

Connecticut Academy of Arts and Sciences, New Haven. Incorporated, 1799. Addison E. Verrill, Pres ; Addison Van Name, Cor. Sec. and Librarian. Publishes "Transactions."*

Field and Forest Club, Southington. W. M. McLaughlin, Pres.; E. R. Newell, Sec.; Dr. J. H. Osborne, Cur.; Mrs. Dr. J. H. Osborne, Cor. Sec.

Meriden Scientific Association. Prof. J. H. Chapin, Ph.D., Pres.; Dr. Chas. H. S. Davis, Sec.*

Middletown Scientific Association. Organized, March 17, 1871. Prof. W. N. Rice, Ph.D., LL.D., Pres.; Prof. H. W. Conn, Ph.D., Cor. Sec.*

New Britain Scientific Association. J. F. Stidham, D.D., Pres.; M. S. Wiard, Sec.*

Waterbury Scientific Society. Organized, October 19, 1868; incorporated July 8, 1869; membership, 70. G. P. Chapman, Pres.; Frederick Wilcox, Treas.

DISTRICT OF COLUMBIA.

Anthropological Society of Washington. Maj. J. W. Powell, Pres.; J. Owen Dorsey, F. A. Seely, Secretaries.*

Biological Society of Washington. Wm. H. Dall, Pres.; Richard Rathbun, F. A. Lucas, Secretaries.*

Philosophical Society of Washington. Organized, March 13, 1871. Asaph Hall, Pres.; G. K. Gilbert and H. Farquhar, Secretaries. Publishes "Bulletins." Seven volumes have been published.

Smithsonian Institution. Organized, 1846. S. P. Langley, Sec.; G. B. Goode, Ass't Sec.; William J. Rhees, Chief Clerk. Museum, Library and Gallery of Art. The publications comprise "Contributions to Knowledge," "Miscellaneous Collections," "Annual Reports."*

ILLINOIS.

Academy of Sciences of Southern Illinois, Carbondale. Organized, Dec. 2, 1876; membership, 100.?

Chicago Academy of Sciences, Exposition Building, Mich. Ave. Organized, 1857; incorporated, 1859. Prof. Edmund Andrews, M.D., LL.D., Pres.; J. W. Velie, M.D., Sec. and Cur. Museum and Library.*

Illinois State Laboratory of Natural History, Champaign. S. A. Forbes, Director.*

Peoria Scientific Association. Dr. E. M. Colburn, Pres.; Dr. Fred. Brendel, Cor. Sec.*

Princeton Acad. of Sci., Princeton. Hon. Simeon Elliott, Pres.; Jacob Miller, Cor. Sec.

Ridgway Ornithological Club of Chicago. Organized, Sept. 6, 1883; incorporated, May, 1884. Geo. Frean Morcom, Pres.; Ruthven Heane, V. P.; H. K. Coale, Sec. and Treas.; Geo. L. Toppan, Curator and Librarian.*

Rockford Scientific Society. Organized, June 13, 1877; active members, 40. M. S. Bebb, Pres.; J. B. Upson, Sec.*

INDIANA.

Brookville Society of Nat. Hist. Incorporated, February, 1882. Amos W. Butler, Sec. Museum and Library. Desires to ex. many duplicate specimens, and asks donations of specimens and publications.*

Indianapolis Lyceum of Natural History. Organized, Oct., 1876. Edward T. Cox, Pres.; Prof. W. Webster Butterfield, M.Sc., M.D., Sec.*

Jeffersonville Natural History Association. Organized, December, 1877. Wm. H. Fogg, Pres.; O. Hobbs, Sec.?

Western Indiana Historical and Scientific Association, Newport. Organized, Aug. 30, 1875; membership, 20. Prof. John Collett, Pres.; H. H. Conley, Cor. Sec. Museum, Collection, and Library.?

IOWA.

Davenport Academy of Natural Sciences, Davenport. Organized, Dec. 14, 1867. Chas. E. Harrison, Pres.; Dr. Chas. H. Preston, Cor. Sec. Library and Museum. Publishes "Proceedings.*

Iowa Academy of Sciences, Iowa City. Organized, 1875. C. E. Bessey, Ames, Iowa, Pres.; C. M. Hobby, M.D., Cor. Sec. Number of Fellows limited to thirty.?

Iowa Natural History Union, Des Moines. Organized, 1877. Wm. Jno. Gill, D.D., A M., Pres.; S. S. Bonbright, Sec.

Iowa State Ornithological Society. J. H. Harvey, Pres.; S. S. Bonbright, Des Moines, Sec.

KANSAS.

Kansas Academy of Science, Topeka. Rev. John D. Parker, Fort Riley, Pres.: E. A. Popenoe, Manhattan, Kan., Sec.*

Scientific Club of the Kansas State Agric. College, Manhattan.*

Topeka Scientific and Literary Club. Prof. J. T. Lovewell, Pres.; Geo. S. Chase, Sec.?

Wyandotte Society of Nat. Hist. W. H. Plank, Pres.; W. H. McCune, Sec., Wyandotte, Kansas.*

KENTUCKY.

Ohio Falls Geological Society, Centre and Walnut Streets, Louisville. Wm. J. Davis, Pres.; J. T. Gaines, Sec. Will exchange Silurian and Devonian fossils for those of other periods.?

Polytechnic Society of Kentucky, Louisville. Instituted, December, 1876. Bennett H. Young, Pres.; E. A. Grant, Sec. Library, Museum, Art Gallery, Laboratory, etc. Desires exchange.*

MAINE.

Portland Society of Nat. History. Incorporated, 1850. Wm. Wood, M.D., Pres.; Prentice C. Manning, Cor. Sec. Cabinet.*

White Mountain Club, Portland. Rev. Dr. Thomas Hill, Pres.; John M. Gould, Sec.*

MARYLAND.

Maryland Academy of Sciences, Baltimore. Organized, 1822. Christopher Johnson, M.D., Pres.; Philip R. Uhler, Cor. Sec.*

MASSACHUSETTS.

American Academy of Arts and Sciences, Boston. Organized, 1780. Joseph Lovering, Pres.; Oliver Wendell Holmes, William Watson, Vice Presidents; Josiah Parsons Cooke, Cor. Sec.; Augustus Lowell, Treas.; Henry Williamson, Haynes, Libr. Publishes "Proceedings" and "Memoirs."*

Amesbury and Salisbury Natural History Society. Organized, 1873. H. S. Leslie, Pres.; Chas. Nayson, Cor. Sec.?

Appalachian Mountain Club. Organized, 1876; incorporated, Apr. 1, 1878. Prof. Alpheus Hyatt, Pres.; Samuel Thurber, Cor. Sec., Roxbury, Mass.*

Arnold Arboretum (Harvard Univ). Chas. S. Sargent, Director; Charles E. Faxon, Ass't in charge of Herbarium. Living collections at Arnold Arboretum, West Roxbury, Boston. Herb. at the residence of the director, Brookline, Mass.

Boston Scientific Society. Organized, May, 1876; 419 Washington St. Prof. Samuel Garman, Pres.; E. E. Norton, Sec. "Science Observer" published by this Society.*

Boston Society of Natural History. Incorporated, 1831. F. W. Putnam, Pres.; Edward Burgess, Sec. Annual Meeting, first Wednesday of May. Library and Collection. Publishes "Proceedings," "Memoirs," and "Occasional Papers."*

Boston Zoological Society, 285 Marlboro' Street. Organized, 1880. F. C. Bowditch, Pres.; Roland Hayward, Sec. Publishes the "Quarterly Journal."

Cambridge Amateur Society of Natural History. Organized, November, 1877. J. A. Osborn, Pres.; Wm. B. Greeley, Sec. Cabinet.?

Cambridge Entomological Club. Established, Jan. 9, 1874; incorporated, March 9, 1877. J. H. Emerton, Pres.; Roland Hayward, Sec. "Psyche," published by this Society, is issued monthly, at $2 per annum, $5 per vol. of 3 years.*

Cape Ann Scientific and Literary Assoc., Gloucester. Organized, 1875. Thomas Conant, Pres.?

Essex Institute, Salem. Incorporated, 1848. Henry Wheatland, M.D., Pres.; George M. Whipple, Sec. Library contains 32,000 volumes. Publishes "Historical Collections" and "Bulletin." Objects, diffusion of knowledge in History, Nat. Hist., Horticulture and Arts.*

Greenfield Nat. Hist. Soc., Greenfield, Mass. C. Ex.

Hanson Nat. Hist. Society. Organized, 1874. Flavel S. Thomas, Sec.?

Harvard Natural History Society. Founded, 1837. W. W. Nolen, Pres.; Edw. C. Mason, Cor. Sec. The Society especially desires to form a coll. of the plants, animals, and minerals of Massachusetts.*

Historical, Natural History and Library Society, South Natick. Incorporated, 1873. G. J. Townsend, M.D., Pres.; Rev. J. P. Sheafe, jr., Cor. Sec. Library and Collection.

Lyceum Nat. Hist., Williams College, Williamstown. Founded, 1835. J. R. Adriance, Pres.; A. H. Burnell, Cor. Sec. Collection.?

Massachusetts Horticultural Society, Boston. Organized. 1829. Henry P. Walcott, Pres.; Robert Manning, Sec. and Lib.; Geo. W. Fowle, Treas. and Supt. of building. The Library contains 5,000 books and 1,700 pamphlets on Botany and Horticulture, and is the best Horticultural Library in the U.S.*

Middlesex Institute, Malden. Organized, 1878. L. L. Dane, Medford, Pres.; F. S. Collins, Malden, Sec.*

Museum of Comparative Zoology, Cambridge. Alex. Agassiz, Director. Publishes "Bulletin" and "Memoirs."*

Nat. Hist. Society of Newton. Chartered, 1873. Prof. J. K. Richardson, Pres.; S. E. Warren, Sec.*

Nuttall Ornithological Club, Cambridge, Mass. Organized, 1873. Wm. Brewster, Pres.; Arthur P. Chadbourne, Sec.*

Peabody Mus. of Am. Archæology and Ethnology, Department of Harvard Univ., Cambridge. Founded, 1866. F. W. Putnam, Peabody, Prof. of Am. Arch. and Eth., Curator.*

Peabody Academy of Science, Salem. Founded, 1867, by George Peabody, of London, and contains Ethnological Coll. East India Marine Soc. (1799), Nat. Hist. Coll. Essex Inst. (1834) as permanent deposits, and large accessions made since 1867 by the trustees. Pubs. Memoirs (2 vols.). Annual reports (19 in 9 numbers). Classes and lectures in botany, zoology, mineralogy, etc. Wm. C. Endicott, Pres.; Edw. S. Morse, Dir.; John Robinson, Treas. in charge of Museum. Special collections, Ethnology in general, and Zool. and Arch. of Essex County, Mass. Museum ranks among the most valuable in the country.*

Springfield Botanical Society. Organized, April 20, 1877. Everett A. Thompson, Pres.; Miss Clara Bell, Sec. Collection.?

Springfield Science Association. Organized, March 12, 1881. Geo. A. Denison, Pres.; E. H. Smiley, Sec.*

Worcester Natural History Society. Organized, Dec., 1852; incorporated, April 16, 1853. Dr. W. L. Raymenton, Pres.; Dr. S. B. Woodward, Treas.; Dr. C. L. Nichols, Cor. Sec. Museum.*

MICHIGAN.

Adrian Agassiz Association. Chapter 687. Adrian, Mich. Edw. J. Stibbins, Sec.

Adrian Scientific Society, Adrian. Incorporated, 1881. E. W. Allis, Pres.; Prof. W. H. Haron, Sec.*

Ann Arbor Scientific Association. M. E. Cooley, Pres.; Chas. K. McGee, Sec.

Detroit Scientific Association. Incorporated, March 21, 1865. J. C. Holmes, Pres. Museum.?

Kent Scientific Institute, Grand Rapids. E. S. Holmes, Pres.; C. A. Whittemore, Sec.*

The Griffith Club of Microscopy, Detroit. W. H. Brearley, Pres.; B. W. Chase, M.D., Sec.?

MINNESOTA.

Minnesota Academy of Natural Sciences, Minneapolis. Organized, Jan. 1, 1873. A. F. Elliott, Pres.; W. H. Leonard, Cor. Sec. Publishes "Bulletin."

Minnesota Historical Society of St. Paul.?

St. Paul Academy of Natural Sciences. Robert Ormsby Sweeney, Pres.; Herbert W. Smith, Cor. Sec. Library and Museum.?

MISSOURI.

Academy of Science, St. Louis. Organized, 1857. Prof. F. E. Nipher, Pres.; Edw. Evere, M.D., Cor. Sec. Publishes "Transactions" and "Proceedings." Has Room, Library and Museum in Wash. Univ. buildings.?

NEW HAMPSHIRE.

Exeter Natural History Society. Organized, Dec. 7, 1874; incorporated, June, 1876. John J. Bell, Pres.; Albion Burbank, Sec. Museum and Library.?

Keene Natural History Society. G. A. Wheelock, Pres.; D. W. Gilbert, Sec.*

NEW JERSEY.

Atco Natural Science Society. Incorporated, 1868. M. J. Skinner, Pres.; A. R. Sloan, Cor. Sec. Library and Museum. Wood and Bot. spec. for ex.?

New Jersey State Microscopical Society. Instituted, April 17, 1871; incorporated, Feb. 16, 1880. Rev. Samuel Lockwood, Freehold, N. J., Pres.; Prof. F. C. Van Dyck, New Brunswick, N. J., Sec. Meets monthly in Geological Hall, Rutgers College, New Brunswick.*

Princeton Acad. of Sci., Princeton. Jacob Miller, A.M., Pres.; F. M. Herrick, Cor. Sec.*

Princeton Science Club. Organized, 1877. Princeton, N. J.*

NEW YORK.

Agassiz Association, Chapter 811, Nyack-on-Hudson, N. Y. Organized in 1884, for the study of the various depts. of Nat. Sci. Meetings are held on the second and fourth Wed. evenings in each month, excepting July and August. G. D. Wilson, Pres.; Miss Emma Partridge, Sec.; J. C. Gregory, Cor. Sec.

Albany Institute. Incorporated, March 12, 1793. Leonard Kip, Pres.; Ernest J. Miller, Cor. Sec. Library and Collection.*

American Chemical Society, Room 1, University Building, Washington Sq., New York City. Incorporated, Nov. 10, 1877. Prof. Chas. A. Goessman, Amherst, Mass., Pres.; P. Casamajor, Brooklyn, N. Y., Cor. Sec. Library. Librarian, Wm. Rupp, New York, N. Y.*

American Astronomical Society. Organized, Jan., 1883. S. V. White, Pres.; G. P. Serviss, Sec., 8 Middah St. Meets first Monday in each month at the Packer Institute, Brooklyn, N. Y. Members, 60 ?

American Geographical Society, New York City.

American Microscopical Society of City of New York, 12 East 22d St. J. B. Rich, M.D., Pres.; O. G. Mason, Sec.?

American Museum of Natural History, Central Park, New York City. Incorporated, 1869. Morris K. Jesup, President. Publishes "Bulletin" and "Annual Report." Library of 12,000 volumes and Museum.*

Brockport Natural History Club. Organized, November, 1875. Cabinet and Library.?

Brooklyn Entomological Society. G. W. T. Angell, Pres.; Wm. Beutenmueller, Cor. Sec. Publishes "Entomologica Americana." Address, Brooklyn, N. Y. Meetings first Tuesday of each month at Saengerbrund Hall, Brooklyn.*

Brooklyn Microscopical Soc. Organized, Feb., 1881. Meetings second and fourth Tuesday in the month. Members, 60. G. D. Hiscox, Sec., 435 Greene Ave.*

Buffalo Microscopical Club. Organized, 1876. James W. Ward, Pres.; Dr. W. C. Barrett, Sec.?

Buffalo Society of Natural Sciences. Organized, Dec. 5, 1861. Lucien Howe, M.D., Pres.; Leon F. Harvey, M.D., Cor. Sec. Museum and Library.?

Central New York Microscopical Club, Syracuse. Incorporated, May 28, 1883. A. Clifford Mercer, M.D., F.R.M.S., Pres.; Newton Hall, 2nd, Sec. Over 40 members.?

Central Park Menagerie, New York City. William A. Conklin, Ph.D., Director.*

Cornell Nat. Hist. Soc., Cornell Univ., Ithaca, N. Y.*

Elmira Microscopical Society. Dr. S. O. Gleason, Pres.; Professor Ford, Ph.D., Vice Pres.; Thad. S. Up de Graff, M.D., F.R.M.S., Sec.?

Jamestown Microscopical Society. Organized, 1873. A. Waterhouse, M.D., Pres.; Prof. S. G. Love, Sec.

Lockport Agassiz Society, 45 Niagara Ave., Lockport. George W. Pound, Cor. Sec.*

Microscopical Society of Canandaigua, New York. Prof. D. Satterthwaite, Pres.; C. T. Mitchell, M.D., Sec.*

Natural Science Association of Staten Island. A. L. Carroll, M.D., Pres.; Arthur Hollick, Cor. Sec. P. O. Box 105, New Brighton.*

New York Academy of Sciences (late Lyceum of Natural History), New York City. Incorporated, April 20, 1818. John S. Newberry, Pres.; A.A. Julien, Cor. Sec. Annual meeting, fourth Monday in February. The publications of the Academy consist of the "Annals," and the "Proceedings.*

New York Entomological Club. A. R. Grote, Pres.; B. Neumogen, Treas.; Henry Edwards, Sec. Meets bi-monthly, 185 East 116th St.?

New York Microscopical Society, 64 Madison Ave., New York City. Organized, November 14, 1877. Rev. J. L. Zabriski, Pres.; Benjamin Braman, Cor. Sec., 44 E. 30th St., New York, N. Y.*

New York Society for Medico-Scientific Investigation, 201 East 23d St., New York. Pres. for 1887, Walter Yeomans Cowl, M.D., 162 W. 24th St.; Sec. for 1887, Malcolm Leal, M.D., "The Albany" 52d St. and Broadway. Library. Desires to ex. medical and scientific books and specimens.*

Rochester Academy of Science. Albert Cronise, Pres.; H. T. Braman, Cor. Sec.

Torrey Botanical Club, New York City. Organized, January, 1873. J. S. Newberry, Pres.; Miss Helena C. Gaskin, Cor. Sec. Publishes "Bulletin."*

Troy Scientific Association. Organized, 1870; incorporated, 1874. R. H. Ward, Pres.; Prof. D. F. Thompson, Cor. Sec.?

Vassar Brothers' Institute, Scientific Section, Poughkeepsie, N. Y. Prof. Leroy C. Cooley, Pres.; Dr. W. G. Stevenson, Cor. Sec.; Prof. W. B. Dwight, Chairman Sci. Section.*

Warner Observatory, Rochester. Lewis Swift, Ph.D., F.R.A.S., Director.*

NORTH CAROLINA.

Elisha Mitchell Scientific Society, Chapel Hill. Library. Semi-annual Journal, F. P. Venable, Sec.*

OHIO.

Agassiz Scientific Association, Delaware. Organized, April 4, 1876. Prof. E. T. Nelson, Pres.; R. E. Hills, Sec.?

Central Ohio Scientific Association, Urbana. Established, October, 1874. S. M. Mosgrove, Pres.; T. F. Moses, Cor. Sec.?

Cincinnati Society Natural History, 108 Broadway. J. Ralston Skinner, Pres.; Wm. H. Knight, Sec. Publishes the "Journal," issued quarterly.*

Cuvier Club, 34 Longrowth St., Cincinnati. Organized, January 1, 1875. L. A. Harris, Pres.; J. J. Glidden, Cor. Sec.*

Kirtland Society of Natural Sciences, Case Block, Cleveland. Organized, March 17, 1869. Dr. E. Sterling, Cleveland, Ohio, Cor. Sec. Library and Museum.*

Licking County Pioneer Historical and Antiquarian Society. Isaac Smucker, Pres.; E. M. P. Brister, Cor. Sec.*

Literary and Scientific Society, Madisonville. Hon. Joseph Cox, Pres.; Charles F. Low, Sec.?

PENNSYLVANIA.

Academy of Natural Sciences of Philadelphia. Founded, March 12, 1812. Joseph Leidy, M.D., Pres.; G. H. Horn, M.D., Cor. Sec.; Edw. J. Nolan, M.D., Rec. Sec. Publishes "Proceedings" and "Journal."*

American Entomological Society, Philadelphia. Incorporated, 1862. Charles A. Blake, Cor. Sec. Publishes "Transactions."?

American Philosophical Society, Philadelphia. Founded, May 25, 1743. Frederick Fraley, Pres.; Pliny E. Chase, Dan. G. Brinton, Henry Phillips, jr., J. P. Lesley, Geo. F. Barker, Secretaries. Publishes "Proceedings" and "Transactions."*

Erie Natural History Society, Erie. G. Guttenberg, Pres.; Miss Sarah Madole, Cor. Sec.?

Lackawanna Inst. of Hist. and Sci., Scranton, Pa. J. A. Pierce, Pres.; R. D. Schimkff, Rec. Sec.; W. A. Wilcox, Cor. Sec.*

Lehigh Valley Microscopical Society. Founded, May 19, 1881. Dr. Fraill Green, Pres.; Dr. Brentano Clemens, Sec.*

Lewisburg (Pa.) Scientific Society. Rev. Dr. J. R. Loomis, Pres.; Dr. Geo. G. Groff, Sec.?

Linnæan Society, Lancaster. Organized, February 15, 1862; chartered August 30, 1865. Prof. J. S. Stahr, Pres.; Dr. H. D. Knight, Cor. Sec. Large Museum and Library.?

Lyceum of Natural History, Marietta. Geo. W. Mehaffey, Pres.; I. S. Geist, Sec. Museum and Library.*

Mineralogical and Geological Sections of A.N.S.P. T. D. Rand, Dir.; A. E. Foote, M.D., Sec. Publishes "Proceedings."

Numismatic and Antiquarian Society, Philadelphia. Founded, Jan. 1, 1858. Daniel G. Brinton, Pres.; Henry Phillips, jr., Sec. Publishes "Proceedings."*

Reading Society of Natural Sciences. Instituted January 1, 1869; incorporated, Nov. 8, 1869. Henry Landis, M.D., Pres.; M. A. Rhoads, M.D., Sec Library and Collection.?

Spencer F. Baird Naturalist Association, Reading. Organized, April 1, 1882. Harry G. Moyer, Pres.; Jno. F. Hoffman, V. Pres.; T. A. Kendall, Sec. and Treas. Museum and Library.*

West Chester Microscopical Society. Prof. G. M. Philips, Pres.; B. H. Warren, Sec.*

West Chester Philosophical Society. D. M. Sensenig, Pres.; J. Newton Huston, Cor. Sec.*

Wyoming Historical and Geological Society, Wilkes-Barré. Incorporated, 1858. Hon. E. L. Dana, Pres.; Sheldon Reynolds, A.M., and S. E. Struthers, Secretaries. Publishes "Proceedings." C.*

Zoological Society of Philadelphia. Incorporated, 1859. Frederick Graff, Pres.; Thos. Hockley, Secretary; Wm. Hacker, Treas.*

RHODE ISLAND.

Providence Franklin Society, 54 No. Main Street. Chartered, 1823. D. W. Hoyt, Pres.; John Daboll, Sec. Annual meeting first Tuesday in January.*

Rhode Island Horticultural Society, Providence. Instituted, Sept. 6, 1845; incorporated, Jan., 1854. Joseph H. Fanning, Pres.; Cyrus C. Armstrong, Treas. Thos. K. Parker, Cor. Sec.*

TEXAS.

Texas Museum. Scientific and Literary Association, San Antonio. Dr. Isidor Lerinthal, Pres.; C. Runge, Sec.?

UTAH.

Museum of Natural History, Salt Lake City. Geo. Reynolds, Curator.*

VIRGINIA.

Jamestown Microscopical Society. Organized, 1873. A. Waterhouse, M.D., Pres.; S. W. Baker, Sec.*
Richmond Microscopical Society. Chartered, 1880. Dr. Henry Froehling, Pres.; Dr. Wm. Gascoyne, Vice Pres.; G. A. Pepley, Sec.; Thomas Christian, Treas.*

GREAT BRITAIN.

[When no other address is given, England should be understood as forming a part of the address.]

Abel, F. A., F.R.S., Royal Arsenal, Woolwich, 39 Welbeck St., London, M.*
Abercrombie, John, M.D., 39 Welbeck St., London. *Mic.*
Abercromby, Ralph, 21 Chapel St., Belgrave Sq., London. *Meteo.**
Aberdare, Henry Austin Bruce, Lord, 1 Queen's Gate, Kensington, S.W.
Abney, Wm. de Wiveleslie, Capt. R. E., F.R.S.E., F.I.C., F.C.S., F.R.A.S., Willeslie House, Wetherby Gardens, So. Kensington, London, S.W.*
Abraham, Phineas S., M.D., Royal College of Surgeons, Stephens' Green, Dublin, Ireland. *Comp. Anat., Physiol.*
Acland, Sir Henry Wentworth Dyke, K.C.B., A.M., M.D., LL.D. (Cantab.), F.R.G.S., Coll. Reg. Med. Soc., Hon. Student of Ch. Ch., Radcliffe. Librarian and Reg. Prof. of Med. in the Univ. of Oxford, Broad St., Oxford.*
Ackland, William, 416 Strand, London, W.C. *Mic.*
Adams, Frederick C., 74 Jermyn St., London, S.W. *Ent.*
Adams, G. F., M. Inst. C.E., Guildhall Chambers, Cardiff, Wales.
Adams, Herbert J., Roseneath, London Road, Enfield. *Ent., Ool.*
Adams, J., care of C. Lane, Halstock, Yeovil, Somerset. *Lepid.*
Adams, John Couch, M.A., LL.D., F.R.S., Lowndean Prof. Ast. and Dir. of the Cambridge Observatory, Cambridge.*
Adams, William Grylls, M.A., F.R.S., Prof. of Nat. Phil., King's College, London, W. C.
Adamson, S. A., F.G.S., 52 Well Close terrace, Leeds. *Geol.**
Addison, Lieut. Gen. Thos., F.R.A.S., Hill House, Melton, Suffolk. *Ast.*
Adie, Richard, care of Alex. Adie & Sons, 37 Hanover St., Edinburgh, Scotland. *Chem.*
Addiscott, C. J., Sydney Villa, St. Bildas Road, Maure Park, Stoke Newington, N.
Adkins, Wm., 431 Oxford St., W. London.
Ager, F. W., Borough Asylum, Ipswich. *Lepid.*
Ainsworth, George, Consett Iron Co., Blackhill, Durham. *Chem.*
Airy, Sir George Biddell, LL.D., M.A., D.C.S., F.C.S., The Royal Observatory, Greenwich, London, S.E. *Ast., Math.**
Aitchison, Jas. Edw. Tierney, Surgeon-Major, M.D., C.I.E., Secretary to the Surgeon-General H. M. Forces, Bengal. 40 Ashburn Pl., Cromwell road, London, S. W.*

Aitken, Capt., Sandfield, Urmston, Manchester. *Geol.*
Aitken, Thomas, M.D., Inverness, Scotland. *Min.**
Aitken, Sir William, M.D., F.R.S., Prof. of Pathology, Army Medical School, Netley, Southampton.*
Alabone, Edwin W., M.D., Lynton House, Highbury Quadrant, London, N. *Mic: Insect Dissections.* C.*
Alcock, Thomas, M.D., Oakfield, Sale, Manchester. *Nat. Hist.*
Aldroyd, M. A., Abbey St., Haversham, Kent. *Geol., Arch., Moll.* C. Ex.*
Alexander, Lieut. General Sir James, 35 Bedford Pl., Russell Sq., London, W.C. *Mic.*
Allbutt, T. Clifford, M.A., M.D., F.R.S., F.Z.S., 6 Park Sq., Leeds.*
Allen, A. H., F.I.C., F.C.S., Consulting and Metallurgical Chemist, 1 Surrey St., Sheffield. *Chem., Geol., Min., Crystall., Lithol., Phys., Elect.*
Allen, Chas. M., Nella Cottage, Wood Green, Middlesex. *Lepid.*
Allen, Daniel, Yarbridge, Isle of Wight. *Mic.**
Allen, F., Chemical Works, Bow Common, E., and 18 Stainsly Road, East India Road, Poplar, London, E. *Chem.*
Allen, Rev. William H., F.R.A.S., 14 Frederick Pl., Plumstead, Kensington.
Allen, W. A., M.S.A., 156 Choumert Road, London, S.E. (Would be grateful for small donations of objects toward School Museum. Very poor school. Fee, 1 d. per week). *Phæn. Bot., Horticulture, Perfumery, Elect., Mic., Geog. Dist., Met.* C. Ex.*
Alma, Tadema, Lawrence R.A., etc., 17 Grove End Road, London, N.W. *Antiquarian.**
Allman, George James, LL.D., F.R.S., Prof. Emer., Nat. Hist., Edinburgh, Ardmore, Dorset and Athenæum Club, London.*
Allman, Geo. Johnston, LL D., D.Sc., F.R.S., Queen's College, Galaway, Ireland. *Math.*
Allpass, Henry, F.R.S.L., 5 The Walk, Ludgarville, Cardiff, Wales. Engaged in completion of Analytical Index of the "Archæologia Cambrensis."
Allport, Samuel, F.G.S., Mason College, Birmingham. *Geol., Lithol.**
Alstone, John, 68, Shepherds Bush Road, W., London.
Ames, George Acland, Union Club, London, S.W. *Mic., Navigation, Music.**
Anderson, John, J.P., F.G.S., Vice Pres. Nat. Hist. and Phil. Soc., Hon. Sec Belfast Soc. for Promoting Knowledge, Holywood, Belfast, Ireland. *Geol., Bot., Ast., Mic.*
Anderson, Joseph, jr., Aire Villa, Chichester. *Lepid., Mic.**
Andrew, John J., L.D.S., R.C.S., Eng. 2, Belgravia Lisburn Road, Belfast, Ireland. *Bot., Mosses, Palæo., Vert., Invert., Mic., Zool., Emb., Comp. and Dental Anat.* C. Ex.*
Andrews, Arthur, Newton House, Blackrock, Co. Dublin, Ireland. *Mic.*
Andrew, F. W., 3 Neville Terrace, Onslow Gardens, S. W.

Andrews, R., 725 Castle St., Hertford. *Bot.**

Angas, George F., F.L.S., C.M.Z. S., 48 Norland Sq., Holland Park, London. *Moll.**

Annandale, Thomas, Prof. Univ., Edinburgh, Scotland.

Anstie, John, B.A., 5 Westminster Chambers, Victoria St., London, S.W.

Anthony, John, M.D., F.R.M.S., 6 Greenfield Crescent, Edgbaston, Birmingham. *Physiol.*, *Histol.* C.*

Archer, F., Little Crosby-road, Crosby, Liverpool. *Ent.*, *Con.*

Archer, Sam'l, Brigade Surg., Major Army Med. Staff, 25 Charles St., London, S.W. *Moll.*, *Crust.**

Archer, Wm., M.R.I.A , 11 South Frederick St., Dublin, Ireland.

Archibald, E. Douglas, Grosvenor House, Tunbridge Wells, Kent. *Geol.*, *Inorg. Chem.*, *Phys.*, *Elect.*, *Meteo.*, *Ast.*, *Eth.**

Argyll, Duke of, K.T., D.C.L., F.R.S., Campden Hill, Kensington, W., and Inverary Castle, Argyllshire.

Armitage, Edward, 3 Hall-road, St. John's Wood, London, N. W. *Ent.*

Armstrong, Sir Alex., K.C.B., M.D., LL.D. (Dubl.), F.R.G.S., late Dir. Gen'l of the Medical Dept. of the Navy, Hon. Physician to the Queen and to H.R.H., the Prince of Wales. D 2 Albany, W.

Armstrong, C.B., D.C.L. (Oxon), LL.D., (Cantab.), etc., etc., Newcastle-upon-Tyne.*

Armstrong, George Frederick, M.A., F.R.S.G., F.G.S., M.I.N.E., Regius Prof. of Engineering, Univ. of Edinburgh, Scotland.*

Armstrong, Henry E., Ph.D., F.R.S., London Institution, Finsbury-circus, London, E.C. *Chem.*

Arnot, William, Chemical Laboratory, 18 Picardy Pl., Edinburgh, Scotland. *Chem.*

Arrowsmith, Wastell, 99 Adelaide Road, Haverstock Hill, N.W.

Ash, Geo. C., 141 Maida vale, W.

Ashbridge, Arthur, 76 Leadenhall St., E.C.

Ashford, Chas., Christchurch, Hampshire. *Structure of British L. and F. W. Moll.**

Ashby, H. T., 8, Bartholomew Road, Kentish Town, N.W.

Ashley, Miss Mary, 16 New King St., Bath. *Ast.**

Atchison, James E. T., M.D., Punjab, East Indies, care of Grindlay & Co., 55 Parliament St., London, S.W.

Atkins, Rev. E., B.Sc., Wyggeston Schools, Leicester. *Phys.*

Atkinson, G. M., 28 St. Oswald's Road, West Brompton, London, S.W.

Attfield, Prof. John, M.A., Ph.D., F.R.S., 17 Bloomsbury Sq., London. *Chem.**

Auld, Henry A., Bank of England, London. *Lepid.*, *Moll.* C.

Austin, W. J., Radnor St., Folkestone. *Lepid.*

Aveline, William Talbot, F.G.S., Oatlands, Wrington, Somersetshire. *Geol.**

Ayrton, Prof. Wm. Edw., Prof. of Applied Phys. in the City and Guilds of London Inst., Central Institution, Exhibition Road, London, S.W.

Babeson, W., St. John's College, Cambridge. *Comp. Anat.*

Babington, Charles Cardale, M.A., F.R.S., F.L.S., F.S.A., Prof. Bot., Univ. of Cambridge, 5 Brookside, Cambridge.

Backhouse, James, York. *Choice plants and fossils.**

Backhouse, T. W., F.R.A.S., West Hendon House, Sunderland. *Ast., Meteo.**

Badcock, J., Queen's Gate, 270 Victoria Park Rd., South Hackney, E. *Mic.**

Bagnall, J. E., 84 Wilton Road, Birmingham. *Phanerogams, Ferns, Mosses.*

Bagshaw, Benjamin, Sheffield. *Genealogy.*

Baigent, R. C., War Office, Pall Mall, London. *Min.*

Bailey, G. H., B.Sc., Grammar School. Bowes *via* Darlington. *Chem.*

Bailey, George Vincent, Headingley, near Leeds, Yorkshire. *Bot., Geol.* C.

Bailey, Rev. Geo., F.R.M.S., Member of The Queckett Mic., The Croydon Mic. and Nat. Hist. Clubs. The Manse, Finching field, Essex. *Mic., Diatoms, Geol., Palæo., Sponges, Con., Ent., Anth., Foraminifera.* C. Ex.*

Bailey, J. W., 75, Broke Road, Dalston, E.

Baily, Wm. H., F.L.S., Acting Palæontologist to the Geol. Surv. of Ireland and Demonstrator in Palæo. to the Royal Coll. of Sci. for Ireland, Moyne House, Moyne Road, Dublin, Ireland. *Palæo.*

Bain, Donald, Wick, Scotland. *Bot.*

Bairstow, S. D., Woodland Mount, Huddersfield. *Lepid.*

Baker, George, Alni Villa, Burton-on-Trent. *Ent.* C. Ex. *British Insects.*

Baker, John Gilbert, Royal Herbarium, Kew.

Baker, Chas., F.R.M.S., 244 High Holburn, W. C.

Baker, Sir Samuel White, Sanford, Orleigh, Newton Abbot, Devonshire.

Baldry, James, Danford, M. Inst., C.E., 2 Queen Sq. Pl., Westminster, London, S.W.

Baldwin, J. W., 38 Dunscar Road, near Bolton, Lancashire. *Lepid.*

Balfour, Isaac B. Sherardian, Prof. Bot., Oxford, England.

Balfour, Thos. G., M.D., Coll. Reg. Med. Soc., Surgeon Gen'l (retired). Acad. Reg. Med. Belg. Soc., Coombe Lodge, Wimbledon Park.

Ball, John, V.P.R.S., 10 Southwell Gardens, South Kensington and Athenæum Club, London, S.W.

Ball, R. S., K.B., LL.D., F.R.S., Andrews Professor of Ast. in the Univ. of Dublin and Royal Astronomer of Ireland, Observatory, Dunsink Co., Dublin. *Ast., Math.**

Ball, Valentine, M.A., F.R.S., F.G.S., M.R.I.A., Dir. Science and Art Museum, Dublin, Home Sec. Zool. Soc. of Ireland. *Geol., Min., Orn.**

Ballard, Dr. W. R., jr., 26 Manchester Sq.

Baly, Joseph S., The Butts, Warwick. *Ent.*

Banister, Richard, Inland Revenue Laboratory, Somerset House, London, W.C. *Chem.*
Banks, W. Mitchell, M.D., F.R.C.S., Prof. Surgery, Univ. College, Ashton St., Liverpool.
Barber, J. T., F.R.A.S., F.R.M.S., Oakfield, Aston-on-Clun, Salop. *Ast.*
Barclay, James, 36 Windsor Terrace, Glasgow, Scotland. *Biology, Micros.*
Barclay, Joseph G., Observatory, Leyton, Essex. *Ast.*
Barclay, Lieut.-Col. Hanbury, F.Z.S., Ashleigh, Dorking. *Orn.*
Barkas, C. E., Newcastle-on-Tyne. *Ent.*
Barkas, Thomas P., F.G.S., Newcastle-on-Tyne. *Diatoms, Palæo., Geol., Elect., Mic., Ast., Anat.*
Barkas, William, 48 Preston Road, Brighton. *Phys.*
Barham, G. T., Danehurst, Hampstead, N. W.
Barkly, Sir Henry, 20 Roland Gardens, South Kensington, London, S. W.
Barlow, J., V.P.R.S., 4 Bath Place, Haggerston, London. *Lepid.*
Barlow, W. H., V.P.R.S., High Coombe, Old Charlton, London, S. E.*
Barnard, Herbert, 33 Portland Place, W.
Barnard, Major R. C., F.L.S., Leckhampton, Cheltenham.*
Barneby, Thos., F.R.A.S., Morton House, Worcester. *Ast.*
Barnes, C. B., 4 Egremont villas, White horse lane, South Norwood, S. E.
Barnes, Henry, Patschull House, Dartmouth Park Avenue, N.
Barnes, John Hickman, C.E., 30 Great George St., London, S. W.
Barrand, Allan T., Sedgehurst, Watford. *Orn.**
Barratt, Thomas, Bell Moor House, Upper Heath, Hampstead, N. W.
Barrett, C. G., 68 Camberwell Grove, London, S. E. *Lepid.**
Barrett, Hamilton, G.E.H., Arthurstown, Co. Wexford, Ireland. *Bot., Zool., Vert., Mam., Orn., Ool.* C. British Birds' Eggs.*
Barrett, Wm. Bowles, F.L.S., 2 Belfield Terrace, Weymouth. *Bot., Dorset Phanerogams and Filices.**
Barrett, Prof. W. F., Royal College Science, Dublin, Ireland. *Phys.*
Barrington, R. M., LL.B., F.L.S., Fassaroe, Bray Co., Wicklow, Ireland. *Phæn. Bot., Meteo., Geog. Dist., Mam., Orn., Ool.* C. Ex.*
Barrow, George, Geological Survey of England, Museum, Jermyn St., London, S. W.
Barrow, Francis, M.A., 3 Phillimore Gardens, London, W. *Ast.*
Barry, Rev. E. J., A.B., Beverly, Yorks. *Ent.*
Bartlett, Edw., L.D.S., M.R.C.S.E., 38 Connaught Square, Hyde Park, London, W. *Ferns, Mic., Protozoa.**
Bartlett, F., 48 Hodley St., Kentish Town, London. *Lepid.*
Bartlett, H., 48 Hodley St., Kentish Town, London. *Lepid.*
Bartlett, Henry C., Ph.D., F.C.S., Laboratory, 39 Duke St., Grosvenor Sq., London, W. *Chem.**

Barton, Stephen, F.E.S., 114 St. Michael's Hill, Bristol. *Ent.**
Bastian, Henry Charlton, M.A., M.D., F.R.S., Prof. of Medicine at University College, London, 20 Queen Anne St., W.*
Baswell, H., Market St., Oxford. *Mosses.*
Batchelor, J. A., 8 Bow Lane, E. C.
Bate, Charles Spence, F.R.S., The Rock, South Devon, 8 Mulgrave Pl., Plymouth. *Marine Zool., Crustacea.* C. Ex.*
Bateman, F., M.D., Norwich. *Psychol., Aphasia and Seat of Speech, Darwinism tested by Language.**
Bateman, James, M.A., 9 Hyde Park Gate, London, W.
Bateman, John F., La Trobe, F.R.S., Abingdon St., London, S.W.*
Bates, E., Assoc. I.C.E., 45, Fentman's Road, Clapham Road, S.E.
Bates, E. F., 18 Melbourne St., Leicester. *Geol., Bot., Biol.*
Bates, F., 32 West St., Leicester. *F. W. Algæ.*
Bates, Fred., 15 Northampton Sq., Leicester. *Coleopt.*
Bates, Henry W., 11 Carleton Road, Tufnell Park, London, N.W. *Ent.*
Bauerman, Hilary, Assoc. M. Inst., C.E., Geologist to the American Boundary Commission, Museum, Jermyn St., S.W., and 41 Acre Lane, London, S.W. *Geol., Min.*
Bayfield, T. G., Magdalen St., Norwich. *Geol., Arch.*
Bayley, Miss E. L., Wilmington Lodge, Hassocks, Sussex. *Lepid.**
Baynes, J., jr., Ph.D., F.I.C., F.C.S., F.R.M.S., Analytical and Consulting Chemist, Assayer, etc., Hull and East Riding Laboratories, Scale Lane, Hull. *Chem.**
Baynes, T., 70 Sunderland Terrace, Ulverstone, Lancashire. *Lepid.*
Beadle, H. A., 4 Victoria Terrace, Kendal. *Lepid.*
Beale, Charles, C.E., Lime Tree House, Rowley Regis, Dudley, Worcestershire. *Geol.* C. Ex. Offers coal measure fossils or Upper Silurian. Wants mound implements or remains.*
Beale, Lionel Smith, M.B., F.R.C.P., F.R.S., Prof. King's College, 61 Grosvenor St., London, W. *Minute Anat., Physiol., Mic., Med.* Treas. R.M.S. of London.*
Beanes, F. E. V., Moatlands, Paddock Wood, Brenchley, Kent. *Analyt. Chem.*
Beardsley, Amos, F. L. S., F.G.S., Grange-over-sands, Lancashire. *Geol., Nat. Hist.* C. Ex. in Suffolk Crag and other strata.
Beaumont, Alfred, Steps Mills, Huddersfield. *Ent.*
Becher, Edward French, Hill House, Southwell. *Birds, L. and F. W. Shells.*
Beck, C., 31 Cornhill, E. C.
Beck, Joseph, F.R.A.S., 68 Cornhill, London, E. C.*
Beckles, Sam'l Husbands, F.G.S., 9 Grand Parade, St. Leonard's.
Beetham, Arthur, Barrister-at-Law, M. 2. M. C., 14 South Square, Gray's Inn, Holborn, London. *Diatoms, Mic.* C. Ex.*
Beddard, Frank E., Prosector to the Zool. Soc. of London, Zool. Gardens, Regents Park, London, N. W. *Vert., Worms.* C. Ex.*

Beddome, Col. R. H., Sispara, West Hill, Putney, London.

Bedson, P. Philips, D.Sc., B.Sc., Prof. Chem., Durham Coll. of Sci., Newcastle-on-Tyne. *Chem.*, *Metall.**

Bedwell, Judge, M.A., Cantab. F.R.M.S., West parade, Hull, Yorkshire.

Beeby, W. H., A.L.S., 14 Ridinghouse St., London, W. *Bot.**

Beesley, Thomas, High St., Banbury, Oxfordshire. *Geol.*

Beetham, Albert Wm., Recorder of Dartmouth, 14 South square, Gray's Inn, London, W. C.

Begg, John, Wick, Scotland. *Ent.*

Bell, Prof. F. Jeffrey, F.Z.S., British Museum, Cromwell Rd., London, S. W. *Comp. Anat.*, *Echinoidæ.*

Bell, James, Ph.D., F.C.S., F.I.C., Laboratory, Somerset House, London, W. C. *Chem.*

Bell, Rev. Thomas, Keig, Aberdeenshire, Scotland. *Ent.*, *Bot.*

Bendix, David, care of Burt, Boulton and Heywood, Prince Regent's Wharf, Victoria Docks, London, E. *Chem.*

Bennett, Alfred W., M.A., B.Sc., 6 Park Village East, London, N. W. Lect on Bot., St. Thomas Hospital, and at Bedford (Ladies) College. *Bot.* C.

Bennett, Arthur, F.L.S., 90 High St., Croydon, near London. *Bot.*, *Potamogetons and Carices.* C. Ex. Desires Potamogetons from all parts of the world. Will send British plants or other Potamogetons in ex.*

Bennett, Francis James, Geological Survey of England, Museum, Jermyn St., London, S. W.

Bennett, Sir Jas. Risdon, M.D., LL.D., F.R.S., 22 Cavendish Sq., London, W.*

Bentley, Robert, Prof., 38 Penywern, Earl's Court, London. *Med.*, *Bot.*, *Org. Materia Medica.**

Berens, Alexander A., 68 Great Cumberland Pl., London, W. *Ent.*

Berjeau, Charles, 137 Hungerford Road, Camden Road, London, N.

Berkeley, Rev. M. J., Sibbertoft, Market Harborough. *Fungi.*

Bernan, F. G., "Brabaret," Tulse Hill, S.W.

Bernays, Albert J., Ph.D., Acre House, Brixton-rise, London, S.

Berney, Fred'k Lee, 61 North End, Croydon. *Orn.*, *Ool.* C.

Berney, John, F.R.M.S., 61 North End, Croydon.

Besant, Wm. Henry, D.Sc., F.R.A.S., Mathematical Lecturer at St. John's College, Cambridge.*

Bessemer, Sir Henry, Denmark Hill, London, S.E.

Bettany, George T., M.A., B.Sc., F.L.S., F.R.M.S., Lecturer on Bot., Guy's Hospital, 2 Eckington Villas, Ashbourne Grove, Dulwich, S.E., London.

Beulah, John, Raventhorpe, Brigg.

Bevan, E. J., 46 Talgarth Rd., West Kensington, London. *Chem.*

Bevan, Rev. J. O., M.A., Assoc. Inst. C.E., F.G.S., F.R.M.S., F.C.P., The Vicarage, Vowchurch, Hereford.*

Beveridge, Robert, M.D., 36 King St., Aberdeen, Scotland. *Phæn. Bot.*, *Zool.*, *Gen. Biol.* C.

Bevington, W. A., F.R.M.S., "Avondale," Coloraine Road, Blackheath, S.E.

Bird, F. E., 33 St. Saviour's Road, Brixton Hill, S.W.
Bickerton, G. A., St. George's Lodge, Queen's Road, Richmond, Surrey.
Bicknell, Percy, F. R. Met. Soc., Beckenham, Kent.
Bidder, Bartholomew Parker, M. Inst. C.E., Wauncelrch, Neath.
Bidder, G. P., M.A., F.R.A.S., Ravensburg Park, Mitcham, Surrey. *Ast.*
Biddulph, Major John, 43 Charing Cross, London. *Orn.* Will exchange Indian, and especially Himalayan birds, for specimens of *Fringillidæ* from other countries.
Bidwell, Edward, 1 Trig Lane, Upper Thames St., London, E. C. *Orn.**
Bidwell, Shelford, M.A., LL.B., Riverstone Lodge, Southfields, Wandsworth, London, S.W.
Biggart, J. W., Chemical Laboratory, 29 Cathcart St., Greenock. *Chem.*
Biggs, Charles J., 58 Wick Road, South Hackney, London. *Lepid.*
Bignell, George C., F.E.S., 7 Clarence Pl., Stonehouse, Plymouth. *Lepidoptera, Ichneumonidæ, Oak-galls.* C. Ex.*
Billington, E. R., Buxton House, Wallasey, Liverpool. *Lepid.*
Billups, T. R., 4 Swiss Villas, Copplestone Road, Peckham, London, S.E. *Ent., Coleopt.*
Binnie, Alex. R., C.E., Heaton, Bradford, Yorkshire. *Ast.*
Binns, E. Knowles, F.G.S., F.R.G.S., 214 Heavygate Road, Sheffield.
Binstead, Charles Herbert, Clergyman, B.A., Aspatria, Carlisle. *Crypt. Plants, Mosses.* C. Ex.*
Birch, R. W. P., M. Inst., C.E., 2 Westminster Chambers, Victoria St., London, S. W.*
Birds, James Adey, B.A., 82 Gloucester Terrace, Hyde Park, London, W. *Geol.*
Birks, Edward, Lecturer on Botany in the Sheffield School of Medicine, Sheffield. *Bot.* C.
Bishop, George, care F. B. Marson, Finsbury Distillery, London, E.C. *Ast.*
Bishop, Mrs., The Platt, Watford. *Bot., Mosses.**
Bisset, J. B., Wynndun Banchory, Scotland. *Desmids.*
Black, Charles, Arbigland, Dumfries, Scotland. *Geol., Bot.*
Blackall, W., 9 Church St., Folkestone. *Lepid.*
Blackie, W. G., Ph.D., LL.D., 17 Stanhope St., Glasgow, Scotland. *Geog.**
Blair, Matthew, Oakland, Paisley, Scotland. *Geol., Min.*
Blake, Henry W., M.A., 8 Devonshire place, Portland place, London, W.
Blake, Rev. J. F., M.A., Prof. Geol. Univ. Coll., Nottingham. *Geol., Palæo.*
Blake, J. Hopwood, Assoc. M. Inst., C.E., Geological Survey of England, Museum, Jermyn St., London, S. W.
Blake, T., Fernside, Kent road, East Molesey, Surrey.
Blanford, Henry Francis, F.G.S., F.Z.S., F.R.M.S., etc., etc., Meteorological Office, 116 Victoria Street, London, S.W.

Blanford, W. T., 72 Bedford Gardens, Kensington, London. *Mam., Herpetol., Moll., Orn., Geol.**

Blatch, William G., 214 Green Lane, Smallheath, Birmingham. *Gen. Ent.* C. Ex.*

Bleach, S. W., Consdale Villas Ave., Acton, Middlesex. *Lepid.*

Blenkinsop, B., Shred Hill, Kenley, Surrey.

Bligh, Edw. H. Stuart, Lord Clifton, Dumpton Park, Ramsgate, F. Zool. Soc., London; M. Brit. Orn. Union, London, M. Norfolk and Norwich Naturalists' Soc. *Orn.**

Blomefield, Rev. Leonard, M.A., 19 Belmont, Bath. *Zool., Bot.**

Blood, Js., 125 Masbro' St., Masbro'. Rotherham. *Lepid.*

Blow, Thomas Bales, F.L.S., Welwyn. *Phæn. Bot., Photog., Geog. Dist., Hymen.**

Bloxham, Geo. W., M.A., Prof. Biol., Trin. Coll., London, Ass't Sec., Anth. Inst., Teddington, Middlesex. *Zool., Comp. Anat., Anth., Chem.*

Blundell, J., Stock Exchange, E.C.

Boase, Henry S., M.D., F.R.S., Seafield House, Magdalen Place, Dundee, Scotland.

Bock, Carl, 19 Fernlea Road, Balham, London, S.W., in care of the Swedish and Norwegian Consul-General, Bangkok, Siam. *Con., Borneo and Siamese Landshells.* C. Ex.

Boden, Charles, 127 Tooley St., Borough, London, S. E. *Lepid.*

Boeddicker, Observatory of Birr Castle, Parsonstown, Ireland. *Ast.**

Bolton, Thos., F.R.M.S., 57 Newhall St., Birmingham.

Bolton, Thos., Microscopists' and Naturalists' Studio, 83 Camden St., Birmingham. *Algæ, Diatoms, Desmids, Mic., Gen. Biol., Worms, Protozoa.**

Bolton, Rev. W. H., Grammar School, Kinver, near Stourbridge. *Bot., Meteo.*

Bond, Francis, M.A., F.G.S., Hull College, Hull. *Geol., Philol.*

Bond, Fred., 5 Fairfield Ave., Staines. *Ent.*

Bond, J. Kinton, B.A., B.Sc., The Corporation Grammar Sch., Plymouth. *Bot.**

Bonney, Prof. T. G., F.R.S., University College, London. *Geol., Petrology.* C.

Bonsfield, Edward C., L.R.C.P., London, 363 Old Kent Road, London, S.E. *Mic., Photo-Mic., Worms, Protozoa.**

Booth, B. C., 137 Kirkwood Road, Peckham, London, S.E. *Lepid.*

Booth, Ed., Pevensey St., Hastings, Sussex. *Lepid.*

Booth, Isaiah, Mining Engineer, Oaks Colliery, Oldham Firwood, Alderley Edge, Manchester.

Borrer, William, M.A., Cowfold, Horsham. *Orn., Ent.*

Bosher, Edward, Bellevue House, Twickenham. *Ent.*

Bostock, Edwin, F.L.S., F.R.M S., The Radfords, Stone, Staffordshire. *Mic., Arach.* C. Ex.*

Boswell, H., M.A., Woodstock Road, Oxford. *Mosses, Hepaticæ.**

Boswell, Dr. Syme, Balmuto, Kirkcaldy, Fife, Scotland. *Bot.*

Boulenger, Geo. A., British Museum (Nat. Hist.), Cromwell Road, London, S.W. *Herpetol., Ichthyology.**

Boulger, G. S., F.L.S., F.G.S., Prof. Nat. Hist., 18 Ladbroke Grove, London, W. *Biol., Geol., Min., Collects esp. Woods; Forestry, Spec. The History of Bot. and Geol.**

Boult, James W., 20 Wainfleet Terra Fountain Road, Beverley Road, Hull. *Lepid.* C. Ex.

Boulton, S. B., 64 Cannon St., London, E.C. *Chem.*

Bouverie, Pusey, S.E.B., Pusey House, Faringdon and 50 Upper Brook St., Grosvenor Sq., London, W.

Bowen, Rt. Hon. Lord Justice Sir Charles Synge, C.Kt., D.C.L., 1 Cornwall-gardens, London, S.W.

Bowman, Fred. H., D.Sc., F.R.S.E., Assoc. Inst., C.E., F.L.S., F.G.S., F.R.A.S., F.C.S., West Mount, Halifax, Yorkshire. *Chem., Elect., Molecular Physics, Spect., Elect. and structure of cotton and other textile fibres.**

Boxer, Edw. Monnier, Major Gen'l, R. A. Upton House near Ryde.

Boyd, Thomas, Surrey Lodge, Hornend Road, Norwood, London, S.E. *Ent.*

Boyd, William C., Cheshunt, Herts. *Ent.*

Boyle, Arthur Robert, Engineer's Office, Central Railway Station, Watson St., Manchester.

Boys, C. V., Physical Laboratory, Normal School of Science, S. Kensington, London, S. W. *Phys.*

Braby, Frederick, F.C.S., Bushy Lodge, Teddington.*

Bradbury, S., Abbats Bromley, Rugely, Staffordshire. *Lepid.*

Brade, J., 7 Percey Terrace, Stratford, London, E. *Lepid.*

Bradley, Henry, 98 Roebuck Road, Sheffield. *Philology.*

Bradley, T., Barton Road, Walton, Liverpool. *Lepid.*

Brady, Dr. George S., 2 Mowbray Villas, Sunderland. *Invertebrate Zoology; Entomostraca, chiefly Copepoda and Ostracoda.* Would exchange specimens of Entomostraca, etc.*

Brady, Henry Bowman, F.R.S., F.L.S., F.G.S, 5 Robert St., Adelphi, London, W. *Recent and Fossil Protozoa, esp. Foraminifera and Radiolaria.* C.*

Braham, Philip, F.C.S., 6 George St., Bath. *Chem., Phys., Crystall.**

Braidwood, P. M., Delamere Terrace, Park Road, South, Birkenhead. *Pathology.*

Brailey, Wm. A., 11 Old Burlington St., London, W. *Mic.* Memb. Council, Ophthalmological Soc.*

Braithwaite, R., M.D., 303 Clapham Road, London. *Mosses.*

Bramwell, Sir Fredk. Joseph, C.E., F.R.S., 37 Great George St., Westminster, London, S.W.*

Bramwell (of Hever) Rt. Hon. George Wm. Wilsher, Lord. Holmwood, Four Elms, Eden Bridge, Kent.

Brebner, James S., Tay St., Dundee, Scotland. *Bot.*

Brett, A. T., M.D., Watford, Herts. *Bot., Fungi, Veg. Palæo., Geol., Zool., Anth., Mam., Worms, Moll.* C.

Brett, John, F.R.A.S., 38 Harley St., London, W. *Ast.*

Brewin, Thomas D., F.R.A.S., 14 Saint Nicholas St., Leicester. *Ast: Mars.*

Bridgman, John B., 69 St. Giles St., Norwich. *Ent.*

Brierley, James, Mem. Soc. Pub. Analysts, Hartley Inst., Southampton. *Analyt. and Gen. Chem.*

Brigg, John, F.G.S., Kildwick Hall, via Leeds. *Geol.* C.*

Briggs, Charles A., 55 Lincoln's Inn Fields, London, W.C. *Ent.*

Briggs, Thomas H., M.A., 55 Lincoln's Inn Fields, London, W. C. *Ent.*

Briggs, T. R. A., F.L.S., Fursdon, Egg Buckland, Plymouth, Devon.*

Brightwen, Mrs. George, The Grove, Great Stanmore. *Bot.*, *Hort.*, *Orn.*, *Ent.**

Brigstock, J. W., "Ferntower," Manor Road, Stoke Newington, N.

Bristow, Henry William, F.R.S., Sr. Director of the Geological Survey of England & Wales, Museum of Pract. Geol., 28 Jermyn St., London, S.W.

Bristowe, John Syer, M.D., LL.D., F.R.C.P., 11 Old Burlington St., London, W.

Brittain, Frederick, Taptonville Crescent, Sheffield. *Bot.*, *esp. Insect-catching plants.* C. Ex. in specialty.

Brittain, Thomas B., Torquay. *Mic.**

Britten, J., Editor of "Journal of Botany," Nat. Hist. Museum, S. Kensington, London.*

Broad, C. S., The Chestnuts, Harlesden, N.W.

Brodie, F., F.R.A.S., 58 Bedford Sq., London, W.C. *Ast.*

Brodie, Rev. Peter B., M.A., F.G.S., Murchison Medalist, 1877, Rowington Vicarage, near Warwick. *Geol.* Ex. for fossil insects.*

Bromley, J. Harrison, Eldwick Crag, near Bingley, Yorkshire. *Geol.*

Brook, George, F.L.S., Lecturer on Comp. Emb., The University, Edinburgh.*

Brooke, Sir Victor A., Bart, F.L.S., Colebrooke, Brookeborough, Co. Fermanagh, Ireland. *Orn.*

Brooke, Sir William Brooke O'Shaughnessy, M.D., 55 Parliament St., London, S.W.

Brooks, Henry St. John, M.D., Trinity College, Dublin, Ireland. *Anat.**

Brooks, Rev. H. S., B.A., Thorrington, near Colchester, Essex. *Philol.*, *Arch.*, *Bot.* C.

Broom, C. E., M.A., F.L.S., Elmhurst, Batheaston, near Bath. *Bot.*, *Mycol.*

Brothers, A., F.R.A.S., 126 Upper Brook St., Manchester. *Photog.*

Brotherston, A., Sheldon Park Road, Scotland. *Bot.*

Brown, Alexander Crum, M.D., Prof. Chem. in the University of Edinburgh, Edinburgh, Scotland. *Chem.**

Brown, Edward, F.L.S., 14 Beatrice Road, Finsbury Park, London.

Brown, Elizabeth, Memb. Liverpool Ast. Soc., Further Barton, Cirencester. *Ast.**

Brown, Fred'k Wm., 35 Walterton Road, St. Peter's Park, Harrow Road, W.

Brown, Geo., 45 Victoria road, Kentishtown, N. W.

Brown, George Dransfield, M.R.C.S., L.S.A., F.L.S., Henley Villa, Ealing, W. *Bot., Palæo., Invert. Anat., Radiates.* C. Ex.

Brown, James Campbell, D.Sc., Prof. of Chem., University College, Liverpool, *Chem., Min.* Ex.

Brown, John, 12 Bedford St., Belfast, Ireland. *Elect.**

Brown, John Allen, F.R.G.S., 7 Kent Gardens, Ealing, London, W. *Geol., Min.*

Brown, John C., LL.D., Prof. Emer., Haddington, Scotland. *Forestry and Econ. Bot.**

Brown, R., 33 Peel St., Toxteth Park, Liverpool. *Bot., Lepid., Coleopt.*

Brown, Robert, M.A., Ph.D., F.L.S., F.R.G.S., Ferslev, Rydal Road, Streatham, London, S.W. *Phys. Geog.*, more especially in its biological and ethnological aspects (spec. Arctic Regions, Northwest America, Morocco and Friesian Islands). Exchange papers, books and maps in relation to above.*

Brown, Wm., B.Sc., 3 Elm Cottages, Middle lane, Crouch End, N.

Brown, W. J., 4, 17 Maple road, Anerley, S. E.

Browne, E. T., Uxbridge Lodge, Uxbridge Road, Shepherds Bush, W.

Browne, James Crichton, M.D., LL.D., 7 Cumberland Terrace, Regent's Park, London, N. W.

Browne, J. W., Frascati, Mason's Hill, Bromley, Kent.

Browne, Montagu, F.Z.S., Curator, Museum, Leicester. *Palæo., Gen. Nat. Hist.* C. Ex.*

Browne, The Ven. Robert W., M.A., Ph.D., F.G.S., Archdeacon of Bath, Wells, Somerset.

Browne, Rev. T. H., High Wycombe, Bucks. *Ent., Mic.*

Browne, W. R., Alder Cottage, Isleworth.

Bruce, Venerable Wm. Conybeare, Archdeacon of Monmouth, St. Woolas Vicarage, Newport, Mon.*

Brunlees, Sir James, F.R.S.E., Past President Inst. C.E., 5 Victoria St., Westminster, London, S. W.*

Brunning, G., 137 Kirkwood Road, Peckham, London, S. E. *Lepid.*

Brunton, T. Lauder, M.D., F.R.S., 10 Stratford Place, London, W. *Pharmacology and Therapeutics.**

Bryant, E., "The Corellis," Anson road, Tufnell Park, N.

Bryant, Is., 41 White St., Bethnal Green Road, London. *Lepid.*

Buchan, Alex., Sec. Scotch Meteo. Soc., 72 Northumberland St., Edinburgh, Scotland. *Meteo.**

Buchanan, Geo., M.D. (Lond.), F.R.C.P., Medical Officer of the Local Government B'd, 24 Nottingham Place, London, W.

Buckland, Miss A. W., Memb., Anth. Inst., 54 Doughty St., London, W. C.

Buckley, F. E., Millerton, Inverness, N. B. *Vert.*

Buckley, Henry, 27 Wheeley's Road, Edgbaston, Birmingham. *Ool.**

Buckley, Thomas E., B.A., Attadale House, Strath Carron, Ross-shire, N. B., Scotland. *Orn.*

Buckney, Thomas, F.R.A.S., M.S.T.E., M.I.M.E., 61 Strand, London. *Timekeepers and Galvanic Chronographs for Observatories.**

Bucknill, John Chas., M.D. (Lond.), Coll. Reg. Med. Socius, Coll. Univ. Lond. Soc. E. 2 Albany, London, W.*

Buckton, Geo. Bowdler, F.C.S., F.E.S., F.L.S., Acad. Sci. Nat. Phila. Corr., Weycombe, Haslemere, Surrey.*

Buffham, Thos. Hughes, Comely Bank Road, Walthamstow. *Algæ, Diatoms, Mic., Ast.* A special collection of Microscopic slides illustrating reproductive organs of Marine Algæ. Ex.*

Bulger, G. E., care Messrs. Wheatley & Co., 156 Leadenhall St., London, E.C. *Orn.*

Bull, Dr. Henry G., Hereford. *Mycology, Pomology.*

Bull, R. E., 85 Milton St., Dorset Sq., London, N.W. *Ent.*

Bunbury, Sir Charles James Fox, Bart., F.R.S., F.L.S., 48 Eaton Pl., Belgrave Sq., London, S.W.

Burder, G. F., M.D., Clifton, Bristol. *Meteo.*

Burge, C. H., Laboratory, Somerset House, London, W.C. *Chem.*

Burgess, James, C.I.E., LL D., F.R.G.S., M.R.A S., Director General of the Archæological Soc. of India, 22 Seton Pl., Edinburgh, Scotland. *Indian Arch., Arch., Geog.**

Burghardt, Dr. C. A., Owens College, Manchester. *Min.*

Burnard, C. F., Plymouth Chemical Works, Plymouth. *Chem.*

Burnell, Edward H., 32 Bedford Row, London, W.C. *Ent.*

Burnett, Ernest, Stogumber, near Taunton, Somerset. *Orn., Physiol., Hygiene and Dietictus.*

Burns, David, Geological Survey of England, Museum, Jermyn St., London, S.W.

Burt, Major T. Seymour, M.R.A.S., Pippbrook House, Dorking, Surrey.

Burton, C.E., F.R.A.S., Rathmichael Glebe, Loughlinstorm, Dublin, Ireland. *Ast.*

Burton, Frederick M., Highfield, Gainsborough.

Bush, H., 420 Old Ford Road, London, E. *Lepid.*

Bush, J. W., F.R.A.S., Observatory, Mapperly, Nottingham. *Ast.*

Butler, Major E. A., Royal Irish Rifles, care Messrs. Cox & Co., Army Agents, Craig's Court, London. *Orn., Ool.*

Butterell, J. D., 2 St. John St., Beverley. *Moll.* C. Ex. Pisidia.

Byron, J. R., Fairfield near Manchester. *Bot., Veg. Palæo., Gen. Biol.*

Bywater, Witham N., 5 Hanover Sq., London. *Mic., Photog., Arch.**

Cadell, Henry M., B.Sc., F.R S.E., Geol. Survey Office, Edinburgh, Scotland. *Strat., Physical.**

Caird, Sir James, K.C.B., F.R.S., 8 Queen's Gate Gardens, London, S.W.

Caithness, James Sinclair, Earl of, 34 Hill St., Berkeley Sq., London, W.

Calver, Edw. Killwick, Capt. R. N., Admiralty Surveyor, Assoc. Inst. C. E., 23 Park-place-east, Sunderland, Durham.

Calvert, M., 72 Caversham Rd., Kentish Town, London, N. W. *Ool.* C.

Cambridge, Frederick O. P., Warmwell Rectory, Dorchester, Dorset. *Lepid.*, *Coleopt.* C. Ex.*

Cambridge, Rev. O. P., M.A., F.R.S., Bloxworth Rectory, Wareham. *Lepid.*, *Arachnida.* C.*

Cameron, A. G., Geol. Surv., Jermyn St., London. *Water Supply.*

Cameron, James, Laboratory, Somerset House, London, W.C. *Chem.*

Cameron, J. MacDonald, Chemical Metallurgical Lab., 52 Lime St., London, E.C. *Chem.*

Cameron, Peter, 31 Willow Bank, Crescent, Glasgow, Scotland. *Ent.*

Campbell, D. C., Ballynagard House, Londonderry. *Lepid.*

Campbell, F. M., F.L.S., Rose Hill, Hoddesdon, Herts. *Ent.*, *Arach.**

Campbell, John MacNaught, Asst. Curator, Kelvingrove Museum, Glasgow, Scotland. *Zool.*, *Arch.*, *Eth.*, *Herpetol.*, *Tax.* C. Ex. Wishes to obtain crania by purchase or ex.*

Canesdale, W. D., M.E.S., 8 Grove Terrace, South Tottenham, Middlesex. *Ent.*

Capper, Henry, Huyton Park, Huyton, near Liverpool. *Ent.*

Capper, Robert, C.E., F.R.G.S., Swansea, S. Wales. *Min.*, *Metall.*, *Phys.*, *Elect.*, *Histol.** •

Capper, Samuel James, F.L.S., Pres. Lancashire and Cheshire Ent. Soc., Huyton Park, Huyton, near Liverpool. *Ent.*, *Lepid.**

Capron, Dr. Edward, Shere, Guildford. *Ent.*, *Bot.*

Capron, J. Rand, F.R.A.S., Guildown, Guildford, Surrey. *Ast.*, *Meteo.*

Carew, R. Russell, Carpenter's Hall, Watford. *Met.*

Carmichael, C. H. E., M.A., 46*a* Coleshill St., Eaton Sq., London, S.W. *Anth.*

Carmichael, Thomas D. Gibson, Castle Craig, Dolphinton. *Ent.*, *Myriopoda.*

Carnelley, Thomas, D.Sc., F.C.S., F.I.C., Prof. Chem., Univ. Coll., Dundee, Scotland. *Org. and Inorg. Chem.*, *Phys.*, *Hygiene*, *Bacteriology.**

Carpenter, J., F.R.A.S., Chester Villa, South St., Greenwich. *Ast.*

Carpenter, Philip Herbert, D.Sc. (Camb.), Eton College, Windsor.

Carpenter, Wm. Lant, B.A., B.Sc., F.C.S., 36 Craven Park, Harlesdon, London, N.W. *Elect.*, *Phys.*, *Chem.*, *Photog.**

Carr, J. W., B.A., F.G.S., Cur. Nat. Hist. Museum, University College, Nottingham. *Palæo.*, *Zool.*, *Bot.* C.*

Carr, W. D., 70 Carholme Road, Lincoln. *Lias Palæo.* C. Ex.

Carrington, Benjamin, M.D., Eccles, near Manchester. *Hepaticæ.*

Carrington, C., Ellershe, Lower Merton, London, S.W. *Ent.*

Carruthers, William, F.R.S., F.L.S., British Museum (Natural History Branch), South Kensington, S.W.

Carteighe, John, 3 Hereford Sq., South Kensington, London, S.W.

Carter, H. J., F.R.S., The Cottage, Budleigh-Salterton, Devon. *Sponges*, *Foraminifera and Infusoria.**

Carter, James, F.R.C.S., F.G.S., 30 Petty Cury, Cambridge. *Fossil Crustacea* (excluding Trilobites).*
Carter, Thomas, LL.B., Mill Hill House, Leicester. *Bot.**
Cartwright, A. J., Quilter St., Bethnal Green, London. *Lepid.*
Cartwright, Prof. Samuel, 32 Old Burlington St., London, W. *Anth.*, *Mic.*
Carulla, F. J. R., The Sharon Chemical Co., Derby. *Chem.**
Casey, John, LL.D., F.R.S., F.R.U.I., Catholic Univ., 86 South Circular Road, Portobello, Dublin, Ireland. *Math.*
Cash, William, F.G.S., 38 Elmfield Terrace, Halifax, Yorkshire. *Bot.*, *Palæo.*, *Zool.* C. Ex. Offers for non-British forms, British species, also scientific apparatus and books.*
Cassal, C. E., Hygienic Laboratory, University College, London. W.C. *Chem.*
Casella, Louis P., F.R.A.S., 147 Holborn Bars, London, E.C.
Caton, Richard, Prof. of Physiol., Univ. Coll., Victoria University, Liverpool, 31 Rodney St., Liverpool. *Gen. Biol.*, *Histol. of Vert.**
Cave-Browne, Rev. J., Detling Vicarage, Maidstone. *Lepid.**
Cavell, Edmund, Saxmundham, Suffolk. *Palæo.*, *spec. Pliocene.*
Cayley, Prof. Arthur, F.R.S., Univ., Cambridge, London.
Chadwick, David, The Poplars, Herne Hill, London, S.E. *Mic.*
Chamberlain, Rt. Hon. Joseph, 40 Prince's-gardens, and Athenæum Club, London, S. W.
Chambers, Geo. F., Northfield Obs., Eastbourne, Sussex. *Ast.*
Chambers, W. Oldham, F.L.S., F.R.I.B.A., Sec. National Fish Culture Assoc., South Kensington, London. *Pisciculture: especial attention to the propagation of food-producing fishes.*
Champernowne, Arthur, M.A., F.G.S., Dartington Hall, Totnes, Devon. *Geol.*, *Palæo.* C. Ex.
Champion, G. C., 274 Walroth Road, London, S. E. *Ent.*
Chance, Edward John, F.R.C.S., F.L.S., F.G.S., Surgeon to the City Orthopœdic Hospital, 59 Old Broad St., London, E.C.
Chapman, T. Algernon, M.D., Burghill, Hereford. *Bot.*, *Ent.* C.*
Charlton, Ernest S., Hesleyside, Bellingham, Hexham. *Ent.*
Charte, A., M.A., M.D., Dir. Nat. Hist. Museum, Dublin, Ireland.
Chase, R. W., 2 Egbaston Road, Birmingham. *Orn.*
Chater, E. M., High St., Watford. *Mic. and Bot.*
Chesney, A., 2 Hope's Court, Port Road, Carlisle. *Lepid.*
Chiene, John, M.D., Prof. of Surgery, Univ., Edinburgh, Scotland.
Childers, Right Hon. Hugh C. E., Athenæum Club, London, S.W.
Chirney, H. G., 139 Seven Sisters Road, London, N. *Lepid.*
Christie, W. H. M., M.A., F.R S., F.R.A.S., Astronomer Royal, Royal Observatory, Greenwich, London, S.E. *Ast.**
Christopher, G., F.C.S., Analytical and Consulting Chemist, 8 Rectory Grove, Clapham, London, S.W. *Chem.*, *Phys.*
Christy, Miller, Chignal St. James, near Chelmsford, Essex. *Bot.*, *Mam.*, *Orn.*, *Moll.**
Chrystal, Prof., Univ., Edinburgh, Scotland. *Math.*
Church, Prof. Arthur Herbert, M.A., F.C.S., F.I.C., Prof. Chem. Royal Acad. of Arts, Shelsley, Ennerdale Road, Kew, Surrey.

Church, H. F., Southgate, London. *Min.*
Clapham, Crochley, M.D., Muriel House, Peak Hill, Sydenham, London, S.E. *Anth., Craniological Section.* C. Skull-forms and Brain-weights of the Insane.
Clapham, Thomas R., Austwick Hall, near Clapham, Lancaster. *Phys., Photog., Ast., Orn.*
Clark, Sir Andrew, Bart., M.D., LL.D., (Aberd. and Edin.) F.R.C.P., Pres. Clin. Soc., 16 Cavendish-square, London, W.
Clark, Frederick Le Gros, F.R.C.S., The Thorns, Sevenoaks.
Clark, J. Gilchrist, Dabton, Thornhill, Dumfries, Scotland. *Min.*
Clark, John, Ph.D., F.C.S., 138 Bath St., Glasgow, Scotland. *Chem.**
Clark, J. A., 48, The Broadway, London Fields, Hackney E. *Chem., Mic., Orn., Ool., Ent., Lepid., Coleopt.* C.*
Clark, J. Edmund, B.A., B.Sc., 20 Bootham, York. *Geol., Ferns, Meteo.**
Clark, Latimer, C.E., 6 Westminster Chambers, Victoria St., London. *Elect.**
Clark, W. E., 9 Commercial Buildings, Leeds. *Orn.*
Clarke, A. H., 16 Furnival's Inn, London, E.C. *Ent.*
Clarke, C., 3 York St., Dublin, Ireland. *Lepid.*
Clarke, Charles Baron, F.L.S., Herbarium, Kew. *Ent.*
Clarke, Hyde, F.S.S., 32 St. George's Sq., London, S.W. *Phys., Meteo., Comp. Philol., Anth.*
Clarke, Rev. Robert, F.L.S., 150 Cromwell Road, London, W. *Nat. Hist.*
Clarke, William Eager, 5 East View, Hyde Park, Leeds. *Orn.*
Clarke, Wm. E., F.L.S., M.B.O.U., The Museum, Leeds. *Palæo., Zool., Geog. Dist., Orn.*
Claxton, W., Tenbury, Worcestershire. *Lepid.*
Clay, Charles, M.D., Lecturer and Author, Obstetric Med. Collector of Theological Literature and Numismatist, Andenshaw Lodge, and 101 Piccadilly, Manchester. C. of 1000 Bibles.
Cleaver, Edw. L., 289 King's Road, Chelsea, London, S.W. *Chem.*
Cleghorn, John Wick, Caithness, Scotland. *Geol., Anth.*
Cleland, John, M.D., Prof. Anat., University of Glasgow, 2 College, Glasgow, Scotland.
Clerk, Henry, 3 Hobart Pl., Eaton Sq., London, S.W.
Clifford-Allbutt, Thos., M.A., M.D., F.L.S., Carr Manor, Meanwood, Leeds.
Clifford, Rev. John, M.A., LL.B., B.Sc., F.G.S., D.D., 51 Porchester Road, Westbourne Park, London, W.*
Clifton, Lord Edw. H. Stuart, Cobham Hall, Gravesend. *Orn.*
Clifton, R. B., Prof. Exper. Phil., Univ. of Oxford, Portland Lodge, Park Town, Oxford.
Clive-Bayley, Miss M., Wilmington Lodge, Hurstpierpont, Sussex. *Lepid.*
Close, Rev. Maxwell H., Newton Park, Blackrock Co., Dublin, Ireland.
Clough, Charles Thomas, B.A., Geological Survey of England, Museum, Jermyn St., London, S.W.

Coates, James, Pitcullen House, Perth, Scotland. *Con.**

Coates, John, Assoc. M. Inst. C.E., 33 Frederick St., Gray's Inn Road, London, W.C.

Cobbold, E. Sterling, Assoc. M. Inst. C.E., F.G.S., Chasewood Lodge, Ross, Herefordshire.*

Cockle, Capt. G., 9 Bolton Gardens, London, S.W. *Ent.*

Cockle, Sir Jas., F.R.A.S., etc., 12 St. Stephens-road, Bayswater, London, W.

Colchester, William, Springfield House, Ipswich. *Geol.*

Cole, Arthur C., F.R.M.S., Microscopist, San Domingo House, 171 Ladbroke Grove Rd., Notting Hill, London, W. *Mic., Gen. Biol., Spec., Bot., Diatoms, Emb., Histol.* See Adv.*

Cole, B.G., Laurel Cottage, King's Pl., Buckhurst Hill, Essex. *Ent.*

Cole, Martin I., Science Teacher and Preparer of Mic. specimens, Lonsdale Chambers, 276 Chancery Lane, London. *Bot., Mic., Gen. Biol., Emb., Histol.**

Cole, W. F., F.Q.M.S., St. Mary St., Weymouth, Dorset. *Mic.*

Cole, William, Laurel Cottage, King's Pl., Buckhurst Hill, Essex. *Lepid.*

Coleridge, Rt. Hon. John Duke, Lord, D.C.L., Lord Chief Justice of England., 1 Sussex-sq., Hyde Park, London, W.

Coles, John, F.R.A.S., F.R.G.S., 1 Saville Row, Burlington Gardens, London. *Geog., Ast., Surveying.*

Colles, Miss, Kilkenny, Ireland. *Bot.*

Collett, Lieut.-Col. H., 23 Pioneers Meean, Meer, Punjaub, India, care of Trafford House, Surbiton Hill, Surrey.

Collier, Edward, 3 Friday St., Manchester. *British and Foreign Land and Freshwater Shells.**

Collingwood, J. Frederick, Science Club, 4 Saville Row, London, W.

Collins, John, F.C.S., F.G.S., etc., The Laboratory, Bradford Buildings, Mawdsley St., Bolton le Moors.*

Collins, J. H., 4 Clarke Terrace, Dulwich Rise, London, S.E. *Chem., Geol. and Min.**

Collins, Walter Hepworth, The Laboratory, Bradford Buildings, Mawdsley St., Bolton le Moors. *Analyt. Chem.**

Colquhoun, James, Tredegar Iron Works, Tredegar, Monmouthshire.

Colsell, George Dannatt, 1 Dermody Rd., East Down, Lewisham. *Hort., Elect., Mic.**

Common, Andrew Ainslie, F.R.S., Treas. R.A.S., 63 Eaton Rise, Ealing, London. *Ast., Celestial Photog.* Ex. Astronomical photographs.*

Conchie, William, Livingstone, Mid Calder, Scotland. *Geol., Bot.*

Conrad, C. C., F.C.S., 23 Well St., Wellclose Sq., London. *Chem., Metall.*

Cooke, A., Spring Vale Liscard, Liverpool. *Ent.*

Cooke, Alfred H., King's College, Cambridge. *Con.*

Cooke, Lieut. Gen. Anthony Charles, C.B., R.E., 22 Ryder St. London.*

Cooke, B., Naturalist, 21 Renshaw St., Liverpool. *Orn., Tax. Ent: Lepid.* C. Ex.*

Cooke, Benj., 103 Windsor Road, Southport, Lancashire. *Ent.*
Cooke, Conrad W., C.E., 2 Victoria Missions, Westminster, London. *Phys. Sci.**
Cooke, J. S., F.R A.S., Springfield Obs., Gomersal, Leeds. *Ast.**
Cooke, M. C., M.A., LL.D., 146 Junction Road, Upper Holloway, London, N. *Fungi, Desmids.* C.*
Cooke, N., Gorsey Hev. Liscard, Liverpool. *Ent.*
Cooke, Stephen, Veterinary College, Glasgow, Scotland. *Chem.*
Cooke, Thomas, 30 Museum St., London, W.C. *Gen. Ent: Lepid.*
Cooke, Thomas, F.R.A.S., Optician, York. *Ast.*
Cooper, Charles, M.D., King St., Leicester. *Bot.*
Cooper, E., 31 Baring St., New North Road, London. *Gen. Ent.: Lepid.*
Cooper, E. F., De Montfort Sq., Leicester. *Bot.*
Cooper, Col. E. H., Markree Obs., Collooney, Ireland. *Ast.*
Cooper, Frank Wm., L.R.C.S., Edin., etc., Leytonstone, London, E. *Bot., Mic., Photog., Arch., Histol.**
Cooper, I. A., 32 Bingfield St., Barnsbury, London, N. *Lepid.*
Copeland, Alfred J., Dell Field, Watford. *Orn., Ent.*
Copeland, Ralph, Ph.D., F.R.A.S., Obs. Dun Echt, Aberdeen, Scotland. *Ast.* Late Editor of "Copernicus."*
Copland, Patrick F., Hillcote, Buckhurst Hill, Essex. *Ent.*
Copperthwaite, W. C., Beechgrove, Malton. *Ent.*
Cordeaux, John, Great Cotes, Ulceby, Lincolnshire. *Orn.*
Corfield, William Henry, M.D., M.A., Prof. Hygiene in Univ. Coll., London, 19 Saville Row, London, W.*
Cornwallis, F. S. W., Linton Park, Maidstone. *Bot., Hort.**
Corry, Thomas H., M.A., Belfast, Ireland. *Bot.*
Cottam, Arthur, 18 Essex Road, Watford. *Coleopt., Diatoms, Ent., Bot.**
Cotterell, William, F.R.A.S., Park St., Walsall, Staffordshire. *Ast., Min.* C.
Cotterill, J. H., 18 Gloucester Place, Greenwich, London, S.E.
Cottrell, John, Royal Inst., Albemarle St., London, W. *Phys., Elect.*
Coverdale, Geo., 24 Fleming Rd., Lorrimore Sq., London, S.E. *Bot., Chem., Mic., Anat., Invert., Histol., Ent: Lepid. of world.* C. Ex.
Cowan, Thomas William, F.G.S., F.R.M.S., Comptons Lea, Horsham, Sussex. *Geol., Nat. Hist., Beekeeping.* Editor of "British Bee Journal."*
Cowan, Rev. William Deans, F.R.G.S., Woodville, Eskbank, Dalkeith, Scotland. *Orn., Ool., Ent: Lepid., Coleopt.* C. Ex.
Cowherd, James, F.L.S., Stony Dale, Grange-over-Sands, Carnforth, North Lancashire.*
Cowie, Thomas R., Riddrie Vale, Parkhead, Glasgow, Scotland. *Bot., Geol.*
Cowper, Rt. Hon. Earl of, Panshanger, Hertford. *Bot.*
Cox, Col. C. J., Fordwich House, Canterbury. *Ent.*
Cox, H. Ramsay, Thornleigh, Forest Hill, London, S.E. *Lepid.*
Coxon, J. L., 27 Barlow Lane, Kirkdale, Liverpool. *Ast.**

Coyle, Denis, 69 Lenham Parade, Greenhill, Derby. *Min.*

Craven, Alfred E., F.L.S.,F.G.S., F.Z.S., F.R.G.S., 65 St. George's Road, London, S.W.*

Crawford and Balcarres, Earl of, M.P., F.R.S., 47 Brook St., London, W., and Dun Echt, Aberdeen, Scotland. *Ast.*, *Phys.*

Crawford, James Coutts, F.G.S., Overton House, Strathaven, Lanarkshire, Scotland. *Geol.* C.

Crawford, W. C., F.R.S., Editor, 1 Lockharton Gardens, Slateford, Scotland. *Physiol. Bot.**

Crawshaw, Edward, 25 Tallington Park, London, N. *Min.*

Creak, Ettrick Wm., Staff Commander R. N., Richmond Lodge, Kidbrooke, Park-road, Blackheath, London, S.E.

Crespigny, Eyre de, M.D., M.R.C.S. (Bombay Medical Service, retired), 64 Tavistock Crescent, Westbourne Park, London. *Bot.* C. Ex. Offers British plants for European and North American.

Creswell, Rev. S. F., D.D., F.R.G.S., F.R.A.S., Northrepps Rectory, S. O., Norfolk.

Crichton, Arthur W., B.A., Broadward Hall, Salop. *Orn.*

Crisp, Frank, LL.B , B.A., V.P.L.S., Sec. R.M.S., 5 Lansdowne Road, London, W. *Mic.**

Criswick, George S., R. Obs., Greenwich, S.E. *Ast.*

Croft, Richard B., Fanhams Hall, Ware. *Crypt. Bot.*

Crofton, Morgan Wm., D.Sc., Fellow of the Royal Univ. of Ireland, 86 Stephen's Green, Dublin.

Croke, J. O'Byrne, M.A., The French College, Blackrock, Co. Dublin, Ireland. *Exper. Physics.*

Croll, James, LL.D., F.R.S., Geol. Survey Office, Edinburgh, Scotland.*

Crombie, Rev. James M., M.A., F.L.S., 12 Coleherne Road, W. Brompton, London, S.W.

Crookes, William, F.R.S., Pres. C. S., 7 Kensington Park Gardens, London, W. and Athenæum Club, S.W. *Chem.*, *Phys.* C.*

Crosbie, Frank, The Chestnuts, Barnet, Herts. *Ent.*

Cross, Chas. F , 46 Talgarth Rd., West Kensington, London. *Chem.*

Cross, Rt. Hon. Richard Assheton, Viscount, G C.B., D.C.L., LL.D., 12 Warwick sq., and Athenæum Club, London, S.W.

Cross, W. J., Waterside, Ely, Cambridgeshire. *Bot.*, *Ent.* Ex.*

Crossfield, Henry Atherton, F.Q.S., 78 King Edward Road, South Hackney, London. *Herpetol.**

Crossfield, Talbot King, 78 King Edward Road, South Hackney, London. *Ent: Lepid.* C. Ex.*

Crosskey, Rev. H. W., LL.D., F.G.S., 117 Gough Road, Birmingham. *Geol. of Glacial Epoch.* C. Ex. Brit. fossils for American fossils.*

Crossley, Edward, M.P., F.R.A.S., Bermerside, Halifax. *Ast.**

Crowfoot, W. M., M.B., Beccles, Suffolk. *Tertiary fossils*, *Ool.*, *Lepid.* C. Ex.*

Crowley, Philip, F.L.S., F.Z.S., Waddon House, Croydon.*

Crowther, Henry, Laurel Grove, Chapel Lane, Armley, Leeds. *Con.*, *Bot.*, *Mic.* C. Ex.

Cruickshank, Alexander, 12 Rose St., Aberdeen, Scotland. *Min.*
Cruise, R., M.R.I.A., Geol. Survey of Ireland, 14 Hume St., Dublin, Ireland. *Geol.*
Cruttwell, Alfred C., F.G.S., West Hill, Frome, Somerset. *Geol.*, *Lithol.* C. Ex.
Cubison, H., 29 Jeffreys Road, Clapham, London, S.W. *Lepid.*
Cumming, John C. E., F.G.S., The Cottage, Tunbridge Wells, and Conservative Club, St. James St., London. *Invert. Palæo.*, *Geol.*, *Phys.*, *Photog.*
Cunnack, James, Coinage-Hall St., Helston, Cornwall. *Bot.*, *Mic.* C. Ex.
Cunningham, D. J., M.D., F.R.S.E., F.R.C.S.I., Trinity College, Dublin. *Human and Comp. Anat.*
Cunningham, Robert O., M.D., Prof. Nat Hist. (Biol.) and Geol., Queen's College, Belfast, Ireland. *Biol.*, *Geol.*
Curling, Thos. Blizzard, F.R.C.S., 27 Brunswick-square, Brighton.
Curnow, John, M.D., 3 George St., Hanover Sq., London. *Anat.*
Curphy, W. S., Chemical Laboratory, 22 Devonshire St., All Saints, Manchester. *Chem.*
Curtis, A. H., LL.D., D.Sc., Assistant Com. Intermediate Education Board, 1 Hume St., Dublin, Ireland. *Math.*, *Phys.*
Cussans, J. E., 150 Junction Road, London, N. *Arch.**
Cushing, Thos., F.R.A.S., India Store Depôt, Belvedere Rd., Lanbeth, London, S.E. *Phys.*, *Elect.*, *Mic.*, *Meteo.*, *Ast.*
Dale, C. W., Glanville's Wotton, Sherborne. *Ent.*
Dale, W. C., 8 Copthall Court, London, E.C. *Lepid.*
Dalgleish, J. J., 8 Athole Crescent, Edinburgh, Scotland. *Orn.*, *Ool.* C. Eggs of rare Laridæ or other sea-birds wanted in exchange.*
Dallas, James, F.L.S., Curator, Albert Memorial Museum, Exeter. *Anth.*
Dallas, John, 21 Alma Sq., Abbey Road, St. John's Wood, London. N.W. *Mic.*
Dallas, Wm. S., F.L.S., Ass't Sec'y Geol. Soc., Burlington House, Piccadilly, London, W. *Palæo.*, *Zool.*, *Ent.**
Dallinger, Rev. W. H., LL.D., F.R.S., F.L.S., Pres. R.M.S., Hon. Memb. Am. Soc. Mic., Prin. and Prof. Wesley College, Sheffield. *Biol.*, *Bot.: Fungi*, *Mic.*, *Emb.*, *Protozoa*, *Infusoria.*
Dalton, W. H., F.G.S., Geol. Surv. Eng. and Wales, 28 Jermyn St., London, S.W. *L. Secondary*, *Geol.*, *and Geol. Bibliography.*
Dambrill-Davies, W. R., Wilmslow, Cheshire, and 101 Piccadilly, Manchester. *Obstetric and Operative Surgery.**
Damon, Robert, Dealer in Nat. Hist., Geol., Con., Min., Weymouth, Dorset. *Geol.*, *Palæo.*, *Min.*, *Zool.* C.*
Darwin, Francis, F.R.S., Univ. Lecturer in Bot., Huntington Rd., Cambridge. *Physiological Bot.**
Darwin, George H., LL.D., F.R.S., Newnham Grange, Cambridge. *Ast.*, *Math.**
Davidson, Rev. G., LL.D., The Manse, Logis-Coldstone, Dinnet, Aberdeen, Scotland. *Diatoms.**

Davidson, J. H., 14 Holloway Road, Harrod Green, Leytonstone, London, E. *Phys.*, *Chem.*

Davies, Ed., Royal Inst., Liverpool. *Chem.*

Davies, G., Clarendon Hotel, Arundel St., Strand, London, W.C. *Mic.*

Davies, Rev. Gerald, Charterhouse, Godalming. Ex. prehistoric specimens for good N. A. and Mexican antiquities.

Davies, Thomas, British Museum (Natural History Branch), South Kensington, London. S.W.

Davies, William, British Museum (Natural History Branch), South Kensington, London, S.W.

Davies, W. H., F.R.A.S., 42 Irvine St., Liverpool. *Ast.**

Davis, H. W., Laboratory, Somerset House, London. W.C. *Chem.*

Davis, J. Barnard, M.D., Shelton, Staffordshire. *Anth.*

Davis, Sir John Francis, Bart., K.C.B., Hon. D. C. L. (Oxon.), Athenæum Club, London, S.W., and Hollywood, Bristol.

Davis, James W., F.G.S., F.L.S., F.S.A., etc., Chevinedge, Halifax. *Geol.*, *spec. Fossil Fishes of Coal Measures.* C. Ex. for those of other formations.*

Dawes, John T., M.E., C.E., F.G.S., Cefn Mawr Hall, Mold, Flintshire, North Wales. *Geol.*, *Min.* C.*

Dawkins, W. Boyd, M.A., F.R.S., F.S.A., F.G.S., Prof. of Geology, The Victoria Univ., The Owens College, Manchester, and Curator Manchester Museum. *Anth.*, *Geol.* C. Ex. Remains of British Bone caves offered for Am. mammals, recent or fossil.*

Dawson, Geo. R., Lockwood St., Driffield. *Ent.**

Dawson, Wm., F.R.M.S., Bury St. Edmunds. *Mic.*, *Ast.* C.*

Day, Robert, Cork, Ireland. *Irish Antiquities.*

Day, St. John V., St. Vincent St., Glasgow, Scotland. *Civil Engineer.*

Dean, W., Lindsey St., Epping. *Lepid.*

Debus, Heinrich, Professor of Chemistry at the Royal Naval College, Greenwich, Guy's Hospital, London, S.E.

Deby, Julien, 31 Belsize Avenue, Hampstead, London, N.W. *Mic.*, *Diatoms*, *Min.* C. Ex.*

Defieux, C. A., 98 Herschel St., Liverpool. *Ast.**

de la Rue Warren, M.A., D.C.L., F.R S., 73 Portland Pl., London. *Electricity*, *Chem.*, *Ast.**

de la Sala, P. P., Col. of Engineers, Sevilla House, Navarino Road, London. *Veg. Chem.*, *spec. rendering wood pliable and non-combustible.* Ex. edible gramineous and leguminous seeds, intertropical woods and their products.

de la Taille des Essarts, Baron A., M.D., 2a Pall Mall, London, S.W. *Mic.*

de Medewe, H. R. B , Carlton House, 169 Amherst Rd., Hackney Downs, N.E. *Bot.*, *Phys.*, *Mic.*

Dendy, Arthur, B.Sc., F.L.S.. Associate of the Owens Coll., Asst. in the Zoological Dept. of the British Museum (Nat. Hist.), Nat. Hist. Museum, So. Kensington, London. *Zool.*, *Gen. Biol.*, *Geog. Dist.*, *Morphol.*, *Emb.*, *Anat.*, *Radiates*, *Sponges*, *Protozoa.**

Denham, Sir Henry Mangles, Admiral, 21 Carlton-road, Maidavale, London, W.

Dennet, F. C., 10 Terminus Terrace, Southampton. *Ast.*

Denning, Wm. F., F.R.A.S., Tyndale House, Ashley Down, Bristol. *Ast.*

Dennis, Rev. B., 8 Coulsan's Terrace, Penzance, Cornwall. *Brit. Con.*

De Rance, Charles E., Geol. Surv. of England, Museum, Jermyn St., London, S.W. *Water Supply.*

Derby, Henry Edw. Stanley, Earl of K. G., M.A., LL.D., Knowsley Park, Prescot, Lancashire.

Derham, Walter, M.A., LL.M , F.G.S., Henleaze Park, Westbury-on-Trym, Bristol.

Derry, F., D.D., LL.D., F.R.G.S., 31 Upper Hockley St., Birmingham. *Nat. Hist.*, *Mic.*

Dessé, Ethelred, M.D. (Lond. et Utrecht), Chir. Doct. (Utrecht), F.R.C.S., 43 Kensington Garden Sq., Bayswater, London, *Mic.*

Devonshire, Wm , Duke of, K.G., M.A., LL.D., F.G.S., Chancellor of the Univ. of Cambridge, Devonshire House, Piccadilly, London, W.

Dewar, James, M.A., Prof. Nat. Exp. Phil., Univ. Cambridge, 1 Scroope Terrace, Cambridge, and Prof. Chem., Royal Institution, London, 21 Albemarle St., London, W.*

Dickinson, Joseph, F.G.S., H.M.'s Chief Inspector of Mines, South Bank, Pendleton, Manchester; and Home Office, Whitehall, London.

Dickson, Alexander, Prof. Bot., University, Edinburgh, Scotland.

Dickson, Prof. Wm., Glasgow, Scotland. *Ent.*

Digby, Chas. R., Studland Rectory, Wareham, Dorset. *Lepid.*

Dillwyn, Lewis Llewelyn, M.P., F.L.S., Hendrefoilan, Swansea, Wales.

Distant, W. L., Russell Hill Road, Purley, Surrey. *Geog. Dist.*, *Anth.*, *Eth.*, *Ethnog.*, *Lepid.*, *Hemipt.* • C. Ex.

Dittmar, Prof. W., LL.D. (Edin.), F.R.S.S., London and Edinburgh, Prof. Chem., Anderson's College, Glasgow, Scotland. *Chem.**

Dixon, Jacob R. L., M.D., 94 Shaw St., Liverpool. *Bot.*, *Zool.*, *Gen. Biol.*, *Emb.*, *Anat.*, *Gen. Ent.*, *Pathology.**

Dixon, Harold R., Fellow of Balliol College, Oxford. Prof. of Chem. in Owens College, Manchester.

Dobbie, J. I., D.Sc., Univ. Coll. of North Wales, Bangor, Wales. *Chem.*

Doble, Edmund M., 12 Mount Ararat Villas, Richmond, Surrey. *Mic.*

Dobson, George Edward, M.A., M.B., F.R.S., Surgeon Major, Army Med. Staff, care of Messrs. Holt, Lawrie & Co., 17 Whitehall Place, London, S.W. *Zool.*, *Comp. Anat.*, *Chiroptera and Insectivora.**

Dobson, H. T., jr., New Malden, Surrey. *Lepid.*

Dodd, B. S., Beech Avenue, Sherwood Rise, Nottingham. *Con.*
Doeg, T. E., Evesham. *Ent., Con., Bot., Orn.*
Donaldson, John, Newport-on-Tay, near Dundee, Scotland. *Bot.*
Donovan, Patrick, J. P., Tralee, Co. Kerry, Ireland. *Mic.*
Dormer, Lord, Grove Park, Warwick. *Ent: Coleopt.* C. of Cincindelidæ, which he wishes to increase by purchase or exchange.*
Douglas, D., 87 Bloomington Road, Leith, N. B., Scotland. *Bot.*
Douglas, John Wm., 8 Beaufort Gardens, Lewisham, London, S.E. *Ent.*
Douglass, Sir James N., C.E., F.R.S., Trinity House, London, E.C.
Dovaston, John, West Fulton, R.S.O., Salop *Mic.*
Dove, Hamilton, London Gas Light Co., Nine Elms, London. *Chem.*
Downes, J., 53 Copenhagen St., Barnsbury, London, N. *Lepid.*
Downes, Rev. W., B A., F.G.S., Kentisbeare, Collompton, Devon. *Geol., Palæo.*
Downing, A. M. W., M.A., Editor "The Observatory, a monthly Review of Astronomy," Royal Observatory, Greenwich, London, S.E. *Ast.**
Downing, W., Whips Cross (near Wood St. Station), Walthamstow, Essex. *Ent: Lepid.*
Dowsett, Arthur, Kingsgate Villa, King's Road, Reading. *Ent.*
Dowson, J. E., M. Inst. C.E., 4 Great Queen St., Westminster. *Metall., Phys., Elect.*
Drage, J. Hy., Tamunk Rd., Croydon. *Orn., Ool.* C.
Drane, Robert, F.L.S., Cardiff. *Phæn. Bot., Anth., Orn.*
Draper, H. N., Temple Road, Rathmines, Dublin, Ireland. *Chem.*
Dresser, Henry E., 6 Tenterden St., Hanover Sq., London, W. *Orn.*
Drew, Frederic, Eton College, Windsor.*
Drew, John Ede, Cornwall House, Penzance. *Min.*
Dreyer, John L. E., Ph.D., Armagh Obs., Ireland. *Ast.*
Dreyfus, Ludwig, 181 Adelaide Road, St. John's Wood, London. *Mic.*
Druce, E. C., Chemics, Northampton. *Bot.*
Druce, Herbert, 1 Circus Road, St. John's Wood, London, N.W. *Ent.*
Drummond, Henry, Lect. on Nat. Sci., Free Church Coll., Glasgow, Scotland. *Geol.*
Drummond-Hay, Henry M., Lieut. Col., Royal Perth Rifles, Seggieden, Perth, Scotland. *Orn.*
Drysdale, John, M.D., 36 Rodney St., Liverpool. *Biology, spec. Monads.**
Ducie, Henry J. Reynolds-Moreton, Earl of, F.G.S., 16 Portman-sq., London, W.
Dudgeon, Patrick, F.R.S.E., Cargen, Dumfries, Scotland. *Min.*
Duer, Yeend, Cleygate House, Esher. *Ent.*
Duffin, W. le Strange, White Church, Cappoquin, Ireland. *Geol.*
Dufty, J. N., F.G.S., M.R.C.P., The Grammar School, Tuxford, Newark. *Vert. Palæo., Geol., Min., Arch., Orn., Ool., Lepid.* C.*

Duggan, Thomas R., F.C.S., M.S.C.I., etc., 32 Narford Road, Upper Clapton, London. *Chem.*, *Metall.*, *Phys.*, *Mic.**
Dunbar, L., Duff. Ackergill Tower, Wick, Scotland. *Coleopt.*
Duncan, Peter Martin, Prof. Geol., King's Coll., 4 St. George's Terrace, Regent's Park Road, London, N.W.
Dunk, William, 111 Camden St., London, N.W. *Mic.*
Dunkin, Edwin, F.R.S., Kenwyn Kidbrooke Park Road, Blackheath, London, S.E. *Ast.*
Dunkin, R., F.R.A.S., 15 Royal Pl., Greenwich. *Ast.*
Dunlop, Andrew, M.D., F.G.S., Consulting Physician, Jersey General Dispensary, 50 David Pl., Jersey. *Geol.*, *Anth.*, *Arch.*, *Eth.*, *Ethnog.*
Dunn, J. T., M.Sc., F.C.S., The School, Gateshead. *Chem.**
Dunnet, John, Wick, Scotland. *Bot.*
Dunning, Joseph W., 12 Old Sq., Lincoln's Inn, London, W.C. *Ent.*
Dunraven, Rt. Hon. Earl of, Adare Manor, Adare, Co. Limerick, Ireland. *Anth.*
Duns, John, D. D., Prof. Nat. Sci., New College, 14 Greenhill Pl., Edinburgh, Scotland. *Zool.*, *Geol.**
Dupré, Dr. Aug., F.R.S., Westminster Hospital, London, W. *Chem.*, *Phys.*
Du Pré, Charles C., 17 Pembroke Gardens, Kensington, W. *Ent.*
D'Urban, W., S.M., F.L.S., M.E.S, Exeter, Devonshire. *Gen. Zool.**
Durham, James, Wingate Pl., Newport Fife. *Geol.*
Durnford, W. Arthur, Birdwell, Barnsley. *Orn.*
Durrad, J. W., F.R.A.S., Sparkenhoe St., Leicester. *Ast.*
Dyer, Wm. T. Thiselton, M.A., C.M.G., F.R.S., F.L.S., Director Royal Gardens, Kew.*
Dymond, C. W., F.S.A., Bath. *Arch.*, *Prehistoric Antiquities.**
Easham, G., Leyland Road, Southport, Liverpool. *Coleopt.*, *Lepid.*, *Hemipt.*
Eaton, Rev. A. E., 51 Park Road, Bromley, Kent. *Ent.*
Eaton, Richard, Mechanical Engineer, Nuttall House, Nuttall, near Nottingham, *Thermo-dynamics and fuel economy*, *Metallurgy.*
Ebury, the Rt. Hon. Lord, Moor Park and 35 Park St., Grosvenor Sq., London, W. *Met.*, *Orn.*
Eddy, James Ray, M.E., The Grange, Carleton, Skipton. *Mic.*, *Min.*
Edkins, W., 12 Charlotte St., London. *Antiquary.*
Edle, J., 40 Goldsmith's Row, Hackney Road, London. *Coleopt.*, *Lepid.*
Edle, J., jr., 37 Dunloe St., London. *Gen. Ent.*
Edle, Thos., 40 Goldsmith's Row, Hackney Road, London. *Ent.*
Edmonds, F. B., 72 Portsdown Road, London, W. *Solar Phys.*, *Meteo.*
Edmonds, John, Kaye Hill, Hochley, Birmingham. *Prac. Mic.*
Edmonds, W. S., 10 Hill St., Rugby. *Brit. and Exotic Ent.**
Edmunds, James, M.D., M.R.C.P., London, etc., 8 Grafton St., Piccadilly, London, W. Medical office of Health and Public Analyst for St. James, London, Senior Physician London Temp. Soc., etc.*

Edmunds, Dr. Lewis H., B.A., D.Sc., LL.B., 1 Garden Court, Temple, E.C., London, St. John's College, Cambridge. *Mathematical Phys.*, *Chem.*, *Elect.*, *Magnetism.**

Edmunds, Thomas Wilcox, 32 Old Change, London, E.C. *Mic.*, *Elect.*, *Photog.*, *Bibliog.*, *Geog. Dist.*, *Arch.* C.

Edmundson, John W., C.E., Electrical Engineer, South Benwell Works, Newcastle-on-Tyne. *Phys.*, *Elect.*

Edwards, James, Rupert St., Norwich. *Hemipt.*, *Arach.* C. Ex.

Egerton, Lieut., Badlesmere Rectory, Faversham. *Orn.*

Elger, Thomas G. E., St. Mary's, Bedford. *Ast.*, *Mic.*

Elgood, John E., 21 Oxford St., Leicester. *Mic.*

Elisha, George, Shepherdess Walk, City Road, London, N. *Lepid.*

Elles, J. W., 34 Peddington, Liverpool. *Coleopt.*

Ellis, Alex. John, B.A., F.C.P.S., F.S.A., 25 Argyll Road, Kensington, London, W.

Ellis, John William, L.R.C.P., F.E.S., 3 Brougham Terrace, Liverpool. *Coleopt.*, *especially Coprophagous Lamellicornes.**

Ellis, William, F.R.A.S., Royal Observatory, Greenwich. *Ast.*, *Meteo.*

Ellis, Wm. H., F.G.S., F.R.Met.Soc., Hartwell House, Exeter, Devon.*

Elsden, James V., 2 Ekowe Villas, Southcote Road, Bournemouth. *Geol.*

Elt, C. H., 41 Gibson Sq., Islington, London, N. *Mic.*

Elwes, H. J., Preston House, Cirencester. *Living monocotyledonous plants*, *Palæarctic and Indian Birds and Lepidoptera.* C. Ex. Special desiderata at present, North American and Arctic butterflies. Good exchange in Indian and European species.*

Elwes, J. W., Otterbourne, Winchester. *Palæo.*

Emerson, W. L., M.D., Stockdale Terrace, Leicester. *Analysis of Water and Food.*

Enock, Fred, Ferndale, Woking, Surrey. Preparer of Insects for the microscope without pressure, retaining all the natural form and color.

Enock, Frederic, Fellow of the Entomological Society, London, 11 Parolles Road, Upper Holloway, London, N. *Mic.*, *Ent.*, *Hymenop.*, *Lepid.*, *Dipt.*, *Coleopt.*, *Hemipt.*, *Orthopt.*, *Neuropt.*, *Arach.*, *Myriopoda.**

Epps, Hahnemann, 95 Upper Tulse Hill, London, S.W. *Bot.*, *Mic.*, *Min.**

Erck, Wentworth, LL.D., I.P., Sherrington, Bray Co., Wicklow, Ireland. *Ast.*

Erichsen, John Eric., F.R.C.S., LL.D. (Edin.), Surgeon extraordinary to the Queen, etc., 6 Cavendish Place, Cavendish Sq., London, W.

Espin, T. H. E. C., B.A., F.R.A.S., F.S.Sc., The Observatory, Wolsingham, Darlington. *Ast.**

Essex, Rt. Hon., the Earl of, Cassiobury Park, Watford. *Geol.*

Esson, Wm., M.A., F.C.S., F.R.A.S., Merton College and 13 Bradmore Road, Oxford.

Etheridge, Robert, F.R.S., L. & E., Palæontologist to the Geological Survey of Gt. Brit., Museum, Jermyn St., London, S.W.

Etheridge, Robert, jr., British Museum (Natural History Branch), South Kensington, S. W. *Palæo.*
Evans, Arthur H., B.A., Clare College, Cambridge. *Orn., Ool.* C. Ex. eggs.
Evans, Caleb, 3 Downshire Hill, Hampstead, London, N.W. *Geol.*
Evans, Franklen George, F.R.A.S., F. R. Met. Soc., J.P., Glamorganshire Llwynarthan, Castleton, near Cardiff, South Wales. *Meteo., Ast., Nat. Hist., Arch.**
Evans, John, D.C.L., LL.D., Treas. R. S., Pres. Soc. Ant., F.L.S., F.Z.S., Pres. Num. Soc., Nash Mills, Hemel Hempstead. *Prehistoric Arch.**
Evans, Dr., Horton Lane, Bradford, Yorkshire. *Moll.**
Evans, Sebastian, LL.D., Heathfield, Alleyn Park, West Dulwich, London, S.E. *Anth.*
Evans, W. Hill, M.D., 58 Horton Lane, Bradford, Yorkshire. *Con.* C. Ex. British shells for Am. Helices and Unionidæ.
Eve, Richard W., M.B., 101 Lewisham High Road, London, S.E.*
Everard, J. B., C.E., 6 Millstone Lane, Leicester.*
Everett, Rev. E., Bugbrook, Weedon. *Lepid.*
Everett, Joseph David, F.R.S., Prof. of Nat. Phil., Queen's College, Lennoxvale, Belfast, Ireland. *Nat. Phil.*
Evers, Dr. H., Dr. Armstrong's Coll., Newcastle. *Steam and Mechanics.*
Ewart, J. Cossar, M.D., Prof. Nat. Hist., Edinburgh, Scotland.
Ewing, Rev. J. A., M.A., Westmill Rectory, Buntingford. *Orn.*
Ewing, Jas. Alfred, F.R.S., Prof. Engineering, Univ. Coll., Dundee, Scotland. *Phys., Elect., Seismology.**
Ewing, T. J., D.D., 3 Crescent Villas, Plymouth. *Orn.*
Eyton, Thomas C., Eyton Hall, Wellington, Salop. *Orn.*
Falconer, Rev. W. A., M.A., The Rectory, Bushey. *Ast.*
Farn, A. B., Dartford. *Lepid.*
Farrar, Ven. Frederic Wm., M.A., D.D. (Cantab.), Archdeacon of Westminster, F.E.S., 17 Dean's Yard, Westminster, London, S.W.
Farre, Arthur, M.D., 18 Albert Mansions, Victoria St., London, S.W.
Faust, Miss Emily, 6 Lime Tree Villas, Bischanger Road, South Norwood, London, S.E. *Mic.*
Fawcett, W., B.Sc., F.L.S., British Museum, S. Kensington, London. *Bot.*
Fayrer, Sir. Jos., K.C.S.I., M.D., F.R.C.P. (Lond.), F.R.S.E., Honorary Phys. to the Queen, 53 Wimpole Street, London, W.
Feilden, Capt. Henry W., R.A., West House, Welles, Norfolk. *Orn., Geol.**
Fergusson, James, D C.L., F.R.S., F.R.A.S., 20 Langham Pl., London, W. *Indian Architecture.*
Fergusson, Rev. John, The Manse, Fern, Brechin. *Mosses, Lichens.* C. Ex.
Ferrers, Rev. Norman MacLeod, D.D., Master of Gonville, and Caius College, Cambridge.
Ferrier, David, M.A. (Aberd.), M.D. (Edin.), etc., etc., 34 Cavendish-square, London, W.

Festing, Edw. Robt., Maj. Gen'l R. E., Ass't Dir. of South Kensington Museum, London, S.W.
Ficklin, A., Norbiton, Surrey. *Lepid.*
Fieldwick, Alfred, jr., 284 Dalston Lane, Hackney, London. *Diatoms, Mic., Ent: Lepid.* C. Ex.
Finch, Dr., Borough Lunatic Asylum, Leicester. *Bot.*
Finzi, John A., 105 Gower St., London, W.C. *Ent.*
Fischer, W. L. F., Emer. Prof. Math., Univ., St. Andrews, Scotland.
Fisher, Harry, 26 Stodman St., Newark. *Bot: Phæn. and Crypt. Plants, Ferns, Mosses, Fungi, Algæ, Inorg. Chem., Photog., Geog. Dist., Lepid.* C. Ex.*
Fisher, Harry, 52 Royal York Crescent, Clifton, Bristol. *Bot: Ferns, Geol.* C. Ex. in Bot
Fish, E. D., 22 North Road, Devonshire Park, Birkenhead. *Lepid.**
Fishwick, Henry, Lieut-Col., F.S.A., The Heights, Rochdale, Lancashire *Arch.**
Fitch, Edward A., F.L.S., F.E.S., Brick House, Maldon, Essex. *Ent.**
Fitch, F., Hadleigh House, Highbury New Park, London, N. *Ent.*
Fitzgerald, Chas E., M.D., Folkestone. *Gen. Nat. Hist.*
Fitzgerald, F., Folkestone. *Moll.*
Fitzgerald, George F., Prof. Expr. Sci., Trinity College, Dublin, Ireland. *Phys.*
Fitzgerald, Julia, Folkestone. *Con.*
Fleming, Ernest L., Borax Works, Old Swan, Liverpool. *Chem.*
Fleming, William J., M.D., 155 Bath St., Glasgow, Scotland. *Surgeon.**
Fletcher, Alfred E., Chief Inspector under the Alkali, etc. Works Act, 5 Edge Lane, Liverpool. *Chem.*
Fletcher, J. E., Happy Land, Worcester. *Ent.*
Fletcher, Lazarus, M.A., British Museum (Natural History), South Kensington, London, S.W.
Fletcher, Thos. Wm., Col., M.A., F.S.A., F.G.S., Lawneswoode House, near Stourbridge, and Carleton Club, London, S.W.
Flower, John, M.A , 6 Fairfield Road, Croydon. *Zool.*
Flower, William Henry, C.B., LL.D., F.R.S., Dir. Nat. Hist. Departments, British Museum, Cromwell Road, London, S.W. *Comp. Anat., Anth.**
Floyd, Thomas, C.E., F.G.S., 3 Victoria Mansions, Victoria St., London, S.W.*
Floyer, Fredk. A., B.A., M.B., Camb., M.R.C.S., Eng., L.S.A., Lond. 23a Sussex Sq., Hyde Park, London, W. *Ool. of Persian Gulf.*
Foord, Arthur H., F.G.S., British Museum (Nat. Hist.), London, S.W. *Palæo.**
Forbes, Prof. George, Anderson's Univ., Glasgow, Scotland. *Ast.*
Forbes, Prof. Geo., M.A., F.R.S., L. and E., F.R.A.S., etc., 34 Great George St., Westminster, London. *Phys., Elect., Ast.**
Forbes, John E., F.G.S., 46 Hyde Road, Manchester. *Geol., Min.* C.

Fordham, H. G., Odsey Granges, near Royston, Cambs. *Geol.**
Forrest, H. E., F.R.M.S., Granville Road, Capthorne, Shrewsbury. *Lower forms of plants and animals. Mic.*
Forster, William, The Hill, Whitely, Surrey. *Orn.*
Forsyth, Andrew Russell, M.A., Fellow and Ass't Tutor of Trinity College, Cambridge.
Foster, Clement Le Neve, D.Sc., B.A., F.G.S., H.M. Inspector of Mines, Llanduno, North Wales. *Geol., Min., Mining.**
Foster, G. C., B.A., F.R.S., Prof. of. Phys., Univ. College, London, 18 Daleham Gardens, London, N.W.
Foster, Herbert Le Neve, Mossend Iron Works, Holytown, Glasgow, Scotland. *Chem. of Iron and Steel.*
Foster, Michael, M.D., Sec. R.S., Prelector of Physiol., Trinity College, Cambridge.
Foster, Sir Walter B., M.D., Senior Prof. Medicine, Queen's College, 14 Temple Row, Birmingham. Pres. Council Brit. Med. Assoc.*
Fowler, G. Herbert, St. Anne's Lodge, Lincoln. *Palæo., Geol.* C. Ex.
Fowler, Rev. G. T., M.A., F.S.A., Durham. *Arch.*
Fowler, Rev. W. W., The School-House, Lincoln. *Ent.*
Fox, Charles, 25 St. George's Rd., Tufnell Park, London, W. *Mic., Photog.*
Fox, Rev. Henry E., M.A.. 30 Warwick Sq., London, S.W. *Orn.*
Fox, St. George Lane, Garden Mansions, Westminster, London S.W. *Phys., Chem., Elect.*
Frail, Prof., University, Aberdeen, Scotland. *Bot.*
Fraine, Henry H., 105 Williams St., New Swindon, Wiltshire. *Tax., Ferns, Mosses.* C. Ex.*
François de Chaumont, F.S.B., M.D., F.R.S., Army Medical School, Netley, Southampton.
Frankland, Edward, Ph.D., D.C.L., LL.D., M.D., F.R.S., late Prof. Chem., Normal School of Science, London, The Yews, Reigate. *Chem.**
Franklin, Ed., 22 Richmond Grove, Barnsbury, London, N. *Ent.*
Franks, A.W., Keeper of Antiquities at the British Museum, 103 Victoria St., London, S.W.
Franks, W. S., F R.A.S., 1 High St., Leicester. *Ast: Star Colors.**
Fraser, A., M.B., F.R.C.S., Owens Coll., Manchester. *Emb. of Vert.*
Fraser, Jno. H., Allaby House, Upper Clapton. *Mic.*
Fraser, Dr. J., Wolverhampton. *Bot.*
Fraser, James Wm., M.D., etc., 16 Brunswick Terrace, Spring Bank, Hull. *Chem., Mic., Photog., Gen. Biol., Histol.* C.
Fraser, Thos. Rich'd, M.D. (Edin.), F.R.C.P., F.R.S. (Edin.), Prof. of Materia Medica and Clinical Med. in Univ. Edinburgh, 37 Melville-street, Edinburgh, Scotland.
Fream, William, B.Sc., F.L.S., F G.S., Prof. Nat. Hist., Coll. of Agric., Downton, Salisbury.*
Freeland, Humphrey William, Chichester, Sussex and Athenæum Club, Pall Mall, London, S.W.

Freeman, J., 10 Brownlon St., Dalston, London, N. *Ent.*
Frere, Geo. Edw., Roydon Hall, Diss, Norfolk.
Friswell, R. J., 10 Clapham Sq., London, E. *Min.*
Frost, Alfred James, Electrician, Librarian Soc. of Telegraph Engineers, 6 Westminster Chambers, Victoria St., London. *Phys.*, *Elect.*, *Mic.*, *Bibliog.*
Frost, Edw. P., The Hall, West Wratting, Cambridgeshire. *Phys.*
Frost, Percival, D.Sc., Fitzwilliam Str., Cambridge.
Fry, Alexander, Thornbill House, Dulwich Wood Park, Norwood, London, S.E. *Ent* *
Fry, C. E., The Little Elms, Watford. *Ent: Lepid.* C. Ex. only in British spec. except the sphinges.
Fry, David, Clevedon, Somerset. *Phæn. Bot.* C. Ex.
Fry, Rt. Hon. Lord Justice Sir Edw., B.A., F.S.A., Fellow of Univ. College, London. Farland House, Long Ashton near Bristol.
Fryer, Herbert F., Chatteris, Cambridgeshire. *Ent.*
Fuller, Rev. Alfred, Pallant, Chichester. *Geol.*, *Orn.*, *Ent: Lepid.* C.
Gadow, H., New Museums, Cambridge. *Comp. Anat.*
Gage, Wm. H., F.R.A.S., Church Rd., West Kirby, Birkenhead. *Ast.*
Gahan, Chas. J., M.A., F.E.S., British Museum (Nat. Hist.), Cromwell Road, London, S.W. *Zool.*, *Ent: Coleopt.**
Gain, William Albert, Tuxford, Newark. *Moll.* C. Ex.*
Gale, James, M.A., Ph.D., F.G.S., etc., Eton Ave., Winchester Road, South Hampstead, London, N. W. *Consulting Elect.* C.*
Galloway, William, M.E., Cardiff, South Wales. *Mining*, *Colliery Explosions.**
Galton, Capt. Sir Douglas, C.B., F.R.S., 12 Chester St., Grosvenor Pl., London, S.W.
Galton, Francis, F.R.S., Athenæum Club and 42 Rutland Gate, Knightsbridge, London, S.W.*
Gamgee, Arthur, M.D., Prof. of Practical Physiol. and Histol., Owens College, Manchester, Fairview, Princes Road, Fallowfield, Manchester.
Gardiner, Henry J., F.G.S., F.R.G.S., Hurstmeade, Eltham. *Geol.*
Gardner, John Starkie, 7 Damer Terrace, Chelsea, London, S.W *Fossil Bot.*, *Tertiary and Cretaceous Geol.*
Gardner, Willoughby, 18 Exchange Buildings, Liverpool. *Ferns Palæo.*, *Geol.*, *Arch.*, *Numismatics*, *Orn.*, *Ool.*, *Ent: Lepid.*, *Coleopt.* C. Ex.*
Garnar, J. H., Blenheim Terrace, Leicester. *Mic.*
Garneys, W., Repton, Burton-on-Trent. *Ent.*
Garrod, Alf. Baring, M.D., Coll. Reg. Med. Socius, Consulting Physician to King's College, Hospital, 10 Harley St., London, W.*
Gascoyne, Rowland, Mining Engineer, Mexborough, Rotherham. *Geol.*, *Min.*, *Gen. Biol.* C. Ex.
Gaskell, Walter Holbrook, M.A., M.D. (Cantab.), Lecturer in Physiol. at Cambridge, Grantchester, Cambridge.

Gaskill, Roger, B.A., North Hill, Highgate, London, W. *Geol.*
Gaskin, Rev. Thos., M.A., F.R.A.S., 7 Pitville Lawn, Cheltenham.
Gatcombe, John, Durnford St., Stonehouse, Plymouth. *Orn.*
Gates, H. Sebastian B., Ord. Prœd., St. Dominic's Priory, Maitland Park, Haverstock Hill, London, N.W. *Coleopt., Collection of British Curculionidæ.*
Gates, William, Taxidermist, Sec. Haggerstone Ent. Soc., 4 Baynes Court, Clerkenwell, London. *Orn., Tax., Lepid.* C. Ex. Entomological apparatus-maker.
Geddes, Patrick, F.R.S.E., Univ., Edinburgh, Scotland. *Biol.*
Gedney, William, Bromley, Kent. *Lepid.*
Gee, Rev. C., D.D., The Vicarage, Windsor. *Naturalist.*
Geikie, Archibald, LL D., F.R.S., L. and E., lately Prof. of Geol. and Min. in Univ. of Edinburgh, Dir. General of the Geol. Surv. of Great Britain and Ireland, 28 Jermyn St., London.*
Geikie, James, LL.D., F.R.S., L. and E., Prof. of Geol. and Min. in Univ. of Edinburgh, Edinburgh, Scotland.*
Gemmill, S. M. B., 20 Tillu St., Glasgow, Scotland *Ast.*
George, Chas. Fred'k, M.R.C.S., S.M., L.S.A., London. Kirton in Lindsey, Lincolnshire. *Mic., Photog., Ent: Hymenop., Lepid., Arachnida, Acarina.* C.*
Gerrard, Edw., 61 College Place, London. *Nat. Hist., Tax., Osteology.* C. Institutions supplied.*
Gervis, Walter Soper, M.D., F.G S., West St., Ashburton, Devon.*
Gibbons, Lieut. J. S., M.D., Southampton. *Con.*
Gibbons, R. T., Ceciltyne, Cavendish Road, Brondesbury, Kilborn, London, N.W. *Lepid.*
Gibbs, Arthur E., Cumberland Road, St. Albans. *Bot.*
Gibbs, John, Chelmsford, Essex. *Bot.*
Gibson, Ernest, F.Z.S., M.B.O.U., 17 Mayfield Garden, Edinburgh, Scotland. *Orn.*
Gibson, George Alexander, M.D., D.Sc., F.R.S.E., F.R.C.P. (Edin.), 17 Alva St., Edinburgh, Scotland.*
Gibson, W. G., Dumfries, Scotland. *Antiquities.*
Gilbert, Joseph Henry, F.R.S., Harpenden, St. Albans.
Gilbertson, Henry, Mangrove House, Hertford. *Mic.*
Gilchrist, Dr. James, Dumfries, Scotland. *Geol.*
Giles, J. J., 44 Guildhall St., Folkestone. *Lepid.*
Gill, James, 2 Beech Mount, Liverpool. *Ast.**
Gill, Wm. Hodgson, Park Cottage, Thwaite Gate, Hunslet, Yorkshire. *Geol.*
Gillett, Alfred, Somerset. *Geol.*
Ginsburg, Christian D., LL.D., Holmlea, Chertsey, Surrey. *Philol*
Gittins, J., Laburnham St., Kingsland Road, London. *Lepid.*
Gladstone, J. H., Ph.D., F.R.S., 17 Pembridge Sq., Bayswater London, W. *Chem., Phys.**
Gladstone, Rt. Hon. Wm. Ewart, D.C.L., Hawarden, Cheshire.
Glaisher, Jas., F.R.S., 1 Dartmouth Pl., Blackheath, S.E.
Glaisher, J. W. L., M.A, F.R.S., Sec. Trinity College, Cambridge *Ast., Meteo., Mic.*

Glaisher, Jas. W. Lee, M.A., P.R.A.S., F.C.P.S., Trinity College, Cambridge.

Glazebrook, Rich'd T., M.A., Sec. C.P.S., Fellow of Trinity College, Cambridge, 7 Harvey-road, Cambridge.

Gledhill, Joseph, F.R.A.S., F.G.S., F.R. Met. Soc., Bermerside Observatory, Skircoat, Halifax, Yorkshire. *Ast.**

Glen, D. Corse, F.G.S., 14 Annfield Pl., Glasgow, Scotland. *Min. Petrology.* C. Ex. rare and fine minerals, ores, rocks and recent shells.*

Glover, G. T., Richardson Bros. & Co., Belfast, Ireland. *Chem.*

Gloyne, C. P., Sparholt Road, Stroud Green Road, London. *Con.*

Godfrey, Rev. N. S., F.R.S., St. Bartholomew Vic., Southsea, Hants. *Ast.*

Godman, Fred'k D., F.L.S., F.G.S., M.E.S., South Lodge, Horsham.

Godman, Percy S., B.A., Muntham, Horsham. *Orn.*

Godwin-Austen, Lieut. Colonel H. H., F.R.S, F.G.S., F.Z.S., F.R.G.S., Shalford House, Guilford, Surrey. *Invert. Palæo., Geol., Zool., Gen. Biol., Geog. Dist., Emb., Anat., Orn., Land Moll. in spirit, esp. slugs.*

Godwin, George, F.S.A., 6 Cromwell Pl., So. Kensington, London, S.W.

Goldsmith, Ky St. B., King's Square, Bridgewater. *Ool.**

Goldthwait, Oliver C., Hon. Sec., Walthamstow, Nat. Hist. and Mic. Soc, Church End, Walthamstow, N.E. *Lepid.* C. Ex.

Golding-Bird, Miss, Swiss Cottage, Lyndhurst. *Lepid.*

Gooch, W. D., C.E., The College, Richmond Hill. *Ent., Anth.*

Goodacre, F. B., M.D., F.Z.S., Wilby Rectory, Attleboro, Norfolk. *Zool.* C. Ex.

Goodman, C. H., Kearsbrook Lodge, Lesness Heath, Kent. *Ent.*

Goodman, John, M.D., 8 Leicester St., Southport. *Identity of Light, Heat, Elect., etc.*

Gordon, Douglas, G. H., F.G.S., Society for Promoting Christian Knowledge, Northumberland Av., Charing Cross, London, S.W.

Gordon, John W., A.I.A., 28 Penbury Grove, Lower Clapton, London. *Phys.*

Gore, George, LL.D., F.R.S., Inst. Scientific Research, 67 Broad St., Birmingham. *Chem., Phys., Electro-Met.**

Gore, John E., F.R.A.S., M.R.I.A., Assc. M.I.C.E., F.R.G.S.I., Hon. Assc. Liverpool Ast. Soc., Beltra Ballisodare, Co. Sligo, Ireland. *Ast., Variable and Double Stars.**

Gore, Richard Thomas, 6 Queen Sq., Bath. *Anth.*

Gorham, Rev. Henry S., Shirley Warren, Southampton. *Ent.*

Goschen, Rt. Hon. George Joachim, M.A., 69 Portland Pl., London, W.

Goss, Herbert, F.L.S., F.G.S., Berryland, Surbiton Hill, Kingston, Surrey. *Ent., Bot.*

Gosse, Philip Henry, F.R.S., V.-P.V.I., M.E.S., Sandhurst, Torquay. *Invert., Lepid., Rotifera.* C. Ex.

Gotto, F., The Terrace, Leighton Buzzard. *Geol.*
Gough, T., B.A., Elmfield College, York. *Bot.*
Grace, Miss, New Ross, Ireland. *Bot.*
Graham, Charles, D.Sc., Univ. College, Gower St., London, W.C.
Graham, N. C., Silwood, Tulse Hill, London, S.W. *Lepid.*
Grainger, Rev. Canon, M.R.I.A., Broughshauer, Co. Antrim, Ireland. *Palæo.*
Grant, Dr. James, Wick, Scotland. *Bot.*
Grant, Jas. Aug., Lieut.-Colonel, C.B., C.S.I., 19 Upper Grosvenor Street, London, W.
Grant, Robert, M.A., LL.D., Regius Prof. Ast., Univ. of Glasgow, Observatory, Glasgow, Scotland.
Grant, W. R. Ogilvie, Natural History Museum, Cromwell Rd., London, S.W. *Ichth.*
Granville, J. Mortimer, M.D., F.G.S., F.S.S., F.Z.S., 18 Welbeck St., Cavendish Sq., London, W. *Psychol.*, *Phys.*, *Neurology*, *Comp. Anat. and Physiol. of Nerves*, *Geol.*, *Chem.*, *Mic.*, *Gen. Biol.*, *Anth.*, *Philol.*, *Myol.*, *Infusoria.*
Granville, Rt. Hon. George Leveson Gower, Earl, K.G., Chancellor of the Univ. of London. Stone Park, Staffordshire.
Graves, Rev. James, B.A., Inisnag Rectory, Stonyford, Co. Kilkenny, Ireland. *History and Antiq. of Ireland.*
Gray, Peter, 24 Josephine Ave., Brixton, London, S.W. *Crypt. Bot.*
Gray, T. P., F.R.A.S., The Lodge, Clapham Road, Bedford. *Ast.*
Gray, Wm., jr., Barton-on-Humber, Lincolnshire. *Ast.*
Gray, William, Belfast, Ireland. *Geol.*, *Arch.*
Green, A. H., M.A., F.R.S., Prof. Geology, Yorkshire Coll., 15 Ashwood Villas, Headingley, Leeds.
Green, J. T., Rumford Pl., Liverpool. *Hymenop.*
Green, N. E., F.R.A.S., 39 Circus Road, St. John's Wood, N.W. *Ast.*
Green, Wm., 9 Castlegate, Berwick-on-Tweed. *Photog.*, *Zool.*, *Arch.*, *Orn.*
Green, W. E., 24 Triangle, Bristol. *Bot: Mycology*, *Bryology esp. Hepatics.*
Greene, Rev. J., M.A., Rostrevor, Apsley Road, Clifton, Bristol. *Ent.*
Greenfield, Prof. W. Smith, University, Edinburgh, Scotland. *Pathol.*
Greenhow, Edw. Headlam, M.D., Coll. Med. Reg. Soc., Consulting Physician to Middlesex Hospital, Castle Lodge, Reigate.
Greenwell, Rev. William, M.A., D.C.L., F.R.S., F.S.A., Durham. *Anth.*, *Ethnology*, *Prehistoric Arch.*
Greg, R. P., F.G.S., F S.A., etc., Coles, Buntingford, Herts. *Min.*, *Arch.*, *Meteoric Ast.*, *Oriental antiquities.* C. Ex. Prehistoric specimens.
Gregory, James R., 88 Charlotte St., Fitzroy Sq., London, W. *Min.**
Gregory, J. Walter, 12 Goulton Rd., Clapton, London. *Invert. Palæo.*, *Geol.*, *Min.* C. Ex.

Gregory, T. Currie, 52 Queen Victoria St., London, E.C. *Engineering*, *Geol.* C.
Gregory, Rt. Hon. Sir Wm. Henry, K.C.M.G., 3 St. George's Place, London, S.W.
Gregson, C. S., Rosebank, Fletcher Grove, Stanley, near Liverpool. *British Lepid.*, *Lycænidæ of the world.*
Grenfell, J. G., B.A., F.G.S., Clifton College, 1 Cecil Road, Clifton, Bristol. *Geol.*, *Chem.* C. Ex. carb. corals for carb. or other Encrinites.
Gresley, William S., M.E., Overseal, Ashby-de-la-Zouch. *Geol. as applied to Mining and Engineering.* C. Ex. coal-measure fossils, etc.*
Grey, Henry, Bengal Staff Corps, care of Messrs. Grindlay & Co., London. *Orn.*
Grierson, Thomas B., Museum, Thornhill, Dumfriesshire, Scotland. *Physiol.*, *Nat. Hist.* C. Ex.
Grieve, G. J. P., Kirkbank, Burntisland, Scotland. *Min.*
Griffin, R. W., A.M., LL.D., ex. S.T.C.D., 1 Harcourt Terrace, and 19 Trinity College, Dublin, Ireland. *Math.**
Griffith, A. F., M.A., 15 Buckingham Pl., Brighton. *Phys.*, *Geol.*, *Anth.*, *Arch.* C. Ex.*
Griffith, F. L., Egypt Expe. Soc., care of Messrs. Thos. Cooke & Son, Cooke's Pavilion, Cairo.
Grime, 112 Waterloo St., Bolton le Moors, Lancashire. *Ent.* C. Ex.
Grimthorpe, Lord, LL.D., 33 Queen Anne St., London, W. *Horology.*
Grindon, Leo H., 20 Cecil St., Greenhays, Manchester. *Gen. Bot.*
Grove, William B., B.A., Queen's College, Birmingham. *Fungi.* C. Ex.*
Grove, The Hon. Sir Wm. Rob't, Knt., M.A., D.C.L., etc., 115 Harley St., London, W.
Grover, Chas., Rousdon Observatory, Lyme. *Ast.*
Groves, James, 16 St. Michael's Road, Stockwell, London. *Bot.*
Groves, J. William, F.L.S., F.R.M.S., Prof. of Botany, King's College, London, 90 Holland Road, Kensington, London, W. *Bot.*, *Mic.*, *Gen. Biol.**
Groves, T. B., F.C.S., St. Mary St., Weymouth, Dorset. *Chem.*
Grubb, Howard, F.R.S., F.R.A.S., etc., Hon. Master Engineering, Univ., Dublin, 141 Leinster Rd., Rathmines, Dublin, Ireland. *Ast.*
Grut, F., 9 King St., Southwark, London, S.E. *Ent.*
Guest, Rev. William, F G.S., Ling Holme, Tunbridge Wells. *Palæo.*, *Geol.*, *Ast.*, *Bibliography*, *Anth.*, *Arch.*
Gull, Sir Wm. W., M.D., 74 Brook St., London, W. *Mic.*
Gunn, John, Dale, Halkirk, Caithness, Scotland. *Geol.*, *Min.*, *Arch.*
Gunn, William, Geological Survey of England, Museum, Jermyn St., London, S.W.
Günther, Albert, C.L.G., A.M., M.D., Ph.D., Keeper Zool. Dept., Nat. Hist. Museum, Cromwell Rd., London, S.W. *Zool.*

Gurney, Rev. Henry P., M.A., 10 Clydesdale Road, Colville Sq., London, W. *Gen. Zool., Reptiles, Fishes.*

Gurney, John H., Northrepps, Norwich. *Orn.* C. Ex.*

Gurney, John H., jr., Keswick, Norwich. *Orn.* C. Ex.*

Guthrie, Alfred Tollbank, Dundee, Scotland. *Nat. Hist., Geol., Bot.*

Gwilliam, G. T., F.R.A.S., 35 Lansdowne Crescent, Bayswater, W. *Ast.*

Gyngell, Walter, 14 Fore St., Wellington, Somerset. *Orn., Ool., Ent., Moll.* C. Ex.*

Haddon, Alfred C., M.A., F.Z.S., Prof. Zool., Royal Coll. of Science, Stephens Green, Dublin, Ireland. *Palæo., Zool., Gen. Biol., Geog. Dist., Emb., Anth., Arch.* C. Ex.*

Hailes, Henry F., 15 Westfield Road, Hornsey, London, E. *Mic.* (*Foraminifera*). C. Ex.*

Hainselin, Henry F., 9 Radnor Pl., Plymouth. *Lepid.* C. Ex.

Hake, H. Wilson, Ph.D., F.I.C., F.C.S., Lecturer on Practical Chem. at the Westminster Hospital Med. School, Westminster, S.W. *Chem.**

Hale, C., Nassau School, Barnes, Surrey. *Lepid.*

Hale, John, 12 Albert Mansions, Victoria St., London. *Palæo., Geol., Elect., Photog., Anth., Arch.* C. Ex.

Halked, W. B., Elmhurst, Aigburth, Liverpool. *Bot., Hort.*

Hall, George Berringer, F.C.S., 134 London Wall, London, E.C. *Geol., Palæo.* C.

Hall, John, M.D., Brown St., Leigh, Lancashire. *Hygiene, Mic.*

Hall, Capt. Marshall, F.C.S., 13 Old Sq., Lincoln's Inn, London, W.C.

Hall, Townshend M., Pilton, Barnstaple, Devon. *Geol. of Devon. Series, and Brit. Min.* C. Ex. Upper Devon. fossils for any Devon. of U. S. or Canada.

Hall, Miss W. L., The Gore, Eastbourne, Sussex. *Bot., Ferns, Algæ, Diatoms, Meteo., Lepid.**

Halliwell-Phillips, James O., 11 Tregunter Road, South Kensington, S.W., and Hollingburg Copse, Brighton.

Hamel, Egbert de, Middleton Hall, Tamworth. *Bot., Inorg. Chem., Mic., Gen. Zool.**

Hamilton, John J., South Barrow, Bickley, Kent. *Mic.*

Hancock, J., Oatland, Walton-on-Thames. *Orn.*

Handford, George C., 224 Kings' Road, Chelsea, London, S.W. *Mic.*

Hanley, Sylvanus, Hanley Road, 27 Hornsey Rise, London. *Con.*

Hannah, Robert, Craven House, Church St., Fulham Road, London, S.W.

Hannay, J. B., Woodbourne House, Helensburg, London. *Min.*

Harbison, Mann, 5 Ravenhill Terrace, Belfast, Ireland. *Geol., Zool.**

Harcourt, Augustus George Vernon, Cowley Grange, Oxford.

Harcourt, Rt. Hon. Sir Wm. George Granville, Venables Vernon, Knt., M.A., 7 Grafton-street, London, W.

Harcourt, Edward William, Esq., M.P., Nuneham Park, Oxfordshire, 42 Princes Gardens, London. *Hort., Agric., Geol., Orn., Ool., Osteol.**

Harding, Geo., F.G.S., The Grove and Fishponds, Bristol. *Ent.**
Hardingham, George G., 83 St. George's Sq., London, S.W. *Mic.*
Hardy, Jas. D., F.R.M.S., etc., 73 Clarence Rd., Clapzon, London. *Mic.**
Hardy, Mitchell C., 6 The Terrace, Farquhar Road, Upper Norwood, London, S.E. *Mic.*
Harford, J. U., Upper Nascot, Watford. *Min.*
Hargitt, E., 1 Bedford Road, Bedford Park, Chiswick. *Orn.*
Hargreaves, James, F.C.S., F.A.S., Widnes, Lancashire. *Thermist and Tech. Chem.**
Hargreaves, John, F.C.S., Widnes, Lancashire. *Technical Chem. and Met.**
Harker, Alfred, B.A., F.G.S., Demonst. in Petrology, Woodwardian Mus., St. John's Coll., Cambridge. *Geol.*, *Min.*, *Crystal.*, *Lithol.* C. Ex.
Harker, Allen, Prof. Roy. Agric. Coll., Cirencester. *Biol.*, *Vermes.*
Harkness, William, F.I.C., F.C.S., F.R.M.S., Laboratory, Somerset House, London. *Mosses*, *Chem.*, *Mic.* C. Ex.
Harland, Rev. A. A., M.A., Harefield Vicarage, Uxbridge. *Nat. Hist.* C.
Harley, George, M.D., 25 Harley St., London, W.
Harley, Rev. Rob't, M.A. (Oxon.), F.R.A.S., etc., etc., 4 Wellington Square, Oxford.
Harmer, F. W., F.G.S., Oakland House, Cringleford, near Norwich. *Phæn. Bot.*, *Ferns*, *Hort.*, *Geol.*, *Moll.* C. Ex.*
Harmer, Sidney F., M.A., B.Sc., Demonstrator in Animal Morphology, Univ. of Cambridge, Fellow of King's College, Cambridge. *Animal Morphology.**
Harper, Alfred, 66 Mansfield St., Kingsland Road, London. *Lepid.*
Harper, Alfred, jr., 66 Mansfield St., Kingsland Road, London. *Lepid.*
Harper, P. H., 30 Cambridge St., Hyde Park Sq., London, W. *Ent.*
Harper, William, 66 Mansfield St., Kingsland Road, London. *Lepid.*
Harris, Ed., Anns Pl., Pritchard's Road, Hackney Road, London. *Lepid.*
Harris, Edward, F.L.S., Rydale Villa, Longton Grove, Sydenham, London, S.E. *Mic.*
Harris, John T., Newton Road, Burton-on-Trent. *Ent.*
Harrison, J., 7 Victoria Bridge, Barnsley. *Lepid.*
Harrison, R. H., 3 Adelphi Terrace, London, W.C. *Electricity.*
Hart, Henry Chichester, B.A., F.L.S., Carrablag, Croaghross, Le Herkemey, Co. Donegal, Ireland. *Bot: Phæn. and Crypt. Plants*, *Ferns*, *Mosses*, *Hort.*, *Vert.*, *Invert.*, *Veg. Palæo.*, *Strat. and Physical Geol.*, *Min.*, *Zool.*, *Gen. Biol.*, *Geog. Dist.*, *Vert. and Invert. Anat.*, *Anth.*, *Arch.*, *Eth.*, *Ethnog.*, *Philol.*, *Vert. Mam.*, *Orn.*, *Ool.* C.*
Hart, Samuel Lavington, M.A., D.Sc., St. John's College, Cambridge. *Physics.*
Hart, Thomas H., Kingsnorth, Ashford, Kent. *Lepid.*, *Coleopt.*
Harting, James E., 22 Regent's Park Road, Gloucester Gate, N.W. *Orn.*

Hartley, W. N., F.R.S., F.I.C., L. and E., Prof. of Chem. and of Applied Chem. Sci. and Art Dept., Royal Coll. of Sci., Dublin, Ireland. *Chem. and Spectroscopy.**

Hartog, Marcus M., D.Sc., M.A., Owens College, Manchester. *Bot., Sapotaceæ, Entomostraca.* C. Will purchase spec.

Hartree, William, Carlton Villas, Blackheath Park, London, S.E. *Mic.*

Hartshorne, Betram F., M.A., 11 Neville Terrace, Onslow Gardens, London, S.W. *Anth.*

Harvie-Brown, J. A., F.R.S.E., F.Z.S., Mem. Brit. Orn. Union, Ex. V. P. Royal Phyl. Soc., Edinb., Cor. Memb. Am. Union, Memb. Permanent Comm. International Orn. Comm. Vienna (section migration), Dunipace House, Larbert, Stirlingshire, Scotland. *Orn., Migration and Dist. of Brit. Birds.* C.*

Harvey, Rev. C. W., Throcking Rectory, Buntingford. *Met.*

Harvey, Enoch, 12 Riverdale, Liverpool. *Bot., Hort.* C. Ex. Orchids, Alpine, Herbaceous and bulbous plants.

Harwood, W. H., Colchester. *Brit. Insects of all Orders, also Bird-skins and Eggs and Nat. Hist. Books. Lepid.**

Hatton, Frank, Royal Coll. of Chem., London, S.W. *Chem.*

Haughton, Rev. Samuel, M.A., M.D., Prof. Geol., Trinity College, Dublin, Ireland. *Geol., Animal Mechanics.*

Hawkins, Bisset, M.D., Coll. Reg. Med. Socius, 9 Brunswick Terrace, Brighton.

Hawkins, Rev. Herbert S., M.A., Beyton Rectory, Suffolk. *Orn.*

Hawkins, L., Hillside, Cornwallis Gardens, Hastings. *Bot: F. W. Algæ.*

Hawkins, R. Leonard, 24 Baker St., London, W. *Crypt. Bot., F. W. Algæ.*

Hawkins, Rev. Wm. Bentinck Latham, M.A., 33 Bryanston-sq., London, W.

Hawkshaw, Sir John, Knt., M.I.C.E., F.G.S., 33 Great George-street, London, S.W.

Hawksley, Thomas, F.R.S., M. Inst. C.E., 30 Great George St., London, S W.*

Hawley, J. P., Forest View, West Willow, Wilts. *Agric., Geol., Min.* C.

Hay, Col. Dummond, Seggieden, Perth, Scotland. *Orn., Bot.*

Hay, Sir John Chas., Dalrymple, Bart., Admiral, K.C.B., D.C.L. (Oxon.), Craigenneoch, Wigtonshire, Scotland.

Hayward, L. R., Devonshire Road, Forest Hill, London, S.E. *Lepid.*

Hayward, Rob't Baldwin, M.A., The Park, Harrow.

Head, J. W., F.G.S., 122 Clapham Park Road, Clapham, London, S.W. C.

Heap, Walter, New Museums, Cambridge. *Comp. Anat.*

Heard, H. C., Hailey Hall, Hertford. *Orn.*

Hearder, G. J., M.D., Job's Well, Carmarthen, Wales. *Ent.**

Hearder, Henry P., M.P.S., Plymouth, Devon. *Chem., Elect.**

Hearder, Wm. S., D.Sc., F.L.S., F.S.A., 195 Union St., Plymouth. *Elect., Mammals, Ichth., Tax., Lepid., Crustacea, Molluscs, Sponges.* C. Ex. rare fish, crustacea.*

Heath, Mrs., 62 Elgin Crescent, Notting Hill, W. *Geol.*

Heath, Thos., B.A., 1st Ass't Ast., Royal Obs., Calton Hill, Edinburgh, Scotland. *Meteo.*, *Ast.**

Heathfield, W. E., 20 King St., St. James, London. *Chem.*

Hebert, E. J., M.A., Geol. Surv. of England, Museum, Jermyn St., London, S.W.

Heddle, M. F., M.D., P. Pres. Geol. Soc. Edin., Pres. Min. Soc. Gt. Britain, Prof. St. Andrew's Univ., Scotland. *Chem.*, *Geol.* C.

Hedworth, Thomas H., Dunston, Gateshead-on-Tyne. *Ool.*, *Moll.* C. Ex.

Helm, H. J., F.C.S., F.I.C., Laboratory, Somerset House, London. W.C. *Chem.*

Henck, J. B., jr., 31 Hildrop Road, London, N. *Phys.*

Henderson, J., 150 Graham Road, Dalston, London, N. *Lepid.*

Hennessy, Henry G., Prof. Applied Math., and Mechanics, Royal College of Science for Ireland, Idrone Terrace, Blackrock, Co. Dublin, Ireland.

Hennessy, W. M., Dublin, Ireland. *Celtic Language and Philology.*

Henrici, Olaus, Ph.D., LL.D., F.R.S., Central Institution, Exhibition Rd., London, S.W.*

Henry-Drage, J., Croydon. *Orn.*, *Ool.*, *Ent.* C.

Henry, George, M.E.S., 38 Wellington Sq., Hastings, Sussex. *Ent.: British Coleoptera, Hemipt., Homoptera, Heteroptera.* C. Ex. Brit. Insects and foreign types of rare "British" preferred.

Henry, Wm. Chas., M.D., F.C.S., F.G.S., Haffield, near Ledbury, Herefordshire.

Henslow, Rev. George, M.A., F.L.S., F.G.S., Prof. Bot., Queen's College and Lecturer on Bot. at St. Bartholomew's Medical School; Examiner in Nat. Sci. for the College of Preceptors, London. Dayton House, Ealing. *Bot.*, *Geol.*, *Min.*, *Physiol.* C.*

Herdman, Wm. A., Prof. Nat. Hist., University Coll., Liverpool. *Zool.*, *Gen. Biol.*, *Morph.*, *Invert. Anat.*, *Histol.*, *Moll.*, *Radiates especially Tunicata.**

Heron, William, C.E., Collooney, Co. Sligo, Ireland. *Bot.*

Herschel, Prof. Alexander Stewart, D.C.L., Hon., Prof. Durham Coll. Sci., Newcastle-on-Tyne. *Ast.*, *Phys.**

Herschel, Colonel John, Roy. F.R.S.*

Herschel, John, Lieut.-Col. R. E., F.R.A.S., Deputy Supt. Grt. Trigonometrical Survey of India, Collingwood, Hawkhurst, Kent.

Hete, John Carroll, The Knowle, Newton-Abbott, S. Devon. *Orn.* C.

Hewett, Sir Prescott Gardner, Bart., F.R.C.S., etc., etc., Chestnut Lodge, Horsham, Sussex.

Heywood, Henry R., 21 Hockley Hill, Birmingham. *Tax.*, *Lepid.* C. Ex. Brit. Lepid. for cocoons of Lepid. of U. S., and showy common beetles. Desires correspondence with butterfly and moth collectors.*

Hich, Rev. J. M., Kinloch Kannoch, Perthshire, Scotland. *Lepid.*

Hick, Thomas, B.A., B.Sc., The Owens College, Manchester. *Bot.*, *Biol.*, *Plant Palæo.**

Hicks, Dr. J. Sibley, 2 Erskine St., Liverpool. *Marine Zoophytes.*
Hicks, Henry, M.D., Hendon Grove, Hendon, London, N.W. *Geol.**
Hicks, Wm. Mitchinson, M.A., Fellow of St. John's College, Cambridge, etc., Endcliffe Crescent, Sheffield.
Hiern, W. P., M.A., F.L.S., Castle House, Barnstaple. *Bot., Math.**
Higgin, Thomas, F.L.S., Tower Buildings, Liverpool. *Photog., Invert. Zool., Sponges, Protozoa, Infusoria.*
Higgins, E. T., M.R.C.S., 24 Bloomsbury St., London, W.C. *Ent.*
Higgins, Rev. H. H., Free Public Museum, Liverpool. *Invert. Zool., Bot.*
Higgs, G., 467 W. Derby Road, Liverpool. *Ast.**
Hill, Rev. Canon, M.A., Sheering Rectory, Harlow, Essex. *Geol.**
Hill, Rev. Edwin, M.A., St. John's College, Cambridge. *Geol., Phys., Meteo.*
Hill, Joseph, Hull. *Meteo.*
Hillhouse, W., M.A., F.L.S., Prof Bot., Mason Science College, Birmingham. Pres. Birmingham Natural History and Mic. Soc.*
Hillman, Henry, 456 King's Road, Chelsea, London. *Ferns, Hort., Plant Palæo., Geol., Zool., Geog. Dist., Anat., Orn., Ool., Osteol., Lepid., Coleopt.* C.
Hillman, Thomas S., Eastgate St., Lewes. *Ent.*
Hime, Thomas W., M.D., Medical Officer of Health, Sheffield. *Biol. and Bacteriology.**
Hinchcliff, Miss, Worlington House, Instow, N. Devon. *Lepid.*
Hinchcliffe, C., 10 China St., Liverpool. *Lepid.*
Hincks, Rev. Thomas, F.R.S., Leigh Woods, Clifton, Bristol. *Hydroida, Polyzoa.**
Hind, John R., F.R.S., Sup't Nautical Almanac, 3 Cambridge Park Gardens, Twickenham. *Ast.*
Hinde, George J., Ph.D., F.G.S., Ivythorn, Avondale Road, South Croydon, Surrey. *Invert. Palæo., Geol., Zool., Sponges.* C.*
Hinde, C. M., Holly Bank Road, Clifton Park, Birkenhead, Liverpool. *Lepid.*
Hippisley, John, F.R.A.S., Stoneaston Park, Bath.
Hirst, Thos. Archer, Ph.D., F.R.A.S., 7 Oxford and Cambridge Mansions, Marylebone Road, London, N.W., and Athenæum Club, London, S.W.
Hobkirk, Chas. C. P., F.L.S., Dewsbury. *Bot: Cryptogams, Musci.* C. Ex.*
Hodge, Harold, Pembroke Coll., Oxford, and 33 Almorah Road, Canonbury, London, N. *Ent., Lepid.* C. Ex.
Hodges, John F., M.D., J.P., Prof. Agric. and Med. Jurisprudence, Queen's Coll., Belfast, Ireland. *Agric., Chem.**
Hodgkinson, J. B., 15 Spring Bank, Preston. *Micro-lepid.*
Hodgson, Alfred E., B.A., Cor. Mem. of the South London Ent. Soc., 57 Brook Green, Hammersmith, London. *Bot., Ent: Lepid., Coleopt.* Author of Sym. list of Brit. Macro-lepidoptera and ex. list of Brit. Coleopt. C. Ex.*
Hodgson, Brian Houghton, F.L.S., Inst. Fr. Corresp., Alderly Grange, Wotton-under-Edge.

Hodgson, Rev. John, M.A., F.G.S., F.S.A., Kinver Vicarage, Stourbridge. *Geol.*

Holden, J. Sinclair, M.D., Sudbury, Suffolk. *Geol.*, *Prehistoric Arch.*

Holland, Rev. B., Stanwick, Higham Ferrers, Northamptonshire. *Lepid.*

Hollis, H. P., B.A., F.R.A.S., Royal Obs , Greenwich. *Ast.*

Holton, Edward, 3 Lansdowne Villas, Nightingale Road, Wood Green, Middlesex. *Ool.*, *Ent: Lepid.*, *Dipt.*, *Coleopt.*, *Neuropt.* C.

Holmes, Edwin A., 149 Essex Rd., Islington. *Diatoms*, *Mic.*, *Ast.*

Holmes, E. W., F.L.S., 30 Arthur Road, Holloway, London. *Mosses*, *Hepaticæ*, *Lichens.*

Holmes, John, Holmsted Roundhay, Leeds. *Arch.*, *Eth.* C.

Holmes, John, F.I.C., Laboratory, Somerset House, London, W.C. *Chem.**

Holt, G. A., 189 Strangeways, Manchester. *Mosses and Hep.**

Home, David Milne, LL.D., O.P.R.F.S., Pres. Edin. Geol. Soc., Vice Pres. Scotch Meteo. Soc., 10 York Place, Edin., and Milne Graden, Coldstream, Scotland. *Meteo* , *Geol.*, *Agric.**

Hopkinson, John, M.A., D.Sc., 3 Holland Villas-road, Kensington, London, W.

Hopkinson, John, F.L.S., F.G.S., F.R. Met. Soc., F.M.S., The Grange, St. Albans. *L. and F. W. Moll.*, *Graptolitidæ*, *Geol.*, *Meteo.**

Hopkinson, Mrs. John, The Grange, St. Albans. *Phæn. Bot.*

Hood, Charles, F.R.S., 10 Leinster Gardens, Hyde Park, London. *Phys.*

Hooker, George, F.Z.S., Nascot House, Watford. *Orn.*

Hooker, Sir Joseph Dalton, K.C.S.I., C.B., M.D., D.C.L., LL.D., F.R.S., F.L.S., late Dir. Royal Gardens, Kew. The Camp, Sunningdale, Berks. *Bot.**

Hoopell, Robert Eli, M.A., LL.D., Byers Green Rectory, *via* Spennymoor. *Ast.*, *Meteo.*, *Arch.*

Hornby, John, 1 Lambeth Road, London. *Chem.*

Horne, Bertram, Hampton Park, Hereford. *Lepid.**

Horne, George, Hampton Park, Hereford. A collector of various living pheasants, also their skins.*

Horne, John, F.R.S.E., F.G.S., Geological Survey of Scotland, Geological Survey Office, Sheriff Court Buildings, Edinburgh, Scotland. *Geol.**

Horne, Robert, Union Terrace, Cheetham Hill, Manchester. *Mic.*

Horniman, F. J., Surrey Mount, Forest Hill, London, S.E. *Ent.*

Horsley, Victor, B.S., F.R.C.S., Brown Prof. of Pathology to the Univ. of London, 80 Park-street, Grosvenor-square, London, W.

Hoskins, Sam'l Elliott, M.D., Coll. Reg. Med. Soc., Soc. Antiq. Norm. Socius, York-place, Guernsey.

Houghton, F.T.S., King Edward's School, Birmingham. *Geol.*

Houstoun, George L., Johnstone Castle, Johnstone, Renfrewshire, Scotland.

Hovenden, Charles W., 95 City Road, London, E.C. *Mic.*
Hovenden, Frederick, 95 City Road, London, E.C. *Anth.*, *Mic.*
Howard, Robert L., Mackerye, Harpenden, St. Albans. *Mic.*
Howard, D., Rectory Manor, Walthamstow. *Chem.*
Howarth, Elijah, F.R.A.S., Public Museum, Sheffield.*
Howchin, Rev. Walter, 9 Frank Pl., North Shields. *Geol.*
Howe, John, The Library, Matlock, Derbyshire. *Geol.*, *Min.*, *Con.*
Howe, Thomas, Normanhurst Court, Battle, Sussex. *Lepid.*
Howell, H. H., Geological Survey of England, Museum, Jermyn St., London, S.W.
Howlett, Rev. Frederick, F.R.A.S., East Tisted Rectory, Alton Hants. *Crypt. Bot: Ferns*, *Mic.*, *Solar Ast.*
Howorth, H. H., Derby House, Eccles, Manchester. *Anth.*
Howse, Richard, The Museum, Newcastle-on-Tyne. *Geol.*, *Palæo.**
Howson, Very Rev. Dean, Chester. *Antiquarian.*
Hoyle, William E., M.A., M.R.C.S., Challenger Expedition Commission, 32 Queen St., Edinburgh, Scotland. *Moll.*, *Osteol.*
Hucklebridge, Henry, 116 Ebury St., London, S.W. *Bot.* Ex. flora of Home Counties for North Eng. and N. B.
Huckett, Thomas, 202 New North Road, Islington, London. *Lepid.*
Hudd, A. E., 96 Pembroke Road, Clifton, Bristol. *Ent.*
Hudleston, Wilfrid H., Oatland's Park, Weybridge, Surrey. *Geol.*, *Min.**
Hudson, Chas. T., LL.D., 6 Royal York Crescent, Clifton, Bristol. *Mic.*, *Rotifera.*
Hudson, Robert, F.R.S., F.L.S., Clapham Common, London, S.W. *Mic.*, *Bot.*, *Zool.*, *Palæo.*
Hudson, W. H. H., M.A., LL.M., Camb., Fellow and Prof. Math., King's College, London, W.C. *Math.*, *Phys.**
Hügel, Baron A. von, Mem. Anth. Inst. of Gt. Br. and Ireland, 4 Earl's Terrace, Kensington, London, W. *Eth.*, *Ethnog.* C. Ex.
Huggins, William, LL.D., 90 Upper Tulse Hill, London, S.W. *Ast.*
Hughes, David Edw., Com. of the Leg. d'Honor, etc., London Joint Stock Bank, 69 Pall Mall, London, S.W.
Hughes, Geo. P., Middleton Hall, Wooler, Northumberland. *Arboriculture*, *Palæo.*, *Geol.*, *Gen. Biol.* C.
Hughes, Theodore H., Geological Survey of India, Calcutta, and St. Nicolas House, Upper Totting, London, S.W.
Hughes, Thomas McKenny, M.A., F.S.A., F.G.S., Woodwardian Prof. Geol., Univ. Cambridge, Trinity College, Cambridge.*
Hughes, W. R., 3 Prince's Gate, E. Prince's Park, Liverpool. *Brit. Lepid.* C. Ex.
Hulke, John W., F.R.C.S., F.G.S., Soc. Phil. Cantab., Soc. Honor. Surgeon to the Royal Lond. Ophthalmic Hospital and the Middlesex Hospital, 10 Old Burlington St., London, W.
Hull, Edward, LL.D., F.R.S., Dir. Geol. Surv. of Ireland, Prof. of Geol. in the Royal Coll. of Sci. for Ireland, 14 Hume St., Dublin, Ireland. *Laurentian Rocks in Ireland, etc., etc.*
Humbert, Charles Francis, Watford, Herts. *Geol.*
Humbert, Sydney, Little Nascot, Watford. *Ent: Coleopt.*

Humphrey, George Murray, M.D., Prof. Anatomy, Univ. Cambridge, Grove Lodge, Cambridge.
Hunt, Arthur Roope, Southwood, Torquay, Devon. *Geol.*
Hunt, Rev. H. G. Bonavia, Mus. B., Warden of Trinity College, London, Trinity College, 13 Mandeville Pl., Manchester Sq., London, W.
Hunter, A. E., Jesus College, Cambridge. *Lepid.*
Hurst, George, F.S.S., F.R.H.S., King's Brook House, St. Mary's, Bedford. *Arch.*
Hurst, John Thomas, Civil Engineer, Raymond Villa, Geraldine Road, Wandsworth, London. *Fungi*, *Geol.*, *Phys.*, *Mic.*, *Gen. Biol.*, *Emb.*, *Protozoa.**
Hutcheson, John C., 8 Lansdowne Crescent, Glasgow, Scotland. *Microscopy.**
Hutchings, W. M., Swansea Zinc Ore Co., Swansea, Wales. *Met.*
Hutchinson, Jonathan, LL.D. (Glasc.), F.R.C.S., etc., etc., 15 Cavendish Sq., London, W.
Hutchinson, J., 4 Strickland Gate, Kendal. *Bot.* C.
Huxley, Thomas Henry, LL.D., Ph.D., F.R.S., F.L.S., Professor of Natural History at the Royal School of Mines, S. Kensington Museum, 4 Marlborough Place, Abbey Road, London, N.W.
Hymers, Rev. John, D.D., F.R.S., Late Fellow of St. John's College, Cambridge, Brandsburton Rectory, near Beverley.
Ibbetson, George Augustus, 19*a* Hanover Sq., London, W. *Mic.*
Ibbetson, Howgate, York. *Bot.* C. Ex.
Ilsley, I. S., 6 Trersthin Terrace, Falmouth, Cornwall. *Marine Zool.*
Ince, Joseph, F.L.S., 11 St. Stephen's Avenue, Shepherd's Bush, London, W. *Mic.*
Inchbald, Peter, The Lodge, Hovingham, York. *Ent.*
Ingall, Charles, 5 Jeffrey's Sq., St. Mary Ave., London, E.C. *Geol.*
Ingall, Herbert, Champion Hill, London, S.E. *Ast.*
Inglefield, Sir Edward Augustus, K.C.B., D.C.L., F.R.S., United Service Club and 99 Queen's Gate, London, S.W.
Irvine, Duncan R., Geological Survey of Scotland, Geological Survey Office, Sheriff Court Buildings, Edinburgh, Scotland.
Irvine, W. B., 17 S. Tay St., Dundee, Scotland. *Nat. Science.*
Isles, James, F.S.A., St. Niniam's, Scotland. *Arch.* C. Ex.
Jackson, A. E. A., 22 Anglesea Road, Ipswich. *Mic.*, *Gen. Ent.* C. Ex.
Jackson, Charles L., F.L.S., F.R.M.S., F.Z.S., Pres. of Bolton Mic. Soc., Hillfold, Bolton. *Palæo.*, *Mic.*, *Zool.*, *Emb.*, *Ichth.*, *Ent.*, *Crustacea*, *Moll.*, *Radiates*, *Sponges*, *Protozoa.**
Jackson, E. Steane, M.A., F.G.S., 3 Trematon Terrace, Ford Park, Plymouth. *Palæo.*, *Geol.*, *Min.*, *Crystall.*, *Lithol.*, *Ast.*, *Anth.*, *Arch.*, *Eth.*, *Ethnog.*, *Philol.*
Jackson, H. Wm., F.A.S., F.G.S., Mem. Royal College of Surgeons, Membre de la Société d'Anthropologie, Paris. *Vert. Palæo.*, *Geol.*, *Phys.*, *Elect.*, *Meteo.* *Ast.*
Jackson, Rev. J. C., M.A., 67 Amhurst Road, Hackney, E. *Ast.*

Jackson, John Hughlings, M.D., Coll. Reg. Med. Soc., Physician to the London Hospital, 3 Manchester-square, London, W.
Jackson, J. P., 9 Canning Place, Liverpool. *Ent: Bees, Coleopt.* C.
Jackson, Wm., 312 Mare St., Hackney, London. *Lepid.*
Jago, James, M.D., F.R.S., Robartes Terrace, Truro. *Medicine, Entoptics, Physiological and Pathological Optics, Acoustics, Mechanics.*
James, G., Abbey St., Birmingham. *Min., Geol.*
James, T. Williams, 23 Old Kent Road, London, E.C. *Lepid.*
Janson, E. W., 35 Little Russell St., Bloomsbury, London, W.C. *Ent.*
Janson, Oliver E., 22 Perth Road, Stroud Green, London, N. *Ent.**
Japp, Francis Robert, M.A., Ph.D., F.I.C., For. Sec. C.S., Ass't Prof. of Chem. in the Normal Sch. of Sci., South Kensington, 27 Woodstock Road, Bedford Park, Chiswick.
Jaques, Edward, Office of Woods and Forests, Whitehall, London, S W. *Geol.*
Jecks, Chas., Lyell House, Clevedon, Somerset. *Geol.*
Jeffares, Israel, M.A., B.A., Hartley Inst., Southampton. *Pure and Applied Math.*
Jefferys, Chas., 15 Warren St., Tenby, Pembrokeshire. *Con., Marine Zool., Ool.**
Jeffrey, Henry Martyn, M.A., The Grammar School, Cheltenham. *Math.*
Jelly, Miss E. C., F.R.M.S., London. Hatchlands, Red Hill, Surrey. *Polyzoa, recent and fossil.* C. Ex.*
Jenkinson, H. I., Keswick, Cumberland. *Min.*
Jenner, J. H. A., High St., Lewes. *Ent.*
Jenner, Sir Wm., Bart., K.C.B., M.D., etc., etc., 63 Brook St., London, W.
Jennings, A. Vaughan, Ass't Demonstrator in Geol., Science School, London, Lecturer on Comp. Anat., Birkbeck Inst., London Science School, So. Kensington, London, S.W. *Bot., Palæo., Geol., Zool.**
Jennings, J. H., High School, Nottingham. *Min., Geol.*
Jeula, Henry, West Combe Lodge, Blackheath, London, S.E. *Mic.*
Jewell, Jos., 3 Mt. Ambrose Terrace, Highway, Redruth. *Min.*
Joass, Rev. Dr., Golspie, Scotland. *Nat. Hist., Arch., Geol.*
Jobson, Henry, 7 Reform Terrace, Tottenham, near London. *Lepid.*
John, Evan, Llantrissant, Glamorgan, Wales. *Ent.*
Johnson, Alice, Newnham College, Cambridge. *Comp. Anat.*
Johnson, Alice, Llandaff House, Cambridge. *Morph., Emb., Anat.**
Johnson, David, F.C.S., F.R.M.S., F.G.S., 52 Fitzjohn's Ave., South Hampstead, London, N.W. *Mic.*
Johnson, Frank, Redruth. *Min.*
Johnson, George, M.D., 11 Saville Row, London, W. *Marine Zoology.*
Johnson, R. C., F.R.A.S., 16 Lord St., Liverpool. *Ast.**
Johnson, Rev. S. J., F.R.A.S., Melplash Vic., Bridport, Dorset. *Ast.*

Johnson, W., 66 Upper Warwick St., Liverpool. *Lepid.*

Jolly, William, F.R.S.E., F.G.S., H.M., Inspector of Schools, Pollokshields, Glasgow, Scotland. *Geol., Bot., Arch., Education, Literature.**

Jones, A. H., Shrublands, Eltham. *Lepid.*

Jones, Chas. Handfield, M.B. (Cantab.), Coll. Reg. Med. Socius, Consulting Physician to St. Mary's Hospital, 24 Montagu Square, London, W.

Jones, Rev. Harry, M.A., Bartonmere, Bury St. Edmunds. *Orn.*

Jones, John Viriamu, Prin. Univ. College of S. Wales, Cardiff, S. Wales. *Phys., Elect.**

Jones, Samuel, 18 Hanover St., Wales. *Min.*

Jones, Thos. Wharton, F.R.S., Ventnor, Isle of Wight. *Physiol.*

Jones, Thomas, 2 Clytha Sq., Newport, Monmouthshire. *Geol.*

Jones, Thomas Rupert, F.R.S., F.G.S., 10 Uverdale Road, King's Road, Chelsea, London, S.W. *Palæo., Geol., Min., Lithol., Anth., Arch., Crustacea, Protozoa.**

Joshua, William, F.L.S., Cirencester. *F. W. Algæ, including Desmids and Diatoms, Lichens, Ferns, Mosses.* C. Ex.*

Joule, James Prescott, D.C.L., LL.D., F.R.S., 12 Wardle Road, Sale, Manchester. *Phys.**

Joynson, J., Waterloo, near Liverpool. *Ast.*

Judd, J. W., Prof. Geol., Royal School of Mines, Science Schools, South Kensington, S.W.

Jukes-Browne, A. J., Geological Survey of England, Museum, Jermyn St., London, S.W.

Kaines, J., M.A., D.Sc., 8 Osborne Road, Finsbury Park, London, N. *Anth.**

Kane, Prof. G. D., Univ. Coll., Sower St., London, W. *Human Anat.*

Kane, Sir Robert, M.D., LL.D., Royal Irish Academy, Dawson St., Dublin, Ireland.

Kane, W. F. De Vismes, M.R.I.A., F.E.S., Sloperton Lodge, Kingstown, Ireland. *Mic., Zool., Geog. Dist., Arch., Orn., Ent., Lepid.* C.*

Kappel, August W., F.E.S., Ass't Librarian at Linnean Soc., 5 Burlington Gardens, Chiswick, London, W. *Bot., Zool., Ent., Lepid.**

Kay, John D., Leeds. *Ent.*

Kay, R , 2 Spring St., Bury. *Lepid.*

Keane, A. H., 19 Westwick Gardens, Kensington Park, London, W. *Ethnology.*

Keeping, H., Woodwardian Mus., Cambridge. *Geol.**

Keith, Rev. James, LL.D., The Manse, Forres, Scotland. *Fungi.**

Kelham, Henry R., Lieut. 74th Highlanders, Maryhill Barracks, Glasgow, Scotland. *Orn.*

Kelly, C., M.D., Worthing. *Hygiene.*

Kempe, Alfred Bray, F.R.S., Crown-Office Row, Inner Temple, London, E.C.*

Kemshead, William Bath, M.A., Ph.D., F.R.A.S., Hanover Villa, Thurlow Park Road, West Dulwich, London, S.E.

Kendall, F., Walthamstow, Essex. *Geol.*
Kennedy, Capt. Alexander W. M. Clark, Knockgray Park, Galloway, N.B., Scotland. *Orn.*
Kennedy, Wm., 40 Carlisle Rd., Londonderry, Ireland. *Phæn. Bot., L. and F. W. Moll.*
Kent, John C., Levant Lodge, Earl's Croome, Worcester. *Chem., Bot., Geol.* C.
Kershaw, Allan E., 3 Tarn Villas, Ilkley, Yorkshire. *Ast., Mic.**
Kershaw, Arthur I., Wetherfield Terrace, Cleckheaton, Yorkshire. *Mic., Ent: Lepid.**
Kerswill, J. B., M.R.C.P., Ed., M.R.C.S., Eng., F.L.S., Fairfield, St. Germans, Cornwall.
Key, The Rt. Hon. Sir Astley Cooper, Admiral, G.C.B., Laggan House, Maidenhead and United Service Club, London, S.W.
Keys, James H., 8 Princess St., Plymouth. *Coleopt.* C. Ex.*
Kidston, Robert, British Museum, South Kensington, London, and Victoria Place, 36, Stirling (Scotland). *Vegetable Palæo.*
Kinahan, G. H., C.E., M.R.I.A., F.R.G.S.I., Geological Survey of Ireland, Ireland. *Geol., Anth., Arch., Eth.**
Kinahan, Gerrard A., 24 Waterloo Road, Dublin, Ireland. *Phys., Geol., Min., Lithol., Inorg. Chem., Metall., Mic.* C.
Kinahan, J. H., Dublin, Ireland. *Geol.**
Kincaid, Col. W., care Alexander Fletcher & Co., 2 St. Helen's Pl., Bishopsgate St., London, E.C. (See India.) *Hort., Geol., Anth., Eth., Arch.*
Kinch, Edward, Prof. Chem., Royal Agric. College, Cirencester. *Agric. Chem.*
Kinder, F., 12 Priam St., Liverpool. *Coleopt., Lepid.*
King, J. J., F.X., 207 Sauchiehall St., Glasgow, Scotland. *Lepid., Neuropt., Coleopt.**
King, J. T., 4 Clayton Sq., Liverpool. *Patents for Inventions.**
Kingzett, Charles Thomas, F.I.C., F.C.S., Analytical and Consulting Chemist, Trevena, Amhurst Park, London, W. *Hygienic and Technical Chem.**
Kirby, W. F., F.E.S., Ass't in Zoological Dept., British Museum, So. Kensington, London, S.W., 5 Burlington Gardens, Chiswick, London, W. *Ent.**
Kirk, Prof. T., F.L.S., School of Agric., Lincoln, Canterbury. *Bot.*
Kirkmam, Rev. Thos. Penyngton, M.A., etc , Croft Rectory, near Warrington.
Kirkpatrick, Randolph, L.R.C.P., London M.R.C.S., Eng , Natural History Museum, Cromwell Road, London, S.W. *Polyzoa, Hydrozoa.**
Klein, Emanuel E., M.D., 5 Longridge Road, Earl's Court, London, S.W.
Knight, Frances A., Brynmelyn, Weston Super Mare. *Photog., Arch., Orn., Ool.**
Knight, John Mackenzie, F.G.S., Architect, Bushwood, Wanstead, Essex, E. *Geol., Mic.*
Knott, George, LL.B., Cuckfield, Sussex. *Ast.*
Knowles, Sir Francis Chas., Bart., M.A., Mayfield, Ryde.

Knowles, J. T., Ballymena, Ireland. *Prehistoric Arch.*
Knowles, W. J., Ballymena, Ireland. *Prehistoric Man in Ireland.*
Knox, Arthur E., M.A., Trotton House, Petersfield, Sussex. *Orn.*
Knubley, Rev. Edward P., M A., M.B.O.U., Staveley Rectory, Leeds. *Biol.*, *Geol.* C. Ex. British birds' skins and British fossil shells.
Kodger, Alex. M., 7 Irelands Lane, Dundee, Scotland. *Osteology.**
Kundell, W. W., Lloyd's, Liverpool. *Elect.*, *Meteo.*
Kuper, Rev. C. A. F., M.A., The Vicarage, Trelleck, Chepstow. *Ent.*
Laby, James, Allerton House, Blackheath, London, S.E. *Geol.*
Ladds, John, 8 Kent Gardens, Castle Hill Park, Ealing, London, W. *Mic.*
Lainson, Mrs., Stafford House, Clevedon, Somerset. *Bot.*, *Geol.*
Laistone, William, Union St., Plymouth. *Lepid.* C. Ex.
Laker, Abbot G., Cluny House, Court Hill Road, Lewisham, London. *Hemipt.*
Lamb, A. C., F.S.A., Lamb's Hotel, Dundee, Scotland. *Antiquities.*
Lamb, Horace, M.A. (Cantab.), Prof. of Pure Math. in the Owens College, Manchester, 106 Palatine Road, Didsbury, Manchester.
Langley, Rev. C. J., M.A., Gt. Berkhampstead. *Bot.*
Langley, J. N., M.A., F.R.S., Trinity College, Cambridge. *Physiol.*, *Histol.**
Lancaster, William James, F.R.A.S., F.C.S., F.G.S., Colmore Row, Birmingham. *Exper. Physics, spec. light of Electricity.*
Lane, C., Odiarne, 2 Bellevue, Clifton, Bristol. *Ent.*
Lane, M. B. H., 90 Junction Road, London. *Ent.*
Lane, William J., 9 Teesdale St., Hackney Road, London. *Lepid.*
Lang, Rev. Gavin, Inverness, Scotland. *Min.* C. Ex.
Lang, Henry C., M.D., 41 Berners St., Oxford St., London, W. *Ent.*
Langdon, Augustin W., M.A., 4 Castle Down Terrace, Hastings. *Con.* C. Ex. Sea-shells, gastropoda only.
Langman, Andrew W. F., Mem. Soc. Arts, Hartley Inst., Southampton. *Engineering Construction.*
Langridge, Herbert A., 2 Sion Villas, Thornton Heath, Surrey. *Geol.*
Lankester, E. Ray, M.A., Prof. Zool. and Comp. Anat., University College, 11 Wellington Mansions, North Bank, N.W.
Lapraik, Wm., F.C.S., F.I.C., Lecturer on Metallurgy at the Nat. Dental Hospital, London, 7 Bond Street, Holpro Sq., W.C.*
Lapworth, Charles, 4 Kinburn Pl., St. Andrews, Scotland. *Palæo.*
Larmor, Joseph, M.A., St. John's College, Cambridge. *Math.*
Lascelles, B. P., M.A., F.C.S., Harrow School. *Chem.*, *Anth.*, *Arch.*, *Eth.*, *Ethnog.* C. Ex.*
Latham, H., Mount Pleasant, Wakefield. *Coleopt.*
Law, H. W., Queen's Gate Terrace, London, S.W. *Lepid.*
Law, Robert, F.G.S., 11 Cromwell Terrace, West Hill Park, Halifax, Yorkshire. *Palæo.*, *Geol.*, *Min.*, *Crystall.*, *Lithol.*, *Arch.* C. Ex.*

Lawes, Sir John Bennett, Bart., LL.D. (Edin.), F.C.S., Inst. Fr. (Acad. Sci.), Corr. Rothamsted, St. Albans.
Lawson, Chas. E., 19 Portsea Pl., Connaught Sq., London, W. *Orn.*
Lawson, M.A., Prof. Botanic Gardens, Oxford. *Bot.: Phanerogams, Musci.* C. Ex. Offers several hundred good recently-gathered specimens of Tasmanian Phanerogamous Plants. Wishes good specimens of mosses from any part of the world, except the U. S., Canada and Europe.
Lawton, William, Victoria Terrace, Derringham, Hull. *Ast., Meteo., Mic., Photog., Zool.* C.*
Layton, C. E., 56 Farringtou St., London. *Phys., Mic.**
Lea, A. S., Trinity College, Cambridge. *Physiol.*
Lea, John Walter, B.A., F.G.S., F.Z.S., 9 St. Julian's Road, Kilburn, London, N.W. *Geol., Zool., Biol.*
Leach, Alfred, Southgate, Wakefield. *Gen. Ent.*
Leach, H. R., Hazeldean, Pinner, Middlesex. *Ool.* C.
Leaf, Charles John, F.L.S., F.S.A., Old Change, London, E.C., and Pain's Hill, Cobham, Surrey.
Learoyd, Samuel, Pres. Huddersfield Literary and Sci. Soc., F.G.S., Sherwood House, Huddersfield. *Min., Precious Stones, Agates, Pearls, Pearl-bearing shells, Con.* Ex.*
Leather, J., Manor Road, Liscard, Liverpool. *Lepid.*
Lebour, G. A., M.A., Professor of Geology in the Univ. of Durham, College of Physical Science, Newcastle-on-Tyne. *Geol.* (*Carbon*). C. Carb. fossils in ex. for foreign spec.
Lecky, R. J., F.R.A.S., 3 Lorton Terrace, Notting Hill, W. *Ast.*
Ledger, Rev. E., M.A., Prof. Ast., Gresham Coll., London.
Lee, Henry, F.L.S., F.G.S., Ethelbert House, Margate. *Ichth., Mam., Zool., Mic.*
Lee, John Edw., Villa Syracuse, Torquay, Devon. *Geol., Arch., spec. Devonian fossils.* C. Ex. for Am. Devon. fossils.
Lee, Thomas, F.R.A.S., Observatory, Kilmarnock, Scotland. *Ast.*
Leech, J. H., Park Villa, Wraxall, Isle of Wight. *Lepid.*
Lees, F. Arnold, M.D., 35 Sankey St., Warrington. *Bot: Mosses, Hepaticæ.*
Lefoy, Gen'l John Henry, F.R.S., 82 Queen's Gate, London, S.W. *Terrestrial Magnetism, Arch.*
Legge, John E., M.A., F.I.C., Gt. Berkhampstead. *Bot., Chem., Phys., Biol.**
Legge, Capt. Vincent, R.A., Aberystwith, Wales. *Orn.*
Leipner, Prof. Adolph, Hampton Park, Bristol. *Bot.**
Lemmon, G. F., 183 St. George's Road, Hastings. *Ast.**
Lendy, Major Auguste Frederic, F.L.S., F.G.S., Sunbury House, Sunbury. *Ent.**
Leonard, Hugh, Geological Survey of Ireland, 14 Hume St., Dublin, Ireland.
Le Strange, Hamon, Hunstanton Hall, King's Lynn, Norfolk. *Orn.*
Le Strange, Paget W., Lieut. Col. Royal Artillery, Guernsey. *Orn.*
Letcher, Thomas H., St. Day, Cornwall. *Min.*
Lett, Rev. H. W., M.A., Lurgan, Ireland. *Mosses, Fungi, Lichens, Algæ, Desmids, Mic.* C. Ex.

Letts, Prof. E. A., Chem. Lab., Queen's Coll., Belfast, Ireland. *Chem.*
Levick, John, Livingstone Rd., Handsworth, Birmingham. *Mic.*, *Gen. Biol.*, *Protozoa*, *Infusoria*.*
Lewin, Geo., F.I.C., Laboratory, Somerset House, London, W.C. *Chem.**
Lewis, A. L., 35 Colebrook Row, London, N. *Anth.*, *Prehistoric Arch.* C. Ex.*
Lewis, Geo., 5 Albert Road, Brighton. *Ent.*
Lewis, J. Harbord, F.L.S., 145 Windsor St., Liverpool, S. *Desmids.* C. Ex.*
Lewis, Richard Thomas, F.R.M.S., Queckett Mic. Club, etc., 28 Mount Park Crescent, Ealing, near London, W. *Crypt. Plants*, *Ferns*, *Phys.*, *Elect.*, *Mic.*, *Ast.*, *Worms.* C. Ex.*
Lewis, Thomas, F.R.A.S., Editor "The Observatory," Ass't Royal Observatory, Greenwich. *Ast.**
Lewis, W. J., 21 Fitzwilliam St., Prof. Min., Camb. Univ., Cambridge. *Min.*
Ley, John H., London Road, Croydon. *Geol.*
Ley, Rev. W. Clement, Ashby Parva, Lutterworth, Leicestershire. *Meteo.*
Lilford, The Lord, Lilford Hall, Oundle, Norths. *Orn.**
Limerick, Chas. Graves, Lord Bishop of, D.D., D.C.L. The Palace, Limerick, Ireland.
Linn, James, H.M. Geol. Surv., Sheriff Court Buildings, Edinburgh, Scotland. *Geol.*, *Arch.* C.
Littleboy, John E., Hunton Bridge, Watford. *Orn.*
Liveing, George Downing, M.A., Prof. Chem., Newnham, Cambridge.*
Livett, H. W., M.D., Wells, Somerset. *Ent.*
Livingstone, Clermont, Tudor Lodge, Snakesbrook, London, E. *Ent.*
Llewelyn, J. T. D., M.A., Ylusgerwn, Neath. *Ent.*
Lloyd, Alfred, F.C.S., Mem. Ent. Soc., The Dome, Upper Bognor, Sussex. *Ent.*, *Chem.*
Lloyd, F. G., Hon. Sec. Hertfordshire Nat. Hist. Soc., Westleigh, Essex Rd., Watford. *Hort.*, *Chem.*, *Mic.*, *Photog.*, *Zool.*
Lloyd, Major John H., Colbrooke Lodge, Bognor, Sussex. *Orn.*
Lobley, James L., 59 Clarendon Road, London, W. *Geol.*
Lockwood, F. W., Belfast. *Arch.*
Lockyer, B., 28 King St., Covent Garden, London. *Lepid.*
Lockyer, J. Norman, F.R.S., 16 Penywern Road, London.
Lodge, Oliver Joseph, D.Sc., F.R.S., Prof. Phys., University Coll. of Liverpool, 21 Waverley Road, Liverpool. *Phys.*, *Elect.*, *Chem.*, *Ast.**
Loewy, B., F.R.A.S., Aberdeen House, Hounslow. *Phys.*, *Terrestrial Magnetism.**
Lofthouse, J. P., Stroud. *Geol.*
Logan, R. F., Spylaw House, Colinton, near Edinburgh, Scotland. *Ent.*
Lohse, Dun Echt Obs., Dun Echt, Scotland. *Ast.*

Lomas, Thomas, 31 Back High St., Middletown, near Manchester. *Ent.*

Lomax, A. E , 56 Vauxhall Road, Liverpool. *Bot.* C. Ex. European wild plants for those of U. S., Asia, Australia and South America.*

Long, Harry Alfred, 52 Jane St., Blythswood Sq., Glasgow, Scotland. *Educationalist.**

Longstaff, George B., South Fields Grange, Wandsworth, London, S.W. *Hygiene.*

Longstaff, George D., M.D., Butterknowle, Wandsworth, London, S.W. *Chem.**

Lovell, Thomas, 128 Hartford St., Stepney, London, E. *Lepid.*

Lovett, Edward, West Burton House, Addiscombe, Croydon. *Marine Zool.*, *Mic.*, *Stone Implements.**

Lovelace, William King, Earl of East Horseley Park, Ripley, Surrey.*

Lovick, Thomas, Metropolitan Board of Works, Spring Gardens, London, S.W. *Geol.*

Lowdon, George, Scientific Instrument maker, 1 Reform St., Dundee, Scotland. *Electrician.*

Lowe, W. H., M.D., Woodcote Lodge, Inner Park Road, Wimbledon Park, London, S.W. *Ent.*

Lowe, Edward J., Shirenewton, Chepstow.

Lowry, Paul J., 61 Hackford Road, North Briston, London, S.W. *Lepid.*

Lowson, D. L., M.A., Clarendon House, 164 Kennington Road, London. *Geol.*

Lloyd, F G., Hon. Sec. Hertfordshire Nat. Hist. Soc., Westleigh, Essex Rd., Watford. *Hort.*, *Chem.*, *Mic.*, *Photog.*, *Zool. Vegetable fibres used for Paper Manufacture.**

Lubbock, Sir John, M.P., High Elms, Down, Kent. *Gen. Ent.*, *Hymenopt.*, *Formicidæ*, *Arch.*

Lucy, W. C., The Winstones, Brookthorpe, near Gloucester. *Water Supply.*

Lumb, George Henry, Piccadilly, Westgate, Wakefield. *Gen. Ent.*

Lumsden, J., jr., Arden House, Alexandria, Scotland. *Orn.*

Lundie, C., Rhymney Railway, Cardiff, Wales.*

Lupton, Henry, The Elms, Chapel Allerton, Leeds. *Ent.*

Lydekker, R., The Lodge, Harpenden, Hertfordshire. *Palæo.*, *Geog. Dist.*, *Vert.*, *Mam.*, *Herpet.**

Lynn, William T., B.A., F.R.A.S., Blackheath, S.E. *Ast.**

Macadam, Stevenson, Ph.D., F.R.S.E., F.C.S., F.I.C., Surgeon's Hall, Edinburgh, Scotland. *Agric. Chem.*

Macadam, W. Ivison, F.C.S., F.I.C., etc., Surgeon's Hall, Prof. Chem., NewVeterinary College, Edinburgh, Scotland. *Chem.*, *Geol.*, *Agric.* C.*

Macalister, Alex., M.A., M.D. (Dub. and Camb.) Prof. of Anat. in the Univ. of Cambridge, Strathmore House, Harvey-road, Cambridge.

MacAlister, Donald, M A., M.D., B.Sc., St. John's College, Cambridge. *Math.*, *Physics*, *Physiol.*, *Pathol.**

Macandrew, J. J., Lukesland, Ivy Bridge, South Devon. *Moll.* C. Ex.

Macaulay, J. J., High Street, Holywood, Co. Down, Ireland. *Mic.*, *Photog.*, *Chem.*

Macdonald, John Denis, M.D., Inspector Gen'l of Hospitals and Fleets, 11 St. James-road, Surbiton.

MacDougald, G. D., 41 Reform St., Dundee, Scotland. *Chem.*

Machin, Wm., 22 Argyle Road, Carlton Sq., London. *Lepid.*

Mackay, Donald, Portnacon, Durness, Scotland. *Bot.*, *Geol.*, *Zool.*, *Geog. Dist.*, *Ichth.* C.*

Mackeson, Henry Bean, Hythe, Kent.

Mackintosh, Daniel, 32 Glover St., Birkenhead.

Mackintosh, Henry W., M.A., Prof. Zool. and Comp. Anat., Trinity College, Dublin. *Mic.*, *Zool.*, *Radiates.*

Mackrell, John, 3 Victoria Road, Clapham Common, London, S.W. *Mic.*

MacLaughlan, John, Louise Terrace, W. Ferry, near Dundee, Scotland. *Bibliography.*

MacLean, W. C., 31 Camperdown Terrace, Great Yarmouth.*

Macmillan, Dr. Angus, Anlaby Rd., Hull. *Diatoms*, *Geol.*, *Anth.*, C. Ex.

Macpherson, Alexander, 3 Great Tower St., London, E.C. *Geol.*

Macqueen, Chas., 4 Osborne Villas, Stroud Green Road, London, N. *Lepid.*

McArthur, John, Belmont Works, Battersea, London, S.W. *Org. and Inorg. Chem.**

McCance, James L., F.R.A.S., F.M.S., Rathfern, Rayner's Road, Putney Hill, London, S.W., and Science Club, Saville Row. *Ast.*

McCarthy, 15 Finchburg Sq., London, E.C. *Mic.*

McClay, James Lynn, Rose Villa, Victoria Mount, Oxton, Birkenhead. *Geol.*, *Arch.* C.

McClintock, Sir Francis Leopold, Admiral, 29 Kensington-gate, Palace-gate, London, W.

McCulloch, Rev. Hugh, The Manse, Buncrana, near Londonderry, Ireland. *Bot.*, *Moll.*

McDonnell, Robert, M.D., F.R.S., Lower Pembroke St., Dublin, Ireland. *Physiol.*

McDowall, H., Fordington Green, Dorchester, Dorset. *Lepid.*

McIntosh, Prof. W. C., M.D., LL.D., F.R S., 2 Abbotsford Crescent, St. Andrews, Scotland. *Annelida*, *Food Fishes*, *Marine Zool.**

McIntosh, William Carmichael, M D., Monthly, Scotland.

McKendrick, John Gray, M.D., LL.D., F.R.S.E., F.R.C.P.E., Prof. of Physiology in the Univ. of Glasgow, 45 Westburne-gardens, Glasgow, Scotland.

McKenzie, Joseph, Vice-Pres. Huddersfield Nat Hist. Soc., Nursery Cottage, Birkby, Huddersfield. *Palæo.*, *Min.*, *Crystal.*, *Crustacea*, *Sponges.*

McLeod, Prof. Herbert, F.I.C., F.C.S., Prof. of Chem. at the Roy. Indian Engineering College, Cooper's Hill. The College, Cooper's Hill, Staines.

McMunn, Chas. Alexander, M.A., M.D., F.C.S., Oakleigh, Wolverhampton. *Biological and Medical Applications of Spectroscope, Physiol. Chem., Zool., Bot., Comp. Physiol.**
McNab, W. R., M.D., Prof. Bot., R. Coll. of Sci., Dublin, Ireland.
McRae, W., Westbourne House, Bournemouth. *Lepid.*
McVie, James, Anchorelle, Kirkendbright, Scotland. *Nat. Hist.*
Maddock, Rev. Henry E., M.A., F.G.S., Patrington Rectory, Hull.*
Maggs, Thomas C., F.G.S., Hon. Local Sec., Palæont. Soc., etc., Mem. Geol. Assoc. and Palæo. Soc., Newlands, Yeovil, Somersetshire. *Geol., Palæo.*
Magnus, Sir Philip, B.Sc., B.A., City and Guilds of London Inst., Exhibition Road, London, S.W.*
Main, I. F., M.A., B.Sc., Clifton. *Math.*
Main, P. T., M.A., St. John's College. *Chem.*
Maine, Sir Henry Sumner, LL.D., K.C.S.I., etc., 27 Cornwall Gardens, London, S.W.
Major, Richard H., F.S.A., F.R.G.S., 51 Holland Road, Kensington, London. *History of Geog. Discovery.**
Makins, W. K., Westhorpe House, Hendon, N.W. *Mic.*
Malcolm, John Wingfield, 7 Stanhope St., Mayfair, London, W. *Orn.*
Malcolmson, Sam'l M., M.D., M.Ch., 55 Great Victoria St., Belfast, Ireland. *Bot., Mic., Zool., Histol., Crust: Ostracoda especially.* C. Ex.
Malet, John C., M.A., Prof. of Math. in Queen's College, Cork, Shanakiel Villa, Sunday's Well, Cork, Ireland.
Maling, C. T., 14 Ellison Pl., Newcastle-on-Tyne. *Geol.*
Mammatt, John E., Bramley, Leeds. *Geol.*
Mann, Harbison, Model School, Belfast, Ireland. *Geol., Zool.*
Manners-Sutton, Hon. Graham, 50 Thurloe Sq., London, S.W. *Orn.*
Manning, Robert, M. Inst. C.E., 4 Ely Pl., Upper, Dublin, Ireland. *Hydrology.**
Mansel-Pleydell, John C., B.A., F.G.S., F.L.S., Whatcombe, Blandford, Dorsetshire. *Gen. Nat. Hist.*
Mantua & Montferrat, H. R. and M.S.H., The Prince of, The Curator of the Museum of, 18 Elgin Road, St. Peter's Park, London, W. Ex. Spec. wanted in Birds, Eggs, Minerals, Fossils, Plants, Seeds, Insects, Botany, Shells and Antiquities.
Marcet, William, M.D., F.C.S., 39 Grosvenor St., London, W.
Markby, J. R., 7 University St., London, W.C. *Geol.**
Markham, Clements Robt., C.B., Sec. R.G.S., etc., 21 Eccleston Sq., London, S.W.
Markin, Chas. J. S., 10 Prince's Park Terrace, Prince's Park, Liverpool. *Mic., Photog., Ent: Lepid.* C.
Marks, Henry S., 15 Hamilton Terrace, London, N.W. *Orn.*
Markwich, Major E. E., F.R.A.S., 13 Upper Eglinton Road, London, S.E. *Ast., Variable Stars.**
Marr, John Edward, M.A., F.G.S., St. John's College, Cambridge. *Geol.*

Marrat, F. P., Free Public Museum, Liverpool. *Con.*, *Min.*
Marriott, John, W. Fleckney, Market, Harborough, Leicestershire. *Geol.*
Marriott, W., Ass't Sec. Royal Met. Soc., 30 Great George St., Westminster, London, S.W. *Meteo.**
Marsden, Herbert Walter, Nat. Hist. Agent, 37 Midland Road, Gloucester. *Orn.*, *Ool.*, *Lepid.* Ex.
Marsh, Henry, Cressy House, Woodsley Rd., Leeds. *Ent: Lepid.*, *Neuropt.* C. Ex.
Marsh, John G., 16 Hanover St., Rye Lane, Peckham, London, S.E. *Ent.*
Marsh, T. E. Miles, C.E., 34 Grosvenor Pl., Bath, and 1 Westminster Chambers, London, S.W.*
Marshall, A. Milnes, Prof. Zool., Owens Coll., Manchester.*
Marshall, John, F.R.A.S., F.G.S., Church Inst., Albion Place, Leeds.*
Marshall, John, F.C.S., etc., etc., Prof. of Anat. to the Royal Acad. of Arts, 10 Saville-row, London, W.
Marshall, John, Belmont, Taunton, England. *Ool. and Albino Eng. Birds.* C.
Marshall, W. P., M. Inst. C. E., 15 Augustus Road, Birmingham. *Mic.**
Marson, Thos., 68 Kirggate, Wakefield. *Ent.*
Marten, E. B., Pedmore, near Stourbridge. *Geol.**
Marth, Albert, Markree Obs., Colloney, Co. Sligo, Ireland. *Ast.*
Martin, J. B., M.A., F.Z.S., 17 Hyde Park Gate, London, S.W. *Anth.*, *Orn.*, *Ool.* C.
Martin, N. Henry, 29 Mosley St., Newcastle-on-Tyne. *Bot.*, *Inorg. Chem.*, *Mic.*
Martin, Richard Biddulph, M.A., Late M.P., Fellow and Late Pres. Inst. of Bankers, Treas. Statistical Soc., F.R.G.S., F.A.I., Chiselhurst. *Anth.**
Martindale, G. E., Liverpool College, Shaw St., Liverpool. Desires to exchange British plants for continental, or European for North American.*
Martindale, Joseph Anthony, Danes Road, Stavely, Kendal. *Lichens.* C. Ex.
Maskelyne, Nevil Story, M.A., M.P., F.R.S., F.C.S., Professor of Mineralogy in the University of Oxford, 112 Gloucester Terrace, Hyde Park Gardens, London, W.
Mason, Philip B., Burton-on-Trent. *Brit. Zool. and Bot.**
Mason, Robert, F.L.S., 6 Albion Crescent, Dowanhill, Glasgow, Scotland. *Bot.* C.*
Masse, G. E., Oak House, Oak Road, Scarborough. *Bot.*
Massey, Gerald, New Southgate, London. *Anth.**
Masson, Orme, A.M., D.Sc., Univ. Edinburgh, Scotland. *Fellow in Chem.*
Masters, Maxwell T., M.D., 41 Wellington St., Strand, London. *Bot.*
Mather, Sidney, Eagley Bank, near Bolton-le-Moors, Lancashire, *Orn.*, *Ool.* C. Ex.*

Mathew, Gervase F., Staff Paymaster Royal Navy, F.L.S., F.Z.S., F.R.G.S., F.E.S., Lee House, Dovercourt, Essex. *Lepid.* C. Ex. Brit. for Exotic Lepid.*
Mathew, Rev. Murray A., M A., Stone Hall, Haverfordwest, Wales. *Orn.*
Mathews, George Ballard, B.A., University College of North Wales, Bangor. *Math.*
Mathews, Wm., M.A., 60 Harborne Road, Birmingham. *Bot.*, *Geol.*
Mathewson, Allan, C.M.S.A., 9 Union Terrace, Constitution Road, Dundee, Scotland. *Geol.*, *Arch.*
Matthews, G., 20 Cropley St., New North Road, London. *Lepid.*
Matthey, George, F.C.S., Cheyne House, Chelsea Embankment, London, S.W.
Maunder, E. W., F.R.A.S., Editor of "The Observatory, a Monthly Review of Ast.," Assistant Superintending the Physical Dept., Royal Obs., Greenwich, London, S.E. *Ast.**
Maw, George, F.L.S., F.S.A., F.G.S., Benthall Hall, Broseley. *Bot.*, *Monograph of Genus Crocus*, *Geol.*, *Sil. Brachiopods.* C.
Max-Müller, F., Oxford.*
May, John W., Arundel House, Percy Cross, Fulham Road, London, S.W. *Ent.*
May, William, Northfield, St. Mary's Cray, Kent.
Mayall, J., jr., 224 Regent St., London. *Mic.**
Maynard, G. N., The Museum, Saffron Walden, Essex. *Bot.*
Maynard, John, East Pool Mine, Redruth. *Min.*
Maynard, Richard, 78 Pendarves St., Tuckingmill. *Min.*
McLachlan, Robert, F.R S., Westview, Clarendon Road, Lewisham, London, S.E.*
Meacham, Fred G., Hampstead, Great Barr, Birmingham. *Geol.* C.
Meade, R. H., Bradford. *Ent: Dipt.*
Medwin, A. George, M.D., L.R.C.P., Lond., F.L.S., M.R.C.S., L.D.S., etc., 34 Bruton St., Berkeley Sq., London, W. *Bot.*, *Ent.**
Medlycott, Ven. W.C.P., Sherborne, Dorset. *Geol.*, *Orn.*, *Con.*, *Mosses*, *Hepaticæ*, *Lichens*, *Algæ.* C.
Meeham, W. H., 446 Kingsland Road, London. *Lepid.*
Meek, Alexander, British Linen Co's. Bank Bldg's, Dundee, Scotland. *Zool.*, *Gen. Biol.*, *Morphology*, *Vert.*, *Invert. Anat.* C.*
Meek, E. G., 56 Brompton Road, London, S.W. *Ent.*
Meiklejohn, J. W. S., M.D., Deputy Inspector General, R. W., 16 Notting Hill Square, London, W. *Bot.* C.
Meldola, R., 6 Brunswick Sq., London, S.W. *Ent.*
Melliss, John Charles, F.G.S., F.L.S., Mem. Inst. C.E., Author of "Purification of Water carried Sewage," "St. Helena, an account of the Nat. Hist. of the Island," etc., 232 Gresham House, Old Broad St., London, E.C.*
Mello, Rev. John Magens, M.A., F.G.S., Member of "Société Scientifique" of Brussels, Local Sec. of Soc. of Antiqs., London, Local Sec. of Victoria Inst., Hon. Member of the Chesterfield and Midland Inst. of Engineers, etc., etc., Mapperly Vicarage, Derby.*

Mennell, Henry Tuke, F.L.S., Croydon. *Phæn. Bot.* C. Ex.

Merivale, Prof. John Herman, M.A., Durham College of Sci., Newcastle-on-Tyne. *Mining.**

Merrifield, Dr. J., F.R.A.S., 7 Hobart Terrace, Plymouth. *Math., Meteo.*

Merry, James S., Swansea, Wales. *Analyt. Chem., Assayer and Mineralogist.*

Metcalfe, Arthur T., F.G.S., Corresponding Member of the Nottingham Naturalists' Soc., Southwell, Notts. *Geol.* (Triassic system), *Gen. Biol., Protozoa.**

Meyrick, E., Ramsbury, Hungerford, Wilts. *Ent.*

Miall, Louis C., Prof. Biology, Yorkshire Coll., 5 Montpelier Terrace, Leeds.

Michael, A. D., F.L., F.Z.S., etc., Cadogan Mansions, Sloane Sq., London. *Acarina.*

Michie, Rev. J. G., Dinnet, Aberdeenshire, Scotland. *Min.**

Middleton, Robert Morton, F.L.S., F.Z.S., Memb. Anth. Inst., Castle Eden, Co. Durham. *Phæn. Bot: Ferns, Palæo., Arch., Orn., Herpetol.* C. Ex.

Midwood, Lieut. H., 74th Highlanders, Aldershot. *Con.*

Miers, E. J., F.L S., F.Z.S., 7 Bellevue Rd., Wandsworth Common, Surrey, London, and Eden Cottage, Beckenham, Kent. *Crustacea.**

Miers, Henry A., M.A., F.G.S., Nat. Hist. Museum, S. Kensington, London. *Min., Crystal., Lithol.**

Miller, Charles, Lynmouth House, Langley Road, Beckenham, Kent. *Lepid.*

Miller, Hugh, Geological Survey of England, Museum, Jermyn St., London, S.W.

Miller, W. J., C.E., 100 Wellington St., Glasgow. *Geol., Metall., Phys., Elect.* C.

Mills, Edmund J , F.R.S., Young Prof. of Technical Chem., Anderson's Univ., 60 John St., Glasgow, Scotland.

Mills, John, 8 St. John's Rd., Clifton, Bristol. *Gen. Bot.*

Mills, Rev. S., Droylsden Rectory, Manchester. *Ast.*

Milward, Miss, Tullogher, New Ross, Ireland. *Bot.*

Mitchell, Sir Arthur, K.C.B., M.D., LL.D., 34 Drummond Place, Edinburgh, Scotland. *Meteo., Anth., Arch.**

Mitchell, Fred. S., Hornshaws, Clitheroe, Lancashire. *Orn., Ool.**

Mitchell, Rev. Hugh, LL.D., Free Church, Manse Craig, Montrose, Scotland. *Geol.*

Mivart, Prof. St. George, Hurstcote, Chilworth, Surrey. *Biol., Comp. Anat.*

Moir, Edward, Newport-on-Tay, near Dundee, Scotland. *Bot., Spec. Alpine Flora.*

Moiser, H. I., South View, York. *Bot., Geol.*

Monck, W. H. Stanley, M.A., B.L., Late Prof. of Moral Philosophy, T.C.D., 13 Belvidere Pl., Dublin, Ireland. *Palæo., Strat. and Physical Geol., Meteo., Ast.**

Moncrieff, Col. Alexander, Easter Road Barracks, Edinburgh, Scotland. *Ordnance Engineering.*

Montalbo, Antonio R., 20 Stanley Crescent, Kensington Park, London, W. *Geol.*
Moore, F., F.Z.S., 110 Oakfield Road, Penge, London, S.E. *Ent.*
Moore, J., 44 Arundel St., Landport, Portsmouth. *Lepid.*
Moore, John Carrick, M.A., F.G.S., 113 Eaton Sq., London, S.W.
Moore, Thomas J., Free Public Museum, Liverpool. *Zool.*, *Palæo.*
More, Alex. G., F.Z.S., F.R.S.E., M.R.I.A., Ex-Curator of the Nat. Hist. Museum in the Sci. and Art Museum, Dublin, Ireland. *Am.*, *Brit. and Europ. Bot.*, *European Rhopalocera.**
Moreton, Frederick Leslie, 21 Ker St., Devonport. *Lepid.* C. Ex.
Morgan, Octavius S., M.A., The Friars, Newport, Monmouthshire.
Morgan, R. T., Wellington House, Clevendon, Somerset. *Geol.*, *Bot.*
Morrieson, Col. R., Oriental Club, Hanover Sq., London, W. *Mic.*
Morris, D., M.A., F.L.S., Ass't Dir. Royal Botanic Gardens, Kew. *Spec. Gramineæ and Orchideæ of the West Indies.* C. Ex.*
Morris, James, 6 Windsor St., Swansea, Wales. *Min.*
Morris, John, M.A., 15 Upper Gloucester Pl., Dorset Sq., London, N.W. *Geol.*
Morrison, Francis R., "Beechwood," Knockholt, near Sevenoaks, Kent. *Geol.*, *Min.*, *Bot.*
Mortimer, R., Fimber, Malton, Yorkshire. *Geol.*
Morton, George H., F.G.S., 209 Edge Lane, Liverpool. *Invert. Palæo.*, *Geol.*, *Min*, *Lithol.* C.*
Morton, Dr. John H., New Brompton, Kent. *Bot.*, *Hort.*, *Mic.*, *Diatoms, Pollens, etc.* C. Ex.
Moseley, H. N., LL.D., F.R.S., F.L.S., F.Z.S., etc., Prof. Human and Comp. Anat., Univ. of Oxford, 14 St. Giles St., Oxford. *Zool.*
Mosley, S. L., Huddersfield, Primrose Hill. *Lepid.*
Moss, John, Wrexham, London, E.C. *Chem.*
Mosse, G. S., Stanford Road, Kensington, W. *Ent.*
Mostyn, Charles, Longwood House, Firby, Huddersfield. *Mic.*
Mott, Basil, A.R.S.M., 90 Chelsea Gardens, Chelsea Bridge Road, London, S.W. *Mining.**
Mott, Frederick T., F.R.G.S., Birstall Hill, Leicester. *Phæn. and Crypt. Bot: Edible Fruits.* C. Ex. Desires information about all edible fruits which are unknown in England. Also correspondence on the working of museums, large or small.*
Moulton, John Fletcher, 2, C.M.A., 74 Onslow Gardens, London, S.W.
Mountcastle, William R., Bridge Farm, Ellenbrook, near Manchester. *Literature.**
Muir, M. M. Pattison, M.A., Fellow and Prælector in Chem., Gonville and Caius College, Cambridge. *Inorg. Chem.**
Muir, Thomas, Beechcroft, Bishopton. *Math.*
Muirhead, Henry, M.D., LL.D., F.F.P.S.G., Bushy Hill, Cambuslang, Lanarkshire, Scotland. *Psychol. and Phys. Phil.**
Müller, Hugo, Ph.D., Pres. C.S., 13 Park-square, East, Regents park, London, N. W.
Muncer, Geo., 4 Martha St., Haggerston, London. *Lepid.*

Mundella, Rt. Hon. Anthony John, F.R.G.S., 16 Elvaston place and Reform Club, London, S. W.

Mundie, J., 22 Watson St., Aberdeen, Scotland. *Tax.*, *Ent.* C. Ex.

Munroe, Henry, M.D., 19 Charlotte St., Hull. *Mic.*, *Med. Jurisprudence:* C. Ex.

Murdoch, James B., Sec. Geol. Soc. of Glasgow, Hamilton Place, Longside, Glasgow. *Zool.*, *Geol.*

Murdoch, J. R., care of Messrs. J. Barran & Co., St. Paul's St., Leeds. *Bryology.*

Murie, Dr. James, Linnean Society, Burlington House, London. *Comp. Anat.*

Murphy, Joseph John, 2 Osborne Park, Belfast, Ireland. Author of "Habit and Intelligence." *Meteo.*

Murry, Adam, Science Club, 4 Saville Row, London, W.

Murray, Mrs., Loughboro' Park, Brixton, London, S.W. *Geol.*

Murray, G. R. M., F.L.S., British Museum, S. Kensington, London, and Examiner in Botany, Glasgow Univ. *Cryptogams.**

Murray, Lieut. H., Tralee, Ireland. *Ent.*

Murray, Rev. Richard Paget, M.A., Baltonsboro Parsonage, Glastonbury. *Ent.*

Musson, C. F., Goldsmith St., Nottingham. *Con.*

Myers, Edward, F.G.S., The Parsonage, Claremont Hill, Shrewsbury. *Geol.*, *Min.*, *Crystal.*, *Lithol.*, *Arch.*

Mylne, Robert William, 21 Whitehall Pl., London, S.W. *Geol.*

Nagel, D. H., Trinity College, Oxford. *Phys.*, *Chem.**

Naidley, Henry, Oxford Military College, 35 Lincoln's Inn Fields, London, W.C. *Geol.*

Napier, Capt. Johnston, Ornamental Pleasure-Garden, Collection and Laboratory, Elm Grove, Salisbury. *Engineering (Military)*, *Chem.*, *Geol.* - C.

Napier of Magdala, Robt., Lord, Field Marshall, G.C.B., G.C.S.I., 38 Cornwall-gardens, South Kensington, London, S.W.

Nares, Sir George Strong, Captain R. N., K.C.B., St. Bernards, Maple Road., Surbiton.

Nash, William C., Royal Observatory, Greenwich, London. *Elect.*, *Meteo.*, *Ast.*

Neave, B. W., 16 Lander Terrace, White Hart Lane, Wood Green, London, N. *Lepid.*

Needham, S. H., F.G.S., F.R.G.S., Mem. Queckett Mic. Club, 5 Mecklenburgh St., Mecklenburgh Sq., London, W.

Neison, Edmund, F.R.A.S., Science Club, 4 Saville Row, London. *Ast.*, *Chem.*

Nelson, John, Wellington St., Dundee, Scotland. *Orn.*

Nesbit, A. A., F.C.S., 38 Gracechurch St., London. *Agric.*, *Chem.* Action of Poisons on Fish, Absorption of Dyes by flowers, Action of poisonous flowers.

Neve, J. R., Kingston-on-Thames. *Bot.*

Nevill, Hugh, Newton Villa, Godalming. *Orn.*

Nevins, Dr. John Birkbeck, 3 Abercromby Sq., Liverpool. *Bot.*, *Sanitary Statistics, Rotatory Storms in British Isles and Voyages in Hudson Bay.**

Nevinson, B. G., 19 Torrington Sq., London, W.C. *Ent.*

Newall, Robt. Stirling, F.R.A.S., Ord. Imp. Bras. Rosae, Ferndene, Gateshead-on-Tyne.

Newcome, Francis D'A., W.C., Feltwell Hall, Brandon, Suffolk. *Orn.*

Newman, T. P., Proprietor of the "Zoologist" (published by Van Voorst, Paternoster Row), and of the "Entomologist" (published by Simpkin, Marshall & Co.), London, 54 Hatton Garden, London, E.C. *Ent., Zool.**

Newton, Alfred, M.A., Prof. Zool. and Comp. Anat., Univ. of Cambridge, Magdalen College, Cambridge. *Orn.*

Newton, Edwin T., Palæontologist to H. M. Geological Survey, Museum, Jermyn St., London, S.W.*

Newton, Richard Bullen, F.G S., British (Natural History) Museum, Cromwell Road, South Kensington, London, S.W. *Invert. Palæo.**

Nicholson, George, Curator Roy. Bot. Gardens, Kew, London, W. *Phæn. Bot., Trees and Shrubs of temperate climate.* C.*

Nicholson, H. Alleyne, Regius Prof. Nat. Hist, Univ., Aberdeen, Scotland. *Nat. Hist., Palæo.**

Nicolson, David, Montpellier House, Wick, Scotland. *Bot.**

Niven, Charles, M.A., Prof. Math., Queen's Coll., Cork, Ireland. *Ast.*

Niven, Wm. Davidson, M.A., Director of studies in the Royal Naval College, Greenwich, London, S.E.

Noble, Andrew, Capt. C. B., F.R.A.S., etc., etc., Jesmond Dene House, Newcastle-upon-Tyne.

Noble, Capt. W., F.R.A.S., Forest Lodge, Maresfield, Uckfield, Sussex. *Ast.*

Norgate, F., Sparkam Vicarage, Norfolk. *Ent., Orn.*

Norman, Rev. Dr., A.M., Rectory Burnmoor, Fence Houses, Co. Durham. *Crustacea, Moll., Polyzoa, Echinoderms, Sponges.* Ex. European for N. A.*

Norman, G., Cluny Hill, Forres, Scotland. *Hemipt.*

Norris, Richard, M.D., Birchfield, Birmingham. *Physiol.**

North, Frederic Wm., F.G.S., M. & C.E., Rowley Hall, Rowley Regis, Staffordshire, and 34 Clements Lane, Lombard St., London. *Civil and Mining Engineering, South African Coal-fields, and in the Midland Counties.*

North, S. W., M.R.C.S., F.G.S., 84 Micklegate, York. *Moll.* C. Ex.

Northbrook, Thos. Geo. Baring, Earl of, D.C.L., G.C.S.I., Stratton, Michelderer, Hants.

Nottidge, Thomas, Ashford, Kent. *Ent.*

Nowers, George P., M.A., Oxon, 14 Hagley Road, Birmingham. *Geol.*

Nunn, C. W., Hertford. *Mic.*

Nurse, C. G., Southgate Green, Bury St. Edmunds, Suffolk. *Lepid.*

Nuttall, R., jr., 14 Westbourne Park Terrace, London, W. *Geol.*

Odling, William M. B., Prof. Chem., Univ. of Oxford, Museum, Oxford.

Ogilvie, A. Graeme, B.A., 20 Carlton Hill, St. John's Wood, London, N.W.

Ogilvie, W. M., Lochee, near Dundee, Scotland. *Bot.**

Ogle, William, M.A., M.D., 10 Gordon St., Gordon Sq., London, W.C. *Bot.*, *Ent.*

Oldham, Chas., 2 Warwick Villas, Chelmsford Road, Woodford, Essex. *Lepid.*

Oliphant, J. C., M.A., 50 Palmerston Place, Edinburgh. *Ast.**

Oliver, Daniel, Prof. Bot., Univ. Coll., London, Royal Gardens, Kew.

Oliver, J. W., 271 St. Vincent St, Birmingham. *Phanerogams.*

Ommanney, Sir Erasmus, F.R.S., The Towers, Yarmouth, Isle of Wight, and United Service Club, London.

O'Mulreuin, R. J., Prof. of Celtic, 17 Carlisle St., S.C.R., Dublin, Ireland. *Agric.*, *Vet. Science.*

Ord, William Miller, M.D., 7 Brook St., Hanover Sq., London, W. *Crystal.*

Orde, Sir John, Bart., Kilmory House, Loch Gilp Head, N. B., Scotland. *Orn.*

O'Reilly, Prof. Jos. P., Royal College of Science, Dublin, Ireland. *Mining and Min* *

Ormerod, Miss Eleanor A., F. R. Met. Soc., etc., Consulting Ent., Royal Agric. Soc. of Eng., Corr. Memb. Ent. Soc., Ontario, Canada, Hon. and Corr. Memb., R. Ag. and Hort. Soc., Australia, etc., Torrington House, St. Albans, England. *Economic Ent.**

Osborne, John Allen, M.D., J.P., Milford, Letterkenny, Co. Donegal, Ireland. *Gen. Biol.*, *Emb. of Invert.*, *Ent: Coleopt.**

Osler, A. Follett, F.R.S., Edgbaston, Birmingham. *Meteo.*

Ovendon, J., 42 Temple St., Stroud, Kent. *Ent*

Owen, Sir Richard, C.B., M.D., D.C.L., LL.D., F.R.S., F.L.S., Assoc. de l'Inst. de France, Sheen Lodge, Richmond Park, East Sheen, London, S.W.

Paget, George E., M.D., Prof. of Physics in Univ. of Cambridge, Cambridge.

Paget, Sir James, F.R.S., 1 Harewood Pl., Hanover Sq., London, W.

Palgrave, Rob't. Harry Inglis, F.S.S., Belton, Great Yarmouth.

Palmer, Thomas, B.Sc., F.C.S., F.R.M.S., Homeleigh, Lower Camden, Chiselhurst. *Mic.*

Parfitt, Edw., Devon. and Exeter Inst., Exeter. *Phæn. and Crypt. Bot.*, *Geol.*, *Meteo.*, *Ent.* C.*

Parish, Hawtayne M., Ashfield House, Mount St., Taunton, Somerset. (To be forwarded to India). *Lepid.*, *Coleopt.* C. Ex.

Parke, George Henry, F.L.S., F.G S., Infield Lodge, Furness Abbey, Lancashire. *Recent and Fossil Moll. and Echinoderms.* C. Ex. British for foreign spec.*

Parker, Rev. Charles J., M.A., Upton Cheyney, Bristol. *Phæn. Bot.*, *Hort.*, *Agric.* C. Ex.

Parker, Major Francis George Shirecliffe, F.G.S., F.R.G.S., A.S.C., L., Westbere House, near Canterbury, Kent.

Parker, James, M.A., Oxford. *Geol.*, *Arch.*
Parker, T., 45 Lower Mosley St., Manchester, and 2 East Hill St., Greengate St., Oldham. *Palæo.**
Parker, Wm. Kitchen, F.Z.S., L.S., etc., Crowland, Trinity Road, Upper Tooting, London, S.W.
Parker, Prof. W. Newton, Univ. Coll., Cardiff, S. Wales. *Zool.*, *Emb.*, *Vert. Anat.* C. Ex.
Parkin, Thomas, M.A., Science Club, 4 Saville Row, London, W. *Orn.*
Parkinson, Rev. Stephen, D.D., Fellow and late tutor of St. John's College, St. John's College, Cambridge.
Parry, Major F. J., Sidney, London. *Ent.*
Parsons, H. Franklin, M.D., F.G.S., London, Local Government Board, Whitehall, London, S.W.*
Parsons, R. Mann, Major Gen'l R. E., Hyde-vale, Blackheath, London, S.E.
Parsons, William, Sergeant R. E., Ordnance-Survey Office, 46 St. George's Road, London, S.W.
Parsons, W. E., 68 Pevensey Road, Eastbourne, London. *Lepid.*
Pascoe, Francis P., Burlington Road, Westbourne Park, London, W. *Ent.*
Paton, James, F.L.S., Curator Kelvingrove Museum and Corporation, Galleries of Art, Glasgow, Scotland. *Bot.*, *Chem.**
Paton, M., 11 Thread St., Paisley, Scotland. *Lepid.*
Pattenden, R., 11 Castle St., Finsbury, London. *Lepid.*
Patterson, R. Lloyd, F.L.S., M.B.O.U., Belfast, Ireland. *Orn.**
Pattinson, John, F.I.C., 75 The Side, Newcastle-on-Tyne. *Analyt. Chem.**
Paul, F. P., Rodney St., Liverpool. *Phys.*, *Mic.*
Paul, John Dennis, Regent Road, Leicester. *Geol.*
Pavy, Frederick W., M.D., F.R.S., Formerly Lecturer on Physiol., Comp. Anat. and Zool., Guy's Hospital, 35 Grosvenor Street, London, W.*
Payne, J. C. Chas., Botanic Ave., The Plains, Belfast, Ireland.*
Peace, Maskell W., F.G.S., Law Clerk and Sec. to Mining Assoc. of Gt. Britain, 66 Piccadilly, London, W. and to South Lancashire and Cheshire Coal Assoc., 18 King St., Wigan.
Peach, Benjamin N., Geological Survey of Scotland, Geological Survey Office, Sheriff Court Buildings, Edinburgh, Scotland.
Peacock, R. A., 41 Osborne Road, Tollington Park, London, N. *Steam*, *Volcanoes and Earthquakes.*
Peal, C. N., F.R.M.S., Fernhurst, Mattock Lane, Ealing, London, W. *Diatomaceæ*, *Polyzoa*, *Echinodermata*, *Invert. Palæo.*, *esp. Corals.**
Pearce, Horace, F.R.A.S., F.G.S., F.L.S., The Limes, Stourbridge, Worcestershire. *Geol.*, *Bot.*, *Arch.* C.*
Pearce, W. G., Bath. *Lepid.*
Pearson, E. Probyn, Belmont Cottage, Lower Breck Rd., Anfield, Liverpool. *Bot: Ferns*, *Hort.*, *Ent: Lepid.*, *Coleopt.* C. Ex.
Pearson, G., 16 Shakespeare Road, South Hackney, London. *Lepid.*

Pearson, Wm. Henry, 15 The Park, Eccles, Manchester. *Fungi*, (*Hepaticæ*). C. Ex.*
Peckover, Algernon, F.L.S., Wisbech, Cambridgeshire.*
Peckover, Alexander, F.S.A., F.L.S., F.R.G.S., Bank House, Wisbech, Cambridgeshire.*
Peek, C. E., Rousdon, Lyme Regis. *Meteorol.*, *Ast.*
Penny, Rev. C. W., M.A., F.L.S., Wellington College, Wokingham, Berks.
Penrose, F. C., F.R.A.S., Coleby Field, Wimbledon, S.W. *Ast.*
Peppe, T. F., F.L.S., Claremont Villa, Cottenham Park, Wimbledon, Surrey. Indian address: Arrah Shahabad, India. *Bot.*, *Agric.* C. Ex.
Percy, Dr. John, F.R.S., 1 Gloucester Crescent, Hyde Park, also Houses of Parliament, London. *Metallurgy of Iron, Steel, Gold and Silver.* C. Wishes to correspond with collectors.
Perkin, William Henry, Ph.D., F.R.S., The Chestnuts, Sudbury, Harrow.*
Perkins, V. R., 54 Gloucester St., South Belgravia, London, W. *Ent.*
Perry, Rev. Jeron J. M., F.R.A.S., St. Paul's Vic., Alnwich, Northumberland. *Ast.*
Perry, John M. E., D. Sc., Prof. of Mechanical Engineering and Applied Mathematics in the City and Guilds of London Technical College, Finsbury, 10 Penywern-road, So. Kensington, S. W.
Perry, S. J., D.Sc., F.R.S., F.R.A.S., F.R.Met.S., Dir. Stonyhurst Obs., Stonyhurst, Whalley. *Terrestrial Mag.*, *Phys.*, *Ast.*, *Meteo.**
Pershouse, Francis, jr., Tor Mohun House, Torquay. *Orn.* C.
Petrie, Capt. Francis W. H., F.G.S., etc., Ed. Journal of Victoria Philosophical Inst. of Gt. Brit., 11 Gloucester Walk, Campden Hill, Kensington, London, W.*
Petrie, W. Flinders, Bromley, Kent. *Metrology.*
Pettigrew, James Bell, M.D., LL.D., F.R.S., Prof. Med. and Anat., Univ. of St. Andrews, Scotland. *Anat.*, *Physiol.*, *Physics.**
Peyton, John E. H., F.R.A.S., F.G.S., 108 Marina, St. Leonards-on-Sea. *Geol.*, *Phys.*, *Ast.*, *Arch.*
Peyton, Rev. W. W., Sec. in Scotland for the Min. Soc. of Great Britain, Fellow of the Bot. Soc. of Edinburgh, Gowanbank, Hill Street, Broughty Ferry, Scotland. *Geol.*, *Bot.*, *Min.**
Phené, J. S., LL.D., 5 Carlton Terrace, Oakley St., London, S.W. *Arch.*, *Anth.*, *Geol.* C.
Philips, T. Wishart, Mem. Phys. Soc., Prof. Nat. Phil., Bow and Bromley Institute, Bow Road, London. *Nat. Phil.*, *Electricity.*
Phillips, William, Canonbury, Kingsland, Shrewsbury. *Mycology: Discomycetes.* C. Ex. British species for those of any other country.
Phipson, Arthur, 3 Gray's Inn Sq., London, W.C. *Ent.*
Pierce, F. N., 143 Smithdown Lane, Liverpool. *British Lepid.* C. Ex.
Plesse, C. H., Analytical Laboratory, Lyon's Inn Chambers, 303 Strand, London, W.C. *Chem.*

Piffard, Bernard, Hill House, Hemel-Hempsted, Herts. *Mic.*, *Morph.*

Piggott, F. T., M.A., 1 Mitre-court Buildings, Temple, London, E.C.

Pigott, G. W. Royston, M.A., M.D., Annandale, Eastbourne, Sussex. *Ent.*

Pilley, John I., Ph.D., F.C.S., F.R.M.S., Lecturer on Chem., Dulwich, London, S.E. *Org. and Inorg. Chem.*, *Gen. Biol.*, *Vert. and Invert. Anat.* C. Ex.*

Pim, Greenwood, M.A., T.C.D , F.L.S., M.R.I.A., Easton Lodge, Monkstown, Co. Dublin, Ireland. *Bot.*, *Crypt Plants*, *Hort.*, *Mic.*, *Photog.**

Pim, H. Bedford, Leaside, Kingswood Road, Upper Norwood. *Ent. esp. Brit. Coleopt.* C. Ex.

Piper, George H., F.G.S., Court House, Ledbury, Herefordshire. *Geol.*, *Palæo.*, *Arch.* C.*

Plant, J., 40 West Terrace, West St. S., Leicester. *Geol.*, *Phys.* C.

Plant, Major John, F.G.S., Curator, etc., Royal Museum and Library, Peel Park, Salford, Manchester.*

Playfair, Lyon, Rt. Hon., Sir K.C.B., F.R.S., LL D., 68 Onslow Gardens, London, S.W.*

Plowman, Thomas, Nystuen Lodge, Bycullah Park, Enfield, London, N. *Vert.*, *Invert.*, *Mic.*, *Zool.*, *Gen. Biol.*, *Morphology*, *Emb.*, *Histol.**

Plowright, Charles B., F.L.S., 7 King St., King's Lynn. *Fungology.**

Plummer, John I., M.A , Orwell Park Obs., Ipswich. *Ast.*

Plunkett, Thomas, Enniskillen, Ireland. *Geol.*, *Arch.*

Pocklington, Henry, F.R.M.S., Memb. British Assoc'n, etc., 20 Park Row, Leeds. *Phæn. Plants*, *Phys.*, *Mic.*, *Photog.* C.*

Pocock, R. Innes, Nat. Hist. Mus., So. Kensington, London, S.W. *Arachnida*, *Myriopoda*, *Crustacea.**

Pode, John D., Slade Hall, Ivy Bridge, Devon. *Antiquarian.*

Poland, John, F.R.C.S., Eng., F.L.S., 16 St. Thomas's St., London, S.E.*

Pole, William, F.R.S., Athenæum Club, London, S.W. *Mech. Science.**

Polwhele, Thomas Roxburg, M.A., Polwhele, Truro, Cornwall.

Ponsonby, J. H., 16 St. James St., London, S.W. *Moll.* C. Ex.

Pontifex, Captain, 9 Pavilion Square, Scarborough. *Geol.*

Porritt, George T., F.L.S., Huddersfield. *Ent.*

Potter, Joseph, 6 Chilterne Road, Bow, London, E. *Lepid.*

Potter, R. S., 2 Vernon Road, Bow, London, E. *Lepid.*

Potts, J., 6 Blenheim Terrace, Norfolk St., Hull. *Lepid.*

Powell, Hugh, 170 Euston Road, Euston Sq., London, N.W. *Mic.*

Power, Dr. I. A., Burton Crescent, London, W.C. *Ent: Coleopt.*

Pratt, David, 398 Mile-end Road, London, E. *Lepid.*

Pratt, Henry, F.R.A.S., 18 Preston St., Brighton. *Ast.*, *Horology*, *Spectroscopy*, *Photography.**

Preece, W. H., C.E., F.R.S., Gothic Lodge, Wimbledon Common, London. *Elect.*

Presland, R. M., M.H.M., N.H.S., 493 & 495 Hackney Rd., London, E. *Zool.*, *Orn.*, *Tax.* C.*

Preston, Rev. T. A., M.A., Thurcaston Rectory, Leicester. *Ent.*, *Bot.*, *Meteo.**

Prestwich, Joseph, M.A., Professor of Geology in the University of Oxford, Shoreham, near Sevenoaks, Kent. *Geol.* (*Quaternary or Tertiary*).*

Price, Bartholomew, M.A., Prof. Nat. Phil., Pembroke Coll., Oxford. *Math.*, *Phys.*

Price, David, 48 West St., Horsham, Sussex. *Ent.*

Priddey, T., Brighton Road, Croydon. *Lepid.*

Prince, Charles Leeson, M.R.C.S., L.S.A., F.R.A.S., F.R.Met.Soc., The Observatory, Crowborough, Tunbridge Wells. *Ast.*, *Meteo.*, *Photog.*, *Arch.*

Prior, Charles M., The Avenue, Bedford and Trinity Hall, Cambridge. *Orn.*

Prior, Geo. Thurland, B.A., Oxford, Bark Place, London, W. *Min.*, *Inorg. Chem.**

Prior, Richard C. A., M.D., F.L.S., 48 York Terrace, Regent's Park, London, N.W. *Phæn. Bot.* C.

Pritchard, Rev. Charles, M.A., F.R.S., F.R.A.S., Savilian Professor of Ast., Univ. of Oxford, 8 Keble Terrace, Oxford.

Pritchard, B., Frankwell Nursery, Shrewsbury. *Lepid.*

Pritchard, Ed., M. Inst. C.E., F.G.S., 2 Storey's Gate, Westminster, and 37 Waterloo St., Birmingham. *Civil and Sanitary Engineer.**

Pritchard, H. B., Chemical Dept., Royal Arsenal, Woolwich, London, S.E. *Chemistry.*

Pritchard, Urban, M.D., Prof. of Aural Surgery, King's College, 3 George St., Hanover Sq., London. *Histol. of Internal Ear.**

Proctor, Richard A., B.A., 76 Warwick Gardens, Kensington, W. *Ast.*

Prouse, Oswald Milton, Assoc. M. Inst. C.E., Westbourne House, Shaftesbury Road, Hammersmith, London, W.

Provis, Richard, Camborne. *Min.**

Puleston, John H., M.P., 7 Dians York, London S.W. *Mic.*

Purdue, John, Ridgeway, Plympton, Devon. *Coleopt.*, *Lepid.*

Purser, John M., M.D., Trinity Coll., Dublin, Ireland. *Physiol.*

Pye, W., Knight's Palace, Cobham, Gravesend. *Geol.*

Pye-Smith, Philip Henry, M.D., B.A., etc., Physician to Guy's Hospital.

Quilter, H. E., 4 Cedar Road, Leicester. *Geol.*, *Bot.*, *Biol.**

Radford, William, M.B., F.R.A.S., Sidmouth. *Mic.**

Rae, John, L.R.C.S., LL.D. (Edin.), etc., etc., 4 Addison-gardens, Kensington, London, W.

Raine, Rev. Canon, M.A., York. *Arch.*

Raisin, Miss C. A., 154 Camden St., London, N. W. *Geol.*

Ralfs, John, Penzance. *Bot: Hepaticæ.*

Ramsay, Alexander, Conductor Scientific Roll, 4 Cowper Road, Acton, London, W. *Phys. Geog.*, *Met.*, *Zool.* Will ex. Sci. Roll with Societies and Authors for their publications.*

Ramsay, Sir Andrew Crombie, Knt., LL.D., F.G.S., etc., etc., 15 Cromwell Crescent, London, S.W.
Ramsay, Prof. Andrew C., LL.D., F.R.S., Dir.-General of the Geol. Surv. of the United Kingdom Mus., Jermyn St., London, S.W.
Ramsay, Capt. R. G. Wardlaw, 74 Highlanders, Whitehill, Rosewell, Scotland. *Orn.* C. Ex. Indian, Malay, Sumatra or Philippine Island birds.
Ramsden, H., M.A., Forest Rise, Walthamstow, Essex, London, N. E. *Mic.*
Ransom, Francis, Examiner to Pharmaceutical Society of Gt. Britain, Hitchin. *Bot.* (*Medicinal*), *Diatoms*, *Org.*, *Meteo.* C. Ex.*
Ransom, William Henry, M.D., The Pavement, Nottingham. *Ent.*
Ransome, Arthur, M.D., M.A., F.R.S., 1 St. Peter's Sq., Manchester. *Physiol.**
Ranyard, A.C., 25 Old Sq., Lincoln's Inn, London. *Ast.*, *Solar Phys.*
Rattray, Richard, Balfour St., Dundee, Scotland. *Mic.*
Rawlinson, Sir Henry Creswicke, K.C.B., D.C.L., Athenæum Club, London, S. W.
Rawson, H. E., 7 Cannon St., London, E.C. *Orn.*
Rayleigh, Lord, Terling Place, Witham, Essex. *Inorg. Chem.*, *Phys.*, *Elect.*
Reade, T. Mellard, C. E., Park Corner, Blundellsands, near Liverpool. *Geol.*
Reader, Rev. H. P., The Priory, Woodchester, near Stroud. *Bot: Mosses*, *Hepaticæ*, *Lichens.* Ex.
Reader, Thos. Wm., M.C.S., 171 Hemingford Road, Islington, London, N. *Palæo.*, *Geol.*, *Mic*, *Con.*, *Moll.* C. Ex.*
Readwin, T. A., Manchester. *Min.*
Redfern, Peter, M.D., Prof. Anat. and Physiol., 4 Lower Crescent, Belfast, Ireland.*
Reed, Sir Edw. Jas., K.C.B., Hextable, Swanley, St. Mary Cray, Kent.
Reed, Dr. J. T. T., Ryhope, Sunderland. *Ool.*, *Con.* Ex. Correspondence invited.*
Rees, Geo. Owen, M.D., F.G.S., etc., Physician extraordinary to the Queen, 26 Albemarle street, London, W.
Reeves, Walter W., F.R.M.S., 32 Geneva Road, Brixton, S.W. *Bot.*, *Phæn. and Crypt. Plants*, *Ferns*, *Diatoms*, *Mic.* C. Ex.*
Reid, Arthur S., M.A. (Cantab.), F.G.S., 12 Bridge St., Canterbury. *Geol.*, *Min.*, *Lithol.*, *Mic.*, *Meteo.*, *Anth.*, *Arch.*
Reid, Clement, Geological Survey of England, Museum, Jermyn St., London, S.W.
Reid, Saville G., Capt. R. E., 14 Medway Villas, New Brompton. *Orn.*
Reid, William, Naturalist, Nairn, Scotland.*
Reinold, Prof. Arnold W., M.A., F.R.S., Royal Naval College, Greenwich. *Phys.**
Rennie, James, 9 Motcombe St., Belgrave Sq., London, S.W.
Reynolds, J. Emerson, M.D., Prof. Chem., Trinity College, 62 Morehampton Road, Dublin, Ireland.

Reynolds, John Russell, M.D., etc., etc., 38 Grosvenor-street, London, W.

Reynolds, Osborne, M.A., F.R.S., Prof. of Engineering, Owens College, Manchester. *Phys.*

Ricarde-Seaver, Major F. Ignacio, F.R.S.E., F.G.S., Assoc. Inst. C.E., M.R.I., Conservative Club, St. James St., London, S. W., Editor-in-chief Journal des Mines, Paris, & 26 rue Cambon, Paris. *Min.*, *Chem.*, *Elect.*, *Phys.**

Richards, Sir Geo. Henry, Knt. Admiral, Vice-President K.C.B., etc., etc., 56 Lexham-gardens, Kensington, W.

Richards, Rev. Walter John Bruce, D. D., St. Mary's Westmoreland Road, Bayswater, London. *Astronomy and Physics.**

Richardson, Benj. Ward, M.D., LL.D., M.A., etc., etc., 25 Manchester Square, London, W.

Richardson, Chas., 4 Northumberland Ave., Putney. *Cryst.*, *Phys.*, *Elect.*

Richardson, C. W., St. John's Grove, Wakefield. *Ent.*

Richardson, Ralph, F.R.S.E., V. P., Edinburgh Geol. Soc., etc., 10 Magdala Place, Edinburgh, Scotland. *Geol.*, *Meteo.*, *Bibliog.*, *Geog. Dist.*, *Moll.* •

Riddell, Chas. Jas. Buchanan, Major Gen'l C.B., Oaklands, Chudleigh, Devonshire.

Ridgway, J. A., F.R.A.S., Beverley. *Bot.*, *Geol.*

Riding, W. S., 36 Euston Sq., London, N. W. *Lepid.*

Ridley, G., 2 Medina Mews, Hove, Brighton. *Lepid.*

Ridley, Henry N., M.A., British Museum, S. Kensington, London. *Orchids.**

Ringer, Sydney, Prof. of Med., Univ. College, London. 15 Cavendish Place, London, W.

Ripon, Geo. Fred'k Sam'l Robinson, Marquis of, K.G., G.C.S.I., C.I.E., D.C.L. (Oxon.), F.L.S., F.R.G.S., 1 Carlton Gardens London, S. W.

Rivers, Lieut-Gen. Fox Pitt, D.C.L., F.R.S., Rushmore, Salisbury, and 4 Grosvenor Gardens, London, Govt. Inspector of Ancient Monuments in Great Britain. *Anth.*, *Arch.* Pres. Anth. Inst. of Great Britain. C. Ex.*

Robarts, N. F., Rosebrae, Glengall Road, Woodford, Essex. *Geol.*

Roberts, George, Lofthouse, near Wakefield, Yorkshire. *Phæn. Bot.*, *Geog. Dist.*, *Migration of Animals*, *Orn.*, *Con.**

Roberts, Isaac, F.G.S., F.R A.S., Kennessee, Maghull, near Liverpool. *Geol.*, *Inorg. Chem.*, *Ast.*, *Mic.**

Roberts, John, M.E., M.M.S., Bryn Crafnant, Trefrin, Llanrwst, North Wales. *Palæo.*, *Geol.*, *Min.*, *Crystal.*, *Lith.*, *Eth.*, *Philol.* C. Ex.*

Roberts, R. D., D.Sc., M.A., F.G.S., Fellow of Clare College, Cambridge. *Phys. Geog.*, *Geol.*

Roberts, Sam'l, M. A. (Lond.) 34 Lady Margaret-road, St. John's College Park, London, N. W.

Roberts, T., Woodwardian Museum, Cambridge. *Geol.*, *Palæo.**

Roberts, Thomas, B.A., F.G.S., St. John's College, Cambridge. *Geol.*

Roberts, William Chandler, F.R.S., Chemist of the Royal Mint, Royal Mint, Tower Hill, London, E.

Roberts, Sir Wm., B A., M.D. (Lond.), Coll. Reg. Med. Soc., Prof. of Med. in Owens College, Manchester, 89 Mosley-street, Manchester.

Robertson, David, F.L.S., F.G.S., Glendale, Uddington, Scotland. *Nat. Hist.*, *Geol.* C. Ex. in Ostracoda and Foraminifera.

Robertson, J. C., M.D., Monaghan, Ireland. *Ast.*

Robinson, Charles, Springfield Lane, Salford, Manchester. *Geol.*, *especially of the coal formations.*

Robinson-Douglas, W.D.; F.L.S., F.R.G.S., F.E.S., Orchardton, Castle Douglas, Scotland. *Coleopt.*, *Brit.*, *and Eur.**

Robinson, F. E., 10 Little Clarendon St., Oxford. *Ent.*

Robinson, Isaac, The Wash, Hertford. *Diatoms*, *Mic.* C. Ex.*

Robinson, Sir Rob't Spencer, Admiral, K.C.B., 61 Eaton-place, London, S. W.

Robinson, Thomas W. U., Hardwick Hall, Sedgefield, Co Durham. *Prehistoric Arch.* C. Ex. for stone and flint implements from Ireland. The Swiss Lake Dwellings, Denmark and North America, etc., etc.*

Robson, Geo., 92 Cranbourne St., Leicester. *Bot.* Ex.

Robson, John E., Ed. "Young Naturalist," 15 Northgate, Hartlepool. *Lepid.* C. Ex.

Rodwell, Geo. F., Science Master in Marlborough College, Wiltshire. *Chem.*, *Phys.*, *Min.* C. of volcanic minerals. Ex.

Roebuck, Wm. Dennison, F.L.S., Sunny Bank, Leeds. *Limacidæ*, of the British fauna, on which subject assistance is particularly desired, as he is preparing a monograph in conjunction with Mr. J. W. Taylor.*

Rogers, Col. Henry T., Royal Engineers, 24 Bassett Road, Notting Hill, London, W. *Ast.*, *Optics.*

Rogers, John, F.R.M.S., 4 Tennyson St., Nottingham. *Bot.*, *Diatoms*, *Org. and Inorg. Chem.*, *Mic.*, *Ent.* C.*

Rogers, Thos , 27 Oldham Rd., Manchester. *Phæn. Bot.*, *Ferns*, *Mosses*, *Algæ*, *Moll.* C. Ex.

Rogers, Wm., Ph.D., Rosemill, near Dundee, Scotland. *Agric. Chem.*

Rogerson, G.R., 5 Cook St., Liverpool. *Ast.*

Rollit, Albert K., M.P., LL.D., D.C.L., B.A., F.K.C.L., F.R.A.S., F.Z.S.S., Thwaite House, Cottingham, E. Yorks and 12 Mark Lane, London, E. C. *Phys.*, *Elect.*, *Zool.*, *Hort.**

Rolph, R. L., Grosvenor Rise East, Waltham, Essex. *Lepid.*

Romanes, Geo. J., M.A., LL.D., F.R.S., 18 Cornwall Terrace, Regent's Park, London, N.W. *Physiol.*, *Psychol.**

Romilly, The Hon. Edward, F.L.S., 6 Atherstone Terrace, Gloucester Road, London, S.W.

Rooper, George, 20 Hyde Park Sq., London, W. *Zool.*

Roper, Freeman Clark Samuel, F.L.S., F.G.S., Palgrave House, Eastbourne, Sussex. *Bot.* C.

Rorie, James, M.D., Royal Lunatic Asylum, West Green, near Liff, Dundee, Scotland. *Con.*, *Physiol.*, *Psychol.*, *Nat. Hist.**

Roscoe, Henry Enfield, Sir, F.R.S., LL.D., D.C.L., M.P., late Prof. of Chem., Owens College, Manchester.*

Rosebery, Rt. Hon. Archibald Philip Primrose, Earl of, Dalmeny Park, Linlithgowshire.

Rosie, Peter, Dempster St., Pulteneytown, Scotland. *Bot.*

Ross, C. C., Penzance. *Min.*

Ross, Captain G. E., Waterside, St. Albans. *Geol.*

Ross, Rev. Wm., F.S.A.S., M.R.I.A., etc., Free Church College, Glasgow, Scotland. *Arch.*, *Philol.*, *Celtic Philology and literature of the Gaidheal.* C.*

Ross, Lt.-Col. W. A., R.A., F.G.S., Acton House, Acton, London, W. *Min.*, *Crystal.*, *Lithol.*, *Chem.*, *Metall.*, *Phys.* C. Ex.

Rosse, Earl of, Birr Castle, Parsonstown, Ireland. *Phys.*, *Elect.*, *Photog.*, *Ast.**

Rothera, G. B., Waverly St., Nottingham. *Ent.*, *Biol.*

Rousselet, Charles, 308 Regent street, London W. *Mic.*, *Zool.*, *Gen. Biol.*, *Anat.*, *Invert.*, *Worms* (*Rotifera*), *Protozoa.**

Routh, Edw. John, D. Sc. (Cantab.), etc., etc. Newnham Cottage, Cambridge.

Routledge, Miss Alicet, Claxeugh, Sunderland. *The Botany and Treatment of Fibres for Paper-making.* C.

Rowbotham, Geo. W., 25 York St., Manchester. *Palæo.*

Rowe, I. Brooking, Lockyer St., Plymouth. *Lepid.* C. Ex.

Rowe, W. L., Devon and Cornwall Bank, Redruth. *Min.*

Rowland-Brown, H., B.A., F.E.S., Orchey Grove, Stanmore, Middlesex. *Lepid.**

Rowlands, W. E., 28 Green Lane, Tuebrook, Liverpool. *Ast.**

Roxburgh, T. J., 120 Harlow St., Liverpool. *Lepid.*

Roy, Chas. Smart, M.D. (Edin.), Prof. of Pathology in the Univ. of Cambridge, Trinity College, Cambridge.

Roy, John, 3 Loanhead Pl., Aberdeen, Scotland. *F. W. Algæ* (*not including Diatoms*), *Desmidæ.* C. Ex. Would prefer specimens preserved in acetate of potash, or otherwise; but, if possible, not dry.

Rücker, Arthur Wm., M.A. (Oxon.), Prof. of Phys., Normal Sch. of Sci. and Royal Sch. of Mines, So. Kensington, Errington, Clapham Park, London, S W.

Rudler, Frederick William, Curator of the Museum of Practical Geology, and Hon. Dir. of the Anth. Inst. of Great Britain and Ireland, 28 Jermyn St., London, S.W. *Geol.*, *Min.*, *Anth.*

Russell, J., 6 Leverton St., Kentish Town, London, N.W. *Lepid.*

Russell, Robert, Geological Survey of England, Museum, Jermyn St., London, S.W.

Russell, Thos. D., Dealer in Fossils, Minerals and Mic. objects, 78 Newgate St., London, E.C. *Palæo.*, *Geol.*, *Min.*, *Lithol.*, *Mic.* C. Ex.*

Russell, Wm. Henry Leighton, A.B., 2 Grove Place, Highgate, London, W.

Russell, Wm. J., Ph.D., F.R.S., Lect. on Chem., Medical School of St. Bartholomew's Hospital, 34 Upper Hamilton Terrace, London, W.*

Rutherford, David Greig, F.L.S., Surrey House, Forest Hill, London, S.E. *Lepid.*
Rutherford, William, M.D., F.R.S., Prof. Physiol., The University, Edinburgh, Scotland.
Rutley, Frank, Geol. Surv. of England, 28 Jermyn St., London, S.W. *Petrol., Freestone and Vitreous Rocks.*
Ryder, E. H., 20 Hammers Terrace, Guilford Road, Greenwich. *Coleopt.*
Sack, Hermann, Ph.D., B.A., B.Sc., 12 Chelsham Rd., London, S. W. *Geol.*
Sadler, Herbert, 32 Manor St., Clapham, London, S.W. *Ast.**
Safford, Samuel Sutherland, Parkshot, Richmond, Surrey. *Genealogy and Heraldry.**
Saise, Walter, Richmond Cottages, Coburgh Road, Montpellier, Bristol. *Chem.*
Salisbury, Rt. Hon. Robt. Arthur, Marquis of, K.G., M.A., etc., Hatfield House, Hatfield, Herts.
Salkeld, Lieut.-Col. J. C., 29 St. James St., London, W. *Geol.*
Salmon, Rev. George, D.D., D.C.L., Trinity College, Dublin, Ireland.
Salomons, Sir David Lionel, Bart., M.A., A.I.C.E., M.S.T.E., Broomhill, Tunbridge Wells, Kent.*
Salvin, Osbert, M.A., Brooklands Ave., Cambridge. *Orn.*
Salway, R. E., 9 Davies St., Berkeley Sq., London, W. *Lepid.*
Samuelson, Sir Bernhard, Bart., M.I.C.E., 56 Princes-gate, London, S.W.
Sandeman, David, Woodlands, Lenzie, Scotland. *Geol.* C.*
Sanders, Gilbert, Albany Grove, Monkstown, Co. Dublin, Ireland. *Marine Bot., Con., Corals of Brit. Shores.* C. Ex. Marine Algæ.
Sanders, G. S., St. Stephens, Canterbury, Kent. *Ent.*
Sanderson, J. S. Burdon, M.D., F.R.S., Waynefiete Prof. of Physiol. in University of Oxford, 50 Banbury Road, Oxford.
Sanford, W. A., Nynehead, Wellington, Somerset. *Zool.**
Sang, John, 6 Chestnut St., Darlington. *Lepid.*
Sarjeant, W. Low, Hon. Sec. Croydon Mic. Club, 7 Belgrave Rd., South Norwood, London. *Mic.**
Saunders, E. Holmesdale, St. Ann's, Mason's Hill, Bromley, Kent. *Ent.*
Saunders, Sir Edwin, 13*a* George St., Hanover Sq., London, W.*
Saunders, Geo. S., Cumberland House, Mount Sion, Tunbridge, Wales. *Econ. Ent.*
Saunders, Howard, 7 Randor Pl., Hyde Park, London, W. *Orn.*
Saunders, Sir Sidney S., Gatestone, Central Hill, Upper Norwood, London, S.E. *Ent.*
Saunders, William Wilson, F.R.S., Raystead, Worthing. *Ent.*
Savile, A. G., B.A., Grosvenor School, Waterloo Crescent, Nottingham.
Savin, Alfred, Cromer. *Geol.*
Savory, Wm. Scovell, M.B., Surgeon to and Lecturer on Surgery at St. Bartholomew's Hospital, 66 Brook Street, London, W.

Sawyer, Frederick Ernest, F.S.A., F.R. Met. Soc., 31 Buckingham Pl., Brighton. *Meteo. and Antiquary.**

Sawyer, George D., F.R.M.S., V. Pres. Brighton and Sussex Nat. Hist. Soc., 55 Buckingham Pl., Brighton. *Mic.*

Schäfer, Edward A., Prof. Physiol., University College, London.

Scharff, Robert, Ph.D., B.Sc., University College, Gower St., London, W. C. *Vert. and Invert. Anat.*

Schaus, Wilhelm, jr., Ormonde Lodge, St. Margarets, Twickenham. *Lepid.* C. Ex.*

Schoolbred, James N., B.A., C.E., 3 Westminster Chambers, Victoria St., London, S.W. *App. of electricity to power, lighting, etc.*

Schorlemmer, Prof. Carl, Organic Chem., Owens College, Manchester.

Schulze, Adolf P., F.R.S.E., 2 Done Gardens, Kelvinside, Glasgow, Scotland. *Microscopy.**

Schunck, Edward, Ph.D., F.R.S., Oaklands, Kersall, Manchester. *Chem., Coloring Matter.*

Schuster, Arthur, Ph.D., F.R.S., Owens College, Manchester.

Sclater, Philip Lutley, Ph.D., M.A., F.R.S., Secretary of the Zoological Soc., 3 Hanover Sq., London, W. *Zool., Orn.* C. Ex. Desires birdskins from S. Am. with exact localities.*

Scott, Sir Arthur B., Bart., 97 Eaton Sq., London, S.W., and Great Barr. Hall, Birmingham.

Scott, John, 1 St. Mildred's Terrace, Bromley Road, Lee, London, S.E. *Hemipt.*

Scott, R. H., Secretary Meteo. Office, 116 Victoria St., Westminster, S.W. *Meteo.*

Scowcroft, W.R., Quarry House, Ormskirk, Lancashire. *Lepid.*

Seabroke, G.M., F.R.A.S., Temple Observ., Rugby School. *Ast.**

Search, C. G., Dorking, Surrey. *Min.*

Searll, H., Rook St., Ashton-under-Lyne, Lancashire. *Bot.* Ex.

Sedgwick, Adam, Trinity College, Cambridge. *Comp. Anat.*

Seebohm, Henry, 6 Tenterden St., Hanover Sq., London, W. *Orn.*

Seeley, Harry Govier, F.R.S., F L.S., Prof. Geog., King's College, London, The Vine, Sevenoaks. *Geol., Geog.*

Segniera, J. T., M.D., F.R.S , Leman St., London, E. *Lepid.*

Selborne, Roundell, Palmer, Earl of, 30 Portland-place, London, W.

Semmour, William, 8 Barry Road, Dulwich, London, S. E. *Min., Geol.* C. Ex. English metallic ores and rocks for Am. minerals or rocks.*

Service, Robert, Sec. of the Dumfriesshire and Galloway Nat. Hist. and Antiq. Soc., Maxwelltown, Dumfries, Scotland. *Orn.* C. Ex. Scottish bird-skins and eggs offered for any foreign ones.

Seton, E. E. T., De Winton, Carberry. *Orn.*

Sewell, Edward, M.A., Methven College, Grange, Carnforth, Scotland.

Shakespear, Lieut.-Col. J. D., Science Club, 4 Saville Row, London, W.

Sharp, David, Bleckley, Shirley Warren, Southampton. *Coleopt.* C.

Sharp, H., 37 Union St., Portland Pl., London. *Lepid.*

Sharp, William, F.R.S., F.G.S., M.D., Rugby, Warwickshire. *Medicine.**

Sharp, William E., New Ferry, Cheshire. *Lepid.*, *Coleopt.* C.

Sharpe, Richard Bowdler, F.S.P., F.Z.S. etc., Senior Assistant, Zoological Department, British Museum, South Kensington, London. W. *Orn.*

Shaw, F. W., Saville St., Wakefield. *Hymenop.*

Shaw, Geo. T., 28 Netherfield Rd., N. Everton, Liverpool. *Bot: Ferns*, *Bibliog.*, *Orn.*, *Ent: Lepid.*, *Coleopt.* C. Ex.

Shaw, John W., Lawefield Terrace, Lawefield Road, Westgate, Wakefield. *Bot: Ferns*, *Mosses*, *Hymenop.* C. Ex.

Shaw, Wm. Forster, Mosshall-grove, North Finchley, London. *Physical and Strat. Geol.*, *Min.*, *Met.*, *Phys.*, *Mic.*, *Bibliog.*, *Arch.*, *Philol.* C. Ex.*

Sheldon, W. G., 46 Kealeston St., Derby. *Lepid.*

Shelford, Wm., M. Inst. C.E , 35*a* Great George St , London, S.W.

Shelley, George E., Capt., late Grenadier Guards, 6 Tenterden St., Hanover Sq., London, W. *African Birdskins*, *Butterflies and Beetles.* C. Ex. a large number of dups. for spec. in above, with locality.*

Shelly, Chas. Edw., B.A., M.B., Cantab., etc., Hertford, Herts. *Bot.*, *Chem.*, *Elect.*, *Mic.*, *Zool.*, *Gen. Biol.*, *Anth.* Desires information as to all cases of heredity and transmission of characteristics of any kind, with special reference to the *sex* of all the individuals.

Shelton, J., Stafford St., New Brompton, Kent. *Bot.*, *Geol.*

Sheowring, G., 22 London Road, Clapton, London, N. *Lepid.*

Shepheard, Thomas, Kingsley Lodge, Chester. *Mic.*

Shepherd, Rev. Charles W., M.A., Trottersclifte Rectory, Maidstone, Kent. *Orn.*

Shepherd, Edwin, 21 Albert Terrace, Clapham Road, London, S.W. *Ent.*

Sheppard, Edward, 18 Durham Villas, Kensington, W. *Ent.*

Sherbrooke, Rob't Lowe, Viscount, G.C.B., LL.D. (Edin.), Sherbrooke, Caterham, Redhill, Surrey.

Shipley, Arthur E., B.A., Christ's College, Cambridge. *Comp. Anat.**

Shone, William, F.G.S., Upton Park, Chester. *Geol.*, *Mic.*, *Arch.*, *Moll.*, *Sponges*, *Protozoa.* C. Glacial Drift Shells.

Shore, T. W., F.G.S., F.C.S., Hartley Inst., Southampton. *Geol.*, *Chem.*, *Anth.*

Short, Frederick, 2 King St., Borough, London, S.E. *Geol.*

Shrubsole, George W., Town Hall Sq., Chester. *Carb.*, *Devon. and Sil. Polyzoa or Bryozoa.* C. Ex. Carb. or Sil. fossils. Wants a specimen of *Archimedes Wortheni.*

Shuttleworth, Edmund, 8 Winckley Sq., Preston, Lancashire. *Tax.*, *Ent: Lepid.* C. Ex.

Siddall, J. D., The Cross, Chester. *Nat. Hist.*

Sieveking, Edw. Henry, M.D., F.R.C.P., F.S.A., LL.D., 17 Manchester Sq., London. *Elect.*, *Mic.*, *Histol.*

Sigsworth, John C., 18 Chaucer Road, Herne-Hill, London, S.E. *Mic., Chem.*

Silber, A.M., 4 Bolton Gardens, South Kensington, London, S.W. *Light and Heat.*

Sillock, H., 22 Randolph St., Camden Town, London, N.W. *Lepid.*

Silver, Lt.-Colonel, Hugh A., H. M. Lieutenancy London, Assoc. Inst. C.E., Memb. Soc. Arts, F.R.M.S., F.R.C.I., F.R.B.S., Hillside, Chiselhurst, Kent. *Mic.*

Silvester, Frank, F.R.M.S., Recorder of Injurious Insects for Hertfordshire, St. Albans. *Geol., Ent.*

Sim, G., jr., 20 King St., Aberdeen, Scotland. *Lepid.*

Simmons, C. W., 8 Gough St., Stainsby Road, Poplar, London, E. *Lepid.*

Simmons, W., 6 New Walk Terrace, York. *Lepid.*

Simms, David, Limayady, Co. Derry, Ireland. *Ast.*

Simon, John, C.B., D.C.L. (Oxon.), etc., Consulting Surgeon to St. Thomas' Hospital, 40 Kensington Square, London, W.

Simpson, Charles T., 14 Cornwall Gardens, South Kensington, S. W. *Mic.*

Simpson, Maxwell, A.B., M.D., LL.D., etc., Queen's College, Cork, Ireland.

Sims, Henry, Cross St., Wakefield. *Gen. Ent.*

Skertchly, S. B. J., Geological Survey of England, Museum, Jermyn St., London, S.W.

Skitton, Mrs. Mary, M.C.T., 21 London Road, Brentford, Middlesex. *Mosses, Algæ, Mic., Moll.* C. Ex.*

Skues, G. E. M., 21 Burton Crescent, London, W.C. *Lepid.*

Sladen, W. Percy, F.L.S., F.G.S., etc., Orsett House, Ewell (Surrey). *Biol., Echinodermata, recent and fossil.* C. Ex.

Slater, Rev. H. H., B.A., Sharrow Cottage, Ripon. *Zool.**

Slater, J. W., Fellow Ent. Soc., Ed. Journ. of Sci., 36 Wray Crescent, Tollington Park, London, N. *Biol. esp. Ent.* C. Ex. Buprestidæ and Cetoniadæ for Cicindelidæ and Carabidæ.*

Slatter, Thomas James, Bank, Evesham. *Geol., Palæo. of Lias and Oolites, Bot., Mic., spec. Lias Palæo.* C. Ex. Liassic moll. and foraminifera for L. Secondary fossils (not chalk) from other localities.

Slaughter, George M., Surgeon-Major, Farningham, Kent. *Orn.*

Sleeman, Rev. Philip, Pembroke Road, Clifton, Bristol. *Polarization of Light.*

Slipper, R. A., The Vicarage, Tuttington, Aylsham, Norfolk. *Lepid., Coleopt.*

Slocombe, F. W., Rockhalls Terrace, Cricklewood, London, N.W. *Lepid.*

Sloper, G. E., Devizes, Wilts. *Geol.*

Sloper, S. W., Devizes, Wilts. *Geol.*

Slugg, J. T., F.R.A.S., Chorlton-cum-Hardy, near Manchester. *Ast.*

Smart, William, 27 Aldgate, London. *Mic.*

Smedley, John H., 10 Beacon Lane, Everton, Liverpool. *Ent.: Lepid.* C. Ex.

Smetham, Alfred, F.C.S., F.I.C., Analytical and Consulting Chemist to the Royal Manchester, Liverpool, and No. Lancashire Agric. Soc., 80 Brunswick St., Liverpool. *Agric., Chem. Geol., Chem., Mic.**

Smith, Abel, Woodhall Park, Watford. *Orn.*

Smith, Rev. Alfred C., M.A., Yatesbury Rectory, Wiltshire. *Orn.*

Smith, Benjamin Leigh, Oxford and Cambridge Club, 74 Pall Mall, London, S W.

Smith, Cecil, B.A., F.Z.S., Memb. B.O.U., Memb. Somersetshire Arch. and N. H. Soc., Lydeard House, Taunton, Somersetshire. *Orn.*

Smith, E., Adelaide Buildings, Liverpool. *Lepid.*

Smith, Edgar A., British Mus., Cromwell Rd., London, S.W. *Con.*

Smith, G. B., 6 Malvern Road, Hornsey, Middlesex. *Ent.*

Smith, G. J., F.R.M.S., 6 Malvern Road, Hornsey, Middlesex. *Geol.*

Smith, Harold, F.M.S., Kenley, Surrey. *Bot., Meteo., Ast.*

Smith, Heywood, A.M., M.D., 18 Harley St., Cavendish Sq., London. *Phys., Gen. Biol.**

Smith, H. Fred., J.P., Hull and Sutton. *Ast.*

Smith, Henley Grose, The Priory, St. Helen's, Isle of Wight. *Diurnal Lepid.*

Smith, M. W., Sundon House, Clifton, Bristol. *Palæo.*

Smith, Rev. W., Beverley. *Bot.*

Smith, Right Hon. William Henry, 3 Grosvenor Pl., London, S.W.

Smith, W.G., F.L.S., M.A.I., etc., Dunstable, Bedfordshire. *Fungi, Anth., Arch.* C.*

Smith, Rev. Canon W. Saumarez, B.D., St. Aidan's Coll., Birkenhead.*

Smith, W. L., Southfield House, Watford. *Bot.*

Smyth, Charles P., F.R.S.E., Ast. Royal for Scotland, Royal Obs., Edinburgh, Scotland.

Smyth, John, jr., M.A., C.E., Lenaderg, Banbridge, Co. Down, Ireland. *Chem.**

Smyth, Samuel Richard, care of J Brodbag, 90 Newgate St., London, E.C.

Smyth, Warington W., M.A., F.R.S., Chief Inspector of Crown Mines, Museum, Jermyn St., London, S W.

Smythe, Wm. Jas., Gen'l R.A., M.R.I.A., Carnmoney, Belfast, Ireland.*

Snell, A. H., The Grange, Harkbridge, Surrey. *Chem.*

Society of Biblical Archæology, W. Harry Rylands, Sec., Library and Offices, 11 Hart St., Bloomsbury, London, W.C., and 9 Conduit St., London, W. *Anth., Arch., Eth., Ethnog., Philol.*

Sollas, W. J., M.A., LL.D., D Sc., F.G.S., Prof. of Geol. in Univ. of Dublin, Trinity College, 4 Clyde Road, Dublin, Ireland.*

Somerville, Alexander, B.Sc., F.L.S., 34 Granby Terrace, Hillhead, Glasgow, Scotland. *Bot., Molluscs.**

Somerville, Rev. James E., M.A., B.D., Mansfield, Broughty Ferry, near Dundee, Scotland. *Nat. Sci., Bot., Zool., Orn., Coleopt., Moll.*

Sorby, Henry Clifton, LL.D., Broomfield, Sheffield. *Mic., Geol., Spectra of coloring matters, Marine researches.*

Sotheby, R. M., Sunny Side, Hastings. *Lepid.*

South, Richard, 12 Abbey Gardens, London, N.W. *Ent: Lepid.*

Southey, William, 38 Windsor Road, Upper Halloway, London, N. *Lepid.*

Southwell, Thomas, F.Z.S., M.B.O.U., 10 The Crescent, Chapel Field, Norwich. *Zool.**

Spalding, R. B., 46 High St., Notting Hill, London, W. *Gen. Ent.*

Spanton, Wm. Dunnett, F.R.C.S.E., Hanley, Staffordshire. *Bot., Mic., Gen. Biol.**

Speers, Adam, B.Sc. (Lond.), Head Master The Sullivan Schools, Holywood, Co. Down, Ireland. *Chem., Phys., Biol., Geol.*

Spence, J. Berger, F.L.S., F.R.A.S., Ellesmere Chambers, King St., Manchester.

Spiller, John, F.C.S., 2 St. Mary's Road, Canonbury, London. *Chem.*

Spink, J., Vine Lodge, Sevenoaks, Kent. *Geol.*

Spon, Ernest, Mining and Civil Engineer, 16 Craven St., Charing Cross, London, S.W. *Geol.*

Spratt, Thos. Abel Brimage, Vice-Admiral, C.B., F.G.S., F.S.A., F.R.G S., Clare Lodge, Tunbridge Wells.

Sprengel, Hermann Johann Philipp, Saville Club, Saville Row, London, W.

Spruce, Dr. R., Coneysthorpe, Malton. *Hepatica.**

Spurling, John, 42 Northgate, Wakefield. *Gen. Ent.*

Stabler, G., Levens, Milnthorpe, Westmoreland. *Mosses, Hepaticæ.* C. Ex.*

Stainton, Henry Tibbats, F.R.S., F.L.S., Pres. Ent. Soc. of London, Mountsfield, Lewisham, London, S.E. *Ent.*

Standish, F. O., 8 St. Paul's Terrace, Cheltenham, London. *Lepid.*

Stanford, John Frederick, M.A., Forest Lodge, North Bank, Regent's Park, London, N.W.

Stanley, Wm F., F G.S., F.R. Met. Soc., South Norwood, London, S.E. Will ex. his work on "Motion of Fluids," for any work on Sci. direct from author, value $2 00.

Stansell, F., 19 Silver St., Taunton. *Ool.* C.

Stark, A. C., Engadine, Torquay. *Orn.*

St. Clair, George, 127 Bristol Road, Birmingham, Author of "Darwinism and Design," "Evil, Physical and Moral,"etc. Lecturer for the Palestine Exploration Fund. *Geol., Anth., Biblical Arch.**

Stead, John E., 3 Zetland Road, Middlesbro-on-Tees. *Metallurgy of Iron and Steel.*

Stebbing, Rev. Henry, D.D., F.R.S., St Nicholas Cole Abbey, London, E.C.

Stebbing, Rev. Thos. R. R., M.A., Ephraim Lodge, The Common, Tunbridge Wells, Kent. *Sessile-eyed Crustaceans.* C. Ex.*

Stephens, Darell, F.G.S., F.L.S., F.Z.S., St. Stephen's, Plympton, Devon.

Steuart, D. R., F.I.C., F.C.S., Chemist to the Broxburn Oil Co., limited, Broxburn, Scotland.

Stevens, George, Alexandria, Scotland. *Chem.*
Stevens, Henry, F.S.A., 4 Trafalgar Sq., Charing Cross, W. C. and Vermont House, 13 Upper Avenue Road, South Hampstead, N.W., London. *Hist. and Bibliog.*
Stevens, J. Edw., 10 Cleveland Terrace, Swansea. *Geol.*
Stevens, John S., 38 King St., Covent Gardens, London, W.C. *Ent.*
Stevens, Samuel, Loanda, Beulah Hill, Upper Norwood, London, S.E. *Ent.**
Stevenson, George Wilson, C.E., 38 Parliament St., London, S.W.
Stevenson, Henry, F.L.S., Mem. B.O.U., Cor. Memb. Am. Orn. Union, 22 Unthanks Road, Norwich. *Zool., Gen. Biol., Emb. and Anat. of Vert., Orn., Ool., Tax.* C. Norfolk birds.
Stevenson, Rev. John, Hon. Sec. Cryptogamic Society of Scotland, Glamis, Scotland. *Mycology.*
Stewart, Samuel A., North St., Belfast, Ireland. *Nat. Hist., Geol.*
Stewart, T. Grainger, M.D., Prof. of Medicine, Univ., Edinburgh, Scotland.*
Stirling, Wm., M.D., Prof. Univ., Aberdeen, Scotland. *Physiol. and Histol. of Vert. and Invert. Animals.*
Stirton, Dr., 15 Newton St., Glasgow, Scotland. *Lichenology.*
Stoate, William, The Colony, Burnham, Somerset. *Ool.* C. Over 2500 species eggs.*
Stoddard, W. Walter, Park St., Bristol. *Min.*
Stoker, J. N., Laboratory, Somerset House, London, W.C.
Stoker, Wm. Thornley, M.D., 16 Harcourt St., Dublin, Ireland. *Anat.**
Stokes, Arthur H., A.M., F.G.S., H.M. Inspector of Mines, Green Hill, Derby. *Geol., Mining.**
Stokes, George Gabriel, Prof., F.R.S., D.C.L., Lensfield Cottage, Cambridge. *Phys., Math.*
Stokes, Paul H., F.L.S., B.A., M.D., sometime Prof. Bot. at Guy's Hospital, Wyombe Court, Bucks.
Stolterfoth, Henry, M.D., M.A., 60 Watergate St., Chester. *Diatomaceæ both fossil and recent.* C. Ex. microscopical slides or materials.*
Stone, Edward James, M.A., F.R.S., Dir. Radcliffe Observatory, Oxford.*
Stone, John Benjamin, J. P., F.L.S., F.G.S., F.R.G.S., Mayor of Sutton-Goldfield. The Grange, Erdington, Birmingham. Will be glad to receive communications from collectors of spec. relating to geographical botany from any part of the world, particularly cryptogamic.*
Stone, Wm. H., M.B., F.R.C.P. 14 Deans Yard, Westminster, Saint Thomas' Hosp., London. *Phys., esp. Acoustics.* C. Ex.
Stoney, Bindon Blood, LL.D., M.I.C.E., M.I.N.A. 14 Elgin Road, Dublin, Ireland.
Stoney, George Johnstone, M.A., D.Sc., F.R.S., 3 Palmerston Park, Dublin, Ireland. *Phys.*
Stopes, Henry Kenwyn, Cintra Park, Upper Norwood, London. *Geol.* C. Ex. Crag shells for stone implements, etc.

Storer, Dr. John, Sydney St., Glasgow, Scotland. *Chem.*
Storrie, John, Curator Cardiff Museum. *Geol.*, *Bot.* C.
Story, Capt. James, F.Z.S., F.B.S., Carlton Club, Pall Mall, London. *Ast.*, *Geog. Dist.*
Strachey, Lieut.-Gen. Richard, F.R.S., India Office; and Stowey House, Chapham Common, W.
Stradling, W. Arthur, M.R.C.S.E., C.M.L.S., etc., Flores, Watford, Hertfordshire. *Ophiology.* C. Ex.*
Strahan, Aubrey, M.A., Geological Survey of England, Museum, Jermyn St., London, S.W.
Straker, E. Havleshaw, Kenly, W., Croydon, Surrey. *Bot.*
Strangways, C. Fox, Geological Survey of England, Museum, Jermyn St., London, S.W.
Struthers, John, M.D., Prof. Anat., Univ., Aberdeen, Scotland.
Strype, William George, C.E., M. Inst. C.E., The Murrough, Wicklow, Ireland. *Agric.*, *Geol.*, *Elect.**
Stuart, Chas. M., M.A., High School, Newcastle, Staffordshire. *Chem.**
Stuart, Graham, Dolgelly, Wales. *Min.*
Stubbins, John, F.G.S., F.R.M.S., Inglebank, Far Headingley, Leeds. *Geol.*, *Mic.*, *Gen. Biol.*
Suffolk, William T., Petersfield, St. Julian's Farm Road, Lower Norwood, London, S.E. *Mic.**
Sully, *James, M.A., Saville Club, 107 Piccadilly, London, W. *Psychol.*, *Æsthetics.*
Sutherland, Dr. Arthur, Invergordon, Scotland, N. B. *Bot.*, *Zool.*
Sutherland, Charles Leslie, Memb. Royal Commission of Agric., Combe, near Croydon, Surrey.
Sutherland, The Duke of, Stafford House, London, S.W., Trentham Hall, Staffordshire, and Cliefden House, Berks.
Sutherland, James, Taxidermist, Sutherland Villa, West Bank, Wick, Scotland. *Orn.*, *Zool.**
Sutton, Wm. D., Upper Claremont, Newcastle-on-Tyne. *Moll.*
Swain, Ernest, A.K.C., F.G.S., 17 Tadmor St., Shepherd's Bush, London, W. *Biol.*, *Geol.**
Swan, David, Spelter Works, Maryhill, near Glasgow, Scotland. *Zinc*, *Metallurgy*, *Metals.* C. Ex. Would like Am. specimens.
Swanston, Wm., F.G.S., 50 King St., Belfast, Ireland. *Geol.* C.*
Swanzy, Andrew, F.L.S., Sevenoaks. *Ent.*
Swarlen, Johnson C., Beverley. *Orn.*
Swinton, A. H., Lansdowne, Dane Park, Ramsgate. *Gen. Sci.*, *Ent.* C. Ex. British insects.*
Sylvester, Jas. Joseph, M.A., D.C.L. (Oxon.), etc., New College, Cambridge.
Syme, George, Beckenham, Kent, Scotland. *Bot.*, *Specialty Conifers*, *Orchids*, *Evolutionists.*
Symes, Richard G., Geological Survey of Ireland, The Rock, Ballyshannon, Co. Donegal, Ireland.
Symonds, Rev. W. S , Pendock Rectory, Tewkesbury. *Geol.*, *Nat. Hist.*

Symons, G. J., F.R.S., Sec. R. Met. Soc., 62 Camden Sq., London, N.W. *Meteorology*. Ex. Met. publications.*

Symons, Wm., F.C.S., 26 Joy St., Barnstaple. *Chem., Elect.**

Tackhadakar, M.A., care of Mr. Lewis, 136 Gower St., London, W.C.

Tait, Lawson, 7 Great Charles St., Birmingham. *Biology*. Ex. slides illustrating gland structure, mounted for microscope.

Tait, P. Guthrie, Prof. Phys., Univ., Edinburgh, Scotland. *Chem., Phys.*

Take, James H., Bancroft, Hitchin, Hertfordshire. *Orn., Ool.* C.

Talbot, T. H., Mount Pleasant, Wakefield *Gen. Ent.*

Tarbock, Robert R., Public Chem. for City of Glasgow, 138 Batle St., Glasgow, Scotland. *Analyt. Chem.*

Tarrant, K. J., Litchford House, Middlesex. *Ast., Double Stars.**

Tatton, W., 15 Doderidge St., Liverpool. *Lepid.*

Taylor, A. O. D., Belfast, Ireland. *Orn.*

Taylor, Beatrice K., Aston Rowant House, Teksworth, Oxon. *Fungi, esp. Tremellinaæ, Hymenomycetes and Gasteromycetes.**

Taylor, Edward C., M.A., 74 Jermyn St., London, W. *Orn.*

Taylor, Geo. C., 42 Elvaston Pl., Queen's Gate, London, W. *Orn.*

Taylor, J. W., Ed. Quarterly Journal of Con., Sovereign Street, Leeds. *Brit. L. and F. W. Shells.**

Taylor, Richard, F.G.S., Science and Art Teacher, Marske-by-the-Sea, Yorkshire. *Bot., Agric., Geol., Chem., Phys., Math., Elect., Biology, Mining, Metall., Geom., Machine construction, Mechanics, Min., Hygiene, etc., etc.* C. Ex.*

Taylor, T. H., George St., Wakefield. *Gen. Ent.*

Teague & Teague, Mining Engineers and Surveyors, Redruth, Cornwall.*

Teall, J. J. H., B.A., 9 All Saints. Nottingham. *Geol.*

Teasdale, Washington, F.R.A.S., etc., Rosehurst, Headingley, Leeds. *Hort., Phys., Mic., Photog., Arch.**

Tebbitt, Walter, Elmhurst, Cavendish Road, Clapham Park, London, S.W. *Mic.*

Tegetmeier, William B , M.B.O.U., F.Z.S., Finchley, Middlesex. *Orn., Mam.*

Tennant, James, West Parade, Stoke-on-Trent. *Min.* C. Ex.*

Tennant, Jas. Francis, Lieut. Gen'l R.E., C.I.E., F.R.A.S., 37 Hamilton-road, Ealing, London, W.

Tennent, R., Edinburgh, Scotland. *Meteo.*

Tennyson, Alfred, Lord, D.C.L. (Oxon.), Poet Laureate, Soc. Reg. Edin. Soc. Honor, Farringford, Freshwater, Isle of Wight.

Terry, William, Peterborough House, Fulham, London, S.W. *Mic.*

Thackeray, W. G., Ass't Royal Observatory, Greenwich. *Ast.*

Thairwall, F. J., 169 Gloucester Road, Regent's Park, London, W. *Arch.*

Theobald, William, late Deputy Superintendent Geological Survey of India, Geological Survey Office, Calcutta; also 50 Harpur St., Bedford, Beds. *L. and F. W. Shells, Reptiles and Coins of India.*

Thomas, E., F.R.S., Athenæum, London. *Indian Numismatics.*
Thomas, Oldfield, F.Z.S., Natural History Museum, Cromwell Rd., London, S.W. *Mammalia.*
Thomas, T. H., 45, The Walk, Cardiff, Wales. *Palæo., Anth., Arch.**
Thomas, W., Abberley House, Worcester Park, Surrey. *Lepid.*
Thomas, Wm., Cook's Kitchen Mine, Camborne. *Min.*
Thompson, Christopher D., The Cottage, Seaton Carew, West Hartlepool. *Orn., Ichth., Tax.* C. Ex.
Thompson, Claude M., M.A. (Cantab.), D.Sc. (Lond.), F.C.S., Prof. Chem., Univ. College, Cardiff, Wales. *Chem.**
Thompson, D'Arcy W., Prof. Biol., University College, Dundee, Scotland. *Morph.* Desires to ex. Zool. material in behalf of Coll. Mus.*
Thompson, Geo. M., F.L.S., Science Teacher, High School, Dunedin. Biol., N. .Z *Crustacea.* C.*
Thompson, Sir Henry, F.R.C.S., 35 Wimpole St., London, W.
Thompson, I. C, F.R.M.S., Woodstock Waverly Rd., Liverpool. *Min.**
Thompson, J. H. Cradley, near Brierley Hill. *Bot.*
Thompson, J. Latham, M. B., F.R.M.S., 19 Charles St., Cardiff, So. Wales. *Pathological Histol. and Ophthalmological Path.**
Thompson, Silvanus P., B.A., D.Sc., Prof. Exper. Phys., University Coll., Bristol. *Elect.* Author of "Elementary Lessons in Electricity and Magnetism, of Dynamo-electric machinery," and of Philipp Reiss, Inventor of the Telephone," and of sundry pamphlets on Apprenticeship Schools and on Technical education. Ex. papers on Exper. Physics.
Thompson, Miss Sophia, Barn Hill, Stamford. *Ent.*
Thompson, W., 183 Stantonbury, Stoney Stratford, Bucks. *Lepid.*
Thoms, W. A., F.R.M.S., Alyth, Scotland. *Fungi.*
Thomson, Allen, M.D., 66 Palace Gardens Terrace, London. W.
Thomson, Andrew, M.A., D.Sc., F.C.S., F.I.C., F.R.S.E., Assistant to Prof. Chem. University College, Dundee, Scotland. *Org. and Inorg. Chem., Met., Agric.**
Thomson, George S., M.D., F.R. Met. Soc., 8 College Road, Clifton, Bristol. *Meteo.**
Thomson, Jas., M.A., LL.D., Prof. of Civil Engineering and Mechanics in Univ. of Glasgow, 2 Florentine-gardens, Hillheadstreet, Glasgow, Scotland.
Thomson, John, Umbank, Perth Road, Dundee, Scotland. *Phys.*
Thomson, Joseph John, M.A. Fellow of Trinity College, and Cavendish Prof. of exper. Phys., Cambridge.
Thomson, Sir Wm., F.R.S., LL.D., D.C.L., etc., Prof. Nat. Philos., The University, Glasgow, Scotland. *Phys., Elect., Math.**
Thorman, Edw., West Ham Gas Works, Stratford, Essex. *Mic.*
Thorn, Thomas, 135 Powmall, Dalton, London. *Lepid.*
Thornewill, Rev. C. F., The Soho, Burnston-on-Trent. *Lepid.*
Thornthwaite, W. H., F.R.A.S., 416 Strand, London, W.C. *Ast.*
Thornthwart, A. Willow, Bridge Road, Canonbury, London, N. *Lepid.*

Thorpe, John, Spring Gardens, Middleton, Manchester. *Lepid.*
Thorpe, Thos. E., Prof. Chem., Yorkshire College, Leeds.
Thorpe, William G., F.R.S., Gloucester House, Larkhall Rise, London, S.W.
Threlfall, J. H., 4 East Cliff, Preston. *Micro-lepid.*
Thuey, Alex., Assoc. M. Inst. C.E., 8 Victoria St., London, S.W.
Thuillier, Sir Henry Edw. Landor, Gen'l R.A., C.S.I., F.R.G.S., 11 Sussex Gardens, Hyde-park, London.
Thurlow, Rt. Hon. Thos. John Hovell-Thurlow, Cumming-Bruce, Lord. Dunphail, Scotland.
Thurnfall, A., Stratford. *Lepid.*
Tickel, J. C., 135 Pournall Road, Dalton, London. *Lepid.*
Tiddeman, R. H., M.A., Geological Survey of England, Museum, Jermyn St., London, S.W.
Tidy, Dr. C. Meymott, Prof. Chem., 3 Mandeville Pl., Manchester Sq., London, W.
Tilden, William Augustus, Prof. Chem. and Metall., The Mason Science College, Birmingham. *Analysis of water.*
Tingle, T., Apothecaries' Hall, Blackfriars, London, E.C. *Mic.*
Todd, Rev. J.W., D.D., Tudor Hall Coll., Forest Hill, London, S. E.
Tomes, Robert F., South Littleton, Evesham. *Geol., Fossil Corals.*
Tomlinson, Rev. S., The Library, St. Patrick's, Dublin, Ireland. *Ast.*
Tompkins, H., 28 Tavistock Sq., London, W.C. *Ent.*
Tomes, Sir John, F.R.C.S. (Eng.), Upwood Gorse, Caterham, Surrey.
Tomkins, Rev. Henry George, Park Lodge, Weston Super Mare. *Arch., Ethnol.**
Tookey, Charles, Museum Pract. Geology, Jermyn St., London, S.W. *Chem.*
Topley, William, Geol. Survey of England, 28 Jermyn St., London, S.W. *Geol.*
Torrens, Elliott, Fisherwick School, Belfast, Ireland. *Phys., Biol.*
Townend, W., West Parade, Halifax, Yorkshire. *Mic.*
Trail, J. W. H., Prof. Bot., Univ. of Aberdeen, Scotland. *Bot., Ent., esp. Galls and Am. Palms.* C. Ex.
Traill, A., LL.D., M.D., 35 Trinity Coll., Dublin, Ireland. *Phys. Geol., Min., Phys., Elect., Meteo., Gen. Biol., Anth., Arch., Eth.*
Traquair, Ramsay H., M.D., F.R.S., Keeper of the Natural History collections in the Museum of Science and Art, Edinburgh, Scotland. *Zool.* Writer of original papers on Fossil Ichthyology and anatomy of fishes.*
Trechmann, Charles O., Ph.D., F.G.S., Hartlepool. *Min., Crystal., Lithol.**
Tregay, W., M.E., Mining Expert, Redruth. *Min., Geol.*
Tren, J. C., 85 Nicholas St., New North Road. *Lepid.*
Tribe, Alfred, 14 Denbigh Road, Bayswater, London. *Chem.*
Tristram, H. B., D.D., F.R.S., The College, Durham. *Orn., Con., Geol., Nat. Hist. of Palestine and Syria.* C.*
Trotter, Coutts, 10 Randolph Crescent, Edinburgh, Scotland. *Comp. Geog.**

Tuely, Nathaniel C., F.L.S., Mortimer Lodge, Wimbledon Park, London, S.W. *Lepid.*

Tugwell, W. H., 3 Lewisham Road, Greenwich. *Lepid.*

Tuke, James H., Hitchin. *Orn.*

Tunley, W. H., Albert Road, Southsea, Portsmouth, Hampshire. *Arch., esp. ancient seal impressions.* C. Ex.

Tunnard, C. C., Factor, Gartarton Cottage, Gartmore, Stirling, N. B., Scotland. *Gen. Nat. Hist.*

Tupman, Major G. Lyon, R.M.A., 1 Vanbrugh Park, Blackheath, London, S.E. *Ast.*

Tupper, Martin Farquhar, D.C.L., Underhill, Cintra Park, Upper Norwood, London, S.E.

Turner, H. H., M.A., B.Sc., Chief Ass't, Royal Obs., Greenwich. *Ast.**

Turner, John, 10 Davenport Stockport, near Manchester. *Moll.* (for Odontophora).

Turner, William, M.B., LL.D. F.R.S., Prof. of Anat, University of Edinburgh, 6 Eton Terrace, Edinburgh, Scotland.

Turtle, J. G., 1 Alfred St., Belfast, Ireland. *Desmids, Diatoms, Hort., Elect., Orn., Mic., Hymen.* C.*

Tye, G. Sheriff, 41 Caroline St., Birmingham. *Con.**

Tyerman, I., Penlee, Tregoney, Cornwall. *Moll.*

Twiss, Sir Travers, Knt., Q.C., D.C.L., F.G.S., 3 Paper-building, Temple, London, E.C.

Tyler, Chas., F.L.S., F.G.S., F.R.M.S., etc., etc., Elberton, New West End, Hampstead, London, N. *Mic.**

Tylor, Edward Burnett, D.C.L., LL.D., F.R.S., Univ. Mus., Oxford.*

Tynam, E. W., C.E., Board of Works Inspector, Gartnamora, Ballinasloe, Ireland.*

Tyndall, John, D.C.L., LL.D., F.R.S., Prof. Nat. Phil., Royal Inst., Albemarle St., London, W. *Phys., Math.*

Ullyett, Henry, B.Sc., etc., Lyell House, Folkestone. *Phæn. Bot., Ferns, Palæo., Ool., Lepid.*

Ullyett, L., Lyell House, Folkestone. *Lepid.*

Umphray, Lerwick, Shetland, Scotland. *Ool.* (*Dealer*).*

Unthank, W. George, 27 St. Mark's Road, Notting Hill, London. *Nat. Hist.*

Unwin, W. Cawthorne, B.Sc., M. Inst. C.E. and M.E., Prof. of Engineering at the Central Institute, City and Guilds of London, 7 Palacegate Mansions, London, W.

Upcher, Henry M., Sheringham Hall, Norfolk. *Orn.*

Ussher, Richard J., Cappagh, Lismore, under Cahir, Ireland. *Orn., Ool.* C. Ex.*

Ussher, W. A. E., F.G.S., Geological Survey of England, Museum, Jermyn St., London, S.W.

Vachell, Chas. T., M.D., 38 Charles St., Cardiff, S. Wales. *Phæn. Bot., Fungi.**

Vacher, Francis, 36 Hamilton Sq., Birkenhead. *Medicine.*

Vandenbergh, William J. V., Ph.D., F.R.A.S., F.M.S., etc., 5 Yale Terrace, Leytonstone, Essex. *Zool.*

Vanner, William, Camdenwood, Chiselhurst, Kent. *Mic.*
Varicas, Lionel, C.E., 24 Chancery Lane, London, W.C. *Geol.*
Vaughan, Howard, 11 Ospringe Road, Brecknock Road, London, N.W. *Ent., Bot.*
Vaughan, P. H., Redland, Bristol. *Ent.*
Veitch, Harry J., F.S.L., Royal Exotic Nursery, King's Road, Chelsea, London, S.W.*
Veley, V. H., M.A., Univ. Coll., Oxford. *Chem.*
Venn, John, Sc.D , Petersfield House, Parkside, Cambridge.
Vereker, Hon. John G. P., Hamsterley Hall, Smith Green, Newcastle-on-Tyne. *Mic., Photog.**
Verini, William, The Ferns, Bushey Heath. *Geol.*
Verrall, G. H., Sussex Lodge, Newmarket. *Ent.*
Vezey, John J., F.R.M.S., 12 Sandbourne Road, Brockley, London, S.E. *Mic.**
Vicars, John, 8 St. Albans Sq., Bootle, Liverpool. *Bot., Mic.* C.
Vickers, T. Edward, Bolsover Hill, Sheffield. *Min.*
Victoria Inst. or Phil. Soc. of Gt. Britain, 7 Adelphi Terrace, Charing Cross, London, W.C. Pres., G. G. Stokes, Pres. of the Royal Soc.; Hon. Sec., Capt. Francis Petrie, F.G.S., etc. *All depts. of Sci. and Phil.**
Vine, G. R., 112 Hill Top, Abercliffe, Sheffield. *Fossil Polyzoa.*
Vinen, Ed. Hart, M.D., F.L S., F.R.M.R., 17 Chepstow Villas, Bayswater, London, W. *Mic., Botany.*
Vines, Sidney H., M.A., Christ's College, Cambridge. *Bot.*
Vivian, Arthur Pendarves, M.P., F.G.S., Glendorgal, St. Columb Minor, Cornwall. *Geol., Min., Met.*
Vivian, Stephen, Llantrissent, Wales. *Min.*
Vivian, William, Llantrissent, Wales. *Min.*
Vize, Rev. Jno. E., M.A., F.R.M.S., Forden Vicarage, Welshpool. *Cryptogams, Mic.**
Waghorn, J. W. W., D.Sc., Royal Naval College, Greenwich. *Phys.*
Wailes, Herbert George, Park Road, Watford. *Geol., Palæo., Min., Chem., Elect., Zool.* C. Ex.
Wain, Thomas, Shrublands, Hersham, Esher, Surrey. *Mic.*
Wainwright, H., Grammar School, Barnstaple. *Bot., Arch.*
Wainwright, Joseph, F.L.S., Springfield Hall, near Wakefield. *Phæn. Bot., Hort., Veg. Palæo.*
Wake, Charles Staniland, M.A.I., Hull. *Anth., Eth.*
Wakefield, Charles M., Belmont, Uxbridge. *Ent.*
Wakeman, W. J., Dublin, Ireland. *Arch. of Ireland.*
Walford, Edwin, F.G.S., Hon. Sec. Banburyshire Nat. Hist. Soc. and Field Club, Banbury, Oxfordshire.
Walhouse, M. J., 9 Randolph Crescent, Maida-vale, London, W. *Anth.*
Walker, A. O., Chester. *Crustacea.**
Walker, Edw., M.A., 9 Dorville-crescent, Ravenscourt-park, Windgate-road, London, W.
Walker, Rev. F. A., M.A., Bourne Villa, Bournemouth, Hants. *Ent.*

Walker, Henry, F.G.S., 30 Leamington Road Villas, Westbourne Park, London, W.

Walker, John Jas., M.A., Cannycot, Willoughby-road, Hampstead, London, N.W.

Walker, J. Watson, Fairfield House, Watford. *Bot.*

Walker, James J., R.N., H.M.S., Hawk, Harwich. *Lepid.*

Walker, William Neish, 2 Hillpark Terrace, Newport, Fife. *Geol.*

Wall, Philip William, M. Inst. C.E., The Grove, Clevedon, Somersetshire.

Wallace, Alexander, M.D., Trinity House, Colchester. *Ent.*

Wallace, Alfred Russel, Frith Hill, Godalming.*

Waller, A. R., 17 Low Cusegate, York. *Phæn. Bot.* C. Ex.

Waller, T. H., 71 Gough Road, Birmingham. *Chem., Microscopic Igneous sections.**

Walpole, T., 17 College St., Spittlegate, Grantham. *Lepid.*

Walpole, The Rt. Hon. Spencer Horatio, M A., D.C.L., Q. C. Trust. Brit. Mus., 109 Eaton-square, London, S. W.

Walsh, Henry, Northgate, Wakefield. *Gen. Ent.*

Walsingham, Lord, F.R.S., Merton Hall, Thetford. *Lepid: Tineidæ.* C. Ex. British and European Tineidæ and Tortricidæ offered for N. A. or other Tineidæ, Tortricidæ and Pterophoridæ, good specimens only.

Walton, Thomas, Hull. *Chem.*

Ward, Christopher, F.L.S., Saville Road, Halifax. *Ent.*

Ward, F. H., Springfield, Tooting, London, S.W. *Ent.*

Ward, William, Cleveland-Cottage, Hill, Southampton. *Mic.*

Wardle, Thomas, F.G.S., F.C.S., St. Edw., St. Leeks, Staffordshire. Desires new or rare species of silk-producing Lepid. with their Cocoons.*

Waring, S. L., The Oaks, Norwood, London, S.E. *Ent.*

Warington, R., Harpenden, St. Albans, Herts. *Chem., Agric.*

Warren, Col. Sir Charles, R.E., G.C.M.G., F.R.S., A.I.C.E., F.G.S., F.R.G.S., care of Cox & Co., Craig's Court, Charing Cross, London.*

Warren, Sir Charles, G.C.M.G., Colonel R. E., 44 St. Georges-road, London, S W.

Warren, Robert, Moyview, Ballina, Co. Mayo, Ireland. *Zool., Orn., Ool.* C. Ex.*

Warren, W., 51 Bridge St., Cambridge. *Lepid.*

Waterhouse, Chas. Owen, British Museum, Cromwell Rd., London, S.W. *Coleopt.*

Waterhouse, F. H., 3 Hanover Sq., London. *Ent. Lib. to Zool. Soc. London.**

Waterhouse, Geo. R., F.Z.S., Curton Lodge, Merter Road, Putney, London, S.W. *Coleopt.*

Waters, Arthur W., F.L.S., care of Mr. West, Royal Mic. Soc., King's College, London. *Bryozoa, fossil and recent.* C.

Waters, W. H., Physiol. Lab., Cambridge. *Physiol.*

Watkins, William, Naturalist, The Hollies, Vicarage Road, Croydon, Surrey. *Lepid., Coleopt.* Ex.*

Watson, Rev. Henry Wm., D.Sc., The Rectory, Berkeswell, Coventry.
Watson, Major H., F.R.A.S., Barracks, Newbridge, Co. Kildare, Ireland. *Ast.**
Watson, Rev. Robert Boog, B.A., F.R.S.E., F.L.S., F.G.S., Free Church Manse, Cardross, Dumbartonshire, Scotland. *Geol.*, *Moll.**
Watson, William, 313 High Holborn, London, W.C. *Mic* *
Watson, Wm. H., F.C.S., F.M.S., Braystones, near Whitehaven, Cumberland. *Chem.*
Watts, Rev. Arthur, F.G.S., etc., Manor House, Shincliffe, Durham. *Physiol.*, *Geol.*, *Veg. Palæo.*, *Bot.* C.*
Way, Thomas, F.I.C., 9 Rupell Road, Kensington, London. *Chem.*
Rotheram-Websdale, George, Castle St., Barnstaple. *Ent: Life History of Insects.*
Weightman, William H., Minster Buildings, Church St., Liverpool. *Lepid.*
Wier, J. Jenner, 6 Haddo Villas, Blackheath, London, S.E. *Ent.*
Weldon, W. F. R., St. John's College, Cambridge. *Comp. Anat.**
Wellcome, Henry S., First Ave. Hotel, London. *Chem.*, *Anth.*, *Arch.*, *Eth.*, *Ethnog.*, *Histol.**
Wellmann, J. R., 14 Portland Pl. North, Clapham Road, London, S.W. *Lepid.*
West, Rev. George Herbert, M.A., Head Master Ascham School, Bournemouth. *Palæo.*, *Geol.*, *Arch.* C. Ex.*
West, Wm., F.L.S., 15 Horton Lane, Bradford, York. *Phæn. and Crypt. Bot.* C. Ex.*
Westendarp, C. H., 19 Stanley Crescent, Kensington Park, London, W. *Geol.*
Western, E. Young, 27 Craven Hill Gardens, Bayswater, London, W. *Ent.*
Westgarth, Wm., 10 Bolton Gardens, South Kensington, London. *Economic, Monetary and Banking.* (Also Hist. of Victoria, Australia).*
Westlake, Ernest, F.G.S., Hon. Cur. Salisbury and S. Wilts Museum, Fordingbridge, Salisbury. *Cretaceous Palæo.*, *Geol.*, *Lithol.*, *Con.*, *Ast.*, *Hymenop.* C. Type spec. of Chalk fossils of Hampshire for ex.*
Westwood, John O., M.A., Walton Manor, Oxford. *Ent.*
Westwood, Oliver J. A., 27 King William St., Strand, London. *Ed. Illust. Science Mo.*, *Meteo.*, *Ast.*
Wethered, Edw., F.G.S., F.C.S., F.R.M.S., Cheltenham. *Geol.*, *Inorg. Chem.*, *Mic.* C. Ex.*
Wharton, Charles B., Hounsdown, Totton, Hants. *Orn.**
Wharton, Henry T., M.A., M.R.C.S., F.Z.S., 39 St. George's Road, Kilburn, London, N.W. *Orn.*, *Bot.*, *Fungi*, *Nomenclature.**
Wheeler, Edwin, The Triangle, Bristol. *Bot.*, *Orn.*, *Ent.*
Wheeler, Francis D., M.A., Norwich. *Elect.*, *Orn.*, *Ool.*, *Lepid.* C. Ex.
Wheldon, John, Scientific Bookseller and Publisher, 58 Great Queen St., London, W.C.

Whewall, James, Saville House, Obs., Halifax. *Ast.*

Whipple, G. M., B.Sc., F.R.A.S.. F.R. Met. Soc., Kew Obs., Richmond, Surrey. *Elect., Photog., Meteo., Ast.**

Whitaker, William, B.A., F.R.S., F.G.S., Assoc. Inst. C.E., Geological Survey of England, Assoc. Soc. Med., Officers of Health, Corr. Ac. Nat. Sci., Philadelphia, 28 Jermyn St., London, S.W. *Geol.**

Whitby, J., 20 Fitzroy St., Liverpool. *Lepid.*

White, A. H. Scott, B.Sc., B.A., F.C.S., Western Terrace, The Park, Nottingham. *Geol., Min.*

White, B., M.D., Perth, Scotland. *Ent., Lepid.*

White, Charles F., F.L.S., F.R.M.S., 3 Amherst Road Castleben, Ealing, London, W. *Bot., spec. Pollens.**

White, F. Buchanan, M.D., F.L.S., Annat Lodge, Perth, Scotland. *Ent., Bot.* C. Ex. hemiptera of the world. Living Alpine and hardy herbaceous plants.

White, James, 244 Sauchiehall St., Glasgow, Scotland. *Phys.*

White, J. Martin, Dundee Naturalists' Society, Balruddery, near Dundee, Scotland. *Phys., Elect.**

White, J. S., 15 Medlock Road, Droylsden, near Manchester. *Coleopt., Lepid.*

White, Jas. W., 52 York Crescent, Clifton, Bristol. *Bot.*

White, Miss Rose, Maisonette, St. Albans. *Bot.*

White, T. Charters, M.R.C.S.E., F.R.M.S., 32 Belgrave Road, London, S. W. *Photo-Micrography, Elementary Microscopic Manipulation, Dental Histology.**

White, Rev. W. F., Stonehouse, Vicarage, Gloucestershire. *Ent.*

White, Wm., The Mall, Clifton, Bristol. *Bot.*

Whitehead, Charles, F.S.A., F.L.S., F.G.S., F.R.G.S., Agricultural adviser to the Lords of the Committee of Council on Agriculture, Barming House, Maidstone.*

Whitelaw, Alex., 87 Sidney St., Glasgow, Scotland. *Chem.**

Whitley, Henry Michell, F.G.S., Assoc. Mem. Inst. C.E., Hon. Sec., Roy. Inst. of Cornwall, Granville House, Ramsden Road, Balham, London, S. W. *Geol., Meteo., Ast., Arch.*

Whitley, N., F. R. Met. S., Hon. Member of R.G.S. of Cornwall, Truro.*

Whittall, J., Assist. Sec. and Librarian of Royal Statistical Society, 9 Adelphi Terrace, Strand, London, W. C.*

Widdas, Charles, 34 Bond St., Leeds. *Geol., Min.* C. Ex. In want of good Agates.*

Widdas, George A., 34 Bond St., Leeds. *Ool.* C. Ex. Desires Eggs of the world. Correspondence invited.*

Wigham, John R., 19 St. George St., Westminster, London. *Lighthouse and General Engineering.*

Wilcolck, Joseph, Northgate, Wakefield. *Coleopt.*

Wild, C. J., 128 Cheetham Hill, Manchester. *Musci, Hepaticæ.*

Wilde, Henry, Rockside, Alderly Edge, Cheshire.

Wilkinson, H. J., 6 Alexandra Terrace, Bishophill, York.*

Wilks, Sam'l, M.D., LL.D. Coll. Reg. Med. Soc., Consulting Physician to Guy's Hospital, 72 Grosvenor street, London, W.

Willacy, Rev. T. R., B.A., F.G.S., The Vicarage, Thorganby, York. *Palæo.*, *Geol*, *Phys.*, *Elect.*, *Meteo.*, *Gen. Biol.*, *Philol.*, *Ent.**

Williams, Alfred, M Inst. C.E., 18 Great George St., London, S.W.

Williams, A. Stanley, 1 Medina Terrace, West Brighton. *Ast.*

Williams, C. H., 25 Portland St., Soho, London, N. *Lepid.*

Williams, E. S., Swansea, S. Wales. *Inorg. Chem.*, *Metall.*

Williams, G., 16 Cambridge Terrace, Hyde Park, London, W. *Ast.*

Williams, Greville, F.R.S., Layfield, Bolingbroke Grove, Wandsworth, Surrey. *Chem.*, *Phys.* C.

Williams, J. T., 23 Old Kent Road, London, S.E. *Lepid.*

Williams, M. W., 18 Kempsford Gardens, London, S.W. *Chem.*, *Phys.*

Williams, W. Carlton, B.Sc., Firth Coll., Sheffield. *Chem.*

Williamson, Alexander William, Ph.D., LL.D, Prof. Emer. of Chem., High Pitfold, Haslemere.*

Williamson, William Crawford, Prof. of Nat. Hist., Anat., and Phys., Owens College, Manchester, 4 Egerton Road, Fallowfield, Manchester.

Willis, James, H.M.'s Inspector of Mines, F.G.S., M.I.M.E., 14 Portland Terrace, Newcastle-on-Tyne.

Wills, A. W., Wylde Green, near Birmingham. *Biol.*, *Mic.*, *Algæ*, *Desmids.* C. Ex.*

Wilson, Alexander Stephen, North Kinmundy, Summerhill, by Aberdeen, Scotland. *Bot.*, *Experimental and Structural, spec. Embryo of Cereal Grasses, and Plasmodiophora brassicæ Wor.* C.

Wilson, Andrew, M.D., Ph.D., 110 Gilmore Pl., Edinburgh, Scotland. *Biol.*, *Zool.*

Wilson, Sir Charles William, Col. R. E., K.C.B., K.C.M.G., D.C.L. (Oxon.), F.R.G.S. Ordnance Survey Office, Southampton.

Wilson, Edward, F.G.S., Cur. The Museum, Bristol. *Geol.*, *Min.*, *Zool.* Ex. Mollusca, Microzoa and Fossils.*

Wilson, Edwin, Nat. Hist. Artist, St. Leonard's, Mortlake, Surrey. *British Coleopt.*

Wilson, George Fergusson, F.R.S., F.C.S., F.L.S., Hetherbank, Weybridge Heath, Surrey.*

Wilson, George, Cross St., Wakefield. *Gen. Ent.*

Wilson, Rev. James Maurice, M.A., F.R.A.S., late Fellow of St. John's College, Cambridge, Clifton College, Bristol.

Wilson, J, 53 Alma Road, Bermondsey, London, S.E *Lepid.*

Wilson, John, LL.D., F.R S.E., F.G.S., etc., Prof. of Agriculture and Rural Economy in the University of Edinburgh, Tunbridge Wells.*

Wilson, Owen S., Cwmffrwd, Carmarthen, Wales. *Lepid.* C. Ex. Eggs of Lepid. desired for figuring species in all their transformations, for publications.*

Wilson, Wright, Crescent, Birmingham. *Zool.*

Wiltshire, Rev. Thomas, M.A., 25 Granille Park, Lewisham, London, S.E. *Geol.**

Winbolt, J. S., M.A., Memb. Inst. C.E., F.G S., 1 Salisbury Villas, Cambridge.*

Windsor-Aubrey, Henry George, Hall Rectory, W. Salisbury. *Mic., Ent. in relation to Mic. preparations.* C. Ex.

Winney, H. J., 1 Shorter's court, Throgmorton street, E.C., London. *Mic.**

Winwood, Rev. H. H., M.A., F.G.S., 11 Cavendish Crescent, Bath. *Geol.* C

With, George Henry, F.R.A.S, F.C.S., Trinity Coll., Dublin, Ireland, Agric. and Sanitary Chemist to the Hereford Soc. for aiding the Industrious, Hereford. *Silver-on-glass specula for Newtonian Telescopes.*

Wonnacott, John, F.G.S., F.R.G.S., F.R.H.S., East Cornwall College, Liskeard. *Geol., Physiol., Animal and Veg. Physiol.* C.*

Wood, Rev. Henry Hayton, M.A., F.G.S., Holwell Rectory, Sherborne, Dorset. *Mosses, Hepaticæ, British, recent and tertiary shells.* C. Ex. Offers British mosses and hepaticæ for foreign.

Wood, Henry Trueman, M.A., Sec.Soc. of Arts, John St., Adelphi, London, W.C.*

Wood, Prof. John, 61 Wimpole St., Cavendish Sq., London. *Human and Comp. Anat.*

Wood, Rev. John George, M.A., Corr. memb. Essex Inst., Salem, Mass., U.S.A., Freeman Lodge, St. Peter's, Kent. *Zool., Anat., Anth., Eth., Tax., Ent.**

Wood, John H., M.B., Tarrington, Herefordshire. *Lepid.*

Wood, Theodore, St. Peter's, Thanet, Kent. *Ent: Brit. Coleopt.* C. Ex.*

Wood, Wm., M.D., 99 Harley St., London. *Psychological Medicine.*

Woodall, John Woodall, M.A., F.G.S., St. Nicholas House, Scarborough. *Geol.*

Woodcock, Reginald C., 28 Abingdon St., London, S.W. *Min.*

Woodgate, John, Richmond Road, New Barnet, Herts. *Ent., Exotic Lepid.*

Wood-Martin, Lt. Col., M.R.I.A., F.R.H.A.A.I., Claveragh, Sligo, Ireland. *Lake Dwellings of Ireland, Hist. of Sligo.**

Wood-Mason, James, Painswick, Gloucestershire. *Gen. Biol., Invert. Anat., Articulates, Lepid., Orthopt., Arach., Crustacea.* C. Ex. (See India.)

Woods, Thos., M.D., Parsonstown. *Chem.*

Woods, W. Fell, 1 Parkhill, Forest hill, S.E. London. *Mic.**

Woodward, Bernard P., F.G.S., F.R.M.S., Librarian Nat. Hist. Mus., 28 Batoum Gardens, London, W. *Land and Fresh-water Mollusca, recent and fossil.**

Woodward, Arthur Smith, British Museum (Nat. Hist.), South Kensington, London, S.W. *Palaeo., Vert., Anat.**

Woodward, B. H., 80 Petherton Road, Highbury, New Park. *Min.**

Woodward, Henry, LL D., F.R.S., British Museum (Natural History Branch), South Kensington, London, S.W.

Woodward, Horace B., F.G.S., Geological Survey of England, Museum, 28 Jermyn St., London, S.W. *English Geol.**

Woodward, Jas., B.Sc., F.I.C., Laboratory, Somerset House, London. *Bot., Org. and Inorg. Chem., Phys., Mic., Gen. Biol.**

Wooler, William, 6 Wolsey Terrace, King Henry St., Mildmay Road. *Lepid.*

Woollcombe, Walter G., M.A., F.R.A.S., F.L.S., Exeter, Devonshire. *Phys., Ast., Chem., Bot., Gen. Biol., Coleopt.* C.*

Woollett, John, 58 Cloudesley Road, Islington, N. London. *Mic.**

Workman, Thomas, Bedford St, Belfast, Ireland. *Arach.* C. Ex. Madagascar and S. A. Desires original papers and notes on Arachnida (Eastern).*

Wormald, Percy C., 2 Clifton Villas, Highgate Hill, London, N. *Ent.*

Worsley, Rev. Thomas, M.A., Master of Downing College, Cambridge.

Worsley-Benison, H. W. S., F.L.S., 25 Grange Road, Canonbury, London, N. *Bot., Mic.*

Worthington, A. M., M.A., Clifton College, Clifton, Bristol. *Capillarity.*

Worthington, Richard, Champion Park, Denmark Hill, S. E. London. *Mic.**

Woundcott, T., Devonshire House, Farnham, Surrey. *Ast.*

Wray, W., F.R.A.S., Laurel House, North Hill, Highgate, N. *Ast.*

Wrey, G. E. B., Addington House, Addington Road, Reading. *Mic.**

Wright, B. M., 54 Guilford St., Russell Square, W. C. London. *Mic.**

Wright, Bryce, M.M.S., F.R.G.S., F.Z.S., 204 Regent St., London, W. *Min., Crystal., Met., Anth., Arch., Eth., Ethnog., Sponges.* C.*

Wright, Charles A., Knight of the Crown of Italy, F.L.S., F.Z.S., Kayhough House, Kew Gardens Road, Kew. *Orn., Bot., etc.**

Wright, Charles R. Alder, D.Sc., 3 Castellain Road, Maida Vale, London, W.

Wright, C. R. A., D.Sc., St. Mary's Hospital, Paddington, London. *Chem., Phys.*

Wright, Perceval, M.D., Trinity College, Dublin, Ireland. *Bot., Zool. (Alcyonaria).**

Wright, J., Backlane, Wakefield. *Gen. Ent.*

Wright, Joseph, F.G.S., 1 Donegal St., Belfast, Ireland. *Foraminifera.* C. Ex. recent or fossil Foraminifera.*

Wyatt, Claude W., Adderbury, Banbury. *Orn.*

Wyatt-Edgell, Arthur, F.G.S., Cowley House, Exeter. *Palæo., Sil. Lamellibranchiata.*

Wyles, Thomas, F.G.S., F.R.Hts.S., Allesley Park Coll., Warwickshire. *Geol., Biol.* C.*

Wynne, A. B., F.G.S., 14 Hume St., Dublin, Ireland. *Geol.*

Yates, Geo. E., F.S.A., Dean, Villa Swinton, near Manchester. *Ancient and barbaric weapons, coins, relics of savage tribes.*

Yates, Robert, 64 Park street, Southwark, London, S.E. *Mic.**

Yockney, Samuel Hansard, M. Inst. C.E., Queen Anne's Gate, Westminster, London, S.W.

Yool, Henry, Oakfield, Weybridge, Surrey. *Mic.*

York, His Grace William Thomson, D.D., Lord Archbishop of. The Palace, Bishopthorpe, Yorkshire.

Yorkshire Philosophical Soc., Museum, York. Hon. Sec., T. S. Noble, F.G.S., F.R.A.S.; Keeper, H. M. Platnauer, B.Sc., A.R.S.M.*

Young, J. T., 27 Hampton Park Road, Hackney, London, E. *Geol. and Stone Implements.*

Young, Morris, Free Museum, Paisley, Scotland. *Ent.*

Young, Robert, 7 Donegal Sq., East Belfast, Ireland. *Arch.* C. Ex.

Young, Frank W., F.C.S., F.R.S.E., High School, 2 Airlie Terrace, Dundee, Scotland. *Chem.*

Young, Jas. Browning, Commander Royal Navy, Present address, 2 Elgin Villas, Rodwell, Weymouth; Permanent address "Admiralty, Whitehall," London, S.W. *Ool.* C. Ex.*

Young, John, M.D., F.R.S.E., Prof. Nat. Hist., Univ. of Glasgow, Glasgow, Scotland. *Geol., Palæo.*

Young, John, F.Z.S, M.B.O.U., 64 Hereford Road, Westbourne Grove, and St. Stephen's Club, London, W. *Orn., Bot.*

Young, Sydney, D.Sc., F.C.S., Prof. of Chem., Univ. College, Bristol.*

Younge, Rev. Duke, Puslinch, Yealmpton, Devon. *Elect.*

Young, William M., 16 Maclise road, West Kensington Park, W. London. *Mic.**

Younghusband, Charles Wright, Royal Arsenal, Woolwich, and Athenæum Club, London, S.W.

Zerffi, G. G., Ph.D., F.R.S.L., F. R. Hist. S., Prof. Art. Hist., South Kensington. Address 8 Warrington Gardens, Maida Hill, London, W. *Sci. of Gen. and Art. Hist.* C.*

BERMUDA.

Peniston, Annie M., Penistons, The Flatts. *Moll.* C. Ex. Shells of Bermuda for those of other localities. Sea-shells preferred, and only good specimens desired.

CENTRAL AMERICA.

COSTA RICA.

Carmigol, San José. *Bot.*

GUATEMALA.

Farfan, Dr. José, Prof. Univ., Guatemala. *Bot.*
Grelck, Juan, Bot. Coll., Guatemala. *Bot.*
Luna, Dr. David, Prof Univ., Guatemala. *Phys., Chem., Bot.*
Peper, E., Guatemala. *Ent.*
Rockstroh, Edwin, National Institute, Guatemala. *Zool.*
Rodriguez, Juan José, Dir. Zool. Mus., Guatemala. *Bot., Gen. Zool.*
Sarg, Francis C., Vice-Consul German Empire, Coban. *Zool., esp. Spiders and Fresh Water Fishes.*
Stoll, De Otto, Guatemala. *Myriopoda.*
Türckheim, Freiherr H. von, Coban, Alto Vera Paz. *Bot., Lepid.* C. Ex.
Yela, Dr. Joaquim, Prof. Univ., Guatemala. *Bot., Nat. Hist.*

HONDURAS.

Thieme, Dr. Carolo, San Pietro. *Bot., Ent., Con.* C. Ex.

NICARAGUA.

Calderon y Arana, Salvador, Leon.
Clay, T. H., Matagalpa.
Downing, Dr. Alex. A., Granada. *Anth.* Ex. for any kind of specimens new to Nicaragua.
Flint, Earl, Rivas. *Antiquarian, Arch.*
Harper, Henry, Granada. *General Science.*
Harper, Col. I. H., Rivas. *Nat. Hist.*
Henry, William, Granada. *Reptiles.*
Janson, E. M., Las Lajas, Chontales. *Ent.*
Levy, Paul, Granada. *Bot.*

SAN SALVADOR.

Ulex, Oscar, San Salvador. *Lepid., Coleopt.* C.

GREENLAND.

Taylor, Joseph Walter, Noungme.

MEXICO.

Aguilar, Panciano, Guanajuato. *Mining Engineer.*
Ajuria, Agustin, Guanajuata. *Mining Engineer.*
Alcacio, Donaciano, City of Mexico. *Bot.*
Alcaráz, Ramon Y., City of Mexico. *Agric.*
Altamirano, Ignatius, M., "La República," City of Mexico.
Altamirano, Fernando, City of Mexico. *Bot.*
Anda, Francisco de, M. E., Manager of the Mint, Guanajuato.
Anda, Luis de, M. E., Assayer of the Mint, Guanajuato.
Anda, Manuel de, M. and C. E., Manrique, 6, City of Mexico. *Strat. Geol., Min., Met., Meteo.*
Andanegui, Juan B., Pinos, Zacatecas. *Min.*
Anguiano, Angel, Tacubaya. *Ast.*
Arevalo, Dr. José S., Morelia. *Nat. Hist.*
Arriaga, José Joaquin, Mem. Mex. Nat. Hist. Soc., City of Mexico. *Bot., Zool.*
Ayme, Luis H., Merida, Yucatan. *Arch.*
Barcena, Mariano, Director del Observatorio Central, Prof. de Geol. and Palæo., Museo Nacional, City of Mexico. *Geology.* C.
Barroeta, Prof. G., M.D., San Luis Potosi. *Phys., Zool., Bot.* C. Ex.
Barroso, Agustin, City of Mexico. *Bot.*
Blanco, Luciano, Guadalajara. *Mining Engineer.*
Blazquez, Prof. Ignacio, Nat. Hist. Coll., Puebla. *Bot.*
Bonilla, J. A., Zacatecas. *Min.*
Calcira, Isidro, Aguas Calientes.
Campa, Luis, Mina de Mellado, Guanajuato. *Mining Engineer.*
Carrillo, M., Engineer, Leon.
Castillo, Antonio del, City of Mexico. *Geol., Palæo.*
Cervantez, Faustino, Calle de la Esampa, 2, Morelos.
Chazaro, M. M., Tlacotalpam. *Bot.*
Chico, Dr. Jesus, Hospital, Guanajuato. *Hygiene.*
Contreras, Manuel, Colegio del Estado, Guanajuato. *Ast.*
Contreras, Juan N., Guanajuato. *Mining Engineer.*
Crespo, Gilberto, City of Mexico. *Min.*
Cubas, Antonio G., City of Mexico.
Dondé, R. Juan, Prof. Pharm., Chem. and Nat. Hist., Calle de los Rosados, No. 48, Merida, Yucatan. *Bot., Zool., Ent: Coleopt., Orn., Chem.* C. Ex.
Dugès, Alfredo, Prof. Nat. Hist., Colegio del Estado, Guanajuato. *Zool., Bot., Vert., especially Reptiles.* C.
Dugès, Dr. Eugène, Tupataro, Guanajuato. *Coleopt.*
Endner, Agustin, Assayer of the Mint, Oaxaca.
Fernandez, Leandro, Mexico. *Ast.*
Fernandez, Vicente, Prof. de Farmacía, Colegio del Estado, Calle de Pocitos del Cereza, Guanajuato. *Meteo.* C. Ex. Mexican birds for those of China and Australia.
Finck, Hugo, Cordova. *Arch., Bot., Geol.*
Flores, Dr. Reyes G., Calle de St. Domingo, Guadalajara. *Bot.*
Fornel, Ing. Manuel, Museo Nacional, Mexico. *Min.*
Garay, Dr. Tiburcio, Colegio del Estado, Guanajuato. *Met.*
Garcia, Dr. Crecensio, Cotija Michoacan. *Nat. Hist., Geol.* C. Ex.
Garcia Icazbalceta, Joaquin, City of Mexico.
Glennie, Francisco, Guanajuato. *Mining Engineer.*
Gonzala, J. Eleuterio, Monterey. *Bot.*

Gonzalez, Jesus, City of Mexico. *Bot.*
Guevara, Ignacio, Guadalajara. *Math.*
Gutierrez, José M., Ameca, Jalisco. *Bot.*
Heinemann, Dr. C., Vera Cruz. *Physiol.*
Herrera, Alfonso, Escuela Nacional Preparatoria ó 2, Calle de S. Juan, 4, City of Mexico. *Bot.*
Huacuja, Francisco F., Botica de San Francisco, Morelia. *Pharmacy Chem.*
Ibanez, Joaquin, Mem. Nat. Hist. Soc., Puebla. *Bot.*
Iparraguirre, Francisco Fernandez, Pharmacien, Guadalajara. *Bot.* C.
Iturbide Gomez, Dr. Luis, C. de la Pila de Zárate, 10, Morelia. *Medicine, Surgery.*
Jimenez, Francisco, Colegio del Estado, Guanajuato. *Phil.*
Johnson, Wm. D., Jr., Diaz, near La Ascension, Chihuahua, Mexico. *Ent.* C. Ex.*
Landero, C. F. de, Ingénieur Geographe et des Mines. Inspecteur des Mines. Prof. de Chimie à l'Ecole des Ingénieurs. P. O. Box 34, Guadalajara. *Min., Chem., Grad., Ast.* C. Ex.*
Lazo de la Vega, J. M., City of Mexico. *Bot.*
Leon, Miguel Velazquez de, M.E., Hacienda de Pabellon, Aguas Calientes. *Mining, Agriculture.* Can procure silver, copper and lead ore samples under an industrial point of view.
Lobato, Flavio, Guanajuato. *Min.*
López, Cárlos M., Aguas Calientes.
Lopez, Dr. Francisco, Calle 63, Morelos. *Meteo.*
Malo, Alberto, F., Rendicion de Pastiti, Guanajuata. *Mech. Engineer.*
Mariano Leal, Leon E. de, Guanajuato. *Chem., Meteo.* C. Ex. Has meteorological data for three years.
Medal, Dr. Melesio, Patzcuaro Michoacan. *Meteo., Bot.*
Médico, Paramo, City of Mexico. *Meteo.*
Mendivil, Cirilo Gomez, Lagos. *Agric.*
Mendoza, Gumesindo, City of Mexico. *Bot.*
Monroy y Salazar, Pedro L., San Luis Potosi. *Min.*
Moreno, Aniceto, Orizaba. *Bot.*
Munoz, Rudolfo, Real del Monte. *Mining Engineer.*
Muro, Luis, Colegio del Estado, Guanajuato. *Min.*
Navia, Severo, Prof. School of Mines, Guanajuato. *Min.*
Ochoa, Juan, City of Mexico. *Min.*
Oliva, Sabino, Guadalajara. *Bot.*
Oluda, Luis, Guanajuato. *Mining Engineer.*
Orages, Pablo, Guanajuato. *Mining Engineer.*
Párres, Joaquin, M. and C. E., Guanajuato. *Geol., Min., Crystal., Lithol., Met., Palæo.* C. Ex. mins. and rocks.
Pascal, Agustiss v., Guadalajara. *Ast., Geol.*
Peñafiel, Antonio, Dr., Dir. général de Statistique de Mexique. *Philologue Mexican et Antiquaire.**
Penzuela, Luis Robles, Calle S. José, Guanajuato. *Mining Engineer.*
Perez, Lalara, Chemist and Druggist, Prof. in the Institute of Science, Calle de Santa Teresa, 18, Guadalajara. *Chemistry and Pharmacy.*
Perez de Arce, Facundo, Guadalajara.
Perez y Arce, Manuel, Chemist and Druggist, Calle de Santa Monica, 4, Guadalajara. *Pharmacy and Chemistry.*
Peza, Juan de Dios, City of Mexico.
Prieto, Raoul, P. O. Box 34, Guadalajara. *Chem., Min., Elect., Ast., Meteo.* C. Ex.*
Puente, Feliciano G., Boticario, Morelos. *Pharmacy.*
Puga, Nicolais, Guadalajara. *Chem.*
Quijano, Ficaro, Mazatlan. *Bot.*

Rables, Dr. Joaquin, Calle Sn. Felipe Neri, 19, City of Mexico. *Surgery.*
Ramirez, Dr. José, Prof. de Zool. en el Museo Nacional y en la Escuela de Agricultura, City of Mexico. *Zool., Mic., Anth.**
Ramirez, Santiago, Calle de Buenavista, 15, City of Mexico. *Mining Engineer.**
Ramos, José, City of Mexico. *Bot.*
Reynoso, Francisco, M.E., Prof. de Fisica en el Colegio del Estado. *Geol., Min., Crystal., Lithol., Met., Physics.* C. Ex.
Reyes, Manuel O., City of Mexico. *Bot.*
Rocha, Ignacio G., Calle de Sopena, Guanajuato. *Mining Engineer.*
Romero, Carlos, Prof. de Géologie et de Paléontologie au Collége, Guanajuato.
Salgado, Dr. Francisco, Colegio del Estado. Guanajuato. *Pathol.*
Sanchez, Jesus, City of Mexico. *Zool.*
Santibañez, Dr. Abraham, Colegio del Estado, Guanajuato. *Anat.*
Sauri, Ricardo, M.D., Merida, Yucatan. *Ent.*
Segura, José, City of Mexico. *Bot.*
Sepúlveda y Lucio, Fernando, Licenciado en Farmacia, Plaze, 6. Farmacia, Villa de Brihnega, Guadalajara. *Botany.* C. Ex.
Silva, J., Zacatecas. *Geol.*
Socket, Sherman G., Corralitos. *Met.*
Sumichrast, Prof., Tehuantepec. *Bot., Zool.*
Tena, Dr. Miguel, Botica de Guadalupe, Catarinas, 16, Morelia. *Bot., Meteo., History.* C. Ex.
Tonel, Jean, Cordova. *Bot.*
Unacuja, Francisco, Zacatecas. *Pharm., Bot.* C. Ex.
Urbina, Manuel, City of Mexico. *Bot.*
Valazco, Sr. José M., Museo Nacional, City of Mexico. *Zool.*
Valle, Felipe, Tacubaya, D.F. *Ast.**
Villada, Manuel, Nat. Museum, City of Mexico. *Bot., Zool.*
Wadgymar, L. A., City of Mexico. *Zool., Orn., Bot.* C.
Weidner, Dr. Frederick, Mazatlan. *Geol.*
Yarate, Francisco P., Zacatecas, *Mining.*

MIQUELON, L'ILE.

Delamare, Dr. E., Ile Miquelon, North Am. *Bot.*, et specialement. *Lichens Sphagnum.**

NEWFOUNDLAND.

Fowler, Great Placentia. *Mining.*
McKendrick, Neil, Great Placentia. *Mining.*
Murray, Alexander, C.M.G., F.G.S., Dir. Geological Survey of St. John's. *Palæo., Geol. Lithol., Chem.* C. Ex.
Somerville, Beverly R., M.D., Western Bay. *Medicine, Arch., Gen. Antiq., Eth.* Correspondence solicted from those desiring rare or current Postage Stamps.*

WEST INDIES.

ANTIGUA.

Nicolson, Dr., Antigua. *Bot.*

BAHAMA ISLANDS.

Saunders, Harry R., Nassau, N.P. *Ferns, Algæ, Sponges, Sea Shells.*

BARBADOES.

Webb, Right Rev. T. W., Prin. Coddington Coll.

CUBA.

Aguiar, Mauricio Alfonzo y, Ingenio Demolido, Santo Cristo. *Lepidoptera.* C.
Aguilera, Cayetano, Rue O'Reilly, 42, Havana.
Aguilera, Manuel Antonio, Rue O'Reilly, 42, Havana.
Babé, Dr., Con. del Museo de Historia Natural de la Acad. de Ciencias médicas, fisicas y naturales, Calle de San Isidro, Havana. *Moll.* C.
Blain, José, San Cristobal. *Bot.*
Cabrera y Martinez, José, Santa Maria del Rosario. *Lepid.*
Casals y Sust, Jorge, Calle de Galiano, 69, Havana. Lepid.
Cisneros, Andrés M. de, Cardenas. *Con.* Ex.
Clerk, Francisco, Rector del Colegio de los Bdoz Escolapios de Guanabacoa. *Min., Moll.* C.
Garro, Felix Suarez, Calle de Manrique, 111, Havana. *Lepid.*
Gundlach, Juan, Ph.D., Ingenio Fermina, Bemba, Island of Cuba. *Mam., Orn., Herpetol., Con., Ent.* C. of the Cuban sp.*
Gutierez, Dr. José Nicolas, Rector de la Univ., Calle del Sol., Havana. *Zool., Moll.* C.
Lachaume, Jules, Dir. of the Acclimatation Garden, Havana. *Bot.**
Latorre, Carlos, Colegio de San Carlos, Matanzas. *Zool.* C.
Martin, Angel, Mauranillo. *Orn.*
Martinez, José Cabrera, Sta. Maria del Rosario, Cotorro, Cuba. *Ent.: Lepid.* C. Ex. Correspondence in French or Spanish.*
Morales, Dr. Sebastian A. de, Calle de Verlarde, 5, Matanzas. *Bot.*
Poey, Dr. Felipe, Calle de San Nicolas, 96, Havana. *Ichth.*
Presas, J. Manuel, Matanzas. *Bot.*
Reinoso, Fernando, Calle de las Animas, 135, Havana.
Santos Fernandez, Dr. Juan, Paseo de Tacon, Carlos III, Quimba de Foca, Havana.
Sauvalle, Francisco A., Havana. *Bot.*
Yradi, José, Cayetano. *Ent.*

CURACOA.

Wills, J., Lainson, care Messrs. Evertez, Curaçoa. *Min.*

DOMINICA.

Nicholls, Henry Alfred Alford, M.D., F.L.S., M.R.C.S., Corr. Memb. N. Y. Acad. Sci., Dominica. *Nat. Hist., Zool., Bot.* C.

GUADELOUPE.

Boname, P., Dir. Agric. Station, Pointe à Pitre. *Bot.*
Colardeau, Dr. St. Felix, Basseterre. *Bot.*

JAMAICA.

Allen, Dr., Kingston. *Polycystina.*
Bancroft, Espeut, William, F. L. S., Spring Garden, Buff Bay, *Bot., Geol., Chem., Elect., Meteo., Zool.*
Bowrey, James John, F.C.S., F.J.C., Gov't Analytical Chemist, Kingston. *Chem., Ent., Gen. Nat. Hist.*
Brennan, J. F., District Engineer's Office, Kingston. *Physical Science.*
Bürger, Herman John, 88 King St., Kingston. *Geol., Min., Nat. Phil., Ast., Meteo.**
Cockburn, N. S., 14 East St., Kingston. *Ent.* C. Ex.
Elliott, Wm. R., Supt. Kings House, Kingston. *Gen. Economic Plants.*
Fawcett, Wm. B., Sc., F.L.S., Director of Public Gardens and Plantations. *Gen. Bot.* (Formerly of Brit. Mus. of Nat. Hist ,London.)*
Gilbert, Wm., Harbour St., Kingston. *Mic.*
Hall, Maxwell, M. A., F.R.A.S., Jamaica, W. I. *Meteo., Ast.**
Harris, Wm., Supt. Botanic Gardens, Kingston. *Palms, Ferns, Orchids*, etc.*
Henderson, Dr. G. C., Gordon Town. *Mic.*
Institute of Jamaica. Founded 1879. The Rev. Alex. Robb, D.D., Chairman; H. Priest, Sec. Museum and Library.*
Mais, Rev. J. L., Walton *Lepid.*
Vendryes, Henry, Solicitor, Kingston. *Con. and Fossils.**

MARTINIQUE.

Thiery, Mons., Martinique. *Maladies de plantes, Gen. Bot.*

PORTO RICO.

Alfan y Baralt, Antonio, San Juan. *Coleopt., Lepid.*
Guillerna, Cesar de, Ingeniero de Montes, San Juan. *Bot.*
Stahl, Dr. Augustin, Rayamon. *Moll.*
Vasconi, Dr. Angel, Ingeniero de Minas, San Juan. *Min., Geol., Palæo.*

ST. THOMAS.

Bryan, C. E., St. Thomas, Collector. *Bot.: Ferns, Mosses, Algæ, Crustacea, Moll., M., L. and F. W. Shells.* C.
Calderon, H. Charles, St. Thomas. *Bot., Herbarium specimens of the Flora of St. Thomas for sale.* Has thoroughly studied the medicinal plants of the Island and will extend researches to other portions of the W. I. Has commenced a medical herbarium and will prepare sets for distribution should sufficient inducement offer. C. Ex.
Eggers, H. F. A. Baron, St. Thomas. *Bot.*

SAN DOMINGO.

Deboux, Dr. J. B., Dir. Med. Sch., Port-au-Prince. *Bot.*
Droit, Prof. J., Medical School, Port-au-Prince. *Bot.*

SANTA CRUZ.

Dahl, Christian, Santa Cruz. *Bot.*

TRINIDAD.

Caracciolo, Henry H., Customs, Port of Spain, Trinidad, W. I. *Mic. Photo., Ent., Lepid., Coleopt., Hemipt., Orthopt., Neuropt.* C. Ex.*
Cort, Dr. J., Port of Spain. *Bot.*
Guppy, R. J. Lechmere, F.L S., F.G.S., Superintendent of Education, Trinidad. *Geol., Con.* C.*
Hart, John Hinchley, Superintendent Botanical Department, Trinidad, W. I. *Bot., Ent., Mic., Algæ, Cryptogamia.* C. Ex.*
Marshall, Rev. T. A., M.A., Golconda Estate near San Fernando. *Ent.*

SOUTH AMERICA.

ARGENTINE REPUBLIC.

Aguirre, Eduardo, Ing. Catedrático de Mineralogía y Geología en la Universidad de Buenos Ayres.*
Ameghino, Dr. Florentino, Vicedirector del Museo Provincial de La Plata.*
Arata, Dr. Pedro N., Catedrático de Química Orgánica en la Universidad y Dir. de la Oficina Química Municipal de Buenos Ayres.*
Balbin, Dr. Valentin, Catedrático de Matematicas superiores en la Universidad de Buenos Ayres.*
Berg, Dr. Carlos, Catedrático de Zoología y de Botánica en la Universidad y de Historia Natural en el Colegio Nacional de Buenos Ayres. Casilla de Correo, 169. *Ent. gen.* C.*
Beuf, Francisco C., Director del Observatorio Astronómico Provincial de La Plata.*
Burmeister, Dr. Hermann, Director del Museo Nacional de Buenos Ayres. *Zool.**
Döring, Dr. Adolfo, Catedrático de Química en la Universidad de Cordova. *Geol, Palæo., and Con.**
Doering, Dr. Oscar, Prof. of Phys. in the Nat. Univ., Pres. of the Nat. Acad. of Sci. of the Argentine Republic. Dir. of the Meteorological Service of the Province of Cordova. Vice-Consul to the German Empire. Cordova. *Phys., Meteo., Terrestr. Magnetism, Geog.**
Frenzel, Dr. Juan, Catedrático de Zoología en la Univ. de Cordova.*
Günther, Guillermo, Maestro Pintor en los Talleres del Ferro-Carril del Oeste en Tolosa (La Plata). *Coll. of Ins.* Ex.*
Hilzinger, Jorge, Preparador, Calle Moreno, 457, Buenos Ayres. *Coll. of Ins.* C.*
Holmberg, Dr. Eduardo L., Catedrático de Historia Natural en la Escuela Normal, etc., de Buenos Ayres, Calle Cerrito, 416. *Arach., Hymenopt., Ichth.* C.*
Kurtz, Dr. F., Catedrático de Botánica en la Universidad de Cordova. C. Ex.
Kyle, F.F.F., Catedrático de Química en el Colegio Nacional y Director Químico de la Casa de Moneda de Buenos Ayres.*
Lynch-Arribálzaga, Enrique, San Antonio de Arcco, Estancie Santa Rosa. *Dipt.* Ex.*
Lynch-Arribálzaga, Felix, Chacabaco (Prov. de Buenos Ayres.) *Coleopt.* Ex.*
Mayano, Carlos Maria, Buenos Ayres. Celebrated Explorer of Patagonia. Lieutenant of the Navy in the Argentine Army.*
Mitre, Gen. Bartolomé, Buenos Ayres.*

Moreno, Dr. Francisco P., Director del Museo Provincial de La Plata. *Anth., Palæo.**
Newberry, Dr. Edward, 125 Calle Florida, Buenos Ayres. *Psych.**
Parodi, Dr. Domingo, Calle Defensa, 185, Buenos Ayres. *Chem.* C.
Puiggari, Dr. Miguel, Catedrático de Química Analítica y Farmacéutica en la Universidad de Buenos Ayres.*
Quiroga, Dr. Atanasio, Catedrático de Química Inorgánica en la universidad y en el Colegio Nacional de Buenos Ayres.*
Roth, Santiago, San Nicolas. *Palæo.* C.*
Ruscheweyh, George, Merch. Calle Tucuman, 500, Buenos Ayres. Poss. of the largest Coll. of Lepidopt. in So. America. Ex.*
Spegazzini, Dr. Carlos, Catedrático de Historia Natural y de Química en el Colegio Nacional de La Plata. *Bot.* C. Ex.*
Thome, John M., Dr., Dir del Observatorio Astronómico Nacional en Cordoba.*
Zeballos, Dr. Estanislao S., Calle Belgrano 1130, Buenos Ayres. *Geog., Arch., Anth.**

BRAZIL.

Alf Georges, Villa Trabel, Rio de Janeiro. *Ent., Con., Vert.*
Bauer, Henrique Ernesto, Ignapc, Provincia, São Paulo. *Min., Mic., Lithol.**
Barbosa Rodrigues, Dr. João, Manáos, Provincia do Amazonas, Dir. Botanical Mus. of the Amazon. *Phæn. Bot., Palms, Orchids, Anth., Arch., Ethnog.* C. Ex.*
Bonninghausen V. V., p. o. box. 775, Rio de Janerio. *Ent., Specialty Lepid.**
Bom-Retiro, Pedreira, Vizconde de, Rio de Janeiro. *Geog., Eth.*
Breistenbach, Dr. Wilhelm, Porto Alegre, Rio Grande do Sul. *Ent.: Orthopt.*
Capanema, Dr. L. S. de, Consul, Rue de San Leopoldo, 1, Rio de Janeiro. *Bot.*
Carvalho, Dr. Pedro A. de, Dir. Hospital Misericordia, Rio de Janeiro.
Cruls, Dr. Louis, Dir. Ast. Obs., Rio de Janeiro. *Ast.*
Derby, Orville A., Dir. of Section of Geol. and Min., Mus. Nacional, Rio de Janeiro. Dir. Com. Geog. et Geol. da Prov. de São. Paulo. *Palæo., Strat. Geol., Min., Lithol.**
De Souza, Dr. Ennes, M.E., Dr. Phil., Prof. Met., Polytech. School, Rio de Janeiro. *Min., Met.*
Dom Pedro II, Emperor of Brazil, Rio de Janeiro. *Ast.*
Freitas, Francisco José de, Sub. Dir. da Sec. de Geol. e Min., Mus. Nacional, Rio de Janeiro. *Palæo., Geol., Min.*
Freire, Prof. Dr. Domingos José, Med. School, Rio de Janeiro. *Org. Chem.**
Gama, Dr. J. Saldanha da, Prof. Bot., Polytech. School, Rio de Janerio. *Bot.*
Glaziou, Dr., Dir. Public Gardens, Rio de Janeiro. *Bot.**
Gorceix, Dr. Henri, Dir. School of Mines, Ouro Preto, Prov. de Minas. *Min., Geol.*
Hahnel, San Paulo, Upper Amazon. *Ent.*
Homen de Mello, Dr. Francisco Ignacio M., Baron de, Rio de Janeiro. *Geol., Eth.*
Lacerda, Dr. J. B., Dir. Zool. Sec., Mus. Nacional, Rio de Janeiro. *Zool., Gen. Biol., Exper. Physiol., Eth.*
Löfgren, Alberto, Morton College, San Paulo. *Bot., Algology, F. W. Algæ.* C. Ex.
Magalhães, Dr. J. V. C. de, Rio de Janeiro. *Geog., Eth.*

Mathan, de, Mare, Pará. *Ent.*
Moreira, Dr. Nicolão, Sub-Dir. Bot. Sec., Nat. Mus., Rio de Janeiro. *Bot.*, *Agric.*
Müller, Fritz, Blumenau, Santa Cattarina.*
Netto, Dr. Ladislau, Dir. General Mus. Nacional, Rio de Janeiro. *Bot.*, *Anth.*, *Arch.*, *Eth.*, *Ethnog.**
Neave, Dr. John, Rue de Principe, 14, San Paulo. *Mycol.*
Peixoto, Dr. J. Rodrigues, Rio de Janeiro. Zoologiste et anthropologiste, attaché au Museo Nacional de Rio Janeiro.*
Penna, Ferreira, Pará.
Puiggari, Dr. Juan I., Apiahy, San Paulo. *Cryptogamia.* C. Ex.
Regnelé, Dr. A. F., Caldas, Minas Geraes. *Bot.*
Ribeiro, Julio, Morton College, San Paulo. *Philol.*
Ringgani, Juan T., Apiahy, San Paulo. *Cryptogamia.*
Rio Branco, J. M. de Silva, Rio Janeiro. *Geog.*, *Eth.*
Rodde & Pape, Dealers, Bahia.
Rodregues, Dr. J. Barbosa, Rio Janeiro. *Bot.*, *Eth.*
Saldanha da Gama, Escola Polytechnica, Rio de Janeiro.
Sequeira, Luis A., Belgian Consul, Pernambuco.
Souza, Fontes, Prof. Dr., Rio de Janeiro. *Geog.*, *Eth.*
Thire, Prof. Arthur, School of Mines, Ouro, Prov. de Minas. *Min.*
Tootal, Albert, Rio de Janeiro. *Anth.*
Wilson, A. H., Pará.

CHILI.

Domeyko, Ignacio, Catedrático de Mineralogia de la Universidad de Santiago. C.
Espic, Juan Edwin, Delicias 269 B., Santiago. *Bot.*, *Mic.*, *Infusoria.*
Leyboldt, Friedrich, Santiago.
Philippi, Federico, Director del Jardin Botanico y Catedrático de la Universidad y del Instituto Nacional, Santiago. *Bot.*, *Ent.**
Philippi, Dr. R. A., Director del Museo Nacional, Santiago. *Zool.*, *Bot.**
Reed, Edwin C., Calle Collegia, Valparaiso.

ECUADOR.

Cordero, Luis, 14 Carabobo St., Cuenca. *Bot*, *Hort.*
Destruge, Dr., Guayaquil.
Flores, A., Quito.
Gomez, Valdez O., Guayaquil.
Herrera, P., Quito.
Larrea, Manuel Angel, Quito.
Matovelle, Julius, Cuenca.
Peralta, Agustin J., 41 Solano Str., Cuenca. *Bot.*, *Hort.*, *Phys.*, *Philol.*, *Ent.* *Sells Coleopt. and Lepid.**

BRITISH GUIANA.

Campbell, W. H., LL.D., Sec. Roy. Agric. and Commercial Soc., Georgetown.
Exley, Percival, B.A., Prin. Queen's Coll., Georgetown. *Orn.*
Francis, E. E. H., F.C.S., Government Analytical Chemist, Georgetown. *Chem.*
Hawtayne, Geo. H., Georgetown. *Zool.*
im Thurn, Everard F., M.A., Pomeroon River. *Anth.*, *Orn.**

Jenman, G. S., F.L.S., Government Botanist, Georgetown. *Bot.*
Russell, Hon. William, Georgetown. *Hydrostatics and Scientific Agric. (Tropical).*
Scard, F. I., F.C.S., Georgetown. *Analyt. Chem.*

DUTCH GUIANA.

Burls, Herbert Thomas, care of M. de Mesquita, Paramaribo, Surinam.

PERU.

Barranca, José S., Lima. *Arch., Nat. Hist.*
Chacaltana, Cesareo, Lima.*
Dibos, Felix, Lima.
Macedo, Mariano, Lima. *Arch.*
Mendiburn, Gen. Manuel de, Lima.
Mesa, Pio B., Cuzco. *Arch.*
Pasapera, Manuel S., Lima.
Quiros, Francis, F.L.S., Lima.
Sanchez Hipólito, Arequipa.

URUGUAY.

Arechavaletea, José, Catedrático de Botanica de la Universidad de Montevideo. *Crypt.* C.
Arteaga, Rudolfo de, Assoc. M. Inst. C.E., Mem. Soc. of Arts of the Geol. Soc. of King's Coll., and of the Scientific and Mechanical Soc. of Manchester, and of the Sociedad Cientifica Argentina, 68 Rincon, Montevideo.
Barrial, Posada Clementé, Montevideo. *Min., Geol., Palæo.*
Fleury, L., M.D., Montevideo. *Surgery.*
Gomez-Ruano, Alberto, Catedrático de Física de la Universidad de Montevideo.
Maeso, Justo, Montevideo. *Geol.*
Mendez, Gualberto, M.D., Montevideo. *Surgery.*
Vidal, Francisco A., M.D., Montevideo. *Surgery.*

U. S. OF COLOMBIA.

Balen, Carlos, Bogotá. *Lepid.*
Perez, Lazaro Maria, Bogotá.
Thiel, Dr. Julius, Panama. *Lepid., Coleopt.* Collects and sells spec. of Nat. Hist.
Zeltner, M. A. de, Panama.

VENEZUELA.

Acosta, Cecilio, Caraccas.
Ernst, A., Caraccas.
Francis, Henry, New Quebrada Mines, care Messrs. Boulton & Co., Puerto Cabello.

PART II.

EUROPE.

AUSTRO-HUNGARY.

Abel, Dr. L., Hochschule für Bodencultur, Wien. *Agric.*
Aberle, Carl, Prof. Dr., Wien. *Bot.*, *Geol.*, *Anthropol.*
Abt, Dr. Anton, Ord. Prof. der Physik an der K. Ung. Franz-Josef Universität, Klausenburg. *Physics.* C.
Achleitner, Carl, Weilbach bei Obernberg. *Coleopt.* C. Ex.
Adolf, Dr. Kunc, Ritter des Franz-Josef Ordens, Csorna. *Physics.* C.*
Albrecht, Ch., Lackstr. 42, Graz. *Min.*, *Shells*, *Coleopt.*, *Lepid.**
Alexi, Dr. A. P., Prof. der Naturwissenschatten am Obergym. zu Nassod; Mitgl. Anthr. Ges., Wien. *Bot.*, *Geol.* C. Ex. offers curiosities of Carpathian flora; Senecillis, etc.
Almásy, Móricz, Wien. *Geol.*
Alth, Dr. Alois v., Prof. Min., University, Krakau. *Geol.*, *Palæo.* C.
Ambrosi, Fr., Dir. Museum, Trent. *Bot.*
Andreis, Johann, Mariehilf 30, Innsbruck. *Lepid.* C. Ex.
Angelis, Joh., Prague, Bohemia. *European Lepid.*
Anker, Ludwig, Bahngasse 13, Budapest. *Lepid.*, *Coleopt.*
Anker, Rudolf, Monor, Pester Comitat. *Lepid.*, *Coleopt.* Ex.*
Antoine, Fr., Dir. Imp. Gar. of Hofburg, Wien. *Bot.*
Aurel, Scherfel W., Azotfaker, Felka. *Bot.*
Ausserer, Anton, Prof. Dr., am I. Staatsgymn. Gratz. *Zool.*, *Arach.*
Babo, A. von, Klosternenburg. *Bot.*
Bach, Dr. József, Szecseny. *Geol.*
Baczó, Gabriel, Prof. an der Hochschule, Zilah. *Bot.*
Barbieux, August, Rothenthurmstr. 18, Wien. *Lepid.*
Barth, Jos., Lagenthal, near Blasendorf. *Bot.* C.
Barth v. Bartenau, Prof. E., Univ., Wien. *Chem.*
Bartscht, Ambros, Hauptstr. 4, Hernals, *Lepid.*
Bauer, Dr. A., Prof. Polytechnicum, Kärnthnerstrasse 20, Wien, I. *Chem.*
Bauer, C., Bot. Gar., Lemberg. *Bot.*
Bauer, Dr. Ernst A., Bohemia, Smichow 567. *Coleopt.* (*Carabic.*, *Ceramb.*), *Dipt.**
Baumler, J. A., Durrmantthorg. 26, Pressburg. *Bot.*
Becher, Dr. Eduard, k. k. Zoolog. Hofcabinet, Wien. *Diptera*, *Mollusca.*
Beck, Dr. Günther, Herrengasse 14, Wien. *Bot.*
Becke, Friedrich, Ph.D., Prof. Min. Univ. Czernowitz, Bukowina. *Petrography.*
Beckerhinn, Dr. C., Hintere Zollamtsstrasse 3, Wien, III. *Chem.*
Behmann, Dr. A., Kozyzowa 21, Krakau. *Bot.*
Belohoubek, A., Prof. Univ., Prague, Bohemia. *Chem.*
Benedikt, Moriz, Prof. Univ., Franciskaner-Platz 5, Wien, I. *Elect.*, *Neurology*, *Anthr.* C. Ex.*
Benedikt, Dr. R., Hochschule, Schwindgasse 18, Wien, IV. *Chem.*
Bennodorf, G., Prof. Univ., Wien. *Arch.*
Benz, Robert von, Sillgasse, Innsbruck. *Phæn. Bot.* C. Ex.

Berecz, Anton v., Dir. K. Ung. höh. Staats-Töchterschule, Gen. Sec. Ung. Geograf. Ges., Redacteur der "Mitth." dies. Ges. seit 15 Jahren, Budapest. *Physics and Geog.*
Bergenstamm, J. Edler v., Tempelgasse 8, Wien, II. *Diptera**
Bermann, Joseph, Secretär d. k. k. Gartenbau-Gesellschaft und Lehrer an der Gartenbau-Schule, Weihburggasse 31, Wien, I. *Botany.* C.
Bernard, Karl, Hochgräfl. Eduard Palffy von Erdödscher, Oberförster in Vacikou bei Preznitz via Pribram, Bohemia. *Coleoptera, Lepid.*
Bertolini, Dr. Stefano de Bargo, Tyrol. *Coleopt.*
Berwerth, Dr. Fritz, Kustos-Adjunkt am k. k. Naturhist. Hofmuseum, Wien. *Min., Petrog.**
Biasioli, Prof. Carl, Dornbirn. *Entomology, Con.* C.
Bidschof, Dr. Friedrich, Asst. der k. k. Sternwarte, Währing bei Wien. *Ast.**
Bielz, Eduard Albert, Pres. d. Siebenbürg. Vereins für Naturwissenschaften, Hermannstadt. *Geol., Min., Zool., Arch., Moll.* C. Ex.
Birkenmajer, Dr. L., Univ., Krakau. *Physics.*
Biró, Ludwig, Reformiter Theolog, Rakos-Palota. *Hymenop., Coleopt.**
Bittner, Dr. A., Univ., Rasumofskygasse 23, Wien, III. *Geol., Palæo.*
Blaas, Dr. Josef, Docent an d. Univ. Innsbruck (Tyrol). *Geol., Petrography.* C. Ex.
Blaha, E., Wien, IV. *Moll.*
Blaha, Konrad, böhm. Sparcape, Prag. *Geol., Hydrol., Palæo.*
Blumentritt, Ferdinand, Prof. an d. Communal-Oberrealschule, Leitmeritz, Bohemia. *Geol., Bibliog., Geog. Dist., Anth., Arch., Eth., Ethnog., Philol.**
Böckh, Johann, Dir. Geologische Anstalt, Budapest. *Geol.*
Bogsch, Prof. Joh., Realschule, Pressburg. *Lepid.*
Bohatsch, Albert, Schreigasse 2, Wien, I. *Coleopt.*
Bohatsch, Otto, Bez., Fleischmannsg. 8, Wien, IV. *Lepid.*
Bohaty, A. Kaden, Brunnersdorf. *Coleopt.*
Böhm, Prof. J., Maysedergasse 3, Wien, I. *Morphology, Syst. Bot., Minerals and Meteorites.* Ex.*
Bolle, D., Görz. *Bot., Chem., Agric.*
Boltzmann, Dr. Ludwig, Univ. Prof., Halbärthgasse 1, Gratz. *Phys.*
Borbás, Prof. Dr. V. de, Dessewffygasse 3, Budapest. *Bot.* C.
Brandowski, A. R., Univ. Prof., Krakau. *Eth.*
Branik, Carl V., Vödritz 30, Pressburg. *Bot.**
Brassai, Prof. S., Univ. Klausenburg. *Math.*
Brauer, Prof. Dr. Friedrich Moritz, Custos am kais. zool. Hofmuseum, Prof. Zool. Univ.; Con. M. I. kais. Akad. d. Wissensch., Wollzeil 23, Wien, I. *Ent., Diptera, Neuroptera, Biology, Crustacea, Phyllopoda.* C.*
Braun, Rev. Ch., S. T. Dr., Mariaschein bei Teplitz, Bohemia. *Ast.**
Bredel J. H., Montanistiker, Privat, v. z. in Peggau, Gratz. *Met., Mic.* C. Ex.
Breidler, Obere, Stubergasse 12, Ottakring bei Wien. *Bot., Specialty, Bryology.**
Breitenlohner, Dr. Jacob, k. k. Hochschule für Bodencultur, Reitergasse 7, Wien, VIII. *Geol., Lithol., Meteo.*
Brezina, Dr. A., Custos. k. k. Naturhist. Hofmus.; Docent Univ., Wien. *Min., Lithol., Crystal., Meteorites.* Ex. minerals and meteorites for the Museum.*
Brock, Ingeneur, Budapest. *Coleopt.*
Brosche, Edward, Spargasse, Prag, Bohemia. *Bot.*
Brücke, Dr. E. W. von, Univ.-Prof. d. Physiol., Währingerstrasse 11, Wien, IX.*

Brühl, Dr. Jul. W., Chem. Lab., Hochschule, Lemberg, Galicia. *Chem.*
Brühl, Prof. K. B., Univ., Wien. *Zootomy, Comp. Anat., Osteol., Mic.*
Brunner v. Wattenwyl, Carl, Wien. *Orthopt.* C.
Brusina, Spiridion, Prof. der Universität und Dir. des Zool. National Museum, Zagreb (Agram), Croatia. *Zool., Palæo.*
Brzorád, I. Rudolph, Mogyorós, Ny-Ujfalu. *Geol.*
Buchmüller, Ferdinand, Burggasse 108, Wien, VII. *Ent.*
Buda, Adam von, Gutsbesitzer, Reapost. Hátszeg, Transylvania. *Orn., Zool., Geol.* C. Ex.
Bühler, Prof. Dr. G., C. I. E., Richardgasse 5, Wien. *Indian Epigraphy. and Law.*
Burány, Johann, Gran. *Palæo., Geol. Min.* C. Ex. Wishes minerals of America for fossils of Hungary.*
Bürgerstein, Dr. Alfred, Gymnasial-Professor, 75 Taborstrasse, Wien. *Physiology of Plants.**
Bürgerstein, Dr. L., Univ., Hörlgasse 15, Wien, IX. *Geol.*
Buza, Johann, Prof. an d. Reform-Hochschule, Sárospatak. *Bot., Diseases of Plants.* C.
Calderoni & Co., Budapest. *Zool., Skelete u. Schädel.**
Cech, Ludwig von, k. ung. Schichtmeister, Schemnitz. *Mountain Geol.* C. Ex.
Celakousky, Dr. Ladislaus, Prof. k. k. Universität, Korngasse 1672, Prag, Bohemia. *Flora of Bohemia.* C. Ex. for flora of America.
Charwath, Dir. d. k. k. Oberrealschule, Troppau. *Lepid.*
Chiari, Dr. H., Univ., Wien. *Pathol., Anat., Histol.*
Chyzer, Dr. Cornelius, S. A. Ujhely. *Arach., Coleopt.**
Ciesielski, Dr. Theophil, Prof. der Botanik an der Universität; Direktor des k. k. Botanischen Gartens, Lemberg. *Botany.* C. Ex. plants of Galicia for foreign.
Claus, K., Prof. an d. Univ., Wien. *Comp. Emb., Osteol., Zootomy.*
Cobelli, Dr. R. de, Rovereto. *Bot., Mycology.*
Csató, Johann von, Vicegespann des Unterweissenburger Comitats, Nagy-Enyed, Transylvania. *Orn., Bot.* C. Ex. Desires American birds and plants for those of Transylvania.*
Czerny, Prof. F. S., Univ., Krakau. *Physical Geog.**
Czerwiakowski, Prof. Dr. de, Krakau. *Bot.*
Czumpelik, Dr. E., Prof. an d. Univ., Wien. *Chem.*
Czyrnianski, E. Prof. an d. Univ., Krakau. *Chem.*
Dadai, Eugen, Dr. der Philol., Assistent an der Universität zu Klausenburg. *Entomostraca.* C. Ex.
Dahlström, Julius, Eperies. *Macro-lepidoptera.*. C. Ex.
Dalla Torre, Prof. Dr. K. von, Innsbruck. *Ent., Hymenop., Zool.*
De Adda, Sándor, Szlatina. *Geol.*
Degen, Arpad, foler von Zelsöhegy, Budapest, Rerepesi-Ut. 8. *Bot.**
Deininger, Emerich v., Prof. an d. kon. Ung. land. Akad.; Leiter der Samencontroll und pflanzenphys, Vers. Stat. Ung., Altenburg. *Bot., Phanerogams and plant culture.* C. Ex.*
Deires, Prof. Franz, Leutschau. *Orography.*
Dékány, Dr. Ráfael, Kecskemet. *Geol.*
Demeter, Dr. Karl von, Prof. am Collegium der Ev. Reform. Maros-Vásárhely. *Bot., Mosses.* C.*
Demuth, Theobald, Ritter, k. k. Finanzrath, Erdbergerstrasse 19, Wien. *Coleopt.*
Derzsi, K. Ferencz, Szekely-Udvarhely. *Geol.*
Deschmann, C. von, Museum, Laibach. *Bot.*
Dessewffy, Graf Nicolaus, Jr., Debreezin. *Coleopt.* C. Ex.
Dexter, Heinrich, Carlsbad, Bohemia. *Lepid.*

Deitz, Sandor, Budapest. *Bot.*
Ditscheiner, Prof. Dr. L., Hochschule, Sterngasse 6, Wien, I. *Phys.*
Dobiasch, Eugen, Gospich, Croatia. *Ent., Zool., Dipt., Moll., Hemipt., Coleopt., Hymen.* C. Ex.*
Doelter, Prof. Dr. Cornelio, Univ., Gratz. *Min., Lithol.**
Döll, E., Realschul-Dir., Wien. *Min., Geol.**
Domalip, Dr. C., Univ., Prague. *Phys.*
Donath, Dr. Julius, Gössergasse 3, Budapest. *Chem., Physiol.**
Dorfinger, Joh., Sallmansdorf near Wien. *Coleopt., Lepid.* C. Ex. Wishes American for European Lepid.*
Drasch, Dr. Otto, Maiffredygasse 2, Gratz. *Physiol., Histol.*
Drasche, Gustav, Wien. *Geol.*
Drasche-Wartinberg, Dr. Richard Baron v. Giselastrasse 13, Wien, I. *Zool., Invert., Anat., Embryology.**
Duda, Ladislaus, Prof. am Gymnasium, Königgrätz, Bohemia. *Ent., especially Hemipt.**
Durège, H., Univ.-Prof., Weinberge, bei Prag. *Math.**
Ebenhochöch, Franz, Rovonczó. *Bot.*
Eberstaller, Dr. Oscar, Gratz. *Anatomy.*
Ebner, Dr. Victor Ritter v., Univ. Prof., Göthegasse 19, Gratz. *Histol., Emb.*
Edelmann, Prof. Dr. S., Steinamanger. *Phys.*
Eger, Dr. L. Breitegasse 9, Wien, VII. *Palæo., Geol., Min., Met., Zool., Emb., Anat., Anth., Eth., Vert., Mam., Orn., Osteol., Ent.* C. Ex.*
Ehrlich, Franz Carl, k. Rath, Linz. *Geol.**
Eichhorn, Dr., Eckelstädt bei Camberg. *Coleopt.**
Eichler, Dr. Gustav, Teplitz. *Coleopt., Lepid.*
Eissen, Dr. Ede, Budapest. *Geol.*
Elekes, Karl, Prof. an der Hochschule, Nagy-Enyed. *Nat. Hist.*
Emich, Gust. v. Emöke, k. k. Truchsess, Franziscanerplatze 7, Budapest. *Lepid.* Buy and exchange.
Entz, Dr. Géza, Prof. der Zoologie und vergl. Anatomie an der k. Universität, Klausenburg. *Protozoa.* C.
Eötvös, Prof. L. Frhr. von, Univ., Budapest. *Phys.*
Erdinger, C., St. Pölten. *Bot.*
Erdody, Sandor, Budapest. *Geol.*
Ernst, Melle, M. Eysn., Thunstr. 10, Salzburg. *Bot.*
Escherich, Prof. G. von, Univ., Czernowitz. *Math.**
Esztrenga, István, Jász Berénv. *Geol.*
Ettingshausen, Prof. A. v., Univ., Gratz. *Phys.**
Ettingshausen, Baron Constantin von, Prof. der Bot., Univ., Laimberggasse 8, Gratz. *Fossil Plants, Tertiary Flora.* C.*
Exner, Prof. F., Univ., Wien. *Phys.**
Exner, Dr. K., Prof. am k. k. Staatsgymnasium, Währingerstrasse 29, Wien, IX. *Phys.*
Exner, Prof. Dr. Sigm., Univ., Wien. *Physiol.**
Eysn, M., Salzburg. *Bot.* Ex. Phanerogams.
Fabian, Prof. O., Univ., Lemberg. *Math., Phys.*
Fabiny, R., Prof. an d. Univ., Klausenburg. *Chem.*
Fabry, Prof. Joh., Mem. Naturwissenschaft-Gesell., Rimaszombat. *Phæn. Bot., Mosses, Fungi, Lichens, Lepid., Coleopt.* C. Ex.*
Feichtinger, Dr. Alexander, Gran. *Gen. Bot., Ent.*, C. Ex.*
Feichtinger, Dr. Sándor, Gran. *Gen. Bot., Ent.* C. Ex.*
Feistmantel, Carl, Smichow bei Prag, Bohemia. *Palæo., Bot.*
Feistmantel, Ottokar, M. D., late Palæontologist Geological Survey of India, now Professor Bohemian Polytech. High School Prague. *Veget., Palæo., Geol., Miner., Geog.**

Fekete, Jos., Bot. Gar., Budapest. *Bot.*
Felder, Dr. C. F. von, Wien. *Coleopt., Lepid.*
Fellner, Oskar, Schottenring 15, Wien, I. *Bot.*
Fellöcker, P. Sigmund, Prior der Benedictiner, Kremsmünster. *Min.*
Fiedler, Joh., Dir. der Zuckerfabrik, Fungbunzlau, Bohemia. *Coleopt.**
Finger, Dr. J., Prof. an d. Polytechnicum, Wien. *Phys.*
Fischer, Samu, Budapest. *Geol.**
Fleischer, Dr., Brünn, Moravia. *Coleopt.*
Fleischer, M. U. Dr., Ant., Brünn, Moravia. *Coleopt.* Ex.*
Fleischl, Dr. E. von Marxow, Prof. der Physiol., Univ., Wien.*
Fodor, Dr. John, Inst., of Anat., Mariastr., Budapest, VIII. *Moll., Coleopt.* C. Ex.*
Fodor, John, M. D., Mariastr. 39, Budapest, VIII. *Anat.*
Förster, J. B., Laderstrasse 20. *Bot., Bryology.*
Foullon, Baron Heinrich v., Adjunkt der k. k. geologischen Reichsanstalt, Wien. *Chem., Crystal.* C. Ex.*
Freyn, J., Beh. aut. Civil-Ingenieur, fürstl. Baurath, Karmelitergasse 15, Prague, III, Bohemia. *Botany, Phanerogams.* C. Ex. Ranunculus not European for European specimens.*
Freyn, Rudolph, Buchbergsthal bei Würbenthal. *Min.* C. Ex.
Fric, V., Wladislawsgasse 21a, Prague, Bohemia. *Min., Geol., Palæo., Zool.* C. Ex.*
Friedenfeldt, Otto Ritter v., Nikolsburg, Moravia. *Coleopt., Lepid.* C. Ex. European for foreign.*
Frisch, Dr. A. Ritter v., Prof. an der Kunst-Acad., Josefstädterstrasse 17, Wien, VIII. *Anat.*
Frischauf, Prof. Dr. Johann, Univ., Gratz. *Math.*
Fritsch, Prof. A., Univ., Prague, Bohemia. *Zool., Palæo.**
Frivaldsky, János, Museum, Budapest. *Ent., Coleopt., Geol., Con.*
Fröhlich, Dr. Prof. Isidor, Univ., Budapest. *Phys.*
Frosch, Louis, Porcellanmaler, Chodau bei Karlsbad, Bohemia. *Lepid.* C. Ex. Will purchase named collections of *Lepid.* from other countries.*
Fuchs, Dr. C. W. C., Meran, Tyrol. *Geol., Lithol., Inorg. Chem.*
Fuchs, Theodor, Custos am k. k. Naturhistor. Hofmuseum, Wien. Leiter der Geol. Palæo. Aletheilung. *Palæo. Geol. (Tertiary).**
Gaiger, Vincenz, Zara, Dalmatia. *Lepid.**
Galantai, Eszterhazy, Mikos, Budapest. *Geol.*
Gallik, Geza G., S. A. Ujhely. *Chemistry, Micro-Chemistry for Physiology, Pathology.* C. Ex.*
Gander, Linz. *Mosses, Hepatica, and Lichens.* C.
Ganglbauer, Ludwig, Custos-Adjunct am k. k. Naturhistorischen Hof-Museum, Wien. *Coleopt., Orthopt.**
Gartner, Anton, Brünn, Moravia. *Lepidoptera.*
Garzarolli v. Thurnlackh, Dr. K., Univ., Gratz. *Chem.*
Gatterer, k. k. Major i. P., Josephg. 10, Gratz. *Coleoptera of Europe.*
Gegenbauer, Prof. L., Univ., Innsbruck. *Math.*
Geiringer, Carl, Napazedl, Moravia. *Bot., Lepid.**
Genersich, Prof. A., Univ., Klausenburg. *Vert. Emb. and Anat., Osteol., Myol., Histol. of Vert.* C. Ex.*
Gerenday, Antal, Budapest. *Geol.*
Geyer, Prof. G. Julius, Iglo. *Pomologg, Meteo.* C. Ex.*
Glowacki, Prof. am Gymnasium, Pettan, Styria. *Bot.* C. Ex.*
Gobanz, Alois, Cavalese. *Coleoptera.*
Godlewski, Emil, Prof. der höheren landwirthschaftlichen Lehranstalt, Dublany, near Lemberg. *Physiology of plants.**
Goldschmidt, Dr. Vict., Wien. *Min.*
Goldzicher, Dr. Wilhelm, Docent an der Univ., Göttergasse 2, Budapest. *Pathol. Anat., Ophthal.* C. Ex.*

De
Di
D

[illegible], János, Budapest. Geol.
[illegible], Sándor, Salgótarján. Geol.
[illegible] Alex. von, Herény, bei Steinamanger. Phys., Meteo., Ast.*
[illegible] Eugen von, F.R.A.S., Herény, Astrophys. Observatorium bei Steinamanger. Phys., Ast., Astrophotogr. C.*
[illegible], Breitegasse 19, Neubau, Wien. Coleopt.*
[illegible], Prof. V., Univ., Czernowitz. Zool., Anat.
[illegible], Heinrich, Kassier und Stadt-Archivar, Eger, Bohemia. Coleoptera, Hemiptera, Hymenoptera.
Graeffe, Dr. Eduard, Inspector k. k. Zool. Stat., Trieste. Zool., esp. Marine Invert., Ent.: Hymenop., Coleopt., Lepid. of Fossil plants of Tertiary, Geogr.*
Graff, Dr. Ludwig von, Prof. d [illegible] Worms.*
Gredler, Vinceuz, Dir. des Privat-Gymnasinms, Bozen. *Coleoptera, Hemiptera.*
Gregus, János, Baroth (Erdely). *Geol.*
Greisiger, Dr. Michael, Szepes-Béla. *Min., Lithol., Orn.* C. Ex.
Gremblich, P. Julius, Gymnasial-Professor, Hall, Tyrol. *Botany, especially Thistles and Willows, Hieracæ and Roses. Conchology.*
Grenzenstein, Béla, Budapest. *Geol.*
Gretzmacher, Gyula, Selmecz. *Geol.*
Grobben, Dr. Carl, Univ., Franzensring, Wien, I. *Zool., Comp. Anat.**
Grosz, Heinrich, Steyr. *Macro-Lepid. of Europe and Asia.* Ex.*
Grüber, Dr. Ludwig, Central-Anstalt für Meteorologie und Erdmagn. Budapest. *Climatology.*
Grünberger, Eduard, k. k. Militair-Apotheke, 9, Trieste. *Coleopt.*
Grunow, Albert, Chemiker, Berndorf, Loebersdorf, near Wien. *Algæ, especially Diatoms.* C. Ex.
Gryglewicz, S., Dir. des Bot. Gartens, Lemberg. *Bot.*
Grzegorzek, Dr., Curate in Bochnia, Galicia. *Diptera.* C. 10,000 spec.*
Guckler, Gyozö, Budapest. *Geol.*
Gudera, Karl, Kalowratring 9, Wien, I. *Native and Foreign birds and animals.*
Guppenberger, Le P. Lamb, Kremenmünster. *Bot.*
Gurlitt, Prof. W., Univ., Gratz. *Philol.*
Gürtler, Herm., Platteis 416, Prague. *Europ. Coleopt., Exot. Lamellicornes.* C. Ex.
Guttenberg, Adolph Ritter v., Prof. an der Hochschule für Bodencultur, Wien. *Bot.* C. Ex.
Guttenberg, Hermann Ritter v., k. k. Forstrath, Trieste. *Min.* C. Ex. Desires minerals from N. Am.
Gyözö, Siepligeti, Kòvul 50, Budapest. *Bot.*
Haberhauer, Joseph, Naturalist, Arpadg. 26, Fünfkirchen.
Haberlandt, Prof. Dr. G. J., Univ., Gratz. *Bot.*
Habich, Otto, Hernals, Stiftgasse 64, Wien. *Macro-Lepid.*
Hackel, Eduard, Professor am Gymnasium, St. Pölten. *Botany, specialty, Gramineæ.*
Haimhoffen, Gustav Ritter Hain, Dir. des k. k. minist. Zahlamts, Florianigasse 2, Wien, VIII. *Hymenoptera.*
Halàcsy, Dr. Eug., Neubaugasse 80, Wien. *Bot.*
Halátz, Colom., Neustift 68, Budapest, II. *Coleopt.* C. Ex.
Hallama, Emil, Prossnitz, Moravia. *Lepid., Coleopt.* C. Ex.*
Hammerl, Dr. H., Univ., Innsbruck. *Phys., Mic.*
Hanaman, Dr. Josef, Dir. der Agric. Station, Lobositz, Bohemia. *Bot., Rubus culture, Meteo.*
Handl, Prof. A., Univ., Czernowitz. *Physics.**
Handlirsch, Adam, M.D., Heugasse 1, Wien, III. *Diptera.* C.*

Handlirsch, Anton, Heugasse 1, Wien, III. *Hymen.* C.*
Hanf, Bl., Pfarrer, Mariahof, Post-Neumarkt, Steiermark. *Orn., Ool.* C.*
Harslinszky, Friedrich, Dir. des evang., Lyceums in Eperjas. *Bot.*
Hasenfeld, Dr. Manó, Budapest. *Geol.*
Hatschek, Dr. Berthold, Zool. Inst. Wien. *Embryology.*
Hauck, F., Via Rosetti 6, Trieste. *Algæ, Desmids, Diatoms.* C. Ex. (of Algæ).*
Hauck, W. Ph., Rettenbenckang., Wien, III. *Phys.*
Hauer, Franz Ritter von, Intendant des k. k. Naturhistorischen Hofmuseums, k. k. Hofrath, Wien. *Geolog., Palaeo.*
Haury, C., Smichow 418, Prague, Bohemia. *Coleopt.: Carabidæ.* Desires to sell collection of Carabus containing 740 spec. and var. from 1757 up to pres. date. Album of Carabus of 41 pictures.*
Hausemann, Franz, Wienergasse 2, Budapest, Hung. *Orn.*
Hausmann, Baron v., Bozen, Tyrol. *Ent.*
Hayek, Dr. Gustav von, k. k. Regierungsrath, Marokkanergasse 3, Wien. *Orn.*
Haynald, Dr. Ludovicus, Cardinal-Archbishop of Kalocsa, Kalocsa. *Bot.*
Hazav, Julius, Müllnergasse 39, Budapest, IV. *Mollusca.* C. Ex.*
Hazslinszky, F. A., Prof., Eperies, Ung. *Phæn. & Crypt. Bot.* C. Ex.*
Hebra, Dr. Hans Ritter von, Docent an d. Univ., Mariannengasse 10, Wien, IX.*
Heckle, Jean, Rösselgasse 16, Saaz, Bohemia. *Palæo., Ent.: Lepid., Coleopt., Hemipt., Crustacea, L. and F. W. Snails.* C. Ex.*
Heeg, M., Circusgasse 33, Wien. *Mic.*
Heger, Franz, Custos am k. k. Naturhistorischen Hofmuseum u. I. Sekretär der Anthropologischen Gesellschaft, Wien. *Eth., Arch.*
Heider, Dr. Arthur Ritter von, Docent f. Zool., Univ., Maiffredygasse 4, Gratz. *Anthozoa, Corals, Radiates.*
Heinzel, Prof. Dr., Agric. Gar., Proskau. *Bot.*
Heller, Camill, Prof. Der. Zoologie an der Universität, Innsbruck. *Crustacea.*
Hellich, Johann, Podĕbrad, Bohemia. *Phæn. Bot., Palæo., Geol., Ent. Dipt., Coleopt.* C. Ex.*
Hellweger, Michael, Innsbruck. *Phæn. Bot., Lepid.* C. Ex.*
Hempel, E. G., Prof. an d. Hochschule für Bodencultur, Wien. *Forestry.*
Hennet, Leopold Ottomar Freiherr von, Oberlandesgerichts-Präsident, Prag. *Mic.*
Hennevogl von Ebenburg, Franz, k. k. Grenzinspector, Reichenberg, Bohemia. *Coleopt., Europ. and Exotic.*
Henning, E. W., Pirkenhamer bei Carlsbad, Bohemia. *Lepid., Coleopt.*
Henschel, G., Prof. an d. k. k. Hochschule für Bodencultur, Reitergasse 17, Wien, VIII.
Hepperger, Dr. Joseph von, Privatdocent für Astronomie an der k. k. Univ. zu Wien.
Herlinger, Franz, Oberplan (Bohemia). *Coleopt., Lepid.*
Herepci, Karl, Prof. an der Hochschule, Nagy-Enyed. *Geol.*
Herman, Otto, Custos am Ungar. National-Museum, Budapest. *Arachnida, Orthoptera.*
Herz, Dr. Norbert, Dir. der Kuffner Sternwarte, Ottakring bei Wien. *Ast.*
Heufler, Ludwig von Hohenbühel, Freiherr, Ansitz Altenzoll, Hall, Tyrol. *Bot.* C. Ex.*
Heyer, F., Darmstadt. *Coleopt.*
Hidegh, C., Prof. an d. Univ., Budapest. *Chem.*
Hilber, Dr. Vincenz, Univ., Gratz. *Geol., Palæo.*
Hirner, Josef, Neubaugasse 70, Wien, VII. *Lepid.*

Hoernes, Dr. Rudolf, Prof. der Geologie und Palæontologie an der Universität, Gratz. C. Wishes to exchange fossils for the same.*
Hoffmann, A. von, Fiume. *Coleopt.*, *Hemipt.* C. Ex.
Hofmann, Dr. Alfred, Chemiker, Orsova. *Chem.*, *Min.*, *Geol.* C. Ex.
Hofmann, Carl, Geologische Anstalt, Budapest. *Geol.*
Hofmann, Prof. K. B., Univ., Gratz. *Med. Chem.*
Hofmann, Rafael, Kirchengasse, Wien, VII. *Mountain Geol.*
Hofmeister, Emil, Smikow 391, Prague. *Eur. Lepid.**
Hofmokl, Dr. Johann, k. k. Primararzt und Docent für Chirurgie an der k. k. Universität, Helferstorferstrasse 9, Wien. *Chirurgy.**
Höhnel, Dr. F. von, Prof. am Polyt. Sch., Wien. *Physiol.*, *Bot.*
Holetschek, Dr. Johann, Adjunct der k. k. Sternwarte, Wien. *Astronomy*, *Meteorol.**
Holuby, T. L., Nemes-Podhragy bei Vâg-Ujhely. *Bot.*
Hoppe, Paul, Gospic, Croatia. *Zool.*, *Ent.: Lepid.*, *Coleopt.*, *Anat.*
Hora, Paul, Bot. Gar., Prague, Bohemia. *Bot.*
Hornig, Dr. E., Hauptstrasse 9, Wien. *Chem.*, *Photog.*
Hornstein, Prof. C., Univ., Dir. der Sternwarte, Prague. *Phys.*, *Elect.*, *Meteo.*, *Ast.*
Horváth, Antal, Pecs. *Geol.**
Horváth, Dr. Géza, Délibábutza 15, Budapest, Dir. de la Station Phylloxérique de l'Etat. *Hemipt.* C.
Horváth, Ignacz, Budapest. *Geol.*
Horváth, Dr. v. Varanuo. *Hemiptera.*
Hostinsky, C., Facset bei Lugos. *Coleoptera.*
Hradczky, Antal, Szepes-Olaszi. *Geol.*
Hübel, Christof, Schulgasse 14, Prague. *Coleopt. and Lepid. of Europe.*
Hudak, Edward, Lehrer, Göllnitz, Zips. *Lepid.* C. Ex.
Hudoba, Gusztáv, Nagy-Bánya. *Geol.*
Huffner, Tivadar, Budapest. *Geol.*
Hugo, May, Favoritenstr. 23, Wien. *Macrolepid.*
Human, Dr., Nationalmuseum, Budapest. *Bot.*
Hundegger, Joseph, St. Valentin auf der Haid, Virstgau, Tyrol. *Bot.* C. Ex. Alpine plants.*
Hunfalvy, Dr. János, Budapest. *Geol.*
Hünninger, Adolf, Director des. Observ., Kalvesa bei Budapest. *Ast.*
Husz, Arnim, Prof. am Evang. Collegium, Esperies. *Coleopt.*, *Macro-Lepid.*
Huter, Rupert, Sterzing, Tyrol. *Phæn. Bot.*, *Ferns*, *Mosses.* C.*
Hüttenbacher, Custos des Fürstl. Fürstenberg'schen Naturaliencabinets, Nischburg, Beraun, Bohemia.*
Inkey, László, Szt. Lörincz. *Geol.*
Ipoly, Fehér, K. Ung. Rath. Studien-Oberdirector, Szegodin. *Phys.**
Iszlai, Dr. Jósef, Budapest. *Odontology.* C. Ex.
Jabornegg-Gámsenegg, Baron de, Dir. Bot. Gar., Klagenfurt. *Bot.*
Jahn, Dr. H. M., Univ., Wien. *Chem.*
Jambory K., Kristinenstadt 182, Budapest, I. B. *Ent.*
Jamnitzky, Lipöt, Budapest. *Geol.*
Janczewski, Dr. Ed. de, Prof. Univ., Krakau. *Bot.*
Janovsky, Dr. J. V., Prof. k. k. Staatsgewerbeschule, Richenberg, Bohemia. *Chem.*
Janka V. v., Nat. Mus. of Hung., Budapest. *Bot.*
Jeleski, Constantin, Conserv. d'Histoire Nat. à l'Acad. des Sciences, Cracovie. *Geol.*, *Lithol.**
Jendrassik, Prof. E., Univ., Budapest. *Physiol.*
Jermy, Gustáv, Bator. *Geol.*, *Bot.*
Jirak, Johann, Holleschwitz bei Prag, Bohemia. *Lepid. of Bohemia.*
Jirus, Prof. Dr. Bohuslav, Univ. Tech., Prag. *Pharmacology and Pharmacognosy.**

John v. Johnesberg, Conrad, Chemist of the k. k. Geolog. Reichanstalt, Wien. *Geol., Lithol., Chem.**
Junker, Rup., Salzburg. *Phæn. Bot., Con.*
Juránvi, Dr. L., Prof. Univ., Dir. Bot. Gar., Budapest. *Bot.*
Jurasky, Johann, k. k. Oberbergrath, Annaplatz 4, neu Prag, Bohemia. *Coleopt. of Europe.*
Kamienski, Dr. Franz, Docent an d. Univ. u. Polyt. Hochschule, Lemberg. *Bot.*
Kanitz, Dr. Aug., Dir. Bot. Gar., Prof. an d. Univ., Klausenburg. *Bot.*
Kanka, Dr Károly, Pozsony. *Geol.*
Karlinski, F. M., Prof. Univ., Krakau. *Math., Ast.*
Karolyi, Dr., Museum, Budapest. *Ichth.*
Karrer, Felix, Sec. des Wissenschaftlichen Clubs, Hauptstrasse 80, Wien, Ober-Döbling. *Geol., Palæo., Rhizopoda.* C.
Kaufmann, Dr. Ernest, Werkarzt der I. k. k. priv. D. D. S. G., Fünfkirchen, Georggrubbe. *Coleopt., Ophilogus.*
Kaufmann, Josef, Rubensgasse 5, Wien, IV. *Coleopt.* C.*
Kávoli, Dr. Johann, Budapest. *Reptiles.*
Keck, Dr. Karl, Editor of Schultz's Herbarium Normale, Aistersheim. *Bot.* C. Ex. for Cal. and South American specimens.*
Kelecsényi, Carl von, Tavarnok, via Nagy, Tapolcsany, Ungarn. *Lepid.* Will buy.*
Keller, Emil, Vág-Ujhely. *Geol.*
Keller, T. B. von, Weiden, Hauptstrasse 78, Wien. *Bot.*
Kempelen, Ludwig v., ob. Donaustr. 29, Wien. *Arachnida.*
Kempelen, R., Pressburg. *Lepid.*
Kerner v. Marilaun, Dr. A. J., Prof. Univ., Dir. Bot. Gar., Rennweg 14, Wien. *Bot.*
Kerner, Jos., Alleestr. 21, Krems. *Bot.*
Kétli, Prof. Carl, Univ., Budapest.*
Kézmárszky, Dr. Tivadar, Budapest. *Geol.*
Kheil, Napoleon M., Prague, Bohemia. *Lepid., Europ. and exotic.* C. Ex.*
Khevenhüller-Metsch, Richard S., Prince of, Wien. *Ent.*
Kirchsberg, Manger von Julius, Goethestr. 7, Gratz. *Coleopt.*
Kittl, Ernst, k. k. Naturhistorisches Hofmuseum, Wien. *Geol., Palæo.* Ex. for Museum.*
Kittner, Theodor, k. k. Bezirksrichter, Kunstadt. *Coleopt.*
Klein, Julius, Prof. Bot., k. u. Josefs-Polytechnicum, Budapest. *Bot., Algæ.* C.*
Klein, W., Prof. Univ., Wien. *Arch.*
Klemencic, Dr. T., Univ., Gratz. *Phys.*
Klemensiewics, Prof. Dr. Rudolf, Gratz. *Experimental Pathol.*
Klemensiewicz, Dr. Stanislaus, Sandecia, Galicia. *Lepid.*
Klément, Robert, Kronstadt, Siebenbürgen. *Photog., Lepid., Coleopt.* C. Ex.*
Klepsch, Advokat, Prague. *Coleopt. and Diptera.*
Klutschak, Prof., Leitmeritz, Gymnasium, Bohemia. *Bot.**
Knapp, Dr. J. A., Museum, Wien. *Bot.*
Knöpler, Dr. Vilm., Marosvásárhely. *Geol.*
Koch, Dr. Anton, Prof. der Mineralogie und Geologie an der k. Ungar. Franz-Josef's Universität, Klausenburg. *Petrogaphy, Geology of Tertiary formations.* C. Ex. Offers Transylvania minerals, espec. Szabóit, Pseudo-brookit. Wishes American minerals.
Koch, k. k. Forstmeister, Carlsbad. *Ent.*
Köcsner, Prof. Jos., Gymnasium, Nyitrd. *Bot.* C.
Kocvan, Ant., Oravitz-Arva. *Orn., Ool.*

Koelbl, Carl, Dr. Phil., Wassagasse 18, Wien. *Crustacea.*
Kohl, Prof. J., Bozen. *Hymenop.*
Kolazy, Josef, k. k. Offic., Kaunitzgasse 6, Wien. *Hymenoptera.**
Kolbenhever, Prof. C., Bielitz, Brünn. *Bot.*
Koller, Prof. Karl, Kesmark, Zips. *Bot.*
Kollesberg, Prof. Dr. Victor Ritter Dantscher v., Univ., Gratz. *Math.**
Kolombatovic, Prof. G., Spalato. *Vertebrates.**
Kondor, Prof. G., Univ., Budapest. *Math.*
Konkoly, Nicolaüs von, Dr. Phyl, Mitgl. der k. Ung. Academie, der Royal Astr. Society, O'Gyalla Sternwarte bei Comorn. *Ast.*
Koovan, Ant. Förss, Oravitz-Arva. *Orn.*
Korcsek, Siegmund, Lehrer an der Töchterschule, Pressburg. *Lepid.*
Koren, Prof. Steph., Lyceum, Szarvas. *Bot.**
Korensky, J., Lehrer der Naturwissenschaften, Smichow, Prag. *Coleopt.**
Kornel, Dr. Chyser, S. a. Ujhley. *Ent., Arachn.**
Kornhuber, Prof. Andreas, Polytec. Sch., Wien. *Zool., Bot.**
Kornis, Count Emil., Herrengasse 66, Budapest, I. *Con., Moll.* C. Ex.*
Körösi, Josef, Dir. Communalstatistischen Bureau, Budapest.*
Kossutanyi, Prof. Dr., Agric. Sta., Altenburg. *Bot.*
Kostein, Joh., p. k. ung. Finanzbeamter, Landstrasse, Beatrixg. 4, B. II., Wien. *Lepid.*
Kosteletzky, Prof. Dr. P. V., Prague, Bohemia. *Bot.*
Kovács, Gyula, Nádasd. *Geol.*
Kövesligethy, Dr. Rudolf, Budapest. *Ast.**
Kowarz, Fred., k. k. Telegraphenbeamter, Franzensbad, Bohemia. *Diptera.**
Kozocsa, Tivadar, Budapest. *Geol.*
Krászonvi, Dr. József, Maria-Nostra. *Geol.*
Kratschmer, Dr. F., Priv.-Docent an der Univ., Wien. *Physiol., Chem., Hygiene.**
Kraus, Carl, Pardubitz, Bohemia. *Nat. Hist.*
Kravogl, Hermann, k. k. Gymnasial-Professor, Bozen, Tyrol. *Bot.* Ex.*
Krecsarevich, Márk, Ujvidék. *Geol.*
Kreissl, Franz Serafin, Heinrichgasse 1, Neu-Prag. *Coleopt.* C. Ex.*
Kreithner, Eduard, Heiligenstadt-Nüssdorf bei Wien. *Zool., Lepid., Macro. and Microlepid.* of Europe. C. Ex.*
Krek, G., Prof. Univ., Gratz. *Philol.*
Kremnitzky, Amandus, Vizakna. *Geol.*
Kremnitzky, Jakob, Vöröspatak. *Geol.*
Kremnitzky, Otto, Vöröspatak. *Geol.*
Krenner, Prof. Dr. Jos., Budapest. *Geol.*
Krenz, Dr. Johann, Univ., Prague. *Bot., Physiol.*
Kreutz, Prof. S., Univ. Lemberg. *Min.*
Kriésch, Johann, Prof. der Zoologie am k. ung. Josefs Polytechnicum, Budapest. *Herpetologie, Ichthyologie, Assistik.**
Kristof, Prof. L., Lyceum of Mademois, Gratz. *Bot.*
Krivany, Johann von, Comitats Obercontroller, Arad. *Geol., Geog.* C.*
Krupa, J., Prof. of Gymnastics, Buczacz (Austrian Galicia). *Spec., Musc., Hepatic, etc.**
Kubacska, Dr. Hugo, Körmöcz. *Geol.*
Kuczynski, Prof. St. L., Univ., Krakau. *Physics.*
Kundrat, Prof. Dr. H., Univ., Wien. *Pathol., Anat.*
Kunc, Dr. Adolf, Prelat, Csorna. *Geol., Phys.**
Kunszt, J., Losoncz. *Bot.* C.*
Kuthy, Desid., Gärtnergasse 16, Theresienstadt. *Coleopt.*
Kutschera, Franz, k. k. Beamter, Reiterg. 12, Wien. *Coleopt.*
Lambel, Dr. H., Univ., Prague. *Math.*
Lambert, Guppenberger, k. k. Gymnasial-Prof., Kremsmünster. *Bot.* C.

Lang, V. v., Prof. Univ., Wien. *Physics, Crystallograhy.*
Langer, Franz, Leinwandfabrikant in Zwittau, Moravia, Austria, Europe. *Lepidoptera.* C. Ex. Lists of duplicates on application.*
Langer, Prof. K., Univ., Wien. *Anat.*
Latre, Dr. Robert, Prof. am Franz Joseph Gymnasiums, Wien. *Zool. Myriopoda.*
Latzl, Prof. Dr. Ed., Wien. *Myriopoda.*
Laube, Prof. Dr. Gustav C., k. k. deutsche Universität, Prague. *Geol., Palæo.* C. Ex.
Lavogler, Prof. Vincenz, Innsbruck. *Zool., espec. Myriopoda.**
Leding, Sandor, Nagy Banya. *Geol.*
Leinner, Anton, Hauptmann in Ruhestand, Hauptstrasse 1, Weinhaus bei Wien. *Astronomy, Selenography.**
Leistner, Wenzl, Altrohlau bei Karlsbad. *Lepid., Coleopt.*
Leitgeb, Prof. H., Univ. Dir. Bot. Gart., Gratz. *Bot.*
Lengvel, B., Prof. Univ., Budapest. *Chem.*
Lenhofsek, Prof. Dr. Jos., Budapest. *Anat.*
Lenz, Dr. Oskar, Africa exploring traveller and Prof. of Geog. in the German Univ. of Prague, Bohemia.*
Leonhard, Otto, Libnoves Zehun, Podebrad. *Coleopt., Lepid.**
Lepkowski, Dr. J., Prof. Univ. Jagellon, Dir. Mus. Arch., Krakau.*
Lerch, Prof. J., Univ. Prague. *Chem.*
Lészav, Dr. László, Szászváros (Erdély.) *Geol.*
Lewandowski, Rudolf, Prof. Dr., Hernals bei Wien. Hauptstrasse 59. *Macro-Lepid., Coleopt., Plants.* Ex.*
Lichtenstern, Baron, Fr., Rovingo, Ystriem. *Algæ.*
Lichtenstern, Franz, Freiherr von, Monfalcone, Gorizia-Gradisca. *Algæ.*
Lieben, Dr. A., Prof. Univ., Wasagasse 9, Wien, IX. *Chem.*
Liebenberg, A. von, Prof. Hochschule für Bodencultur, Wien. *Bot., Veg. Anat.*
Liebermann, Prof. Dr. Leo, Chef der Chem. Staats-Versuchsstation, Rottenbillergasse 23, Budapest. *Chem., Met., Gen. Biol.**
Liedermann, Josef, Bau-Ingenieur der Herrschaft Münkacs. *Geol.* C. Ex. Offers Trachyte, Alunite, Sandstone (Dragomite), for interesting natural subjects.
Lielegg, Prof. A.. Gärtnerstrasse 35, Wien, III. *Phys.*
Linder, O., Schwarzenbergstrasse 17, Wien. *Geol.*
Linhart, Prof. G., Agric. Acad., Ungarisch Altenburg. *Pathol., Bot., Fungi.* C. Ex.*
Linnemann, Prof. E., Univ., Prague, Bohemia. *Chem.*
Lippich, Prof. F., Univ., Prague. *Phys., Math.*
Lippmann, Prof. E., Univ., Wien. *Chem.*
Lóczy, Prof. Lewis de, Geol., Polytechnicum, Budapest. *Strat. and Physical Geo.* C. Ex.*
Lojka, Prof. Hugo, Josefplatz 10, Budapest. *Lichenology.* C. Ex. Desires only good spec.*
Lorenz, Dr. Ludwig Ritter v., Beatrixgasse 25, Wien, III. *Zool., Orn., Worms, Radiates.**
Loschmidt, Prof. J., Univ., Wien. *Physical Chem.*
Löte, Ludwig, Prof. an der Hochschule. Nagy Enyed. *Phys.*
Löw, Dr. Franz, Wieden, Hauptstr. 47, Wien. *Hemipt. and Galls.*
Löw, Paul, Wieden, Hauptstr. 47, Wien. *Hemipt.**
Loyka, Gustav, Privatdocent, Budapest. *Lichenology.*
Ludwig, Prof. Ernst, Allgem. Krankenhaus, Wien. *Chem.*
Lukas, Dr. F., Kruman, Bohemia. *Bot., Phys.*
Lutter, János, Budapest. *Phys., Nat. Phil.*
Lutter, Dr. Nándor, Dir. am Gymnasium, Budapest. *Math.**
Lützow, Prof. K. v., Univ., Wien.. *Arch.*

Mach, Prof. Dr. Ernst, Univ., Weinberggasse, Prague, II, Bohemia. *Physics.*
Mácsay, Dr. Istvyn, Zajescár (Szerbia). *Geol.*
Madarassy, L., Staatsanwalt, Kecskemet. *Ent.*
Madarász, Dr. Julius von, Custos-Adjunct der Zoologischen Abtheilung am Ungar. National-Museum, Budapest. *Orn., Singing Birds.* C. Would like to ex.*
Maderspach, Livius, Bergingenieur, Rosenau (Rozsnjó). *Mining, Geol.* C. Wishes American minerals in ex. for Hungarian iron and zinc.
Magyari, Dr. Charles, Physician, Hagy Enyed, Transylvania. *Bot.*
Makowsky, Prof. Al., Polytech. Schule, Thalgasse 25, Brünn. *Bot.*
Malesevics, Prof. Emil, Staatsgymnasium, Losoner. *Zool., Bot.*
Malfatti, Johann, Innstrasse, Innsbruck. *Hort.*
Maloch, Acad. Maler, Michaelsgasse 438, Prague. *European Lepid.** C. Ex.
Maly, Fr., Imp. Gar. of Belvedere, Wien. *Bot.*
Maly, Prof. Dr. Rich., Deutsche Univ. in Prag. *Chem.*
Mann, Josef, am k. k. Zool. Cabinet, Canal 17, Wien, III. *Lepid.**
Marchesetti, Dr. Ch. de, Dir. am Naturhist. Museum, Trieste. *Bot.*
Marenzeller, Dr. Emil Edler von, Custos am k. k. naturhist. Hofmuseum Tulpengasse 5, Wien. *Zool.* Ex. Echinoderms, Worms.*
Margó, Th. Prof. Univ., Budapest. *Zool., Histol.*
Margules, Dr. M., Univ., Wien. *Phys., Electro-Magnetism.*
Marschall, Augustus Frederick, Count, Chamberlain to H. M. the Emperor of Austria, Wollzeile 33, Wien. *Nat. Sci. in gen.*
Martin, Prof. L., Univ., Klausenburg. *Math.*
Martoufi, Dr. L., Prof. Gymnasium, Szamosujvár. *Geol. Palæo.* C. Ex. Foraminifera, Meteorites of Mócs and Transylvania Minerals.
Matyaosovszky, Jakab, Budapest. *Geol.*
Mayer, Prof. S., Univ., Prague. *Histol.*
Mayr, Alfons, Innrain 40, Innsbruck. *Anat.*
Mayr, Prof. Dr. Gustav, Landstr., Hauptstr. 75, Wien. *Hymenoptera.*
Mayr, Matth., Prof. Gymnasium, Hall. *Cicadæ.*
Medgyesi, Béla, Kolozsvár. *Geol.*
Mednyánszky, Le Baron, Dénis Chambellan de S. M. I. and R. A., Rapovicz, Nyitra. *Phæn. Bot., Palæo., Geol., Min., Lithol., Met., Arch.* C.*
Menyhárt, Ladislaus, Prof., Kalocsa bei Budapest, Ungarn. *Bot.*
Merkl, Eduard, Rěsicza, South Hungary. *Coleopt.* C. Ex.*
Mertens, Prof. F., Univ., Krakau. *Math.*
Mertha, Hans, Beamter a. ob. Gerichtshofe, Wien. *Coleopt.**
Metzger, Anton, II, Rothkreuzg. 8, Wien. *Lepid.*
Micklitz, Franz, k. k. Oberförster, Radmansdorf, Oberkraim. *Coleopt.* C. Ex.*
Mihâldy, István, Bakony-Szt-László. *Geol.*
Mikalhovitz, Prof. Dr. Gera, Universtät, Budapest. *Anat.*
Miklosich, Dr. Franz, Prof. Univ., Wien.
Mikosch, Dr. Carl, Realschulprofessor. Privat Docent an der Universität, 66 Währingstrasse, IX, Bez, Wien. *Anatomy of Plants.*
Miller, Ludwig, Adj. im k. k. Ackerbau-Ministerium, III, Salmgasse 11, Wien. *Coleopt.*
Mocsary, Alexander, Assistent am National-Museum. Budapest. *Ent., Hymenop.*
Moeller, Dr. Josef, Prof. an der Universität, Innsbruck.*
Mojsisovics, Dr. Edm. von, k. k. Oberberg. Chefgeol.; k. k. Geol. Reichsanst., III., Reisnerstrasse 51, Wien. *Geol., Palæo., Trias of the Alps.*
Mojsisovics von Mojsvár, M. D. August, k. k. ausserord. Professor de

Zoologie an der technischen Hochschule, Sparbersbachgasse 25, Gratz. *Mam.*, *Osteol.*, *European Orn.*, *Zool.*, *Dist.*, *Anat. of Reptiles and Birds.**
Molisch, Dr. Hanns, IX., Mariannengasse 12, Wien. *Physiol. of Plants.*
Molitor, Edmund, Orsova. *Coleopt.*, *Lepid.*, *Bot.*, *Min.* C.
Monti, Dr. Alois, Rosengasse 8, Wien, I.*
Moser, Dr. Carl, Prof. in Triest. *Cave animals.*
Much, Dr. M., k. k. Conservator u. Mitglied der Central-Commission für Kunst- u. historische Denkmal, etc., Josefgasse 6, Wien, VIII. *Prehistoric Arch.*, *Palæo.* C.
Müller, Ferdinand, Brünn, Moravia. *Coleopt.*
Müller, Florian, Pfarrer in U. Siebenbrunn, Marchfeld, Moravia.
Müller, Dr. Johann, Prof. Univ., Innsbruck. *Philol.*
Müller, Josef, Karlsgasse 418, Smichow, Prague. *Lepid.*, *Coleopt.*
Mulser, Ant., Bozen (Tyrol). *Amphibia.**
Munganast, Emil, Markstrasse 15, Linz. *Coleopt.* C. Ex.
Murmann, Le P. O. A., Convent of St. Benoit, Melk. *Bot.*
Murr, Josef, Dr. Phil., Fallmerayerstrasse, Innsbruck. *Phæn. Bot.* C.*
Natterer, Ludwig, II., Kleine, Stadtgutgasse 3, Vienna II. (Austria). *General Sciences.* C. Ex.*
Neithardt, Ant., Chodan bei Karlsbad. *Bot.*
Netoliczka, Dr. Eugen, Prof. der Physik an der Landes-Oberrealschule, Gratz. *Physiological Optics.* *Color blindness.**
Netuschill, Franz, k. k. Jäger-Oberlieutenant, Com. bei Astronomical Section k. k. Militair-Geog. Institute, Wien. *Ent.* C. Ex. Wishes Coleoptera of N. America and N. Asia.
Nevole, M., Prof. Univ., Prague, Bohemia. *Org. Chem.*
Nickerl, Dr. Ottokar, Pres. der Ent. Section der physiokratischen Gesell., Wenzelsplatz 16, Prague, Bohemia. *Lepid.*, *Coleopt.**
Niessl, De Meyendorf, Prof. G. Polytec. Sch , Brünn. *Bot.* : *Mycol.*
Niesnser, Leonhard, Lehrer, Zwittau, Moravia. *Nat. Hist.*
Nossalek, Karl, Karolinenthal 258, Prague. *Lepid.*, *esp. Noctuidæ.*
Novák, Ottomar, Ph.D., Prague. *Invert. Palæo. Geol.**
Nowicki, Dr. Max, Prof. der Zool., Universitat, Krakau. *Diptera.*
Nurnberger, Heilige Geistgasse 12, neu Troppau. *Lepid.*, *Coleopt.*
Obermayer, Prof. A. v., Favoritenstrasse 21, Wien, IV. Laborat., Technische Militair Acad., VII. Stiftgasse 2. *Phys.**
Obersteiner, Dr. Heinrich, Prof. Univ., Doebling, Wien. *Anat. of Vert.*, *Neurology*, *Histol. of Vert.**
Ochorowicz, Dr. J., Univ., Lemberg. *Psychol.*, *Nat. Phil.*
Odstreil, Dr. J., Gymn. Prof., Teschen. *Lepid.*
Oellacher, Dr. Jos., Prof. Univ., Innsbruck. *Histol.*, *Emb. of Vert.**
Olszewski, Prof. K., Univ. Krakau. *Chemical Analysis.*
Oppenheim, Dr. Samuel, Asst. der k. k. Sternwarte, Währing bei Wien. *Ast.**
Oser, Dr. J., Prof. Hochschule, Kärntherstrasse 45, Wien, I. *Chem.*
Osnaghi, Ferdinand, Trieste. Dir. nautische Academie, *Meteo. Oceanography.**
Ossikowsky, Prof. J., Univ., Klausenburg. *Med.*, *Chem.*
Pacher, David, Ober-Vallach. *Bot.*, *Coleopt.*
Palisa, Alais, Adj. der k. k. Sternwarte, Triest. *Ast.*, *Lepid.**
Palisa, Dr. Johann, Adj. der k. k. Sternwarte, Währing bei Wien. *Ast.**
Pantocsek, Joseph, Doctor der gesammten Heilkunde, Tavarnok, Nagy Tapolcsány. *Bot. Phanero gams*, *Cryptogams.* C. Ex. and buy Ranunculaceæ, Violaceæ, Scrophulariaceæ, Crepis, Hieraceium, and Ferns. *Living and Fossil Diatoms.*
Parädy, Colomann, Prof., Klausenburg. *Zool.* C. Ex. "Süsswasser-Turbellaria."

Paszlavszky, József, Prof. Realschule, Föreáliskola, Budapest, II. *Zool.*, *Cynipida*, *Hymenop.* C. Ex.*
Pavel, Joh., National Museum, Budapest. *Lepid.*
Pebal, Dr. Leopold Edler v., Prof. Univ., Halbärthgasse 5, Gratz. *Chem.*
Pech, N., Mondscheing 844, Budapest, Taban. *Lepid.*
Peïker, Libor, Schuldirector, Trieste. *Min.*
Pelikan von Plauenwald, Anton, Vice-Pres. des k. k. n. öst. Finanz-Landes-Dir., Fleischmarkt 7, Wien. *Coleopt.*
Pelzeln, August von, Imp. Zool. Museum, Schönlatergasse 13, I. Wien. *Orn.*, *Mam.**
Penck, Prof. Dr., Wien. *Geographie*, *Geol.*
Pernter, Dr., Gymnasial Prof., Trient (Tyrol). *Bot.*
Petersen, B., Prof. Univ., Prague, Bohemia. *Arch.*
Petvicsko, Eugen, Prof. Ober-Gymnasium, Neusohl. *Zool.*, *Local Coleopt.*
Peyl, Theodor, Inspector der k. k. priv. Riunione Adriatica di Sicurta, Prague, III., Thomasgasse 13. *Zool.*, *Gen.*, *Biol.*, *Ent.*, *Coleopt.*, *Myriop.**
Peyritsch, Prof. Johann, Univ., Innsbruck. *Bot.*
Pfaundler, Prof. Dr. Leopold, University, Innsbruck. *Phys.*
Pfeiffer, P. Anselm, Benedictines, u. k. k. Gymnasial-Prof., Kremsmünster. *Geol.* C.*
Pfund, Dr., Assistent am Naturaliencabinet, Prague, Bohemia. *Ent.*
Pichler, Dr. Adolf, Prof. Mineralogie u. Geognosie, Universität, Innsbruck. *Geol.*
Pichler, Prof. Johann, Prossnitz, Moravia. *Ent.*, *Herpetol.*, *Worms.* C. Ex.
Pichler, Thomas, Lienz. *Bot.* C.
Pilar, Prof. Dr. G., Univ., Agram. *Geol.*
Pilati, Don Silvio, Vice Dir. am Collegium Vigilianum, Roveredo. *Coleopt.*
Piotrowski, Prof. G., Univ., Krakau. *Physiol.*, *Histol.*, *Emb.*, *Mic.*
Pipitz, Dr. F. E., Goethestrasse 7a, Gratz (Steiermark). *Coleopt.* Ex.
Pisko, Prof. Dr. Franz Josef, Dir. Realschule, Margarettenstrasse 7, Wien, IV. *Chem.*, *Phys.**
Plason, Dr. Victor, Postg. 22, Wien., I. *Coleopt. of Europe and Exotics.*
Plósz, Prof. P., Univ., Budapest. *Physiol.*, *Pathol.*, *Anat.*
Poetsch, Dr. Randegg. *Bot.*, *Lichenology.*
Pokorny, Emanuel, Präfect am k. k. Theresianum, Wien. *Lepid.*
Polák, Karl, Vladislavgasse 21, Prague, Bohemia. *Phæn. of Europe*, *Hieracium*, *Carex of the World.* C. Ex.*
Polansky, Anton, Palais d'Este, Brünn. *Lepid.*, *Coleopt.* C. Ex.*
Polinsky, Emil, Budapest, II., Lánchid-tér. *Coleopt.* Ex.
Porcius, Florian, Naszod-Rodna (Transylvania). *Bot.* C. Ex. Phanerogams of Transylvania for others.*
Pöschl, Ede, K. Bányatanácsos és Akademiai tanár. Selmeczbánya.*
Posepny, Franz, Prof. School of Mines, Pribram, Bohemia. *Geol.*
Preyss, Dr. J. Georg, k. k. Medicinalrath, V. P. des Wiener medic. Doctors Collegiums, III, Salesianergasse 8, Wien. *Anth.* C. Ex.
Pribram, R., Prof. Univ., Dir. Chem. Lab., Czernowitz. *Chem.**
Prihoda, Mor., Engelgasse 4, Wien. *Bot.*
Primics, Dr. Georg, Custosadj., Landesmuseum zu Kolozsvar. *Petrography und Mantangeblozic.**
Prochaska, Leop., Hainburg a Douan. *Coleopt.**
Puchta, Dr. A., Univ., Prague. *Math.*
Pulszky, de, Dir. Nat. Mus. of Hung., Budapest. *Bot.*
Puluj, Dr. J., Prof. Univ., Prague. *Phys.*
Pungur, Julius, Zilah (Szilágyer-Comitat). *Orthopt.**
Purjesz, Dr. Sigmund, Docent, Univ., Budapest, Geschichte der Medecin. *Bibliog.*, *Anth.*, *Arch.*, *Ethnog.**

Puschmann, Prof. Dr. Theodor, Wien, IX. *Bibliog.*, *Gen. Biol.*, *Arch.*, *Eth.*, *Ethnog.*, *Philol.**
Rabl, Dr. Carl, Anatom. Inst., Wien. *Emb.*, *Anat.**
Radziszewki, R., Prof. Univ., Lemberg. *Chem.*
Raimann, E., Prof. Landes-Oberrealschule, Kremsier, Moravia. *Chem.*
Rathav, Prof. Emerich, Klosterneuburg. *Bot.*
Ratzenbeck, Franz, M. D., Goldgasse 2, Prague. *Phys.*
Rauch, Fr., Imp. Gar., Laxenburg. *Bot.*
Rauscher, Dr. Rob., Museum, Linz. *Bot.*
Rebel, Hans, Dr., Helfertorferstr. 9, Wien, I. *Bot.*, *Micro-Lepid.* C. Ex.*
Rehmann, Dr. A., Prof. Univ., Lemberg. *Bot.*, *Bryol.*
Reinisch, Dr., Prof. Univ., Wien. *Egypt.*
Reinitzer, F., Univ., Prague. *Bot.*, *Physiol.*
Reitter, Edmund, Mödling bei Wien, Ungargasse 12. *Coleopt.**
Rejtö (Renner), Adolf, Diplom. Prof., Assistent am k. Forstakademie, Schemnitz. *Bot.*, *Diseases of Plants.*
Ressman, Dr. S., Rosenbühl, near St. Veit, Kärnthen. *Moll.**
Réthy, Prof. M., Univ., Technische Hochschule, Budapest. *Math.**
Reuss, Dr. August, Ritter von, Prof. der Ophthal., Wallfischgasse 4. Wien, I. *Phæn. Bot.* C.*
Richter, Joh. Anton, Rechbauerstr. 28, Gratz, II. *Macro-Lepidoptera.* Ex.
Richter, Dr. Karl, Taborstrasse 17, Wien. *Bot.* *Ex. for European plants.**
Richter, Lajos, Kaufmann, Budapest, Andrassy Ut 3. *Bot.*, *Coleopt.*, *Lepid.*, *Diptera*, *Hymenoptera*, *Neuroptera*, *Orthoptera*, *Conch.*, *Hemiptera.* C. Ex. Wishes pressed plants, insects, land molluscs, and postage stamps from all parts of the world.*
Riess, Carl, Hermanstadt, Siebenburgen. *Molluscs.*
Rinnböch, J. C., Simmeringstr. 14, Wien, Austria. *Mic.* (Diatoms and other slides), *Photo.* (Stereograms on glass and Lantern slides). C. Ex.*
Robic, Sim., Ulrichsberg bei Zirklach. *Coleopt.*
Roesler, Prof. Dr. L., Klosterneuburg. *Chem.*, *Phys.*, *Bot.*
Rogenhofer, Alois Friedrich, Custos am k. k. Zool. Hofcabinet, Josefstadterstr. 19, Wien. *Lepid.*, *Hymenop.**
Rogner, Prof. Dr. Johann, Gratz. *Ast.*
Rohon, Dr. Josef, Zool. Inst., Wien. *Anat.*
Rollett, Dr. Alexander, Universitäts-Professor, Harrachgasse 21, Gratz. *Physiol.*, *Histol.**
Romani, Ant. von, Gleisdorf bei Gratz. *Moll.*
Romer, Rev. Dr. F. F., Museum, Budapest. *Arch.*
Ronniger, Ferdinand, Rothenthurmstr. 15, Wien, I. *Bot.*
Rösler, Prof., Klosterneuburg, Wien. *Chem.*
Rostafinski, Dr. Jos. Thom. de, Prof. Univ., Dir. Bot. Gar., Straszewskistrasse 11, Krakau. *Bot.*
Roth, Samuel, Dr. Prof., Leutschan. *Geol.*
Rothe, Dr. Carl, Prof. Staatsrealschule, Wien, VII. B. *Chem.*, *Min.*
Rozsay, Emil, Prof. Gymnasium, Pressburg. *Coleopt.*, *Lepid.*
Rozsay, Dr. Josef, Budapest. *Geol.*
Ruffiny, Jeno, Dobsina. *Geol.*
Rumpf Prof. Johann, Gratz. *Min.*, *Geol.*
Rupertsberger, Mathias, Mühldorf. *Coleopt.*, *Biol.**
Rybár, István, Budapest. *Geol.*
Safarik, Prof. A., Weinberge. 422, Prague. *Ast.**
Safcsásk, Julius, Derno, Grubenverwalter, Görmör. *Geol.*, *Min.* C. Ex.*

Sajfhelyi, Frigyes, Budapest. *Geol.*
Sajo, Carl, Ungvar. *Coleoptera, Hymenoptera, Hemiptera, Diptera.*
Sajokaroly, Prof. Nat. Sci. Ungvar. *Ent.*
Sándor, Prof. Johann, Spáspváros Broos. *Min.*
Sarvicki, Dr. Emil, Gymnas. Prof., Lemberg. *Phys.*
Saxlehner, Arpad, Budapest. *Coleopt.*
Schafarzik, Ferencz, Budapest. *Geol.*
Schaitter, Ignaz, Rzeszow, Galicia. *Gen. Zool.* C. Ex.*
Scharschmidt, Jules, Klausenburg. *Bot., Algæ.*
Schaschl, Joh., Buchscheiden near Feldkirch (Kärnthen). *Coleopt.* C.*
Schätterer, Heinrich, Carlsbad, Bohemia. *Lepid.*
Schauer, Ernst, Brody bei Pieniaki. *Phæn. Bot., Mam., Orn., Ool.* C.*
Schedl, Arnulf, Benediktiner Prof. am Obergymnasium in Gran (Esztergorn). *Zool., Bot., Min.* C. Ex.
Schenk, S. L., Prof. Univ., Wien. *Embryol.*
Schenzl, Dr. Guidó, Dir. Ung. Central Anstalt für Met. und Erdmagn., Budapest, I. *Meteorology, Terrestial Magnetism.*
Scheüthauer, Prof. Gust., Budapest. *Pathology, Anatomy.*
Schiavuzzi, Dr. Bernardo, Monfalcone, Gorizia-Gradisca. *Orn., Ool., Tax.* C. Ex.*
Schiffner, Victor, Assistent Bot. Gar., Prague. *Bot., Min.*
Schindler, Franz, Prof. Neutitschein, Mähren. *Bot., Agric.,* C. Ex.*
Schindler, Hermann, Weissenhof b. Kloptan. *Meteo.*
Schirnhofer, P., Gerhard, Capitular Stiftshofm. des Cistercienser Stiftes Lilienfeld, gen. Sec. v. k. k. Gartenbau-Ges. in Wien, u. Lehrer an deren Gartenbau-Schule, I. Wienburggasse 31, Wien. *Pomology.*
Schlachta, Lajos, Máramaros-Sziget. *Geol.*
Schlangenhausen, Dr. Fridolin, Feldhof, bei Gratz. *Zool., Gen. Biol. Anth., Herpetol., Tax.**
Schmarda, Dr. Ludwig, Acad., Wien. *Moll., Vermes, Zoophytes.*
Schmidt, Alexander, Custos-Adjunkt am National Museum, Budapest. *Mineralogy, esp. Crystallography.*
Schmidt, Anton, Lehrer, Leipa in Böhmen. *Bryol.* C. Ex.*
Schmuck, J. von, Schwaz. *Bot.*
Schneider, Gustav, Bergwerksbesitzer und Director, Schmölnitz. *Phys. Chem., Geol., esp. Nat. Hist.* C.
Schneller, August, Schondorfergasse, Pressburg. *Bot.*
Schoepke, Prof. Hugo, Bruneck. *Bot.*
Scholtz, Dr. A., Univ., Budapest. *Math.*
Schott, Prof. F., Univ., Innsbruck. *Pathol., Anat., Histol.*
Schram, Dr. Julian, Asst. an der Univ., Lemberg. *Chem.**
Schrauf, Dr. Albrecht, Prof. Min. Universität, Waltergasse 3, Wien. *Mineralogy.*
Schröder, Rezsö, Selmecz. *Geol.*
Schreiber, Dr. Egid, Dir. der Staatsrealschule, Görz. *Amphib., Reptil. Coleopt.**
Schröckenstein, Franz, Neuburgasse 72, Wien, VII. *Geol.* C. Ex.*
Schroff, Dr. Carl D. R. von, Prof. Emer., Gratz.
Schuch, Prof. Dr., Rákosgrabengasse 14, Budapest. *Bot.*
Schuchter, Karl, Fallbachstrasse 4, Innsbruck. *Geol.*
Schulek, Dr. Vilmos, Budapest. *Geol.*
Schuller, Prof. Alois, Budapest. *Experimental Physics.**
Schulzer, von Müggenburg, Capt., Vinkovce. *Bot.: Mycology.*
Schuster, Max, Ph. D. Privat-Docent der Univ., Wien, I. Grillparzerstrasse. *Min. Petrog.**
Schvarcz, Dr. Julius, F. G. S., M. del. Acad. Hon., Stuhlweissenburgh. *Geol., Anth.*
Schwab, Ad., Mistek (Moravia). *Orn., Coleopt.*

Sándor, Gothard, F.R.A.S., Hereny bei Steinamanger. *Phys.*, *Astr.* C.*
Schwackhöfer, F., Prof. Hochschule für Bodencultur. *Agric.*, *Chem.*
Schwanda, Prof. M., Univ., Wien. *Physics.*
Schwarz, Dr. Franz, Breslau, Assistent an Bot. Gart. *Physiol.*
Schwarz, Dr. Frank, Universität Breslau, Schlesien. *Bot.*
Schwarz, Dr. Heinrich, Technische Hochschule, Gratz, Steyermark. *Tech. Chem.**
Schwarz, L., Bot. Gar., Krakau. *Bot.*
Schwerer, János, Pancsova. *Geol.*
Schwöder, Adolf, Müglitz, Moravia. *Gen. Bot.*, C. Ex.*
Sebestyén, Pál, Budapest. *Geol.*
Sebesy, Alajos, Szombathely. *Geol.*
Seeger, Dr. Hall, Tyrol. *Ent.*
Seligmann, Prof. Dr. Franz, R. Univ., Wien.
Semsch, Carl Bruno, Ph.D., Henmarks Münzarms, Wien, III. *Chem. Met.**
Senek, Dr. István, Selmecz. *Geol.*
Senhofer, Prof. K., Univ., Innsbruck. *Chem.*
Sersawy, Dr. V., Univ., Wien. *Analyt. Chem.*, *Mechanics.*
Seydler, Prof. A. Univ., Prague. *Ast.*, *Phys.*
Seigmeth, Karl, Inspector der Ung. N. O. Bahn, S. A. Ujhely. *Geol. Topography*, *Geog.* *C.*
Sigmund, Alois, Gymnasium, Landskron, (Böhmen). *Petrography.**
Simek, Adolf, Bezirksecretär, Weisswasser (Bohemia.) *Coleopt.*, *Lepid.**
Simettinger, Michael; Bergingenieur, Annenstrasse 29, Gratz. *Geol. Min.*, *Palæo.* C. Ex.*
Simkovics, Lajos, Ph.D., Prof. Nat. Hist. in Lyceum at Arad, Oberrealschule, Melyutca 2, Arad. *Phytography and Taxonomy.* C. Ex. Offers plants of Transylvania and Hungary, and wishes those of Russia, Roumania, Bessarbia, Bukovina, Galicia, Szerbia, Bosnica, Rumenia, Purcia, Caucasus.
Simic, Wladimir, Demetergasse, Agram. *Bot.**
Simony, Prof. O., Hochschule für Bodencultur, Wien. *Phys.*, *Math.*
Skalitzky, Dr., Karmeliterg. 24 Prague, Bohemia. *Coleoptera, esp. Staphylinidæ.*
Skofitz, Dr. Alex., Mühlgasse 1, Wien. *Bot.**
Skraup, Prof. Dr., Universität, Gratz. *Chem.**
Solcz, Gyula, Prof. an der Berg- und Forstakademie Forstrath, Schemnitz. *Forestry.*
Sommaruga, E., Fhr. v., Ph.D., Prof. Univ., Wien. *Chem.*
Spaeth, Dr. Franz, Kohlmessergasse 3, Wien. *Coleopt.* C. Ex. Desires Coleopt., esp. Longicornes and Chrysomelites from all parts of the world.*
Speiser, Prof. Fr., Kalocsa.*
Spitaler, Rudolf, Asst. der k. k. Sternwarte, Währing bei Wien. *Min.*, *Photog.*, *Meteo.*, *Ast.* C. Ex.*
Srdinko, Josef, Ingenieur, Inselgassse 1447, Prague. *Europ. Lepid.*
Srnka, Anton Kön, Landesbeamter, Kleinseite 259, Prague. *Lepid.*, *Ithomidæ*, *Heliconidæ.* Will buy and exchange.*
Stache, Dr. Guido, Wien. *Geol.*
Standfest, Dr. Franz, Gratz. *Geol.*
Stanecki, Th., Prof., Univ., Lemberg. *Phys.*
Staub, Prof. Dr. Moriz, Kerepeserstrasse 8, Budapest, VII. *Bot.*, *Spec. Phytopaloæ.*
Stecker, Anton, Brenntegasse 7½, Prague, Bohemia. *Arachnida.*
Stefan, Freiherr von Washington, Schloss Pöls, Past Wildon, Stiermark. *Orn.*, *Acclimatization and Geog. Dist. of Birds.* Ex.*
Stefan, Dr. Jos., Sec. R. Acad. Sci., Wien. *Bot.*, *Phys.*, *Meteo.*
Steffek, Dr. Adolf, Atillag. 647, Taban, Budapest.

Steffell, Dr. Adolph, Budapest, Corvinplatz. *Lepid. and Stamps.*
Steidl, Lad., Muth-Ring 2, Budapest. *Lepid.*
Steigerwald, Karl V., Chotebor, Bohemia. *Orn., Ent., Lepid.* Sale and exchange of Coleopt.*
Stein, Prof. Dr. F., sen., Prague, Bohemia. *Anat., Zool., Vermes.*
Stein, Dr. R., Chodau bei Karlsbad. *Ent., esp. Lepid., Hymenop., Neuroptera.*
Steindachner, Dr. Franz. Acad., Wien. *Herpetol., Ichth.*
Steiner, Dr. Prof. Julius, Klagenfurt, *Lichens.* C. Ex.*
Steinhausz, Julius, Bergverwalter, Peggau. *Min.* C. Ex. Witherite, Barite, Zincblende, Galenite, Hydrozisecite, Cerusite, etc.
Steinitz, Wenzel, Elisabethplatz 19, Budapest. *Ent., Bot., Herpetol., Protozoa, Entomozoa, Malacozoa, Min., Geol.* C. Ex.
Stessel, Dr. Lajos, Tánió-Szele. *Geol.*
Stofella d'alta Rupe, Prof. Dr. Emil, Univ., Alserstrasse 26, Wien, VIII. *Pathol., Therapeutics.**
Stolz, O., Prof., Univ., Innsbruck. *Math.**
Stossich, Prof. Mich., Gymnasium, Fiume. *Bot.*
Strasser, Gabriel, Benedictiner u. Director der Sternwarte, Kremsmünster *Ast.*
Streintz, Prof. Heinrich, Univ., Gratz. *Phys.**
Strobl, Franz, Oberlehrer an der Bürgerschule, Linz. *Coleopt.*
Strobl, Franz Peter, Witten, bei Innsbruck. *Phæn. Bot., Lichens, Mosses, Hepaticæ.*
Strobl, Prof. P. Gabriel, Melk. *Bot., Ent.* C. Ex. Coleoptera, Diptera, and Hymenoptera for those of N. and S. America.
Struska, J., Soc. Hort., Gratz. *Bot.*
Studnicka, Prof. F., Univ., Prague. *Math.*
Stur, Dionys, Acad. Sci., Rasumoffskygasse 3, Wien. *Palæo., Bot.*
Stussiner, J. A., Wienerstrasse 15, Laibach (Krain). *Pselaphidæ and Scydmænidæ, Coleopt. Orthoptera and Moll.* C. Ex*
Subic, Prof. S., Univ., Gratz. *Meteo.*
Sukup, Julius, Napagedl, Moravia. *Lepid.* C. Ex.*
Svácha, F., Bürgerschullehrer, Deutschbrod (Bohemia). *Coleopt., Lepid.**
Svoboda, Dr. Rudolf, Leitomischl. *Coleopt.**
Szabó, Prof. Dr. Joseph, Univ., Budapest. *Geol., Min., Lithol.* C. Ex.*
Szaniszlo, Dr. A., Prof. Agric. Sch., Univ., Klausenburg. *Anthropoda, Bot.*
Scâsz, Dr. Etienne, Gymn., Miko. *Bot.*
Szécsi, Zsigmond, Prof. Berg- u. Forstakademie, Schemnitz. *Bot., Agric.*
Szepligeti, Prof. V., Joseph-Ringstr. 50, Budapest. *Bot.*
Sziklay, Ludwig, Piseke Süttö. *Bot.*
Szilniczky, Jakab, Selmecz. *Geol.*
Szily, Coloman, Prof. Polytechnicum, Budapest. *Phys.*
Szinnyei, Otmár, Univ. Library Building, Budapest. *Moll. and Numismatica.* C. Ex.*
Szombathy, Josef, Custos am k. k. Naturhistorischen Hofmuseum, Sigmundsgasse 8, Wien, VII. *Anth., Arch., Osteol.**
Szontagh, Dr. Nic., Bad Neú-Schmecks, Uj Tàtrafüred. *Phæn. Bot., Meteo.* C.*
Szontaghà, Dr. Tamil, Budapest. *Geol**.
Sztehlo, Surel, Ravacsonvigasse 9, Budapest. *Bot.*
Takoits, János, Dir. Telegraphs, Budapest. *Physics.*
Tallatschek, Ferencz, Petrozsény. *Geol.*
Talsky, Prof. Jos., Neutitschein, Moravia. *Orn.*
Tangl, Dr. E., Prof. Univ., Czernowitz. *Bot.**
Tarbaky, István, Rector und Prof. Berg- und Forstakademie, Bergrath, Schemnitz. *Mechanics.*

Tatar, M., Bot. Gar., Prague, Bohemia. *Bot.*
Tauscher, Dr. J. Aug., Eresin. *Bot.* C.
Tedlik, Dr. Anvos, Prof. der Phys. in Univ. at Budapest from 1840 to 1879. Now pensionist in Raab.*
Teichmann, Prof. Med. L., Univ., Krakau. *Anatomy.*
Tekete, Lajos, Forstrath und Prof. an der Berg- und Forstakademie, Schemnitz. *Forstbotanik.**
Teller, Dr. Friedr., k. k. Geolog. Inst., Wien. *Geol.*
Terren, Andreas, Körmöczbánya. *Ent.: Lepid., Coleopt.* C.*
Tery, Dr. Ódön, Selmecz. *Geol.*
Teschler, Georg, Prof. Staats-Oberrealschule, Körmöczbánya. *Nat. Hist., Chem., Lithol., Anat., Herpetol., Histol. of Vert., Odontol.* C. Ex. Trachyto, Opal.*
Thalhammer, Prof. Johann, Kalocsa bei Budapest, Ungarn. *Ent.**
Than, Prof. Karl, Budapest. *Chem.*
Thanhoffer, Prof. Dr. Ludwig, Budapest. *Phys., Min.*
Thümen, Felix Baron, Görz, österreich. Küstenland. *Mycology (Systematic), Agric. and Forestry, Bot.* C. Ex.*
Tief, Wilhelm, Prof. am Gymnasium zu Villaich. *Zool., Diptera.**
Tiesenhausen, Baron von, Bozen, Tyrol. *Con., Coleopt.* Ex. Land and F. W. Shells.*
Toldt, Prof. C. Univ., Prague. *Anat. and Emb. of Man.*
Tolinszky, Béla, 105½, Budapest, II. *Bot.*
Tomaschek, Prof. Ant., Polytech. Sch., Brünn. *Bot.*
Torma, Fräulein Sofie von, Szaszvaros (Broos), Transylvania. *Anth., Geol., Palæo., Arch., Eth.* C.*
Török, Prof. A., Univ., Klausenburg. *Anat.*
Török, Dr. József, Debreczen. *Geol.*
Toth, Dr. M., Kalocsa, bei Budapest.*
Toula, Dr. Franz, Prof. der Mineralogie u. Geologie, an der k. k. technischen Hochschule, IV., Wien. *Geol.**
Trusz, Simeon, Lehrer am k. k. Gymnasium, Buczacz (Galizien). *Syst. Bot.* C.*
Tschapeck, H., 18 Morellenfeldgasse, Gratz. *Moll., Coleopt.*
Tschermak, Dr. Gustav, k. k. Hofrath, Prof. Min., Univ., Wien. *Min.*
Tschörch, Franz, Wien, k. k. Institut. *Coleopt.* C. Ex.*
Tschudi, Dr. Johann J., Baron von, Jacobshof, post Edlitz.*
Tschusi zu Schmihtoffen, Victor Ritter von, Villa Tännenhof, bei Hallein, Salzburg, Chairman of Comm. for Ornithological Obs. in Austro-Hungary. *Orn., esp. Orn. of Austria and Hungary.* C. Ex. Birds of Austro-Hungary, esp. of the Alps.*
Türk, Rodolf, k. k. Min.-Secretär, Lagerg. 1, Wien. *Coleopt.*
Udranfky, Larzlo, Budatinfsolna, Rutka. *Bot.**
Ulanowski, Adam, Zwierzynieckagasse 8, Krakau. *Coleopt.**
Ulbricht, Prof. Dr. R., Agric. Sta., Altenburg. *Chem., Bot.*
Ultzman, Dr. Robert, Docent Universität, Wien, VIII. Bezirk, Alserstrasse 7.
Urbantschitsch, Dr. Victor, Docent, Kolowratring 4, Wien, IV. *Osteol.**
Valvi, Dr. J., Univ., Klausenburg. *Math.*
Vangel, Eugen, Batthyánigasse 59, II. Bezirk, Budapest. *Lepid., Cynipidæ, Neuropt.* C. Ex.*
Vécsey, József, Budapest. *Geol.*
Vejdovsky, Franz, Ph.D., Prof. of Zool., University, Prague, Bohemia. *Zool., Gen. Biol., Emb. of Invert., Comp. Anat., Worms, Protozoa, Fresh-Water Sponges Coccidæ, Psyllidæ.* C.*
Velenovsky, Dr. Josef, Böhmische Universität, Prague. *Phæn. Bot., Mosses, Plant, Palæo., Morph. and Systematic Bot., Veg. Palæont. of Bohemia.* C. Ex.*

Venturi, Dr. G., Trento, Tyrol. *Bot.: Bryol.* C. Ex. European mosses for American.
Vetter, Ad., Imp. Gar., Schoenbrunn, near Wien. *Bot.*
Vlantken, Max, Dir. des Geolog. Institut, Budapest.
Vleck, William, Bürgomeister, Weinberge-Prague. *Lepid., Europ. and exotic.*
Vogel, Fit, k. k. Hofgartner, Laxenburg, bei Wien. *Macro- and Micro-Lepid.*
Vogl, Franz, Lehramtscandidat Trüban. *Zool.*
Vogl, Prof. C. v., Leitmeritz. *Isopoda.**
Vogrinz, Gottfried, k. k. Prof. am II. Deutschen Gymnasium in Brünn (Mähren). *Ethnol., Philol.*
Voss, Prof. W., Laibach. *Bot., Mycology.*
Vrba, Prof. K., Univ., Prague. *Min., Crystal.*
Vuchetich, Ruszkabánya. *Bot.* C.
Vukotinovics, Lajos, Agram, Croatia. *Bot.*
Waagen, Wilhelm, Ph.D., Prof. Polytechnicum, Mariengasse 2, Prague, II. *Invert. Palæo., Strat. Geol., Min.* C. Ex.*
Wagner, Coloman, Gymnasial-Prof. und Adj. der Sternwarte, Kremsmünster. *Physics, Magnetism.*
Wagner, Dr. Daniel, Budapest. *Geol.*
Wagner, Ladislas v., Prof. k. technischen Hochschule, Budapest. *Bot., Hort., Agric., Veg. Palæo., Chem., Geol., Lithol., Org. Chem.* C. Ex.*
Wajgiel, Leop., Prof. Gymn., Kolomea. *Arachnida.*
Waldner, Univ., Gratz. *Bot.*
Waltenhofen, Prof. Dr. A. von, Wien. *Electricity, Magnetism.**
Walter, August, Grumden. *Coleopt.* C. Ex.
Walz, Lud., Bot. Gar., Klausenburg. *Bot.*
Wangel, Eugen, Budapest. *Lepid.*
Wartha, Vincens, Ph.D., Prof. k. Polytechnicum, Budapest. *Geol., Chem., Met., Photog.* C. Ex.*
Wassmuth, Prof. A., Univ., Czernowitz. *Phys., Math.*
Weber, Robert, Wien. *Coleopt.*
Weichselbaum, Dr. A., Priv.-Docent, Univ., Wien. *Pathol., Histol., and Anat.*
Weidel, H., Prof. Univ., Wien. *Chem.*
Weiler, Prof. J., Innsbruck. *Lepid.*
Weinek, Dr. Ladislaus, Prof. Univ. Prague, Bohemia, Dir. der k. k. Sternwarte. *Met., Ast.**
Weinzierl, Dr. Th. Ritter von, Docent, Vorstand der Samen-Control Stat., Herreng. 13, Wien. *Physiol. of Plants, etc.**
Weiss, Prof. Dr. Edmund, Dir. k. k. Sternwarte, Währing, Wien. *Ast. Math.*
Weiss, Dr. G. A., Prof. Univ., Mem. d. k. Academie, Prague. *Bot., Physiol.**
Weisz, Tádé, Zalathna. *Geol.*
Weselsky, Ph.D., Prof. emer., Saar, Moravia. *Chem.*
Weyr, E., Prof. Univ., Wien. *Math.*
Wierzejski, Anton, Phil. Dr., Docent an der Universität, Krakau. *Zool., Crustacea, Comp. Anat.*
Wiesbaur, Johann B., S. J., Prof. der Naturgeschichte, Mariaschein, Böhmen. *Bot.: Phanerogams, Violaceæ.**
Wiesner, Dr. J., Prof. Univ., Alservorstadt, Türkenstr. 3, Wien. *Bot., Physiol., Anat.*
Wieszner, Adolph, Selmecz. *Geol.*
Wihlidal, Josef, Schwefelgasse 461, Prague, Bohemia. *Lepid.*
Wilckens, M., Prof. Hochschule für Bodencultur, Wien. *Zoology.**
Willdauar v. Wildhausen, F., Prof. Univ., Innsbruck. *Philology.*

Wilhelm, Dr. Karl, Privat-Docent, k. k. Hochschule für Bodencultur, Skodagasse 17, Wien, VIII. *Bot.**
Willigk, Prof. E., Univ., Prague, Bohemia. *Chem.*
Willkomm, Dr. Heinrich Moritz, Prof. Syst. Bot. d. k. k. Univ., Dir. d. k. k. Bot. Garten, Prague, Bohemia. *Bot., Geog. Dist., Flora of Spain.* C. Ex.*
Witlaczil, Dr. Emanuel, Wien, III., Sofienbruckengasse 3. *Zool., Anat., Emb.**
Wittinger, János, Budapest. *Geol.*
Wohlbach, Ernst, Mädchenbürgerschule, Linz. *Coleopt.*
Wohner, Franz, k. k. Naturhistor. Hofmuseum, Privat-Docent an der Univ., Wien. *Geol., Palæo.**
Wolff, Gabriel, Thorda. *Bot.* C.
Woloszczak, Dr. Eust., Bot. Gar., Wien. *Bot.*
Wumner, August, Maximilianplatz 14, Wien. *Zool.*
Xanthus, János, Budapest. *Coleopt.*
Zanctzky, Paul, Gömör. *Bot.*
Zavadskv, Dr. Alexander, Stry, Galicia. *Coleopt., Lepid.*
Zechenter, Adolph, Yánoshegy. *Min., Ent.*
Zechenter, Dr. Gustav, Kremnitz, k. ung. Bergwesensarzt. *Geognosy. Min., Bot.* C. Many spec. to ex.*
Zeissl Dr. Maximilian, von, Docent für Syphilis und Hausteraupheiten, I, Kohlmarkt 26, Wien.*
Zelbr, Karl, Phil. Dr., Asst. der Sternwarte, Währing, Türkenschanze, Wien. *Astronomy.**
Zelinka, Dr. Karl, Assistent am Zoolog. Institut der Universität, Gratz. *Zool. Rotatoria.*
Zeller, Fritz, Postg. 20, Wien. *Ent.*
Zenger, Chas. V., F.R.A.S., Prof. Nat. Phil. and Ast., Observatory T. R. Bohemian Polytechnic School, Wienbergg. 570, Prague. *Nat. Phil., Ast.* Would like to ex. solar and lunar photographs for objects in the same line.*
Zepharovich, Dr. Victor L. Ritter von, Oberbergrath, Prof. der Mineralogie an der k. k. Universität, Prague. *Min., Crystal.* C.*
Zimeter, A., Prof. an der k. k. Oberrealschule, Steyr. *Bot.* C. Ex.
Zitkovsky, L. v., Prof. Univ., Wien. *Nat. Hist.**
Zmurko, Prof. W., Univ., Lemberg. *Math.*
Zoch, Dr. Ivan, Gym.-Dir., Bosna Serajevo. *Phæn. Bot., Phys., Elect.**
Zoeltvay, Brogdán, Lehrer, Varannó. *Zool., Orthoptera.* C. Ex. native for foreign.
Zotta, Vict. v., Univ.-Laboratorium, Prague. *Chem.*
Zsedényi, Otto, Szelakna. *Geol.*
Zsigmondy, Béla, Budapest. *Geol.*
Zsigmondy, Wili., Budapest. *Geol.*
Zuber, Dr. Rudolf, Asst. an der Univ., Krakau. *Geol.*
Zuckerkandl, Prof. E., Univ., Gratz. *Anat.*
Zulkowsky, Prof. K., k. k. Inst., Brünn. *Chem.*
Zwanziger, G. Ad., Klagenfurt. *Palæo., Bot.*
Zwiflhofer Franz, Spargasse, Prague, Bohemia. *Mic.**

AZORES.

Arruda Furtado, Francisco d', St. Michael's Island. *Malacology, Con.* C. Ex. Offers L. shells of Azores, Europe and America for L. and F. W. shells of all parts of the world.*
Gomes Machado, Dr. Carlos Maria, Directeur du Musée National, Professeur au Lycée National de l'Ile St. Michael, St. Michael's Island. *Zool.* C. of the museum. Ex.

BELGIUM.

Baguet, Pr. Chs., rue des Joyeuses-Entrées 6, Louvain. *Bot., spec. Flora of Belgium.**

Ballion, Jean, Gand. *Invert. Palæo., Zool., Anth., Orn., Ent., Moll.* C. Ex.*

Barrow, 85 rue Royale Sainte-Marie, St.-Josse-ten-Noode. *Mic.*

Bauwens, rue Schmitz 19, Koekelberg (Brussels). *Bot., Con.*

Bayet, Ernest, rue Joseph II. 58, Brussels, Belgium. *Geol., Min., Palæo.* C. Ex.*

Becker, Leon, rue Godecharles, Ixelles. *Arach.*

Bemmel, Charles van, rue St.-Lazare 25, St.-Josse-ten-Noode, near Brussels. *Coleopt.*

Berchem, François, Ing., Chef Dir. hon. des Mines, rue Pepin 32, Namur. *Min., Geol.*

Bergé, Albert, Membre de la Societé Entomologique de Belgique, rue de la Poste 122, Schaerbeek, near Brussels. *Ent.: Coleopt., esp. Buprestidæ and Lamellicorns.* C. Ex. Coleopt. of Belgium for Buprestidæ and Lamellicorns.

Bernardin, Prof., Curator of the Commercial and Industrial Museum, College of Melle, near Ghent. *Technol., Bot., Zool.* C. Ex.*

Bilharz, Oscar, Moresnet, near Herbesthal. *Geol.*

Blanchart, Camille, rue Vautier 6, Ixelles. *Geol.*

Boë, Adolphe de, F. R. A. S., Antwerp. *Ast.**

Bommer, J. E., Prof. University, rue de la Chancellerie 18, Brussels. *Ent.: Lepid.*

Bonaert, Baron Raoul, rue Marie-Thérèse 85, Brussels.

Bormans, Auguste Ernest de, rue de Constantinople 21, St. Gilles, Brussels. *Ent., Orthoptera.* C. Ex. Orthoptera of all countries, especially of the Dermaptera, of which have prepared a general monograph.

Bouhy, Victor, rue Darchis 58, Liege. *Geol.*

Boulanger, Eugène, Place du Marché, Châtelet. *Geol.*

Bourdon, Dr. Jules, Place St.-Pierre 21, Liege. *Coleopt.*

Bovie, Alphonse, rue des Fabriques 2, Brussels. *Coleopt.*

Branquart, Jules, rue du Grand Hospice 1, *bis*, Brussels. *Coleopt.*

Breithof, Nicolas, Prof. Univ., rue du Canal 54, Louvain. *Geol.*

Bremer, Capt., rue du Trône, Ixelles. *Lepid.*

Briart, Alphonse, Morlanwelz. *Geol., Palæo.*

Bustin, Oscar, rue des Guillemins 23, Liege. *Geol.*

Candèze, Léon, Glain, near Liege. *Ent., Sphingidæ, Bombycidæ.* C. Ex.*

Cannart, d'Hamale, Fr. de Malines. *Bot.*

Capronnier, J. B., rue Rogier 251, Schaerbeek. *Ent.: Lepid.**

Carbonnelle, Rev. P. Ignace, rue des Ursulines 14, Brussels. *Math.**

Carion, François, rue Névraumont 55, St.-Josse-ten-Noode. *Coleopt.*

Carnoy, Dr. J. B., Prof. Univ. Louvain, Marché aux Grains 11, Louvain. *Bot., Mic., Cellular Biology.**

Casse, Dr. J., rue de Ligne 39, Brussels. *Mic.*

Casteele, Dr. van de, rue de l'Ouest, Liege. *Arch.**

Chalon, J., St.-Jervais, near Namur. *Bot.*

Chandelon, Joseph, Prof. Univ., rue Darchis 14, Liege. *Geol.*

Chandelon, Théodore, rue St. Gilles 86, Liege. *Geol.*

Charles, E., rue Joseph II. 49, Brussels. *Mic.*

Charlier, Dr. Eugène, Faubourg St. Gilles 19, Liege. *Coleopt., Geol.**

Chaudron, Joseph, rue Joseph 11, Brussels. *Geol.*

Chavanne, Dr. Joseph, African Explorer, address Institut National de Géographie, Brussels. *Meteo., Climatology.**

Chevron, Laurent, Prof. Agric. Sch., rue Notre-Dame 306, Gembloux. *Geol.*
Chirion, Rev. P. Julien, rue des Récollets 13, Louvain. *Ast.*
Clavareau, Camille, Waret-la-Chaussée, Province of Namur. *Lepid.*
Cloquet, Norbert, M.D., Feluy. *Arch., Geol., Palæo.*
Closon, Jules, Liege. *Bot., Hort.*
Cogels, Paul, Deurne, near Antwerp. *Geol., Palæo., Biblioq.* C.*
Coppez, Dr., Boulevard du Jardin Botanique 24, Brussels. *Mic.*
Cornet, J. F., Chaussée de Wavre 263, Brussels. *Bot.*
Corput, Dr. B. Ed. van den, Prés. de la Comm. méd. du Brabant, Prof. à l'Université, 19 Avenue de la Toison d'or, Brussels. *Therapeutics.* C. Ex. Library of 20,000 volumes, Nat. Hist. objects, medical portraits, about 3,000 autographs, antiquities, etc.*
Coubeaud, Eugène, 17 rue des Paroissiens, Brussels. *Bot., Palæo., Geol., Min., Crystal., Lithol., Zool., Vert., Articulates, Ent.* C., esp. of Belgium. Ex.*
Coyon, Armand, Prof. Collège, Dinant. *Bot., Ent., Zool.*
Crépin, François, Dir. Jardin Bot., rue de l'Esplanade 8, Brussels. *Coleopt., Bot. Veg., Palæo.*
Crick, Dr. Charles, Thuillies, Hainaut. *Coleopt.*
Crocq, Dr. J., Prof. Univ., rue Royale 110, Brussels. *Geol., Mineralogy, Palæo.* C. Ex. minerals and rocks of Europe for those of all parts of the world.*
Cuylits, Jacques, rue Leys 14, Antwerp. *Zool.*
Dallemagne, rue de la Poste 46, Brussels. *Mic.*
Dastot, Dr. Adolphe, Chirurgien honoraire de l'Inst. Ophtalmique Provincial, Mons (Belgique).*
Davreux, Paul, Sec. Mus. Indus. at Brussels, 14 rue Lefrancq, Schaerbeek. *Geol.*
De Bonnier, rue de la Blanchisserie, Brussels. *Mic.*
De Caters, Le Baron Constantin, rue Gérard 2, Antwerp. *Zool.*
De Ceuleneer, Dr. Adolf, l'Univ., rue des Champs 85, Gand. *Biblioq., Anth., Arch., Eth., Ethnog., Philol.**
De Cort, Hugo, rue de l'Arbre 79, Bénit. *Gen., Zool. Con.*
De Cuyper, Charles, Prof. Univ. of Liege, rue Mercelis 80, Brussels. *Geol., Ast., Math.*
Deheen, Pierre, rue de Joie 54, Liège. *Phys., Chem.**
De La Fontaine, Jules, Univ., Ghent. *Coleopt., Lepid., Hymenop., Dipt.*
Delacre, Ambroise, 80 Montagne de la Cour, Brussels. *Mic.* C. Ex.*
De la Vallée, Prof. Poussin, rue de Namur 190, Louvain. *Geol., Min.*
Delecosse, Dr., rue de l'Hôpital 14, Brussels. *Mic.*
Delsaulx, Rev. P. Joseph, Prof. Phys., rue des Récollets 11, Louvain. *Phys., Math.**
Delstanche, Dr. Charles, rue du Commerce 11, Brussels. *Mic.*
De Moffarts, Ferdinand, Chateau de Stré par Huy. *Coleopt.* C. Ex.*
De Mot, Alfred, rue des Bouchers 46, Brussels.*
Denys, Jos., rue des Joyeuses Entrées 20, Louvain. *Anat., Pathol., et Bactériol.**
Depaire, J. B., Prof. Univ., rue Royale 54, Brussels. *Mic.*
De Pitteurs Hiegaerts, Ch., Zepperin, Limbourg. *Mic.*
De Puyt, Emil, Naturalist, Pres. Société des Sciences, des Arts, et des Lettres du Hainaut, Mons.
De Reul, X., rue de Robiano, Schaerbeek. *Geol.* C.
Despret, Félix-Léon, rue du Bouchain, Ath, Hainaut. *Ent., Coleopt.*
Destrée, rue au Beurre 49, Brussels. *Mic.*
Devis, Paul, Quai Mariemont 2, Brussels. *Bot.* C. herbs of Belgium.
Dewalque, François, Prof. Ordinaire de Chimie Industrielle à l'Université, 26 rue de Joyeuses-Entrées, Louvain. *Chem., Min.* C. *

Dewalque, Gustave, Prof. ordinaire de Minéralogie, de Géologie et de Paléontologie à l'Université, 17 rue de la Paix, Liège. *Min.*, *Geol.*, *Palæo.* C. Ex. Desires fossils, espec. Devonian, and offers Minerals and Fossils of Belgium.*
De Winter, J. Jacques, rue Van Straelen 50, Antwerp. *Zool.*
Dietz, François, 40 Marché aux Chevaux, Antwerp. *Coleopt.* C. Ex.*
Dietz, François, rue van Bloer 8, Antwerp. *Ent.*, *Coleopt.*
Dollo, M. L., Aide.Naturaliste au Musée Royal d'Histoire Naturelle de Belgique, Brussels. *Vert.*, *Palæo.*
Donckier, de Donceel, Ch. rue Mandeville 128, Liege. *Lepid.**
Donckier de Donceel, Henri, Mus. hist. nat., rue Malibran 109, Ixelles. *Coleopt.*
Donckier, Charles, Chokier, near Flemmalle. *Geol.*
Dubois, Dr. Alphonse, Conservateur au Musée royal d'histoire naturelle, Brussels. *Mam.*, *Orn.* Ex.*
Dugniolle, Maximilien, Prof. Univ., 57 Compure, Ghent. *Geol.*
Duliat, Jules, rue de Montigny, Charleroi. *Geol.*
Dupont, E., Dir. R. Mus. Nat. Hist. rue de l'Arbre Bénite 19, Ixelles, near Brussels. *Geol.**
Du Pré, Dr. Gaston, rue Pépin 13, Brussels. *Coleopt.**
Durand, Théophile, rue Lambert le Bègne 12, Liege. *Geol.*
Dusart, E., rue du Chatelain 7, Brussels. *Mic.*
Du Trien de Terdonck, Joseph, Chateau de Meuysenhuis, Malines. *Hort.*, *Lepid.*, *Coleopt.* C. Ex.*
Duvivier, Antoine, rue du Progrès 98, Schaerbeek. *Ent.: Coleopt.*, *Physoph. du globe*, *Orn. gen.* C. Ex.*
Engels, Charles, Anseremme, near Dinant. *Coleopt.*
Errera, Dr. Léo, Prof. à l'Université, 1 rue Stephanie, Brussels. *Bot.**
Eugène, S., Naturalist, rue de l'Enseignement 19, Brussels. *Coleopt.*
Faly, Joseph, Boulevard Charles-Quint, Mons. *Geol.*
Fayn, Joseph, 22 Avenue Rogier, Liege. *Geol.**
Férage, Emile, Dinant. *Chem.*, *Mic.*
Fettweiss, Maurice, rue de Limbourg 19, Verviers. *Coleopt.*
Firket, Adolphe, rue Dartois 28, Liege. *Min.*, *Geol.*
Firket, M., rue de la Paix 17, Liege. *Min.*, *Geol.*
Foettinger, Alexandre, Dr. en Sci. Nat., Dr. en Médecine, Chirurgie et Accouchments; Conservateur des collections zoologiques à l'Univ. de Liège. *Mic.*, *Zool.**
Folie, François, Dir. de l'Obs. royal, Brussels.*
Fologne, Egide, rue de Namur 12, Brussels. *Lepid.*
Foudu, Nicolas, Hôtel de la Toison d'or, Leuze (Hainaut). *Lepid.*, *Coleopt.*
Fontaine, J. C., Cultivateur, Papignies (Belgium). *Birds, Insects, Lepid. of Belgium.* C. Ex. of Nat. Hist. subjects of Belgium for those of other countries.*
Forir, H., Ingénieur répétiteur à l'école du Mines, 75 rue Haut-Laven, Liège.*
Fraipont, Prof. Julius, Université, Liège. *Zool.*, *Paléon. et. Anthr. préhistorique.**
Frederic, Victor, rue de Lausanne 60, St.-Gilles, near Brussels. *Lepid.*
Frère, Emile, rue Delannoy, Brussels. *Mic.*
Fromont, Edmond, Docteur en Medecine, Rue de la Victoire 179, St.-Gilles, near Brussels (Belgium). *Coleopt.* (*Carabites*, *Calosomites*, *Cychrites*) *of the entire world.* Ex.*
Fuisseaux, Georges de, rue Blanche 20, St.-Gilles, near Brussels. *Coleopt.*
Fuisseaux, Henri de, rue Blanche 20, St.-Gilles, near Brussels. *Coleopt.*
Gautier, l'Abbé, Institut St.-Agnace, Antwerp. *Coleopt.*

Gedoelst, Dr. Louis M., rue d'Ecosse 77, St.-Gilles, Brussels. *Mic., Gen. Biol., Histol.**
Ghysen, Dr. H., Univ., Liege, rue Pints en Sock 73, Liege. *Chem.**
Gilkinet, Alfred, Prof. Univ., rue Renkin 13, Liege. *Geol.*
Gillon Auguste, Prof. Univ., rue Beckmann, Liege. *Geol.*
Gilson, Gustave, Prof. Univ., Louvain. *Zool., Comp. Anat., Embr.**
Giron, Alfred, rue Goffart 16, Ixelles. *Lepid.*
Goret, Léopold, rue Ste.-Marie 19, Liege. *Geol.*
Gouttier, H., Braine-l'Alleud (Brabant). *Lepid.*
Graindorge, Joseph, Prof. Phys. and Math., Univ., rue Paradis 92, Liege. *Geol.*
Gravet, Fred, Louette-St.-Pierre, near Gedinne, Province of Namur, *Bryology.* C. Ex.*
Gravis, Dr. A., Prof. de Botanique à l'Univ., Directeur du Jardin botanique de Liège (Belgium).*
Greiner, Adolphe, Quai Neuf 10, Seraing. *Geol.*
Guibal, Théophile, rue des Groseilleirs 43, Mons. *Geol.*
Habets, Alfred, rue des Carmes 9, Liege. *Geol.*
Hans, Louis Evban, near Herrenhut. *Moll.*
Hanuise, Prof. l'Ecole des Mines du Hainaut, Brussels. *Geol.*
Harzé, Émile, rue de Trèves 76, Brussels. *Geol.*
Hayez, Fr. R. Acad., rue de l'Orangerie 16, Brussels. *Math.* C.
Heger, Dr. Paul, Prof. Univ., rue des Drapiers 35, Brussels. *Mic.*
Hennequin, Major E., Prof. à l'Ecole de Guerre, des Côteaux 121, Schaerbeck, Brussels. *Cartographie, Geol., Phys. Geog.* Carte Géologique de l'Europe à l'échelle de 8.000,000, d'après A. Dumont, 1875, avec notice. Nouveau tirage chromolithographique (1876), de la carte Géologique de la Belgique et des contrées voisines par A. Dumont, avec notice explicative.
Hennuy, Léon, rue St.-Pierre 10, Dinant. *Ent.: Coleopt., Bot.*
Hock, Gustave, Prof. Athenæum, Boulevard Beauduin de Jerusalem 27, Mons. *Geol.*
Hooreman, Ch., Observatory, Brussels. *Ast., Meteo.*
Houzeau, J. C., Dir. Roy. Obs., Brussels. *Ast.*
Houzeau de Le Have, Auguste, Mons. *Geol.*
Jacob, L., Makoy & Co. Liege. *Bot.* C. of plants.*
Jacobs, Dr. J. Ch., rue des Ursulines 28, Brussels. *Coleopt., Dipt., Hymenop.*
Janson, Paul, Place du Petit Sablon 18, Brussels. *Mic.*
Jochams, F., Inspecteur général des Mines, rue de Staasart 100, Ixelles. *Geol.*
Joly, A., Prof. Univ., rue de Parnasse 38, Brussels, Est. *Chem., Min.*
Joris, Dr., rue des Alexiens 19, Brussels. *Mic.*
Jorissen, Armand, rue Sur-la-Fontaine 108, Liege. *Geol.*
Jorissenne, Dr. Gustave, Boulevard de la Sauvenière 130. Liège, *Pathol., Physiol., Bot., Geol.* C. of plants, rocks, and fossils of Belgium.*
Julin, Ch., Prof. Univ., rue Bassenge 46, Liège. *Mic., Anat., Compar. Emb.**
Kerchove de Denterghem, Count Oswald de, ex-Gov. of Prov. Hainaut, Membre de la Chambre des Représentants de Belgique, Gand. *Bot., Coleopt., Agric.* C. Palm-trees and coal-fossils.*
Kerremans, Ch., Captain of Belgian Army, 58 rue du Lac, Brussels. *Coleopt., Spec. Buprestidæ.**
Kick, Dr. J. J., Prof. Univ., rue St.-Georges 28, Ghent. *Bot.*
Kirkpatrick, R. S., rue de la Croix 66, Ixelles. *Mic.*
Koltz, J. P. J., Agent forestier, Luxembourg. *Bot.: Phanerogams and Cryptogams.* C. Ichth., Mollusques. Ex.*
Kupfferschlaeger, Isidore, Prof. Emer. Univ., rue du Jardin Botanique 18, Liège. *Chimiste.**

Lagnesse, Emile, rue d'Enghien 3, Mons. *Geol.*
Lagrange, Observatory, Brussels. *Ast.*
Lallemand, Amédée, rue Berckmans 12, St. Gilles, near Brussels. *Lepid.*
Laloux, Henri, Membre effectif de la Société Royale de Botanique de Belgique, Avenue Logier 14, Liège. *Bot.* C. Offers plants of the flora of Belgium, and desires F. W. Algæ, and plants of all species from America.
Lamal, Alphonse, Marché-aux-Cuirs 5, Malines. *Coleopt.*
Lamarche, Oscar, Pres. du Tribunal de Commerce, rue Louvret 70, Liège. *Ent.*, *Lepid.*, *Exotics of Europe.* C. Ex. books and insects.
Lambert, Guillaume, Prof. Univ. of Louvain, Boulevard de l'Observatoire, 50, Brussels. *Geol.*
Lambrichs, Edmond, rue Kessels 66, Schaerbeek. *Ent.*, *Lepid.*
Lameere, Auguste, Ph.D., Chaussée de Charleroi 121, Brussels. *Whole Zool.*, *Ent.*, *Longicornia.* C. Ex.*
Lammens, Dr. F., rue Dupont 65, Brussels. *Mic.*
Lancaster, Albert Benoit Marie, Metéorologiste-inspecteur à l'Observatoire Royal de Bruxelles, rue Royale Ste.-Marie 129, Schaerbeek, near Brussels. *Meteo.*, *Ast.**
Leboucq, H., Compure 155, Ghent. *Anat.*, *Comp. Histol.*
LeBrun, Arthur, Dinant. *Bot.*
Lecatte, Louis, rue Linnée 79, St.-Josse-ten-Noode. *Lepid.*
Ledent, Prof. Com. Coll., Verviers.
Lefevre, Th., Secrétaire de la Société Royale Malacologique de Belgique, rue du Pont Neuf 10, Brussels. *Tertiary fossils.* C. Ex. shells of Belgium for those of the U. S.
Lejeune, J., Chaussée d'Ixelles 119, Ixelles. *Mic.*
Le Mek, Frederic, 5 rue de Persil, Brussels. *Math.*
Lemonnier, Alfred, rue de Quatre Fils Aymon, Mons. *Lepid.*
Le Paige, Dr. Ch., Prof., Univ., Liege.
Liagre, Charles, rue d'Egmont 46, Malines. *Ent.*, *Lepid.*
Liagere, Gen. J. B. J., Sec. Acad. Roy. Sci., Brussels. *Bot.*
Linden, J., rue du Chaume, Ghent. *Bot.*
Lubbers, L., rue du Berger 26-28, Ixelles, Brussels. *Bot.*, *Hort.*
Macar, Julien de, Quai des Pêcheurs 39, Liege. *Geol.*
MacLeod, Dr. Julius, Assistant à l'Université, Visscherij 43, Ghent. *Zool.*, *Anat.*, *Embryol.* C. Ex. Offers Coleoptera, Hemiptera, Arachnids and Molluscs of Belgium, and wishes foreign Arachnids and Molluscs.
Mahaux, Dr., Prof. Univ., rue Thérèsienne 8, Brussels. *Mic.*
Malherbe, Renier, Ingénieur, rue Dartois 14, Liege. *Geol.*
Malaise, C. H. G. L., Prof. à l'Institut Agricole de l'Etat Belge, Membre de l'Academie Royale, Gembloux. *Min.*, *Geol.* C. Ex. Offers Archæological objects of Belgium, Silurian, Devonian and Carboniferous fossils. Wishes Cambrian and Silurian fossils, and minerals of America.
Malpertuis, Lucien, rue du Poincson 39, Brussels. *Coleopt.*
Marchal, E. Botanic Garden, Brussels. *Mic. and Mycology.**
Maréchal, Jules, Méry-Tilff, Prov. of Liege. *Ent.*, *Coleopt.**
Marloye, Auguste, Dinant. *Min.*, *Geol.**
Martens, Dr. Ed., Prof. Univ., rue Marie-Thérèse 27, Louvain. *Bot.*
Masius, V., Prof. *Pathol. and Therapeutics*, Univ. of Liege.
Mélise, Louis, rue Faider 16, St.-Gilles, near Brussels. *Coleopt.*
Mélot, Albert, Chaussée de Charleroi 12, St.-Gilles, near Brussels. *Coleopt.*
Melsens, Louis H. F., rue de la Grosse-Tour 17, Brussels. *Phys.**
Mertens, Albert, rue Marie de Bourgogne 32, Brussels. *Coleopt.**

Mertens, Gaston, rue Marie de Bourgogne 32, Brussels. *Coleopt.**
Meunier, A., Collège Juste, Lipse, Louvain. *Bot.*
Michelet, Gustave, rue Pascale 6, Brussels. *Ent.*
Michels, Galerie du Roi, Bruxelles. *Zool., Mam., Orn.* C.
Michels, Louis, Naturalist, Galerie du Roi 19, Brussels. *Ent.: Coleopt.*
Michiels, Charles, Canal des Récollets 21, Antwerp. *Zool.*
Michót, Norbert Louis, Abbé, Mons, Hainaut. *Bot., Geol., Con., Fossils, Min.* C.
Miedel, Joseph, rue des Prébendiers 6, Liege. *Coleopt.*
Miller, Prof. Henry, Place de l'Industrie 30, Brussels. *Mic.*
Minette, Charles, avenue Rogier, Liege. *Bot.*
Moerenhout, Victor, Membre des Sociétés Entomologiques de Belgique et de France, à Comblain-au-Pont, Prov. de Liège. *Coleopt., Lepid.*
Morel, Armand, rue Joseph II. 10, Brussels. *Coleopt.*
Morette, Emile, rue Kevenveld 23, Ixelles. *Neuropt.*
Mori, Alfred, rue Belliard 83, Brussels. *Lepid.*
Morren, Dr. Edouard, Prof. ord. de Bot. à l'Université, Boverie 1, Liège. *Bromeliaceæ and Flora of S. America.* C. Plants of S. America.
Mourlon, Charles, rue de Ruysbroeck 61, Brussels. *Elect.*
Mourlon, Dr. Michel, Agregé à l'Université, Conservateur au Musée Royal d'Histoire Naturelle, Membre de l'Academie des Sciences de Belgique, rue Belliard, Brussels. *Stratigraphical Geol., Upper Devonian.* C. Ex. for the Museum.*
Muller, F., rue du Beau Site 2, Brussels. *Bot.*
Niesten, L., Royal Observatory, Brussels. *Astronomy.*
Nerom, Prosper van, rue St.-Guidon, Anderlecht, near Brussels. *Coleopt.*
Noblet, Albert, avenue d'Avroy, Liege. *Geol.*
Nuel, J. P., Prof. de Physiol. et d'ophthalmologie à l'Université de Liège.*
Pâque, E., S. J., rue des Récollets 11, Louvain. *Phæn. and Crypt. Bot.* C. Herbs of Belgium.*
Paternotte, Jean, rue Alphonse Vanden Peereboom 23, Brussels.
Paternotte, L., rue Alphonse Vanden Peereboom 23, Molenbeek-St.-Jean, near Brussels. *Coleopt.*
Pelseneer, Paul J., Doct. en Sci. Nat., rue du Gentilhomme 17, Brussels. *Compar. Anat. of Moll.* Wishes Gymnos. Pteropoda in ex. for other animals.*
Perard, Louis, Prof. Univ., rue du St.-Esprit 93, Liege. *Geol.*
Peteau, Antoine, rue Royal 173, St.-Josse-ten-Noode. *Lepid.*
Petermann, Dr. Arthur, Directeur de la Station Agricole Expérimentale, et Prof. à l'Institut Agricole de l'Etat, Gembloux. *Agricultural Chem., Mic.**
Petit Bois, Gustave, rue Louvrex 97, Liege. *Geol.**
Picard, Edmond, avenue Toison d'Or 47, Brussels. *Mic.*
Pierret, Emile, rue du Progrès, 132, Schaerbeek. *Hemipt.*
Piré, Louis, rue Keyenveld, 111, Ixelles. *Bot.*
Piret, Adolphe, Directeur du Comptoir Belge de Paléontologie et de Mineralogie, Tournay. *Carb. Palæo.* C. Ex. Solicits correspondents in America.*
Pitteurs, Dr. Charles de, Zepperen, near Ordange, Limbourg. *Chem., Nat. Phil., Mic.*
Plateau, Felix, Prof. à l'Université, Dir. du Musée, Boulevard du Jardin Zoologique 64, Ghent. *Zool., Comp. Anat.* C. Desires especially Myriapods.*
Pletinckx, Jules, avenue de la Toison d'Or 70, St.-Gilles, near Brussels. *Coleopt.*
Pré, G. du, chaussée St. Pierre 99, Etterbeck, Brussels. *Ent.: Coleopt.*
Preudhomme de Borre, Alfred, Con. Musée Royal d'Hist. Nat., rue de Dublin 19, Ixelles. *Bibliog., Zool., Gen. Biol., Geog. Dist., Articulates, Ent.: Coleopt.**

Prinz, W., Chaussée de Wavre 263, Brussels. *Geol.*, *Min.*, *Lithol.*, *Mic.**
Proost, Sec. Soc. Roy. Agric., Place Royale, Brussels. *Mic.*
Puls, Jacques Charles, Pharmacien, Place de la Calendre 4, Ghent. *Diptera*, *Hymenop.*, especially *Formicidæ* of the world. C. Ex.
Purves, John, Chaussée de Charleroi 91, Brussels. *Geol.*
Pynaert-van-Geert, Ed., Prof. d'Horticulture, Ghent. *Hort.*, *Arboriculture*, *Pomology*. C. Ornamental Plants and Fruit Trees. Ex. with botanical collectors of all countries.
Pyro, Joseph, Prof. Agric. Inst., Gembloux. *Geol.*
Quaedvlieg, Louis, Vise (Liege). *Lepid.*
Quetelet, Ernest, Ixelles.
Ramy, Albert, rue Dupont 56, Schaerbeek. *Mic.*
Renard, A. F., Cons. Musée Royal d'Hist. Nat. de Belgique, 426 Ave. Brugmann, Uccle. *Geol.*, *Min.*, *Lithol.**
Renson, G., rue de la Poste 192, Brussels. *Mic.*
Reul, Gustave de, Grand rue 75, Jambs. *Geol.*
Robie, Francois, Pres. Agric. and Hort. Union, Forest, near Brussels. *Ent.*
Roelofs, Paul J., Klipsteeg 22, Antwerp. *Coleopt.* C. Ex.*
Roelofs, Willem, Ancien Président de la Soc. Entomologique, Chaussée de Haecht 218, Brussels. *Ent.*: *Coleopt.* (Circulionidæ); Geographical Distribution.
Roffiaen, Francis, rue Godecharle 16, Brussels. *Moll.* C.
Royer, Emile, rue Neuve 25, Brussels. *Coleopt.*
Ruhl, François, rue Rogier 12, Verviers. *Coleopt.*
Rutot, Aimé, Mus. Nat. Hist., Brussels, rue du Chemin de fer 34, St. Josse-ten-Noode. *Geol.**
Sauveur, Jules, rue Juste-Lipse 40, Brussels. *Ent.*: *Coleopt.*
Schmitz, Chr., S. J., Prof. Nat. Hist., Coll., La Baix, Namur. *Bot.*
Segvelt, Edm. van, Boulevard des Arbalétiers 96, Malines. *Coleopt.*
Sélys Fauson, Baron Fred. de, Quai Manelis, Liege. *Geol.* C.
Sélys-Longchamps, Baron Edmond de, Sénateur, Mem. de l'Académie Royale de Belgique, Boulevard de la Sauvenière 34, Liege. *Orn.*, *Mam.*, *Neuropt.**
Siegen, Pierre-Mathias, Luxembourg. *Geol.*
Société des Naturalistes Dinantais, Dinant; Pres., Prof. Amand Coyon; Sec., Edmond Bruyuinx; Conservator, Gustave Flostroy. *Bot.*, *Zool.*, *Min.*, *Geol.* C. Ex. the products or objects of our country for those of others.*
Spring, Walter, Prof. Univ., rue Paul Devaux 1, Liege. *Geol.**
Stas, J. S. St.-Gilles, near Brussels. *Chem.*
Stevens, Agap, Chaussée d'Ixelles 242, Ixelles. *Lepid.*
Stevens, René, rue Malibran 127, Ixelles. *Coleopt.*
Stuckens, Maurice, rue Haute 130, Ghent. *Vert.*, *Anat.*, *Moll.**
Swaelmen, J. Vander, The Lily Nursery, Ghent. *Bot.*, *Hort.* C.*
Terby, François, Docteur en Sciences, Membre de la Société Royale Astronomique de Londres, rue des Bogards 96, Louvain. *Phys.*, *Ast.* C. of drawings of Planets, esp. Mars, Venus, Jupiter. Ex. Publications on Astronomy, esp. for the Observ. of Planets.*
Thibault, Chev. Edouard de, Place Dailly 13, Schaerbeek. *Lepid.*
Thirot, Edouard, rue de l'Orient 19, Etterbeek, Brussels. *Ent.*: *Hymenop.*, *Lepid.*, *Dipt.*, *Coleopt.* C. Ex.*
Thiroux, Eugène, Boulevard de la Senne, 101, Brussels. *Ent.*, *Coleopt.*
Thomas, E. rue de la Tribune 2, Brussels. *Ent.*, *Coleopt.*
Thomas, E., 12 rue de Progrès, St.-Josse-ten-Noode. *Ent.*
Tirlinck, J., Prof. Normal School, rue des Quatre-Vents 74, Molenbeek-St.-Jean, near Brussels. *Coleopt.*
Tosquinet, Dr. Jules, Médecin principal de l'armée, rue d'Ecosse 4, à St.-Gilles, Brussels. *Ent.*: *Hymenop.*, *Ichneumonidæ.**

Tras, C. R. P., Prof. Coll. La Paix, Namur. *Geol.*
Trasenster, Louis, Prof. Univ., Quai de l'Industrie 9, Liege. *Geol.*
Troostembergh, Max de, Place St.-Jacques 22, Louvain. *Ent.: Coleopt.*
Van Bambeke, Ch., rue Haute, 5 Ghent. *Ent.*
Van Bastelaer, Désiré Alexandre Henri, Memb. l'Acad. Royale de Méd., et de l'Acad. d'Arch. de Belgique, rue de l'Abondance 24, Brussels. *Bot., Arch., Pharm., Chem., Hyg.**
Van Beneden, Edouard, Prof. à l'Université, rue des Augustins 43, Liege. *Embryology, Comparative Anat., Zool.* C. of the University. Ex. Wishes to receive Tunicates, esp. Ascidians.*
Van Beneden, Pierre Joseph, Prof. l'Université, 93 rue de Namur, Louvain. *Zool., Comparative Anat., Animal Palæo.* C.*
Vanden Born, l'Abbé H., Hasselt. *Diatoms.*
Van den Branden, Constant, rue de la Madeleine 69, Brussels. *Ent.: Phytophaga of the globe.* C. Ex.*
Vanden Broeck, Ernest, Mus. Nat. Hist., rue de Terre-Neuve 102, Brussels. *Geol., Foraminifera.**
Vandendaele, Henri, Mem. Société Royale Malacologique de Belgique, Renaix. *Invert. Palæo. of the Tertiary, Crustacea, Moll.* C. Ex.*
Vanden Heuvel, Em., rue de Laeken 118, Brussels. *Mic.*
Vanden Oberlee, Louis, rue des Tianneurs 41, Antwerp. *Zool.*
Vanderberghe, Emile, Roulers. *Lepid., Coleopt.*
Vander Kindere, Marcel, rue de Livourne 64, Brussels. *Ent.: Lamellicornes.*
Vandernoot, Louis, rue de la Croix de Pierre 12, St.-Gilles, near Brussels. *Coleopt.*
Vandresse, Paul, rue Fyon, Verviers. *Coleopt.*
Van Ertborn, Baron Octave (Winter), rue des Lits 14, Antwerp. (Summer), Aertselaer, near Antwerp. *Ast., Geol.**
Van Heerswinghels, rue du Persil 4, Brussels. *Mic.*
Van Heurck, Dr. Henri Prof. de Botanique, et Directeur du Jardin Botanique, rue de la Santé, 8, Antwerp. *Bot., Mic., Diatoms.* C. Herbarium of the globe, 70,000 specimens. Ex. Diatoms. Author, and editor of "Synopsis des Diatomés de Belgique," containing an Atlas with 140 photo-lith. prints, 3,000 figures. Price, 140 francs. or $28.*
Van Houtte, L., Gentbrugge. *Bot.*
Van Hulle, H. J., Ghent. *Bot.*
Vanlair, C., M.D., Prof. Univ. of Liege. *Gen. Biol., Histol. of Vert.**
Van Leynzeele, rue de Laeken 94, Brussels. *Mic.*
Van Scherpenzeel, Thim. Jules, rue Nysten 34, Liege. *Geol.*
Van Tricht Rev. P. Victor, Prof. Nat. Sci., Coll. N. Dame de la Paix, Namur. *Phys., Meteo. Con.* C. Ex.*
Van Volxem, Dr. T., Prof. Univ., rue Belliard 4, Brussels. *Mic.*
Vaughan, E., Boulevard Central 46, Brussels. *Mic.*
Vaux, Adolphe de, rue des Anges 15, Liege. *Geol.*
Vekemans, Jacques, Directeur de la Société Royale de Zoologie, Antwerp. *Zool.**
Velge, G. Lennick.-St.-Quentin. *Geol.* C.
Verbessem, Albert, avenue du Jardin Zoologique 36, Ghent. *Coleopt.*
Vincent, Gérard, Nat. Hist. Mus. of Brussels, rue Granvelle 95, St. Josse-ten-Noode. *Geol., Palæo.* C.
Von Gehuchten, Arthur, Prof. d. Anat., Louvain. *Anat.**
Vos, André, de, Univ., Liege. *Bot.*
Wehenkel, Dr., Prof. Univ., rue d'Allemagne 49, Brussels. *Mic.*
Wesmael, Prof., Nimy, near Mons. *Bot.*
Weissenbruch, Paul, rue du Princon 45, Mollenbeek-St-Jean. *Mic.**
Willain, D., Trivières, near Braquegnies, Hainaut. *Ent., Coleopt.*

Wilmart, Dr. Prof. Univ., rue d'Assaut 26, Brussels. *Mic.*
Wiot. Fr., Liege. *Bot.*, *Hort.**
Wissinger, Camil, Ingénieur et Chimiste, rue Hôtel des Monnaies, St.-Gilles, Brussels. *Chem.*, *Elect.**
Witmeur, Henri, Prof. Univ. and Polytec. Sch. rue d'Ecosse 14, Brussels *Geol.*
Wytsman, P., rue de Neuchâtel, 17, St.-Gilles, near Brussels. *Coleopt. esp. Cetonidæ.* Ex. with those desiring coleopt. from Belgium.

CORSICA.

Antommarchi, Prof. P., College, Paoli. *Bot.*
Burnouf, Charles, Dir. College, Paoli. *Bot.*
Dupuis, l'Abbé, Ajaccio. *Coleopt.*
Orticoni, Calvi. *Coleopt.*
Rèvélière, Eugène, Porto-Vecchio. *Coleopt.*

DENMARK.

Aaren, J. C., Prof., Aabybro. *Bot.*, *Philol.**
Aggersborg, N. N., Copenhagen. *Bot.*
Andersén, A., Havrehed, Ideusc. *Bot.*
Andersen, N., Astens. *Bot.*
Baagöc, J., Apotheker, Nœstved. *Phæn. Bot.*, *Hort.*, *Orn.* C. Ex.*
Bartholin, C. T., Copenhagen. *Bot.*
Bauer, Chr. A. P., Cand. Pharm., Rudkjöbing. *Ichth.*, *Reptilia und Amphibia.* C.
Becher, A., Rosendalsag 1, Copenhagen *Bot.*
Bergh, L., Thorshavn, Strömöe. *Bot.*
Bergh, Prof. Dr. Rudolph, Phys. to the "Vestre Hospital" of Copenhagen, Stormgade 19, 2. Copenhagen. *Zool.*, *lower animals.**
Bergstedt, N., Bodilsker pr. Nexoe. *Bot.*
Bing, Direct, 37 Pilestræde, k., Copenhagen. *Math.*
Boas, Dr. J. E. V., Copenhagen. *Zool.**
Bohr, Dr. Christian, Physiol. Lab, Bredgade 62, Kjöbenhavn. *Gen. Biol.*
Borries, T., St. Kongarsgade 90, Copenhagen. *Bot.*
Borst, L., Medoeden pr. Skjorbak. *Bot.*
Boysen, J. H. H., Ravnsborggade 6, 2, Copenhagen. *Bot.*
Branth, Rev. J. S. Deichmann, Sneptrup, near Skanderborg. *Lichenology*, *Geol.* C. Lichens. Wishes lichens from So. temperate climates, and can offer Boreal and Arctic in Ex.*
Bremer, W., Copenhagen. *Bot.*
Bruhn, C. A., Aarhuus. *Bot.*
Christensen, J. P., Roonsberggade 6, Copenhagen, N. *Physics*, *Bot.*
Collin, Jonas, Rosendalsvei 5, Copenhagen. *Zool.**
Dohlmann, Sophus, 5 Sophievei, Copenhagen V. *Lepid.* C.*
Fausböll, J., Hassing pr. Thisted. *Bot.*
Feilberg, C., Osterbrogade 52, Copenhagen. *Bot.*
Feilberg, Rev. H. F., Darum Præstegaard, near Bramminge Station. *Bot.*, *Philol.*, *Danish Dialects.* Publisher of a Dictionary of Western Danish dialects, 13 sheets printed and published.*
Flindt, H., Fredriksberg Runddel, V. Copenhagen. *Bot.*
Fraas, V., Valby pr. Helsinge. *Bot.*

Friderichsen, K., Hadersley, Slesvig. *Bot., esp. Rubi.* C. Ex.
Friedrichsen, Th., Bot. Gar., Copenhagen. *Bot.**
Friis, J. J. L., Taudloy, Hjoring. *Bot.* C. Ex.*
Gelert, Otto, C. L., Ribe. *Bot., Rosaseæ.* C. Ex.*
Gjeding, Marie, Frederiksörs. *Bot.*
Gram, Dr. J. P., Linnésgade 16, A., Copenhagen. *Math.**
Grönlund, Chr., Mouradog 17, V., Copenhagen. *Bot.*
Haas, Andreas Bang, Norresogade 37, Copenhagen. *Lepid.*
Hallas, Y., Sonderborg. *Bot.*
Halstebræ, O., Copenhagen. *Bot.*
Hannover, A., M.D., Prof. Gl., Kongevej 91, Copenhagen, V.*
Hansen, Carl, Docent at the Roy. Ast. School, Copenhagen. *Bot., Cultivated Plants and Trees.* C. Ex. European Plants, Fruits, and Fir Trees for foreign.*
Hansen, Dr. Emil Chr., Vorstand des Physiologischen Laboratoriums, Carlsberg, Copenhagen. *Physiology of Plants.**
Hansen, J. J., Faaborg. *Bot.*
Hansen, Dr. P. C. V., Sortedamsgade 7, Copenhagen, N. *Math.**
Hansen, R. A., Nautensgade 46, Copenhagen. *Bot.*
Heiberg, C. C. B., Norrebros, Copenhagen, N. *Bot.**
Helveg, L. O., Redacteur, Copenhagen. *Bot.**
Hempel, P., Friesenborg pr. Hammel. *Bot.*
Henningen, W., Thüresengade, Copenhagen. *Bot.*
Henningsen, A., Nyard, Stege. *Bot.*
Henningsen, Valdemar, Regentsen, Kjöbenhavn, Denmark. *Phæn. and Crypt. Bot., Veg. Palæo.* C. Ex.*
Hildebrandt, Paul, Svaneapothiket, Horsens. *Bot.: Cyperaceæ, Ferns, Mosses, Lichens.* C. Ex.*
Hjorth, A. L., Ronne. *Bot.*
Hohlenberg, J. S., Norregade 17, Copenhagen. *Naut. Meteo.*
Holm, Th., Cand. phil. bot., 89 Vestervold, Copenhagen. *Anat., Morphology, and Systematic Bot.* C. Ex. Cypreaceæ.*
Holst, E. Möller, Frederiksberg Allé, Copenhagen. *Bot.*
Hörring, A. F., Frodriksborggade 26, 1, Copenhagen. *Bot.*
Hüüs, Uhr, Sötröp pr. Hasley. *Phæn. Bot., Fungi., Algæ., Mic.*
Jacobsen, E., Copenhagen. *Bot.*
Jacobsen, H., Hæsede pr. Ronnede. *Bot.*
Jacobsen, Dr. J. C., Carlsberg ved Copenhagen. *Bot.*
Jensen, Arnold, Lieutenant Royal Navy, Sölvgade 28, Copenhagen. *Phys., Geographical Dist.* Corresponds in English.*
Jensen, Chr., Hvalsö Apothek, Hvalsö Station. *Mosses.* C. Ex.*
Jensen, F. A. D., Copenhagen. *Geol.*
Jenssen-Tusch, Harald, Col., Frederiksberg, Bredegade 21, Copenhagen. *Bot.* C.
Jeppesen, Forstander for Stabg. Hojskole, Ulfborg Station. *Danish Bot., esp. Fungi and Characeæ.** *C.* Offers plants and seeds for foreign, esp. from the tropics.*
Jeppesen, J. Kr., Faarup pr. Aabybro. *Phæn. Bot., Ferns, Mosses.* C. Ex. Offers Phanerogams and Cryptogams of No. Europe, and wishes plants from all foreign lands.*
Jeppesen, Gjedved, Horsens. *Bot.* Ex. Mosses.*
Jerseld, Dr., Torrden. *Bot.*
Johansen, Aalborg. *Bot.*
Johnsén, N., Prosto. *Bot.*
Johnstrup, Fr., Prof. u. Director des Mineral-geogn. Museum der Universität, Copenhagen. *Min., Geol.**
Jörgensen, Alfred, Director of laboratory for Mic. and Zymotechnical analysis, and preparation of absolutely pure yeast, Vesterbrogade

268, Copenhagen V. Cable address, "Zymotecnic, Copenhagen." *Technical Microscopy.*
Jörgensen, H. G. Fredriksberg Allé, 17, 1, V. Copenhagen.
Jörgensen, P., Odense. *Bot.*
Jörgensen, Dr. S. M., Prof. an der Universität, Gothersgade 156, Copenhagen. *Chem.**
Kiærskou, Hjalmar, Prof. à l'école Polytechnique Inspecteur, du Musée Botanique de l'Univ. Botanical Gardens, Copenhagen. *Filices, Brassica, and Tech. Microscopy.**
Kjor, A. J., Rudkjoburg. *Bot.*
Kloecker, A., Cort Adelersgade 10, Copenhagen, K. *Bot.* C. Ex.
Krabbe, Dr. Harald, Lehrer der Anatomie u. Physiologie bei der k. Veterinärschule, Monradsvej 19, Copenhagen. *Vet. Anatomy, Helminthology.**
Lange, Prof. Dr. Johan, Lehrer in Botanik bei dem königl. Veterinär und Ackerbauschule, Thorvaldsens Vej 5, V. Copenhagen. *Bot.* Wishes N. American plants, espec. trees and shrubs in ex. for N. European and Greenland plants.*
Langkhilde, R. C., Silkeborg. *Bot.*
Larsen, Kronprinsessegade 18, Copenhagen. *Bot.*
Larsen, A., Fredriksværk. *Bot.**
Lassen, Prof. Dr. J., Nörregade, 32, 3, Copenhagen. *Bot.*
Leth, T., Sahl pr. Bjerringbro Station. *Bot.*
Lind, N., Aalborg. *Bot.*
Löffler, Doc., Frederiksberg Allé 22, V. Copenhagen. *Geog.*
Lorenz, Prof. Dr. Ludvig, V. Copenhagen. *Math.*
Lotze, Gustav, Pres. Pharm. Assoc. of Denmark, Dir. Mus. of Antiquities, Odense. *Bot., Hort., Min., Arch.* C. Ex. Am. Antiquities for corresponding coll. of Danish in silex.
Lowzow, A. G., Slettegaard pr. Helsinge. *Bot.*
Lund, Samsöe, Bot. Gardens, N., Copenhagen. *Bot.*
Lutken, C., Lykkesholin Allé, Copenhagen. *Bot.*
Lütken, Christian, F., Dr. Phil., Prof. Zoöl. and Dir. of Dept. of Vert. in the Zoölogical Museum, Univ. Copenhagen, Nörregade 10, Copenhagen. *Gen. Zool., Palæo., Ichth., Cœlenterata, Echinoderms, Parasitical Crustacea.**
Madsen, H. P., Copenhagen. *Bot.**
Matthiessen, H. J., Kioge. *Bot.*
Meinert, Dr., 20, Bülowsvej, V. Copenhagen. *Zool.*
Michelsen, C., Larslystrade 9, Copenhagen. *Bot.*
Möller, Fabricius, Ribe. *Bot.*
Möller, Hans Jacob, Nörrebros Apothek, Copenhagen, N. *Chem.**
Möller, S., Norre Sundby. *Bot.*
Möller-Holst, E., Harsdorfsvej 7, V. Copenhagen. *Bot.**
Moltke, E. G., Norager pr. Ruds Vedby. *Bot.*
Mortensen, H., Johnstrup pr. Ballerup. *Bot.*
Müller, Dr. P. E., Sorö. *Zool.**
Nielsen, P., Orslov. pr. Skjelskor. *Bot.*
Nyeland, S., Vilvorde pr. Charlottenlund. *Bot. Gardening.*
Ottesen, L. O. C., Jagtvej 81, N. Copenhagen. *Bot.*
Overgaard, Gjettrup pr. Thisted. *Bot.*
Panum, Dr. Peter L., Prof. Physiol., Univ., Copenhagen.
Paülsen, A., Dir. d. Dänischen Meteor. Inst. *Phys.*
Pechyle, Dr., Observatory, K. Copenhagen. *Ast.*
Pedersen, N., Norager Vaaseskov pr. Ruds Vedby. *Bot.*
Pedersen, R., Klerkegade 9, 1, Copenhagen. *Bot.*
Petersen, A., Copenhagen. *Bot.*
Petersen, E., Graasten, Haberslev. *Bot.*

Petersen, E. A., Copenhagen. *Bot.*
Petersen, E. P. F., Copenhagen. *Bot.*
Petersen, K. T., Copenhagen. *Bot.*
Petersen, Nicolai Emil, Sölleröd, near Holte. *Bot.* C.
Petersen, O. G., Gothersgade 154, N. Copenhagen. *Bot.*
Petersen, P., Tandernpskole, Fjerritslev. *Bot.**
Petersen, Dr. Peter C. J., Polytec. School, Copenhagen. *Math.*
Petersen, S., Slotsbjergby pr. Slagelse. *Bot.*
Petit, E., Harsdorfsvej, V. Copenhagen. *Bot.*
Philipsen, F., Fredricia. *Bot.*
Piper, H. A. T., Copenhagen. *Bot.*
Poulsen, D. T., Roeskildevej, Kjöbenhavn. *Bot.*
Poulsen, H. F., Vester, Egitsborg pr. Præsto. *Bot.*
Poulsen, J. C., Odense. *Bot.*
Poulsen, Viggo A., Rosenvængets Hovedvei 29, Copenhagen. *Bot.*
Rasch, C., M. D., Graabrodretory 5, Copenhagen, K. *Bot.*, *Marine Algæ.* C. Ex. Wishes Algæ in ex. for N. European Algæ.*
Rasmussen, H., Karleby pr. Nykjöbing p. F. *Bot.*
Raunkjor, C., Berchs Kollegium Kjöbenhavn. *Bot.*
Reck, A., Hallingszode 40, Kjöbenhavn. *Bot.*
Riise, A. H., Fredriksberg Alle 12, V. Copenhagen. *Bot.*
Reimeri, D., Aabeuraa. *Bot.**
Rink, Dr. Hinrich J., Keysergade 3, Christiania. *Geol.*, *Ethnol.**
Rosenberg, Caroline, Hofmansgade pr. Odense. *Bot.*, *Algæ.*
Rosenvinge, L. Kolderup, Frederiksborggade 41, Copenhagen. *Bot.: Algæ.**
Rossing, Fredriksberg Allé 36, 2, V. Copenhagen. *Bot.*
Rostrup, E., Docent, Copenhagen, V. *Bot.: Fungi.**
Rostrup, O., Kjöbenhavn, V. *Bot.*
Rothe, Tyge, Dir. Royal Gardens, Rosenberg, Copenhagen. *Bot.*, *Culture of plants.*
Rudmose, N., Ferslev pr. Roeskilde. *Bot.*
Rung, G. A., St. Kongensgade 85, Copenhagen. *Meteo.*
Rützou, Sophus, Cand. Pharm., Norregade 20, Copenhagen. *Bot.*, *Mic.*
Salomonsen, Dr. Carl Jul., Höjbroplads 9, Copenhagen, Prof. of Medical Bacteriology, Univ. of Copenhagen.*
Schiellerup, Dr. Hans C. F. C., Prof. Ast., Observ., Copenhagen.
Schmidt, A., Copenhagen. *Bot.*
Schmidt, Vald., Frederikshavn. *Bot.*
Schultz, A. C., Admiral, Læssöesgade 6, Copenhagen. *Bot.: Ferns.*
Schütz, C., Helsingör. *Bot.*
Seehusen, V. L., Copenhagen. *Bot.*
Smith, Otto, Lerchenborg, near Kallundborg. *Bot.* C.*
Steenstrup, Dr., Japetus S., Prof. Univ., Copenhagen. *Zool.*, *Geol.**
Steenstrup, K. I. V., Forhaabningsholms Allé, 10-2, Kjöbenhavn, Asst. Min. et Geol. Museum, Copenhagen, esp. Geol. of Greenland.
Stockfleth, V. P. T., Osterbrogade 31, Copenhagen. *Bot.*
Storm, V., Odense. *Bot.*
Svendten, F., Holbergsgoer, Kjöbenhavn. *Bot.*
Thiele, Prof. Dr. Thorvald, Nicolai, Observatoriet, Copenhagen. *Ast.**
Thorsen, M., Stege, Moen. *Bot.*
Topsoe, Dr. Haldor, Inspecteur Royal des Fabriques, Prof. à l'Académie Militaire, Copenhagen, V. *Chem. Crystal.**
Trier, S. M., Rosenborggade 3, Copenhagen. *Bot.*
Tychsen, Dr. Camillo, Dir. der Staats-Lebensversicherungs-Anstalt, Savanholmsvei 1, Copenhagen. *Math.*
Vestesen, B. Q., Mynstersvej 4, V. Copenhagen. *Bot.**
Vilandt, Dr. Hans N. P., Ribe. *Bot.*, *Lycopodiaceæ.* C.*

Wandel, C. F., Copenhagen. *Geog., Zool.*
Warming, Prof., Joh. Eug. Bülow, Ph.D., Dir. Botan. Garten, Copenhagen. *Ptorphologie Phan. Bot., Arctic Plants.**
Wiinstedt, Dr. St., Kongeisgade, 93, 1, Copenhagen. *Bot.*
Zahrtmann, Hans, Hornslet, near Aarhus. *Bot., Insect fertilization.*
Zeuthen, Prof. Dr. Hieronymus, G., Univ., Copenhagen. *Math.**

FINLAND.

Ahlquist, Dr. August E., Prof. Univ. Helsingfors. *Finn. and Hung. Language.*
Alcenius, O. Wasa. *Bot.*
Arppe, Prof. Dr. Adolph E., Universität, Helsingfors. *Chem.*
Arrhenius, Dr. Axel, Asst. Bot. Mus., Univ., Helsingfors. *Phan. Bot.* C. Ex.*
Aschan, C. A., Kuopio. *Orn.*
Asp, Prof. Dr. Georg, Kyrkotorget 3, Helsingfors. *Anat.*
Aspelin, Dr. Eliel, Univ., Helsingfors.
Aspelin, Dr. Prof. Johan Reinhold, Museum Finn. Ugr. Arcnæologie, Commission, Arch. Société Ard. Univ., Helsingfors. *Arch., Ethnog.**
Backman, H. Dr. Med., Ympilaks. *Nat. Hist.*
Becker, Prof. Dr. F. J., Universität, Helsingfors, *Physiol., Chem., Pharm.*
Bergroth, E. Evald, Forssa, Finland. *Ent., Hem., Tipulidae.* C. Ex.*
Biese, Ernst, Asst. in Phys. Univ.-Laborat., Helsingfors. *Phys., Elect., Meteo.**
Blom, E. W., Helsingfors. *Bot.: Phanerogams.*
Blomquist, A., Director, Evois, Forstwissensch.
Bomansson, J. O., Aland, Saltrik (n. Sund). *Bot.: Mosses.*
Bonsdorff, Dr. Prof. Ernst, Tavastehus. *Math.*
Bondsdorff, Dr. Evert-Jules, Prof. Emer. Uskela, Salo.
Borenius, Prof. Dr. Heinrich G., Universität, Helsingfors. *Math.*
Brander, Casimir Evald Wilhelm, Ikalis, Parkano. *Phan. Bot., Hort., Orn., Ool.* C. Ex.*
Brenner, M., Schuldirector., Helsingfors. *Bot.**
Brotherus, Dr. F. V., Helsingfors. *Bot.: Mosses.**
Brotherus, V. F., Dr., Helsingfors. *Bryol.**
Collin, Dr. Otto, Lehrer, Tawastehus *Phan. Bot., Orn., Ool.*, C. Ex.*
Donner, Prof. Anders, Dir. Sternwarte, Helsingfors. *Ast.**
Donner, Prof. Dr. Otto, Universität, Helsingfors. *Philol., Anth.**
Elfving, Fredrik, Privat-docent des Botanischen Museums, Helsingfors. *Physiol.*
Elmgren, Prof. Dr. Sven-Gabriel, Universität, Helsingfors.
Envald, R., Kand., Helsingfors. *Ent.*
Estlander, Prof. Dr. Charles G., Universität, Unionsgatan 45, Helsingfors, *Arch., Philol.**
Faust., J., Ingénieur, Andrégatan 13, Helsingfors. *Coleopt.*
Freudenthal, Prof. Dr. Axel-Olof, Universität, Helsingfors. *Philol.**
Frosterus, Prof. Dr. J. G., Helsingfors, *Univ. Hist.*
Furuhjelm, Hjalmar, Director of the Corps of Mining Engineers, Helsingfors.*
Furuhjelm, J. E., Lector, Evois. *Nat. Hist.*
Furuhjelm, Victor de, Helsingfors. *Coleopt.*
Gronfeldt, G., Björneborg. *Nat. Hist.*
Gylling, Hjalmar, Ph.D., Staats-Geolog., Helsingfors. *Geol., Min., Crystal., Lithol.* C. Ex.*

Hällsten, Prof. K. G., Helsingfors. *Physiol.*
Heikel, A. O., Kand., Helsingfors. *Arch.*
Heimbürger, W., Boulevardsgatan 15, Helsingfors. *Coleopt.*
Hellstrom, F., Dr. Med., Gamla Karleby. *Bot.*
Hisinger, Edward, Dr. Phil., Baron Fagervick, Station de Karis. *Bot., Fungi, Algæ, Min., Orthop., Neuropt., Hort., Agric.**
Hjelt, Dr. Eduard, Prof. Universitäts, Laboratorium, Helsingfors. *Chem.*
Hjelt, Hj., Lector, Wasa. *Phæn. Bot.**
Hjelt, Otto E. A., Dr. Med., Prof. emeritus an der Univ. zu Helsingfors, *Pathol., Anat.**
Hollmén, H., Helsingfors, Cardes Kaserm. *Bot.*
Krohn, Dr. Julius L. F., Univ., Helsingfors. *Mythol.*
Homén, E. A., Th. Dr. Med., Helsingfors. *Path., Anat.*
Hougberg, Dr. Emil, Helsingfors. *Orn., Ool., Arach., Moll.* C. of Moll. Ex.*
Hult, R., Dr. Phil., Univ. Docent of Geog., Helsingfors, *Phys. Geol., Phys. Geog. and Bot. of Finland.**
Ignatius, Dr. Charles E. F., Statistical Office, Helsingfors. *Philol., Statistics.**
Inberg, I., Ingen., Borga. *Geog.*
Iverus, Ivar D., Strömfors. *Ent., Bot.*
Karsten, Dr. P. A., Mustiala. *Bot.: Mycology.*
Kihlman, Dr. Oswald, Docent an der Univ. in Helsingfors *Fungi.**
Lemström, Prof. Dr. Charles-Selim, Universität. Helsingfors. *Phys., Elect., Meteo.**
Leopold, C., Dr. Med., Tammerfors. *Bot., Phæn.**
Levänen, Sakris, Docent, Univ., Helsingfors. *Math., Ast.**
Lindberg, Dr. S. O., Prof. Bot., Botanic Garden, Helsingfors. *Bot., Mosses, Hort., Mic.* C. Ex.*
Lindelöf, Dr. Laurent-Leonard, Helsingfors. *Math.*
Malmgren, Prof. Dr. André-Jean, Inspector of Fisheries, Helsingfors. *Zool., Fishery.**
Mela, A. J., Helsingfors. *Vert., Moll.**
Mellin, Dr. Hj., Helsingfors. *Math.*
Moberg, Prof. Dr. Adolph, Universität, Helsingfors. *Physics.*
Neovius, Dr. Prof. E. R., Helsingfors. *Math.*
Nordenskiold, Nils Karl, Direktor Meteorologische-Magnetische Observatorium, Helsingfors. *Meteo. and Terrestrial Magnetism.*
Nordquist, O., Alexandersgatan 7, Helsingfors. *Zool., Vert., Crust.*
Norrlin, Dr. Johan Petter, Prof. an der Universität, Helsingfors. *Geography and Topography of Plants, Flora of Finland, especially Hieracia and Cladoniæ.* C.*
Nylander, Dr. Edwin, Knopio. *Phæn. Bot., Lichens, Hort., Agric., Moll.* C.*
Palmén, Prof. D. J. A., Helsingfors. *Zool., Comp. Anat.**
Pippingskold, J. A. J., Dr. Prof., Helsingfors. *Gynakol.**
Reuter, Odo Morannal, Ausserord. Prof. in Zool. an d. Univ., Helsingfors. *Hemipt. Collembola, Thysanoptera in spirits.* C. Ex.*
Rindell, Dr. Arthur, Prof., Chem. Landw. Inst., Mustiala. *Inorg. Chem.* C. minerals of Tammela. Ex.*
Runeberg, J. W., Dr. Prof., Helsingfors. *Med.*
Saelan, Dr. Th., Prof., Helsingfors. *Bot.**
Sahlberg, Dr. John Reinhold, e. o. Prof. Ent., Albertsgatan 32, Helsingfors. *Ent.: especially Coleoptera, Hemiptera, and Lepid.* C. Ex.*
Saltzman, F., Dr. Prof., Helsingfors. *Surgery.*
Sandman, Jon A., Magister, Helsingfors. *Bot., Zool., Oöl.* C. Ex.*
Schulman, Hj., Kand., Helsingfors. *Orn.*
Siemssen, Gustav, Helsingfors, *Oöl.**

Schulten, Dr. August, Docent, Helsingfors. *Inorg. Chem.**
Schulten, M. W., Dr. Prof., Helsingfors. *Surgery.*
Sievers, Rich., Dr. Med. Helsingfors. *Zool.*
Silén, F., Forstmeister, Kittila. *Bot.*
Solitander, Carl Probus, Helsingfors. *Geol., Met.**
Spoof, A. R., Dr. Med. and Chir., Abo, Finland. *Gen. Biol., Vert., Anat., and Emb., Public Health; Acari, Worms.**
Spoof, Wald., Secret. refer., Helsingfors, Finland. *Birds and Fishes.**
Sundell, Prof. A. F., Helsingfors. *Phys.**
Sundman, N., Kand. Med., Helsingfors. *Orn.*
Sundvik, E., Dr. Prof., Helsingfors. *Physiol., Chem., Pharmacologie.**
Tengström, Dr. J. M. J., Lojo. *Lepid.**
Unonius, K., Lector, Helsingfors. *Bot.**
Wahlfors, Dr. Kr., Docent, Helsingfors. *Chem.*
Wainio, Dr. Edw., Docent, Helsingfors. *Lichenol., Topography of Plants, Flora of Lapland.* C.
Warén, E., Dr. Med., Helsingfors. *Zool.*
Wiik, Prof. Fred. Joh., Helsingfors. *Crystal, Min., Geol.*
Willebrand, Prof. Dr. Canut-Felix de, Universität, Helsingfors. *Nat. Hist.*

FRANCE.

Abbadie, Antoine T., Mem. Acad. Sci., Rue de Bac, Paris. *Geog. and Navigation.**
Abeilhé, Edouard, Marciac (Gers). *Coleopt., Palæo., Orn.*
Abeille, de Perrin Elzéar, place les Palmiers 11, Hyères (Var). *Coleopt., Hymenop.*
Abria, Jérémie J. B., Quai de Bacalan, Bordeaux. *Phys.*
Alain, L., rue de Châteaudun 23, Paris. *European Lepid.*
Alanore, Pres. Med. Soc., Clermont-Ferrand. *Bot.*
Albert, Ampus, near Draguignan. *Bot.*
Alexandre, Auguste, rue Brezin 4, Montrogue (à Paris). *Coleopt.*
Alexandre, Paul, rue de l'Ecusson 31, Alençon. *Coleopt.*
Alix, Place St.-Vincent, Blois. *Coleopt.*
Allard, Ernest, rue Paradis-Poissonnière 2, Paris. *Coleopt.*
Allard, Gaston, La Maulevrie, Route des Ponts-de-Cé, near Angers. *Coleopt.*
Allard du Plantier, rue des Quatre-Chemins, Voiron. *Coleopt.*
Alléon, Comte, rue St.-Dominique 85, Paris. *Coleopt.*
Allin, rue Rousselet 31, Paris. *Ent.*
Alluard, Prof. E., Faculty of Science, Clermont-Ferrand 22, Place de la Taude, Clermont. *Phys.**
Amadieu, Tours (Indre-et-Loire). *Ent.*
Amans, Dr., Montpellier. *Mécanique Animale.**
Amblard, Dr. Louis, rue Paulin 14 *bis.* Agen. *Coleopt.*
Ancey, Felix, 34 rue Montée de Lodi, Marseille. *Coleopt., Hymenop., and Mollusks of the world.* C. Ex. Offers an immense number of duplicates. Wishes to get spec. from Central and Western U. S., and generally those from any country but Europe. Corrrepondence solicited.*
Andouard, Ambr., Prof. Ec. de Médecine, Nantes. *Bot., Chem.**
Andoynaud, Prof. Alfred, 25 boulevard de l'Hôpital, Montpellier. *Agric.*
André, Prof. Charles, Lyon. *Astronomy.*
André, Edouard, rue Chaptal 30, Paris. *Botanique, plants de l'Amérique du Sud.**

André, Edmond, Ingénieur boulevard Bretonnière 21, Beaune (Cote-d'or). *Hymenop.* C. Hymenoptera of the world. Editeur-Directeur de la librairie spéciale des sciences naturelles, publié périodiquement des catalogues d'ouvrages et de brochures neufs et d'occasion sur l'histoire naturelle; col. d'invert. pour l'enseignement.*
André, Ernest, rue des Promenades 17, Gray (Haute-Saône). *Ent.: Hemiptera and Formicariæ of the world.* C. Ex. Formicariæ of Europe for foreign.*
Angot, A., Bureau Central Meteor., Paris. *Phys.**
Antessanty, l'Abbé Gabriel d', Lyceum, Troyes. *Coleopt.*
Anthouard, Léon, Sauve. *Bot.*
Apréval, d', Brunoy (Seine-et-Oise). *Lepidopt., Nat. Hist.**
Aragon, Amédée, Perpignan. *Coleopt.*
Arbaumont, Jules d', membre de l'Académie de Dijon, rue Saumaise 43, à Dijon. *Bot.**
Arcelin, Adrien, Collaborateur de la carte géologique detaillée de la France, Archiviste Paleographe, St. Sorlin (Saône et Loire). *Palæo., Geol., Mic., Photog., Anth., Arch., Ethnog.* C.*
Archambaud, Gaston, 141 rue Notre-Dame, Bordeaux. *Orn.*
Argod, Albert, Membre de la Société Entomologique de France, Crest (Drôme). *Coléoptères de l'Europe et circa Coléoptères cavernieoles du monde entier.**
Arnaud, Charles, Membre á Vie de la Soc. Botanique de Erance, Layrac, par Agen (Lot-et-Garonne) *Bot.* C. Ex. for European plants only.*
Arnaud, H., Avocat, rue Froide 23, Angoulême (Charente). *Geol., especially Cretaceous.* C. Ex. for Chalk.
Artigue, Felix, 28 rue Laseppe, Bordeaux. *Palæo.*
Artique, Henri, 30 rue de Cheverus, Bordeaux. *Bot.*
Artufel, Boulevard du Musée 1, Marseille. *Coleopt.*
Arvet-Touvet, Gières (Isère). *Bot.: Hieracia.**
Association pour les Echanges entre Musées Scolaires et cantonaux, honorée d'une Subvention Ministérielle, 11 rue Soufflot, Paris. (Bureau du Journal pédagogique de l'Ecole). Pres., J. Saint-Martin; Sec.-fondateur, Paul Berton. C. Ex. of all manufactured products.
Aubert, Maurice, cours Larayette 56, Toulon. *Coleopt.*
Aubert, Joseph André Marius, Aide-Naturaliste au Muséum, Boulevard de la Corderie 34, Marseille (Bouches-du-Rhône). *Carcinology, Crustacea, Edriophthalma (Amphipoda, Isopoda),* de toutes les parties du monde.*
Aubouy, A., Secrétaire redacteur de la Société d'Horticulture et d'Histoire Naturelle de l'Hérault, et Botaniste, rue de la Gendarmerie 2, Montpellier. *Bot.* C. Herbs of France and plants of Europe, especially of Switzerland and Belgium. Ex.
Aumonier, Jacques-Marie, rue Sainte-Placide 58, Paris. *Geol.*
Auvert, Georges, Château le Grand-Fort, St.-Denis-en-Val, near Orleans. *Phæn. Bot., Anat., Ent., Coleopt., Moll., Comparative Physiol.**
Auzoux, Dr. Hector, St. Aubin-d'Ecrosville, near Neubourg. *Coleopt.*
Azam, Ch., rue de l'Observance 60, Draguignan. *Ent.: Coleopt.*
Bacle, Louis, Ingénieur des Mines, ancien élève de l'Ecole Polytechnique, Villa Péreine Asnières (Seine). *Phys.**
Baer, Gustave-Adolphe, Cité Bergère 1 *bis*, Paris *Coleopt.*
Bayer, I., 9 rue Laffitte, Paris. *Fossils.* C.
Baillon, Henri, Prof. à l'Ecole de Médecine, rue Cuvier, Paris. *Bot.*
Bailly, Louis, Beller (Ain). *Geol., Min., Anth.* C. Ex.*
Baizamor, J., rue Jouben 4, Paris. *Mic.*

Balbiani, Prof. d'Embryogénie, Collège de France, 18 rue Soufflot, Paris. *Ent.*, *Embryology*.
Balguerie, Alfred, Ingénieur, ancien Prés. de la soc. Linnéenne de Bordeaux, cours du Jardin public 84, Bordeaux. *Palæo.*, *Con.*, *Petrography*, *Min.**
Barallier, Dr., Dir. Bot. Gar., Rochefort. *Bot.*
Barbat, Pierre-Michel, Châlons. *Coleopt.*
Bardin, Louis, l'Abbé, Prof. Geol. Univ., libre d'Angers, rue de la Préfecture 19, et à Sièches (Marne-et-Loire). *Geol.*, *Palæo.* C. Ex. Tertiary fossils of Touraine and Anjou for foreign, especially American.*
Baril, A., Nigré, par Loulay. *Bot.*, *Orn.*
Barla, Jean Baptiste, Consul Hon. de l'Empire du Brazil, Tancien V. Consul de la Repub. Orientale de l'Uruguay, Dir. du Musée d'Histoire Naturelle, Place Garibaldi 6, Nice. *Bot.*, *Mycology*, *Ichth.* C. Ex. meridional plants, orchids, mushrooms.*
Barnsby, David, Prof. Sch. Med., Quai du Ruan St. Anne 36, Tours. *Bot.*
Baron, G., Avenue de St.-Cloud 85, Versailles. *Coleopt.*
Barrandon, A., Conservateur du Jardin des Plantes, Montpellier (Hérault). *Bot.* C. Ex, Offers plants of S. France, and wishes plants of America.
Barraud, Jules, 31 Cours du Jardin-Public, Bordeaux. *Orn.*
Barrère, Félix, Place Marcadieu 24. Tarbes. *Coleopt.*
Barrillos, M. Ch., Instituteur-Naturaliste, Limalonges (Deux-Sèvres). *Shells.**
Barrois, Charles, Dr., Maître de conférences à la Faculté des Sciences, rue Solferino 183, Lille. *Geol.*
Barrois, Dr. Jules, Directeur du Laboratoire maritime, Villefranche-sur-mer (Alpes maritimes). *Embryology.*
Barrois, Dr. Théodore, Licencié Sciences-Naturelles 37 rue de Lannoy, Lille (Fives). *Moll.*, *Crustacea*, *Echinoderms.*
Barthélemy, Aimé, Professeur à la Faculté. *Zool.*, *Bot.*, *Chem.*
Bataillard, Paul, Archiviste de la Faculté de Médecine de Paris, rue Notre Dame des champs 119 *bis*, Paris. *Eth.*, *Met.* C.*
Baudon, Dr. A., Mong de l'Oise. *Moll.*
Baudrimont, Dr., rue St-Rémy, Bordeaux. *Palæo.*
Bavay, Prof. à l'École de Médecine Navale, Grand rue 45, Brest. *Conchology*, *Herpetology*, *Helminthology.* C. Ex. L. and F. W. Shells.*
Beaudoin, Victor, Péronne. *Coleopt.*
Béchamp, Dr., Univ. Cath., 8 rue Beauharnais, Lille.
Becquerel, Ed., 57 rue Cuvier, Paris. *Phys.*
Bedel, Louis, rue de l'Odéon 20, Paris. *Coleopt.*
Bedorez, Prof. Lyceum, 60 rue de Flore, Le Mans. *Phys.*
Bellerade, Bial de, Place Henri IV., Bordeaux. *Coleopt. Entomology.* C. Ex.*
Bellier de la Chavignerie, E., Naturaliste, rue St. Louis 35, Evreux (Eure) France. *Ent.: Lepid. and Coleopt.* C. Ex. First-class specimens.*
Belloc, Emile, 105 rue de Rennes, Paris. *Algæ*, *Desmids*, *Diatoms*, *Mic.* C. Ex.*
Belon, Prof. Paul, rue du Plat 25, Lyon (Rhone). *Coleopt.* C. Lathridiidæ and Longicorns of the globe. Ex.
Beltremieux, Conrad, Chevalier de la Légion d'Honneur, rue des Fondères 48, La Rochelle (Charente-Inférieure). *Geol.*, *Palæo.*, *Zool.* Ex.
Beltremieux, Edouard, 42 Jardins, Rochelle. *Geol.*

Benoist, Emile, rue de la Franchise 6, Bordeaux. *Palæo.*
Benoit, Dr. R., Pavillon de Breteuil par Saint-Cloud (Seine-et-Oise). *Phys.*
Bénouville, Léon, rue de Seine 53, Paris. *Ent.: Neuropt.*
Bérard, Charles, La Garde, near Montlieu. *Coleopt.*
Berchon, Dr. Ernest, Médecin principal de lière Classe de la Marine, et Directeur du Service Sanitaire en retraite, de la Gironde des Landes, des Basses Pyrénées, et de la Charente Inf., (Gironde). Château Cordeillan, près Pauillac, Gironde. *Zool., Geol., Anth., Arch., Med.* C. Ex.*
Berdoulot, Jules, Miremont. *Coleopt.*
Berger, Eugène-Louis, rue Berthollet 17, Paris. *Coleopt.*
Berger, Dr. Jules, Dir. de l'Ecole de Médecine, rue Lafayette 5, Grenoble (Isère.) *Coleopt.*
Bergon, Paul, 40 Boulevard Haussmann, Paris. *Diatoms.**
Berher, Dr. E., Epinal. *Bot.*
Bernard, Prof., Cluny (Saône-et-Loire). *Chem.*
Bernard, Henri, Gonneville par Criquetot-l'Esneval (Seine-Inférieure. *Gen. Bot.: spec. Algæ.* C. Ex.*
Bernard, Dr. Marius Blaise, Quai Saint-Peirre 2, Cannes. *Anth.* C.
Bernard, Pharmacien-major, La Rochelle (Charente Inférieure). *Mycology.*
Bernard de Montessus, Ferdinand, Dr., Prés. Soc. des Sciences Naturelles de Saône-et-Loire, et de la Société française d'Orn. à Lyon. Châlon-sur-Saône (Saône-et Loire); Musée d'Orn. d'Europe etc., à Châlon. *Palæo., Geol., Min., Orn., Ent., Lepid., Coleopt.* C. Ex.*
Bernardin, Camille, Brie-Comte-Robert. *Bot.*
Bernault, Abbé, rue des Bouillis 25, Blois. *Palæo.*
Berne, Dr. Paul, A.B, B.Sc., 63 boulevard St.-Germain, Paris. *Zool., Anth., Hist.* C.
Berthelot, Marcelin P. E., Mem. Acad. Sci., rue Mazarine 3, Paris. *Phys.**
Berthoule, rue de Seine 87, Paris. *Pisciculture.*
Berthoumieu, V., Bayet par St. Pourcain (Allier). *Bot., Ent., Lepid. Hymenopt.* (special, *Ichneum*), *Phanerog, and Crypt.* C. Ex. (chiefly Ichneum. and Crypt.). French spec. for American.*
Bertin, Dir. Normal School, rue d'Uim 45, Paris. *Phys.*
Bertin, J., rue de la Petit-Porte 5, Rouen. *Ent.: Coleopt.*
Bertot, Pharmacien. Bayeur (Calvados). *Bot.*
Bertrand, Prof. Dr. Ch. Eug., Grande Route de Béthune 17, Loos, near Lille. *Bot.*
Bertrand, Manel, Ingénieur au Corps des Mines, rue St. Guillaume 29, Paris. *Geol.*
Bescher, Auguste, rue Royale-St.-Honoré 8, Paris. *Coleopt.*
Bescherelle, Em., 11 rue Thiers (Clamart) Seine. *Bot.**
Béthune, Albert, rue Jeanne-d' Arc., Reims. *Con., Ent.: Coleopt., Geol.**
Bétis, Louis, rue du Faubourg du Temple 19, Paris. *Coleopt.*
Bezancon, Dr. Alph., rue de Tournons 29, Paris. *Palæo., Con.*
Bial de Bellerade, Merignac (Ou Tarre), near Bordeaux (Gironde). *Ent. Coleopt., Phytophages.* C. Ex.*
Bignon, Louis, Lassay. *Ent.: Coleopt.*,
Bigot, J. M. F., Officier de l'Instruction Publique etc., Mem. Soc. Ent. de France, rue Cambon 27, Paris. *Ent., Dipt.**
Bioche, Alphonse, rue de Rennes 57, Paris. *Geol.*
Blanc, Edouard, Cercy-la-Tour. *Coleopt.*
Blanc, Marius, quai du Canal 22, Marseille. *Coleopt., Lepid., Hemipt.*

Blanchard, Emile, Memb. Acad. Sci., rue de l'Université 34, Paris. *Ent.: Coleopt.*
Blanchard, J., Bot. Gar., Brest. *Bot.*
Blanchard, Dr. Raphaël, Prof. Agrégé à la Faculté de Médecine, Sec. Général de la Soc. Zool. de France, rue Monge 59, Paris. *Comp. Anat., Physiol., Vert., Palæo., Zool.**
Blanche, Dr. Prof. Emmanuel, Boulevard Canchois, Rouen. *Bot.*
Blandeau, Dr. Dijon. *Ent.*
Blaud, Ch., St.-Germain-de-Prinçay, par Chantonnay. *Coleopt.**
Blavet, A., Président de la Société d'Horticulture, Etampes, (Seine-et-Oise). *Bot.* C. Ex.*
Blavy, Alfred, rue Barallerie, Montpellier. *Mic.*
Bl. de Paravicini (Vicaunt de), 54 quai de Billy, Paris. *Gasteropods, Cephalopods.* C.
Bleicher, Prof., Nancy. *Nat. Hist., Geol., Palæo.*
Bleuse, Léon, 36 rue de Paris, Rennes. *Coleopt.* Offre des livres d'histoire naturelle.*
Blonay, Roger de, rue de Larochefoucauld 23, Paris. *Coleopt.*
Blondeau, Dr., rue Buffon 21, Dijon. *Coleopt.*
Boban, Eugene, Antiquaire, Avenue d'Orleans 122, á Paris. Collections à vendre d'Antiquités du Mexique et d' Archéologie Préhistorique de France et Autres.*
Bois Désiré, rue Cuvier 57, Paris. *Bot.*
Boissal, Prof. Emile, Lycée de Montluçon (Allier). *Geol., Min., Palæo., Marine Con.* C. of 5,000 specimens. Ex. fossils and minerals of France for the same, or F. W. Shells of other countries.
Bompar, Dr. Felix, Portets, Gironde. *Bot.*
Bompart, rue des Huguenots 17, Orleans. *Coleopt.*
Bonaparte, Prince Rol., Cour de la Reine, Paris. *Anth., Eth., Arch.*
Bonnafont, Dr. T. P., rue Mogador 3, Paris. *Otology, Chirurgy.*
Bonnaire, Baron Archille, rue St. Méry 114, Fontainebleau. *Coleopt.*
Bonneuil, Vicomte Roger de, rue St.-Guillaume 31, Paris. *Coleopt.*
Bonnier, Gaston, Prof. à la Sorbonne, rue Amyot 7, Paris. *Bot.**
Bonnier, Jules, 75 rue Madame, Paris. Sous-dir. du laborat. de Zool. de Wimeraux. *Crustacés décapodes, Schizopodes, Cumaces, et Amphipodes.* Ex.*
Bonnière, Néron, Place Saint Gervais 83, Rouen. *Bot.**
Bonvouloir, Vicomte Henri de, Boulevard St.-Germain 215, Paris. *Coleopt.*
Bony, Vicomte G. de, rue de Passy 84, Paris. *Ent.: Coleopt.*
Bordère, Instituteur, Botaniste, Gèdre, Luz-St.-Sauveur, Hautes-Pyrénées. *Bot.* C.*
Bordier, Dr., Saillans, près Vif. *Anth.*
Bornet, Ed., Quai de la Tournelle 27, Paris. *Bot., Algæ.**
Bossert, Observatory, Paris. *Ast.**
Bouat, Gustave, Secrétaire de l'Académie d'Aix-en-Provence. *Bot.**
Boucard, Adolphe. Voyageur-Naturaliste, Officier d'Académie, Chevalier de l'ordre royal de la Conception, 13 rue Guy de la Brosse, Paris. *Palæo., Ethnog., Orn., Ent., Coleopt.* C. Buy, sell, or exchange.*
Brame, Prof. Dr. Ch., Tours. *Chem.*
Brabant, Edouard, Cambria. *Bot.**
Bovis, François, rue Rondelet 10, Paris. *Ent.: Lepid., Coleopt.*
Bouchard, Prof. Dr., rue de Rivoli 174, Paris.*
Bouché, l'Abbé, Curé à St.-Maurice l'Exil, par le Péage (Isère). *Ent.: Coleopt., Lepid.* C.*
Boudier, Emil, Place du Marché, Montmorency. *Coleopt.*
Bouju, Alphonse, rue de la République 82, Rouen. *Coleopt.*
Boulay, l'Abbé. D.Sc., Prof. à l'Université Catholique, Boulevard Vaubau

127, Lille (Nord). *Bot.* C. Ex. Mosses and Vegetable Fossils.*

Boullet, Eugène, Place Faidherbe à Corbie (Somme). *Lepid of the world.* C. Many duplicates for ex.*

Bourgeois, Jules, ancien Président de la Société Ent. de France, 38 rue de l'Echiquier, Paris. *Ent.: Coleopt. of Europe, Foreign Malacodermata.* C. Coleoptera of Europe and Malacodermata of the globe, ex. or buy.*

Bourgougnon, Claudius, Memb. Soc. Bot. de France, Chassignet par Chantelle (Allier). *Bot., Agric.* C. Ex.

Bourguignat, Réné, rue des Ursulines, St. Germain en Laye (Seine-et-Oise). *Con.*

Bouriez, E., fils, Grande-Place 6, Tourcoing. *Lepid., Sericulture.*

Bourlet de la Vallée, Fondateur et Directeur du Jardin Bot. du Hâvre, Graville (Seine Inférieure). *Bot.**

Bourru, Dr. H., rue de la Forêt, Rochefort, S. M. *Nat. Sci., Clinique Medicale.**

Boursier, Ch., rue de la Poissonnerie 26, Nancy (Meurthe et Moselle). *Lepid., Minerals, Fossils.* C. Ex. Lepidoptera and Fossils

Boury, Eugène de, Membre de plusieurs Soc. Savantes. Théméricourt par Vigny (Seine et Oise) *Eocene Fossils, Mathildia, Scalaria, Acirsa,* recent and fossil. Living shells from Gulf of Gascoyne et fossils du bassin de Paris for ex. contre Scalaria, livres traitant des Scalaria, etc. Scalaria and eocene fossils of Alabama, America.

Borsselier, Officier de marine, rue du Rempart 47, Rochefort sur Mer. *Geol., Palæo.* C. Ex.*

Bouteiller, Prof. Ed., Provins. *Ent., Coleopt., Bot.*

Bouthery, Dr. Charles Auguste, Langeais. *Coleopt.*

Boutillier, Louis Roucherolles le Vivier (Seine Inférieure). *Geol., Palæo., Min., Conch.*

Bouvet, G., Pharmacien, rue Lenepreu 32, Angers. *Bot.**

Bouvier, A., Naturalist, Bourg (Ain), (formerly 55 Quai des Grands Augustins), Paris. *Orn., especially African Mam., Anthropods, Malacol.* C. 90,000 birds. Ex. and sell.

Brand, F. V., Archiac (Charente Inférieure). *Bot., Geol., Ent.: Lepid., Coleopt.* C. Ex.*

Brandenburg, 1 rue de la Verrerie, Bordeaux. *Apiculture.*

Branly, Edouard, D.S., M.D., Prof. Phys., l'Institut Catholique de Paris, avenue de Breteuil 42, Paris. *Phys.**

Bras, Dr. A., Villefranche de Rouerque (Aveyron.) *Bot.*

Brechemin, Louis, rue du Val-de-Grâce 18, Paris. *Coleopt.*

Brévière, L., Port Ste. Marie (Lot-et-Garonne). *Con., Bot.*

Briard, Dr. E., 36 rue des Carmes, Nancy. *Bot.**

Brillouin, Prof. Marcel, Maître de Conférence à l'Ecole Normale Supérieure, Paris. *Phys., Elect. Hydrodynamique.**

Briquel, C., rue de Viller 32, Luneville. *Coleopt.*

Brisout de Barneville, Henri, Saint-Germain-en-Laye. *Coleopt.*

Brisout de Barneville, Charles, rue de Pontoise 15, Saint-Germain-en-Laye. *Coleopt.*

Brissaud, Prof., Lyceum Charlemagne, rue Mazarine 9, Paris.

Brochon, E. Henri, 25 rue du Temple, Bordeaux. *Geol.*

Brochon, H., Pres. Soc. Linéenne, Bordeaux. *Bot.*

Brongniart, Charles, Muséum d'Histoire Naturelle, rue Guy-de-la-Brosse 8, Paris. *Zool., Palæo., Bot.* C. Fossils of the Carboniferous, Insects, and Fishes. Ex.*

Brown, Robert, 39 Pav des Chartroéns, Bordeaux. *Ent.*

Brown-Sequard, Charles Edouard, M.D., Collège de France, Paris.

Brun, l'Abbé, Grand-Rue, Nogent-sur-Seine. *Coleopt.*

Brun-Buisson, Dr., rue Sermorens, Voiron (Isère). *Coleopt.*, *Lepid.*
Brunaud, Paul, 3 rue Saint-Vivien, Saintes. *Bot.*
Bucaille, E., Membre des Sociétés Géologiques de Normandie, de France, du Nord, etc., rue St.-Vivien 132, Rouen (Seine-Inférieure). *Geol.*, *Palæo.* C. Fossils of Normandy. Ex. Fossils, Echinoids, Brachiopods.*
Buchillot, M., Rheims. *Orn.*, *Herpetol.* Ex.*
Bucquoy, Dr. E., 14 rue Foy, Perpignan. *Con.*
Buffet, Paul, 99 rue d'Aboukir, Paris. *Ent.: Lepid.*
Buquet, Lucien, St.-Placide 52, Paris. *Coleopt.*
Bureau, Charles Albert, Pharmacien, Administrateur du Musée, rue St.-Aubert 7, Arras. *Lepid of Europe*, *Sericulture.* C. Ex.
Bureau, Edouard, quai de Béthune 34, Paris. *Coleopt.*, *Bot.*
Bureau, Dr. Louis, 15, rue Gresset, Nantes. *Orn.*
Busch, G., rue Beaurepaire 12, Boulogne-sur-Mer. *Coleopt.**
Buysson, Henri du, Château du Vernet, Brout-Vernet (Allier), l'hiver: Toulouse, 33 rue de Rémusat. *Ent.*, *Coleopt.* (*spec. Elatenidae*). *Dipt.*, *Hymenopt.*, *Bot.*, *Phanerog.* C. Ex. Fr. specimens for American. Desires entomological correspondents in Am. and other parts of the world.*
Buysson, Robert du, Château du Vernet, Broût Vernet (Allier). *Bot.*, *Ent.*, *Hymenopt.* (*special, Chrysididæ of the world*), *Crypt.* C. Ex. French specimens for Amer.*
Cabanne, Paul, Géomètre, Aide - Naturaliste au Muséum, Bordeaux. *Palæo.*, *Geol.*, *Min.*, *Lithol.*, *Anth.*, *Arch.* C. Ex.*
Cacussel, Frédéric, Dir. des Postes et Télégraphes, Drônx, Valence. *Gen. Ent.*, *Palæo.**
Cahours, Auguste A. T., Mem. Acad. Sci., Paris. *Chem.*
Caille, A., Bot. Gar., Bordeaux. *Bot.*
Cailletet, Louis, Institut, Châtillon-sur-Seine. *Bot.*, *Min.*
Caix de Saint-Aymour, Vicomte Am., Château d'Ognon, près Barbery (Oise), and rue de Milan 11, Paris.
Cantagrel, Polytechnic School, boulevard Malesherbes 145, Paris.
Capus, G., rue de Buffon 53, Paris. *Bot.*
Caralp, Préparateur de Géologie et Minéralogie à la Faculté des Sciences, rue des Chapeliers 15, Toulouse. *Geol.*
Cardon, Ch., rue du Rempart 3, Tours. *Coleopt.*
Cardot, Jules, Agriculteur, Stenay (Meuse). *Bot.* C. Ex. Musci of Europe for those of the world, and especially of America.*
Carez, Dr. Léon, avenue Hoche 36, Paris. *Geol.*
Carlet, Dr. Gaston, Prof. à la Faculté des Sciences et à l'Ecole de Médecine, rue Villars 3, Grenoble (Isère). *Biol.*, *Zool.**
Carnot, Adolphe, Ingénieur en chef des mines; Inspecteur de l'Ecole supérieure des mines; Prof. à l'Ecole des mines et à l'Institut agronomique, boulev. St.-Michel 60, Paris. *Agric.*, *Min.*, *Geol.*, *Chem.**
Caron, A. D., rue Joinville 22, Havre. *Coleopt.*
Caron, E., Rubempré. *Bot.*
Caron, Victor, St.-Amour (Jura). *Palæo.*
Carpentier, Ernest de, Clos-Barrey, Commune de Dosnon par Orcis-sur-Orbe. *Sylviculture.*
Carpentier, Léon, Secrétaire de la Société Linnéenne du Nord de la France, rue de la Pâture 16, Amiens. *Mic.*, *Palæo.*, *Ent.: Coleopt. of Somme-et-Oise*, *Parasites of Insects.*
Carret, l'Abbé A., Prof. Inst. of Chartreux, Lyons. *Coleopt.*
Carrière, E. A., rue de Vincennes, Montreuil-sous-Bois (Seine). *Bot.*
Carthailac, Emile, Dir. de la Revue; Matériaux pour l'histoire primitive de l'homme; Dir. du Laboratoire d'Anth. de Toulouse, rue de la Chaine 5, Toulouse. *Anth.*, *Arch.*, *Eth.*, *Ethnog.* C. Ex.*

Casthelaz, John, rue Ste.-Croix-de-la-Bretonnerie, Paris. *Chem.*
Castillon, Gérard de, Membre de la Société Entomologique de France et de Suisse, Château de Parron, par Mézin (Lot-et-Garonne). *Coleopt.* C. Ex. native specimens for European and foreign.*
Caton, Prof. J., rue des Cultivateurs 7, Pau. *Coleopt.*
Caulle, Pierre, rue Berchet 3, Sédan. *Coleopt.* C. Ex.*
Cauvet, Dr. D., Prof. à la Faculté de Médecine, rue Franklin 33, Lyon. *Bot.*, *Nat. Hist.*
Cavaillé, Augustin, chemin de Madame, Viroflay (Seine-et-Oise). *Coleopt.*, *Lepid.*, *Myriopods*, *Reptiles.* C. Ex. Offers Lepidoptera and Coleoptera of Europe for Reptiles and Myriopods.
Cavaillé-Coll, Aristide, avenue du Maine 15, Paris. *Phys.**
Cayol, Marius, rue des Moines 50, à Batignolles, Paris. *Agric.*, *Coleopt.*
Cazalis de Fondouce, Paul, rue des Etures 18, Montpellier. *Geol.*, *Arch.*, *Anth.* C.*
Certes, A., Inspecteur général des Finances; Prés. de la Soc. Zool. de France, rue de Varennes 53, Paris. *Physiol.*, *Infusoria and Protozoa.**
Cessac, le Comte Pierre de, Château de Mouchetar, Guérct (Creuse). *Geol.*
Chaignon, Vicomte L. de Cuiseaux. *Geol.*, *Min.*
Chaix, J. St.-Etienne, Loire. *Bot.* C. Ex.
Chalande, Henri, Membre de la Soc. d'Histoire Naturelle de Toulouse, rue des Couteliers 46, Toulouse. *Bot.*, *Con.* C. Ex. Wishes plants and shells of all countries.
Chalande, Jules, Membre de la Soc. d'Histoire Naturelle, rue des Couteliers 51, Toulouse. *Ent.: Coleopt.*, *Reptiles.* C. Ex. Coleoptera of France for those of all countries.*
Chambovet, rue du Vieux-Montaux, St.-Etienne. *Coleopt.*
Champenois, Amédée, Inspeteur des forêts, Autun (Saone-et-Loire). *Coleopt.*, *Hemipt.* C. Ex.*
Chanay, Pierre, Secrétaire de la Soc. Linéenne et de la Soc. Botanique de Lyon, Cour d'Herbouville 12, Lyon. *Bot.: Phanerogams*, *European and foreign*, *Ent.: Coleopt. and Hemipt. of Europe.* Foreign Lamellicorns and Sternoxes. C. of herbs and insects. Ex. Desires correspondents, especially in Europe and America.
Chanrion, l'Abbé, Prof. Seminary of L'Argentière, Duerne. *Coleopt.*
Chantre, Ernest, Sous-Dir. Mus. Sci. Nat., Prof. d'Anth., Secrét. gén. Soc. Anth., 37 Cours Morand, Lyon. *Palæo.*, *Geol.*, *Anth.**
Chaper, Maurice, Mineralogical Society, rue St. Guillaume 31, Paris. *Con.*, Ex. Fossils Marine L. and F. N. Shells.*
Chappui, Maurice, rue Bausset 14, Vaugirard, Paris. *Coleopt.*
Charbonneaux, Emile, rue du Bourg St.-Denis 98, Reims (Marne). *Ent.: especially Coleopt.* C. 1,500 species. Ex. Coleoptera of Reims for those of all countries, especially Carabidæ and Longicornes.
Chardon, Gabriel, Bureau du Télégraphe, Bone (Algérie). *Coleopt.**
Charguerand, A., Jardinier en chef á l'Ecole Vétérinaire, Alfort (Seine). *Bot.* C.
Charpentier, A., Prof. de Phys. et Méd. à l'Univ., Nancy. *Phys.*
Charpy, Victor, Ancien Notaire, Saint-Amour (Jura). *Moll.* C. Ex. L. and F. W. shells of France and foreign.*
Charreyre, Jules, 7 Place de l'Eglise St. Michel, Marseille. *Bot.*, *Physiol.*
Chatin, Gaspard A., Mem. Acad. Sci., rue de Rennes 129, Paris. *Bot.*
Chatin, Prof. Dr. Joannes, boulevard Saint-Germain 128, Paris.
Chaumont, E., 14 rue Moutyon, au premier. *Geol.*, *Org. Chem.*, *Elect.*, *Photog.*, *Ast.* C. Ex.
Chauvet, Gustave, Notaire, Secrétaire de la Société Archéologique de la Charente Ruffec (Charente). *Arch.* C. Arch., especially of the valley of the Charente.*

Chérot, A., Polytechnic School, quai de Billy 10, Paris.
Chervin, Dr. Arthur, Dir. of the Paris Inst. for the cure of Stammering, avenue Victor Hugo 10, Paris.*
Cheux, Albert, rue Delaâge 47, Angers. *Meteo.*, *Ast.*, *Min.*, *Ent.*; *Lepid.*, *Geol.*, *Palæo.* C. Ex.*
Chevalier, E. l'Abbé, E. Armency (Haute-Savoie). *Bot.*, *Coleopt.*
Chevreux, Edouard, le Craisic, Loire Inférieure. *Zool.*, *Amphipode Crust.*
Chineut, Armand Lucien, Officier d'Académie, rue Lacépède 34, Paris. *Nat. Hist.*, *Ent.* C. Insects of all kinds, principally Lepidoptera. Ex.
Chiron,-du Brossav, rue Ménage 19, Angers. *Coleopt.*
Chomienne, Léon, Pharmacien, cours de l'Intendante 27, Bordeaux. *Geol.*
Chouillou, Edouard, quai du Havre 13, Rouen. *Chem.*
Claudon, Edouard, Ingénieur, boulevard d'Enfer 6, Paris. *Chem.*, *Min*; Microbiologie.*
Clément, A. L., rue Lacépède 34, Paris· *Coleopt.*
Clément, Stan. 7 rue Maison-Carrée, Nîmes. *Con.*, *Orn.*
Clet, Jean, quai de Brosses, Grenoble. *Coleopt.*
Clin, Dr. Ernest M., rue Racine 14, Paris. *Chem.*
Cloizeaux, Prof. Alfred Des, Muséum, rue Monsieur 13, Paris. *Min.*
Clos, Dominique, Prof. de Botanique à la Faculté des Sciences, Directeur du Jardin des Plantes, allée des Zéphirs 2, Toulouse, *Bot.* C.*
Collet, Alfred, Lieutenant de Vaisseau, Répétiteur à l'Ecole Polytechnique 151, Boulevard Magenta, Paris. *Ast.* *Geodesy.**
Collier, E. rue Limas 10, Avignon, *Bot.*, *Palæo.*, *Geol.*, *Anth.*, *Arch.*, *Hymen.*, *Coleopt.*, *Hemipt.*, *Moll.* C. Ex.*
Collignon, Dr. René, Aide-Major de 1ère classe au 1er Bataillon de Chasseurs à Pied, Verdun sur Meuse (Meuse). *Anth.*, *Craniology.* C. Ex. ancient and modern, against American of any kind, or the crania of Oceanica.
Collot, Prof. Louis, Faculté des Sciences, Dijon. *Geol.**
Combes, Jacques Ludomir, Chevalier de l'Ordre de Charles III., Officier de l'Académie Château de la Dausse, Monflanquin (Lot-et-Garonne). *Geol.*, *Palæo.*, *Arch.* C. Ex·
Comerford-Casey, Rev. G. E., M.A., F.L.S., Nice.*
Comme, Jean, rue Belleville 15, Bordeaux. *Bot.*
Condamy, rue des Bazines 33, Angoulême. *Truffles and Mushrooms.*
Constant, A., Golfe-Juan (Alpes-Maritimes). *European Lepid.*, *spec. Microlepid.**
Coppet, De, Louis C., Ph.D., Villa Irène, aux Baurnettes, Nice. *Crystal.*, *Chem.*, *Phys.**
Copineau, Charles, Doullens (Somme). *Bot.**
Coquerel, A., rue du Thym, Impasse Leroy, Caudebec-les-Elbeuf. *Ent.*, *Coleopt.*, *Bot.*
Corbière, Prof. F., L., des sciences naturelles au Lycée. Cherbourg. *Bot.**
Coret, Simon-Paul, rue Malissier 7, Puteaux. *Coleopt.*
Cornil, Prof. 183 boulevard St. Germain, Paris.
Cornu, A., Memb. d. l'Acad. des Sci., Ing. en chef des mines, Prof. à l'Ecole Polytechnique, rue des Ecoles 38, Paris. *Phys.*
Cornu, Maxime, Professeur de Culture au Muséum d'histoire naturelle, 27 rue Cuvier. Paris.
Cosserat, Prof. Léon, Grande-Place 21, Armentières. *Geol.*
Cossigny, Ch. de Courcelles, par Clérey (Aube) *Geol.**
Cossmann, Ing. du service technique du Nord Ry., 17 rue St. Vincent de Paul, Paris. *Invert.* C. Ex. Desires Tertiary of the U. S. in Ex. for Parisian Tertiary.

Cosson, Ernest Saint-Charles, Mem. Acad. Sc., rue La Boëtie 7, Paris. *Bot.**
Costa de Beauregard, le Comte Paul, Ravine, near Chambéry. *Coleopt.*
Coste, Dr. Ulysse, avenue de Toulouse 3, Montpellier.
Cotard, Charles, Polytechnic School, 60 rue de la Chaussée d'Antin, Paris.*
Cotteau, boulevard St. Germain 17, Paris. *Palæo.* (*Echinodermata*).
Coudère, Prof., A. J., Camonil Rodez (Aveyron). *Mam.*, *Orn.*, *Tax.*, *Bot.*, sires a few Am. correspondents. Cor. in Eng. and German. C. Ex.
Couette, Maurice, rue Volney 2, Angers. *Coleopt.*
Coulet, Auguste, Dourbes, near Digne. *Coleopt.*
Coulon, Léon, rue Lombarderie 36, Dieppe. *Coleopt.*
Courage, l'Abbé Emile, rue Casimir-Périer 15, Paris. *Coleopt.*
Courtois, Henri, Château de Muges, par Damazan (Lot-et-Garonne). *Phys.*, *Ast.*
Coutures, Georges, rue Palais-de-lOmbrière 18, Bordeaux. *Coleopt.*, *Otaphylimidæ*, *Claricornes.* C. Ex.
Couturier, Albert, 2 rue du Calvaire, Sagny-sur-Marne. *Phys.*, *Elect.*, *Chem.*
Cove, Capt. C. H., St.-Paul-de-Fenouillet. *Coleopt.*
Crampon, l'Abbé, rue Neuve 26, Amiens.
Crocy, W., 3 rue Bergeret, Bordeaux. *Ent.: Coleopt.*
Croissandeau, Jules, rue du Bourdan blanc 15, Orléans. *Metal.*, *Coleopt.*, etc. C. Ex. Franç. et Corse psélaphieurs du globe.*
Crosnier, Julien, rue d'Illiers 54, Orléans. *Con.*
Crosse, Hippolyte, Directeur du Journal de Conchyliologie, rue Tronchet, 25, Paris. *Con. Palæo.* C.
Crouzil, Dr., de l'Ecole de la Dalbade, Toulouse. *Coleopt.*, *Moll.*
Crozel, Georges, place de l'Hotel de Ville, Vienne (Isère). *Geol.*, *Palaeo.*, *Crustacea.* C. Ex. L. F. W., and marine Shells, Fossils and Mins. of France to exchange. Correspondence solicited.*
Curie, Jacques, rue de la Visitation 2, Paris. *Chem.*
Daffry de la Mounoye, Adalbert, rue du Cherche Midi 11, Paris. *Ent.: Coleopt.*, *Dipt. et Aviculture.**
Dagincourt, Dr. Emmanuel, Licencié ès Sci. Nat., Sec., de la Société Géol. de France, etc., 15 rue de Tournon. *Vert.*, *Palæo.*, *Min.*, *Lithol.*, *Inorg. Chem.*, *Metall.*, *Mic.*, *Arch.* C.
D'Agnel, Z. rue Muiron 10, Mourillon, Toulon. *Coleopt. Geol.**
Daleau, François, Bourg-sur-Gironde. *Anth.*, *Arch.*, *Eth.*, *Palæo.* C. Nearly 30,000 specimens. Ex. L. and F. W. shells of France and New Caledonia for specimens of Archæology and Ethnography.
Damour, Augustin A., Mem. Acad. Sci., rue Vignon 10, Paris.
Darasse, Léon, rue Simon-Lefranc 21, Paris. *Chem.*
Dareste, Camille, M. D., D. Sc., Dir. Lab. de Tératologie à l'Ecole pratique des hautes études, Paris. *Teratology.*
Darlu, Prof., Lyceum, Bordeaux. *Phil.*
Darves, Antoine, rue des Ecoles, St. Jean de Maurienne (Savoie). *Coleopt.*
Dat, Charles, quai des Violettes 4, Amboise. *Coleopt.*
Daubree, G. Auguste, boulevard Saint-Germain 254, Mem. Acad , Sci., Paris. *Min.*, *Geol.**
Daurel, J., Président de la Société d'Horticulture de la Gironde., Allées de Tourny 25, Bordeaux. *Bot.**
Dautzenberg, Philippe, rue de l'Université 213, Paris. *Con. and tertiary Foss.* Desires exchanges.*
David, Dr., 23 rue Amelos, La Rochelle. *Bot.*
David, l'Abbé, Armand, Ancien Missionnaire en Chine, rue de Sèvres 95,

Paris. *Orn.*, *Coleopt.*, *Lepid.* C. Ex. Offers Coleoptera and birds of China.
Davy, Marie, Montsouris. Paris. *Meteo.*, *Ast.*
Debat, Louis, Mem. Soc. Botanique de Lyon, place Perrache 7, Lyon. *Crypt. Bot.*, *Mosses of France*, *Mic.* C. Ex.
Debray, Ferdinand, Prof. à l'école des Sci., Alger. *Fungi*, *Algæ.* C. Ex.
Decharme, Doct. ès Sc., Chevalier de la Legion d'honneur, Prof. de Physique de l'Univ. (en retraite), Officier de l'Instruction Publique, rue Laurendeau 82, Amiens. *Phys.**
Decœne-Racouchot, Alfred, Antoine (Luzy). *Coleopt.**
Defargues, Capt., boulevard des Iles-d'Or 2, Hyères. *Coleopt.*
Defaud, Gabriel, Clermont-Ferrand. *Coleopt.*
Degrange-Touzin, A., rue de Temple 24, *Bis.*, Bordeaux. *Geol.*, *Min.* C. Miocene fossils in ex. for fossils and minerals.
Dehérain, P. P., Prof. au Muséum d'Histoire Naturelle, rue d'Argenson 1, Paris. *Vegetable Physiol.*, *Agric.* C. Ex.
Delaby, Edmond, rue Neuve 10, Amiens. *Coleopt.*
Deladerrière, Emile, Avocat, rue Capron 8, Valenciennes (Nord). *Zool.*, *Ent.*, *Palæo.*, *and Botany of France.* C. Vert., Invert. (Insects, Mollusks, etc)., Plants and Fossils of France. Ex.
Delafond, Frédéric, Ingénieur en chef des Mines à Châlon-sur-Saône. *Geol.*
Delagrange, Charles, Imprimeur, Besançon (Doubs). *Ent.*: *Coleopt.*, *Lepid.* C. Ex.
Delahaye, Jules, rue Brezin, 15 Montrouge, Paris. *Lepid.*
Delahaye, Victor, rue de la Republique 84, Rouen.
Delaire, Bould, St. Germain 135, Paris. *Geol.*
Delalande, H., rue St.-Georges 34, Rennes. *Coleopt.*
Delamair, Henri, Jarnac. *Ent.*, *Coleopt.*, *Lepid.*
De Lapparent, 3 rue de Tilsitt, Paris. *Geol.*
Delarue, Pierre, rue d'Auteuil 6, Paris. *Coleopt.*
Delattre, Edmond, boulevard du Prince-Eugène 63, Paris. *Coleopt.*
Delauney, Felix-Julien, Cherbourg. *Coleopt.*
Delavoie, rue Gambetta 35, Rochefort sur Mer. *Lepid.* C.
Deleveau, Prof. Paul, Lyceum, Orleans. *Chem.*
Delfortrié, rue de Pessac 66, Bordeaux. *Palæo.*
Delherm de Larcenne, Prof. d'Histoire Naturelle, Gimont (Gers). *Coleopt.*, *Hymenop.*, *Bot.* C. Ex.
Delort, Prof., Saint-Flour, Cantal.
Deloynes, Paul, rue de la Course 113, Bordeaux. *Bot.*
Delplanque, P., Préparateur à la faculté de Méd., Lille. *Tératology.*
Délugin, A., Pharmacien, rue Denis Papin 33, Blois (Loire-et-Cher). *Coleopt.* C. Ex.*
Demaison, Charles, Ingénieur Civil, rue Rogier 9, Reims. *Ent.*: *Coleopt.* C. Ex. Coleoptera of France, Algiers, Egypt, and Syria.
Demaison, Louis, Archiviste Paléographe, rue Cérès 21, Reims. *Ent.*: *Lepid.* C. *Birds and rept.**
De Maricourt, G. René du Mesnil, homme de lettres, Villemétrie près Senlis (Oise). *Anth.*, *Arch.*, (*prehist.*)*
Demarque, Firmin, Cubzac-d'Aude. *Coleopt.*
De Mortillet, Adrian, St.-Germain-en-Laye (Seine-et-Oise). *Anth.*, *Arch.* C. Ex.*
Denans, Albert, rue Château Redou 29, Marseille. *Moll.* C. Ex.
Denis, Fernand, rue Mautrec 1, Bordeaux. *Bot.*
De Payan-Dumoulin, Grignan (Drôme). *Palæo.* C.
Depuiset, Alphonse, Naturalist, rue des Saints-Pères 17, Paris. *Lepid.*

Derbès, Prof., rue Reynard 35, Marseille. *Bot.*
Derenbourg, Prof. Hartwig, boulevard Saint-Michel 39, Paris. *Palæo.*
Dermigny, C., Péronne. *Coleopt.*
Dert, L., rue de l'Eglise St.-Seurin 16, Bordeaux. *Coleopt.*
Deruelle, J., rue de Vaugirard 199, Paris. *Bot.*
Desbrochers de Loges, Jules, Naturaliste, Ardentes, near Châteroux (Indre). *Descriptive Entomology, Coleoptera of the ancient world N. of Africa, Curculionidæ, Brenthidæ, and Cassididæ of the globe.* C. Ex.
Deschamps, E., rue Jean-Cousin 3, Sens. *Coleopt.*
Deschange, Emile, Longuyon (Meurthe-Moselle). *Lepid., Sericulture.* Sell, buy or ex. Lepidoptera, Cocoons, Caterpillars, and Eggs of all countries.
Des Gozis, Maurice, place de l'Hôtel-de-Ville, Montluçon (winter in Paris.) *Coleopt.* Hymenopt, Hemipt, and Orthopt in France.
Deslongchamps, Prof. M. E. Caen (Calvados). *Bot., Coleopt.*
Desmarest, Eugène, Aide Naturaliste, Muséum, rue Cuvier 57, Paris. *Coleopt.*
Designolle, Paul, rue du Bac 40, Paris. *Orn., Lepid., Coleopt.* C. Ex.
Dessaignes, Victor, Vendôme. *Chem.*
Destermes, Prof., Collège, Figeac. *Coleopt.*
De Seynes, Jules, 15 rue Chanaleilles, Paris. *Bot.*
Detaille, Charles, 38 boulevard St. Germain, Paris. *Phys., Ast.**
Detalle, P., Senonches. *Coleopt.*
De Tarlé, Adolphe, 57 rue Volney, Angers. *Lepid.*
Détroyat, Arnaud, Membre de la Société Geologique de France, Bayonne. *Archæology* (local). C.
Deussault, Philibert, Dessinateur Géographe, rue des Lombards 12, Paris. *Geog.**
Devaulx de Chambord, R., rue du Cerf-Volant 5, Moulins. *Coleopt.**
Devouzy, Emile Désiré Vervins. *Coleopt.*
Deyrolle, Emile, Naturalist, rue de la Monnaie 23, Paris. Dir. du *Naturaliste*, revue illustrée des sciences naturelles. *Zool., Geol., Bot., Mic.* C. of Coleoptera, Conchology, Lepidoptera, Mammals, Birds, Reptiles, Fishes, Osteology. *Fossils, Min., Rocks.**
Deyrolle, Henri et Cie., place Denfert-Rochereau 20, Paris. *Ent., Coleopt. Lepid.* Vente et achat.*
Dezanneau, Dr. Alfred, Prof. School Med., Angers. *Bot.*
Didier, Gerardmer (Vosges). *Ent., Bot.* C.
Dieulafoy, Prof. Dr. Georges, rue Caumartin 16, Paris. *Med.*
Dillon, Charles Auguste, Tonnerre. *Coleopt.*
Dognin, Paul, Villa de la Réunion 16, Auteuil, Paris. *Lepid.*
Doiy, Inspec. primaire, rue des Dix Moulins 90, Rochefort-sur-Mer. *Geol., Bot.* C. Ex.*
Dollé, Maurice, rue Chenizelles 2, Lyon. *Coleopt.*
Dollfus, Adrien, rue Pierre-Charron 35, Paris. *Crustacea, esp. Isopoda.**
Dollfus, Gustave, rue de Chabrol 45, Paris. *Geol., Palæo., Con.*
Dollfus, René, rue Spontini 1, Paris. *Coleopt.*
Donnadieu, Prof. A. L., D. S., Lyon. *Zool.*
Dor, D. Henri, Prof. honoraire de l'Université de Berne (Suisse), quai de la Charité 2, Lyon. *Ophthalmology, Entomology.* C. Coleopt. of Europe.
Dorey, Paul, Sables-d'Olonne. *Coleopt.*
Douat, Muséum, Lyon. *Zool.*
Douin, Louis, Normal School, Draguignan. *Coleopt.*
Douliot, Henry, Mus. d'Hist. Nat, 63 rue de Buffon, Paris, Préparateur de Bot. (Anat.), 25 rue Bréa, Paris. *Bot.**
Doumerc, Jean, rue Corail 1, Montauban. *Geol.*

Doumerc, Paul, Montauban. *Geol.*
Doumet-Adanson, Nap., Pres. Hort. Soc., Cette. *Bot.*
Douvillé, Henri, Ingénieur des Mines, Prof. de Paléontologie á l'Ecole des Mines, boulevard St.-Germain 207, Paris. *Palæo., Geol.*
Doze, Raymond, rue Bonneau 15, Montpellier. *Coleopt.*
Droguet, M. A., fils, Lambelle (Côte du Nord) *Ent.*
Dromineau, Dr., rue des Augustins, Rochelle. *Hygiene.*
Drouaux, G., rue Sery. Havre. *Geol.*
Druilhet-Lafargue, boulevard de Cånderån 173, Bordeaux. *Horticulture*
Dubalen, P. E., Pharmacien, St.-Sever (Landes). *Bot., Orn., Arch., Geol., Malacology, Parasites.* C. Ex. L. and F. W. Molluscs. Fossil Molluscs of the Tertiary of the basin of the Adour.
Dubin, J., Prof., Auch. *Coleopt.*
Du Bois, rue Madeleine, Blois (Loire-et-Cher). *Bot.: Bryology.*
Dubois, Albert, rue Richaud 14, Versailles. *Ent.: Coleopt.*
Dubois, Prof. Edmond, rue Cozette 29, Amiens. *Phys., Nat. Hist.*
Dubois, Michel, rue Pierre l'Hermite 24, Amiens. *Ent.: Coleopt., Hemipt.*
Dubreuil, E., Montpellier. *Bot., Con.*
Dubreuilh, William, Lormont. *Bot.*
Duchartre, P., Mem. Acad. Sci., rue de Grenelle 84, Paris. *Bot.*
Duclaux, Prof. Emile, rue Malebranche 15, Paris. *Agric.*
Dufour, Edouard, rue de l'Héronnière 6, Nantes. *Bot.*
Dugas, Albert, St.-Maurice-d'Exil, near Vienne. *Coleopt.*
Dujardin-Beaumetz, Dr., rue de Rennes 66, Paris..
Dumesnil, H., rue du Faubourg du Temple 59, Paris. *Coleopt.: Ent., Lepid.*
Duneau, Ed., Orleans. *Bot,*
Duparc, Georges, quai du Louvre 30, Paris. *Coleopt.*
Dupart (Abbé), Prof. Petit Séminaire de St. Méen (Ille-et-Vilaine). *Con.*
Duponchelle, Dr. P., Maître de Conférences à la Faculté de Méd., Lille. *Zool.*
Dupont, Louis, rue des Bernardins 36, Paris. *Ent., principally Lepid.* C. Ex. especially with Naturalists of America. Wishes Lepidoptera of N. America in ex; tor Insects of Europe, especially Coleoptera and Papilio.
Dupuy, G., Angoulême. *Ent.: Lepid.**
Dupuy, Léon, Prof. Lyceum, rue Vital-Carles 13, Bordeaux.
Duque, J., rue Guileraud Moissac (Tarne-et-Garonne). *Arch., Bibliog.*
Duquesne, A., Pont-Audemer (Eure). *Bot., Zool., Orn.* C. Ex.*
Durand, Albert, rue de Limoges 3, Versailles. *Coleopt.*
Durand, Prof. Eugène, Montpellier. *Agric.*
Dureau, Alexis, rue des Saints Pères 49, Paris. *Medicine, Teratol., Anth.*
Durien de Maissonneuve, E., rue David-Johnston 39, Bordeaux.
Dutertre, Emile, boulevard Montparnasse 88, Paris. *Geol.*
Dutreux-Pescatore, Aug., Château de la Celle-St.-Cloud, near Bougival (Seine-et-Oise). *European Lepid.*
Duval, Antonin Gaulmier, Manufacturier, Chevalier de la Légion d'Honneur, rue Pints-Gaillot 31, Lyon. *Agric.*
Duverger, Joseph-Alexandre, Dax. *Coleopt.*
Duvivier, Sec. Hort. Soc., rue de Grenelle 84, Paris.' *Bot.*
Ebrard, Sylvain, Firminy. *Ent., Lepid.**
Edwards, Alphonse M., Mem. Acad. Sci., Paris. *Anat., Zool.*
Elphège, Prof. Seminary, Sainte-Anne-d'Auray. *Coleopt.*
Emery, Prof. H., rue Verrerie 35, Dijon. *Bot.*
Eprémesnil, Le Comte d', rue de Lille 41, Paris. *Bot.**

Ervert, Dr. Jacquet, cours Lafayette 3, Lyon. *Ent.* C. Ex. Wishes Coleoptera of Europe and the Hemispheres.
Etienne, Pharmacien, Gournay (en Bray, Seine Inférieure), *Gen. Bot., esp. Mosses of Normandy.*
Eudes-Deslongchamps, Eugène, Prof. Faculté des Sciences, rue de Geole 28, Caen. *Palæo., Geol., Zool., Anat., Eth., Ethnog., Vert., Mam., Orn., Ool., Herpetol., Ichth., Crustacea, Moll., Radiates, Sponges.* C. Ex. Will ex. circulars of Museum of Caen for publications of other Scientific Soc.
Euthymer, Le Frère, Inst. des Petits-Frères de Marie, St. Genis-Laval près Lyon. *Coleopt., Min., Geol., Arch., Con.*
Fabre, J. H., Prof. Lycée, Orange. *Coleopt.*
Fabre-Domerque, Dr. ès-Sci., 20 rue de la Clef, Paris. *Mic., Protozoa.**
Faguct L. Auguste, Avenue des Gobelins 26, Paris. *Bot.*
Fairmaire, Léon, rue du Bac 94, Paris. *Coleopt., Hymenop., Hemipt. of Europe.* C. Ex.
Fallot, Dr., rue Cardinal Lemoine 67, Paris. *Geol.*
Fallou, Jules, rue des Poitevins 10, Paris. *Coleopt., Lepid., Hymenop.*
Fallou, René, rue des Poitevins 10, Paris. *Coleopt., Lepid.*
Falsan, Albert, Officier de l'Instruction publique, Saint-Cyr-au-Mont-d'Or (Rhône). *Geol., Min., Photog.* C.
Farlé, M. de, rue Volney 57, Angers. *Lepid.**
Farjasse, Maurice, rue Denfert-Rochereau 89, Paris. *Con., Geol.*
Fauconnet, Mary-Louise, Autun. *Coleopt., spec. Longicornes of the World.* C. Offers Coleopt. of Europe for Longicornes from all countries.
Faure, H., Mem. A.R.S., rue l'Oiseau, Moulins-sur-Allier. *Ent., Coleopt., Bot.* C. Ex. Coleopt. of New World desired for those of Central France.
Faure, l'Abbé P., Supérieur du Petit Séminaire du Rondeau, Grenoble. *Bot.* C. Ex. 3,100 specimens of the Société Dauphinois for other specimens and publications.
Fauvel, Albert, rue d'Auge 16, Caen. *Coleopt.* C. of Staphylinidæ of the United States Ex. for the Coleoptera of America.
Favarcq, L., rue de Vernay 48, St.-Etienne. *Coleopt.*
Fayol, Henri, Directeur des Louillires de Commandry (Allier). *Geol., Palæo.*
Fée, Prof. Dr. Félix, à Nantes.
Félissis-Rollin, Jules, rue de Rennes 72, Paris. *Coleopt.*
Fellot, Louis, Château de Pierrefilant Rivolet, near Villefranche (Rhône). *Mam., Orn.* C. Ex.
Féminier, Gabriel, Alais. *Bot., Lithol.*
Ferlay, Marius, Notaire, Montmeyran, (Drôme). *Bot.**
Fermond, Ch., rue Pasquier 28, Paris. *Bot.*
Figuier, Prof. Dr., Bordeaux.
Fernique, l'Abbé, rue de Vaucanson 4, Paris. *Coleopt., Mic.*
Ferry, Dr. René, St. Dié (Vosges.) *Mycology.*
Feuilleaubois, M., rue de Heuville 12, Fontainebleau (Seine-et-Marne). *Fungi.* C. Ex.
Fière, Paul, Mem. Correspondant de la Ste. Fse. de Numismatique et d'Arch; de l'Assoc. Fse. pour l'Avancement des Sciences; de la Soc. d'Anth. de Paris, de l'Académie Delphinale, Voiron (Isère). *Palæo., Ant., Arch.* C.
Filhol, Prof. H., boulevard St. Germain 90, Paris. *Palæo.*
Fines, Dr. E., Dir. de l'Observatoire, Perpignan, Pyrénées-Orientales. *Meteo.**
Finot, Adrien, Capitaine d'Etat, Major en retraite, rue St. Honoré 27, Fontainebleau (Seine-et-Marne). *Ent., esp. Orthopt.* C. Ex.

and buy. Offers Orthoptera of France and Algeria, and desires to buy or ex. Orthoptera of the whole world.*
Fischer, Dr. Paul, Museum of Nat. Hist., Jardin des Plantes, Paris.
Fizeau, Armand H. L., Mem. Acad. Sci., rue de la Vieille-Estrapade 3, Paris. *Physics.*
Flahault, Charles, Prof. de Botanique à la Faculté des Sciences, Montpellier. *Crypt. Bot., Vegetable Anat., Physiol.**
Flahault, Evariste, Ingénieur, 17 route du Montferrand, Clermont-Ferrand (Puy de Dôme). *Geol., Palæo.* C. Rocks and fossils. Ex. Offers eruptive and volcanic rocks of Auvergne, fossils and rocks of France and Belgium, and wishes tertiary fossils and rocks of other basins, vegetable fossils of all the formations.
Flammarion, Camille, Avenue de l'Observatoire 36, Paris. *Ast.*
Fleutiaux, Edmond, rue Malus 1, Paris. *Coleopt.*
Flourens, G., Haubourdin, near Lille. *Chem.*
Foex, Prof. Gustave, Faubourg Saint-Jacques 29, Montpellier. *Agric.*
Folin, Marquis Léopold de, Directeur des "Fonds de la Mer," Membre de plusieurs Académies et Sociétés Savantes, rue d'Espagne 18, Biarritz. *Mollusca, Rhizopoda.* C. Ex. publications with other scientists.
Folus, Marquis de, Biarritz. *Arch.*
Fontaine, Arnaud Louis, Broglie (Eure). *Bot.: Mosses, Lichens, Algæ.*
Fontaine, Hippolyte, rue Drouot 15, Paris. *Phys.*
Fontan, Alfred, Castres, Tarn. *Min., Geol., Con.*
Foucard, Jardin Botanique de la Marine à Rochefort (Charente-Inférieure).*
Foucart, Alfred, Naturalist, rue Blancs-Mouchons 45, Douai. *European Lepid., Micro-Lepid.* C. Ex.
Foucaud, Mem. de la Soc. Botanique de France, Jardin Botanique de la Marine à Rochefort (Charente-Inférieure.)*
Foulquier, G. A., rue St.-Sepulcre 1, Marseille. *Coleopt.*
Fouqué, Prof. au Collège de France, rue Humboldt, 23, Paris. *Geol., Petrog., Min.*
Foureau, Fernand, Fredière-Saint-Barbant, near Mézières (Haute-Vienne.) *Geol.*
Fournier, Alphonse, Musée de Niort, rue des Fassér St. Jean 25, Niort (Deux-Sèvres). *Gen. Nat. Hist.*
Friant, Prof., rue de l'Hospice, Nancy. *Zool.*
Francezon, Paul, Alais (Gard). *Chem.*
Franchet, A., rue Monge 111, Paris. *Bot.*
François, fils (Ph.), Château de la Vienne, near Grand-Pressigny. *Coleopt.*
Francq, Léon, Officier d'Académie, Lauréat de la Société d'Encouragement, 54 rue de Châteaudun, Paris *Physics and Mechanics.*
Fraucicl, Edmond, cours d'Alsace-et-Lorraine 105, Bordeaux. *Bot.*
Fray, J. P., Aumônier à l'École Normale, Bourg (Ain). *Bot.* C. Ex.
Fréminville, Paul de, Château de l'Aumusse, Pont-de-Veyle (Ain). *Ent., Min., Con.* C. Ex.
Fremy, Edmond, Mem. Acad. Sci., Dir. Mus., rue Cuvier 33, Paris. *Chem.*
Frère, Louis, rue de l'Ange, Perpignan. *Coleopt.*
Fridrici, Edmond, Berneuil, Guise-la-Motte. *Coleopt.*
Friedel, Charles, Mem. Acad. Sci., rue Michelet 9, Paris. *Phys., Chem.*
Fromentel, Dr. Henry-Joseph-Edouard-Dieudonné de, Gray (Haute-Saône), *Physiol.* "Les Synalgies ou Sympathies douloureuses."*
Fromentel, Dr. Louis Edouard Gourdan de, Gray, (Haute-Saône.) *Met., Nat. Hist., Palæo., Mic., etc., etc.**
Frossard, le Pasteur, rue de la Verrerie 11, Bordeaux. *Bot., Min.*
Fübrel, Capitaine d'Artillerie, au Pont-de-Mielin, par Servance (Haute-Saône.) *Min., Petrology.*

Fuchs, Ingénieur en chef des Mines, Prof. à l'Ecole des Mines 9, rue des Beaux Arts, Paris. *Geol.*
Fumouze, Dr., rue du Faubourg-St.-Denis 78, Paris. *Coleopt.*
Fuzier-Herman, L., Château de la Houssière, par Ligneil. *Coleopt., Orn.**
Gabillot, Joseph, quai des Célestins 5, Lyon. *Coleopt.*
Gaborit, Adrien, Pharmacien, place du Marché-Neuf 2, Angoulême (Charentes). *Lepid.* C. Ex.
Gaché, Dr., quai de Brosses, Grenoble. *Coleopt.*
Gadeau de Kerville, Henri, rue Dupont 7, Rouen. *Zool.**
Gage, Dr. Léon, rue de Grenelle-St.-Germain 9, Paris *Coleopt.*
Gahineau, Ernest, rue de la République 212, Sotteville-les-Rouen (Seine-Inférieure). *Bot., Geol., Min.**
Gaillard, Henri, rue du Cherche-Midi 34, Paris. *Coleopt.*
Gainet, Abbé, Traves (Haute-Saône). *Geol.* C.
Galipe, Dr., rue Sainte-Anne 48, Paris. *Nat. Hist.*
Gallé, C., Soc., avenue de la Garenne 2, Nancy. *Bot.*
Gallé, Emile, Sec. Gén. de la Société Centrale d'Horticulture, 2 avenue de la Garenne, Nancy. *Bot.* C. Ex. Wishes seeds of the living plants of the United States, indicating the names and localities of species offered.*
Gallé, Ernest, Cour du Château 12, Creil. *Con., Ent.: Coleopt.**
Gallois, Dr. Ernest, place de l'Etoile 2, Grenoble (Isère). *Fungi.*
Gallois, Joseph, rue de Bellay 92, Angers (Marne-et-Loire.) *Palæo., Ent.: Coleopt.* C. Ex. especially Silurian and Devonian fossils.*
Gallois, Marc, La Verpillère (Isère.) *Bot.*
Gallot, Prin. du Coll. de Charmes (Vosges). *Con.*
Gambey, avenue Casimir 10, Asnières (Seine). *Coleopt.* C. European and Caledonian. Ex.
Gandillot, Arthur, rue Clausel 22, Paris. *Coleopt.*
Gandoger, Arnas (Rhône). *Phaner. Bot.**
Garat, J., place Fondandège 7, Bordeaux. *Bot.*
Gariel, Charles M., Prof. à l'Ecole de Médecine, rue Jouffroy 39, Paris. *Phys. Elect.*
Garin, E., quai Saint-Clair, Irigny. *Ent.: Coleopt.*
Garlin-Soulandre, Prof., rue Saint-Firmin 18, Montpellier. *Math.*
Garneau, Ferdinand, Alais. *Geol., Min.*
Garnier, l'Abbé Alphonse, rue de l'Hôtel de-Ville 18, Troyes *Coleopt.*
Garnier, E., St.-Mème-les-Carrières. *Coleopt*
Garrigou, Dr. Joseph Louis Felix, rue Valade 38, Toulouse (Haute Garonne). *Geol., Chem., Anth.* C.
Gascard, Boisguillaume, près Rouen. *Ent., Geol.*
Gashet P. A., rue des Remparts 40, Bordeaux. *Coleopt.*
Gatien, le Frère Ernest, Impasse Godefroy-de-Bouillon, Clermont-Ferrand, *Coleopt.*
Gatine, L., rue des Rosiers 23, Paris. *Chem.*
Gaube (du Gers), Dr. J., rue Ste Isaure 23, Paris. *Biol.**
Gaudion, Henri, ave. St. Pierre 38, Beziers, Hérault. *Con., Moll.*
Gaudry, Albert, Prof. Nat. Hist. Museum, rue des Saints-Pères 7, *bis*, Paris. *Palæo.*
Gaugnet, J. Elie, Officier d'Académie, Mem. de la Soc. Polytech, de France, rue de Seine 36, Paris.
Gaulle, Jules de, rue Notre Dame des Champs 36, Paris. *Ent. Hymenop.**
Gauthiot, Charles, Sec. Gén. de la Société de Géog. Commerciale, boulevard Saint-Germain 63, Paris.
Gautier, Gaston, Place St.-Just, Narbonne. *Bot.: Bryol.*

Gautier, Hubert, rue Neuve, Langres. *Coleopt.*
Gavoy, Louis, rue de la Préfecture 5, Carcassonne. *Coleopt.*
Gebin, Joseph Jean Baptiste, Villa du Point du Jour, Remiremont (Vosges). *Coleopt., especially Carabidæ.* C. Ex. Desires to buy American Calosomæ, Carabidæ, and Cychri.*
Génévier, Gaston, Nantes. *Bot.*
Geoffroy St. Hilaire, Albert, Zool. Gardens of Acclimatation of Paris. *Zool., Living Animals.**
Georges, Emile, Luneville. *Phæn. Bot.* C.
Gérard, Cl. Alb., Con. des Hypothèques, Belfort. *Bot.* C. Ex.*
Géraud-Mousset, rue du Lac 11, St. Mandé (Seine). *Eur. Lepid.*
Gérin, Léopold, Carcasonne 109, Faubourg Erivalle. *Ent.* C. Ex.
Gernez, Prof., Lyceum Louis-le-Grand/rue Médicis 17, Paris. *Phys.*
Gervais, d'Aldin, Péronne. *Coleopt.*
Giard, Alfred, Prof. á la Faculté des Sciences de Lille, Directeur de la Station Zoologique de Wimereux, 181 Bd. St. Germain, Paris. *Embryology of Invert. Cunicata Rhizocephala and Epicarida.* Ex. Spec. preserved in Alcohol.*
Giard, Alfred, Prof., á l'Ecole Normale Supérieure, 45 rue d'Ulm, Paris. Dir. du laborat. de Zool. de Wimeraux (Pas-de-Calais). *Annilides, Ascidies, et Crustaces. Champignons, parasites des Insectes.**
Gilbert, Marc, care Dr. Gilbert, rue Serg 41, Havre. *Geol., Orn.* C. Ex. European birds and fossils for foreign.
Gillet, C. C., rue de l'Adoration 23, Alencon. *Bot.: Mycol.*
Gillot, Dr., 5 rue du Faubourg Saint-Audoche, Autun. *Bot.* C.
Girardot, L. A., Prof, d'Histoire Naturelle au Lycée, Lons-le-Saunier (Jura). *Geol., Prehistoric Arch., Bot.*
Giraud, Théodore, quai d'Albret 15, Lyon. *Coleopt.*
Giraudias, Louis, Receveur de l'Enregistrement, Foix (Ariège), *Bot.* C. Ex. Plants of western France in exchange for foreign and those of eastern Europe and the Mediterranean.*
Giraux, Dr. H., Châlons-sur-Marne. *Ent.*
Girerd, rue de l'Hôtel-de-Ville 3, Lyon. *Con.*
Glastien, Joseph, Prof., St.-Etienne. *Bot.**
Gobert, Dr. Emile, rue de la Préfecture 2, Mont-de-Marsan. *Ent.: Coleopt.*
Godard, Jules, rue de Paris, Perigueux. *Bot.*
Godefroy, Eug., rue de la Montagne, St.-Geneviève 8, Paris. *Bot.*
Godefroy, Léon, Professeur des Sciences au Petit Séminaire, La Chapelle, St. Mesmin. *Geol., Min., Con., Ent.* C. Ex. Offers shells and Coleoptera for foreign.
Goossens, Th., rue du Faubourg St.-Martin 171, Paris. *Lepid.*
Gosselet, Prof. J., rue d'Autin 18, Lille. *Geol.*
Goualt, Albert, rue Cuvier 57, Paris. *Bot.*
Gouley, Albert, rue Vilaine 19, Caen. *European Lepid.*
Gounelle, Emile, rue de Rennes 115, Paris. *Agric., Coleopt.*
Gourdon, Maurice, Villa Maurice, Luchon. *Coleopt.*
Goure de Villemontée, Gustave, Prof. Normal School, Cluny. *Coleopt.*
Gourg, Georges, rue de Montmoreau 41, Angoulême. *Coleopt.*
Goussard, Blois (Loire-et-Cher). *Coleopt., Bot.*
Goutay, Edouard, rue de l'Horloge 32, Riom. *Coleopt.*
Grancher, Prof. Dr., rue Beaujour 36, Paris*
Grandeau, Louis, Directeur de la Station Agronomique de l'Est, Doyen et Prof. de Chimie Agricole à la Faculté des Sciences, Prof. de l'Ecole Nationale Forestière, rue du Faubourg Saint-Jean 24, Nancy (Meurthe-et-Moselle).
Grand'Eury, Corr. de l'Institut, cours St. André 23, St. Etienne. *Bot., Vegetable Palæo.**

Grangeneuve, Maurice, Avoue, Licencié, 82 cours de Tournay, Bordeaux (Gironde). *Min.* C.
Granger, Albert, boulevard de Talence 330, Bordeaux (Gironde). *Con.* C. Ex. Shells of the coast of the Mediterranean, and shells and fossils of the Gironde, for L. and F. W. shells.
Grenier, Dr. A., rue de Vaugirard 55, Paris. *Ent.: Coleopt.*
Grilat, R., rue Rivet 19, Lyon. *Ent.*
Grisard, Jules, Sec. de la Revue des Sciences Naturelles appliquées, Soc. Nationale d'Acclimatation de France, rue de Lille 41, Paris. *Bot., Hort., Bibliog., Arch.**
Gronier, rue de Foy 6, *bis*, St.-Quentin. Aisne. *European Lepid.*
Grossouvre, Albert, de, Ingénieur au Corps National des Mines, Bourges. *Geol., Palæo.**
Groult, Edmond, Fondateur des Musées Cantonaux Lisieux (Calvados).*,
Guebhard, Dr. Adrien, Préparateur à la Faculté de Médecine de Paris, rue de Chartres 12, Neuilly-sur-Seine. *Phys , Palæo.*
Guédel, Dr., cours-St.-Bruno 10, Grenoble. *Coleopt., Lepid., Hymenop.*
Guérin, Eugène, 13 rue de Strasbourg, Le Mâcon (Sâone-et-Loire). *Coleopt.* C. Ex.*
Guerne, Jules Germain de, rue Monge 2, Paris. *Zool., especially Invertebrates.* C. Ex. Marine invert. of the coast of France for those of the Atlantic, with remarks upon the localities. Faune pélagique.*
Guerry-David, Cross of Legion of Honor, rue de l'Arsenal 58, Angoulême. *Coleopt.**
Guertin, Emile, Chinon. *Coleopt.*
Guester, Daniel, pavé des Chartrons 35, Bordeaux. *Malacol.*
Guevel, Georges, Houdan (Seine-et-Oise). *lants, Grasses.*
Guiard, Abbé V., rue de Baveux 26, Caen. *Bot.*
Guieysse, Prof. Camonil, Rodez (Aveyron). *Ent., Coleopt., Hemipt., Orn., Mam., Min., Bot., Lepid.* C. Ex. Coleoptera of France for those of foreign. Corresponds in Eng. and German.*
Guignard, Dr. Léon, 19 rue Linné, Paris. *Bot.*
Guilbert, Robert, rue de Buffon 24, Rouen. *Coleopt.*
Guillard, Dr. J. A., Prof. à la Faculte de Médecine; Redacteur et gérant du Journal d'histoire naturelle de Bordeaux et du Sud-Ouest, et des Annales d'histoire naturelle de Bordeaux et de Sud-Ouest, Bordeaux. *Bot.*
Guillaumin, Charles, rue de Buffon 15, Paris. *Con., Geol., L. and F. W. Shells and fossils.* C. Ex.
Guillemin, A., Orsay près Paris (Seine-et-Oise). *Ast.*
Guillibert, Hipp., Avocat à la Cour, Secrétaire de l'Académie des Sciences, Arts, et Agriculture et Belles-lettres, rue Saint Claude 3, Aix. *Bot.* Culture of vineyards. C. Ex. plants and slips.
Guinard, E., Montpellier. *Mic.*
Guinon, E., Directeur de la Station Agronomique, rue de Déols 33, Châteauroux (Indre), *Geol.* C. Minerals and fossils of Indre.
Guriaud, Dr. L. avenue de la Gare 39, Nice (Alps Maritimes). Summer address, Montauban (Tarn-et-Garonne). *Anth., Bot.* Ex.
Hahn, Dr., rue Saint Placide 31, Paris. *Zool , Ent., Bot.*
Hallez, Paul Professeur à la Faculté des Sciences, rue St. Gabriel 92, Lille (Nord). *Zool.* C. Ex. Lower animals in alcohol, particularly Turbelleria.*
Halloy, Léon d', rue Porte-Paris 23, Amiens. *Coleopt.*
Hamonville, Baron Louis d', Conseiller-Général au Château de Manonville, par Noviant-aux-près, Meurthe-et-Moselle. *Orn., Ool., Con.* C. Buys or exchanges Trochilidæ in skin. Ex. birds' eggs of Europe and shells of France for exotics. *Spec. Cypselidæ, Hirundinidæ, Paradiseidæ.**

Hamy, Dr. Ernest, Conservateur du Musée, d'Ethnographie de Paris· Aide-Naturaliste chargé de Cours au Muséum, rue de Lübeck, 40, Paris, *Anat.*, *Anth.*, *Ethnog.*, *Geog.**
Hanra, Prof. D., Châlons. *Bot.*, *Geol.*
Hanry, Hipp., Luc. *Bot.: Bryol.*
Hardy, E., rue Bonaparte 19, Paris. *Chem.*
Harlé, Eug., Fontaine par Senlis (Oise). *Min.*
Harmand, Dr., Mus. French Col., Paris. *Bot.*
Hauquelin, Dr. A. T. F., Prof. d'Hygiène á l'Ecole professionnelle Vaucanon, Mem. de la Société des Sciences Naturelles du Sud-Est, Grenoble (Isère). *Bibliog.*, *Zool.*, *Anth.*, *Moll.* C. Ex.
Haut-Saintamour, Adolphe, Gravelle, Ste. Henosine, near Havre. *Coleopt.*
Hayes, Joseph, Commissaire de la Marine en Retraite, Fromenteau, Jurasy (Seine-et-Oise). *Geog.*
Hébert, Prof., Memb. Acad. Sci., rue Garancière 10, Paris. *Geol.*, *Min.*
Heckel, Dr. Edouard Prof à la Faculté des Sciences et à l'Ecole de Médecine, Dir. du Jardin Botanique, cours Lieutaud 31, Marseille. *Bot.*, *Fungi*, *Mic.*, *Teratology*, *Physiol.*, *Con.*, *Materia Medica.* C. Ex.
Heilman, J, Muséum, Cannes. *Bot.*, *Min.*, *Con.*
Hélot, Dr. Paul, Chirurgien en chef de l'Hospice général, rue Saint-Nicolas 32, Rouen.
Hémard, Hippolyte, Pont-à-Mousson. *Lepid.*
Henneguy, Dr. Louis Félix, rue de Sommerard 17, Paris. *Zool.*, *Emb.*, *Ent.: Protozoa*, *Infusoria.*
Hénon, Adrien, quai d'Auteuil 132, Paris.
Hénon, Escombres, Pourru-St. Rémy. *Coleopt.*, *Lepid.*
Henrivaux, J., Chimiste, Directeur de la Glacerie, membre de plusieurs sociétés savantes et industrielles, St.-Gobain (Aisne).*
Héribaud, Prof, Clermont-Ferrand. *Bot.*
Hérincq, F., Conservateur des Galéries de Botanique au Muséum d'Histoire Naturelle, Paris. *Bot.*, *Cultivated Plants.*
Hermite, Charles, Membre de l'Institut, 2 rue de la Sorbonne, Paris. *Ast.**
Héron, Daniel, rue d'Alger 8, Paris. *Coleopt.*
Héron-Rover, rue de Cléry 22, Paris. *Batraciens.**
Hervé, F., Morlaix. *Ent.*, *Coleopt.*
Hervé, Mangon, Membre de l'Institut, Paris.*
Hervier, Joseph, Grande rue de la Bourse 31, Saint-Etienne (Loire), *Bot.*, *Phanerogams and Vascular Cryptogams.* C. Exchange herbs of Europe for Phanerogams of Europe and France.
Hette, F., rue de Mons 107, Valenciennes, *Neuropt.*, *Coleopt.*, *Lepid.*, *Con.*
Hickel, Robert, Hautefeuille 9, Paris. *Coleopt.*
Hiller, Dr. Albin, Prof. à la Faculté des Sciences, 7 rue de Lorraine, Nancy. *Chem.**
Hirn, Prof. l'Abbé Georges, Rougemont, near Belfort. *Bot.*
Hollande, D. S., Dir. de l'Ecole préparatoire à l'enseignement supérieure; Prof. au Lycée, Chambéry (Savoie). *Geol.*, *Phys.**
Hommey, Dr., rue Potin, Sées. *Bot.*, *Bryol.*
Honnorat, Ed.-F., Naturaliste, quartier des Sieyes, Eigne (Basses-Alpes). *Ent.: Coleopt*, *Ool.*, *Herpetol.*, *Palæo.* C. Ex. Reptiles, Coleoptera, and Crinoids of France for foreign specimens.
Hopperhorn, 282 St.-Jacques, Paris. *Cocoons and Min.**
Houllet, R., rue Cuvier 57, Paris. *Bot.*
Houry, Alphonse, Mer (Loir-et-Cher), Entomologiste. *Gen. Ent.*, *Tax.*, *Photog.*, *Geol.*, *Min.*, *Orn.*, *Herpetol.*, *Con.* C. Ex. Coleopt., Lepid., Hymenop., Hemipt., Dipt., etc.*

Hovelaque, Prof. Abel, rue de l'Université, Paris. *Anth.*
Hovelacque, Maurice, rue des Sablons 88, Passy, Paris. *Bot., Palæo., Geol., Min., Lithol.* C. Ex.*
Hubcrson, Gabriel, rue Laromiguière 2, Paris. *Coleopt., Bot.*
Hue, place Centrale 3, Fontainebleau. *Coleopt.*
Huet, A. de Naturaliste chargé de la Ménagerie, Nat. Hist. Muséum, Paris. *Zool.**
Huet, Louis, place Richebé 7, Lille (Nord). *Chem.**
Hugues, Rév. Gustave, rue du Marché 7, Bergerac, Dordogne. *Min., Bot., Geol., Palæo.**
Humnicki, Valentin, rue Neuve-St.-Aignan 4, Orléans. *Coleopt.**
Husnot, Th., Cahan, Athis. *Bot.: Bryol.*
Huyard, Henri, rue Sauteyrou 55, Bordeaux. *Chem.*
Hy, Abbé Félix-Ch., Prof. Cath. Univ., Angers. *Bot.*
Illaret, Antoine St. Ferme, Monsegur (Gironde), Membre de l'Association Française pour l'Avancement des Sciences; de la Société Nationale d'Encouragement à l'Agriculture; de la Société d'Agriculture de la Gironde.
Itasse, Léon, rue du Faubourg Montmartre 56, Paris. *Coleopt.*
Jablochkoff, rue de Naples 52, Paris. *Phys.*
Jackson, James, Librarian Société de Géographie, boulevard St.-Germain 184, Paris.*
Jacquet, Dr. Ernest, cours Lafayette 3, Lyon. *Ent.: Hemipt., Coleopt.* C. Ex.
Jacquemet, Edouard, Voiron (Isère). *Phæn. Bot., Fungi, Algæ, Invert., Palæo., Lithol., Gen. Ent., Crustacea, Moll., Radiates, Sponges.*
Jacquot, Inspecteur-Général des Mines, Dir. de la Carte Géologique, 83 rue de Monceau, Paris. *Geol.*
Jannel, Charles, Géologue de la Cie. des Chemins de fer de l'Est, à Paris.*
Jannettaz, Edouard, Maître de conférences à la Sorbonne, Aide naturaliste au Muséum d'histoire naturelle, rue Linné 9, Paris. *Min.*
Jannettaz, Prof., Nat. Hist. Muséum, Paris. *Min.*
Jannin, Eugène, rue des Saints-Pères 5, Paris, *Coleopt.*
Janssen, Pierre Jules, Astronome-physician, Membre de l'Institut de France et du Bureau de Longitude, Directeur de l'Observatoire d'Astronomie Physique, Meudon (Seine-et-Oise). *Phys. Astronomy**.
Jarlan, Emile Louis, Membre de la Société Entomologique de la Gironde et du Sud-ouest de la France, rue Frère 16, Bordeaux (Gironde). *Lepid.* C. Ex.
Jarris, l'Abbé Pierre, Professeur de Philosophie au Collège Sainte-Marie. St.-André-de-Cubzac (Gironde). *Bot., Ent.* C. Ex.
Javal, Dir. Opthal. Lab. of La Sorbonne, rue de Grenelle 58, Paris. *Phys.*
Jean, J., Castelbosc, near Alirac, Canton de Montreal. *Coleopt.*
Jeanbernat, Dr. Ernest, rue de Musée 5, Toulouse.
Jekel, Henri, Naturalist, rue de Dunkerque 62, Paris. *Coleopt.**
Jollet, André, La Mothe-St.-Heray. *Coleopt.*
Joly, Charles, rue Boissy d'Anglas 11, Paris. *Hort.*
Joly, Dr. Marie Auguste Emile, Licencié des Sciences, Lauréat de l'Institut de France, officier d'Academie. *Entomology (Anatomy, Physiology), Orthoptera, Ephemeridæ of Europe.* C. Ex. Wish Larvæ and Nymphæ of Ephemeridæ.
Joly, Nicolas, Prof. honoraire à la Faculté des Sciences de Toulouse, Cor. Mem. Inst. de France, rue des Amidonniers 52, Toulouse (Haute-Garonne). *Zool., Gen. Biol., Emb., Anat., Arch., Animal and Human Palæo.*
Jolyet, Dr. F., Prof. à la Faculté de Méd., Bordeaux. *Physiol.*

Jouan, H., Cherbourg. *Zool., Anth., Bot.**
Joubert, Prof. Collège Rollin, rue Violet 67, Grenelle, Paris. *Phys.*
Jourdain, Leopold, rue Lafayette, Grenoble. *Palæo., Min.**
Jourdan, P., rue de la Course 121, Bordeaux. *Coleopt.*
Jourdes, Raymond, Courteilles, par Verneuil-sur-Avre. *Bot.* C. Ex.
Jordan, Al., rue de l'Arbre Sec 40, Lyon. *Bot.* C.
Jousseaume, Dr., rue de Vanves 4, Paris. *Zool., Con.*
Jousset, E., rue Lafayette 1, Rochefort. *Bot.*
Jousset de Bellesme, Physiologiste, Directeur des Services de Pisiculture de la Ville de Paris, Château de St. Jean à Nogent-le-Rotron (Eure-et-Loire) France.*
Juignet, Dr. R. J. Coudray-Macouard, Saumur. *Coleopt.*
Juliany, Joseph, rue des Marchands 16, Manosque (Ba. Alpen). *Coleopt., Lepid., Con.**
Jullian, Camille, boulevard du Nord 15, Marseille. *Hymenoptera, Hemiptera.*
Jullien, Jean, rue de l'Université 2, Paris. *Chem.*
Jumeau, Gaston, Mem. Soc. Zool. de France, rue Rôtisserie, Béziers, (Herault). *Geol., Min., Crystal., Herpetol., Moll.* C. Ex.
Jungfleisch, Prof. School Phar., rue des Ecoles 38, Paris. *Phys.*
Jurien de la Gravière, Vice-Admiral J. P. E., Mem. Acad. Sci., Paris *Geography and Navigation.*
Kercado, A., Comte de, place Pay-Berland 30, Bordeaux. *Con.*
Kerhervé, A., rue des Beaux Arts 4, *bis*, Paris. *Ent.: Coleopt.*
Klincksieck, Paul, 15 rue de Sèvres, Paris. Librairie Ancienne et Moderne de Sci. Nat., Physiques et Mathématiques.*
Kœchlin, Camille, avenue Ruysdael 4, Paris. *Coleopt.*
Kœchlin, Edmond, à Saint Denis, Ile de la Réunion. *Ent.: Coleopt.*
Kœchlin, Emile, Ingénieur 52, rue du Four St. Germain, Paris. *Ent.: Lepid., Coleopt.*
Kœhler, R., rue de Metz 17, Nancy. *Emb , Echinoderms.**
Kórgnies, Emile, Manroil, par Honnechy Nord. *Bot.*
Koenig, rue de Pontoise 26, Paris. *Phys.*
Koziorowicz. Edouard, Annecy. *Coleopt.*
Krafft, Prof. Eugène, Lyceum, Périgueux. *Math.*
Künuholtz, rue St. Guilhem 23, Montpellier. *Con.*
Kühnholtz-Lordat, Achille, Administrateur des Mines de Graissessac, Montpellier. *Min., Con.* C.
Künckel d'Herculais, Jules, Aide-Naturaliste au Muséum, Paris. *Ent., Anatomy of Articulate Animals.* Ex. publications relating to entomology.
Künstler, J., Bordeaux. *Infusoria.*
Labbé, Louis, rue du Temple 17, Bordeaux. *Bot.*
Labbé, Paul, rue de Choiseul 15, Paris. *Coleopt.*
Laboratoire de la rue des Fabres, Marseille. *Biol., Hist.*
Laboulbène, Prof. Dr. Alexandre O., boulevard St. Germain 181, Paris. *Gen. Ent.*
Lacaille, à Balbec (Seine inférieure). *Bot., Ent., Geol.*
Lacatte, l'Abbé, Seminary. Autun. *Coleopt.*
Lacaze-Duthiers, Prof. Félix J. H. rue de la Vieille-Estrapade 7, Paris. *Anat., Zool.*
Lacroix, Alfred, Membre de la Société de Minéralogie de France, 11 rue Cujas, Paris. *Min.* C. Ex. Wishes crystallized minerals.*
Lacroix, Eugène, 35 rue St. Joseph, Lyon. *Geol.*
Lacroix, Francisque, Conservateur du Musée d'histoire naturelle de Mâcon (Saône-et-Loire). *Bot., Min., Con.* C.*
Lafaury, Dr. Clément, Saugnac-les-Dax (Landes). *European Lepid.*
Lafosse, Ferdinand, La Garde, near Montlieu. *Coleopt.*

Lagrenée, Mme. Georges, Château de Frocourt, près Beauvais (Oise). *Ornithology*. C. Ex.
Laguesse, Prof. Dr. Dijon. *Bot.*
Lahaussois, Charles, rue Biot 22, Paris. *Entomology especially Hymenoptera and Coleoptera.* C. Ex. Coleoptera of France for those of other countries.
Lair, E., Grande-rue, Amboise. *Coleopt.*
Lambert, Dr. Paul, Château de la Gagneric, Semblançay (Indre-et-Loire). *Ent.: Coleopt.* C. Ex.
Lambert, Francis, Grand Serre (Drôme). *Agric., Geol.*
Lambin, Charles, rue St.-Antoine 164, Paris. *Coleopt.*
Lami, Stanislas, Villemetrie, Senlis. *Coleopt.*
Lamothe, Louis, quai de la Monnaie 18, Bordeaux. *Hort.*
Lamotte, Henri, Chantelle. *Ent., Lepid.*
Lamy de la Chapelle, Edouard, Botaniste, Membre de la Société Botanique, rue du Saint-Esprit 17, Limoges (Haute-Vienne). *Mosses, Hepaticæ, Lichens.* C. Especially Cryptogams. Ex.
Lajoye, Abel, rue Ruinart-de-Brimont 9, Reims. *Ent.: Coleopt., Mineralogy.*
Lancelevée, Th., rue St.-Etienne 29, Elbeuf-sur-Seine. *Coleopt., Lepid., L. and F. W. Shells. Bot.* C. Ex. Offers especially specimens of the Province of Normandy.
Lancereaux, Dr. Etienne, Prof., Agrégé à la Faculté de Médecine, Médecin de l'Hôpital de la Pitié, Mem. de l'Académie de Médecine, etc., rue de la Bienfaisance 44, Paris. *Anat., Pathol., Syphilis.*
Lancereaux, Eugène, Château du Thiel, Chauvigny. *Coleopt.*
Landolt, Dr. Edmond, rue Volney 4, Paris. *Ophthalmology.**
Landry, F., 77 rue Denfert, Rochereau. *Math.*
Lanessan, Prof. Dr. de, rue des Halles 13, Paris. *Bot.*
Langlois, Maurice, rue Soufflot 24, Paris. *Coleopt., Lepid.*
Langrand, Charles, rue Raze 18, Bordeaux. *Coleopt.*
Lantier, Dr. Etienne, Cannay (Nièvre). *Medicine, Surgery.* C. Ex.*
La Perraudière, Raoul de, rue des Fosses, Laval. *Coleopt.*
Laplanche, Maurice C. de, au Château de, Laplanche Luzy (Nièvre). *Agric., Myc., Ent.: Coleopt.* C. Ex.*
Laporte, Ernest, rue Laroche 83, Bordeaux. *Coleopt.*
Laporte, E., Capt., Navarreux. *Coleopt.*
Laporte, Prof., rue Mouneyra 71, Bordeaux. *Geom.*
Lapparent, Prof. de, Catholic Univ., rue Tilsit 3, Paris. *Geol.*
Larcher, Ad., rue Claude Bernard 82, Paris. *Bot.*
Laroix, Maron, Saône-et-Loire. *Bot., Min.*
Larralde d'Arencete, Martin, Lourdes (Hautes-Pyrénées). *Lepidoptera.*
Larrey, Le Baron F. H. Mem. l'Inst., rue de Lille 91, Paris.
Lartet, Prof. Louis, rue du Pont de Tounis 14, Toulouse (Haute-Garonne). *Palæo, Geol., Anth., Arch.* C. Ex.
Lataste, Evard, Cadillac-sur-Garonne. *Ent.: Coleopt., Con.*
Lataste, Fernand, 7 avenue des Gobelins, Paris. *Batrachians, Reptiles in Alcohol, Mammiferous in Alcohol or in Skins with craniums,* in exchange for French, European, or Algerian.*
Laugel, Auguste, Ex-Secrétaire de la Société Géologique de France, 19 rue de la Ville l'Evêque, Paris.
Lanois, P. E., l'Hôtel-Dieu, Reims. *Coleopt.*
Lauret, Frédéric, Millau (Aveyron). *Geol., Min.*
Lauzanne, Henri de, Château de Porzantrez, près Morlaix (Finisterre). *Lepid, Moll.*
Lavallée, Alphonse, Président de la Société Nationale d'Hort. de France, Société Nationale d'Agric. de France, rue de Penthièvre 6, Paris, et Château de Segrez, near Boissy-sous-St.-Yon (Seine-et-Oise).

Bot. C. 6,000 specimens trees and shrubs. Ex. Large herb. of phænerogams.
Lavarde, Roset de, en Château d'Eutumia, en Paramé, près St. Marlo. *Minéraux et Mollusques.* C.*
Lawton, Edouard. quai des Chartrons 95, Bordeaux. *Orn.*
Lavné, C., place Morand 9, Lyon. *Coleopt.*
Le Blanc, Dr. F., place Perière 5, Paris, *Therapeutics.*
Leboeuf, Charles, Membre de la Société Entomologique de France, rue de Tallyrand 19, Reims. *European. Coleopt.: Carabidæ, Dytisidæ, Hydrophilidæ, Silphidæ, Lamellicorns, Cleridæ, Longicorns.* C. Ex.
Le Bon, Gustave, rue Vignon 29, Paris. *Anth.* C. Ex. for Crania.*
Le Bouteiller, Edmond, rue Malatiré 32, Mont-St.-Aignan, near Rouen. *Coleopt.*
Le Breton, Andre, ex-Sec. de corr. de la soc. des Amis des Sc. Nat. de Rouen; Ancien Vice-Sec. de la session Mycologique à Paris, 1877, Membre de la soc. Botanique de France. Membre Fond. de la soc. Zoologique de France. Membre Fondateur de la soc. Mycologique de France, etc., etc., boulevard Canchoire 43, Rouen (S. I.). *Mycologie* (principally de Normandie). Ex. et Achat d'ouvrages et de Mémoires sur la Mycologie générale et particulière.*
Le Brun, Marcel, rue du Cloître de St.-Pierre 28, Troyes. *Ent.: Coleopt.*
Le Châtelier, Ing. du Corps National des Mines, rue Notre Dame du Champs 73. *Phys., Chem.*
Leclerc, A., Dir. du Laboratoire de Recherches de la Compagnie Générale des Voitures, rue du Ruisseau 91, Paris. *Alimentation Rationnelle du Cheval.*
Leclerq, Eugène, Prof. Collége du Quesnoy (Nord). *Geol.*
Lécouflet, Emile, rue d'Ecosse 1, Dieppe. *Coleopt.*
Lefèvre, Edouard, rue du Bac 112, Paris. *Ent.: Coleopt.*
Legrand, Antoine, Bourges (Cher). *Coleopt.*
Le Grand, Gustave, avenue du Parc-de-Bercy 3, Charenton. *Coleopt.*
Legrix de la Salle, Charles, place Dauphine 13, Bordeaux. *Ethnog.*
Leguay, Louis, Officier d'Académie, rue de la Sainte-Chapelle 3, Paris. *Anth., Arch.* C.
Le Jariel, G., Curé de Jublains (Dept. de la Mayenne). *Coleopt.*
Le Jolis, Dr. August F., Cherbourg. *Bot., Algæ.*
Lelaurin, Henri, Institution St.-Vincent, Senlis. *Coleopt.*
Lelièvre, Ernest, Entreponts 22, Amboise. *Herpetol, Ent.: Coleopt., Lepid., Hemipt., Bot.*
Lelong, l'Abbé, rue St.-Hilaire 13, Reims. *Coleopt.*
Leloup, Charles, avenue des Gobelins 25, Paris. *Coleopt.*
Lemaire, préparateur à la Faculté des Sci., Nancy. *Bot.*
Lemaire, Eugène, Fondateaur de la Société Linnéenne de la Charente-Inférieure, Con. Musée, Royan-les-Bains. *Bot., Marine Algæ.* C Local Algæ, shells, plants, archæology. Ex.
Lamaire, Henri, rue Violet 54, Grenelle, Paris. *Coleopt.*
Le Mesle, G., rue du Grain-d'Or 6, Blois. *Geol.*
Lemetteil, Membre de la Société Zoologique de France à Bolbec (Seine-Inférieure). *Orn., Ool.*
Lemoine, Prof. Dr., boulevard des Promenades 49, Reims. *Palæo.*
Lemoine, Julien, rue de Fougères 3, Rennes (Ille-et-Vilaine). *Con.*
Le Monnier, Prof., rue de la Pépinnière, Nancy. *Bot.*
Lemoré, Eugène, rue Guichard 2, Passy, Paris. *Coleopt., Con.*
Lenhardt, Prof. Franz, Faculté de Montauban. *Phys. and Nat. Sci.*
Lennier, G., 2 rue Bernardin de St. Pierre, Havre. *Geol., Palæo.*
Lenoel, Dr., rue de la République 34, Amiens. *Nat., Hist.*
Lepeintre, Henri, rue de l'Annonciation, Passy, Paris. *Ent.; Coleopt., Bot*

Lepileur, Dr. Louis, rue de Castellane 12, Paris. *Coleopt.*
Leprieur, C. E., rue des Ecoles 38, Paris. *Coleopt.*
Le Riche, J. B., Instituteur à Gézaincourt, près de Doullens (Somme). *Ent., Hymenop., Apidæ.*
Leroy, Eugène, Prof. au Collége Libre, Lachapelle-sous-Rougement. *Lepid., Coleopt.* C.
Le Roy, Gustave, rue de Tournai 47, Lille. *Geol., Ent.; Lepid.*
Lescuver, F., Saint-Dizier (Haute-Marne). *Orn.*
Léséleuc, Dr. Augustin de, rue Voltaire 40, Brest (Finisterre). *Ent.; Coleopt.* C. Ex. Coleoptera of all countries, especially of France, Algiers, Spain, Portugal, Italy, for those of the United States and Mexico.
Le Sénèchal, Raoul, Corbon, in Cambremer. *Coleopt.*
Lesseps, Ferdinand de, Mem. Acad. Sci., Paris.
Letacq, l'Abbé, Vicaire à Ecouché (Orne). *Bot.*
Letellier, Prof., en retraite, rue Desgenettes, Alençon. *Geol.**
Lethierry, Lucien, Membre des Sociétés Entomologiques de Belgique et de France, rue Blanche 46, Faubourg St. Maurice, Lille. *Ent.; Coleopt., Hemipt., Hymenop.* C. Ex. Offers Coleoptera and Hemiptera of all countries, especially of Europe and of north of Africa, and wishes Coleoptera, Hemipteras and Hymenoptera of America.*
Letourneux, Tacite, rue J. J. Rousseau 5, Nantes. *Bot.*
Levasseur, Prof. E., Mem. de l'Inst., Collège de France, rue Monsieur-le-Prince 26, Paris.*
Levassort, Georges, rue du Vieux-Colombier 4, Paris. *Ent.: Coleopt., Bot.*
Léveillé, Albert, rue St.-Placide 42, Paris. *Coleopt.*
Léveillé, Prosper, Chaussée de Clignancourt 30, Paris. *Coleopt.*
Levoiturier, J. A., rue du Glaieul 36, Elbeuf. *Coleopt.*
Lhotellerie, Juba, rue de Sévigné 12, Paris. *Moll.* C. Ex.
Lhotte, H., 4 rue St. André, Rouen. *Macro-Lepid.: Micro-Lepid et chenilles préparées.**
Liebenberg, Alfred de, rue Lacharrière 15, Paris. *Coleopt.*
Lieury, rue du Petit Salut à Rouen. *Mycology.*
Lieutaud, Dr. Em., Prof. Sch. Méd., boulevard de Lices 19, Angers. *Bot.*
Ligner-Armand, Eugéne, rue Boucher-de-Perthes 17-19, Abbevillle. *Coleopt.*
Lignier, Prof. de Bot. à la Fac. des Sc. de Caen (Calvados). *Bot.**
Limur, F. Comte de, Membre de la Société de Minéralogie de France, Officier de l'Ordre de la Rose du Brésil, President de la Commission Météorologique du Morbihan, Hôtel de Limur (Nannes), Morbihan. *Min., Geol, Arch.* C. Ex. Wishes minerals and rocks of the United States.
Lionnett, G., Vice-Président de la Société Géologique de Normandie, Havre. *Con., Geol., Rocks, Fossils and Minerals.* C. Ex
Lippmann, Gabriel, Membre of French Acad. of Sci., Prof. at the Sorbonne, 108 boulevard St. Germain, Paris. *Phys., Elect.**
Lirondelle, Prof., Lyceum, Douai. *Geol.*
Livon, A., rue Péiries 17, Marseille. *Orn., Ent.: Lepid.*
Lizambard, l'Abbé Charles, Château de Gizeux. *Coleopt.*
Lloyd, James, rue François-Bruneau 15, Nantes, Loire-Inférieure. *Bot.**
Lluch y Diaz, José Maria, Toulouse. *Geog.*
Locard, Arnould, Ingénieur Civil, quai de la Charité 38, Lyon. *Palæo., Moll.* C. Ex*
Lœvy, Maurice, Dir. Obs., Mem. Acad. Sci., rue Cassini 6, Paris. *Astronomy.*
Lombard, Abbé, Curé de Goncelin (Isère). *Bot., Coleopt.*

Lombard, C., Hôpital, Banon. *Coleopt.*
Lombard, Félicien, rue Monge 60, Paris. *Coleopt.*
Longchamps, Prof. G. de, Prof. de Mathematiques Spéciales, Lyceum of Charlemagne, rue de l'Estrapade 15, Paris. *Math.**
Looz, Georges Comte de, Château d'Avin, near Avennes. *Geol.*
Loret, Henri, rue Barthez 4, Montpellier. *Bot.*
Lortet, Dr. Louis, Directeur du Muséum des Sciences Naturelles, Palais St. Pierre, place des Terreaux, Lyon. *Palæo., Ichth., Crypt.* C. Ex.
Lory, Charles, Dir. Agric. Station, Grenoble. *Bot., Min.*
Louis, Adrien, Ressinaud, near St.-Rambert-en-Bugey (Ain). *Bot., Phanerogams, Cryptogams, Mosses, Hepaticæ, Lichens, Mushrooms, Algæ of Europe.* C. Ex. Offers Phanerogams and Cryptogams of Europe in exchange for the same, native and foreign.
Lucand, Capt., rue St.-Christophe 8, Autun (Saône-et-Loire). *Bot.* C. Author of "Mushrooms of France," price 30 francs per fasicle.
Lucante, A., Sec.-Gen. de la Soc. française de Bot., Courrensan, near Gondrin. *Coleopt., principally Cavernicoles. Bot.**
Lucas, Henri, Mus. Nat. Hist., rue Cardinal Lemoine 9, Paris. *Zool.*
Lucas, Hippolyte, Entomologique Muséum, rue Monsieur-le-Prince 10 Paris. *Ent.: Coleopt.*
Lugo, Auguste de, Bagnères-de-Bigorre. *Bot.*
Lusson, Prof., Officier d'Acad., rue A. d'Orbigny, Rochelle. *Phys., Bot., Nat. Sci.*
Luys, Dr. Jules, Membre de l'Académie de Médecine, rue de Seine 23, Ivry (Seine).
Mabille, Paul, Agrégé de l'Université, rue du Cardinal Lemoine 75, Paris. *Ent.: Lepid., Neuropt., Lepid. of Africa, Hesperia of the globe.* C. Ex. Hesperia of all parts of the world.
Macquerys, S., Rouen. *Ent.*
Mager, Henri, Publiciste Géographe, 11 rue d'Aboukir, Paris. *Geog.* Is interested in all questions pertaining to colonization. Collects all documents of the regions which were colonized by Frenchmen, and the centres actually inhabited by Frenchmen.*
Magne, Dir. Veterinary Sch., Alfort. *Bot.*
Magnien, Lucien, Prof. d'Agriculture du Departement de la Côte-d'Or, rue St.-Martin 2, Dijon. *Agric.**
Magnier, Charles, Dir. Bot. Gar., St.-Quentin. *Bot.*
Magnin, Ant., (*olim* Sec. Bot. Soc., Lyon,) Prof. à la Fac. des Sci., Besançon. *Bot.**
Magnin, Jules, rue Honoré-Chevalier 3, Paris. *Coleopt.*
Magon, J., Conservateur du Musée d'Hist. Nat., Marseille. *Zool., Ichth., Lepid.*
Maillard, Dr. Gustave, de la société Géologique suisse, conservateur et bibliothécaire du Musée d'Annecy (France), à Annecy (Hte. Savoie) France. *Min., Geol., Petrology, Prehist. Arch., Anth., Numis., Con., Eth., Bibliog., Photog. Sigilligraphia.* C. Ex. Minerals, French and foreign; fossils, tertiary, cretaceous, jurassic, liassic; Rocks.*
Maillard, Prof. Dr. Aug., rue du Petit-Potet 34, Dijon. *Bot.*
Maillot, Prof. Eugène, Montpellier. *Agric., Lepid., Bot.* *
Maisonneuve, Dr. Paul, Prof. de Zoologie à la faculté libre des Sciences, rue Volney 5, Angers.*
Malosse, Dr. Thre., Agrégé des Facultés de Médecine et des Ecoles Supérieures de Pharmacie, rue Marceau 2, Montpellier.*
Mancag, l'Abbé, Caen (Calvados) *Ent.*
Manceau, l'Abbé, Cenon-la-Bastide. *Con.*
Manes, Adolphe, Capt., Saujon. *Coleopt.*

Mangin, Lieut.-Col., boulevard des Invalides 18, Paris. *Phys.*
Mangon, Charles F. Hervé, Mem. Acad. Sci., rue Saint-Dominique, Paris. *Agric., Meteo., Chem.*
Manuel de Locatel, Le Comte Alfred de, Château de Gonflans, Albertville. *Coleopt.*
Maquenne, Dr., aide-naturaliste au Muséum, rue Cuvier 97, Paris. *Chem.**
Marchais, Ernest, Saint Jean d'Angély (Charente Inférieure). *Min., Ool., Tax., Ent.* C. Desires exchanges.
Marchand, Eugène, Chemist, Mem. de l'Académie de Médecine, Fécamp (Seine Inférieure). *Agric., Chem., Hyg., Phys., Meteo.**
Marchand, Dr. Léon, Prof. Cryptogamia, École Supérieure de Pharmacie de Paris, Thiais (Seine). *Bot.**
Marcotte, Félix, Muséum, rue Ledien 34, Abbeville. *Coleopt.*
Mareine, Remirement (Vosges). *Geometry, Min.*
Marès, Dr. Paul, boulevard St. Michel, Paris. *Geol., Bot.*
Marey, Dr. Etienne J., boulevard Delessert 11, Paris. *Phys.**
Marie, Edouard Auguste, Commissaire adjoint de la Marine, en retraite, Officier d'Académie, Chevalier de la Légion d'Honneur, 1 rue Christine, Paris. *Con., Bryol.* C. living shells. Ex. Offers shells of New Caledonia, shells and mosses of Nossibé, near Madagascar, and of Mayotte.*
Marin, François, rue des Overs 2, Lille. *Mam., Orn.*
Marion, E., Dijon. *Palæo.*
Marmottan, Dr., rue Desbordes-Valmore 31, Passy (Paris). *Ent.: Coleopt., Bot.*
Marquet, Léon, rue Vieille-du-Temple 15, Paris. *Chem.*
Marseul, Silvin de, Directeur du Journal Entomologique l'Abeille, boulevard Pereire 271, Ternes-Paris. *Ent.: Coleopt of Europe, N. of Africa and Asia, Heteromera, Apates, and Histeridæ of the entire world.* C., 30,000 species. Ex. Coleopt. of the ancient world, especially, of France and Algiers, also will exchange publications*
Marsoo, Dr. Jules, à Orthes, 47 rue St. Gilles et à Salies de Béarn. *Palæo., Geol.*
Marsy, Comte Arthur de, Compiègne (Oise). *Geog.*
Martin, Aug., rue de la Pomme 7, Toule.
Martin, Dr. Henri Charles, rue Ste.-Claire 4, Passy, Paris. *Coleopt.*
Martinet, Léon, rue Sainte-Hélène 35, Irigny. *Bot.*
Martins, Prof. Ch., Dir. Bot. Garden, Montpellier. *Bot.*
Marty, Gustave, Officier d'Academie, Commandeur de l'Ordre Royal d'Isabelle la Catholique, boulevard de Strasbourg 67, Toulouse. *Min.**
Marzel, M. L., Ollioules (Var). *Coleopt.**
Mascart, Prof. E., Coll. France, Dir. Bureau Central Météor., Paris. *Phys.*
Masson, E., Oisemont. *Coleopt.*
Masson, Edmond, Meux, in Compiègne. *Coleopt.*
Mathan, René de, Albi. *Coleopt.*
Mathieu, A., rue Girardet 10, Nancy. *Coleopt., Bot.*
Mathieu, Dr., Villa Adriana, Cannes. *Con.*
Maufras, Emile, Notaire, Membre de la Société d'Anthropologie de Paris, Pons (Charente-Inférieure). *Geol., Anth., Arch., L. and F. W. Shells.* C. Ex. Fossils of Chalk, Flint, L. and F. W. Shells of S.E. of France.
Mauppin, Alfred, Membre de la Société Entomologique de France, 155 boulevard St.-Germain, Paris. *Coleopt. of Europe.* C. Ex. insects of France for those of other countries.
Maurein, V., Dir. Bot. Gar., rue de Gand 30, Lille. *Bot.*

Maurel, Auguste, Villard-des-Dourbes. *Coleopt.*
Maurice, Charles, Licencié ès Sciences Naturelles, Château d'Attiches par Pont à Marcq (Nord). *Gen. Zool., Emb., Lepid.* C. Ex.
Maurice, Jules, Licencié ès Sciences Naturelles, Château d'Attiches par Pont à Marcq (Nord). *Gen. Zool., Embryology, Hymenopt., Dipt.* C. Ex.
Maury, Paul, Dr. ès Sci. Nat., 63 rue de Buffon, Paris. *Bot.**
Maxwell-Lyte, F., Faubourg-Saint-Honoré 30, Paris. *Chem.*
Mayet, Valéry, Prof. de Zoologie générale à l'Ecole d'Agriculture, 3 rue Urbain V., Montpellier. *Ent.*
Mege, J. L. E., Curé, Villeneuve by Blaye (Gironde). *Shells, Coleopt. Lepid.* C. Especially European and foreign Lepidoptera. Ex. Specimens of France, Algiers, New Caledonia, and China.
Mégin, J. P., Pres. Soc. Ent. de France, Vincennes. *Ent., Acariologue.**
Melier, Camille (fils), rue Ste.-Catherine 6, St.-Etienne. *Coleopt.*
Ménard, l'Abbé, Saint-André-de-Cubzac (Gironde). *Ent.*
Ménard, St. Yves, Médecin Vetérinaire, Dir. adjoint du jardin Zoologique d'Acclimation, Prof. d'Hygiene Industrielle et d'Histoire Naturelle appliquée à l'Ecole centrale des Arts et Manufactures, rue Charles Lafitte, Neuilly-sur-Seine.*
Mene, Dr., rue Ordinat 29, Paris. *Bot., Hort.*
Mensignac, Edouard de, rue de la Rouselle 67, Bordeaux. *Bot.*
Mer, Emile, avenue Duquesne, Paris. *Bot.*
Merkl, Joseph, Rennes. *Coleopt.*
Mesmin, Louis, Morthemer, near l'Hommaizé. *Coleopt.*
Mestre Gaston, rue de la Chaine 4, Toulouse. *Ent.: Coleopt.*
Meugy, rue Madame 77, Paris. *Geol.**
Meyer, L. E., rue de la Cloche 13, Rochelle. *Philol., Meteo., Nat. Sci.*
Meyer, Samuel, La Rochelle. *Nat. Sci.*
Meyran, Octave, rue de l'Hôtel de Ville 39, Irygny. *Bot.*
Michard, Adrien, Pharmacien de Ire Classe, Ex-interne des Hôpitaux, Lauréat de l'Ecole de Paris, 88 rue Godefroy, Puteaux (Seine). *Ent.* C. Ex. Wishes insects of America.
Michaud, Engène, ave. de la Gare Mouttuion allier. *Coleoptera.*
Michel, Henry, 9 ave. de l'Observatoire, Paris. *Lepid.*
Michel-Lévy, Ingénieur au Corps des Mines, rue d'Aumale 22, Paris. *Geol., Min., Petrog.*
Miciol, E., Morlaix. *Bot.*
Migneaux, Jules, à Billancourt (Seine). *Nat. Hist. Artist.*
Millardet, Prof. de Bot à la Faculté des Sciences, Bordeaux. *Bot.*
Millot, Paul, place Saint-Jean 51, Nancy (Meurthe et Moselle). *Bot., Phanerogams.* C. Ex. Plants of Lorraine and Algeria for Graminiæ of France.
Milne-Edwards, Prof. Alphonse, rue Cuvier 57, Paris. *Zool., Nat. Hist.*
Mimont, de, Château de la Houssaye, in Fontenay, Trésigny. *Coleopt.*
Mingaud, Galien, St.-Jean-du-Gard. *Coleopt., Bot.*
Miot, Henri, Officier de l'Instruction Publique, Membre à vie de la Société Entomologique de France, Correspondant du Musée royale d'Histore Naturelle de Belgique, Juge au tribunal civil de Beaune, (Côte-d'Or). *Economic Ent.* C. Ex.*
Missol, rue Montorgueil 19, Paris. *European Lepid.*
Mocquard, Dr. François, Elève d'Ecole Pratique des Hautes Etudes, boulevard Saint-Germain 36, Paris. *Anatomy of the Crustacea.*
Mocquerys, Emile, rue de la Préfecture 28, Evreux. *Coleopt, Hymenop.*
Moleyre, Muséum Entomologique, Paris. *Ent.: Coleopt.*
Momméja, Jules, Faubourg Sapiac, Montauban. *Arch.*
Monaco, S. A. S., Le Prince Albert de, 16 rue St. Guillaume, Paris. *Meteo., Zool., Gen. Biol., Geog. Dist., Icth. Crustacea, Worms,*

Moll., *Radiates*, *Sponges*, *Protozoa*, *Hydrography and Maritime Zool.*, *Navigation*, *Deep sea sounding and dredging*. C. Ex.*
Mondom, R. P., Prof. Collège Saint-Marie, Saint-Chamond. *Coleopt.*
Moniez, Dr. R., Prof. à la faculté de médecine de l'Etat, à Lille. *Cestoidæ.* C. Ex.
Monnier, Fred., rue des Cornillons 11, Châlon-sur-Saône. *European Lepid.*
Monod, Prof. Dr. Charles, Chirurgien des Hôpitaux, rue Cambacéries 12, Paris.
Monod, Léon, Pouilly-par-Inor, Meuse. *Agric.*
Monod, Robert, rue d'Aumale 19, Paris. *Bot.*: *Bryol.*
Monnot, Edouard, Lyceum, Mans. *Coleopt.*
Monoyer, Prof. M. E. Y., Lyon. *Phys.*
Mons, A., rue Vergniaud, 49 Bordeaux. *Coleopt.*
Montagne, J. B., rue de Sambre-et-Meuse 56, Paris. *Coleopt.*
Montillot, Louis, rue du Cherche-Midi 84, Paris. *Coleopt.*
Moquin-Tandon, Prof. Gaston, Toulouse. *Zool.*, *Emb.**
Morand, Abbé Laurent, Curé de Maché, Chambery (Savoie). *Geol.*
Moreau, Pharmacien, Blois (Loir-et-Cher). *Bot.*
Moreau, Ferdinand, rue Mondenard 35, Bordeaux. *Orn.*
Morel, Ambroise, 63 rue Claude-Bernard, Paris. *Coleopt.*
Morel, Officier de l'Inst. Publique, etc., Mirecourt, (Vosges). C. *Arch.**
Morgan, Jacques de, Ing. des Mines, Dir. gen. des Mines, d'Akhtala (Caucase). Memb. des Soc. Géog., Géol., et Zool. de France, 7 avenue de Villars, Paris. *Geol.*, *Palæo.*, *Con.**
Morière, 40 rue de Bayeux, Caen. *Geol. Bot.*
Morisse, A., Octeville, canton de Montivilliers, Seine Inférieure, France. *Coleopt.*, *Geol.*, *Min.**
Moritz, Naturalist, rue de l'Arbre-Sec. 46, Paris. *Coleopt.*
Motelay, Léonce, Membre de la Société Botanique de France, et Archiviste Bibliothécaire de la Soc. Linnéenne de Bordeaux, etc., etc., cours de Gourgue, Bordeaux. *Bot.* C.*
Mors, Louis, Ingénieur Civil, rue de Solférino 4, Paris. Coleopt., *Hymenop.*, *Con.* Ex. and buys, asks lists and prices.
Mouchez, Ernest A. B. C., Amiral, Mem. Acad. Sci., Dir. Observatory Paris. *Astronomy.**
Mougel, J. B., Vagney, (Vosges), *Orn.*, *Ool.* C. Ex. in Europe only.
Moulière, Auguste, rue Rennaise, Laval. *Geol.*
Mouillard, l'Abbé, Réminiac, in Carentoir. *Coleopt.*
Mouillefarine, Ed., rue Saint-Anne 46, Paris. *Bot.* Ex. in plants of all countries.*
Moureau, Prof. G., cours Saint-Jean 141, Bordeaux, *Bot.*, *Lepid.*, *Coleopt.* C. Ex. for first-class specimens.
Mouret, Georges, Mem. Soc. Géologique de France, rue St. Martin 84, Perigueux. *Geol.* C. Ex.*
Moutte, Edouard, Naturaliste prèparateur, Lycée de Constantine. *Moll.*, *Tax.*
Moyet, l'Abbé, Prof. Petit Seminaire, Grenoble. *Palæo.*, *Con.*, *Biol.*
Mühl, Georges, Au-Bourget-lez-Paris. *Osteol.*, *Tax.*
Mulsant, l'Abbé, Prof. Coll., Saint-Chamond. *Coleopt.*
Mussat, Emile, Prof. à l'Ecole Nationale de Grignon, boulevard St. Germain 11, Paris. *Bot.* Ex. plants of Europe and Algeria for those of N. A.
Musset, Charles, Prof, Fac. Scien. de Grenoble (Isère). *Bot.*, *Phys.*
Nadaillac, Marquis de, Ancien Préfet, rue d'Anjou-Saint-Honoré, Paris. *Anth.*, *Arch.*
Nadar, Paul, rue d'Anjou-St.-Honoré 51, Paris. *Coleopt.*
Nansouty, Max de, rue Saint-Martin 2, Paris. *Chem.*

Nansouty, Général de, Vansinat, Bagnères-de-Bigorre. *Meteo., Con.*
Nanteuil, Roger de, avenue de Villars 10, Paris. *Coleopt.*
Narcillac, le Comte de, boulevard des Italiens 6, Paris. *Coleopt.*
Naudin, Charles, Mem. Acad. Sci., Paris, Dir. du Laboratoire botanique de la Villa Thuret, Antibes (Var). *Phæn. Bot., Hort., Agric., Meteo., Gen., Biol., Philol., Arboriculture.* C.*
Négrié, M. Joseph, rue fond audège 59, Bordeaux. *Coleopt.**
Nerville, F. de, Ingénieur des Télégraphes 116, boulevard Haussmann, Paris. *Phys. Con., Geol., Min., Ent.* C. Ex.
Neumann, L., Château, Fontainobleau. *Bot.*
Neyra, Romain, Tronche, near Grenoble (Isère). *Bot.* C. Ex.
Neyraud, Marcel, Montferrand, near Bordeaux. *Coleopt.*
Nickles, René, rue de Rennes 59, Paris. *Geol., Min.*
Nicolas, André, rue Jean Réveil, Pau (Basses Pyrénérs.) *Longicornes d'Europe, Dorcadions du globe, Carabides d'Europe, Carabides vrais du globe.**
Nicolas, J., Sec. Hort. Ass., rue Passet 10, Lyon. *Coleopt.*
Nicolle, Dr. Prof. Medècine de l'Hospice général, place Rougemare 7, Rouen.
Niel, rue Herbière 28, Rouen. *Mycology.**
Niveit, Prof. Ingénieur-en-Chef des Mines, rue du Bac 97, Paris. *Geol.*
Nodier, Dr., rue Saint-Uhel 2, Lorient. *Ent.: Coleopt.**
Noel, Fr., rue Désirée 36, St.-Etienne. *Coleopt.*
Noel, Paul, Chimiste, rue Panguy 15, Boisguillaume, near Rouen. *European Lepidoptera.* C. Ex. Lepidoptera for minerals and fossils.
Noguey, Gustave, rue Chai-des-Farines 14, Bordeaux. *Orn., Palæo.*
Norguet, Anatole de Mardre de, rue Jemmapes 61, Lille. *Coleopt.*
Normand, Ch., 51, rue des Martyrs. *Geog.*
Noroy, Ch., rue Mexico 63, Havre. *Chem.*
Nou, Michel, Naturalist, Vernet-les-Bains. *Coleopt., -ot.*
Noualhier, Maurice Laborie, near Limoges. *Coleopt.*
Noulet, Dr., Prof. Sch. Med., rue Nazareht 15, Toulou . *Bot.*
Nonry, Prof. Hâvre (Seine inférieure). *Geol.*
Nugue, l'Abbé A., à Couptrain (Mayenne), Coleopt Desires to know some one who will exchange American beet s (Coleopt). for French ones. Writes both English and French *
Nylander, Dr., passage des Thermopyles 61, Paris. *Crypt, Bot. Lich.*
Oberlender, place St. Paul 32, Rouen. *Ent.*
Oberthür, Charles, Rennes (Ille-et-Vilaines). Ent. Lepid., A les collections complètes de Boisduval, de Guenée, de Graslin, *de Constant Bar, Xa.* Publie Les Etudes d'Entomologie, ouvrage avec planches coloriées, exclusivement devoué aux Lépidoptéres; Ex. of Lepid. from all parts of the world.*
Oberthür, René, Rennes (Ille-et-Vilaine). *Ent.: Coleopt.* C. Ex. Offre pour échange des Coleopt. de toutes les parties du monde. A les collections de Chaudoir (Carabicidæ), Steinheil, Rosenhauer, Thorey, Wehncke (Hydrocauthares), Mniszech (partim), von Harold, etc. Publie *les Coleopterorum* novitates.*
Odier, Georges, Polytec. School, rue St.-Lazare 93, Paris. *Coleopt. Hemipt., Lepid.*
Oehlert, D., Conservateur de la Bibliotheque, et du Musée d'Histoire Naturelle, 29 rue de Bretagne, Laval. *Palæo.**
Olive, G., rue Montgrand 14, Marseilles. *Orn., Herpetol., Ent., Con., Bot., Geol., Palæo., Min.*
Oliver, l'Abbè, Dreux, Eure-et-Loire. *Astronomy.*
Olivier, Ernest, château des Ramillors près Moulins (Allier). *Bot., Zool., Ent.* C. of Botany and Zoology of France, Entomology of Europe.

Asia, and Africa. Ex. animals, birds, and plants of France, insects of Europe, and of the north of Africa. Has his grandfather's (G. A. Oliver) collection. Will buy Lampyrini and Melvidae of the globe.*
Olivier, H., Autheuil (Orne). *Lichenology, Mosses.* C. Ex. Lichens of Orne and Calvados for those of other countries.
Olivier, Louis D., Sc. 90 rue de Rennes, Paris. *Mic., Bot.*
Ollier de Marichard, Vallen, Ardèche. *Arch.*
Orbigny, Henri de, rue des Beaux-Arts 12, Paris. *Coleopt.*
Ortlieb, Jean, Croix, near Roubaix. *Chem., Geol.*
Osmont, Auguste, Controleur des Douanes, rue de Geole 29, Caen (Calvados). *Ent.: Lepid., Calosoma, Carabus, Chychrus.* C. Ex. Specimens, Carabus, Colosoma, Chychrus, Catocala.
Oster, rue Bonaparte 59, Paris. *Malacology.*
Oustalet, Muséum, rue Bonaparte 52, Paris. *Coleopt.*
Ozanon, Charles, St.-Emiland, Conches-les-Mines. *Bot.* C.
Pandellé, Louis, rue du Lycée 17, Tarbes. *Coleopt.*
Panescorse, Fréd., Allées d'Azemas, Draguignan. *Palæo., Con.*
Paquet, René, rue de Vaugirard 34, Paris. *Orn.*
Parat, rue de l'Arsenal, Rochefort-sur-Mer. *Bot.*
Pardo de Tavero, T. H., 36 boulevard Pereire, Paris. *Philol.*
Parfait, Capt. de frégat, rue des Fonderies, Rochefort sur Mer. *Marine Zool.*
Passet, Jules, rue Miromesnil, 60. *Gen. Ent.* C. Ex.
Passy, Frédéric, rue Labordère, Neuilly-sur-Seine.
Passy, P. Ed. Howard, rue Labordère 6, Neuilly-sur-Seine. *Physiologie du langage.**
Pasteur, Joseph, rue de Sèze 17, Lyon. *Coleopt.*
Pasteur, Louis, Mem. Acad. Sci., rue d'Ulm 45, Paris. *Min.*
Patouillard, N., Pharmacien, Fontenay Sous Bois, près Paris. *Fungi (exotic).**
Patou, Jules, la Chapelle Moche (Orne). *Lepid.**
Patry, Gabriel, au Marché neuf près Bernay (Eure). *Orn.*
Paulin, Médecin-Vétérinaire, St. Dizier (Haute Marne). *Palæo.* C.*
Péchiney, A., Salindres (Gard). *Chem.*
Pellat, Ed., rue de Vaugirard 77, Paris. *Geol.*
Pellet, H., Officier d'Académie, Laboratoire de Chimie Scientifique, Industrielle et Agricole, 5 rue Fénelon, Paris. *Chem.*
Pelletan, Dr. Jules, Prof. Histol. et Mic., Univ. de Paris, rue de Berne 14, Paris. Dir. du Journal de Micrographie. *Bot., Chem., Mic., Zool., Gen. Biol., Emb., Anat., Articulates, Gen. Ent., Crustacea, Worms, Moll., Radiates, Protozoa, Infusoria.* C. Ex.*
Pelletier, Horace, Madon près Blois. *Bot., Ent.**
Peltier, Edmond, Commerçant, rue de Monsieur 18, Reims (Marne). *Ent.: Coleopt.* C. Ex. Insects of Reims for those of other countries.
Penchynat, Dr., Port Vendres (Pyrénées-Orientales). *Con.*
Penet, Léon, Con. Mus. d'Histoire Naturelle, Grenoble (Isère). *Min., Geol., Petrog., Con., Bot., Zool., Arch.*
Pennès, J. A., rue de Latran 2, Paris. *Chem.*
Pennetier, Dr. Georges, Directeur du Muséum d'Histoire Naturelle, Rouen. *Zool.*
Perez, J. S., Prof. Zool. à la Faculté des Sci., Bordeaux. *Hymen.**
Périer, Alexandre, Bélesta. *Coleopt.*
Perier-Lefranc, Louis, Fabricant de Couleurs, quai d'Issy 21, Issy (Seine). *Lepid.*
Perrens, Prof. Dr., route de Bayonne 72, Bordeaux. *Bot.*
Perrier, Eugène le Baron de la Bâthie, Prof. d'Agric., Albertville (Savoie). *Bot., Hort.*

Perrier, François, Général Directeur de l'Académie de Science, 138 rue de Grenelle, Paris. *Géographie et Navigation.**
Perrier, Prof., Muséum, rue des Saints-Pères 19, Paris. *Zool., Moll.*
Perrin, Abeille de, rue Marengo 56, Marseille. *Coleopt., Hymenop.*
Pesier, Edmond, Valenciennes. *Chem.*
Pestre, A. P., Prof. de Sciences Physiques et Naturelles, Institution St. Joseph, Montluçon (Allier). *Bot., Coleopt.*
Pestre, Rev. P., rue de Vaugirard 104, Paris. *Coleopt., Bot., Min., Roches.**
Peticlerc, Paul, Membre de plusieurs sociétés savantes, rue du Collège 4, Vesoul (Haute-Saône). *Geol., Palæo.* C. Ex. Possède de nombreux doubles de Fossils Jurassiques et Cretacées et désire entrer en relation d'échanges avec des amateurs étrangers parlant français.
Petit, Eugène, Naturaliste préparateur, rue Porte-Neuve 47, Pau. *Zool. of the Pyrenees.* C. Ex.
Petit, Paul, Ancien Pharmacien, Officier d'Académie, 17 boulevard St.-Germain, Paris. *Diatoms of all countries and F. W. Algæ of France.* C.
Petrucci, Ch. Raphael, Ingénieur Economiste, 38 avenue St. Pierre, Béziers (Héraulte). *Geol.*
Peyron, Ed., rue de Lodi 47, Marseille. *Coleopt.*
Philibeaux, Gustave, Bligny-sur Ouche. *Coleopt.*
Picard, Lieut.-Col. Francis Louis, Langres (Haute Marne). *Palæo., Stra Geol., Min., Crystal., Lithol.* C.
Pichez, Dr. Ernest, rue Alcide d'Orbigny, La Rochelle. *Medicine, Ent.*
Pichon, St.-Armand-sur-Fion. *Bot.: Mycol.*
Pierre, Prof. Isidore, Dir. Agric. Station, Caen. *Bot.*
Pierrat, D., Naturalist, Gerbamont, near Vagney (Vosges). *Zool., Orn., Ool., Tax., Bot., Ent.: Orthopt.* C. Ex. Mounted birds or skins, dried plants, Orthoptera.*
Pierson, Henri, 7 rue Pierre-Lescot, Paris, ou à Brunoy (Seine-et-Oise). *Mic., Photog., Ent., Hemipt., Orthopt., Neuropt.* C. Ex.
Pignol, Jules, Frueder, rue des Deux Boules 7, Paris. *Ent., Zool.*
Pillet, Louis, Place St. Leger, Chambéry (Savoie). *Arch., Palæo., Geol., Min.*
Pinart, Alph. L., Chargé de Mission dans les deux Amériques, care of the France Geographical Co., Paris, Marquise, Pas-de-Calais. *Arch., Eth.*
Pinel, Fernand, rue Lenotre 20, Rouen. *Orn.*
Pinot, R. P., Convent of Coublevie, in Voiron. *Coleopt.*
Pissot, Abbey de Longchamps, in Neuilly. *Coleopt.*
Place, Henri de, Château de la Rive, Ste.-Gemmes-sur-Loire. *Coleopt.*
Place, Louis de, Angers. *Coleopt.*
Planchon, Prof. J. E., Montpellier. *Coleopt., Bot.*
Planchon, Prof. Gustave, boulevard St.-Michel 139, Paris. *Bot.*
Planté, Gaston, rue des Tournelles 56, Paris. *Phys.*
Poiranet, Georges, 20 rue Cuvier, Paris. *Crypt. Bot.*
Poirier, J. Muséum, avenue du Maine 43, Paris. *Zool.*
Poisson, Jules, Muséum, rue de Buffon 63, Paris. *Bot.**
Polle-Deviermes, Léon, rue de la Ferme-des-Mathurins 18, Paris. *Coleopt.*
Pollet, Charles-Louis-Joseph, Généalogist, rue de Tourneville 33, Havre. *Coleopt.*
Pomerol, B., Rédacteur de la Revue, Matériaux pour l'Histoire de l'Homme, 36 rue des Ecoles, Paris. *Prehistoric Archæology, Palæontology.*
Ponche, Narcisse, rue Constantine 6, Amiens.
Poncin, l'Abbé, Mem. Soc. des Sciences Naturelles du Sud-Est, rue d'Italie 125, Tour-du-Pin (Isère). *Coleopt.*

Poncin, Prof. à l'Externat, rue des Vieux-Jesuits, Grenoble. *Coleopt.*

Ponsd'hauterive, Leopold, Estaing, d'Aveyron. *Moll.* C. Birds, Animals, L. and F. W. Molluscs. Ex. for foreign.*

Ponson, A., fils, quai de la Guillottière 20, Lyon. *Coleopt.*

Pontarlier, Charles, Prof. en retraite, la Roche-sur-Yon (Vendée). *Phæn. Bot.*

Ponte, Dr., cours Senozan, Voiron (Isère). *Coleopt., Lepid.*

Populus, Dr., Coulanges-la-Vineuse. *Hemipt., Coleopt.*

Porte Orieulx, J. de la, Ingénieur Civil des Mines 38, rue de Fleurus, Paris. *Geol., Min., Palæo.* C. Ex.

Portevin Hippolyte, Ingénieur Civil, ancien Elève de l'Ecole Pôlytechnique, rue de la Belle-Image 2, Reims. *Min.* Wishes specimens of ores of iron, with indications of uses for which they are employed.*

Potel, Maurice, 69 rue de Rennes, Paris. *Myriopods.*

Potier, Prof., Polytechnic School, boulevard St.-Michel, Paris. *Phys., Geol.*

Pouchet, Georges, Professeur d'Anat. comp. au Muséum d'Histoire Naturelle, 10 rue de l'Eperon, B'd St.-Germain, Paris. *Comparative Anatomy, Histology.**

Poucnet, Eugéne, Landorff (Lorrain). *Coleopt.*

Poujade, Gustave Arthur, Muséum, rue des Ecoles 15, Paris. *Ent.: Coleopt., Lepidop.**

Poujol, A., Corinthe-de-Cognin, near Chambéry. *Coleopt.*

Poussielgue, J. Belmont, Tramonet, Pont de Beauvoisin. *Coleopt.*

Poussier, Alfred, Pharmacien, 47 rue d'Amiens, Rouen. *Geol., Bot., Pisicul., Anthropology.**

Power, Gustave, St.-Auen-de-Thoubreville (Eure), near Bouille (Seine-Inférieure). *Coleopt.*

Pozzi, Dr. Samuel, Prof. Agrégé à la Faculté de Paris, place Vendôme 10, Paris. *Anat., Anth.*

Prarond, Ernest, Abbeville (Somme).

Prazmowski, rue Bonaparte 1, Paris. *Phys.*

Prié, J., Poulignen (Loire-Inférieure). *Crustacea, Moll.*

Prillieu, Edouard, Inspecteur général de l'Enseignement agricole, Professeur à l'Ecole Centrale des arts et manufacture et à l'Institut agronomique, rue Cambacères 14, Paris. *Bot.**

Prulière, Naturaliste préparateur, rue Contellerie 4, Marseille. *Mam., Orn., Herpet., Ichth., Ent., Crustacea, Moll., Zoophytes Cephalopods, Lower Invert., Echinoderms.**

Puton, Dr. J. B. Aug., Remiremont (Vosges). *Ent.: Hemipt., Coleopt.,* C. Ex. Hemiptera.

Pyot, Victor, Gien. *Coleopt.*

Quædvlieg, Louis, Naturalist, rue de la Goutte-d'Or, Aubervilliers. *Ent.: Lepid., Bot.*

Quatrefages de Bréau, Jean Louis Armand de, Membre de l'Institut, Prof. au Muséum, Paris. *Zool., Anth., Osteol., Photog.* C. of the Muséum. Ex. Crania.*

Quélet, Dr., Hérimoncourt (Doubs). *Bot., Mycol.*

Quétin, Eugène, rue de Bruys 9, Marseille. *Coleopt.*

Quinquarlet-Debony, Félix, Maison Prado, Carnac (Morhiban). *Hemipt., Galls.*

Quinquand, Dr., rue d'Odéon 5, Paris. *Fungi, Organic Chem., Mic., Gen. Biol., Anth., Coleopt., Protozoa, Infusoria.*

Rabaud, Alfred, rue Paradis 101, Marseille. *Geog.*

Rabourdin, Prof. Lucien, rue Labodrée, 8 Neuilly (Seine.) *Ethnog. Anth., Prehistoric Arch.*

Ragain, Prof. Gustave, Lyceum, rue de Ségalier 42, Bordeaux.

Ragonot, Emile L., Banquier, quai de la Rapée 12, Paris. *Micro-lepidoptera of the World.* Will determine European micro-lepid. Desirous of receiving Phycidæ from all parts of the world for naming. Ex. Will be glad to receive publications on mic.
Rambaud, Delphin, Loulay, St.-Jean-d'Angely (Charente-Inférieure). *Orn., Tax., Lepid.* C. Ex.
Rames, Dr. J., rue d'Aurcignes, Aurillac, Cantal. *Geol.*
Ramond, A., rue des Ecoles 38, Paris. *Bot.*
Raoult, Dr. Charles, Raon-l'Etape. *Coleopt.*
Raspail, Eugène, Gigondas (Vaucluse). *Geol., Arch.*
Rataboul, Joseph, Moissac (Tarn-et-Garonne). *Diatoms.* C. Ex.*
Raveret-Wattel, rue des Acacias 20, Paris. *Pisciculture.**
Ravoux, Alfred, Pharmacien, Nyons, Drôme. *Coleopt.*
Rawlings, Ed., rue Boissière 26, Paris. *Con.*
Ravet, Prof., Bordeaux. *Phys.*
Raynaud, Dir. Telegraph Lines, boulevard Saint-Germain 60, Paris. *Phys.*
Rebond, Dr., St., Marcellin. *Bot.**
Reclus, Prof. Dr., rue des Saints-Pères 9, Paris.
Regimbart, Dr. Maurice, rue de la Petite Cité 4, Evreux (Eure). *Entomology and Coleoptera of Europe and of the basin of the Mediterranean, especially Dytiscidæ, Grinidæ, Hydrophilidæ, Parnidæ and Heteroceridæ of the Globe.* C. Ex. Coleoptera of Europe in exchange for specimens indicated above.
Réguis, Sec. Bot. and Hort. Soc. of Provence, place St.-Michel 12, Marseille. *Bot.*
Réguis, Dr. J. M. F., Naturalist, Allauch, near Marseille (B. du Rhône). *Vert., Palæo., Zool., Vert. Anat., Mam., Orn., Herpetol., Ichth., Histol. of Vert.* C. Ex.
Reich, Louis, Arles-sur-Rhône. *Agric.*
Reinwald, C., Libraire-Editeur, rue des Saints-Pères 15, Paris. *Publication of French Scientific Works, and records of Experimental and General Zoology.**
Remy, Jules, Ancien Naturaliste-Voyageur, Louvercy, near Mourmelon (Marne). *Bot.* C. Plants from all parts of the world except the Sandwich Islands. Ex. Offers Ferns of Australia in exchange for American.
Renard, Adolphe, Prof. de Chimie à l'Ecole Supérieure des Sci., rue du Contrat Social 37, Rouen. *Chem.*
Renaud, J. B., cours d'Herbouville 21, Lyon. *Ent.: Coleopt., Hemipt.*
Renauld, F., Commandant du Palais de Monaco, France. *Mosses.* C. Ex. for American Mosses.*
Renault, Dr. B., Muséum, rue de la Collégiale 1, Paris. *Bot., Palæo.*
René, Ad., St. André-de-Cubzac (Gironde). *Coleopt., Lepid.*
Renémesnil, Pierre de, Chef de Division à la Mairie de Caen, rue de l'Eglise St.-Julien 12, Caen (Calvados.) *Ent. Coleopt.* C. Ex.
Renou, E., Observatoire du Parc, St.-Maur (Seine). *Meteo.**
Renouard, fils, Alfred, Ingénieur, Secrétaire-général de la Société Industrielle du Nord de la France, et de la Société des Agriculteurs du Nord, rue Alexandre Leleux 46, Lille (Nord). *Agriculture, Textiles of tropical countries.*
Revelière, G., rue Volney 45 Angers (Maine-et-Loire). *Mineraology, Geology, Palæo.* C. Ex. Minerals and rocks of Bretagne.
Revelière, Jules, Receveur de l'Enregistrement, rue Volney 45, Angers (Maine-et-Loire). *Coleoptera of Europe and of the basin of the Mediterranean.*
Reverchon, Elisee, Bollène (Vaucluse). *Bot.*
Reverchon, L., Mazan. *Bot.*

Revil, Pharmacien, Place du Marché Couvert, Chambery (Savoie). *Arch.*, *Palæo.*, *Geol.*
Revon, Louis, Muséum, Annecy. *Bot.*
Rey, Celestin, Econome au Petit Séminaire, Grenoble. *Coleopt.*, *Lepid*
Rey, Timothée, Nissan, near Béziers (Hérault). *Birds and Mammals.* C.
Rey-Lescure, faubourg du Moustier 8, Montauban. *Geol.*
Reynard-Lespinasse, Avignon. *Con.*, *Geol.**
Reynaud, Lucien, rue de Vendôme 235, Lyon (Rhône). *Lepidoptera.* C. Ex.
Ribadieu, Ferdinand, cours d'Albret 83, Bordeaux. *Arch.*
Richard, attaché anx collections de l'Ecole Nat. des Chim., rue Guy la Crasse 11, Paris. *Min.*
Richard, Alfred, cours St. Bruno 2, Grenoble (Isère). *Phæn. Bot.*, *Coleopt.*
Richard, Jules, Ancien Procureur de la République, 31 rue de Magenta, Poiters (Vienne). *Phanerogams*, *Lichens.* C. Ex. Lichens of France for those of America.*
Richard, Jules, Licencié ès-sciences physiques et naturelles, 16 rue St.-Guillaume, Paris. *Echinoderms.* C. Désire échanger entomostracés d'eau douce.
Richard, l'Abbé, Pierre, Vicaire-Général, hydrogéologue au Seminaire-Montlieu (Charente-Inférieure). *Geol.* C.
Richemond, Louis de, Officier de l'Univ., rue Verdière 23, Rochelle. *Arch.*, *Philol.*, *History.**
Richer, Dr., rue Saint-Jacques 98, Amiens. *Nat. Hist.*
Richer, Henri, rue de l'Odéon 12, Paris. *Coleopt.*, *Orn.*
Richer, Henri, rue St.-Pierre 3, Chartres. *Coleopt.*
Richet, Prof. Ch., Dir. de la Revue Scientifique, 15 rue de l'Université, Paris. *Physiol.*, *Gen. Biol.*
Rigaux, Henri, rue de l'Hôpital-Militaire 112, Lille. *Geol.*
Rigaud, Léon de, Ingénieur des Mines, Chimiste, Naturaliste Photog., 54 quai de Billy, Paris. Invest de missions Scientifiques par l'ex-gouvernement impérial de France, en Bulgarie, Asie-Mineure, Australie, et N. Caledonie, etc.
Risler, Charles, rue de l'Université 39, Paris. *Chem.*
Risler, Edmund, Dir. Nat. Agric. Station, Paris. *Bot.*, *Agric.*
Risler, Eugène, boulevard Haussmann 168, Paris. *Agric.*
Riston, Victor, Malzeville, near Nancy. *Geol.*, *Palæo.* C. Ex.
Rivals, l'Abbé de, Mouleau, near Arcachon (Gironde). *Coleopt.* C. Longicorns of the globe. Ex.
Riveau, Charles, Prof. Libre, Genouillé (Charente-Inférieure). *Gen. Nat. Hist.*, *especially Botany*, *Entomology.* C. Ex. plants and insects.
Rivière, Em., rue de Sèvres 139, Paris. *Arch.*
Rizaucourt, Jean-Baptiste, rue de la Rotonde 63, Marseille. *Coleopt.*
Robin, Charles, boulevard Saint-Germain 94, Paris. *Coleopt.*
Robin, H. A., Préparateur de la Faculté des Sciences, 38 rue d'Ulm, Paris. *Mammology*, *Annelids*, *F. W. Turbellaria*, *Anatomy.* C. Ex. Mammals in alcohol, Annelids, and Turbellaria.
Roche, I., care M. H. Mager, rue d'Aboukir 11, Paris. *Exploration du Brésil.*
Rochebrune, Prof. de, Nat. Hist. Muséum, Paris. *Zool.*
Rocher, Maximin, Montlouis, near St.-Julien-l'Ars. *Coleopt.*
Rodier, Prof. Emile, rue Mazarin 61, Bordeaux. *Gen. Biol.**
Rolland, E., rue de Rennes 66, Paris. *Phys.*
Rolland, Fernand, Surgères. *Ent.: Coleopt.*
Rolland, Victor, rue Surcouf 1, Paris. *Orn.*, *Algæ.* C. Ex. Offers French Algæ for those from all parts of the world.

Roset, Henri, Pharmacien, Chimiste, Membre de l'Académie Nationale, rue Jehan-Foucquet 5, Tours. *Mollusca.* C.
Rossignol, L., rue de Bercy 151, Paris. *Coleopt., Lepid., Shells.**
Rottenstein, Dr. Johann B., Paris.
Roüast, Georges, rue du Stat. 32, Lyon. Mollusques terrestres et marins du globe entier. *European Lepid.* C. Ex.*
Roubalet, L., rue St.-Georges 12, Nancy. *Coleopt.*
Rouchy, Jn., l'Abbé, Membre de plusieurs sociétés savantes, Vicaire, Ségur (Cantal). *Bot., Min., Ent.* C. Ex. Offers plants and minerals of the central part of France.
Rouget, Prof. Ch., Nat. Hist, Museum, Paris. *Phys.*
Rouguie, Aumonier de l'asile d'aliénés de Leyme à Lachapelle. *Ent.* C. Ex. Coleoptera.
Roujon, Prof. A., Clermont-Ferrand. *Bot.*
Roumeguère, Dr. C., Rédacteur en chef de la Revue Mycologique, rue Riquet 37, Toulouse. Vente et échange des Exsiccata contre des publications de la même nature. *Crypt. Bot., Bibliog., Mycology.* C. Ex.*
Rovon, Con. Mus., Annecy (Haute-Savoie). *Bot., Palæo., Geol., Min., Vert., Moll., Arch., Eth.*
Royer, Charles, rue des Encommencés, Langres (Haut-Marne) *Coleopt., Lepid.* C. Ex.
Royer, Madame Clémence, Prof. publiciste, avenue des Ternes 82, Paris. *Palæo., Geol., Chem., Phys., Gen. Biol., Anth., Arch., Eth., Ethnog., Philol.*
Rouquier, l'Abbé, Leyme, La-Capelle-Marival. *Coleopt.*
Rousseau, Charles, rue Fondandège 47, Bordeaux. *Ent.: Coleopt.*
Rousseau, Em., rue des Ecoles 44, Paris. *Chem.*
Rousseau, P., boulevard St.-Germain 258, Paris. *Chem.*
Rousselet, L., boulevard Saint-Germain 126, Paris. *Arch.*
Roussille, Albert, Professeur de Minéralogie et Géologie à l'Ecole Nationale d'Agriculture, Grignon, Neauphle le Château (Seine-et-Oise). *Min.* C. Ex. Fossils of Grignon.
Rouville, P. de, Prof. de Géol. à la Faculté des Sci., Montpellier. *Geol.*
Roux, rue de Pessac 31, Bordeaux. *Zool.*
Roux, H., Pres. Bot. and Hort. Soc. of Provence, Marseille. *Bot.*
Rouy, Georges, Vice-Prés. de la Société Botanique de France, Rédacteur au Naturaliste, Directeur du Comptoir Parisien d'Echange de plantes, 66 rue Mozart, à Paris. *Phæn. Bot.* C. 19,000 species; 90,000 specimens.*
Rouzard, Henri, Docteur es Sciences, Maître de Conférences à la Faculté des Sciences, Montpellier. *Zool., Anat., Comp. Histol., Embryol.**
Roze, Ernest, rue Claude Bernard 72, Paris. *Bot.**
Ruchillot, Naturaliste Préparateur et Directeur du Muséum, Rennes. *All branches, especially Mam., Orn., and Lepid.* C. Ex.
Rucquoy, Alfred, Favat. *Con.*
Rufino, José Cuervo, 3 rue Meissonier, Paris. *Philol.*
Rupin, E., Brive. *Bot.*
Sabatier, Prof., rue Barthez 1, Montpellier. *Con.*
Sabatier, Armand, Prof. Zool. à la Faculté des Sciences, Dir. Station Zoologique de Cette, Montpellier. *Bibliog., Zool., Gen. Biol., Emb., Anat, Osteol., Myol., Histol. of Vert., Articulates, Arach., Worms.*
Sagnier, Henri, rue de Rennes 152, Paris. *Agric.*
Sagot, Dr. P. A., rue des Godrans 30, Dijon. *Bot.*
Saint-Exupéry, Le Comte de, rue du Gouvernement Saint-Quentin. *Geography.*
Saint Gal, M. J., Prof. de Botanique à l'Ecole Nationale d'Agriculture de

Grand-Jouan Nozay (Loire-Inférieure). *Bot., Sylviculture, Agricultural Ent.* C.*
Saint-Hilaire, Albert Geoffroy, Directeur du Jardin Zoologique d'Acclimatation, Neuilly-sur-Seine. *Zool.* C. *
Saint-Lager, Dr., Librarian Bot. Soc., cours Gambetta 8, Lyon. *Bot.**
Saint-Légier, M. Ed. de, Château d'Orignac par St.-Ciers du Taillon, (Charente Inf.). *Coleopt.**
Saint-Pierre, Camille, Montpellier. *Agric.*
Saint-Quentin, Prof. Collège, Péronne. *Coleopt.*
Saint-Remy, Georges, Préparateur suppléant à la Faculté des Sciences, Nancy (Meurthe-et-Moselle). *Emb. of Invert* *
Saint-Quentin, C., terrasse St.-Pierre 10, Douai. *Coleopt.*
Saint-Saud, Comte d'Arlot de, Château de la Valouze, par La Roche-Chalais, Dordogne. *Arch.**
Sallé, Auguste, Naturaliste, ruy Guy de la Brosse 13, Paris. *Coleopt. of America, L. and F. W. Shells, Orn.* C. Ex.*
Salleron, J., rue Pavée en Marais 24, Paris. *Phys.*
Salles, L., 3 rue Daval, Paris. *Trochilidæ.* C. Ex.
Salmon, Philippe, Vice-Prés. de la Commission des Monuments Mégalithiques, rue le Pelletier 29, Paris. *Palæo.* C.
Sancey, Louis, rue Neuve 26, Besançon. *Ent.: Coleopt., Lepid.*
Sand, Maurice, Baron Dudevant, Château de Nohant, near La Châtre. *Coleopt.*
Saporta, Le Marquis Gaston de, Aix. *Bot., Geol., Palæo.**
Saquet, H. R. R., connu sous le pseudonyme anagramme Nérée Quépat, 34 rue Vaugirard, Paris. *Orn.*
Sarromejean, B., Cacarens, near Lannepax. *Coleopt.*
Saury, E. J., rue des Frères, Aurillac. *Coleopt.*
Saury, Jules, rue Pont-Hérisson 8, Limoges. *Coleopt.*
Sauvage, Dr. Emile, Dir. de la Station agricole de Boulogne. *Ichth., Herpet.*
Sauvage, Louis, Corbie (Somme). *Agric.*
Sauvinet, Ernest, 15 rue de Buffon, Paris. *Préparateur au Muséum de Paris.*
Sauze, Dr. La Mothe, 1st, Héray (Deux-Sèvres). *Bot.*
Savatier, Dr., rue Matho, Beauvais (Charente-Inférieure). *Bot., Orn.*
Savatier, Ludovic, Médecin en chef de la Marine, Lorient (Morbihan). *Bot.*
Savioz, Naturalist, Chamonix. *Coleopt.*
Savoye, Emile, rue du Bleumouton 4, Lille. *Geol.*
Sazerat, Marc, Place St.-Pierre, Limoges. *Coleopt.*
Scalabre, Ferdinand, Naturalist, Ham. *Coleopt.*
Schlernitzauer, Jules, rue St.-Denis 221, Paris. *Coleopt.*
Schlumberger, rue du Bailliage 14, Rouen. *Foreign Orchids.*
Schlumberger, Ch., 94 *bis*, rue du Four St.-Germain, Paris. *Geol., Palæo. (Foraminifera).*
Schlumberger, Gustave, Pau. *Coleopt.*
Schmitt, Prof. Ernest, Lille. *Chem.*
Schneider, Prof., Poitiers. *Bot., Zool.*
Schutzenberger, Prof., Collège de France, rue Claude Bernard 53, Paris.
Sebert, Lieut.-Col. Marine Artil., boulevard de Courcelles 17, Paris. *Phys.*
Sédillot, Maurice, Membre des Sociétés Entomologiques de France, Belgique, etc., 20 rue de l'Odéon, Paris. *European and Exotic Coleopt., principally Hydrocanthus, Erotylidæ, Trogostidæ, Cleridæ, Heteromera.* C. Ex.
Seize, Pierre, Hôpital St.-Martin, rue de Récollets 8, Paris. *Coleopt.*
Selle, de, avenue de Villars, Paris. *Geol.*

Sénac, Dr. Hippolyte, Ussel par Chantelle (Allier). *Coleopt.**
Sénéchal, Maoue Le, Préparateur de Zool. à la Faculté des Sci. de Caen (Calvados). Con. du Musée d'Hist. Nat. de la dite Faculté. *Spec., faune des eaux saumâtres.* Desires to correspond with Boston Naturalists.*
Senneville, Gaston de, rue de Grenelle-St.-Germain 52, Paris. *Coleopt.*
Sépulchre, Joseph, Maubeuge (Nord). *Geol.*
Serre, Gaston de, rue Las-Cases 8, Paris. *Geol.*
Serrin, V., boulevard St.-Martin 1. Paris. *Phys.**
Servain, Dr., rue des Champs St.-Martin 49, Angers. *Con.*
Siépi, Pierre, Naturaliste-Préparateur au Muséum d'Hist. Nat. de Marseille, et de l'Ecole de Médecine, rue Pavillon 7, Marseille. *Mam., Orn., Herpetol., Ichth., Ent., Tax.*
Signoret, Victor, rue de Rennes 46 (place St.-Germain-des-Près), Paris. *Hemipt.*
Silva, R. D., Prof. Chargé de Cours in the Central School of Arts and Manufactures, Prof. of Analyt. Chem., Municipal School of Industrial Phys. and Chem. of Paris, 26 rue de la Harpe, Paris. *Org., Chem.**
Simon, Eugène, ancien Président de la Société Entomologique de France, Président de la Société Zoologique de France, avenue du Bois-de-Boulogne 56, Paris. *Arachnology.* C. of Arachnids, with the exception of Acari. Ex.
Simon, J., Redon (Ille-et-Vilaine). *Geol.*
Sinéty, Le Marquis de, Vice-Prés. Société d'Acclimatation de France, rue de Lille 19, Paris.
Société Centrale de Produits Chimiques, 42-44 rue des Ecoles, Paris. *Chem., Phys., Met.* C. Ex. Organic Chemistry and Mineralogy.*
Société des Amis des Sci. Nat. de Rouen. Etudie la Zool., la Bot., la Min., et la Géol. de la Normandie. Publie les Bulletins, échange les publications.
Société Géologique du Nord, 1 rue des Fleurs, Lille (1870). Contains memoirs and important publications.
Société Linnéenne du Nord, Amiens. Contains valuable works on various branches of Natural History.
Société Populaire d'Etudes Diverses, Alexandre Gahineau, rue Lemoine 72, Président, Sotheville-les-Rouen (Seine-Inférieure). *Natural Sciences in general, and their applications. Phys., Anat., Ent., Anth., Palæo.* C. Ex. Mineralogy, Geology, Ethnology, Zoology. Botany.*
Soland, Aimé de, rue de l'Hôpital, Angers. *Bot.*
Solles, rue d'Albret 20, Bordeaux. *Con.*
Sollier, Marius, Longchamps 83, Marseille. *Con.*
Songeon, André, rue de Roche, Chambrey (Savoie). *Geol., Phys.*
Soubervan, Prof. J. Léon, Montpellier. *Bot.**
Souché, Baptiste, Pamproux (Deux-Sèvres). *Bot., Palæo., Anth., Arch.,* C. Ex.
Souchon, Abel, Bureau des Longitudes, Paris. *Astronomy.*
Sourbien, M. E., rue St.-Lucien 35, Carcassonne (Aude). *L. and F. W. Shells, Ent.: Coleopt., Lepid., Hemipt., Orthoptera.*
Southomar, L., rue de la République 12, Lyon. *Ent.*
Souverbie, Dr., Saint-Martin, Dir. Mus., Cité Bardineau 5, Bordeaux. *Con.*
Souvolle, Alexandre de Breuil, de Château de Souvolle, Dunle-Palletau. *Coleopt.*
Stableau, rue Guilleminot 29, Plaisance. *Coleopt.*
Staes, Dr., Croix (Nord). *Geol.*

Stephan, E., Observatoire, Marseille. *Ast.**
Stephan, J. M. E., Dir. Obs., Marseille. *Ast.*
Strobl, Hermann, rue de Paris 101, Valenciennes (Nord). *Chem.**
Sury, l'Abbé J., Dir. Seminary, Reims. *Coleopt.*
Sylvain, Ebrard, Aciéries-d'Unieux, Loire. *Ent.: Zool.* C.
Tabuteau, Lieut.-Col. A. O., 93d Highlanders, 192 boulevard St. Germain, Paris.
Tallon, Raoul, rue de l'Horloge, Riom. *Coleopt.*
Talrich, Jules, boulevard St. Germain 97, Paris. *Anat.*
Tardieu, Jules, rue de Brettes, Limoges. *Coleopt.*
Tarniquet, Félix, Sec. Soc. d'Etude Sciences Naturelles, Béziers, Hérault., *Mic.*
Tarriel, E., rue St. Gervais 6, Rouen. *Ent., Coleopt.*
Tarry-Camille, Officier vétérinaire, 4 rue de l'Abbé de l'Epée, Versailles (Seine-et-Oise). *Lepid.*
Tassel, Raoul, Elbeuf. *Coleopt.*
Taton-Baulmont, Edouard Louis, rue St. Jacques 152, Paris. *Coleopt.*
Taylor, Arthur, Pontgibaud (Puy-de-Dome). *Min.*
Téallier, Clermont-Ferrand. *Agric.*
Teisserenc de Bort, Léon, Chef du Service de Météo. Générale au Bureau Central Météorologique, Sec. Général de la Société Météorologique de France, rue des Grands Augustins 7, Paris.*
Telesphore, F., Joseph Vermet 34, Avignon. *Coleopt., Bot.*
Ternant, A. L., Manager and Electrician of Eastern Tel. Co., Prés. de la Société Scientifique Industrielle de Marseille, V. P. de la Société de Statistique, boulevard Longchamp 62, Marseille. *Phys.*
Terrier, Prof. Dr., rue Pigale 22, Paris.
Tesseron, Yres-Augustin, Crazannes (Charente Inférieure). *Bot., Ast.*, C. Ex.*
Tessier, Lucien, Kichompré, near Gérardmer. *Coleopt.*
Testoud, A., Cour d'Appel, Grenoble. *Coleopt., Lepid.*
Teulade, Marc, rue Peyras 10, Toulouse. *Geog., Nat. Hist.*
Teullières, Prof., rue Dupuis-Vendôme 9, Paris. *Coleopt., Nat. Hist.*
Therry, J. J., rue Mercière 50, Lyon. *Crypt. Bot., Mycol.*
Theurier, A., Place des Pénitents 8, Lyon. *Chem.*
Thiébaut, Ch., rue Traverse 53, Brest. *Bot.*
Thierry, Agric. Inst. of Rhône, Ecully, near Lyons. *Bot.*
Thierry-Mieg, Paul, rue des Mathurins 51, Paris. *Ent.: Lepid., Hesperidæ, Noctuidæ, Phalænidæ, of all parts of the world.* C. Ex.
Thiviæ, Xavier, à Geriandmer (Vosges). *Bot., Entom., Min.*
Thoinet, Dr., Rue St. Clément 44, Nantes. *Bot.*
Tholin, Rev. P. A., Prof. Collège, La Seyne. *Coleopt., Bot.*
Tholin, R. P.; Institution St. Vincent, Senlis. *Coleopt.*
Thomson, James, rue de Presbourg 8, Paris. *Coleopt.*
Thoulet, Prof., Chaude le Lorrain 16, Nancy. *Min.*
Tichit, Instituteur public, Bigose, Canton de Saint-Chély-d'Apcher (Lozère). *Coleopt., Dipt., Hemipt., Orthopt., Neuropt., Hymenopt., Con., Bot.**
Tillet, Paul, Ex-Professeur de Sciences Naturelles, place des Minimes, Lyon (Rhône). *Bot., Ent : Coleopt.* C. Ex.
Tilman, Victor, Dir. Sup. Sch., rue des Lombards 2, Lille. *Geol.*
Timbal-Lagrave, Ed., rue Roumiguière 15, Toulouse. *Bot.*
Tissandier, G., avenue de l'Opéra 19, Paris. *Chem.*
Tisserand, François-Félix, Mem. Acad. Sci., Paris. *Ast.*
Toffart, Auguste, Lille. *Geol.*
Topinard, Dr. Paul, rue de Rennes 105, Paris. *Anthr.**
Torre, Carlo della, rue Monge 60, Paris. *Coleopt.*
Toulouse, Adolphe-Bertrand, rue Ferbos 31, Bordeaux. *Bot.*

Tourlet, E. H., Chinon. *Bot.*
Tournier, J., Prof. au Collège Choissy (Ain). *Geol., Min., Arch.* C. Ex. Fossils of France for foreign specimens.
Trécul, Auguste A. L., Membre Acad. Sci., Hôtel de Londres, rue Linné, Paris. *Bot.*
Trédille, Prosper, boulevard de Nantes 11, Angers (Maine-et-Loire). *Marine and F. W. Algæ, Desmids, Diatoms.* C. Ex.
Trémeau de Rochebrune, Naturaliste, à Angoulême. *Coleopt.*
Triana, Joseph, actuellement Consul-Général des Etats-Unis de Colombie, en France, ancien Membre de la Commission Corographique de la Nouvelle Grenade (E. U. de Colombie), 10 boulevard d'Enfer, Paris. *Bot.*
Tribidez, Théodore Auguste, Aumônier de la Flotte Française, 37 rue de Thillois, Reims (Marne). *Min., Con.* C.
Tromelin, G. le G. de, Château de Roselin, Finisterre, près Quimper. *Geol.*
Trouessart, Edouard Louis, Docteur en Médecine, Officier de l'Instruction Publique, 118 ave. Victor Hugo, Paris. *Crypt. Plants, Bacteria, Palaeo., Vert., Invert., Mic., Biblio., Zool., Geog. Dist., Vert., Mam., Acarida.* C. Ex.*
Truchot, Prof., barrière d'Issoire 4, Clermont-Ferrand. *Agric., Bot.*
Trutat, Eugène, Conservateur du Muséum de Toulouse, Membre de la Commission des Monuments Mégalithiques, au Ministère de l'Instruction Publique, rue des Prêtres 3, or Jardin des Plantes, Toulouse (Haute-Garonne). *Palæo.* (Glacial Epoch.)
Tulnasne, Louis R., Mem. Acad. Sci., Paris. *Bot.*
Tuniot, Adolphe, rue Macquart 17, Reims. *Invert., Palæo., Lepid., Moll.* C. Ex.*
Turquin, Georges-Hippolyte, Laon. *Coleopt.*
Tuskiewitz, Dr. Diomède, Le Vigan. *Bot.*
Ulysse, Nicolas Hector, Conducteur des Ponts et Chaussées, rue Velonterie 9, Avignon (Vaucluse). *Ent., Geol., Con., Arch., Prehistoric Bot.* C. Ex.
Umhang, Jean, Directeur du Collége Libre, Lachapelle s. Rougemont (Belfort). *Lepid., Coleopt.* C. Ex. Lepidoptera of France for those of other countries.
Uzac, Alfred, 50 cours d'Aquitaine, Bordeaux (Gironde). *Coleopt., Lepid.* C. Ex. or buy Curculionidæ or Carabidæ, especially European Carabus.
Vachal, A. L. McJoseph, Argentat (Corrèze). *Hymenop.**
Vacher, Georges, Comte de Lapange, rue le Goff 6, Paris, Prof. de droit et de sociologie, etc. *Phæn. Bot., Palæo., Geol., Mic., Gen. Biol., Anat., Anth., Mam., Histol. of Vert., Ent.* C. Ex.*
Vaillant, Prof. Dr. Léon, Polytechnic School, rue de Cursol 38, Bordeaux. *Zool.*
Valenciennes, A., avenue de Paris 317, Saint-Denis.
Valentin, Juge, Montelimar, Drôme. *Arch.*
Valla, J., Professeur au Séminaire de l'Argentière, Ducrne (Rhône). *Coleopt.* C. Ex.
Vallantin, Dr. Henri, rue d'Austerlitz 65, Angoulême. *Orn., Lepid.* C. Ex.
Vallée, Gaston, place Saint-Marie 7, Rouen. *Orn.*
Vallée, Marcel, rue de la Gravière 17, Châlons. *Bot.*
Vallette, René, rue des Carmes 1 *bis*, Poitiers. *Coleopt.*
Vallois, Félix, rue de la Savonnerie 12, Rouen. *Bot.*
Vallot, Joseph, avenue d'Autin 61, Paris. *Geol., Bot.*
Van Kempen, Charles, rue St.-Bertin, Saint-Omer, Pas de Calais. *Zool., Vert., Mam., Orn., Ool.* C. Ex.
Van Tiéghem, Philippe E. L., rue Vauquelin 29, Paris.

Varenne, E., Rouen. *Bot.*
Vastel, Emy, rue du Quatre Septembre 91, Sotteville les Rouen. *Ent.*
Vaulogé, Marcel, rue Jean Burguet, Bordeaux. *Ent.: Coleopt.*
Vauthier, J. L., rue de Buffon 35, Paris. *Zool.*
Vaussenat, C. X., obs. du Pic de Midi, Bagnères-de-Bigorre. *Min.*
Vayssière, Albert, Faculté des Sciences, Marseille. *Zool.*
Velain, C. H., boulevard Saint-Germain 50, Paris. *Geol.*
Vendryes, rue de Madame 34, Paris. *Bot.*
Verchère, Ernest A., rue de Cuire 86, Argentière (Duerne). *Coleopt.*
Verdin, Ch., Constructeur d'Instruments de Précision pour la Physiologie, Officier d'Académie, 6 rue Rollins, Paris.*
Verlaque, l'Abbé, La Seyne, near Toulon. *Coleopt.*
Verlot, B., à Verrière-le-Buisson (Seine-et-Oise). *Bot.**
Verlot, J. B., Grenoble. *Bot.*
Verne, Jules, boulevard Longueville 44, Amiens.
Verneuil, Préparateur au Muséum, 34 rue Dauphin, Paris. *Chem.*
Vesque, Dr. Julien, Chef de Travaux à l'Institut Agronomique, Aide-Naturaliste au Muséum, rue de Mirbel 4, Paris. *Anat., Vegetable Physiol.*
Vétu, Louis, rue St.-Joseph 23, Argentière (Duerne). *Coleopt.*
Vialla, Louis, rue des Grenadiers, Montpellier. *Agric.*
Viallanes, Dr., 9 rue du Val de Grâce, Paris. *Zool., Anat. of Anthropods.**
Viallanes, Dr. Alfred, Prof. School Medecine, Dijon. *Bot.*
Vian, Jules, rue des Petits-Champs 42, Paris. *Orn.**
Viaud-Grand-Marais, Prof. Dr., place St.-Pierre 4, Nantes. *Bot.*
Vibert, le Frère, par Sauveterre, Aveyron. *Coleopt. à Pradinas.**
Vidal, Olivier, rue Naujac 212, Bordeaux (Gironde). *Coleopt.*
Vié, Léonce, Sijan (Aude). *Con.*
Vieillard, Alphonse, Monaco. *Coleopt.*
Vieillard, Eugène, Dir. Bot. Gar., rue St. Jean 245, Caen. *Bot.*
Vignal, Louis, 28 avenue Duquesne, Paris. *Geol., Con.**
Viguier, Dr. Maurice, Faubourg St. James, Montpellier. *Molluscs, alive and fossil.*
Villard, L., rue Royale 33, Lyon. *Coleopt. of Europe, Longicorns of the world.* 8,000 species. Ex. Coleoptera for first-class specimens of native and foreign Longicorns.
Ville, Prof. Georges, rue de Buffon 43 *bis*, Paris. *Nat. Hist.**
Ville, Jules, cour des Casernes 33, Montpellier. *Chem., Phys.*
Villery, Edouard, rue du Moulin-à-Vent 23, Sotteville-les-Rouen (Seine-Inférieure). *Geol., Min., Ent.*
Villot, Ernest, Ing. en chef des mines, Marseille. *Geol.*
Villot, Naturaliste, La Bajatière, Grenoble. *Zool., Geol.**
Vilmorin, H., boulevard St.-Germain 149, Paris. *Bot.**
Vinot, Prof. J., cour de Rohan, Paris. *Ast., 24me Année.* *
Vion, René, à la Bibliothèque Communale, Amiens. *Nat. Hist.**
Virieu, Wilfrid, Marquis de, 60 boulevard La Tour, Maubourg, Paris. *Coleopt.**
Vivier, Alfred, 26 rue Bazoges, La Rochelle. *Mechanics, Min., Meteo.*
Vlasto, Ernest C. E., bg. bd. Haussmann. *Geol., Chem., Phys.* C. Ex.*
Voisins, Comte Georges Gilbert des, 12 allée des Capucines, Marseille. *Bot., Hort., Photog.* C. Ex.
Werlein, Ivan, 11 rue Git-le-Cœur, boulevard St.-Germain, Paris. *Geol., Min., Crystal., Inorg. Chem., Phys., Mic.* C. Ex.
Westphal-Castelnau, Villa-Louise, Montpellier. *Coleopt.*
Wilm, Dr., boulevard Montparnasse 82, Paris. *Chem.*
Wimy, Dr. Alfred, Bazaine-sur-Vesles (Aisne). *Anth., Palæo., Arch.* C. Ex. and sell.
Wingarter, Ch., Bot. Gar., Rochefort. *Bot.*

Witz, Georges, place des Carmes 46, Rouen. *Chem.*
Wohlgemuth, Jules, Cgre. des Belemnites au Pont d'Essey, près Nancy. *Geol., Min., Crystal.* C.
Wynde, Henry Zylof de, rue des Blancs Mouchons 39, Douai (Nord). *Orn.* C. Ex.
Xambeu, Capitaine au 22me d'Infantérie, Montélimar (Drôme). *Coleopt.* C. Ex. Insectes de tous ordres, principalement Longicornes exotiques. Désire se mettre en relations avec des entomologistes du Nouveau Monde pour l'échange de tous les ordres d'insectes.
Yver, P., Briare. *Coleopt.*
Zeiller, Paul, Sous-Directeur des Cristalleries Baccarat, rue de Viller 92, Luneville (Meurthe-et-Moselle). *Ent., Lepid., Bot.* C. Offers cones of Europe and ferns of Vosges for those of America. Will ex. Lepid. of Europe for those of foreign countries.
Zeiller, René, Ingénieur en chef au Corps National des Mines, rue du Vieux Colombier 8, Paris. *Vegetable Palæo., Geol., Bot.**
Zuber-Hofer, Charles, place Wagram 1, Paris. *Coleopt.*

GERMANY.

Abbe, Prof. Ernst, Math. and Phys., Univ., Jena; Dir. of Ast. Observ. *Specialty, Geom. and Analyt. Optics, Optical and Astronom. Instruments.**
Abendroth, Dr. R., Hohestr. 11, Leipsic. *Coleopt.*
Abendroth, Prof. Dr. W., Schrorrstr. 25, Dresden. *Coleopt.*
Ackermann, Dr., Kölnstr. 21, Cassel. *Coleopt.*
Ackermann, Prof. Th., Univ., Halle. *Pathol. Anat.*
Adami, Carl, Lehrer an der Höhern Stadtschule, Altenkirchen, Reg. Bez. Coblenz. *Orn., Ool., Mic., Bot.* C. Ex.
Adelmann, Dr. Georg B. von, Prof. Emer., Berlin.
Ahles, Dr. Wilhelm E., Prof. Botany and Pharmacy, Polytechnic School, Stuttgart.
Ahrbeck, Hanover. *Coleopt., especially Lamellicorns.*
Albers, G., Senator, Hanover. *Coleopt., esp. Lucanid.* C.*
Alberti, R., Hildesheim. *Bot.*
Albrecht, Dr., Oberschulrath, Strasburg.*
Albrecht, Dr. P., Docent, Univ., Königsberg. *Emb. of Vert., Osteology, Comp. Anat.*
Albrecht, Prof. Dr. Th., Sectionschef im königl. Preuss. geodätischen Institut, Wichmannstrasse 12c, Berlin, W. *Astronom. Geography.**
Albrich, L., Karuthstr. 11, Breslau. *Lepid.* C. Ex.
Aldenhoven, C. T. F., Vorstand des Herzogl. Sächs. Kunst-Cabinets und Director des Herzogl. Museums zu Gotha. *Arch.*
Aldendorf, H., Frauenstr., Münster. *Lepid.* C. Ex.
Aldendorf, H., Jr., Frauenstr., Münster. *Lepid.* C. Ex.
Althaus, Ernst, Oberbergrath at the Royal Mining Court, Breslau. *Mining and Metallurgy.*
Altum, Prof. Dr., Eberswalde. *Forest Zool., Ent.*
Ambronn, Dr. H., Botanical Institute, Leipzig. *Bot.*
Ammon, Dr. Ludwig von, Privatdocent der Technischen Hochschule und kgl. Bergamts-Assessor, Ludwigsstr. 16, Munich. *Palæo., Geol.*
Andrae, Prof. C. J., Univ., Bonn. *Veg. Palæo.*
Andreae, Dr. Prof., Univ., Heidelberg. *Geol., Palæo.**
Angelrodt, Carl, Nordhausen. *Bot.: Ferns, Mosses. Fungi, Lichens, Algæ, Bibliog., Gen. Ent., Moll.*
Angersbach, Ch., Mittelseestr. 7, Offenbach am Main. *Lepid.**

Anschütz, Dr. Richard, Chem. Inst., Popplesdorf, bei Bonn. *Chem.*
Ansorge, Bruno, Auenstrasse, Breslau. *Phæn. Bot.: Mosses.* C. Ex.
Arnold, Carl, Ph.D., Memb. Chem. Lab. der k. Thierärztlichen Hochschule, Hannover.*
Arnold, Dr. F., Sonnenstrasse 7, Munich. *Lichens.**
Arnold, Prof. Georg, Mannheim. *Lepid.*
Arnold, Prof. J., Univ., Heidelberg. *Pathol., Anat., and Histol.*
Aron, Dr. H., Docent Univ., Berlin. *Phys.*
Aron, Theodor, Univ., Bonn. *Pharm.*
Arzruni, Dr. A., Min. Museum, Berlin. *Min.*
Ascherson, Dr. P., Prof. Univ., Körnerstr. 9, Berlin. *Bot.*
Askenasy, Prof. E., Univ., Heidelberg. *Bot.**
Assmann, A., Asst. Zoological Mus., Breslau. *Ent.*
Assmann, Dr. Richard, Meteor. Inst., Berlin. *Meteo.**
Aubers, Prof. Dr. Hermann, Rostock. *Gen. Biol., Embryol., Physiol.*
Auerbach, Dr. Felix, Prof. Meteo., Royal Univ., Breslau.
Auerbach, Dr. Leop., Prof. Univ., Breslau. *Physiol.**
Augustin, Hauptlehrer, Höchsdorf bei Lützenburg. *Coleopt.*
Autenrieth, T. u. G., Stuttgart. *Coleopt.*
Baader, Friedrich, Frankfort-on-Main. *Geol.*
Babo, Prof. L. von, Univ., Freiburg. *Chem.*
Babo, von, Ph.D., Weinheim bei Heidelberg. *Ent.*
Bachmann, Otto, Königl. Reallehrer, Laborat. für Mikroskopie, Landsberg am Lech, Bavaria. *Con.* C. Ex. Wishes to receive shells of any kind in ex. for any Microscopic preparations.
Bachmann, Prof. P., Academy, Münster. *Math., Analyt. Mechanics.*
Bachstein, Ernst, Gr. Brüdergasse, Dresden. *Lepid.*
Backhaus, Hermann, Poniatovskystrasse 7, Leipsic. *Lepid.*
Baden, Dr. F. A. F., Blücherstrasse 33, Altona (Holstein). *Coleopt.* C. Ex.*
Baenitz, Dr. C., Königsberg. *Bot.*
Baeyer, A., Prof. Univ., Munich. *Chem.*
Bail, Dr. Carl A. T., Prof. Real-Gymnasium, Dir. of the Nat. and Philos. Society, Dantzig. *Bot.**
Baldamus, Dr. Eduard, Coburg. *Orn., Biol., Caliology, Ool., Ferns, Orchids.* C. Ex.
Balzer, H. C., Sonderburg. *Physics.*
Bansa, Gottlieb, Frankfort-on-Main. *Ast.*
Banse, F., Gymnasiallehrer, Prälatenstr. 2, Madgeburg. *Coleopt.*
Barbiche, René-Théodore, Curé à Bionville (Lorraine-Allemande). *Bot., Phanerogams and Cryptogams, especially Mosses, Lichens, Mushrooms, Pseudoneuroptera, Odonata, L. and F. W. Shells.* C. Ex. Offers plants, odonats, and L. and F. W. shells of Lorraine for the same from all parts of Europe.
Bardeleben, Prof. Dr. Karl, Jena. *Vert. Emb., Vert. Anat., Anth., Vert., Mam., Osteol., Myol., Histol. of Vert.*
Barnewitz, A., Brandenburg on the Havel. *Bot.*
Bartels, Carl, Bahnhofstr. 22 Cassel. *European Coleopt.*
Barth, Dr. Max, Dir. Kaiserl. Landwirth. Versuchs-Station, Rufach (Alsace). *Chem.**
Barthel, F. Th., gr. Johannisstr. 9, I, Hamburg. *Lepid.* C.
Bary, A. de, Prof. Univ., Strasburg (Alsace). *Bot.**
Basler, Dr. W., Offenburg, Baden. *Moll.*
Bastelberger, Lieut. Max, Knoblochgasse 17, Strasburg. *Europ. Macrolepid.*
Bastian, Dr. Adolph, Dir. Eth. Museum, Berlin.
Bau, Alexander, 4 Hermannplatz, Berlin. *Lepid., Coleopt., Diptera.* C. Ex. and sell. Will buy Insects of all parts of the world. Priced catalogues free.*

Bau, Arminius, 3 Lachmannstr., Berlin. *Dipt., Hemipt.**
Bauer, Prof. G., Univ., Munich. *Math.*
Bauer, G. H., Chemiker and Botaniker, Neuenburgerstrasse 15, II, Berlin. *Chem., Bot.* C. Ex.*
Bauer, J. Nic., Lehrer, Mosen bei Weida. *German Coleopt.* C. Ex.
Bauer, Prof. M., Univ., Königsberg. *Min.*
Bauernfeind, Dr. C. M. von, Prof. Polytechnic School, Munich.
Baum, Dr. Wilhelm, Prof. Univ., Göttingen.
Baumann, Prof. E., Univ., Berlin. *Physiol., Chem.*
Baumert, Georg, Ph.D., Privatdocent an der Univ., Halle. *Chem.*
Baumgarten, Prof. Dr. P., Univ., Königsberg. *Pathol. Anat. and Bacteriology.**
Baumstark, Prof. F., Univ., Greifswald. *Chem.*
Bausch, Leopold Vors Sand des, Lehrer am Gymnasium, Garten Caen. *Dendrology, Bot.*
Bebber, Dr. Wilhelm Jacob van, Seewarte, Hamburg. *Meteo.*
Beckers, G., Seminarlehrer, Rheydt. *Lepid., Hymenop., Dipt.*
Beetz, Prof. Dr. W. von, Polytechnic School, Munich. *Physics.**
Behn, Dr. Th., Hamburg. *Coleopt.* C. Ex.
Behrens, Wilhelm Julius, Dr. Phil., Redacteur des Botanischen Centralblattes und der Zeitschrift für Wissenschaftliche Mikroskopie und für Mikroskopische Technik, Göttingen. *Bot., Physiol., Biol., Anat.* C.
Behrmann, Dr. Carl, Director Elsfleth. *Ast., Meteo., Deviations of the Compass.*
Beiuling, Prof. Dr., Gymnasial-Oberlehrer, Breslau. *Gen. Ent.*
Beling, Theodor, Seesen am Harz. *Phæn. Bot., Dipt., Coleopt.* C. Ex.*
Bellevoye, Ad., rue du Tour-du-Cloître 5, Metz (Lorraine). *Ent.: Hemipt. and Coleopt.*
Benecke, Prof. Berthold, Univ., Königsberg. *Photog., Anat. and Emb. of Vert., Ichth.*
Benecke, Dr. E. W., Professor Universität, Strasburg (Alsace). *Geol., Palæo.*
Bentfeld, Guissan, near Eutin. *Mycol.*
Berendt, Dr. Gottlieb, Landesgeolog u. Prof. a. d. Univ., Dessauerstrasse 35, Berlin, S. W. *Geol.*
Berlepsch, Graf Hans von, Schloss Berlepsch, bei Witzenhausen (Hessen-Nassau). *Orn.* C. Bird-skins, especially of S. and Central America.
Bernstein, Dr. Julius, Univ., Halle. *Phys.*
Bernthsen, Prof. Dr. A., Mannheim L., 14, 4. *Chem.**
Bernuth, von, Freienwalde. *German Insects.*
Berthold, Dr., Docent, Univ., Göttingen. *German Flora.*
Bertkau, Dr. Philipp, Prof. extraord., Bonn, Maurflach 4. *Anth.**
Bertram, Rev. W., Brunswick. *Bot., Mosses.**
Besnard, Dr. Anton F., Munich. *Bot.*
Bessiger, Max, Höhestr. 19, Leipsic. *Lepid.*
Beutell, Albert, Breslau. *Chem., Min.*
Beuthin, H., Dr., St. Georg, Steindamm 144, III, Hamburg. *Coleopt.* C. Ex.
Beyer, Dr., Hauptstrasse 8, Dresden. *Coleopt.* C. Ex.
Beyrich, Prof. Dr. Heinrich E., Univ., Berlin. *Min.*
Bezold, Dr. Wilh. v., Prof. Dir. d. Königl. Institut, Berlin. *Meteo.**
Biedermann, Prof. Dr. Rud., Royal Univ., Mitgl. des Kaiserl. Patentamts, Berlin. *Chem.**
Bieger, Docent, Langendorf, bei Rehmsdorf. *Macro-lepid.* C. Ex.
Birnbaum, Dr. K. Hofrath, Prof. Polytechnicum, Carlsruhe. *Chem.*

Birnbaum, Prof. K., Univ., Leipsic. *Agric.*
Birner, Dr. H. F. W., Regenwalde. *Agric. Chem.*
Bischof, G., Wiesbaden. *Lepid.*, *Bot.*
Bischoff, Dr. C., Docent Univ., Würzburg. *Org. and Physiol. Chem.*
Bischoff, Prof. Dr. Theodor L. W. von, Munich. *Anat.*, *Phys.*
Bissinger, Carl, Dr. Phil., Mannheim. *Lepid.*
Blankenhorn, Dr. Adolph, Professor der Universität, President der Deutsch. Weinbauer, Carlsruhe (Baden). *Grapes and Grapevines.* C. Ex.
Blasius, Dr. Rudolf, Docent, Technische Hochschule, Präsident des permanenten internationalen ornithologischen Comités, Brunswick, Tetrithor-Promenade 25. *Orn.**
Blasius, Dr. Wilhelm, Prof. Technische Hochschule, Dir. Bot. Gar. und Mus. Nat. Hist., am Fallerslebenthore 4, Braunschweig. *Zool.*, *Mam.*, *Orn.*, *Osteol.*, *Mic.* C. Ex. Wishes mammals and birds o all countries, especially in spirit, skeletons, or skins.*
Blees, Carl, Schifferstrasse 74, Frankfurt a. Main. *Lepid.* C.
Bleisch, Dr Stehlen. *Diatoms.*
Blisse, Herm., Lehrer, Brandenburg. *Coleopt.* C. Ex.
Blochmann, Dr., Privatdocent und Assist., Heidelberg. *Zool.*, *Emb.**
Blochmann, Dr. R., Docent, Univ., Königsberg. *Tech. and Analyt. Chem.*
Blomeyer, Prof. A., Univ., Leipzig. *Agric.*
Blum, J., Frankfurt-am-Main. *Moll.*
Blunschli, J. C., Heidelberg.
Bodewig, Dr. C., Schildergasse 96, II, Köln. *Chem. and Min.**
Boecker, Heinrich, Mikroskopisches-Institut, Wetzlar. *Mic.*, *Macro-Lepid.* C. Ex. Wishes exotic Lepidoptera for microscopic objects.*
Boedeker, Prof. C., Univ., Göttingen. *Chem.*, *Chem. Geol.*
Boettger, Dr. Oskar, Seilerstrasse 6, Frankfurt-am-Main. *Palæo.*, *Invert.*, *Herpetol.*, *Moll.* C.*
Boguslawski, Prof. Dr. Georg v., Hydrograph an der Kaiserl. Admiralität, Berlin. *Hydrography*, *Meteo.*
Böhm, Dr. A., Anat. Inst., Königsberg. *Embryology.*
Böhne, Albert, Hohestr. 5, Leipzig. *Lepid.*
Bois-Reymond, Prof. P. du, Univ. Tübingen. *Math.*
Bolau, Dr. Heinrich, Director des Zoologischen Gartens, Hamburg. *Zool.*, *especially mammals and birds.**
Bolle, Dr. C., Leipziger Platz 14, Berlin. *Bot.*
Bolhorst, Georg, Stadteich, 178, Hamburg. *Min.* C.
Bollinger, Prof. O., Univ., München. *Pathol. Anat.*
Booch-Arkossy, Hans, Erdmanstrasse 2, I, Leipzig. *Lepid.*, *Prepared Larvae.*
Borcherding, Fr., 9 Bremerstr., Vegesack bei Bremen. *Zool.*, *Gen. Biol.*, *Geog. Dist.*, *Anat.*, *Moll.* C. Ex.
Born, Dr. G., Docent, Univ. Breslau. *Emb. of Vert.*
Born, Max, Mathildenstr. 6, Dresden. *Coleopt.*
Bornträger, Prof. A., Univ., Heidelberg. *Chem.**
Borsch, Prof. Dr., Flottwellstr. f., Berlin, W. *Geod.*
Borst, L., Lehrer, Medolden, bei Sherrebeck (Schleswig-Holstein). *Bot.*, *Gramineæ*, *Trindadeæ*, *Cyperadeæ.**
Bortsch, Dr. Eugen, Breslau. *Bot.*, *Min.*
Bösenberg, W., Hamburg. *Arach.* C. Ex.*
Bosse, Th., Apotheker, Gandersheim. *Coleopt.* C.*
Boström, Dr. E., Docent, Univ., Freiburg. *Pathol. Anat.*, *and Histol.*
Böttingen, Dr. Carl, Karlstrasse 38, München. *Chem.*

Bouché, J., Botanischer Garten, Bonn. *Bot.*
Brade, Alexander, Forst (Nieder Lausitz), Preussen. *Ent.: Hymenop., Lepid., Coleopt.* C. Ex.
Brandenburger, Joh., Seminarlehrer. *Bot., Ent.*
Brandt, Anton, Jakobstr. 7, Eisenach. *Coleopt.**
Bratuscheck, Prof. E., Univ., Giessen. *Phil.*
Braun, Prof. C. F., Univ., Tübingen. *Phys.**
Braune, Prof. Chr. W., Univ., Leipzig. *Osteol., Anat.*
Braungardt, Dr., Prof. Bot., Agric. Acad., Weihenstephan.
Brauns, Prof. David, Ph.D., M.D., Univ., Halle. *Geol., Min., Palæo.**
Braune, Oberlehrer, Schwerin (Mecklenburg). *Coleopt.*
Brefeld, Dr. O., Eberswalde. *Bot.*
Brehmer, Dr. W., Lübeck. *Bot.*
Brehmer, Dr. Gustav A., Görbersdorf, bei Friedland. *Med.**
Breitfeld, Alexander, Breslau. *Bot.*
Brenning, Maj. Th., Wittenberg. *Coleopt.* C. Ex.
Brenske, Ernst, Rittergut Warchau bei Gr. Wusterwitz, Reg. Bez. Magdeburg. *Coleopt., Melonthidæ.* C. Ex.
Bretschneider, F., Gymnasiallehrer, Holzminden. *Ent.*
Brinkmann, A., Oberlehrer, Walle, bei Bremen. *Hymenop.*
Brischke, Hauptlehrer, Zopport. *Hymenop.*
Britzelmeyer, Dr., Augsburg. *Mycol.*
Brock, Dr. Johannes, Privat-Docent, Göttingen. *Vertebrates, Mollusca, Zool.**
Brockmüller, Heinrich, Fleischbeschauer, Königsstrasse 16, Schwerin. *Bot., especially Cryptogams.* C. Ex. Offers Phanerogams and Cryptogams of Mecklenburg, and wishes plants from all foreign lands.
Bruhl, Prof., Lemberg. *Phys., Chem.*
Brunn, Dr. A. von, Docent, Univ., Göttingen. *Osteol., Anat.*
Brunn, Prof. H., Univ., München. *Arch.*
Bruns, Prof. Dr. Heinrich, Dir. Sternwarte, Leipzig.
Brussow, Victoriaschule, Fürstenstr. 14, Berlin. *Lepid.*
Buchal, Gustav, Patschkau (Schlesien), *Lepid.* C. Ex.
Buchenau, Prof. Dr. Franz, Director der Realschule, Bremen. *Bot., Juncaceæ, Butomaceæ, Juncaginaceæ, Mismacea, Morphology, German Flora.* Ex.
Buchinger, Prof., Strassburg (Elsass-Lothringen). *Bot.* C. Ex.
Buchka, Dr. C., Docent, Univ., Göttingen. *History of Chemistry.*
Büchner, Ludwig, Prof. Dr., Holgesstrasse 14, Darmstadt. *Gen. Biol., Anth.**
Buchner, Prof. L. A., Univ., München. *Pharm. Chem., Toxicol., Pharm.*
Buck, Dr. Emil, Konstanz (Baden). *Bot., Mic., Zool., Protozoa, Infusoria.*
Bucking, Dr. Hugo, Prof. Min. Petrog. und Kryst., Dir. des Min. u. Petrogr. Inst. der Univ., Strassburg. *Min., Crystal., Lithol.**
Buckler, Carl, Eisenberge, Sachsen Altenburg. *Lepid., Coleopt.* C. Ex.*
Buddeberg, Dr., Director der Realschule, Nassau. *Coleopt.**
Budge, Dr. A., Docent, Univ., Greifswald. *Osteol.*
Budge, Prof. Dr. Ludwig J., Univ., Greifswald. *Anat.*
Bunsen, Prof. Dr. R., Univ., Heidleberg. *Chem.*
Burchardt, Dr., Director des Gymnasiums, Bückeburg. *Coleopt.*
Bürck, Dr. Alphons, Schwarzach in Baden. *Lepid.* C. Ex.
Burbach, Otto, Professor der Zoologie, Director des Herzogl. Naturalien-Cabinets zu Gotha.*
Bürger, Rector, Altes Fischerufer 40, Magdeburg. *Ent.*
Bürger, Julius, Hainstr. 2, II, Leipzig. *Nat. Hist., Hydropath.**
Burghardt, Dr., Warmbrunn. *Coleopt.*

Burkhardt, Dr. A., Besselstr. 17, Berlin. *Lepid.*
Burkhardt, Dr. G., Alexandrinenstr 82*a*, Berlin. *Lepid.*
Burmeister, Heinr., Arnstadt. *Lepid.*
Bütschli, Prof. O., Univ., Heidelberg. *Zool.*
Buttner, R., Burgstrasse, Potsdam. *L. and F. W. Mollusca.* C. Ex. Offers plants and shells of Northern Germany for those of other lands.
Cabanis, Dr. Jean, Professor, Herausgeber des Journal für Ornithologie, Alte Jacobstrasse 103*a*, Berlin, S. W. *Orn.*
Calix, O., Blumenstr. 25, Berlin, E. *Coleopt.* C.
Callenberg, Emil, Lippstadt. *Orn.*
Cantor, Prof. G., Univ., Halle. *Math.*
Cantor, Prof. Dr. Moritz, Univ., Heidelberg. *Math.*
Carriere, Dr. J., Docent Univ., Strassburg. *Histol. of Animals.*
Carus, Jul. Victor, M.D., Ph.D., D.C.L., Professor Universität, Gellertstrasse 7, Leipzig. *Zool., Comp. Anat.**
Caspary, Prof. R., Univ., Königsberg. *Bot., Mic.*
Chauvin, Fräulein Marie von, Freiburg im Breisgau. *Zool., Gen. Biol., Ent., Neuropt.* C.*
Christiana, Dr. A., Prof. Univ. Berlin.
Christoffel, Prof. E. B., Univ. Strassburg. *Math.*
Chun, Prof. Zool., Leipzig. *Zool.*
Cichorius, Paul, Gotha. *Bot., Lepid.* C.
Claisen, Dr. L., Docent, Univ., Bonn. *Chem.*
Clark, Jas., M. A., A.N.S.S., Botanisches Institut, Tübingen. *Morph., Physiol., Bot.* Wants in ex. seeds and specimens of the Gentianaceæ from all parts of the world.*
Clasen, Dr. F. W., Gymnasiallehrer, Rostock. *Ent.*
Claudon, Albert, Membre de la Société d'Histoire Naturelle, rue Saint-Jean 5, Colmar (Alsace-Lorraine). *Bot., Geol., Coleopt., only Carabus, Buprestidæ, Cetonidæ, Longicorns.* C. Ex. Plants of Colmar and Alsace, Geological specimens, and Coleoptera as above.
Claus, Prof. A., Roy. Univ. Freiburg, Breslau. *Chem.*
Clausius, Rudolph, Professor an der Universität und Geheimer Regierungsrath, Bonn. *Physics, especially heat and electricity.*
Clauss, Königslutter, Brunswick. *Macro-lepid. of Germany and Helvetia.*
Cohen, Prof. Dr. Emil, Univ., Greifswald. *Min., Petrography.**
Cohn, Prof. Dr. Ferdinand, Univ., Schweidnitzer Stadtgraben 26, Breslau. *Bot.*
Cohn, Dr. Hermann, Prof. Univ., Schweidnitzer-Stadtgraben 16*b*, Breslau. *Ophthal., Phys., Elect., Hygiene.**
Cohnheim, Prof. J., Univ., Leipsic. *Pathol. Anat. and Histol.*
Compal, Maj., Hanover. *Lepid.* C. Ex.
Conwentz, Dr. H., Director des West Preuss. Provinzial-Museums, Danzig. *Vegetable Palæo., Bot.**
Cornelius, Prof. Dr. Carl Sebastian, Halle (Saxony). *Physics, Elect., Meteo.**
Cornelius, Heinr., Kasernenstr. 20, Düsseldorf. *Lepid.**
Cotta, Bernhard v., Freiburg (Baden). *Geol.*
Credner. Ph.D., Präs. d. Geog. Gesellsch., Prof. Univ., Greifswald. *Geog.**
Crüger, Dr. C., Hohenfelde bei Hamburg. *Lepid.*
Crumbach, Prof. Gustav, Düsseldorf. *Coleopt.*
Curtius, Prof. E., Roy. Univ., Berlin. *Arch.*
Czeczorzinski, Adolf, Neudorfstrasse 63, Breslau. *Lepid. and Hymenopt.**
Czeczorzinski, B., Holteistrasse 12, Breslau. *Lepid.**

Eppelsheim, Friedrich, Grünstadt, Rheinpfalz. *Lepid.* C.
Erdmann, Prof. Dr. E. O., Lichterfelde, bei Berlin. *Chem.*
Erichsen, H., Flensburg. *Orn.*, *Ool.*
Erné, rue des Orphelins, Mülhausen (Alsace). *Coleopt.*
Eulenburg, Prof. Albert, Hindersinstrasse 12, Berlin. *Pathol. of nervous diseases.*
Euneper, Prof. A., Univ., Göttingen. *Math.*
Ewald, Dr. A., Docent Univ., Heidelberg. *Histol.*
Ewald, Prof. C. A., Univ., Berlin. *Physiol.*
Eyffinger, Georg, Wasserweg 34, Frankfort-on-Main. *Lepid.* C. Ex.
Eyrich, Dr. L., Mannheim. *Moll.*
Faber, Carl, Sr., Stuttgart. *Coleopt.*
Faber, Carl, Jr., Stuttgart. *Coleopt. of Europe and China.*
Fack, Lehrer, Mühlhausstr., Kiel. *Coleopt.*
Fager, Hermann, Grossherzoglicher Hofgarteninspector, Eisenach (Saxony). *Bot.*
Falkenberg, Dr. Paul, Univ., Göttingen. *Bot.*
Farwick, B., Docent, Cleve. *Ent.*
Faubel, J., Lehrer, Coslin. *Coleopt.*, *Lepid.*
Faudel, Dr., rue de Blés 8, Colmar (Alsace). *Nat. Hist.*
Faust, Henry, Jr., Uerdingen-on-the-Rhine. *Meteo.*
Fechner, Prof. Dr. Gustav T., Univ., Leipsic. *Physics.*
Feddersen, Dr. Berend Wilhelm, Carolinenstrasse 9, Leipsic. *Physical Sciences, especially Electricity.**
Fehr, Dr. M., Docent, Univ., Heidelberg. *Chirurgie.**
Felsche, Carl, Chaussée-Str. 2, Reudnitz near Leipsic. *Coleopt.**
Fesca, Dr. M., Docent, Univ., Göttingen. *Agric.*
Fettig, l'Abbé, Matzenheim (Alsace). *Gen. Ent.*, *Coleopt.*, *Lepid.*, spec., *Micro-lepid.*
Feussner, Prof. W., Univ., Marburg. *Analyt. Mechanics*, *Phys.*
Fickert, Dr. C., Gymnasial-Oberlehrer, Strasburg. *Arach.*
Fick, Prof. A., Univ., Würzburg. *Physiology of Man.*
Fieberg, Dr. E., Michaelkirchplatz 19, Berlin, S. O. *Chem.*
Fiedler, Dr. Alfred, Geh. Med.-Rath., Königl. Leibarzt, Dresden. *Medicine.* Collection of Prehistoric antiquities.
Fietz, Carl, Schulinspector u. D. in Steinau a. d. Oder, Schlesien. *Bot.*, *Moll.* C.*
Fikentscher, Zwickau. *Coleopt.* C. Ex.
Finger, Dr. Aug., Frankfort-on-Main. *Anth.*
Fingerling, Max, Windmühlenstr. 37, Leipsic. *Lepid.*
Finkler, D., Prof. Agric. Acad., Poppelsdorf bei Bonn, and Prof. of Medicine, Univ., Bonn. *Physiol.**
Fischer, Lödischehofstr. 16, Magdeburg. *European Macro-Lepid.* C. Ex.
Fischer, Lehrer, Töchterschule, Merseburg. *Ent.*
Fischer, Prof. Dr., Schwerinstr. 21, Berlin, W. *Geod.*
Fischer, Dr. Alfred, Zeiterstrasse 37, Leipsic. *Bot.*
Fischer, Dr. Emil, Chem. Lab., Akademie, Munich. *Chem.*
Fischer, Dr. Heinrich, Professor Universität, Freiburg (Baden). *Min.*, *Mic.*, *and Arch.*
Fittbogen, Dr. J., Dahme. *Bot.*
Fittica, Dr. Friedrich Bernhard, Cor. Memb. N. Y. Acad. Sci., Prof. a. d. Universität, Marburg (Marburg-on-the-Lahn). *Chem.**
Fittig, Prof. R., Univ., Strasburg (Alsace). *Chem.*
Flemming, Dr. Walther, Prof. der Anatomie, Dir. des Anatomischen Instituts, Düsternbrook 55, Kiel. *Anat.*, *Histol.*, *Morphology, and Biology.**
Flückiger, Prof. Dr. F. A., Strasburg (Alsace-Lorraine). *Pharmacy, etc.**
Flügel, Dr. Felix, Agent Smithsonian Institute, Leipsic.

Flügge, Dr. C., Prof. Univ., Breslau. *Hygiene.**
Focke, Dr. Wilh. Olbers. Wall 206, Bremen. *Bot. Rosaceæ, esp. Rubus, Hybridization.* C. Ex. European Phanerogams for foreign Rosaceæ.*
Foerster, Arnold, Prof., Aix-la-Chapelle. *Coleopt.*
Follmann, Dr. O., Poppelsdorf bei Bonn. *Palæo.*
Forst, Adolf, Maschstr. 14, Brunswick. *Lepid.*
Förster, Prof. Dr. W., Univ., Lindenstrasse 9, Berlin. *Bot., Ast.*
Forwerg, Seilergasse 9, Dresden. *Coleopt.*
Fraas, Dr. Oscar, Prof. am Königl. Naturalien-Cabinet, Stuttgart. *Palæo., Arch.* Ex. Wishes Miocene Mammals for those of Nebraska.
Frank, A., Längswitz-Vorstadt 294, Arnstadt. *Ent.*
Frank, Prof. Bernhard, Ph.D., Landwirth, Hochschule, Philippstrasse 8, Berlin. *Crypt. Bot.: Fungi, Agric.*
Franke, Emil. Oberlehrer, Briez. *Bot., Gen. Biol., Phil.*
Franke, R., Gymnasiallehrer. Bad Kösen. *Coleopt.* C.*
Frantz, Richard, Bad Kösen. *Ent., Coleopt. (Ceramb.).* C. Ex.*
Franz, Dr. Julius, Observator der Universitäts-Sternwarte, Königsberg. *Astronomy.**
Fraustadt, Dr., Ordentlicher wissenschaftlicher Lehrer an der höheren Bürgerschule, II., Breslau. *Phæn. Bot., Anatomy of plants.* C.*
Frege, Prof. G., Univ., Jena. *Analyt. Mechanics, Math.**
Frenzel, Dr. A., Freiberg. *Chem., Min., Orn.*
Frerichs, Prof. Dr. Fr. Theod., Director der Med. Klinik der Univ., Geheim ob. Med. Rath. im Ministerium, Bismarckst. 4, Berlin, N. W.
Fresenius, Dr. Carl Remigius, Geheimer Hofrath u. Prof. Director des Chemischen Laboratoriums, Wiesbaden. *Inorganic, Technical and Analytical Chemistry.**
Fresenius, Prof. Heinrich, Ph.D., Vorsteher d. agriculturschem Versuchsstation; Docent, Chem. Lab., Wiesbaden. *Agric., Chem.**
Fresenius, Wilhelm, Ph.D., Docent, Chem. Lab., Wiesbaden. *Crystal., Chem., Phys.**
Freyer, Jacobskirche 25, Augsburg. *Lepid.*
Freyhold, Dr. A. von, Adenau. *Coleopt., Lepid.**
Freytag, Prof. Poppelsdorf, bei Bonn. *Chem.*
Fricke, Dr. Carl W., Docent, Univ., Kiel. *Mic., Odontol.**
Fricken, Dr. Wilhelm, Königsberg. *Coleopt.*
Fridrici, Edmond, Con. du Mus. d'Histoire Naturelle, 25 rue de l'Evêché, Metz (Lorraine), *Geol., Min., Moll.* C. Ex.
Friedel, Ernst, Stadtrath von Berlin und Dirigent des Märkischen Provincial Museums, Köllnisches Rathhaus, Breitestr. 20, Berlin C. *Ichth., Con., Anth.*
Friederichen, L., Generalsecretair der Geographischen Gesellschaft, Neuerwall, 61, I, Hamburg. *Geog., Cartog., Navigation.**
Friedländer, Dr. C., Docent, Univ., Berlin. *Histol.*
Frief, Gustav, Breitestrasse 37, Breslau. *Lepid.*
Friese, Heinrich. Kirchenstrasse 1, Schwerin. *Gen. Biol., Hymenop., Apidæ, Dipt., Coleopt.* C. Ex.
Friren, Auguste Marie Joseph, Prof. de Sciences au Petit-Séminaire, Montigny-les-Metz (Alsace-Lorraine). *Palæo.* C. Ex. Fossils of Metz for Brachiopods and Echinoderms.
Fritsch, Dr., Krausnickstr., Berlin. *Coleopt.*
Fritsch, Dr. Karl von, Prof., Director des Kön. Akademischen Mineralogischen Museums, Halle (Saxony). *Geol.* C. Ex. Offers German Petrifactions of various formations in ex. for Anthozoa, Echinoderms, Crustacea, Vertebrates.
Fritsch, Dr. Carl W. G. F. von, Prof. Min. Geol., Univ., Halle.
Fritsch, Prof. G., Univ., Berlin. *Comp. Anat. of Vert., Mic., Hist.*

Fritze, R., Apotheker, Rybnik, Ober-Schlesien (Prussia). *Bot., Culture of Alpine plants.* C. Ex. Offers living Alpine plants in ex. for those of the mountains of America and Himalaya.
Fromme, Prof. C., Univ., Giessen. *Magnetism, Galvanism.**
Frommann, Prof. C., Univ., Jena. *Emb. of Man, Histol.*
Frommholtz, Neue Friedrichstr. 47, Berlin. *Lepid.*
Froriep. Dr. August, Prof., Univ., Tübingen. *Histol. of Vert., Emb. and Anat. of Vert.**
Frocht, A., Apotheker, Hamburg. *Bot.*
Fuchs, A., Bornich, bei St. Goarshausen, *Lepid.* C. Ex.
Fuchs, Dr. Ernst, Lehrer und Vorstand agriculturwissen. Laboratoriums der Landwirthschaftlichen Scuhle, Kappen (Schleswig-Holstein). *Analytic Chemistry and Botany.* C. Ex. Phanerogams and Mushrooms *
Fuchs, Prof. L., Univ., Heidelberg. *Math.*
Fugner, K., Prof. Normal School, Witten-on-the-Ruhr. *Coleopt.*
Funck, F., Bot. Gar., Leipsic. *Bot.*
Funk, Dr., Dir. Bot. Gar, Bamberg. *Bot.*
Funk, N., Dir. des Zool Gartens, Cöln.*
Fürbringer, Prof. Dr. Paul, Krankenhaus, Friedrichshein, Berlin, N. *Lepid* C. Ex.*
Furtwängler, Prof. A., Roy. Univ., Berlin. *Arch.*
Futh, Prof. Louis, Königsberg, Neumark (Preussen). *Con., Bot.* C. Ex. L and F. W. shells, and F. W. Algæ of Germany for foreign.
Gabriel, Dr. S., Docent, Univ., Berlin. *Analyt. Chem.*
Gad, Dr. J., Prof a. d. Univ., Berlin. *Physiology of the nervous system.**
Gaedechens, Prof. R. Univ., Jena. *Arch.*
Gaehtgens, Prof. C., Univ., Giessen. *Med. Chem., Pharm.*
Gaffron, Dr. Eduard, Lippstadt, Westfalen. *Zool.*
Galle, Prof. Dr. J. G., Königl. Univ., Breslau. *Ast.**
Gänge, Christian, Privat-Docent, Univ., Jena. *Phys., Chem.**
Ganser, Dr. S., Docent, Univ., München. *Anat.*
Garcke, Dr. August, Prof. an der Universität und Custos am Königl. Botanischen Museum, Friedrichstr. 227, Berlin. *Pharmac., Bot.**
Gasser, Dr. E., Prof. Univ., Marburg. *Anat.**
Gaule, Dr. Med. J., Docent, Univ., Leipzig. *Histol.*
Gegenbaur, Prof. Dr. Carl, Univ., Heidelberg. *Anat.**
Geheeb, Adalbert, Apotheker, Geisa, Sachsen-Weimar. *Bryology.* Brazilian Mosses. C. Ex. mosses of Europe, Brazil, Africa, Australia, East Indies, etc.
Geiger, Carl, Ulm (Würtemberg.) *Lepid., Coleopt.*
Geilenkenser, E., Lehrer, Baustr. 57, Elberfeld. *Coleopt.* C. Ex.*
Geilenkeuser, Prof. Guillaume, Elberfeld. *Coleopt.*
Geinitz, Prof. E., Univ., Rostock. *Geol., Mic., Min., Physiol.*
Geinitz, Prof. Dr. H. B., Dir. R. Min. Museum, Geheimer Hofrath, Dresden. *Geol., Palæo., Min.**
Gentzke, Dr, Präs. Seidenbauvereins, Bützow. *Ent.*
Genzmer, Halberstadt. *Ent.*
Georgens, Dr. Daniel, Berlin. *Anth.*
Gerber, Regensburg. *Coleopt.*
Gercke, G., Schroederstrasse 7 Hohenfelde, Hamburg. *Dipt.*
Gerhard, Bernhard, Arndtstrasse 53, Leipzig. *Lepid.*
Gerhards, Felix, Landgrafenstrasse 14, Berlin. *Bot.*
Gerhardt, Prof. Dr. Carl I., Gymnasium, Eisleben.
Gerhardt, Julius, Lehrer, Liegnitz. *Phæn. Bot., Fungi, Coleopt.* C. Ex.*
Gerichten, Dr. E. von, Docent, Univ., Erlangen. *Chem.*
Gerike, H., Heuscheuer, Carlsberg. *Coleopt., Lepid.* C. Ex.*

Gerlach, Joseph von, Prof. der Anatomie, Universität, Erlangen. *Photography, Anat.* Anatomy of the eyes.
Gerlach, Leo, Erlangen (Baiern). *Emb., Anat., Histol. of Vert.* C.
Gerland, Prof. Dr. Georg, Univ., Strasburg. *Geog.*
Gerndt, Dr. Leonhard, Oberlehrer, Römerstrasse 21, Zwickau (Sachsen). *Geographical distribution of plants.*
Geromont, Fr., Winkel-am-Rhein. *Chem.*
Gerstäcker, Prof. A., Univ., Greifswald. *Ent., Zool.*
Gerstenberger, C. Glob., Königsbrückerpl. 4, Dresden. *Diatoms.*
Gerstl, Max, Frauenhoferstr. 12, München. *Lepid., Coleopt.*
Gesell, Alexander, k. ung. Bergrath, Chemnitz. *Mountain Geology.*
Geuther, Prof. Dr. Anton, J. G., Univ., Jena. *Chem.**
Geyler, Dr. Hermann T., Friedberger Landstrasse 107, Dir. Bot. Gartens, Frankfurt am Main. *Palæo., Bot., Lepid., cur. et exot.**
Gierke, Prof J., Univ., Breslau. *Physiol., Histol.*
Gies, Prof. Dr. W., Fulda. *Bot.*
Giesbers, Charles, Düsseldorf. *Coleopt.*
Gieseler, Prof. Agric. Acad., Poppelsdorf bei Bonn. *Phys.*
Gieseler, H., Inspector Bot. Gartens, Göttingen. *Bot.*
Glan, Dr. Phil., Privat-Docent a. d. Universität, Sebastianstr. 75, II, Berlin. *Phys., Meteo.*
Glitz, Th., Osterstr. 35, III, Hannover. *Lepid.**
Goette, Dr. Alexander, Prof. Univ., Strassburg, Elsass. *Zool., Comp. Anat., Evolution.**
Goeze, Dr. Edm., Bot. Gartens, Greifswald. *Bot.*
Goldfuss, Otto, Halle. *Moll.*
Goll, Pfarrer, Boetsingen, Baden. *Mosses and Lichens.*
Goltz, Prof. Dr. Friedrich L., Univ., Strassburg (Elsass). *Gen. Biol.*
Goppelsroeder, Prof. Dr. Friedrich, Mülhausen (Elsass). *Chem., especially Elect. Chem.**
Gordan, Prof. Dr. P. A., Univ., Erlangen. *Math.*
Goring, Anton, Waldstr. 38c, Leipzig. *Lepid.*
Gossare, W., St. Pauli, Hamburg. *Carabidæ.*
Götte, Prof. A., Univ., Rostock. *Zool.*
Gottsche, Dr. Carl M., Altona. *Bot.: Hepaticæ.*
Grabbe, Heinrich, Candidatus philosophiæ, Lickwegen bei Bückeburg. *Geol., Palæo.* C. Ex. Offers petrifactions from N. German territories.
Graetz, Dr., Prof. a. d. Univ., München. *Phys.**
Gräser, L., Hamburg. *Lepid.* C. Ex.
Greeff, Prof. Dr. Richard, Univ., Marburg. *Zool., Anat.*
Grenacher, Prof. H., Univ., Göttingen. *Zool.**
Greve, Dr. Eduard, Oldenburg. *Zool., Ichth.*
Greve, Dr. Ludwig, Oldenburg. *Zool., Ent.*
Griepenkerl, Prof. F., Univ., Göttingen. *Agric.*
Griewank, Dr. Kreisphysicus, Bützow (Mecklenburg). *Medicine, Bot., Coleopt.* C. Ex. Plants of northern and central Germany for European.
Grohé, Prof. F., Univ., Greifswald. *Pathol. Anat.*
Grönland, Dr. Johann, Acad., Dahme. *Bot., Mic.*
Groth, Prof. E., Univ.. Strassburg (Elsass). *Phys., Chem.*
Groth, Dr. P., Prof. Univ. u. Conservator d. Min. Sammlung d. Stacke, München. *Min., Crystal.**
Gruber, Dr. A., Prof., Univ., Freiburg. *Zool.**
Gruber, Prof. Dr. August, Freiburg. *Invert., Zool., Gen. Biol., Protozoa, Infusoria.**
Gruenhagen, Prof. Dr. A. W., Univ., Königsberg i. Pr. *Physiol.**
Gucheidlen, Prof. R., Univ., Breslau. *Physiologie und Hygiene.**
Gümbel, Prof. Dr. Carl W., Univ., Munich. *Geognosy.*

Gumppenberg-Pöttmes, Karl Freiherr v., Louisenstr. 20, II, Munich. *Lepid.**
Gurlt, Dr., Bonn. *Geol.*
Gürich, Dr. Georg, Asst. Bot. Garten, Breslau. *Bot., Geol., Min.*
Gutberlet, Dr. Const., Würzburg. *Nat. Philos.*
Gutheil, A., Dörnfeld bei Königsee. *Coleopt.*
Gutzeit, Prof. Dr. H., Univ., Jena. *Pharm., Chem.*
Gysser, Aug., Cattenon, bei Dienenhofen. *Moll.*
Haas, Dr. H., Strassburg. *Fossil Brachiopoda.*
Haas, Otto, Burtscheid bei Aix-la-Chapelle. *Lepid.*
Haase, Dr. Erich, Asst. Zool. Mus., Univ., Dresden. *Myriap., Coleopt.**
Habelmann, P., Köpnickerstr. 140, Berlin. *Coleopt.*
Hache, Mittelstr. 17, Berlin. *Lepid.*
Haeckel, Prof. Dr. Ernst, Univ., Jena. *Zool.*
Hagen, Dr. B., Schiller str. 35, München. *Hymenop.*
Hagena, Prof. Karl, Marienstr. 15, Oldenburg. *Bot.: Phanerogams, Fungi.*
Hagenbeck, Carl, Thiergrosshandlung, Dealer in large animals, supplies Menageries, etc., St. Pauli, Hamburg.*
Hagenbeck, Christian, Vogelgrosshandlung, St. Pauli, Hamburg.*
Hagens, von, Marienstrasse 8, Düsseldorf. *Coleopt.*
Hahn, H., Schrotdorferstr. 14, Entomol. Museum, Magdeburg. *Coleopt.**
Hähn, Johannes, Präsident des Geflügel-Züchter-Vereins, Halberstadt. *Orn.*
Hahn, Otto, Reublingen Wiert. *Meteo.*
Hahne, A., Wasseralfingen bei Aalen. *Lepid.*
Halfar, A., Wissenschaftliche Sec. der Königl. geol. Landesanstalt, Invalidenstr. 14, III, Berlin, N. *Palæo., Strat. Geol.*
Hallas, V., Cand. Pharm., Sonderburg. *Bot.*
Hallier, Prof. Dr. Ern., Stuttgart. *Bot.**
Hamdorf, Dr., Oberlehrer, Guben. *Coleopt.*
Hammeran, Dr. Adam, Frankfort-on-Main. *Eth.**
Hansen, Dr. Bot. Inst., Erlangen. *Bot.*
Harnack, Prof. Erich, Univ., Halle. *Pharm., Physiol., Chem., Hygiene.**
Harrach, Graf Ernst, Kl. Krichen, bei Lüben. *Agric., Mic., Zool., Orn., Ool., Ent.: Coleopt.* C.*
Hartnack, Prof. Dr. E., Potsdam. *Mic.*
Hartwig, Dr. E., Sternwarte, Bamberg. *Ast.**
Harz, Dr. C. O., Prof. der k. Centralthierarzneischule und Docent der Bot. an d. Technischen Hochschule, München, Mitglied der kais. Gesell. d. Nat. zu Moskau. *Bot.*
Hartlaub, Dr. Carl J. G., Bremen. *Orn.*
Hartmann, Leop., Wördlingen. *Photog., Lepid.**
Hartig, Dr. Robert, Universitäts Prof. ordin. und Vorstand des Forstbotanischen Instituts, Georgenstr 3b, München. *Forest Bot. and Pathol. of Plants.* C.*
Haskarl, Dr. Justus Karl, Mitglied der Königl. Akademie zu Halle, Sachsen, Vierpagweg, Cleves. *Bot.* C. Ex. plants of Germany for those of America.
Hasse, Prof. Dr. Carl, Univ., Breslau. *Anat.*
Hasse, W. A., Witten (Westphalen). *Bot.* C. Ex.
Hassel, Otto, Helmstedt, Braunschweig. *Ent.*
Hauchecorne, Wilhelm, Dir. d. k. Bergakademie, Berlin. *Geol.*
Haupt, Dr., Inspector Nat. Cabinet, Bamberg. *Moll., Bot.*
Haupt, Dr. W. Albert, Chemnitz. *Bot.**
Hauser, Friedrich, München. *Ent.*
Hauser, Dr. Gustav, Asst. Pathol.-Anat. Inst., Erlangen. *Zool., Gen. Biol., Emb., Anat., Osteol., Myol., Histol. of Vert., Articulates, Ent.*

Hausknecht, Prof. C., Weimar. *Bot.*
Haverkampf, Fritz Ronsdorf, bei Elberfeld. *Lepid.* C. Ex.
Hechel, Wilhelm, Lehrer an der Höheren Töchterschule, Brandenburg an der Havel. *Systematic and Geographical Bot., Equisetum.* C.
Hedenus, Th., Neureudnitz bei Leipzig. *Lepid.*
Hegelmaier, Dr. Christian F., Prof. Bot., Univ., Tübingen.
Hegewald, H., Cantor in Hakenstedt bei Erxleben. *Coleopt.* C. Ex.
Heiden, Prof. Edouard, Pommritz. *Bot.*
Heidenhain, Prof. R. P. H., Univ., Breslau. *Physiol., Histol., Mic.*
Heidenreich, Inspec. Bot. Gar., Münster. *Bot.*
Heidepriem, Dr. F., Dir. Agric. Stat., Köthen. *Bot.*
Heidorn, Dr., Calculator der Königlichen Sternwarte, Göttingen. *Ast., Meteo.*
Heiland, Lehrer, Winterkasten bei Lindenfels. *Ent.*
Heiland, G., Lyohen bei Brandenburg. *Bot.* C. Ex.
Heimburg, H. v., Moltkestrasse 8, Oldenburg. *Con.*
Heincke, Dr. Friedrich, Oldenburg. *Zool., Ichth., Gen. Biol., Geog. Dist., Fishery.**
Heinrich, Prof. Reinhold, Dir. der Landwirthschaftlichen Versuchs-Station, Rostock.
Hell, Dr. C., Prof. am Polytechnicum, Stuttgart. *Chem.*
Heller, Prof. Dr. Arnold, Kiel. *Mic., Gen. Biol., Histol. of Vert., Arach., Worms, Pathology.**
Hellmann, Dr Gustav, Königl. Meteorologisches Institut, Berlin, S. W. *Meteo.* Library. Ex.*
Hellriegel, Prof. Dr., Bernburg. *Bot., Agronomy.*
Hellwald, Friedrich von, Tölz in Bayern. *Anth., Ethnograph.**
Helm, Otto, Poggenhof 88, Dantzic. *Coleopt.*
Helmholtz, Prof. H., Roy. Univ., Berlin. *Phys., Math.*
Helms, Alwin, Burggarten No. 1, Hamburg-Borgfelde. *Sells Ferns, Lycopods and eggs of birds from New Zealand.*
Hempel, C. Ed., Chemnitz. *Bot.*
Henke, C. K., Saupsdorf (Saxony). *Zool.*
Henke, Prof. Ph. W. J., Univ., Tübingen. *Anat., Osteol.*
Henle, Prof. Dr. F. G. J., Univ., Göttingen. *Anat.*
Henneberg, Prof. Dr. W., Göttingen. *Agric. Chem.**
Henning, Louisenstr. 54, Berlin. *Lepid.*
Hennings, P., Roy. Bot. Museum, Berlin. *Bot.*
Henning, R., Kl. Plauenschestr. 37, Dresden. *Coleopt.**
Hensen, Prof. Dr. Victor, Univ., Kiel. *Phys.*
Herber, Wiesbaden. *Coleopt.* C. Ex.
Herbst, Prof. H. F. W., Univ., Göttingen. *Physiol.*
Hering, Prof. Dr. Edward A. von, Stuttgart.
Hering, Prof. Dr. Hermann, gr. Wollweberstrasse 29, Stettin. *Ent.: Lepid.* C. Ex.
Hermann, Fried., Karlstr. 13, Munich. *Dipt.*
Hermann, R., Proskau. *Bot.*
Herpell, Gustav, St.-Goar-on-the-Rhine. *Bot.: Mosses and Fungi.* C. Ex.*
Herrmann, Dr. F., Docent, Univ., Wurzburg. *Analyt. Chem.*
Herter, Dr. Erwin, Privat-Docent, Univ., Johannisstrasse 3, Berlin. *Org. Chem., Gen. Biol., Anth., Physiol.*
Hertwig, Prof. B., Univ., Jena. *Anat., Physiol.*
Hertwig, Prof. R., Univ., Königsberg. *Zool.*
Hertz, Dr. M., Prof. Philol., Roy. Univ., Breslau.
Hess, Prof. A. E., Univ., Marburg. *Math.**
Hesse, P., Backerstrasse 20, Nordhausen am Harz. *Moll.* Ex. European land shells for slugs from any part of the world.
Hett, Emil, Frankfort-on-Main, Neue Kraine 23. *Lepid.* C.

Hetzer, Gerh., Nordstr. 4, Dresden. *Coleopt.**
Heydemann, Prof. H., Halle, Saxony. *Arch.*
Heyden, Dr. Lucas von, Königl. Preuss. Major, Schlosstrasse 54, Bockenheim, near Frankfort-on-Main, Prussia. *Entomology, especially Coleoptera of Europe, N. Africa, Asia, and Siberia.* C. American Carabus, Cychrus, Calosoma desired for European.
Heydenreich, Osnabrück, Regierungsrath. *Lepid.* C. Ex.*
Heyn, Karl, Plantagenstrasse 5, Berlin, N. *Lepid.* C. Ex.
Heyne, I. A., Jun., Kaufmann, Hamburg, Bockmanstr. 51. *Bot.*
Heyne, Ernst, Hospitalstr. 2, Leipsic. *Lepid. and Coleopt.**
Heyneman, D. F., Pres. d. Deutsch. Malacozool. Gesell., 53 Schifferstr., Frankfort-on-Main *Moll.*
Heincke, F., Dr. Phil., Oldenburg. *Zool., Gen. Biol., Geog. Dist., Ichth.*
Hiendlmayr, Anton, Schwanthalerstrasse 10, III., Munich. *Hymenop., Dipt.* C. Ex.
Hild, Eduard, Königl. Universitäts Gärtner, Kiel, Schleswig-Holstein. *Bot.*
Hildebrand, Prof. F., Univ., Freiburg. *Bot.*
Hildebrandt, Carl, Ph.D., Gymnasiallehrer, Eichendorffstr. 4, Berlin, N. *Phys., Elect., Meteo., Orn.*
Hilgendorf, Dr. Franz M , Zool. Mus., Berlin.*
Hilger, Prof. A., Roy. Univ., Erlangen. *Chem.*
Hillenbrandt, Heinr., Fulda. *Nat. Philos.*
Hiller, Demminerstr. 2, Berlin. *Coleopt.*
Hilpmann, G., Schwabach, bei Nuremburg. *Ent.: Lepid.*
Himly, Prof. C , Univ., Kiel. *Chem.*
Himstedt, Dr. F., Docent, Univ., Freiburg. *Analyt. Mechanics.*
Hinneberg, Dr., Apotheker, Docent an der pharmazeutischen Lehranstalt Eimsbüttler Chaussée 171S, Hamburg. *Syst. Bot., Florist.*
Hinrichsen, Prof. N., Schleswig. *Bot.*
Hintz, Dr. Ernst, Docent am Chemischen Laboratorium, Wiesbaden. *Chem.*
Hirn, Gustave Adolphe, Correspondant de l'Institut de France, boulevard du Hohlandsberg 10, Colmar (Alsace). *Philosophy, Physics and Mechanism.**
Hirschfeld, Prof. G., Univ., Königsberg, Prussia. *Arch., Meteo.*
Hirt, L., Prof. Dr., Teichstr. 7, Breslau. *Gen. Ent.*
Hirzel, Christoph Heinrich, Ph.D., Prof. Univ., Leipsic, Plagwitz, bei Leipsic. *Chem.*
His, Prof. W., Univ., Leipsic. *Anat., Histol., Emb. of Vert., Mic.*
Hitzig, Prof. Dr. Eduard, Halle. *Mental Sci., Neurology, Physiol.**
Hoas, Dr. H., Univ., Kiel. *Palæo., Geol.*
Hochstetter, W., Bot. Gardens, Tübingen. *Bot.*
Hoeme, Alphonse, Oberblasewitz bei Dresden. *Bot.* C.
Hoffmann, Prof. H., Univ., Giessen. *Bot.*
Hoffmann, Dr. Julius, Stuttgart. *Lepid.**
Hoffmann, Dr. O., Steinmetzstr. 15, Berlin. *Bot.**
Hofmann, Prof. A. W., F. R. S., Univ., Berlin. *Org. Chem.*
Hofmann, Ernst, Ph.D., Prof, Custos K. Naturalien-Kabinet, Stuttgart. *Biol. of Ent.* Exchanges for the Museum.*
Hofmann, Dr. Franz Adolf., Prof. und Dir. des Hygienischen Instituts der Univ , Emilienthstr. 15, Leipsic. *Geol., Meteo., Gen. Biol.*
Hohl, Prof. Univ., Tübingen. *Math.*
Holbein, Frau Alma, Apolda. *Lepid.*
Holdefleiss, Prof. F., Univ., Breslau. *Agric. Chem.*
Hollandt, W., Rechtsanwalt, Lessingsplatz 10a, Brunswick. *European Eggs.* C. Ex.

Holler, Dr., Kgl. Bezirksarzt, Memmingen (Bavaria). *Bryology.* C. Ex. Mosses, especially of Bavaria, Central Tyrol, and Switzerland.
Höllmer, Hollenbeckerstr., Münster. *Lepid.* C. Ex.
Holtz, G., Bot. Garden, Hamburg. *Bot.*
Holtz, L., Bot. Gardens, Greifswald. *Bot.*
Holtz, W., Ph.D., a. o. Prof. an der Univ., Greifswald. *Phys.**
Holzapfel, Dr. E., Prof. a. d. Technische Hochschule, Aix-la-Chapelle. *Palæo.*, *Geol.**
Hölzer, Dr., Univ., Göttingen. *Agric. Chem.*
Holzhaus, Oberlehrer, Unteroffizierschule, Marienberg. *Coleopt.*
Holzmüller, Gustav, Ph.D., Hagen. *Phys.*, *Elect.*, *Ast.*
Homann, G., Kurfürstenstr. 12, Berlin. *Ent.*
Höme, Alfons, Brühlsche Terrasse Dresden. *Coleopt.*, *Lepid.*
Homeijer, Maj. Alex. von, Greifswald in Pomerania. *Orn.*, *Lepid.* C. Ex.*
Honeyer, E. F. von, Pres. der Allgem. Deutschen Ornithologischen Gesellschaft, Stolp in Pommern. *Histol. of Vert.* C. 7000 birds. *Palæo.* Ex.*
Honrath, Eduard G., pres. of the Berl. Entomol. Verein, Unter den Linden 3, Berlin, W. *Ent.: Lepid.* C. Ex.*
Hopffgarten, Baron v., Mülverstedt bei Langensalza. *Coleopt.*
Hoppe, Paul, Brusaue, near Gospic, Süd-Kroatien. *Zool.*, *Ent.: Lepid.*, *Coleopt.* C. Ex.
Hoppe, Prof. Dr. R., Docent, Univ., Berlin. *Math.*, *Phys.**
Hoppe-Seyler, Dr. Felix, Prof. Medicine, Univ., Strassburg. *Geol.*, *Org. Chem.*, *Gen. Biol.*
Höpstein, Alte Ulrichstr. 4, Magdeburg. *European Macro-lepid.* C. Ex.
Horstmann, Prof. A., Univ., Heidelberg. *Chem.*
Hosäus, Dr. A., Oberlehrer am Real-Gymnasium, Eisenach. *Agric Chem.**
Hösius, Prof. A., Academy, Münster. *Palæo.*, *Min.*
Hötte, Rothenburg, Münster. *Lepid.* C. Ex.
Huber, Johannes C., M. D., Memmingen, Bayern. *Mosses*, *Bibliog.*, *Worms.* C. Ex.
Huber, Dr. K., Docent, Univ., Leipsic. *Pathol. Anat.*
Hübner, Dr. Prof. Hans, Dir. Chem. Laborat., Univ., Geismar Chaussée 17, Göttingen. *Chem.*, *Phys.*
Hüfner, C. G., M.D., D.Sc., Prof. Univ., Tübingen. *Physiol.*, *Chem.*
Hülsen, R., Staykowo, near Czarnikau. *Bot.*
Hülsen, Prof. Rudolf, Bohne, near Gr. Wudicke (Prussia). C. Ex.
Hunger, Emil, Stallschreiberstr. 26, Berlin, S. 14. *Bot.*, *Cyperaceæ and Gramineæ.* C. Ex.
Huntemann, Johann, Oldenburg. *Bot.*, *Zool.*, *Coleopt.*, *Formicidæ.* C. Ex.*
Hupp, Charles, Düsseldorf. *Coleopt.*
Ihering, Dr. Hermann von, Leipsic.. *Moll.*
Ihle, Aug., Rietschelstr. 8, Dresden. *Lepid.* C. Ex.
Ihle, Rich., Rietschelstrasse 14, Dresden. *Coleopt.* C. Ex.
Ijima, Isao, Thalstrasse 1, 1 Etage, Leipsic. *Zool.*, *Emb. of Nephelis.* C.
Ilse, Inspector of Forests, Hagenau. *Bot.*
Imbach, Philipp, Lörrach (Baden). *Chem.*
Insel, Krausnickstr. 3, Berlin. *Ent.*
Jack, J. B., Constance. *Bot.: Hepaticæ.*
Jacobi, A., Wildeshausen. *Ent.*
Jacobsen, Oscar, Universitäts-Professor, Rostock (Mecklenburg). *Chem.*
Jacoby, Dr. N., Wendisch, Buchholtz, W. Berlin. *Coleopt.*
Jaennicke, Fred, Mayence. *Ent.: Dipt.*, *Bot* *
Jaensch, Dr. Theodor, Rathenowerstr. 87, Berlin, N. W. *Bot.* (*esp. Anat.*

and Phys. of Plants) *Ent.*: *Lepid. and Coleopt.* C. Ex. Desires Coleopt. and living cocoons and eggs of foreign Lepidoptera in exchange for German. Also woods and seeds especially of Leguminosæ and climbing plants.*
Jaeger, Dr., Prof. a. D., Stuttgart. *Zool.*, *Anth.**
Jannasch P., Prof. Dr., Univ., Göttingen. *Chem.**
Jenssen, Dr. Chr., Sec. K. Landwirthschafts-Gesell., Hannover. *Bot.*
Jesnitzer, Rector, Zanow (Stettin). *Coleopt.*
Jessen, Dr. C., Prof. Univ., Greifswald, Kastanien Allée 69, Berlin. *Bot.*
Jetschin, Robert, Patschkau, Germany. *Conchology.* C. Ex. European L. and F. W. shells in exchange for those of all lands.*
Jickeli, C. F., Jr., 17 Weingartenstr., Würzburg. *Moll.*
Jölly, J., Prof. Univ., Würzburg. *Eth.*
Joseph, Gustav, Dr. Med. et Phil., Pract. Arzt u. Docent a. d. Univ., Breslau. C. Ex.*
Jössel, Prof. J. G., Univ., Strasburg. *Anat.*, *Mic.*
Jost, Carl Fried., Privatier, Mannheim. *Lepid.*
Jühlke, Dir. des Kgl. Gartens, und Director der Landesb.-Schule und Gärtner-Lehranstalt, Potsdam. *Bot.**
Jülfs, Christian, Lehrer an der Grossherzoglich Oldenburgischen Navigationsschule, Elsfleth-on-the-Weser. *Bot.* C. Ex. Plants of N. W. Germany for foreign.*
Jung, Carl, Siebenhufenerstr. 26, Breslau. *Lepid.**
Jürgens, Dr. E., Docent, Univ., Halle. *Math.*
Just, Prof. Dr. Johann L., Carlsruhe.
Kabath, H., Schuhbrücke 27, Breslau. *Bot.*
Kaemerer, Prof. Dr. Herman, Nuremburg. *Chem.*, *Geol.*, *Met.*
Kaibel, Prof. Dr. G., Roy. Univ., Breslau. *Philol.*
Kaiser, Dr., Elberfeld. *Zool.*, *Geol.*
Kaiser, Dr. E., Friedenstrasse 27, Berlin. *Mic.*
Kammerer, Dr. Robert, Stuttgart. *Coleopt.*
Karsch, Prof. Dr., Münster. *Bot.*
Karsch, Dr. Ferdinand, Custos of the Zool. Museum, of the Roy. Univ., Strelitzerstr. 13, Berlin, N. *Ent.*: *Coleopt.**
Karsten, Prof. Dr. Gustav, Univ., Kiel. *Phys.*
Kasper, J., Reichenbergerstr. 125, Berlin. *Coleopt.*
Katenkamp, Dr. Heinrich, Delmenhorst, Oldenburg. *Bot.*: *Lichens.*
Katter, Dr. F., Putbus (Rügen). *Ent.*
Kayser, Dr., Ansbach. *Bot.*: *Bryology.*
Kayser, Prof. E., Invalidenstrasse 46, Berlin. *Geol.*
Kayser, Dr. H., Prof. Technische Hochschule, Hannover. *Spectrum Analysis.**
Kegebein, R., Greifswald. *Ent.* C. Ex.
Keitel, G. T. Naturalist, Nicolai-Kirchhof 9, Berlin, C. *Lepid.*, *Coleopt.*, *and all branches of Nat. Hist.* C. Ex.
Kekulé, Prof. A., Roy. Univ., Bonn. *Chem.*
Kekulé, Prof. R., Roy. Univ., Bonn. *Arch.*
Keller, Adolf, Reutlingen. *Ent.*
Kellner, Forstrath A., Pres. Thür. Ent. Vereins, Gotha. *Coleopt.*
Kemmler, Donnstetten, near Urach. *Bot.*
Kerl, Prof. B., Bergakademie, Wichmannstrasse 1, Berlin, W. *Chem. und Met.**
Kessler, F. F., Cassel, bei Frankfort-on-Main. *Physics.*
Kessler, Dr. Hermann F., Polytechn. School, Cassel. *Bot.*
Kessner, Bürgerschullehrer, Zwickau. *Coleopt.*
Ketteler, Prof. E., Roy. Univ., Bonn. *Physics.*
Kieffer, l'Abbé J. J., Prof. d'Histoire Naturelle au Coll. de Bitche (Lorraine). *Teratology of plants and galls.* C. Ex.

Kienitz, Dr. M., Eberswalde. *Bot.*
Kiepert, Prof. H., Roy. Univ., Berlin.
Kinkelin, Dr. F., Zeisselstrasse 7, Frankfort-on-Main. *Geol., Palæo.**
Kirchoff, Dr. Alfred, Odentlicher, Prof. der Erdkunde an der Univ., Halle (Saxony). *Meteo., Geog. Dist., Anth., Eth., Ethnog.*
Kirchner, Dr. Oscar, Hohenheim, near Stuttgart. *Bot.*
Kirchhoff, Chief Gardener to Prince de Fürstenberg, Donaueschingen. *Bot.*
Kirchoff, Prof. Gustav, Univ., Berlin. *Phys.*
Kirsch, Theodor, Custodian, Zool. Mus., Dresden.
Kittel, Prof., Passau. *Coleopt., Hemipt., Dipt., Orthopt., Hymenop., Lepid.*
Klaeger, H. Oranienstr. 178, Berlin. *Coleopt.**
Klaeger, O., Wilhelmstr. 114, Berlin. *Coleopt.**
Klatt, Dr. F. W., Eimsbuttel, Augustastrasse 8. *Bot.: Compositæ, Trideæ.*
Klebs, Dr. G., Strasburg.
Klein, Dr. B., Docent, Univ., Marburg. *Math.*
Klein, Prof. Dr. C., Univ., Göttingen. *Min., Crystal.*
Klein, Prof. F., Univ., Göttingen. *Math.**
Klein, Dr. Herm. J., Director der Wetterwarte der Kölnischen Zeitung, Besitzer eines Astronomischen Privat-Observatoriums, Cologne. *Ast. and Meteo.* Topography of the upper surface of the moon.*
Klein, Dr. Otto, Neues Chem. Lab., Tübingen, *Chem.*
Kleiner, Robert, Dresden-Albertstadt. *Lepid.*
Klemm, Curt, Moschelstr. 13, Leipsic. *Lepid.*
Klercker, Dr. John E. F., Asst., Univ. of Tübingen. *Physiol.**
Klinger, Dr. Heinr., Privat-Docent an der Universität, Bonn-on-the Rhine. *Chem.*
Klippert, Grünestrasse, Vegesack. *Orn., Ool.**
Klipstein, Prof. Dr. v., Giessen (Upper-Hesse). *Geol., Palæo.* C. Ex. Offers petrifactions and minerals of the Alps and W. Germany for those of N. America.
Klocke, Prof. F., Roy. Univ., Marburg. *Min., Crystal.*
Klotz, Dr. C. E., Sidonienstr. 16, Leipsic. *Ent.*
Klunzinger, Dr. Carl Benjamin, Ord. Prof. der Zool., Anth., und Hygieine am Königl. Polytech., Moserstrasse 7, Stuttgart, Würtemberg. *Zool., Ichth., Corals, Crustacea.* C.*
Knapp, Friedrich, Gotha. *Bot., Lepid.* C.
Knauth, Johannes, Dr. Nordstr. 35, Dresden. *Coleopt.* C. Ex.
Knebd, Dr., Sternstrasse, Breslau. *Phanerogams.*
Knoblauch, August, Zeil 54, Frankfort-on-Main. *Moll.*
Knoblauch, Prof. Dr. Carl Hermann, Präs. d. kais. Leop. Carol. Deutsch Akad., Univ., Halle. *Phys.**
Knoche, Richard, Hanover. *Con.* C.*
Knop, Prof. W., Univ., Leipsic. *Chem.*
Kny, Dr. Leopold, Prof. a. d. Univ. und Landwirthsch. Hochschule, Keithstr. 8, Berlin, W. *Bot., Bot. Physiol.**
Kobell, Prof. Dr. Franz X. W. Ritter von, Univ., Munich. *Min.*
Kobelt, Dr. Wilhelm, Schwanheim, bei Frankfort-on-Main. *Moll.*
Kobitzsch, F., Albertstr. 37, II., Leipsic. *Lepid.*
Kobold, Hermann, Dr. Phil., Observator, Strassburg. *Ast.**
Koch, Rector, Perleberg. *Macro. et Micro-Lepid.* C. Ex.*
Koch, Dr., Wöhrd, bei Nürnberg. *Arach., Coleopt.*
Koch, E. E., Agriculturist, Güstrow. *Moll.*
Koch, Dr. K. R., Prof. Univ., Freiburg. *Mechanics.**
Koch, Prof. Dr. L., Univ., Heidelberg. *Bot., Anat.*
Koch, Rud., Münster. *Gen. Ent.*
Koch, Victor von, Brunswick. *Moll.*

Koch, de Wolestein, Dr. Robert, Regierungsrath, Berlin. *Bot.*
Koechlin, Joseph, quai du Ballage, Mülhausen (Alsace). *Coleopt.*
Koechlin, Oscar, Chimiste, Dornach, near Mulhouse (Alsace). *Ent., principally Coleopt.* C. Coleoptera and Hemiptera.
Koehne, Dr. Emil, Realgymnasiallehrer, Goebenstr. 31. *Bot.* Wishes Lythraceæ.
Koenig von Warthausen, Richard F., Leop. Acad., Warthausen bei Biberach. *Ool., Moll., Bot., Arch.*
Koenike, F., Gr. Johanisstrasse 60, Bremen. *Zool., Hydrachnia.*
Koenike, F., Lehrer, Bremen. *Arach., Hydrach.**
Kohlmann, Reinhard, Vegesack, near Bremen. *Higher Mushrooms (Hymenomycetes), Orn., Con., Min.* C. Ex. East India shells and higher mushrooms, fresh or dry, shells (Cypræa, Strombus, Voluta, etc.). Wishes crystallized minerals.*
Kohlrausch, Dr., Lüneburg. *Lepid.*
Kohlrausch, Prof. F., Univ., Würzburg. *Phys.*
Kohlrausch, Dr W., Docent, Univ., Strasburg. *Phys.*
Kolb, E., Kisslegg. *Bot.: Bryol.*
Kolb, Max, Bot. Gardens, Munich. *Bot.*
Kolbe, Hermann J., Custos Zool. Museum d. Univ., Berlin, N., Strelitzerstr. 51. *Invert. Palæo., Emb. and Anat. of Invert., Ent., Coleopt., Orthopt., Neuropt.* C. Ex.*
Kölliker, Prof. Dr. August A. von, Univ., Würzburg. *Anat.*
Koltze, W., Gertrudenstr. 11, Hamburg. *European Coleopt.**
Könen, Prof. A. v., Göttingen. *Palæo., Geol.*
König, Französischestr. 48, Berlin. *Lepid.*
Königs, Dr. W., Docent, Univ., Munich. *Chem.*
Königsberger, Prof. L., Heidelberg. *Math.*
Konow, Fr. W., Pastor, Fürstenberg, Mecklenburg. *Bot., Con., Min., Ent.: esp. Hymenoptera, Tenthredinidæ.* C. Ex.*
Kopp, Dr. Hermann F. M., Univ., Heidelberg. *Chem.*
Köppen, Dr. W., Seewarte, Hamburg. *Meteo., Geog. Dist.*
Korb, Max, Marsstrasse 39, Munich. *Ent.: Lepid., Coleopt.* C. Ex.*
Korn, C., Lehrer, Blaue Beilstr. 16, Magdeburg. *European Macro-lepid.* C. Ex.
Körnich, Eduard, Meissen. *Lepid.* C. Ex.
Körnicke, Prof. Dr. Friedrich August, Docent der Botanik an der Königlichen landwirthschaftlichen Akademie, Poppelsdorf bei Bonn. *Bot.* Wishes samples of grain for sowing, and maize in whole ears. Especially interested in diseases of plants.*
Körnig, Adolf, Breslau. *Bot., Eth., Ethnog.*
Korschelt, Eugen, Leipzig. *Ent.: Emb.*
Körte, Prof. G., Univ., Rostock. *Arch.*
Kortum, Prof. H., Univ., Bonn. *Math.*
Kossmann, Prof. Dr. R., Univ., Heidelberg. *Zool.**
Köster, T. E., Elsfleth-on-the-Weser. *Navigation and Astronomy.*
Köstlin, Prof. Dr. Otto, Stuttgart.
Kothe, Alb., Graveur, Hollmannstrasse 31, Berlin. *Lepid.*
Kraatz, Gustav, Ph.D., Pres. Ent. Gesell. Linkstrasse 28, Berlin. *Ent.: Coleopt.* C. Ex.
Krabbe, Dr., Bot. Inst. am Guitgarten, Berlin. C. *Plant Physiol.*
Kraepelin, Dr. Karl, Hammerbrookstr. 17, Hamburg. *Bot.*
Kraetzer, Dr. J., Mem. Malacozool. Gesell., Frankfort a. M., Untermain-Anlage 7. *Bot., Palæo., Geol., Min., Crystal., Lithol., Moll.* C. Ex. Recent and fossil Moll., the latter particularly from the Alpine Triasic, Cretaceous and Tertiary formations.*
Kramer, Ludwigsdorf bei Gilgenburg. *Coleopt., Lepid.* C. Ex. for European and exot. Lepid.

Kraucher, Dr. Oscar Paul, Carolinenstrasse 20, II., Leipzig. *Zool.*, *Ent.: Hymen.*, *Lepid.*, *Coleopt.* C. Ex.*
Krantz, Dr. August, Rheinisches Mineralien-Comptoir, Coblenzerstrasse 121, Bonn. *Min.*, *Palæo.*, *Petrography.* C. Ex. minerals and fossils.*
Kranz, Dr. C. A., Karlstr. 21, Munich *Ent.*
Kraske, Dr. P., Prof. an der Univ., Freiburg.*
Kraus, Dr. Carl, Lehrer der Landwirthschaftlichen Schule und Vorstand der Samencontrolstation, Triesdorf, Bavaria. *Physiol. of Plants.**
Kraus, Prof. Dr. Gregor, Univ., Halle (Saxony). *Bot.*
Krause, Dr. Arthur, Mariannenplatz 19, Berlin. *Chem.*, *Bot.*
Krause, Dr. Aurel, Zossenerstr. 19, Berlin. *Palæo.**
Krause, Franz, Altenburg, Saxony. *Lepid.*, *spec. Micro-lepid.*, *Coleopt.* C. Ex.*
Krause, Prof. M., Univ., Rostock. *Math.*
Krause, Prof. W., Univ., Göttingen. *Histol.*
Krauss, Prof. Dr. Ferdinand von, Stuttgart. *Nat. Hist.*
Kraut, Prof. Dr. K., Welfenschloss, Hanover. *Chem.*
Krauze, Dr. Hermann, Hanover. *Bot.*
Krechscher, Prof. F., Frieberg. *Bot.: Algæ.*
Kreglinger, Karl, Privatgelehrter, Stephanienstrasse 44, Carlsruhe (Baden) *Con.*
Kretzer, J. F., Mülheim-on-Main. *Moll.*
Kricheldorff, Ad., Oranienstr. 135, Berlin. *Coleopt.*, *Lepid.*
Kriechbaumer, Dr., Findlingstrasse 18, Munich. *Ent.: Hymenoptera*, *Diptera.*
Krieghoff, Edmund, Atlenfeld bei Gross-Breitenbach. *Lepid.*, *Coleopt.* C. Ex.
Kries, Prof. J. von, Univ., Freiburg. *Physiol.*
Kroener, Präparator, Naturhist. Mus., Strasburg. *Europ. Lepid.*
Krohn, Prof. Dr. August D., Bonn.
Kronecker, Prof. H., Univ., Berlin. *Physiol.*
Kropp, R., Prof., Weiswasser. *Ent.*
Krüger, Prof. A., Univ., Kiel. Dir. der Sternwarte. *Ast.**
Krukenberg, C. F. W., Dr. Ph., Med. et Chir., Prof. der Physiologischen Chemie a. d. Gesammt. Univ., Jena. *Physiol.*, *Chem.*, *Comp. Physiol.*
Krümmel, Dr. Otto, Seewarte, Hamburg. *Hydrography*, *Geog.*, *Meteo.*
Kubary, Joh., Hamburg.
Küch, Dr. W., Potsdamerstrasse 69, Berlin. *Geol.*, *Petrography.*
Küchenmeister, Dr. F., Dresden.
Kügler, Dr., Zeil, Frankfort-on-Main. *Bot.*
Kuhlmann, Victor, Seestrasse, Dresden. *Coleopt.*, *Lepid.* C. Ex.
Kühn, Prof. Dr. Gust., Agricultural Chemist, Mockern, near Leipsic.
Kühn, Heinr., Blasewitz zu F. in Niederlausitz (Sachsen). *Coleopt.*
Kühn, Prof. Dr. Jul., Univ., Halle-on-the-Sale. *Bot.*
Kühn, Prof. P. Kaspar, Custos Mus., Ottobeuren. *Phæn. Bot.: Algæ*, *Moll.* C.
Kuhn, Dr. M., Friedenau bei Berlin, Fregestr. 68. *Bot.*, *Ferns.**
Kühne, Ludwig, Petersteinweg 13, Leipsic. *Lepid.*
Kühne, Prof. W., Univ., Heidelberg. *Physiol.*
Külz, Prof. E., Univ., Marburg. *Physiol.*
Kummer, Prof. E. E., Roy. Univ., Berlin. *Math.*
Kummer, Prof. Paul, Münden (Hanover). *Bot.*, *especially Mosses*, *Lichens and Fungi.* C.
Kundt, Prof. A., Univ., Strassburg. *Phys.*
Kunkel, Dr. A., Docent, Univ., Würzburg. *Med.-Chem. Analysis.*
Kuntze, Albert, Altmarkt 7, Dresden. *Phæn. Bot.*, *Diptera.* C. Ex.
Kuntze, Dr. Otto, Leipsic. *Bot.*

Kunze, Lieut. Carl, Weistritz bei Schweidnitz. *Lepid.*
Kunze, Prof. Dr. Carl L. A., Weimar. *Math., Phys.*
Kunze, Dr. Joh., Lutherstrasse 10, Eisleben. *Bot., Mycol.*
Kunze, Prof. Max, Acad., Tharandt, near Dresden. *Moll.*
Küpffer, Prof. Dr. Carl, Univ., Munich. *Anat.*
Kurtz, Dr. Fritz, König. Augustastr. 50, Berlin, W. *Syst. Bot., Phytogeog., Phytopalæo.* C. Ex. European plants for Phanerogams from all parts of the world, including Ferns, Lycopodiaceæ, and Equisetaceæ.
Kützing, Prof. Dr. F. T., Nordhausen. *Bot., Algæ.**
Kutzleb, Ph.D., Halle. *Agric.*
Kutzleb, Victor, Ph.D. *Agric.* C. Ex.
Kuwert, Gutsbesitzer, Wernsdorf, near Tharau, in old Prussia. *Coleopt., Lepid.* C. Ex. Wishes Lamellicorns and Cerambycidæ in ex. for Coleoptera of Germany.
Lackowitz, A. W., Schönhauser Allée 57, Berlin. *Bot.*
Lademann, Thilo., Westend bei Charlottenburg. *Moll., Bot.*
Ladenburg, Prof. A., Univ., Kiel. *Chem.*
Lagenbühl, F., Wiesbaden. *Coleopt.*
Lahmann, Albert Heinr., Sohn, Brill 8, Bremen. *Lepid.*
Lamers, Guillaume, Jägerhofstr. 1, Düsseldorf. *Coleopt.*
Lamp, Dr. E., Observator, Königliche Sternwarte, Kiel. *Ast.*
Landauer, Robert, Einhorn Apotheke, Würzburg. *Bot.* C. Ex.*
Landois, Prof. H., Univ., Münster. *Orn., Mic.*
Landois, Prof. Dr. L., Dir. Physiol. Inst., Univ., Greifswald. *Physiol.*
Landolf, Prof. L., Univ., Berlin. *Phys., Chem.*
Landolt, Prof. Dr. Hans, Prof. Chem., Landw. Hochsch. und Univ., Berlin. *Chem.**
Lang, Dr. Arnold, Prof. à l'Univ. de Jena. *Vermes.**
Lang, O., Univ., Göttingen. *Geol., Lithol., Mic.* Ex.
Lange, A., Annaberg. *Coleopt.*
Lange, Ernst, Neukirkhof 32, Leipsic. *Lepid.* C. Ex.
Länge, F. A., Ulm. *Lepid.* C. Ex.*
Langendorff, Dr. O., Docent, Univ., Königsberg. *Physiol., Histol.*
Langhans, Dr., Lehrer, Gewerbeschule, Fürth. *Coleopt.*
Langsdorf, W. v., Breisgau (Baden). *Ent.*
Lanz, Herman, Friedrichshafen on Lake Constance. *Lepid.* C.
Lapowitz, Dr. Konrad, Asst. Bot. Garten, Breslau. *Bot.*
Lappe, Neudietendorf bei Gotha. *Moll.*
Laspeyres, Dr., Prof. H., Universität, Bonn am Rhein. *Geol., Min., Lithol.**
Latschenberger, J., Prof. Med., Univ., Freiburg. *Physiol., Toxicology, Hygiene.*
Lattermann, Georg, Dr. Phil., Molkenmarkt 5, Berlin. *Min.**
Laubenheimer, Prof. A., Höchst am Main (bei Frankfurt am Main). *Chem.**
La Valette Saint-George, le Baron von, Prof., Bonn. *Coleopt.*
Legel, Rud., Dönienstr., Leipsic. *Coleopt., Lepid.**
Lehmann, F. X., Karlsruhe. *Moll.**
Lehmann, Hugo, Bohrauerstr. 11, Breslau. *Lepid.* C. Ex.
Lehmann, Dr. Johannes, Prof. a. d. Universität, Breslau. *Min.* C.
Lehmann, Dr. R., Prof. Acad., Münster in Westphalia. *Geog.**
Lehmann-Filhés, Dr. Rudolf, Docent der Astronomie an der Königl. Universität, Landgrafenstr. 4, Berlin, W. *Ast.*
Lehmann, Udo, Neudamm, Prov. Brandenburg. *Ent.**
Leichtlin, Max, Eigenthümer eines Botanischen Privatgartens, Baden-Baden. *Bot., Introduction of new and rare plants.* C. Ex. Wishes correspondents abroad.*
Leimbach, Prof. Dr. Gotthelf, Präsident u. Redacteur der "Irmischia,"

Sondershausen, Thüringen. *Phan. Bot.: Ferns, Plant Palæo., Geog. Dist.* C. Ex. European orchids for those not of Europe.
Lemke, Auguststr. 93, Berlin. *Lepid.*
Lentz, Prof. Dr. L., Königsberg. *Coleopt., Lepid.*
Lenz, Dr. Heinrich, Conservator am Naturhistorischen Museum, Lübeck. *Zool.* C. Ex.*
Lepsius, Prof. Dr. C. R., Darmstadt. *Geol.*
Letzner, K., Rector emer., Vorwerksst. 5, Breslau. *Coleopt.**
Leuckart, Rudolf, Prof. u. Kgl. Sächs. Geheimer Hofrath, Zoologisches Institut, Thalstr. 15, Leipsic. *Zool.*
Leyden, Prof. Dr. Ernst, Univ., D. d. 1. med. Klinik, Berlin. *Pathol., Therap* *
Leydig, Prof. F. von, Univ., Bonn. *Emb., Anat., Histol.*
Lichtenstein, Dr. Eduard, Berlin.
Liebe, Dr. Th., Kürassierstr. 2, Berlin, S. W. *Bot.**
Lieberkühn, Prof. Dr. Nathanael, Univ., Marburg. *Anat.*
Liebermann, Prof. C., Roy. Univ., Berlin. *Chem.*
Liebisch, Dr. Theodor, Prof. der Mineralogie Krystallographie, u. Petrographie an der Univ., Göttingen. *Min., Crystal., Petrog.**
Liepe, Lehrer, Eberswalde (Brandenburg). *Coleopt.*
Lill, Dr. Med., Johannisplatz 4, Würzburg. *Coleopt.**
Limpricht, G., Palmstrasse 21, Breslau. *Bryol.*
Limpricht, Heinrich, Prof. der Chemie an der Universität, Greifswald *Chem.*
Lincke, Lehrer, Höhere Bürgerschule, Stettin. *Dipt.*
Lindemann, Adolf F., F.R.A.S., Hôtel Graf, Durkheim (Bavaria).
Lindemann, Prof. F., Univ., Königsberg i. Pr. *Math.**
Lindley, W. H., Civil Engineer, Member of the Institution of Civil Engineers (London), Fellow of the Geographical Society (London), Stadtbaurath, Frankfort-on-Main, 29 Blittersdorffsplatz, Frankfort-on-Main. *Sanitary Engineering.**
Linnaea Institution for Nat. Hist. (Dr. Aug. Müller), Berlin, Invalidenstr. 38. Large stock of Nat. Hist. objects. Catalogues sent free on application.*
Lipschitz, Prof. R., Roy. Univ., Bonn. *Math.*
List, Dr. Edmund, Würzburg. *Chem.**
Listing, Dr. Johann Benedict, Prof. of Natural Philosophy in the University, Göttingen. *Optics, Math., Geol., Meteo.*
Littke, H., Klosterstr. 56, Breslau. *Ent.: Lepid., Coleopt.* C. Ex.
Liweh, Dr., Asst. Min.-Geol. Inst., Univ., Erlangen (Bavaria). *Min., Crystal.**
Loebbecke, Th., Conchilien-Museum, Düsseldorf. *Living shells.*
Loew, Dr. E., Lützowstr. 51, Berlin. *Bot.*
Loew, Dr. Oscar, Karlstrasse 29, Munich. *Org. Chem., Gen. Biol.*
Loewig, Prof. Dr. C. J., Roy. Univ., Breslau. *Chem.*
Loffler, E., Lehrer, Niemeierstr. 6, Halle a. S. *Coleopt., Lepid.**
Lohse, Dr. Oswald Königlich Astrophysikalisches Observatorium, Potsdam. *Coleopt., Astro-Physics and Astro-Photography.**
Lommel, Eugen, Ph.D., Prof. Univ., München. *Phys.**
Lorey, Prof. T., Univ., Tübingen. *Agric.*
Loritz, Heins, Gera. *Lepid.*
Loritz, Dr. N., Berlin. *Moll.*
Löso, Dr., Lützowstr. 51, Berlin.
Lossen, Prof. Dr. Karl August, Invalidenstrasse 44, Berlin, N. *Geol., Lithol.*
Lossen, Prof. W., Univ., Königsberg. *Chem.*
Löw, Dr., Wichmannstrasse 3, Berlin, W. *Geod., Ast.*
Lüdecke, Otto, Ph.D., Prof. der Mineralogie, Univ., Halle; Sec. Naturwissenschaftlichen Vereins; Mit-Redakteur der Zeitschrift für

Naturwissenschaft. *Geol., Min., Crystal., Anth.* Ex. American minerals for old German specimens.*
Lüders, Edward, Lauterberg-on-Harz. *Moll.*
Ludwig, Prof. C., Univ., Leipsic. *Physiol.*
Ludwig, Prof. Dr. Friedrich, Gymnasial-Oberlehrer, Greiz. *Bot., Biol.**
Ludwig, Hubert, Dr. Phil., Prof. Zool. und vergleichenden Anat., Univ., Bonn am Rhein. *Zool., Gen. Biol., Geog. Dist., Emb., Anat., Vert., Mam., Orn., Herpetol., Ichth., Arach., Myriopoda, Crust., Worms, Moll., Radiates, Sponges, Protozoa, Infusoria.* C. Ex.*
Luerssen, Dr. Gerh. Christian Friedrich, Prof. der Botanik an der König. Forstacademie zu Eberswalde. *Vascular Cryptogams, Ferns and their allies.* C. 30,000 specimens of Ferns. Ex. Ferns of Polynesia, Asia, and Europe for those of the globe, especially of America.*
Lüllnitz, A., Ritterstr. 41, Coeslin. *Coleopt.* C. Ex.*
Luschan, Dr. F. von., Asst. Dir. Ethnographical Museum, Berlin.*
Luther, Prof. E., Univ., Königsberg. *Ast.*
Lützjohann, A. T. F., Bützow, *Phæn. Bot., Geol., Chem., Lepid., Dipt.* C.
Maack, Heinr., Hamburg. *Lepid.* C. Ex.
Maassen, Peter, Elberfeld. *Lepid.* C. Ex.
Macker, Dr. Emile, Colmar (Upper Alsace). *Lepid.*
Machleit, Turnlehrer, Lüneburg. *Lepid.*
Maercker, Prof. M., Univ., Halle. *Agric. Chem.*
Magnus, Hugo, Prof., Univ., Breslau. *Phys., Gen. Biol., Anth.*
Magnus, Dr. P., Prof. Bot., Univ., Blumeshof 15, Berlin, W. *Bot.**
Maier, Prof. R., Univ., Freiburg. *Gen. Pathol., Anat. and Histol., Hygiene.*
Malherbe, Judge, Metz.
Maltzan, Baron Hermann von, Invalidenstrasse 38, Berlin. *Conchology, espec. geog. distribution of animals.* C. Ex. Marine shells.*
Mangoldt, Hans von, Prof. a. d. Königl. Technischen Hochschule zu Aachen. *Math.**
Mann, F., Osterstr. 41, Greiz. *Lepid.**
Mann, F. W., Kaiserstrasse 16, Frankfort-on-Main. *Lepid.* C. Ex.
Marchand, Prof. F., Univ., Giessen. *Pathol. Anat. and Histol.*
Marck, Dr. v. d., Hamm. *Min.*
Märkel, G., Leuben, bei Lommatzsch. *Ent.*
Marmé, Prof. Dr. Wilhelm, Göttingen.
Marquart, Dr. Louis C., Bonn.
Marshall, Dr. W., Docent, Univ., Leipsic. *Ent., Vert. Palæo., Zool.**
Marsson, Dr. Theodor, Greifswald, Pommern, Prussia. *Bot., Palæo., Chem.* C.*
Martens, Dr. E. von, Prof. Zool., 35 Kurfürstenstr., Berlin, W. *Moll.**
Martini, W., Sömmerda. *Micro and Macro-Lepid.*
Martini, Ingénieurlieutenant, Pionierkaserne, Berlin. *Ent.*
Marx, Conrad, Rosenweg, Dresden. *Coleopt., Lepid.* C. Ex.
Mathiotte, Ferdinand, Remilly (Lorraine). *Lepid.* C. Ex.
Matthan, Carl, Brandenburg. *Coleopt.*
Matthiessen, Prof. L., Univ., Rostock. *Phys.*
Matuschka, v., Kreuzkirche 4, Breslau. *Coleopt.*
Maus, Wilh., Wiesbaden. *Lepid.* C. Ex.
Mayer, Prof. A., Univ., Leipsic. *Math.*
Mayer, C., Dir. Bot. Garden, Grand-Ducal, Carlsruhe.
Mayer, Dr. C. E. Louis, Privat-Docent, Schützenstr. 73-74. Berlin, S. W. *Lepid.* C. Ex.*
Mayer, C. E., Donaueschingen. *Coleopt.*
Mayer, W., Apotheker, Tübingen.*
Mayr, Prof. A., Univ., Würzburg. *Ast., Anth.*

Mayr, Dr. Heinrich, Asst. am forstbotanischen Inst., Amalienstrasse 67, Munich. *Pathol. of Plants, Forest Bot.*
Medicus, Prof. L., Würzburg. *Analyt. Chem.*
Meinheit, C., Harburg. *Lepid.* C. Ex.
Meinheit, Karl, Dortmund. *Ent.: Lepid.* C. Ex. Lepid of Spain and S. France for those of N. Germany.
Meisel, K., Güterbahnhofstrasse, Dresden. *Ent.*
Meissner, Prof. Dr. Georg C. F., Univ., Göttingen. *Physics.*
Melchert, Gustav, Dir. des Allgemeinen Ent. Tauschvereins für Europe, Dessau. *Ent.: Lepid., Coleopt.* C. Ex.
Melde, Prof. F. E., Univ., Marburg. *Mechanics, Physics, Optics, Math.*
Melsheimer, Marcellus, Ober-Förster, Linz-on-Rhine. *Bot., Zool.**
Menderf, H., Barby. *European Macro-Lepid.*
Mengelbier, Wilh., Aix-la-Chapelle. *Lepid.*
Merbitz, Jul., Leisnig i. S. *Lepid. Spec. präp. Raupen.**
Mering, Dr. J. von, Docent, Univ., Strasburg. *Pathol., Physiol., Chem.*
Merkel, Prof. Friedrich Siegmund, Dir. Anat. Inst., Rostock. *Emb., Anat., Anth.*
Mess, Eduard, kgl. Regierungsrath, Staatsanstalts-Dir., Sonnenstr. 27, München. *Ent.: Lepid., Coleopt., Living Reptiles.**
Messer, C., Reallehrer, Bremen. *Bot.**
Metzger, Dr. Prof. der Zool. an der Königl. Forstakademie, Münden. *Zool., Moll., Crustacea.* Offers Marine Invert. of North Sea.
Metzner, Carl, Josephinengasse 19, Dresden. *Coleopt.*
Meyer, Dr. Georg, Luisenstrasse 3, Königsberg. *Geol., Palæo.*
Meyer, Dr., Docent, Oldenburg. *Ent.*
Meyer, Dr. Adolf B., Dir. Zool., Anth. Eth. Mus., Dresden. *Vert., Geol. Dist., Eth., Anth., esp. East Indian Archipelago.*
Meyer, Prof. E. S. Chr. von, Univ., Leipsic. *Chem.*
Meyer, Ferdinand, Telegraphenbeamter, Colmar (Upper Alsace). *Malacology, especially of Germany.* C. Ex. European Helices for those of North America.
Meyer, Dr. Frz., a. o. Prof. Univ., Tübingen. *Math.**
Meyer, Dr. Lothar, Prof. Chem., Univ., Tübingen. *Chem.*
Meyer, Prof. Dr. O. E., Roy. Univ., Breslau. *Phys.**
Michael, A., Waldenburg (Silesia). *Moll.*
Michaelis, Prof. Dr. A., Polytechnicum, Carlsruhe.
Michel, Prof. A., Mühlhausen. *Ent.*
Michow, Dr., Steinthorwall 47, Hamburg. *Ent.*
Mieg, rue des Bons-Enfants, Mulhouse (Alsace). *Geol.*
Mieg-Kroh, Mathieu, Prés. du Comité du Mus. historique de Mulhouse (Alsace). *Geol.**
Milcke, F. W., Charlottenstr. 79, Potsdam. *Coleopt.*
Miller, Dr. Conr., Essendorf (Würtemberg). *Moll.*
Miller, Prof. W. D., A.B., D.D.S., 2 Hausvoigtei Platz, Berlin. *Oral Sci., Mic., Chem.; special study, Dental caries.* C.
Miller, Wilhelm von, o. Prof. der Chemie und Conserv. des Chem. Labor. an der technischen Hochschule, München. *Chem. Geol., Chem.*
Minks, Dr. Arthur, Breitestrasse 53-54, Stettin. *Bot.: Lichens (Anatomy and Morphology).**
Minnigerode, Prof. Dr. Bernhard, Greifswald. *Math.*
Moebius, Prof. Dr. Karl A., Berlin, Dir. Zoological Museum. *Zool., Comp. Anat.**
Moeckel, Elisabethstr. 55, Berlin. *Lepid.*
Moehring Herm., Schlosstr. 25, Dresden. *Coleopt.* C. Ex.
Möller, Ludwig, Redakteur von Möllers Deutscher Gärtner-Zeitung, Erfurt, Thüringen. *Phæn. Bot., Fungi, Hort., Carpology.* C. Ex.*

Möller, Max, Ingenieur, Berlin, N. *Meteo. Mechanics.*
Möller, J. D., Präparator für Microscopie, Wedel, Holstein. *Diatoms.**
Monsterberg, Major von, Bamberg. *Moll.*
Moritz, Neue Königstr. 5, Berlin. *Ent.*
Moritz, Dr., Berlin. *Chem.**
Morsbach, Dr. Ad., Dortmund (Westphalia). *Coleopt.*
Möschler, H. B., Krönförstchen, bei Bautzen. *Lepid.**
Mossler, C. G., Director des Geflügelzucht Vereins, Gotha. *Orn.*
Moulin, Le Comte du, Bertholzheim, near Neuberg-on-the-Danube. *Bot.*
Mühll, Prof. K. von der, Univ., Leipsic. *Phys., Math.*
Mühlwenzel, B., Carlsstrasse 43, Breslau. *Lepid.*
Müller, Carl, Sidonienstr. 40, Leipsic. *Diatoms.**
Müller, Clemens, Holzhofgasse, Dresden. *Coleopt.*
Müller, Dr. G., Astrophysikalischen Observatoriums, Potsdam. *Ast.*
Müller-Thurgau, Dr. Herman, Geisenheim. *Bot.**
Müller, J. F., Bot. Garden, Giessen. *Bot.*
Müller, Prof. Dr. Johan W., Univ., Jena. *Anat.*
Müller, Dr. N. F. C., Prof. der Botanik, Münden (Hanover). *Physiological Botany.*
Müller, Dr. Wilhelm, Greifswald. *Ent., Crustacea.* Caterpillars in ex. for South American bat. Ostracoda in exchange.*
Munk, Prof. H., Univ., Berlin. *Physiol.*
Naegeli, Prof. Dr. Ch. Guill. von, Univ., Augustenstrasse 15, Munich. *Bot.*
Narr, Dr. F., Prof. Univ., Munich. *Mechanics.**
Nasse, Prof. H., Univ., Marburg. *Physiol.*
Nasse, Prof. O., Univ., Rostock. *Pharm., Physiol. and Pathol. Chem.*
Nathanson, A., Hamburg. *Lepid.*
Naumann, Bürgerschullehrer, Zwickau. *Coleopt.*
Naumann, Prof. Al., Univ., Giessen. *Chem., Met.*
Naumann, Dr. F., Géra. *Bot.*
Neesen, Prof. Friedrich, Ziethenstrasse 6c, Berlin, W. *Phys.**
Nehring, Alfred, Prof., Ph.D., Pres., etc., Zool. Sammlung der Kgl. Landwirthsch. Hochschule, Berlin. *Vert. Palæo., Zool., Geog. Dist., Vert. Anat., Anth., Vert., Mam., Osteol.* C. Ex.
Nehrkorn, Adolph, Oberamtmann, Riddagshausen, near Brunswick. *Orn., especially Ool.* C. 3,200 species. Ex. eggs from all countries.*
Nerz, Fidelis, Geschäftsführer des Physical. Mech. Instituts von M. Th. Edelmann, Munich. *Physical Science.*
Nessler, Prof. Dr. Jul., Dir. Stat. Agron., Carlsruhe. *Chem.*
Netto, Prof. E., Univ., Strasburg. *Math.*
Neugebauer, Emil, Forst (Nieder Lausitz). *Ent.: Hymenop., Lepid., Coleopt.* C. Ex.
Neumann, Prof. C., Univ., Königsberg. *Pathol., Anat., and Histol.*
Neumann, Prof. K., Univ., Leipsic. *Math.*
Neumayer, Prof. Dr. Georg, Director der Deutschen Seewarte, Hamburg. *Geography, Magnetism, Meteorology, Hydrography.**
Nicolai, Dr. A., Greussen, bei Erfurt. *Ent.*
Niepraschk, J., Dir. Botanic Gardens, Hort. School and Fresh and Salt Water Aquarium, Cologne. *Bot., Phys., Chem., Hort., Meteo., Zool., Min.* Herbarium. Coll. of wood, seeds, artificial fruits, and Minerals.*
Nies, Dr. August, Docent, Grossh. Realschule, I. orden, Mainz. *Nat. Sci., Min.*
Nies, Prof. Dr. Friedrich, Kgl. Acad., Hohenheim, Wurttemberg. *Min., Geognosis.**
Neitschmann, Seidelstr. 3, Berlin. *Lepid.*
Nitsche, Prof. Dr. H., Tharand. *Zool.*

Nitschke, Particulier, Breslau. *Lepid.*
Nitschke, Prof. Dr. Th., Münster. *Bot.*
Nobbe, Dr. Fred, Tharand. *Bot.*
Nöldeke, Celle. *Bot.*, *Geol.*
Noll, Prof. Dr. F. C., Editor of the "Zool. Garten" 96 Oederweg, Frankfort-on-Main. *Zool.**
Nördlinger, Prof. Dr., Forstrath von, Univ., Tübingen. *Bot.*, *Zool.*, *Wood Technol.*
Northagel, Prof. D. Hermann, Univ., Jena. *Pathol.*
Nöther, Prof. M., Univ., Erlangen. *Math.*
Nötling, Dr. Fritz, Docent der Paläontologie und Geologie an der Universität, Königsberg, Prussia. *Palæo.*, *Geol.*
Nuhn, Prof. A., Univ., Heidelberg. *Osteol.*, *Anat.*
Nussbaum, Dr. Joh. Nep. Ritter von, k. b. Geheimrat, Universitäts Professor, Munich, Bavaria.*
Nussbaum, Prof. M., Univ. Bonn. *Anat.*
Nüsslin, Prof. Otto, D. Sc. Polytechnicum, Carlsruhe. *Zool.*, *Ichth.*, *Entomology*, *Protozoa.* C. Ex.
Obenauf, Gustav, Zeitz bei Leipsic. *Lepid.*, *Coleopt.* Will buy and exchange.*
Oberbeck, Prof. Dr. Anton, Univ., Halle. *Phys.*
Oberndorfer, Rudolf, Lehrer der Universität der Naturkunde und k. Landschule, Günzburg. *Ent.*, *especially Coleopt.*, *Malocology.* C. Ex. Wishes first-class specimens of L. and F. W. shells from all countries.
Oebbeke, Dr., Director d. Geol. Inst. u. Conservator d. Min. Sammlung, Prof. Univ., Erlangen (Bavaria). *Min.*, *Crystal.*, *Petrog.*, *Geol.*, *Palæo.**
Oertzen, von, Brunn, bei Neubrandenburg. *Lepid.*
Oettel, Aug., Karmeliterstrasse 2, Munich. *Ent.*
Olbocter, Mellen, bei Dramburg. *Coleopt.*, *Lepid.*
Olearius, Alfred, Mem. Naturhistor. Vereins, Elberfeld. *Ent.: Lepid.* C. Ex.
Olearius, Robert, Harburg. *Lepid.* C. Ex.
Oppenheim, Prof. Dr. H., Blumeshof 1, Berlin, W. *Ast.*, *Photog.**
Oppenheim, Paul, Heidelberg. *Lepid.*
Oppermann, C., Mittelschullehrer, Zerbst, Anhalt. *Coleopt.* C. Ex.*
Orth, Prof. A., Univ., Berlin. *Org. Chem.*, *Bot.*
Orth, Prof. J., Univ., Göttingen. *Pathol. Anat. and Histol.*
Osann, Dr. A., Heidelberg. *Geol.*, *Min.*
Ost. H., Univ., Leipsic. *Histol.*, *Chem.*
Osten Sacken, Baron Charles Robert, Heidelberg. *Dipt.* C. Ex.*
Osterbind, Aug., Dr. Med., Fedderwarden, Wilhelmshaven. *Ent.*, *Orn.**
Ostwald, Prof. Dr. Wilhelm, Brüderstr. 34, Leipzig. *Chem.*, *especially chemical affinity.**
Otting, Count Max, Wiesenfelden. *Moll.*
Ottmer, Julius, Dr. Philol., Prof. und Vorstand des Mineralogischen Cabinets der Herzogl. tech. Hochschule, Braunschweig. *Min.*, *Geol.*, *Palæo.*
Paasch, Dr., Stralauerbrücke 4, Berlin. *Coleopt.*
Pabst, Prof. Dr. Moritz, Chemnitz. *Phæn. Bot.*, *Geol.*, *Chem.*, *Phys.*, *Lepid.* C. Ex.
Pagenstecher, Dr. Arnold, Taunustrasse 22, Wiesbaden. *Lepid.* C. Ex.
Pagenstecher, Prof. Dr. Heinrich A., Dir. Zool. Mus., Hamburg. *Zool.**
Pape, Prof. C., Univ. Königsberg. *Phys.*
Pappenheim, Dr. Samuel, Univ., Giessen, Berlin. *Math.*
Passavant, Th., Oberlindaue 78, Frankfort-on-Main. *Hymenop.*, *Dipt.*
Pasch, Prof. M. Paul, Unter den Linden 64, Berlin. *Coleopt.*, *Lepid.*
Paulisch, R., Fruchtstr. 77, Berlin. *Coleopt.*

Paulsen, P., Königstrasse 21, Flensburg. *Ool.*
Pauly, Dr. A., Veterinärstr. 5, Munich. *Ent.*
Pauly, Peter August, Ph.D., Privat-Docent Kgl. Univ., Hess-Strasse 54, II, r., Munich. *Zool.*
Pausch, Prof. A., Kiel. *Anat.*, *Anth.*
Pazschke, Dr. O., Leipzig-Reudnitz. *Fungi.*
Penzoldt, Prof. Franz, Univ., Erlangen. *Pathol.*
Perlenfein, G., Gr. Eschenheimergasse 76, Frankfort-on-Main. *Bot.*
Perring, W., Bot. Gardens of the Univ., Berlin. *Zool.*, *Bot.*
Pertsch, Dr. Wilhelm, Geh. Hofrath u. Director der Herzogl. Landes-Bibliothek zu Gotha. *Arch.*
Peter, Dr. Albert, Bot. Gardens, Munich. *Bot.*
Peters, Dr., Neu-Strelitz. *Ent.*
Peters, A., Salzdahlumerstrasse, Brunswick. *Lepid.*
Peters, Dr. C. W. F., Univ., Kiel. *Ast.*
Petersen, Hartwig, Hamburg. *Moll.**
Petersen, Dr. Theodor, Frankfort-on-Main. *Chem.*, *Geol.**
Pethö, Gyula, Munich. *Geol.*
Petri, Dr. Camillo, Strassburg. *Fossil Brachiopoda.*
Petry, Arthur, Schwanthalerstr. 67, Munich. *Ent.*
Petsch, Gustav, Wiesbaden. *Lepid.*
Pettenkofer, Prof. Dr. Max von, Univ., Munich. *Hygiene.*
Petzholdt, Dr. Alexander, Prof. Emeritus, Wirklicher Staatsrath, zur Zeit, Freiburg, Baden.
Pfaffzeller, Franz, Munich. *Ent.*
Pfeffer, Georg, Ph.D., Naturhistorisches Museum, Hamburg. *Anat.*, *Ichth.*, *Osteol.*, *Crustacea*, *Moll.*, *Radiates.*
Pfeffer, Prof. W., Univ. Leipzig, Director des botanischen Instituts und des botanischen Gartens.*
Pfeiffer, Eisenberg. *Lepid.* C. Ex.
Pfitzer, Prof. Dr. E., Dir. Bot. Garden, Heidelberg.
Pfitzner Dr. W., Strassburg. *Anat.*
Pfleiderer, Prof. E., Univ., Tübingen. *Phil.*, *Anth.*
Pflüger, Prof. E. F. W., Univ., Bonn. *Physiol.*
Pfützner, J., Alexandrinenstr. 37, Berlin. *Lepid.*
Philippi, Prof. A., Univ., Giessen. *Arch.*
Physikalische Gesellschaft, B. Schwalbe, Corresponding Secretary. C. Georgenstrasse 30-31, Berlin.*
Pietsch, Dr., Glogau. *Coleopt.*
Pinkert, Ernst, Zool. Garten, Leipzig.
Pinner, Adolf, Ph.D., Univ., Berlin. *Chem.**
Pinzger, Prof. Dr., Reichenbach. *Bot.*
Pirngruber, G., Gaisach bei Tölz. *Ent.*
Pitsch, Gymnasial-Oberlehrer, Stettin. *Coleopt.*
Planck, Dr. Max, Privat-Docent a. d. Kgl. Universität, Barerstrasse 48, II, Munich. *Physics.*
Planeth, Dr. H., Schwerin, Mecklenburg. *Con.*, *Min.*
Planitz, v. d., Neidschütz bei Naumburg. *Ent.*
Pochhammer, Prof. L., Univ., Kiel. *Math.*
Podlech, Theodor, Brandenburg. *Orn.*, *Coleopt.* C. Ex.
Pohlig, Dr. J., Docent, Univ., Bonn. *Geol.*, *Palæo.**
Polakowsky, Dr. H., Augustastr. 49, Berlin. *Flora of Costa Rica.**
Poleck, Dr. T., Prof. Chem., Roy. Univ., Breslau.*
Pollack, Wilhelm, Kaufmann, Südefelderstrasse, Münster. *Ent.*: *Lepid.* C. Ex.
Pollmann, Dr., Agric. Acad., Poppelsdorf bei Bonn. *Apiculture*, *Geog.*, *Bot.*
Polstorff, Prof. C., Univ., Göttingen. *Chem.*
Pompetzki, Josef, Breslau. *Gen. Science.*

Poppe, Albrecht, Vegesack near Bremen. *Zool.* (*Acar.*, *Pedicul.*, *Coppepoda*).
Poscharsky, G. A., Curator Royal Bot. Gardens, Dresden. *Bot.**
Post, Prof. Dr. J., Technische Hochschule, Hanover. *Chem.*
Posth, F., Bischwiller. *Ent.: Lepid.*
Potonie, Dr. Henry, Dorotheenstr. 42, Berlin, N. W. 7. *Bot.**
Pott, Dr. Rob., Docent, Univ., Jena. *Agric.*, *History of Chem.*
Pougnet, Eugène, Landorff (Lorraine). *Bot.*, *Chem.*, *Phys.*, *Bibliog.*, *Arch.*, *Tox.*, *Osteol.*, *Myol.*, etc. C. Ex.
Prantl, Dr. Karl, Professor der Botanik an der k. Forstlehranstalt, Aschaffenburg. *Bot.*, *Filices.* C.*
Prazmowski, Dr. Adam, Hohestr. 11, Leipsic. *Bot.*
Preiss, Dr. Johann A. L., Herzberg-on-Harz. *Bot.*
Preuss, Wilhelm Heinrich, Navigation-Lehrer, Elsfleth. *Physical Science, Biology.* C. Ex. Beetles of the North of Germany for others.*
Preussing, Dr., Benburg. *Bot.* C. Ex.
Preyer, Thierry William, Prof. Univ., Jena. *Physiol. Chem.*, *Physiol.*, *Gen. Biol.*, *Emb.*, *Psychology.*
Preyer, W., Professor Universität, Jena. *Physiology of Embryology.*
Pricbisch, Telegraphen-Secretär, Leipsic. *Dipt.*, *Bot.**
Pringsheim, Dr. A., Docent, Univ., Munich. *Math.*
Pringsheim, Dr. N., Professor, Königin-Augustastr. 49, Berlin, W. *Bot.*, *Phys.**
Progel, Dr. A., Waldmünchen. *Bot.*
Prym, Prof. F., Univ., Würzburg. *Mathematics.*
Püngler, Pet. Jac., Aix-la-Chapelle. *Lepid.*
Purckhard, Joh. Tar Ludw., Frankfort a. M., Dominikanergasse 8, *Lepid.* C.
Puttrich, Dr. Ludwig, Brühl 64, Leipsic. *Lepid.*
Putze, H., Uhlenhorst, Hamburg. *Lepid.*
Quapp, Dr., Leer. *Coleopt.*, *Lepid.*
Quedenfeldt, Frobenstr. 29, Berlin. *Coleopt.*
Quellhorst, Fr., Lehrer, Poststr., Nienburg a. Weser. *Coleopt.*, *Lepid.**
Quenstedt, Prof. F. A. v., Univ., Tübingen. *Geog.*, *Nat. Hist.*
Quincke, Prof. G., Univ., Heidelberg. *Optics*, *Elect.*
Raddatz, Ad., Director der höhern Bürgerschule, Rostock. *Dipt.*
Rademann, Malchin (Mecklenburg). *Ent.*
Radicke, Prof. G., Univ., Bonn. *Math.*
Rabt Rückhard, Dr. Hermann, Genthinerstr. 5a, Berlin. *Mic.*, *Emb. and Anat. of Vert.*, *Anth.*, *Eth.**
Radlkofer, Dr. Ludwig, Universitätsprofessor, ordentliches Mitglied der Königl. bayerischen Academie der Wissenschaften, München (Bavaria). *Bot.**
Rammelsberg, Prof. E., Roy. Univ., Berlin. *Chem.*
Ramsay, Prof. Dr. Wilhelm, Schönebergerstrasse 10, Berlin. *Chem.*
Ranke, Dr. J., Docent, Univ., Munich. *Gen. Nat. Hist.*
Rassmann, gr. Plauenschegasse 9, Dresden. *Coleopt.* C. Ex.
Rath, Prof. Gerhard von, Bonn. *Geol.*, *Min.*, *Crystal.*, *Lithol.* C. Ex.
Ratibor, Herzog Victor von, Durchlaucht, in Rauden und Corsey, (Schlesien), Mem. Ent. Vereins, Berlin. *Ent.**
Rathke, Prof. B., Halle (Saxony). *Org. Chem.*
Rathke, Carl, Alexandrinenstrasse 41, Berlin, S. *Chem.*
Rau, Dr., Hohenheim, near Stuttgart. *Bot.*
Rauber, Prof. A., Univ., Leipsic. *Anat.*, *Emb.*
Rechten, G., Lehrer, Stade, (Hannover). *Coleopt.*, *Lepid.**
Recklinghausen, Prof. F. von, Univ., Strasburg. *Pathol. Anat. and Histol.*
Reess, Prof. Dr. Max F. F., Univ., Erlangen. *Bot.**

Rehm, H., M.D., Ratisbonne. *Bot., Lichenology, Mycology, Ascomycetes,* for all Discomycetes, Editor Ascomyc. exes. fasc. XIX. will be continued.*
Reiber, Ferdinand, 8 Kronenburgerstrasse, Strasburg. *Photog., Bibliog., Arch., Ent.: Coleopt., Hemipt.* C. Ex.*
Reiber, Ferdinand, Faubourg de Saverne 8, Strasburg (Alsace). *Coleopt., Hemipt.**
Reichardt, Prof. Dr. Edward, Univ., Jena. *Chem.*
Reichenbach, Prof. Dr. H. G., Dir. Bot. Garden, Hamburg. *Orchids.*
Reichenow, Dr. Anton, Wissenschaftlicher Assist. am. Kgl. Zool. Mus. und Schriftführer der Allgemeinen Deutschen Ornithol.-Gesellschaft zu Berlin, Grossbeerenstrasse 52, Berlin, S. W. *Orn., Herp.**
Reichert, Prof. Dr. Carl B., Univ., Berlin. *Anat.*
Reichlin-Meldegg, Frh. Gustav von, Munich. *Coleopt., Lepid., spec. Micro-lepid.*
Reinecke, Lehrer, Gernrode. *Coleopt., Lepid.* C. Ex.
Reinhard, Dr. Hermann, Präsid. d. Landes-Medicinal-Collegium, Johannisstrasse 14, Dresden. *Hymenopt.**
Reinhardt, Küchengartenstr. 11, Neureudnitz, bei Leipsic. *Lepid.*
Reinhardt, Dr. O., Oranienstr. 45, Berlin, S. *Moll.*
Reiff, Rep. Univ., Tübingen. *Math.*
Reimers, D., Aabenraa, Sleswick. *Bot.*
Rein, G. G., Ph.D., Prof. of Geog. in the Univ. of Bonn.*
Reinke, Prof. J., Univ., Göttingen. *Bot., Mic.*
Reinsch, Paul Friedrich, Erlangen, Bavaria. *Mic., Bot., Geol., Paleo.* Ex. Phanerogams and Cryptogams (including Algæ) of Europe, Mic. sections of coal, minerals, and rocks.*
Reiss, Dr. Wilhelm, Potsdamerstrasse 69, Berlin, W. *Geol., Eth., Geog.*
Rehnisch, Prof. Dr. Julius Eduard, Göttingen. *Phys., Gen. Biol., Anth.**
Remak, Dr. Ernst, Privat-Docent, Univ., für Nerven-Pathologie, Mauerstrasse 40, Berlin. *Pathol.*
Rennert, Carl, Mühlenbach 24, Cologne-on-the-Rhine. *Org. Chem.*
Reichenau, Lieut. Wilh. von, Conservator des Museums, Mainz. *Lepid.*
Reichenbach, Heinrich, Frankfort-on-Main. *Zool.*
Rensch, Rector, Nostizstrasse 14, Berlin. *Bot.*
Renz, Dr. Wilh. Theodor, Kgl. Baderarzt und Geheimer Hofrath und Vorstand u. Cus. der Anstalt, Baden-Baden. *Balneology, Neurol., Electricity.* C. Ex.
Rëttig, E., Inspector Bot. Gardens, Jena. *Bot.**
Reusch, Prof. Dr. F. E. von, Univ., Tübingen. *Bot.*
Rey, Eugene, Ph.D., Flossplatz 11, Leipsic. *Mam., Orn., Ool., Lepid., Moll., Radiates, Sponges, Protozoa.* C.*
Reye, Dr. Theodor, Prof. Univ., Strassburg. *Math.*
Rhone, A., Webervorstadt 34, Zittau. *Nat. Hist.*
Ribbe, Carl, Zöllnerstr. 23, Dresden (at present in the East Indies). *Ent., Lepid., Coleopt., Moll., Birds, nests, eggs.**
Ribbe, Heinrich, Zöllnerstr. 23. Dresden. *Mam., Orn., Ool., Gen. Ent., Moll.* C. Ex.*
Richter, Dr., Pankow, n. Berlin. *Coleopt.*
Richter, Fritz, Eppelsheim, Grünstadt. *Lepid.*
Richter, Otto, Leipsic. *Lepid.*
Richter, Paul, Lehrer, Aeussere Hospitalstrasse 7. *Bot., Algæ.* C. Ex. Algæ of all kinds for F. W. Algæ.
Richter, Prof. V. v., Univ., Breslau. *Chem.*
Richter, Waldemar, Wettinerstr. 43, Dresden.
Richters, Ferd., Ph.D., Oberlehrer, Frankfort-on-Main. *Crustacea.**

Richthofen, Prof. Dr. Ferdinand Baron von, Berlin W., 117 Kurfürstenstrasse.*
Riecke, Prof., Göttingen. *Phys.*
Riedel, Ferd., Sulz am Neckar. *Lepid.* C.*
Riemann, Dr. Carl, Gorlitz. Dealer in all kinds of natural curiosities. C. Desires to buy and Ex.*
Riemenschneider, C., Bartüsserstrasse 11, Nordhausen. *Moll.*
Riessland, Rob., Badergasse, Dresden. *Coleopt.* C. Ex.
Rindfleisch, Prof. G. E., Univ., Würzburg. *Pathol. Anat.**
Rindfleisch, A., Askanischestr. 47, Dessau. *Lepid.* C. Ex.
Rinecker, Prof. Dr. Franz von, Univ., Würzburg. *Syphilis, Dermatology, Psychiatry.*
Ritter, Jr., Wiesbaden. *Lepid.*
Ritthausen, Prof. H., Univ., Königsberg. *Chem.*
Roder, Adolf, Wiesbaden. *Lepid.*
Röder, Victor von, Hoym (Anhalt). *Diptera.*
Rodig, C., Mikroscopisches Institut, Wandsbeck. 6. Hamburg.*
Rodewald, Dr. H., Inst. Physiol., Göttingen. *Bot.*
Roemer, Ferdinand, Royal University, Breslau, Prussia. *Geol., Palæo.* C. Ex. Palæozoic and other fossils of Europe for North American specimens.*
Roeper, Dr. Johann A. C., Director Botanical Gardens, Prof. Univ., Rostock.
Roessler, Dr. Adolf, Wiesbaden. *Local Lepid.* C. Ex.
Roger, Dr. O., Schwandorf. *Coleopt.*
Rohde, Dr. Emil, Oberlehrer Striegauerpl., Breslau. *Chem.*
Rohde, G., Hohenregstr. 10, Pottsdam. *Coleopt.**
Rohde, Walther, Albrechtstr. 7, Magdeburg. *Ent.*
Rohleder, J. O., Gopliz, Leipsic. *Mam., Orn.*
Rohn, Dr. K., Docent, Univ., Leipsic. *Math.*
Rohrmann, Bernstadt (Silesia). *Moll.*
Rohweder, J., Husum. *Orn., Ool.**
Röll, Dr. Julius, Lehrer an der höh. Mädchenschule, Darmstadt. *Bot., Mosses of Thüringen.* C. Ex. Mosses of Germany for those of America.
Römer, Prof. F., Univ., Breslau. *Min., Geognosy, Palæo.*
Römer, W., Hildeschcim. *Palæo., Arch.*
Röntgen, Prof. W. C., Univ., Giessen. *Phys.*
Rosanes, Prof. J., Univ., Breslau. *Math.**
Rose, Dr. Edmund, Mariannenplatz 3, Berlin, S. O. *Phys., Anat.* C.
Rose, F., Prof., Univ., Strasburg (Alsace.) *Chem.*
Rosenberger, Prof. A., Univ., Halle. *Math., Ast.*
Rosenberger, Dr. Johannes A., Docent, Univ., Würzburg. *Mic., Osteol. Mycol., Chirurgy.*
Rosenbohm, Eug., Bot. Gardens, Königsberg. *Bot.*
Rosenbuch, Prof. H. F., Univ., Heidelberg. *Min., Geol., Petrography.*
Rosenhain, Prof. J. G., Univ., Königsberg. *Math.*
Rosenthal, Prof. I., Univ., Erlangen. *Physiology.*
Rossbach, Prof. Dr. A., Roy. Univ., Berlin. *Philol., Arch., Hist.*
Rossi, K. Gustave de, Neviges. *Coleopt.*
Rostock, Michael, Lehrer em., Dretschen, jetzt Gaussig bei Seitschen. *Neuropt., Bot.* C.*
Roth, Prof. G., Univ., Strasburg. *Math.*
Roth, Prof. Dr. Justus, Univ., Berlin. *Min., Geol.*
Roth, Insp. Bot. Gardens, Muskau (Silesia.) *Bot.*
Roth, H. L. C., Dr. Phil., Frankfurt a. M., Rhönstrasse 57. *Lepid.* C.
Rottenbach, Prof., Meiningen. *Bot.*
Roux, Dr. W., Prof., Univ., Breslau. *Menschliche Anatomie u. Entwickelungmechanik.**

Rudel, Wilhelm, Ohlauerstr. 68, Breslau. *Lepid.*
Rüdorff, Prof. Dr., Polytechnicum, Berlin. *Chem.*
Rüdinger, Prof. N., Univ., Munich. *Anat.*
Rudow, Dr. F., Perleberg. *Orthopt.*, *Hemipt.*, *Hymenop.*
Ruge, Dr. G., Docent, Univ., Heidelberg. *Osteol.*, *Anat.*
Rügheimer, Dr. L., Docent, Univ., Kiel. *Chem.*
Rühe, Robert, Klavier und Mikroskopir-Lampen-Fabrik, Landsberg a. W. *Coleopt.*, *Lepid.**
Rühter, Dr. Reinhardt, Director, Hofrath, Saalfeld. *Geol.*, *Palæo.* C.
Rümker, Georg, M. A., Director der Sternwarte, Reichs-Prufungs-inspector für die Nautischen Prufungen der Deutschen Handels-Marine, Abtheilungs-Vorstand der Deutschen Sternwarte, Hamburg. *Astronomy and Navigation.* C. Library of Astronomical and Nautical works.
Rummer, Prof. F., Univ., Heidelberg. *Math.*, *Mechanics.*
Rupp, Lehrer, Schweidnitz. *Coleopt.*
Rüss, Karl F. O., Ph.D., Bellealliancestrasse 81, Berlin, S. W. *Orn.* C. Herausgeber der "Isis" und der "Gefiederten Welt." Verfasser des "Lehrbuch der Stubenvogelpflege," "Abrichtung und Zucht," etc.*
Rüst, Dr., Gr. Eicklingen, bei Celle. *Ent.*
Rüst, Dr. D., Sedanstrasse 22, Hannover. *Palæon.*, *Mic.*, *Spec. Radiolaria.* Ex.*
Saalmüller, Max, K. Pr. Oberslieutenant a. D., Bockenheim (near Frankfort-on-Main), Obere Königstrasse. *Ent.*, *Lepid.*, *Europ. Exot.*, including *Microlep.*, partic. Madagascar. C. Ex.*
Ruthe, R., Bärwalde. *Bryol.*
Rutter, Dr., Neustadt. *European eggs.* C. Ex.
Saalschütz, Prof. L., Univ., Königsberg. *Math.*
Saare Dr., Invalidenstrasse 42, Berlin, N. *Agric.*, *Chem.*
Sachs, Prof. Dr. Jul. von, Univ., Dir. Bot. Gardens, Würzburg. *Bot.*
Sachse, C., Altenkirchen, Reg. Bez. Cobleny. *Ool.* Wishes to sell his Collection of 8,000 eggs; many rare specimens.*
Sachsse, Dr. Rob., Univ., Leipsic. *Bot.*, *Chem.*
Sadebeck, Prof. Dr. Richard, Prof. der Bot. und Dir. des Bot. Mus. und des Laboratoriums für Waarenkunde, Präs. Gesell. f. Bot. Steinthorplatz, Hamburg. *Physiology and Anat. of plants*, *Morphology*, *Mycology*, *Bot.**
Saderbeck, Dr., Prof. in dem Königl. Geodesischen Institut, Steglitzerstr. 4*f*, Berlin, W. *Geodesy.*
Saifert, J., Bot. Gardens, Erlangen. *Bot.*
Salkowski, Prof. Dr. E., Patholog. Inst. der Kgl. Charité, Berlin. *Chem.*
Salkowski, Prof. H., Akad., Münster. *Chem.**
Salm-Salm, Prince zu, Anhalt, Westphalia. *Moll.*
Salmin, St. Pauli, Hamburg. *Lepid.*
Salomon, C., Bot. Gardens, Würzburg. *Bot.*
Samter, Dr., Director, Königsberg. *Ent.*
Sandberger, Prof. C. L. F., Univ., Würzburg. *Geol.*, *Min.*, *Palæo.*
Sander, Dr. Julius, Belle-Alliancestrasse 15, Berlin, S.W. *Physiology and Medicine.*
Sanio, Carl Gustav, Ph.D., Lyck (Ost-Preuss.). *Bot.: Phæn.*, *Crypt. and Mosses.**
Sauber, A., Hamburg. *Lepid.* C. Ex.
Saulcy, Fél. de, rue Chatillion 3, Metz. *Coleopt.*
Schaaffhausen, Prof. Dr. Hermann, Univ., Bonn. *Palæo.*, *Geol.*, *Micr.*, *Biol.*, *Anat.*, *Anthr.*, *Arch.*, *Ethn.* C.*
Schabert, J. W., Sec. Soc. Hort. of Hamburg, Altona, Eimsbüttel Sandweg 25*b*, Hamburg. *Bot.*
Schacko, Gustav, Waldemarstrasse 14, Berlin, S.O. *Moll.*, *Mic.*, *Fora-*

minifera, Anat., Ostracoda, recent and fossil. C. Ex. samples of deep-sea sounding.*
Schade, Harmstr. 18, Kiel. *Coleopt., Lepid.*
Schaeffer, Prof. H., Univ., Jena. *Math., Physics.*
Schäfer, Calbe. *European Macro-lepid.* C. Ex.
Schäffer, Prof. Dr. Carl J. T. H., Univ., Jena. *Math. and Phys.*
Schafhäutl, Prof. C. F. v., Univ., Munich. *Geog., Petrog.*
Schapler, Obergärtner, Baumschulen, bei Altona. *Coleopt., spec. Curcul.*
Schasz, Dr. E., Radebeul-Dresden. *Gen. Lepid.*
Schattemann, A., Rückertsstr., Schweinfurt. *Lepid.**
Schauf, Dr. Wilhelm, Phonstrasse 119, Frankfort-on-Main, *Geol., Min.*
Schaufuss, Camillo Festiv, Chef der Firma: L. W. Schaufuss sonst E. Klocke. Naturalienhandlung, Dresden. *Zool.* C. Ex. for insects and shells.*
Schaufuss, Dr. Ludwig Wilhelm, Ritter, Director des Museums Ludwig Salvator, near Dresden. *Zool.* Wishes to sell shells and beetles. Wishes foreign *Pselaphidæ and Scydmænidæ.**
Schauinsland, H., Dr., Dir. der Städtischen Sammlungen für Naturgeschichte und Ethnog., Bremen. *Zool.**
Scheffer, Carl Gust., Frankfort a. M., Thiergarten 39. *Lepid.* C.
Scheibler, Dr. C., Prof. der Chemie und Herausgeber der Neuen Zeitschrift für die Rübenzucker-Industrie, Buchenstrasse 6, Berlin, W.*
Scheidel, Seb.-Al., Gärtnerweg 60, Frankfort-on-the-Main. *Coleopt.**
Scheiffele, J., Gymnasiumstrasse 10, I, Stuttgart. *Coleopt., Larvæ.*
Schellack, C., Hochmeisterstr. 4, N. Berlin. *Lepid.**
Schellhass, Prof. v., Landshut (Bavaria). *Chem., Nat. Hist.*
Schenk, Prof. Dr. August von, Univ., Leipsic. *Bot.*
Scherenberg, Grohn, near Vegesack. *Orn.*
Schering, Prof. E., Univ., Göttingen. *Math., Phys., Analyt. Mechanics.**
Schieck, F. W., Halleschestr. 14, Berlin (S.W. II.). *Coleopt.**
Schiefferdecker, Dr. P., Docent, Univ., Rostock. *Emb.*
Schick, Dr. Oscar, Professor am Gymnasium, Weimar. *Math., Phys.*
Schiefferdecker, Dr., Königsberg. *Coleopt.*
Schilde, Johannes, Bautzen. *Lepid.* C. Ex.
Schiller, Carl, Bautzuerstr. 28, Dresden. *Mosses, Algæ. Diatoms, Desmids, Ent.: Hemipt., Neuropt.* C. Ex.*
Schilsky, J., Schönhauser-Allée 39*a*, Berlin. *Ent. Coleopt.**
Schindler, Bahnexpeditor in Regensburg. *Gen. Ent.*
Schirm, Dr. J. W., Wiesbaden. *Lepid.*
Schirmer, Engelufer 12, Berlin. *Ent.*
Schirmer, F., Bahnhofstr., Wiesbaden. *Moll.*
Schirmer, H. L. W., Charlottenburg. *Gen. Ent.*
Schirmer, Hermann, Mannheim in Baden. *Lepid.*
Schiwon, Berthold, Breslau. *Lepid.*
Schlechtendal, Dr. D. v., Halle. *Plant Diseases, Insect Galls, Hymenopt.* C. Ex.
Schlemm, Dr. Oscar, Rastenburg. *Moll.*
Schlickum, J., Winningen. *Bot.*
Schlieben, Major von, Alberstadt, Dresden. *Ent.**
Schliephacke, Dr. Karl, Waldau, near Osterfeld, Merseburg (Prussia). *Bryol., Mosses. C.* Ex.
Schlömilch, Prof. Dr. Oscar, Dresden. *Math.**
Schlosser, Glückstr. 1, Munich. *Lepid.*
Schuberg, August, Akademienstrasse 28, Karlsruhe. *Zool.*
Schlumberger-Dollfus, Jean, Guebwiller, Alsace. *Coleopt.*
Schlüter, Prof. Dr. Clemens, Bonn. *Palæo., Geognosy.*
Schlüter, Wilhelm, Naturalist, Halle-on-Saale. *Zool., Vert., Mam., Orn., Ool., Tax., Osteol., Moll.* C.*
Schmetzer, Carl, Hospitalstr. 22, Leipsic. *Lepid.*

Schmid, Anton, Regensburg. *Micro-lepid., Larvæ.*
Schmid, P., Hallischestr. 8, Merseberg. *Coleopt.**
Schmidt, Klosterfelde, bei Basdorf. *Ent.*
Schmidt, Oberlehrer, Hamburg, St. Georg Kreuzweg 4. *Syst. Bot.*
Schmidt, Obergartner, Flottbecker Baumschule, bei Hamburg. *Coleopt., Curculionidæ.*
Schmidt, Pfarrer in Zülzefitz, bei Labes. *Coleopt., Con.* C. Ex.
Schmidt, Prof. A., Univ., Heidelberg. *Geol., Min.*
Schmidt, Adolphe, Aschersleben. *Diatoms.*
Schmidt, Prof. Ernst, Ph.D., Univ., Halle. *Chem.*
Schmidt, Franz, Zelle'scher Weg, Dresden. *Lepid.*
Schmidt, Georges, rue de Bâl 23, Colmar (Alsace). *Coleopt., Dipt., Hemipt., Hymenop., Bot.* C. Ex.*
Schmidt, Dr. Heinr., Docent, Wismar. *Coleopt.*
Schmidt, Rev. Johannes, Gollwitz, bei Brandenburg. *Coleopt.* C. Ex. Histeridæ.*
Schmidt, Prof. Dr. J. A., Univ., Heidelberg. Mittelstr. 37, Hamburg. *Bot.*
Schmidt, Dr. Maximilian, Dir. Zool. Gardens, Berlin.
Schmidt, Prof. Dr. O., Thierarzneischule, Stuttgart. *Chem.*
Schmidt, O., Weimar. *Moll.*
Schmidt, Prof. Osc., Univ., Strasburg. *Zool., Mic.*
Schmidt, Dr. Otto, Oberlehrer, Breslau. *Math., Phys.*
Schmidt, Rev. Theodore, Klosterfelde, Potsdam. *Coleopt.* C. Ex.
Schmidtlein, Dr. Richard, Asst. am Zool. Inst., Leipsic. *Zool.**
Schmiedeknecht, Dr. Otto, Gumperda bei Kahla, Sachsen-Altenburg. Large coll. of European Hymenop. Sells or Ex. Desires exotic Hymen.
Schmidt, Prof. Dr. R., Polytechnicum, Dresden. *Chem.*
Schmitz, F., Prof. Dr., Greifswald. *Bot.*
Schmolling, Strasburg. *Lepid.*
Schneidemühl, Georg K., Theirarzeneischule, Hanover, Prussia, *Histol., Anat., Ent.*
Schneider, Prof. Dr. A., Roy. Univ., Breslau. *Zool.*
Schneider, Prof. E. R., Univ., Berlin. *Phys.*
Schneider, Dr. Karl, Jr., Berlin. *Geol.*
Schneider, Dr. Oscar, Portikusstr. 4, Dresden. *Physical Geography, Coleopt.* C. Ex. European Caucasian beetles for foreign amber and insects of all countries.
Schneider, Dr. W. G., Breslau. *Mycology.*
Schneider, Lehrer, Frankfort-on-the-Main. *Coleopt.*
Schöbel, Pfarrer, Ottmuth, Krappitz (Upper Silesia). *Lichens, Phanerogams.*
Schoder, Prof., Dir. Meteo. Central Station, Stuttgart. *Meteo.*
Schoeler, Prof. Dr. Heinrich Leopold, Karlstrasse 2, Berlin. *Physics, Optics, Anth., Ophthalmology.*
Scholz, Prof. M., Univ., Greifswald, *Min.*
Schönfeld, v. Major, Neuthenstr. 11, Mainz. *Coleopt.* C.*
Schönfeld, Prof. E., Roy. Univ., Bonn. *Ast., Math.*
Schöppe, Eisenberg. *Lepid.* C. Ex.
Schottelius, Prof. M., Univ., Marburg *Pathol. Anat. and Histol.*
Schottky, Dr. F., Docent, Univ., Breslau. *Math.*
Schrader, Dr. Carl, Observator der Hamburger Sternwarte, Hamburg. *Astronomy.*
Schramm, Max von, Margarethenstr. 36, I, Breslau. *Geog.*
Schreiber, C., Lehrer, Markt 8, Bitterfeld. *Coleopt.* C. Ex.
Schreiber, M., Esslingen (Württemberg). *Gen. Ent.* C. Ex.
Schreiber, H., Ilfeld a. Harz. *Lepid.**
Schreitmuller, Professor, Poliergasse 8, Dresden. *Lepid.* C. Ex.

Schroeder, Dr. Ernst, Prof. a. d. Techn. Hochschule, Carlsruhe in Baden. *Math., Logic.**
Schröder, Regierungsstr. 4, Cöslin. *Coleopt.* C. Ex.
Schröder, Richard, Dr. Phil., Rector des Realprogymnasiums 6, Naumberg a. Saale. *Moll.* C. Ex.*
Schroederstift, Ed. Otto, 29, Louisenstrasse, II, Hamburg. *Bot.*
Schroeter, Dr. Julius, Breslau. *Mycol.*
Schröter, Prof. Dr. H. E., Univ., Breslau. *Math.**
Schröter, Walter, Mannheim in Baden. *Lepid.*
Schuchardt, Carl, Sandstr. 2, Darmstadt. *Coleopt.*
Schuchardt, Dr. Theodor, Manufacturing Chemist, Dealer in minerals, Supplier of new and rare medicinal products, Gorlitz. *Bot., Min., Chem.* C. Ex.*
Schüle, W., Dir. der Kais. Obst- und Gartenbau-Schule, Grafenberg bei Brumath (Elsass). *Bot., Zool., Pomol.**
Schulgin, Dr., Univ., Gaisbergstrasse 14, Heidelberg. *Gen. Zool., Emb., Brachiopoda.*
Schülter, Prof., Univ., Bonn. *Geol.*
Schultes, Dr. J. H., Schwanthalerstr. 41, Munich. *Bot.*
Schultheiss, Benj., Königstr. 43, Munich. *Coleopt.*
Schultz, Prof. Dr. A., Roy. Univ., Breslau. *Arch.*
Schultz, Dr. A., Finsterwalde. *Bot.* C.
Schultz, Dr. G., Docent, Univ., Strasburg. *Chem.*
Schultz, Gustav, Ph.D., Baerwaldstrasse 7, Berlin, S. *Chem.*
Schultze, Prof. Dr. Hugo, Brunswick. *Bot., Chem.*
Schultze, Maj., Mayence. *Coleopt.*
Schultze, Prof. Dr. Bernhard, Univ., Jena. *Gynæcology.**
Schulz, Dr. Jac., Plauen (Vogtland). *Ent.*
Schulze, Prof. Dr. Franz Eilhard, Schellingstr. 9, Berlin. *Zool., Anat., Sponges.* C. Ex.
Schulze, H., Lorengstrasse, Breslau. *Mosses.*
Schulze, Max, Jena. *Bot.*
Schumann, Dr., Reichenback. *Bot.*
Schumacher, Dr. E., Geologische Landesanstalt, Strasburg. *Geol.*
Schumann, Dr. Ch., Breslau. *Bot.*
Schumann, Karl, Dr. Phil., Kustos am König. Bot. Mus. zu Berlin. *Phæn. Bot., Geog. Dist.*
Schunke, Lottumstr. 25, Berlin. *Ent.*
Schupplie, Theodor, Beilau, near Neisse, Silesia. *Bot.*
Schur, Dr., Docent, Univ., Leipsic. *Math.*
Schur, Wilhelm, Prof., Dir. of Obs., Göttingen. *Ast.**
Schurig, Heinrich, Neustadt 3, Halle. *Ent.*
Schurtz, Dr., Zwickau. *Gen. Ent., spec. Orthopt.*
Schwabe, Dr., Stadt Remda, bei Rudolstadt. *Ent.*
Schwalbe, Prof. Dr. Gustav, Univ., Strassburg. *Anat.*
Schwan, Rud., Halle-on-the-Saale. *Bot.*
Schwanert, Dr. Hugo, Prof. Chem., Universität, Greifswald. *Chem.*
Schwartz, Dr., Hallisches Ufer 2e, Berlin. *Diatoms.*
Schwarz, Prof. H. A., Univ., Göttingen, Weender Chaussée, 17 A., *Math.**
Schweiger, Jac., Custos am Maximiliansmuseum, D, 283, Augsburg. *Lepid., Larvæ.* C. Ex.
Schweizer, Wilhelm, Zeitz, I. *Lepid.*
Schwendener, Dr. S., Prof. Univ., Mathäikirchstr. 28, Berlin. *Bot.**
Schwerber, Josef, Lehrer, Gönnersdorf, bei Niederbreisig. *Coleopt.* C. Ex.
Schwoder, Heinrich, Ottmachau. *Coleopt., Lepid., Hemipt.* C. Ex.
Schwoerer, Philippe Auguste Emile, Ingénieur, Secrétaire de M. G. A. Hirn, Colmar (Alsace). *Phys. and Mechanism.**

Scriba, Apotheker in Winnweiler (Bavaria). *Ent.*
Scriba, W., Wimpfen-on-Neckar (Hesse-Darmstadt). *Coleopt.*
Seehaus, Prof. C., Stettin. *Bot.*
Seeliger, Dr. H., Sternwarte, Munich. *Ast.*
Segnitz, Prof. Dr. Gottfried von, Schweinfurt. *Bot.*
Seibert, Hermann, Eberbach-on-the-Neckar (Baden). *Zool.*, *Moll.*, *Palæo.*, *Geol.*, *Min.*, *Anth.* C. Ex. Offers Molluscs from this place, and various forms of Nepheline from Katzenbuckel, and wishes Shells and Minerals.
Seibert, Wilhelm, Wetzlar. *Optics*, *Mushrooms.**
Seibt, Prof., Dr. Phil., Zietenstrasse 18, Berlin, W. *Geol.**
Siedel, Heinrich, Chemnitz. *Bot.*
Seidlitz, Dr. Georg, Königsburg, Prussia. *Coleopt. of Europe.**
Seidel, Prof. Dr. Ludwig, Univ., Munich. *Math.*, *Ast.*
Selenka, Prof. E., Roy. Univ., Erlangen. *Anat.*, *Moll.*
Sell, Prof. Dr. E., Univ., Markthallen A, Berlin, N. W. *Chem.*
Selling, Prof. E., Univ., Würzburg. *Math.**
Semper, Prof. Dr. C., Würzburg. *Moll.*
Semper, Georg, Altona, Prussia. *Indo-Austral. Lepid.*
Sendtner, Ludwigstr. 2, Munich. *Lepid.*
Senft, Dr. Carl F. F., Eisenach. *Bot.*
Seubert, Karl F. O., Privatdocent, Univ., Tübingen. *Inorg. Chem.*
Seubert, Prof. M., Carlsruhe. *Ent.*
Seyffer, Dr. C., Stuttgart. *Ent.*
Sharlok, Gartenstrasse 22, Graudenz, W. Prussia. *Bot.* C. Wishes to buy and sell.
Sickmann, Fr., Lehrer a. d. höhern Privatschule, Province Hannover. *Hymenop.*, *aculeata.* Ex.*
Siebert, Prof. Dr. Fred. L. J., Univ., Jena.
Siemssen, C. A., Lübeck, *Min.*
Simon, Hans, Kaufmann, Stuttgart. *Carabus*, *Ent.* C. Ex. Desires only Paussiden, Pselaphus, Scydmanen, and Mastigus. Will buy and exchange.*
Singer, Prof. Dr. J., Ratisbonne. *Bot.*
Sintenis, P., Kupferberg i. Schlesien, Preussen. *Bot.* C.*
Snell, Prof. C., Univ., Jena. *Math.*
Sochting, Dr., Potsdamerstr. 120, Berlin.
Sodtmann, J. G. J., Pöseldorf, bei Hamburg. *Ent.*
Sohncke, Prof., Dir. Meteo. Central Office, Carlsruhe. *Meteo.*
Solereder, Hans, Dr., Asst. am Bot. Laborat. der Univ., Knöbelstr. 12, Munich. *Bot.**
Solger, Prof. Bernhard, Univ., Greifswald. *Emb.*, *Gen. Biol.*, *Anat.*, *Histol. of Man and Vert.**
Solms-Laubach, Prof. H., Univ., Göttingen. *Bot.*
Sommer, Prof. F., Univ., Greifswald. *Histol.*, *Mic.*, *Comp. Anat.*
Sonnenburg, von, Moosburg. *Coleopt.*
Sorauer, Prof. Dr. Paul, Proskau. *Bot.*
Sorhagen, Dr., Realschullehrer, Hamburg. *Lepid.*
Soyaux, Herman, Stade, Province Hannover. *Bot.*, *Hort.*, *Tropical Agric.*, *Meteo.*, *Anth.*, *Eth*, *Ethnog.*, *Ent.* C.*
Spangenberg, Dr. Fr., Prof. der Zool., a. d. Forstlehranstalt, Arschaffauburg (Baiern). *Zool.*, *Anat.**
Spengel, Dr. J. W., Prof. der Zoologie u. vergl. Anat. der Univ., Dir. des Zool. Inst., Giessen. Editor "Zoological Year-book." (Gustav Fischer, Jena). *Zool.**
Speyer, Dr. Ad., Rhoden, bei Arolsen. *Macro-lepid. of Europe and N. A.* C. Ex.
Spieker, Prof. Dr. Th., Postdam. *Bot.*
Spiess, Ernst, Prof. Chemie, Realgymnasium, Nuremberg. *Chem.*

Spiessen, Prof. August von, Königl. Preuss. Observatorium, Wiesbaden (Hessen-Nassau.) *Systematic Bot. and Geognosy.* C. Ex. German plants for those of other countries.
Spihlmann, A., Parkallee 10, Hamburg. *Bot.*
Spirgatis, Prof. H., Univ., Königsberg, Prussia. *Chem.*
Sprengel, Prof., Bonn. *Bot.*
Sprung, Dr. Adolf, Kön. Preussisch. Meteor. Institut., Berlin. *Meteo.**
Stachelhausen, Dr. Gustav, Barmen. *Coleopt.*
Städel, Prof. W., Univ., Tübingen. *Chem.*
Stahl, Dr. Ernst, Prof. Univ., Jena. *Bot.*
Stahlschmidt, Prof. Polytechnicum, Aix-la-Chapelle. *Chem.*
Standen, Richard S , 15 Schweigerstr., Dresden. *Ent.**
Standfuss, Gustav, Lissa i. Schlesien. *Lepid.* C. Ex.*
Stanke, Wilh., Kunstgartner, Breslau. *Lepid.*
Stannius, Dr. F. H., Prof. Emer., Rostock.
Stark, J., Gewürzmühlenstr. 5, Munich. *Coleopt.**
Staudinger, Otto, Ph.D., "Villa Diana," Blasewitz, bei Dresden. *Lepid., Coleopt.*
Steger, Ph.D., Breslau. *Bot., Palæo.*
Stegmann, Prof. F. L., Univ., Marburg. *Math.*
Stein, B., Inspector of the Botanic Gardens. Breslau. *Lichens., Hort., Alpine Plants.*
Stein, J. P. E. Fedr., Ph.D., Custos Zool. Museum, Brandenburgerstrasse 34, Berlin. *Gen. Ent.*
Steinach, W., Munich. *Moll.*
Steinbrinck, Dr. C., Lippstadt. *Bot.**
Steinmann, Dr. Gustav, Prof. der Geol. und Min., Freiburg (Baden). *Geol., Palæo.* C. Ex. Fossils and Foraminifera.*
Stelzner, Dr. Alfred, Professor, Kgl. Bergakademie, Freiberg (Saxony). *Geol., Min.**
Stenzel, Prof. Dr. Carl G. W., Realschuloberlehrer, Phlauer Stadtgraben 26, Breslau. *Bot., Palæo.**
Stephani, F., Leipsic. *Hepaticæ.* Ex.
Stern, Prof. M. A., Univ., Göttingen. *Math.*
Sterzel, Dr. J. F., Chemnitz (Saxony). *Palæo., Bot.*
Sterzing, H., Thüringen. *Bot.* C.
Steudel, Dr. Wilhelm, Stuttgart. *Lepid.*
Stickelberger, Prof. L., Univ., Freiberg. *Math.*
Stieber, alte Jacobstr. 93, Berlin. *Lepid.*
Stieda, Dr. Ludwig, Prof. der Anatomie a. d. Universität, Königsberg i. Pr. *Anat., Emb., and Histol. of Vert., Anth.* C. Ex.*
Stiefel, Henry C., Ph.D., 38 Koselstr., Frankfort-on-Main. *Chem.*
Stimming, Gustav, Brandenburg. *Coleopt., Lepid.*
Stizenberger, Dr. E., Constance. *Bot., Lichens.*
Stöckhardt, Prof. Dr. Ernest Theodor, Counsellor of Ministerial Department of Agric. and Industry, Pensionary, Weimar. *Agric., Zool., Anth.**
Stöckhardt, Prof. Dr. Julius A., Tharand. *Chem.*
Stockmayer, Domänenpächter in Lichtenberg, bei Oberstenfeld (Würtemberg. *Lepid.* C. Ex.
Stoeber, Otto, Dortmund, Burgwall. *Bot., Orn., Ool., Tax., Lepid., Coleopt.* C. Ex.*
Stoehr, Hans Adam, Schriftsteller und Redacteur, Dresden, Rietschelstrasse 9. *Lepid., Coleopt.*
Stoelting, Bergen, a. d. Dumme. *Lichens.*
Stohmann, Prof. F. K. A., Univ., Leipzig. *Chem.*
Stohr, Dr. Med. Ph., Docent a. d. Univ., Würzburg. *Histol.*
Stoll, Eugen, Uhlandstr. 72, Tübigen. *Lepid.*
Stollwerck, Prof., Uerdingen, Rhine-Province. *Ent.*

Straehler, A., Görbersdorf. *Bot.*
Strasburger, Dr. C., Prof. Bot., Univ., Bonn.
Strasburger, Prof. Dr. Eduard, Univ., Jena. *Bot., Coleopt., Lepid.*
Strasser, Hans, Prof. Extraord., Freiburg. *Anat., Orn.*
Strebel, Herm., Hamburg. *Arch., spec. Mexikanisches.**
Streckfuss, Melchiorstr. 18, Berlin. *Lepid.*
Streng, Prof. August, Ph.D., Giessen. *Geol., Min., Crystal., Lithol.* C. Ex.
Stricker, Dr., Breslau. *Lepid.*
Stricker, Dr. Wilhelm, Frankfort-on-Main. *Anth.*
Stroebert, Dr. Oscar, Mem. Zool. Section for Westfalen and Lippe, Düsseldorf. *Zool., Anat. of Insects.* C. Ex.
Stromeyer, Aug., Annestrasse 2, Hanover. *Chem.**
Strubell, Bruno, Rentier, Schwindstrasse 9, Frankfort-on-Main. *Con.* C. Ex. L. and F. W. shells of Germany for others.
Strübing, Louisenstr. 4, Berlin. *Ent.*
Struck, Carl, Gymnasiallehrer, Custos d. von Maltzanschen Museums für Meckl., Waren (Mecklenburg-Schwerin). *Bot., Zool.* C.
Struckmann, Carl, Dr. Phil., Amstrath, Hanover. *Palæo., Geol., Geog. Dist., Anth., Mam.* C.*
Struve, Oscar, Dr., Zeitzerstr., Leipsic. *Lepid.*
Stübel, Dr. Alphons, Feldgasse 17, Dresden. *Geol., Volcanic Geog. of South America.* C.*
Sturm, Prof. R., Academy, Münster. *Math.**
Sussdorf, Prof. Dr. Julius G., Dresden. *Chem., Phys.*
Sutor, Dr. August, Meingen (Thüringen). *Con.**
Sy, Eugene, Jägerstr. 40, Berlin. *Coleopt.*
Sybel, L. v., Univ., Marburg. *Arch.*
Sydow, Paul, Lehrer, Dirigent des Berliner Botanischen Tauschvereins, Dennewitzstr. 34, Berlin, W. *Crypt. Bot.* C. Ex. Filices.
Tancré, Rudolf, Anclam, Pomerania. *Orn., Ool., Lepid.* Will sell European and Siberian birds, skins and eggs. Also Siberian butterflies.*
Taschenberg, Dr. Ernst Ludwig, Prof., Inspector a. Zool. Mus., Halle. *Zool., Ent.*
Teicher, Theodor, Landeshut. *Ent.: Lepid.* C. Ex.
Tenckhoff, Dr., Paderborn. *Moll.*
Tesch, Carl, Carlstr. 32, Brunswick. *Lepid.*
Tesch, Iwan, Doventhordeich 20, Bremen. *Lepid.*
Tetens, Herm., Altona. *Lepid.* C. Ex.
Thaer, Prof. A., Univ., Giessen. *Mic.*
Thalenhorst, F. G. Adolf, Grindelhof 32*a*, Haus 6, Hamburg. *Lepid.* C. Ex.
Thamm, Grüssau, bei Landeshut. *Lepid.*
Thate, Alexander, Botanical Inst., Leipsic. *Chem.*
Thiele, H., Mem. Ent. Vereins, Frobenstr. 16, Berlin, W. *Lepid.*
Thieme, Dr., Templinerstr. 4, Berlin. *Coleopt.*
Thiemer, G., Hamburg. *Ent.*
Thierfelder, Prof. A., Univ., Rostock. *Pathol. Anat. and Histol.*
Thiesen, Dr. M., Docent, Univ., Berlin. *Terrestrial Phys.*
Thoma, Prof. Richard, Heidelberg. *Mic., Vert. Anat., Histol. of Vert.* C. Ex.
Thomae, Prof. J., Univ., Jena. *Math.*
Thomas, Dr. Carl, Prof. Emer., Wiesbaden.
Thomas, Dr. Friedrich August Wilhelm, Prof. und Oberlehrer an der Herzogl. Realschule, Ohrdruf, bei Gotha. *Phytopathology.* C.*
Thomé, Dr. O. W., Cologne. *Bot.*
Thomé, Prof. W., Univ., Greifswald. *Math., Mechanics.*
Thorey, G., Hamburg. *Coleopt.*

Thum, E. S., Institut für Mic., Leipsic, Brüderstr. 35. *Diatoms, Foraminifera, Sponges, etc.* Catalogue free.*
Thuns, Neudorf, bei Nimptsch. *Lepid.*
Thurau, F., Fischerbrücke 15, Berlin. C. *Lepid.**
Tieffenbach, Mariannenstr. 43, Berlin. *Neuroptera, Orthoptera.*
Tiemann, Prof. F., Roy. Univ., Berlin. *Chem.*
Tillmanns, Dr. H., Docent, Univ., Leipsic. *Surgery, Anat., Pathol.*
Timm, J., Lehrer, Griefenberg. *Lepid.*
Titzenthaler, Franz, Viaduct 2, Dresden. *Ent.: Lepid., Coleopt., Hemipt.* C. Ex. Will buy Ent. Works.*
Tollens, Prof. Dr. Bernhard, Dir. Lab. of Agric. Chem. of the Univ., Göttingen. *Org. and Inorg. Chem., Agric.*
Torge, Otto, Schönberg bei Lauban. *Ent.*
Trapp, Hermann, Chemiker, Kaichen in der Wetterau. *Lepid.*
Traube, Dr. Morritz, Breslau. *Bot.*
Treichel, Alexander, Agrosoph., Hoch-Paleschken, post Altkirchen (West Prussia). *Bot. Ethnol. præhist., Philat.* C. Ex. Offers plants and stamps, postal and fiscal.*
Treu, Lebrecht, Klosterstrasse 35, Munich. *Coleopt., Con.**
Treuge, J., Reallehrer, Münster. *Coleopt.* C. Ex.
Triess, Fred., Kl. Metzigstr. 21, Strasburg. *Hymenop.* (*Alsace*).
Trinker, Jos., Stuttgart. *Lepid.*
Troeltsch, Dr. Anton Friedrich, Freiherr von, Professor der Ohrenheilkunde an der Universität, Würzburg. *Ool.* C.
Trost, Theodor, Frankfort-on-Main. *Moll.*
Tschirch, Dr. Alexander, Docent der Bot. an der Univ. und der Königl. landwirthschaftlichen Hochschule, Assistent am Pflanzenphysiologischen Inst., Birkenstr. 73, Berlin, N. W. *Histol., Physiol., Chlorophyl., Pharmacognosie.**
Tubeuf, Dr. Carl, Freiherr, Asst. am forstbotanischen Inst., Munich, 53 Schellingstr. *Pathol. of Plants, Forest Bot.**
Türckheim, Freiherr v. Geheimerath, a. D., Mahlberg, Baden. *Lepid., Coleopt.**
Uechtritz, R. von, Klosterstr. 84, Breslau. *Bot.*
Uhde, Dr. Carl W. F., Brunswick. *Anth., Mic.*
Uhle, Dr. R., Museum, Dresden. *Eth.*
Uhlworm, Dr. Oscar, Director der Stadtbibliothek, Redacteur des "Botan. Centralblattes," der "Bibliotheca Botanica" und des "Centralblattes für Bacteriologie und Parasitenkunde," Terrasse 7, Cassel. *Bot.* C. Ex.*
Uloth, Dr. W., Friedberg. *Chem., Bot.*
Urban, Dr. Ignatz, Custos des Königl. Botanischen Garten, 5, 2 W., Berlin, Sponholzstrasse 37, Friedenau, near Berlin. *Bot.**
Uslar, Prof. L. v., Univ., Göttingen. *Chem.*
Van Werveke, Dr. Leopold, Strasburg. *Strat. Geol., Lithol.**.
Varendorf, von, Arensberg (Westphalia). *Coleopt.*
Vatke, W., Leipzigerstr. 2, Berlin, W. *Phæn. Bot.* C. Ex.
Venus, C. E., Serrestr. 12, Dresden. *European Coleop. and Micro-lepid*
Vetter, Dr. Benjamin, Fridensplatz 1, Blasenitz. *Zool., Emb.*
Vetter, Ch., Grosse Pleichen 32, Hamburg. *Bot.*
Vettin, Dr. F., Bernburgerstrasse 24, I, Berlin. *Meteo.*
Vieordt, Prof. K. von, Univ., Tübingen. *Physiol.*
Vigelius, August, Selters. *Lepid.*
Vigener, A., Bieberich-am-Rein. *Bot.*
Virchow, Dr. H., Univ., Berlin. *Anat.**
Virchow, Hans, Berlin. *Human Anat.**
Virchow, Prof. Dr. Rudolph, Univ., Berlin. *Anat.*
Vocke, Ad., Nordhausen. *Bot.*

Vogel, Dr. Med., Pract. Arzt, Wandsbecker Chaussée 83, Hamburg. *Mycology.*
Vogel, Paulshütte, bei Schoppinitz. *Ent.*
Vogel, Prof. A., Jägerstrasse 7, Munich. *Chem.*
Vogel, Prof. Dr. H. C., Dir. des Astrophysikalischen Observatoriums, Potsdam. *Coleopt., Ast. and Astro-physics.**
Vogel, Prof. Hermann W., Ph.D., Kurfürstenstr. 124, Berlin, W. *Chem., Phys., Photog., Spectrum-analysis.* C. Ex.
Vogler, Prof. A., Univ., Bonn. *Physical Geog.*
Voigt, O., Volkmarsdorf, bei Leipsic. *Coleopt.* C. Ex.
Voigt, Prof. W., Univ., Königsberg. *Math., Phys.*
Voigtländer, Prof. Dr. Carl F., Univ., Munich. *Phys.*
Voigtländer, Fr. von, Wolfenbüttlerstrasse 4, Brunswick. *Lepid.*
Voit, Carl von, Professor der Physiologie an der Universität, und Vorstand des Physiologischen Instituts und der Physiolog. Sammlung des Staats, Munich. *Phys.*
Volhard, Prof. J., Roy. Univ., Halle a. d. Saale. *Chem.**
Voller, Dr. Aug., Hornerweg 54, Hamm, near Hamburg. *Phys.*
Vom Rath, Prof. G., Roy. Univ., Bonn. *Min.*
Vormann, Dr., Münster (Westphalia). *Hymenop.*
Wackerzapp, Omar, Wallstrasse 48, Aix-la-Chapelle. *Macro-lepid.*
Wacquant-Geozelles, Theodor, Freiherr von, Major auf Sophienhof, bei Oerzen. *Macro-lepid.* C. Ex.
Waentig, Paul, Zittau. *Lepid.*
Wagener, Prof. Dr. Guido R., Univ., Marburg. *Osteol.*
Wagener, B., Friedrichsstr. 11, Kiel. *Coleopt., Spec. Cassid., Brenth.*
Wagenmann, G., Kirchstr. 21, Lahr i. Baden. *Lepid.**
Wagner, Dr. Balthasar, Docent, Fulda. *Ent.*
Wagner, Dr. Franz von., Asst. der Zool. Inst. der Univ., Strassburg (Elsass). *Zool., Vermes, Entwickelungsgeschichte.**
Wagner, Prof. Dr. Herman, Univ., Göttingen. *Geog.**
Wagner, Prof. Dr. Moritz F., Dir. Eth. Mus., Munich.
Wahle, Linkstr. 10, Berlin. *Lepid.*
Wahlländer, Dr., Puttkammerstr. 16, Berlin. *Coleopt.**
Wahnschaff, Dr., St.-Paulisternstr. 5, Hamburg. *Bot., Bryol.*
Waldburg-Zeil-Trauchburg, Carl J. Graf von, Schloss Zeil, Algäu (Würtemberg). *Bibliog., Arch., Orn.* C.
Walderdorf, Graf von, Hauzenstein. *Lepid.*
Waldeyer, Prof. A., Univ., Berlin. *Anat.**
Waldeyer, Prof. Dr. H. W. G., Univ., Berlin. *Anat.**
Waldeijer, W., Prof. Anat. und Dir. des Anatomischen Inst. der Univ., 35 Lutherstr., Berlin, W. *Emb., Anat.**
Waldner, Henry, Secretär der Botanischen Vereins, Alsace-Lorraine, Wasselnheim. *Bot.* C. Ex. Native herbs for European.
Wallach, Prof. O., Roy. Univ., Bonn. *Chem.*
Walser, Dr., Praktischer Arzt, Schwabhausen, near Dachau, Upper Bavaria. *Con., Moll.* C. Ex. Buys and sells. Wishes all kinds of Marine shells, especially of the Atlantic Ocean, in exchange for European.
Walther, Dr. Al., Baireuth. *Bot., Bryol., Mycol.**
Walther, J. Ph., Mannheim. *Lepid.*
Wangerin, Prof. A., Univ., Halle. *Math.*
Warburg, Prof. E., Univ., Freiburg. *Experimental Phys., Math. Phys.**
Warburg, Marcus, F.R.A.S., Magdalenenstrasse 50, Hamburg.
Warlée, Ferd., Hamburg. *Ent.*
Warnstorf, Carl, Lehrer, Neuruppin (Prussia). *Bryol.* C. Ex. Mosses.
Weber, Stadtgärtner, Frankfort-on-Main. *Bot.*
Weber, Gustav, Lehrer Töchterschule, Burtscheid, bei Aix-la-Chapelle. *Coleopt.*

Weber, Prof. H., Univ., Königsberg. *Math.*
Weber, Prof. H. A. von, Univ., Tübingen. *Agric.*
Weber, Prof. Leonhard, Univ., Breslau. *Phys., Elect., Meteo., Effects of Lightning, Photometry.**
Weber, Prof. Dr. Wilhelm E., Univ., Göttingen. *Phys.*
Weberbauer, Otto, Landeck. *Mycol.*
Websky, Prof. Martin, M.D., Royal Univ., Lützower Ufer 19*b*, Berlin, W. *Min., Crystal.*
Weddige, A., Univ., Leipsic. *Chem.*
Wedekind, Ludwig, Ph.D., Prof. Math., Karlsruhe, Baden. *Math.**
Weierstrass, Prof. C., Roy. Univ., Berlin. *Math.*
Weigelt, Dr. Curt, Kaiserl. Dir. an D., Thurmstr. 2A, Berlin, N.W. *Angewandte Chimie, Bakteriologie.**
Weigert, Prof. C., Univ., Frankfort-on-Main. *Pathol. Anat. and Histol.*
Wein, Dr. Ernst, I. Assistent der Königl. Landwirth, Sammlungstrasse, Munich (Bavaria). *Agric. Chem.*
Weiler, Prof. Dr. August, Ritterstrasse 18, Carlsruhe (Baden). *Math., Ast.*
Weinland, Dr. David F., Esslingen (Würtemberg). *Moll., Meteo.*
Wiepken, C. F., Oldenburg, Grossherzogthum. *Orn.*
Weise, J., Sec. Ent. Gesell., Kastanien-Allée 100, Berlin. *Ent.: Coleopt.* C. Ex.
Weiske, Prof. Hugo, Ph.D., Univ. *Chem., Gen. Biol.*
Weismann, Dr. August, Prof. d. Zoologie, Freiburg (Baden). *Zool.*
Weiss, Dr. Ch. Ernst, K. Landesgeolog u. Docent der Bergakademie, Berlin, N. W., Louisenplatz 2, or N. Invalidenstrasse 44. *Geol., Min.* C. Ex. mineral and fossil plants of all formations.
Weiss, Frankfort-on-Main. *Coleopt.*
Weissflog, E., Strehlenerstr. 7, Dresden. *Diatoms.**
Welcker, Prof. H., Univ., Halle. *Anat., Emb.*
Wenzel, Prof. E., Univ., Leipsic. *Physiol., Anat., Mic.*
Wenzig, Th., Schlossstrasse 10, Steglitz, bei Berlin. *Bot.**
Werner, L., Adolf, Schäferstrasse, Dresden. *Lepid.*
Wertermaier, Dr., Bot. Inst. am Gurtgarten, Berlin. C. *Bot.*
Weskamp, A., Paderborn. *Coleopt., Lepid.* C.*
Westermaier, Dr. M., Feilnerstr. 3, Berlin, S. W. *Bot.*
Westhoff, Dr. Fr., Privatdocent f. Zool., Münster, Westf., ausserord. Assistent am Zool. Institut daselbst. *Zool.**
Westphal, Dr., Pionierstr. 12*a*, Berlin, S. W. *Geod.*
Westphal, Major Cuno, Kl. Ziegelgasse 14, Dresden. *Coleopt.*
Westphal, Dr. Carl, Prof. p. ord. Univ., Kaiserin Augustastrasse 59, Berlin, W. *Neurology, Trythetrie.**
Wetckamp, Wilhelm, Lippstadt. *Bot.*
Wetzler, A., Günzburg (Bavaria). *Moll.*
Weyer, Prof. Dr. Georg D. E., Univ., Kiel. *Math., Ast.*
Weyl, Dr. Theodor, Lützowstrasse 88, Berlin. *Physiol. Chem., Physiol.**
Weymer, G., Kleeblattstr. 58, Elberfeld. *Lepid.*
Wichelhaus, Prof. Dr. H., Univ., Georgenstrasse 33, Berlin, N.W. *Chem.*
Wibel, Ferdinand, Dr. Phil., Dir. of Chemical State Laboratory of Hamburg, Domstrasse 5, Hamburg. *Min., Inorg., Anth., Arch.**
Wiebel, Prof. Dr. Carl W. M., Domstrasse 5, Hamburg. *Phys., Chem.*
Wiedemann, Prof. Dr. Ernst Eilhard G., Universität, Erlangen. *Phys.**
Wiedemann, Heinrich Gustav, Geheimer Hofrath und Professor an der Universität, Leipsic. *Phys.**
Wiedersheim, Prof. Dr. Robert, Freiburg. *Vert. Palæo., Zool., Gen. Biol., Vert. Emb., Vert. Anat., Anth., Osteol., Neurology, Myol., Histol. of Vert.*
Wiedmer, Potsdamerstr. 105, Berlin. *Ent.*
Wiegmann, Fritz, Jena. *Moll.*

Wiepken, C. F., Dir. des Grossherzogl. Nat. Hist. Mus., Oldenburg Grossherzogthum. *Moll.*
Wiese, Dr. H., Docent, Univ., Göttingen. *Physical Diagnosis.*
Wieseler, Prof. F., Univ., Göttingen. *Arch.*
Wiesenhutter, Ober-Lichtenau bei Lauban. *Ent.*
Wigand, Dr. Julius W. A., Prof. Bot., Univ., Marburg. *Bot., Mic., Orn.* Ex.
Wildt, Dr. Eugène, Dir. Agric. Inst., Posen (Prussia). *Bot.*
Will, Lieut. Fried., Gabelsbergerstr. 28, Munich. *Coleopt., Biol.*
Will, Prof. H., Univ., Giessen. *Chem.*
Willgerodt, Prof. K. F., Royal Univ., Freiburg. *Chem.*
Wilsdorf, Max, Dir. der Landwirtschaftschule, Chemnitz. *Bot.**
Wiltheiss, Dr. E., Docent, Univ., Halle. *Math.*
Winkler, A., Geh. Kriegsrath a. D., Schillstr. 16, Berlin, W. *Bot., Morphology, Biology.* C.*
Winkler, Dr. Clemens, Prof. der Chem. an der K. Sächs. Bergakademie, Freiberg, Sachsen. *Inorg. Chem., Met.**
Winnecke, Prof. A., Univ., Strasburg. *Ast.*
Winnertz, Joh., Crefeld. *Dipt.*
Winter, Georg, Ph.D., Ed. Hedwigia and Rabenhorstii Fungi exsiccati, Leipzig, Lessingstr. 18. *Fungi.* C. Ex.
Winter, Dr. H., Brandenburg-on-the-Havel. *Bot.*
Wislicenus, Prof. J., Univ., Würzburg. *Chem.*
Witt, Otto N., Ph.D., 33 Lindenallée, Westend, bei Berlin. *Diatoms, Chem., Mic.* C. Ex.*
Witte, Landesgerichtsdirector, Freiburgerstr. 26, Breslau. *Lepid.* C.*
Wittich, Prof. W. von, Königsberg. *Physiol.*
Wittmack, G., Hamburg. *Lepid., Biol.* C. Ex.
Wittmack, Dr. Louis, Prof. an der Universität und an der landwirthschaftlichen Hochschule, Custos des Museums der landw. Hochschule, General-Secretär d. Vereins z. Beförd. d. Gartenbaues, Invalidenstrasse 42, Berlin, N. *Agric., Hort. and Technical Bot.* Offers agric. and forest seeds, woods, fibres, etc., in exchange for samples of the food of the Indians for the Museum.
Wittrich, Dr. W. H. von, Prof. Phys., Univ., Königsberg.
Wocke, Dr. Felix, Jr, Breslau. *Lepid.*
Wocke, Georg, Breslau. *Lepid.*
Woitschach, Dr. Georg, Freistadt. *Geol., Min.*
Wolf, Dekan, Dinkelsbühl (Bayern). *Coleopt., Lepid.* C. Ex.*
Wolf, Dr. Wilhelm, Oberlehrer der Königl. Landwirtschaftschule und Vorstand des Agriculturchemischen Laboratoriums, Döben. *Agric. Chem.*
Wolff, Dr. Griesheim, Frankfort-on-Main. *Hygiene. Chem.*
Wolff, Prof. Dr. E. von, Hohenheim, near Stuttgart. *Bot.*
Wolff, Dr. Max, Docent, Prof. Univ., Behrenstrasse 57, Berlin. *Mic.* C. Ex.
Wollny, Dr. Ewald a. ö. Prof. der Landwirthschaft an der K. technischen Hochschule, Nymphenburgerstr. 20, Munich (Bavaria). Redacteur der "Forschungen auf dem Gebiete der Agrikultur," Physik (Centralblatt für Bodenphysik, Agrar-Meteorologie und Pflanzenphysik), Agric., Physiology of plants, Physics of Soil, Agricultural Meteorology.*
Wollny, Robert, Niederlössnitz, bei Kützschenbroda, Dresden. *Bot., Algol.*
Wolschke, Oscar, Altenburg. *Ent.* C. Ex.
Wollschlaeger, Amtsgerichtsrath, Ortelsburg (Ost. Pr.). *Coleopt., Lepid.* C.*
Woronin, Dr., Mainzerstr. 24, Wiesbaden.
Wortmann, Dr. F., Strasburg (Alsace-Lorraine). *Bot.*

Wroblewski, Dr. S. von, Prof., Univ., Krakau. *Phys.**
Wüllmer, Adolph, Prof. Phys., Aix-la-Chapelle.
Wünsche, Dr. Otto, Oberlehrer am Gymnasium an Zwickau (Saxony). *Bot., Natural History.**
Wunschmann, Dr., Templinerstr. 10, Berlin. *Bot.*
Wüstnei, Realschullehrer, Sonderburg. *Coleopt., Hymenop., Hemipt.* C. Ex.
Wutzdorf, H., Kupferschmiedestrasse 11, Breslau. *Lepid.*
Wydler, Dr. Heinrich, Gewesener Prof. d. Botanik in Berne, Switzerland, und in Gernsbach, Grossherz (Baden). *Morphology, Bot.*
Zabel, Hermann, Königl. Gartenmeister, Münden (Hanover). *Dendrology, Spiræ, Lonicera.* C.
Zahn, Lehrer am Seminar zu Gotha. *Geol., Min., Ent.*
Zech, Prof. Dr. Paul H. von, Stuttgart. *Phys.*
Zeiller, Carl, Lüneburg (Hannover). *Gen. Ent.* C. Lepid and Coleopt. for sale and ex.*
Zeller, Dr. E., Stuttgart. *Bot., Algæ.*
Zeller, Wilhelm, Bot. Gardens, Tübingen. *Bot.*
Zenker, Prof. Dr. F. A., Univ., Erlangen. *Anat.*
Ziegler, Prof. Dr. Ernst, Tübingen. *Pathol. Anat., Gen. Pathol.*
Ziegler, Dr. H. Ernst, Freiburg i. B. *Zool., Emb.**
Ziegler, Dr. Julius, Frankfort-on-Main. *Bot.**
Zierow, Belle-Alliancestr. 88, Berlin. *Ent.*
Zietz, Amandus, Cur. Zool. Mus., Kiel. *Invertebrates. Ichth.* C. Ex.
Zimmer, Aug., Ringenhain, bei Neukirch. *Lepid., Neuropt.* C. Ex.
Zimmermann, C., Hamburg. C. Ex.
Zimmermann, Dr., Holzappel, Rylz, Wiesbaden. *Bot.**
Zimmermann, Dr. Oscar Emil Reinhold, Oberlehrer an der Realschule, I. Ordnung, Bernsbachstr. 15, I. Chemnitz (Saxony). *Mycology.* C. Ex. Desires first-class specimens of mushrooms and lichens for good microscopical preparations.
Zimpel, W. A., Kaufmann, Hamburg, Graumannsweg, 3. *Bot.*
Zincke, Th., Univ., Marburg. *Chem.*
Zincken, Carl Friedrich, Georgenstr. 18, Leipsic. The geol. horizonts of the fossil carbons; the fossil hydrocarbons.*
Zirkel, Prof. F., Univ., Leipsic. *Min., Mic.*
Zittel, Prof. Carl A., Univ., Munich. *Palæo., Geol., Emb. and Anat. of Vert., Sponges.* C. Ex.
Zöllner, Prof. J. K. Fr., Univ., Leipsic. *Physics, Astrophys.*
Zopf, Dr. W., Barutherstr. 13, Berlin. *Bot., Physiol.*
Zopt, Dr. A. W., Invalidenstrasse 42, Berlin, N. *Mycol.*
Zorn, Dr. W., Docent, Univ., Heidelberg. *Org. Chem.*
Zschock, Otto v., Liegnitz, Prussia. *Ent.: Coleopt.**
Zuhlke, August, Lehrer, Calbe (Saxony). *Lepid.* C. Ex.
Zuntz, Prof., Landwirthschaftliche Hochschule, Invalidenstr. 42, Berlin, N. *Physiol.*
Zurn, F. A., Univ., Leipsic. *Mic.*
Zwenger, C., Univ., Marburg. *Chem.*

GREECE.

Anagnostackis, A., Prof. Univ., Athens. *Oculist.**
Aphertoulis, Th., Prof. Univ., Athens. *Pharmacology. Bot.**
Arctaeus, Th., Prof. Univ., Athens. *Surgery.**
Argyropoulos, T. A., Prof. Univ., Athens. *Exper. Phys.**
Boussackis, C., Prof. Univ., Athens. *Physiology.**
Caramitsas, G., Prof. Univ., Athens. *Clinique.**

Cassimati, Stylianus J., D.C.L., Ex-Pres. of the Greek Parliament, Athens. *Anthropology, Laws, Politics.**
Chadgidackes, G. N., Prof. Univ., Athens. *Math.**
Chadgimichalis, M., Prof. Univ., Athens. *Special nosology.**
Cockides, D. K., Prof. Univ., Athens. *Ast.**
Crinnus, G. A., Prof. Univ., Athens. *Chem., Syntagology.**
Cristomanus, Prof. Univ., Athens. *Chem.*
Deliganius, C. P., Prof. Univ., Athens. *Clinique, Path.**
Heldreich, Prof. Th. de, Dir. Bot. Gardens, Athens. *Bot., Zool., Anth.* C. Ex.
Holzmann, Timoléon, Athens. *Bot.* C. Desires plants.*
Joannou, P., Prof. Univ., Athens. *Epidemrology, Syphilitology.**
Kalligas, Prof. P., Speaker of the Greek Parliament, Athens.
Kloetzcher, H., Royal Gardens, Athens. *Bot.*
Krüper, Dr. Theobald J., Conservator Univ. Museum, Athens. *Zool., Geol.* C. Ex. Coleopt., Hemipt., etc.
Kyriakos, P. G., Prof. Univ., Athens. *Medical Encyclopædia.**
Kyzickinas, A., Prof. Univ., Athens. *Math.**
Laccon, B., Prof. Univ., Athens. *Math.**
Lochiòs, J., Prof. Univ., Athens. *Exper. Physiology, Comp. Anat.**
Mackas, G. A., Prof. Univ., Athens. *Path., Therapeutics.**
Maugiunas, S., Prof. Univ., Athens. *Surgical Path.**
Maurocordato, Alexander, rue de l'Académie, Athens. *Coleopt.*
Mitzopoulos, Prof. E., Athens. *Nat. Hist.*
Munter, Ludvig, Tator, near Athens. *Zool., Lepid.*
Orphaaides, D. G., Prof. Univ., Athens. *Clinique.**
Papaioannou, L., Prof. Univ., Athens. *Anat.**
Poniropoulos, Eutache, Prof. de Botanique à l'Ecole Normale, Prof. des Sciences Naturelles au Collège Royale, Athens. *Bot.*
Rosseels, L., Athens. *Chem., Geol.*
Schliemann, Dr. Henry, Athens.
Schmidt, Dir. of Obs., Athens. *Ast.**
Stephanus, C., Prof. Univ., Athens. *Math.**
Stroumbas, D., Prof. Univ., Athens. *Phys.**

HELIGOLAND.

Gätke, Heinrich, Sec. to Gov. Heligoland. *Orn.*

HOLLAND.

(*See* NETHERLANDS.)

ICELAND.

Gröndal, Prof. Benedikt, Reykjavik (via Leith, Scotland. Membre du Congrès international des Américanistes, membre du Comité international permanent Ornithologique à Vienne. *Zool.**
Thorvaldur, Modruvellir, pr. Akureyri (via Leith, Scotland).

ITALY.

Abetti, Prof. A., Padua. *Ast.**
Acri, Prof. Francesco, R. Univ., Bologna. *Phil.*
Adami, G. B., Maggiore, Verone. *Malacol.*

Albini, Prof. G., Naples. *Physiol.*
Alfieri di Sostegno, Carlo, Presidente del Consiglio e Superintendente dell' Istituto, Florence
Amiciò, Juan d', Geol Mus., Roy. Univ., Bologna. *Geol., Con.*
Andres, Angelo, Prof. Dr., Museo Civico, Milano. *Mic., Bibliog., Zool., Gen. Biol., Radiates.* Ex.*
Angelo, Senna, Milano, Via Fiori Oscuri, N. H. *Cheiroptère of the whole world.* C. Ex.*
Antonmarchi, Paul Martin, Mem. de la Soc. des botanists de France, Pietza de Verde. Cervione (Corsica). *Phan. Bot.*
Arcangeli, Prof. Dr. Jean, Dir. Bot. Gar., Pisa. *Bot.*
Archibald, A. B., Via Montebello, 15 p. p., Florence. *Coleopt.*
Ardissone, Francesco, Professeur de Botanique à l'Ecole Royale Supérieure d'Agriculture, Milan. *Marine Algæ.* C. Algæ of the Mediterranean. Ex.*
Armitago, E., Via Ripetta, Palazzo Campana, Rome. *Bot.* C.
Bagatti, Dr. O., Advocate, Parma. *Fossil shells of the Tertiary Period.**
Baglietto, Fr., Voltri, near Genoa. *Lichenol., Bot.*
Balsamo, Dr. Franc., Naples. *Bot.*
Barbaglia, Prof. Dr. G. A., Univ., Pisa. *Pharm. Chem.*
Barbera, Prof. Luigi di Minervino, R. Univ., Bologna. *Phil.*
Barbera, Prof. Luigi di Minervino, R. Univ., Bologna. *Phil.*
Barbo, Conte Gaetano, Via San Damiano 24, Milan. *Ent.*
Bargagli, Pierre, Via dei Bardi 1, Florence. *Ent., esp. Cetonides. Coleopt.* C.
Bargellini, Dr. Démètre, Via Guelfa 1, Florence. *Mycol.*
Baroni, Giov., Borgo la Croce 53, Florence. *Coleopt., Lepid.*
Bastianini, J., Florence. *Bot.*
Batelli, Dr. Andrea, Arezzo. *Bot.*
Battistini, Attilio, Rome. *Physiology.*
Baudi di Selve, Flaminio, Via Bavetti 18, Turin. *Ent.: Coleopt.**
Beccari, Odoardo, Prof., R. Museo di Storia Nat., Via Romana 19, Florence. *Bot.**
Beccari, Dr. Orlando, Via degli Archibusieri 8, Florence. *Bot.*
Beccari-Incisa, di S. Stefano, Gen. Luigi, Via Giannone 5, Turin. *Ent.*
Bechi, Prof. Emilio, Roy. Inst. Tech., Florence. *Chem.*
Bellardi, Prof. Luigi, R. Mus. Zool., Turin. *Ent.: Diptera.*
Belli, Saverio, Torino, Amedeo-Avogadro 8. *Syst. Bot.*
Bellonci, Dr. Giuseppe, Prof. Università, Bologna. *Comp. Anat., Emb.**
Bellucci, Dr. E., Bot. Gar., Portici, near Naples. *Bot.*
Bellucci, Joseph, N.H.D., Prof. Univ., Perugia. *Anth., Arch., Ethnol., Ethnog.* C. Ex. Desires especially objects of prehistoric Arch.*
Belluzzi, Dr. Cesare, Mem. Acad. Sci., Bologna.
Beltrami, Prof. Eugenio, Pavia. *Math., Phys.*
Beltrani, Vito, Licata, Sicily. *Botany: Cryptogams, Mycology.*
Beni, Dr. Carlo, Tuscany. *Orn.*
Benvenuti, Leo, Este. *Arch.**
Berenger, J. M. Adolph de, Inspecteur Général des Forêts en retraite, jadis professeur d'Histoire Naturelle et d'Economie forest. à l'Ecole forest. de Vallombrosa (Tuscany). *Bot.* C. Ex.*
Bergamasco, Camillo, Casal Beltrame (Provincia di Novara). *Ent.*
Berlese, Dr. Antonio, Firenze, R. Instituto Botanico del l'Univ. di Padova, Via Romana 19. *Acari, Myriopoda, Scorpions, Fungi.**
Berti, Prof. Leonida, Mem. Acad. Sci., Bologna.
Berthold, Dr. G., Zool. Station, Naples. *Bot., Zool.*
Betta, Antonio, Via S. Bartolommeo 228, Pavia. *Ent.: Coleopt.*
Bianca, Joseph, Avola, Sicily. *Bot.*
Bicchi, Prof. Dr. C., Lyceum, Dir. Bot. Gar., Lucca.
Billi, Dr. Luigi, Via de' Servi 15 p. t., Florence. *Acari, Ent.*

Biondi, Antonio, Member of the R. Horticultural Society, Agronome, Via dei Serragli 115, Florence. *Bot.* C. Ex. for European Flora.
Bizzozero, Giacomo, Con. du Jardin Botanique, Padua. *Bot.* C. Plants of the Flora of Venice. Ex. Offers Phanerogams and Vascular Cryptogams, Venice, in exchange for those of Europe.
Blaserna, Prof. Pietro, Rome. *Phys.**
Boccaccini, Prof. C., Lyceum, Cuneo. *Bot.*
Boldrini, Dr. Luigi, Castel d'Ario (Mantovano). *Ent.*
Bombicci, Luigi, Via Zamboni 34, Bologna. *Min.**
Bombicci-Porta (Comm. Chev.) Louis, Prof. de Minéralogie et Directeur du Cabinet Minéralogique de l'Université Royale, Bologna. *Min.* C. 36,000 (116 meteorites) specimens in the University. Ex. Offers mineral crystals of Italy and Meteorite, Alfrianello 1883, in exchange for those of other countries.*
Bonardi, Dr. Edoardo, R. Univ., Pavia. *Chem., Geol., Lithol.*
Bonizzi, Prof. Paolo, Modena. *Orn.*
Borzi, Dr. Antonio, Professeur de Botanique à l'Université Royale et Directeur du Jardin Botanique, Messina, Sicily. *Bot., Algæ, etc.* C. Ex. Desires to exchange plants of Sicily for Algæ, Quercus, and Salia of America.
Bosi, Prof. Federico, R. Univ., Bologna.
Bottini, Dr. Antonio, Marchese, Pisa. *Bryol.**
Bozzo, Prof. G., Sec. R. Acad. Sci., Palermo, Sicily. *Bot.*
Bracciforti, Prof. Alberto, Via Diritta 130, Piacenza. *Ent.*
Brandt, Dr. Karl, Bibliothécaire de la Station Zoologique, Naples. *Protozoa.*
Brioschi, Francesco, Dir. Inst. Tech., Milan. *Math.*
Briosi, J., Prof. Univ., Dir. Crypt. Station, Parè. *Phys., Path., Bot.**
Brizi, Dr. Orestes von, Sec. Acad. Sci., Arezzo.
Brizio, Prof. Edoardo di Torini, R. Univ., Bologna. *Arch.*
Brogi, Sigismondo, Naturaliste à la Royale Acad. des Fisiocritici, Piazza S. Agostino 5, Siena. *General Sciences.* C. Buys, sells, and exchanges Natural History objects, except Botanical specimens.*
Brugnoli, Prof. Dr. Giovanni, Mem. Acad. Sci., Bologna.
Bruno, Dr. F., Bot. Gar., Turin. *Bot.*
Bruschi, Prof. Al., Univ., Perugia. *Bot.*
Bubani, Dr. Pietro, Bagnacavallo (Emilia). *Bot.* C. Ex.
Cacciatore, Gaetano, Palermo, Sicily. *Ast.*
Cafici, Yppolito, Catania. *Geol., Palæo.*
Calderini, Prof. Pietro, Varallo. *Ent.*
Callegari, Ferdinando, Campo della Guerra, Venice. *Ent.*
Caluri, Olivio, Pisa. *Ent.*
Calzolari, Cesare, R. Univ., Bologna.
Camerano, Dr. Aggregato, Lorenzo, Assistente al. R. Museo Zoologico, Turin. *Zool.**
Cammarota, Gaetano, Rome. *Ent., Bot.*
Canepa, J. B., Bot. Gar., Rome.
Canestrini, Prof. Giovanni, Univ., Padua. *Anth., Ichth., Arach.* C. Ex.
Canestrini, Riccardo, Dr. Nat. Hist., Padua. *Ent., Arach., Bacteriol.**
Canevazzi, Silvio, R. Univ., Bologna.
Cantoni, Prof. Gaetano, Dir. Agric. Station, Milan. *Bot.*
Cannizzaro, Prof. Stanislao, Senatore Istituto Chimico della Regia Università di Roma, Via Panisperna, Rome. *Chem.*
Capellini, Giovanni, Via Zamboni 59, Bologna. *Palæo., Strat. Geol., Lithol.*
Cappannelli, Giuseppe, Cortona. *Ent.*
Capranica, Stefano, Rome. *Phys., Chem.*
Carega, Francesco, R. Univ., Bologna. *Agron.*

Carestia, l'Abbé Ant., Riva Valdobbia (Varallo). *Bot.*
Carlucci, M., Avellino. *Bot.*
Carpegna, Count Guido, Rome. *Ent.*
Carpene, Prof. A., Conegliano. *Bot.*
Carrara, Guido Luigi, Lucca. *Coleopt.*
Carruccio, Prof. Antonio, R. Univ., Modena. *Ent.*
Caruel, Teodoro, Professeur de Botanique et Directeur du Jardin et du Musée Botanique, de l'Institut des Etudes Supérieures, Florence. *Bot.**
Casorati, Prof. Felix, Università, Pavia. *Mathematical Analysis.*
Cassani, Comm. D. Giacomo, Prof. Emerito nella Regia Univ. di Bologna.*
Castelfranco, Prof. Pompeo, Milano. *Palæo.*
Casstelli, Dr. Federico, Livorno. *Malacol.*
Castelli, David, Professore straordinario di Lingua ebraica, R. Istituto, Florence.
Castracane degli Antelminelli, Conte Alessandro, Piazza delle Capello 50, Rome. *Silk Culture, Diatoms.* C. Ex.
Cattaneo, Dr. Achille, Pavia. *Bot.*
Cattaneo, Giacomo, Dr. Nat. Sci., Socio dell' Istit. Lomb. e della Soc. Ital d. sc. nat., Prof. agguinto nella Univ., Pavia (Lab. d'Anat. comp.). *Mic., Gen. Biol., Protozoa, Moll., Comp. Histol.**
Cavanna, Dr. Guelfo, Sec. Société Entomologique, al Regio Museo, Via Romana 19, Florence. *Arach., Hemipt., Comp. Anat.* Ex. Myriopods, Spiders, and Hemiptera for the R. Museum.
Cavara, Dr. F., Asst. à l'Inst. Bot. de Parè. *Palæo., Crypt. Bot.**
Cavazzi, Dr. Alfredo, R. Univ., Bologna.
Cazzuola, Ferd., Bot. Gar., Pisa. *Bot.*
Ceccoti, N., Bot. Gar., Parma. *Bot.*
Cerletti, Prof. G. B., Conegliano. *Bot.*
Cernello, Dr. V., Univ., Palermo, Sicily. *Bot.*
Ceselli, Prof. Luigi, Rome. *Palæo.*
Chiamenti, Dr. Alex., Presidente del Comisio Agricolo, Chioggia. *Bot., Moll.* C. Ex.
Chierici, Prof. Gaetano, Reggio Emilia. *Palæo.*
Chiovenda, Umberto, Domo d'Ossola. *Ent.*
Ciaccio, Prof. Giuseppe, v. Mem. Acad. Sci., Preside della Facoltà di Scienze, Bologna. *Math., Phys., Anat.**
Cianchettini, Dr. Giulio, R. Univ., Museo Zoologico, Via della Crocetta 3, Genoa. *Zool., Crustacea.*
Cicone, Dr. Lepoldo, Univ., Naples. *Phys.*
Citarda, N., Bot. Gar., Palermo, Sicily. *Bot.*
Cocchi, Prof. Igino, Florence. *Geol.*
Cocconi, Prof. Girolamo, Mem. Acad. Sci., Bologna. *Bot.*
Cogollo, Girolamo, Vicenza. *Ent.**
Colasanti, Giuseppe, Professore di Chimica Fisiologica, R. Univ. di Roma. *Physiology.**
Coletti, Prof. Dr. Ferd., Univ., Padua. *Bot.*
Colognesi, Prof. Alfonso, Mem. Acad. Sci., Bologna.
Comes, Dr. Orazio, Prof. R. Scuola Sup. Agric., Portici (near Napoli). *Veg. Pathol.*
Concestabile, Giancarlo, Perugia. *Arch.*
Console, Prof. Dr. Michelangelo, Via Stobile 281, Univ., Palermo, Sicily.
Conti, Augusto, Professore ordinario di Filosofia teoretica e morale, R. Istituto di Studi Superiore, Florence. *Phil.*
Coppi, Dr. Francisco, Gorzano par Maranello. Publications, Monog. et Iconog. Terramara di Gorzano, etc. *Invert. Palæo., Lithol., Moll.* C. Ex.*
Corsi, Arnaldo, Rue Volfondo, Florence. *Min.*
Corti, Dr. San S. B. A. de, Turin. *Bot.*

Cossa, Alfonso, Prof. Chem., Roy. Ind. Mus., Turin.
Costa, Prof. Achille, Dir. Roy. Mus. Zool., Naples. *Ent.*
Cremona, Luigi, Prof. Math., Univ., S. Pietro in Vincoli 5, Rome. *Math.**
Crespellani, Dr. A., Modena. *Palæo., Arch.*
Cristofani, H., Pisa. *Bot.*
Cugini, Prof. Dr. G., Univ., Bologna. *Physiol., Bot.*
Curo, Antonio, Bergamo. *Lepid.**
D'Achiardi, Antonio, Prof. Univ., Pisa. *Min.*
Dal-Fiume, Camillo, Badia Polesine (Veneto). *Orn., Ent.**
Dalle Donne, Gaetano, R. Univ., Bologna.
D'Amato, Dr. Fred., Inst. Tech., Teramo. *Bot.*
Damry, Naturalist, Ozièri, Sardinia. *Coleopt., Hemipt., Dipt., Hymenop., Orn. of the Islands in the Mediterranean.* C. Ex. for Hyrocanthus, Polpicorns, Pselaphidæ, Scydmæmidæo of Europe.
D'Ancona, Cesare, Docteur ès Sciences, Prof. de Palæo. du R. Inst. di Studi Superiori di Firenze, Piazza d'Azeglei 14, Florence. *Palæo., Living Malacology.* Ex. for Mus., Fossils and L. & F. W. Shells.*
D'Apel, Luigi, R. Univ., Bologna. *Phil.*
De Betta, Edoardo, Verona. *Zool.*
DeGasparis, Annibale, Dir. Roy. Obs., Naples. *Ast.*
De Gregorio, Marquis Antonio, Dr. Nat. Sc., Via Molo, Palermo, Sicily. *Invert. Palæo., Geol., Fossils of the Tertiary Period, Living Mediterranean Mollusca, Secondary fossils, Corals of Jura and Lias.*
De Gregorio, Giacomo, Doct. Litt., Via Molo, Palermo, Sicily. *Philol.* African languages, Neolat. dialects.
Dehnhardt, Alfred, Bot. Gar., Naples. *Bot.*
Dei, Apelle, Secrétaire de la Commission Ampélographique de Sienne, Via dei Tufi 1, Siena (Tuscany). *Orn., Ent., Comp. Anat.* C. Offers birds' skins and insects of the orders of Coleoptera, Hemiptera, and Lepidoptera in exchange for Neuroptera, especially Termitidæ.*
Della Valle, Prof. Dr. Antonio, Regia Università, Gabinetto di Zoologica, Modena. *Copepo da Normal Amphipoda, Compound Ascidians.*
Del Gaizo, Modestino, Univ., Naples. *Phys.*
Del Magus, Norberto, Milano. *Malacol., Ent.*
Delpino, Federigo, Prof. Bot., R. Univ., Bologna. *Biol.**
Delponte, Prof. G. B., Turin. *Bot.*
Del Prete, Raimondo, Viareggio, Toscane. *Malacol.* C. Ex.*
Denza, Padre Francesco, Dir. del Osservatorio del Real Collegio Carlo Alberto, Moncalieri, Dir. generale della Società Meteo. Italiana, Turin.*
De Paolis, Prof. Riccardo, R. Univ., Bologna. *Geom.*
De Sanctis, Leone, Prof. Zool., Rome.
De Silvestri, Prof. Antonio, Torino. *Zool.*
De Stefani, Dr. Carlo, Prof. de l'Inst. des Etudes Supérieures, Firenze. *Geol., Malacol.**
Devincenzi, G., Senator, Giulianova. *Agric.*
De Zigno, Baron Achille, Padua. *Geol.*
Diblassi, Prof. Dr., R. Lyceum, Palermo, Sicily. *Bot.*
Di Stefano, Dr. Giovanni, Via Aloro 14, Palermo, Sicily. *Palæo., Con.*
Doderlien, Prof. Pietro, Palermo. *Zool. Palæo.*
Dodero di Giustino, Agostino, Genoa. *Coleopt., esp. Psilaphidæ and Scydmæneidæ.* C.
Dohrn, Prof. Dr. Anton, Zoological Station, Naples. *Zool.**
Donati, Prof. Luigi, R. Univ., Bologna. *Math.*
Doria, Marquis G., Museo Civico di Storia Naturale, Genoa. *Vertebrates.*
Dorna, Alessandro, Dir. Roy. Ast. Obs., Turin.
Dufour, Luigi, Via Balbi 15, Genoa. *Bot., Algol.*
Eisig, Dr. Hugo, Stazione Zoologica, Napoli. *Annelids.**
Emery, Carlo, Prof. di Zoologia nella R. Università, Bologna. *Comp.*

Anat., *esp. of Vertebrates*, *Entomology*, *Natural History of Ants.* C. Ex. Offers European and Exotic Ants for other species, and copies of his works against analogous publications.*
Eugénie, Filipperi, Cours Tintori 43, Florence. *Coleopt.*
Fabretti, Prof. Ariodante, Univ., Turin. *Arch.*
Failla-Tedaldi, Luigi, Castelbuono, Palermo, Sicily. *Ent.*
Fanelli, Brandimarte, Sarteano, Siena. *Ent.*
Fanzago, De Filippo, Prof. nell' R. Univ., Sassari. *Myriopoda*, *Acari*, *Zool.* C. Ex.
Fea, Leonardo, Civ. Mus., Genoa. *Ent.**
Federici, Antonio, Prof. di Botanica nel' Università, Urbino. *Bot.*
Felici, Riccardo, Prof. Phys., Pisa.
Fenzi, E. O., Pres. Hort. Soc., Via S. Gallo 10, Florence. *Bot.*, *Ent.: Lepid.*
Ferranti, Vincenzo, R. Univ., Bologna. *Phil.*
Ferrari, Enrico, Via Ormea 20, Torino. *Bot. sist.**
Ferrari, Pietro, 40 Via Consolazione, Genoa. *Hemipt.*
Ferrero, Avv'to, Francesco, Torino, Via St. Francesco d'Assisi 29. *Bot.*, *Anat.**
Ferrero, Prof. U., Dir. Agric. Station, Caserta. *Bot.*
Ferrini, Rinaldo, Inst., Milan. *Phys.*
Ferrucci, Prof. Michele, R. Univ., Bologna.
Fiaschi, Tito, Segretario Capo e per la Sezione di Filosofia e Filologia, Florence. *Phil.*, *Philol.*
Filipperi, Eugenia, 43 Corso Tintori, Florence. *Ent.: Coleopt.**
Filippi, Angelo, Professore straordinario di Medicina legale, R. Istituto, Florence.
Filopanti, Prof. Quirico, Mem. Acad. Sci., Bologna.
Fiori, Andrea, Prof. Storia Naturale, Liceo, via Indiquendenha 22, Bologna. *Orn.* (*Italien*) *Coleopt.* (*Europe*). C. Ex. of Coleopt.*
Fiorini, Matteo, Via Mazzini 37, Bologna. *Geodesy.*
Fontana, Giuseppe, Sec. R. Univ., Bologna. *Geol.*, *Palæo.*, *Con.*
Fornasini, Carlo, Geol. Museum, Bologna. *Foraminifera.**
Forsyth, Major Dr. C. J., 2 Via Senese, Florence. *Palæo.*, *Mammifères.* Ex. of Mammifères tertiares et quaternaires.*
Francolini, Massimiliano, Rimini. *Ent.*
Francs, Dr. Pasquale, Univ., Naples. *Min.*, *Geol.*
Franke, Dr. Max, Messina, Sicily. *Bot.*, *Physiol. of plants.*
Freda, Dr. Giovanni, R. Liceo Genovesi, Naples. *Min.*
Freda, Prof. Dott. Pasquale, Dir. dèlla R. Stazione chimico agraria di Roma et du journal périodique "Le Stazioni sperimentalia agrarie Italiane."*
Gamberini, Pietro, Prof. à l'Université, rue des Beaux Arts 15, Bologna. *Dermatology.* C. Offers "Treatise on Maladies of the Tongue."
Garbocci, A., Pisa. *Bot.*
Gasco, Prof. Francesco, R. Univ., Genoa. *Zool.*
Gelardo, Prof. Dr., Inst. Tech., Palermo, Sicily. *Bot.*
Gemmellaro, Prof. Dr. Carl, Univ., Catania, Sicily. *Min.*, *Geol.*
Gemellaro, Prof. Gaetano Giorgio, Roy. Univ., Palermo, Sicily. *Min.*, *Geol.*
Gennarelli, Achille, Professore ordinario di Archeologia, R. Istituto, Florence. *Arch.*
Gennari, Prof. Dr. P., Univ., Cagliari, Sardinia. *Bot.*
Gentile, Prof. Giacomo, R. Inst. Tech., Porto Maurigio. *Bot.*
Gestro, Dr. Rafiaello, Museo Civico di Storia Naturale, Genoa. *Coleopt.**
Gherardi, Com., Dir. Inst. Tech., Florence.
Giacomelli, Prof. Enrico, Mem. Acad. Sci., Bologna.
Gianelli, Giacinto, place Victor Emanuel 21, Turin. *Lepidoptera.* C. Very desirous to buy or exchange *Lepid.*, especially Tortricidæ.*

Gibelli, Camillo, Torino, Via Ormèa 40. *Coleopt.**
Gibelli, Dr. Giuseppe, Professore di Botanica nella R. Università, Dir. del R'o. Orto botanico, Torino. *Bot.**
Giesbrecht, Dr. Wilhelm, Stazione Zoologica, Naples. *Zool.*, *Crustacea.**
Giglioli, Henry Hillyer, Prof. Zoology and Comp. Anatomy of Vertebrate Animals, and Director Zool. Mus., R. Univ., Florence. *Zool.*, *Anat.*, *Palæo.* *and Geogr. Dist. of Vertebrates*, *Anth.*, *Ethnol.* C. Ex. Italian Vertebrates in exchange for Vertebrates and Ethnological objects from any part of the world.*
Ginori, March Carlo, Via dei Ginori 11, Florence. *Ent.**
Giordano, Felice, Inspector Gen. of Mines, 105 Via dell' Archetto, Olla Pilotta, Rome. *Geol.*
Giordano, Prof. Jos. Camille, Inst. Tech. Tarsio, Naples. *Bot.*, *Bryol.*
Giovanetti, Carlo, R. Univ., Bologna.
Giovanni, A. Phil., Bot. Gar., Bologna. *Bot.*
Gioran, Prof. Augustin, Lyceum, Verona. *Phys.*, *Bot.*
Giudici-Albergotti, March. de, Angiolo Lorenzo, Arezzo. *Ent.*
Gonzaga, Ferrante, Palazzo Gonzaga, Mantova. *Ent.*
Gotti, Prof. Alfredo, Mem. Acad. Sci., Bologna.
Govi, Gilberto, Prof. Phys., Naples.*
Grandi, Dr. Giacomo, Mem. Acad. Sci., Bologna.
Grassi, Giov. Batt., Rovellasca, Como. *Zool.*
Grattarola, Prof. G., Piazza S. Marco, Florence. *Min.**
Gregorio, Rigo, Torri del Benaco, Verona.
Gribodo, Giovanni, Ingénieur Assistant à l'Université, rue Accademia Albertina 5, Turin. *Hymenop.* C. Ex. Very desirous to buy or exchange Hymenoptera, esp. Chrysides and Evanides.
Groves, H., Borgognissanti 15, Florence. *Bot.*
Gualandi, Dr. Francesco, Mem. Acad. Sci., Bologna.
Gualandi, Dr. Giovanni, Mem. Acad. Sci., Bologna.
Guicciardini, Count Pietro, Via dei Guicciardini 17, Florence.
Guidi, Louis, Prof. d'Histoire Naturelle à l'Institut Technique, Pesaro (Marches). *Bot.*, *Geol.* C. Ex.
Inzenza, Prof. Dr., Univ., Palermo, Sicily. *Agric.*, *Mycol.*, *Bot.*
Issel, Prof. Arturo, R. Univ., Genoa. *Geol.*, *Min.*, *Malacol.*
Jatta, Antoine, Ruvo di Puglia. *Bot.*: *Lichenol.*
Jervis, Cavaliere Guglielmo, Conservatore del Reale Museo Industriale Italiano, Turin. *Geol.*, *Min.*, *Lithol.**
Johnston-Lavis, H. J., M. D., M.R.C.S., L.S.A., F.G.S., Palazzo Caramanico, 7 Chiatamone, Naples. *Palæo.*, *Geol.*, *Chem.*, *Mic.*, *Meteo.*, *Gen. Biol.*, *Geog. Dist.* C. Ex.
Keeler, Prof. Dr. Ant., Univ., Padua. *Agron.*, *Bot.*
Kminek-Szedlo, Giovanni, R. Univ., Bologna.
Koenig, Dr. Fr., Dir. Oenolog. Versuchstation, Asti. *Agric.*, *Org. Chem.*, *Min.*, *Meteo.*
Lanzi, Dr. Matth., Via Cavour 6, Rome. *Bot.*, *Mycol.*
Lepori, Dr. Cesare, Prof. R. Univ., Cagliari, Sardinia. *Ent.*
Levier, Dr. Emile, Borgo San Frediano 16, Florence. *Bot.*, *Phanerogams*, *Bryology*. C. Ex. Offers Phanerogams and mosses of Italy, Corsica, Spain, and Portugal for mosses of America.
Libassi, Prof. Le Père, Seminary, Palermo, Sicily. *Bot.*
Licopoli, Prof. Dr. Cai., Lyceum Victor-Emanuel, Naples. *Bot.*
La Bianco, Salvatore, Stazione Zoologica. Naples. *Preservation of Marine Animals.*
Lemoigne, Dr. Alessio, Milano. *Zool.*
Lodi, Achille, Dr., Scienze Naturali, R. Soceo Mareo Foscarini, Venezia. *Crypt. Bot.**
Lodi, Prof. Fortunato, R. Univ., Bologna.
Lo Jacono, Michel, Lib. Doc. de Bot., Con. des Herbiers du Jardin Bot.,

Piazza Sto. Spirito 5, Palermo, Sicily. *Phytog., Organog., Monog. of Genera Trifolium, Orobanche, e Art. des Plantes Sic.* C. Ex.
Lombroso, Cesare, Prof. di Medicin legale, Torino. *Anth.* C. Ex.
Lorenzini, Demetrio, Poretta. *Coleopt.**
Lorenzona, Prof. A., Dir. Osservatorio, Padua. *Ast.*
Loreta, Prof. Pietro, Mem. Acad. Sci., Bologna.
Macchiati, Dr. Luigi, Prof. di Storia Naturale nel R. Istituto Tecnico Modena. *Bot. generale, Diatome, Afidi.**
Macchiavelli, Leopoldo, R. Univ., Bologna.
Maestri, Ulisse, Capitano del 25, Fanteria, Naples.
Maggi, Dr. Leopoldo, Prof. Univ., Pavia. *Anat.*
Maggiorani, Carlo, Prof. Emer , Rome.
Magnaguti-Rondinini, Cte. Antoine, Mantua (Lombardy). *Bot., Con.* C. Ex. Offers specimens of plants and mushrooms of Central Europe and the Mediterranean, especially of Algeria.
Magretti, Dr. Paolo, Canonica d'Adda (Prov. di Bergamo). *Gen. Zool., Hymenop.**
Majocchi, Prof. Domenico, R. Univ., Parma. *Mycol.*
Major, C. J. Forsyth, Porto Santo Stefano, near Orbetello, Toscana, Italy. *Palæo., Vert., Mammals, Herpetol., Geographical Dist'n.* Corresponds in Eng., French, German or Italian. C. Ex.*
Malfatti, Giovanni, Professore di Scienze Naturali, Milan. *Ent.: Orthopt., Fossil Insects.* C. Ex. Offers Orthoptera of Lombardy and Italy for foreign.
Malinoerni, Alexis, Quinto-Vercellere, near Vercelli. *Bot.*
Manganotti, Prof. Ant., Lyceum, Mantua. *Bot.*
Manganotti, Dr., Sec. Acad., Verona. *Bot.*
Mantegazza, Prof. Paolo, Pres. Anth. Soc. of Italy, Via Gino Capponi 3, Florence. *Anth., Eth., Ethnog.* C. Ex.*
Manzoni, Count Angelo, M.D., 32 Via Barberia, Bologna. *Geol., Palæo.* C. Ex. especially Echinoderms and fossil sponges.
Marchi, Prof. Pietro, Via degli Alfani 50, Florence.
Marcucci, Dr. E., Borgo Tegolaja 48 pp., Florence. *Bot.**
Martelli, Ugolino, 8 Via della Forca, Florence. *Bot.* Ex.*
Massalongo, Dr. Charus, Prof. de Bot. à l'Université, et Directeur du Jardin Bot., Ferrara. *Bot.: Cryptogams.* C. Ex. Hepaticæ of Europe for those of America.*
Massarenti, Prof. Carlo, Mem. Acad. Sci., Bologna.
Masini, J., Siena. *Bot.*
Matteuzzi Federico, R. Univ., Bologna.
Mattirolo, Dr. Oreste, Torino, Piazza Bodoni 5. *Bot.: Fungi, Anat.**
Mauri, P., Bot. Gar., Rome. *Bot.*
Mayer, Dr. Paul, Stazione Zoologica, Napoli.
Meli, Romolo, Prof. Min. and Geol. in R. Technical Inst., Prof. of Geol. and Ass't in Museum of Geol. in R. Univ., Rome. *Fossils and Recent Shells.* C. Ex.*
Mella-Arborio, Count Charles, Vercelli. *Bot.*
Meneghini, Giuseppe, Prof. Geol., Univ., Pisa. *Bot.*
Meyer, E., Stazione Zoologica, Napoli. *Annelids.*
Millosevich, Elia, Vice Direttore dell' osservatorio astronomico del Collegio, Rome. *Ast.*
Moleschott, Jacopo, Professore di Fisiologia nella Sapienza di Roma. *Physiol.*
Molfino, Gio. Maria, Advocato Professore di Fisico, Genoa. *Ent.*
Molon, Dr. Francesco, Vicenza. *Geol.*
Moni, Olinto, Bagni di Lucca. *Coleopt.*
Montanari, Prof. Antonio di Meldola, R. Univ., Bologna.
Monterosato, Marchese di, 14 Via Carella, Palermo, Sicily. *Con.*
Morescotti, Prof. Angelo, R. Univ., Bologna.

Morettini, Al., Perugia. *Bot.*
Mori, Prof. Ant., Dir. del Giardino botanico della R. Univ. di Modena. *Bot.**
Moriggia, Aliprando, Professore in Istologia e Fisiologia, Via Fontane 4, Rome. *Physiol.*, *Emb.*
Mosso, Angelo, Prof. Physiol., Roy. Univ., Turin.*
Nallino, Prof., Dir. Agric. Station, Udine. *Bot.*
Negri, Dr. A., Padua. *Geol.*, *Palæo.*
Negri, F., Cassale-Monferrato. *Bot.*, *Mic.*, *Diatoms.*
Nencioni, J., Bot. Gar., Pisa. *Bot.*
Nicolis, Cav. Enrico de, Verona. *Geol.**
Nicolucci, Giustiniano, Prof. d'Anthropologie à l'Université, Salita Stella 35, Naples. *Anth. and Prehistoric Arch.* C. Ex. Offers ancient and modern skulls of Italy, and prehistoric objects in exchange for the same from America and other countries.*
Nicotra, Dr. Léopold, Messina, Sicily. *Bot.**
Ninni, Count, Dr. Alessandro, Membro del Comitato direttivo del Civico Museo, St. Lorenzo 3392, Venice. *Fauna Veneto : Vert.*, *Orthopt.*, *Parasita.* C. Ex.
Nobile, Prof. A., Capodimonte, Naples. *Ast.*
Omboni, Giovanni, Prof. de Géologie à l'Université Padua. *Geol.*, *Palæo.* C. Director of the Museum of Geol. of the Univ.*
Orsi, Dr. Paolo, Roma. *Palæo.*
Paganucci, Luigi, Professore ordinario di Anatomia descrittiva, R. Istituto, Florence.
Palmieri, Prof., Obs. Vesuviano, Naples.*
Pantanelli, Prof. Dr. Dante, R. Univ., Modena, Prof. de Geol. *Diatoms*, *Invert. Palæo.*, *Geol.*, *Moll.*, *Radiates*, *Protozoa.*
Paoli, Cesare, Prof. ord. della Paleografia e della Diplomatica, R. Istituto, Florence.*
Paolucci, Prof. L., Inst. Tech., Ancona. *Bot.*
Papasogli, Prof. J. P., Inst. Tech., Alessandria. *Bot.*
Parona, Corrado, Prof. Zool., Anat. and Comp. Phsiol., Univ., Cagliari, Sardinia. *Zool.*, *Thysanura*, *Worms*, *Protozoa*, *Infusoria.*
Parona, Dr. Charles Fabricius, R. Univ., Pavia. *Palæo.*, *Moll. of Trias*, *Lias*, *Jura*, *Mioc. and Phoc*).*
Parona, Dr. Ernesto, Dir. des Hôpitaux Fatebenefratelli, Milan. *Helmintology.**
Pasquale, F., Inst. Tech. e R. Univ., Naples. *Bot.**
Pasquale, Prof. Dr. J. A., R. Orto Botanico, Naples. *Bot.**
Pasqualini, Prof. A., Dir. Agric. Station, Forli.
Passerini, Dr. Giovanni, Prof. di Botanica, Rettore della R. Università, Parma. *Bot.: Phanerogams*, *Mycology*, *Ent.*, *Aphides.* C.
Paulucci, Marchesana, Florence, Villa Novoli. *Moll.*
Pavesi, Prof. Dr. Pietro, Dir. del Museo di Zoologia nella R. Università Pavia. *Zool.*, *Geog. Dist.*, *Ichth.*, *Arach.*, *Entomostraca.* C. Ex.*
Pelliccioni, Gaetano, R. Univ., Bologna. *Phil.*
Penzig, Prof. Dr. Otto, Direttore del R. Orto Botanico dell' Univ. di Genova. *Bot.* (*Anatomy*, *Morphology*, *Mycology*, *Teratology.*) C. Ex. European plants.*
Pepoli, Count Carlo, R. Univ., Bologna.
Perazzi, Commendatore C., Councillor of State, Rome.
Peroglio, Prof. Celestino di Palestro, R. Univ., Bologna. *Geog.*
Peracca, Dott. Mario G., Asst. aggiunto al R. Museo Zoologico, Turin. *Zool.**
Perreau, Pietro, Bibliotecairo della Reale Biblioteca, R. Istituto, Parma.
Pescetto, Capt. Federigo, Turin. *Lepid.*
Piana, Dr. Gian-Pietro, Prof. di Patologia generale e Anatomia Patologica,

R. Scuola Sup. di Med. Veterinaria, Milano. *Pathol.*, *Helminthology.**
Piccardi, Carlo, Bot. Gar., Sassari. *Bot.*
Piccioli, Ferdinando, Aggreg. al R. Museo, via Romana 19, Florence. *Coleopt.*, *Hymenop.*
Piccone, Dr. Antoine, Dr. agrégé à l'Univ., Professeur d'Histoire Naturelle, R. Lycée Cristoforo Colombo, Corso Paganini 67, Genoa. *Bot.: especially Algology.* C. Ex. Algæ of the Mediterranean for those of other localities.*
Pieri, Count Antonio dei Marchesi Nerli, Taverne d'Arabia, Siena.
Pigorini, Prof. Luis, Dir. Arch. Mus., Rome. *Arch.*
Pigorini, Prof. Pietro, Parma. *Ast.*, *Meteo.*
Piccitore-Marrott, Jacques, Dr. en Jurisprudence et en Sciences Naturelles, Via Alacqueda 129, p. p., Palermo, Sicily. *Ent.: Lepid.*, *Coleopt.*, *Shells.* C. Ex. Coleoptera and Lepidoptera of Europe only.
Pini, Napoleone, Ragioniere, Via del Crocifisso 6, Milan. *Coleopt.*
Piolti, Giuseppe, Dr. Nat. Sci., Asst. al Museo Mineralogico dell' Univ. di Torino, Via Arsenale 6, p. 3, Turin.
Pirona, Dr. J. A., Udine. *Bot.*
Pirotta, R., Bot. Gar., Rome, Prof. Bot., R. Univ. *Bot.**
Pirotta, Prof. Dr. Romualdo, R. Lyceum, Alessandro. *Bot.*, *Mycol.*
Pivazzoli, Ed., Imola. *Ent.: Coleopt.*
Pizzi, Prof., Vicebibliotecario della R. Biblioteca, Mediceo-Laurenziana, Florence.
Pizzoni, Guido, Prof. Università di Bologna. *Pathol.*
Pochettino, Prof. J., Inst. Tech., Rome. *Bot.*
Poggi, cav. Vittorio, Maggiore, Paria. *Arch.**
Pollonera, Carlo, R. Museo Zool., Turin. *Moll.*, *Terr. fluv. Europa.* Ex.*
Portis, Dr. Alessandro, Prof. de Geol. à l'Ecole Polytechn., Via Gioberti 20, Roma. *Palæo.*, *Strat. Geol.*, *Vert. Anat.*, *Anth.*, *Osteol.**
Pozzolini, Enrico, Via dei Pilastri 31, Florence. *Ent.*
Prada, Prof. Dr. Teodore, Pres. Inst. Tech., Pavia. *Ent.*, *Coleopt.*
Puini, Carlo, Professore Ordinario di Storia e Geografia dell' Asia Orientale, R. Istituto, Florence. *Geography.*
Pullé, Francesco L., Professore di Storia comparata delle Lingue classiche e di Sanscrito, R. Università, Padua.
Quadri, Dr. Achille, Prof. Zool. and Comp. Anat., R. Univ., Siena. *Gen. Ent.*
Raffaele, D. F., Stazione Zoologica, Napoli. *Ichth.**
Ragona, Dr. D., Obs., Modena.*
Ragusa, Enrico, Dir. Naturalista Siciliano, Via Stabile 89, Palermo, Sicily. *Coleopt.*, *Lepid.*
Ranieri, Dr. Peni, Villa di Grignano, Prato. *Hort.* C. Ex.
Razzaboni, Cesare, Bologna. *Math.*
Regalia, Ettore, Florence. *Anth.**
Respighi, Lorenzo, Prof. Ast., Dir. Ast. Obs. of Campidoglio, Rome.
Rezzio, Dr. Giuseppe, Univ., Palermo, Sicily. *Comp. Anat.*
Ricasoli, Vincent, Via Ricasoli 7, Florence. *Bot.*
Riccardi, Prof. Pietro, Mem. Acad. Sci., Bologna. *Geom.*
Riccò, Cav., Prof. Annibale, Palermo. *Ast.*, *Phys.*
Ridolfi, Marchese L., Via Maggio 13, Florence. *Ent.*
Riggio, Giuseppe, Via Pergole 88, Palermo, Sicily. *Con.*
Rigo, P., Torri del Benaco, Garda. *Bot.*
Rizzoli, Prof. Francesco, Pres. Acad. Sci., Bologna.
Roncati, Prof. Francesco, R. Univ., Bologna.
Rosa, Dr. Daniele, Museo Zoologico, Turin. *Zool.**
Rossetti, Francesco, Prof. Phys., Roy. Univ., Padua.

Rossi, Dr. Prof. Arturo, Padua per Passagno. *Geol., Palæo., Lithol.* C. Ex.
Rostan, Dr. Edouard, San Germano di Pinerolo, Piedmont. *Plants of the Alps.* C. Sells plants of Europe, 25 fr. a hundred specimens. Postage at expense of the purchaser.*
Ruffini, Prof. Ferdinando, Mem. Acad. Sci., Bologna.
Saccardo, Pier-Andrea, Prof. de Botanique et Directeur du Jardin Botanique de l'Université de Padoue, Padua. *Bot., especially Mycology.* C. Ex.
Sacchetti, Dr. Gualtiero, Mem. Acad. Sci., Bologna.
Sacchi, Carlo, Dr. Sci. Nat., 9 Via Chiassi, Mantova. *Mic.*
Sacchi, Cattaneo, Maria, laureata in Sc. Nat., Lab. d'Anat. Comp., dell' Univ. di Pavia. *Mic., Histol., Gen. Biol.**
Sacco, Dr. Frederic, Prof. of Palæo., Univ. of Turin, Museo Geologico, Turin. *Palæo., Invert., Geol., Strat., Tertiary, Anth.**
Salinas, Prof. Antonio, Dir. des fouilles et du Musée National, Palermo. *Arch.*
Salvadori, Prof. Tommaso, Roy. Zool. Mus., Turin. *Orn.**
Santagata, Prof. Domenico, Mura di Porta Mazzini 1, Bologna. *Chem.*
Santalena, Prof. Giov. Treviso, Seminara. *Geol.*
Santoni, Prof. Milziade, Camerino. *Arch.**
Sapeto, Giuseppe, Professore di Arabo nel R. Istituto Tecnico, Genoa.
Saporetti, Antonio, Mem. Acad. Sci., Via Zamboni 33, Bologna. *Ast.*
Sansoni, Dr. Francesco, Prof. de Min. à l'Univ., Pavia. *Crystalog.**
Savastano, Dr. Luigi, Prof. d'Arboriculture, R. Scuola Sup. d'Agriculture Portici (near Naples). *Bot., Pathologie végétale.**
Saverio, Dr. Belli, Asst. Lab. Bot., Univ., Torino. *Bot., Phanerog.* (*Trifolium Hieracium*).*
Savi, Dr. Adolfo, R. Mus. Nat. Hist., Pisa. *Ent.*
Scacchi, Arcangelo, Prof. Univ., Naples. *Min.*
Scaffai, L., Florence. *Bot.*
Scandellari, Dr. Gaetano, Mem. Acad. Sci., Bologna.
Scarabelli, Giuseppe G. F., Imola. *Geol., Palæo.**
Schiaparelli, Giovanni, Dir. R. Obs. of Brera, Milan. *Ast.*
Schiemenz, Dr. P., Stazione Zoologica, Napoli, Librarian. *Mollusca.**
Schiff, Hugo, Prof Chem., Istituto di Studj Superiori, Univ. di Firenze, 3 Via Gino Capponi, Florence. *Chem., Bibliog.* C. of Lab.*
Schiff, Dr. Rob., Laborat. Chimico dell' Univ., Modena *Chem.*
Secco, Chev. Andrea Bassano, Venice. *Geol.*
Seguenza, Prof. Giuseppe, Univ., Messina, Sicily. *Geol.*
Semmola, Eugenio, Istituto tecnico a Tarsia, Naples. *Phys.*
Sertoli, Prof. E., Milano. *Histol.*
Severini, Anselmo, Professore ordinario di Lingue dell' estremo Oriente, R. Istituto Superiore, Florence.
Siacci, Francesco, Prof. Math., Roy. Univ., Turin.
Siemoni, G. C., Rome. *Agric., Bot.*
Simonetti, Dr. T., Dir. School Agric., Caltagirone, Sicily. *Bot.*
Siragusa, Francesco Paolo Camillo, Prof., pareggiato all' Università, Via delle Pergole 33, Palermo, Sicily. *Bot. and Veg. Physiol.**
Société Technique, rue des Benci 4, Florence. *Gen. Ent.*
Solla, Dr. R., Prof. R. Forest Acad., Vallombrosa (Toscana). *Bot.**
Sommier, Stephen, Lungarno, Secret. Soc.d'Anthrop., Corsini 2, Florence. *Bot.**
Sordelli, Ferdinand, Museum, Milan. *Palæo., Bot., Herpetol.**
Soverini, Dr. Carlo, Mem. Acad. Sci., Bologna.
Spence, Guglielmo, Via degli Strozzi, Palazzo Corsi, Florence. *Ent.: Lepid.*
Spezia, Giorgio, Prof. Univ., Turin. *Min.*
Spica, Prof. Pietro, Laborat. Chimico-farmaceut.dell' Univ., Padua. *Chem.**
Stefanelli, Prof. Pietro, Via Pinti 57, Florence. *Lepid.*

Stoppani, Antonio, Prof. de Géologie à l'Institut des Etudes Supérieures et Directeur du Museo Civico à Milano. *Palæo.*, *Geol.*, *Terrestria Phys.* C.
Strobel, Dr. Pellegrino, Prof. à l'Univ., etc., Parma. *Malacology*, *Paleth-nology*, *Palæo.**
Strüver, Giovanni, Prof. Univ., Rome. *Min.*
Tacchini, Pietro, Direttore dell' Osservatorio del Collegio Romano, Roma. *Ast.**
Tanari, March. Luigi, Via Palestro 3, Florence. *Ent.*
Tapparoni-Canefri, Dr. Cesar, 21 Via San Quintino, Turin. *Moll.*
Taramelli, Dr. Torquato, Prof. de Géologie à l'Université, Pavia. *Geol. of secondary formations of the Alps and Appenines.* C. Fossils of the Alps. Ex.
Tardy, Placido, Roy. Univ., Genoa. *Math.*
Targioni-Tozzetti, Ad., Prof. di Zool. ed Anat. degle animali invert., Inst. Studi Superiori di Firenze, Via Romana 19, Firenze. *Anat. and Zool. of Invert.*, *Homoptera*, *Crust.*, *Orthopt.*, *Anat. of Insects*, *Econom. Ent.*
Taruffi, Prof. Cesare, Mem. Acad. Sci., Bologna. *Anat.*
Tassi, Prof. Att., Univ., Siena. *Bot.*
Tempel, W., Obs., Arceti, Florence. *Ast.*
Tenchini, Prof. Lorenzo, R. Univ., Parma. *Anat.**
Tenore, Prof. Gaetano, Napoli. *Min.*
Tenore, Prof. Dr. Vincent, Naples. *Bot.*, *Zool.*
Terraciano, Dr. N., Dir. R. Garden, Caserta. *Bot.*
Terreni, Maggior Fortunato, Via dell' Orivolo 35, Florence. *Ent.*
Terrenzi, Guiseppe, Narni (Ombrie). *Palæo.* C. Ex.
Testi, Francesco, R. Univ., Modena. *Ent.*
Teza, Prof. Emilio, R. Univ., Bologna.
Thomassi, Dr., Florence. *Chem.*, *Phys.*
Thorell, Prof. Dr. Tamerlan, Museo Civico, Genoa. *Arach.* (See Sweden).*
Tocco, Felice, Prof. ordinario di Storia della Filosofia, R. Istituto di Studi Superiori, Florence. *Phil.**
Todaro, Prof. Agostino, Senator del Regno, Direttore del Orto Botanico, Palermo, Sicily. *Bot.* C. Ex. Flora of Sicily.
Todaro, Prof. Antonio, Formaggi 10, Palermo, Sicily. *Bibliog.*, *Bot.*
Todaro, Prof. Francesco, Rome. *Anat.*
Tommasi, Dr. Prof. Annibale, Udine. *Palæo.*, *Geol.**
Tommasi, Anselmo, Castelgoffredo. *Malacol.*
Tommasi-Crudeli, Conrad, Director of the Hygienical Inst. of the University, Via Quattro Fontave 94, Rome. *Experimental Pathology, especially infections and malaria.*
Tommasi, Prof. Salvatore, Naples.
Tornabene, Prof. Fr., Univ., Dir. Bot. Gar., Catania, Sicily. *Bot.*
Traverso, G. B., Civ. Mus., Genoa. *Min.**
Traverso, J., Pavia. *Bot.*
Trevison di S. Leon, Count Vittore, Monza, near Milan. *Bot.*
Trinchese, Salvatore, Prof. Comp. Anat., Roy. Univ., Naples. *Zool.*
Trineber, Prof. Univ., Naples. *Zool.*
Trois, Henry Philippe, Conservateur des Musées zoologiques et anatomiques de l'Institut Royale des Sciences, Palais Ducale, Venice. *Ichth.*, *Anat. of fishes*, *Angiology of inferior vertebrates*, *Anatomy of marine invertebrates.* C. Ex. Offers duplicate anatomical preparations of vertebrates, especially marine fishes, turtles, cephalopods, etc.*
Turrini, Prof. Giuseppe di Avio, R. Univ., Bologna. *Phil.*
Ulivi, Giotto, Doyen, Campi-Bisenzio (Tuscany). *Ent.*, *Nat. Hist. of Bees*, *Hymenop.*

Uzielli, Prof. Gustave, Scuola d'Applicazione per gli Ingegneri, Turin. *Min.*, *Geol.**
Valenziani, Avv. Carlo, Professore di Lingue e Letterature dell' Estremo Oriente nella R. Università, Rome.
Valerga, Abate Pietro, Prof. Coll. Internazionale, Turin. *Bibliog.*, *Philol.*
Valiante, R., Ponterorvo 90, Naples. *Bot.*
Varijeo, Prof. Antonio, Bergamo. *Geol.*
Verdiani, Giuseppe, Volterra. *Ent.*
Verdiani-Bandi, Arnaldo, San Quirico d'Orcia (Siena). *Ent.*
Verdiani-Bandi, Luigi, Rocca d'Orcia (Siena) *Coleopt. of Europe.* C. Ex. Coleoptera of Europe, especially of Italy, for Coleoptera of the world, but prefers Pselaphidæ, Cerambycidæ and Chrysomelidæ.
Verson, Prof E., Padua. *Bot.*
Villari, Imilio, Via delle Belle Arti, Università, Bologna. *Phys.*
Villari, Pasquale, Senatore, Memb. del Cosiglio Superiore, Prof. ord. di Storia Moderna, Pres. del' Sezione di Lettere, R. Istituto Superiore, Florence.*
Vimercati, Comte Professeur Guido, Directeur de la Revue Scientifique indus., Membre de la Société Entomologique Italienne, Lungarmo Zecca, Villino 2, Florence. *Ent.: Coleopt.*, *Moll.*, *Fossils et Minéraux de l'Ile d'Elbe.* C. Ex.*
Vinciguerra, Decio, Civ. Mus., Genoa. *Ichth.*
Vismara, Francesco, Civ. Mus., Milan. *Hemipt.*
Vosmaer, Dr. G. C. J., Asst. Stazione Zoologica, Naples. *Sponges.**
Winterberg, Dr. E., Rome. *Ast.*
Zanetti, Dr. Arturo, Prof. Nat. Hist., Tech. Sch., Via de Conti, Florence. *Anth.*
Zersi, Prof. Elias, R. Lyceum, Bergamo. *Bot.*
Zigno, Baron A. de, Venice. *Bot.*, *Palæo.*, *Ichth.*
Zona, Dr. T., Forli. *Ast.*
Zoological Station (Stazione Zoologica) at Naples. *Marine Zool.* Prof. Anton Dohrn, Director. Assistants, Dr. Hugo Eisig, *Annelids*: Dr. Wilh. Giesbrecht, *Crustacea*; Dr. Paul Mayer, *Anthropods*; E. Meyer, *Annelids*; Dr. F. Raffaele, *Pisces*; Dr. P. Schiemenz, *Mollusca*; Dr. G. C. J. Vosmaer, *Sponges.**
Zouoli, Prof. Francesco, Milano. *Comp. Anat.*

MALTA.

Brickenden, Major Richard Thomas William Lambert.
Gulia, Dr. Gavin, Valetta. *Ichth.*
Warton, Capt. R. G., 10th Regiment.
Zeraffa, Prof. Stefano.

NETHERLANDS.

Abeleven, Th., H. A. J., Sec. Bot. Soc., Nijmegen. *Bot.**
Aghina, Vinc. Mar., High St., Schiedam. *Bot.*, *Ent.: Lepid.*, *Coleopt.*
Albarda, Dr. William, Ginneken, near Breda. *Ent.: Lepid.*, *Coleopt.* *Neuropt.*, *Sponges*, *Protozoa.* C.
Albarda, J. Herman, Leeuwarden. *Neuropt.*
Andreæ, Dr. J. L., Sneek. *Chem.*
Ankum, Dr. A. H. van, Groningen. *Chem.*

Ankum, Dr. H. J. van, Prof. Univ., Groningen, *Zool.*, *Ent.*
Annëns, Harmens W., Analytical Chemist, Spuistraat 146, Amsterdam. *Chem.*, *Mic.**
Aronstein, Dr. L., Breda. *Chem.*
Baas, A. G. de, Beestraat 151, Leiden.
Backer, J., Oosterbeek, near Arnheim. *Coleopt.*
Baehr, Dr. G. F. W., Prof. Polytechnic College, Delft. *Math.*
Baelde, C. H. L., Hoozewoerd 99, Leiden.
Bakhoven, Dr. G. H. Leignes, Kampen. *Chem.*
Bakhuis-Roozeboom, Dr. H. W., Asst. Lab., Univ., Leiden. *Inorg. Chem.**
Bakhuijzen, Dr. H. G. van de Sande, Prof. Univ., Leiden. *Ast.*
Ballot, Dr. C. H. D. Buijs, Prof. Univ. and Director of the Royal Dutch Meteorological Institute, Utrecht. *Phys.*, *Meteo.**
Baumhauer, Dr. E. H. von, Sec. of the Dutch Society of Science. Haarlem. *Chem.* C. Ex. publications on Natural Science of Netherlands for others.
Behrens, Dr. Th. H., Prof. Polytechnic College, Delft. *Min.*
Beijerinck, Dr. M. W., Bacteriologist, Delft. *Bot.*, *Plant galls.* Ex. Wishes living American Rosegalls, with living Wasps (Rhodites).*
Bemmelen, A. A. van, Dir. der Rotterdamsche Diergaarde, Pres. der Nederlandsche Dierkundige Vereeniging, Rotterdam. *Gen. Zool.**
Bemmelen, Dr. J. F. van, Assistant at the Zoological Laboratory, Utrecht. *Zool.*
Bemmelen, Prof. Dr. J. M. van, Dir. Lab., Univ., Noordeinde 50, Leiden. *Inorg. Chem.**
Berg, F. J. van den, Ex-Prof. Polytechnic School, Delft. Address, Rotterdam, Mauritsweg 37. *Math.**
Berg, J. C. van den, Breestraat 72, Leiden. Havendijk, Goringen.
Berlin, Dr. W., Prof. Emer., Univ., Amsterdam. *Zool.*
Bierens de Haan, Prof. Dr. D., Univ., Rapenburg 26, Leiden. *Math.*
Bijleveld, Dr. R. Th., Jr., Rapenburg, Leiden. *Gen. Ent.*
Binnendijk, Dr. J., Amsterdam. *Physiol.*
Bisschop van Tuinen, K., Lehrer a. Reichs Höhere Bürgerschule und das Gym., Zwolle. *Phæn. and Crypt. Bot.*, *Lepid.*, *Coleopt.* C. Ex.*
Bleekrode, Dr. L., The Hague. *Phys.*
Boeke, Dr. J. D., Alkmaar. *Chem.*
Boer, Dr. P. de, Prof. Univ., Groningen. *Bot.*
Boerlage, Dr. J. G., Con. Roy. Herb., Leiden. *Bot.*
Bohnensieg, G. C. W., Librarian of Teijler's Museum, Haarlem. *Bot.*
Bosscha, Prof. Dr. J., Sec. of Dutch Soc. Sci., Haarlem. *Phys.**
Braam, Houckgeest, Dr. J. P. van, Prof. Univ., Groningen. *Anat.*
Brandt, A. van den, Venlo. *Coleopt.*
Brants, Dr. A., Jr., Buitensingel, Arnheim. *Lepid.*
Bremer, Dr. G. J. W., Rotterdam. *Chem.**
Breukelman, M., Delfthaven. *Lepid.*
Brink, G. van den, Hortulanus at the Univ., Utrecht. *Bot.*, *Hort.*
Broek, Dr. J. H. van den, Nijmegen. *Chem.*
Brondgeest, Dr. P. Q., Lecturer, Univ., Utrecht. *Physiol.*
Brutel de la Rivière, P. M., Leiden. *Engineer.*
Bruijn, L. de, Delft. *Ent.*
Bückmann, Dr. H. W. C. E., Amsterdam. *Physics.*
Buijsman, M., Middleburg. Publishes a general analytical herbarium, and
Burg, Prof. Dr. E. A. van der, Dir. Pharm. Lab., Univ., Langebrug 87, Leiden. *Pharm.*, *Toxicol.*
Burger, Dr. C. P., Leeuwarden. *Math.*
Burgersdijk, Dr. L. A. J., Deventer. *Zool.**
Buse, Dr. L. H., Renkum, near Arnheim. *Bot.*
Büttikofer, J., Conserv. of the Royal Mus. of Nat. Hist., Leiden. *Zool.**

desires to come into relation with all botanists for the sake of getting collaborators. Also wishes all meteorological reviews and publications, especially of Australia and South America. *Bot.*, *Phæn. Plants*, *Meteo.**
Calker, Dr. F. J. P. van, Prof. Univ., Groningen. *Min.*
Calkoen, H. J., Amsterdam. *Bot.*
Cankrien, A., Boompjes, Rotterdam. *Lepid.*
Cattie, Dr. J. Th., Arnhem, Holland. *Zool.*, *Bot.*, *Vergl. Anat.*, *Mic.**
Cleeff, Dr. G. Doijer van, Amsterdam. *Chem.**
Cobet, Prof. Dr. Carel Gabriel, Univ., Rapenburg 2, Leiden. *Antiquities*, *Palæography.*
Conrad, J. F. W., The Hague. *Engineer.*
Costerus, Dr. J. C., 10 Oosteinde, Amsterdam. *Bot.**
Crok, C., Bloemist, Cupelstraat I, 18, Utrecht. *Bot.*, *Hort.*
Dekhuijzen, Dr. M. C., Asst. Physiol. Lab., Univ., Maarsmansteeg 9, Leiden. *Physiol.*
De Leeuw, Dr. F. Leo, Wemeldinge. *Pisciculture*, *Agric.**
De Man, Dr. J. G., Middleburg. *Crustacea*, *Lower Animals.**
De Vries, Dr. Hugo, Prof. Univ., Amsterdam. *Physiol.*, *Bot.**
Dibbits, Dr. H. C., Prof. Univ., Utrecht. *Inorg. Chem.**
Diesen, G. van, The Hague. *Engineer.**
Dissel, Dr. E. F. van, Leiden. *Engineer.*
Donders, Dr. F. C., Prof. Univ., President of the Royal Academy of Science, Utrecht. *Physiol.* C. Ex.
Du Bois, Henri, E. J. G., Dr. Phil. Nat., 47 Bezuidenhout, The Hague. *Phys.*, *Elect.**
Eeden, F. W. van, Haarlem. *Bot.*
Eeden, W. van, Jr., Langebrug 107, Leiden.
Eek, A. van, Raamstraat 9, Leiden.
Egeling, C., Guldensteeden, Zeist. *Chem.*
Ekama, Dr. H., Amersfoort. *Phys.**
Engelmann, Dr. Th. W., Prof. Univ., Utrecht. *Physiol.*, *Histol.*, *Gen. Biol.*
Enklaar, Dr. J. E., Heerenveen. *Chem.*
Enschedé, Dr. W. A., Emeritus Prof., Univ., Groningen. *Math.**
Erbrink, J. F. G. W., N. Z. Voorburgwal, over de Kolk, Nr. 62, Amsterdam. *Gen. Ent.*
Everts, Dr. E. J. G., The Hague. *Ent.* C.
Fijnje van Salverda, H. F., Nijmegen. *Engineer.**
Fokker, Dr. A. J. F., Zierikzee. *Ent.: Hemipt.*, *Coleopt.* C. Ex. Offers Coleopt. and Hemipt. of Holland for European Hemipt. Wishes to buy European Hemipt., or to ex. Coleopt. and Hemipt. of Holland for them.
Fokker, Dr. A. P., Prof. Univ., Groningen. *Hygiene.*
Forster, Dr. J., Prof. Univ., Amsterdam. *Hygiene.*
Franchimont, Prof. Dr. A. P. N., Dir. Lab., Univ., Rapenburg 104, Leiden. *Org. Chem.*
Franckenberg en Proschlitz, W. M. S. C. van, The Hague. *Math.**
Fürbringer, Dr. M., Prof. Univ., Amsterdam. *Anat.*
Geer, Prof. Dr. P. van, Univ., Rapenburg 81, Leiden. *Math.*
Giltay, Dr. E., Asst. Bot. Lab., Univ., Breestraat 72, Leiden.
Giltay, J. W., Delft. *Physics.*
Gorkum, K. W. van, Baarn. *Bot.*
Graaf, W. de, Noordeinde 123, The Hague. *Micro-Lepid. and Avesindi Genae.**
Graaf, H. W. de, Hoogewoerd 123, Leiden. *Zool.*
Gratama, Dr. W. D., Gymnasium, Delft. *Chem.*
Grinwis, Dr. C. H. C., Prof. Univ., Utrecht. *Math.*, *Phys.**
Groneman, Dr. F. G., Groningen. *Phys.*

Groneman, H. J. H., Arnheim. *Math.*
Grotendorst, E. J., The Hague.
Grothe, D., Prof. Polytechnic College, Delft. *Technology.*
Grothe, W. K., Zeist. *Ent.*
Gunning, Dr. J. W., Prof. Univ., Amsterdam. *Chem.*
Guye, Dr. A. A. G., Prof. Univ., Amsterdam. *Otology.**
Haan, Dr. D. Bierens de, Prof. Univ., Leiden. *Math.*
Haar, D. ter, Nijmegen. C. *Lepid.*
Haga, Dr. H., Delft. *Phys.*
Halbertsma, Dr. T., Prof. Univ., Utrecht.*
Harst, L. J. van der, Veterinary College, Utrecht. *Physiol. of plants.*
Harting, Dr. P., Emeritus Prof., Kampen. *Zool.*
Hartogh, Heijs von Zouteveen, Dr. Hermann, Assen Drente. *Palæo., Geol., Min., Chem., Anth., Prehistoric Arch.*
Hasselt, Dr. A. W. M. van, The Hague. *Toxicology. Arach.*
Hasselt, W. van, Amsterdam. *Meteo.*
Hennekeler, Dr. A. van, Amsterdam. *Phys.*
Hensgen, C., Asst. Lab., Univ., Oude Vest 19, Leiden. *Inorg. Chem.*
Hertz, Dr. H., Prof. Univ., Amsterdam. *Pathol.*
Heusch de la Zangrije, Baron Oscar de, Strabeek, near Valkenburg (Limburg). *Coleopt.*
Heylaerts, Dr. F. J. M., St. Jansstr. A. 503, Breda. *Lepid.* C. Ex.*
Heynsius, Prof. Dr. A., Dir. Physiol. Lab., Univ., Nieusteeg 21, Leiden.
Hoek, Dr. P. P. C., First Sec.-Lib., Neth. Zool. Soc., Leiden. *Zool., Emb. and Anat. of Invert., Crustacea, Fishes.**
Hoff, Dr. J. H. van't, Prof. Univ., Amsterdam. *Chem.**
Hoffman, Prof. Dr. C. K., Dir. Zool. Lab., Univ., Oude Singel 20, Leiden. *Zool.*
Hoffmann, Prof. J. J. P., Leiden. *Ent.*
Honert, J. van der, Schipperstraat 26, Amsterdam. *Ent.*
Hoogewerff, Dr. S., Rotterdam. *Chem.*
Hoorweg, Dr. J. L., Utrecht. *Phys.**
Horst, Dr. R., Conservator Mus. Nat. Hist., Nieuwsteeg 2, Leid n. *Invert., esp. Worms.* Ex.*
Hubrecht, Dr. A. A. W., Prof. Univ., Utrecht. *Zool., Comp. Anat., Emb.**
Huet, Prof. Dr. G. D. E., Univ., Hooigracht 67, Leiden. *Med., Klin., Pharm.*
Huisman, Dr. A., Utrecht. *Osteol.*
Huizinga, Dr. D., Prof. Univ., Groningen. *Physiol.*
Imans, Dr. M., Utrecht. *Ent.*
Janse, J. M., Dr., Asst. Bot. Univ. of Leiden, Oude Rijn 14, Leiden. *Bot., Physiology, Anat., Biol.**
Jentink, Dr. F. A., Director of the Museum of Natural History, Leiden. *Zool., Mammalia.**
Joncheere, J. C. J. de, Voorstraat, D 368, Dordrecht. *Lepid.*
Jonkman, Dr. H. F., Univ., Utrecht. *Bot.*
Jordens, D. J. R., Sassenportewal, F 3471, Zwolle. *Lepid.*
Julius, Dr. V. A., Delft. *Phys.**
Kamerlingh, Dr. H., Asst. Phys. Lab. of the Polytechnic School, Delft.
Kamerlingh, Prof. Dr. Onnes, Dir. Phys. Cab., Univ., Oude Singel 6, Leiden. *Phys.*
Kan, Dr. C. M., Vice-Pres. of Dutch Geogr. Soc., Prof. in Geog. at the Univ. of Amsterdam. Sarphalistraat 88.*
Kappers, Dr. J. A., Sappemeer. *Chem.*
Kapteijn, Dr. J. C., Prof. Univ., Groningen. *Math.*
Kapteijn, Dr. W., Prof. Univ., Utrecht. *Math.**
Kate, Dr. H., Sr., 48 Javarhart, The Hague. *Anth., Eth., Geol.*

Kerbert, Coenraad, Ph.D., Manager Aquarium, Royal Zool. Soc. Amsterdam. *Zool., Gen. Biol., Ichth., Worms, Parasites.*
Kerkhoven, W. O., Twello. *Ent.*
Keijzer, Dr. Y., Middleburg. *Zool., Moll.*
Kinker, J., Keizersgracht 580, Amsterdam. *Diatoms.* C. Ex.*
Klobbie, E. A., Plein 4, The Hague. *Org. and Inorg. Chem.*
Kobus, J. D., Wageningen. *Bot.* C. Ex.
Koning, Dr. P. de, Anat. Cab., Univ., Rapenburg 21, Leiden. *Anat.*
Kooijker, Dr. H. A., Prof. Univ., Groningen. *Clin.*
Koppeschaar, Dr. W. F., The Hague. *Chem.*
Korteweg, Dr. D. J., Prof. Univ., Amsterdam. *Math.*
Korthals, Dr. S. W., Haarlem. *Bot.*
Kuhn, Dr. C. H., Prof. Univ., Amsterdam. *Anat.*
Koster, Dr. W., Prof. Univ., Utrecht. *Anat.*
Kramps, Dr. J. M. A., Breda. *Chem.*
Lacoste, Dr. C. M. van der Sande, Amsterdam. *Bot., Bryol.*
Laer, Dr. J. R. E van, Utrecht. *Geol.**
La Fontijn, N., Vlissingen. *Ent.*
Lansberge, Dr. J. W. van, Brummen. *Ent.: Coleopt.* C.
Ledden Hulsebosch, M. L. Q. van, Apotheker, Nieuwendijk 17, Amsterdam. *Microscopic Cryptogams, Fungi.* C. Ex. native cryptogams for those of other countries.*
Leesberg, A. F. A., Jan-Hendrickstraat 9, The Hague. *Coleopt.* C. Ex.
Leemans, Dr. Conradus, Dir. Royal Netherlands Mus. of Antiq., Leiden. *Arch., Eth., Ethnol., Philol.*
Leeuwen, Professor Dr. J. van, Jr., Noordeinde, Leiden. *Lepid.*
Legebeke, Dr. G. J., Prof. Polytechnic College, Delft. *Math.*
Lith, Dr. J. P. T. van der, Prof. titul., Utrecht. *Psychiat.**
Lobry van Troostenburg de Bruijn, C. A., Asst. Lab., Univ., Houtstraat 5, Leiden. *Org. Chem.*
Lodeesen, J. W., Tulpstraat 6, te Amsterdam. *Lepid. indigena.**
Logeman, W. M., Haarlem. *Phys.*
Loghem, W. van, The Hague.
Loman, Dr. J. C. C., Leidschekade 96, Amsterdam. *Zool.**
Loncq, Dr. G. J., Emeritus Prof., Univ., Utrecht. *Pathol.*
Loos, Dr. D. de, Leiden. *Chem.*
Lorentz, Dr. H. A., Prof. Univ., Leiden. *Math., Phys.**
Lorie, Dr., Privat Docent, Geological Museum, Utrecht. *Invert. Palæo., Strat. and Phys. Geol.**
Lotman, Gerbrand, Rozengracht 152, Amsterdam. *Chem., Hort.**
Lubach, Dr. D., Kampen. *Zool.*
MacGillavry, Prof. Dr. Th. H., Univ., Garenmarkt 9, Leiden. *Pathol. Anat., Hygiene.*
Martin, Dr. K., Prof. Univ., Dir. Roy. Geol. Mus., Leiden. *Geol., Min., Palæo.*
Maurissen, A. H., rue de Tongres, Maestricht. *Insects d'Europe.*
Mayer, Prof. Dr. Adolf. E., Director of the Government Establishment for Experiments in Agriculture. *Agricultural Chem.*
Medendach de Rooij, A. B. van, Weerdjesstraat, Arnheim. *Lepid.*
Mees, Dr. R. A., Prof. Univ., Groningen. *Phys.*
Meilink, Dr. B., Kampen. *Phys.*
Mellink, Dr. J. F. A., Assen. *Bot., Anat.*
Meyer, Dr. G. van Overbeek de, Prof. Univ., Utrecht. *Hygiene*
Meijeringh, Dr. W., Arnheim. *Chem.*
Meulen, Dr. B. van der, Winschoten. *Chem.*
Michaëlis, Dr. G. J., Arnheim. *Math.**
Michaëlis, N. T., The Hague. *Engineer.*

Middendorp, Dr. H. W., Prof. Univ., Groningen. *Pathol. Anat., Pathol.**
Modderman, Dr. R. S. Tjaden, Prof. Univ., Groningen. *Chem.*
Moens, Dr. Isebree, Geos. *Physiol.*
Molengraaff, G. A. F., Phil. Nat. Doct., Assist. at the Botanical Lab., Utrecht. *Bot., Geol.*
Moll, Dr. J. W., Utrecht. *Bot.**
Mollinger, Godefroi, Mem. de la Société d'acclimation de France, Wageningen. *Lepid.* C. Correspondence desired with collectors in the United States and Canada *for the purchase or ex. of hibernating pupæ of America, Rhopaloceres and Heteroceres.*
Mourik, P. van, Utrecht. *Math.*
Mulder, Dr. E., Prof. Univ., Utrecht. *Org. Chem.**
Neervoort van de Poll, J. R. H., Amsterdam. *Ent., Coleopt.* C. Ex.
Obbes, Dr. F. N., Hilversum. *Ent.*
Onnes, Dr. H. Kamerlingh, Prof. Univ ,Leiden. *Phys.*
Oudemans, Dr. A. C., Prof. Polytechnic College, Delft. *Chem.*
Oudemans, Dr. C. A. J. A., Prof. Univ., Sec. of the Royal Academy of Science, Amsterdam. *Bot., Mycol.**
Oudemans, Dr. J. A. C., Dir. of Observatory, Prof. Univ., Utrecht. *Ast.**
Oudemans, Jzz. Dr. A. C., Cons. Zool. Mus., Mitglied der Niederländischen Entomologischen Gesellschaft der Niederl. Zool. Gesellschaft, und des Niederl. Naturwiss. Congresses, zu Haag.*
Oudemans, Johannes Theodorus, Ass't. in Zool. a. d. Univ., Sarphatistraat 78, Amsterdam. *Hymenopt.* C. Ex.
Pekelharing, Dr. C. A , Prof. Univ., Utrecht. *Pathol., Physiol.*
Pesch, A. J. van, Prof. Univ., Amsterdam. *Math.*
Plaats, Dr. J. D. van der, Veterinary College, Utrecht. *Chem.*
Place, Dr. T., Prof. Univ., Amsterdam. *Physiol.*
Plemper van Balen, B. A., Hortulanus at the Univ., Amsterdam. *Bot. Hort.* Ex.
Pleyte, Dr. W., Curator Arch. Mus., Rapenburg 84, The Hague. *Arch.*
Plugge, Dr. P. C., Prof. Univ., Groningen. *Pharmacy and Toxicology.*
Pollen, François, P. L., A. L. M. et Phil. Dr., Vice Consulat Impérial d'Allemagne, Scheveningen, The Hague. *Hort., Palæo., Geol., Min., Lithol., Metal., Bibliog., Gen. Biol., Geog. Dist., Anth., Vertebrates, Tax., Osteol.* C. Ex.
Putnam-Cramer, W. I. C., Velp, bei Arnheim. *Ent.: Lepid.* C. Ex.
Ras, P. H. J. J., Jr., Huize Rijnstein, Arnheim. *Ent.*
Rauwenhoff, Dr. N. W. P., Prof. Univ., Utrecht. *Anat. and Physiol. of plants, Cryptogams.**
Rees, Dr. J. van, Assistant at the Physiological Laboratory, Amsterdam. *Physiol., Zool.*
Riemsijk, Dr. A. D. van, Assayer General at the Royal Mint, Utrecht. *Chem.*
Rijke, P. L., Prof. Emer., Univ., Hooigracht 13, Leiden. *Phys.*
Rink, Dr. H. J., Prof. Univ., Groningen. *Math.*
Ritzema Bos, Dr. J., Agricultural College, Wageningen. *Economic Zoology, Injurious Insects* and other lower animals, and plant diseases caused by them.*
Ritsema, C. Czn., Mus. Nat. Hist., Rapenburg 94, Leiden. *Articulates.**
Robbers, Dr. J., Gymnasium, Utrecht. *Math.*
Rombouts, Dr. J. E., Amsterdam. *Entomology.*
Rombouts, Dr. J. G. H , Groesbeek. *Ent.*
Romburgh, Dr. P. van, Asst. Lab., Univ., Kaiserstraat 28, Leiden. *Org. Chem.*
Romeny, Dr. J., Dordrecht. *Chem.*
Roo van Westmaas, Dr. E. A. de, Jr., Huize Daalhuigen, Velp. *Lepid.*
Roos, P. F. van Hamel, Dr. of Nat. Phil., Rédacteur en chef de la Revue

Internationale des Falsifications, 146 Spuistraat, Amsterdam. *Chem.*, *Mic.**
Rossum, Dr. A. J. van, Kastanjelaan, Arnheim. *Ent.*
Roijen, Dr. A. E. van, Haarlem. *Chem.*
Ryke, D. P. L., Emeritus Prof. Univ., Leiden. *Phys.*
Saltet, R. H., Doct. Med., Singel 318, Amsterdam. *Hygiene.* *
Salverda, Dr. M., The Hague. *Zool.*
Sande, Bakhuyzen, Dr. E. F. van der, Privatdocent, Ast. Obs., Univ.. Leiden. *Ast.*
Sänger, Dr. W. M. H., Prof. Univ., Groningen.*
Scheffer, Dr. J. D. R., Veendam. *Chem.*
Schepman, M. M., Rhoon, near Rotterdam. *Moll.*
Schepmann, W. A., Invangh, Rhoon. *Lepid.*
Schill, J. F., Amsterdamsche veerkade 25, The Hague. *Palæo.*, *Bibliog.*, *Zool.*, *Sponges.* C. Ex.*
Schmeltz, J. D. E., Cur. Ethnog. Museum, Leiden. *Ethnog.*, *Ethnol.*, *Anth.*, *Zool.*, *Geog. Dist.**
Schols, Dr. C. M., Prof. Polytechnic College, Delft. *Math.*, *Geod.**
Schoute, Dr. P. H., Prof. Univ., Groningen. *Math.*
Schubärt, Dr. J. W., Utrecht. *Ent.*
Seelheim, Dr. F., Utrecht. *Chem.*
Seipgens, Emile, Normal School, Leiden. *Coleopt.**
Serrurier, Dr. L., Dir. R. Ethnog. Museum, Leiden. *Anth.*, *Arch.*, *Ethnog.*
Sirks, Dr. J., Deventer. *Phys.*
Six, G. A., The Hague. *Coleopt.*
Smeets, J. A., Keeper of the Government Herbarium, Leiden. *Bot.*
Snellen, Dr. Herman, Prof. Univ., Utrecht. *Ophthal.*
Snellen, Dr. Maurits, Director of the section "Land-observations" of the Royal Dutch Meteorological Institute, Utrecht. *Meteo.**
Snellen, P. C. T., Wynhaven 45, Rotterdam. *Lepid.* C. Ex.
Snijders, Dr. A. J. C., Zutphen. *Chem.*
Snijders, J. A., Prof. Polytechnic College, Delft. *Math.*
Stadt, Dr. H. van de, Arnheim. *Meteo.*, *Phys.**
Stenfert Kroese, Dr. H. P. T., Arnheim. *Math.*
Stieltjes, F. J. J., Jr., Asst. Ast. Obs., Leiden. *Ast.*
Stoeder, W., Prof., Univ., Amsterdam. *Pharm.*
Stokvis, Dr. B. J., Prof. Univ., Amsterdam. *Pathol.*, *Physiol.*
Stolk, J. van, Zeemansstraat, Rotterdam. *Lepid.*
Stortenbeker, W., Goes. *Theoretic Chem.**
Suringar, Prof. Dr. W. F. R., Dir. Bot. Lab., Univ., Nonnensteeg 1, Leiden. *Bot.*
Swarts, Dr. Th., Univ., Ghent. *Chem.*
Swierstra, K. N., Amsterdam. *Coleopt.*
Talma, Dr. S., Prof. Univ., Utrecht.*
Thomas, Dr. A. E. Simon, Prof. Univ., Leiden. *Obstet.*
Tordens, D. J. Rudolf, Mem. of the Ent. Soc. of the Netherlands, Zwolle. *Lepid.* C. Ex.*
Tuyl van Scrooskerken, F.L.S., Buitensingel, Arnheim. *Ent.*
Ubaghs, Musée Casimir, Maestricht. *Geol.*, *Palæo.*, *Con.*, *Prehistorie Arch.* C.
Uijen, H., Priemstraat, Nymwegen. *Lepid.* C.
Valeton, Dr. Th., Leeraar in Plant. en Dierkunde, Groningen. *Mic.*, *Olacineæ.**
Van Haren Norman, Dr. Dirk, Oosterstraat 5, Utrecht. *Vert. Emb.*, *Anat. and Hist.*
Ven, Dr. E. van der, Director of Teijler's Museum, Haarlem. *Phys.*
Verbrugge, B., Leuvenhaven 209, Rotterdam. *Coleopt.*
Verloren, Dr. C. M., Schöthorst, near Amersfoort. *Coleopt.*

Verster van Wulverhorst, F. A., Administrateur Mus. Nat. Hist., Rapenburg 40, Leiden.*
Veth, Prof. D. P. J., Univ., Papenstraat 6, Leiden. *Phys. Geog., Indian Archipel.*
Veth, Dr. H. J., Boezemsingel 118, Rotterdam. *Coleopt.* C. Ex. European for N. American specimens.*
Waals, Dr. J. D. van der, Prof. Univ., Amsterdam. *Phys.*
Wakker, J. H., Amsterdam. *Bot., Fungi.*
Wall, Dr. N. van de, Amsterdam. *Chem.*
Weber, Dr. Max., Prof. Zool., Amsterdam. *Mam.*
Wefers, Bettink, D. H., Prof. Univ., Utrecht. *Pharm.*
Went, Dr. F. A. F. C., 95 Heerengracht, Amsterdam. *Bot.**
Westerman, Dr. G. F., Director of the Royal Zool. Soc., "Natura Artis Magister," Amsterdam. *Zool.**
Weijtlandt, A. J., Rijswijk, near The Hague. *Coleopt.*
Wichmann, Dr. C. E. A., Prof. Univ., Utrecht. *Min., Geol.*
Wilterdink, J. H., Ast. Obs., Leiden. *Ast.*
Winkler, Dr. T. C., Director of Teijler's Museum, Haarlem. *Palæo.**
Wirtz, Dr. A. W. H., Director of the Veterinary College, Utrecht.*
Witte, H., Nonnensteeg 6, Leiden. *Hort.*
Wulp, F. M. van der, Sec. Dutch Ent. Society, Trompstraat 154, The Hague. *Ent.: Dipt.* C. Ex.*
Wurfbain, Dr. C. L., Prof. Univ., Amsterdam. *Surgery.*
Wurtbain, Joan G., Huize Heuven, Worth-Reden. *Zool., Gen. Biol., Geog. Dist., Mam., Orn., Ool., Herpetol., Ichth., Tax.* C. Ex.
Wybe, Dr. J. W. van, Zool. Dr., Alemetoo.
Wijsman, H. P., add. Bacteriol. Laborat., Preddhefe Fabrik, Delft.*
Zaaijer, Dr. J., Leeuwarden. *Phys.*
Zaaijer, Prof. D. T., Dir. Anat. Cab., Univ., Rapenburg 16, Leiden.* *Anat., Emb.*
Zeeman, Dr. J., Amsterdam. *Pathol.*

NORWAY.

Ammitzböll, Dr. Ivar., Christiania. *Ent.*
Åstrand, Prof. J. J., Observatory, Bergen. *Ast.*
Berner, Director C. C. Museum, Bergen.
Bjerknes, Prof. Dr. C. A., Universitas Regia Fredericiana, Nordal Bruns Gade 5, Christiania. *Math.**
Blytt, Axel, Prof. Bot., University Christiania. *Bot., Geog. Dist. of plants.**
Broch, Prof. J. P., Christiania.
Broch, Prof. O. J., Christiania.
Brunchorst, J., Dr. Phil., Curator of Mus., Dir. of "Naturen," Magazine of Nat. Sci., Bergen. *Bot. (Physiology), Fungi.**
Bryhn, N., Dr. Med., Hönefors. *Bryol.* C. Ex.*
Carstens, Prof. M. C., Trondhjem.
Collett, Robert, Prof. of Zoology, and Director of the Zoological Museum of the University, Christiania. *Vertebrates.**
Cornelіussen, O. A. Senjens, Nikkelvek. *Min.*
Dahll, Dr. Tellef, Ingénieur en chef des Mines, Kragerö. *Geol., Min.* C. Ex.
Danielssen, Dr. Daniel Cornelius, Chief Physician, President of the Museum, Bergen. *Marine Invertebrates.* Ex. for the collection of the Museum.*
Dons, W., Universitas Regia Fredericiana, Christiania.
Esmark, Fraulein Birgithe, Lækkeveien 11, Christiania. *Malaco-Zoology.*
Esmark, Prof. M., Universitas, Christiania. *Zool.*

Fearnley, Prof. C., Universitas, Christiania. *Ast.*
Foslie, M., Con. Mus., Tromsö. *Algology.* C Ex.*
Friele, Herman, Dir. of the Museum, Bergen. *Malacol.* C.*
Friis, Prof. J. A., Christiania.
Geelmuyden, H., Universitas Regia Fredericiana, Christiania. *Ast.*
Grieg, James, Conservator am Bergens Mus. *Zool* *
Guldberg, Prof. Dr. Cato M., Universitas Regia Fredericiana, Christiania. *Math.**
Hagemann, Axel, Forstkandidat, Saltdalen pr. Bodö. *Arctic Coleoptera.* C.*
Hagerup, F., Universitas Regia Fredericiana, Christiania.
Hansen, G. A., Oberarzt, Bergen. *Annelids.*
Helland, A., Universitas, Christiania. *Geol.*
Hjortdahl, Prof. Th., Universitas, Christiania. *Chem.*
Holst, Elling, Universitas Regia Fredericiana, Christiania.
Jensen, Olaf S., Jernbanegaden 7, Christiania. *Anat.*, *Histol.*
Kaurin, Chr., Opdal. *Bot.*, *Bryology.*
Kiær, Frantz, Christiania. *Bryology*, *Hepaticæ.* C. Ex. European and foreign mosses and liverworts in exchange for European and foreign.
Kindt, Dr. C., Trondhjem. *Bot.: Lichens.*
Kjerulf, Prof. Dr. Th., Universitas, Christiania. *Geol.*
Landmark, A., Fischerei Inspector, Christiania. *Orn.**
Landmark, Rev. J. R., Flakstad. *Bot.* C. especially of Arctic Zone.*
Lie, Prof M. S., Christiania.
Lorange, Anders, Conservator at the Museum of Bergen, Bergen.*
Lütke, Rev. M. F., Bergen.
Moe, Dr., Botanical Gardens, Christiania. *Bot.*
Mohn, Prof. Dr. Henrik, Meteorologisk Institut, Christiania. *Meteo.*, *Phys.*, *Geog.*
Münster, Prof. E. B., Universitas, Christiania.
Nansen, Fridtjof, Curator Mus., Bergen. *Zool.*, *Histol.**
Nicolaysen, Prof. J., Christiania
Nielsen, Dr. Yngvar, Universitas Regia Fredericiana, Christiania. *Ethnog.*, *Geog.*
Nordvi, A. G., Christiania. *Orn.*, *Ool.* and all Norwegian and Swedish minerals. Sells Northern bird-skins and eggs, skeletons and skulls of Lapps from heathenish tombs in Lapland, Norway. For sale by me only.*
Norman, J. M., Forstmeister, Laurvig. *Arctic Norwegian phanerogamic Flora*, *Lichenology.* C. Ex.*
Nijhus, O., Land. real, Tromsö. *Bot.*
Pettersen, Karl, Dir. Mus., Tromsö. *Geol. of N. Norway.**
Pihl, O. A. L., F.R.A.S., Christiania.
Reusch, H. H., Christiania. *Geol.*
Sandberg, Georg Sognepræst, Sydvaranger Præstegaard, Finmark. *Ent.* C.
Sars, G. O., Universitas, Christiania. *Zool.*, *spec. Crustacea*, *Pycnogonida and Mollusca.*
Schiotz, Prof. O. E., Universitas, Christiania. *Phys.*
Schjott, Prof. P. O., Universitas Regia Fredericiana, Christiania. *Phil.*
Schneider, Jacob Sparre, Con. Mus., Tromsö. *Ent.: Arctic Lepid.*, *Crustacea*, *Moll.*, *Geog. Dist.* C.*
Schöyen, Dr. W. M., Christiania. *Lepid.*
Schübeler, Dr. F. C., Dir. Bot. Gardens, Christiania. *Bot.*
Sexe, Prof. F. A., Christiania.
Slater, H. H., F.C.S., Brettnaes, Loffoden. *Chem.*
Stenersen, Dr. L., Universitas Regia Fredericiana, Christiania.
Storm, Joh., Prof. of English and Romance, Christiania. *Philology.**
Tromholt, Sophus, Bergen. *Meteo.*, *Ast.: Auroræ.*

Unger, Carl R., Prof. Universitas, Christiania.
Waage, Prof. P., Universitas, Christiania. *Chem.*
Winge, Prof. E., Christiania. *Anat.*
Worm, Müller, Prof. Dr., Universitas, Christiania. *Physiol.*, *Physiol. Chem.**
Wulfsberg, Niels G., F.M.D., Ph.D., Universitas Regia Fredericiana, Christiania. *Bot.*, *Chem.*

PORTUGAL.

Albuquerque, Manoel d', Ingenieur Civil, rue du Rozario 70, Oporto. *Bot.*
Alvarenga, Dr. Peter F. da Costa, Prof. Med. Coll., Lisbon. *Bot.*
Arruda Furtado, Francisco d', Museum da Escola Polytechnica, Lisbon. *Malacology*, *Con.* C. Ex. Offers shells of Azores, Europe, and America for L., F. W., and marine shells of all parts of the world.
Barbosa, Joaquim Casimiro, Jardin Botanique, Massarellos 42, Oporto. *Bot.*
Barboza du Bocage, José Vicente, Dir. Mus. Hist. Nat., Lisbon. *Orn.*, *Herpetol.*, *Eth.*, *Geol.*
Cotter, J. C. Berkeley, Attaché à la Commission Géologique, 148 R. da Procissão, 1º, Lisbon. *Paleont. of the Tertiary formation.**
Breyner, Luiz de Mello, Dir. R. Gar., Lisbon. *Bot.*
Capello, João Carlos de Brito, Directeur do l'Observatoire do Infante D. Luiz, Escola Polytechnica, Lisbon. *Meteorology and Terrestrial Magnetism.*
Carreiro, Bruno S. Travares, Univ., Coimbra. C. *Bot.*
Carvalho Monteiro, Antonio Augusto de, D S., LL.D., Memb. of many Sci. Soc., rua do Alecrim 70, Lisbon. *Lepid. of the globe.* C. Ex. Offers European, Brazilian, and African (from Portuguese colonies), spec. for those of Madagascar, India, China, Ceylon, Australia, N. Am., etc.*
Castro Freire, Dr. Antonio de, Coimbra. *Bot.* C. Wishes to sell plants, especially Phanerogams. *
Chaperon, G., Polytec. Sch., Place Decazes 40, Lisbon.
Choffat, Paul, attaché à la Commission géologique, 113 rua do Arco a Jesus, Lisbon. *Geol.*, *Palæo.* C. of the Jurassic and cretaceous formations.
Coelho, Joseph M., Prof. Min., Polytec. Sch., Lisbon.
Corvo, João de Andrade, Prof. Polytec. Sch., Dir. Bot. Gar., Memb. de l'Inst. de Paris, Lisbon, *Bot.**
Coutinho, Pereira, Agric. Inst., Lisbon. *Bot.* C.
Da Costa Simões, Dr., Prof. Phys., Univ., Coimbra.
Daveau, Jules Alexandre, Inspecteur des Jardins Botaniques de l'Ecole Polytechnique et de l'Ecole de Médecine, Lisbon. *Bot.*, *Ent.* C. Ex. Offers plants of Portugal in exchange for plants of the region of the Mediterranean.*
Delgado, Joaquin Filippe-Nery, Directeur de la Commission des travaux géologiques, 113 Rua do Arco a Jesus, Lisbon. *Geol.**
Ficalho, Prof. Comte de, Lisbon. *Bot.*
Freire, Antonio Castro, Univ., Coimbra. *Bot.* C.
Giraldes, Albino, Museo Zoológico, Coimbra.*
Girard, Albert (of New York), Attaché au Musée Zoologique, Museum d'Histoire Naturelle, Ecole Polytechnique, Lisbon. *Ent.: Neuropt.*, *Orthopt.*, *Hymenopt.*, *Lamellicorns*, *Tenebrides.* C. Ex.
Gomes, Bernardino Barros, Lisbon. *Bot.* C.

Henriques, Dr. Julio A., Prof. de Botanique à l'Université, Coimbra. *Bot.* Ex. plants of Portugal for the herbarium of the Botanical Gardens.*
Luzo da Silva, Prof. Augusto, Lyceum. *Crypt. Bot.*
Mariz, Dr. Joaquin de, Naturalist, Botanic Gardens of the University, Coimbra, S. Bento. *Bot.*, *Nat. Phil.*
Mattozo, Fernando, Prof. à l'Ecole Polytechnique. Mus. de Zool., Lisbon. *Emb.*, *Herpetol.*, *Arach.*, *Myriopoda*, *Crustacea.*
Meirelles Guedes Couto Garrido, Prof. Antonio de, Coimbra. *Bot.*
Mello Breyner, Louis de, Directeur en chef des Jardins de Sa Majesté le Roi de Portugal, Palais Royal d'Ajuda, Lisbon. *Bot.* C. Orchids. Ex. Orchids of Portugal for foreign, and also for other plants and seeds.*
Mello Pereira Caceres, Manoel d'Albuquerque, Oporto. *Bot.* C.
Moller, Adolpho Frederico, Inspecteur du Jard. bot. à l'Univ., Coimbra. *Bot.: Phanerogams and Cryptogams, especially Mushrooms.* C. Ex. plants of Portugal for those of Europe.
Newton, Isaac, Oporto. *Crypt. Bot.* C.
Nixon, P. C., Fellow of Roy. Mic. Soc., Memb. Geologists' Assoc., Memb. of Queckett Mic. Club, of London, Oporto, Portugal. *Geol.*, *Min.*, *Met.*, *Mic.*, *Photog.*, *Meteo.* C. Ex. in Photog.*
Oliveira, Jose Duarte de, Jr., Ed. Hort. Journal, Oporto. *Bot.*
Padrão, Dr. Affonso Dias, Bougado, Oporto. *Bot.*, *Moll.* C. Ex.
Padrão, Antonio, Bougado, Oporto. *Phæn. Bot.*
Paula e Oliveira, Francisco, attaché à la Commission Géologique, 113 Rua do Arco a Jesus, Lisbonne. *Anthropol.**
Paulino d'Oliveira, Manoel, Prof. à l'Université, Coimbra. *Ent.* C. Ex. Insects of Portugal, Brazil, Angola, India, and Macall.
Penaud, Emile, rue de Mandé, Lisbon. *Bot.*
Pereira da Costa, Dr. Francisco Antonio, Dir. Mus. d'Histoire Naturelle, section minéralogique, rue S. Roque 22, Lisbon. *Geol.*, *Min.*, *Palæo.*
Pereira Guimarães, Antonio Roberto, Aide-Naturaliste au Muséum d'Histoire Naturelle, rua do Machadinho 20, Lisbon. *Ichth.*
Reis, Jayme Batalha, Prof. in the Gen. Agric. Inst. of Portugal.
Ribeiro, Carlos, Acad. Sci., Lisbon. *Geol.*
Rodriguez Miranda Junior, Manuel, Ingeniero de puentes, calzadas y minas, Miembro de la Sociedad de Ingenieros y Arquitectos civiles, Catedrático de Geologia y Mineralogia aplicadas al laboreo de minas en el Instituto industrial, C. de Cedofeita 468, Porto.*
Salles Gomes Cardozo, Dr. Francisco de, Prof. Polytec. Acad., Dir. Bot. Gar., Oporto. *Bot.*
Santos, Fernando Mattozodos, Prof. de Zool. à l'Ecole Polytechnique, rua do Sol do Rato 59, Lisbon.
Schmitz, E., Oporto. *Bot.* C. Ex.
Veiga, Estacio da, S.P.M., Gentilhomme à la Cour de S. M. Très-Fid., Commandeur de l'Ord. d'Elisabeth la Cathol. en Espagne, Memb. de l'Acad. R. des Sciences et de la Société de Géogr. de Lisbonne, de l'Institut et de la Soc. Broterienne de Coimbra, de l'Imp. Instit. Archeol. German. de Rome, de la Soc. Franç. d'Archéol., de l'Acad. R. d'Hist. de Madrid, de la Soc. Econom. de Malaga, de l'Acad. d'Archéol. de Belgique, de l'Inst. Archéol et Géograph. de Pernambuco; n. à la ville de Tavira, Algarve. Aut. en Bot. de: 1. Plantas de la Serra de Monchique (Algarve). Lisbonne, 1866-1869. 2. Catalogue méthodique des plantes crypt. et phanerog. des environs de Mafra, au N. de Lisbonne, 1875, inéd. 3. Orchidées de Portugal, Lisbonne, 1886.
Villa Major, Vicomte de, Univ., Mem. Acad. Sci., Coimbra. *Bot.*

ROUMANIA.

Bottea, C., Str. Pitar Mosu 5, Bucharest.
Brandza, Dr. D., Prof. de Bot. à l'Univ., Dir. du Jard. Bot. et Membre de l'Académie, Strada Fôntânei 14, Bucharest. *Bot.* C. Ex. plants of Roumania for others.
Fêtu, Prof. Dr. A., Univ., Dir. Bot. Gar., Yassy, Moldavia. *Bot.*
Gotteland, André, Bot. Gar., Bucharest. *Bot.*
Grecesco, Dr. D., Professeur à la Faculté de Médecine, Strada Diaconeselor 8, Bucharest. *Bot.* C. Ex. plants of Roumania.
Hepites, S., Dir. Met. Inst., Bucharest.*
Licherdopol, Prof. J. P. (Bura), Chaussée Dorobanti, Bucharest. *Geol., Bot.* C. Ex. fossils and rocks of all countries.*
Michali, Ignat, Tirgu-Jiu. *Gen. Ent., Lepid.*
Montandon, Arnold, Administrateur du Domaine Royal de Sinaia, Valachie Brosteni Folticeni, Moldavia. *Ent.: Hemipt.* Desires Hemiptera of all countries, determined or not, in exchange for Hemipt. Coleopt., shells collected in the Carpathians.
Rauss, Dr. Louis, Prof. de Médecine Opératoire à la Faculté de Médecine, Yassy.
Sabba, Prof. Stefanescu, Bucharest. *Geol., Palæo.* C. Shells and fossils. Ex. shells of Roumania for those of America.*
Stefansen, Gregoriu, M.A.R., Membre des Socs. Géol. et Min. de France, Dir. du Bureau Géol. Roumaine, Prof. de Geol. i Min. la Univ., Directore allu Museum de Istoria Naturala din Bucuresti, Strada Verde 8, Bucuresti. *Min., Geol.**

RUSSIA.

Adamowicz, Dr. Adam F. R. von, Prof. Emer., Wilna.
Akinine, J., St. Petersburg. *Coleopt.*
Alexandrowicz, Prof. J., Universität, Warsaw. *Bot.*
Alexeyeff, Pierre, Prof. Univ., Kiew. *Chem.* C. Ex.*
Alphéraky, Sergius, Taganrog. *Lepid.* C. Ex.
Albrecht, Wilhelm, St. Petersburg. *Lepid.*
Albrecht, Robert, St. Petersburg. *Lepid.*
Arnold, Nicolas, Gory. *Ent.**
Backlund, Dr. Oscar K., Sternwarte, Pulkowa, bei St. Petersburg. *Ast.*
Balassaglo, Waldemar, St. Petersburg. *Coleopt.*
Basarow, Dr. A., Univ., Kiew. *Chem.*
Basileswsky, Victor, St. Petersburg. *Ent.*
Batalin, Dr. Alexander, Botanical Garden, St. Petersburg. *Phytophysiology and cultivated plants.*
Baumgarten, Théodor, Warsaw. *Coleopt.*
Beck, Dr. Alexander, Prof. am Baltischen Polytechnicum, Riga.*
Becker, A., Organist, Sarepta. *Bot., Ent.**
Beggrow, Théodor, St. Petersburg. *Lepid.*
Békétoff, Prof. André, Universität, Dir. Botanical Gar., St. Petersburg. *Bot.: Morphology, Phytography.*
Beilstein, Prof. F., Tech. Inst., St. Petersburg. *Chem.*
Berdau, Prof. Dr, F., Varsovie, Polognerusse, rue Wspólna 57.*

Berg, F., Realschuldirector, Riga. *Zool.*
Bidder, Prof. Dr. F. H. von, Universität, Dorpat. *Physiol., Pathol.*
Biel, Dr. Johannes, Handelshaus Stoll u. Schmidt, St. Petersburg. *Analyt. Chem.**
Bispen, Théodor, Moika 40, Qu. 41, St. Petersburg. *Lepid.**
Bobretzki, Prof. Dr., Univ., Kiew. *Zool., Emb.*
Bobyleff, D. Bobylew, Prof. der Universität, St. Petersburg.*
Boettcher, A., wirkl. Staatsrath, Prof. Emeritus, Univ., Dorpat. *Pathol., Anat., and Histol.**
Bogdanoff, Anatole, Moscow. *Ent.*
Bogdanow, Anatole, Prof. Dr., Univ., Moscow. *Zool., Anth.**
Borgmann, T., Privat-Docent der Universität, St. Petersburg. *Phys.*
Borodin, Prof. J., St. Petersburg. *Bot.*
Böthlingk, Otto, Imp. Acad. Sci., St. Petersburg.
Bouniakofski, Victor, Vice-President Imp. Acad. Science, St. Petersburg.
Bramson, Constantin, Gymnasial Professor, Ekaterinoslaw. *Lepid., (especially Lycænidæ, Zygænidæ, Arctiadæ), Coleopt., Hymenop.* Ex. and for sale.*
Brandt, Dr. Alex., Prof. Zool. and Comp. Anat., Univ., Veterinarnaja 11, Charkow. *Emb., Anat., and Histol. of Vert.**
Brandt, Dr. Edouard, Imperial Medico-Chirurgical College, St. Petersburg. *Ent.*
Braun, Prof. Dr. Max, Imp. Universität, Dorpat. *Zool., Emb., Con.* C. Ex. Offers Balearic shells and emb.-mic. preparations of reptiles and birds.
Bredichin, Prof. Dr. Th., Director der Sternwarte, Moscow. *Ast.* C. Ex. Annals of the Observatory of Moscow, 10 volumes, for publications of American observatories.
Brückner, Prof. Dr. Alex., Imp. Univ., Dorpat. *Hist.**
Brunner, Prof. Dr. Bernhard, Imp. Univ., Dorpat.
Brunner, Prof. R., Univ., Dorpat. *Agric.*
Bruttan, Andreas, Imp. Univ., Dorpat. *Bot.*
Büchner, Eugen, Conservator am Zool. Mus. der Kaiserlichen Acad. der Wissenchaften zu St. Petersburg. *Mammals.**
Bührig, Dr. H., Comptoir der Verwaltung des Teutellewschen Chemischen-Fabrik, Fonarni 3, St. Petersburg. *Chem.**
Buhse, F. A., Ph.D., Cus. Nat. Hist. Mus., Pres. Soc. Hort., Riga. *Bot.: Plants of Persia.*
Bunge, Nicolaus, Prof. Technischen Chem. a. d. Univ., St. Vladimir, Kiew. *Chem.**
Cettingen, Prof. Dr. Arthur v., Imp. Univ., Dorpat. *Phys.*
Chatiloff, Joseph, Goover, Toula Novossill. *Zool.*
Christoph, Hugo Th., Custos Ent. Samm. d. Grossfürsten Nicolai Michailowitsch Aptekarsky, Pereulok 4, St. Petersburg. *Lepid.*
Clausen, Thos., Dorpat. *Ast.*
Cronebeerg, Dr. Alex., Moscow. *Ent.: Arach.*
Cybulski, H., Bot. Gar., Warsaw. *Bot.*
Dobroslavine, Dr. Alexis, Prof. de l'Hygiène Publique, Acad. Imp. de Med. Milit., St. Petersburg. *Meteo., Infusoria.* C. Ex.
Dolgew, W., Yaroslav. *Bot.*
Dragendorff, Dr. Georg, Prof. an der Universität, Kaiserl. Russischer wirkl. Staatsrath und Ritter. *Pharmacy, Phyto-Chemistry.* C. of the University. Ex.
Dybowsky, Dr. W., Niankow. *Moll.*
Dziedzicki, Dr. Harry, Chlodna St. 21, Poland. *Diptera, Nematocera.*
Egoroff, N., Prof. der K. Universität, Warsaw. *Phys.*
Eichwald, Dr. E. M., St. Petersburg.

Ender, Ernst, Imp. Botanic Gardens, St. Petersburg. *Bot.*
Enninghaus, Dr. Prof Hermann, Dorpat. *Anth.*
Fadejeff, Dr. A. de, Prof. an der Akademia, Moscow.
Erschoff, Nicolas, Wassili Ostrw. 12, Line 15, St. Petersburg. *Lepid.* C. Ex.*
Famintzin, Prof. A., Universität, und Mitglied d. kaiserlichen Akademie d. Wissenschaften zu St. Petersburg. *Bot.*, *Anat.*, *Physiol.*
Fischer, von Waldheim, Prof. Dr. Alex., Moscow. *Bot.*
Fixen, Carl, St. Petersburg. *Lepid.*
Gadolin, Gen. Axel, Imp. Acad. Sci., St. Petersburg. *Min.*, *Crystal.*, *Phys.*
Ganin, S., Warschau. *Anat.*, *Emb.*
Glasenapp, Maximilian, Prof. am Polytechnicum, Riga. *Chemische Technologie*, *Waarenkunde*, *Photog.**
Glassenapp, Serge von, Prof. der Astronomie, Dir. der Sternwarte der kais Universität, St. Petersburg, und Dekan der Mathematischen Facultät. *Ast.**
Glausen, Dr. Thomas, Prof. Emer., Imp. Univ., Dorpat.
Gobi, Dr. Christopher, Prof. an der Universität, und am Berg-Corps zu St. Petersburg. *Bot.: Fungi, Morphology.* Algæ of Baltic and White Seas, Flora of Valdai Hills, Europe and Russia.
Golofkinsky, Prof N., Universität, Odessa. *Min.*
Goronowitsch, L. N., pract. Arzt, Kaiserliche Naturforschende Gesellschafts zu Moskau. *Zoomorphologie.**
Grimm, Dr. Oscar von, St. Petersburg. *Ichth.*, *Biol.**
Grönberg, Prof. Th., Riga. *Phys.**
Gruber, Prof. Dr. Wenzel, Academie, St. Petersburg. *Anat.*
Günther, Alex., Petrosavodsk. *Coleopt.*, *Lepid.*, *Hemipt.**
Gustavson, Prof. Gabriel, Academie, Petrowsk, near Moscow. *Org. Chem.*
Hasselberg, Dr. Bernhard, Alterer Astronom, K. Sternwarte, Pulkowa, bei St. Petersburg.*
Hausmann, Prof. Dr. Richard, Prof. Imp. Univ., Dorpat. *Hist.*
Helmling, Prof. Dr. Peter, Imp. Univ., Dorpat. *Math.*
Herder, Dr. F. G. von, Bot. Gardens, St. Petersburg. *Bot.*
Heseltus, N., Privat-Docent der Universität, St. Petersburg. *Phys.*
Hoyningen-Huene, Baron Friedrich, Lechts (Estland). *Ool.*, *European Lepid.* C. Ex.*
Hueber, Alex., St. Petersburg. *Lepid.*
Jakowleff, Basil, Astrakhan. *Hemipt.*
Jaroshefski, W. A., University, Kharkoff. *Diptera.*
Jeremejen, P. de, Sec. Min. Soc., St. Petersburg.
Jegorow, Tiflis, Georgia. *Bot.*
Johanson, Mag. Edwin Adolf, Collegienassessor, Oberlehrer der Naturwissenschaften, Chemiker der Pharm. Gesell., Redacteur der. Zeitschrift für Russl.; früher Privatdocent in Dorpat, u. Assistent von Prof. Dragendorff, gegenwärtig Director der Mineralwasser-Anstalt in Riga (Wöhrmann's Park), Russland. *Analyt. Chem.**
Karpinski, A., Inst. Nouvelle-Alexandrie. *Zool.*
Kauffert, B., Universität Bot. Gardens, St. Petersburg. *Bot.*
Keussler, Eduard v., Riga.
Kiesevitzky, Prof. G., Riga. *Math.*
Klimenko, E., Docent, Univ., Odessa. *Chem.*
Klinge, Johannes Christoph, Privatdocent, Directorgehilfer am Bot. Garten, Oberlehrer der Naturwissenschaften, Magister der Botanik, Dorpat. *Comparative Morphology.* Ex. specimens of Equisetæ and Carex.*

Klossovsky, Alexander, ordentlich Prof., Univ., Odessa. *Phys. Geog.**
Knowe, Karl F., Nicolajeo.
Knüpffer, Paul, Dorpat. *Mic., Zool., Lepid.* C. Ex.*
Kokscharow, Nicolaus von, Pres. Min. Soc., St. Petersburg.
Kokujeff, N., Jaroslawl. *Coleopt.* C. Ex.
Kononowitsch, Alex., ausserordentlicher Prof. Univ. Odessa, Dir. Obs., Odessa. *Ast.*
Köppen, Alexis, Berg-Department, St. Petersburg. *Met., Geol.*
Köppen, Friedrich Th., St. Petersburg. *Ent., Geog. Dist. of plants and animals, Gen. Biol.*
Korotneff, Dr., Univ., Moscow. *Zool., Emb.*
Kovalewsky, Prof. Alexander, Universität, Odessa. *Zool.*
Kowalski, Marion, Kazan. *Ast.*
Kowalski, T., Red. Gar.-Pol., Warsaw. *Agric.*
Koknen, N., Yaroslav. *Ent., especially Coleopt.* C. Ex. Offers Russian Coleopt. and wishes Colybidæ, Dermestidæ, Bruchidæ of all the world.
Kroneberg, Dr., Univ., Moscow. *Zool.*
Krutizki, P. J., Universität. *Bot.*
Krylow, P., Bot. Gar., St. Petersburg. *Bot.*
Kuhlberg, Dr. A., St. Petersburg. *Chem.*
Kuhlberg, Ch., St. Petersburg. *Chem.*
Küster, Dr. Carl F. von, St. Petersburg.
Lagorio, Prof. Dr. Alex., Warsaw.
Lahnsen, Prof. T., Custos am Museum der Kais. Berginstitutes, St. Petersburg. *Geol.*
Lang, Heinrich, St. Petersburg. *Lepid.*
Lemberg, Dr. J., Docent, Univ., Dorpat. *Chem.*
Ligin, Valerian, Pres. Math. Sec. der Neurussischen Naturforscher-Gesell., Prof. ordinarius an der Universität, Odessa. *Mechanics.*
Lindeman, Dr. K., Prof. an der landwirthschaftlichen Acad., Moscow. *Ent.**
Lindemann, Eduard, Wissenschaftlicher Secretair der Sternwarte, Pulkowa, near St. Petersburg. *Ast., especially Photometric.**
Lindstedt, Prof. Dr. Andres, Imp. Univ., Dorpat. *Theoretical Mechanics.*
Lothner, E., Abo in Finland. *Agric. Chem.*
Manderstjerna, Alex., Weiska 1, Warsaw. *Coleopt.*
Markownikoff, Prof. V., Univ., Moscow. *Chem.*
Masing, Dr. E., Docent, Univ., Dorpat. *Pharm.*
Maximowicz, Charles John, Ord. Member Imp. Acad. and Botanist at Imperial Botanic Garden, St. Petersburg. *Bot., Phytography and Phytogeography, Flora of E. and Central Asia and Russia.* Ex. especially desired, either for Academy or Botanic Gardens, U. S. Carices and Salices, authentically named. Offers in return dried plants from Russia, Siberia and Turkestan.*
Meinshausen, Charles F., Dir. Bot. Mus., Acad. Sci., St. Petersburg. *Bot., Phytography.* Flora of St. Petersburg, Carices of Russia.
Mendelejeff, St. Petersburg. *Phys., Chem.*
Menschutkin, Nicolas, Prof. Chem., Kaiserliche Univ., St. Petersburg.*
Mereschkowski, Univ., St. Petersburg. *Zool., Emb.*
Meyer, Dr. Leo., Imp. Univ., Dorpat. *Vergl. Grammatik.**
Middendorff, Dr. Alexander von, Livland, über Dorpat. *Zool., Ethnog.*
Miklucho-Maclay, Michael, Berginstitut, St. Petersburg. *Petrog., Geol.*
Milaschewitz, Dir. Gymnasium, Militopoll. *Geol.*
Moeller, Prof. Dr. Valerian von, St. Petersburg.
Montéverdé, N. A., St. Petersburg. *Bot.*
Morawitz, Dr. Ferdinand, Vosnesenskaja, n. 40, St. Petersburg. *Ent.*

Moritz, Dr. Arnold, Meteor. Obs., Dorpat. *Meteo., Phys., spec. Terrestrial Magnetism.*
Mühlen, Max von Zur, Jacobstr. 25, Dorpat. *Zool., Neuropt., Formicidæ, Tenthredenidæ.**
Nassanoff, Prép. Université, Moscow. *Zool.*
Nedzelsky, Ant., Sebastopol. *Bot.*
Neugebauer, Prof. Dr. Ludwig A., Académie, Warsaw.
Nolcken, Baron, Gen. Major a. D., Tichtendahl. Brief address: Riga, Thronfolger-Boulevard 6. *Macro- and Micro-Lepid.* C. Ex.*
Nowakowski, Dr. Leon, Privat-Gel., Lublin. *Bot., Mycol.**
Nusbaum, Joseph, Warschau. *Embryol.*
Nyrén, Dr. Magnus, K. Sternwarte, Pulkowa bei St. Petersburg. *Ast.*
Obert, J., St. Petersburg. *Coleopt.*
Oettingen, Dr. Arthur von, Prof. der Physik an der Universität, Dorpat, *Meteo., Phys. Sci., Acoustics.*
Oettingen, Dr. Georg v., Prof. Emer., Imp. Univ., Dorpat.
Onljanin, Dr., Université, Moscow. *Zool., Emb.*
Ortwald, Prof. Dr. W., Riga. *Chem.*
Osnobichine, J., Simbirsk. *Ent.*
Osterloff, Friedric, im Polnischen Bank, Warsaw, Poland. *Coleoptera, spec. Curculionidæ.*
Ouljanin, Univ., Moscow. *Zool., Emb.*
Ousjanikoff, Mem. de l'Académie, St. Petersburg. *Zool.*
Ovsiannikoff, Philipp, Akademiker, St. Petersburg. *Anat., Physiol.*
Perepelkine, Alexis, Secrétaire de la Société Impériale d'Agriculture, Smolensky boulevard, Hôtel d'Ecole d Agric., Chancellerie de la Société, Moscow. *Technical Zool.*
Perepelkine, Constantin, Moscow, Nemetzky Oulyza Posslannikow pereoulok, Maison Delssale. *Zool.*
Perijaslavzew, Dr., Directrice Laboratoire de Zool., Sebastopol. *Zool., Emb.*
Petersen, Wilhelm, Conservator am Mus., Reval (Estland). *Lepid. of the World.*
Peterson, Wilh., Dorpat. *Macro. and Micro-lepid.*
Petzboldt, Dr. Alex., Prof. Emer., Mitau.
Pleske, Th., Conservator am Zool., Museum der Kaio, Akademie der Wissenschaften, St. Petersburg. *Orn.**
Podwyssotzki, Dr. V., Docent, Univ., Dorpat. *Pharm.*
Pohrt, Nicolai, Ingénieur, Chemiker, Polytechnikum Versuchsstation, Riga. *Chem.**
Pouzilo, Michel, Rostow. *Coleopt., Lepid.*
Popoff, Prof. A., Lab. Univ., Warsaw. *Chem.*
Portschinsky, Joseph, Sec. Ent. Soc. of Russia, St. Petersburg. *Dipt.*
Posse, C., Docent an d. Universität, St. Petersburg. *Math.*
Prendel, Romulus, Cur. Min. Mus., Univ., Odessa. *Geol., Min., Lithol.*
Radde, Dr. Gustav Ferdinand Richard, Dir. d. Kaukassichen Mus. u. dir. Off. Bibliothek, Tiflis (Georgia). *Bot., Zool.**
Radoszkoffski, Pres. Entomological Society, St. Petersburg.
Regel, Dr. Eduard A., (Geheimrath), Dir. des Kais. Botanischen Gartens, St. Petersburg. *Bot.: Dendrology, Hort., Flora Turkestanica, Sibirica, etc.**
Reinhardh, Prof. Universität, Odessa. *Bot.*
Renard, Dr. Carl von, Geheimrath, Excellenz, Präsident der Kaiserlichen Naturforschenden Gesellschaft, Moscow. *Nat. Hist., especially Ethnog., Anth., Eth., Mam., Orn.*
Repiachow, Prof. Dr., Univ., Odessa. *Zool.*
Reyher, Dr. Carl, 6 Osernoij-Pereulok, St. Petersburg. *Chirurgy.**
Reyher, Dr. Gustav, Emeritus Docent der Universität, Dorpat (Livonia). *Medicine and Therapeutics.*

Rischawi, Prof. L., Universität, Odessa. *Bot.: Vegetable Physiol.**
Romanowski, Col., School of Mines, St. Petersburg.
Rosenberg, Prof. Dr. Alexander, Imp Univ., Dorpat.
Rosenberg, Prof. Dr. Emile, Imp. Univ., Dorpat. *Comp. Anat., Emb. Histol.**
Rudolph, R., Bot. Gar., Odessa. *Bot.*
Russow, Prof. Dr. Edmond, Universität, Dir. des Botan. Gartens, Dorpat. Russ. Kaiserl. wirkl. Staatsrath, Excellenz, Orden. Wladimir III. Cl., Anna II. Cl., Stanislaus II. Cl.; corr. Mitglied der Academie in St. Petersburg: Ehrenmitglied und ord. Mitglied zahlr. Gesellschaften. *Anat., Physiol., Morphologie, Systematik (Sphagnaceæ).**
Sabanisew, W., Yaroslav. *Malacology.*
Sack, Arnold, Dr., Kuznetczny Per. 5, St. Petersburg. *Zool.**
Sagemehl, Maxmilian, Dorpat.
Sarkewitch, Anastasius, Prof. de l'Université, Charkow.
Salensky, Prof., Universität, Kasan. *Emb.*
Salensky, Dr., Université, Odessa. *Zool., Emb.*
Scharrer, W., Tiflis, Georgia. *Bot.*
Schell, Jul., Wilna. *Bot.*
Schmalhausen, Profess. a. d. Universität, Kiew. *Bot., Vegetable Palæo.*
Schmidt, Prof. Dr. Alex., Imp. Univ., Dorpat. *Physiol.*
Schmidt, Prof. Dr. Carl, Imp. Univ., Dorpat. *Chem.*
Schmidt, Friedrich, Academie der Wissenschaften, St. Petersburg.*
Schnabl, Johann, M.D., N. 59 Krakauer Vorstadt, Warsaw, Poland. *Dipt. Brachycera.**
Schöne, Dr. Emil, Prof. der Chemie an der Land- und Forstwirthschaftlichen Akademie, Petrowskoye Rasumowskoye, near Moscow. *Chem.*
Schrenk, Dr. August von, Dorpat.
Schwarz, Prof. Dr. Ludwig, Imp. Univ., Dorpat. *Ast.*
Schweder, Director des Stadtgymnasiums, Riga. *Zool.*
Schwedoff, Dr. Theodor, Prof. Univ., Odessa. *Phys.**
Scrobichewsky, L., Dir. Gartenbau-Schule, Ouman. *Bot.*
Selheim, G., St. Petersburg. *Bot.*
Selivanoff, Alexis, Skopine (Gov. Riasane). *Myriopoda.*
Semiradzki, Joseph, Imp. Univ., Dorpat.
Setschenoff, Prof., Univ., St. Petersburg. *Zool.*
Sievers, Gustav, Tiflis. *Gen. Ent.*
Simonoff, Director Observatory, Kasan.
Sintenis, F., Oberlehrer, Dorpat. *Lepid., Coleopt., Dipt.* C.*
Slosarski, A., Univ., Warsaw. *Zool.*
Smirnow, Michail, Tiflis, Hahn Strem, Huns Tamashew. *Bot.*
Sochotsky, T., Prof. der Universität, St. Petersburg. *Math.*
Sokoloff, Observatory, Moscow.
Sommer, Alfred Richard, Schlossberg 7, Dorpat. *Zool., Foraminifera.*
Sorokin, Prof. N. W., Universität, Dir. Botanical Gardens, Kazan. *Bot.*
Stelling, Edward, Physikalisches Central-Observatorium, W.O., 23, L. H. 2, St. Petersburg. *Meteo.*
Strauch, Dr. A., Dir. der Zool. Mus. der Kaiserlichen Acad. du Wissenchaften zu St. Petersburg. *Reptilia und Amphibia.**
Struve, Prof. Dr. H., Staatstrath, Tiflis.
Struve, Otto, Director Observatory, Pulkowa, St. Petersburg. *Ast.*
Szedinszy, N., Charkow. *Bot.*
Szokalski, Dr. Victor F., Warsaw.
Taczanowski, W., Univ., Warsaw. *Zool.*
Tchebichef, Academy, St. Petersburg.
Tchébicheff, Prof. Pafnutij, St. Petersburg.
Tchihatchev, Feodar, Petersburg-Moskauer Handelsbank, St. Petersburg. *Geol., Petrogr.*
Teich, C. A., Kreislehrer, Riga. *Ent.*

Thoms, Prof. George, Riga. *Agriculturchemie, Physiology, Chemie Samenkunde, laudio, Versuchswesen.**
Tichomiroff, Univ., Moscow. *Zool.*
Timiriasef, Prof. Dr. C., Academy of Agriculture, Petrowski, near Moscow. *Physiol. of Plants.*
Trautschold, Dr. Hermann, Prof. Geol. und Min.,Petrowskische Ackerbau- und Forst-Akademie, near Moscow. *Geol., Palæo., Min.* C.
Treffner, Edward, Imp. Univ., Dorpat.
Twelvetrees, W. H., Voskrensky Zavod, near Meleus, Orenburg.
Ulianin, B., Prof. Univ., Moskau. *Emb.*
Umoff, Prof. Dr. Nikolaus, Univ., Odessa. *Phys.*
Unterberger, Prof. Dr. Friedrich, Imp. Univ., Dorpat.
Urbanorvicz, Felix, Warschau. *Embryol.*
Verigo, Prof. Alexander, Universität, Odessa. *Chem.*
Vesselofski, Sec. Acad. Imp. des Sciences, St. Petersburg.
Viohniakov, Nicholas, Gagarinstr., Moscow. *Palæo.*
Volck, Dr. Wilhelm, Imp. Univ., Dorpat.
Waga, Prof., Warsaw. *Gen. Ent.*
Wagner, Prof. Dr., Univ., St. Petersburg. *Zool., Emb.*
Wahl, Prof. Dr. Eduard von, Imp. Univ., Dorpat.*
Watecki, A., Univ., Warsaw. *Zool.*
Weihrauch, Prof. Dr. Carl, Imp. Univ., Dorpat. *Phys. Geog., Meteo., Math.**
Wiedemann, Dr. Ferdinand Johann, Akad. der Wissenschaften, St. Petersburg. *History and Language of the Finns.**
Wianin, Dr. Basolius, Moscow. *Mic., Zool., Invert. Emb., and Anat.*
Wiezemsti, Prof. Dr. Adam, Imp. Univ., Dorpat.
Wild, Dr. Heinrich, Wirkl. Staatstrath, Mitglied der Academie der Wissenschaften, und Director des physikal Central-Observatoriums, St. Petersburg. *Physics, especially Meteorology and Terrestrial Magnetism.**
Wischnegradsky, Alexis, Lab., Univ., St. Petersburg. *Chem.*
Woeikof, Alex. J., Ph.D., Imp. Geog. Soc., St. Petersburg. *Meteo.*
Wolff, Prof. Dr. R. Reinh., Polytechnische Schule, Riga. *Bot.*
Wroblewsky, Dr. E., Lab., Tech. Inst., St. Petersburg. *Chem.*
Ziloff, Prof. Université, Varsovie. *Phys.**
Zinger, Prof. Universität, Moscow.
Znatowicz, Br., Univ., Warsaw. *Chem.*
Zograff, Conserv. à l'Univ., Moscow. *Zool.*

SERVIA.

Touyorritch, T., Prof. Geol., Univ. de Belgrade, Serbie. *Palæo., Geol.*
Zujović, J. M., Prof. de Min., Geol. et Palæo. à la Faculté des Sci. de Belgrade, Kraynjevacka uldae, 12, Serbie. *Palæo., Geol., Min., Lithol.* C. Ex.

SPAIN.

Abela y Sainz de Andino, Eduardo, C. de Felipe V, 2, Madrid.
Adan de Yarza y Torre, Ramon, Ingeniero de Minas, Bilbao. *Mineralogia, Geologia y Paleontologia.**
Adaro, Luis, Mining Engineer, Gijon. *Geol., Min.*
Alea, Francisco, Nat. Sci. Mus., Madrid.

Almera, Jaime, Presbítero, Licenciado en Teología, Catedrático de Geología en el Seminario conciliar, C. de Sellent. 3, 3.º, Barcelona.*
Alonso Martinez, Adriano, Licenciado en Medicina y Cirugía, ex-Ayudante premiado del Hospital de San Juan de Dios, Alumno del Doctorado. C. del Conde de Aranda, 3, entresuelo, Madrid. *Antropologia*.*
Alvarez Alvistur, Louis, Agronome, Délégué du Ministère de Fomento pour l'Etude des infirmités des plantes, de l'Académie Royale de Sciences et lettres, rue Alcalá, 48, 3.º, Madrid. *Ent.: Hymenop.*
Amo, Dr. Mariano del, Grenada. *Bot.*
Andrés y Montalvo, Tomás, Doctor en Ciencias naturales, Madrid.*
Andrés y Tubilla, Tomás, Sec. Soc. Linnean Matritense, C. de Santa Clara, 3, Madrid. *Bot.*
Angulo y Suero, Francisco, Farmacéutico militar, Plaza del Dos de Mayo, 3, 1º. centro. *Bot.**
Antiga, Pedro, Plaza de Sta. Ana, 4, Barcelona. *Gen. Nat. Hist.**
Anton y Ferrandiz, Manuel, Doctor en Ciencias, Professor auxiliar de la Universidad Central, Ayudante por oposición del Museo de Ciencias naturales, C. de Villalar, 5, 2.º, Madrid. *Moluscos Zoófitos y Antropologia.**
Aranzadi y Unamuno, Telesforo, Vergara (Guipúzcoa), ó Jacometrezo, 1, 3.º Madrid.*
Arce y Jurado, José, C. de Recoletos, 13, 3.º, Madrid. *Bot.*
Arcimis, Augusto T., Prof. de la Institucion Libre de Enseñanza, Serrano, 58, 3.º, Madrid. *Ast., Meteo.**
Areitio y Larrinaga, Alfonso Maria de, Bilbao. *Min., Geol., Palæo.*
Arellano y Ballesteros, Antonio, Director y Fundador del Colegio de Sordo-mudos y de Ciegos, C. de Juan de Aragon, 15, principal, Zaragoza.*
Ariza, Dr. Antonio, Lugue, Cordova. *Ent.**
Artigas, Dr. Prinitios, San Lorenzo del Escoria, Prof. á la Escuela de Ings. de Montes.*
Asensio, Ildefonso, Doctor en Medicina, C. de la Montera, 29, 3.º izquierda, Madrid. *Malacología.**
Asnero y Villaescusa, Dr. Vicente, C. del Principe, 15, 2.º, Madrid.
Atienza y Silvent, Meliton, Catedrático de Agricultura en el Instituto, C. de la Victoria, 13, 2.º, Málaga.*
Autran, Isidoro, C. de Villamagna, 4, 2.º, Madrid.*
Autran, Isidoro, Substitut du Procureur Royal au Conseil d'Etat, 50, Calle de Serrano, Madrid. *Micrography.* C.
Avila, Pedro, Ingeniero de Montes, Escorial.*
Azcárate, Cabildo, Ingeniero Agrónomo y Catedrático de Fisiografía en la Escuela de Agricultura, C. de Goya, 25, Madrid.*
Barandica, Torcuato, Ingeniero de la fábrica de Bolueta, Bilbao.*
Barceló y Combis, Francisco, Catedrático de Física en el Instituto, Palma de Mallorca.*
Barrial Posada, Clemente, Propietario, Director del Museo de Historia natural y Catedrático de Geología y Paleontología de la Universidad católica libre y del Colegio del Salvador, explorador geológico, Hotel de la Concordia, Montevideo. *Min., Geol., Paleont.**
Bayod y Martinez, Dr. Martin, Fuencarral, 37, 3. , Madrid.*
Bellido, Patricio, Ingeniero de Montes, Zaragoza.*
Bello y Espinosa, Domingo, Doctor en Jurisprudencia, San Cristóbal de la Laguna (Tenerife).*
Benavides, José R, de la Academia de Medicina, C. de Atocha, 103, 2.º izquierda, Madrid.*
Benet y Andreu, José, Doctor en Ciencias naturales, C. de la Montera, 9, 3.º izquierda, Madrid.*

Bofill, Arturo, Cortes, 297 y 299, 3.º, Barcelona. *Bot.*, *Con.*, *Fossils of the Miocene and Pliocene.**
Bolivar, Ignacio, Prof. d'Entomologie à l'Univ., Olóraga, 16, Madrid. *Ent.*, *gen. and specific, Orthopt. du monde entier, Hemipt. d'Europe.**
Bolivar y Urrutia, José Maria, Licenciado en Medicina, C. del Carbon, 2, 2.º, Madrid.*
Bolós, Ramon, Farmacéutico, Naturalista, C. de San Rafael, Olot (Gerona). *Bot.**
Bonet, Prof. Magin, Calle Caboza, 24, Madrid. *Chem.*
Boscá, Eduardo, Licenciado en Ciencias y en Medicina, Catedrático de Historia natural, Jardín Botánico, Valencia. *Reptiles de Europa.**
Boscá, Fernando, Valencia. *Bot.*
Botella y de Hornos, Federico de, Inspector general del Cuerpo de Minas, C. de San Andrés, 34, Madrid.*
Brehm, Reinaldo, Calle de Goya, 5, Madrid. *Orn.*
Breñosa, Rafael, Ingeniero de Montes de la Real Casa, San Ildefonso (Segovia.)*
Brochard, Belmonte (Cuenca). *Coleopt.*
Buen, Odonde, Quera, Zaragoza. *Bot.*
Buen y del Cos, Odon, Licenciado en Ciencias naturales, Madrid. *Bot.*, *Crustacea*, *Redaccion de las " Dominicales del libre pensamiento."**
Cabello-é-Ibanez, Barcelona. *Chem.*
Cáceres, Francisco S. de, Plaza de Zubarán, 6, Sevilla. *Bot.*
Cadevall y Diars, Juan, Doctor en Ciencias naturales, Licenciado en Ciencias exactas, Director del Colegio modelo, Tarrasa.*
Calavia, Salvador, Arande dol Conde, Madrid. *Bot.*
Calderon, José Angel, Ingeniero civil, Fuencarral, 51, 3.º, Madrid.*
Calderon, Prof. Salvador, Inst., Madrid. *Bot.*
Calderon y Arana, Laureano, C. de Carretas, 14, bajo, Madrid.*
Calderon y Arana, Salvador, Doctor en Ciencias, Catedrático de Historia natural de la Facultad de Ciencias de la Universidad, Sevilla.*
Calleja y Ayuso, Francisco de la, Farmacéutico Talavera de la Reina.*
Calleja y Sanches, Dr. Julian, Plaza de Matute, 9, 2.º, Madrid.
Cámara y Cámara, José Maria, Ayora (Valencia).*
Campion y Aristeguieta, Ricardo, Perito mercantil, Plaza de Guipúzcoa, San Sebastian (Guipúzcoa). *Ent.**
Canovas, Cobeno Francisco, M.D., Prof. Inst. Lorca. *Palæo.*, *Bot.*, *Nat. Hist.*, *Arch.*, *Ichth.* C. Ex.
Cánovas, Francisco, Catedrático de Historia natural en el Instituto, Murcia. *Paleontologia y Estudios prehistóricos.**
Caparros y Fernandez, Alfonso, Caravaca (Murcia), ó C. de Silva, 16, Madrid. *Ent. general.**
Carbó, Narciso, Presidente de la Sociedad Económica barcelonesa de Amigos del País, Vicepresidente de la Academia de Ciencias naturales de Barcelona, Catedrático de Terapéutica y Farmacología en la Universidad, C. de la Union, 15, Barcelona.*
Cardona y Orfila, Dr. Francisco, C. del Horno, 23, Mahon, Balearic Isles. *Malacology*, *Ent.*, *Palæo.* C. Ex. Offers Molluscs, Fossils, and Coleoptera of Minorca for those of other countries.
Carurrc, Manuel, Colegiata, 8, Madrid. *Coleopt.*, *Orthop. of Europe.*
Casas y Abad, Serafin, Doctor en Ciencias naturales, Licenciado en Medicina y Cirugía, Catedrático de Historia natural en el Instituto, Huesca.*
Castel, Cárlos, C. de Hortaleza, 44, 3.º, Madrid.*
Castellarnau y de Lleopart, Joaquin María de, Ingeniero Jefe de Montes, Segovia. *Micrografía.**
Castelló y Sanchez, Vicente, Licenciado en Farmacia, C. del Sacramento, 2, Farmacia, Madrid.*

Castro y Duque, Jacinto, Escorial. *Comp. Anat., Lepid.*
Caule, Dr. H. Priato, Sta. Barbara, 7, Madrid. *Moll.*
Cazurro y Ruiz, Manuel, Doctor en Derecho, C. de la Colegiata, 8, 1.º derecha, Madrid. *Coleópteros y ortópteros de Europa.**
Centeno, D. José, Ingeniero Jefe de Minas, Manila.*
Cervelli, Rev. P. Luis, San Gervasio, 20, 1.º, Barcelona. *Con.*
Cervera, Rafael, de la Academia de Medicina, C. de Jacometrezo, 66, 2.º derecha, Madrid.*
Cervera y Baviera, Julio, Capitan de ingenieros, C. del Arenal, 4, Hotel de Oriente, Madrid.*
Cerviño, Antonino, Licenciado en Teología, vice-Rector, Director y Catedrático del Seminario, Tuy.*
Chape, Prof. Dr. Juan Bautista, Cádiz. *Nat. Hist., Bot.*
Chaves, Antonio, Bot. Gar., Barcelona. *Bot.*
Chia, Manuel, C. de la Paja, 31, Barcelona.*
Chicote y del Riego, Dr. César, San Bernardo, 41, Madrid. *Ent.* C. Hemiptera of Europe. Ex. good native specimens for those of Egypt and of Russia.
Chil y Naranjo, Gregorio, Director del Museo canario, Las Palmas, Gran Canaria.*
Codina y Länglin, Ramon, Socio residente del Colegio de Farmacéuticos de Barcelona, numerario de la Academia de Ciencias naturales y de Artes de la misma, de la Academia de Medicina y Cirugía, Doctor en Farmacia, C. de San Pablo, 70, Barcelona.*
Codorniu, Ricardo, Ingeniero de Montes, Cartagena.*
Colmeiro (Excmo. Sr. D. Miguel), Caballero Gran Cruz de la Orden de Isabel la Católica, de las Academias de Medicina, y de Ciencias exactas, físicas y naturales de Madrid, Doctor en Ciencias y en Medicina, Catedrático de Botánica y Director del Jardin Botánico, C. del Barquillo, 8, 2.º izquierda, Madrid. *Bot.**
Colvée, Pablo, Doctor en Medicina, Plaza de Mirasol, 1, Valencia.*
Comerma, Andrés A., Ingeniero de la Armada, Ferrol.*
Compañó, Manuel, Ciudad Real, Lorenzo del Escorial. *Bot.*
Corminas, Enrique, Calle Milano, Barcelona. *Phys.*
Coronado, Francisco, Calle Serra 18, 2.º, Barcelona. *Con.*
Corral y Lastra, Rafael, Farmacéutico, Socio corresponsal del Colegio de Farmacéuticos de Madrid, Individuo de la Academia Nacional de Agricultura, Industria y Comercio de Paris, de la Sociedad Linneana matritense y de la de Higiene, Plazuela de la Media Luna 4, principal, Santander.*
Cortadelles, Jacundo, Burgos. *Con.*
Cortázar, Daniel, Ingeniero de Minas, C. de Jorge Juan, 19, Madrid.*
Cortazar, de, Calle Isabel la Catolica, 25, Madrid. *Geol.*
Cortes y Morates, Balbino, Pres. du Conseil d'Agric. du département de Madrid, C. de Campomanes, 6, Madrid.*
Cortes, Juan Francisco, Agric. Sch., Madrid. *Bot.*
Coscollano y Burillo, José, Licenciado en Ciencias naturales, C. del Cardenal Toledo, 10, Córdoba.*
Costa, Dr. Antonio Cipriano, Claris, 7, Barcelona. *Bot.*
Couder, Gerardo, Ingeniero de Montes, Avila.*
Crespí, Antonio, Licenciado en Farmacia, C. de San Felipe, 4, Palma (Mallorca).*
Cruz Manso de Zúñiga y Enrile, Victor, C. de la Aduana, 4, Madrid. *Bot.*
Cuesta, Dr. Segmido, Ayala, 7, 2.º, Madrid. *Ingénieur forestier.**
Cuní y Martorell, Miguel, Individuo de la Real Academia de Ciencias naturales y Artes, C. de Codols, 18, Barcelona.*
De Alós, Luis F., Calle Bassa S. Pédro 31, 1.º, Barcelona. *Numis.*
De Barnola, Rafael, Calle Escedellero, 5, 7, 9, 1.º, Barcelona. *Numis.*
Delás y de Gayolá, Francisco de Sales de, Condal, 20, Barcelona. *Bot.**

De Mazarredo, Carlos, Ingeniero de Montes, Claudio Coello, 12, pral., Madrid. *Arach.*, *Myriododa.* C.*
De Siscar y de Montolin, Ramon, Calle Puertaferessa, 21, 1.º, Barcelona. *Numis.*
Diaz Cueto y Teran, Emeterio, Molledo (Santander).
Diez Ulzurrun, Pablo, Farmacéutico, C. Imperial, 1, principal, Madrid.*
Dionisio, Martin Ayuso, C. E., Inst., Pamplona. *Agric.*, *Meteo.*
Don Domingo Sanchez del Arco, Domingo. *Bibliog.*
Dorronsoro, Bernabé, Ayudante de la Facultad de Farmacia en la Universidad, C. de Fuencarral 3, 3.º, Madrid.*
Egea y Tortosa, Márcos, Doctor en Medicina y Cirugía, Subdelegado del partido de Velez-Rubio, condecorado con la cruz de epidemias, Socio académico profesor del Liceo artístico y literario de Granada, y de la de Amigos del País de Lorca, Velez-Rubio (Almería).*
Ehlers, Guillermo, Banquier, Muralla del Mar 27, 2.º, (Oficina, 17, Plaza del Rey), Cartagena. *Ent.: Coleopt.* C. Cicindelidæ and Carabidæ. Buys and exchanges specimens of all countries.*
Erice y Murua, Tomás, Ingeniero de Montes, Individuo de la Comision científica de la fragata *Blanca*, Hernani (Guipúzcoa).*
Escalera, Justino, Farmacéutico, Gijon. *Bot.*
Escalante, José, Doctor en Ciencias naturales, Catedrático de Historia natural y Secretario del Instituto, C. del Cubo, 8, 2.º derecha, Santander.*
Espejo, Zoilo, Ingeniero Agrónomo, Catedrático propietario y Subdirector de la Escuela superior de Ingenieros Agrónomos, C. de Fuencarral, 97, principal, Madrid.*
Espluga y Sancho, Faustino, Licenciado en Ciencias de la Zoológica de Regensburgo, etc., etc., C. de Silva, 40 y 42, principal izquierda, Madrid.*
Fabié, Excmo. Sr. D. Antonio Maria, Consejero de Estado, C. de San Onofre, 5, 2.º derecha, Madrid.*
Falcon y Lorenzo, Antonio, Ingeniero de Montes del distrito forestal, Plaza del Arzobispo, 9, Valencia. *Bot.*
Fatigati, Prof. Serrano, Ciudad Real. *Bot.*
Femenias Aledo, G., rue Moreras, Mahon (Baleares). *Bot.: Marine Algæ.* C.
Fernandez Cuesta, Nemesio, C. de Tragineros, 22, 3.º, Madrid.*
Fernandez de Castro, Angel, Ingeniero de Montes, Inspeccion de Montes, Manila (Filipinas).*
Fernandez de Castro, Excmo. Sr. D. Manuel, Inspector general del Cuerpo de Ingenieros de Minas, C. de Jorge Juan, 23, 1.º, Madrid. *Min.*, *Geol.*
Fernandez, Francisco, Guadalajara. *Bot.*
Fernandez Losada, Excmo. Sr. D. Cesáreo, Caballero Gran Cruz de la Orden de Isabel la Católica, Gran cordon de la de Metjidié, Comendador de número de la de Cárlos III, condecorado con la Cruz de primera clase de Beneficencia y con otras de distincion por méritos científicos y de guerra, Socio de varias corporaciones cientificas nacionales y extranjeras, Inspector, Médico Mayor del Cuerpo de Sanidad Militar, Doctor en Medicina, Plaza del Progreso, 5, 2.º, Madrid.*
Fernandez-Minguez, Dr. Cesar, Farmacéutico Militar, Aduana, 21, Madrid.*
Fernandez Molina, Dr. Ramon, Campanario (Badajoz).
Fernandez Rodriguez, Mariano, Doctor en Ciencias y en Medicina, ex-Profesor auxiliar y ex-Secretario del Instituto del Noviciado, C. de Pontejos, almacen de papel, Madrid.*
Ferrand, Julio, Ingeniero Jefe de la 1.ª seccion de Vía y Obras de los ferrocarriles andaluces, C. de Infanzones, Estacion de San Bernardo, Sevilla.*

Ferrand, Julio, Oficina del Ferrocarril de Malpartida a Placencia, Valencia de Alcántara.
Ferrandiz, Dr. Manuel Anton, Aide-Naturaliste au Muséum d'Histoire Naturelle, Madrid. *Moll.*, *Zoophytes.* C.
Ferrari, Cárlos, Doctor en Farmacia, Plaza de San Ildefonso, 4, Madrid.*
Ferrer, Cárlos, Ronda de la Universidad, 16, 1.º, Barcelona.*
Ferrer y Viñerta, Enrique, Doctor en Medicina, Catedrático de Clínica quirúrgica en la Universidad, C. de Ballesteros, 7, Valencia.*
Flores y Gonzalez, Roberto, Escuela Normal, Oviedo.*
Formica, Corsi Coronado, Dr. Antonio, Ronda de S. Pedro 185, Barcelona. *Anat.*
Fortanet, Ricardo, C. de la Libertad 29, Madrid.*
Frades, Luis G., D.S. Catedrático de Física y Química y Director de la Estacion Meteorológica en la Univ. de Oviedo, Instituto Provincial Oviedo. *Meteo.*
Fruan, Alfredo, Gijon, Oviedo. *Diatoms.*
Fuente y Gonzalez, Eduardo de la, Médico, Villarejo del Valle (Avila).*
Galdo, Excmo, Sr. D. Manuel María José de, Caballero Gran Cruz de la Orden de Isabel la Católica, Doctor en Ciencias, Catedrático de Historia natural en el Instituto del Noviciado, C. de Hortaleza, 78, 2.º, Madrid.*
Garcia Cardiel, Ricardo, Travesía de San Mateo, 4, Madrid. *Coleopt.*, *Dipt. of Europe.*
García de Meneses, Ricardo, Licenciado en Medicina y Cirugía. C. de Vida, 2, Sevilla. *Geol.**
Garcia, Frejo, Dr. José Antonio, Fuencarral, Madrid.*
Garcia Mercet, Ricardo, Farmacéutico de Sanidad Militar, Hortaleza, 126, 2.º izquierda, Madrid. *Coleópteros y dípteros de Europa.**
García Rendueles, Rufo, Ingeniero de Caminos, Gijon.*
García Solana José, Médico, C. del Conde de Aranda, 9 principal, Madrid.*
García y Alvarez, Rafael, Catedrático de Historia natural en el Instituto, Granada.*
García y Arenal, Fernando, Ingeniero de Caminos, Gijon.*
Gaspar y Loste, Francisco, C. de las Hileras, 7, 2.º, Madrid. *Orthopt.*, *Ent. general.**
Gerona y Vilanova, Dr. Ignacio, Barcelona.*
Ghersi, Francisco, Cadiz. *Bot.*
Gila y Fidalgo, Félix, Segovia. *Petrografia.**
Gil y Flores, Manuel, Puerta del Sol, 5, Café de Levante, Madrid (also, Loranca de Tajuna, Guadalajara. *Palæo.*, *Geol.*, *Min.*, *Crystal.*, *Lithol.*, *Moll.*, *Radiates*, *Sponges.* C. Ex.
Gogorza y Gonzalez, José, Ayudante del Museo de Ciencias naturales, C de Serrano, 78, 4.º izquiérda, Madrid. *Himenopteros.**
Gomer Pamo, Dr. Juan Ramon, Prof. de la Universidad Farmacéutica, Santa Isabel, 5, Madrid.*
Gomez Carrasco, Enrique, C. de Santiago, 18, 2.º, Madrid. *Ent. general.**
Gomez y García, Manuel, Ingeniero Agrónomo, C. del Arenal, 18, principal, Madrid.*
Gomez Machado, Cárlos María, Rector del Liceo Nacional de Ponta Delgada, Isla de San Miguel (Azores).*
Goñi y Armendariz, Antero, C. de la Montera, 3 principal, Madrid.*
Gonzalez y Canales, Prof. Dr. Vicente, Dir. Bot. Gar., Santiago. *Bot.*, *Nat. Hist.*
Gonzalez Fragoso, Romualdo, Licenciado en Medicina, C. de Felipe III, 8, 3.º derecha, Madrid. *Musgos.**
Gonzalez de la Pena, Pablo, Dir. Agric. Sch., Madrid. *Bot.*
Gonzalez de Velasco, Eduardo, Commandante de Artillería, Fábrica de Trubia (Oviedo).*
Gonzalez Linares, Augusto, Catedrático de Historia natural en la Facultad

de Ciencias en la Universidad, Director del Laboratorio de Zool. marino, Valladolid.*
Gonzalez, Mariano, Agric. Sch., Madrid. *Bot.*
Gonzalez Marti, Dr. Ignacio, Encomienda. 9, Madrid.
Gonzalez, R. P. D. Juan Crisóstomo, Profesor en las Escuelas Pias de San Antonio Abad, C. de Hortaleza, Madrid.*
Gonzalez Velasco, Dr. Pedro, Mus. Antropol., Madrid.
Gonzalo y Goya, Angel, Doctor en Ciencias naturales, Catedrático de Historia natural en el Instituto, Plaza de la Verdura, 7 principal, Salamanca.*
Gorriz y Muñez, Ricardo José, Milagro, Navarre. *Gen. Ent.: Hymenop., Coleopt.*
Graëlls, Dr. Mariano de la Paz, Profesor de Anatomía Comparada y Fisiología, Consejero de instruccion publica, Calle de la Bota, 2, Madrid. *Comp. Anat., Physiol., Zool., Bot., Ent.* C. Ex.
Grau y Agudo, José María, Licenciado en Farmacia, C. de Meson dé Paredes, 10, principal, Madrid.*
Grau, Victor, Doctor en Medicina, Las Palmas, Gran Canaria.*
Gredilla y Gauna, Apolinar Federico, Doctor en Ciencias, Ayudante por oposicion del Museo de ciencias naturales, C. de Leganitos, 23, Madrid.*
Greenhill, Tomás Arturo, Ingeniero civil, Asociado del Instituto de Ingenieros civiles de Lóndres, C. de la Vírgen de las Azucenas, 3. 2.º, Madrid.*
Greus y Martinez, Domingo, Plaza de Santa Catalina, Valencia.
Guerra Estope, Jaime, Ronda de San Pedro, 70, Barcelona.*
Guirao y Navarro, Angel, Catedrático de Historia natural, C. de Atocha, 103, 105 y 107, Madrid.*
Gutierrez Solano, Dr. José, C. Conde de Avanda, 9, Madrid.*
Hidalgo, Dr. Joaquin Gonzalez, Roy. Acad. Sci., Calle de Cadiz, 9, 3.º derecha, Madrid. *Con.* C. Ex. shells of Spain for L. and M. shells of other countries.
Ibañez, Francisco Antonio, del Comercio, Vocal de la Junta de Pesca del Departamento de Cádiz, Socio corresponsal de la Sociedad Protectora de Animales y Plantas de la misma ciudad, Muralla del Mar, 43, Cartagena. *Bot., Malacol., Ictiología.**
Iglesia, Dr. Santiago de la, Calle Real, 61, principal, Ferrol. *Mic. Preparations.**
Iñarra y Echeverria, Fermin, Profesor auxiliar, por oposicion, de la seccion de Ciencias fisico-químicas y naturales en el Instituto del Cardenal Cisneros, C. de Gravina, 14, 3.º, Madrid.*
Inchaurrandicta, Rogelio, C. de la Princesa, 7, Madrid. *Min., Geol.*
Irastorza, José, Farmacéutico, San Sebastian (Guipúzcoa).*
Izquierdo y Rodrigues Espeira, Dr. Luis, Farmacéutico militar, Hortaleza, 106, Madrid. *Bot.**
Jimenez de Cisneros, Daniel, Catedrático de Historia natural del Colegio, Caravaca (Murcia).*
Jimenez de la Espada, Márcos, C. de Valenzuela, 6, 4.º izquierda, Madrid. *Mamíferos, aves, reptiles y batracios.**
Jimenez de Pedro, Justo, Doctor en Medicina, Licenciado en Farmacia, Director de los baños de Uberuaga de Ubilla (Marquina), C. de la Magdalena, 1, 2.º izquierda, Madrid.*
Lacasa, Manuel, Vera (Almería). *Geol.*
Lacoizqueta, José Maria de, Presbítero, Navarte (Navarra). *Bot.**
Laguna, Máximo, Ingeniero de Montes, C. del Clavel, 2, 3.º centro, Madrid. *Bot.**
Landerer, José J., Tortosa. *Geol. y Paleont.**
Lara, José Perez, Jerez de la Frontera. *Bot.*
Lanzarote, Joaquin, Propriétaire, Commandeur, San Judas, 3, Murcia. *General Sciences, Agric.*

Larrinúa y Azcona, Angel, Doctor en Derecho, Plaza de las Escuelas, 1, 2.o, San Sebastian (Guipúzcoa). *Ornith., Coleopt.**
Lauffer, Jorge, Miembro de la Sociedad de Historia natural de Augsburgo, de la Entomológica de Munich y la Escuela de Veterinaria, C. de San Bernardo, 75, principal, Madrid.*
Lázaro é Ibiza, Blas, Doctor en Farmacia, Licenciado en Ciencias, Ayudante del Jardin Botánico, C.de Monteleon,18, 3.o izquierda,Madrid. *Bot.**
Lemus y Olmo, Eugenio, Director regente de la Calcografia nacional, C. del Arco de Santa Maria, 35, 2.o derecha, Madrid.*
Lizambard, Abbé, Consulat de France, San Sebastian. *Ent.: Coleopt.*
Lizarán Paterna, Fernando, C. de la Bodega, 1, Lorca (Murcia).*
Lleó, Antonio Maria, Presbítero, Doctor en Sagrada Teología, Bachiller en la Facultad de Ciencias, Catedrático de Física y Química en el seminario central, Valencia.*
Lletget, Pedro, Catedrático de la Escuela de Farmacia en la Universidad, C. de Hortaleza, 54 y 56, 3.o, Madrid.*
Lopez Cainzares, Dr. Baldomero, Peninsular, 4, Madrid. *Ent.**
Lopez Cepero, Adolfo, Chiclana (Cádiz). *Ent., Coleopteros de Europa.**
Lopez Dóriga, José, Doctor en Ciencias y en Medicina, Catedrático supernumerario del Instituto, Oviedo.*
Lopez, Juan, Doctor en Farmacia, Profesor auxiliar del Instituto, C. de Lucería, 16, Murcia.*
Lopez de Quintana, Diego, C. de la Independencia, 8, 3.o, Zaragoza. *Min., Geol.*
Lopez de Silva, Estéban, Doctor en Medicina, Licenciado en Ciencias naturales, C. de Ferraz, 52, bajo, Madrid.*
Lopez Lezcano, Francisco de, C. de Carretas 9, 3.o, Madrid. *Coleopt.*
Lopez Seoane, Ilmo. Sr. D. Victor, Abogado, Comisario Regio de Agricultura, Industria y Comercio, del Congreso internacional de Antropología y Prehistoria, de las Sociedades Imp. y Real Zool.-bot. de Viena, Senkenb. de Francfort, Geolog. y Zoolog. de Francia, Entom. de Francia, Bélgica, Suiza, Berlin, Stettin, fundador de la de Alemania y otras, Coruña. *Vert.**
Lorenzana, Augusto E., Licenciado en Farmacia, Caballero de la Orden de Cárlos III, Redondela (Pontevedra). *Min.**
Loscos, Francisco, Castelserás. *Bot.*
Lozano, Dr. Eduardo, Barcelona.*
Lozano, Isidoro, C. Mayor 108 y 110, 4.o ,Madrid.*
Mace, Dr. Emilio, Puerta de Sto. Domingo, 18 dupl., Madrid. *Ent.**
Machado, Antonio, Doctor en Ciencias y en Medicina, Catedrático de Malacología y Actinología en la Facultad de Ciencias de la Universidad, C. de Felipe III, 8, 3.o, Madrid.*
Machado, Prof. Dr. Antonio, Dir. Bot. Gar., Seville. *Bot., Nat. Hist.*
Macho de Velado, Jerónimo, Doctor en Ciencias, Catedrático de la Facultad de Farmacia en la Universidad, Comendador ordinario de la Orden de Isabel la Católica, C. de Carranza, 21, 2.o izquierda, Madrid.*
Mac-Lennan, José, Ingeniero, Portugalete (Bilbao).*
Macpherson, Guillermo, Consul de Inglaterra, C. de la Exposicion, 2, Barrio de Monasterio, Madrid. *Geol.**
Macpherson, José, C. de la Exposicion 4, Barrio de Monasterio, Madrid. *Min., Geol.**
Maffei, Eugenio, Ingeniero de Minas, C. de Mendizábal, 2, Madrid.*
Maisterra, Miguel, Catedrático de ampliación de la Mineralogía en la Facultad de Ciencias, Director del Gabinete de Historia natural, C. del Olivar, 3, 2.o izquierda, Madrid.*
Marin Martinez, Ceferino, Abogado, Lorca (Murcia).*
Marin y Sancho, Francisco, Licenciado en Farmacia, C. de la Luna, 28, 30 y 32, 2.o izquierda, Madrid.*

Marqueta y Morales, Valentin, Madrid.*
Martí y de Lleopart, Francisco Maria de, Licenciado en Derecho civil y canónico, C. de Santa Ana, 8 principal, Tarragona.*
Martin de Argenta, Vicente, Doctor en Ciencias y en Farmacia, Socio del Colegio de Farmacéuticos de Madrid, Catedrático de la Facultad de Ciencias, C. de Hortaleza, 86, Madrid.*
Martin del Amo, Eduardo Jacobo, Licenciado en Farmacia, Director del Colegio del Baztan, C. de la Estacion, Vitoria.*
Martinez Añibarro Rives, Dr. José M., Dir. du "Bureau Scientifique," Fomento, 34, Madrid. *Chem.* C.
Martinez Añibarro Rives, Juan, Officier d'Artillerie, Lain Calvo 20, Búrgos. *Pyrotichnic Philosophy.*
Martinez Añada, Andrés, C. de Saurin, 4, Murcia. *Orn., Min.*
Martinez, Luis Arcadio, Ingeniero ogrónomo, Secretario de la Junta de Agricultura, Industria y Comercio, Catedrático de Agricultura en el Instituto, Huelva.*
Martinez de Pison, Venancio, C. de Preciados, 6, 2.o, Madrid. *Geol., Palæo.*
Martinez Vigil, Ilmo. Sr. Fr. Ramon, Obispo de la diócesis, ex-Catedrático de Historia natural en la Universidad de Manila, Oviedo.*
Martinez y Angel, Antonio, Doctor en la Facultad de Medicina, C. de Fuencarral, 56, principal, Madrid.*
Martinez Molina, Excmo. Sr. D. Rafael, Caballero Gran Cruz de la Orden de María Victoria, de la Academia de Medicina, Doctor en Ciencias, Catedrático jubilado de la Facultad de Medicina en la Universidad, C. de Atocha, 133, principal, Madrid.*
Martinez y Saez, Francisco de Paula, Catedrático de Zoografia de los vertebrados en la Facultad de Ciencias de la Universidad, Plaza de los Ministerios 5, 3.o izquierda, Madrid. *Coleopteros de Europa.**
Martorell, Dr. Francisco, Rambla de Sta.-Mónica, 33, 1.o, Barcelona. *Ent.*
Martorell y Cuni, Jerónimo, Commerciante, Plaza de Medinaceli, 1 bis, 1.o, Barcelona. *Agric.**
Martorell y Peña, Manuel, Rambla de Santa Mónica, 33, 1.o, Barcelona. *Coleopt., Hemipt., Hymenopt., Orthopt., Lepid., Dipt.* C. Ex.
Masferrer y Rierola, Mariano, Barcelona.*
Masferrer y Arquimbau, Dr. Ramon, Plaza de Don Miguel, 1, piso 2.o, Catalodia (Vich). *Bot.* C.
Masferrer, Mariano, Pra. de Sta. Ana, 4, Barcelona. *Gen. Nat. Hist.*
Mavorga y Garcia, Antonio, C. Mayor, 43, Madrid. *Bot.*
Mazarredo, Cárlos, Ingeniero de Montes, C. de Claudio Coello, 12, Madrid. *Aracnidos.**
Mederos y Manzanos, Pedro, San Lorenzo (Gran Canaria).*
Medina y Ramon, Dr. Manuel, Goyeneta, 27, Sevilla. *Gen. Ent., Hymenop.**
Mercado y Gonzalez, Matías, Licenciado en Medicina y Cirugía, Médico cirujano titular, Nava del Rey (Valladolid). *Ent.**
Miralles de Imperial, Clemente, Rambla de Estudios, 1, Barcelona.*
Mir y Navarro, Manuel, Catedrático de Historia natural en el Instituto, Barcelona.*
Mojados, Eduardo, Ingeniero de Caminos, Professor en la Escuela del Cuerpo, C. de Valverde, 30 y 32, 3.o izquierda, Madrid.*
Mompó y Vidal, Vicente, Licenciado en Ciencias naturales, Perito agrónomo, Individuo de la Sociedad de Agricultura Valenciana y de la de Amigos del País de Santa Cruz de Tenerife, Catedrático de Historia natural en el Instituto, Albacete. *Ornitologia**
Monjo Monjo, Prof. P., Place Principe, Mahon. *Moll.*
Monsalud, Marqués de, Almendialejo (Badajoz). *Agric.*

Monserrat y Archs, Juan, Licenciado en Medicína, Secretario general de la Sociedad Botánica Barcelonesa, C. del Hospital, 47, Barcelona. *Bot.**
Mora, Manuel C. de las Córtes, 38, Cáceres. *Coleopt.*
Moragas, Ucela y, Ricardo, Farmaceutico de la Sociedad Española de Historia Natural, El Prado, Madrid. *Bot.*
Moragues é Ibarra, Ignacio, C. de San Francisco, 18, Palma (Mallorca). *Coleópteros y Moluscos.**
Moragues y de Manzanos, Fernando, Presbitero, C. del General Barceló, Palma (Mallorca). *Coleópt.**
Moreno, Prof. Eugenio Prieto, Agric. Sch., Madrid.
Moreno y Gonzalez, Rufino, Farmacéutico militar. *Bot.**
Moriana, Sr. Conde de, Fuencarral, 55, principal izquierda, ó en Las Fraguas (Reinosa).*
Muller, Daniel, Paseo Gracia, 123, 4.o, Barcelona. *Ent.: Coleopt.*
Munita y Alvarez, Dr. Vicente Hortaleza, 87 Madrid. *Botanique.**
Muñoz Cobo y Arredondo, Luis, Licenciado en Ciencias naturales y en Derecho, Director y Catedrático de Historia natural en el Instituto, Jaen.
Muñoz del Castillo, Dr. José, Prof. à la Faculté des Sciences de l'Université, Alfonso, 1.o, 43, 20, Saragosse. *Ampelography.*
Nieto Serrano, Excmo. Sr. D. Matías, Secretario perpetuo de la Academia de Medicina, Ronda de Recoletos, 11, Madrid.*
Nogués, A. F. Ingeniero civil, ex-Professor de Geología y Explotación de minas, C. de Colon, 36, Sevilla. *Geologia y Mineralogia, Explotacion de minas.**
Noreña Gutierrez, Antonio, C. del Carmen, 39, 2.o, Madrid.*
Ochoa y Echagüen Luis, C. de Oriente, 10, 2.o, derecha, Vitora.*
Olavide, Excmo. Sr. D. José, Caballero Gran Cruz de la Orden de Isabel la Católica, de la Academia de Medicina, Doctor en Medicina, C., de Alcalá 40, Madrid.*
Ouis, Dr. Mauricio Carlos, Santa Engracia, 23, Madrid. *Gen. Nat. Hist.**
Orio, Prof. Dr. Antonio, Madrid. *Bot., Min.*
Osorio y Zavala, Amado, Doctor en Medicina y Cirugía, Vega de Rivadeo. Oviedo.*
Ortiz y Landauri, Antonio, C. de Bailén, 6, Caballerizas, Madrid. *Zool.*
Padilla, Juan, Doctor en Médicina y Cirugía de la Escuela de Paris, Las Palmas, Gran Canaria.*
Paer Valero, Dr. Antonio, Calle de la Paciencia 5, Cordova. *Ent., Orthopt.**
Palacios y Rodriguez, José de, Farmacéutico, Plaza de Santa Ana 11, Madrid.*
Pantel, José, S. J., Monasterio de Uclés, Tarancon (Cuenca). *Coleópteros, Ortópteros.**
Pastor, Prof. Dr. Pascual, Dir. Bot. Gar., rue St. Michel 12, Valladolid.
Paul y Arozarena, Manuel José de, C. de San Eloy, 34, 2.o, Sevilla.*
Pedrals y Moliné, Arturo, Calle Aucha, 7, 4.o, Barcelona. *Numis.*
Perez Arcas, Laureano, de la Academia de Ciencias exactas, físicas y naturales de Madrid, Catedrático de Zoología en la Facultad de Ciencias de la Universidad, C. de las Huertas 14, 3.o, Madrid *Peces y coleópteros de Europa.**
Perez de Arce, Facundo, Licenciado en Ciencias naturales, Catedrático de Historia natural en el Instituto, Guadalajara.*
Perez de Arrilucea, Andrés, Licenciado en Ciencias naturales, Catedrático de Agricultura en el Instituto, Segovia.*
Perez-Hidalgo y Perez-Rincon, Adolfo, C. de Arriaza, 7, 2.o izquierda, Madrid.*
Perez Lara. José María, Jerez de la Frontera, Cádiz. *Botánica.**
Perez Ortego, Enrique, Doctor en Ciencias, C. de Atocha 36, Madrid.*

Perez Maeso, José, C. de Quintana 8, 3.º derecha, Madrid. *Botánica.**
Perez Minguez, Prof. Dr. Luis, Valladolid. *Bot., Nat. Hist.*
Perez San Millan, Mauricio, Doctor en Farmacia, Catedrático de Historia natural en el Instituto, Burgos.*
Pieltain y Bartoli, José María, Abogado, C. de Alcalá, 65, 3.º izquierda, Madrid. *Bacteriologie, Physiologie.**
Plannellas, Giralt, Dr. José, Dir. Bot. Gar., Barcelona. *Nat. Hist., Bot.*
Planellas Llanos, Alejandro, Catedrático de la Universidad, C. de Pelayo 7, Barcelona.*
Pomata et Gisbert, Eladio, Officier du 3c corps de Topographes, Polan, (Toledo). *Mineralogy, Geol., Bot.* C. Ex. Desires engraved lithographs of natural history objects and botanical specimens.
Pombo, Antonio, Socio fundador del Ateneo científico, literario y artístico de Vitoria, Licenciado en Farmacia, Doctor en Ciencias naturales, Catedrático de Historia natural en el Instituto, C. del Arca, 1, 2.º, Vitoria.*
Pons y Soler, Juan, Mahon. *Con., Palæo.* C. Ex. shells of Europe and fossils of Minorca for shells of all the world and ancient rocks.
Prado y Sainz, Dr. Salvador, Plaza de San Ildefonso, 6, Madrid. *Min., Orthopt.**
Présser, Ernest, C.E., Mem. Inst. Med. (London), Salesas 4, Madrid.
Prieto y Caules, Francisco, Ingeniero primero de Caminos, Canales y Puertos, Director de las obras del puerto, Málaga. *Geol., Malacol.**
Prieto y Prieto, D. Manuel, C. del Turco, 8, 3.º, Madrid. *Zool., Comp. Anat., Physiol.*
Puig y Larraz, Gabriel, Ingeniero de Minas, C. de Pavia, 2, 2.º, Madrid.*
Puiggarí, Juan, Barcelona. *Bot.*
Purai y Baroja, Dr. Benjamin, Princesa, 22, Madrid. *Bot.**
Quiroga y Rodriguez, Francisco, Doctor en Ciencias y en Farmacia, Ayudante por oposicion del Museo de Ciencias naturales, C. de Castelló, 8, principal, Madrid. *Min., Geol., Cristal.**
Ramon Gomez Pamo, Juan, Pres. Soc. Linnean Matritense, Madrid.
Ramor y Mallafré. Dr. Eduardo, Barcelona.*
Reyes y Prosper, Eduardo, Licenciado en Ciencias naturales, C. de San Bernado, 56, 2.º derecha, Madrid. *Dibujo científico, Cristalografía, Micrografía.**
Reyes y Prosper, Ventura, Doctor en Ciencias naturales, C. de San Bernardo, 56, 2.º, derecha, Madrid. *Ornitología y Malacología.**
Ribera, Marqués de la, C. de Serrano 6, 2.º, Madrid. *Min.*
Rich, Wm., Jr., Mining Engineer, Rio Tinto Mines, Spain.*
Rico y Jimeno, Tomás, Catedrático de Historia natural en el Instituto, Coruña. *Geol.**
Riera Viltraret, Antonio, Barcelona.*
Rio, José, Ingeniero de Montes, C. de Tetuan, 20, 2.º derecha, Madrid.*
Rioja y Martin, José, Auxiliar de la Facultad de Ciencias, C. de San Francisco, 28, principal, Valladolid.*
Ripoche, Diego, Tafira (Gran Canaria).*
Rivera, Emilio, Doctor en Ciencias naturales, Catedrático de Historia natural en el Instituto, Plaza de la Aduana, Valencia.*
Rivera, Excmo. Sr. Marqués de la, Consejero de Estado, Miembro de la Sociedad Geológica alemana, C. de Puerta Cerrada, 5, Madrid. *Min.**
Rivero, Excmo. Sr. D. Roque Leon del, Inspector general de segunda clase del Cuerpo de Ingenieros de Montes, de los de la Real Casa, Socio fundador de la Geográfica de Madrid, de la Central de Horticultur y de Mérito de la Protectora de Animales y Plantas, Caballero Gran Cruz de Isabel la Católica, Comendador de la de Cristo de Portugal, y Caballero de la de Cárlos III. Invierno, Villalar, 6, 1.º izquierda ; verano, San Ildefonso (Segovia).*

Roca y Carchan, Ignacio, Calle Gigantes, 6, 2.o, Barcelona. *Ent.*
Roca y Vecino, Santos, Licenciado en Ciencias naturales, Puerta de Segovia, 1, principal, Madrid. *Min.**
Rodriguez Aguado, Enrique, Doctor en Medicinia, Professor auxiliar de la Facultad de Ciencias, C. del Reloj, 1 y 3, principal, Madrid.*
Rodriguez de Cepeda, Excmo. Sr. D. Antonio, Decano y Catedrático de la Facultad de Derecho en la Universidad, Valencia.*
Rodriguez Mourelo, José, C. de la Reina, 27, 2.o, Madrid.*
Rodriguez Nuñez, Eduardo, Licenciado en Farmacia, Socio corresponsal de la Linneana matritense, Numerario del Gabinete cientifico, C. del Castillo, 32 y 34, Santa Cruz (Tenerife).*
Rodriguez Risueño, Emiliano, C. de la Cruzada, 3, Madrid.*
Rodriguez y Femenías, Juan J., C. de la Libertad, 48, Mahon (Menorca). *Bot.**
Rodriguez y Perez, Felipe, Socio del Gabinete científico (ciencias naturales), Gabinete instructivo y Sociedad naturales, Professor en el Colegio de segunda enseñanza, Torrelavega (Santander).*
Roger y Gil, Enrique, Licenciado en Filosofía y Letras, Cuartel provincial, Lorca (Murcia). *Estudios geológicos y prehistóricos.**
Roig y Torres, Prof. Raphael, Barcelona. *Phys.*
Roman, Maximiliano, Abogado, C. de la Gorguera, 5, bajo, Madrid.*
Romero y Alvarez, Julio, Ingeniero de Montes, C. de Alcalá 36, principal, Madrid.*
Romero y Garcia, Pedro, Doctor en Medicina, Licenciado en Ciencias naturales, Catedrático supernumerario y Secretario del Instituto, Socio corresponsal de la Linneana matritense, Huesca. *Bot.**
Rubio, Federico, Doctor en Medicina, C. de las Torres, 4, Madrid.*
Ruiz, Casaviella, Juan, Licenciado en Farmacia, Caparroso (Navarra).*
Ruiz de Angulo, Bonifacio, Farmacéutio, Vitoria.*
Sainz Gutierrez, Pedro, Catedrático de Organografía y Fisiología vegetal en la Facultad de Ciencias de la Universidad, C. de la Salud, 11, 3.o, Madrid. *Physiol. vegetal.**
Salarich y Jimenez, José, Médico del Hospital de Santa Cruz de la Ciudad de Vich, Socio corresponsal de la M. I. Academia de Medicina y Cirugía de Barcelona, Corresponsal laureado de la Económica barcelonesa de Amig s del País, honorario del Círculo literario de Vich, Plaza Mayor, 31, Vich.*
Salvañá, Joaquin Maria, C. de Aribau, 11, 3.o, Barcelona.*
Sanchez Cabezudo, Federico, Doctor en Farmacia, Carriches (Toledo).*
Sanchez Comendador, Antonio, Catedrático y Decano de la Facultad de Farmacia en la Universidad, Barcelona.*
Sanchez y Sanchez, Domingo, Ayudante de la Comision de la Flora forestal, Manila (Filipinas).*
San Martin, Basilio, de la Academia de Medicina, C. del Lobo, 27, 2.o izquierda.*
San Millan y Alonso, Rafael, C. de San Lorenzo, 15, Madrid.*
Santistéban, Mariano, Instituto, Travesia del Fúcar, 14, Madrid.
Sanz, Prof. Serafin, Dir. Bot. Gar., Grenada. *Bot.*, *Nat. Hist.*
Sanz de Diego, José, Prof., C. de San Bernardo, 15, Madrid. *Math.*
Sanz de Diego, Maximino, Naturalista-comerciante, de objetos y libros de Historia natural, de utensilios para la recoleccion, preparacion y conservacion de las colecciones, cambio y venta de las mismas en todos los ramos, C. de San Bernardo, 94, principal, Madrid.*
Saura, Santiago Angel, C. del Duque de la Victoria, 14, Barcelona. *Ent.*, *Malacol.*
Secall é Inda, José, Ingeniero de Montes, Ronda del Corpus, 7, Salamanca.*
Seebold, Teodoro, Ingeniero civil de la Sociedad de Ingenieros civiles de Paris, representante de la casa F. Krupp, Comendador de la Orden

de Cárlos III, Caballero de varias órdenes extranjeras, C. de la Estufa, 3, 3.º, Bilbao. *Lepid.**

Seoane, Dr. V. Lopez, Coruña. *Bot., Vert., Invert. of Europe.*

Sepúlveda, José, Farmacéutica, Premiado con medalla de Honor de la Exposicion Farmacéutica, de oso de la Enconómica Matritense y Premio especial de la Direccion de Beneficencia y Sanidad por sus artículos botánicos, Brihuega. *Farm. Bot.**

Serra, Julio, Teniente de Estado Mayor, C. de la Salud, 21, principal izquierda, Madrid.*

Serrano Fatigati, Enrique, Catedrático de Química del Instituto del Cardenal Cisneros, C. de las Pozas, 17, Madrid.*

Serrano, Dr. Matias N., Madrid.

Serrano y Pla, Eduardo, Ingeniero Jefe de Montes, Plaza Moscas, 1, Valencia.*

Silvela, Luis, Universidad, C. de Pizarro, 19, 2º, Madrid.

Socorro, Marqués del, Academia de Ciencias, C. de Jacometrezo, 41, Madrid.

Solano y Eulate, José María, Marqués del Socorro, Catedrático de Geología en la Facultad de Ciencias, C. de Jacometrezo, 41, Madrid. *Min., Geol.**

Sorela y Faxardo, Luis, C. de Santa Engracia, 21, Madrid.*

Suarez, Sergio, Ingeniero, Inspector facultativo de Hacienda, C. del Prado, 3, 2.º, Madrid. *Bot., Ent.**

Sureda y Villalonga, Juan, Palma. *Geol.*

Texidor, Dr. Juan, Barcelona. *Bot.*

Tió y Salvador, R. P. D. Dionisio, Colegio de PP. Escolapios, Ronda de San Antonio, Barcelona.*

Torrepando, Sr. Conde de, Ingeniero de Montes, C. de Ferraz, 48, hotel, Madrid.*

Torres y Perona, Tomás, Catedrático de Química orgánica en la Facultad de Farmacia, Socio corresponsal del Colegio de Farmacéuticos de Madrid, Farmacia de San Gabriel, Manila.*

Tremols y Bórrell, Federico, Catedrático de Química inorganica aplicada de la Facultad de Farmacia en la Universidad, C. de Córtes, 214, 2.º, Barcelona. *Bot.**

Truan, Alfred, Gijon, Dir. des Verreries de Gijon. *Diatoms, Photomicography.**

Ubach y Soler, Antonio, Propietario agricultor, Administrador del Banco, Tarrasa. *Zootecnia agrícola.**

Uhagon, Federico de, Marquina (Vizcaya).*

Uhagon, Serafin de, Miembro de las Sociedades Entómologicas de Francia y de Berlin, C. de Piamonte, 2, 2.º, Madrid. *Coleópteros de Europa.**

Valdés y Pajares, Juan, C. de la Amnista, 12, 2.º, Madrid. *Orn. of Spain.*

Valero y Castell, Blas, Bot. Gar., Valencia. *Bot.*

Valduvi y Vidal, Francisco, C. de la Luna, 36, 3.º, Madrid. *Hymenop.*

Valle y Ortega, Tomás, C. del Caballero de Gracia, 24, 3.º, Madrid.

Vayreda y Vila. Estanislao, Licenciado en Farmacia, Besalú, Sagaró (Gerona). *Orn., Bot.**

Vazquez Avoca, D. Rafael, San Marco, 26, Madrid (en hiver). Mascanones, 14, Cordova (en été).*

Vazquez y Lopez Amor, Antonio, C. de la Biblioteca, 2. Madrid.

Velasco, Jesús, Plaza de Bilbao (Vitoria).*

Velaz de Medrano, Fernando, Ingeniero de Montes, Soria.*

Vergara, Mariano, Avocat, ex. Deputé, ex-Prefect, Prof., Univ., Madrid, Plaza de Santa Barbara. *Gen. Sci., Agric., Bibliog.*

Vidal, Dr. Ignaz, Prof. Univ., Valencia. *Physiol.*

Vidal y Quadras, Manuel, Calle Cristina, 1, 2.º, Barcelona. *Numis.*

Vidal y Soler, Sebastian, Ingeniero de Montes, Jefe de la comision de la Flora y Mapa forestal de Filipinas, Manila.*
Vié, Louis, Nat. Sci. Mus., Madrid.
Vicites de Andrade, Vicente, Juez de la instancia, Barbastro. *Zool.*
Vila y Nadal, Antonio, Ayudante en la Facultad de Ciencias, Santiag Galicia.*
Vilanova y Piera, Juan, de las Academias de Medicina y de Cienc exactas, físicas y naturales, Doctor en Ciencias y en Medicina, Catedrático de Paleontología en la Facultad de Ciencias de la Universidad, C. de San Vicente, 12, principal, Madrid. *Geol.*, *Palæo.**
Vincente, Nemesio, Ingeniero de la Armade, Cartagena.
Vizcarrondo, Julio, 11, Calle de Villabar, Madrid.
Vizcaya y Conde, Atilano Alejandro, C. de Fomento, 40, 3.o, izquierda, Madrid.*
Xavier de Castro, Prof. Dr. Francisco, Madrid. *Bot.*
Yañez, Excmo. Sr. D. Teodoro, Catedrático de la Facultad de Medicina de la Universidad, C. de la Magdalena, 19, principal, Madrid.*
Zabalburu, Mariano, C. del Marqués del Duero, 7, Madrid.*
Zapater y Marconell, Bernardo, Albarracin. *Lepid.*, *Bot.* C.
Zerolo, Tomás, Villa de la Orotava, Tenerife.*
Zubía, Ildefonso, Doctor en Farmacia, Licenciado en Ciencias naturales, Comendador de la Real Orden de Isabel la Católica; Caballero de Carlos III y Catedrático del Instituto, C. Mayor, 147, Logroño. *Bot.**

SWEDEN.

Abelin, H. A., Prof., M.D., Stockholm. *Med.*
Adlerz, E., Lektor (Oberlehrer), Ph.D., Örebro. *Bot.*: *Bryol.* C. Ex.
Adlerz, Dr. Gottfrid, Asst. am Zootomischen Inst. der Univ. zu Stockholm. *Ent.*, *Anat.**
Adlerz, Henning, Ph. Lic., Stockholm. *Zool.**
Af Klercker, Dr. John E. F., Botanischen Institut, Tübingen. *Anatomical and Physiological Bot.**
Agardh, Jacob, Prof. Emer., Ph.D., Lund. *Bot.*, *Algology.*
Ahlstrand, J. A., Ph.D., Bibliothekar, Stockholm. *Nat. Hist.*: *Bibliog.*
Ahlner, K., Ph.D., Lehrer, Wexiö. *Algology.**
Ahlrat, A. T., Kalmar. *Ent.*
Aehrling, Ewald, Ph.D., Lehrer, Arboga. *Bot.*
Åkerberg, B. F., Ph.D., Upsala. *Math.*
Åkerhielm, M., Baron, Lehrer d. Agric., Ultuna, Upsala. *Agric.*
Åkerman, A. R., Prof. Metall., Royal High School, Stockholm. *Metallurgy.*
Alén, J. E., Ph.D., Göteborg. *Chem.**
Alin, Edward, Kandidat, Upsala. *Invert. Palæo.*, *Photog.*, *Histol. of Man*, *Moll.* Offers fossils from the upper Silurian beds of Gotland. Wishes portraits of illustrious men.
Almén, Aug. T., Ph. u. Med. Dr., Generaldirektor, Stockholm. *Med. Chem.*
Almqvist, Sigfr., Ph.D., Lektor, Joh. ö. kyrkogata 22, Stockholm. *Bot.* Lichens of the fam. Graphidæ, Japanese Lichens, Swedish Hieracia. C. Ex.
Almstrom, R., Rörstrand, Fabrikant, Stockholm. *Chem.*
Anderson, O. Fr., Upsala. *Bot.*, *Algæ.**
Andersson, F., Ph.D., Lektor, Halmstad. *Mat.*, *Phys.*
Andersson, A. E., Ph.D., Lektor, Kristianstad. *Nat. Hist.*

Andersson, C. G., Sater. *Ent.*
Andersson, Gunnar, Lund. *Bot.* C.*
Engström, C. A., Prof. Royal Tech. High School, Stockholm. *Hydraulic and Mechanical Engineering.*
Ångström, Dr. Knut, Laborator u. Director des Phys. Instituts der Hochschule in Stockholm. *Phys.**
Ankarcrona, Jak. W., Lyckeby. *Ent., Bot.*
Annell, Gustaf, K. M. K. Inst., Stockholm. *Histol.*
Appellöf, Ad., Ph.Kand., Upsala. *Zool., Moll* *
Areschoug, Fredr. Wilh. Chr., Ph.D., Prof., Lund. *Bot.*
Arnell, H. W., Ph.D., Lektor, Jönköping. *Bot., Bryol.* C. Ex.
Arrhenius, J., Ph.D., Prof., Stockholm. *Agric. Econ.*
Atterburg, Alb., Ph.D., Vorsteher d. chem. Station für Landwirthschaft u. Gewerbe, Kalmar. *Chem.*
Aurivillius, Carl W. S., Docent d. Univ., Phil. Dr., Upsala. *Zool., Crustacea.**
Aurivillius, Christopher, Ph.D., Prof. d. Wiss. Acad., Dir. Ent. Mus., Stockholm. Ent.
Bäcklund, Alb. Vict., Ph.D., Prof. Lund. *Mech.*
Backman, C. J., Ph.D , Lektor, Lulea. *Bot.*
Bager, Ernst, Malmö. *Ent.*
Bahr, L. v., Vorstand der Samenkontrollstation Hjortsberga, Hjortsberga Mölnbo. *Bot.*
Barnekow, Fabian, Freiherr, Ströö. *Ent.: Lepid.*
Bergendal, D., Ph.D., Docent, Lund. *Zool.**
Berger, Alex. Fredr., Ph.D., Docent, Upsala. *Math.*
Berggren, Sven, Ph.D., Prof., Lund. *Bot., Bryol of New Zealand.*
Bergin, P. G., Dr. Adj., Vorstand der Samenkontrollstation, Wenersborg, *Bot.*
Bergman, Gustaf, Med. Dr., Docent i Epidemiologi och Allmän helsovårdslära vid Universitetet i Upsala.*
Bergstrand, C. E., Ph.D., Prof , Stockholm. *Agric., Chem.*
Bergstrand, J. O., Ph.D., Vorsteh. d. chem. Stat. Westerås. *Agric., Chem.*
Berlin, Mac, Ph.D., Lektor, Jönköping. *Nat. Hist., Math.*
Berlin, Nils J., M. u. Ph.D., late Generaldirektor, Stockholm. *Chem.*
Billbergh, Thure, Ph.D., Lektor, Westerås. *Phys., Math.*
Billmansson, S. R., Ph D., Nora. *Bot.*
Björkén, John, M.D., Adj. d. Universit., Upsala. *Ophthalmol.*
Björling, Carl F. E., Ph.D., Prof., Lund. *Math.*
Björlingsson, Gust. V., Kalmar. *Chem.*
Björnström, Fredrik J., Ph. u. M.D., Medicinalrath, Prof., Stockholm. *Psychiatr., Bot.*
Blix, Prof. M. G., M.D., Lund. *Physiol.**
Blomberg, Albert, Ph.D., Stockholm. *Geol.*
Blomberg, Olof Gotthard, Pastor, Ekènsholm. *Lichen.* C. Ex.*
Blomstrand, Christian Wilh., Ph D., Prof., Lund. *Chem., Min.**
Blüm, C. A., Dir. d. Samenkontrollanstalt, Linköping. u Vorsitzer d. Samenkulturverein in Ostgothland. *Econ. control of seeds, Carpology.**
Bohlin, Carl, Assist. d. astron. Observ., Stockholm. *Astron.**
Boman, Claës Eric, Rektor. u. Lektor, late Capt., Malmö. *Math., Phys.*
Börtzell, J. E. Algernon, Intendent, Stockholm. *Geol.*
Bovallius, Carl E. A., Ph.D., Docent, Upsala. *Carcinol., Comp. Emb.* C. Ex. Scandinavian Crust. and Mollusca for Amphipoda, etc.*
Brattstrim, J., Ph.D., Rector vid Trans Schartaus, praktiska Handelsinstitut i Stockholm.*
Broberg, Joh. Val., M. u. Ph.D., Bibliothekar, Stockholm. *Med. History.*

Brögger, W. C., Prof. d. Univers., Clara Strandgata 11, Stockholm. *Geol., Min.*
Broman, J. F., Direktör Vorstand der Samenkontrollstation, Ope., pr. Brunflo. *Agric. Bot.*
Broström, C. M., Upsala. *Algology.*
Brunnström, J. A., Ph.D., Lehrer, Karlshamn. *Nat. Hist.*
Brusewitz, Emil, Münzdirektor, Stockholm. *Chem., Met.**
Bruzelius, N. G., Ph.D., Rektor, Ystad. *Ethnog.*
Busch, J. A. W., Bergmeister, Söderköping. *Mining.**
Carlberg, P. A., Bergwerkbesitzer, Ställdalen. *Mining.*
Carlson, A. F., Bjaf. *Ent.*
Carlson, J., Upsala. *Bot.*
Carlsson, C. Ph., Ph.D., Bergmästare, Falun. *Mining.*
Carlsson, Oscar, Stockholm. *Techn. Chem.*
Carpelan, Gustaf T., Stockholm. *Ent.*
Cederström, Carl, Ph.D., Freiherr, Rittergutbesitzer, Carlstad. *Zool., Arch., Ethnog.* C.
Cederwall, Edo. Wilh., Ph.D., Lektor, Göteborg. *Bot., Nat. Hist., Chem.*
Ceiller, D. C., Kopparberg. *Metall.*
Charlier, C. W. L., Ph.D., Docent, Upsala Observatory. *Astronomy.**
Christensen, R., Univ., Lund. *Bot.*
Clason, Prof. Dr. Edward Claes Herman, Roy. Univ., Upsala. *Anat., Hist.*
Cleve, P. T., Ph.D., Prof., Upsala. *Chem., Mic., L. and F. W. Shells.* Ex.
Crattingius, A T., Forstmeister, Örbyhus. *Zool.*
Collinder, E., Ph. Kand., Lehrer, Sundsvall. *Bryology.*
Cramér, H. J. C., Ph.D., Lektor, Wisby. *Math.*
Cronander, A. W., Ph.D., Lehrer, Upsala. *Chem.*
Cronvall, Axel Jul. A., Ph.D., Semin. Lehrer, Linköping. *Meteor.**
Curman, Carl, M.D., Prof., Stockholm. *Meteor.*
Dahlander, G. R., Prof., Stockholm. *Phys.*
Dahm, Oscar E. L., Kalmar. *Ent.*
Dalén, J. E., Ph.D., Lektor, Östersund. *Nat. Hist.*
Danielsson, C. F., Ingenieur, Linderberg. *Mining.*
Daug, Herman Theodor, Ph.D., Prof., Upsala. *Math.**
De Geer, Gerard, State Geologist, Geolog. Byrån, Stockholm. *Geol., Glac.**
De Laval, Patrik F. H., Ph.D., Lehrer, Stockholm. *Malacol.*
Dellwiks, C. A., Direktor, Stockholm. *Metall.*
Dillner, Göran, Ph.D., Prof., Upsala. *Math.*
Düben, Gustaf W. J., von, M.D., Prof., Stockholm. *Anat., Ethn.*
Dunér, Prof. Nils Christofer, Ph.D., Observatory, Lund. *Ast.**
Dusén, K. F., Ph. Dr., Docent der Bot. an der Univ., Upsala. *Bot.* Sphagnaceæ. C. Ex. fine specimens of Scandinavian Sphagnaceæ for others.*
Edgren, Per Adolf, M.D., Sodza Humleggardsgaten 10, Stockholm. *Ent.*
Edlund, E., Ph.D., Prof., Königl. Academie der Wissenschaften, Drottninggaten 94, Stockholm. *Phys., Electr.*
Eggertz, Carl M. U., Ph.D., Lektor, Karlskrona. *Ent.*
Eggertz, Victor, late Prof., Stockholm. *Metall., Chem.*
Ekeberg, Hans J., Apotheker, Göteborg. *Ent., Moll.*
Ekelund, A. F., Ingénieur, Stockholm. *Mining, Metall.*
Ekholm, Nils Gustaf, Lehrer, Ultuna, Upsala. *Meteor.*
Eklund, J. E., Vorsteher d. Bergschule, Falun. *Mining, Metall.*
Ekman, Fredrik Laurenz, Ph.D., Prof. Tekniska Högskolan, Stockholm. *Chem., Technol., Hydrography.**
Ekman, Gustaf, Ingénieur, Stockholm. *Hydrography.*
Ekstrand, Ake Gerhard, Ph.D., Docent, Upsala. *Chem.*
Ekstrand, Carl Richard, Ph.D., Lektor, Göteborg. *Mech.*

Elander, S. U., Upsala. *Chem.*
Elgenstierna, C. J. R., Postmeister, Nora. *Bot.* C.*
Elmqvist, C. F., Ph.D., Lehrer, Örebro. *Bot.* C.
Enell, Henrik, Apotheker, Alingsås. *Chem.*
Engelhart, Carl David, Stockholm. *Phæn. Bot., Ferns.* C. Ex.
Engström, B. A., Ph.D., Lehrer, Kalmar. *Nat. Hist.*
Engström, Folke August, Ph.D., Docent, Lund. *Ast.**
Engström, Nils, Ph D., Lehrer, Alnarp, Akarp. *Geol., Min., Chem.*
Erdmann, Edvard, Geolog, Amanuens. d. geol. Mus., Stockholm. *Geol.* Coal Mines and Quaternary deposits.*
Eriksson, Prof. Jacob, Ph.D., Pflanzen Physiologie der Kgl. Land bau Academie, Stockholm. *Bot* *
Eurén, Assist. d. Zool. Mus., Upsala. *Invert. Zool.*
Eurenius, Dr. Axel Gustaf Julius, Ph.D., Lektor, Norrköping. *Mathematics.*
Eurenius, M. C. J., Ph.D., Lektor, Malmö. *Zool.**
Ewert, A. W., Ph.D., Lektor, Göteborg. *Chem.*
Fagerholm, John Alfred, Ph.D., Lektor, Visby. *Math.*
Falk, Maths, Ph.D., Lektor, Upsala. *Math.*
Fegraeus, Torbern, Upsala. *Geol., Min.**
Fernqvist, Erik Bernhard, Lektor, Örebro. *Chem., Geol.*
Fineman, Carl Gottfried, Assist. Met. Obs., Upsala. *Meteo., Phys.*
Floderus, Manfred M., Ph.D., Rektor, Upsala. *Phys., Math., Ent., Bot.**
Fogelmarck, Prof. Fredrik Emil, Ph.D., Stockholm. *Math.*
Forssell, Dr. K. B. J., Karlstad. *Lichens.* C. Ex. lichens of Sweden and Norway for those of other countries.*
Forssman, L. A., Ph.D., Cancellierath, Stockholm.
Forsstrand, Carl W., Ph.D., Asst. at the Royal Library of Stockholm. *Zool. Literature and Geog. Dist.**
Fredholm, K. A., Ph.D., Rektor, Lulea. *Min., Geol.* C. Ex. Offers Swedish and Norwegian minerals and rocks from Lapland.*
Fries, Rob., M.D., Göteborg. *Bot., Fungi.*
Friesen, Joh. Otto, von, Ph.D., Lehrer, Nya Elementarskolan, Stockholm. *Bot., Zool.*
Friesen, Sixten von, Ph.D., Rektor, Stockholm. *Phys.*
Fristedt, Prof. Dr. Robert Fredrik, Roy. Univ., Upsala. *Pharmacology and Medical Nat. Hist.*
Fürst, Carl Magnus, Universitetet, Lund. *Anat.*
Gadamer, H., Forstmeister, Råstätt, Jönköping. *Ent.* C. Ex. Wishes Carabidæ, especially Cicindela, Carabus, Proctorus, Calosoma, Buprestidæ, Chrysomelidæ, Cryptocephalus, Cassida, Cryptus, Melolontha.
Gadde, Dr. F. O., Lund. *Malacology.*
Gelertsen, H., Lehrer, Ultuna, Upsala. *Hort.*
Geologiska Föreningen, Stockholm, 1888. Pres., State Geologist, Eduard Erdmann: Sec., Dr. Eugène Svedmark.*
Goës, Axel, M.D., Kisa. *Prophylactic Medicine, Invert., Gen. Biol., Rhizopoda.**
Grönvall, A. L., Ph.D., Lektor, Malmö. *Bot., Bryol., Nat. Hist.* C.
Gumælius, Otto, Mining Engineer, Rocklunda, Walla. *Geol.*
Gyldén, J. A. Hugo, Ph.D., Prof. Astr. Observatorium, Stockholm. *Astr.*
Gyllencreutz, Richard, Med. Kand., Upsala. *Bot.*
Hackwitz, von, Gustaf O. D., Ph. Kand., Lehrer, Wenersborg. *Orn., Ent.* C.
Hagelin, J.W., Ph.D., Stockholm. *Bot.*
Haglund, C. J. Emil, M.D., Practischer Arzt, Norrköping. *Hemipt. of the entire world.* C. Ex.
Haij, Julius B., Upsala. *Ent.*

Håkansson, Johan Fredrik, Ph. Kand., Lehrer, Pictå. *Bot.*
Hallenberg, G. F., Ph. Kand., Lehrer, Visby. *Agric.*, *Chem.*
Hallstrom, Dr. M. F., Falun. *Nat. Hist.*
Hamberg, Hugo Emanuel, Ph.D., Stockholm. *Meteo.*
Hamberg, N. P., M.D., Prof., Stockholm. *Chem.*
Hammargren, Tullius, Ph.D., Pfarrer, Carlskoga. *Ornithol.*
Hammarsten, Olof, M.D., Prof., Upsala. *Physiol. Chem.**
Hansson, C. A., Stromstad. *Ichthyol.*
Hartman, Robert, Ph.D., Lehrer, Gefle. *Bryol.* C.
Hazelius, Arthur, Ph.D., Lektor, Stockholm. *Archæol.* C.
Hedberg, Per Gustaf, Falun. *Ent.*
Hedbom, K. J., Ph. Kand., Upsala. *Bot.*, *Zool.* C. Ex.
Hedell, L. E., Upsala. *Zool.*
Hedenius, Per, M.D., Prof., Tradgärdsgatan 8, Upsala. *Pathol.*, *Morbid. Anat.**
Hedberg, Dr. Johan, August, Linköping. *Math.*
Hellbom, P. J., Ph.D., Lehrer, Örebro. *Bot.*, *Lichens.**
Henning, E., Upsala. *Hymenomycetes.*
Henschen, Salomon Eberh., M.D., Prof. *Pathol.*, *Anat.*
Hermelin, C. A., Freiherr, Morrtullsgasse 12, Stockholm. *Ent.*
Hildebrand, Hans O. H., Ph.D., Reichsantiquar, Stockholm. *Archeol.*
Hildebrandsson, Hr. H. Hildebrand, Dir. Meteo. Observatory, Prof. Roy. Univ., Upsala. *Meteo.* Ex. Observations.
Hjeltstrom, S. A., Ph.D., Lektor, Sundsvall. *Meteo.*
Hofberg, Dr. Herman, Stockholm. *Ent.*
Hofgren, Gottfried, Kassör, Hornsgatan 43B, Stockholm. *Lepidopt.* C.
Högbom, A. G., Licentiat, Upsala. *Geol.**
Holm, Gerhard, Ph.D., Docent, State Geologist, Geolog. Byrån, Stockholm. *Geol.*, *Palæo.*, *Silver.**
Holmgren, August E., Lektor, Artillerigatan 26, Stockholm. *Ent.*, *Ornithol.* C.
Holmertz, C. G. G., Direktor, Stockholm. *Orn.*
Holmgren, Frithiof, M.D., Prof., Upsala. *Physiol.*
Holmgren, Kart Albert, Ph.D., Prof., Lund. *Phys.*
Holmström, L. P., Ph.D., Lehrer, Hvilan, Lund. *Geol.**
Hulting, Johan, Ph.D., Lehrer, Norrköping. *Bot.*, *Lichens.* C. Ex.*
Hultgren, John, Örebro. *Ent.*
Huss, M., M.D., late Prof. and Generaldirect., Stockholm. *Med.*, *Bot.* C.
Hylten-Cavallius, Gustaf Erik, Lund. *Bot.: Phanerog. and Ferns.* C. Ex.*
Tamm, A., Doctor, Stockholm. *Med. Chem.*
Igelström, L. T., Bergskonduktör, Sunnemo, Wermland. *Min.* Ex. rare Swedish Minerals. C. Ex.
Ihre, O. A., Ph.D., Lehrer, Örebro. *Chem.*, *Phys.*
Indebeton, Johan Conrad, Apotheker, Avesta. *Bot.*, *Malacol.*, *Min.*, *Ent.*, *Moll.* C. Ex. Offers Salices of Scandinavia for those of other countries.
Iverus, J. Edo., Dn., Medicophil. Kand., Lehrer, Linköping. *Min.*, *Chem.*, *Zool.*, *Osteol.*, *Bot.*
Jäderin, Edward, Lector, Technische Hochschule, Stockholm. *Ast.*, *Geodesy.**
Jäderholm, Prof. A. O. G., M.D., Stockholm. *Med.*
Janson, Jons, Stockholm. *Geol.*
Jochnich, C. Walter, Ph.D., Lektor, Carlberg, Stockholm. *Phys.*
Johanson, C. J., Smålands Station, Upsala. *Bot.*, *Mycol.* C. Ex.*
Johanson, Carl Hans, Ph.D., Lektor, Westerås. *Ent.*
Johanson, Dr. Nils Abraham, Direktör der höheren Realschule, Gothenburg. *Bot.*, *Math.*

Jolin, Severin, Dr., Rörstrandsgatan 32, Stockholm. *Chem.*
Jönsson, B., Ph.D., Docent, Lund. *Bot.*
Jönsson, Johan, Skåne. *Ent.*
Juhlin-Dannfett, Herman, Ph.D., Lehrer, Ultuna, Upsala. *Diatoms, Agric.* C. Ex. Gives slides containing Swedish Diatoms in ex. for foreign samples.
Jungner, Johan Richard, St. Petri Kyrkogata 7, Lund. *Phæn. Bot., Mosses.* C. Ex.
Kahlmeter, T., Ph.D., Stockholm. *Phys.**
Karsberg, P. L., Krigskassör, Stockholm. *Mycol.*
Key, Axel, M.D., Prof., Editor des "Nordiskt Medicinskt Arkiv," Stockholm. *Pathol., Anat.* C.
Key-Åberg, Dr. Algot, Prof. Karol. Inst., Stockholm. *Forensic medicine.**
Keyser, Carl Johan J., Ph.D., Lektor, Norrköping. *Chem.*
Kinberg, J. G. H., M.D., Prof., Stockholm. *Zool., Comp. Anat. and Osteol., Archæological Zool., spec. Orn.* C. Ex. N. European and Greenland birds and publications for birds of N. America; Scolopacidæ, Anserinæ, Œdemia, Sterninæ and publications.
Kindberg, Nils Conrad, Ph.D., Lektor, Linköping. *Bot., Bryol., Zool.* C. Ex. Offers mosses and flowering Alpine plants.*
Kjellman, F. R., Ph.D., Prof., Upsala. *Bot., Algology and Arctic Phæn. Flora.* C. Ex. Scandinavian Marine Algæ. Desires esp. Fucoideæ.*
Kjellstedt, Lars, Lektor, Borås. *Mech.*
Klason, Peter, Ph.D., Lund. *Chem.**
Kolmodin, L., Ph.D., Lehrer, Wisby. *Zool.*
Kolthoff, Gustaf, Konservator, Upsala. *Orn., Lepid.* C.*
Kolthoff, Johan A., Mellerud. *Ent.*
Kowalevski, Sophie, née Carvin-Krukovski, Prof. Dr., Stockholm. *Math.*
Krok, Jonas M., Ph D., Lektor, Jönköping. *Math.*
Krok, T. O. B. N., Lehrer, Stockholm. *Bot.* C.
Kurck, C., Baron, Petersburg, Smedstorp. *Geol.*
Læstadius, C. P., Ph.D., Lehrer, Umea. *Bot.* C.
Lagerheim, G., Stockholm. *Bot.**
Lagerstedt, Nils Gerhard Wilhelm, Ph.D., Lehrer, Stockholm. *Bot., Diatoms.* C.
Lalin, C. J., Ph D., Lehrer, Stockholm. *Bot.* C.*
Lamm, O., Stockholm. *Chem.*
Lampa, Sven, Preparator, Drottninggatan 19, Stockholm. *Coleopt., Lepid.* C. Ex. Offers Swedish Lepidoptera, Coleoptera and eggs; wishes Longicorns and Bombyces.
Lang, John Robert Tobias, Ph.D., Prof., Lund. *Chem.*
Leche, Dr. Wilhelm, Prof. der Zoologie an der Hochschule, Stockholm. *Morphology of Vertebrata.* Desires Mammals in alcohol.*
Leffler, Johan A., Dr. Phil., Stockholm. *Bot.* (*Rosæ, Spingulariæ*), *Phæn. Plants.**
Liedzén, Sven, Lektor, Borås. *Chem., Geol.*
Lilljeborg, Wilhelm, Ph.D., Prof. Emer., Upsala. *Zool.**
Lindblad, Dr. Mathias Adolph, Stockholm. *Mycology.**
Lindblad, Wilhelm, Stockholm. *Vert.: Mammals and Birds.*
Lindskog, Nat., Ph.D., Docent Mech., Upsala.*
Lindström, Axel Fr., Geolog, Stockholm. *Geol.* C.
Lindström, Gustaf, Prof., keeper of Palæo. Dept., State Museum, Stockholm.*
Lindström, Gustaf, Asst. Mineralogical Dept., State Museum, Stockholm.*
Lindeberg, Carl Johan, Ph.D., Lektor, Göteborg. *Bot., espec. Hieracia and Rubi.* C.
Lindgren, Erik, Dir. Roy. Agric. Acad., Experimentalfältet, Albano, near Stockholm.*

Lindgren, Hjalmar, Med. Dr., R.N.O., L.L.F.S., Prof. der Anat., Dir. der Anat. u. Histol, Lund.*
Lindhagen, Arvid., Ph.D., Stockholm. *Ast.**
Lindhagen, Daniel Georg, Ph.D., Prof., Sec. Roy. Acad. Sci., Stockholm. *Ast.**
Lindman, C. F., Ph.D., Lektor, Strengnäs. *Math.*
Lindman, Lektor, Stockholm. *Bot.**
Linnaea. An Internat. Bot. Association for the exchange of dried plants, Lund, Sweden.*
Linnarsson, E. J. S., Adjunct., Skofde.*
Littorin, S. H., Wara. *Ent.*
Ljungman, Dr. Axel W., M.P., Lilldal, Orost and Tjörn. *Echinoderms, Fishes, spec. Nat. Hist. of the Herring.*
Ljungström, Ernst, Dr., Doc. Univ., Lund. *Bot., Mycol.* Deutsche Corresp. erwünscht.*
Lönnberg, C. J. E, Ph D., Norrköping. *Bot.* C. Ex. Offers Swedish Phanerogams and Mosses for those of North America.*
Lönnberg, Einar, Kand. Ph., Upsala. *Zool.**
Lovén, Christian, M.D., Prof., Sec'y Roy. Agric. Acad., Stockholm. *Physiol., Agric.**
Lovén, Sven, M. u. Ph.D., Prof. Academy of Sciences, Stockholm. *Zoology: Invertebrates, Echinoderms.* C. of the State Museum. Ex. Northern and Arctic marine invertebrates for other invertebrates and echinoderms.
Löwegren, G., Gartendirektor, Göteborg. *Bot., Hort.* C. Ex.
Lübeck, Henrik G., Karlskrona. *Ent.*
Luhr, A. E., Westerås, Springstad. *Bot.* C. Ex.*
Lundberg, B., Sternam, Skara. *Coleopt., Lepid.*
Lundberg, C. W., Forstmeister, Aby. *Orn., Ent.* C.
Lundberg, J. B., Axevalla. *Ent.*
Lundberg, Rudolf, Ph.D., Superintendent of fisheries in the Baltic and the fresh waters in Sweden, Stockholm. *Ichth.**
Lundbohm, Hjalmar, State Geologist, Stockholm, Geologiska byrån. *Geol.**
Lundell, N. P., Stockholm. *Bot.*
Lundgren, Sven Anders Bernhard, Ph.D., Prof., Lund. *Geol., Palæo.*
Lundgren, W., M.D., Upsala. *Physiol.*
Lundin, Axel, Unnayrd. *Ent.*
Lundquist, Carl Gustaf, Ph.D., Prof., Upsala. *Mech.*
Lundquist, P. F., Asele. *Bot.* Desires to exchange genus Rosa.*
Lundstrom, Axel Nicolaus, Ph.D., Docent, Upsala. *Bot.: Salices, Biology.* C. Ex. Offers Salices from Northern Europe and literature on the same for that of other countries.
Lyttkens, August, Dir. Vorstand der Samenkontroll-Station, Nydala pr. Halmstad. *Phæn. Bot., Agric.* C. Ex. seeds, plants, and woods.*
Lyttkens, I. A., Ph D., Norrköping. *Phonetics.**
Lyttkens, E., Vorsteher d. Chem. Stat., Halmstad. *Agric. Chem.*
Malm, Dr., Inspector of Sea-fisheries, Göteborg. *Ichth.**
Malmberg, Fredrik Salomon, Capt., Nautic. Meteo. Bureau, Stockholm. *Meteo.**
Malmberg, Mauritz, M.D., Jönköping. *Med. Bot.*
Malmstedt, Anders Magnus, Ph. Kand., Lehrer, Linköping. *Phys., Meteo.*
Mankell, Otto A., Artillerigatan 18, Stockholm. *Ent.*
Martensson, S., Upsala. *Coleopt.*
Meves, Andreas F. A. J., Grefthureg 18, Stockholm. *Ent.*
Meves, Wilhelm, Konservator, Kammakareg 35, Stockholm. *Orn., Ool., Lepid.* C. Ex. in Ool.

Mittag-Leffler, Prof. Dr., Redacteur von Acta Mathematica, Gösta, Stockholm. *Math.**
Moberg, Dr. Johan C., Stockholm. *Geol., Palæo.*
Molér, Dr. T. C. V., Västeras. *Bot.*
Möller, A. M., Ph.D., Lektor, Helsingborg. *Nat. Hist.*
Möller, Carl, Gutsbesitzer, Wedelsbäch. Stehag, Skåne. *Orn., Ool., Coleopt., Lepid.* C. Ex. Offers first-class specimens of skins, beetles, butterflies, and birds of Sweden for those of North America.*
Möller, Didrik Magnus Axel, Ph.D., Prof., Dir. Obs., Lund. *Ast.*
Möller, Dr. Gustaf Fredrik, Trelleborg. *Ent.: Hymenop., spec. Ichneumonides.**
Möller, Julius, Ph.D., Docent, Lund. *Math.*
Montelin, C. O. U., Ph. Kand., Lehrer, Wexiö. *Bot.**
Montelius, Gustaf Oscar Augustin, Ph.D., Asst. Mus. Antiq., Stockholm. *Archeol.*
Mortonson, Anders S., Upsala. *Ent.: Coleopt.*
Munktell, H., Falun. *Chem., Metall.*
Murbeck, Sv., Amanuensis Univ., Lund. *Bot., Phan.* Ex., especially Cerastia and Stellaria.*

Nathorst, Alfred Gabriel, Ph.D., Prof., Acad. of Sciences, Stockholm. *Palæo.: Fossil plants.**
Nauckhoff, Gustaf, Ph. Dr., Grångesberg. *Mining, Geol., Min.**
Naumann, Carl Fredrik, M. et Ph.D., Prof. Emer., Lund. *Anat.*
Neander, N. E., Ph.D., Lehrer, Lund. *Nat. Hist.*
Nerander, Teodor, Karol. Inst., Stockholm. *Physiol.*
Nerén, C. Harald, M.D., Skeninge. *Ent., Gen. Biol., Mic.* C.
Neuman, Rektor, Carl, Borås. *Ent., Acari.* C. Ex. Acari., etc.
Neuman, L. M., Ph.D., Lektor, Sundsvall. *Bot., Phanerog. and Ferns.* C. Ex. Viola, Rubus, Potamogeton, Sparganium.*
Nilsson, Dr. Alb., Docent, Upsala. *Bot.**
Nilsson, L. F., Ph.D., Prof., Dir. Inst. of Agric. Chem. and Physiol., Stockholm. *Agric. and Inorg. Chem.*
Nilsson, N. Hjalmar, Dr., Docent, Bot. Garten, Lund. *Phan. Bot., Hort.**
Nilsson, S. J., Ph.D., Lehrer, Göteberg. *Bot.*
Nisser, M., Grubeningeniör, Falun. *Min., Metall.*
Norblad, J. A., Dr., Rörstrand, Stockholm.
Nordenskjöld, Prof. Adolf E., Baron, Academy of Science, Stockholm.
Nordenstrom, Prof. Gustaf, Stockholm. *Mining.*
Nordenström, Henning, M.D., Linköping. *Med., Nat. Hist.*
Nordin, Isidor, Stockholm. *Ent.*
Norlund, Gustaf Adolf, Prosektor, Upsala. *Anat.*
Nordstedt, Dr. C. F. Otto, Lund. *Bot.: esp. Algæ, Diatoms.*
Norstedt, Otto, Ph.D., Lund. *Bot.:* Characeæ and Algæ. *Desmids.**
Nordstedt, Dr. Otto, Keeper at the Bot. Mus. Univ., Editor of Botaniska Noticeer. *Bot., Characeæ, Desmids, Freshwater Algæ.* C. Ex.*
Nordström, F. G., Dir. der K. Landwirtsch. Inst., Ultuna, Upsala. *Agric.*
Nordström, Simon, Ph.D., Expéd. Secret., Stockholm. *Ent.*
Nordström, Th., Ph.D., Sala. *Min., Metall.*
Nyberg, Yngve, Ph.D., Lektor, Norrköping. *Phys., Math.*
Nyberg, Ingemar, Mining Engineer, Säfsjö. *Mining, Metall.: Cobalt and Copper.*
Nylander, Oscar, Dir. d. chem. Stat., Shara. *Agric. Chem., Mycol., Hort., Agric., Geol., Phys., Elect., Mic.*
Nyman, C. F., Acad. of Sciences, Stockholm. *Bot.*
Nyman, Erik, Stud., Linköping. *Bryol., Min.* C. Ex.*
Öberg, P., Ph.D., Persberg. *Min., Geol.*

Öberg, Victor, Dr., Lehrer, Hernamo. *Geol.*
Odenius, M. W., M. u. Ph.D., Prof., Lund. *Anat.*
Ohrvall, Hj., M.D., Upsala. *Physiol.*
Olbers, Alida, University, Stockholm. *Anat.*, *Bot.**
Olsson-Gadde, M. O. A., M. u. Ph.D., Lund. *Nat. Hist.*, *Med.*
Olsson, Peter, Ph.D., Lehrer, Norrköping. *Bot.*, *Bryol.* C. Ex.
Olsson, Dr. Peter, Lektor, Östersund. *Zool., especially Pisces, Crust., Copepoda, and parasitic Vermes.* C.*
Pahl, Carl Nicolaus, Ph.D., Lektor, Umeå. *Phys.*, *Chem.*
Paykull, S. R., Ph D., Fabriksbesitzer, Stockholm. *Chem.*, *Min.* C. Ex. minerals.
Persson, J., Hessleholm. *Bot.*, *Mosses.**
Petersson, Oscar Victor, M.D., Prof., Upsala. *Med.*
Pettersson, Otto, Ph.D., Vorst. d. chem. Labor. d. Univ., Stockholm. *Chem.*, *Phys.*
Pfannenstiel. Ernst, Ph.D., Upsala. *Math.*
Pihl, A., Direktor, Stockholm. *Bot.*, *Hort* *
Porat, von, Carl O., Ph.D., Lehrer, Jönköping. *Ent.*
Post, von, Hampus A., Ph.D., Prof., Ultuna, Upsala. *Myol.*, *Hort.*, *Geol.*, *Lithol.*, *Geog. Dist.*, *Ent.: Arachnida.*
Post, Mats. v., Vorstand der Samenkontrollstation, Nyköping. *Bot.*
Quennerstedt, Aug. Wilhelm, Ph.D., Prof., Lund. *Zool.*
Rääf, C. G. S., Ph.D., Lektor, Carlskrona. *Math.*, *Nat. Hist.*
Rådberg, Karl Frithiof, Ph.D., Lektor, Wenersborg. *Math.*
Ramberg, J., State Railways Office, Gothenburg. *Oöl.* C. Ex. Sells.*
Redelius, Otto Wilhelm, Pfarrer, Hallingeberg. *Bot.: Ferns, Mosses, Hort.* C. Ex.
Réhn, G., Chr., Kopparberg. *Met.*
Retzius, Magnus Gustaf, M.D., Prof., Stockholm. *Med.*, *Hist.*, *Antiquity of Man.*
Reuterman, C. O., M.D., Carlskoga. *Bot.*
Rogstadius, A. W. F., Ph D., Lektor, Nyköping. *Math.*, *Phys.*
Rosén, P. G., Ph.D., Prof., Stockholm. *Phys.*
Rosenberg, Johan Olof, Ph.D., Prof., Stockholm. *Chem.*
Roth, C. D. E., Museum, Lund. *Ent.*
Rubenson, Robert, Ph.D., Prof., Stockholm. *Meteo.*
Sahlén, Anders J., Ph.D., Lektor, Skara. *Nat. Hist.*
Sandahl, Oskar T., M.D., Prof., Vasagatan 8, Stockholm. *Ent.*, *Pharm.**
Sandin, Emil, Göteborg. *Zool., esp. Coleopt.* C. Ex.*
Sandström, J., Dr., Upsala. *Anat.*, *Hist.*
Sandström, V., Direktor, Vorstand der Samenkontrollstation, Falun. *Bot.*
Santesson, Dr. Birger, Bergingenieur, Geologiska Byrån, Stockholm. *Geognosy.**
Santesson, Gustaf Henrik, Ph.D., State Geologist, Geol. Bureau, Stockholm. *Geol.*, *Chem.**
Säve, Gunnar A., Ph.D., Lehrer, Jönköping. *Chem*, *Phys.*
Scheutz, Nils Johan, Ph.D., Lektor, Wexiö. *Bot. Esp. Rosæ and Ranunculaceæ.* C. Ex.
Schlyter, Carl Oscar, Landesgerichts-Präsident, Hudiksvall. *Phæn. Bot.* C. Ex.
Schmalensee, v., C. G., Stockholm, Geologiska Byrån. *Palæo.**
Schultz, Herman, Ph.D., Prof., Dir. Obs., Upsala. *Ast.**
Seth, K. A., Ph. Kand., Lehrer, Upsala. *Bryol.* C. Ex.
Setterberg, Carl, Dr., Stockholm. *Chem.*
Sillén, Leopold, Apothecker, Hedemora. *Bryol.* C. Ex.
Sillén, W. O., M.D., Öland. *Bot.* C.
Sjögreen, Carl M., Hastholmen. *Ent.**

Sjögren, Dr. C. Anton H., Mining Engineer, Filipstad. *Min.*, *Palæo.*, *Geol.*, *Crystal.*, *Lithol.* C. Ex.
Sjögren, S. A. Hjalmar, Prof., Upsala. *Min.*, *Geol.*, *Crystal.*
Sjöstrand, Dr. Gustaf S., Linköping. *Phys.*, *Math.*
Skånberg, Alexander, Lektor, Stockholm. *Phys.*, *Chem.*
Smitt, Fredrik Adam, Prof. Dr., Dir. of the Dept. for Vertebrates, Royal Mus of Nat. Hist. *Vert.*, *Palæo.*, *Gen. Zool.*, *Emb.*, *Anat.*, *Vert.*, *Tax.*, *Osteol.*, *Myol.*, *Histol. of Vert.*
Söderblom, Anders Leonard Axel, Ph.D., Docent, Upsala. *Math.*
Soderlund, Dr., Upsala. *Marine Zool.*
Spångberg, Jacob, Ph.D., Lektor, Gefle. *Ent.*
Stahre, Ludwig, Apotheker, Stockholm. *Chem.*, *Pharm.*
Stalhammar, Hjalmar, Göteborg. *Ent.*
Starbäck, Carl, Ph. Kand., Upsala. *Bot.*, *Mycology* (*Ascornyceten*).*
Starck, Ernst Manfred, Polytechnicum, Örebro. *Mech.* Has published 1250 problems of the mechanics of rigid bodies.
Stenberg, Isak Ludvig, Ph.D., Lektor, Malmö. *Ent.*
Stenström, K. O., Ph. Kand., Upsala. *Bot.**
Stenström, O. E., Direktor, Gårdsjö, Borgvik. *Ent.* C. Ex.
Sterner, Carl Gustaf, Lektor, Malmö. *Chem.*, *Geol.*
Steffenburg, Alrik, Ph.D., Falun. *Zool.*
Stolpe, H., Ph.D., Nat. Mus., Stockholm. *Eth.*, *Anthrop.*, *Archæol.**
Stolpe, Mats, Geolog., Stockholm. *Geol.*
Strandmark, P. W., Ph.D., Lektor, Helsingborg. *Nat. Hist.*
Stridsberg, F. G., Degerfors, Wermland. *Metall.*
Ströhm, Svante G. M., Lehrer, Oscarshamm. *Ent.*
Strokirk, C. G., Ingenieur. Vorstand der Chem. Station, Hernosand. *Chem.* *Bot.*
Strömfelt, H. Graf, Docent, Stockholm. *Bot.*, *Algæ.**
Stuxberg, Dr. Anton, Keeper of the Zool. Dept., Museum, Gothenburg. *Zool.*, *esp. Myriopoda*, *Crustacea.* Wishes to buy extra-European Reptiles and Batrachia. C. Ex.*
Svedmark, L. Eugène, Ph.D., Geolog, Stockholm. *Geol.*
Svenonius, Dr. Fredr., Geologiska Byrån, Stockholm. *Geol.*, *Min.*
Svensson, Dr. Nils, Westervik. *Phys.*, *Chem.*
Svensson, P., Adjunct, Hernösand. *Bot.**
Swederus, Dr. Magnus Bernhard, Adjunct, Cathedral Sch., Upsala. *Zool.*, *Moll.*, *esp. Tunicata.*
Tamm, Dr. A., Stockholm. *Metall.*, *Chem.**
Tenow, S. W., Ph.D., Lehrer, Carlstad. *Nat. Hist.*
Thalén, Tobias Robert, Ph.D., Prof., Upsala. *Phys.*, *esp. Spectral Analysis.*
Thedenius, C. G. H., Tanum, Hörby. *Bot.*, *Cotyledoneæ and Heteronomeæ*, *Lepid.*, *Coleopt.*
Thedenius, Knut F., Lektor, Kvarngatan 34, Stockholm. *Ent.*, *Phæn*, *Bot.*, *esp. Bryol.* C.
Théel, J. Hjalmar, Ph.D., Prosektor, Upsala. *Zool.*, *Annelida*, *Polychæta Gephyrea*, *Holothuridæ.*
Theorin, Per Gustaf E., Ph.D., Lektor, Falun. *Bot.*, *Zool.*, *Chem.*
Thomson, Carl Gust., Ph.D., Adjunkt d. Univ., Lund. *Ent.*
Thorburn, Robert M., F.R S., Uddevalla. *Con.* C. Ex. Offers Post-glacial shells from raised beaches.*
Thorell, T., Tamerlan Theod., Ph.D., Prof., Upsala (Present residence: Museo Civico, Genoa). *Zool.*: *Arachnida.* C.*
Thudén, Carl J. A., Ph. Kand., Lektor, Halmstad. *Zool.*, *Geol.*, *esp. Rhizopods from the glacial epoch.* C. Ex. Rhizopods from the chalk and other formations. Localities must be accurate.
Tiberg, H. V., M.E., Grufvedisponent, Långbanshyttan. *Min.* C. Ex.

Tidblom, A. W., Ph.D., Rektor, Borås. *Phys., Meteo., Math.**
Tigerstedt, Robert, A.A., M.D., Prof. der Physiologie, Carol. Inst., Stockholm. *Physiol.**
Tiselius, Gustaf August, Ph.D., Lehrer, Jakobs Schule, Stockholm. *Bot. esp. Potamogeton.* C.
Torell, Otto Martin, Ph.D., Prof., Director Geol. Surv., Stockholm. *Geol.*
Torin, Karl J. L., Lehrer, Skara. *Zool.*
Törnebohm, Dr. Alfred Elis, Practical Geologist, Lecturer on Min. and Geol., Technische Hochschule, Stockholm.*
Törnqvist, Dr. Sv. Leonh., Lund. *Geol., Palæozoic Fossils of Sweden.* C.
Törnsten, Adolf, Ph.D., Norrköping. *Phys., Math.*
Tranberg, Gustaf, Stockholm. *Ent.*
Trybom, Filip, First Assistant of Fisheries, Stockholm. *Ichth., Ent., Carcinology.* C.*
Trysen, Alb. O., Bergmeister, Lulea. *Mining.*
Tullberg, Tycho, Ph.D., Prof., Upsala. *Zool.**
Ullén, Fredr. Aug., Major, Göteborg. *Math.*
Virgin, Carl F. S., Ph.D., Rektor, Örebro. *Math., Phys.*
Wåhlander, Herman Rudolf, Ph.D., Lektor, Hernösand. *Math., Phys.*
Wahlstedt, L.J., Ph.D., Lektor, Christianstad. *Nat. Hist., esp. Characeæ.* C. Ex. Fine specimens of European, esp. Swedish Characeæ, for foreign.
Wahrenberg, E. A., Dr, Upsala. *Math., Phys.*
Walmstedt, E. U., Lehrer, Stockholm. *Bot.* C.
Walmstedt, L. E., Ph.D., Prof Emer., Upsala. *Min., Geol.*
Wallengren, Hans D. J., Pastor Farhult, Mjöhult. *Lepid., Vascular plants.* C. Ex. Offers Scandinavian plants for foreign, esp. for those of N. Am. and Europe. First-class specimens.
Wallis, Curt, M.D., Prof. Stockholm. *Pathol., Anat.*
Warenius, Benjamin, Malmö, S. Nygatan 56. *Ent.* Offers Swedish Coleoptera.
Wenström, Wilh., Ingeniör, Nora. *Mining.*
Werner, A., Stockholm. *Bot., Hort.*
Westberg, C. F., Bergmeister, Nora. *Mining.*
Westerlund, Carl Agardh, Ph D., Lehrer, Ronneby. *Zool., Malacol.* C. Ex. First-class specimens, esp. Palæo-Arctic Fauna.
Westöö, Oskar A., Lehrer, Wisby. *Bot.*
Wetterdal, Gustaf Ludv., Ingeniör, Falun. *Mining.*
Wetterhall, J. Erland, Ph. Kand., Lehrer, Upsala. *Ent., Bryol.*
Wiborgh, Joh. G., Lektor, Stockholm. *Metall., Mining.*
Wiksell, K., Dr., Upsala. *Math.*
Widman, Oscar, Ph.D , Docent, Upsala. *Chem.*
Wijkander, August, Ph.D., Prof., Göteborg. *Phys., Meteo., Ast.**
Wikström, Ernest, Edsvalla. *Ent.*
Wilander, H. M., Ingeniör, Handtverkerg. 31*a*, Stockholm. *Min., Geol.* C. Ex. Offers Swedish minerals for those of America.*
Wille, N., Dr. e. o. Prof., Univ. of Stockholm. *Bot., esp. Algol., Anat., Physiol.**
Wingqvist, K. R., Nykroppa. *Mining, Metall.*
Wingdahl, Askersund. *Ent.: Coleopt.*
Winslow, A. P., Ph.D., Lehrer, Göteborg. *Bot. esp. Rosæ and Salices.* C. Ex. Wishes first-class specimens in ex. for Swedish.
Wirén, A., Dr. Ph., Docent der Zoologie, Upsala. *Zool., Anat., Annelida.**
Wiström, Johan Alfr., Ph.D., Ritter von Wasa orden, Lehrer, Hudiksvall. *Ent.: Lepid. and Coleopt., Bot.**
Wittrock, Veit B., Ph.D., Prof., Stockholm. *Bot., esp. Algol., Morphol.*

Wrede, Fabian J., Baron, Lieut.-Gen., Ph.D. Honor., Stockholm. *Phys.*
Yhlen, von, Gerhard, Inspector of Sea Fisheries, Göteborg. *Zool.*; *Ichthyol.*
Zeipel, von, Ewald Victor, Univers. Adjunkt, Lund. *Math.*
Zetterlund, C. G., Vorstand der Agrikulturchemischen-Station und Samenkontroll-Antstalt zu Örebro. *Agric.*, *Chem.**

SWITZERLAND.

Abeljanz, Prof. H., Univ., Zürich. *Chem.*
Aeby, Dr. Chr., Prof. Univ. und Thierarzneischule, Berne. *Histol.*, *Comp. Anat.*, *Zool.*
Ador, Prof. E., Geneva. *Chem.*
Amberg, Prof. Bernhard, Lucerne. *Phys.*
Amsler, Prof. Jacob, Schaffhausen. *Phys.*, *Math.*
Anderegg, Prof. Dr., Chur. *Bot.*
Andreä, Fleurier. *Bot.*
Anneler, E., Basel. *Chem.*
Arnet, Prof. Xav., Lucerne. *Math.*, *Phys.*
Asper, Prof. G., Univ., Zürich. *Zool.*
Autran, Eugène, Charmilles, Genève. *Hemiptères paléarctiques.**
Bachmann, Prof. Dr. Isidor, Berne. *Geol.*
Bachmann, J. J., Stettfurt. *Chem.*
Bader, Pharmacien, Geneva. *Bot.*
Baltzer, Dr. A., Prof. Geol., Hottingen-Zürich.
Barbey, William, Valleyres sous Rances (Vaud). *Bot.* C.*
Barbezat, Paul Emile, Neuchâtel. *Phys.*
Barth, Place Neuve, Geneva. *Coleopt.*
Baur, J., Lehrer, Biel. *Math.*
Bazzigher, Lucius, Chur. *Lepid.*
Becker, Dr. Ferd., Basel. *Chem.*
Bedot, Maurice, Geneva. *Zool.*
Bellenot, Gust., Neuchâtel. *Ent.*
Benteli, F., Berne. *Lepid.*
Benteli, R., Berne. *Lepid.*
Bernoulli, Dr. Wilhelm, Schartlingasse 4, Basel. *Phæn. Bot.*, *Ferns.* C. Ex. Desires correspondents.*
Bertsch, Prof. Hrch., St. Gall. *Phys.*, *Chem.*
Biaudet, Dr., Bex. *L and F. W. Shells.* Ex.
Bieler, Avenue Agassiz, Lausanne. *Mic.*
Billwiller, Robert, Zürich. *Meteo.*
Bischoff, Prof. Henri, Lausanne. *Chem.*
Blaser, Dr. C. G. E., Docent, Univ., Berne. *Math.*
Bloesch, Basel. *Coleopt.*, *Lepid.*
Boedecker, Martin, Bremerschlüssel, Zürich. *Min.* C. Ex.
Boeschenstein, A., Schaffhausen. *Coleopt.**
Bollinger, J., Basel. *Nat. Hist.*
Bonnet, Marc, Carouge, near Geneva. *Lepid.*
Bonstetten, Aug. von, Ph.D., Berne. *Chem.*
Boos, Prof. Dr. Heinrich, Univ., Basel. *Palæo.*
Böschenstein, Alfred, care of Kühne & Co., rue de la Fosse aux Ours, Geneva. *Coleopt.*, *Hemipt.*
Boucart, Paul, Geneva. *Coleopt.*
Bourgknecht, L., Pharmacien, Freiburg. *Chem.*
Bouvier, Dr. Louis, Lancy, near Geneva. *Bot.*

Brélaz, Prof. George Louis, Lausanne. *Chem.*
Bridler, Prof., Chur. *Math.*
Brot, Dr., Route de Malagnou 6, Geneva. *Con., L. and F. W. Shells.*
Brügger, Prof. Ch. G., Chur. *Bot., Zool., Min., Meteor., Geog.**
Brun, Prof. J., Univ., Geneva. *Mic.*
Brunner, Apotheker, Diessenhofen, Thurgau. *Ent.*
Brunner, Dr. Heinrich, Prof. de Chimie et Dir. de l'Ecole de Pharmacie à l'Académie, Lausanne. *Chem.* C.
Brünnow, Dr., F.F.E., F.R.A.S., Maison Beauval, Vevay.
Bucherer, Emil, Basel. *Nat. Hist.*
Bugnion, Dr. Edouard, Prof. d'Anatomie, Lausanne. *Anat., Pathol., Helminthology, Coleopt.* C.
Bulacher, Karl, Ph.D., Basel. *Chem.*
Bumann, Dr. Max., Freiburg. *Chem.*
Burckhardt, Prof. Dr. Fritz, Munsterplatz 15, Basel. *Phys., Physiol.*
Burkhardt, Prof. G. A., Laufen, Jura (Canton Berne).
Burnat, Emile, Nant-sur-Vevay. *Bot.*
Buser, Robert, Aarau. *Bot.*
Calloni, Silvio, Prof. Nat. Hist., Pazallo près Lugano.
Canderay, Jul., Lausanne. *Phys., Elect.*
Chaix, Prof. Paul, Geneva. *Phys., Geog.*
Chappuis, F. L. A., Pharmacien, Boudry. *Bot.*
Chappuis, P., Ph.D., Basel. *Phys.*
Chavannes, Rev. Sylvius, Lausanne. *Geol.*
Chevrier, Frédéric, Rentier, Beau-lac, near Nyon (Vaud). *Coleopt., Hymenop.*
Christ, Dr. H., rue St. Jacques 5, Basel. *Systematic and Geographical Botany, Canarian flora, Carex, Pinus, Rosa, Entomology:* Rhopalocera and Zygænidæ of Central Europe.*
Christener, J. Adolf, M.D., Berne. *Geol.*
Christersson, J., Hernösand. *Agric. Chem.*
Colladon, Prof. Daniel, Univ., Geneva. *Phys.*
Corcelle, Ch., 6 rue de Mont Blanc, Geneva. *Ent.: Lepid., Bot.*
Cornu, Felix, Basel. *Chem.*
Coulon, Louis de, Neuchâtel. *Orn.*
Cramer, Prof. Dr. C., Dir. Bot. Garden, Polytechnic Sch., Adlerburg, Zürich. *Bot.*
Cuénoud, Prof. Sam., Lausanne. *Math.*
Dapples, Charles, Lausanne. *Phys.*
De Candolle, Dr. Anne C. P., rue Massot 11, Geneva. *Bot.*
De Candolle, Prof. Alphonse, L.P.P., Cours St. Pierre 3, Geneva. *Bot.* C.
Decoppet, Casimir, Lausanne. *Chem.*
Decrue, Prof. David, Geneva. *Phys., Math.*
Delabar, Prof. Gangolf, St. Gall. *Phys., Math.*
Denzier, Prof. W., Univ., Zürich. *Math.*
Deseglise, Alfred, rue Thalberg 4, Geneva. *Bot.*
Dobeli, Sam., rue de Carouge 17, Geneva. *Coleopt.*
Dodel-Port, Dr. Arnold, Prof. Bot. à l'Université, Zürich. *Bot., Darwinism.*
Dodel-Port, Madame Carolina, Prof. Bot. à l'Université, Zürich. *Bot.*
Doge, François, La Tour-de-Peilz (Vaud). *Palæo., Geol.* C.
Dor, Dr. Henri, Vevay (Vaud). *European Coleopt.*
Duby, Dr. J. E., rue de l'Evêché 5, Geneva. *Bot.*
Duby de Steiger, Dr. Johann S., Geneva. *Bot.*
Ducommun, Prof. J. C., Berne. *Bot.*
Ducret-Dufour, Moudon (Vaud). *Coleopt.*
Dufour, Dr. Phil., Asst. in Bot., Polytechnicum, Zürich.
Dufour, Arthur D., Capitaine, Moudon (Vaud). *Coleopt.* C. Ex.

Dufour, Prof. Charles, Morges. *Phys.*
Dufour, Henri, Prof. de physique à l'Académie, Lausanne. *Phys. et Météo.**
Dufour, Prof. Louis, Lausanne. *Phys.*
Dunant, Victor, Geneva. *Geol., Min.*
Du Plessis, Dr. G., Montchoisi, near Orbe. *Coleopt.*
Dürr, Prof. Henry, Lausanne. *Chem.*
Eichleiter, Antal, Rohrschach. *Geol.*
Engelmann, Dr. Theod., Apotheker, Basel. *Min., Microscopic preparations, Diatoms, and Foraminifera.* C.
Escher, Dr. J. J., Zürich. *Bot.*
Escher-Kündig, Zürich. *Ent.*
Fankhauser, Lehrer, Berne. *Bot.*
Fasel, Vincent, F.R.A S., Maison, Turin. *Bot.*
Fatio, Dr. Victor, rue Massot 4, Geneva. *Zool., Gen. Biol., Geog. Dist., Vert. Anat., Mam., Orn., Ool., Herpetol., Ichth., Hemipt.* C.
Favrat, Prof. Louis, Lausanne. *Bot.*
Favre, Alphonse, Correspondant de l'Institut de France, rue de Granges 6, Genève.*
Favre, Antonin, Freiburg. *Zool.*
Favre Augustin, Place St. Gervais 15, Geneva. *Lepid.*
Favre, Emile, Chanoine du Gd. St. Bernard, Martigny-Ville (Valais). *Bot.* C. Offers rare plants of Valais and of the valley of Aosta, particularly Hieracium.
Favre, Ernest, 6 rue des Granges, Geneva. *Geol.*
Fellenberg, Dr. Edmund von, Berne. *Geol., Min., Chem.*
Fenn, Dr., Schaffhausen. *Coleopt.*
Fischer, Dr. L. von, Prof. Bot., Univ., Berne.
Fischer-Sigwart, Apotheker, Zofingen. *Bot., Geol.*
Flesch, Dr. M., Prof. Univ., Zürich. *Anat.*
Fol, Prof. Dr. Herm., Geneva. *Emb.*
Forel, Auguste, Prof. Univ., Dir. Heilanstalt Burghölzli, Zürich. *Ants, Biol. of Insects, Anat. of Brain of Vertebrates.* C. Ex. Formicariæ of the world for other Formicariæ of the world, or will purchase.
Forel, Dr. F. A., Prof. à l'Académie de Lausanne, Morges. *Phys. and Nat. Hist. of Lakes and Glaciers.**
Forster, Prof. A., Univ., Berne. *Phys., Meteo.*
Forster, Prof. Dr. E. M., Berne. *Phys.*
Frey, Prof. Dr. Heinrich, Prof. Medical Science, Univ., Zürich, Oberstrasse 17, Zürich. *Zool., Histol., Mic.*
Frey-Gessner, E., Conservateur des Collections Entomologiques, Musée d'Histoire Naturelle, Geneva. *Ent.: especially Swiss Hemipt., Orthoptera, Mellifera, and Chrysides.* C. Ex.
Gauthier, L., Chateau d'Œx. *Ent.*
Gautier, Prof. Alf., Geneva. *Ast.*
Gautschi, rue de Bourg, Lausanne. *Optics.*
Geiger, Dr. F., Basel. *Bot.*
Geiser, Prof. K. Frdr., Hottingen-Zürich. *Math.*
Gerber-Baerwart, Armand, Basel. *Chem., Geol., Coleopt.*
Gerber-Keller, J., Basel. *Chem., Geol.*
Gibollet, Victor, Juge en Tribunal, Neuveville (Berne). *Bot.* C.
Gilléron, Dr. V., Instituteur, Rosengartenweg 5, Basel. *Geol., Palæo* C.
Girard, Dr. Ch., Berne. *Emb.*
Girardet, François, Morges. *Bot.*
Girtanner, Dr. A., St. Gall. *Orn.*
Girtanner, Dr. Karl, St. Gall. *Bot.*
Godet, Charles, Neuchâtel. *Ent.*

Godet, Prof. Paul, Neuchâtel. *Coleopt.*
Golaz, Charles, Bex. *Bot.*
Goll, Dr. Fr., Docent, Univ., Zürich. *Pharm.*
Goll, Hermann, Conserv. d. Mus. Zool., Ave. de la Gare, Lausanne. *Geol., Min., Mic., Zool., Ichth.* C.
Goppelsroeder, Dr. Friedrich (Brubachstrasse 14, Mülhausen in Alsace, Germany), Prof. der Chemie, Basel. *Chem.*
Gouvernon, Victor, Aux Bois (Berne). *Bot.*
Graebe, Prof. Dr. C., Ecole de Chimie, Univ., Geneva. *Chem.*
Graf, Dr. J. H., Docent, Univ., Berne. *Phys., Math.*
Grangier, Prof. L., Freiburg. *Geol.*
Grivel, Fréd., Aubonne (Vaud). *Chem.*
Grubenmann, Prof. U., Frauenfeld. *Chem.*
Gruet, Emile, Renan. *Orn., Ent.: Lepid.*
Gruet, Jules, Propriétaire, Renan. *Orn., Ent.* C. Ex. eggs and chrysalids of Lepidoptera.
Gruner, R. Sigrist, Berne. *Gen. Ent.*
Grüninger, Dr. K., Basel. *Chem.*
Grützner, Prof. P., Univ., Berne. *Physiol.*
Guédat-Frey, Jules, Tramelan-Dessus. *Ent.: Lepid.*
Guillaume, G., Neuchâtel. *Ent.*
Guinet, Auguste, Employé de Commerce, Route de Carouge 64, Plainpalais, near Geneva. *Bot.: Bryology.* C.*
Gutzwiller-Gongenbach, Prof. A., Basel. *Geol.*
Hagenbach-Bischoff, Dr. Edward, Prof. de l'Université, Basel. *Phys.*
Haemi, Prof., Berne. *Agric.*
Hall, Marshall, Veytaux-Chillon. *Geol., Chem.*
Haller, Dr. G., Privatdocent, Puthus 222, Berne. *Zool., Bot.* C. Ex.
Hartmann, Prof. F., Thierarzneischule, Berne. *Osteol.*
Heer Tschudi, Lausanne. *Coleopt.*
Hegetschweiler, Dr. Charles, Riffersweil (Zürich). *Mosses and Lichens.*
Heim, Albert, Prof. Dr. am Schweizerischen Polytechnicum und an der Universität in Zürich. *Geol.* C.
Hemming, Joh. Jul., Privatdocent, Zürich. *Geol.*
Hermann, Prof. L., Univ., Zürich. *Physiol.*
Herzen, Alex., Villa Montalegre, Lausanne. *Physiology.*
Hess, Prof. Clemens, Frauenfeld. *Phys.*
Hipp, Dr. M., Neuchâtel, Dir. of the telegraph works. *Elect.**
Hirsch, Prof. Ad., Ph D., Neuchâtel. *Math., Phys.*
Hofmeister, Prof. Hrch. B., Zürich. *Phys.*
Hofmeister, Prof. J. R., Univ., Zürich. *Phys., Opt., Mag.*
Hoffmann, Edward, Basel. *Chem.*
Honegger, J. J., M.D., Maneggstr. 5, Zürich. *Anat. of brains of vertebrates.**
Hoppe, Prof. I., Univ., Basel. *Pharm., Physiol.*
Horner, Jak., Ph D., Zürich. *Math.*
Hoscus, F. Hermann, Basel. *Min.* C. Ex., buys or sells.
Hotz, Dr. Rud., Basel. *Geog.*
Huguenin, Prof. Dr. C. Gust., Riesbach-Zürich. *Ent.: Bot.*
Humbert, Dr. Prof. Alois, Onex, near Geneva. *Lepid., Myriopoda.*
Imhoft-Falkner, Basel. *Ent.*
Imhof, Emil, Ph.D., Zürich. *Zool.*
Immermann, Prof. Dr. Hermann, Univ., Basel. *Pathol.*
Ischer, Gottfr., Mett, bei Biel. *Geol.*
Iselin, Hrch., Basel. *Min., Geol.*
Isler, Henri, Ph.D., Lausanne. *Chem., Phys.*
Jaccard, Prof. H., Aigle. *Ent., Bot.*
Jack, Joseph B., Constance. *Crypt. Bot.: Hepaticæ.*

Jacob, B., Fabricant d'horlogerie, Corcelles, near Neuchâtel. *Bot.: Pnanerogams, Ent.: Coleopt. and Ants.* C. Ex.
Jaeggi, Jacob, Polytechnicum, Zürich. *Bot.* C.
Jenner, E., Berne. *Lepid., Coleopt.*
Jenner, J., Cus. Museum, Berne. *Ent.*
Joclin, H., Basel. *Geol.*
Jonquière, Prof. D., Univ., Berne. *Pharm.*
Joos, Dr. Emil, Schaffhausen. *Min.*
Jordan, Et., Pharmacien, Neuchâtel. *Bot.*
Joris, Etienne, Orsières (Valais). *Coleopt.*
Kaufmann, Rob., Reallehrer, Rorschach. *Geol.*
Keller, Dr. Conrad, Docent de Zoologie à l'Université, Zürich. *Comparative Anatomy, Microscopy.* C. Ex. Offers mounted objects, especially of Zoophytes, anatomical preparations, and microscopical invertebrates.
Kenel, Ferdinand, Porrentruy (Berne). *Coleopt.* C. Ex.
Kenngott, Prof. Dr. Adolph, Univ., Zürich. *Min.**
Killias, Dr. E., Naturforsch. Gesell., Chur. *Bot., Ent.*
Kinkelin, Prof. Herm., Ph.D., Basel. *Math.*
Klaye, Dr. J. A., Basel. *Chem.*
Klebs, Prof. E., Univ., Zürich. *Pathol., Pathol. Anat. and Histol.*
Kleiner, Prof. A., Univ., Zürich. *Phys.*
Knecht, Henri, Rosengartenweg 3, Basel. *Coleopt.*
Kober, Dr. J., Basel. *Zool.*
Koby, Prof. Fréd. Louis, Porrentruy. *Geol.*
Koch, Joh. Rud., Lehrer, Berne. *Math.*
Kollbrunner, Emil, Frauenfeld. *Geol.*
Kollman, Prof. Dr. J., Basel. *Anat., Emb., Anth.* Desires crania of Indians in ex. for European, especially Switzerland, Embryos of Teleosts, Selachians, and Reptiles, well preserved for microscopical dissection.
König-Christerer, R., Berne. *Coleopt.*
Konrad, Emil, care Hubler & Schaffroth, Burgdorf (Berne). *Gen. Ent.*
Köser, F., Lehrer, Zürich. *Bot.*
Krafft, Prof. Dr. Fr., Prof. Univ., Basel. *Org. Chem.*
Krebs, C. Frd., Lehrer, Gymnasium, Winterthur. *Math., Phys.*
Krieger, W., Botanic Gardens, Basel. *Bot.*
Kübler, J. Jak., Ph.D., Neftenbach. *Mic., Nat. Hist.*
Kündig, Dr. Theod., Basel. *Chem.*
Kurz, Dr. Emil, Burgdorf. *Phil.*
Labhard, Dr. Hildebrand, Männsdorf, bei Zurich. *Ent.*
Lacroix, Pierre, rue de Candolle, Geneva. *Coleopt.*
Landolt, H., Sparenberg, Engstringen (Zürich). *Ent.*
Lang, Prof. Franz, Solothurn. *Geol.*
Langhans, Prof. Th., Univ., Berne. *Pathol. Anat., Parasites.*
La Roche, J., Basel. *Geol.*
Lee, Arthur Bolles, D., aux Devens par Bex con de Vaud, Suisse. *Zool.*
Léonard, Ad., 1 Bourgfelderstrasse, Basel. *Ent.: Lepid.*
Lippe, G. Leonhardskirchplatz 3, Basel. *Lepid.**
Leutwein, Charles, Diemer. *Min., Geol.*
Lenesche, L., Rolle. *Bot.*
Lenthner, Dr. Fr., Basel. *Zool.*
Liliencron, C. Frdr. von, Apotheker, Zürich.
Lindt, Dr. W., Berne. *Lepid.*
Lerch, Dr. Jules, Couvet. *Bot.*
Liechty, Prof. Dr. Paul, Aarau. *Phil.*
Liechty, Louis, Frauenfeld. *Chem.*

Loriol, Percival de, rue des Chanoines, Geneva. *Lepid.*, *Echinoderms*, *Geol.*
Lossier, Louis, Geneva. *Chem.*
Luchsinger, B., Prof. Univ. und Thierarzneischule, Berne. *Pharm.*, *Toxicol.*, *Physiol.*, *Emb.*, *Histol.*
Lude, Prof. Alexis, Lausanne. *Phys.*
Lunel, Alph., Grand Bureau 477, Geneva. *Ent.*
Lunel, Godefroy, Dir. du Musée, Bastions, Geneva. *Vert. Mam.*, *Orn.*, *Herpetol.*, *Ichth.*, *Tax.*
Lunge, Prof. Dr. Georg, Polytechnicum, Zürich. *Chem.*
Lüschen, Hermann, Zofingen. *Bot.*
Lusser, Fr. Vital, Ingénieur, Aviolo. *Geol.*
Maillard, Gust., Mus. 2 A., Valentin, Lausanne. *Geol.*
Mallet, Ch., Geneva. *Bot.*
Marguet, Prof. P. Jules, Lausanne. *Phys.*
Marignac, Jean C. G. de, Geneva. *Chem.*
Märki, Charles, rue Caroline, Carouge. *Coleopt.*
Masson, Mademoiselle Rosine, Lausanne (Vaud). *Bot.* C. Ex. Offers plants of Switzerland, especially Phanerogams and Filices of the Alps.
Matthey, F., Délémont. *Geol.*
Mauler, Eugène, Laboratoire de Microscopie, Travers, Neuchâtel. *Mic.*, *Diatoms*, *Algæ*, *Histol.* C. Ex. buys, and sells. Offers microscopic preparations, and wishes algæ and diatoms of the Pacific coast.
Mayer, Prof. Karl, Ph.D., Hottingen-Zürich. *Geol.*, *Palæo.*
Mayser, Dr. Paul, Heilausalt Burghölzli, Zürich. *Anatomy of the Brain of Fishes.*
Menzel, Prof. Dr. A., Gymnasium, Fluntern, bei Zürich. *Hymenop.*
Merz, Prof. V., Univ., Zürich. *Org. Chem.*
Meyer, Prof. A., Univ., Zürich. *Math.*
Meyer, Dr. Arnold, Horn. *Bot.*
Meyer, Prof. Dr. Carl, Basel. *Phil.*
Meyer, Georg, Geneva. *Coleopt.*
Meyer, Dr. Georg Hermann von, Prof. Anat., Fluntern, bei Zürich. *Vert. Anat.*, *Anth.*, *Eth.*, *Ethnog.*, *Vert.*, *Osteol.*
Meyer, Prof. H. von, Univ., Zürich. *Osteol.*, *Anat.*
Meyer, Leopold, Schaffhausen. *Ent.*, *Hymenop.*
Meyer, Dr. Richard, Prof. an der Kantonschule, Chur. *Chem.*
Meyer, Prof. Victor, Ph.D., Polytechnicum, Zürich. *Chem.*
Meyer, Dr. W., Observatory, Geneva. *Ast.*
Meyer-Darcis, Georges, Mem. Swiss Ent. Soc., Wohlen (Argovie). *Bot.*: *Ferns*, *Mosses*, *Lichens*, *Zool.*, *Ent.*, *Coleopt.* C. Ex. Buprestidæ. Desires American ferns for European mosses.
Meyer-Dür, Burgdorf, Berne. *Ent.*: *Neuropt.*
Micheli, Marc, Crest-Jussy, near Geneva. *Bot.*
Miescher, Prof. Dr. Friedrich, Sr., Univ., Augustinergasse 21, Basel. *Pathol.*, *Anat.*
Miescher, Prof. F., Jr., Univ., Basel. *Physiol.*, *Physiol. Chem.*
Miescher-Rürch, Prof. Dr. Fr., Basel. *Zool.*
Möllinger, Prof. Otto, Fluntern, bei Zürich. *Phys.*, *Math.*
Monnier, Prof. Denis, Geneva. *Chem.*
Montmollin, Aug. de. Neuchâtel. *Geol.*
Morthier, Dr. Paul, Corcelles, near Neuchâtel. *Bot.*: *Phanerogams and Cryptogams.* C. Ex.
Mösch, K., Ph.D., Dir. d. Zoolog. u. Con. d. Geolog. Sammlungen am Polyt. u. d. Univ., Oberstrass-Zürich.
Mousson, Prof. Alb., Hottingen-Zürich. *Phys.*

Mühlberg, Fritz, Prof. der Kantonschule, Con. des Kantonalen Naturhistorischen Museums, Aarau. *Bot.*, *Palæo.*, *Strat. Geol.*, *Min.*, *Lithol.* C. Ex.
Müller, A., 195a, Junkerstrasse, Berne. *Ent.*
Müller, Prof. Dr. Albert, Prof. Universität, Basel. *Min.*, *Geol.* C.
Müller, Dr. Fr., Basel. *Zool.*
Müller, H., Zürich. *Bot.*
Müller, Prof. Dr. Johann, Univ., Dir. Bot. Gar., Boulevard des Philosophies 8, Geneva. *Bot.*
Müsi, Prof. Maur., Freiburg. *Zool.*
Mylius, Adalbert, Basel. *Chem.*
Natural History Society of Basel. Pres. Prof. H. Vöchting, Sec., Dr. A. Riggenbach, Basel.
Naville, J., Vernier, près Geneva. *Chem.*
Nencki, Prof. Dr. M., Univ., Berne.
Nicoud, Louis, Chaux-de-Fonds. *Orn.*
Niederhäusen, Prof. H. von, Berne. *Zool.*
Nienhaus, C., Basel. *Chem.*
Nitzchner, Botanic Gardens, Geneva. *Bot.*
Nothrop, Prof. H. E., Inst. Thudicum, Pregny, Geneva.
Nuesch, Prof. Dr. J., Erziehungsrath, Schaffhausen. *Bot.*, *Zool.**
Odier, James, rue de la Cité 24, Geneva. *Coleopt.*
Oetli, Prof. Jacq., Lausanne. *Phys.*
Oltramare, Prof. Gabriel, Univ., Geneva.
Ortgies, Ed., Botanic Gardens, Zürich. *Bot.*
Ott, Carl, Lib. Naturforschenden Gesell., Kirchgasse 31, Zürich. *Phys.*, *Elect.*, *Meteo.*, *Bibliog.*
Parent, François, rue Montblanc, Geneva. *Lepid.*
Paul, Moritz, adjoint au Musée d'Hist. Nat., Geneva. *Lepid.*, *Neuropt.*
Perrenoud, Dr. P., Docent, Univ., Berne. *Pharm.*
Perrot, Dr. Adolphe, Geneva. *Chem.*
Perty, Dr. J. A. Maximilian, Prof. Nat. Phil., Zool., Berne.
Pestalozzi-Hirzel, Pelikan, Zürich. *Lepid.*
Piccard, Prof. Dr. Julius, Bernoullistrasse 18, Basel. *Chem.*
Pictet, Raoul, Prof. Univ., Geneva. *Phys.*
Pittier, H., Château d'Oex. *Geog. Dist. of Plants.*
Planta, Dr. Ad. von, Reichenau. *Chem.*, *Phys.*
Plessis, Prof. Dr. G. du, Orbe, near Lausanne. *Zool.*
Plüss, Dr. Benj., Basel. *Nat. Hist.*
Plüss, Dr. N., Basel. *Phys.*, *Chem.*
Potter, Place Neuve 4, Geneva. *Coleopt.*
Privat, Eugène, 18 Chemin du Mail, Geneva. *Bot.*, *Orn.* C. Ex. Wishes to exchange eggs of birds for the eggs of Swiss specimens, or plants of the Swiss Alps.
Probst, Botanic Gardens, Solothurn. *Bot.*
Rambert, Prof. E., Lausanne. *Bot.*
Rapin, Daniel, Route de Carouge, Geneva. *Bot.*
Rätzer, A., Siselen (Berne). *Lepid.*
Rausch, Arthur, Schaffhausen. *Ent.*
Rebstein, Prof. Jakob, Zürich. *Math.*
Rechberg, Schulthess A. V., Zürich. *Hymenopt.*, *Bombus Vernidæ.* C. Ex.*
Renevier, Prof. Eugène, Lausanne. *Geol.*
Rey, Gustave, Prof. de Sciences Naturelles du Collège, Vevay. *Geol.*
Reymond-le-Brun, Gust., Berne. *Zool.*
Rhiner, Joseph, Schwytz. *Philol*, *Bot.*
Rhyner, Adolf, Chaux-de-Fonds. *Geol.*
Riedmatten, Prof. P. Marie de, Sitten. *Chem*

Riggenbach, Dr. Albert, Assistent am Bernoullianum (Universitäts Observatory), Sec. Naturforschende Gesellschaft zu Basel, Basel. *Ast.*, *Meteo.*
Riggenbach-Stehlin, F., Freiestrasse, Basel. *Ent.: Coleopt.*
Ris-Schnell, Frd., Lehrer, Berne. *Math.*
Rive, Lucien de la, Geneva. *Phys.*
Romieux, Henry A., 27 Florissant, near Geneva. *Bot.* C. Ex. Phanerogams, especially Hieracium.*
Rossi, Camille, St. Moritz. *Ent.*
Rossi, Rev. P., Hôpital Grand-St.-Bernard. *Coleopt.*
Roth, Pros. Dr. Moritz, Univ., Basel. *Pathol.*, *Anat.*
Rotheli, Prof. J., Solothurn. *Math.*
Rothenbach, J. Emil, Küssnacht (Zürich). *Bot.*
Rothen, T., Berne. *Elect* *
Rothpletz, August, Ph.D., Zürich. *Geol.*
Rougemont, Henri de, Neuchâtel. *Crustacea.*
Rudin, Joh., Basel. *Nat. Hist.*, *Ast.*
Rutimeyer, Dr. Ludwig, Prof. Comp. Anat., Univ., Rennweg 2, Basel.
Rütimeyer, Prof. Dr. M., Basel. *Comp. Anat.*, *Geol.*
Salis, Frdr. von, Chur. *Geol.*
Salis, Rob. von, Chur. *Geol.*
Salis, Uliss. Adalbert von, Marschlins, *Bot.*
Sandoz, Pharmacien, St. Imier (Berne). *Bot.*
Sarasin, Edm., Geneva. *Geol.*
Sarasin, Edouard, Geneva. *Phys.*
Saussure, Ferdinand de, Cité 24, Geneva. *Linguistique.**
Saussure, Henri de, Cité 24, Geneva. *Zool.*, *Eth.*, *Vert.*, *Anth.*, *Geol.*, *Volcanoes*, *Prehistorical Hydrology*, *Agric.**
Schacht, Dr. Siders, (Wallis). *Coleopt.*
Schaffer, Dr. F., Docent, Univ., Berne. *Chem.*
Schalch, A., Basel. *Geol.*
Schalch, Ferd, Ph.D., Schaffhausen. *Geol.*
Schardt, Hans, rue de l'Ecole Industrielle 4, Lausanne. *Palæo.*, *Strat.* *Geol.*, *Moll.* C. Ex.
Schärmli, Karl, Thun. *Geol.*
Schenk, Bernh., Eschenz. *Bot.*
Scherrer-Engler, B., St. Gall. *Geog.*
Schiff, Prof. Maurice, Geneva. *Physiol.*
Schindler, Dr., Cus. Ent., Samml., Zürich. *Ent.*
Schindler, Fräulein Anna, Con. Naturalienkabinet, Glarus. *Hemipt.*, *Coleopt.*
Schinz, Prof. Emil., Ph.D., Fluntern, bei Zürich. *Phys.*
Schläfli, Prof., Ludwig, Berne. *Math.*
Schlatter, Theodor, St. Gall. *Bot.*
Schlosser, Gottl., Lehrer, Interlachen. *Phys.*
Schmid, Walther, Basel. *Coleopt.*
Schmidely, August, rue Argand, Geneva. *Bot.*
Schmidhauser, Joh., Lehrer, Basel. *Math.*
Schneebeli, Prof. H., Ph.D., Zürich. *Phys.*
Schneider, Gustav, Naturalienhändler, Zoologisches Intstitut, Basel. *Con.*, *Vert. and Invert. in Spirits.* C. Ex. Niederlage von Mikroskopischen Präparaten und conservirten Merethieren der Zoologischen Station in Neapel.*
Schnetzler, Prof. Jean, Lausanne. *Bot.*
Schoch, Dr. G., Dir. des Coll. Ent. du Musée d'Hist. Nat., Plattenhof Fluntern, Zürich.
Schönholzer, Prof. J. G., Berne. *Math.*
Schröder, Dr. G., Basel. *Phys.*, *Chem.*

Schröter, Dr. Carl, Polytechnicum, Zürich. *Bot.*
Schnetzler, Prof. J. B., Lausanne. *Bot.*
Schulze, Prof. Dr. Ernst, Polytechnicum, Zürich. *Chem.*
Schumacher, H., Berne. *Ent.*
Schwab, Alfred, Berne. *Min.*
Schwarzenbach, Prof. V., Univ., Berne. *Chem.*
Seitz, Dr. Johannes, Plattenstrasse 7, Hottingen-Zürich. *Medicine.**
Severin, A., Botanic Gardens, Berne. *Bot.*
Sidler, Prof. Georg, Berne. *Math., Ast.*
Sidler, W., Rev. P., Einsiedeln. *Phys.*
Siegfried, H., Zürich. *Bot.*
Sire, Eugène, Chaumont. *Bot.*
Soret, Prof. Charles, Univ., rue Beauregard 6, Geneva. *Min., Geol.*
Soret, Louis, Prof. Univ., rue Beauregard 2, Geneva. *Phys.*
Spiess, Charles, Pharmacist, Porrentruy (Berne). *Ent.: Coleopt., Lepid., Rearing larvæ.* C. Ex. only specimens in first-class condition. Many Alpine specimens on hand. Foreign correspondence invited.
Stadler, Dr. August, Zürich. *Phil.**
Stähelin-Bischoff, B., Basel. *Ent.: Coleopt.*
Standfuss, Max, Ph.D., Custos am Museum des Polytech., Zürich. *All kinds of Insects.* C. Ex.*
Stapff, Dr. Friedrich Moritz, Ingenieur, Geolog der Gotthardbahn, Airolo. *Practical Geol.*
Stein, C. W., St. Gall. *Geol.*
Stierlin, W. G., M.D., Schaffhausen. *Ent.*
Stizenberger, Dr. Ernst, Constance. *Bot.*
Stockar-Escher, Kaspar, Hottingen-Zürich. *Geol.*
Stöklin, Em., Freiburg. *Bot.*
Stoll, Dr. Otto, Privat docent an d. Universität, Linthenbergasse 24, Zürich. *Ent., Moll. Myriopods.*
Streng, H., Civil and Sanitary Engineer, Schulhaus, Oberstrass, Zürich. *Geog. Statics applied to Nat. Sci. and Statistics.* Correspondence desired.*
Studer, Dr. Waldkirch, bei Gossau. *Ent.*
Studer, Prof. Bernhard, Berne. *Moll., Min., Geol.*
Studer, Hch., Kilchberg, Zürich. *Chem.*
Studer, Prof. Th., Dir. Zool. Mus., Univ., Berne. *Zool.: Geog. Dist., Radiates.*
Sulger, Hans, Basel. *Min., Ent.: Coleopt.*
Sulzberger, Prof. Jakob, Frauenfeld. *Bot.*
Suppiger, Jk., Triengen. *Bot.*
Suter, Dr. Prof. Heinr., Aarau. *Math.*
Täschler, Max, St. Fidèn, S. Gall. *Lepid., Coleopt.*
Tauber, Dr. E., Docent, Univ., Zürich. *Physiol., Chem.*
Thorrmann v. Graffenried, Fr., Berne. *Geol.*
Thury, Prof., Univ., Geneva. *Bot.*
Tournier, Henri, Villa Tournier, Peney, near Geneva, et rue Croix d'Or 18, Geneva. *Ent.: Coleopt., Hymenop., Dipt., Hemipt.* C. Ex.
Trächsel, Ph.D., Berne. *Geol.*
Tribolet, Maurice, D.S., Prof. Acad., Neuchâtel. *Palæo., Geol., Min., Crystal., Lithol.*
Tripet, Fritz, Neuchâtel. *Bot.* C. Ex.
Turenne, Marquis de (26 rue de Berri, Paris), Gwatt, near Thoum.
Uhlmann, Dr., Münchenbuchsee (Berne). *Gen. Ent.*
Unzeitig, Dr., Docent, Univ., Berne. *Chem.*
Venetz, François, Ingénieur, Sitten (Wallis). *Ent.*
Vernon, Antoine, care M. Monnet, La Plaine, near Geneva. *Chem.*
Vilmar, Ch. C., Freiburg. *Bot.*

Vionnet, P. L., Etoy (Vaud). *Geol.*
Vittel, Edouard, Yverdon. *Chem.*
Vochting, Prof. Dr. H., Univ., Basel. *Bot.*
Vogler, Dr. C. Hch., Schaffhausen. *Ent.*
Vogt, Dr. Adolf, Ordentl. Prof. der Hygiene und Sanitäts-Statistik an der Hochschule, Spitalgasse 178, Berne. *Hygiene, Epidermology.*
Vogt, Prof. Carl, Geneva. *Geol.*
Volz, Dr. Ed., Interlachen. *Bot.*
Walner, Maison Guedin, Geneva. *Lepid.*
Wartmann, Dr. B., St. Gall. *Bot.*
Wartmann, Prof. E., Geneva. *Phys.*
Wattenwyl, von, Berne (Stadt). *Coleopt., Lepid.*
Wattenwyl-von-Montbenay, Frd. von, Berne. *Geol.*
Weber, Prof. A., Univ., Zürich. *Analyt. Chem.*
Weber, Prof. H. F., Zürich. *Phys.*
Weber, Prof. Dr. Robert, Neuchâtel. *Phys.*
Wegelin, H., Birschofszell, Schweitz. *Bot.*
Weilenmann, Dr. A., Univ., Zürich. *Phys.*
Wild, Dr. C.
Witte
Wirz, *Phil.*
Wolf, Murithienne, Soc. de Bot. du Valais, ffers rare plants of Valais and Aosta, Cogsne.
Wolf,
Wolf, Sternwarte, Zürich. *Ast.*
Wolfe ürich. *Ent., Diatoms.*
Wolfer, Observatory, Zürich. *Ast.*
Wuilleret, Lieut.-Col. Henri, Freiburg. *Chem.*
Wurstemberger, Arnold R. C. de, Dr., Zürich. *Geol., Min., Chem. Phys., Elect.* C. Ex.*
Wyss, Dr. H. von, Docent, Univ., Zürich. *Pharm.*
Yung, Dr. Emile, Geneva. *Zool.*
Zaggi-Meyer, I., Zürich. *Bot.*
Zeller, Rudolf, Balgrist, Hirslanden, Zürich. *Lepid., Biol. of Lepid.*
Ziegler, Dr. James M., Basel. *Geog., Geol.*
Zimmerman, E., Notaire, Vrège (Valais). *Ent.: Coleopt.*
Zimmermann, Ern., Visp. *Bot.*
Zollikofer, Casp., Marbach (St. Gall). *Bot.*
Zollikofer, G. J., St. Gall. *Meteo.*
Zschokke, Fritz, Aarau. *Zool.*

TURKEY (IN EUROPE).

Beszédes, Kálmán, Constantinople. *Geol.*
Hoyland, C. W., Constantinople.
Lacoine, Emile, Civil Engineer, Constantinople. *Phys.*
Paspati, Dr., Constantinople.

ASIA.

CEYLON.

Dixon, Alex. C., B. Sc. (Lond.), F.C.S., &c., Colombo. *Geol.*, *Cinchona Alkaloids.**
Ferguson, W., F.L.S., Colombo. *Bot.*, *Herpetol.*
Mackwood, Frank M., M.L.C., Colombo. *Ent.*, *Lepid.* Ex. Offers India species, and wishes perfect specimens, 2 males and 2 females of each species of Diurnal Lepidoptera.
Nock, W., Supt. Gardens, Hakgala. *Bot.: Ferns.*
Phear, Sir John Budd, M.A., Chief Justice of the Supreme Court of Ceylon, Colombo.
Roosmalecoeq, Andrew Henry, Ceylon Civil Service, Colombo.
Thwaites, G. H. K., Ph.D., Peradeniya. *Bot.*
Trimen, H. M. B., F.L.S., Dir. Royal Botanic Gardens, Peradeniya. *Bot.*

CHINA.

Bretschneider, Dr. Emile, Attaché à la Légation Imp. de Russia, Pekin. *Bot.*
Carrall, James W., F.G.S., Lond., &c., Office of Customs, Shanghai, *Geol.*, *Mining.**
Collin de Plancy, V., Pekin. *Herpetol.*
Doberck, William, Ph.D., Observatory, Hong Kong. *Ast.*, *Double Stars*, *Meteo.*
Ford, Charles, Supt. Botanic Gardens, Hong Kong. *Bot.*
Girinon, Garde d'Artillerie, Saigon, Cochin China. *Coleopt.* C. Ex.
Hance, Dr. Henry F., H.B.M. Acting Consul, Canton. *Bot.: Chinese flora.**
Heude (Rev. Père), Zika-wei, near Shanghai. *Zool.*, *Bot.* Ex.
Holdsworth, Edward, Shanghai. *Ent.*
Hungerford, D. S. G., H.B.M. Army, Hong Kong. *Moll.*
Little, Louis L., F.R.A.S., Shanghai.
Palmer, Maj. H. S., F.R.A.S., Govt. House, Hong Kong.
Sampson, Theophilus, Schoolmaster, Canton. *Bot.**
Schmacker, B., Carlowitz & Co., Shanghai. *Moll.* Ex.*
Stevens, Capt. G. R., F.R.A.S., Hong Kong.
Styan, F. W., care Messrs. R. Anderson & Co., Shanghai. *Orn.*, *Oöl.**

CYPRUS.

Euclide, Dr., Leucosia.

INDIAN EMPIRE.

Aitchison, J. E. T., M. D., Surg-Maj., Agra, N. W. Province. *Bot.*
Anderson, John, M. D., F.R.S., Superintendent Indian Museum, Calcutta. *Vertebrates, Ethnol., Arch.*
Andy, Senjee P., M.D., Madras.
Archer, Samuel, M.D., Surgeon-Major, Singapore. *Con.*
Barker, Robert Arnold, M.D., Bograh (Bengal).
Bellen, H. W., Bombay.
Bettington, Albemarle, M.R.A.S., of the Bombay, Civil Service, Bombay.
Biddulph, John, Capt. 19th Hussars, Gilgit (Cashmere). *Orn.*
Bidie, S. G., Gov. Central Mus., Madras. *Zool.*
Bombay Museum, Byculla (Bombay).
Bose, P. N., B.Sc., Lond., Geological Survey Office, Calcutta.
Brown, Capt. Alexander Burton, R.A., F.R.A.S., Fort Canning, Singapore.
Calvert, John M., Inst. C.E., Kulu (Punjâb).
Cameron, J., F.L.S., Supt. Govt. Garden, Bangalore. *Bot.**
Cammiade, Gilbert Henry, Madras.
Campbell, W. H., M.A.B.D., Cuddapah, Madras. *Lepid.*
Cantley, N., Supt. Botanic Gardens, Singapore. *Bot.**
Carrington, R. C., F.R.A.S., Indian Marine Survey, Calcutta.
Cattell, W., Surgeon 10th Hussars, Raoul, Pindu, Simla (Punjâb).
Chambers, Charles, Colāba Observatory, Bombay.
Chambers, Frederick, F.R.S., Colāba, Bombay. *Meteor., Magnetism, Meteo. Reporter for Western India.; Dir. Gov. Obs., Bombay.**
Clarke, Col. Sir Andrew, Calcutta.
Cline, G. W., L.L.D., The Currency Office, Fort St. George, Madras.
Cole, Major H. H., Royal Engineer, Simla (Punjâb). *Architecture and Archæology.*
Cole, W. H., M.A., F.R.A.S., Dehra.
Coles-Hardinge, J. J., Honorary Secretary Phayre Museum, Rangoon (Burmah).
Cooke, Samuel, M.A., Assoc. M. Inst. C.E., F.I.C., F.G.S., F.R.G.S.I., Cor. M.R.H.S., Professor of Chemistry and Geology in the College of Science, Poona (Bombay). Ex. of Min. desired.*
Cooke, Theodore, LL.D., M.A., F.G.S., Principal of the Coll. of Sci., Poona (Bombay.) *
Dique, W. F., Royfettale, Madras. *Tax. and Gen. Nat. Hist.*
Dreyer, C. H., Librarian Indian Museum, Calcutta. *Hymenopt.*
Drummond, Capt. Henry, Bengal Army, Bengal.
Duthie, J. F., B.A., F.L.S., Dir. Botanical Dept. Northern India, Saharanpur (N. W. Prov.). *Bot.**
Dymock, Dr., Govt. Med. Storekeeper, Bombay. *Materia Medica.**
Eatwell, W. T. B., M.D., Surgeon Bengal Army, Oriental Club (Bengal.)
Eliot, John, M. A., Meteo. Reporter to Govt. Bengal, Calcutta.
Fedden, Francis, A.R.S.M., F.G.S., Geological Survey of India, Imperial Museum, Calcutta (care of Agnew Fedden, Solicitor, Bristol, Eng.)*
Fischer, Robert, B.L., F.R.S.L., F.A.S.L. (Barrister-at-Law, Lincoln's Inn), Madura, Madras. *Anth.**
Fleet, J. F., C.I.E., Bombay Covenanted Civil Service, care of Messrs. Purvis & Son, Elphinstone Circle, Bombay; address in England, care of Messrs. Purvis & Co., Imperial Buildings, Ludgate Circus,

London, E. C. *Archæology, Indian Epigraphy.* Joint proprietor and editor of the *Indian Antiquary.*
Foote, R. B., Geological Survey of India, care of Messrs. Arbuthnot & Co., Madras.
Foulkes, Rev. T., Retired Chaplain, Salem, Madras.*
Fraser, O. H., Assistant to the Superintendent, Indian Museum, Calcutta. *Vertebrates.*
Fuller, I. B., Sec. to Govt. Agric. Commission, Central Provinces. *Agric.*
Furnell, Michael Cudmore, M.D., F.R.C.S., Madras. *Gen. Biol., Anth., Eth.*
Government Central Museum, G. Bidie, M.B., Surgeon Maj., Superintendent, Madras. *Phæn. Bot., Zool., Anth., Eth., Mam., Oöl., Lepid., Coleopt.* C. in Mus. Ex.
Grey, Dr. W., First Physician, Sir J. Jeejebhoy Hospital, Bombay. *Bot.*
Griesbach, C. L., Geological Survey of India, Geological Survey Office, Calcutta.
Grigg, H. B., Spring Garden, Madras. *Anth.*
Hederstedt, H. B., F.R.G.S., Lucknow.
Henderson, J. R., M.B., F.L.S., Prof. of Zoology, Christian College, Madras. *Herpetol., Crustacea (Paguridæ), Mollusks, Radiates.* C. Ex.*
Hennessey, John B., M.A., Great Trigonometrical Survey of India.
Hill, Dallus, Ahmedabad, Guzerat.
Hope, C. W., C.E., care of Messrs. Gillanders, Arbuthnot & Co. *Ferns.*
Hungerford, Richard, Surgeon-Major, Rangoon, Burmah. *Con.*
Indian Museum, Dr. J. Anderson, F.R.S., Superintendent, Calcutta. *Vert., Invert., Arch., Eth.*
Jack, Alexander, Capt. Bengal Native Infantry, Bengal.
Kaye, Ernest St. G., Jessore, Bengal. *Ent.*
Ketchen, Lt.-Col. W. D. B., Hony. Secretary Trevandrum Museum and Public Gardens, Travancore.*
Kincaid, Col. W., Sehore, Central India. *Hort., Geol., Anth., Arch., Eth.*
King, George, M. B., LL.D., F.R.S., Director Royal Botanic Garden, Calcutta. *Bot., Phæn. Plants.**
Lackersteen, M. H., M.D., Surg. H. M. Bengal Army, Bengal.
Lang, Col. Arthur M., Chief Engineer, Rangoon, Burmah. *Ent.: Lepid.* C. Ex. only in India and Malay.
Lawder, A. W., C.E. Rohilkund and Kumaon Railway, Naini Tal, N.W. Province.
Leith, Edward Tyrrell, Barrister-at-Law, High Court, Bombay. *Anth.*
Lisboa, Dr. J. C., Girgaum, Bombay. *Bot.*
Logan, D., Penang (Straits Settlement). *Anth.*
Lyall, Sir Alfred, K.C.B., Lieut.-Gov., Allahabad. *Anth., Philol.*
Lynn, Edwin, Hyderbad, Deccan (Bengal). *Anth.*
Mallet, F. R., Superintendent, Geological Survey of India, Geological Survey Office, Calcutta. *Geol., Min.**
Mann, Gustav, Conservator of Forests, Shillong, Khasi Hills, Assam. *Bot. and Forestry.*
Marshall, Major G. F. L., R.E., Secretary of the Agent of the Governor General, Mount Abu, Rajpootam. *Orn., Lepid. (Rhopalocera).**
Medlicott, Henry Benedict, M.A., F.R.S., Director of the Geological Survey of India, Geological Survey Office, Calcutta.
Mirza, Mehdy Khan, Chudder Ghout, Hyderabad (Deccan).
Mootoosawmy, P. S., F.L.S., Tanjore, Madras. *Bot., Plant Palæo., Zool., Emb., Anat.*

Mysore Government Museum, Supt., J. Cameron, F.L.S., Curator, B. Santappale, Bangalore.*

Nevill, G., Assistant to the Superintendent, Indian Museum, Calcutta. *Mollusca.*

Nicéville, L. de, Calcutta. *Lepid.* Offers to ex. Arabic Rhopalocera, or books on the same, for his "Butterflies of India, Burmah and Ceylon."*

Nicholas, G. J., Trekenning House, Oude.

Noble, B., Phayre Mus., Rangoon, Burmah. *Specialty, Ent. of Burmah.* In charge of collection of Museum.*

Nurising, Row., Esqr., A.V., F.R.A.S., F.R.G.S., Daba Gardens, Vizagatapam.*

Oldfield, Richard C., care Messrs. Kettlewell & Bullen, Calcutta.

Olpherts, Wybrandts G., East Indian Railway Company, Calcutta.

Ouchterlony, J., Lieut. Madras Engineers, Madras.

Parish, Hawtayne M., Calcutta. *Lepid., Coleopt.* C. Ex.

Parsick, Edmund A., Kolhapore, Poona (Bombay).

Pedley, Dr., Supt. Museum, Rangoon. *Tax.*

Pogson, Isis, Met. Obs., Madras.*

Pogson, Norman, F.R.A.S., Dir. Obs., Madras.

Poole, Major M. C., Sandoway (Burmah).

Pringle, E. H., F.R.A.S., Mangalore, South Canara.

Rivett-Carnac, J. H., C.I.E., F.S.A., Bengal Civil Service, Allahabad (Bengal). *Anth., Arch., Eth., Ethnog., Philol.* C. Will ex. Indian stone implements.

Rogers, Alexander, Bombay Civil Service, Revenue Commissioner, Northern Division, Bombay.

Saise, Walter, D. Sc., M. Inst. C.E., F.G.S., Kurhurbaree Collieries, E.I. Railway, Giridih (Bengal, via Bombay).*

Scott, Douglas A., Lieut. R.E., Roorkee (N. W. Prov.).

Schwender, L., Government Electrician, Telegraph Department, Calcutta. *Telegraphy.*

Sealy, Alfred Forbes, M.A., Cochin, S. India. *Orn., Ent.*

Sclater, Wm. L., B.A., F.Z.S., Deputy Supt., Indian Museum, Calcutta. *Zool., Mam., Radiates.**

Smithe, J. Doyle, Government Commissioner, Madhapoor (Punjâb), (care Messrs. King & Co., 65 Cornhill, London, E.C., Eng.).

Sorabjee, Khan Bahadur Bomanji, Assoc. M.I.C.E., Civil Lines, Poona.

Syed, Ali, B.A., H.H., The Nizam's Revenue Survey, Aurangabad (Deccan).

Sylvester, John Henry, Bombay.

Temple, Capt. R. G., B.S.C., Mussoorie, N.W. Prov. *Indian Folk-lore.*

Tennant, James F., The Mint, Calcutta.

Theobald, Albert G. R., M.A.A.A.S., N.S.A.T., Forest Department, Collegal., Coimbotore, Madras. *Nat. Hist.: Mammals, Birds, Reptiles, Fishes, Insects, etc.* C.

Theobold, Wm., Jr., Rangoon (Burmah).

Vyse, Griffin W., Assoc. M. Inst. C.E., Executive Engineer, P.W.D., Multân (Punjâb).

Waldie, David, Barnagore Chemical Works, 3½ Hastings St., Calcutta. *Chem.*

Waller, John E. H., C.E., Rohilkund and Kumaon Railway, Naini Tal, N.W. Province.

Waterhouse, Maj. James, Surveyor-Gen.'s Office, Calcutta.

Whitty, I. J., M. Inst. C.E., Kurhurballee Collieries, E.I. Railway, Giridih (Bengal, via Bombay.)

Wilson, William H., Ph.D., F.I.C., F.C.S., Professor of Physical Sciences, in the Presidency College, Madras.*

Wood-Mason, James, Prof. Comp. Anat., Medical Coll., Deputy Indian Museum, Calcutta. *Gen. Biol., Invert. Anat., Articulates, Lepid., Orthopt., Arach., Crustacea.* C. Ex.
Woodrow, George Marshall, Lecturer in Botanical College of Sci., Poona *Bot.* C. Ex. Offers specimens of Indian plants of the Deccan for those of other countries.*
Wynne, Arthur Beavor, Geological Survey of India, Punjâb.
Yule, J. H., Lieut. 11th Regt., Poona (Bombay). *Orn.*

JAPAN.

Berson, Prof. Gustav F., Univ., Tokio. *Phys., Mech.*
Bertin, Louis Emile, Ingénieur de la Marine, 66 Shiba Koentii, Tokio.
Bisset, James, F.L.S., Yokohoma. *Bot.*
Boeddinghaus, C. E., Nagasaki. *Coleopt., Lepid., Shells, etc.* Collection of beetles and shells.*
Custance, Prof. J. D., Tokio. *Min.*
Dybowski, Prof. Alexandre, Univ., Tokio. *Phys.*
Eldridge, Stuart, A.M., M.D., Ph.D., Yokohama.
Fukuda, Riosaku, 52 Ichibaucho, Tokio. *Chem.* C.
Fujesawa, Chikara, University of Tokio, Tokio. *Phys.*
Hikorokurō, Yoshida, Rigakushi, Ph.D., Fellow Chem. Soc., Membre Soc. Chem. Industry, Assistant Prof. of Chem. in the Scientific College, Imperial Univ., Tokio.*
Hida, Mitsuzo, 8, Imayawakoji Ichióme, Tokio. *Chem.*
Hotta, Reutaro, University of Tokio, Tokio. *Met.*
Imai, Prof. Iwawo, Univ., Tokio. *Met.*
Ishido, Toyota, Tokio-Daigaku. *Chem.*
Ishikawa, Chiyomatsu, Tokio Univ., Tokio. *Zool., Emb.* C. Lepidoptera and Coleoptera.
Ishikawa, Iwao, Hiogo. *Chem.*
Ishimatsu, Sadamu, Fukuoka. *Chem.*
Isone, Tokusaburo, Fukuoka. *Chem.*
Ito, Prof. Keisuke, F.R.S., Prof. Bot., Univ., Tokio, 14, Masagochio, Hongo, Tokio. *Gen. Bot., Zool.*
Ito, Shinrokuro, Rigakushi, 11 Hisakatamachi, Koishikawa, Tokio. *Chem. Tech.**
Ito Tokutaro, 14, Masagochio St. Hongo, Tokio. Now in the Univ. of Cambridge, Eng. *Bot.: Jap. Ranunculaceæ, Mosses, Lichens, Zool., Ichth., Ent. of Japan.*
Iwakawa, Tomotaro, Normal School, Tokio, *Zool., Emb.*
Iwata, Nakazwa, 13, Tuskudo, Hachimanche, Tokio. *Chem.*
Jacobs, Frederic, Yokohama.
Janibana, Kakusaburo, University of Tokio, Tokio. *Chem.*
Kada, Teiichi, Geol. Society of Japan, Tokio. *Geol.*
Katayama, Yempei, Agric. and Com. Dept., Komaba. *Physics.*
Kawano, Shachio, Kumanoto. *Mining.*
Kilkuchi, Dairoku, M.A., B. A., Prof. Tokio University, Tokio. *Math.*
Kitamura, Yataro, Rigakushi, 42, Chitosecho, Hongo, Tokio. *Chem., Chem. Geol.*
Kobayashi, Kiochi, Tokio. *Chem.*
Kochibe, Tadatsugu, Nagasaki. *Geol.*
Kōga, Prof. Moritaro, Univ., Tokio. *Phys.*
Kōga, Yoshimasa, Shizuoka. *Chem.*
Koma, R., care Japanese Post Office, Yokohama.

Kotô, Bunjiro, Shimane. *Geol.*
Kuhara, Mitsuru, Okayama. *Chem.*
Masuda, Reisaku, B.Sc., University of Tokio, Tokio. *Engineering.*
Matsubara, Shinnosuke, 106, Mikumicho St., Zushima, Tokio. *Zool.*
Matsui, Naokichi, Ph.D., University of Tokio, Tokio. *Chem.*
Matsumoto, Osamu, 5, Sarugakucho, Tokio. *Chem.*
Mayr, Heinrich, Prof. Dr., Univ., Tokio. *Forest Bot.**
Milne, Prof. John, Imperial College of Engineering, Tokio, Yokohama.
Miyazaki, Michimasa, University of Tokio, Tokio. *Chem.*
Moriya, Monoshiro (R.G.), Okamaya. *Chem.*
Nakamura, Kiohei, Rigakushi, 54, Tahara, Mikawa, Aichikew, present residence, Nagasaki Shihan-Gakko, *Phys.*, *Math.*
Nakazawa, Iwata, Ishikawa. *Chem.*
Namba, Masashi, Okayama. *Phys.*
Nerika, K., Agric. and Commercial Dep't. College. *Zool.**
Netto, Prof. Curt., Univ., Tokio. *Min.*, *Met.*
Nishi, Matsujiro, University of Tokio, Tokio. *Geol.*, *Mining.*
Nobutani, Teiji, Tokio. *Phys.*
Okins, Tadao, University of Tokio, Tokio. *Engineering.*
Okada, Ichizo, Imperial Branch Mint, Tokio. *Mining.**
Ota, Kuejizo, Chingakko, Shidsnoka. *Chem.*
Potter, Frederick Antony, B.Sc., Nagasaki. (Also, 88 Tower Hill, London, E.C.)
Sakurai, Jioji, F.C.S., University of Tokio, Tokio. *Chem.*
Sameshima, Susumu, Niigata. *Phys.*
Sasaki, Chiujiro, Prof. of Zool. in the Agricultural and Dendrological College of Tokio.*
Sakurai, Fusaki, Ishikawa. *Phys.*
Sembon, Yoshitaka, Tokio. *Phys.*
Sugiura, S., F.C.S., University of Tokio, Tokio. *Chem.*
Takanose, Munenori, Shiga. *Phys.*
Takasu, Rokuro, Tokio. *Chem.*
Takamatsu, Toyokichi, Tokio. *Chem.*
Takayama, Jintaro, 9, Tamuramachi, Shika, Tokio. *Chem.*
Takeo, Massauobo, Komaba Agricultural College. *Chem.*
Tanaka, Yoshiwo, 72, Hongo Kinsuke-Cho., Tokio. *Nat. Hist.**
Taniguchi, Noosada, B.Sc., University of Tokio, Tokio. *Engineering.*
Terao, Hisashi, Fulkuoka. *Phys.*
Toyota, Shinye, Hiroshima. *Phys.*
Uno, Tadahiro, Shizuoka. *Chem.*
Utsunomiga, Saburo, 10, Eujimichiogochome, Tokio. *Chem.*
Wada, Yuji, Meteorologist, Tokio Observatory.*
Watanabe, Jiunichiro, Komaba Agricultural College. *Chem.*
Watanabe, Wataru, R.G., Ass't Prof. of Mining in University, Tokio, Daigaku, Tokio. C. (For three years will be in Freiburg, Germany.) *Mining and Met.*
Watanabe, Yeijiro, Nagasaki. *Chem.*
Watanabe, Yuzura, Sakai. *Chem.*
Yamagawa, Kenjiro, Ph.B., Prof. of Physics, University of Tokio. *Phys.*
Yamaguchi, Hauroku, University of Tokio, Tokio. *Engineering.*
Yamaoka, Prof. Giro., Univ., Tokio. *Chem.*
Yamasahita, Denkichi, Suitama. *Geol.*
Yataba, Mumekichi, Akita. *Phys.*
Yatabe, Prof. Riokichi, B.Sc., Univ., Tokio. *Bot.*
Yoshida, Hikorokuro, Hiroshima. *Chem.*

TURKEY (IN ASIA).

Blanche, M., Beyrout, Syria. *Bot.*
Gillman, Henry, U. S. Consul, Jerusalem, Palestine. *Bot.*, *Bibiliog.*, *Anth.* C.*
Mariya, Dr. Michael, Tripoli, Syria. *Bot.*, *Mic.*
McCraith, Dr. J., Smyrna.
Peyron, J., Beyrout. *Bot.* C.
Porter, Prof. Harvey, B.A., Beyrout. *Bot.: Compositæ*, *Arch.**
Post, Dr. George E., Prof. Syrian Protestant College, Beyrout, Syria. *Bot.* C.*
Van Dyck, Dr. C. V. A., Beyrout, Syria. *Ast.*, *Meteo.*
Van Dyck, Dr. William T., Beyrout, Syria, *Zool.*, *Gen. Biol.*, *Osteol.*, *Mic.* C. Ex.*
Zohrab, Dr., Broussa.

AFRICA.

ALGERIA.

Battandier, Prof. A., Med. Sch., 9 rue Desfontaines Mustapha, Algiers. *Ent.**
Bourlier, Prof. Dr. A., 6 Boulevard de la République, Algiers.
Bourlier, Prof. Dr. Charles, Algiers.
Bruch, Prof. Dr. Edmoud, Algiers.
Chairy, Prof. Charles, Lyceum, Algiers. *Phys.*
Debeaux, Dr. O., Military Hospital, Oran. *Bot.*, *Con.* C. Ex. plants and living shells from all parts of the world.
Dunando, Prof. Gaëtan, rue René-Caillé, 4, Algiers. *Bot.*
Feuillet, Prof. Emile, Bibliothécaire du Gouvernement Générale, rue Micheles 40, Mustapha (Algiers). *Bibliog.*, *Anth.*, *Eth.*, *Philol.*
Godefrin, School of Sciences, Algiers. *Bot.*
Guillemin, Prof., Maire d'Alger, à l'Hôtel-de-ville, Algiers.*
Hagenmuller, Dr., Bône. *Bot.*
Hanonne, Gabriel, Algiers. *Chem.*, *Nat. Hist.*
Hemon, Adrien, Prof. au Lycée, Passage Ruennais, Constantine. *Coleopt.*, *L. and F. W. Shells.* C. Ex. Offers Coleoptera and Molluscs of Algeria, for those from all parts of the world, excepting Europe.
Lallemant, Ch., Arba, Algiers. *Ent.: Coleopt.*, *Bot.*, *Herpetol.*, *Malacology*, *Nat. Hist.**
Lamey, Adolphe, rue d'Isly, 4, Algiers. *Coleopt.*
Lejeune, L. P. D., St. Eugène of Algiers. *Coleopt.*
Montillot, Anatole-Louis, rue de la Lyre 48, Algiers. *Coleopt.*
Olivier, G., Bône. *Coleopt.*
Oudry, Capt., Biskra. *Zool.*
Papier-Marengo, Alex., Prés. d'Académie d'Hippone, Bône. *Geol.*, *Palæo.* C. Ex.
Papier-Marengo, Alex., Prés. d'Académie d'Hippone, Bône. *Geol.*, *Min.*, *Palæo.* C. Ex.
Pomel, Auguste, Directeur de l'Ecole supérieure des Sciences, professeur de Géologie, rue Rovigo 104, Algiers. *Geol.*, *Palæo.*, *Bot.* C. Ex. Offers cretaceous and tertiary fossils, and wishes Paleozoic and Triassic fossils.
Ramel, Prosper, Naturalist, Algiers.
Richard, E., El Biar, near Algiers. *Coleopt.*
Rivière, Ch., Dir. Gardens Hamma, Algiers. *Bot.*
Schmitt, Algiers. *Bot.*
Sorbier, Prof. Jules, Lyceum, Algiers. *Phys.*
Stepham, Prof. Dr. E., rue Rovigo 18, Algiers.
Texier, Dr. Louis, Algiers.
Thevenet, Prof. Antoine, Lyceum, rue de la Lyre 40, Algiers. *Math.*
Trabut, Prof. Dr. Louis, Med. Sch., Cité Bisch 52, Algiers. *Nat. Hist.*, *Bot.*
Trollier, Prof. Dr., rue Lamoricière 1, Algiers.
Warion, Dr. Camille, Oran. *Coleopt.*
Vieusse, Dr., Military Hospital, Tlemcem.
Viguier, Prof. Dr., Algiers.
Vollot, Prof., Lyceum, Algiers. *Math.*

ANGOLA.

Brand, George, .MA., Her Majesty's Consul, Angola, W. Africa.

CANARY ISLANDS.

Bello y Espinosa, Dr. Domingo, San Cristóbal of Laguna (Teneriffe).
Bethencourt y Alfonso, Juan, Plaza de la Constitucion, 2, Santa de Teneriffe (Teneriffe).
Hildebrand, Dr. H., Orotava. *Bot.*
Maffiote La-Roche, Miguel, Plaza del Hospital del Rey, Santa Cruz de Teneriffe (Teneriffe).
Masferrer, Ramon, Santa Cruz de Teneriffe (Teneriffe). *Bot.*
Rodriguez Nuñez, Eduardo, C. de San José, 35, Santa Cruz de Teneriffe (Teneriffe).
Rodriguez y Perez, Felipe, C. de Jesús Nazareno, 28, Santa Cruz de Teneriffe (Teneriffe). *Malacol.*
Wildpret, Orotava. *Bot.*

CAPE COLONY.

Amphlett, G. T., Standard Bank, Cape Town. *Ent.**
Appel, Ph.D. (Send by London, Livingstone Congo Society). *Ast.*, *Geog.*
Atherstone, William Guybon, M.D., M.R.C.S., Grahamstown.
Bairstow, S. D., F.L.S., P.O. Box 204 (repeat letter if no reply), Port Elizabeth. *Hymenop.*, *Coleopt.*
Barber, Mrs. M. E., George Town. *Ent.*
Bolus, Harry, F.L.S., Cape Town. *Orchideæ.**
Brady, J. H., M. A. (Oxon.), Department of Public Education, Cape Town. *Coleopt. and Orthopt.**
Danekelman, Alexander von, Ph.D. (send by Intern. Afric. Assoc.), Vivi Station. *Meteo.*
Eddie, L. A., F.R.A.S., Oatlands, Grahamstown. *Ast.*
Finlay, W. H., F.R.A.S., Royal Obs., Cape Town. *Ast.**
Gill, David, H.M. Astronomer, Royal Obs., Cape of Good Hope.*
Goodger, Arthur, St. Andrew's College, Grahamstown.
Harford, Henry C., Cape Colony. *Ent.*
Kilgour, G., F.R.G.S., Dutoitspan, Kimberley, Griqualand West.
MacLea, J. H., Botanic Gardens, Graaf Reinet. *Bot.*
MacOwan, Peter, F.L.S., Prof. Bot., South African Coll., Dir. Bot. Gar., Cape Town. Cur. Cape Govt. Herbarium. *Herb. Home Austro-Africa, 6 cent issued.**
Morgan, Conwy Lloyd, Diocesan College, Rondebosch, Cape Town.
Oats, Francis, F.G.S., Kimberley, Diamond Fields.
Peringuey, L., Asst.-Cur. S.A. Museum, South African Coll., Cape Town. *Coleopt.**
Pinchin, Robert, Assoc. M. Inst. C. E., Government Surveyor, Port Elizabeth.
Rous, Slowman, P.O. Box 200, Port Elizabeth. *Coleopt.*, *Moll.* C. Ex.
Share, Com. J. M., F.R.A.S., Cape Town.
Shaw, Prof. John, Ph.D., M.A., South African College, Cape Town. *Geol.**

Tidmarsh, Ed., Botanic Gardens, Grahamstown. *Bot.**
Trimen, Roland, F.R.S., F.L.S., Cur. of South African Museum, Cape Town. *Ent.: Lepid.**
Tyson, William, Dale Coll., King William's Town. *Bot.* C. Ex. only South African plants.*
Watson, J., F.R.G.S., Cape Town.
Wilson, Supt. of St. George's Park, Port Elizabeth. *Bot.**

CONGO.

Duparquet, Le P., Landana.*
Sims, A., M.B., C.M. (Aberd.), American Baptist Missionary Union, Leopoldville, Stanley Pool, The Upper Congo. *Med., Geog., Zool., Bot., Meteo.**
Techuel, Dr. Loesche, Stanley Pool (send by Intern. Afric. Assoc.), *Geog., Ast., Meteo., Geol.*

EGYPT.

Gaillardot, Dr. C., Dir. Medical School, Cairo. *Bot.*
Gastinel-Bey, Dir. Botanic Gardens Hospital, Cairo. *Bot.*
Letourneux, A., Alexandria. *Bot.*
Mustapha, Ibrahim, Alexandria. *Chem.*
Planta, Alexandria. *Bot.*
Schweinfurth, Prof. Dr. George August, Cairo. *Bot.* C. Ex. Egyptian and Tropical African Flora.*

FERNANDO PO.

McCormack, J., Fernando Po.

GAMBIA.

Sherwood, Dr. W. H., Bathurst, Gambia.

MAURITIUS.

Caldwell, W. James, Asst. Superintendent of Desjardin's Museum, C.M. Z.S. *Bot., Phæn. and Crypt. Plants, Ferns, Mosses, Fungi, Zool., Mammals, Orn., Ichth., Tax., Crustacea, Mollusks, Radiates, Sponges.* C. Ex.*
Capeyron, A. Leonce, Port Louis. *Con.* C.
Daruty de Grandpré, J. M. R. Albert, Superintendendent of Museum of Botanical Gardens, Sec. of Royal Soc. of Arts and Sciences, Pres. of Soc. of Acclimation, Port Louis. *Nat. Sci., Biol., Bot., Zool.,* C. Ex.*
Horne, J., F.L.S., C.M., R.B.S.L., &c. Author of "A Year in Fiji," &c., Mauritius. *Bot.**
Meldrum, Charles, M. A., F.R.S., Alfred Obs., Port Louis.
Owen, Lieut.-Col. John Fletcher, Port Louis.
Powell, Lewis, M.D., Civil Medical Service, Port Louis.
Robillard, V. de, Port Louis. *Bot., Palæo., Zool., Emb., Mam., Orn., Ichth., Gen. Ent., Moll., Radiates, Sponges, Protozoa, Infusoria.* C. Will sell spec.

NATAL.

Bainbridge, John, Jr., Klip Kraal, Ladysmith.
Behreno, Carl, F.R.A.S., Durban.
Callaway, Rev. H., Springvale.
Marwick, E. L., F.R.A.S., Ordnance Dept., Pieter Maritzburg.
Perrin, James, Pieter Maritzburg.
Ridley, William, Natal Government Railways, Durban.
Sutherland, Dr. P. C., Surveyor General, Port Natal.
Wathen, G. Henry, Natal.
Wood, J. Medley, A.L.S., Supt. Natal Bot. Gar., Durban. *Bot.: Ferns, Fungi.**

REUNION ISLAND.

Cordemoy, Jacob B., St. Denis. *Bot.*
Potire, M. J., Dir. Bot. Gar., St. Denis. *Bot.*

SAINT HELENA.

Ianisch, H. R., F.R.A.S., Governor of St. Helena. *Ast.*

SENEGAL.

Thibeaudeau, St. Louis. *Con., Herpetol.*

SIERRA LEONE.

Rosenbusch, T. A., Freetown.

YORUBA.

Mills, Henry, Abbeokuta (Egba).

ZANZIBAR.

Kirk, Dr. John, C.M.G., H.M. Consul-Gen. and Political Agent, Zanzibar. *Bot.*

OCEANICA.

AUSTRALIA.

NEW SOUTH WALES.

Barkas, Dr. W. J., Warealda. *Physiol., Medicine, Palæo.*
Bennett, G., M. D., F.R.C.S., England, F.L.S., F.Z.S., Hon. Member of the Geog. Soc. of Rome, &c., Sydney, N. S. Wales.*
Bensusan, S. L., Exchange, Pitt St., Sydney.
Brazier, John, F.L.S., C.M.Z.S., Curaçoa House, 82 Windmill St., and Australian Museum, College St., Sydney. *Con., Eth., Numis., Bryozoa.* C.*
Brazier, Miss Sophie M. S., Curaçoa House, 82 Windmill St., Sydney. *Con., Postage Stamps.* C.*
Brazier, Amelia Rossiter, Curaçoa House, 82 Windmill St., Sydney. *Con.* C.*
Brazier, Eleanor Rossiter, Curaçoa House, 82 Windmill St., Sydney. *Con.* C.*
Brooks, J., F.R.G.S., Woollahara, Sydney. *Ast., Geog., Surveying.**
Campbell, Frederick Alexander, C.E., Tamworth. *Strength of materials, timber in particular.*
Clemesha, R., Redfern, Sydney. *Lepid.* C.
Conder, W. J., Survey Office, Sydney. *Ast., Surveying.*
Cox, James, M.D., Hunter St., Sydney. *Con.*
Cracknell, E. C., M.I.C.E., Eng., Supt. of Telegraphs, George St., Sydney.*
De Vis, Chas. W., Sydney. *Fishes.*
Dixon, W. A., F.C.S., Chemical Laboratory, School of Arts, Sydney.
Fairfax, James R., Herald Office, Hunter St., Sydney.
Fischer, C. F., M D., M.R.C.S., Eng., L.R.C.P., Lond., F.L.S., Lond., etc., Macquarie St., Sydney. *Zool., Bot.*
Garran, Andrew, LL.D., Herald Office, Hunter St., Sydney.
Gilliatt, H., Sydney. *Anth.*
Glasgow, S., Sydney.
Goodwin, A. P., Lismore, Richmond River. *Orn. and Eth.**
Haswell, W. A., M.A., D.Sc., Lecturer on Zool., Univ., Sydney. *Zool.**
Hewitt, Thomas, Observatory, Sydney. *Mic.*
Hunt, Robert, The Mint, Sydney.
James, John William, care of Mr. F. Smith, 13 Queen's Pl., Sydney.
Jennings, William E., Sydney.
Jones, P. Sydney, M.D., College St., Sydney.
Josephson, Joshua Frey, Sydney.
Kyngdon, Francis B., 69 Darlinghurst Road, Sydney. *Mic., Agric.**
Kindersley, S. W., 10 Bridge St., Sydney. *Geol.*
Laure, Louis T., M.D., 131 Castlereagh St., Sydney.
Leibius, A., Ph.D., M.A., F.C.S., Royal Mint, Sydney. *Inorg. Chem., Met.**
Liversidge, Archibald, F.R.S., F.C.S., Prof. of Chemistry and Mineralogy in the University of Sydney, Sydney. *Chem., Min.* C. Ex. minerals.
MacDonald, W. J., F.R.A.S., Bank of N. S. Wales, Sydney. *Ast.*

Mackenzie, John, F.G.S., Government Examiner of Coal Fields, Newcastle. *Min., Geol.* C. Ex. Offers coal, Cannel coal, Boghead mineral, tin, galena, copper, and other ores; also, fossil flora and fauna, for similar specimens from the Northern States.
Maclay, The Hon. William, F L.S., Elizabeth Bay, Sydney. *Ichth., Ent. especially Coleopt. Zool.**
Marshall, Henry, Angaston, Adelaide, So. Australia. *Evolution.**
Masters, George, Richmond Villa, Elizabeth Bay, Sydney. *Orn.*
Moore, C., F.L.S., Botanic Gardens, Sydney. *Bot., Hort.**
Moore, W. Gosling, Sydney.
Morell, G. A., C.E. and Architect, Office, 156 Pitt St., Sydney. *Engineering, Sanitary Science, and Architecture.* C. Ex. tin and ores (lode and steam) from New England (N.S.W.) tin mines.
Morse, E. K., Sydney. *Phæn. Bot., Palæo., Geol.**
Olliff, A. Sidney, F.E.S., Member Soc. Ent. de France, Australian Museum, New South Wales. *Ent., especially of Australia.**
Pedley, Percival R., 48 Wymard Sq., Sydney. *Mic., Polyzoa.* C. Ex raw material of Marine Polyzoa.
Ramsay, Ed. P., LL.D., F.R.S.E., M.R.I.A., F.L.S., F.G.S., F.R.G.S., etc., Curator Australian Museum, Sydney, N. S. W., Fellow Royal Imp. Zoological Bot. Soc., Vienna, Hon. Member Royal Soc., Tasmania, &c., &c. *Gen. Zool.**
Ratte, Felix, M.E., Australian Museum, Sydney. *Min. and Lithol.**
Roberts, Alfred, Bridge St., Sydney.
Rolleston, Christopher, C.M.G., Univ., Sydney.
Russell, Henry Chamberlain, B.A., F.R.S., F.R.A.S., F.R.M.S., Government Astronomer, Sydney Observatory, Sydney. *Ast., Meteo.**
Scott, Rev. Wm., Bungendore, Sydney.
Stephen, Evelyn A. H., Sydney. *Psychometry.*
Stephen, G. Milner, F.G.S., F.R.S., Sydney. *Min., Psychol.* C.
Stephens, W. J., M.A., Prof. Nat. Hist., Univ., Sydney.
Swan, J., New Town, Sydney.
Tebbutt, John, F.R.A.S., Observatory, Windsor.
Tenison-Woods, Rev. J. E., 533 Elizabeth St., Sydney. *Bot., Palæo., Strat. Geol., Bibliog., Ichth., Moll., Radiates.**
Thorpe, J. A., Shirley, Glenmore Road, Sydney. *Orn.*
Travers, S. Smith, New Town, Sydney.
Whitelegge, Thomas, Australian Museum, Sydney. *Mic., Bot.: Bryology.**
Wilkinson, Charles S., Government Geologist, Sydney.
Woolls, Rev. W., Ph.D., Richmond. *Australian Bot.*
Wright, Horatio George A., M.R.C.S., Eng., L.S.A., Lond. 2 Carlton Terrace, Wynyard Sq., Sydney. *Mic.**

SOUTH AUSTRALIA.

Adamson, D. B., Angas St., Adelaide.
Anderson, John, Port Lincoln. *Coleopt. of dist.**
Bednall, W. T., Adelaide. *Con.*
Blackburn, Rev. Thomas, B.A., Vicarage, Woodville, Adelaide. *Coleopt. especially of Australia.* C. Ex.*
Brown, John Ednie, F.L.S., Conservator of Forests, Government offices, Adelaide. *Forest Culture.* Desires correspondence upon this subject.
Chalwin, Thomas, St. John St., South Terrace. Adelaide.
Cloud, Thomas C., Wallaroo Smelting Works, Wallaroo. *Chem. Geol., Min.*

Crawford, Frazer Smith, Photolithographer, Surveyor-Gen. Office, Adelaide. *Insects and Fungi injurious to food plants.* Ex. Mic. specimens, wishes correspondence.
Fletcher, Rev. W. R., North Terrace, Kent Town, Adelaide.
Goyder, George Arthur, Mineralogist, Government Survey Office, Adelaide. C. Ex.*
Goyder, G. W., Surveyor, Gen. Govt. Offices, Adelaide.*
Guest, Edward, Balhamah. *Coleopt., Lepid.*
Haacke, J. W., Ph.D., Cur. Museum, Adelaide. *Zool.*
Hosking, J , Brown St., Adelaide
Lamb, Prof. Horace, Univ. of Adelaide, Adelaide.
Miethke, Rudolf, Victor Harbor. *Birds' Eggs, Coleopt.**
Mohan, John H., Archer St., North Adelaide. *Hort.*
Neumann, T. C., Wallaroo. *Min.*
Rutt, Walter, C.E., Engineer-in-Chief's Office, Adelaide.
Schomburgk, Dr. R., Dir. Botanic Gardens, Adelaide. *Bot., Hort.**
Tate, Ralph, Prof. of. Nat. Science, Adelaide. *Con., Tertiary Palæo., Bot.* C. Ex. Wishes minerals and tertiary fossils; those suitable for lecture illustrations preferred.
Tepper, J. G. Otto, F.L.S., Norwood, care of Messrs. E. S. Wigg & Son, Booksellers, Adelaide. *Geol., Bot., Ent.* C. Ex. plants and insects in special cases. The latter for the Public Museum only.*
Todd, Chas., M.A., C.M.G., F.R.A.S., F.R.M.S., F.S.T.E., &c., Postmaster Gen., Supt. of Telegraphs and Govt. Astronomers, Obs., Adelaide.*

QUEENSLAND.

Bancroft, Joseph, M.D., Brisbane. *Diseases of Plants.* Human Filaria. Contributions to Pharmacy from Queensland.*
Bailey, Frederick Manson, F.L.S., Colonial Botanist, Brisbane. *Bot.**
Bernays, Lewis Adolphus, F.L.S., F.R.G.S., House of Parliament, Brisbane. *Economic Bot.*
Cockle, Sir James, Brisbane.
De Vis, C. W., M.A., Queensland Museum, Brisbane. Ex.*
Gray, Rev. W., Townsville, North Queensland. *Elect.*
Gregory, Augustus C., Surveyor Gen., Brisbane.
Gulliver, T. A., F.L.S., Elect. Telegraph Manufac., Townsville, Northern Queensland. *Bot., Ferns, Agric., Plants, Zool., Orn., Ent., Coleopt., Hort.* C. Ex.*
Hartmann, C. H., F.R H.S., M.B.V. (Berlin), Toowoomba. *Bot. and Pomology.* C. Ex. Offers Australian and many varieties for those of America and Europe, and sells Fern impressions. *Phæn. and Crypt. Bot.*
Jack, Robert Logan, Gov't Geologist for Queensland, Townsville, North Queensland. *Palæo., Geol.* C. Ex., especially silver and lead ores.*
Mar, I., Gov't Analyst, Brisbane. *Chem.*
McConnel, David C., Cressbrook, Ipswich. *Geol., Mic., Moll.* C.
Miskin, W. H., Brisbane. *Lepid.: Exotic Diurnal Sphingidæ, Uranidæ, Saturnidæ.* C. Ex.
Musgrave, Anthony, Brisbane. *Ichth.* C.
Plant, C. F., F.R.A.S., Townsville, North Queensland.
Ringrose, R. C., Charters Towers, N. Queensland. *Geol., Min., Con.**
Scortechini, The Rev. Benedict, LL.B., F.L.S., Logan Village. *Phæn. Bot., Ferns, Mosses, Fungi, Lichens.*
Staiger, K. T. S., F.L.S., Brisbane. *Analyt. Chem.*
Steiger, J., Edmund St., South Brisbane. *Geol.*
Tregaskis, R , Charters Towers. *Min.*

VICTORIA.

Allen, Harry B., M.D., Univ., Melbourne. *Anat., Pathol.*
Barnard, W. H., School of Mines, Ballarat.
Barton, R., Royal Mint, Melbourne. *Chem., Metall.**
Bear, Naturaliste Preparateur, 46 Park St., East Emerald Hill, Melbourne. *Mam., Orn.*
Blackett, C. R., F.L.S., Gertrude St., Fitzroy, Melbourne. *Chem.*
Bosisto, Joseph, Chemist, Richmond, Melbourne. *Chem.*
Browning, J. H., M.D., et Ch. B., J.P., Health Officer and Superintendent Quarantine Station, Victoria.*
Campbell, A. J., H. M. Customs, Melbourne. *Ool.**
Challen, Peter R., Electric Telegraph Office, Melbourne.
Clarke, James, Royal Society, Melbourne.
Clarson, W., F.L.S., Melbourne, and 70 Pitt St., Sydney, N.S.W. *Bot., Hort., Mic.*
Coles, Alfred, Taxidermist and Furrier, 220 Elizabeth St., Melbourne. *Zool., Tax.* C. Ex.
Dendy, Arthur, M.Sc., F.L.S., Associate of Owens College, Demonstrator and Asst. Lecturer in Biology in Univ. of Melbourne. *Zool., Gen. Biol., Invert., Sponges.**
Dobson, Arthur Dudley, F.G.S., Member Institution of Civil Engineers, Warrnambool, Victoria.*
Ellery, R. L. J., F.R.S., F.R.A.S., Government Astronomer, Observatory, Melbourne. *Ast.*
Flude, Assayer, School of Mines, Ballarat. *Chem.*
Foord, Geo., Royal Mint, Melbourne. *Metallurgical and Technical Chem.**
Fowler, Thomas Walker, C.E., Melbourne University, Associate Royal Society of Victoria, Caunban, Hawthorne, Melbourne. *Civil Engineering, Physics, Railway Engineering.*
French C., Melbourne. *Ent.*
Gibbons, Sydney W., 5 Collins Street, E. Melbourne. *Chem., Mic.*
Grut, Percival de Jersey, English, Scottish, and Australian chartered Bank, Melbourne. *Political Economy.*
Guilfoye, William R., F.L.S., Curator of the Botanic Gardens. *Bot. and Landscape Gardening.* C. Ex. Wishes herbarium and vegetable products of any kind for a Museum of Economic Botany now being established in the Gardens.
Halford, George B., M.D., Prof. Physiol., Univ., Melbourne.
Hayter, Henry Heylyn, C.M.G., Government Statist of Victoria, Melbourne. *Statistical Research.* Statistical publications of Australia in exchange for similar works respecting other countries.*
Heinecke, F. W., Harkaway, Berwick. *Chem.*
Holmes, W. E, Tel. Eng. Office, Railway Dept., Spencer St., Melbourne.
Howden, J. M., Messrs. Lyell & Gowan's, 46 Elizabeth St., Melbourne.
Howitt, Alfred William, F.G.S., F.L.S., Warden of the Goldfields, Sale, Gippsland. *Geol. and Anth.* C. Ex. Igneous and Metamorphic rocks.*
Johnson, William, Government Analytical Chemist, Melbourne. *Chem.*
Kernot, W. C., M.A., C.E., Pres. of Roy. Soc. of Victoria, Melbourne University. *Civil Engineering.**
Kershaw, William, Univ., Melbourne. *Bot.*
Kirkland, John Booth, Chem., Met., and Physiol. Laboratories, Univ., Melbourne. *Phys., Chem.*
Kirkland, John Drummond, M B., Ch.B., Medical School, Prof. University, Melbourne. *Chem., Met.*
Langtree, C. W., Sec. for mines and water supply, Ex.-Pres. of the Vic-

torian Inst. of Surveyors, Chief Mining Engineer, Melbourne, Victoria. *Geol., Strat. Phys., Min., Met., Elect., Meteo., Ast.* C. Ex.*

M'Coy, Frederick, F.R.S., Prof. Nat. Sci., Univ., Dir. Nat. Mus., Melbourne. *Palæo., Nat. Sci.*

McGillivray, Dr. P. H., F.L.S., Sandhurst. *Mic., Polyzoa.*

McGowan, Samuel Walker, Telegraphic Engineer, Chief Inspector of Telegraphs and Postal Service, Melbourne. *Elect. and Magnetism as applied to Telegraphic processes.*

Maciver, R. W. E., 27 Queen St., Melbourne. *Min.*

Maclean, C. W., Dept. Ports and Harbors, Walsh St., Melbourne. *Engineering.**

Maplestone, Charles M., Portland. *Mic., Polyzoa, Palates of Mollusca.* C. Ex. Offers named species of Polyzoa, and wishes the same or named American Diatoms.

Moerlin, Carl, Obs., Melbourne. *Ast.*

Moffat, W. T., Romsey, Victoria. *Phæn. Plants, Ferns, Mosses, Algæ Desmids, Diatoms, Mic., Gen. Biol., Protozoa, Infusoria.* C. Ex.

Mueller, Baron Ferd von, M.D., Ph.D., K.C.M.G., F.R.S., F.L.S., F.G.S., F.C.S., etc., Melbourne. *Bot., Mural industries, Chem., Palæo.**

Murray, Reginald A. F., Mining and Geological Surveyor, Department of Mines, Government Offices, Melbourne. *General Field Geology, Auriferous deposits.**

Nevins, A. E., F.R.A.S., Mercantile Marine Service, Melbourne.

Newbery, J. Cosmo, B. Sc., C.M.G., Industrial Museum, Melbourne. *Chem.**

Nicholas, Williams, Mining Department, Melbourne.

Oddie, James, Pres. School of Mines, Ballarat.

Patching, H. S., 110 York St., W., Emerald Hill, Melbourne.

Ralph, Dr. T. S., Kew, near Melbourne. *Mic.*

Rawlinson, Thomas, Granite Terrace, Fitzroy.

Scourfield, R., Messrs. Scourfield & Coultas, Swanston St., Melbourne.

Smibert, George, Technological Museum, Public Lib., Melbourne.

Smith, Prof. Mica, School of Mines, Ballarat. *Chem., Phys.*

Stirling, James, F.C.S., F.L.S., Geological Survey, Omeo. *Bot., Geol., and Meteo. of Australian Alps.* C. Ex.*

Stitt, J. G. B., 142 Latrobe St., Melbourne. *Min.*

Sutherland, Alex., M.A., Carlton Coll., Royal Park, Melbourne. *Inorg. Chem., Phys.*

Taylor, Mrs., Benny Hill, Camperdown.

Thureau, G. A. H., 14 Victoria Chambers, Sandhurst.

Turner, Joseph, Observatory, Melbourne. *Ast.*

Verdon, Sir George F., Melbourne.

White, E. J., Obs., Melbourne. *Meteo.*

Wilson, Sir Samuel, Oakleigh Hall, East St. Kilda, Melbourne.

Worcester, T., Nolan St., Frankston, Victoria. *Palæo., Moll.* C. Desires to exchange Australian fossils and shells.*

BORNEO.

Becher, H. M., The Borneo Company, Saráwak.

Gray, H. M., The Borneo Company, Kuching, Saráwak.

Houghton, Dr. E. P., Saráwak.

Posewitz, Dr. Theodor. *Geol.*

JAVA.

Binnendijk, S., Bot. Gar., Buitenzorg. *Bot.*
Burck, Dr. W., Adj.-Dir., Bot. Gar., Buitenzorg. *Bot.**
Gogh, J. van, Vice-Admiral Royal Navy, Batavia.
Ludeking, Dr. E. W. A., Batavia.
Maier, P. J., Batavia.
Mertens, Dr. K. H., Batavia. *Chem.*
Moens, J. C. Bernelot, Dir. Govt. Cinchona Plantations, Bandong. *Bot.*
Nooten, Dr. J. C. C. W., Buitenzorg. *Bot.*
Piepers, M. C., Batavia. *Lepid.* Fine collection of Lepidoptera of Java, in care of M. Snellen, Wynhaven, 45, Rotterdam, Netherlands. Desires to ex. Lepidoptera of Java for those of other tropical countries of the Old World, and diurnals of the entire world. Desires especially Lycænides.
Ploem, Dr., Sindanglaia.
Renesse, Dr. J. J. van, Batavia. *Chem.*
Sluiter, Dr. C. Ph., Prof. Nat. Hist., Gymnasium Willem III., Meester Cornelius, Batavia. *Invert. Anat., Worms, Radiates.*
Stok, Dr. van der, Dir. Meteo Obs., Batavia. *Meteo.*
Treub, Dr. M., Dir. Bot. Gar., Buitenzorg. *Bot.**
Treysmann, J. E., Buitenzorg. *Bot.*
Verbeek, R. D. M., Buitenzorg. *Min.*
Waitz, Dr. F. A. C., Batavia.

NEW CALEDONIA.

Layard, Edgar Leopold, C.M.G., F.Z.S., H.B.M. Consul, Nouméa. *Orn. of N. Caledonia and N. Hebrides, L. and F. W. Shells, Ferns.* C. Ex. Offers L. and F. W. shells and ferns from many countries, especially from N. Caledonia; wishes shells in *triplicate* where possible.*
Montrouzier, R. P., Nouméa. *Con., Ent., Bot.*
Rossiter, R. C., Nouméa. *Molluscs.*
Savés, Théophile, Nouméa. *Con., Ent., Orn. L. and F. W. Shells and insects.* Would like to sell.

NEW ZEALAND.

Barclay, H. V., F.R.A.S., Wanganui.
Barkas, Fred., F.C.S., Science Associate of Durham Univ., Lecturer on Chem., Canterbury Coll. School of Agric., Lincoln. *Agric., Chem.*
Bickerton, A. W., Christ Church, Canterbury. *Chem.*
Brown, Capt. Thos., M.E.S., Lake Takapuna, Auckland. *Ent.* C. Ex. Offers New Zealand insects for S. American Coleoptera.
Brewer, H. Molyneux, F.L.S., Wanganui, Wellington. *Fish Culture.**
Buchanan, John, Botanist to Geological Survey, Museum, Wellington.
Buller, Sir Walter Lawry, K.C.M.G., D.Sc., F.R.S., F.L.S., Wellington. *Orn.*
Campbell, W. D., Assoc. M. Inst., C. E., F.G.S., Auckland. *Geol. and Psychol.**

Cheeseman, T. F., Cur. Museum, Auckland. *Bot.*
Cox, Samuel Herbert, F C S., F.G.S., Assistant Geologist and Inspector of Mines for the Colony of New Zealand, Colonial Museum, Wellington. *Geol. and Mine Engineering.*
Craig, Eric, Princes St., Auckland. *Bot.*, *Ferns.* New Zealand ferns and curios.*
Curl, S. M., M.D., F.L.S., M.N.Z.I., &c., &c., Greatford, Rangitikei, Wellington. Specially interested in anything connected with medical science, Economic Bot., and Acclimatization; also interested in Ethnology, Philology, and the migration of men in pre-historic times. Author of various papers to learned societies upon Botany, Geology, Palæontology, Ethnology, Polynesian and Melanesian migrations, etc., and various works upon medical subjects, Life, &c' Published in separate volumes.
Drew, S. H., Wanganui. *Palæo.*, *Orn.* Ex. N. Z. Tertiary Fossils dan birds' skins for any object of Biol. C.*
Duigan, James, F.G.S., Wanganui.
Dutton, Rev. D., F. R A.S., Sydney St., Wellington.
Enys, John Davies, F.L.S., Trelissick, Canterbury.
Fereday, Richard William, Christ Church, Canterbury. M.E.S. *Ent.*: *Lepid.* C.
Fraser, Rev. Charles, M.A., F.G.S., Christ Church, Canterbury.
Hector, Sir James, K.C.M.G., M.D., F.R S., Dir. of the Geological Survey of New Zealand, Curator of the N. Z. Museum, Naturalist, Wellington. *Geol.* C. Ex. Wishes casts of fossil Cetaceæ in exchange; also, Rhoetic fossils for the Museum, for those of any branch.*
Helms, Richard, Greymouth. *Coleopt.*, *Land and Fresh Water Moll.*, *Crypt. Bot.*, *esp. Filices, and other Nat. Hist. objects.* Ex. and sell.
Hutton, Frederick Wollaston, F.G.S., Prof. Geology, Canterbury College, Christchurch, Canterbury. *Strat. and Phys. Geol.**
Kirk, Thos. Wm., Asst. Curator Col. Mus., Wellington. *Moll. Crustacea.*
Kitchener, Arthur B., F.G.S., Royal School of Mines, London. The Grange, Waihemo, Otago. *Mining Engineer, Geol. of Otago.* C.
Lambert, S. J., F.R.A.S., Auckland.
Mair, Capt. G., F.L.S., Officer in charge of native affairs, Tauranga.
Mair, Robert, Wharyarei, Auckland. *Bot.*
Mair, Major W. G., Auckland. *Bot* *
Mantell, Walter Baldock Durrant, Wellington. *Geol.*
Martin, Josiah, Model Training School, Auckland.
Maskell, W. M., F.R.M.S., Wellington. *Mic.*, *Bot.*, *Zool.*, *F. W. Algæ*, *Homoptera.* C. Ex.*
Meyricke, Edw., Warwick House, Armagh St., Christchurch, Canterbury.
Murray, A., Coromandel Valley.
Parker, Prof. Thos. Jeffery, Univ. of Otago.*
Petrie, D., M.A , F.L.S., Dunedin. *Bot.**
Potts, T. H., Christchurch, Canterbury. *Bot.**
Robson, C H., Napier. *Nat. Hist.* C.
Scott, Prof. J. H., Univ., Otago. *Anat.**
Sloman, J. F , F.R.A.S., Auckland College, Auckland.
Stratford, Dr. S., Auckland.
Thomson, Geo. M., F.L.S., Science Teacher, High School, Dunedin. *Biol.*, *N. Z. Crustacea.* C.
Tomlinson, W., F.R.A.S., Auckland College, Auckland.
Travers, W. T. L., F.L.S., Wellington *Bot.*
Ulrich, G. H. F., The University, Dunedin, Otago.

PHILIPPINE ISLANDS.

Botet, Dominigo, Zamboanga.
Möllendorf, Dr. O. F. von, Consul, Imperial German Consulate, Manila, *Zool., L. and F. W. Shells.* C. Ex. Offers Chinese and Philippine L. and F. W. Mollusca, and wishes L. and F. W. shells of other countries.*
Noralcda, Bernardino, Universidad, Manila. *Gen. Science.*
Prado, Norbeto, Universidad, Manila. *Gen. Science.*
Sebastian, Vidal y Soler, Manila, Jardin Botánico. *Geol. Bot.*
Sivilla, Julian, Universidad. *Gen. Science.*

SANDWICH ISLANDS.

Bailey, Edward, Wailuku. *Cryptogams: Mosses, especially Lichens and Algæ, Diatoms.* C. Ex. Desires Australian Ferns.
Baldwin, D. D., Asst. Principal Labrainaluna Seminary, Lahaina, Macie. *Bot., Mosses and Ferns, L. and F. W. Shells.* C. Ex. only in L. and F. W. shells.*
Barton, Geo. H., Government Surveyor, Honolulu. *Geol., Min.* C.
Cummings, O. S., M.D., Honolulu. *Histol.*
Dole, S. B., Honolulu. *Lichens. Orn.*
Haydon, Asa, Punuhou School, Oahu. *Lepid.*
Kurbary, Joh. S , care H.B M. Consul, Ponape, Honolulu. *Anth., Orn.*
Lydgate, John M., Laupahoehoe. *Pteridologist.*
Wetmore, C. H., M.D., Hilo. *Ferns, Fishes.*
Scientific Society, Honolulu, Geo. H. Barton, Pres., Honolulu.

SOCIETY ISLANDS.

Garrett, Andrew, Huahine, South Pacific, via Tahiti, Photographer and Collector of Nat. Hist. *Photog., Ichth., Moll.* C. of Shells. Ex South Sea Shells.*

TASMANIA.

Abbott, F., Jr., Hobart.
Agnew, Dr., Sec. Roy. Soc., Hobart.
Barnard, James, Hobart.
Beddome, C. E., Hobart. *Con.* Ex.
Beddome, Lieut. Charles E., Hill Grove, near Hobart. *Moll., also Postage Stamps.* C. Ex. Boëville, Davey St., Hobart.
Dobson, His Honor Justice, Hobart.
Harrop, Edward D., Launceston.
Hinsby, George Kilmer, Pharmaceutical Chemist, Hobart, Tasmania. *Bot., Crypt. Plants, Ferns, Algæ, Chem., Orn., Ool., Tax., Moll.* C. Ex.*

obert M., F.L.S., Government Statistician, 2 Davey St., Hobart.*
Palæo., Geol., Meteo., Ichth. C.
illiam V., Col. R. A., Military Barracks, Hobart. *Orn.* C.
exchange Australian sea-birds for American.*
Villiam, Hobart. *Con.*
C., Hobart.*
illiam F., F.R.S.T., Launceston. *Zool., Orn., Moll.* C. Ex.
, William E., Bushy Park, New Norfolk. *Meteo.* Meteoro-
al tables, especially rainfall and evaporation.
gustus, Launceston. *Ent., Bot., Con., &c.**
Thomas, M.A., F.G.S., Dir. of Education, Hobart. *Geol.**
., F.G.S., Government Geological Surveyor. Hobart.

APPENDIX TO UNITED STATES AND CANADA.

ALLISON, HENRY, Ft. Worth. *Invert. Palæo.* C. Ex. **Tex.**
ANDREWS, SUMNER, 76 Garden St., Lawrence *Min.* C. Ex.* **Mass.**
ANGELMAN, JOHN, 13 Spring St., Newark. *Ent., Lepid.** **N.J.**
BAKER, H.J., Oakville, Ont. *Orn.* **Canada.**
BAKER, WM. EMERSON, 278 Commonwealth Ave., Boston. *Bot., Hort., Chem., Phys., Elec., Mic., Zool., Anat., Ichth.* **Mass.**
BARNUM, ELIPHALET C., Denmark, Lewis Co. *Mosses, Palæo., Geol., Min., Ool.* C. Ex. **N.Y.**
BEERS, J. M., 126 E. Water St., Elmira. *Geol., Min., Arch., Orn., Ool.* C. Ex. **N.Y.**
BEHRE, CHAS. H., Atlanta. *Herpetology.* **Ga.**
BETZ, CHRIS., 221 W. Kinney St., Newark. *Ent., Lepid.** **N.J.**
BINNSON, JULUIS, 290 Washington St., Newark. *Ent., Lepid.** **N.J.**
BISCHOFF, CHS., 66½ 17th Ave., Newark. *Coleopt.** **N.J.**
BOTSFORD, ANSON H., Freedoni Station, Portage Co. *Arch., Fossils and Minerals.* C. Ex. **Ohio.**
BRAYMER, F. H., M. D. North Granville. *Palæo., Geol., Min., Orn., Crystall., Con.* C. Ex.* **N.Y.**
BREHM, HERRN, 483 Springfield Ave., Newark. *Ant., Lepid.** **N.J.**
BROWN, W. W., Rock Falls, Whiteside Co. *Ferns, Mosses, Fungi, Min., Crystall., Lithol., Zool., Orn., Ool., Herpet., Ichth., Tax., Coleopt., Sponges.* C. Ex. **Ill.**
CATLIN, H. A., Box 271, Richmond. *Bot.: Tuberoses, Ferns, Geol.* **Va.**
COLLIER, G. H., Prof. Chem., Oregon Univ., Eugene City. *Chem., Oregon Trees.* **Ore.**
COLTON, BUEL P., Ottawa. *Bot., Mic., Zool., Gen. Biol., Geog. Dist., Morph., Emb., Anat., Histol.* **Ill.**
CROSSCUP, GEO. W., 702 Chestnut St., Philadelphia. *Engraver of Scientific Illust., Photog.* **Pa.**
DANMAR, WILLIAM, P. O. Station E., Brooklyn. Sends free copies of "The Tail of the Earth" on application. *Chem., Phys., Ast.** **N.Y.**
DAVIS, WM. H., 134 So. 5th St., Reading. *Bot., Geol., Arch.* C. Ex. **Pa.**
DEEMS, FRANK MELVILLE, M.D., Ph.D., 429 W. 22d St., New York City. *Fungi, Invert. Palæo., Mic., Gen. Biol., Anat., Histol.* **N.Y.**
DIETZE, ERNEST, 30 Broome St., Newark. *Lepid.** **N.J.**
DOLL, JACOB, 55 Graham Ave., Brooklyn, E. D. *Lepid.** **N.Y.**
DUGANNE, Rev. HIRAM C., 127 Garham St., Lowell. *Bot.: Ferns, Hort., Geol.* **Mass.**
EAGLE, CLARENCE H., 129 East 30th St., New York City. *Zool., Orn., Ool.* C. Ex. **N.Y.**
EGBERT, H. V., A. M., Asst. Ast., Washburn Univ., Madison. *Ast.** **Wis.**
FAULKNER, CHAS. S., 48 East 22d St., New York City. *Ool.* C. Ex. **N.Y.**

FELLOWS, CHAS. S., 330 Temple Court, Minneapolis. *Gen. Nat. Hist., Crustacea.* C.* Minn.
FERRIS, J. H., Joliet. *Ferns, Moll.* C. Ex.* Ill.
FINLEY, E. B., Adj.-Gen. of Ohio, Bucyrus. *Palæo., Geol., Chem., Geog. Dist., Anat., Anth., Eth., Ichth.* Ohio.
FORD, S. W., Schodack Landing, Columbia Co. *Palæo.* N.Y.
FOULKES, JAS. F., Box 314, Oakland. *Chem., Mic., Meteo.* Cal.
GARRISON, J. B., M.D., 313 East 72d St., New York. *Elect., Anat.** N.Y.
GAUL, Dr. R. C., Reading. *Min.* C. Ex. Pa.
GEHRET, GEORGE, 647 Mulberry St., Reading, Bucks Co. Desires minerals from all parts of the world. Can offer minerals from Penn. and Africa in cabinet and museum specimens. Correspondence desired. *Min., Ool., Tax.* C. Ex.* Pa.
GILBERT, A. C., San Antonio. Dealer in Mexican and Indian Curiosities, Minerals, Fossils, Furs, Shells, Cactuses, etc.* Tex.
HARTMANN, LEOPOLD, Big Casino, 68 Congress St., Houston. *Lepid.* Also all kinds of insects to order.* Tex.
HAYDON, WALTON, F.R.G.S., East Selkirk. *Diurnal Lepid., Bot., Folk Lore of American Indians.* Manitoba.
HERPERS, HENRY, 18 Crawford St., Newark. *Lepid.** N.J.
HESS, JOHN, 311 W. Kinney St., Newark. *Coleopt.** N.J.
HODGES, FRANK L., Clayton, Clayton Co. *Geol., Min., Arch.* C. Ex.* Iowa.
HOWDIN, JAMES C., M.D., Sunnyside, Montrose, N.B. C.* Canada.
JONES, GEO. M., 14 Mandeville St., Utica, Ed. "Collector." *Min., Orn., Ool.* C. Ex.* N.Y.
KEISER, JAMES, Reading. *Min.* C. Ex. Pa.
KENDALL, W. J. A., 847 Green St., Reading. *Ool.* C. Ex. Pa.
LYFORD, TAYLOR C., P. O. Box 782, Spencer. *Geol., Min., Lithol., Elect., Photog., Ast., Zool., Geog. Dist., Anat., Vert., Arch., Mam., Orn., Ool., Herpetol., Ichth., Tax., Osteol.* C. Ex.* Mass.
MALLEIS, WM. B., Portland. *Orn.* Ex* Oregon.
MOYER, HARRY G., 333 Moss St., Reading. *Min.* C. Ex. Pa.
MUHLENBURG, N. A., Reading. *Chem., Min.* C. Ex. Pa.
PALM, CHAS., 172 East 64th St., New York. *Lepid.** N.Y.
PAMMEL, L. H., Shaw School of Bot., St. Louis. *Phæn. Bot., Fungi.* C. Ex. Mo.
PILSBRY, H. A., Conservator Conchological Section, Philadelphia Acad. of Sci. Desires alcoholic gasteropoda and shells from all countries. Offers American and foreign mollusca and publications of Conchol. Sec. Phila. Acad. C. Ex.* Pa.
PRICE, C. WESLEY, Plymouth, Wayne Co. *Stamps, Coins, Minerals.* C.* Mich.
PRICE, T. S., Borden, Fresno Co. *Min., Ast., Bibliog., Eth., Philol.* C. Ex. Cal.
PULVER, H., Rednersville, Prince Edward's Co., Ont. *Woods.* Canada.
PURINTON, GEO. D., Prof. of Biology, Univ. of the State of Missouri, Columbia. *Bot., Min., Chem., Orn., Tax.* C. Ex.* Mo.
RENNINGER, JOHN S., M.D. Marshall, Lyon Co. C. Ex.* Minn.
RICKSECKER, L. E., Santa Rosa, Sonoma Co. *Coleopt. and other insects of western N. A. for sale.** Cal.
ROBINSON, W. F., Prin. School No. 4, Elizabeth. *Min., Inorg. Chem., Ent., esp. Lepid., Coleopt., Con.* C. Ex.* N.J.
RUTTLE, WM., 1597 Scott St., Covington. *Ferns.* C. Ex. Ky.
SATTUCK, JOSEPH, Nashua. *Ent.: Lepid., Dipt., Coleopt.* C. Ex. N.H.

SCHEBNIKOW, ERNEST, P. O. Box 3540, New York. *Min.*, *Crystal.*, *Arch.* C. Ex.* N.Y.
SCHUMAN, THEO., 63 Whitehall, Atlanta. *Chem.* Ga.
TOWNSEND, CHAS. H., Smithsonian Institution, Washington. *Gen. Nat. Hist.*, *Orn.* C. D.C.
TUGANZA, J. A., Britt, Hancock Co. *Geol.*, *Min.*, *Mic.*, *Orn.*, *Tax.* C. Ex. Iowa.
UDDEN, J. A., A.B., Lindsborg, McPherson Co. *Local Flora.* C. Ex.* Kan.
WADSWORTH, M. E., A.M., Ph.D., Director Michigan Mining School, Prof. of Min., Petrog. and Geol., Michigan Mining School, Houghton. *Geol.*, *Strat.*, *Phys.*, *Min*, *Crystall.*, *Lithol.* C* Mich.
WAHL, WM. H., Ph.D., Franklin Inst., Philadelphia. *Chem.*, *Geol.*, *Min.*, *Electro-Metal.* Pa.
WHITE, Dr. F. D., L.B., 97 Connersville, Fayette Co. *Arch.*, *Photog.*, *Num's.* Ind.
WOLFF, J. E., Instructor in Harvard College, Cambridge. *Geol.*, *Phys.*, *Strat.** Mass.

APPENDIX TO INTERNATIONAL DIRECTORY.

Adami, G. Batta, Maggiore nel 51 Reggimento Janleria dell' Esercito Italiano, Brescia, Italy. *Moll.* C. Ex.

Albers, Alida, University, Stockholm, Sweden. *Phæn. Bot.*

Ault du Mesnil (d'), 1 rue de l'Eauette, Abbeville, France. *Geol., Arch. Préhist.* C.*

Biro, Louis, Station phylloxérique hongroise, Budapest, Austro-Hungary. *Hymen., Neuropt., Myriopoda.*

Brooks, Wm. P. B. S., Prof. of Botany and Agriculture, Sapporo Agr. College, Sapporo, Japan. *Bot., Phæn. Plants, Ferns, Hort.* C. Ex.*

Cann, Eugène, Trith-Saint-Léger (Nord), France. Copépodes libres et parasites. Ex.*

Charpy, Léon, Membre de la Société minéralogique de France et de la Société Paléontologique (Suisse), Bibliothécaire et Conservateur du Musée d'Annecy (Haute Savoie) à Annecy (Haute Savoie), France. *Min., Geol., Petrology, Prehist. Arch., Anth., Numis., Con., Eth., Bibliog., Photog., Sigilligraphia.* C. Ex. Minerals, French and Foreign; fossils, tertiary, cretaceous, jurassic, liassic; rocks.

Chatellier (du), à Kernuy, près Pont l'Abbé, Finisterre, France. *Antiq.* C.*

Claúdi-Hausen, R. A., Vodrofsvej, 46, Copenhagen, V., Denmark. *Phæn. and Crypt. Bot., Ferns, Zool.*

Cousens, Henry, Poona, India. *Ind. Arch.*

Ducrost, curé de Solutre (Saône et Leire), France. *Arch. Préhist.**

Ebenhöch, Franz Xaver, infulirter Abt von Tomāj, Capitular der Raaber Domkirche, Consistorialrath und Mitglied der Prosynodal-Prüfungs-Commission, Corresp. Mitglied der kön. ungar. Central Commission zur Erforschung u. Erhaltung mittelalterlicher Baudenkmale, Professor der Kunstarcheologie am Raaber Priester-Seminar. Raab, Ungarn. *Ornith. und Botanik.**

Finger, Dr. Aug., gr. Pfingstweidstrasse, Frankfurt-a.-M., Germany.*

Fornier, conseiller à la cour, Rennes, France. *Antiq.* C.*

Gaillard, à Plouhamel, Morbihan, France. *Antiq.**

Gibson, Eugène, Chimiste, à Jette St. Pierre, Brussels. *Chem. Org., Gen. Biol.**

Gudden, Bernh. v., Director der Kreisirrenanstalt, München, Germany. *Anatomy of the brain of the Vertebrate.*

Hamark (abbé), à l'Oratoire, Rennes, France. *Géol., Arch. Préhist.* C.*

Hieronymus, Prof. G., Sabethstrasse 1, Breslau, Prussia, Germany. *Bot.*

Holeczek, Adalbert, Domanen-Administrator, Hilicsy bei Dawiderny, Bukowina, Austro-Hungary. *Lepid., Dipt., Coleopt.**

Hüninger, Adolf, Kalocsa, Austro-Hungary. *Meteo., Ast.**

Ilosvay, Lajos, Prof. Dr., Phil. Dr., Chem. exper. Prof., Polytechnic um Budapest, Austro-Hungary. *Chem., Org., Inorg.**

Johnston-Lavis, H. J., M.D., M.R.C.S., B. ès Sc., L.S.A., F.G.S. Consulting Physician and Surgeon to Messrs. Sir Wm. Armstrong, Mitchell & Co.'s Works, Pozzoli. Palazzo, Caramanico, 7, Chiatamone, Naples, Italy. *Palæo., Geol., Min., Chem., Mic., Meteo., Gen. Biol., Geo. Dist.* C. Ex.*

Juel, Oscar, University, Stockholm, Sweden, *Fungi*, *Coleopt.*
Junowicz, Dr. R., Sereth, Bukowina, Austro-Hungary. *Anat. of plants.**
Karsten, Dr. C. G. W. Hermann, Prof. der Wiener Universität, Austria. *Bot.**
Kerviler, ingénieur, Saint-Nazaire, France. *Arch.**
Kremnetzky, Dr. Otto, Schemnitz, Austro-Hungary. *Phys.*
Lebenonte, pharmacien, place du Lice, Rennes, France. *Geol.* C.*
Leder, Hans, Mëdlung bei Wien, Austria. *Coleopt.*, *Hemipt.*, *Orthopt.*, *L. and F. W. Moll.**
Lestourbeillon (comte de), 1 rue Sully, Nantes, France. *Antiq.**
Linnarsson, Ernst, Skofde, Sweden. *Bot.* Grows and exchanges living plants from northern regions.*
Maillard, curé de Thorigné-en-Charnie, Mayenne, France. *Arch. Préhist.* C.*
Maria, Michel, Dir. en Med. et en Chir., Tripoli, Syria, Turkey. *Phæn. Bot.* C. Ex.
Maricourt, Baron de, La Thierraye, par Souday (Loire et Cher), France. *Anth.*, *Arch.*, *Orn.*, *Ool.*, *Lepid.*, *Coleopt.* C. Ex.*
Marktanner-Turneretscher, Gottlieb, Langegasse 16, Wien, VIII., Austro-Hungary. *Chem.**
Nemethy, Dr. Karl., Schemnitz, Austro-Hungary. *Geog.*
Oman, J. C., Prof. of Nat. Sci., Govt. College, Lahore, India. *Geol.*, *Zool.**
Palacky, Jan., Ph.D., Prof. Univ., Brentegasse, 34, Prague, Austro-Hungary. *Geog. Dist. of Animals and Plants, living and fossil.*
Petersén, Peter, Lehrer, Tanderup Skole, Fjerrilsler, Denmark. *Bot. Phys.* C. Ex.
Pott, Emil, Dr. Phil., Docent an der Kgl. Hochschule in München. Präs. des Deutschen Hopfenbauvereins, München, Germany. *Hort.*, *Agric.*
Ráthgeb, A., Schemintz, Astro-Hungary. *Min.*, *Geol.*, *Minerals*, *Rocks.* Ex.*
Rialan au Pratel, Vannes, Morbihan, France. *Antiq.**
Römer, Julius, Kronstadt, Siebenbürgen, Austro-Hungary. *Phæn. Bot.* C, Ex.
Schell, Wilhelm, Dr. Phil., Prof. am Polytechnicum zu Karlsruhe, Baden, Germany. *Phys.*, *Elect.*, *Ast.*, *Bibliog.*
Schmidt, Anton, Bürgerschullehrer, Leipa in Böhmen, Austro-Hungary. *Mosses*, *Moll.* C. Ex.*
Smith, Charles Michie, F.R.S.E., F.R.A.S., Prof. Phys. Sci., Christian College, Madras, India. *Physical*, *Phys.*, *Elect.*, *Photog.*, *Meteo.*, *Ast.**
Stelling, Edward, Director des Magnetisch-Meteorologischen Observatoriums in Irkutsk, Russia.*
Stockbridge, H. E., B.S., Ph.D., Consulting Chemist to Japanese Government, Sapporo, Japan. *Geol.*, *Lithol.*, *Inorg. Chem.**
Weiner, Dr. Christian, Prof. an der Polytechnischen Schule, Karlsruhe, Baden, Germany. *Math.*
Wetterhan, D., Baslerstrasse 6, Freiburg, Br. Grossherz. Baden, Germany. *Bot.*
Zfanndler, Leopold, Dr. Ph., Prof. Phys. an der Univ., Innsbruck, Austro-Hungary. *Phys.*
Zujovic, T., Prof. Geol., Univ. de Belgrade, Serbie. *Palæo.*, *Geol.*

The Best and Seasonable Books.

On Butterflies.

THE BUTTERFLIES OF NEW ENGLAND. Colored Plates. This new book, by C. J. Maynard, will prove a most useful work for all collectors and students of Lepidoptera. Full descriptions of all the species, and 232 life-size colored plates. Quarto. Cloth, 7.00

On Spiders.

SPIDERS: THEIR STRUCTURE AND HABITS. By J. H. Emerton. Fully illustrated. 1 vol. 12mo. Cloth, 1.50

THE SPIDERS OF THE UNITED STATES. By N. M. Hentz. With twenty-one copperplate illustrations. 8vo. Pamphlet. $3.00. Cloth, 3.50

On the Microscope.

GUIDE TO THE MICROSCOPE IN BOTANY. Translated from the German of Dr. Julius Wilhelm Behrens by Rev. A. B. Hervey. Illustrated. 1 vol. 8vo. Cloth, 5.00

On Wild Flowers.

AMERICAN WILD FLOWERS. A most comprehensive volume on the well-known flowers of our fields and woods. The text is by Prof. George L. Goodale, of the Botanic Gardens at Cambridge, and the 51 magnificent colored plates by Mr. Isaac Sprague. Quarto. Cloth (in box), 15.00

On American Mosses.

MANUAL OF THE MOSSES OF NORTH AMERICA. With six fine copper plates illustrating the Genera. By Leo Lesquereux and Thomas P. James. 1 vol. 8vo. Cloth, 4.00

On American Lichens.

A SYNOPSIS OF THE NORTH AMERICAN LICHENS. Comprising the Parmeliacei, Caldoniei and Cœnogoniei. By Edward Tuckerman, M. A. 1 vol. 8vo. Cloth, 3.50

On Histology.

BOTANICAL MICRO-CHEMISTRY. An introduction to the study of Vegetable Histology, for the use of students. By V. A. Poulsen. Translated by Prof. William Trelease. 1 vol. 12mo. Cloth, 1.00

On Ferns.

FERNS IN THEIR HOMES AND OURS. By Prof. John Robinson. Illustrated with 8 Lithographs and other plates and illustrations. 1 vol. 12mo. Cloth, 1.50

On Fresh Water Algæ.

FRESH WATER ALGÆ OF THE UNITED STATES. Complemental to the *Desmids of the United States*. By Rev. Francis Wolle. The new work comprises a description of all the known fresh-water algæ of the country, nearly 1300 species, with 157 plates, giving over 2000 figures colored after nature. 2 vols. 8vo. Cloth, 10.00

On Mushrooms.

MUSHROOMS OF AMERICA. Edible and Poisonous. With text and 12 colored plates illustrating the families. Edited by Julius A. Palmer. In portfolio or chart form, 2.C0

On Marine Algæ and Sea Weeds.

MARINE ALGÆ OF NEW ENGLAND and Adjacent Coast. By W. G. Farlow, M. D. 15 plates. 1 vol. 8vo. Cloth, 1.50

SEA MOSSES: A Collector's guide, and an Introduction to the Study of Marine Algæ. By A. B. Hervey, A. M. 20 colored plates. 1 vol. 12mo. Cloth, 2.00

On Desmids.

DESMIDS OF THE UNITED STATES and list of American Pediastrums. By Rev. Francis Wolle. With 1100 illustrations in 53 colored plates. The best manual of desmids published. 1 vol. 8vo. Cloth, 5.00

Minerals, Scientific and Medical Books, Shells, Fossils, Birds, Eggs,

And all objects of Natural History, are bought, sold and exchanged by

A. E. FOOTE, M.D.,

No. 1223 Belmont Avenue, Philadelphia, Pa.

(Professor of Chemistry and Mineralogy; Fellow of the American Association for the Advancement of Science; Life Member of the Academy of Natural Sciences, Philadelphia, and American Museum of Natural History, Central Park, N. Y. City.)

Specimens sent to any part of the world by mail. Specimen copy of the illustrated monthly, "Naturalist's Leisure Hour," of 32 pages, sent free. Subscription, 75 cents a year. For Club Rates and Premiums, see each monthly issue.

I received the highest award given to any one at the Centennial Exposition of 1876, and the only award and medal given to any American for "Collections of Minerals."

My Mineralogical Catalogue of 100 pages is sent post-paid on receipt of 25 cents; heavy paper, 50 cents; bound in cloth, 75 cents; half sheep, $1.00; half calf, $1.25; cloth, interleaved, $1.00; half sheep, interleaved, $1.25; half calf, interleaved, $1.50; (price-list alone, 16 pp., 3 cents). It is profusely illustrated, and the printer and engraver charged me about $1,100 before a copy was struck off. By means of the table of species and accompanying tables, most species may be verified. The price-list is an excellent check list, containing the names of all the species, and the more common varieties, arranged alphabetically and preceded by the species number. The species number indicates the place of any mineral in the table of species; after it will be found the species name, composition, streak or lustre, cleavage or fracture, hardness, specific gravity, fusibility and crystallization. I have very many species not on the price-list, and some that I had in 1876 are no longer in stock.

Collections of Minerals for Students, Amateurs, Professors, Physicians, et al.

The collections of 100 illustrate all the principal species and all the grand subdivisions in Dana and other works on Mineralogy; all the principal Ores, etc., etc. The collections are labeled with printed labels, that can only be removed by soaking. The labels of the $5.00 and higher-priced collections give Dana's species number, the name, locality, and in most cases, the composition of the Mineral; the $5.00, and higher, are also accompanied by my Illustrated Catalogue and table of species.

I have now over forty tons, and over $50,000 worth of Minerals, mostly crystallized, in stock. It is well recognized that my prices are lower and my specimens better labeled than those of any other dealer in the country. This is mainly due to the immense stock I carry (the largest of minerals of any in the country) and my system of printed labels attached to the specimens.

Catalogue of 2,500 species of Shells, made for me by George W. Tryon, Jr., who has labeled nearly all my shells, 3 cents; printed on heavy paper, with genus label list, 10 cents. I have purchased one or two of the most celebrated collections known, and have now over 2,000 pounds, 3,000 species, and 30,000 specimens of Shells and Corals in stock. Catalogue of Birds, Eggs, Eyes, Skins, etc., etc., 3 cents. Catalogues of Books, 16 pp., each 3 cents. Medicine, etc., 48 pp., 5 cents. (Please specify exactly what class of books you wish catalogues of.)

Send for the *Naturalist's Leisure Hour,* giving full particulars. Specimen copy free. You will confer a double favor by handing this to some physician or other person interested in science.

Please mention where you saw this.

CIRCULAR TO COLLECTORS.

I wish to increase the number of my correspondents, among those persons, who are interested in science as students and collectors.

I desire also to add to my private collections first-class specimens in Natural History, such as

MARINE, LAND and FRESH WATER SHELLS, FOSSILS, BIRDS' EGGS and NESTS, MINERALS, CRYSTALS, GEMS and PRECIOUS STONES.

Prehistoric relics of the stone and bronze ages.

POTTERY AND GLASS, Ancient and Modern.

ETHNOLOGY.

Arms, Implements, Dress, Jewels, Tools, Hunting and Fishing Utensils, Pipes and Utensils for use of Tobacco and other Narcotics, and for Beverages; Toilet Articles, Trinkets and Ornaments; Idols and Images, Charms and Religious or Political Symbols; Basketry; Shoes, and other Foot-wear; Gloves and other Hand-wear; Hats and other Head-covering; Utensils and Processes for making Fire; Sculptures, Carving, Metal Work, Embroideries, Musical Instruments, Etc., Etc.

Persons having such articles, and willing to sell the same for cash, will please send a descriptive list with prices.

On the other hand, I can serve those making collections, with many similar articles from the United States and elsewhere, lists of which will be sent on application.

Address,

FREDERICK STEARNS (Personal),

371 LAFAYETTE AVENUE, - - DETROIT, MICH., U. S. A.

ROYAL MALACOLOGICAL SOCIETY OF BELGIUM.

CATALOGUE ILLUSTRÉ

DES

COQUILLES FOSSILES

De l'Éocene des Environs des Paris.

PAR

M. COSSMANN,

INGÉNIEUR CIVIL.

Membre de la Société royale malacologique de Belgique, de la Société Géologique de France et de la Société Paléontologique suisse.

Thanks to the profusion of fossil shells contained in the various Tertiary deposits of the Paris Basin, the *Description des animaux sans vertèbres* de DESHAYES took a most important position among works on Eocene mollusca, and for a time exhausted the subject. But the riches of the Paris Basin seem in this respect inexhaustible, and since 1865, fresh discoveries have continually been made, collections enlarged, new genera have taken their place in families, and existing genera have been enriched with numerous species unknown to DESHAYES. Many of these have been described in different scattered publications but more were without description. It became necessary after 20 years to do for the *Animaux sans Vertèbres* of from 1856–1865, what DESHAYES had himself done for his *Description des Coquilles fossiles* de 1837, that is to say, describe the new species, bring together the scattered descriptions of others, and introduce those reforms into the nomenclature required by the progress of science. It is this work that M. COSSMANN has achieved.

It was no small matter to undertake to reform such a work as DESHAYES'; but the author set to work courageously and has met with a success that must satisfy the most exacting, due no doubt to the vast collections at his disposal, which comprised beside his own and those of many private friends, the great collection DESHAYES at the Ecole des Mines and the other public collections of Paris. The very flattering approval of *MM. P. J. Van Beneden*, Prof. of Zoology at the University of Louvain, of *G. Dewalque*, chief of the Faculté des Sciences and Prof. of Geology at the University of Liège; of *A. Briart*, chief engineer at the collieries of Mariemont, all members of the "Académie royale des Sciences" of Belgium; as well as a most commendatory report of *M. H. Crosse*, editor of the *Journal de Conchyliologie* of Paris, places the *Catalogue Illustré* of M. COSSMANN in the front rank of scientific works of the age, rich as it has been in the publication of remarkable works in both hemispheres.

NOTICE TO SUBSCRIBERS.

The *Illustrated Catalogue of Fossil Shells from the Eocene of the Paris Basin* is published in 4 parts, comprising 1000 pages of text and about 35 plates. The first 2 are published; the 3rd is in the press. The subscription of *60 francs* for the complete work is payable, *30 francs* with order for first 2 parts and *15 francs* on receipt of notice that each of the 2 remaining parts are ready.

When the Publication is completed, the price will be raised to 80 francs.

Order by letter, accompanied by postal order, for France, from M. COSSMANN, 17 Rue St. Vincent de Paul, Paris, and for all other countries M. TH. LEFÈVRE, Secrétaire de la Société royale Malacologique de Belge, 10 Rue du Pont-Neuf, Brussels.

Lightning Source UK Ltd.
Milton Keynes UK
UKHW011009111218
333786UK00009B/573/P

9 780260 067296